A HISTORY OF ANCIENT PHILOSOPHY

A HISTORY OF ANCIENT PHILOSOPHY

FROM THE BEGINNINGS TO AUGUSTINE

Karsten Friis Johansen

Translated by Henrik Rosenmeier

London and New York

First published in English 1998
by Routledge
11 New Fetter Lane, London EC4P 4EE

Simultaneously published in the USA and Canada
by Routledge
29 West 35th Street, New York, NY 10001

First published in Danish 1991
as Den Europæiske Filosofis Historie : Antikken
by Nyt Nordisk Forlag Arnold Busck, Copenhagen

Typeset in Garamond by Routledge
Printed and bound in Great Britain by
TJ International Ltd, Padstow, Cornwall

British Library Cataloguing in Publication Data
A catalogue record for this book is available from the British Library

Library of Congress Cataloguing in Publication Data
Friis Johansen K. (Karsten)
[Den Europæiske Filosofis Historie. Antikken. Danish]
A history of ancient philosophy: from the beginnings to Augustine
Karsten Friis Johansen. Translated by Henrik Rosenmeier.
Includes bibliographical references and index.
1. Philosophy: Ancient – History. I. Title
B115.D36F7513 1998

F180-dc 21 97–45072 CIP

ISBN 0–415–12738–6

This book was awarded the Amalienborg Prize by Her Majesty the Queen of Denmark and His Royal Highness the Prince Consort.

No serious person will ever commit serious matters to writing.

(Plato)

CONTENTS

—•◆•—

— Contents —

PART V: HELLENISTIC PHILOSOPHY

PREFACE

———— •◆• ————

The present work spans the history of ancient philosophy from the earliest Greek thinkers to Augustine. It was first published in Danish in 1991, and the English edition does not differ in any essential respect from the original version.

The book addresses itself to readers who are principally interested in surveying the first millennium of Western thought as well as to those chiefly seeking direct access to the primary sources. To meet the requirements of the latter a detailed reference apparatus is integrated in the text.

The aim has been to link the respective parts of the book in such a manner that an overall picture emerges in which there is emphasis on the many interrelationships between different trends. The underlying supposition, that 'ancient thought' constitutes a coherent whole, albeit one with many variations, does of course have its limitations; it represents but one writer's views and presuppositions.

The book was inspired in equal measure by Anglo-Saxon and continental scholarship. In addition, I have had the benefit of discussions with Danish colleagues and friends over many years. I beg them all to accept my sincere thanks.

With admirable patience and engagement Henrik Rosenmeier, the translator, brought his expertise and stylistic sensibility to bear on the work. The book was a difficult one to translate, and without Dr Rosenmeier's great contribution it is unlikely that the plans for translation could have been realized. We worked in close collaboration – one that I take pleasure in remembering. Johnny Christensen, Troels Engberg-Pedersen, and Fritz Saaby Pedersen most kindly read individual sections, mainly with an eye to terminology. Major portions of the book were reviewed by Eric Jacobsen from a stylistic and linguistic viewpoint. The invaluable assistance of all these persons is gratefully acknowledged.

The Danish edition was published by Nyt Nordisk Forlag Arnold Busck, and I am pleased to acknowledge my indebtedness to Søren Hansen for his unflagging support.

Special thanks are extended to Malcolm Schofield of Cambridge University who recommended the book to Routledge for publication of the English edition.

I am also indebted to Routledge for undertaking to publish this book, to Richard Stoneman, and to the two anonymous readers who provided useful comments on several chapters. Of course I alone remain responsible for any errors and shortcomings.

The translation was made possible by grants from the Carlsberg Foundation and the Velux Foundation, and I am most grateful for their generous support.

Last but not least I should like to express my sincere and respectful gratitude to Her Majesty the Queen and His Royal Highness the Prince Consort who awarded the Amalienborg Prize to the original Danish version as a work in the humanities written in Danish and deserving of international dissemination.

Karsten Friis Johansen
Copenhagen
October 1997

INTRODUCTION

———•◆•———

Ancient philosophy, the basis of Western thought and science, evolved in the course of almost one thousand years. In the sixth century BC that process was begun in which we still find ourselves: the attempt at a rational explanation of the world and of man's place in the world.

The earliest period – until just past the middle of the fifth century BC – was economically, socially and politically a period of crises, but at the same time a period which opened up for foreign influences provoking thinkers and poets to seek for some order behind all changes, an order that could be grasped by human thought. With the victorious conclusion of the Persian wars, Athens became the political and cultural centre of the Greek world. Still, the owls of Minerva do not take flight until dusk. Socrates' work was carried out during a period of decline, and Plato and Aristotle were not the ideologists of democratic, imperialist Athens. They brought earlier thought to a conclusion, created a conceptual apparatus that has left its impress on all subsequent Western philosophy, and assigned man a place in society and the cosmos at the moment when the era of greatness had been lost irretrievably, and the city state was in decay. The old Greek world finally lay in ruins when Alexander the Great forged his world empire. From then on political decisions were made by distant monarchs, and individual man was left to find his own proper place. Still, new philosophical systems were formulated – Epicureanism and Stoicism – and philosophy was still a universal explanation of the world; but the emphasis was on ethics, and it was in this period that philosophy and science began to pursue their own paths.

By the second century BC the Romans had become the rulers of the entire Mediterranean area. They adopted Hellenistic culture and with it Greek philosophy. The old philosophical schools were continued in Roman times and culminated during the late Empire (from the third century AD) in Neoplatonism. But times had changed. Religious movements from the Orient appealed to a far wider circle than philosophy ever did, and with the advent of Christianity a confrontation and cultural fusion took place, which are unparalleled in our history. Antiquity was over, but its thought survived.

There are breaks during this long evolution – but also continuity. Each period had its own features, but there was also recourse to the tradition, which in a sense never became the past. The fundamental idea that originally made philosophy an especial mode of interpreting the world was never left behind: man can understand the world as a whole and thereby know himself. Ancient thought always aimed at an all-comprehending view – even when moving to the limits of rationality. The universal aim was never abandoned, not even as the several separate disciplines gradually evolved. And confidence in the possibilities of human thought was maintained, even when reflections began about the basis of knowledge. The world was considered a rational, orderly whole, and in many cases the cosmic order was taken to be moral order as well.

The strength of ancient philosophy is the formulation of basic fundamental positions – materialism, idealism and scepticism, rationalism, and empiricism, to use modern labels – and of basic fundamental problems, which may belong within the purview of a given period, but which at the same time have constituted the underlying fabric of a thousand-year old tradition and have served until recently as paradigms. But ancient thought was always speculative, and in a manner of speaking it lacked a counterpart. Individual sciences, such as mathematics and medicine, achieved significant results; but from social and ideological points of view one cannot in Antiquity – as in our times – speak of science as an established authority that ties down philosophical reflection decisively. In Antiquity one could choose one's own philosophical position as one today chooses one's outlook on life or political party. But in so doing, one had also chosen a certain view of the physical world and of man's moral obligations.

Already in Plato there is awareness of the tradition. Since his time, philosophy has been tied up with its own history. This history has often served as a self-evident background; yet just as often philosophers have deliberately sought to return to the ancients, and in every case something new has been the outcome. Until the end of the eighteenth century the relationship with the tradition was in a certain sense free of problems. One could discuss with a colleague from Antiquity – more or less as Aristotle had debated with his forerunners – which is to say not out of interest in a distant past, but out of interest in subject matters beyond differences in time. A direct relation to Antiquity has not died out, as can be seen for example in Hegel, Kierkegaard, Nietzsche, or Heidegger, and not infrequently among analytical or Marxist interpreters. Still, towards 1800 AD emerged what has been called historical consciousness. Primarily thanks to Herder, the view came to prevail that man is a creature of history and that history accordingly has no meaning beyond itself. It follows from Herder's basic thought that every cultural phenomenon – hence also philosophy – exists only in a historical dimension and that every age must be judged on its own presuppositions.

But this causes the historian's debate with the past to be far more reflected than it had formerly been. He is obliged to respect an alien mode of thought but is also tied to his own presuppositions. Furthermore, for the historian of philosophy the problem becomes even more acute, because philosophy is both fixed in a certain time and seeks universal validity. The history of philosophy is both philosophy and history and will always express the interpretation of a particular age of a particular past, and the historian of philosophy must consider both the atemporal and historical perspectives – not necessarily in such a manner that he incessantly recites his own hermeneutical credo, but so that in his mind's eye he envisages a timeless problem emerging in a historical context. Strictly speaking, this requires superhuman abilities but also a certain craftsman's understanding of what it is that a given text does not say.

All these difficulties become especially clear in the history of ancient philosophy. It is a period with relevance for us, because it is the basis for all subsequent Western thought. Yet, there is both in time and in culture such a great distance between us and Antiquity that ancient ways of confronting problems are often not immediately understandable, even if the problems discussed may be today's problems as well. The philosophy of such a period does not become understandable by mere paraphrase. To gain access to the conceptual world of the past with the conceptual apparatus of our own time requires considerable balance – and that not least with respect to the philosophy of the earliest period.

THE EVIDENCE

It may be appropriate to begin with some comments on the philological background for the interpretation of ancient texts, both with respect to the very nature of technical-philological work and to the kinds of surviving sources. The latter is connected with the question of Antiquity's understanding of itself.

The literature of Antiquity is but a torso to us. Major parts have been lost, and the first printed editions of ancient texts in the Renaissance were based on transcripts of transcripts made throughout the long period since the originals were written. Surviving manuscripts are rarely older than the ninth century AD, and hence we must take into account that in the long history of transmission, errors have crept into the texts, which can never be detected. Thanks to the finding of papyri, none of which are older than c.350 BC, texts have been found, which are unknown in the manuscript transmission – for example Aristotle's treatise on the constitution of Athens and a number of Epicurean papyri. But a papyrus has usually been preserved only in fragments, and its age is not a guarantee of a better text than that which perhaps also has been indirectly transmitted in medieval transcripts, and which perhaps has been derived from an authorized edition from Antiquity. Thus the few preserved Plato papyri have seldom occasioned corrections in the manuscript transmission.

The philologist is confronted with considerable difficulties concerning transmission and textual criticism. The classical philologist's ever more refined techniques make our editions more reliable than the first to be printed, but we shall never have access to a wholly authentic text. By means of a systematic registration of obvious errors that recur and by the dating of manuscripts, etc., the mutual interdependence of surviving manuscripts can be accounted for with greater or lesser probability, and in fortunate cases it is thereby possible to reconstruct – perhaps also identify – the source of the surviving manuscripts (the *archetypus*). Such a source can, for example, be a lost manuscript from the early Middle Ages, but it can never be identified with the author's text.

Nor was it possible in Antiquity to be certain that one held an authentic text in one's hand that had been approved by the author. No two manuscripts are identical, and at that time there was often a significant difference between a reliable text and a 'pirate edition' (cf., e.g. Plato *Parm.* 128 D). A 'sound' text from earlier Greek Antiquity will — as it presents itself to us — stem from philological editing in Hellenistic times (third–second century BC). It is during this period — first and foremost in Alexandria — that the foundation of philological technique was laid down, not least with respect to establishing a reliable Homeric text. From marginal notes, which at some time have been absorbed in the transmission and copied in extant manuscripts, one can surmise something of the 'working methods' of the Alexandrian philologists. Measured by modern standards, they worked in a rather arbitrary manner, and their methods of textual criticism were not always exemplary. Yet they accomplished a great task by preserving the existing transmission and by finding their way to the soundest text, and they had so much respect for the well-transmitted text that they followed the sensible philological principle of listing proposed textual emendations as notes rather than incorporating them in the text itself.

A standard of editorial technique was thereby introduced, which also influenced ancient editions of renowned philosophical texts, although the Alexandrians did not primarily concern themselves with this genre. What and how much was transmitted varies greatly from one philosophical writer to another. All that Plato published with a greater public in mind seems to have been preserved, and our Plato text can be assumed to depend on an authorized edition arranged for by the Academy (third century BC?). What has been preserved for us by Aristotle evidently goes back to an edition of lecture notes from the first century BC. Epicurus' letters have been preserved as quotations in another writer (Diogenes Laertius). Our Plotinus goes back to a posthumous edition by Porphyry, but there are traces of an older and less sound Plotinus text.

In other words, every philosophical or literary treatment of ancient texts is fundamentally dependent on comprehensive philological reconstruction, but the dependence is mutual. No ancient text can be interpreted without a basis of philology and textual criticism, and no text can be determined without interpreting its contents.

What has been lost over the course of time is owing not only to external circumstances but to changing tastes and interests as well. Furthermore, the tendency in late Antiquity to allow anthologies and compendia to take the place of the original texts has been fatal. To us Plato and Aristotle are the dominant figures in Greek thought. But such a picture was determined upon already during Antiquity. It is not accidental that from pre-Hellenistic times only complete texts by these two men have been preserved. Therefore we may easily get a distorted understanding and overlook the fact that there are important connective lines that by-pass these two giants. Several of the so-called Presocratics were presumably lost already early on, soon after the age of Aristotle. Subsequently only random quotations were known, and hence quotations from late Antiquity are often quotations of quotations. The fundamental works of such major Hellenistic schools as Epicureanism and Stoicism are also known only fragmentarily, but entire, more readable works from the later tradition have been preserved (Lucretius in the case of Epicureanism; Seneca, Epictetus, and Marcus Aurelius in the case of Stoicism), and the debate between the Hellenistic schools is amply reflected in Cicero. But with respect to major parts of the philosophy of Antiquity, we only have recourse to quotations and accounts in later authors, and, of course, this makes work with philological reconstructions even more difficult. One is left with loose ends taken out of context, and one must take into account the bias of the author who is quoting someone else.

Plato's and Aristotle's attitude to the tradition to which they belonged is decisive for our knowledge of it. They – and the students of Aristotle – have determined the understanding of the development of philosophy. Both saw themselves as solvers of problems raised in earlier thought. Yet they had different ways of confronting the problems.

Plato does not wish to provide information about the Presocratics. He makes use of them instead. He is interested in rethinking the problems posed by his predecessors in order to formulate principal philosophical positions – not in paraphrasing particular doctrines. Some of his interpretations – for example his view of Heraclitus and Parmenides as counterparts, or his contrast of materialism with idealism – have remained. But certainly it would be a misunderstanding to read, for example, his *Parmenides* as a source for what Parmenides did, in fact, mean.

Unlike Plato's, Aristotle's historical view was systematic. He considers earlier positions as the raw material of philosophy on a par with empirical observation. Almost all his treatises therefore commence with a survey in which he – often in great detail – summarizes, quotes, or criticizes his predecessors. Thus the entire first book of the *Metaphysics* is a historical examination with an aim to conceptual analysis, and it has remained a normative 'history of philosophy' for times far later than Antiquity. It follows from Aristotle's procedure that he treats earlier thinkers in terms of his own conceptual apparatus. He asks about the meaning that lies behind their – often stumbling – attempts to arrive at those truths that it was possible for Aristotle himself to formulate, precisely because the attempts had been made. This is not simply arrogance, for in his discussions of the development of problems Aristotle takes his predecessors seriously – far more so than is the case with so many other great men of philosophy. If one wishes to evaluate Aristotle as a source, one must recollect that he had access to just about the entire earlier philosophical tradition, that he carefully gathered and preserved a very voluminous historical material, but that he gathered and retold it in his own context.

To a large extent, Epicureanism and Stoicism must be thought of as reactions to problems stated and discussed by Plato and Aristotle. But at the same time these schools seek a tie to Presocratic views, reinterpreted without much regard to a historical perspective. A Hellenistic philosopher makes use of the tradition, as Plato and Aristotle did. But no Epicurean or Stoic had Plato's or Aristotle's interest in a debate with the past. Historical material encapsulated in Hellenistic philosophy is often so masked as to be unrecognizable. Something of an exception, however, is the late Sceptic Sextus Empiricus (c.200 AD) who provides extensive and exact quotations especially with epistemological contents. The Platonist Plutarch (c.100 AD) and the physician Galen (second century AD) can also be significant philosophical sources.

In late Antiquity the long philosophical tradition was viewed through Neoplatonic glasses or was attacked from a Christian point of view. Several Church Fathers transmitted quotations, often these were second-hand. But as a rule the Neoplatonists had profound familiarity with the tradition. Among the late Neoplatonists there is special reason to single out Simplicius, who lived as late as the sixth century AD and represents a special genre, that of the Aristotelian commentators. He was dependent on the Aristotelian tradition, but at the same time had access to sources that were still available in his time. Thanks to him, many Presocratic fragments have been preserved. He quotes precisely, and his commentaries are often valuable – which is also true of other Aristotelian commentators. Simplicius is a good example showing that a late source is not necessarily a bad source. At a time when literature only existed in an often very limited number of manuscripts, a writer's access to books, i.e. where he lived, can be more decisive than his dates.

A special genre is the so-called doxography. On this genre as well, Aristotle has indirectly left his mark. Aristotle's student, the philosopher and botanist Theophrastus, shared his teacher's historical interest and wrote a comprehensive work on the history of natural philosophy. Of this, the section on perception has survived. In his ordering and evaluation of the material Theophrastus is dependent on Aristotle, and his work served as the basis for many later compendia that included Aristotelianism and Hellenistic philosophy. Some of these have been preserved. Theophrastus was still a historian of problems, although more rigid and dogmatic than Aristotle. The doxographic tradition followed Theophrastus' systematics and arranged the material according to philosophical beliefs (*doxai*), not according to persons or schools – under such headings as matter, space, time, causes are furnished the views of the different schools. But no quotations are provided, nor any commentaries and philosophical criticism. A transition has taken place to compendia-like surveys for the use of busy readers who value easily obtained ready information.

A variant of this genre arranged the matter according to individuals within the particular schools, apparently with greater interest in the external history of the schools than in their doctrines. The ordering principle is the concept of *diadochē*, the 'line of succession' – which is to say the succession of leaders within a school. This genre also followed Aristotelian impulses, but the method could – especially with respect to the Presocratics – lead to sterile systematization.

Finally, philosophers – and other writers – were treated biographically. But we should not think of biographies in the modern sense. Originally this genre probably bore the stamp of Aristotle's interest in typical modes of life, but from quite early on it seems to have degenerated into anecdotes and *chronique scandaleuse*. Biographical interest naturally goes hand in hand with interest in chronology, and here – for better or worse – a work by Apollodorus (second century BC) has been influential. He cannot have had much knowledge of the oldest philosophers' exact dates but worked out a strict sequel in which a teacher was succeeded by a forty-years-younger student who 'had heard him'. The method does not inspire confidence.

Most of the works in these genres have been lost, but they were the basis for the only 'history of philosophy' of Antiquity that did survive, written by Diogenes Laertius (presumably in the first half of the third century AD). Formally Diogenes writes in the *diadochē* genre, but he also diligently uses doxographical and biographical matter, and he quotes energetically – sometimes charmingly, rarely carefully, and never profoundly. To us it can sometimes be an advantage that he serves up his material in its raw state. He shares his contemporaries' interest in the well-turned unreliable anecdote, their reverence for a grand past and the clever sayings of wise men. It has been said that to him history is broken down into stories. He did not have philosophical insight. But by a quirk of fate his work has been preserved, and down through the centuries it has probably been more influential than any other history of philosophy. He is a second-hand source, although often primary in the current historical sense, which is to say primary in relation to other preserved sources.

Accordingly, the imperfect but varied source material can be divided into three groups:

1 Independently transmitted texts – where one must always take the special nature of the transmission into account.
2 Quotations in other authors – where one must take the transmission of these authors into account and bear in mind that the quotations are out of context and are employed for a specific purpose.
3 Accounts in other authors (*testimonia*) – where one must likewise take the bias of these authors into account.

The delimitation between the two last groups is not always easy to establish, for it can often be difficult to know what is quotation and what is paraphrase, and the matter is even more difficult in Antiquity where one is often quoted from memory. With respect to the earliest thinking, it may be a help that some Presocratics wrote in verse, which is not so easily distorted, and also that genuine textual fragments often can be identified by special dialect features. But it holds good for the fragmentarily transmitted philosophers – for example the Presocratics and the older Stoics – that the distinction in modern standard editions between fragment and testimony not infrequently must be viewed with some reservation. The distinction often depends on the editor's discretion.

Warnings of this sort are the immediate consequence of general principles of textual criticism and source criticism. To these must be added the interpretative difficulties. Antiquity was itself able to furnish histories of problems – often of high standard – and collections of material – sometimes on a most unambitious level – but hardly a history of philosophy in the modern sense. The modern historian of philosophy must combine an Aristotle's preoccupation with problems with a Diogenes' simple eagerness to collect facts, and he must in addition bring to his task that sympathy and historical distance, which at happy moments have been the hallmarks of humanistic scholarship.

Until about 1800 AD 'history of philosophy' was by and large confined to doxography. Hegel's history of philosophy was epochal in being the first treatment written from a consistent philosophical position. Zeller's *Die Philosophie der Griechen* (1st. ed., 1844–52) is the first work to unite philosophical interpretation with philological method. The subsequent years can boast of many examples of philosophical-systematic analysis and of genetic method – which is to say that special emphasis is placed on influences and historical sequels. To this must, of course, be added investigations from social or psychological points of view.

The following pages have not been written with the view that philosophy follows a necessary and autonomous course or that the past must be judged in light of what could and would endure. The general cultural and social background will, to some extent, be considered – especially in the earliest period and at the transition from Antiquity to Christianity – but this book is primarily a presentation of the history of philosophy. It does not pretend to be a history of science or a general history of ideas.

PART I

PRESOCRATIC PHILOSOPHY

——•◆•——

1

MYTH, POETRY AND PHILOSOPHY

——— •◆• ———

Greek philosophy arose during the sixth century BC. Like us, the Greeks asked themselves how it all came about. Aristotle ties this to the problem of the nature of philosophy (Aristot. *Met*. 980 a 21 ff.). Philosophy builds on experience, though it is not experience. Experience deals with the particular, philosophy or science with the universal. The practical man – for example, the artisan – knows what he has to do in a given situation. The theoretician or philosopher knows the causes, for he not only knows *that* this or that is the case, he also knows *why*. Practical discoveries, Aristotle continues, are the first to appear in the development of mankind. It is not until the material needs have been met that it becomes possible for someone to devote himself to speculation. This happened in Egypt where the priesthood had enough time to study mathematics. Aristotle further notes that theoretical speculation is at all times more highly regarded, because its aim is not some practical application. In fact, theoretical knowledge, just as the life of a free man, has its purpose in itself.

These Aristotelian considerations about the philosophy of history and sociology of knowledge are telling, even though they are not, strictly speaking, dependent on his definition of the nature of philosophy. To Aristotle, as to Plato, philosophy comes about because men wonder and without prejudice try to come up with rational explanations. What existed before philosophy was what Aristotle called theology, which is to say, mythology. But mythological explanations are not rational (cf. 1000 a 5 ff.). If the philosopher abandons his belief in rationality and order, he must surrender to chaos and the dark night of the 'theologians' (1071 b 26; 1072 a 18).

Philosophy originated only in few locations – in Greece, India and China – and it came about much later than religion. Poetic and religious interpretations of life seem to be universal human endeavours. Religion provides an explanation. Just as is the case with philosophy, it does not take the world to be what it pretends to be; yet it does not provide some distant explanation of 'given' phenomena that are reducible to universal causes. At the same time as religion is an interpretation of life, it is a way of life. By living in a society and in relation to nature men live in a relationship with the divine, and this relationship is not to be explained but to be experienced and confirmed. This has been described as not being an objective relation to a 'this' but as a personal one to a 'Thou'.

The relation of man to god is confirmed at the festival that ensures that the gods still sustain natural order and that the world will not fall back into chaos and the power of the demons. At the festival gods and men meet each other, and the proto-drama is presented and repeated in which the gods – by annihilating the demonic powers – secured or created an orderly world. This occurs by cultic and ritual acts, by sacrifice, and by means of the language of the festival, the myth that relates the beginning of the world (Greek: *archē*), 'that time', which is both primordial time and the present which in the feast recreates the first drama. Cult, rite, and myth are the basic elements of primitive religion, in the religions of the Mediterranean and thereby in Greek religion as well. And these elements continued to live until the advent of Christianity. In Athens, Delphi, and throughout the Greek world the festival drama endured, even though poets and philosophers by and by spoke about god, the world and man in quite a different language. It was only slowly that the old, traditional religion came to be thought of as empty ceremony. The fact that the old religion had so much vitality is connected with its dependence on institutionalized practice, on action, and on its not containing a systematized theology. Greek religion is free of dogma. The myth is an account which early came to balance subtly on the borderline between faith and fable. It is not an authorized, intellectual, religious verity. Therefore a Greek poet or thinker was able to have his own personal, sublime view of god and at the same time he could with the clearest conscience in the world participate in the cultic festival – the cult can continue to be the traditional expression of that which a community of men has in common and which thought cannot grasp. But if religion is not revealed theology, the cult is precisely a social affair: to omit sacrifices is therefore the same as disavowal of the community of both god and state.

Greek religion is polytheistic. This does not mean that the mythological host of closely related gods, each with his own official area of responsibility, provide an adequate picture. A god resides in a sanctuary, be it Zeus, Apollo, or Athena, but remains first and foremost 'the god', yet also a god who protects a special area of life and permits the worship of a related god – often in the same sanctuary. But only a rationalizing mythology will attempt to specify the tasks of the individual gods. The god is – to use an awkward modern expression – a personification, which means that he is both a person and a power. Probably this is why proclaimed atheists are so rare in the Greek world. To deny the existence of Aphrodite, for example, would be absurd, for it would be tantamount to denying the existence of the erotic.

The basic elements of Greek religion that have been sketched in the preceding correspond with what is known about other religions in the Mediterranean area. But the common features allow for many possible variations, and there are many latent lines of development. The great exception is, of course, the development of the Jewish religion. To the Jews there is only one God, Jahve; He speaks to His people through the prophets; as we are told in Genesis, He created heaven and earth out of nothing by an act of will, but He is Himself transcendent, beyond created nature.

Otherwise in Egypt and Babylonia. In Amenhotep IV's (Achenaton's) famous hymn to the sun (fourteenth century BC) the sun and the god are one, and in the ritual Babylonian poem of creation *Enuma elish* (second millennium BC) both the world and the gods are created from the primordial waters, the male Apsu and the female Tiamat.

In Egypt the king was the god's representative, and in both Egypt and Babylonia the priesthood had powerful social and political positions. Under such circumstances it was possible to develop and refine mythical thinking. Yet major departures would hardly have been possible.

In the Greek world, on the other hand, no powerful priesthood evolved, nor did an official mythology. This provided opportunities as probably nowhere else for a development and change of the ancient mythical way of thinking. Mythical thought is poetical, and if the tie between myth and cult is loosened, poetry can arise in its own right. This happened with Homer. The *Iliad* and the *Odyssey* are epic works of poetry in which the well- and deliberately-composed story is the superior consideration – superior to religion as well. In Homer the gods live in the Olympic skies, are eternal, happy and 'easy-living', but also angry, cunning, in discord and with human virtues and vices on a grand scale. In the universe of the epic it is first and foremost the task of the gods to participate in the action – the battles of Troy, the return of Ulysses. They rarely show themselves to men, but the poet allows his auditors to look over his shoulder so that we can see what the gods are up to and why things happen as they do. Thereby the gods get each his own face, but undeniably become a little less divine. This is not to say that Homer is irreligious, but only that an epic poet does not write theology. Nevertheless, the Homeric Pantheon was to occupy a significant place in the minds of the Greeks. All Greeks knew Homer, and the connection between the old festive religion and the Homeric Pantheon is a unique Greek phenomenon. Through Homer other religious ideas were transmitted as well: the ancient thought of water as the progenitor of everything – in Homer the river Okeanos, which floats around the world (Hom. *Il.* XIV 200; 244; cf. *Enuma elish*) and the thought of fate – *moira* or *aisa* – the lot that is accorded every man at birth (cf. *Il.* XX 127; *Od.* VII 196). Yet, at the same time, it is not a named god, but the Divinity or the guardian genius (*ho daimōn*) who guides the steps of man (cf. XI 61). The epic poet communicates and reshapes the religion he lives in; but he does not systematize it.

But it is also possible to proceed from myth to mythology, to what might be called a quasi-rational interpretation of life. An example has been mentioned from Babylonian culture of mythological poetry that is still tied to the cult and thereby expresses an 'official' view. On Greek soil, Hesiod (probably c.700 BC) gave shape to his own personal mythology in the poem the *Theogony* (the Origin of the Gods).

Of the genesis of the world he writes:

> Verily first of all did Chaos come into being, and then broad-bosomed Gaia [earth], a firm seat of all things for ever, and misty Tartaros in a recess of broad-wayed earth, and Eros, who is fairest among immortal gods, looser of limbs, and subdues in their breasts the mind and thoughtful counsel of all gods and all men. Out of Chaos, Erebos and black Night came into being; and from Night, again, came Aither and Day, whom she conceived and bore after mingling in love with Erebos. And earth first of all brought forth starry Ouranos [sky], equal to herself, to cover her completely round about, to be a firm seat for the blessed gods for ever. Then she brought forth tall

> mountains, lovely haunts of the divine nymphs who dwell in the woody mountains. She also gave birth to the unharvested sea, seething with its swell, Pontos, without delightful love; and then having lain with Ouranos she bore deep-eddying Okeanos.
>
> (Hes. *Theog.* 116 ff.; trans. G.S. Kirk)

Subsequently the gods enter the world, father and son, until the coming of Zeus and his descendants who defeated the Titans, the enemies of the gods.

There are many rational elements in these lines. The question posed is what came first – Chaos, the chasm, which in its indefiniteness makes it impossible to ask what was before 'first'. Then appear the two principal regions of the world: earth (Gaia) and the underworld (Tartaros) and Eros, the power that makes creation and procreation possible. Next the darkness of the underworld (Erebos) and Night are born, and they beget their contrast, the day and pure air (Aither). Thereafter the world – as we know it – appears gradually: heaven or the vault of heaven (Ouranos), the mountains, the sea (Pontos), and the primordial river (Okeanos).

This is different from Genesis where God created the world. There is no distinction between gods, nature, and power; and earth, underworld, Eros, day and night are 'concepts' or rather 'persons' of the same order. Yet things are orderly nevertheless. There is not only a rational before and after; there is also a causal explanation voiced by the sexual language and cosmic procreation. The world is explained through its beginning and birth (cosmogony), and the birth of the world explains the nature of the world.

So much for the rational. But there is an equally important non-rational aspect. Hesiod's mythological explanation of the world is irrational in so far as he cannot be contradicted. He is not disposed to argue for or against. His words are their own authority, which finds its poetic expression in its not being Hesiod who speaks, but the Muses through Hesiod – just as the Muse speaks through Homer.

It is never the case that one mode of thinking suddenly is succeeded by another. Hesiod had his successors in his role as mythological systematist, for example Pherecydes from Syros (sixth century BC), a contemporary of the oldest philosophers. But he was influential considerably later than the sixth century. Like Homer, Hesiod became an integral part of Greek education – not only as a poet one could consider in aesthetic terms, but as a teacher to whose message one had to respond.

Hesiod also had long-lasting influence in another way. His cosmogony and theogony were continued by the mystical-religious movement, Orphism, but in a new context. As has become clear, Greek religion had several faces, and the world of the Pantheon did not consist exclusively of noble super-human figures spicing their blessed lives with Homeric family fights. Occupying a special position in the Pantheon was Demeter, the goddess of fertility, whose cult in Eleusis became a mystery cult for the initiated. And Dionysus had his own very special place among the gods. He was the god of wine, but above all of the irrational in man, of chaotic feelings and uncontrolled instincts, the wish for death, and the yearning for unification with the divine. Dionysus also had his own secret cult for the initiated – apparently an ecstatic cult without fixed rituals, unlike Demeter's mysteries at Eleusis. The worship of Dionysus was a clear contrast to the typical cultic religion and to the Homeric Pantheon, and it is no mere accidental stroke of genius when Nietzsche speaks of the Apollonian and the Dionysian as opposite poles in the Greek attitude to life. The Greeks themselves felt the contrast, and probably wise religious politics were behind the introduction of the cult of Dionysus in Apollo's shrine at Delphi.

Greek mysticism was no more of a private matter than was official religion, and the mystic conduct of life was channelled into congregations, the mystery cults. Yet the purpose was the redemption of the individual. It is difficult to distinguish between the various mystical-religious currents. Worship of Dionysus was, for example, integrated in Orphism, so named after the mythical singer Orpheus who journeyed to the Underworld in order to conquer Death. But soon Orphism also became connected with Pythagoreanism, which is why this particular movement has been especially important with respect to the history of philosophy. Orphism probably arose in the sixth century and must be considered as a manifestation of general religious protest. There are but few early – indirect – sources (the poet Pindar, for example), and the Orphic literature that has survived, which sought to systematize the movement's world of thought, is late. Because of its ideas about the origin of the world and of the gods, it has ties back in time to Hesiod; but among other things speculations about a 'cosmic egg' (cf. Aristoph. *Av.* 693 ff.) suggest that there was a wish to amplify the analogy between cosmogony and the birth of a living being. More important, though, is the connection with the worship of Dionysus, for it is by its interpretation of man's relation to the divine that Orphism is clearly opposed to traditional religious views. Orphism is an individualistic and dualistic religion of redemption for the initiated. Man is an individual composed of good and evil. The human soul is not – as to the mind of the ordinary Greek – tied to his body and this world. The soul, the real man, is a stranger visiting the body – Plato reports the Orphic creed that the body is a prison, and Euripides asks – probably inspired by Orphism – whether that which we call death is life and life death (Plat. *Crat.* 400 C; Eur. frg. 833 Nauck). Life is a punishment for misdeeds in a former existence, but man has a hope of happiness in the beyond. By spiritual and bodily purification the soul may posthumously achieve salvation and be united with the godhead. In an Orphic text from the fourth century we are told about him who has escaped the circuitous transmigration of the soul: 'Happy and blessed. You shall become a God instead of a mortal' (*Orph.* frg. 32 C Kern). From a philosophical point of view, it is the Orphic understanding of the soul and its life after death that is of special interest. Seen in its social context, Orphism is one among many religions of salvation with a special appeal to those who are unsuccessful in this life.

In fact the new religious currents also reflect profound changes in the structure of Greek society in the sixth century. Already in the eighth century, Greek colonies were founded as off-shoots from the mother states throughout the Mediterranean. But in the sixth century these developments accelerated – economically, socially, and politically. Money economy replaced natural economy. In a number of city states trade and crafts became more important, but the typical city state – the *polis* – continued to be a city with adjacent agrarian areas. The increasing amount of trade did, however, result in new farming practices: cultivation of grain crops was replaced by the planting of vineyards and olive trees, and thus a city state was no longer able to supply its own foodstuffs. The deeply rooted Greek ideal of the city state as an autonomous unit had to be realized in a new way, and the lack of economic stability led to considerable social upheavals. The need for cheap labour led to an increase in the number of slaves, and in the classic Greek city state the free (but rarely idle) citizen's existence was dependent on slavery – often the number of slaves exceeded the number of citizens. But the balance between the social classes shifted in another way as well. The owners of capital – the *nouveaux riches* – outranked the old rural nobility and the smallholder. Naturally all this had political consequences. Sparta, which continued to be an agrarian state, preserved its ancient aristocratic government – the oligarchy. But the development in Athens was in many respects typical for the new city states. First a political compromise was attempted in order to correct social shortcomings (Solon). Next the social losers allied themselves with a powerful family (the Pisistratides), and one-man rule – tyranny – was established. Towards the end of the century this led to another reaction whereby tyranny was succeeded by democracy, the form of government in which the political and judicial powers are invested in the male citizens. There is some inner logic in the transition from oligarchy to tyranny, from tyranny to democracy, and this sequence of events lies behind later Greek theory of state, although it was considered in moral rather than social categories (Plato and Aristotle).

The social and political changes led, of course, not only to new religious movements but also to a new moral and intellectual focus and to reflection about norms that formerly more or less had been taken for granted. In the present chapter myth, poetry, and philosophy are dealt with as separate modes of interpreting existence. In the sixth century not only poetry, but philosophy as well, became emancipated without being severed suddenly from religion. In literature one poet after another comes forth and speaks in his own name. In lyrical poetry Sappho, for example, voices her own wholly personal feelings; her own mental states, her experience of love and nature are worlds unto themselves. But other poets – for example, Solon, Theognis, and Simonides – presented problems for debate. In Homer's idealized world the hero's moral obligations and privileges are consonant with his social status as a matter of course. But Homer is also able to distance himself from his ethics of nobility, and, for example, in the development of Achilles' character he reveals new norms. And in a world in which the norms have changed, justice or happiness are no longer concepts that are immediately given by things and society as they are. They call for reflection and the question of a higher justice. Here there are, to be sure, also connective lines back – to Hesiod, for example. But Solon and Theognis are typical of the sixth century. They speak from personal experience, but they do so with the authority of the wise man – Solon as the acknowledged sage and Theognis as the worldly wise critic. Their mode of expression depends on the *gnome*, which is to say the general apophthegmatic rule of life couched in imperatives or categorically. We know such concise rules of life from the maxims that are attributed to the 'Seven Wise', among whom Solon belonged, and whom the Greeks considered the forerunners of philosophy – maxims such as 'nothing to excess', 'know thyself', and 'let not your tongue precede your reason'. An example from Solon shows the combination of worldly wisdom and general reflection. First he prays to the gods for riches and honour and for his remaining a friend to his friends and foe to his foes. Then he proceeds:

> I do indeed want to have money, but to come by it unlawfully I will not allow, for the punishment for that will come afterwards in any case. The wealth granted by the Gods becomes man's enduring possession from cornerstone to ridgepole. But that which man strives for by hubris does not come in an orderly way. It follows only reluctantly, led by the deeds of injustice and mingled with ruinous infatuation.
>
> (Solon frg. 1,7 ff. Diehl)

One can juxtapose this serene conservative confidence in justice as being what it was with Theognis' protest:

> How can it be just, King of the Gods, that the man who refrains from injustice and neither transgresses nor breaks his word, but is just, still does not reap the rewards of justice? – How then can other mortals, looking towards him, have respect for the Gods?
>
> (Theogn. 743 ff.)

If one goes forward in time, one finds argumentation and debate. In a poem quoted by Plato in the *Protagoras*, Simonides (who died in 468 BC) debates with the old sage Pittacus: Pittacus said that it is difficult to be truly noble, but *I* say that only the gods can have that privilege.

Such poems can be considered from many points of view. They can, of course, be read purely aesthetically – but that was not the intention. They may be read as expressions of social struggles of the time. They may also be said to deal with moral philosophy. It is suggestive that in older days the philosopher's task was to speak of the nature of the world. But it was in the poet's domain to speak of what is good and evil, justice and injustice, and hence it may seem somewhat arbitrary when current histories of philosophy ignore the older poets.

Next to the poetry in which the sage speaks as an individual stands another Greek poetic tradition that in a remarkable way retains its affiliation with religion. This is the choral lyric and – subsequently – tragedy. In the choral lyric, which we know from all the way back in the seventh century (Alcman), poetry is recited by a chorus to the accompaniment of music and dance on the occasion of a religious festival. Often there is no question of cultic poetry or cultic act, but the religious tie vests the poem with special loftiness, and the poet's thought acquires a special dimension thanks to the chorus. The very mode of presentation makes the poet's I into a universal I. The religious dimension is further emphasized by the special occasion to which the poem applies: it is placed in a sort of eternal perspective by the narrative of a myth. This is best known from the greatest poet of choral lyrics, Pindar (c.518–438), who in his poems praises the victors at the games tied to the religious festivals (the cult of Zeus at Olympia, for example). Pindar connects a specific occasion with a mythical subject, which, so to speak, makes the moment eternal and thereby imparts to his thoughts on life, death, or justice an authority thus transcending his own person. This tradition survives in the choral songs in tragedy, but tragedy contains spoken verse as well, which is delivered by actors speaking as individuals. It has been said that in this way tragedy unites two aspects of early Greek poetry. As we know, tragedy prefers to take its matter from known myths and is performed in connection with worship (the cult of Dionysus in Athens).

It will appear from this brief survey that old Greek poetry did not primarily aim at an aesthetic experience. The poet is a sage and a teacher who speaks – or pretends to utter – the truth. It must have seemed all the more scandalous that the teacher *par excellence*, Homer, in fact told of something far from truthful – of the gods, for example. Already Hesiod seems to have protested against Homer, and in Pindar there is a brief passage about true and false poetry (Pind. *Ol*. I 28 ff.): Many things are wondrous, and in legends among mortals that transgress truth stories spiced with manifold lies may lead astray. The gracefulness of song can charm mortals with its sweetness and make that credible which is not. But the days to come are the best witnesses; and it is fitting for man to speak well of the gods. – The idea of the poet as the prophet of truth was decisive for Plato's criticism of the false poet.

And then philosophy emerged as a genre in the sixth century. The first philosophers wrote in prose, and thereby a good deal has been said. Like Solon and Theognis they speak on their own behalf; they do not disguise themselves as spokesmen of higher powers; they speak of a subject matter using reason as their criterion; and they can be contradicted. As previously mentioned, the oldest philosophers leave wisdom of life to the poets and speak about the world. But – to remember Aristotle – what makes them philosophers is that they do not confine themselves to asking what the world is; they ask why it is what it is. And they do not refer to some superterrestrial power or person; they do not speak of the god but of the divine; and to them it is the world that is divine. They abstract and generalize, and they draw conclusions from a general thesis. But although their subject is everything in nature – from thunder and lightning to the primary substance of the world – they speak as philosophers and not as men of science. It is reasonable for us to say that (natural) science consists in the formulations of theories based on experience, which may be confirmed or disproved experimentally, while philosophy concerns itself with that which transcends experience or that which is a precondition for experience, and therefore a philosophical theory can only be tested *as* theory or argument. But the distinction between philosophy and science did not exist to the Presocratics. The word *philosophia* itself, love of wisdom, is used as the common designation as late as Hellenistic times. The Presocratics, of course, proceed from immediate observation, but on that basis they are able to generalize with amazing daring, which is at once both their strength and their weakness. Their theories are speculative, and they would never have been able to verify them by experiment, even if they had wanted to do so. Their subject is nature and their mode of thought philosophical, which means that reason is their sole criterion of truth. This confident belief that the real is rational and the rational real is in itself precisely as irrational as a mythological account of the world. And in the sixth century nobody could know whither it might lead. Of course it is possible to see the Presocratics as the forerunners of science, but that would at best be a one-sided interpretation. Is it more correct to use the cliché that the Presocratics took the step from *mythos* to *logos*, from myth to reason?

The early thinkers reacted against mythology, not against religion, and the transition from *mythos* to *logos* was not a sudden one. It was perhaps never completed. Far down in history religious concepts remain a part of the philosophers' ideas. Many Presocratics apparently considered themselves as the seers and prophets of a new era, and it has been maintained that the earliest thinking should be considered primarily as a new form of non-institutionalized religion. Nor should one believe that philosophical argumentation came into existence fully fledged with the first philosopher. Deliberate philosophical argumentation was only developed gradually, and the *gnome* – i.e. the unproved general maxim – is characteristic of Heraclitus as well as Solon. The birth of philosophy does not coincide with the birth of the argument, but it is possible to speak of philosophy whenever a thought process calls for argumentation and might be presented as an argument, which could be contradicted.

It has also been maintained that the first philosophers basically ask about the same as do the poets and mythologists. They asked what the world is and how and why it has become what it is. But neither poets nor philosophers thought – as the Jews – that the world had been created from nothing. Many of the philosophers' answers are variations on very ancient religious themes. When the first 'philosopher', Thales, maintains that everything is derived from water, there are undoubtedly lines back to Hesiod, to Homer (Okeanos) and to many of the old Mediterranean religions (cf., e.g. the *Enuma elish*), and many of these lines have been identified in recent years. But the dispute about whether the first philosophers were champions of reason or shamans and prophets is to little purpose, unless one distinguishes between the questions asked by the Presocratics and the answers they provided. The real problem is whether Thales had a different frame of reference than Hesiod's and whether he thought in a different way.

If it is correct to maintain that the Greek philosophers of the sixth and fifth century began to think in a novel way, this implies an important thing: that the early phase of Greek thought is the only period in the history of Western culture during which philosophy was free of tradition and special terminology. Many of the Presocratics' problems may seem remote and strange to us. But they ask their questions about the world directly, daringly, and immediately, and – as in no other period – we are able to follow the evolution of philosophical language and its emancipation from religious language, the language of poetry, and everyday speech.

2

IONIAN NATURAL PHILOSOPHY

——— •◆• ———

The birthplace of philosophy, Miletus, was from the beginning of historical times a Greek settlement on the south-western coast of Asia Minor (Ionia). In about 600 BC it was one of the most flourishing trading cities of the Greek world, the mother city of a number of colonies and with trade relations with the Near East, the Black Sea, Egypt, and southern Italy. It was a wealthy and cosmopolitan city, politically independent and unencumbered by rigid traditions. Nevertheless, the city was forced in the middle of the sixth century to acknowledge the formal sovereignty of first the Lydians and later the Persians. But until the revolt against the Persians and the destruction of Miletus in 494 (the beginning of the Persian wars), the city occupied a privileged position. Prosperity and political independence do not, of course, automatically lead to cultural flowering, but it is clear that liberty and the close connections with other cultural spheres were necessary preconditions. It is no accident that Miletus was also the home of the first historians and geographers. A typical 'scholar' from Miletus wrote in prose, which means that he imparted information or presented theories without obligation to religious authorities or literary conventions. He was practical and engaged in politics, but he was above all curious – without an aim to gather riches and without visions of mastering nature with technical means. His curiosity was directed at the world around him – from the minutest to the largest. He was naturalistically inclined, and other religions were only of ethnographic interest to him – expressions of the strange customs of other peoples. What was most remarkable about a philosopher from Miletus was that he sought causal explanations.

In the two major cultural regions with which Miletus had relations, Egypt and Babylonia, no philosophy ever arose, even though they had evolved a fairly advanced practical mathematics – in both cases due to the requirements of their societies. Egyptian mathematics came about owing to the need for technical rules for surveying, accounting, stock taking, etc., and accordingly Egyptian mathematics had a clearly empirical character. A famous mathematical document, *Papyrus Rhind* (c.1600 BC), is apparently a sort of instruction book with concrete problems and presupposed procedures for solutions. After the middle of the second millennium, it does not seem as if Egyptian mathematics developed much further. In contrast to the Egyptian, somewhat cumbersome, additive decimal system, the

Babylonian system was a sexagesimal positional system, which probably helped to advance Babylonian mathematics to a higher level. The Babylonians employed equations of the second degree as well as arithmetical and geometrical progressions, and their use of fractions was more refined than the Egyptians'. As early as about 1700 BC they made tables with sets of integers that can be assigned to the sides of a 'Pythagorean triangle'. In astronomy the Babylonians reached far greater achievements than the Egyptians. They were familiar, for example, with the retrograde movements of the planets, and without knowing the cause they were able to predict solar eclipses. But astronomy was not pursued for its own sake. In their origin astronomy and astrology are inseparable – the purpose in both cases being the prediction of future events. It was – for example, for the sake of the making of a calendar – important to be able to predict the time of the new moon; it was important to be able to predict eclipses; and it was natural to imagine that all events on earth were dependent on events in the heavens. At the same time, the celestial bodies were thought to be divine, and hence the development of astronomy was far from being a process of secularization.

It applies generally to Egyptian and Babylonian mathematics that advanced methods and advanced practical techniques were developed. Nevertheless, if one cannot speak of a science in a strict sense, this is owing to the lack of logical proof and to the lack of generally formulated problems and generally formulated theorems. The demands of a real mathematical science were in Greece, for example, formulated by Plato in the beginning of the *Theaetetus*, in which he calls for a general theory of incommensurables instead of proofs that this or that magnitude is incommensurable. It is also to Plato that the self-conscious claim is attributed that everything the Greeks have taken over from foreigners has been brought to greater perfection (*Epin.* 987 D).

Thales – the first philosopher (from the beginning of the sixth century) – learned from both Egyptian mathematics and Babylonian astronomy. It is said of him – as of so many early Presocratics – that he visited Egypt. In the history of science he won great fame by predicting a solar eclipse in 585 BC, which he was able to do thanks to Babylonian calculations – and he was indeed only able to predict the likelihood of an eclipse within a certain period. He could measure the height of a pyramid by comparing the shadow of the pyramid with that of man, and he was able to measure a ship's distance from the coast, which means that he must have known that two triangles with one side and adjacent angles of equal size are congruent (cf. KRS 79–80). He is also credited with knowledge of other theorems, for example, that the diameter divides a circle in two halves of equal size, or, that an angle in a semi-circle is right. Supposing this information to be correct, it can be maintained that Thales was interested in solving practical problems based on theoretical mathematical knowledge. But what were his theoretical intentions? It is remarkable that the theorems attributed to Thales are quite elementary; they are intuitively evident, and they had been known in the Orient for centuries. In other words, he did not discover anything new, nor was he able to formulate any real proof. Perhaps the most likely explanation of his contribution is that he consciously wanted to offer generalized formulation of intuitively valid sentences. If this is so, then his originality consists of not being satisfied with rules of thumb, and his interest in general 'theorems' can then be considered parallel with an interest – which goes beyond mathematics – to discover general causal connections. For example, he explained the floods of the Nile by claiming that the strong northerly winds force the river waters backwards – an evident attempt to provide a causal explanation by means of hypothesis instead of a mythological one. Admittedly Thales did not verify his hypothesis, and he was, alas, wrong – even though he did think scientifically. Another example is Thales' claim that the magnet has a soul. Probably this is not some animalistic reminiscence, for his argument is clearly rational: by its own force the magnet can move, just like beings that have souls.

As will have been seen, the transmission allows us only glimpses, and we do not even know whether Thales wrote anything. In Antiquity a number of good anecdotes about him were current, but they merely show that nothing was known, which allowed all the more space for the invention of tales about this wonderful sage who was counted among the 'Seven Wise': sometimes he was the absent-minded thinker who fell into a well because he was watching the stars and sometimes the brilliant engineer who altered the course of the River Halys so that the Lydian army could reach safety. Still, not knowing anything about the man is not the same as saying that the opinions ascribed to him are mere fabrication. Aristotle did not know all that much, but he knew enough to single out Thales as the first philosopher, because he thought rationally.

Thales' principal philosophical thesis is that water is the source of everything. Aristotle carefully considered what this might mean. In the first book of the *Metaphysics* (983 b 6 ff.) he says that the earliest philosophers only supposed material principles as causes for everything. A principle (*archē*) is, in their view, that of which everything consists, from which it comes-into-being, and wherein it also perishes. It is the substance that remains even though the properties change. The substance in itself is, in other words, eternal; in an absolute sense there is nothing that comes-into-being or perishes. This corresponds with our (Aristotle's) maintaining that Socrates continues to be Socrates, even though he changes properties. There must accordingly be one or several basic elements, from which other things come-into-being.

Aristotle continues that it was Thales who founded such a philosophy. Thales maintained that water was the principle of everything and therefore he thought that the earth rests on water. Aristotle goes on to imagine some reasons for supposing water to be the principle of everything, for example that food contains water, or that the semen of living beings is moist. And, finally, he points out that the old 'theologians' also thought everything came-into-being from water.

From this one can immediately conclude that Thales extended his interest in causal explanations to include the question of the cause of the world as a whole and that he thought naturalistically, not mythologically. It is likewise evident that Aristotle did not have a text to rely on, that he is only able to guess at Thales' reason for choosing water as 'principle', and that he distinguishes between Thales' rational explanation and the 'theologians'' explanation, even though water in both cases figures as the progenitor of the world. It can also be seen that Aristotle uses his own terminology in his account. The word 'principle' (*archē*) may be a special Aristotelian term, but it is a common Greek word, which in a religious context means the beginning or the progenitor of everything, and quite early on – perhaps even as early as with Anaximander – it was used as a special philosophical term. Yet it is clear that Aristotle's use of the causal concept is anachronistic. Aristotle himself distinguishes between four 'causes' or ways of describing a given subject (the material, the formal, the efficient, and the final causes – cf. pp. 285 and 319). His thesis in the first book of the *Metaphysics* is that the oldest thinkers only 'knew' the material cause – and this is clearly unhistorical, if only because the concept of matter itself presupposes concepts about something non-material with which it can be contrasted.

Aristotle illustrates Thales' main thought with an example, which, although unhistorical, is still to the purpose. The example is the Aristotelian thought about the substance – Socrates, for example – that remains even though its properties change. According to Aristotle's understanding, this is also the case with Thales' basic stuff, water. Partly, this is the stuff of which all things in the world are really composed, even though things are different at first sight. The basic stuff is a constant or invariable behind seeming changes. Partly, water is in a temporal sense that from which everything came-into-being at some point in primordial times and that in which it will perish at some future point.

It is implicit in this that Thales did not distinguish between the question of what the world is (ontology or cosmology) and how it arose (cosmogony). If one peels Aristotle's special terminology away, he is probably in all essentials correct in his interpretation. It places Thales in the context of the religious tradition, and philosophically it connects him to his alleged successors, Anaximander and Anaximenes.

A detail can perhaps allow us a glimpse into Thales' way of thinking. Earth floats on water – and so the basic stuff is on this very day 'the carrier' of our world. But, as Aristotle remarks elsewhere (*De caelo* 294 a 28), whereupon does water rest? To this Thales might suitably reply that the basic stuff is distinguished from all other stuffs by being infinite, and that Aristotle's problem accordingly is a pseudo-problem. This would correspond with Hesiod's being explicitly on guard against the question of what was before 'first', and such a reply would be in agreement with Anaximander.

Both as a mathematician and natural philosopher Thales was clearly in search of rational statements and general explanations. However, it is not otherwise possible to distinguish the connecting lines between Thales, the mathematician, and Thales, the natural philosopher. It is not until Anaximander that we are confronted with a cosmology with mathematical focus. As a natural philosopher, Thales continued ancient religious ideas, but within a new frame of reference. He has no use for gods in a drama of creation, but there is, none the less, a religious dimension to his world. It is suggestive that he is said to have stated that everything is filled with gods.

According to tradition, Anaximander (who died c.545 BC) was a student of Thales, and it is in any case clear that they belong to the same intellectual milieu. Like Thales, Anaximander was an active man, a politician with practical concerns – for example, he introduced the solar clock from the Orient in the shape of a vertical stick placed in the earth (a gnomon).

In Anaximander we meet the voracious interest of the time in everything worth knowing about things in heaven and on earth. He is a metaphysician, geographer, natural historian, astronomer, and meteorologist all at once and also interested in mathematics. But in the end, what is most important is that all these 'subjects' seem to be incorporated in one comprehensive view, and also that we can trace the contours of a certain line of thinking.

Anaximander may well have been the first writer of Greek prose. Later on his work was given the standard title *On Nature*, and it was certainly available to Aristotle and his students. One sentence – the oldest in the history of Western philosophy – has survived. All interpretations of Anaximander rely on the reading of this sentence, which has occasioned almost endless scholarly scrutiny. In its entirety, the sentence goes like this: 'And the source of coming-to-be for existing things is that into which destruction, too, happens according to necessity; for they pay penalty and retribution to each other for their injustice according to the assessment of time' (Anaximan. DK B1; trans. G.S. Kirk).[1]

This passage does not argue – it postulates something. First a universal law is couched as a gnome. Then follows a description of the transition of things into each other. It is clear from other information about Anaximander that his 'existing things' probably refer primarily to contrasts such as hot/cold, dry/moist – although he does not distinguish, for example, between the property of heat and that which is hot. The cosmic processes are considered a contest between contraries, and it has been pointed out that this position later led to the classical Greek doctrine of the four elements. Anaximander considers this contest from a legal or moral point of view; a thing takes form, or a thing becomes, for example, hot. This means that the thing realizes one potentiality at the expense of another; in a manner of speaking, it takes something away from another thing. Yet the cosmic order is just. In due time, the thing will be punished, for it will cease to be, or it will cease to be hot. One might then imagine that what is constant behind the apparently chaotic changes in the world – which the philosopher looks for – precisely is the just course of the world, and hence that the constant is inherent in the process.

But this is not an interpretation without problems, for Anaximander also imagined a basic stuff, which he called *to apeiron*, the infinite or the boundless. This is that from which the heavens and the world come-into-being; it is the principle (*archē*) for everything; it is eternal; it surrounds everything; and it governs everything. Thus it partly has functions traditionally accorded the gods, and partly it seems to fulfil the same purpose as Thales' water: it is that from which the world came-into-being and that which the world really is. Still, it is different from Thales' basic stuff. Water is a known stuff occurring in nature. But what about the infinite, *to apeiron*? Aristotle offers several explanations. One of the arguments he advances (Aristot. *Phys*. 204 b 28) goes to show that the basic stuff cannot be identical with a natural stuff, for as it is infinite it would in the course of time have swallowed up all stuffs that are finite. There is a more theoretical formulation (203 b 4 ff.): any natural stuff whatsoever must be finite – i.e. limited and changeable. But the limited and the changeable logically presuppose a principle or a basic stuff, which is unlimited and infinite. A known stuff is finite in time and space, but it is also qualitatively limited by being x and not not-x. Thus it has both quantitatively and qualitatively a limit, *peras*.

---

1   It has been debated whether the first part of the passage renders the very words of Anaximander – as is here supposed (still, cf. p. 25).

Linguistically, Anaximander hence characterized his basic stuff negatively as that which has no limitation, *to apeiron*. Put in modern terms, this means that the basic stuff is infinite in time and space and is not conceptually delimited. The reasoning points to an abstract metaphysical conceptualization and thereby to a new, revolutionizing philosophical way of thinking. But it is conceptual thinking encapsulated in object-thinking. It is characteristic for early Greek thought that it makes the use of what we call concepts, but that a concept is not considered as a concept; it is considered as a reality, a sort of thing, which is merely radically different from other things. Accordingly, Anaximander cannot have been satisfied with a concept which points to a process of natural law whereby things in nature 'pay penalty and recompense to each other for their injustice according to the assessment of Time'. The things must, in fact, come-into-being from and perish in *to apeiron*, a stuff without quality and limitation, which surrounds and governs our world. Inasmuch as our world as a whole is also finite, there is nothing to prevent the existence of an infinite number of worlds in time or space, and such a view has, in fact, been attributed to Anaximander. If so, one might consider this interpretation of the fragment: it is concerned with the relation of things or worlds to *to apeiron*. The things come-into-being from *to apeiron*, but their very existence is an 'injustice' for which they must pay the penalty by perishing in *to apeiron*. Yet this view (*e.g.* presented by Nietzsche in *Die Philosophie im tragischen Zeitalter der Griechen*) is not a problem-free reading either, for the fragment declares that the things 'pay retribution to each other'.

Hence the conclusion must be that *to apeiron* has a double function. It is the basic stuff existing outside our world, from which worlds are created, and in which worlds disintegrate. But at the same time, it is a basic stuff lying behind the changes in the world: one thing is changed into another, but this is only a modification of the same basic stuff. It is worth remembering that the first part of the fragment contains a general maxim – which corresponds with Aristotle's characterization of the first philosophers' general understanding of the basic stuff, or the principle. Then follows an application of the maxim to one area: the transition of things into each other in our world. But the maxim can with equal justice be applied to worlds in their relation to *to apeiron*, and this relation is equally important to Anaximander. The fragment we have before us may have been pieced together from two fragments, in any case it seems to operate on two levels; that which is simple to Archaic thought, looks extremely complicated when expressed in modern language.

The theory of *to apeiron* is a theory of the necessary connection between contraries, and it is revolutionary, because it introduces a metaphysical concept, even though that concept has been reified. The theory follows the old tradition by saying both something about the origin of the world (cosmogony) and about its structure (cosmology) at the same time. But it is a further testimony to Anaximander's originality that at this stage of his system he is able to keep the two issues separate. We have but few possibilities of finding out whether and how Anaximander argued. But we are able to see that to a considerable extent he illustrated his thoughts by means of models, which means that his presentation largely consisted of analogies.

The missing link in the description of the origin of the world – or of worlds – must have been the qualitative transition from a metaphysical substance to properties and things. How does one get from *to apeiron* to the primary property objects, the hot, the cold, etc.? Apparently Anaximander solved the problem by letting some 'seeds' separate themselves from *to apeiron* (cf. KRS 118–21). From these seeds the hot and the cold, for example, came-into-being. It is not an elegant solution to interpolate a middle link, but the theory is interesting because it suggests a biological model. The world is considered a living being, and, like living beings, it comes about by a birth. The thought can be seen as a parallel to 'the cosmic egg' in Orphic cosmogony.

The primary property objects – i.e. 'elements' with 'properties' – are then placed in the sequence of earth, sea, mist, and fire. Fire takes the form of a series of wheels at the extreme edge of the firmament. These wheels are enveloped in mist or steam, but there are 'breathing holes' in the mist – and these holes we conceive of as stars! Meteorological phenomena are, like the astronomical ones, explained by the primary 'elements' – rain, for example, comes about because of the sun's effect on the moisture that evaporates from earth, lightning because winds and clouds (air and moisture) clash with each other. Earth was at first covered with moisture, but as the moisture gradually evaporated, earth became visible. This agrees with the thought that the first living beings lived in water. According to Anaximander, man has come-into-being from other species of animals, and he came late, for, unlike other animals, man requires a long time before he can feed himself. In a modern presentation it is impossible to do anything other than to leave the strangely and the acutely thought in these theories to stand side by side (cf. KRS 133–7).

When Anaximander comes to his second principal question, the structure of the universe (cf. 122–8), he employs mathematical models. The earth is a cylinder, the breadth of which is three times its height, and we live on one of the cylindrical planes. As mentioned, the heavenly bodies are large wheels, which we see as holes through steamy mists. The sequel, seen from earth, is the surprising one of fixed stars, moon, sun, and beyond the sun, one must imagine *to apeiron*. Our sources have nothing to say about the planets. The somewhat uncertain transmission seems to suggest that the diameters of the heavenly wheels were respectively nine, eighteen, and twenty-seven times greater than the diameter of earth. Anaximander's actual knowledge of astronomy does not appear to be equal to the Babylonians', and, while it is possible for us to understand what lies behind the biological model in his cosmogony, it is not easy to divine what lies behind the arithmetical series he assigned to his cosmological model. The decisive point is *that* he made use of a mathematical model. He did the same as a geographer. Anaximander was the first Greek to make a map of the world – in the form of a circle (one of the cylindrical planes), in which four 'world regions' are made up of four sections of equal size of a circle.

There is one point in Anaximander's cosmology where we can discern an original way of reasoning. Earth is to be found in the centre of the world, and it does not move, for there is no reason for that which is in the middle to move in one direction rather than another. There is considerable distance from Thales' earth resting on infinite water to this version of an economic principle: the simplest explanation is chosen, as there is no reason to do otherwise.

Anaximander's abstract-metaphysical insight was in a sense his weakness. The transition from a metaphysical substance to physical 'property objects' – the hot, the cold, etc. – was not easy to explain as long as the metaphysical concept was still considered a stuff, albeit of a special kind. Apparently it is this problem that Anaximander's student Anaximenes (who died near 525 BC) sought to solve. The outcome is a system that signals an advance in physics and a decline in metaphysics.

The metaphysical nature of Anaximander's basic stuff appears directly by the term 'the infinite', *to apeiron*. It is telling that Anaximenes uses *apeiron* as a predicate, for he uses it *about* his basic stuff. But the basic stuff in itself is a physical stuff, air. It is a principle (*archē*), and from it comes-into-being everything that was, everything that is, and everything that shall be. When air is diluted, fire comes-into-being, and when it is condensed, it becomes at first wind, then clouds, then earth, then stone (cf. 139–41). Like the other Presocratics, he did not think of demonstrating his theory by experiment. Yet he does refer to an everyday observation: if you exhale air from a wide-open mouth, it will be warm; and if you compress your lips, the flow of air will be cooler. Condensation leads to cooling.

Accordingly, Anaximenes presented an orderly series of physical states: fire, air, wind, clouds, water, earth, stone. So doing, he makes the theory of basic stuff physically relevant: qualitative changes are explained by their being referred back to quantitative changes. This is an initial step on the road to a mechanical understanding of nature – even though Anaximenes did not go the whole way. His basic stuff is still divine and eternal. It is the real essence of the world, and – just as Anaximander says of his *apeiron* – Anaximenes says of air that it governs and surrounds the world. His thinking introduces this difficulty: air is both the basic stuff and a stuff on a par with others in the cosmic process. If so, why could not one of the other stuffs be basic stuff? Neither Anaximander nor Anaximenes could have been content with identifying the constant, which they look for, with a process of natural law. The warrant that the world follows an immanent law is to them some kind of substance, and the theory is still intended to explain coming-into-being, existence, and essence for individual things as well as the whole world all at once.

Anaximenes 'discovered' the human soul. Yet an Orphic dualism was utterly foreign to the Ionian naturalist philosophers. Anaximenes considers man as but a small copy of the world at large. The soul is air and governs us, as it does the world (Anaximen. DK B2). There is no chasm between mind and outside world.

In his scientific thought, Anaximenes – like Anaximander – did not distinguish between astronomy and meteorology. But he never reaches the elegance and consistency that mark Anaximander's world picture and his use of models. He conducts his thoughts by loose analogies – as for example when he says that the earth is sustained by air, because it is flat as a leaf.

Ionian natural philosophy was quickly succeeded by other ways of thinking that posed new philosophical problems. Yet the enduring influence of Anaximander should not be underestimated, and it is not an unknown phenomenon in the history of philosophy that old ways of thinking continue to have their own lives and remain relatively unaffected by the fact that subsequent great thinkers – the usual heroes in the history of philosophy – considered them antiquated. As late as about 440 BC Anaximenes had a disciple, Diogenes of Apollonia, who in clear terms formulated the fundamental position of the old Ionians. He declares (Diog. Apol. DK B2) that all existing things come from one and the same thing and *are* one and the same thing.

The reason is that if the things in the world, which appear to be different, were not in a fundamental sense identical, it would not be possible for one to merge with another: earth could not become plants, and living beings could not come-into-being. Everything is differentiated from the same and returns to the same.

Everything indicates that Aristotle was essentially right in his general characterization of the Ionian natural philosophers. Each has his own face, but they move on the same horizon. Their interest is on the physical world. They inherited many questions from the mythological tradition, but their questions were posed in a new way. The Ionians inquire about a universal substance behind the seemingly chaotic changes in the sensory world. In their own way they thereby formulate the main problem of Greek philosophy: what is being? They seek the 'real' reality behind the seeming – and thereby the constant of matter, so to say – and they seek for regularity. These two things are seen as one; regularity is not bound to the natural processes themselves but to a substance lying behind them. A modern law of nature establishes a dependence which makes it possible to predict a future state on the basis of a present state – it does not reveal what the world 'really' is. But it is this that the Ionians wish to explain by their theory that any transition is only a seeming modification of something basal. One can only fantasize about how the history of philosophy might have looked, if the first philosophers had asked about process or function instead of 'things'.

The Milesians' confidence in the possibilities of human cognition is boundless. They are unfamiliar with special epistemological problems, and, similarly, they do not debate special ethical problems. Their visions within natural philosophy and their certainty that the physical world is an orderly world dominate all their thought. Their strength lies in generalizations and conclusions from quite general statements. To us these are hypotheses lacking verification – to the Ionians, however, they are theses – the correctness of which must be evident, once understood. The form of argumentation one senses in Anaximander and Anaximenes is from analogy – a feeble form of argumentation that demonstrates a truth rather than proving it.

The three Milesians left two special problems behind them, which later times must consider unsolved. In the first place, a substance-thinking that does not distinguish between things and properties must inevitably lead to logical problems. Plato puts the problem clearly (*Soph*. 242 D ff.): if the world 'really' is for example, the hot or the cold, how then do the three entities 'world', 'hot', and 'cold' 'really' relate to each other? Yet, the problem emerged far earlier than that – in Heraclitus and Parmenides.

The second question is: how can a stuff account for change and motion? This question was also crystallized in the later Presocratic tradition. Yet it was no problem for the Milesians themselves who did not distinguish between stuff and motive force. Original matter changes or moves by itself, a view that was later accorded the learned appellation hylozoism, i.e. that matter is alive. This is why Aristotle is both right and wrong in calling the natural philosophers materialists. They can only think in terms of stuff, but stuff is not in contrast with something else. This animation of matter can probably be explained by a still lingering religious dimension in the Milesians' way of thinking. There are no all-powerful gods doing as they please with the world, but the world is rational and the world is divine.

3

HERACLITUS

———— •◦• ————

Heraclitus (c.500 BC) was a loner among the earliest Greek philosophers. He came from Ephesus which, like Miletus, was a prosperous Ionian commercial city on the west coast of Asia Minor. Hence he belongs geographically and culturally to a milieu corresponding with that of the three Milesians. But in chronological terms he comes after both Pythagoras and Xenophanes whom he mentions. That he is dealt with here before those is because his philosophy can best be considered in relation to that of the old natural philosophers, even though he was in no way their pupil. He reinterpreted their ways of presenting problems, and he reacted against them. The mutability of things was a given fact to the Milesian thinkers. Their problem was not how things change nor why they change exactly as they do. It was the very circumstance *that* things *do* change that was explained by something unchangeable behind it. This was Heraclitus' point of departure, but he saw things in a new perspective, and thereby he demolished the older framework. It is at the same time characteristic of Heraclitus – as it is of Parmenides, his younger contemporary – that he struggles to make language express the new that was on his mind.

In politics, Heraclitus was an aristocrat by both birth and inclination. But Ephesus was governed democratically, and, while the three Milesians seem to have felt at home in their city, Heraclitus reacted contemptuously against a society that was not as it ought to be and against a world that had gone awry. His fellow citizens, the Ephesians, had best hang each other man for man, for they had evicted Hermodorus, the best of their men. Their motto was: nobody among us shall be better than anyone else (Heracl. DK B121). Elsewhere (49), Heraclitus says: 'One counts for me as 10,000, if he is the best', and he resigned an hereditary religious office in protest. His thought of the crowd as a tyrant anticipates Plato's. But like Plato, Heraclitus did not get stuck in ordinary conservative protest. Instead he found a truer world behind that which the crowd in its ignorance takes for reality. This may be interpreted as the aristocrat's recompense for political impotence, and Heraclitus participates in the older poets' search for absolute norms instead of a current justice that has turned out to be accidental and man-made. Seemingly, he is still moving on a political plane when he finds that it agrees with nature's order for some men to be free and for others to be slaves (53), or, that there is a universal law behind the plurality of laws – which has been seen as a universal justification by natural law of his own political orientation. But regardless of the extent of his political motivation, there are more profound dimensions in Heraclitus' thought. Where Anaximenes includes the human soul in an universal cosmology, Heraclitus goes in the opposite direction, so to speak, and 'discovers' perspectives in his own soul. As he puts it, he has explored his inner self (101), but so doing he found a law of universal validity.

Behind Heraclitus' words lies an unspoken 'one thing is necessary'. Therefore all human fussing and all human opinions are children's play (70), and he is filled with contempt for acknowledged 'lords' among poets and thinkers: Homer, Hesiod, Pythagoras, or Xenophanes. What he turns against is 'the learning of many things' instead of the one thing that is worth knowing. And although he does not directly refer to the Milesians, his attitude towards them is not difficult to surmise: they have identified a problem – *the* problem – but they have not solved it, and they have lost themselves in unimportant knowledge of many things. It is no accident that Heraclitus' interest – for example, in astronomy and meteorology – is quite modest.

About 125–30 fragments of Heraclitus' work have been preserved. Apart from one sentence, which seems to have introduced his work, all the fragments have the same linguistic feature: they are gnomes. Therefore one ought not to expect the work as a whole to have a continuous, argumentative character. It must have consisted of a series of brief and pregnant maxims. It has already been mentioned that the gnome is an ancient and cherished form of expression, yet nobody exploited the stylistic possibilities of the gnome or aphorism with Heraclitus' subtlety. His choice of linguistic expression is deliberate. The truth is to be found in the soul; yet the depth of the soul cannot be fathomed (45). Truth hides itself (123), and the sage – Heraclitus – does as does the god at Delphi: he says nothing, he conceals nothing, but he gives a sign (93). This means that Heraclitus acts like the poet: he shows, but he does not prove. The gnome is well suited to his purpose. Like the poem, it says something precisely, but often in an image, and it provides associations for the initiated reader that go beyond what is explicitly said. It is not without reason that Heraclitus was called 'the Obscure'. He wants to be obscure, and he wants to address the initiated.

A frequently cited gnome (60) states: 'The path is one and the same, upwards and downwards'. From time to time this sentence has been interpreted in different ways. It can be understood allegorically, for example, as an image of the passing life of the individual or of mankind; but probably the point is that it should be taken as a general truth, which the initiated can use for himself in whatever context he finds pertinent. The adage has precisely the same function today.

Heraclitus exploits the possibilities of poetic language. A poetic comparison can – for example, in Homer (cf. Hom. *Il.* XVII 132) – merely be a momentary illustration, or it can – for example, in Pindar (Pind. *Ol.* I 1 ff.) – balance on the edge of some 'theory'. Heraclitus goes further and lets his comparisons express a universal connection, but he does so without formulating himself in general terms.

In the introduction to his work, Heraclitus speaks of his key concept of *logos* – a word I shall leave untranslated for the moment:

> This is Logos, but men never comprehend it, neither before they have heard it, nor afterwards. Everything occurs according to this Logos, and yet they are to be compared with inexperienced ones as soon as they experience such

words and things as I set forth, when I distinguish every thing according to its nature, and declare how it is. Still, the others do not know what they are doing when they have woken up, as they forget what they did when they slept.

(Heracl. DK B1)

A contraction of the quotation will reveal a certain thought structure:

Everything occurs according to the Logos I describe – nevertheless, people understand nothing;
people understand nothing – although they hear;
they are awake – although they are as if asleep.

This is a refined application of the comparison: the ordinary person when awake relates to true insight, as does the sleeper to the man who is awake; a is related to b as b is to c. In subtle fashion antithesis is here combined with analogy: the opposition between a and b is analogous with the opposition between b and c, and thereby a connection is suggested behind the opposites.

If one turns from phrase to content, another subtlety is clear, for Heraclitus' mode of expression is a precise image of the actual ordering of the world: an ordered system in which the opposites are the outward manifestation of a hidden, inner connection. Heraclitus calls insight into this connection *logos*. In Greek it means both the spoken word and what is meant, and it has connotations such as proportion, order, reason, and rational cause or rational principle. Heraclitus plays on all these meanings. In the quotation *logos* means Heraclitus' own words, the cosmic order, and the law that explains the contrasts. This law is universal, also in the sense that it is common and immediately accessible to the man who uses his reason – and yet men live as if each had his own private understanding (2, cf. 114 – Heraclitus is punning on similar words: *xynon*, common, and *xyn nōi*, with reason). This idea is connected to an embryonic epistemology: eyes and ears are good witnesses, but only for the man who has reason and arms himself with the common (cf. 55; 107; 114). Furthermore, there is a built-in judgement of the crowd that hears, but fails to understand; the fool is there, but he is not present (34).

The idea of polar opposites can assume different forms. To the same thing can – in modern language – be attributed opposite predicates: the sea is healthy for fish, harmful for men (61), or – with a somewhat varied expression – mules prefer chaff to gold (9). In other words, chaff and gold are each by themselves both worthless and valuable. Or, as in the introductory quotation, the opposites can be placed in a proportional scheme: man is as childlike before god as the boy before the man (79); the wise man is before god as is the monkey before the wise (83); or: sickness makes health a boon; hunger satiety; weariness rest (111). While Heraclitus often prefers merely to point out the unity in opposites, he is also able to draw a general conclusion: life is death; waking sleeping; youth age, for the former becomes the latter, the latter the former (88). Here the logical aspect of Heraclitus' law makes its appearance. Of course he does not maintain that life is identical with death. He maintains the dialectical thesis that a concept implies its opposite: life implies death both logically and in fact, and it is therefore 'the same as' death. The thought – that a concept can be defined by its negation – was in the fullness of time developed further by the Neoplatonists and Hegel. It implies a very profound problem in the concept of identity itself: A is only A by virtue of not-A. With his flair for punning, Heraclitus is able to put the thought in this way (48): the name of the bow is life, its deed death (Greek *biós*: bow, *bíos*: life).

There are other – they might be called ontological – aspects of Heraclitus' law. He can illustrate the crowd's failure to understand unity in difference with the backward turning of the bow or the lyre (51). He can speak of the unapparent harmony that is stronger than the apparent (54), or about nature's love of hiding herself (123) – like the god at Delphi that reveals and conceals truth in his oracular language. And in one of the few places in which he attempts to conclude in general terms (10), we are told that wholes are bound to not-wholes; what is brought together to what is brought apart; harmony to discord: of everything one, of one everything. This may be read as an argument against Anaximander's thesis: everything returns in time to that from which it came.

The hidden harmony, the truth in the depth, is god. In Heraclitus' concept of god the contrast between the hidden and the apparent can also be seen. He rejects traditional religion and turns his own insight into true religion. Using an expression, which from ancient times was attributed to the godhead, he declares that everything is steered (41). The worship of the crowd is pure folly: to be purged of blood guilt or pray to a statue as if one were conversing with a house (5). But that one wisdom will and will not consent to be called by the name of Zeus (32). The true Zeus, or the god, is precisely the harmony between opposites: god is day and night, winter and summer, war and peace, satiety and hunger (67). If one does not perceive the hidden connection, one will call something just and something unjust. But to god everything is beautiful, good, and just (102), in later ages (for example, Plotinus and Leibniz) this became a frequently employed argument for the justification of the godhead (a theodicé argument): the meaning with the world and with life lies in the whole; what may seem unjust – if considered in isolation – is meaningful in a larger perspective.

The inner harmony lies behind the external contrasts, or – to use Heraclitus' harsh language – the common is war, right is strife, and all things happen by strife and necessity (80). Strife – the father and king of all things (53) – is a cosmic concept, but is at the same time the precondition for human society: some are free and some are slaves. When Heraclitus speaks of strife as the law of life and ties it to the concept of necessity, it is probably justified to discern a hidden polemic against Anaximander. To Anaximander, injustice is necessarily counterbalanced by the assessment of time, but to Heraclitus strife and inequality are justice and necessity. To him strife and harmony are two sides of the same issue. It is only when he is unilaterally regarded as the philosopher of strife and contrasts that he comes to stand as the absolute counterpart to Parmenides, the philosopher of unity.

Not all changes occur between polar opposites, nor do all contrasts arrange themselves in pairs. Yet Heraclitus generalized his law of constancy in changes. Everything is subject to change, not only when compared to other things, but in itself, and everywhere it holds true that A implies not-A. According to tradition Heraclitus is also credited with the slogan, 'everything is in flux'. We are unable to trace this tradition further back than to Plato (Plat. *Crat.* 402 A), but we can discern the basis – which has been preserved in three different versions (Heracl. DK B 12; 49 a; 91) – of the idea that we cannot twice enter the same river. We ourselves have changed, and the river changes, as it steadily consists of new currents of water. Clearly, here Heraclitus exemplifies a universal law that approximates the law of change between antitheses: both we and the river are changed – just as, for example (126), the cold becomes hot, the hot cold, the moist dry, and the dry moist. The image of the river raises a new side of the problem of identity: how can we justifiably speak of an entity in time and space as 'the same', and how can we claim that it maintains its identity when it notoriously changes itself from one moment to the next? In a special context, Plato (Plat. *Theaet.* 179 E ff.) lets Heraclitus defend the view that nothing preserves its identity, that every thing is everywhere and at any moment subject to change. In other words: there is no river – only coursing waters. Against this, Plato offers the criticism that any change presupposes that something changes, for otherwise we cannot speak of 'every thing' as changing.

There is much to indicate that Plato's criticism is (deliberately?) slanted and that Heraclitus might in fact have agreed with him. Heraclitus does not annul the concept of life in saying that life presupposes death. Nor does he cancel the concept of the river, but he maintains that it can only be understood as a tensional relation between the river as a unity and as changing elements, the coursing waters. It seems probable that the same thought lies behind this aphorism: there is a new sun every day (Heracl. DK B6). This can hardly be called an astronomical theory, but only another example of the relation determined by natural law between difference and identity: we do identify the sun, and yet it is not the same as yesterday's.

The river image is hardly to be interpreted as an embryonic theory of atoms. Its point is that in and by the existence of 'something' in time, it is in one respect different from itself and yet, in another, identical with itself. A river may change in a moment, a stone may be worn down in the course of centuries – and yet both river and stone exist. So, to maintain the identity of the thing despite its change may be a paradox, but it is no absurdity.

Heraclitus both narrowed down and expanded the field of problems of Ionian natural philosophy. As has been mentioned, he is not interested in detailed scientific speculations, but concerns himself with something other and more than the external world. The soul, human life, its conditions, and its norms – for example right and wrong – preoccupy him, but all from one point of view: the unity and the connection behind plurality and change. When he speaks of unity he most often uses the expression *logos*, which may be reproduced as both law and insight into law; he may also say harmony, and he may say god. The concept of *logos* – that reason, which at the same time is law, norm, and governing principle – has a long history in Greek thought, and in spite of all differences, Heraclitus would in his own way have been able to subscribe to the initial words of The Gospel According to St John (1, 1): 'In the beginning was the Word (*logos*), and the Word was *with* God, and the Word *was* God'. If one concentrates on the conceptual aspect of *logos,* he certainly went beyond the Milesians by thinking abstractly. He speaks of processes that are in conformance with natural law, but unlike the Milesians he does not seem forced to assign the process to an element. The problem is in fact more complicated than that – among other things, because to Heraclitus there was no sharp distinction between abstract and concrete.

It may seem surprising that fire, according to the doxographical tradition, to Heraclitus was the basic stuff, as water was to Thales, *to apeiron* to Anaximander, and air to Anaximenes. In one sense or another, fire was basic stuff, but apparently Heraclitus reinterpreted the concept itself. For the time being, and in modern language, we can say that fire represents the physical side of the concept of *logos*. Like *logos* fire (the thunderbolt) governs everything (Heracl. DK B64), and clearly there are in Heraclitus' understanding of fire as basic stuff some consonant religious conceptions of fire as a purgatory force, or of light as the giver of life. But the religious background cannot account for the function of fire – at most it can only throw light on it.

Fire can appear in a comparison: god is everything, just as is fire that is mixed with incense and takes its name from each individual fragrance (67). But fire is not merely an image. God is everything, everything is harmony, everything is strife, and everything is fire. In elevated style Heraclitus says: 'None of the Gods and no man created this world. It was ever, is ever, and ever it shall be: an eternal living fire, which is kindled in measures and extinguished in measures' (30). In part fire is everything, and in part it guarantees – just as does *logos* – that the cosmic process proceeds regularly. It is kindled and extinguished 'in measures', a universal law, which can be exemplified by the sun that will not exceed 'its measures', for otherwise it will be caught up with by the goddesses of revenge, the ministers of justice (94).

In one of his beloved analogies Heraclitus says that everything can be exchanged for fire and fire for everything, like goods for gold and gold for goods (90). In this case fire is probably not to be thought of as basic stuff in the 'old-fashioned' sense. Rather, the analogy states that fire is a measuring unit like money in exchange for goods.

In cosmic format Heraclitus speaks of 'the turnings' of fire (31): first it becomes sea; of the sea one half becomes earth, the other becomes 'burner', and earth again turns into sea in the same ratio (*logos*) as before it became earth. In other words: fire $\rightleftarrows$ water $\rightleftarrows$ earth. It is evident that the subject is the cosmic process as a whole and a general application of the thesis that everything occurs 'in measures'. The Stoics, who considered Heraclitus a sort of spiritual ancestor, went further and took this text to mean that the world – after certain periods – disintegrates in fire and thereupon comes into being once again, which is an interpretation derived from the Stoic idea of a 'cosmic conflagration' (*ekpyrōsis*), which is thought to occur when the once determined cosmic process has been concluded. Following this, the same process will be repeated. But Heraclitus probably did not think of a cyclic cosmological process. To him 'this world' is eternal, and he does not speak of a process that points towards a final ending. The same 'turnings' take place constantly; what he has in mind are simultaneous processes.

Inasmuch as the world is eternal, Heraclitus is not – as the Milesians – in need of a cosmogony. The world was not created at some point in primordial times from fire, and fire does not surround the world as some infinite reservoir. But apparently fire has the same dual function to Heraclitus as did air to Anaximenes: it seems to work in the cosmic process as a link in a chain at the same time as it is basic stuff. With

Anaximenes this is simply awkward; but Heraclitus seems to think more subtly. At any time all things can 'turn' into fire. This may be understood in a physical or literal sense: there is an interaction between fire and other elements, and at any time all things can be devoured by fire. Like *logos*, fire is hidden in the thing. But it can also be read as an image, for fire is like a process. It is its nature to be moved and changed – and thereby it is an image of motion and change: it glows, emits flames, and is extinguished 'in measures'. Heraclitus speaks of the world both as *being* fire and as being *like* fire. Fire is at once stuff, state, and symbol. It is not for nothing that Heraclitus is a poet-philosopher, and he has his reasons for wishing to 'show' that which cannot be said directly. To a poet an image can be both reality and symbol, and poetical insight sustains itself, in a manner of speaking, on the tension between what is said and what is meant.

All this means that the connection between fire and *logos* hardly allows of rational explanation. It is only a half-truth that fire stands for something physical and *logos* for some abstract natural law. Both concepts show the connection between what we would call the physical and the non-physical. And this connection is rediscovered in both the macrocosm and in the human microcosm, in ontology and anthropology. Man is a member of the macrocosm, but individual man is responsible for himself and is not an innocent victim of external powers – man's own character is his genius, *daimōn* (cf. 119). *Logos* is the common and is understood by the wise man. But the wise man is also he who – quite literally – has fire inside himself; he has a dry soul (118); it is the death of the soul to become water (36); and the drunkard raves in ignorance because his soul has become moist (117).

Wisdom is insight into the common *logos*. But the soul's dependence on 'the common' also shows up on the concrete level. The fool lives as if he had his own insight. He lives as if asleep. For in his sleep man kindles his own small light instead of that of the senses, and he is prevented from breathing the divine *logos* (26; A 16).

Heraclitus is also a loner in the sense that he did not immediately have pupils. Nevertheless, he influenced medical science and was parodied in fifth-century Sicilian comedy (Epich. DK B2). Plato mentions some extreme Heracliteans, although they may very well have been invented to serve special Platonic purposes. One, however, is known: Socrates' contemporary, Cratylus, who outdid Heraclitus' river image by proclaiming that it was even impossible to enter the 'same' river once, and he finished his philosophical career by refusing to say anything at all. He confined himself to moving his finger (Aristot. *Met.* 1010 a 7 ff.) – for nothing is permanent. This is not the last time that Heraclitus was to be made banal.

Plato used Heraclitus as he pleased; but he knew very well also that it was Heraclitus who spoke of unity behind all changes (Plat. *Symp.* 187 A; *Soph.* 242 E). The Stoics also exploited Heraclitus for their own purposes. In a longer perspective he was to Hegel – and thereby also to Marx – the founder of dialectics. But Heraclitus himself, the obscure, hides behind his *Wirkungsgeschichte*; his special unification of poetry and thought could not very well live on.

4

THE PYTHAGOREANS

——— •◆• ———

The philosopher Pythagoras once visited Phlius. The king marvelled at his wisdom and asked what sort of man he was. Pythogoras replied that he was a philosopher. Life is like a market at the great festivals, he said, some come to win, others to barter. But there are others who consider this nothing; they come to study and contemplate life – they are lovers of wisdom, philosophers, and this was how the word arose. The small anecdote (Cic. *Tusc. disp.* V 9; cf. Aristot. Προτρ. B 18 Düring) speaks of a new human ideal.

Pythagoreanism arose shortly before Heraclitus in the western part of the Greek world, in Southern Italy. It was a philosophical movement which – thanks to Plato – was to have indirect influence spanning two millennia. What is novel in the movement is that the Pythagoreans tied a philosophical-scientific position to a religious one and to a certain conduct of life. They behaved as initiates in a mystery cult, but can at the same time be called rationalists. Where the Ionians' interest applied to 'things' as physical entities, the Pythagoreans concerned themselves with the formal features of the essence of things, and they initiated a new mode of thinking, the deductive one. One of the difficulties with the Pythagoreans is to understand the connection between the rational and the mystical.

Yet this is not the only difficulty. The founder of the school, Pythagoras, whose historical existence is undeniable even though he appears to have left no writings, quite early became shrouded in a mist of legends. In analogy with mystery cults, the doctrines of the school were kept secret, Pythagoras himself was considered some sort of demi-god, and all views and discoveries were attributed to him ('he said so himself'). The Pythagorean Philolaus (c.430 BC) was the first to write in his own name, but the fragments with which he is credited should most likely be considered fraudulent. The school has a lengthy history, but those who after Plato called themselves Pythagoreans were heavily influenced by Plato's reshaping of Pythagoreanism and are therefore very doubtful sources for the early history of the school. This applies, for example, to the biographies of Pythagoras that were written by the Neoplatonists Porphyry and Iamblichus (c.300 BC); later sources on Pythagorean mathematics must also be regarded with considerable scepticism. As there are no direct quotations at all from earlier Pythagoreanism, we must have recourse to Plato and Aristotle. Plato is a difficult source to use, because he presupposes that we already know what Pythagoreanism is. Hence Aristotle is our principal source. Aristotle deals frequently and in considerable detail with the Pythagoreans, but within his own conceptual frame, and it is characteristic that he never refers to Pythagoras himself, but speaks only of the 'Pythagoreans' – which is to say fifth-century Pythagoreanism. 'The Pythagoreans' will in the following first and foremost denote the Pythagorean philosophy that Aristotle knew. It clearly contained older elements as well, but a sharp distinction between various stages preceding Plato cannot really be established. All in all, any presentation of early Pythagoreanism should be considered hypothetical.

We do, though, know something about Pythagoras – about his life and work and about the entire vision that lies at the root of what was later developed.

Pythagoras (c.570–497 BC) came from Samos, off the coast of Asia Minor. Like Heraclitus he was an adherent of aristocracy, and it should probably be seen as a protest against the tyranny on his native island that he emigrated to Croton in Southern Italy in about 530. Here he founded a religious community and apparently governed the city with a firm hand. This led to resistance, and he spent the last years of his life in a neighbouring city. But in the first half of the fifth century the Pythagoreans seem to have played a significant political role in Southern Italy, until the opponents once more attacked and killed most of the leading Pythagoreans in a fire. Only very few escaped and settled elsewhere in the Greek world. The resistance is not hard to understand. The Pythagoreans made absolute ethical and religious demands, and everything indicates that they did not tolerate political opposition. Behind this political attitude surely lay an ideological motive. In Greek 'aristocracy' means rule by the best, and the Pythagoreans wished the rulers to be a moral and intellectual elite. It is tempting to imagine that Plato's ideal state was inspired by Pythagoreanism – also because the Pythagoreans apparently lived a communal life. Their societies were religious, political, and economic communities to which women also seem to have had access. Prior to admission there was lengthy moral and ascetic training.

Some Pythagoreans may have felt the duality of the original ideology, and in any case tradition distinguishes between 'acusmatics' (those who follow the master's moral and religious commandments) and 'mathematicians' (those interested in philosophy-mathematics). Yet the fundamental Pythagorean vision unites the two aspects.

A series of secret prescriptions (*symbola*: signs), said to come from Pythagoras himself (cf. Diog. Laert. VIII 17 ff.; 33 ff.), has been transmitted. It is, for example, decreed that one must not eat beans, step across a lever, urinate against the sun, nor turn around as one leaves one's native country. There are further prescriptions for worship and purgation and bans on the eating of meat. Such prescriptions have a strange, primitive character with elements of taboo, magic, and ritual rules, the closest parallels to which can be found in the mystery religions. In later Pythagoreanism everything possible was done to interpret the rules symbolically, but strictly speaking there is nothing to prevent the assumption that from the outset Pythagoras' rules were of symbolic significance, sometimes so that a prescription can be understood as a cryptogram for a certain doctrine. Bans and ritual rules may have been elements in ascetic training, an outward expression of a certain conduct of life, and a sign that the soul is preparing to meet the divine. Or, one can suppose that old prescriptions deliberately have been used to channel the religious feeling towards an ideological goal. There was probably not a sharp demarcation between token and meaning.

We know the main features of the religious ideology of Pythagoreanism and know that there are close connections with Orphism, indeed so close that on many points it is impossible to distinguish. Like the Orphics, the Pythagoreans had a dualist view of the relation between soul and body and believed in the immortality and transmigration of the soul (cf. KRS 260–61). The soul was related to the divine, and the soul who in this life realizes its divine nature by the conduct of a 'purified' life (*katharsis*: purification) will be reborn to a better life, while the bad soul will be punished with a worse existence (for example, as an animal). Behind the doctrine of the transmigration of souls lies in part a belief in a relationship between all living – i.e. animated – beings, hence the vegetarian prescriptions, and in part a yearning for a union with the divine. But what separates the Pythagoreans from the Orphics and makes Pythagoreanism not only a religious but also a philosophical movement is that the divine is not a god but cosmic order itself (*kosmos* originally means order and hence an orderly world). It is man's task to gain insight into the cosmic order and thereby become 'well ordered' himself, *kosmios*; for insight is the highest form of purification. The Pythagorean ideal of science is thus intimately connected with a moral and religious task, and thinking is an existential practice. This fundamental view colours the Pythagorean tradition down through the centuries.

It is said of Pythagoras (Iambl. *Pyth.* 115) that he discovered the existence of a certain ratio between the pitch and the length of the string on a lyre, which can be expressed as a relation between integers. Thus the octave is expressed by the relation 1:2 (half of the string), the fifth by the relation 2:3, and the fourth by the relation 3:4. It must have been a revolutionary discovery that the basic musical intervals turned out to be reducible to something quantitative and exact – the numbers – and with the customary Presocratic penchant for daring generalization Pythagoras concluded that this reductional procedure has universal validity: all things are numbers. This sentence expresses the insight into the nature of *kosmos*, and it has both scientific and 'magical' consequences. In science the discovery led to the mathematical concept of nature, but the scientific vision is closely connected with numerical mysticism: the number 10, for example – the sum of the basic numbers 1, 2, 3, and 4 – was considered a sort of key both to the sequence of numbers and to the universe. To a Pythagorean it must have been a confirmation of the relation between man and *kosmos* that the basic mathematical concepts, the numbers, are both mental phenomena and constitutive in the macrocosmos.

The sentence 'all things are numbers' is the Pythagoreans' answer to the search of all the Presocratics for a constant, which was later expressed by means of the question: what is being? But the answer undeniably differs from that of the Ionian natural philosophers. Numbers are not a stuff; but what are they then? Aristotle clearly had difficulty in interpreting the ontological status of numbers in the Pythagoreans (cf. Aristot. *Met.* 985 b 23 ff.; 987 b 11; 1080 b 16). He can say both that in their view everything is numbers and that everything imitates numbers. That he is in doubt is owing to his own thinking of numbers as abstract entities and things as material entities. But such a distinction was not available to the Pythagoreans, and they distinguished no more than did the Milesians between thing and property. To them a thing can be identified with its essential and constitutive property. To the extent that a phenomenon can be reduced to or described by a number, it 'is' therefore number. A number is neither a concept nor a thing, but the mark of the being of the thing.

It has caused some confusion that the Pythagoreans used a geometrical numerical notation, in which the unit is indicated by a point (for example, represented by a pebble), and that they apparently assigned spatial extension to the point. But it probably does not mean – as has been supposed – that they considered a numerical unit as a sort of physical atom. For example, they reproduced the venerable number 10 with the following figure (*tetraktys*):

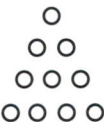

This illustrated that 10 is the sum of the basic numbers 1, 2, 3, and 4 (cf. Sext. Emp. *Adv. math.* VII 94). That such a pattern of points 'is' the number 10, means in modern terms that it depicts or reproduces the number 10, and that there is no difference between physical and mathematical reality. Yet a number can be 'depicted' or appear in several ways, and it has an infinite number of functions. The discovery of the definite ratios between the length of the string and the pitch shows already that the Pythagoreans were not primarily interested in the numerical unit as a point, but were interested in proportions or relations between numbers.

The Pythagorean theory of numbers most likely evolved from simple manipulation with amusing numerical relations, illustrated by patterns of points, in which the idea was that the same pattern can be read in two ways and thereby reveal a hidden 'correlation' (cf. Aristot. *Phys.* 203 a 10). A *tetraktys* can thus both be read as the sum of the first four numbers and so that the lines are added successively, whereby a series of 'triangular' numbers appears (1, 3, 6, 10 etc.). At a more advanced level, such numerical combinations led to the establishment of the arithmetical, the geometrical, and the 'harmonious' proportion and of arithmetical and geometrical progressions. Plato's contemporary, Eudoxus, was able to expand the Pythagorean doctrine of proportion by his general theory of proportion which is equally valid for commensurables and incommensurables, known from the fifth book of Euclid's *Elements*.

The remarkable thing about these discoveries is that the Pythagoreans worked with general formulations and with variables – in modern notation expressed by letters. The same applies to the Pythagorean theorem. As has been mentioned, it had been known for centuries that in a triangle, for example with the sides 3, 4, and 5, there will be one right angle. The opposite theorem – that in such a triangle the side opposite the right angle will be the longest – had likewise been known. It satisfied the Pythagoreans' predilection for numerical magic and mathematical thinking to formulate a general proof that the square of the hypotenuse equals the sum of the squares of the other two sides. Their proof is unknown, but the following proposal appears likely (reproduced from Thomas Heath, I, 149):

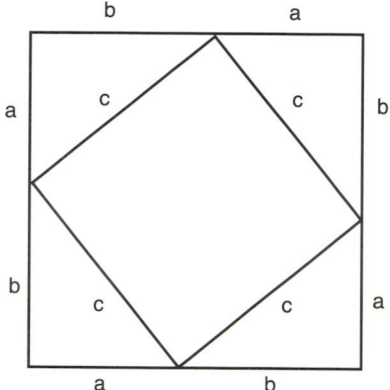 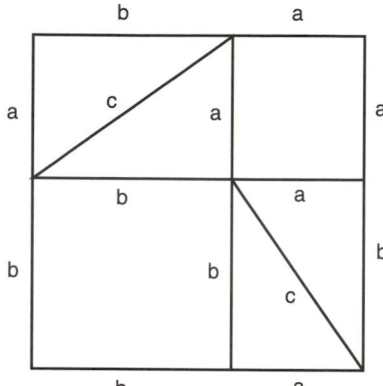

The two squares with the side a + b are equal. As the four triangles with the sides a, b, and c are also equal in the two figures, it follows that c^2 must equal $a^2 + b^2$. The proof presupposes the general axiom that if equals are subtracted from equals, the remainders are equal.

In a sense the proof is intuitive (*demonstratio ad oculos*) but is at the same time — like the preceding examples — generally valid, and it is an expression of a new way of thinking, the deductive or axiomatic, in which the truth of derived sentences, theorems, is deduced from the truth of an axiom. Yet another example is the theorem, which tradition ascribes to the Pythagoreans, that the sum of the angles in a triangle is equal to two right angles. We do not know to what degree the Pythagoreans met the classical demands of an axiomatic system: consistency, completeness, and sufficiency. But the deductive scientific ideal itself is apparently something new in comparison with the status of mathematics in Thales and Anaximander.

However, it is not plane figures alone that are determined by number. Three-dimensional bodies can also be determined by numerical figurations. According to Platonizing sources (cf. *Theol. arith.* p. 82 de Falco; Sext. Emp. *Adv. math.* III 19; Diog. Laert. VIII 25, Alexander Polyhistor), the Pythagoreans are said to have constructed the simplest stereometric bodies, the pyramid and the cube, by gradual 'addition' of a new dimension. Thus two points constitute the straight line, three, the triangle, and four, the pyramid (the four basic numbers). A point 'in motion' is a line, and similarly the line 'creates' the square, and the square the cube. Most sources are late, but it is probably in agreement with genuine Pythagorean thinking that more complex figures and bodies can be derived from less complex ones and that figures and bodies in the last analysis are 'created' from unity. This way of thinking is philosophical rather than mathematical, even though it is through a mathematical procedure that the Pythagoreans — if tradition has it rightly — constructed the five so-called regular polyhedra — regardless of the fact that these polyhedra were accorded cosmological significance by Plato and probably others before him.

If we wish for a more down-to-earth picture of how a physical body could be thought to 'be' a number we could mention that the Pythagorean Eurytus maintained that a man's number can be determined – say, as 250 (cf. Aristot. *Met.* 1092 b 8). It is, of course, nonsense to suppose that every point/unit is a physical atom. But it does make sense if one imagines Eurytus drawing connecting lines between 250 points that are so located that a picture of a human being emerges. To a Pythagorean something not-physical must also be essentially determined by number. Justice, for example, is 'four', because the square is delimited by four equal sides and can be divided into equal parts. In other words: in a square each gets what is coming to it! The method in the madness is, of course, that everything should be quantifiable – the readiness to generalize is unquestionable.

Everything can be determined quantitatively. Numbers and numerical relations 'are', which is to say that they are the principles for everything. Now, according to Aristotle, the Pythagoreans also asked about the principles for numbers, meaning that they asked what it is that enables numbers to determine things formally. Their irreducible principles were 'limit' (*peras*) and 'unlimited' (*apeiron*), or finite and infinite. These concepts are principles, not predicates, but they have the same pseudo-abstract character as *to apeiron* in Anaximander, and he most certainly provided inspiration, even though the concepts are placed in another context. For Anaximander finite entities are derived from *to apeiron*, and they come-into-being or are destroyed in constant interaction, while *to apeiron* is the basic stuff that endures and governs everything. The Pythagoreans, on the other hand, are dualists. The concepts of *peras* and *apeiron*, seemingly, function to a greater degree as metaphysical principles than as metaphysical substances, and they contribute equally to the characterization of any subject: a thing, a moral value, or a mathematical concept has each its own place in some order; but an order presupposes both something ordering and something ordered, something limiting and something unlimited. The idea can be illustrated with an example from music: a given pitch is a 'limitation' of the musical scale – considered as a continuum. A number is similarly a 'limitation' of an indefinite quantity, and a thing is a 'limitation' of an indefinite stuff. The theory is most persuasive when it comes to the division of a continuum into a discontinuous series (for example, the series of numbers). Yet, clearly the aim was universal: everything can be described by numerical ratios, and the principles of numbers must therefore be the principles of everything.

The basis for this account of the Pythagorean doctrine of principles is Aristotle (985 b 23 ff.), but it is necessary to remember that Plato provided the theory with a more subtle metaphysical form, and that Aristotle may have been influenced by it. Something indicates that the Pythagoreans had difficulties with formulating a coherent theory. In any case, in Aristotle as well, other speculations about the basic pair of opposites are transmitted, which cannot immediately be made to agree with the theory that has been outlined. Some Pythagoreans have juxtaposed ten pairs of opposites (986 a 22 ff.):

limit	unlimited
odd	even
one	plurality

right	left
male	female
at rest	in motion
straight	bent
light	darkness
good	bad
square	oblong

As it presents itself to us, such a table may be a manifestation of the need in later times to bring order to older modes of thought – always in the name of the holy number 10 – and if so, the intention did not quite succeed. Nor does the table agree with the theory that is paraphrased above. According to that, any entity depends on an interplay between finite and infinite, while the ten pairs of opposites divide the world into 'entities' that are either limited or unlimited. But there is another essential difference. The first theory makes *peras* and *apeiron* into principles for numbers and numbers into principles for phenomena. The thought of opposite pairs is an expression in a different language of the fundamental Pythagorean vision of ordering principles in all areas of existence. What lies behind seems not to be the formulation of an abstract-mathematical theory, but an older 'symbolic' way of thinking that views all existents as an interplay between something positive and something negative. 'Limit' and 'unlimited' are most likely the basic pair, but it was of no concern whether the remaining pairs logically could be derived from the first.

Finally, the concepts of *peras* and *apeiron* can appear in physical connections, which is to say as a kind of stuff. According to the vague information we have about Pythagorean cosmogony (cf., e.g. Aristot. *Phys.* 213 b 22 ff.), the world came into being when the unlimited that surrounds 'heaven' (i.e. the universe) was 'breathed in' and limited to a world of distinct entities. In the orderly world the unlimited is associated with the void that separates 'limited' physical bodies; for the later philosophical development it was to have consequences that the Pythagoreans accordingly accepted the existence of a void. Furthermore, there are evident agreements with the cosmogonies of Ionian natural philosophy – this applies to the original substance outside the universe as well as to the 'breathing in' that guarantees agreement between the macrocosmos and the world of man.

It is a flickering picture that the transmission of Pythagorean numerical ontology and cosmogony yields us, and only on a few points is it possible to uncover tendencies to an evolution of thought. The vision of numbers as the essence of things is clearly connected with the thought of the limited and unlimited as fundamental principles. Apart from that, we must content ourselves by registering different patterns of ideas, which do not simply make up an overall unity.

In two areas we are able with certainty to refer Pythagorean theories and ways of thought to some time well into the fifth century. This applies to astronomy and to the question of incommensurables. There exists an astronomical system, attributed to Philolaus, and definitely not older than his time (cf. KRS 446–7). According to this system, earth is not the centre of the universe. That is the so-called central fire. There are in all ten heavenly bodies: central fire, the 'counter-earth', the earth, the moon, the sun, and the five known planets, and the entire universe is surrounded by the sphere of the fixed stars. The nine celestial bodies move in concentric circles around the central fire, but both central fire and counter-earth are invisible from the inhabited area of earth. There is no reliable basis in the sources for the often advanced contention that Philolaus thought the earth spherical. Naturally the theory commands interest because it makes earth a planet, and although the central fire — not the sun — is considered as the centre of the universe, it is clearly a precursor of Aristarchus' heliocentric hypothesis and — in a wider perspective — of Copernicus' system. Whether it is earth, sun, or central fire that is placed in the centre of the universe, we are confronted with a simple ideal model with its roots back in Anaximander, one which, after the Pythagoreans, had to be significantly modified and expanded, but which decided the development of astronomy all the way down to Kepler: the idea of a spherical universe, in which the celestial bodies move in circles. Naturally, the circular motion explains the steady repetition of astronomical events, but it also reflects the idea of the sphere as the perfect expression of the finiteness of the universe.

The theory is a typical Pythagorean blend of science and mystical speculation. The central fire and the counter-earth seem among other reasons to have been introduced to explain eclipses. It was already known (by Empedocles and Anaxagoras) that the moon reflects the light of the sun, whereby it was possible to explain lunar eclipses correctly. The Pythagorean theory, of necessity of a later date, then supposed that not only the moon and the planets but the sun as well receive their light and so the counter-earth was a convenient explanation of otherwise inexplicable eclipses: the counter-earth, which was placed between the central fire and earth, could by its intervention shade the light from the central fire. But there are also other motivations for this cosmology. Aristotle sarcastically remarks that the Pythagoreans without regard for observable facts introduced central fire and counter-earth in order to arrive at the magical number 10. There is, of course, no empirical basis either for the tenacious Pythagorean idea of 'the harmony of the spheres': when the heavenly bodies move they emit a harmonious sound that we cannot hear because we are accustomed to it from birth! (cf. Aristot. *De caelo* 290 b 12). But the idea follows from the Pythagorean presuppositions: as 'all is numbers', there must be a connection between harmonious numerical relations in the theory of music and in astronomy.

The Pythagorean ideal of science presupposes that all relations can be expressed as relations between integers. Therefore it was no less than catastrophic when it was discovered some time in the second half of the fifth century that incommensurables exist. Thereby the entire basis of Pythagorean thought was gone, and apparently this also caused the gods to become angry. According to legend, at any rate, the Pythagorean who betrayed the secret died in a shipwreck (cf. Eucl. *El.* X sch.). What occasioned the abandonment of the Pythagorean basic thesis was probably the discovery that the diagonal and the side in a square are incommensurable — but it may also be that some Pythagoreans, for example reflected on the fact that only certain numerical sets can be assigned to the sides of a 'Pythagorean triangle'. That the scandal occurred so relatively late is probably owing to the Pythagorean preference for geometrical rather than arithmetical proofs. It cannot immediately be 'seen' that the diagonal and the side of a square are incommensurable. But, as so often in the history of science, the collapse proved fruitful. During the eventful period in

Greek mathematics towards the end of the fifth and the beginning of the fourth century the discovery in part had the consequence that the existence of incommensurables, which could not be expressed by the traditional numerical concept, was proved step by step. Yet the discovery of incommensurables is not just identical with the discovery of irrational numbers, and Greek mathematics tried to solve the difficulties by using the geometrical concept of quantity without formulating a more advanced numerical concept. In part, the discovery provided the Pythagoreans with the occasion to employ a special method of proof, the indirect proof (or the *reductio ad absurdum* proof). For if one supposes that side and diagonal in a square relate to each other as two mutually prime integers, the same number will be both even and odd. The indirect proof hence consists of the demonstration that a given presupposition will lead to absurd consequences, and therefore the presupposition must be false.

If we place the main emphasis on what from a modern point of view must be considered enduring gains in Pythagoreanism, we must, for example, credit it with the development of deduction and indirect proof, two forms of proof that are important in both logic and mathematics; with the theorems that with greater or lesser certainty can be attributed to the Pythagoreans; and, not least, with the establishment of mathematics as science and of the four basic mathematical disciplines of arithmetic, geometry, astronomy, and the theory of harmony or music. But it should not be overlooked that the Pythagorean vision with its special fusion of mysticism, ethics, philosophy, and science retained its influence all the way down to the breakthrough of modern natural science. This long line of development will not be pursued in this chapter; but it should be repeated that Plato – probably especially due to the mathematician Archytas from Tarentum – was heavily influenced by Pythagoreanism and that he influenced later developments to such a degree that it is most often futile to try to distinguish between Platonism and Pythagoreanism. Plato's *Timaeus* absorbed and reinterpreted a number of Pythagorean ideas and remained almost throughout the entire Middle Ages a bible of natural philosophy. But Plato's later metaphysics also continued a Pythagorean inspiration, against which Aristotle reacted strongly.

A younger contemporary of Pythagoras, the physician Alcmaeon of Croton (c.500 BC), was probably not a member of the Pythagorean brotherhood, but apparently he combined the inspiration from Pythagoras with empirical research of great originality. He transferred the Pythagorean thought of harmony to medical science. Good health was to him the harmonious relation between bodily functions, and sickness was caused by some disproportion (Alc. DK B4). The sparse information we otherwise have about Alcmaeon suggests that he must have been an – often overlooked – key figure in the history of both philosophy and science: he was probably the first to carry out dissection, he discovered the connection between eye and brain, and studied the physiology of the individual senses. Apparently he connected this with an epistemological concern; he distinguished between sensation and reason and voiced a 'scepticism' that is reminiscent of that of his older contemporary, Xenophanes (Alc. DK B1).

5

THE ELEATICS

———— •◆• ————

XENOPHANES

Like Pythagoras, his contemporary, Xenophanes (c.570–475 BC) is a connective link between the eastern and western parts of the Greek world. He left his home town of Colophon in Ionia in Asia Minor and settled in Southern Italy where he spent his long life as a poet and rhapsode. His poems – not all of which are philosophical – leave the impression of a straightforward, civilized gentleman, aware of his own worth, a person who thought about life in his own way. As a theologian and epistemologist his achievement is significant, because he asked questions about what had until then been left unformulated.

The thinking of the Milesians contained an indirect distancing from traditional religious views. The Pythagoreans gave shape to a religion of their own. Xenophanes was a philosopher of religion and thereby explicitly chose sides in the conflict between that which had been transmitted and the new; subsequently Heraclitus incorporated a critical philosophy of religion in his doctrine of *Logos*. It is not unusual to regard Xenophanes as the Feuerbach of Antiquity, as one who considered current religious conceptions as human projections. Yet he is no atheist, but he is indignant on behalf of the godhead: Homer and Hesiod permit the gods to steal and commit adultery and fraud (Xenophanes DK B 11); black people imagine that the gods are flat-nosed and black; the Thracians imagine they are blond or redheads. Indeed, if animals could draw, horses would depict hippic and cows bovine divinities.

Such an attack on anthropomorphic representations of deities voices a theory about the relativity of religious conceptions. Still, the divine cannot be relative. It must be absolute, and Xenophanes tries to describe the absolute. 'There is one God, the greatest amongst gods and men, although in no way resembling mortals in either body or thought' (23), he declares – and like later Greek philosophers, he apparently sees no 'theological' problem in speaking about gods, provided only that they are not mistaken for the one god. The one god is wholly vision, wholly thought, wholly hearing, and he remains without motion in the same place, because it is not fitting that He wander hither and thither; effortlessly He governs everything by his thought (24–6).

Ever since Aristotle – who did not have a high opinion of Xenophanes – it has been asked whether this meant that Xenophanes was a pantheist. Does he identify god with the world or part of the world, or is his concept of god transcendent? One should probably couch the questions differently. If his views are compared with those of Ionian natural philosophy, the similarities become evident: god governs the world, as did the basic stuff for the Milesians, and the world is rationally ordered; god is reason. These two things are connected, for if the world is not chaotic but rationally ordered, it must follow that reason governs; reason is not some neutral disinterested insight but rather a power. Xenophanes does not ask – as the Milesians do – to what stuff one can attribute cosmic government. He takes a step backwards and asks what is understood by that reason and insight that govern the world, and if that question is asked in absolute terms, its wording is: what is god? Now, it has previously been pointed out that early Greek thought did not distinguish sharply between a conceptual world and a world of objects, between ideal and material, or between metaphysics and physics, but problems are nevertheless dealt with which to us presuppose such a distinction. When Xenophanes speaks about god, he must use a pseudo-material language: god does not move hither and thither. But one should note that he uses this language in a negative way – he speaks about what god does not do.

We human beings are not god. If we assume an absolute being, we are in fact unable to describe it. Throughout the Platonic-Christian tradition the absolute is expressed in figurative language by attributing absolute characteristics to god which we know but imperfectly – or by negation. This is exactly what Xenophanes does: god is neither this nor that: he is wholly vision, thought, and hearing.

Xenophanes draws a consistent inference from this: god has absolute knowledge; man's knowledge is only relative. Just as he emancipated the philosophy of religion from natural philosophy, so Xenophanes is the first to pose a clear-cut epistemological problem; he does not ask what we know, but whether we know rightly. Xenophanes is often considered the first sceptic. This can be misunderstood, for there is an objective truth, and god's knowledge is absolute. Xenophanes' 'scepticism' pertains to the limits of human knowledge. We have only hypothetical knowledge; god knows absolutely (cf. 35). And although we may by luck stumble on the truth, we cannot know, because we humans can only form opinions. The gods have not revealed everything to us; yet, by seeking, we may improve our knowledge (cf. 34; 18). With sure skill Xenophanes here distinguished between knowledge – the cognition that is always true – and opinion – the cognition that may be true or false and which does not itself have criteria for verification at its disposal.

Xenophanes was a theologian and an epistemologist. Natural philosophy was of no interest to him, but he was indeed able to think in terms of 'science'. He points out that the existence of ocean fossils on dry land shows that ocean and land alternate constantly (A 33) – thus anticipating Nicolaus Steno.

Probably it was Plato who made Xenophanes the spiritual father of Parmenides and hence of the Eleatics (Plat. *Soph.* 242 D). Whether or not there was a teacher–student relationship between the two, this was probably justified. Parmenides' theory of knowledge is unthinkable without Xenophanes' as a starting point; but while Xenophanes searches for the absolute as a theologian, Parmenides does so as a metaphysician. What most profoundly ties the two together is their demand for unity and their abstract way of questioning. Both ask about that which others implicitly took for granted.

PARMENIDES

Parmenides came from Elea, an Ionian settlement on the west coast of Southern Italy, and was – as is appropriate for a Presocratic of the old school – politically active. He is praised for the legislation with which he is said to have provided his native city. His chronology is uncertain. Plato's dialogue, the *Parmenides*, is the most reliable source, and according to it Parmenides was born in about 515 and died soon after 450.

According to more or less reliable sources, Parmenides was an adherent of Xenophanes or an apostate Pythagorean. In any case he must have been inspired – positively or negatively – by both sources. What is far more important is that he encompassed the entire earlier tradition. He must of course have been familiar with Hesiod's mythological way of thinking; he knew Ionian natural philosophy; and he was most likely acquainted with Heraclitus. Like Socrates he broke new ground, and after him philosophy looked different. The post-Parmenides generation were wholly under his influence; Plato was profoundly influenced by him – especially in his later works; and it was still a matter of course to Aristotle to settle with Parmenides before proceeding to his own position.

The old philosophers' problem was to describe how our world came to look as it does and what it 'really' is. They looked for an invariable, and each had his own answer. Now, what Parmenides does is to penetrate to the presuppositions for such questions. He does not ask what 'the world' is, but what 'being' is. His answer is perhaps the most radical of any in the history of philosophy: only that is, which can be thought of without contradiction; but anything other than being can only be thought of in terms of contradiction; it 'is' one thing but 'is' not the other. The conclusion is that only being is; 'the world' is an illusion – to which Aristotle appended the comment (Arist. *De gen. et corr.* 325 a 16) that Parmenides sacrificed facts for the sake of the argument, something close to madness.

Xenophanes wrote in verse – which was his profession. Parmenides also wrote in verse, but in his case probably by preference. While Xenophanes was in doubt about the possibilities of human cognition, Parmenides – like Heraclitus – was not in doubt that he – unlike the mob – possessed the truth. But while Heraclitus spoke about the truth known to *him*, Parmenides received the truth as revelation, and hence it was natural for him to choose the same mode of expression as Hesiod's. In the proem to his poem Parmenides describes his journey from the abodes of darkness to light. The Sun's daughters guide his chariot and with gentle words moved the Goddess of Justice to open the gate that separates the paths of Day and Night. There the Goddess received him, taking him by the hand, saying: Thou art welcome! No evil fate, but law and justice set you on this path – for it is remote from the path of men; you shall learn everything, the unshakeable heart of well-rounded truth as well as the opinions of mortals, in which there is no true persuasion (Parm. DK B 1).

Whoever writes in such a way is not only a poet-philosopher who has mastered his famous colleague Hesiod's art so that he too can pass on a truth that nobody can contradict. He is a visionary poet whose imagery lives in its own sphere, one who surely has received a revelation that is superior to everyday experience. The visionary exaltation sustains the entire poem, however strange it may seem to the modern reader that strict logical thought is presented as revelation. But in Parmenides' time there was not yet an insurmountable chasm between poetry and thought, nor between rhetoric and strict knowledge, nor, probably, between philosophy and religion. The forceful argument and the reality it uncovers gave Parmenides a mystical insight that, in his own words, imparts to his words the force of persuasion – they are not only, by and large, true (cf. 2, 4: the path of persuasion 'follows' truth). Nor is it accidental that in the poem – not only in the proem – semi-divine persons occasionally appear whom one can only with difficulty make conform with a systematic interpretation. There are, for example, Justice and Necessity who guarantee that necessity really is necessary (cf. the Goddesses of Revenge, the ministers of justice in Heraclitus). Like Pythagoras, Parmenides has experienced the mysticism of thought, and this applies to his way of expressing himself as well as to his philosophy as a whole.

We should not ask who Parmenides' goddess is. But she has given him a table of contents. Parmenides is both to experience 'the well-rounded truth' (*alētheia* – 'well-rounded' anticipates the content of the poem) and men's 'opinions' (*doxai*). Thereby the two ways of cognition are indicated, which Xenophanes distinguished between – in Parmenides' words, two paths; that which is to be known is 'being' – but in a certain sense it will – as in Heraclitus – turn out that subject matter and method are closely connected. At a later time the poem was given the usual trivial title *On Nature*. Apart from the proem, it consisted of two parts, one on truth, one on opinions. Fortunately, so much has been preserved – especially in Simplicius – not least of the first part that we have a reasonable idea of the argument.

'The Path of Truth' is the essential part. Like Heraclitus, Parmenides has so much on his mind that he has difficulty making the language obey him – his style is pointed, it has its own knotty grace, and is a rewarding study for anybody interested in the interplay between language and thought. At times he uses wholly modern forms of argumentation; at times his way of thinking seems alien. One characteristic feature – familiar from contemporary poetry – is that the argument is non-linear, but in a manner of speaking radiates from certain recurrent key concepts. Parmenides himself comments ably on his thinking, saying that it does not matter to him where he begins; he shall always come back (5). This does not mean that his views appear helter-skelter. He emphasizes that one must judge with reason (*logos*) as criterion (7, 5), not with sensation.

'The Path of Truth' began with the goddess distinguishing between 'two paths' (2), there being no other paths to be recognized. One declares: ' "Is" and "not to be" is impossible' – this is the Path of Truth. The other declares: ' "Is not" and "not to be" is necessary'. But this path is impassable, for one can neither know nor express not-being.

Formally a fully valid disjunction is established between two irreconcilable theses, and it is clear that Parmenides is fully aware of the way he is arguing.

With respect to contents, it is natural to ask what are the grammatical subjects of the two theses. The translation looks strange, because modern languages demand a subject, while 'is' and 'is not' linguistically are complete sentences in Greek, which is to say that the subject normally appears from the context – but here there seems not to be any context. Fortunately, Parmenides himself comes to the rescue. Elsewhere (6, 1) he says: being is, nothing is not. In other words, it is not a question about something (an object) that is or is not; being is its own subject, and the statement 'is' is hence equivalent to the apparently tautological 'being is'. Such a tautology is analytically true and expresses a truth independent of experience, an a priori truth that is valid for all 'possible worlds'. It appears later that all earlier thinkers in Parmenides' opinion transgressed against the fundamental sentence 'being is', but it also appears that he does not consider the sentence void of content.

Parmenides exploited the possibilities in the Greek language of formulating what Hegel would call a 'speculative' sentence, that is, a sentence in which subject and predicate coincide and which therefore at once does away with the question of what is spoken of that is or is not. When Parmenides wishes to express his 'subject', he is free to use participle or substantivized infinitive interchangeably – 'what is' and 'being'. By means of his apparent tautology he establishes the existence of 'is' (being), and, correspondingly (cf. B2, 7), he concludes his way to a nothing that is not. He hypostatizes being and does not distinguish between the concept and that for which the concept stands. He is deliberately able to follow a strict logical method, but his logic is a logic of being, which is to say that there is no distinction between ontology and logic nor between subject matter and method.

So far, this is an analysis with a logical and linguistic point of departure. But two points have been left out of consideration. In the first place: what signification does Parmenides attribute to the word 'is', and why will he only speak of being and not of things that are? In the second place: the sentence '[being] is not' is false, because one cannot know not-being. Why this argument?

Later in his poem (6; 7) Parmenides unexpectedly introduces a third path. He or the goddess repeats that there are two paths and warns against the path of not-being that is false. But then there is a third path, which apparently not only is false but also absurd. Nevertheless,

> the ignorant mortals wander aimlessly on this path, two-headed. For bewilderment reigns in the wandering thought in their hearts, they are driven along, deaf and blind, dazed, a witless mob who believe that to be and not to be are the same and not the same: to them everything follows a backwards turning path [cf. Heraclitus' 'backward turning'].

Probably in continuation of this, Parmenides repeats his warning: one must not allow oneself to be compelled by the thought that not-being is, nor by habit and experience, (the third path); instead of sensation (the 'aim-less eye, the echoing sound, and the tongue'), one must trust to reason. He who possesses reason will know that he can capture the diversified by means of thought – as we are told in a fragment, the context of which is uncertain (4).

The third path is a logical absurdity, because it both says 'is' and 'is not'. But this third path – habit and experience – is the one we all travel. We maintain that a thing is, and at the next moment that it is not. We say that something 'is' black and that it 'is not' white – in other words, we say both 'is' and 'is not'. But Parmenides also attacks the whole earlier philosophical tradition. Heraclitus had built his entire philosophy around the unity behind the contrast 'is' and 'is not', and a linguistic detail (see above) suggests that Parmenides especially had him in mind, even though his attack was formulated in general terms. The Ionian natural philosophers maintained, for example, that the world apparently is as it is, but that it is in reality, for example, water or air – it is and it is not. But if what is is water, then it is not air – and if so, what is it then that is identified with something else? In Parmenides' view the philosopher in other words thinks more illogically than the man in the street, because he has at his disposal an absolute concept without using it absolutely. One must follow logic and reason; ergo the world is – both as it appears immediately and as the philosophers interpret it – an illusion, for there is no world of things with changing properties nor a world that both is as it appears and something else behind it. Only being is.

In other words, Parmenides demands partly that a sentence always be true and partly that the word 'is' have one and only one meaning. From modern points of view it is often maintained that Parmenides fails to distinguish between 'is' in its existential and copulative meanings; the sentences 'x is', 'x is black', and 'x is not white' are not at odds with one another – still from modern points of view. Parmenides, of course, does not know of this distinction; but this does not mean that he reasons primitively. Apparently he distinguishes between 'is', used absolutely, and 'is' with incomplete application, which is to say in subject-predicate sentences (x is y). Now, any empirical subject-predicate sentence states something about something that might be different, and therefore it does not honour Parmenides' strict demands for constancy and self-identity. Every sentence that attributes a property to a thing is absurd, and, even more rigorously, every sentence about a thing is absurd, because a thing both 'is' (this and that) and 'is not' (this and that). Thereby existential sentences about things also become vulnerable. All that is left is the absolute use of 'is' in the sentence 'being is', in which subject and 'predicate' stand for the same and in addition only such sentences as may follow from it.

This means that Parmenides stands as the initiator of that long, speculative tradition, which without recourse to experience investigates being as an absolute concept. But he is more radical than that: that any sentence about a thing is absurd implies for him that the concept of thing is absurd, and that things simply do not exist. This thought, which directly cancels out the whole empirical world, became a well-nigh insurmountable challenge to the generations that followed him. Today it may also constitute a challenge, if one for example asks what 'is' means in a copulative sentence. Ever since Aristotle (Aristot. *Phys.* 186 a 22), Parmenides has often been summarily dismissed and blamed because he hypostatized and failed to acknowledge that a word may have several meanings or that a concept may have several instances. But this is a *petitio principii*, which presupposes that the empirical world is given and that a thing has properties.

It will be seen that to Parmenides expression, concept, and reality are closely connected. In the opening disjunction he maintained that it is untrue that being is not, because one cannot know or speak about not-being. To Parmenides 'is' denotes both being and truth. At one point (Parm. DK B3) he says (the exact translation is disputed):[1] 'Thought and being are the same'; elsewhere (8, 34) he similarly identifies thought with its object and calls thought the expression of being. With this, Parmenides does not say that thought constitutes the world and that we accordingly construct our world, but rather that thought is a manifestation of being; it is known or true being. This implies that a sentence that has been validated by reason immediately points towards a 'true' reality; being is a necessary precondition for thought, and correct thinking is a sufficient precondition for being. There are, of course, false sentences – as was made abundantly clear. But Parmenides conceives of cognition as a direct contact with the object of cognition. When I know, I know x, not some statement about x. In a wider historical perspective, Parmenides is the author of the concept of ontological truth and the thought that absolute knowledge and absolute being coincide. In regard to this point he had profound influence on Plato and, indirectly, for example on Anselm of Canterbury and Hegel.

The sentence 'being is' is accordingly no mere tautology. 'To be', according to ancient Greek thought, means the same as 'to be something', and being therefore implies more than mere existence. The sentence is informative, and the content Parmenides seeks to deduce from it can be seen in a long surviving fragment (8). He speaks of being as having many 'signs', and it seems natural to the modern reader to read this so that from the very concept of being one can deduce a series of fixed predicates of being. In this long passage there is a series of partial arguments that clearly can be described as deduction or *reductio ad absurdum*, but on the whole – and from modern points of view – the passage defies logical analysis. What in one partial argument may function as a premise, appears in the next as a conclusion, and Parmenides seems to have been true to his principle: it matters not where he begins, for he will come back. Apparently there is mutual dependence between the several 'signs', which should be obvious to anybody who thinks his way through the concept of being, and there is in fact no question of deduction but of conceptual analysis. What the 'predicates', which Parmenides attributes to the absolute, have in common is that they express something perfect, or that they deny: being is imperishable, indivisible, unchangeable, and perfect; this sort of predicate was the only one he acknowledged. In other words, Parmenides follows Xenophanes. In the following, some key predicates and a few partial arguments will be emphasized.

Being is, not-being is not. It follows from this (8, 3 ff.) that being is eternal; it neither comes into existence, nor does it perish. This is demonstrated in two ways. In the first place by means of an indirect proof: being could only come into existence from not-being, but being cannot come into existence from not-being, nor can it perish in not-being – which is implicitly an application of the principle that 'nothing will come from nothing' (*ex nihilo nihil*) and its correlative, 'nothing perishes in nothing', a principle that actually by unspoken consent had been presupposed in all earlier thought. In the second place, Parmenides uses the same form of argument that Anaximander had used in order to prove that the earth is the centre of the universe:

---

1   The current English translation – 'the same thing is there to be thought of and to be' – is linguistically possible, but seems to introduce a special 'thing' besides thought and being.

there is no reason for being to arise at one particular moment rather than any other. Thereby Parmenides has hardly cancelled the concept of time, but he has shown that being is eternal, that it is unchangeable *in* time: 'Thus becoming has been extinguished and perishing unheard of'. He also accounts for being as a spatially coherent unity. Nothing can arise from not-being: therefore nothing can come into being or exist 'next to' being, which must be indivisible, homogeneous, and preclude the existence of something not-being (a void) that would separate being from being. Just as being as a continuum, so to speak, fills both time and space, it is implicit that one cannot conceptually imagine anything other than being.

An unchangeable time-space continuum is, like Xenophanes' god, without motion (8, 26 ff.), for motion is change and presupposes a something 'next to' absolute being. It follows from the concept of perfection that being must be self-sufficient; it is confined in itself, which Parmenides expresses by saying that it remains in itself, kept in great bonds of 'Necessity'. This may surprise, but on Parmenides' premises it is a consistent conclusion that being is finite or limited. It applies to this argument, as it does to all of Parmenides' thought, that the formulation has a general aim, even though it does contain a pointed sting aimed at the Pythagoreans: a dualism – between limited and unlimited, rest and motion, filled space and empty space – is irreconcilable with the concept of being as absolute. An absolute entity must be finite; beyond the limit there is nothing.

With his conclusion about the immovable being Parmenides reaches a high point. As suggested, his concept of being may be considered a continuation and a metaphysical 'translation' of Xenophanes' concept of god, the one immovable god who is all thought. Against this background it is not particularly strange that Parmenides – immediately following his demonstration that being is imperishable, indivisible, unchangeable, and one – places one of his passages about the identity of being and thought (8, 34 ff.). His general epistemological position has been discussed. Here it should be noted that he considers thought the direct consequence of the perfection of being. Were thought not 'identical with' being, there would be something next to being. In other words, Parmenides does not exclusively consider cognition as the relation of a subject to an object, but primarily as something ontological. Opposed to true knowledge stands what mortals conceive of as true, but which in fact are merely 'names'.

Parmenides concludes his lengthy description of being (8, 42 ff.) with a finale that may surprise the modern reader. He says that being is like a 'well-rounded ball'. Being is in fact limited, and being everywhere it impinges equally on being – any point on the surface of a ball is equidistant from the centre, and the ball is therefore the perfect tri-dimensional body.

What immediately strikes the modern reader is that Parmenides on the one hand conceives of being as a quite abstract, metaphysical notion, placing it on the other hand in time and space and describing it in concrete terms. Is he speaking about concept or thing; is he a materialist or an idealist? Without doubt the question is anachronistic, and there is a certain – although imperfect – analogy with the problem of Heraclitus conceiving of fire as a stuff or his not doing so. It would be a strange materialism to deny the validity of sense-perception and the existence of the world of sense and to point to reason as the sole source of knowledge. On the other hand, the concrete-materialistic language is undeniable, even though it should be noted that Parmenides is aware that he uses figurative language: being is *like* a ball. In fact he makes more acute a problem, which had been latent in the tradition since Anaximander. Being functions as a concept – and *qua* concept it must be finite – although in early thought everything is considered – more or less directly – temporal and spatial. Plato is the first to speak of being beyond time and space, and Aristotle is the first who decisively liberates himself from the idea of concept as a 'thing' of superior order. The concept is used, before it is understood as a concept. It is no accident that Parmenides, besides being an astute logician and profound metaphysician, is a visionary poet who, so to speak, watches his concept take form. There is nothing nonsensical in the depiction of being concluding in the 'well-rounded truth', which the goddess proclaimed as she began her revelation. Still, it did raise problems.

Having depicted the truth, the goddess proceeds with 'deceitful words' to describe the opinions of mortals (8, 53 ff.) – apparently on the grounds that Parmenides should not be less favoured than other mortals when they discuss the visible world, its construction, and coming into being. Nevertheless, here as well Parmenides generalizes his argument and does not present it as his own or the goddess' theory which one may, if so inclined, compare with other theories. His discourse applies to what mortals have made up their minds to opine – this probably refers to 'the third path' – as it has to be formulated, if need be. If one accepts a world of sense, then one concept is not a sufficient explanation. It is necessary – as it was, for example, for the Pythagoreans – to base it on a dualistic view and account for the changeable world of sense as a shift or interplay between contraries that – as for example in Heraclitus – mutually presuppose each other. To Parmenides crucial pairs of contraries are light versus darkness and dense versus rare.

On this basis he apparently explained the construction of both the world and man. Not many fragments from the second part of the poem have been preserved, and so Parmenides' precise views are unclear, and, against the background of the then general ideas, they do not seem to have been particularly original. Here only a few details will be mentioned. Parmenides' cosmology was a system of concentric rings consisting of light and darkness and an 'admixture'. Probably there is a connection between this system and late Pythagorean cosmology. But it would appear that Parmenides is special in allowing a female divinity to reside at the centre of the universe. It is she who is responsible for world order and sees to the propagation of mankind by Eros – but she is, of course, a quite different goddess from the goddess who provides Parmenides with his revelation.

Man also functions properly on the basis of the right 'admixture' of contraries. This holds for human cognition as well. The cognition spoken of in the 'Path of Truth' is a function of true being; the cognition that man has recourse to in his world of seeming depends on his physical constitution (16).

What is more interesting than these details is the question of why the goddess also instructs Parmenides about the false world and false cognition; the reason cannot merely be to get the upper hand in a debate. The reason must be that Parmenides deliberately sought to let the contrast between the true and the false world remain unexplained. There is not, nor can there be, any connection between deductive, a priori, rational knowledge and cognition by sense-perception, which always depends on hypotheses and which therefore at most has conditional validity. Yet, thereby not all is said. Given the intimate connection Parmenides sees between cognition and its object, it is also impossible to imagine any reconciliation between the world that reason knows and the world accessible to sensation. There is a true and a false world, not one world intelligible by different methods. The contrast is not to be explained away; it is to be demonstrated.

Parmenides is a milestone in Greek thought as a logician, epistemologist, and metaphysician – to him three aspects of the same thing. He argued according to a fixed logical pattern; he reflected on the relation between cognition and reality; and as a metaphysician he introduced the idea of absolute being. He accomplished all this by thinking his way through the conceptual presuppositions of all earlier thought in such a way that he invalidated the earlier tradition from within. He left philosophy in a dilemma – which probably was exactly what he intended. Either all further philosophy must be abandoned and the paradox be acknowledged that all pure, rational thought leads to mysticism, or else reason and experience must be combined in order to create new ways of thought.

It appears that Parmenides' system became the subject of debate at once. The epistemological and metaphysical perspectives in his thought probably did not make their mark until Plato. What preoccupied the generation after Parmenides were two questions especially: one was whether it was possible to combine reason and experience and another the ontological status of the Parmenidean concept of being – what could be done with a unity existing in time and space and yet one which could not be sensed, which is indivisible and without motion?

Parmenides' own pupils, Zeno and Melissus, took part in this debate, but apparently did so with the main goal of defending and explaining their master; Zeno acted upon the motto that attack is the best defence. Their relatively restricted aim in no way makes them secondary figures. They speak the language of a new generation, and Zeno at any rate has been provocatory even down to our own day. They abandoned Parmenides' visionary, poetical style and placed some of his basic views in a new light.

ZENO

Zeno was born in c.490 BC in Elea, Parmenides' native city. According to Plato (*Parm.* 127 D ff.) he wrote a book with the intention of defending Parmenides' One Being, showing that it will lead to absurd consequences to assume the existence of a plurality; what has been preserved of this work only confirms the characterization. It is perhaps worthwhile to note that the emphasis has been changed from being to unity.

Seemingly the work was strictly constructed and consisted of a lengthy series of arguments, identically structured, in which the opponent's views are assumed as premises, which are then shown to imply contradictory conclusions. The most important of the surviving fragments disprove the existence of plurality and motion, but in fact they deal with the same questions. They are closely tied to Parmenides' claim that being is indivisible and without motion, and the form of argument (*reductio ad absurdum*) had likewise — as previously mentioned — been employed by Parmenides. What is original in Zeno are profound analyses of such concepts as divisibility, continuum, and infinity as well as his subtle application of the indirect proof. In both areas there is an evident, close connection with contemporary mathematics, even though we know so little about the development of mathematics that we cannot decide whether it was mathematics or philosophy that contributed more.

It is often claimed that Zeno attacked 'the Pythagoreans' who in their turn supposedly had reacted against Parmenides. On certain points the Pythagoreans are doubtless the targets, but, like his teacher and all other Presocratics, Zeno was arguing in general terms, and without doubt his attack was aimed at all those who supported the existence of plurality or motion. A general presupposition for Zeno's polemics is most likely the discovery of incommensurables — which must have been unknown to Parmenides.

An argument against plurality will prove that plurality will be both infinitely large and infinitely small. This argument has been preserved by Simplicius (Zeno DK B1–2) who mixed paraphrase with quotations and apparently also moved the individual links in the argument around. (The following is based on Herman Fränkel's reconstruction.) The main structure of the argument may be reproduced as follows:

Any given plurality must be divisible and hence consist of parts.

a)   If every single part is indivisible, it cannot have extension; but that which has no extension, does not exist. It can neither augment nor diminish something existing, if added or subtracted.
b)   If every single part is divisible, it has extension, and its individual parts must also be divisible and have extension — and so forth *ad infinitum* so that there will be no final part.

Conclusion: a plurality will be both so small that it has no extension and so large that it is infinite.

Each of the two limbs leads to a conclusion, which the opponent is unwilling to accept (*modus tollens*), and the whole argument is a *reductio ad absurdum*, because it leads to a self-contradictory conclusion. Yet it should be noted that this is only the case if both limbs are accepted and if the argument is not taken to be a disjunction.

It goes without saying that the truth of an argument does not depend merely on the form of the argument but on the truth of the premises as well. The argument presupposes some premises that can be formulated as follows:

1   The sum of an infinite number of entities of arbitrary, small extension is infinitely large.
2   The sum of an infinite number of entities without extension is 0.
3   If a division of a given, finite entity were 'carried through', the result would be 0.

There is reason to believe that these hidden 'axioms' were considered true at the time. The first and the third are false, but views such as those gave impetus to work with infinitesimals in Greek mathematics and thereby to the earliest historical presupposition for the emergence of the infinitesimal calculus of the seventeenth century.

It is probably immediately evident that the plurality which Zeno 'does away with' as easily can be considered mathematical as physical – a section of a line, for example, is 'non-existent' if it consists of an infinite number of points without extension, and infinitely large if it consists of an infinite number of points with extension. But it is worthwhile to emphasize that Zeno is fighting against an understanding of existence, which he himself does not share, and that he finds the current concepts of plurality and unity self-contradictory. The uncertain transmission suggests (2) that he himself would acknowledge an entity without extension, and if this is true, it means that he performed a radical change vis-à-vis his master on a point, which to his contemporaries must have seemed equally unclear.

The logical difficulties in connection with divisibility are tied to the logical discrepancy between a continuum and a discontinued series. This part of the problem emerges especially in an argument in which Zeno maintains that a plurality consisting of unities must be both limited (finite) and unlimited (infinite), and that this is logically contradictory. The argument (3) is formally constructed like the preceding one and states that a plurality a) must consist of as many parts as it actually consists of – the parts must in other words in principle be countable just as is a given series of integers. But b) there will always be something 'between the parts' – a continuum consists of an infinite number of parts. Consequently a plurality is both finite and infinite.

Motion is a sort of change that presupposes a continuum divisible in time and space, and Zeno's famous four arguments against motion are therefore an expansion of the problem of continuity versus discontinuity. The four arguments in which Zeno would demonstrate that motion is impossible have been preserved in a paraphrase by Aristotle (Aristot. *Phys.* 239 b 9 ff. = Zeno DK A25–8) and can be reproduced as follows:

(a) It is impossible to traverse a finite course (a stadium), because the runner must first traverse half of the course and then one half of the next half, etc. – *ad infinitum.*

(b) In a race between Achilles and a tortoise (one fast and one slow runner) in which the tortoise has an advance lead, Achilles will never catch up with the tortoise, because when Achilles has arrived at the tortoise's starting point, the tortoise will have moved to another point; when Achilles reaches this, the tortoise will once more have moved, etc. – *ad infinitum.*

(c) If time is composed of moments, an arrow in flight will at any given moment be at rest.

(d) (Here a generally accepted modern reconstruction is reproduced, which corrects Aristotle's version.) Assume three rows of objects of equal size that move in relation to each other as follows:

1.   AAAA   2.   AAAA   3.   AAAA

       BBBB   BBBB   BBBB

        CCCC   CCCC   CCCC

It will be seen that the A-row is at rest, and it will be assumed that the two other rows move at the same speed. On the presupposition that time and space are composed of minimal units, that every object represents a minimal unit in space, and that each B and C pass 1 A in 1 minimal unit in time, 1 B will in its final position have passed 2 A's in 2 time units, but at the same time 4 C's in 4 time units. Consequently 2 minimal units will equal 4 minimal units in both time and space, and 'the half will equal the double'. Accordingly the relativity of speeds precludes absolute minimal units.

The interpretation adhered to here[2] implies that the four arguments have been constructed symmetrically: (a) and (b) presuppose that motion is continuous, (c) and (d) that motion is discontinuous; (a) and (c) pertain to one object in motion, (b) and (d) to the relation between several objects in motion.

In his discussion of Zeno's paradoxes, Aristotle is partially dependent on Plato's *Parmenides*. In his comments on the first argument against motion (*Phys.* 233 a 21; cf. 263 a 4 ff.), he maintains that Zeno confuses two senses of the infinity of a continuum, for there is a difference between infinity of extension and infinite divisibility, and infinity in time presents a correspondingly ambiguous concept. A finite course (the stadium) is run through in finite time, but the same course is infinitely divisible, and infinite divisibility must be connected with infinite time, which is to say that a division will never be finished. According to Aristotle, Zeno makes a mistake by correlating a finite course with an infinite concept of time.

From mathematical points of view, it is possible to develop Aristotle's criticism further thanks to modern infinitesimal calculus and theory of sets, and the axioms of Zeno and his contemporaries can be refuted, in the sense that it can, for example, be demonstrated that the sum of the infinite geometrical progression $1/2 + 1/4 + 1/8 + 1/16 \ldots + 1/n$ converges toward the limit 1, and it can mathematically be calculated when Achilles catches up with the tortoise. The concept of infinity then current is too primitive (cf. Aristotle), and the same logic does not apply to integers as to real numbers. The series of integers is a discontinuous series in which each number has an immediate predecessor and an immediate successor, but a continuum of numbers cannot be made an object of a counting procedure.

Zeno's paradoxes can be resolved with the aid of a modern mathematical conceptual apparatus. But this is not, for example, to say that the opposites finite/infinite

---

2   An alternative reading distances itself partially from Aristotle and denies that arguments (c) and (d) presuppose temporal and spatial minimal entities. In that case the argument (c) will claim that what holds true for a given moment in a temporal sequence holds true for the whole sequence; argument (d) will claim that motion is not relative to one fixed standard.

and continuous/discontinuous can be resolved as a philosophical problem. Zeno raised the problem, and – as is characteristic of an Eleatic – he thought that whatever is conceptually self-contradictory does not exist.

One further argument by Zeno attacks the existence of space (Zeno DK A24). On the supposition that space can be defined as that in which something is, one can go on to ask what contains space; thus one would be caught in an infinite regress. It is unclear whether Zeno was aware that the concept of space might be defined differently.

MELISSUS

Melissus from Samos (roughly contemporary with Zeno) popularized the thoughts of the Eleatic School and came to be treated as the favourite whipping-boy of the opponents. He did not possess Zeno's incisive dialectical intellect, and Aristotle considered him negligible. He might seem to be an epigone, but he is of interest because he shows how Parmenides' thoughts were formulated in the next generation and especially how they had to be modified. To Melissus, as well as to Parmenides, being must be a perfect unity filling both time and space entirely. If there were any being next to being, it would lead to logical absurdities (Melis. DK B5–6), and, similarly, being cannot be thought to have any beginning or conclusion in time – Melissus explicitly formulates the principle of *ex nihilo nihil* (1).

Being is infinite in time: 'It is, it always was, and it always will be' (2). This certainly agrees with Parmenides, but it is an innovation that Melissus also considers being as spatially infinite (3). So doing, he freed himself from Parmenides' quasi-spatial imagery and warded off the troublesome question of what there is 'outside of being'. On the other hand, he also weakened the conceptual finiteness of being as well as the metaphysical thought that being impinges on nothing.

Melissus goes on to declare that being is incorporeal (9). In other words, he distinguishes between material and immaterial modes of being. But how can something immaterial have spatial extension? If being were thought of as a 'concept', it would of course not exist in time and space. Melissus did not go that far. Strictly speaking, it is not necessary either; it is quite possible to imagine something incorporeal with spatial extension – a 'force' might for example be thought of in this way. Hence Melissus' position is interesting in showing that Parmenides' imagery compelled the second generation of the Eleatics to formulate and solve a latent problem – although without abandoning the thought that being exists *in* time and space.

In two lengthy fragments (7 and 8) Melissus shows his ability to formulate current 'catch phrases' in the standing debate. In the first (7, 7) we are told that 'a void does not exist, for a void is a nothing, and a nothing does not exist'; and inasmuch as a void is a precondition for motion, motion does not exist. In the second (8, 2 ff.) Melissus says that if there – *per impossibile* – should exist a plurality, each part of this plurality must be equipped with the properties of Eleatic unity. These statements were to have consequences that must have been upsetting for any orthodox Eleatic.

6

POST-PARMENIDEAN
NATURAL PHILOSOPHY

The major figures in the middle of the fifth century BC – Zeno, Melissus, Empedocles, Anaxagoras, Leucippus – were roughly contemporary and the leading figure among the Atomists, Democritus, only a little younger. All of them react to Parmenides – although their mutual relations cannot be accounted for in detail. There is no chronological succession in which each individual philosopher reacts against his predecessor; all were confronted with the same set of problems and must be thought of as reflecting a wide-ranging contemporary debate. Zeno and Melissus stuck to Parmenides' fundamental position, denying the existence of plurality and hence of the physical world. For the others the task must be to respect Parmenides' logic but at the same time 'to save the phenomena', so that philosophy still could be a reflection about the cosmos; thus doing, they rehabilitated the earlier natural philosophy, but allowed the metaphysical perspective in Parmenides to fade into the background. Empedocles constitutes a direct reaction against Parmenides. Anaxagoras and the Atomists, furthermore, took into account such theoretical-mathematical problems as divisibility and continuity versus discontinuity. So doing they – directly or indirectly – provided 'answers' to Zeno's paradoxes, and it seems natural to imagine a distinction between the thinkers who came before and after the discovery of incommensurables.

To these philosophers the problem must not only have been the saving of the phenomena without conflicting too much with Parmenides. Like Melissus, they must have found it necessary to interpret Parmenides' concept of being, but, unlike him, they interpreted it materially: the physical world was real and corporeal. As previously discussed, Parmenides indirectly occasioned the distinction between material and immaterial, even though being at the same time continued to be conceived of as being in time and space. This had far-reaching consequences. The last Presocratics were not only able to make a few adjustments; a new frame of reference was available, and, for this reason as well, it was impossible simply to continue the old tradition of natural philosophy. The old 'hylozoistic' view gave way to a distinction between stuff and force. Being was understood materially, but something must cause it to change and move.

EMPEDOCLES

Empedocles, from the Doric colony Acragas (Agrigento) at Sicily, probably lived from c.490 to c.440 BC. By birth he was an aristocrat, by inclination a democrat. As a philosopher he must be viewed as a participant in the debate occasioned by Parmenides. Yet, by his cast of mind, he should rather be considered as a second Pythagoras, and he is as interesting to the historian of religion as to the historian of philosophy. He was not only a poet, thinker, student of nature, and physician, he was also a miracle maker, prophet, and poseur. He has been called 'the last shaman', but to pose as a prophet and combine philosophy, science, and mysticism was probably more problematic for him than for Pythagoras, his great model. He overplayed his role a bit, and made up for it by a well-developed flair for publicity.

A considerable number of fragments of two poems by Empedocles has survived: one is on natural philosophy (*On Nature*), one is religious (*Purifications*). It can be difficult to harmonize details in the two poems, but there is no doubt among modern scholars that they should be considered two sides of one overall view. Like Pythagoras, Empedocles would have considered thinking and knowledge of nature some sort of purification or revelation, and it is the prophet who speaks in both poems. The poem about natural philosophy, addressed to Pausanias, probably an adherent, begins (Emp. DK B 111) with an assurance that the poem will provide Pausanias with remedies against misfortune and old age, enable him to halt the wind, cause rain and drought, and recall the dead from Hades. The poem *Purifications* is addressed to Empedocles' fellow citizens, and in the introduction (112) he presents himself as an immortal among mortals crowding around him to learn of the path to gain, to hear prophecies, and to seek cures.

In *Purifications* Empedocles relies on many sources: on ancient accounts – known from Hesiod – of a by-gone golden age from which man has fallen, on Xenophanes' concept of god, and on common Greek religious ideas. But above all the poem is influenced by the Orphic-Pythagorean tradition. Empedocles believes in the kinship of everything living, the transmigration of souls, and in release from the hardships of this world. The immortal soul is not to be understood as life-principle (*psychē*) but as the real self, the divine in man (*daimōn*). Empedocles accepts Orphic dualism literally: the physicist can describe living and breathing man; the prophet can show spiritual man the way back to his home in the beyond; and to him who has the prophet's eyes, this world is a cave barred from above, a place void of pleasure where murder, envy, and all manner of corruption prevail (120–21).

Long ago – in the golden age – it was the Goddess of Love who ruled (128, cf. the goddess in the second part of Parmenides' poem). But man fell because of bloodshed and the eating of the flesh of his fellow man, by bearing false witness, or by sowing discord. Reincarnation is the punishment for the fall. By divine decree the fallen soul roams from one element to another (115); Empedocles himself has been boy, girl, bush, bird, and fish (117). But after millennia of roaming, man – like Empedocles – becomes a sage, singer, physician and prince (146); finally, redeemed man is accepted among the immortals (147). It is not clear whether this means that the *daimōn* of individual man is immortal or whether man is united with the divine – which, as mentioned, is depicted exactly as is Xenophanes' god: he has no limbs; with fleet thoughts he hastens over the whole world (134).

Most likely this lack of clarity is not accidental. If the man who is freed from the cycle of reincarnation is united with a cosmic consciousness, it makes little sense to ask about individual man's immortality – it is not man's real nature to be an individual. *Purifications* is a mystical-religious poem which proclaims man's kinship with the divine beyond the world that we believe is real. The poem does not advocate any philosophical doctrine. Also for this reason one should be on guard against comparing Empedocles' two poems too pedantically. There are both resemblances and apparent discrepancies; but in spite of the prophetic tone, each has its own language.

Parmenides was a 'dualist' in the sense that behind the illusion that appears as reality lies a world accessible to thought. Empedocles' 'dualism' is of a different sort. Man's true home is the divine, but our everyday object-world is real enough and can be known rationally. To a far higher degree than Parmenides, he is able – in the poem *On Nature* – to exchange his basic concepts for deities and a causal chain of events for divine will ('broad oaths', 115); yet one should not expect to arrive at a system among his divinities. But it is evident that his errand is rational, and hence it is clear that he had to confront Parmenides directly.

Empedocles leaves us in no doubt about that. Like Parmenides he has paid a visit to a goddess who has revealed the truth to him, in so far as it can be comprehended by men (3), and there are deliberately sought-for verbatim concurrences. Empedocles emphatically agrees that nothing arises from nothing and that nothing perishes in nothing; being is homogeneous and there is nothing next to being (11–12). But reason is not man's sole source of knowledge; in evident opposition to Parmenides, Empedocles maintains that one should also trust the senses and closely consider their testimonies against each other (3). On the basis of the general view at the time this implies that the object of sensation, the material world, is real. Thereby Parmenides' concept of being has been interpreted materialistically, and it follows from Empedocles' concessions to Parmenides that matter is imperishable and homogeneous and that nothing exists 'next to'; hence a void does not exist. But sense-perception teaches us that matter is in motion; consequently motion must take place by the exchange of place of physical bodies – as when, for example, one throws a stone into the water. It is also apparent from sensation that several physical objects exist. Inasmuch as Empedocles wishes to rehabilitate the physical world and translate Parmenides' concept of being to materialism, he must in other words maintain against Parmenides that motion and plurality exist.

Hereafter the problem must be how to make Parmenides' demand for constancy agree with the existence of plurality and motion. Like his contemporaries, Empedocles never dreamed of finding constancy or regularity in motion itself; it must be found in the stuff. He agrees with Parmenides that nothing can come into being from nor perish in nothing, but he distinguishes between absolute and relative becoming and perishing (cf. 11). In an absolute sense matter is unchangeable. What to us looks like changes are relative changes; matter can be mixed and separated in different proportions (8). The constancy behind is what Empedocles calls the four 'roots' (6; 17; 21) – in later terminology the four elements, i.e. earth, water, air, and fire that were sometimes given colourful names of deities. In themselves these elements are unchangeable; what men call birth is a special mixture of elements, death a separation (9). It is characteristic that Empedocles hereby in part systematizes an ancient tradition – the thought of basic 'property-things' that goes back to Anaximander – and in part adjusts the erstwhile conceptions to the new philosophical situation created by Parmenides. Because the elements can be mixed and separated, they must presumably exist as some sort of particles, each of which is qualitatively unchangeable: the theory of the mixing of the elements is thus an expression or mark of quantification, and a comparison has often been made with the role of the elements in modern chemistry. It is interesting that Empedocles, for example, determined bones, blood, and flesh as certain proportions between the elements (96; 98).

The next problem that arises is that of the cause of motion – mixture and separation – and of the occurrence of changes according to a relatively fixed pattern. Here Empedocles refers to what we would call two forces, Love and Strife (cf. 17; 22; 26), which affect the stuff, the four elements, in such a way that love unites the elements and strife separates them – in Aristotelian terms: the stuff is the material, the force the efficient cause. But in Empedocles Love and Strife have a remarkable ontological status not immediately compatible with Aristotelian or modern views. Sometimes the forces can be reified and described almost as if they were two additional elements. But the point is that they must affect the elements and that therefore they are to be found everywhere. Empedocles puts it this way (17; 19): Strife is apart from the elements, although of equal weight; but Love is among them, equal in length and breadth. In modern terms: Love and Strife coexist with the elements. To us such forces are abstract; to Empedocles they were to be found everywhere in the world, filling space, even though indivisible. The parallel with Melissus' understanding of being is a striking one, and it reveals a mode of thinking that is typical of the time.

By naming 'the forces' Love and Strife Empedocles succeeds in uniting two views, which to us can only be aligned with difficulty. On the one hand Love and Strife appear as forces of attraction and repulsion in an apparently mechanical system. On the other hand they are concepts of value that connect the human sphere with the cosmos; when all is said and done, the world is not merely mechanically ordered; coming into being is good, perishing is evil. The same duality underlies the second part of Parmenides' poem.

Empedocles' doctrine of elements and stuff and force is probably his most important philosophical contribution. But he goes beyond merely presenting a theory that legitimates a constancy while at the same time explaining change. A man is born, comes to a high point, grows older, and dies. The same applies to the cosmos as a whole. Just as, for example, the seasons change, so the world traverses a repeated cycle (cf. especially 35; 17), which – after Aristotle (cf. *Phys.* 250 b 26 ff.) – traditionally has been divided into four phases. In the first phase Love rules absolute – which is to say that it unites all the elements in a spherical mass (cf. Parmenides). But by means of a vortex, somewhat unclearly described, Strife – in the second phase – gains admittance and separates what is united. In the third phase Strife holds complete sway and keeps the elements separate; but thereupon they are once again reunited – in the course of the fourth phase – until one is back at the beginning. The whole thought of a cycle is, so to speak, a chronological unfolding of the dialectics between unity and plurality. But against the four-partite scheme – in which the world is at rest in the first and third phases and in motion and subject to change in the second and fourth phases – Aristotle argues (*Met.* 985 a 23 ff.) that in this way Love separates (the elements) while Strife unites (the elements). From a purely mechanical point of view this criticism is justified, but it ignores the normative aspect: it is 'good' that everything is united in Love.

But there are more difficulties. According to traditional understanding, we live in world-phase two, and accordingly we are – in analogy with Empedocles' religious poem – well on our way from a golden age towards the abyss. Phase four on the other hand should, so to speak, be a counter-world on the way from Strife to Love, and Empedocles is quite reticent about this phase. All in all, he does not speak very clearly about the cosmic cycle – it can be difficult to single it out from the lesser cycles (the lifespan of a man, for example; cf. Emp. DK B 17) – and modern scholarship is sceptical with respect to Aristotle's schematic interpretation. At least in this respect Empedocles was greater as a poet than as a thinker, and details will probably remain obscure. Here resignation is a virtue.

Empedocles had a very broad 'scientific' field of interests – the traditional subjects (cosmogony and cosmology) aside, he stressed biology and physiology – and he must have possessed considerable intuition. For example, he assumed that light is a 'moving body' which travels at great but finite speed (A 57). To this should be added a rich flair for paedagogical analogies. Earth is motionless in the centre of the world, because heaven rotates with such great speed that earth is prevented from moving – just as water in a cup would be at rest if the cup were moved with sufficient speed (Aristot. *De caelo* 295 a 17) – and respiration functions in the same way as a water pipette (a *clepsydra*); the blood is pressed back leaving space for air, just as liquid and air exchange places in a pipette (Emp. DK B 100). This hardly proves that Empedocles conducted experiments, but rather that he had a well-developed flair for finding analogies.

The world has come into being (cf. A 30) by the separation of the elements from the original unity because of a vortex. Thereby the elements were accorded each its own region with earth in the centre, and a fixed star sphere was formed, which shrouds a light and a dark hemisphere (day and night). Details are unclear, but it is evident that the universe – in accordance with current Greek thought – is finite, and the idea of a separation of the elements from an original homogeneous mass continues the tradition from Anaximander.

The emergence and development of life seem subject to accident – or to 'the survival of the fittest', as it is called by modern interpreters who have generously seen Empedocles as a precursor of Darwin. Originally everything living arose from earth in the form of scattered limbs, etc., which then were joined to become the strangest monsters – men with heads of oxen, for example. Then creatures were formed without separate organs, limbs, sexual members, etc.; finally come the creatures we know who are formed by procreation, where the male and the female strive to be reunited with their lost halves – if we are to believe the parody that Plato in the *Symposium* puts in Aristophanes' mouth. The sequence that is depicted here is owing to a doxographical reconstruction (72, Aetius), and modern attempts to adjust it to the cosmic cycle are in a manner of speaking reconstructions of the second order. The preserved fragments (cf. B57–62) provide vivid descriptions of the various phases, but do so without allowing us to follow a clear course of development. The whole imaginative theory is clearly also a continuation of Anaximander, although it is adjusted to Empedocles' conceptual frame (mixture and separation of elements) and spiced with fantastic mythical creatures. Furthermore, it apparently mattered to Empedocles that nature through 'trial and error' had 'tested' all possibilities for life.

Imagination and stringent thought are perhaps more firmly joined in Empedocles than in any other Presocratic. Behind lies the universal theory of elements that provides a mechanical explanation of the kinship and bond with all parts of the cosmos. Empedocles' epistemology is an interesting example of the application of the theory of elements. Steadily 'effluences' or particles are emitted from physical bodies, which can be absorbed in passages or pores in other bodies. This is a general physical theory, which more closely describes how elements are mixed or separated. Applied to sense perception, it means that sense organs are 'passages' specially fitted to receive 'effluences' from outside, so that sight, for example, is able to receive colour (cf. Plat. *Meno* 76 C ff.). But it is not only the forms of the sense organs but also their material constituency that make sensation possible. Empedocles follows the principle of 'like seeks like' (cf. Theoph. *De sens.* 7 ff.), which means that earth in the sense organ senses earth; with fire, fire is sensed, etc., and inasmuch as blood is an equal mixture of all elements, it is the seat of thought. Cognition is therefore an interplay where related elements are united with Love as the driving force. Only concerning sight do we have a closer description preserved – as so often in Empedocles in the form of analogy (Emp. DK B84).

It is characteristic for Empedocles, as for his whole generation, that cognition exclusively is explained by a physical theory and that it is made dependent on physical contact. The question of the validity of cognition is not asked; the act of cognition itself is an adjunct of a physical process, and therefore no further epistemological problems are raised.

Cognition is a physical process, and man – like all creatures and objects – is a perishable material entity. How can this be reconciled with the picture of the world and man's immortal soul as they appear in the second poem, *Purifications*? Strictly speaking, it is not reconcilable, and, as mentioned, in a certain sense it should not be. Beyond the physical world that can be rationally described lies a world that does not permit of analysis by reason, which is where real man belongs. Nevertheless, there are, of course, points of contact, not in doctrines but in themes. In both worlds Love is the good force; both in the physical-rational and mythical worlds there is a cycle, a paradisiacal golden age, a fall, and a return. And in both worlds everything has kinship with the universe; the self-identity of the rational deity corresponds to physical interaction.

A dualism such as Empedocles' could hardly have been imagined after the middle of the fifth century, and yet it was – in a different form – to have consequences in Plato and Aristotle. Of more direct and enduring importance was Empedocles' scientific doctrine of the elements. It was employed by Plato in the *Timaeus*, was taken over by Aristotle, and for the physician Galen (second century AD) it constituted the basis for the doctrine of the four bodily fluids. By these paths Empedocles was to remain influential throughout late Antiquity and the Middle Ages.

ANAXAGORAS

Like Empedocles, Anaxagoras (c.500–428 BC) took up Parmenides' challenge. He was slightly older than Empedocles, but according to Aristotle his philosophical activity occurred later, which can also be seen in his philosophy: he was preoccupied with the problem of divisibility and continuity, familiar from Zeno's paradoxes and Melissus, but apparently unknown to Empedocles. Anaxagoras was from Ionian Asia Minor (Clazomenai), and this was evidently of some importance. He never behaved like a prophet or miracle maker but resumed the matter-of-fact Ionian curiosity of the past – and he wrote in prose. The tradition makes him the heir of Anaximenes, and his philosophy should be seen as a revival of the old project of natural philosophy on the premises advanced by the Eleatics and the development of mathematics. The principal task must be to get a conceptual grasp of the problem of change.

With Anaxagoras philosophy entered Athens. He is said to have stayed in Athens for thirty years and to have had close contact with Pericles; assuming that tradition is correct, he was forced into exile because of an accusation of godlessness that should be viewed as part of the opposition's struggle with Pericles for power.

Apparently Anaxagoras' oeuvre was limited to one work of relatively modest extent. Most of the fragments are preserved by Simplicius.

Anaxagoras' answer to Parmenides is close to Empedocles'. It is wrong to speak of becoming and destruction in an absolute sense. Every change depends on mixture and separation (Anaxag. DK B17). Thus there is something that in a Parmenedean sense remains constant (3: it is impossible for what is to cease to be), but this does not preclude that 'things', understood relatively, become and perish. The question then is: what is the constant? To Empedocles the answer was quantitative entities – roots or elements; Anaxagoras' constant is qualitative. It is implicit in this that Anaxagoras, unlike Empedocles does not reduce the plurality of things to a limited – and arbitrary – number of elements; he undertakes no reduction whatsoever; 'everything is in everything'.

To understand this it is necessary to look at Anaxagoras' reaction to the problem of divisibility, continuity, and infinity. It is likely but not certain that he was acquainted with Zeno. In any case he was acquainted with the 'axioms' Zeno presupposes, and in many cases it is informative to place Anaxagoras and Zeno quotations next to each other. Anaxagoras denies that the sum of an infinite number of entities of arbitrarily small extension is infinitely large; an infinite series can accordingly converge towards a limit. And he denies that a division of a finite entity can be 'carried through' to 0; a given entity is accordingly infinitely divisible. Already this – which removes some of the presuppositions for Zeno's paradoxes – indicates remarkable insight. But some of the conclusions that Anaxagoras draws from this also show an intuitive understanding of the logic of the concept of infinity, which apparently failed to find support in contemporary mathematics.

According to Zeno (Zeno DK B1) any divisible entity would be both infinitely large and infinitely small, which to him was an absurd conclusion. But the conclusion is meaningful to Anaxagoras (Anaxag. DK B3): there exists no minimal part of the small; there is always something smaller; and there is always something larger than the large, because the large is numerically equal to the small, and in itself each thing is both large and small. Concerning the latter he adds (5): everything is neither larger nor smaller than everything; it is always of equal size. Here Anaxagoras once again accepts a conclusion that Zeno found absurd (Zeno DK B 3): everything has a finite size, even though it is infinitely divisible.

The infinitely large and the infinitely small are equal, which is to say that there is no numerical concept that in an absolute sense can be assigned to infinite quantities. Consequently the whole world is numerically identical with any given thing – a finite magnitude – and in that sense it holds true that 'everything is in everything'.

By combining his insight into the problem of infinity and divisibility with empirical observation Anaxagoras is then able to construct a physical theory, which – to judge by the transmission – had a firm inner logic, but which seems so alien to us that he is one of the most difficult Presocratics to understand. But it is without doubt correct, as has been said, that it is logically possible that the world is constructed as Anaxagoras imagined. His theory may be said to build on two presuppositions: the thought of infinite divisibility and the sentence 'everything is in everything'.

The thought of infinite divisibility implies to Anaxagoras that a stuff can be divided infinitely without changing qualitatively – Aristotle says (*Phys.* 187 a 25) that while Empedocles calculated with four basic elements, Anaxagoras did so with an infinite number of *homoiomerē* (an Aristotelian term designating entities that consist of uniform parts). Understood in this way, all naturally existing stuffs – stones, gold, water, flesh, bones – are basic elements to Anaxagoras. But as in the good old tradition, he did not distinguish between things and properties nor between substance and quality; colours or smells, for example, are also 'basic stuffs' – this should not be taken to mean that a blue object is partially blue and partially object; rather the blue is just as irreducible a phenomenon as are the object itself and its other properties. Anaxagoras cannot stop with minimal entities, be they Empedocles' elements or Democritus' atoms. His theory is not a particle- or corpuscular theory, but a theory of continuum; his physics is not quantitative but qualitative; and all stuffs or properties exist on equal footing.

But of course Anaxagoras cannot finish by finding that each object is what it is, regardless of how much it is divided. Everything is in everything also in the sense that everything has a share (*moira*) in everything (Anaxag. DK B 6); nothing can exist separately; in all things there is a qualitative plurality, in the large and in the small. Accordingly, every object contains 'seeds' (*spermata*) of everything (4), as Anaxagoras calls it with an expression borrowed from biology. We find empirically that, for example, food turns into hair, flesh and bones (cf. A 46). But hair does not come into being from not-hair (nothing comes into being from nothing); therefore hair must already be present in food, but in so small quantities that it cannot be sensed (cf. B10; Aristot. *Phys.* 187 a 26 ff.). This does not mean that hair is present in food as particles that can be removed by a mechanical process; it is the proportional relation between different stuffs in the food that is changed as the food is ingested so that some of it is preserved in the organism and some of it is separated off. So, like Empedocles, Anaxagoras takes apparent changes in stuffs to be proportional changes, although within a different conceptual frame, for to him quantity is not a quantity of minimal units but a quantity in which something qualitative preponderates over something else – and this preponderance can be changed. By a successive change of this preponderance any empirical object can be changed into any other one, and hereby Anaxagoras has provided Anaximenes' old theory of the transition of the stuffs into each other with a subtle underpinning. It is not in disagreement with his concept of infinity that the ingredients in infinite quantities vary proportionally.

Traditionally it has been seen as a problem that all parts of a thing qualitatively are identical with the whole thing, while every thing at the same time contains ingredients of everything else. But the disagreement only arises if one identifies the ingredients in a thing with particles or minimal units – which was precisely what Anaxagoras did not do. On the other hand, apparently another problem arises. If everything has a share in everything and contains the 'seed' for everything else, no stuff seems able to appear as pure. This is to say, for example, that hair is both hair and not-hair. This must mean that a 'pure' stuff is an abstraction, in so far as it will always be present empirically in a mixture with other stuffs. Hair should thus come into existence by a preponderance of 'pure' hair in a mixture with everything else. This is not stated in the Anaxagoras-fragments that have survived, but it must be the logical consequence.

Inasmuch as it is a fact that there are things in the world that change and that nothing comes from nothing, it must be presupposed that everything is in everything, and the most likely explanation for this is that this is the way it has always been. None the less, Anaxagoras cannot rid himself of the then current general idea that the orderly world was created from a disorderly one. Originally everything was so mixed that an imagined observer would have been unable to distinguish one stuff from another (Anaxag. DK B1; 4). To this very day everything is in everything, but one can distinguish one thing from another, because the thing is determined by the dominance of a given property. Therefore something must have occurred between the original state and the present one, and accordingly Anaxagoras resumes the ancient Ionian thought of a cosmogony. He is in need of a starting point in which chaos becomes cosmos, but unlike Empedocles he does not need a cyclical development. Furthermore, as the world in its original state consisted of the same ingredients as in the present, Anaxagoras, unlike Anaximander, is not compelled to provide an inexplicable transition from 'metaphysical stuff' to physical stuff.

The process, whereby Anaxagoras imagines the several stuffs and 'things' as having become separated off from the original mixture, is – as with most fifth century thinkers – a vortex (9; 12; 15) that reinforces itself with extraordinary speed. This motion, the basic features of which are reminiscent of the separation of the elements in Empedocles, satisfies the principle of 'like seeks like' and explains that what is heavy will seek towards the centre of the vortex (the earth); one exception seems to be that the celestial bodies are flung away from the centre of the vortex by means of some sort of centrifugal force. Details concerning the rotating motion and Anaxagoras' universe will not be dealt with here. We should merely note that the motion takes place in perpetuity and that Anaxagoras' universe is expanded as the vortex gradually comprises an ever larger area. The question whether it is possible to think of several vortexes and hence several worlds is ambiguously answered (cf. 4).

In his cosmogony Anaxagoras is confronted with the same principal question as was Empedocles: what causes motion to commence? A problem like that did not exist for the older Ionian tradition; but to Anaxagoras the vortex had to be a purely mechanical process with a necessary first cause. Anaxagoras' answer is reason or mind (*nous*). Reason (cf. 11–14) sets the cosmic process in motion and thereby controls its course; but for this very reason it must be outside the process and be independent of the mixing of the stuffs. Animated beings partake in a special way in *nous*, even though it is everywhere. It is finer than everything else, it is without limit (*apeiron* – cf. Anaximander), and it knows the past, present, and future (cf. Xenophanes' concept of god).

In a certain sense Anaxagoras' concept of *nous* fits in with the tradition, although now in the conceptual frame of a later time. Like Empedocles, he needs a force that is separate from a stuff, but characteristically the force itself is rational and not, as in Empedocles, a projection of human feelings (Love and Strife), and Anaxagoras does not conceive of a cyclic interplay between two forces aiming in opposite directions. When he speaks of *nous* as being outside the material 'mixture' and yet ubiquitous, it is perhaps the clearest and most subtle expression in his age of the search for something incorporeal that is operative everywhere in a world of time and space. Aristotle praises Anaxagoras for his concept of reason – he was a sober person compared with his predecessors (Aristot. *Met.* 984 b 13).

Anaxagoras' concept of *nous* expresses three ideas that are closely connected:

1   the cosmic course is causally and rationally determined (in modern terms: any sequel in the world is subject to natural laws); therefore:
2   reason is to be found not only in man but in the whole world, and
3   reason governs the world.

Against this background it may be doubted whether Plato – and Aristotle after him – was right when they claim that Anaxagoras' causal concept is purely mechanical and 'blind' (*Phaedo* 97 B ff.).

Apparently the question of the relation between human and cosmic reason was only partially posed by Anaxagoras. Like all late Presocratics he entertains a theory of the physiology of sensation (Theoph. *De sens.* 27), which shows him to be a better empiricist than Empedocles – we sense by contrasts; the sense of touch registers, for example, best what is warmer or colder than the organism itself. But the senses are weak, and sense-perception has only limited validity (Anaxag. DK B21). The principal question of the validity of rational cognition is not asked by Anaxagoras – and inasmuch as man simply partakes in universal reason, he probably never felt the need to ask it.

On the other hand, he has quite precise ideas about how reason can be used for scientific cognition; he is most likely the first thinker whom we can credit with having conscious principles of scientific method – and it is possible that he himself would stress his 'scientific' theories more than their philosophical basis. On a large scale we have seen his procedure in the construction of a universal theory of natural philosophy: an interplay between mathematical-logical speculation and an empirical acknowledgement that there is in any case a world that is subject to apparent change. His methodological attitude to an empirical material can be seen in his statement that 'through the phenomena that which is hidden can be seen' (21a). This is a manifesto that does not refer to simple inductive gathering of material or to empirical generalization. Empirical facts provide inspiration for the formulation of a theory, the validity of which depends on whether it explains the facts satisfactorily. Such a methodological position may be reminiscent of modern science, but is different because it is also applicable to areas where empirical verification or disproof in principle is impossible; systematically controlled experiments are missing. Anaxagoras may, however, have taken the first step on this path as well. He has shown that air is a stuff by tying up a sack and finding that it cannot be flattened (Aristot. *Phys.* 213 a 22). Is this merely a reference to everyday observation (like Empedocles' clepsydra) or is it a primitive experiment?

But Anaxagoras cannot have felt himself obliged to verify his scientific views by experiments. Some of the results he obtained – for example, his explanation of solar and lunar eclipses – are correct; some, presented with the like authority, are wrong (cf. Anaxag. DK A42). What is decisive is the view of the world that lies behind all Anaxagoras' thought. The world can be explained rationally and by means of causes, and man, earth, and the universe beyond earth are subject to the same laws. Socrates had good reason – in Plato's *Apology* – to distance himself from a man who thought that the sun, the moon, and the stars are merely stones.

As a rule, the great names, the seminal philosophers with new ideas, are singled out, but this may cause those lesser lights to be overlooked who perhaps to a higher degree characterize the ordinary milieu of the time. Here mention will be made of two lesser thinkers who both belong in the wake of Anaxagoras; both are eclectics, but such persons may in their time have seemed to be the spokesmen more than any others of the strange natural philosophy that turned the world upside down (cf. Aristoph. *Nub.*, here p. 120).

Archelaus of Athens is mentioned as an Anaxagoras student. Apparently he especially stressed cosmology and biology; whether he understood the profundity in his teacher's thinking shall be left unsaid. His fame rests first and foremost on the claim that he had been Socrates' teacher – there is some indication that Socrates, in fact, did fraternize with the godless natural philosophers. Diogenes of Apollonia sought on a less sophisticated level than Anaxagoras to join the old Ionian natural philosophy with the new currents of the time, and, as has been mentioned, he formulated a justification for the Ionian thought of a basic stuff. Like Anaximenes he thought of air as basic stuff but was not unaffected by the distinction of more recent date between force and stuff, and therefore he associated air with Anaxagoras' principle of force, reason, and thus introduced a teleological principle (Diog. Apol. DK B3). Back of the grand systems of the time one senses many attempts to create a whole out of random bits of thought. And there was no established science to restrain the free flight of thought.

THE ATOMISTS

The third – and perhaps most significant – reaction against the Eleatics was Atomism, the first consistent mechanical-materialistic philosophy. It was founded by Leucippus who probably was a little younger than Zeno, and it was further developed by Democritus of Abdera in Thracia (presumably c.460 to c.370 BC). The basic features of Atomism probably go back to Leucippus who must have been faced with the same task as Anaxagoras – to 'save the phenomena' – but at the same time must respond to the Eleatic challenge and take sides in the debate about divisibility and continuity, which presumably is connected with the discovery of incommensurables. Leucippus wrote two works, *The Great World System* and *On Mind*, but was soon outshone by Democritus. It seems that the works of the two writers were quickly combined, and it was Democritus' formulation of Atomism that became known. Democritus' oeuvre was – both with respect to size and subject matters – as voluminous as that of Aristotle, but fragments aside, we must make do with a long list of the titles of his works (Diog. Laer. IX 45 ff.), which around the time of the Birth of Christ were ordered into groups: ethical writings, writings on natural philosophy, writings on 'causes' (of natural phenomena), mathematical writings, writings on music, literature, and language, technical writings (on medicine, agriculture, etc.). In this classification there are not a few titles that provoke our curiosity – *The Cornucopia*, *On the Underworld*, *On Fighting in Armour*, for example. Probably the main works were *On Tranquillity* and *The Little World–System*, which was either a summing up of Leucippus' work or dealt with the human world as a 'small world'.)[1] It must also be observed that Democritus was the first to write an independent theoretical work on method, the *Kanōn* (guideline). But first and foremost one notes his all-devouring scholarly interest. Nothing was alien to Democritus; he resumed the old Ionians' interest in technical and practical problems, but it was a novelty that a philosopher wrote separately about ethics, epistemology, mathematics, and the liberal arts. Even the division into 'disciplines' was something new. Democritus was not only bound to fifth century, post-Parmenidean problematics; he was apparently also influenced by medical science, was a contemporary of the Sophists, a little younger than Socrates, and as a very old man he may have read Plato. Despite his dates, it makes sense to consider him the last 'Presocratic', but he is also a man of the new era. We know of nothing concerning the relative chronology of his works, but it seems reasonable to think that his interest in mathematics and ethics came fairly late. Nevertheless, he himself probably considered his work one system; we are unable to point to a development. Close to three hundred fragments have been preserved, but by far the greatest number are brief ethical rules of conduct – and some are perhaps even spurious. We have very scant direct source material on Democritus' natural philosophy and epistemology, but there are several indirect sources, first and foremost Aristotle who valued Democritus highly, and Theophrastus and Sextus Empiricus. Plato apparently received impulses from Democritus, although he fails to mention him. Democritus must have been a more productive person than the forty years older Anaxagoras, but by his cast of mind he is reminiscent of him; he was influenced by him, and that even though Anaxagoras and the Atomists came up with diametrically opposite answers to the same questions.

The Atomists as well 'translated' Parmenides' concept of being to materialism,

---

1   In this case the subject may have been the civilization of man or man as a 'little *kosmos*'. The term microcosmos would seem to go back to Democritus (cf. Dem. DK B34).

but, contrary to Anaxagoras' theory of a continuum, the atomic theory is a corpuscular theory, which – once more contrary to Anaxagoras – implies that there is a difference between the macroscopic and microscopic levels. The basic elements of the theory are a plurality of indivisible particles of the same stuff – atoms – which constantly move in the void (cf. Aristot. *De gen. et corr.* 324 b 36 ff.). But each of these particles is, like being in Parmenides, unchangeable and indivisible, and so the demand for constancy is maintained, while motion and change at the same time are explained purely mechanically. Leucippus in Aristotle's words (325 a 23) entertained a theory that was in agreement with the phenomena. But beyond that the atomic theory was speculative. It holds for the Atomists as well as Anaxagoras that at the base of the theory there is only one empirical element: there is a world in motion and change; the rest is theorizing on the basis of the contemporary discussion about divisibility and indivisibility.

We are able fairly closely to reconstruct the rise of the theory. Melissus had found that void is a precondition for motion but that void does not exist, and hence motion does not exist either. And he had maintained that every member of a plurality must be like Parmenides' unity. The Atomists take him at his word. There exists a plurality of unchangeable unities in motion in a void; it is true that void is a necessary precondition for motion, but void does exist. The more precise theoretical reasons are found reproduced in Aristotle (316 a 15 ff.) and turn out – as in Anaxagoras – to be a response to the 'axioms' that Zeno attacked. The Atomists are, however, less radical than Anaxagoras in their answers. Inasmuch as the universe is infinite, the sum of an infinite quantity of entities – not of arbitrarily small extension but of minimal extension – is infinitely large. It is furthermore accepted that the sum of an infinite quantity of entities without extension is 0 and that a division 'carried through' would result in 0. But such a division is, in fact, impossible – for there is a world of things. Actually there has to be a limit to divisibility, which can only be the case because indivisible minimal entities exist: the atoms that must be compact and impervious. Hence there is nothing to prevent the existence of atoms of considerable size; but in that part of the universe which we know, they must be supposed to be of minimal size, which is to say below the threshold of sensation.

Thus, with one concession to experience, the basis of the theory is theoretical-deductive. But if one proceeds to the properties and behaviour of the atoms, conclusions by analogy from the macroscopic world are allowable. Atoms are small bodies below the threshold of sensation behaving like bodies in our world. They have extension and form; they move and are moved. They distinguish themselves from each other not by different stuff but by form – *idea* – and mutual position (cf. *Met.* 985 b 4 ff.), and they have all imaginable forms, which must allow of mathematical description – they may be round, edged, hooked, convex, concave, etc. (Dem. DK A37), so that they can become entangled with each other and thereby successively form macroscopic bodies, which – depending on the atomic configuration – can be more or less porous. Accordingly the difference between macroscopic bodies can partially depend on the forms of the atoms, partially on the quantity and distribution of cavities in the body.

The atoms are called the being or the compact. Contrary to this is the void, also called nothing. It would be an anachronism to ask whether the Atomists assumed the existence of absolute or relative space; to them space is the unfilled vacuum in which atoms exist and move; and as motion is an empirical fact, the void, the precondition for motion, must exist. But they are aware that hereby they attribute to the void a strange ontological status, which Democritus points out through the paradox that 'nothing exists'. To Parmenides, nothing was a metaphysical negation of being; to the Atomists the void is a physical precondition for the position and motion of bodies. In both cases it is a question of a limiting concept that can only be negatively characterized. It should be noted that the Atomists' concept of the void is different from the view of space as a 'container', which Zeno attacked.

To the Atomists such concepts as a gravitational and inertial mass are unknown, nor were they better acquainted with forces working from a distance. One atom can only move another by direct contact, by pushing or shoving or by the infiltration of atoms into each other so that visible bodies are formed for briefer or longer periods. The void is a necessary but insufficient condition for motion, and motion must therefore be a fundamental factor without need of further explanation. The three principal elements in Atomism – atoms, the void, and motion – have always existed, and to Aristotle's regret (Aristot. *Met.* 985 b 19; cf. KRS 577–82) the Atomists therefore have no need – as did Empedocles and Anaxagoras – to consider how motion was started originally. A mathematical description of motion (kinematics) was beyond their ken.

The theory of atoms is first and foremost a theory of physics, but like all Presocratics the Atomists evidently considered their theory universally applicable. This raises the question whether an atom is physically or mathematically divisible. The argument that a division of a physical body must cease at an arbitrary point is a purely physical argument, which still opens for the possibility of mathematical divisibility – which must also be implicit in the thought of the different shapes of the atoms (an atom can, for example, consist of a ball and a 'hook'). The problem has been a prominent one in modern debates; nor can it have been neglected by the Atomists. They were familiar with Zeno's paradoxes, and, measured by contemporary standards, Democritus possessed considerable mathematical knowledge. Often it is presented as if Democritus were either an adherent of a physical or a theoretical atomism. It seems likely that this alternative is misleadingly formulated. Democritus appears to have considered geometry as the science whereby physical bodies are measured, not as a science about idealized entities. Thus a stereometric body can be thought of as a model that in all respects is analogous with physical bodies – and which consequently as a 'quasi-body' must consist of minimal parts. Apparently Democritus for example (Plut. *De comm. not.* 1079 E) considered a cone as constructed in 'steps' – cylinders of minimal height with steadily decreasing diameters invisible to the eye. He is considered a precursor of the method of exhaustion of Greek mathematics (Eudoxus, Euclid, and Archimedes), which builds on decreasing, arbitrarily limiting values instead of infinitesimals. Such a method is in principle not incompatible with 'theoretical' Atomism. Besides, it should be remembered that the theoretical understanding of irrational numbers was only in its infancy in Democritus' old age. It could be imagined that there was a limited number of 'basic' irrational numbers corresponding with 1 as the basic number in a series of natural numbers.

It appears from the preceding that the Atomists – Democritus at any rate – were preoccupied with questions of method. From the Eleatics they accepted the axiom, then agreed on by all, that nothing comes into being from nothing, as well as the axiom that the void is a necessary precondition for motion. Leucippus added the statement: 'Nothing comes into being by chance, but everything for a reason and by necessity' (Leuc. DK B2). We shall return to the Atomists' concept of necessity. Here it should only be pointed out that it excludes external forces (gods, Empedocles' Love and Strife, Anaxagoras' reason). Some of the Atomists' methodological principles have been mentioned. As with Anaxagoras, the theory depends on a combination of deductive reasoning with the one empirical fact that the world exists. Hereafter, conclusions by analogy from the visible to the invisible are also permitted, and on this point Democritus has acknowledged his debt to Anaxagoras by expressly adhering to the principle of 'through the phenomena that which is hidden can be seen'. This methodological rule was then quite subtly counter-balanced by 'the principle of sufficient reason', a principle of economy with roots in the earlier tradition (Anaximander and Parmenides), which apparently was used with greater methodological proficiency by Democritus, which is to say only in those areas in which a sure conclusion is impossible either empirically or on the Atomists' theoretical basic premises. The principle can be formulated: there is no greater reason for q than for p; therefore p – for example: there is no reason that atoms should not have all shapes; there is no reason that not-being should not 'exist' just as well as being.

By means of these methodological principles the theory of atoms was developed with the express aim to quantify qualities. As in Anaxagoras, there is much that may look modern: inferences by analogy from the visible to the invisible, the principle of economy, and the combination of deduction and empiricism. None the less, the strength of the theory lies in the speculative rather than in the empirical; systematically planned experiments are missing, and Democritus seems to have been satisfied, if only a good causal explanation were not contradicted by immediate observation. His interest in gathering facts was enormous, and he preferred to discover one cause to becoming King of the Persian Empire (Dem. DK B118). The following 'causal explanations' can be considered typical: thunder comes about when an irregular atomic combination compels a surrounding cloud downwards, and lightning is due to the collision of clouds, whereby fire atoms gather in a void and break through (A93). Natural phenomena are explained by atomic motions. Still, in spite of greater awareness of method, no important, essential progress had been made since the days of Ionian philosophy.

In a mechanical theory one cannot – as Anaxagoras did – use reason to explain why the world looks ordered, that it is a cosmos. That we actually live in a structured world must be explained mechanically. The universe is infinite, eternal, and populated by atoms in constant motion; atomic constellations are constantly formed and dissolved. In such a universe coordinated atomic motions can appear anywhere and at any moment, which can form a relatively stable system of particular structures that under certain conditions can be further stabilized by a self-increasing process. In this way a world – a cosmos – comes into being and numberless worlds of different appearance can arise and perish in the universe (40). Hence the Atomists, after all, like the other natural philosophers, need a cosmogony, which in the initial stage is accidental but subsequently follows a regular course. We know Leucippus' cosmogony from a quite confused report (Diog. Laert. IX 31). Several details seem fairly archaic, but what is important is that Leucippus relied on the standard fifth century model of a vortex, which in analogy with whirlwinds and whirling waters allows what is heavy to seek towards the centre, what is light away from the centre. Such a vortex makes it possible to speak of weight – which is to say that especially compact atomic constellations seek towards the centre of the system. Despite the lack of clarity in the doxographic tradition, the concept of weight is only meaningful in ordered worlds, not in the primordial state (cf. KRS 573–6). The theory of the vortex also allows the Atomists to entertain the ancient theory that 'like seeks like', which holds good for both the organic and inorganic world: doves seek doves, just as similar grains of corn in a sieve and pebbles on the beach seek each other (Sext. Emp. *Adv. math.* VII 116). Thus the Atomists operate with two levels: a primordial state and ordered worlds within the universe; in an ordered world, a cosmos, special laws pertain that are superimposed on the basic laws in the primordial state.

These special laws within an ordered world must have given rise to certain kinds of things that have resemblance, things with a certain structure, including 'things' (living beings) that can create other things of the same kind. Plato and Aristotle are not satisfied with this – a principal point in their criticism is that Atomism cannot furnish a reasonable account of the structure or essence of things (cf. Plat. *Tim.* 52 D ff.; Aristot. *De gen. et corr.* 317 a 17 ff.; *De part. an.* 642 a 27). Therefore Aristotle blames Democritus for not having provided adequate definitions of essence; he makes do with ostensive definitions – we can point out a man, and a man is 'what we all know' (640 b 30; cf. Sext. Emp. *Adv. math.* VII 265); in that case there is, opines Aristotle, no difference between a man and a corpse.

Mental life, including sense perception and intellectual cognition, must on the premises of the atomic theory be explained mechanically-materially. The soul, whose task it is both to perceive and to keep the vital functions going, consists – like fire – of small round, and therefore easily moving atoms (cf. Aristot. *De an.* 405 a 11) which enable it to be 'present' everywhere in the body – a strange combination of ancient Greek ideas of the soul as a vital principle with the doctrine of atoms; it might be added that it is an unsatisfactory combination in so far as psychic phenomena are simply reduced to a 'body inside the body' (cf. 409 b 3). Every cognitive act depends of necessity on physical contact between soul and the surrounding world. The mechanism behind intellectual cognition is unclear, but we are better informed about sense perception. It is due to motion from the sense object mediated by the sense organ and transmitted to the soul. Following Empedocles, the Atomists believe that effluences – or minimally thin images *(eidōla)* – are emitted from physical objects (cf., e.g. Leuc. DK A30). These images resemble the object, even though visual images, of course, must decrease in size on their passage from object to eye (this is, among other things, probably the cause of the complex account of the mechanism of sight, Theoph. *De sens.* 50). These images, which of course are atomic structures, encounter another atomic structure, the sense organ, and on this depends the sense image we perceive with the soul. In his search for 'causes' of individual sensations Democritus does not seem to have pursued a methodological course. Sweet taste is owing to large rounded atoms, harsh taste to small hard-edged atoms (Dem. DK A129) – in other words to objective properties in the physical object. But in principle it is true that we do not sense the thing directly, only motions in the sense organ.

This, of course, has far-reaching epistemological consequences – as it does for any physical-causal theory of sensation, and Democritus clearly realized this. He says (B9) that in fact we do not perceive anything exactly but only that which changes in accordance with the body's disposition and the atoms piercing and offering resistance – 'the truth lies in the deep' (117), and Aristotle quotes him as saying that either there is no truth, or it is hidden from us (Aristot. *Met.* 1009 b 11). Such statements were later taken to be expressions of scepticism (Sext. Emp. *Adv. mat.* VII 135 ff.) or as a claim that 'the phenomenon is the truth' (Aristot. *De an.* 404 a 27; *Met.* 1009 b 12). These are not conflicting interpretations. Our sensory experiences are true *qua* sensory experiences (phenomena), but sensation does not necessarily provide a true experience of things as they are. Sensory experiences are representations which justly have been compared with *ideas* in John Locke. To use an expression, e.g. from Locke, the secondary sense qualities are subjective – what one man experiences as sweet is experienced as bitter by another.

But not all cognition is sensation, and next to the subject-dependent sense experience there is an objective, cognizable reality. As Democritus says in compact but ornate style: 'by convention: sweet and bitter; by convention: hot and cold; by convention: colour; in truth: atoms and void' (Dem. DK B9; cf. 125). We can 'see what is hidden through the phenomena', and we know that atoms and the void have objective existence – we can (in partial disagreement with Locke) know both the atom and its 'primary', which is to say its objective qualities (shape, extension, etc.), but we cannot know this reality through sensation. Sensation is 'obscure', but there exists a 'true' cognition, reason, which takes over where sensation gives up (cf. 11).

Rational cognition must be primary – or else the entire deductive basis of the atomic theory would disappear, and of course one cannot sense atoms. But what legitimates it? This was no problem for Anaxagoras; to him reason was a cosmic reality in which man had a share. But to a materialistic philosophy of the Democritus type the priority of rational cognition creates problems. In a fragment (125) he lets the senses address reason: 'Wretched mind. From us you take your certainty, and yet you would overthrow us? – Our defeat will be your downfall'. We do not know what Democritus let reason reply. But judging from our whole picture of him, his epistemological position may approximately be summarized as follows: all cognition depends on physical events – atomic motions – and sense-perception is clearly a consequence of a physical, causal course of events. Everything considered, rational cognition presupposes a physical basis, but it is apparently not causally dependent on it. Although we do not know whether or how Democritus solved the problem, it is clear that he did ask the question of the validity of cognition independently of the question of the physical pre-conditions for cognition. He is the first to emancipate epistemology from ontology.

To Anaxagoras – as to the whole earlier tradition – man is a citizen in a rational world; if one knows the cosmic order, one knows oneself. In Atomism man is confronted with a world governed by mechanical necessity (*anankē*). Is man thereby in the power of external forces – forces that he perhaps does not know? The answer depends to a large extent on the implications of the atomistic concept of necessity. According to Aristotle and the tradition building on him, the Atomists sometimes maintain that everything occurs by chance and sometimes that everything occurs of necessity (cf. Aristot. *Phys.* 196 a 24; *De gen. an.* 789 b 2). This is because Aristotle, like Plato, had returned to the old thought of a rational world order. Both had a dual causal concept: mechanical causes (necessity) were subordinate to teleological and rational causes. Seen in relation to a teleological cause, necessity and chance must coincide. But the Atomists' world did not look like that. Already Leucippus identified necessity with a rational cause, but not with a teleological cause or an active principle. According to this view, chance must be a 'hidden' cause, which is to say an unknown necessity (cf. *Phys.* 195 b 35).

The atomistic concept of causality seems related to laws of nature in a modern sense. Most often it has been inferred that the Atomists were rigid determinists, and thereby Democritus was confronted with the familiar problem whether determinism is compatible with free will and thereby with ethics as well. The question seems a fatal one, for Democritus in fact worked out an ethics building on the acceptance of free will, but it is posed on doubtful premises. Modern science relies implicitly on the thought of predictability: from knowledge of a given initial state, a sequential course of events must be predictable. But concepts such as predictability and physical determinism were not formulated in Greece until the Stoics; they were unknown concepts to Democritus. To this must, of course, be added that atomic events to him escape observation and that mathematical laws of motion were unknown to him. That everything has a rational and necessary cause therefore means to him only that events are owing to atomic motions, but not that they can be specified in advance. Democritus does not know natural laws, only general rules, and a special sequence of events is in principle not predictable. It is, for example, possible that man may actively participate in a causal chain of events. In other words, ethics is possible, but it would be strange if there were not some closer connection between Democritus' ethics and his philosophy in general.

At first glance there seems to be no systematic unity in Democritus' ethical fragments. They all seem like practical rules for the conduct of life, couched in popular terms; some are a little flat, some rather common-place, and some reveal a good-hearted appreciation of the brighter sides of life (for example, Dem. DK B230: 'A life without festivals is a long road without inns').

In politics Democritus was a moderate democrat. He advocates a state of law in which the individual can develop freely in a greater community (251–3). Nature decides that the strongest must rule (267), but they should serve the whole and the poor so that solidarity and concord, or the common will (*homonoiē*) come to replace personal considerations (255; cf. 245); but the state must have sanctions at its disposal against internal enemies (258). Such a state of law is apparently a link in a natural process in which man has learned by observing his natural kin: from the spider we learned to weave, from the swallow to build houses, and from the birds to sing (154).

Democritus' ethics was agent-centred, and some basic thoughts and key concepts recur. Happiness lies not in cattle or gold, but the soul is 'the dwelling of one's genius' (171; cf. Heraclitus). Just acts must stem from an inner urge and psychic harmony rather than the coercion of laws (174; 181), and the good does not consist in avoiding injustice, but rather in shunning it (62).

The aim of a man's life is well-being or tranquillity (174; 191). Such psychic calm will, of course, provide pleasure, but not all pleasures endure – certainly not immoderate pleasure. Pleasure may differ from one person to another, even though what is good and true is common to all men (69). In this respect a parallel to Democritus' epistemology has been suggested: what is immediately experienced – the phenomenon – is not, simply, objective truth or the real.

Most likely this is not the sole connection with Democritus' epistemology and physics. Although one can nowhere in Democritus' ethical fragments find the words 'necessity' and 'atom', this may be due to a later interest in preserving general apophthegms – at this point in history the gnome, so to speak, had degenerated into popular maxim, because there was now another vehicle: the philosophical-scientific argument; at any rate Democritus' theoretical argumentation has not been preserved. The word 'chance' does, however, appear in the sense of unknown necessity (cf. 197).

It is likewise clear that tranquillity depends on physical balance (191). Peace of mind thus, apparently, has both psychic and physical signification. To psychic harmony corresponds physical harmony, in which the elements of the soul are not violently agitated. On such a psycho-physical balance man can himself have influence. By education and insight man can be re-formed (here a word is used, which in the physical fragments means change in atomic configurations), and by re-forming himself man is enabled, as we are told, to form his own nature (33). Once more, this must be understood both physically and psychically. The man who re-forms his physical nature becomes wise; he comprehends the sequence of events, which to the fool seems only a play of coincidence (197). Thanks to his insight into the macrocosmic series of events that are beyond man's influence, Democritus' sage can fashion his own life as a balance between nature and civilization. Hence, when he speaks of man as a microcosmos, this probably has special meaning. In the primordial chaos, basic general laws apply; in the ordered macrocosm there are further laws; man in his microcosmos can legislate for himself through insight into how he can adjust himself to the macrocosmic order. It holds true for the individual and also for democratic society, the cosmos in which the citizens freely contribute to the common good (259; cf. 248 ff.). Such a cosmos is dependent on man-made institutions such as language (26).

The weaknesses in Democritus' justification of 'free will' are apparent to the modern reader, but to Democritus – who later was considered a great 'magician' – it is no more strange that man thinks and acts than that magnets attract other bodies or that gods, who exist even though they do not interfere in the cosmic order, are always happy. Special atomic compositions have special talents, and Democritus' ethics is not at odds with his mechanical view of the world. Man is both a product of nature and alienated from external nature. To Plato and Aristotle – who, as has been mentioned, revived the old tradition – the purpose of human life is dependent on a teleological universal order. Democritus represents a humanism in which man creates his own purpose.

In its origin Atomism – as were Empedocles and Anaxagoras – is tied to the Eleatic provocation in the middle of the fifth century. And even though the answers that were offered to Parmenides, the great challenger, differed widely, there are still, apart from the main issues, clear agreements, not least between Anaxagoras and the

Atomists — one may think of details such as the vortex theory or of similarities in methodological views. But in his epistemology, his ethics and humanity Democritus is also related to the Sophists — the most prominent Sophist, Protagoras, came from his home town — and to those many currents in Greek intellectual life which towards the end of the fifth century concerned themselves with man's place in the world.

Apparently Democritus headed a school in Abdera. But it led a withdrawn existence until about 300 BC, when Epicurus in the context of Hellenistic thought reassumed Democritus' doctrine of atoms and his ethics. This, however, is not to say that Democritus was without influence in the fourth century. In implicit polemics against him Plato in the *Timaeus* formulated an alternative mathematical atomism, and Aristotle, himself an adherent of a continuum physics, considered Democritus a worthy competitor. If, after all, one would adopt a theory of particles, Democritus' physical Atomism would in his view be preferable to Plato's mathematical one. What Aristotle finds missing in Democritus' materialism is a satisfactory explanation of structure and order — form in Aristotle's language.

The connection between Democritus and modern atomic theory is tenuous. There is an indirect connection with the reappearance of atomism in the seventeenth century (Gassendi, Boyle). Yet it should not be overlooked that Democritus' atomic doctrine was natural philosophy on a par with other speculative systems, whereas modern atomic physics builds on a long development in the natural sciences.

7

MEDICAL SCIENCE

——— •◆• ———

Parmenides' criticism of the presuppositions of earlier natural philosophy had led to conceptual and methodological clarification and to the formulation of two possible explanations of the cosmos: a theory of a continuum and a theory of particles. But the competing schools could agree about very little, and it is small cause for wonder that a general scepticism prevailed concerning philosophical explanations altogether. Such scepticism was voiced by the Greek physicians. One theory might be as good as the next, and what was the use of occupying oneself with 'things in heaven and below the earth', they asked (cf. Hipp. *Nat. hom.* 1; *Vet. med.* 1). The protest by Greek medicine against philosophy is the first revolt of empiricism against rationalism.

Towards the end of the fifth century BC Greek medicine had undergone a not insignificant development. Next to mathematics it was the only specialized science, and it had been developed with relative independence of philosophy. Towards the end of the century the great master of medicine, Hippocrates (born c.460), lived on the Isle of Cos near the coast of Asia Minor, where he apparently directed a 'school' or guild of physicians. We know little about his personal contribution, but thanks to the authority he enjoyed in his own time and later, a considerable number of writings were attributed to him. The 'Hippocratic writings' that have been preserved are far more numerous than the preserved Presocratic fragments – several of them must have been written in the fifth and fourth century (most likely none before 440 BC), but some are of a much later date; it is possible that some of the oldest were written by Hippocrates himself. There are considerable differences between the individual treatises both in points of view and method – there are also different medical 'schools' – and it is a likely hypothesis that the 'Hipppocratic writings' actually were a medical library. But in spite of differences it is possible to focus on some common features that cause these writings to be of interest also in the history of philosophy.

The Hippocratic writings are in part directed against magic, in part against philosophy – and yet it goes without saying that behind the criticism, a philosophic influence can be traced to a greater or lesser extent. The oldest writings clearly belong in a general, late fifth-century context, and such names as Heraclitus, Empedocles, Anaxagoras, and Democritus are obvious in the background.

The physicians' criticism of philosophy applies to natural philosophy in general, but first and foremost to tendencies to make medicine itself speculative

(Empedocles). The author of one of the oldest pamphlets ridicules what he calls 'hypotheses' (*Vet. med.* 1), and with this he does not mean hypotheses in the modern sense – assumptions that can be verified or falsified – but what the word originally means in Greek: presuppositions or basic principles, which is to say postulates. Such a 'hypothesis' is, for example, that everything consists of 'the hot and the cold' – a typical way of thinking in natural philosophy. A physician cannot cure his patients with such a prescription, and the author also finds that the concepts are unclear in themselves (14). In the first place, they are not absolute. There is nothing that is hot or cold 'in itself' without participating in some other 'form' (*eidos*), as he puts it, using terminology that among other things throws interesting light on the pre-history of Platonic terminology. In the second place: food and drink may be hot or cold; but one cannot speak of the hot 'in itself' but should rather say what it is that is hot. With this implicit distinction between substance and property the empiricist has provided an astute contribution to the contemporary philosophical debate – one needs only to think of the 'property things' that still appear in Anaxagoras. Nor is he satisfied with such general questions as 'what is a man?' (20 – most likely a dig at Democritus). One must ask what this and that person is in relation to what he eats and drinks and does besides. In the same way, cheese is not simply deleterious, but may be so for a particular person with a special constitution and in a special situation.

In another of the oldest treatises (*De arte* 2; 11) the author squarely attacks the ontological preoccupations of the fifth century. Only that which is visible to the eyes and knowable by reason ('the mind's eye') can exist, and only by a combination of these means of cognition can one understand the true 'form' (*eidos*) of things. The writer is profoundly influenced by the philosophy of his day – the two forms of cognition we know from Democritus, indeed also in the way that rational knowledge must rely on the soul's inner vision. But the philosophical influences are more far-reaching. Simple sensory observation is not sufficient; it must be supplemented by rational cognition of 'the hidden', the real causes for example of the symptoms of sickness. Anaxagoras' formula ('through the phenomena the hidden can be seen', cf. Anaxagoras and Democritus) apparently gained wide acceptance as a scientific programme. But the physicians had much better possibilities than the natural philosophers for realizing such a programme of empirical research. In a late compilation (*Praec.* 1) there is a sophisticated account of the relations between reason, experience, and sense observation – which probably does owe something to Aristotle.

It appears that philosophers and physicians did not ensconce themselves, each in his own fortress. No empirical science can confine itself to mere registering of facts, and Greek medical science was not without commitments to theory, which is to say that certain ideas of man's constitution and the world order were presupposed. Everything in the world has natural causes, and of course this goes for sickness as well. But nature is – as in the earlier tradition of natural philosophy – itself divine. The author of an interesting dissertation on epilepsy (*Morb. sac.* 1) emphasizes that 'the holy sickness' has natural causes and that hence it is well-nigh blasphemous to consider this sickness more holy than others. Of course the physician should observe the concrete symptoms of disease, but he is to take into account the overall state of health of his patient (cf. Plat. *Leg.* X 903 C) – and his psychic and social circumstances as well – and it is important to know that man's physical and psychic constitution is dependent on climatic and geographic circumstances (cf. Hipp. *De aëre* 1 ff.). Key concepts in Hippocratic medicine – which explicitly are attributed to Hippocrates himself (Plat. *Phaedr.* 270 C; cf. *RP* IV 444 D) – are nature (*physis*) and force (*dynamis*). Every phenomenon – men, food, stuffs, and diseases – has its own nature and a special force affecting other natures in a special way – and the good physician of old always knew this, as we are told in a polemical argument against the flighty philosophers (Hipp. *Vet. med.* 14). These natures and forces are not to be found in isolation; but good health – and stability in the world altogether depend on a harmonious interplay of 'natures' and 'forces' (cf. Alcmaeon). In the *Symposium* Plato has the physician Eryximachus deliver a brilliant presentation of this entire way of thinking (Plat. *Symp.* 185 E ff.). Nature strives everywhere for a harmonious blend of dissimilar forces and elements, and the physician's task is to assist nature. Eryximachus himself mentions Heraclitus, and he is probably also thinking of Empedocles when he speaks of Eros as the driving force. Those two did in fact leave their marks on the Hippocratic writings.

The notion of the harmonious blend was accorded a special formulation in the doctrine of the bodily fluids (in the later tradition, blood, phlegm, black and yellow bile became canonical), which thanks to Galen came to dominate medicine for centuries. According to this pathology of the humours, sickness consists in an imbalance of the bodily fluids. The theory expands Empedocles' doctrine of the four elements, but it is odd that the same author at the same time considers the theory of the elements empty speculation and wholeheartedly embraces the theory of the four bodily fluids (Hipp. *Nat. hom.* 1; 4). In this case the Hippocratic call for empirical and verifiable observation is clearly at odds with the need for a general theory.

But in details the combination of experience and theory was quite sober. The Greek physicians' impact on the history of thought does not rest on visionary ideas but on a conscious attempt to construct an empirical science. By close observation it was possible to accumulate a reliable empirical basis so that attempts at theoretical explanations were constantly verifiable. In the Hippocratic writings there are precise rules of observation (cf., e.g. *Hum.* 2), and admirably exact patients' journals have been preserved (cf. *Epid.* 1, 26) on the basis of which diagnoses can be made even today. The aim was especially precise diagnoses and prognoses, and the physician's task was not least a preventive one – thus according with the principle of 'aiding nature'.

Not surprisingly, it was the physicians and not the philosophers who worked with experiments. It is, to be sure, a matter of opinion at what moment one can speak of experiments in the true sense. Rigorous demands of arranged experiments under ideal conditions are hardly fully met until the breakthrough of modern natural science, and hence the borderline between experiment and analogy with everyday observations is in Antiquity often left up in the air (cf. Empedocles and Anaxagoras). No science was in principle bound to experiments, but there are several examples of physicians undertaking arranged experiments and arranged observation. For example, the development of the chicken embryo was investigated by the piercing on each succeeding day of an egg from the same nest (*Nat. puer* 29). The following example testifies at any rate to good intentions (*De corde* 8): it is to be shown that a minimal amount of liquid pervades the lungs when one drinks. The proof: one takes a thirsty pig and lets it drink water to which dye has been added. Thereupon the pig is slaughtered, and one finds that the dye is present in the lungs.

Despite the physicians' protest against the philosophers' speculativeness, there is a close connection with the late Presocratics' research programme, and in another way as well the flowering of medical science towards the end of the fifth century is typical of the era. The humanist and individualist view of man that inspired Democritus to his ethics also pervades the Hippocratic writings. Unconditional respect for individual man shows itself in practice, for example in the scrupulous patients' journals; the ethical position is finely voiced in the Hippocratic oath, in which we among other things hear:

> Into whatsoever house I enter, I shall come to help the sick, and I shall desist from all deliberate injustice and harm, also from sexual intercourse with women and men, free and slaves. And whatever I see or hear in my task or outside in human life, which should remain hidden, I shall be silent about, and I shall keep such things as holy secrets.
>
> *(Jusj.)*

PART II

THE GREAT CENTURY
OF ATHENS

8

PERICLES' ATHENS

———— •◆• ————

In 490 BC the Athenians defeated the Persians at Marathon. In 480 the Persian fleet was defeated at Salamis. Although the Persian Wars were not formally concluded until 449, the generation who had witnessed these two fateful battles was marked by unparalleled national and religious exaltation; to the Athenians it was the gods who had interfered and granted freedom to their city. Before 480 Athens had been a somewhat old-fashioned agrarian society still fairly unaffected by the new cultural currents in Ionia. Now the city claimed its place as a leading naval power, and for fifty years Athens' dominant position was maintained with increasing brutality. From about the middle of the century Pericles was the uncrowned king of democratic Athens, and also in cultural matters he conducted imperialistic politics. Philosophers, historians, and rhetors (for example Anaxagoras, Herodotus, and Protagoras) took up residence in Athens for brief or sustained periods, and the flowering of Attic tragedy is indissolubly tied to this age of greatness. It was concluded abruptly by the debilitating Peloponnesian War (431–404) with Sparta, the rival city, which led to the total defeat of Athens and to moral and political dissolution, embodied in the brilliant opportunist Alcibiades and the tyrants' régime ('the thirty tyrants') put in power by Sparta in 404 BC.

The official ideology during the era can, for example, be encountered in the fusion of myth and nationalism of the Parthenon sculptures, but also in the eulogy of Attic democracy, which Thucydides has Pericles deliver on the occasion of the burial of warriors at the outset of the Peloponnesian War (Thuc. II 35 ff.).

Pericles does not mention the gods. The greatness of Athens has been created by the Athenians themselves and their noble ancestors who dwelt on the land from time immemorial. The fundament of the state is democracy, which is to say that a majority governs for the good of all; all have equal rights before the law; and those with the necessary qualifications are elected to the public offices so that even the poor participate in government. All have insight in communal affairs, and, without distrust, the city is open to strangers. Flourishing trade allows the citizen to enjoy the goods brought from abroad, and he can take pleasure in beauty, wisdom and public festivals. A free state is an independent state, and the citizen is his own master; hence Athens is an example to all of Hellas, and hence those who fell sacrificed their lives for the common good; awareness of this will offer the greatest support for those they left behind.

Now, it may be easy enough to praise the Athenians in Athens, as we are told in a parody by Plato (Plat. *Menex.* 235 D), and such an ideological manifestation as Pericles' funeral oration does of course demand a confrontation with reality. Pericles' Athens builds on several earlier developments. In the general opinion – both in the fifth and fourth centuries – Solon was considered the great father of his nation. He had forged the ancestral constitution, and he was the incarnation of the old ideals of justice, which were stubbornly proclaimed – no matter how much their meaning had changed. It was only unwillingly that it was remembered that it was Pisistratus, 'the tyrant', who had created the basis for Pericles' imperialism and cultural politics. It was the golden age of Solon that became incorporated in the myth of democracy.

It appears from Pericles' oration that freedom of speech and equality before the law were highly valued democratic ideals. But in political terms, democracy – the rule by the people – was limited to adult male citizens; when Athens was at her height this meant probably some 40,000 or 45,000 citizens out of a total population of close to 300,000. These citizens held the legislative and judiciary powers, and, despite Pericles' utterances about qualifications, most public offices were filled by lot for one year at a time. Representative democracy was unknown, and hence it was 'the people' who – at least formally – held full sovereignty. But such a political system presupposed professional politicians who had all their time to dispose of, and this may explain why leading politicians until the Peloponnesian War began – Pericles, for example – were recruited from the noblest and most wealthy families. Thucydides notes (Thuc. II 65) that Athens was only a nominal democracy; *de facto* the city was ruled by its first citizen, Pericles.

Women had no political rights, nor did other important population groups. Immigrants – the Metics – had no civil rights and could not own land, although they were often wealthy. A considerable portion of the city's trade was in their hands. Athens was – as Pericles claims – open to all. Furthermore, the economy depended on the use of cheap slave labour, and the number of slaves increased steadily during the fifth century (the probable number being close to 80,000). Yet, although personally unfree, the slaves were not entirely without personal, private rights and did live under quite varying circumstances.

The right of citizenship belonged to the old families – regardless of social status – and hence there was a strange contrast between a seemingly radical political democracy and a social conservatism, in which the ideal of a state of farmers and artisans was still sustained. The different political, economic, and social lines criss-crossed each other. Still, economic prosperity was dependent on foreign labour resources and unchecked imperialism towards 'the allies' of Athens who had no claim to citizenship but did pay tributes.

The realities of democratic Athens were a strange mixture of liberty, equality, and suppression. Pericles' speech is propaganda. Still, propaganda is only effective when it appeals to ideals that people actually believe in. The Periclean ideal came to inspire the myth of later times about Attic democracy, and such crucial concepts as liberty and independence for the state and the individual (autarchy) laid the ground for later theories of state, among them not least the Aristotelian. At the time it was intimately tied to an embryonic humanist view that perhaps was more nobly formulated by strangers such as Democritus and Protagoras than by Pericles – the ideologue in charge. Yet it should not be forgotten that the Periclean order allowed for considerable freedom of speech which also made serious debate possible.

9

TRAGEDY AND VIEW OF HISTORY

———— •◆• ————

In his *Poetics* (Aristot. *Poet.*1451 b 5) Aristotle says that poetry is more philosophical and hence loftier than the writing of history; for poetry – tragedy – deals with what might happen, because it is possible or probable, which is to say universal, history with what has happened, the particular. Most likely not very many human beings will find themselves in such extreme conflicts as Oedipus or Antigone. But the tragic hero is a human being who is larger than life-size; he has a particular character, and it must, as Aristotle says, be probable or necessary that he acts as he does as he is struck down by a fate greater than himself. The action of a tragedy takes place on the mythical, supra-human level, but the hero's feelings and passions must be universally understandable and must therefore appeal to all. When Aristotle compared poetry or tragedy to the writing of history, he probably never thought of an absolute contrast, for history is not exclusively an accidental chain of events. To both Aristotle and the Greeks in general, history harbours a meaning behind the general sequence of events, which it is the historian's task to disclose. Like the epic poet the historian has a tale to tell; the tale has a moral point to make, and it is notable that historical writing was considered a literary genre in Antiquity.

The philosopher seeks to argue or convince about some truth; the epic poet and his heir, the historian, tell of events; the tragic poet presents an action. Behind the myth lies the tragic poet's real 'subject', always something moral and religious; it may to modern eyes be political, but if so, it is raised above the mundane and hence has no specific target. To this extent the tragic poet continues in the poetic tradition, but he never speaks in his own name, as does for example Solon or Theognis. He cannot be identified with his characters, nor can one simply read his 'message' in the general reflections of the chorus. It is his task to present a conflict and pose a problem in an action, and it would be to misunderstand tragedy as a genre if one were to read it as a theory that might just as well have been formulated philosophically. Nor can one speak of *the* tragic mode, for the three great tragic poets, Aeschylus, Sophocles, and Euripides, are too different for that; each of the tragedians has his own moral and religious universe, which finds expression in the tragic conflict. Tragedy conveys ideas and therefore belongs not only in literature but also indirectly in the history of philosophy. Tragedy circles around one question that was only later to be taken up directly by philosophers: man's place in a world he does not master, his responsibility for the actions he has been compelled to perform, and his possibility of understanding himself and retaining his moral integrity in misfortunes that exceed the measures of everyday life. The tragic hero is not necessarily a moral saint, nor a sinner, but rather a man who is constrained to err, either by compulsion or from ignorance – to use a formula from Aristotelian ethics. The dramatic conflict differs in the three tragic poets and from tragedy to tragedy, but it is a common characteristic that Greek tragedy balances between the subjective and the objective, between the hero's character and an ominous sequence of events on which he has but little influence. The drama consists in whether this or that individual can come to terms with the world as it is. Tragedy is rarely a revolt against world order, but rather an attempt to come to understand it through experience.

Already Homer's world was divided into two levels, the human and the divine. The life of the gods is not subject to the vicissitudes of fate; the gods live their own lives in perpetual happiness; yet they also move along with men and have their protégés among them; they decide about man's life, but man cannot know of the gods' decision, of fate. In the old ethics of nobility this does not lead to bitterness or resignation; it leads to acceptance of the conditions granted by the gods, to an awareness that man should not strive for something beyond his lot but should act according to his nature. A nobleman can be known by his wealth and power, but to the outer splendour correspond inner marks such as pride, courage, justice, and generosity. A late, almost anachronistic spokesman of this view of life is Pindar. In his encomia one only senses indirectly that we no longer live in the legendary heroic world, and his patrons who paid for the praise – for example the pragmatic tyrants of Sicily – probably had no objection to being praised as mythical nobles.

But Pindar knows the distinction between gods and men (Pind. *Nem.* VI 1). The nobleman knows very well that the gods grant two misfortunes for each favour; but he knows how to bear it and turns the fairer side out (*Pyth.* III 81). Pindar's nobleman is what he is by virtue of his nature; he who must learn to be wise sways back and forth with a listless mind (*Nem.* III 41). In such a world man can only unfold his nature; he cannot develop. The tragic hero, on the other hand, is not simply himself; he becomes himself. He is in the hands of outside powers that can form or destroy him; he does not become a real hero until he has come to know himself and acts accordingly.

The oldest of the great tragedians, Aeschylus (c.525–456 BC), is a dramatic thinker who far more profoundly than Pindar speculates on man's place in the world. In his case one can more justly than in the case of Sophocles and Euripides speak of a message built into the dramatic action itself, which can burst out with an 'I have not the others' faith' in the choral commentary on the action. He seeks to make peace between the worlds of gods and men and to unite the reflected demand for justice – already known from Solon and Theognis – with the old gloomy religious concepts of offence, guilt, and fate.

A man is what he does. He takes upon himself guilt and responsibility through action, but at the same time he acts like a puppet in a game he does not know. The powers that confront man are the gods, fate (*moira*) or necessity (*anankē*). And man has his *daimōn*, his guardian or tutelary genius. If this word is translated into what to us is rational language, it designates the personification of man's fate or the fate of his house, which is to say that a *daimōn* sets down the limit for individual man's potential acts; the *daimōn* can protect, warn, or bring disaster. In the philosophical tradition man was by Heraclitus and Democritus held responsible for his action through a kind of identification of soul with *daimōn*. In Aeschylus the thought of responsibility is expressed poetically rather than rationally. He who from *hubris* or blindness (*atē*) strives to exceed what is allotted to him and wants to become something other than what he is will be haunted by a fearsome *daimōn* – as happened to Xerxes who wanted to lay Hellas in ruins (Aesch. *Pers.* 724) and as also happened to the blood-stained House of Atreus (*Ag.* 1468 ff.).

Such a transition between concept, personification, and godhead is not unknown in the philosophical tradition and has its ancestry both in Homer (see p. 13) and popular religion. But in Aeschylus the seeming vagueness is meaningful. Man is indeed confronted with unknown powers, which objectively might be called necessity, subjectively fate or guilt, and from a religious point of view, the gods. But the thought is always of a limit to human understanding, which can only be crossed through the experience of life and through the interference of the very same powers.

Seemingly man acts blindly in such a universe. The same act can be necessary, dutiful, and bring about guilt. Man cannot act against the larger order, but he can accept his fate, and therein lies, in the final analysis, the seeds of justice – Aeschylus' theodicy, so to speak. But the individual also carries with him the fate of his house, which is to say the offence, the guilt, and the call for revenge that attach themselves to the house. The dramatic conflict in Aeschylus often arises from the fight between the mythical demand for blood revenge where one misdeed begets another and the demands of a new age for higher justice and higher morality; the hero's moral dilemma is accordingly that he can do nothing but accept the role prescribed by the old norms – and thereby incurs a guilt that cannot be washed away. Aeschylus' answer is often called a reconciliation, which is to say that he does not exchange one set of norms for another, but by a collaboration between gods and men he elevates the family quarrel to a matter of state.

This is the main theme of the *Oresteia*, a trilogy performed shortly before Aeschylus died. Behind the solution of the conflict between old and modern norms lies a profound reconciliation of blind fate to higher justice and higher morality, which is learned through suffering. The chorus knows Zeus as the executor of justice, but he is a remote and harsh god – 'Zeus, whoever he may be; I call him by that name, if it is dear to him to be so named', as we hear in the famous hymn to Zeus (*Ag.* 160). The gods are splendidly enthroned, but their bounty is cruel. Zeus it is who has shown mortals the way to wisdom by setting down his own law: learn through suffering (176 ff.).

The chorus also turns against the old adage that unbounded happiness begets insatiable misery:

> I have not the others' faith,
> but think alone.
> The sinful act
> will in the end beget more sin,
> the spitting image of its kin.

Yet fortune always blesses
the home of justice with fair issue.

(Ag. 757 ff.; cf. Eum. 538ff.)

Life is not, as in the popular belief, a constant change between happiness and misery, for guilt begets guilt, and justice begets justice. There is also a goodly distance from Pindar's praise of the race of nobles to Aeschylus' general law and general morality, which respect neither person nor rank:

But justice shines in smoky shacks;
she only honours purity of heart.

(Ag. 774–5)

Sophocles' (496–406 BC) universe is also peopled by gods and men; the gods are everywhere, but the gods' plans are not accessible to men, and any thought of the joint efforts of gods and men – as in Aeschylus – to bring about a new moral and judicial order is quite alien to Sophocles. He can let the chorus or his characters voice spontaneous piety, a confidence that divine laws warrant the higher justice, and in this respect it may be instructive to compare Aeschylus' hymn to Zeus with the encomium on Zeus that is offered by the chorus in *Oedipus Rex*:

O, may it be my lot in life
always to keep reverend purity
in all my thoughts and deeds.

(Soph. OT 863 ff.)

By his laws god is great, he does not age, and 'champion for me is God; I shall not let Him go' (881). A like confidence in divine laws as superior to human ones is voiced by Antigone, herself the incarnation of 'the purity of the heart' of which both Aeschylus and Sophocles speak:

Not today, nor yesterday – eternally
they live; none knows when they arose.

(Ant. 456–7)

But man is not privy to the laws of the gods. He is the plaything of what is characteristically called 'necessary chance' (*Aj.* 485; cf. Democritus on these concepts), and most often the gods appear cruel, as the vengeful deities of old, the enforcers of law, or as dangerous, possessive powers. The deeply tragic in the Sophoclean drama, which permits of no reconciliation – as in Aeschylus – is that life to the eye of man never 'works out right'. Suffering and an incomprehensible series of misfortunes that conform with a gruesome inner logic are facts that neither are explained nor defended. Sophocles shows this by a subtle dramatic technique, which perhaps a little obliquely has been called tragic irony – which is to say that what apparently occurs is not what actually occurs. Oedipus, for example, wants to rid his city of a curse; but so doing, he flings himself upon misfortune. Each of the characters has his own understanding of the events; the chorus have their own; and the audience have their awareness of what is hiding behind appearances. Sophocles' tragic irony is neither sceptical nor sarcastic but a simple demonstration of life's own ambiguousness.

The reactions of the chorus to the events in *Antigone* are clear examples of such a fumbling human understanding of life; step by step it is gainsaid by the dramatic development. At each of the phases of the drama the reflections of the chorus are double-sided and ambiguous, opaque to the chorus itself. The first *stasimon*, for example (*Ant.* 332 ff.), lauds human wisdom ('nothing in the world is as great as Man'); man has made himself the master of the sea and earth, and he is the master of language and thought – *if* only he does not sin against the laws of the city and the laws of the gods. Without knowing it, the chorus has thus formulated the unsolvable and the disastrous conflict of the tragedy.

Man has options, but if he has chosen, he has surrendered to an unknown fate, and perhaps his choice was indeed predetermined by fate. Misfortune and the tragic conflict come from the outside, but the focus has been shifted to the hero himself; the tragic hero is alone with his moral suffering. In Aeschylus higher powers fight among themselves with the hero as the defenceless – almost anonymous – victim; in Sophocles the hero is the man who solely on account of his character (cf. *Philoct.* 902; 1310) may take suffering upon himself. In this consists his real freedom.

Sophocles' most famed tragedies, *Antigone* and *Oedipus Rex* deal with the curse of the Thebian Labdacides. In obedience to the god's law Antigone buries her brother, and thus she defies the law of the city and King Creon. But the tragedy does not deal – as in Aeschylus – with the conflict between two sets of norms; its subject is two people's reactions to this conflict. Both Creon and Antigone perish – but Creon is destroyed by his defiant pride; Antigone wins, but victory costs her life.

In terms of the mythical chronology *Oedipus Rex* is earlier. Where the hero in Aeschylus (Orestes) acts under coercion but fully aware of the guilt he takes upon himself, Oedipus does not know that he has killed his father and married his mother. Objectively, he has committed a crime, but subjectively he is blameless; yet the punishment is his. It has often been pointed out that Sophocles nowhere exploited tragic irony to greater effect than in his *Oedipus Rex*. Oedipus is the good and wise king; he has solved the riddle of the Sphinx but does not know his own; as the good king he is, he is more anxious than anybody to discover the guilt that lies over the city; but the greater his efforts, the more tightly he ties the noose around his own neck; seeing, he is blind. When he realizes the truth he blinds himself. In *Oedipus Rex* as well the protagonist must take upon himself the conflict between the welfare of his city, which Oedipus uncompromisingly acknowledges, and the unfathomable ways of the god.

Sophocles' hero accepts the fact that life is ambiguousness and suffering; he is no repentant sinner, but meets his misfortune with reverence for the divine that he does not understand and remains true to himself.

It is sometimes said that the question of free will is not posed in the fifth century. The reader of Sophocles will doubt such a claim. To Sophocles freedom and necessity are not opposed to each other, and he does not demand a world order in which the blameless avoids punishment. His view of man's role is presented poetically and with the poet's distance. But it might have been translated into a philosophical theory.

There are points of resemblance with the Stoics' subtle unification of physical determinism and ethical freedom through acceptance.

It is not unusual to look for contrasts and parallels between Sophocles and Herodotus – 'the father of history' – who was his contemporary (485/80–430/25 BC) and who told of the customs and history of peoples, culminating with the greatest event, the Persian Wars. Herodotus' narrative talents require no comment, nor is there any doubt that to him history is meaningful. History is a drama, and even a minor chain of events in Herodotus' account is often a carefully constructed dramatic unit. But the more specific implications in Herodotus' 'view of history' are difficult to spot for a modern reader in search of a consistent theory. Yet one can point out that many contemporary currents converge in Herodotus: the inquisitiveness and reserved scepticism of Ionian natural philosophy, the epic tradition, tragedy, a simple, somewhat old-fashioned religiousness closely related to popular belief, and a reliance on the gods' always true but veiled oracular utterances – especially the wisdom of the Delphic god. An agnostic and subtle rationalism thrives in Herodotus side by side with deep piety. A rational account is probably sufficient, but it is prudent to believe in a higher government behind it. What keeps the work together is not a considered theory of history, but first and foremost delight in a good tale with a good point. Nevertheless, even the smallest anecdote has a perspective: the vicissitudes of human life, unfathomable fate – necessity, a god or *daimōn* – changing good fortune to misfortune and overthrowing the proud. On a grand scale this is what happened when the great Persian realm was defeated by Greece. Man can only seemingly choose; he does not know the consequences of his choice – the King of Persia chose insolently to bring tiny Hellas to her knees, but thereby he chose his own downfall. The Delphic 'know thyself' accordingly means to Herodotus: respect your limitation and know that you are only a man. Nor is it good for man to know his fate, for he has no power to ward it off (cf. Her. IX 16).

Fate and necessity have as much significance for Herodotus as for Aeschylus and Sophocles, and Herodotus also knows that the punishment of fate clings to the family, although it may not be effectuated until the fourth or fifth generation, as happened to the great King Croesus who failed to heed the wise Solon's warning and completed his own destruction by misinterpreting the Oracle's answer (I 32 ff.). It is not accidental that this paradigmatic tale can be found in Book One, nor that it is structured like a tragedy in which the net is inescapably tightened and the protagonist acts in blindness. The tale of Croesus can rise to tragic pathos, and a minor character, Adrastus, elevates himself to the stature of tragic hero; he takes his own life after he has acted as the instrument of fate by mistake having killed the king's son (I 45).

But Herodotus' belief in fate is more closely akin to popular belief than is tragedy; he is hardly a profound thinker, and therefore he is perhaps more informative about what was usually thought at the time. Prosperity and happiness are omens of misfortune; they provoke the jealousy of the gods and bring down punishment on the miscreant – nobody knows when. It was against such a belief in fate that Aeschylus turned, and to Sophocles as well the human tragedy takes place at another level. He is familiar with blind fate, but he does not know of jealous gods; the tragic depends on inner human suffering not on the edifying or terrifying that lies in seeming good fortune ending in misfortune.

Aeschylus, Sophocles, and Herodotus, each in his own way, interpreted an Archaic view of life, a religious realism, in which remote gods are the masters of man but do not thereby provide him with much occasion for optimism. But there were quite different currents in the century, and they became prevalent in the later years of the great age. This is a rationalism where the gods have departed the human arena, where man is master in his own house, and is considered a natural being who by his reason has created a civilized world. This rationalism manifests itself, among other things, in a view of history characterized by faith in the future and a cultural optimism inspired, we must believe, by the general optimism of the Periclean golden age. Ionian philosophy constituted the scientific presupposition.

From the historian Diodorus Siculus, who lived as late as the first century BC, a passage has been preserved on the development of the universe and man (Diod. Sic. I 7 ff.), which in spite of some terminological retouching, clearly reveals itself as a survival of fifth-century thought. It has – probably incorrectly – been attributed to Democritus; there are, to be sure, agreements with his view of civilization (on this, see p. 76), but the section summarizes a line of thought we meet elsewhere as well, and probably it had several sires. The basic thought is that there has been gradual progress towards the natural and cultural world as we know them. Heaven and earth have come into being by a separation of the elements, set in motion by a vortex – the standard explanation of fifth-century natural philosophers. The first living beings arose in water, but by and by they also adapted themselves to life on land. Man is such a living creature. Thus he is considered from a purely biological point of view as an animal among other animals. The first men led a miserable, unprotected existence. But common needs bred common interests; language made communication possible and, above all, the formation of a society to meet common needs. Man's finest tools were his hands, language, and his acumen. It is clear that this development is viewed positively. There is no question of a vanished golden age, but of progress made by man himself, and it is worth noticing that language and the establishment of a community are decisive pre-conditions for the development of technical skills.

Plato has the great Sophist Protagoras present another version (Plat. *Prot.* 320 C ff.; on this, see p. 105); behind Plato's ironic and cunning style we may probably believe that it is actually Protagoras who speaks. Protagoras uses the frame of myth or fable, but he himself remarks that this should not be taken too seriously. We are not told how the universe came into being; but we learn that the gods bade Prometheus (he who thinks ahead) and Epimetheus (he who has hindsight) create the animals out of earth and fire and equip them with suitable properties. Epimetheus eagerly took the initiative. He created each species of animal, provided each with natural protection, pointed out sources of nourishment, and allotted to each certain forms of behaviour. But when he came to man he had used up his whole supply of natural talents. Then Prometheus interfered and stole fire and technical skill from the gods – for which he was, as it happened, punished later. Then man began to acquire necessities and nourish himself with crops from the land; he cultivated the land and created language. But something was amiss; men were constantly in quarrels and fights, because they were without justice and morality. Zeus then commanded Hermes to furnish them with these, for he feared what might otherwise happen.

Thus men were able to found societies, and while people in other respects have unequal talents, all partake of justice and morality so that they can share in governing – as the democratic Protagoras concludes.

The decisive elements and the utilitarian tendency are also included in Protagoras. Although he does not concern himself with cosmology, he is all the more interested in the development from natural – biological – conditions to god-given – read: manmade – social institutions, including divine worship. And it is quite fitting that precisely Protagoras emphasizes that ethical norms are the basis for political life. The myth reveals his personal modifications of the theme.

We know something about the effect of these theories on their time. Apparently they were old enough to have called for reactions by the 'archaic' tragedians. The tragedy of *Prometheus Bound* has been transmitted as written by Aeschylus. Surely Prometheus, the benefactor of mankind, symbolizes man's progress, but the myth is no external embellishment. Prometheus' description of his benefactions to men (Aesch. *Prom.* 436 ff.; cf. 226) constitutes a close parallel to Diodorus Siculus' account and to Plato's *Protagoras*. But the main theme of the tragedy is that Prometheus – humanity? – from excessive pride has offended Zeus and hence must be punished. Here we meet the cruel Zeus; but it is possible that Zeus and Prometheus were reconciled in a subsequent tragedy, in analogy with the idea of the reconciliation in the *Oresteia*. Sophocles' reaction, the choral song in *Antigone* lauding the greatness of man, has already been discussed: man is great – *if* only . . . .

Opposed to the evolutionary hypothesis stand Plato and Aristotle, the idealists. To them the world and man are without temporal beginning, and there is a metaphysical background for human norms and institutions. The theory is parodied and undermined, so to speak from the inside in Plato's *Republic* (*RP* II 369 A ff.). Aristotle's reply can be seen in the beginning of his *Politics* (*Polit.* 1252 a 24 ff.).

A rationalist and naturalistic view of humanity and civilization does, of course, not necessarily have to take the form of an optimistic belief in progress. If the gods, fate, or providence depart from the world, the vicissitudes of life will remain – in the then current mode of thought: the subtle interplay between necessity and chance, all that is alien to man. Democritus represents a confident belief that human reason can provide insight into enigmatic nature and thus make it possible to create a worthwhile human life. Thucydides and Euripides were also rationalists, but their trust that the majority of people will act rationally was not very great.

Thucydides, who died shortly after 400, was the historian of the Peloponnesian War and the first historian to formulate and deliberately use source criticism. He belongs to the circle of empirical rationalists who in natural philosophy are represented by Anaxagoras and Democritus and in medicine by the Hippocratic school. Like them he seeks 'truth in the deep', which is to say that he looks for the hidden causes of chains of external events in a world in which the gods do not participate. That such an objective truth exists is taken for granted, but it is not always possible to arrive at more than the probable. Visions or speculations that cannot be verified – such as, for example, the theory of evolution, which takes the history of the world back to the formation of the universe – are of no interest to Thucydides. But if one succeeds in gaining insight into the true sequence of events, one has realized the necessity of what at first sight appears as chance. The parallel with Democritus is evident, and it is clear that necessity neither signifies logical necessity nor absolute predictability – once again as in Democritus and the physicians. The insight of the historian and the politician is basically the same and provides political experience. To use an Aristotelian formulation: it is an insight into what happens for the most part. Therefore one does not everywhere need to blame chance, as Thucydides has Pericles announce (Thuc. I 140). Cause, insight, probability, and necessity are key words in Thucydides.

Understanding of a particular sequence of events depends on critical examination of available sources. But in the final analysis the historian's knowledge is insight into man's general nature, which is constant (I 22). The proper understanding of a series of events – the Peloponnesian War, for example – is universally applicable and paradigmatic, and hence Thucydides is able to describe his own work as a possession for ever (ibid.). The balance between the particular and the universal is reflected in the form of the work. The universal only appears indirectly in Thucydides' account, but in the orations that he assigns to his 'historical' persons, he follows the epic tradition in so far as the motives for actions are furnished in the form of general reflections about a concrete situation.

The driving force in the political process and in human nature is power. Whoever has power will use it, and whoever does not must submit. In his account of the psychology of power Thucydides is almost always objectively descriptive, as in the famous dialogue between the Athenians and the Melians, which precedes the Athenians' brutal subjugation of the Isle of Melos, which had wished to remain neutral (V 84 ff.; cf. the debate on the siege of Mytilene, II 35 ff.). It is characteristic of Thucydides that the dialogue takes the shape of a debate on general principles. The Athenians leave the Melians with the choice of subjugation or destruction. It has always been self-evident that the law of might prevails, so they say, and justice prevails only among equals. If the Melians are realistic they will choose the lesser evil, which will be helpful for both sides. The Melians, of course, know very well that they are trapped. Their argument is not about justice and morality but about the changeable fortunes of war, and so they maintain that in the long run brutality will bring its own punishment. This is an uncertain hope, reply the Athenians – tantamount to gambling with realities. When the Melians refuse, all male inhabitants are executed, and the women and children are sold as slaves.

Yet the Melians were vindicated. Thucydides knows the irony of fate and masters contrasting effects as subtly as any Sophocles. A few years later ensued the decisive defeat of the Athenians in Sicily (415–13 BC) and the equally brutal fate of the surviving Athenians. In wartime the true face of human nature shows itself, as Thucydides shows elsewhere (III 81 ff.) in one of the few passages in which he directly voices the moral indignation that normally lies between his lines. Reason cannot – as in Democritus – justify morality; in the real world the sole refuge of morality is indignation, resignation, or sympathy.

This concealed dual view probably contributes to the construction of Thucydides' work as if it were a tragedy. And as does Herodotus (the tale of Croesus), Thucydides sounds his basic theme almost in the beginning of his work. It is often said that Pericles is Thucydides' hero; he has the statesman's insight and knows that politics build on power, even though power should only be brought to bear when it has been consolidated. His successors did not have that insight, and so things must go wrong – the events at Melos and Sicily are Thucydides' version of the old *hubris* motif. Pericles delivers his funeral oration at the outset of the war. Thereafter misfortunes set in: the great plague and the first military confrontations. When Pericles once again addresses the Assembly of the People (II 60 ff., especially 63–4), he no longer speaks of the democratic ideals; now we see the tough Pericles who makes the Athenians stick to the power politics that they had embraced once and for all. Is this the wise statesman who understands political necessity, or is his mask slipping?

In Thucydides man has a relatively large measure of freedom. Freedom is dependent on insight, although not on insight into the good. And the measure of chance or of the incalculable (*tychē*), which will also determine human life, is not lessened by people most often being without insight. The history of mankind is the history of folly.

The last of the great tragedians, Euripides (ca. 485–406 BC), marks a break with the two earlier tragedians both with respect to form and content; but his cast of mind is reminiscent of Thucydides'. His basic position is rationalistic, but he is not confident that reason is able – even in smallest measure – to master the irrational forces of life. He has Thucydides' distant objectivity and repressed passion, fights for psychological insight, and is perhaps more than Thucydides influenced by the contemporary rhetoric, by the Sophists, and by the philosophers. Thus he can present a psychological conflict dialectically and is, so to speak, able to toy with philosophic catchwords; his poetry is experimental, at times absurd (*Helena*), at times affected, but never preachy.

It cannot be surprising that the characters in such a poet's work do not have Aeschylus' or Sophocles' confidence in the gods. Euripides' gods err as much as his characters do, and like humans they are subject to blind chance (*tychē*), good fortune or misfortune. When the gods nevertheless interfere and resolve the dramatic conflict, it has sometimes been interpreted as dramatic inability and sometimes – probably with greater justice – as the especially refined irony of the absurd.

Euripides may let his characters – not the chorus – appeal to Zeus; but it is Zeus – the unknown god – who fades into nothing. Zeus, whoever you are – we hear this with clear address to Aeschylus – you who sustain the earth and have your throne on earth; you the unfathomable, whether you be nature's necessity or human reason, I appeal to you; soundlessly you walk on your path and guide men's fortunes towards justice (Eur. *Troad.* 884 ff.; cf. *Her. fur.* 1263 ff.; *Hel.* 1136 ff.).

But Euripides can also let his characters ask whether it is not *tychē* that is god rather than Zeus (*Hec.* 488 ff.), or he can let them pray to Tychē (*Io* 1512 ff.) – a modern reader unfamiliar with Greek 'personification' of concepts may thus be surprised that scepticism about the gods creates yet another god, as it were.

The new democratic times can be seen in the embourgeoisement of Euripidean drama; within the mythical frame, which by and large is still observed, the atmosphere is far from mythical; plain ordinary people may appear, and the protagonist in the *Medea* – a barbarian woman – pleads the lot of suppressed woman (*Med.* 230 ff.). But it is characteristic of Euripides that his democratic outlook is dominated by its less pleasant side: no mortals are free; we are bound to money, chance, a political majority, and to legal decrees (*Hec.* 864 ff.). And mythical 'heroes' – and gods – are 'ordinary', also in the sense that they have no tragic format: the hero is not up to his task and is unable to win by taking his own fate upon himself. 'The pure of heart' are few in Euripides (Hippolytus, Io, Iphigenia), and often they stand on the outside – whether by chance or choice. Man becomes great in crime or madness; an example is Medea who kills her children because she is rejected in love. But Euripides does not judge his heroes; Medea was violated, and, although her misdeeds are boundless, they are not groundless.

Euripides is the poet of passion; erotic conflicts, which play a less prominent part in Aeschylus and Sophocles, are with him a principal theme and gave offence to his contemporaries. He circles around the pathology of the human psyche, which he lays bare and observes with hitherto unknown empathy, indirectly often with sympathy, and not seldom with melodramatic effects. And there is a great distance from Euripides to the Socratic maxim that 'virtue is knowledge'. Euripides' guilt-ridden – and great – women know very well what they do. Medea knows that her triumph is her suffering (*Med.* 764 ff.), and Phaedra can begin her self-analysis with the consideration that we know what is just and right but do not act accordingly (*Hipp.* 377 ff.).

What most frequently interests Euripides is the dramatic situation, the passions in themselves, and their inner logic rather than the development of character. Yet he also made experiments with respect to this. That is the case, for example, with Iphigenia, the protagonist in *Iphigenia in Aulis*, performed posthumously.

Euripides' 'message' lies in the psychological analysis itself, in the uncovering, as it were, of irrationality by reason; reason can analyze but never master passion. *The Bacchae* – also performed soon after the poet's death – portrays religious madness, the ecstatic worship of Dionysus, in which the female worshippers of the god – the Bacchae – identify themselves with Dionysus (Bacchus) by devouring his flesh. That is to say that they become one with nature – with its grace and its brutality. The Bacchae flee from rational deliberation, from every distinction between good and evil, and – perhaps the essential point – they flee from themselves and surrender to pure instinct (cf. *Bacch.* 862 ff.). Euripides exploits fully the contrast between mild happiness and wild madness (677 ff.; 1043 ff.) united in the god, beyond good and evil. The tragedy culminates with the King – representing reason's scepticism – being torn asunder by the Bacchae among whom is his own mother who carries home her son's head in triumph. When she awakens from drunken stupor she realizes what she has done and returns to reason's curse. As transmitted to us, her final words are: 'Let others dance to Bacchus' (1387).

Euripides himself never has the last word. In his last play he lets characters and chorus praise and damn the triumphant Dionysus, the irrational and repressed. This is one commentary on what has been called the period of rationalist enlightenment in Greek intellectual history.

10

THE SOPHISTS

———•◆•———

Events in the course of the intellectual history of the fifth century BC followed swiftly upon each other. Yet, as always in a transitional period, breaks and connective lines criss-cross each other. Concepts such as necessity, chance, or fate could still be applied to alien and unknown powers even after the secular breakthrough. And rational insight was not necessarily an insight bridging man's little world and nature's macrocosm. It is possible to observe a relatively uniform rationality in the science of the age – Democritus, Hippocrates, Thucydides – but the concept of insight had already for some time been acquiring a new content. No longer was the object mere speculative insight into the nature of the world, but far more man's insight into his own nature, his own powerlessness, or his own possibilities.

Without doubt the Sophists – the 'wise' men – were the first and foremost to voice the rationalism and humanism of the age, a strong confidence in man's autonomy and in his capacity to understand and give new shape to the civilization he himself had created. To the Sophist, man's worth – and success – depend on knowledge and 'education', not on birth or privilege.

Sophistry is not a philosophical school but an intellectual movement that manifests itself in philosophy and science, rhetoric and politics, anthropology and paedagogics. There are certain shared intellectual *leitmotifs*, even though Sophists did not necessarily think alike. The Sophistic movement is closely tied to Periclean democracy in Athens and to the individual citizen's need for knowledge, political skill, and forensic training in a community based on direct democracy and oral procedure – abilities that provided him with hitherto unknown possibilities for social ascent. This notwithstanding, one should not imagine that Sophistry was a popular movement. The Sophists' task consisted rather in the education of a political elite, and they never had the broad popular appeal of the tragedians – nor did they presumably want it. Socrates' fate and Aristophanes' comedies show that the ordinary Athenian lived – and wanted to live – relatively unaffected by the new style of life. New-fashioned ideas might call for a derisive laugh and in extreme cases for aggression, whenever upper-class hotheads wanted to turn morality, religion, or politics upside-down. Very likely the average complacent Attic citizen was a quite telling conservative factor. In the first place it seemed irritating that the Sophists charged fees for their teaching; according to old-fashioned ideals no fee was required for making people 'good'. Furthermore, they did not – as far as one could judge – believe in anything, but did turn black into white. Nor did they seem to belong anywhere. The Sophists came from all corners of the Greek world, cosmopolitans going from place to place as 'travelling salesmen in intellectual food' (Plat. *Soph.* 223 E). Thus, in his confrontation with the Sophists, Plato could rely and play on popular animosity.

Our sources are sparse. Few fragments have been preserved, and – such major contributions as those of Protagoras aside – we must suppose that the majority of the Sophists' works were lost at a fairly early point. The reason may very well be that Plato and Aristotle considered them enemies and non-philosophers; because of this they were excluded from the doxographic tradition and to this very day play quite a drab role in the history of philosophy. Our most important source, about Protagoras at any rate, is Plato. In contrast to the other Sophists, he apparently considered Protagoras a worthy opponent who should be justly dealt with; hence it seems possible to form a reasonably correct picture of at least the principal figure among the Sophists – based on the chief opponent of the movement.

Many have felt that the Sophists are in need of rehabilitation. In part, their supposedly liberal tolerance and pragmatic attitude to life appeal to interpreters who themselves are not afraid to assist our uncertain knowledge (Popper on 'the great generation'). In part, the original contribution of the Sophists is indisputable in epistemology and linguistics and in cultural and moral philosophy. They debated such questions as the validity of cognition, the relation of language to reality, the concept of truth, and the dependence of moral norms on human nature and individual civilized societies. Their sphere of interest is in other words far more intimately connected with human activities than the tradition of the earlier natural philosophers. Their proper place is in a particular political context, but their teaching of practical and formal skills is closely tied to their scientific and philosophical theories.

One historic precondition for the Sophistic moment is rhetoric, which emerged as a special genre in Sicily during the fifth century. In then current Greek rhetoric, the distinction is made between three types of orations: the forensic oration, the purpose of which is to present arguments about a past sequence of events; the political oration in which the argument is about how events ought to occur; and the occasional oration – Pericles' funeral oration, for example – that appeals to emotions and in veiled fashion may plead a cause, even though not directly calling for a decision or action. According to rhetorical theory, all three categories imply a close interplay between case, speaker and audience. The speaker is not merely to impart information; his speech is an act, and therefore he must know both the case itself and his audience, know his goal, and how to exploit a favourable situation. For this technical skill is required; but thereby a series of epistemological and moral problems presents itself as well.

In a forensic oration one rarely finds oneself able to present unambiguous proof. In the great majority of cases the argument must be based on probability. In one of the oldest rhetorical manuals (written by Corax, now lost, the example in Aristot. *Rhet.* 1402 a 17; cf. Plat. *Phaedr.* 273 B) the following – fictive – case is produced: a big, strong man and a small, weak man have been at fisticuffs. Who began it? The small man ought, of course, to claim that he, being the smaller, would never attack his better; the big man ought, on the other hand, to maintain that exactly because people will point to him as the guilty one, he would never be stupid enough to attack. Legal arguments have grown from such, mostly fictional, concrete cases. Using exempla the speaker can acquire a technique of argumentation so that in analogous situations he has an arsenal of typical arguments – 'loci' – to have recourse to or 'seek out' (*inventio* in Latin rhetorical terminology). This form of argumentation differs from the deductive proof that was familiar to the Pythagoreans and the Eleatics and from the paedagogical persuasion that characterized so many Presocratics. The issue is probability, not truth. Thucydides – who was influenced by the Sophists – resembled them, but to him probability was an approximation to truth. The seemingly innocent tale of the fight between the big and the small man actually contains explosive philosophical matter, for not only can we never arrive at pure objective truth; but a human institution, the tribunal, determines the truth by judicial decision. Accordingly, man establishes truth as well as justice. In a political oration the argument turns on probability and expediency. Here as well it is man who can do things with words. What, then, is the relation between truth, probability, and expediency?

Epistemologically the Sophists could find support in Parmenides. To him thought and being were the same, which means that true thinking is known or true being; all words about the not-being are mere empty names figured out by mortals (Parm. DK B8,38). But what if man creates truth, and true thinking still expresses true being? Such a question could occasion the Sophistic slogan that one cannot think what is not (cf. Plat. *Euthyd.* 286 A; *Theaet.* 167 A; 189 A). Therein lies a twist of the concept of knowledge; knowledge is made subjective and relative and is not merely a theoretical affair; it is instead a practice and a knowledge of what is useful. He who propagates his knowledge is a paedagogue, demagogue, and 'psychagogue' – he is an educator, a political leader, and he 'guides souls'. Hence cognition cannot be separated from the imparting of knowledge; it is probable that it was under Sophist influence that the word *paideia* – education – at this time assumes the sense of formation of character.

Although the several aspects of the Sophistic movement are connected, of course individual Sophists cultivated their own spheres of interest. The grand old father-figure of the movement, Protagoras (c.490–20), covered the entire field with all the questions of epistemology and moral philosophy that have been hinted at in the preceding; to this should be added that he evidently was a paedagogue *par excellence*. He came from the outskirts of the Greek world – Democritus' home town of Abdera in Thracia – but by mid century he was so well known that in 444 he helped the Athenians with the making of laws for their colony of Thurioi in Southern Italy. Among other prominent first-generation Sophists was Gorgias (c.483–376), a student of the Sicilian rhetors, who among other things developed a technique of formal argumentation and is well-known as a reformer of Greek prose style; others were Prodicus (c.470 to after 400) and Hippias (c.480–10) who primarily were inclined to scientific study. It is apparent that the Sophists' contribution to what we call the humanities was significant, even though neglected by Plato and hence by posterity. Plato has described his Sophist opponents with great care, and his flair for staging a confrontation is effective: loyal generosity, harsh sarcasm, or the barbed witticism that sticks. He lets the Sophists emphasize that they are not dry scholars remote from the world as were the old natural philosophers; they are often consulted by important people (cf. *Hipp. Maj.* 281 C). The *Protagoras* dialogue takes place in the house of the rich Athenian Callias immediately before the Peloponnesian War; here almost all the bigwigs are assembled, and Protagoras is portrayed as the uncrowned king, while Prodicus and Hippias must submit to their role as caricatured secondary characters (*Prot.* 314 E ff.; cf. 337 A ff.). The main concern is quite clearly the meeting between the two great educators of Hellas: Protagoras and Socrates. Gorgias is conspicuous for his absence. He did not reach Athens until 427 and is accorded a dialogue of his own, in which the master himself is dealt with politely and condescendingly; the attack on his disciples is all the more biting.

The Sophists were educators and provided wealthy young people of Athens with a welcome supplement to the elementary schooling in gymnastics and the musical disciplines (reading, arithmetic, and music) – a mixture of elementary teaching proper and building of character, for example through the reading of famous classics. The Sophists could carry this education further, for example through allegorical interpretation of the poets, which made the literary heritage topical and socially relevant. But of course this was not all. They taught in private or in public, acted as legal or political consultants, or lectured at great assemblies, for example at the Olympic Games. It is not surprising that their written work often mirrored the verbal form; they wrote not only scholarly monographs, but also declamations and allegorical representations (cf. Protagoras' 'myth') or guides to debating techniques. It appears, for example, from Plato's *Protagoras* (cf. 320 C; 329 B; 334 E; 338 D) that there were formalized rules about lengthy and brief speeches and about questions and answers in a debate. This met the needs of a more or less innocent competitive mentality; but the more profound purpose is training in 'the art of contradiction' – *antilogikē*. This kind of technique was seen as a common feature of the Sophists (cf., e.g. *Soph.* 232 B), but it rested on a theoretical foundation.

PROTAGORAS

One of Protagoras' writings – a manual or collection of exempla – deals with 'the art of contradiction' (*antilogikē*), and it is Protagoras who is supposed to have said that two opposite arguments – *logoi* – can be furnished about any given case (*Prot.* DK B6 A; Diog. Laert. IX 51), and that what counts is 'to make the weaker case the stronger' (cf. Aristot. *Rhet.* 1402 a 23; Aristoph. *Nub.* 112 ff.). Such slogans can, of course, be taken as instructions in lawyers' tricks – to turn right into wrong – but in themselves they reveal no more than that an assertion about a case can be negated and that it is possible to argue from a seemingly weak position. That this is not only possible but legitimate is owing to the actual ambiguity of reality. Plato's Protagoras advances several relativistic views: some foods are beneficial for man but not for animals; something is good for animals but not for plants, etc. (Plat. *Prot.* 334 A ff.). And it appears from a work, probably by a student – the so-called *Double Arguments* from c.400 (DK, no. 90) – that such listings had become fashionable. The author of this not very stimulating small pamphlet has many trite instances to comment upon: the same can be both good and evil, just and unjust; he only rarely borrows a genuine point from contemporary discussions, for example that a statement about contingent states of affairs may be true at one time and false at another (4, 2). But relativistic or sceptical points of view were after all not new in the philosophical tradition – one needs only to think of Xenophanes and Heraclitus. The new lies in Protagoras' epistemology.

The most famous Protagoras quotation left to us – the so-called *homo mensura*-thesis (Prot. DK B 1; cf. Plat. *Theaet.* 152 A; *Crat.* 386 A; Sext. Emp. *Adv. math.* VII 60) – was the beginning of his main epistemological work, *The Truth*, which has a bellicose sub-title, translatable as 'the Knock-Out Arguments'. The quotation is in typical fifth-century style: compact, pompous, and well-nigh untranslatable. Still, it seems reasonable to translate it as follows: 'Man is the measure of all things, of the being of things that are, of the not-being of things that are not'. This is open to many possible interpretations.

Our principal source is Plato's interpretation in the *Theaetetus* dialogue. Plato himself indicates indirectly (cf. *Theaet.* 152 C; 155 D; 166 A) that in his further argumentation he will proceed beyond the historical Protagoras; but in his opening presentation of the thesis, he is probably by and large fair (but see p. 221) – and we have no option other than to rely on his representation. According to Plato it is implicit in Protagoras' thesis that things are to me as they appear to me, to you as they appear to you, and 'appears to' should be interpreted as 'is perceived by'. The same wind, for example, appears cold to me, warm to you; ergo it is cold to me and warm to you. Now, the word 'appear'[1] can partially mean that something (a sensory object) appears to somebody (something red 'appears to person x') and partially that it appears to x *that* this and that is the case. The latter meaning implies a judgement that can pertain to a sensory situation (it appears to me that the wind is cold) or, for example, to political or moral circumstances (it appears to me that this or that is good). Later in Plato's discussion (165 E ff.) it becomes evident that Protagoras' thesis included all these meanings of 'appear'; but it is likely that he – as Plato presents it – considered perceptual judgements basic in relation to beliefs or valuations. In any case, it will hold good that what appears, appears *to* someone, that a judgement will be made *by* someone.

Actually, every word in Protagoras' thesis is debatable. Today it is taken for granted that Plato is right in claiming that 'man' stands for individual persons, and that an earlier-presented (Neo-Kantian) interpretation of 'man as species' is an anachronism; but this of course does not preclude some sort of conventionalism, as we know from Democritus' epistemology: it has become conventional to designate this or that sensory quality as 'red', for example. It is likewise certain that 'measure' signifies 'standard' or 'criterion'. Man himself is the judge of his impressions. However, it is not immediately certain what status 'things' – and properties – have in Protagoras' theory. Yet he cannot have been an adherent of what we today would call phenomenalism according to which only that exists that is perceived, the phenomenon, (*esse est percipi*); consequently he is exempt from worries about what

---

1   Greek: *phainesthai* – cf. 'phenomenon': what appears; more recent derivations: phenomenalism, phenomenology.

happens to the table when one does not sense it. Such a way of thinking would indeed also be an anachronism, contradicted by Plato's example, in which the objective existence of the wind is undoubted, and contradicted by the wording of the quotation, which implies that man is judge of the nature of something that in a vague sense is present or absent – independently of human minds. It follows from this that 'is' does not stand for existence but for mode of being – which is in agreement with general fifth-century thought, in which the existential 'is' is not set apart: 'to be' means to be something (cf. Parmenides).

But does this then mean that the wind in itself is both warm and cold, that one person perceives one quality in the thing, another the opposite – which would be reminiscent of Anaxagoras' view – or does it mean that it is neither warm nor cold; that sense qualities are dependent on the perceiving subject – Democritus' view? At first sight it looks as if both possibilities can be argued; the former seems to find some support in Sextus Empiricus (*Hyp. Pyr.* I 217) who – in Aristotelian terms and clearly influenced by Plato's *Theaetetus* – took Protagoras to mean that the physical object potentially possesses the properties that appear when the object is sensed.

But actually the question is meaningless on Protagoras' premisses. What is radical in his pragmatic theory of perception seems indeed to be that he refrains from this type of question. It is sufficient to know that there is a wind; what is decisive is how each of us perceives it. This is no solipsism, for we do not, each of us, have our own private wind, and we can meaningfully tell each other how we perceive the wind; in modern terminology: we can describe the wind phenomenologically. But in other respects the theory is extremely far-reaching – whether or not Protagoras himself realized all the consequences. In the first place, it is essential that a distinction is made between physical object and sense object. My judgement of the sense object is naturally true – if I sense a cold wind, it is true that I sense a cold wind. The relative and subjective consists in my being unable to say something true about the nature of the physical object. In the second place, the theory implies that Protagoras makes the act of perception primary in relation to the perceiving subject and the perceived object – subject and object are constituted by the very act of perception. Whether or not Protagoras reflected on these consequences, he certainly must have realized that he breaks away from the earlier philosophical tradition. He protests in the name of common sense against theories that claim that the world is entirely different from what it appears to be. But he does more than that. Where the aim of all earlier efforts had been to proceed from the phenomenon to a constant and 'true' reality behind it, to Protagoras human truth is inherent in the phenomenon itself, in immediate experience – regardless of the reality behind it. Accordingly it is experience that determines men's actions.

Two consequences can be drawn from this. In the first place (cf. Plat. *Theaet.* 157 E ff.), that which appears in dreams is as true as that which occurs when one is awake, and the sick man's view of the world as well as that of the 'abnormal' is as true as the healthy or 'normal' man's. In the second place, Protagoras must take an agnostic or negative view of phenomena that cannot be sensed. It is, for example, not correct that a tangent only touches a circle at one particular point (cf. Aristot. *Met.* 998 a 1), for nobody has ever seen it – in any case, an interesting glimpse into the discussion apparently then being conducted for or against idealized geometry (cf. here p. 72 on

Democritus). It is in this light that one ought also to see the famous fragment (Prot. DK B 4), which offers a welcome impression of Protagoras' subtle sense of humour: 'I cannot know whether the Gods exist or not, nor what shape they have. There is much to prevent it: the obscurity of the matter and the brevity of human life'.

Relativism and subjectivism characterize not only Protagoras' theory of perception but in a wider sense also his theory of beliefs. Here as well, we can only have recourse to Plato's *Theaetetus* (165 E ff.), where Socrates on behalf of Protagoras delivers a 'defence oration' intended to justify political and moral decisions. Once again we have no means of verifying Plato's version. But apparently Plato takes pains to come up with a sympathetic report; the theory presented is coherent and carefully worked out. To us it is Protagoras' own theory.

It is true not only of all perceptual judgements but of judgements of any kind that they are true in so far as they express a person's experience. There are accordingly no false judgements; every judgement – and every position – is as true as any other. Yet, not every judgement is equally expedient, and the concepts of true/false ought therefore to be replaced by the concepts of the expedient/inexpedient. The expert can persuade you that his view is more expedient than that of others, and hence he can make his judgement true for the person he persuades – the physician is in this sense an expert on health and sickness, the farmer on the tilling of his soil, and the wise man, 'the Sophist', can persuade you that his view of justice and morals in the long run will be profitable to the individual and society. In other words, the theory has political consequences. Positive law and the body of laws and moral norms, written or unwritten, and valid in a given state, are 'true' or just for that particular state for as long as they are valid – law and morality are relative to particular societies. So, just as the concept of truth is relative, so is the concept of justice. But an expert – the Sophist – will be able to decide if the prevailing norms are also expedient; accordingly he may persuade the state to change its norms. So Protagoras' theory does not imply slavish acceptance of any social system whatever, but presupposes that a state that functions properly makes decisions based on qualified debate. The state has need of qualified educators and statesmen – of Sophists.

This essentially pragmatic theory justifies the slogans that have been attributed to Protagoras among others, and which in brief indicate Sophistic practice: 'it is impossible to contradict' and 'one cannot say a nothing'; every assertion immediately expresses some individual experience. But for every assertion there is a corresponding counter-assertion; in this sense it is possible to contradict and possible to make the weaker case the stronger – provided that one can convince of probability and expediency.

At the same time, the theory colours Protagoras' version of the fifth-century evolutionist view of history, as set forth in the myth of Plato's *Protagoras* (320 C ff.; here p. 94). As mentioned earlier, the theory of evolution itself had several adherents in its day; but here there is reason to focus on some special Protagorean features. As the ideologue of democracy he is first and foremost interested in elucidating the basic political process. Man is a creature of nature but also a product of civilization, and he has turned himself into a civilized being by organizing the production of life's necessities, by giving shape to his society and its religious and political institutions, and by communication in language. Still, perhaps the most important precondition for cultural and civic life is a sense of justice and morality – of a system of norms and customs that prevent men from falling back into a Hobbes-like state of nature with every man at war with every man. The contrast between nature on the one hand and conventions and norms on the other – *physis* opposed to *nomos* were the phrases used – is crucial here, as it clearly was to all Sophists. Man cannot change his biological nature, but law and morality are human creations and consequently they can be changed. In Sophistic discussions *physis* and *nomos* were apparently often thought of as absolute opposites. But Protagoras looked more deeply – man is, to be sure, master in his own house and can thus determine the principles that must be valid in a given society. But it would appear from the myth that it is determined by nature *that* man is only able to live within the institutional frameworks and with certain rules of moral and political conduct. In this sense *nomos* is derived from *physis*; it is, in a manner of speaking, that part of nature on which man has influence. It says much that Plato lets another Sophist, Callicles (*Gor.* 483 E), speak of nature's own *nomos*.

The naturally given ability, which is a precondition for the establishment of society in general and more especially for a democratic society is in Greek called *aretē* – a concept that comprehends virtue, skill, and ability,j in other words, the ability that makes for a well-functioning person. In conformance with his entire, basically pragmatic position, Protagoras must consider this a means rather than a goal – *aretē* is the means to arrive at expedient, universal human welfare. It is not possible to furnish a strict definition from Protagoras' position, but it is possible to describe how the concept works. Inasmuch as virtue *par excellence* is political virtue and the constitution *par excellence* is the democratic one, virtue must – as stated in the myth – be distributed among all men, not as a fully developed skill but as an ability. Therefore virtue can be learned – a favourite topic of contemporary discussions – and therefore there is a need for teachers of virtue – as Athens, for example, needed Protagoras. And, as virtue – *aretē* –is common to all and not dependent on special talents, there is good sense in a general forming of character or an all-round education, and it makes sense for the state to expect each citizen to educate himself in civic virtue. Nobody scoffs at people who by nature's hand are poorly equipped for special trades, yet everybody can and ought to have insight in the common affairs – as Pericles himself had noted in his funeral oration. The state is entitled to sanctions against anybody who offends against his civic duties; it is characteristic of Protagoras that he considers punishment an educational measure. His view of *aretē* as common and teachable shows a reflected position with respect to the relation between expert knowledge and the right to participate in the making of decisions in a democracy.

In modern terms, Protagoras' thinking may be called pragmatic, naturalistic, and humanist rationalism. Furthermore, to judge by Plato – and no ancient source disagrees with him – there must have been quite imposing unity in his philosophy, which on the basis of a relativistic and subjectivistic epistemology constructs a political philosophy and an ideology of democracy. But this whole fabric of thought is, of course, open to criticism. There are grounds for imagining a quite close connection between Protagoras and Democritus, by thirty years his junior and a fellow-citizen from Abdera. Democritus' epistemology is perhaps in part formulated as an answer to Protagoras. In many ways the two resemble each other. Their ethical and political ideals are closely related, and both have optimistic confidence in reason as educator.

Epistemologically they were faced with analogous problems, and there appears to be a certain external resemblance between Protagoras and Democritus' 'sceptical' fragments – 'the truth lies in the deep'. As has been mentioned, Democritus also had a 'sceptical' methodological principle, in the preceding called 'the principle of sufficient reason'. But he employed this principle very restrictively; in general it holds true that we are not exclusively referred to the phenomenon, for thanks to reason we have the possibility of arriving at absolutely certain knowledge of the physical world and objective norms of morality. Therefore it is interesting to learn that Democritus explicitly criticized Protagoras' general scepticism (Plut. *Adv. Col.* 1109 A) and, in so doing, he also criticized the relativization of the concept of truth. He seems to have been the first to apply the so-called self-refuting argument to the *homo mensura* thesis (Sext. Emp. *Adv. math.* VII 389): if it is true that man is the measure of all things, the opinion of those who maintain that Protagoras' thesis is false is also true.

Plato's criticism – in both the *Theaetetus* and *Protagoras* – is to a large extent indirect. And at decisive points he generalized his criticism so that it applies to any relativistic and subjectivistic philosophy rather than specifically to Protagoras – which, as stated, he indicated himself. These wider perspectives will be dealt with in another context. Yet at this point, it is possible to single out a special Platonic criticism of Protagoras. With respect to epistemology, Plato has no objections to the claim that the individual's perceptual judgements are true *qua* perceptual judgements (Plat. *Theaet.* 179 C) – to me the wind is cold, if I feel that it is cold. Otherwise it is important for him in the *Theaetetus* to reduce Protagoras' theory of perception to mere phenomenalism. If the theory of perception really implies that the wind only exists for me or you, of course it cannot also exist in itself. Thus no ontology is possible; and an epistemology without an ontological foundation will in Plato's view lead to absolute fluctuation that would make knowledge itself impossible. These are perspectives that go beyond the historical Protagoras. Yet Plato is probably right, in the sense that there is something muddled about Protagoras' view of the relation between physical object and sense object. He both speaks about and does not speak about the physical object.

When Protagoras' epistemological relativism is expanded to apply to all kinds of judgement, Plato's criticism becomes more pointed. In part he employs Democritus' self-refuting argument (171 A ff.), and in part he points out that according to common sense expert knowledge does in fact exist, and it is considered competent, because it is able to predict future events with relative certainty: the physician, for example, is a better judge of disease than his patient, not because he is better at persuasion but because he knows (178 B ff.). If this were not the case no one would be wiser than anybody else and Protagoras no wiser than a pig (161 C). These arguments, conducted *ad hominem*, seem to imply a more essential critical point. To Protagoras wisdom does not consist in insight into truth but depends on ability to convince of the expedient. But what is the criterion for expediency? More generally: can one do without an objective concept of truth? Apparently Democritus and Plato presuppose that Protagoras claimed a special status for his *homo mensura* thesis in the sense that it is absolutely true that truth is relative. If so, Protagoras is of course directly defeated by the self-refuting argument. If he also considers his own thesis relative – that is to say as a report about what he, Protagoras, means – but at the same time claims that he can convince others of the 'expediency' of the thesis – it is a question whether he does not implicitly presuppose that something is objectively true. It is this question that is stated between the lines of Plato's criticism.

Plato's indirect criticism in the *Protagoras* follows the same paths. To Protagoras *aretē* was a means, not a goal, and the concept could only be defined as a means to achieve the expedient. Here Plato also attacks Protagoras' relativism. It must be possible in an absolute sense to account for what *aretē* is. It presupposes insight into absolute norms, and if such insight is impossible, virtue cannot be taught – as Protagoras had maintained (cf. *Prot.* 361 A). Plato's criticism of Protagoras is everywhere an indirect reference to an absolute concept of truth and a set of absolute norms. His final answer to Protagoras is: god is the measure of all things (*Leg.* IV 716 C).

Aristotle amplifies and clarifies the criticism that is latent in Plato's *Theaetetus* (*Met.* 1005 b 35 ff.; cf. 1009 a 6 ff.). Every argument presupposes at least the validity of one basic logical principle, the principle of contradiction. If everything is true, nothing is true, and argument is consequently impossible. To this should be added that every argument presupposes understandable language, which is to say that a valid and unambiguous inter-subjective means of communication exists. By the very fact that Protagoras is arguing, he presupposes logic and language as an objective standard. He presupposes what he denies.

GORGIAS

Rhetoric is the discipline that makes the word active, which enables man to act and change his own world by 'making the weaker case the stronger'. It presupposes technique and it presupposes reflections on the relation between truth and probability, between knowledge and belief, and between what is and what seems to be. Rhetoric is also a psychological discipline, for the rhetor's word is intended to affect certain people in a particular set of circumstances. As we have seen, Protagoras was able to provide a theoretical justification for rhetoric. Gorgias' field was formal rhetoric, and it may at first sight look as if he confined himself to teaching the technique of argumentation. Plato lets a student of Gorgias declare that Gorgias only wanted to train skilful rhetors; moral questions did not interest him (*Meno* 95 C). He allows Gorgias himself to declare that the subject of rhetoric is words and nothing else (*Gor.* 449 D ff.) and that rhetoric is superior to all other disciplines, because it subjugates everything voluntarily, not by force (*Phil.* 58 A).

Thanks to two fictive model speeches that have survived, we are able to form an impression of Gorgias' technique; these are speeches with paradigmatic argumentation applicable in analogous cases. One (Gor. DK B 11 a) is a legal tour de force: a defence oration, in which all the classical arguments for the innocence of the accused are presented and tied to an appeal to the judges' better selves. It would appear that there is little philosophy in this, but if one reads the other speech (11), one may get suspicious. This is a defence of Helen, the *femme fatale* of myth, who let herself be abducted by Prince Paris and thereby occasioned the Trojan War. The rhetor wants to rehabilitate the beauteous Helen. That she allowed herself to be abducted may be owing to fate, the bidding of necessity, or the will of the gods; she may have been compelled, or perhaps she let herself be charmed by words or was ensnared by love. In any case, she was a helpless victim. Helen was innocent, and her fate was not due to her guilt but to misfortune.

Here the tragic view of life is turned upside-down. The incalculable and unknowable powers of life (fate: *tychē*; necessity: *anankē* and gods), and whatever else would relentlessly make a tragic hero utterly guilty are ameliorating circumstances for which Helen is not responsible. One is tempted to ask whether she could be held responsible for anything at all. Furthermore, the speech cunningly becomes a commentary on itself, as it were. Truth must out, by means of the word, but the very force of words is the temptation that excuses Helen. Speech is treacherous, we are told (11, 8 ff.); by unnoticeable means the word can persuade one about anything whatsoever, as can be seen in poetry or incantations, which produce affect and illusion, fear and misery, joy and comfort. One seldom has knowledge; hence the word can persuade and create confidence, seduce, and affect – as all would know who are familiar with a court of law or a philosophical debate. In other words: Gorgias' speech claims to lay bare the pure, unadulterated truth about Helen in words; yet we also learn that words are not reality; it is the essence of words to create their own world and their own truth: belief instead of reality, illusion instead of facts. Words are the drugs of the soul (11, 14). Where Protagoras maintains that everything is true, Gorgias insists that nothing is true.

Apparently Gorgias quite deliberately disguises himself with an ambiguousness that turns illusion into reality. Word and reality are incommensurable, and man's world is the world of the word. It was evidently therefore that Gorgias was fascinated with tragedy, the pure illusion where the deceiver (the tragedian is more honest than he who does not deceive; the deceived (the audience) are wiser than the undeceived (23). In general form he stated his ambiguous insight in this way: unknowable is the being that does not achieve seeming; feeble is the seeming that does not achieve being (26).

Gorgias wrote a philosophical treatise, which later was given the revealing dual title of *On the Not-being or on Nature*. It has survived as a summary (3 (Sext. Emp. *Adv. math*. VII 65 ff.); cf. [Aristot.] *MXG* 979 a 11 ff.). Here he maintains three theses:

1   Nothing exists.
2   If something exists, it is unknowable.
3   If it is knowable, it cannot be communicated.

The argumentation in support of the first thesis is especially informative. It has two parts. First it is stated that the not-being does not exist, for being is not not-being. Next it is stated that being does not exist, which can be accounted for by a series of *reductio ad absurdum* arguments that conclude that being can neither be eternal nor created, nor both; that it can neither be one nor many. It is evident that here Gorgias is defeating the Eleatics with their own weapons. But it is also remarkable that he – as perhaps the first to do so – distinguishes precisely between reality, cognition, and the communication of cognition. Among interpreters it has become traditional to ask whether this treatise is a parody or is seriously meant. This is probably due to an ingenuous misapprehension of the diabolical philosopher of illusion. If the problem were solvable, the illusion would be dissolved, and reality is an illusion. It is not without justification that Plato in the *Sophist* (*Soph*. 268 C) defines a Sophist as an artist of illusion 'who produces all sorts of phantoms in words'. And perhaps it would not have been unwelcome to Gorgias that in Plato's universe he is the grand seducer. If Protagoras was the honourable man of Sophistry, Gorgias was its Mephistopheles.

THEORIES OF LANGUAGE

It is natural that the Sophists who literally sustained themselves by the power of the word to quite a special degree took an interest in language. They concerned themselves with what we call philology and literary interpretation (as did for example Protagoras and Hippias); linguistic and epistemological deliberations were fundamental – not only to Protagoras and Gorgias. Theses such as 'one cannot say a nothing' and 'one cannot contradict', which is to say that false judgements are impossible, were apparently common property (the latter thesis has been attributed variously to Protagoras, Prodicus, and Antisthenes), and, as has been mentioned, in the final analysis it rests on a reinterpretation of Parmenides. Such slogans imply that language has reference, that it deals with something real, but in themselves they say nothing about whether the 'real' is objective or subjective, nor whether the 'real' really is an illusion. Furthermore, they say nothing about whether language is created by man, whether it exists by 'convention' or according to 'nature' (*nomos* versus *physis*). Behind the current formulas one could entertain other views of the nature and function of language than Protagoras' and Gorgias'. It was, for example, possible to resolve the whole problem into a game. How this could be carried out was shown by Plato in the *Euthydemus*, in which two brothers, Euthydemus – a historical person of whom we know little – and Dionysodorus, demonstrate to Socrates that they can refute or prove anything whatsoever. Their theoretical ballast was the theses just quoted (*Euthyd*. 284 A; 286 C) supplemented with a third (286 A): every object is unambiguously designated by one word – a principle that in a sense also has been 'borrowed' from Parmenides. Against this background the two brothers can carry out what is really a quite simple strategy: every time they themselves say something, they designate something real and say something true. When the opponent says something else, he does not speak falsely but 'says a nothing', which means that he is not saying anything at all. The principle of 'one object – one word' is so turned around that ambiguous designations are treated as if they were unambiguous, as for example in the following inference (301 D): it is proper for a cook to cut up, skin, and roast; if one cuts up and skins the cook, he gets what is proper for him. Or (298 D): your dog has pups; it is a parent; it is yours; ergo it is your parent – a handsome *secundum quid* fallacy. Stubbornly but unsuccessfully Socrates tries to maintain that words can have several meanings (293 C ff.). In the *Cratylus* (*Crat*. 386 D) Plato formulated Euthydemus' standpoint in this way: all designations at all times belong to all things in equal measure.

Plato's account is of course a parody, but it had a historical background. Protagoras' 'art of contradiction' could be defended, and so in a way could Gorgias' scepticism. Euthydemus' 'theory' is a mere play in words and with linguistic principles: a technique of refutation for refutation's own sake – eristics, Plato calls it. Especially sly is the application of the principle of one designation for each object, which can legitimate any fallacy. For it was the very purpose of the principle to avoid ambiguous expressions. Probably it goes back to Prodicus who wanted to determine 'the proper use' of words (cf. *Euthyd.* 277 E) and who hence concerned himself with the difference between apparently synonymous expressions (cf. *Prot.* 337 A; *Crat.* 384 B). The theory must rest on the presupposition that there is a naturally given, ideal language – hence language does not depend on convention. The elements of language are the words, and as apparently no distinction is made between parts of speech, every word must refer to one thing or one reality. No distinction is made between meaning and reference, and regardless of how Prodicus understood the concept of 'thing' or 'reality', he must therefore – unlike Gorgias – have thought that language can express cognition of reality. The theory also establishes coherence between the slogans. He who uses language correctly cannot 'say a nothing', and one cannot contradict, but only speak of different things.

The most advanced version of this way of thinking is owing to Antisthenes (c.455–360). He was originally a student of Gorgias and later an enthusiastic follower of Socrates. Plato's and Aristotle's philosophy of language is probably partly a reaction against Antisthenes; they make up our – scant – source material, even though Plato does not cite Antisthenes as the author of the theory. It can be characterized as a picture and element theory. In modern language it can tentatively be reproduced as follows (cf. Aristot. *Met.* 1024 b 32; Plat. *Theaet.* 201 D ff.): it is the function of language to depict reality. Reality is composed of elements that cannot be further analysed and are only accessible to perception; for each real element there is a corresponding, adequate designation, the word or the name. Accordingly, the minimal linguistic unit functions as a proper name in such a way that there is formal identity between thing and name. But as an element cannot be analysed, as perception can only occur or not occur, and as a name can only be adequate or inadequate, no account can be provided of the minimal elements of reality. They cannot be made the subject of true or false statements, and consequently not of predication either, for in a predicative sentence there is not identity between subject and predicate, and an elementary subject cannot be several things at the same time. If 'man' and 'good' are elementary designations, 'the man is good' is thus an illegitimate statement; we can only assign to the real man the word 'man' and to that which is good the word 'good' (cf. Plat. *Soph.* 251 B, which is here taken to refer to Antisthenes). The elements of reality can accordingly only be defined ostensively, perhaps by reference to the object x as 'resembling' the object y (Aristot. *Met.* 1043 b 23 ff.).

Now, states of affairs or composite real objects actually do exist; they consist of elements, and to these there are corresponding statements composed of names or words. To a composite object there is a corresponding statement so that a composite object can be described and defined by an enumeration of elements. Such an enumeration is hence true or false (Plat. *Theaet.* 201 D ff.; cf. 206 E ff.; Aristot. *Met.* 1043 b 23 ff.). If 'man' is a composite, it is accordingly legitimate to say 'man is x, y, and z', etc., where x, y, and z stand for elements.

This linguistic theory also belongs in the Parmenidean tradition in so far as it considers language as a direct function of reality. But – unlike Protagoras', Gorgias', and Euthydemus' – Antisthenes' linguistic theory is clearly anti-relativistic: it implies an objectively true ontology and the existence of objectively true statements. As the oldest detailed and specific linguistic theory, it is quite advanced, albeit that it is unclear what ontological status Antisthenes accorded his elements – what an 'elementary thing' is; nor is it clear if and how he distinguished between universals and particulars – linguistically, conceptually, or really. And the ontological frame that precludes language from being considered as something other than a sum of names narrows down the possibilities of explaining actual linguistic phenomena. Inasmuch as all elements of language directly name real elements, it is, according to the theory, not possible to state about x that this or that is the case, but only to state the border-line case of x consisting of a, b, and c. Normal predicative sentences and essential definitions accordingly seem precluded, unless properties can be considered 'elements'. Finally, negative existential statements and false statements are similarly precluded – they are not enumerations of actual elements and, consequently, not-statements. Plato had to rid himself of a cumbersome heritage before he could present a theory of predication in the *Phaedo* and a theory of negative and false statements in the *Sophist*. Thus Antisthenes' linguistic theory above all had the – not inessential – significance that it must provoke reaction. But with respect to one point perhaps he left something for Plato and Aristotle to inherit: the idea of the direct 'grasping' of an object as the precondition for language and discursive thought. It ought also to be mentioned that the basic thought of language as a system of elements or names can be found again down through the history of philosophy (Hobbes, Wittgenstein's *Tractatus*).

LATER SOCIAL THEORIES

Linguistic and epistemological theory and social philosophy are the two main poles in Sophistic thought, and Protagoras was a pioneer in both fields. But his relativism could lead anywhere. Just as the current semantic formulas could leave room for quite different views, so within social philosophy the opposition of nature (*physis*) and convention (*nomos*), whose author is unknown, could be interpreted either humanistically and optimistically – as did Protagoras himself – or nihilistically, so that might was identified with right. We know this whole lively discussion only fragmentarily, but we are nevertheless able to realize that it is an important presupposition for the discussion in later times of the relation between natural law and positive law, written or unwritten laws, or of a social contract, and of the justification of morality.

In general, nature was not considered neutral; rather, the idea was that nature makes certain demands of human behaviour – from nature's 'is' follows an 'ought to' for man – whereas men's own conventions may be discussed and are changeable.

Protagoras himself saw no absolute contrast between *nomos* and *physis*. It is inherent in man's nature that he must form societies in order to survive, that social institutions are hence contractually dependent, and that a conventional system of norms must prevail in every society. Still, nature does not prescribe which norms should prevail. Good and evil are made relative, just as true and false are – what is in fact morally right is something determined by society; but it is determined by nature that something is expedient, that something else is not. This view may be open to criticism, if one, as Plato does, calls for fixed moral standards; yet it also allows for questions in other respects.

The oldest known explicit formulation of the principle of a social contract comes from Hippias (Xen. *Men.* IV 4,13) and develops Protagoras further. According to Hippias, law and justice (*nomos*) rely on agreements between citizens who determine what is to be done and not to be done. Another development of Protagoras' thought is to be found in an anonymous text from the end of the fifth century (*Anonymus Iamblichi*, DK, no. 89, 402, 21 ff.), in which it is claimed that *nomos* – and hereby also virtue, *aretē* – are inescapable pre-conditions for man's being able to take care of himself: virtue pays off. But it could be argued that also nature's law, the unwritten laws, perhaps god's law, have positive contents – according to Xenophon (*Mem.* IV 4,19 ff.) Socrates and Hippias agree on that view. And it could be argued that positive, man-made law is artificial, perhaps even deleterious, and that one ought only to respect what nature herself prescribes.

The entire problem is summarized by Aristotle (*Rhet.* 1373 b 1 ff.). Anybody who argues about right and wrong must know that there is a special and a universal law. The special law – whether written or unwritten – applies to a particular society. Universal law is nature's law binding on all men. Characteristically, Aristotle ties this to the literary tradition and quotes the famous lines from the *Antigone* about eternally valid laws.

With this Aristotle said something quite essential: the discussion of written and unwritten laws is not in a wider perspective bound to the Sophists' conceptual world. In the fifth century it was no longer possible to believe (as had Solon and Heraclitus) that human law ideally can be derived from some higher order. In Aeschylus, Sophocles, and Herodotus divine laws are vastly superior to human ones and are only momently, if ever, knowable. In the wake of the secularization process, the idea of an eternal order vis-à-vis a human one is no longer special for the Sophists either. In one of the Hippocratic treatises (Hipp. *De aëre* 14) we are told that ethnic differences depend on nature or convention. Further reference could be made to such different persons as Pericles and Democritus.

Confronting such ideals of written or unwritten laws or of man's capacity for cultivating nature stands a much harsher interpretation of the relation between *nomos* and *physis*. *Nomos* is a mere outer shell, and stripped of all varnish man's nature is un-nature. That might is right is all too clear in the Melian dialogue in Thucydides or in a tragedy by Euripides on the lot of the Trojan women after the fall of Troy (*Troades*).

It is against this broad background that one should see the Sophistic discussion. It is not surprising that all positions – from humanist idealism and utilitarianism to egoistical thirst for power – appear to be represented. As has been mentioned, it is a fundamental idea that nature herself is the basis for morality; and so a modern reader eagerly looks for a formulation of man's natural rights, for a law of nature declaring that all men are equal – not merely, as in Pericles' Athens, all male citizens. Here it is customary to refer to Hippias, for surely he was an advocate of a 'social contract' and the principle of unwritten laws, and he was known as perhaps the most cosmopolitan of the Sophists. In Plato's *Protagoras* (337 C) he tells those present that they are all of the same family, companions, and fellow citizens according to nature, not according to law (*nomos*). And he adds that what concurs with nature is related, but that law is man's tyrant and violates nature. It is possible that this is a declaration of human rights, but strictly speaking it may just as well mean that those who are present – the elite or the Sophists – are naturally related. The principle of unwritten, natural laws does not directly imply a principle of natural rights.

How complicated the threads are that meet in the debate on *nomos* and *physis* can best be seen in the Sophist Antiphon (second half of the fifth century; he may be identical with the author of some paradigmatic orations in the manner of Gorgias that have survived). In a papyrus fragment (Ant. DK B44) he says that nature has equipped us all alike, whether barbarians or Greeks. Everybody can provide himself with life's necessities, be he barbarian or Greek, for we all breathe through our noses and mouths and eat with our hands. – Nor is it unambiguously stated here that all men are equal, but only that from nature's hand they have been granted the same external conditions. Furthermore, it is clear from what he says earlier that he has another errand.

He takes *nomos* and *physis* to be absolute opposites. Justice consists in not transgressing against the law. But the prescriptions of law are artificial (literally: an addendum); but what nature prescribes is on the other hand necessary. Therefore it pays to observe the law when there are witnesses present; but nature's prescriptions must always be followed. Most frequently the law is in conflict with nature. What is useful according to nature makes one free and brings pleasure.

Antiphon's view of life has been called hedonistic. He agrees with the anonymous author of the text mentioned above (*Anonymus Iamblichi*) that the individual ought to act in his own interest. The disagreement concerns the question whether law or nature in principle is the better guide. That Antiphon in a brief fragment (61) distances himself from anarchy is one of the riddles of the transmission.

Although the Stoics are the first to maintain the equality between all men as a principle, one should not imagine that such thoughts were wholly unfamiliar around 400. Aristotle tells us (*Pol.* 1253 b 20) that there are 'some' who think that slavery is unnatural and unjust – that it is owing to convention rather than nature. The terminology suggests that those 'some' were Sophists, and in fact we do know the name of a Sophist, Alcidamas, who – as late as 360 – expressly declared that slavery was unnatural (*Rhet.* 1373 b 18 sch.). But we do know somewhat more about the discussion of the position of women, even though we must here go outside the Sophists' narrow circle. Euripides has Medea speak against the suppression of women, and in three comedies (*Lysistrata*, *Thesmophoriazusae*, *Ecclesiazusae*) Aristophanes lets women settle their own affairs; in the *Lysistrata*, which was performed in a catastrophic year in the Peloponnesian War (411) this is partly peace propaganda; in *The Popular Assembly of Women* (*Eccl.*, from the late 390s) a utopia is proposed of a communist society with economic community and equality between men and women (cf. especially Aristoph. *Eccl.* 581 ff.); there are striking points of similarity with Plato's *Republic*, which, regardless of how they otherwise are to be explained, show that Plato's thoughts of women's position were not conceived in a void. It is true that one ought not directly to identify dramatists with their characters, and Euripides and Aristophanes were probably no male blue-stockings. Yet we are told something about contemporary thoughts, which in all likelihood were fostered in the Sophistic milieu. It is characteristic that thoughts concerning the rights of suppressed population groups appear randomly and unsystematically; they have apparently not been formulated in any general manifesto on human rights.

What above all occupies Sophistic social theories is man's possibility of achieving optimal welfare within the framework that nature and man himself have created. Antiphon relies on natural instincts and turns against *nomos*. The like could lead to romantic utopianism, moral nihilism, or to an *Umwertung aller Werte*. Plato had two Sophists to express the ideology of power that was all too well known in Athens towards the end of the century.

The first is Thrasymachus who in Book I of the *Republic* (*RP* I 336 B ff.) is the vulgar spokesman for the 'might is right' thesis. Although he does have a theory, he is inclined to take refuge in boisterous argumentation when faced with Socrates' teasing irony. It is his thesis that justice is that which benefits the strong (338 C), and the strong are the establishment or the government. Whether it is a question of one-man rule, aristocracy, or democracy, the rulers will legislate in their own interest, and then justice is what is required of the subjects who must make a virtue of necessity and act in the interest of the powerful (339 B). It may happen that rulers on occasion will care for their subjects; but this is hypocrisy, for the ruler is like the shepherd who tends and feeds his flock from self-interest (343 B ff.). So, the truly powerful is he who can act unjustly without any restriction, as Thrasymachus somewhat illogically puts it, for the powerful should be above justice and injustice. His ideal figure is the tyrant, and not – as with Antiphon – the clever man who violates the law when nobody is looking; he is instead the man who is above the law and risks nothing by enforcing his wishes. Thrasymachus does not mention the concepts of *nomos* and *physis*, although of course they could be applied; *nomos* would then be fraud and *physis* the self-assertion of the stronger.

In fact Thrasymachus is a historical person, and a fragment by him (Thras. DK B8) has survived, which may give pause for thought – also perhaps about the way Plato used his sources. In this fragment we learn that the gods do not interest themselves in men, for otherwise they would not ignore the greatest human good: justice; after all, it is a fact that man makes no use of this virtue. – The historical Thrasymachus may not have been such a moral nihilist as he appears to be in Plato's version. He may have been a frustrated idealist who scorns prevailing ideals, because they are not adhered to – a caricature of Thucydides, as it were. And furthermore, it should be noted that Plato's Thrasymachus did not – as was the Sophists' wont – express an opinion about how society ought to be constructed; he only spoke about how it actually is. His point: the law as violator of the weak is of course real enough and was indeed debated among contemporaries (cf. Xen. *Mem.* I 2,40 ff.).

In the *Gorgias* Plato lets another Sophist, Callicles, use the language of power. It is probable that Callicles was likewise a historical person, although we only know of him from Plato. There are agreements between Thrasymachus and Callicles, but there are also striking differences. Callicles relies quite explicitly on an opposition between *nomos* and *physis* and is in that respect comparable with Antiphon; he also has a real theory of natural law concerning how the ideal society should be ordered (Plat. *Gorg.* 482 C ff.). Laws were made by men; they are not – as in Thrasymachus – made by the strong but by the weak who thus express their resentment; they are a defence mechanism against the strong who ought to rule according to nature's order. Laws are therefore not only unnatural but expressions of a slavish nature that would cripple and obstruct natural self-expression. The laws regiment young people and make them follow a false ideology. Still, it is nature's law that the strong is the ruler and that he is also economically superior to the weak:

> On the day when that man steps forth who has the necessary power within him, you will see how he shakes off all these chains, breaks out, and frees himself. He will trample all our scribblings, spells, and incantations as well as all our unnatural ordinances under foot; he, whom we thought our slave, will stand up and appear as the lord, and natural justice will shine like the sun in full splendour.
>
> (484 A)

Callicles' theory is not complicated, although he himself is a quite complex figure. As a person he is an idealist; he is no moral nihilist but wishes to subordinate morality to life or nature and not to subordinate true human nature to pseudo-morality. To this extent it is understandable that he has been compared with Nietzsche over and over again. But his moral indignation is linked to a quite primitive ideology of power that has little to do with Nietzsche.

Regardless of how much or how little Plato caricatured Thrasymachus and Callicles, it is clearly his intention to uncover 'the ideology' behind a corrupt society of power and thereby indirectly to raise the question of the justification of a non-egoistical morality. But his errand was not merely theoretical. Callicles argues on Sophistic premises and uses Sophistic slogans. Thus he is a modern; but his revolutionary ideology is actually not very far from a political conservatism, which otherwise has very little to do with philosophy or with the Sophists. Such conservatism we know from a pamphlet on the constitution of the Athenians from the third quarter of the fifth century that erroneously has been attributed to Xenophon. The aristocratic author (cf. [Xen.] *Resp. Ath.* I 1 ff.) attacks democracy using an old-fashioned, somewhat hackneyed vocabulary that has its roots in Solon. Morality and politics are one: it was the 'good' (= the wealthy; cf. aristocracy: government by the best) who ought to rule, but in fact the 'bad' (= the poor) rule: they conspire and profit from being so many. Such an ultra-conservative way of thinking later entered into an unholy alliance with the Sophist ideology of power; Plato witnessed this during the ominous terror regime instigated by the Thirty Tyrants; its leading figure was Plato's uncle Critias who belonged to Sophistic circles. We learn (Lys. XII 5 ff.) that the Thirty had a moral-political programme: they wanted to purge the city of injustice and guide the citizens back to virtue and justice; but in fact they instituted tyrannical power. Tyrants have of course often legitimated their politics by means of old-fashioned moral precepts and a lofty ideology; it is well known that they have also frequently believed in their own propaganda. The strange mixture of moral pathos and out-and-out egoism that characterizes Plato's Callicles and perhaps Thrasymachus as well is in a higher sense not unhistorical. Plato had seen a Thrasymachus or a Callicles in action for himself.

If one takes an overall view of Plato's picture of the Sophists, it is evident that he wanted to demonstrate that uncontrollable and dangerous consequences naturally will follow from the wise, good-natured, and benevolent Protagoras' relativism. When he was an old man Plato (*Leg.* X 888 E ff.) summarized his criticism of the natural philosophers and the Sophists in one passage: there are people who believe that everything depends on nature, chance, or on man-made conventions; nature is blind, and all that is man-made – including justice – is owing to conventions that have only relative validity. Such a way of thinking, in which nature is without reason and human societies are not governed by absolute values given by nature, makes man rootless and leads to the greatest misfortune, as we are told.

11

SOCRATES

——— •◦• ———

In 399 Socrates was sentenced to death by a popular tribunal in Athens and executed. He was approximately 70 years old. For decades he had been a fable to the Athenian population, but the trial and execution became an epochal event that left its impact not only on the history of Greek philosophy but on the entire history of Western thought. All later centuries have in fact reacted to Socrates as his friends and 'students' did: he has served as a magnet, he has inspired and initiated, and men have seen their own attitudes to life mirrored in the legendary ironist who wrote nothing.

It is probably impossible to penetrate beyond the Socrates of legend, although it is possible to sense a historical point of departure for the most important of the legends about Socrates, which was Plato's.

Socrates was an Attic citizen. He did not feel himself called to a political career, although he carried out his civic duties, for instance as a soldier. At the outset, he was probably not without means, but towards the end of his life he was apparently more or less destitute. His life's task was philosophical discussion. Teasing, disturbing, fascinatingly ugly, and yet with a special aura he walked the streets and lanes – so tradition presents him. But we should not forget that his 'public' was identical with the Sophists' and that his 'students', like the Sophists', were wealthy young men in need of an education. Several became involved with Socrates in erotically-tinged friendships.

We are reasonably well informed of the outer circumstances surrounding Socrates' trial. We know the names of the three prosecutors – the poet Meletus, officially the main prosecutor: the democratic politician Anytus, probably the real principal; and the rhetor Lycon. As late as in the Roman Empire the indictment was said still to be accessible in the archives of Athens; Socrates was accused of not acknowledging the official gods and of introducing new deities (*daimonia*) and, furthermore, of corrupting the young. A death sentence was demanded (Diog. Laert. II 40; cf. Xen. *Mem.* I 1,1; Plat. *Apol.* 24 B). By a fairly narrow majority the tribunal found the accused guilty (39 A; Diog. Laert. II 41). Before sentence was pronounced, Socrates was, in accordance with Attic law, entitled to propose his own punishment; according to Plato's account (*Apol.* 37 A; cf. a slightly different version, Xen. *Apol.* 23), he proposed with ironic awareness of his own worth that he be awarded a civic honour:

free meals in the town hall. Thereupon a greater majority sentenced him to death. The sentence was not effectuated at once, for, in conformance with tradition the Athenians must first send a religious delegation to Delos; until then no execution could take place. Plato used this interval to allow two dialogues to be enacted as conversations between Socrates and his friends in the prison: the *Crito*, in which the law-abiding Socrates refuses to avail himself of an actual possibility to escape, and the *Phaedo*, in which Plato lets him formulate his spiritual testament.

In formal terms there is nothing strange about the trial; such a vague indictment was possible according to Attic law. Godlessness does not primarily signify heretical religious views; but one could be pronounced godless if one transgressed against the state cult – and from the end of the fifth century such trials are well known in Athens, the stronghold of free thought (Anaxagoras, Alcibiades, perhaps Protagoras). Godlessness was thus a crime against the state and could easily be linked to real political motives. The trial took place a few years after the end of the Peloponnesian War and the restoration of a democratic regime, and everything suggests that Socrates was considered politically suspect. His association with such politically dubious aristocrats as Alcibiades and Critias was notorious; from a fourth-century rhetor (Aeschin. I 173) we learn in plain terms that the Athenians executed Socrates, the Sophist, because he had taught Critias. It is also telling how anxious the Socratics were to clear Socrates of accusations of collusion, especially with Alcibiades – who had been responsible for the defeat of Athens in Sicily. A general amnesty forbade indictments for crimes committed prior to 403/02 in order to prevent debilitating legal encounters. Consequently, Socrates' indictment is not formally political and must aim at his activities in the last years of his life. Yet such a formal limitation did not mean that the prosecutors were prevented from referring to earlier events.

It should be added that a general dislike of new ideas combined with the catastrophic mood of the day may have triggered mass hysteria and a demand to give the odd ones their come-uppance. In Plato's *Apology* (18 A ff.) Socrates emphasizes that he really must defend himself against two accusations: one is the actual indictment; the other, an unofficial one, is far more important: the town gossip of older date, which he ironically formulates as a sworn indictment: 'Socrates is purported to be guilty of useless concern with what is under the earth and in heaven, of making the weaker case the stronger, and of instructing others in this' (19 B). Then he alludes to Aristophanes' caricature of him in *The Clouds*, performed in 423 – as other comic writers had done as well. What began in comedy ended in disaster.

ARISTOPHANES' SOCRATES

Aristophanes' comedy has been preserved and is our only contemporary source. It confirms Socrates' fictional indictment, for quite literally it makes him the whipping-boy of all the novel: natural philosophy (things under the earth and in heaven) and Sophistry (making the weaker case the stronger). But thereby not everything has been said.

The plot of the comedy is simple. A lowly and naïve peasant – a type close to Aristophanes' heart – is on the verge of being ruined thanks to his son's extravagant habits. In his misery he turns to Socrates who, *ad modum* Pythagoras, lives with his disciples in a small, shut-off world, a 'speculatorium', as one translation has it. In fact, what he wants to know is how to cheat his creditors, and he has heard that from Socrates one can learn how to make the weaker case the stronger (Aristoph. *Nub.* 112 ff.). Among much else besides, he is indeed permitted to attend a dialogue between the logos of justice and the logos of injustice (889 ff.) – i.e. the good old customs versus new-fangled immorality. He is initiated in the mysteries, which is to say that he is subjected to Socrates' insistent technique of questioning (344 ff.) and learns dialectics and grammar ('the proper use of words') as well as natural philosophy; for example: how far can a flea jump – Socrates, always with his head in the clouds but unwashed and bare-footed, and his lean and hungry disciples do in fact not own much else besides their fleas and their 'philosopha'. Still, the peasant is a little slow on the up-take, so he sends his son instead, and he is such an adept pupil that he goes home and beats up his father – for it is just to return the beatings one has been given oneself; it is merely owing to *nomos* that one must not beat one's parents (1400 ff.). When he also wants to beat up his mother, it becomes too much for the good father, and he burns down the speculatorium – just as of old when Pythagoras' community was destroyed by fire. The comedy ends with the peasant's curse: 'You have mocked the Gods' (1509) – a harsher conclusion than usual for a comedy.

When the peasant arrives at the speculatorium he meets Socrates suspended in a basket up in the air (244 ff.) – the airy outside must correspond with the airy inside, and in his basket he can get close to his gods, the clouds.

These clouds grant us ready wit, dialectics, and reason (*nous*) as well as fantasy and prevarication, deceit and trickery (317). And the prophet of the clouds, Socrates, is able to explain what happens in the clouds themselves – for example thunderstorms, the favourite subject of all good old Presocratics (377 ff.).

Aristophanes' Socrates is everything that appears dangerous and ridiculous to the common citizen: natural philosopher, Sophist, ascetic – in short, an intellectual. The subjects of *The Clouds* are blasphemy and corruption of youth – exactly as they were in Meletus' indictment twenty-four years later. – But how dangerous was Socrates in 423? It is related that at the end of the performance he stood up to allow all to see the original (Ael. *Var. hist.* II 13); it is also related – in Plato' *Symposium* – that Socrates and Aristophanes met and drank as the best of friends.

In a comedy it is difficult to distinguish between the author's and the audience's idiosyncrasies. Socrates is made responsible for all modern wickedness; but an able caricaturist must both exaggerate and hit home. Aristophanes' Socrates argues sophistically – as he does in Plato; he is interested in 'the proper use of words' – as he undeniably is in Plato who – ironically? – makes him a student of Prodicus (*Prot.* 341 A; *Charm.* 163 D); he is presented as a Pythagoras redivivus – as in Plato's *Phaedo*. As presented in *The Clouds*, natural philosophy is a mish-mash of contemporary epigone philosophy, probably first and foremost as represented by Diogenes of Apollonia and Archelaus. And there is other familiar stuff, for example the fashionable theory of a cosmic vortex and the explanation of thunderstorms. But when Socrates' disciples, Xenophon and Plato, come to defend him (Xen. *Men.* I 11 ff.; Plat. *Apol.* 19 C; 26 D), it is of the utmost importance to them to distance Socrates from the natural philosophers – and yet Socrates did, even according to Plato, have a period of natural philosophy (*Phaedo* 96 A). Considering the times, it would be strange if this had not been the case.

This might occasion some further airy hypotheses. But it is more important that Aristophanes is aware of Socratic ignorance and the maxim 'know thyself', Socrates' personal signature (Aristoph. *Nub.* 842), for this is neither Sophistry nor natural philosophy but the crucial Socratic message familiar from all pro-Socratic sources. Furthermore, Aristophanes is perfectly familiar with Socratic dialectics and 'midwifery' (137) – of course with the addition of Socrates' visible oddities.

XENOPHON'S SOCRATES

Aristophanes knew the man he attacked; he knew the milieu he came from and the sort of attack his public expected; he also knew that Socrates was dangerous. But of course the slanted perspective of comedy is no analysis of Socrates' thought. Everything else about Socrates was written under the impact of the trial. The man who was a fable in his lifetime became a myth at his death. At some point in the 390's a now lost pamphlet against Socrates appeared. It was in the form of a fictional indictment, written by a Sophist, Polycrates. Most likely the pamphlet attacked Socrates primarily for anti-democratic views, and even as late as in the fourth century AD it provoked a counter-attack (Lib. *Decl.* I). The 390s also saw a significant number of pro-Socratic writings – as direct reactions to the trial or as answers to Polycrates. Plato presumably began writing at this time, but a number of other Socratics wrote defences of their teacher, for example, Antisthenes, Aeschines of Sphettos and – somewhat later – Xenophon. In Antiquity Aeschines was considered the most reliable source, though the few fragments left to us do not make closer evaluation possible. Xenophon probably did not belong to Socrates' intimate circle of friends. All these writings constituted a special genre – the Socratic dialogues (*logoi*) – which Aristotle (Poet. 1447 b 11; cf. *Rhet.* 1417 a 20; [Plat.] *Ep.* XIII 363 A) considered a special, mixed genre, formally fictional and dramatic but with factual contents. The fact that Socrates' students all chose to represent him in direct form, in conversation, immediately shows that Socrates' thinking was tied up with his personality. Representation could not simply take a doctrinal form; every student recorded his own version of the great challenge. While all the others tried to draw a moral, only Plato allowed Socrates to remain on his own as challenger and enigma. Now, a writer of fiction – and the dialogue genre is deliberate fiction – has a considerable degree of freedom with respect to his subject; in a manner of speaking the reporting form is part of the fiction. Finally, the author of course does not have to rely only on personal recollections – Xenophon, for example, informs us that he has consulted other Socratics (cf. Xen. *Apol.* 1 ff.), and it is more than likely that he had read Plato, at any rate the *Apology* and the *Symposium*. Given this, it does not seem easy to leave myth behind and come to terms with Socrates, the man himself.

Xenophon (c.430–355) was an officer. After a varied military career, he retired as a Peloponnesian squire, and most of what he wrote probably dates from his retirement. He was a historian (*Hellenica*; *Anabasis*), wrote a sort of historical novel about his ideal king, Cyrus (*Cyropaedia*), wrote about hunting and horsemanship, and, finally, about Socrates: an imagined defence oration (*Apol.*) a charming account of a drinking bout in which Socrates participated (*Symposium*), and a dialogue in which Socrates – the ignorant one – allows himself to be instructed about one of Xenophon's pet interests, agriculture (*Oeconomicus*). But his most important Socratic work by far is the *Memorabilia*, a work of recollection and commemoration of Socrates. It begins with a refutation of the indictment (probably also of Polycrates), but the major part of the work constitutes a series of loosely connected, anecdotal episodes that fictionally purport to reproduce Socrates' conversations – of course with the intention of showing the absurdity of convicting such a man. To have the well-turned anecdote characterize a person became a favourite mode of presentation in Hellenistic times.

Xenophon's Socrates is far more practical-minded than Plato's and has no objection to advise in big and small matters. But there is an inner coherence in the portrait of Socrates who always says 'the same about the same' (Xen. *Mem.* IV 4,6; cf. Plat. *Gor.* 490 E). Xenophon has always come up short when compared with Plato, and it has become a bad habit to call him dull, boring, or simple-minded. Actually, he is an excellent raconteur with an astute flair for the ironic or sly point. Behind his moralizing façade one can sense hidden amusement, and, for example in a conversation with Critias and another of the Thirty Tyrants, he recreates Socratic irony as ably as did Plato (Xen. *Mem.* I 2,31 ff.): the Tyrants have been wanting to get at Socrates with a law forbidding the practice of 'the art of argumentation'. Socrates seeks them out, because he is confused about what is and is not allowed. – Is it good or bad arguments that he may not use? Is there an age limit applying to the people he may talk with? May he not ask young people where Critias lives? – He is curtly told to stop his endless babbling about cobblers, masons, and blacksmiths. – Also when this has a bearing on justice and piety? asks the innocent Socrates.

To Xenophon's Socrates, knowledge begins with self-knowledge; just as in Aristophanes and Plato, he obeys the Delphic command to 'know thyself' (IV 2, 24; III 9,6). He shows his interlocutors that they know nothing; this holds true, for example, for Glaucon, Plato's brother, who has political ambitions but has to concede that he knows nothing about politics. Similar rough treatment is accorded Euthydemus, no less, who ends up quite embarrassed (IV 2 ff.); Plato's Socrates was less successful. According to Xenophon, Socrates did not pretend to be a teacher (I 2, 3); he was effective through discussions and by his own example (cf. I 4, 1). 'Virtue is knowledge' – another apophthegm, familiar from Plato – is also guiding for Xenophon's Socrates. All virtues depend on knowledge (III 9, 5), and such knowledge comes about in discussions showing up imagined knowledge (IV 6, 1) and aims to arrive at the true definition of the virtues (I 1, 16); Xenophon knows that it is inherent in the Socratic method patiently to come back to the point of departure whenever a discussion gets off the track.

But Xenophon's Socrates was no revolutionary, and his portrait of Socrates actually concludes that the trial was one big misunderstanding. However, as the good conservative he is, he cannot conceal that Socrates, for example opposed the Athenian practice of selecting officials by drawing lots (I 2, 9). But otherwise, Socrates is the dutiful Athenian citizen. He sacrificed to the gods like all sensible people (I 1, 2), and the strange divine voice that guided him – *to daimonion* – was just a parallel to the oracular answers that all believe in. In all respects his aim was to make his young interlocutors useful citizens.

Although Xenophon's Socrates claims to be ignorant, that ignorance does not go very far. He knows himself, others and life's practical realities well enough; when asked, he is well able to define the several virtues (IV 6, 1 ff.). And his purpose suits well with the old-fashioned morality advocated by, for example Xenophon. He wants to turn the young into gentlemen (*kalokagathoi*, i.e. 'handsome and good', cf. e.g. I 1, 16), and this is connected with a utilitarian view – the good is good for somebody, and, after all, people do aim at their own advantage (III 9, 4); he who acts morally with insight will gain honour and fame (IV 2, 28), and the good man is friend to his friends and enemy to his enemies (II 6, 35).

This entire moral position fits in handsomely with a general view of man's role in the world and is inspired by old-fashioned religiosity. Socrates would not be concerned with natural philosophy, even though he was of course familiar with it. For it cannot be man's task to concern himself with things that transcend human measure, and nobody can imagine that man can subjugate nature. A man is to find his place in nature's order, which is rational, and he must know that in a real sense only the gods are wise. It is the task of the god – for example by oracles – to intimate what will happen or not happen; it is man's task to learn and experience within this framework (I 1, 3 ff.). The discourse with Euthydemus concludes in confident teleology: nature and the gods have ordered the world in the best possible way (IV 3, 1 ff.).

Xenophon's *Memorabilia* is an invaluable key to the Attic ideal of a gentleman – just as Aristophanes voices the ideals and aversions of the middle class, the peasants and the petite bourgeoisie. In the end the difference between their views of life is not overwhelmingly great; yet their views of Socrates are diametrically opposite. To Aristophanes he was a dangerous modernist, to Xenophon he was wise and pious, basically a conformist citizen who was never dangerous. The difference between Xenophon's and Plato's figures of Socrates lies on a different plane. There are many outward points of similarity, themes that are repeated like headings: piety, questioning technique, searches for definitions, the refutation of pseudo-knowledge, 'know thyself', etc. But as soon as one begins to fill in the headings, the chasm appears. This is apparent already in the evaluations of Socrates' attitude to the trial. Without regard to the consequences, Plato's Socrates stands for what he is; he can do nothing else. Xenophon's Socrates, on the other hand, adjusts himself to the events, because he is destined to die soon in any case (Xen. *Apol.* 8; *Mem.* IV 8, 8). A reader of Xenophon may well wonder what Socrates really wishes to achieve with his endless questions, his ignorance, and his call for self-knowledge, since he is after all able to speak straight about straight questions. Plato's Socrates, however, is a paradox who does not meet the reader with deed or advice. He asks, not as a means to something but because it is his nature to do so. He is not ignorant from a motive of paedagogical benevolence; he is simply ignorant. His irony – dissimulation, as it really means in the Greek – is not form, but nature; he takes away from people the lie they live by, and thereupon leaves them to pursue their own course. The Platonic Socrates is at once conservative and revolutionary, and he opens up for religious, metaphysical, and logical perspectives – to Xenophon a *terra incognita*.

A reconstruction of the 'historical Socrates' based on Xenophon and Plato is impossible, unless one is satisfied with the surface or the smallest common denominator. Here normal principles of source criticism cannot be applied. In Xenophon's favour it has been argued that he, the unoriginal of the two, could not have made anything up; in Plato's favour, that one genius understood the other. Such arguments refute themselves, because the premises are naïve and because it is overlooked that the Socratic writings belong to a fictional genre that does not aim at a historically correct report. Each author has his own idealized Socrates. It avails little to bring in the Socratics who are only fragmentarily transmitted or, for example, Aristotle's assessment.

PLATO'S SOCRATES

It has justly been stressed that one can very well imagine hysterical people and Banausians putting to death such a provocative person as Plato's Socrates; but Xenophon's Socrates would probably have been allowed to live peacefully. It is also true that the other contemporary views of Socrates basically become understandable through Plato – not the other way around. Which is probably to say that Plato was the one who best understood Socrates' errand, but not that he confined himself to reporting the 'historical' Socrates. In his dialogues Plato so identified himself with his Socrates figure that distinction between the two is impossible. It is often imagined that in his so-called early dialogues he depicted Socrates roughly as he was but that later he used him as his 'spokesman'. This is a perilous view that presupposes that a life-like characterization must be correct, apart from the fact that it compels the Plato interpreter to lay down arbitrary dividing lines in Plato's oeuvre. It is, for example, something of a myth that the Platonic Socrates from a certain, demonstrable point in time begins to become interested in 'the doctrine of ideas'. It may be instructive to compare Plato's Socrates with, for example, Plato's Protagoras. Both are created by Plato on a historical basis. But with respect to Protagoras he has to maintain a certain objective distance that enables him to evaluate and think his way through positions he does not share; consequently he signals when and how he departs from the 'historical' Protagoras. Otherwise Socrates is from the outset of his own flesh and blood. As stated in a letter attributed to Plato (*Ep*. II 314 C), this is a Socrates who 'has become young and beautiful'. We can follow the evolution of Plato's Socrates and see how he, so to speak, evolves from a fifth-century outlook into one of the fourth century; but throughout there is a synthesis between Plato and his Socrates. At certain points, when Plato intimates some distance, he does so in order to denote the extent of the Socratic inspiration, not to mark a distance from the 'historical' Socrates.

We do know something about Socrates' life. We have some cues that point back to Socrates, the philosopher; otherwise we only know him from the impact he made and as a legend. Hence the several versions of Socrates must stand side by side as variations on a theme. Although we can only draw the outlines of the 'historical' Socrates, we do know something about the Socrates of history: he is identical with Plato's Socrates.

Yet there is one place where Plato provided – if not a photographic likeness of Socrates – a picture of the Socrates he wished us to accept as the historical portrait. Socrates' defence oration – the *Apology* – was probably written in the 390s. It is without doubt a fictional forensic speech, but this fiction had to be more restricted than in a dialogue, for otherwise the *Apology* would have failed its purpose and would have been one which contemporary eye witnesses to the trial at once could have refuted as make-believe. We can read the *Apology* in two ways: as a contribution to the debate immediately following on Socrates' execution or as a portrait of the Socrates who influenced Plato and was permitted to evolve and grow in the course of Plato's long life as a writer.

The *Apology* introduces us directly to a person. It is an account that is effective by its simplicity; but behind the simple lies something quite complicated. The individual cannot be separated from the ideal, and what Socrates has to say cannot be separated from what Socrates is. A forensic speech is not philosophy, but the attitude that the Socrates of the *Apology* expresses could be formulated in religious and philosophical terms.

The *Apology* is carefully organized. In the part of the oration that leads up to the sentencing, Socrates first turns against his informal accusers, the oldest and most dangerous, who consider him a natural philosopher and a Sophist (*Apol.* 18 A ff.). Surprisingly quickly he denies having anything whatsoever to do with natural philosophy (19 C; cf. 26 D, where he expressly distances himself from Anaxagoras). Confronted with the accusation that he is a Sophist, he executes a characteristic surprise manoeuvre. He is indeed 'wise' – *sophos* – but in a manner quite different from the Sophists: his wisdom is 'human wisdom'. The god in Delphi, no less, can testify to it; for he has provided the oracular answer that nobody is wiser than Socrates (20 E ff.). Like Xenophon's Socrates, Plato's also knows that the god does not err and that divine wisdom exceeds man's by far. As in Xenophon, he also knows that it is man's duty to explore truth as far as possible. There the similarity with Xenophon ends. According to the *Apology* Socrates now tries to find someone wiser than himself, and to that end he questions in turn a number of politicians, poets, and artisans. All entertain high opinions about their own wisdom, but Socrates' probing questions show it to be pseudo-knowledge. What the god wanted to say is that human wisdom is worth next to nothing and that Socrates is the wisest, because he knows that he knows nothing (23 A).

Socrates meets the 'new' indictment – the formal one of the seduction of youth and the introduction of new 'deities' – with yet one more surprise manoeuvre, employing the very form of argumentation that he is accused of (24 B ff.). He cross-examines Meletus and leads him by the nose, not as a correct logician but in such manner that the prosecutor himself demonstrates his ignorance about the education of youth and religion – once again showing up pseudo-knowledge.

Hereupon Socrates formulates his true mission (28 A ff.). He has – somewhat wilfully – understood the oracular answer to mean that his wisdom consists in doing what he has always done: confronting his fellow citizens with the demand for self-knowledge. Hence he is in the service of the god when he questions all and sundry and irritates like a gadfly from whom nobody can feel himself safe. He has never been anyone's teacher (33 A); his task is to make every man realize that his worth as man and citizen depends on his taking care of his soul and striving for its becoming as good as possible (29 E; 30 B; cf. 36 C). The good man is only to heed justice, nothing else (28A; cf. 31 B); wrong is never right (cf. *Crito* 49 A), and the good man can never be harmed by a worse one (*Apol.* 30 C; cf. 40 D). This could never have been uttered by Xenophon's Socrates. It is a new ideal of man that breaks with the old moral precepts, *kalokagathia*. The good man is not he who asserts himself and obtains external goods by following virtue. The highest virtue for the individual is to follow a categorical imperative without regard to outward success.

Following the conviction, but before the sentencing (35 E ff.), when Socrates has the opportunity of proposing his own punishment, he insists that he would be disobedient to the god if he were to attempt to avoid the consequences of his acts, for example by going into exile, and then he offers his provocative proposal: he merits free meals at the town hall.

The last part of the speech (38 C ff.) – after the sentence – can have no historical foundation. Here Socrates first addresses the judges who have found him guilty. They may deprive him of life, but they will gain nothing from this; after him others will follow (Plato?) who more forcefully will make them face the question of how they conduct their lives. Addressing the judges who have voted for his innocence he speaks about death. No one can fear death, for nobody knows whether it merely means the end of life or a new and better life; he plays with the idea of a life after death, in which he, Socrates, can test heroes of the past and ascertain whether their wisdom is true or a sham. Accordingly Socrates is an agnostic – it has been alleged. Yet he acted in the belief that the good man is always in the hands of god.

In the *Apology* Socrates' message is voiced in two statements. One says: an unexamined life is not worth living (38 A). The other is the last sentence of the *Apology*: I go to death, you go to life. Nobody but the god knows whose lot is the better (42 A).

Plato continued the *Apology* with a brief dialogue, the *Crito*, in which Socrates' old friend, Crito yet again attempts to persuade him to flee. Socrates refuses, and in an allegory he lets the laws themselves explain why (*Crito* 50 A ff.): as a citizen Socrates cannot avoid his responsibility to the law and the society to which he has submitted himself. It is men who have abused the law, but flight would be tantamount to disavowing the law itself. Plato's Socrates is submissive to both the god's command and the city's law; when they conflict, he can only choose death – as a sort of Antigone of philosophy. The small dialogue does not lose itself in subtle deliberations, but then as now it is a telling commentary on the discussions for or against *nomos*.

The *Apology* is cunning, ironic, and double-edged. Considered as a – fictional – forensic speech it is brilliant. Socrates was probably not guilty of 'treason', but his ties to politically suspect persons could hardly be explained away. In such a situation he can naturally not act as an adherent of either aristocracy or democracy. Instead he refers to his having once defied the democrats and once the Thirty Tyrants (*Apol.* 32 B ff.), and he stresses that it was a democrat, Chaerephon, who had received the famous oracular answer. In other words, Socrates was above parties – in his situation, the best possible defence. Nevertheless, he has always obeyed the city laws; for example, he fulfilled his military obligation – an effective ploy by the Socrates who claims that he will not appeal to the judges' emotions (34 B ff.). The *Apology* as a whole begins with a shrewd exploitation of a somewhat hackneyed theme (17 B ff.): the just man who is unfamiliar with rhetoric but knows only the truth and only can speak as he usually does, an artlessness with a sting to it, as it turns out later during the cross-examination of Meletus; Aristotle (Aristot. *Rhet.* 1419 a 8) singles out precisely Meletus' examination as a specimen of professional forensic rhetoric. But what is decisive is that Socrates stands forth as an unblemished person – and here he also lives up to Aristotle's *Rhetoric* (1418 a 37 ff.): it is more important to show oneself an honest man than to argue subtly. From what we know, Socrates at one time had been interested in natural philosophy – consequently he dismisses this accusation contemptuously and without argumentation. And the purpose of showing up Meletus is to suggest that Socrates' *daimonion* is not in conflict with official worship – which is why this point in the indictment should be withdrawn. Socrates' defence oration occupies a handsome place in the tradition of Gorgias, the arch-enemy – also when he reminds the judges that they must judge solely according to the law (*Apol.* 35 C).

But exactly by following the rhetorical apparatus to the letter, Socrates topples the cardhouse in order all the more effectively to distance himself from the entire trial and in a way to outdo the prosecutors. It is a provocation for him to speak plainly and directly as he usually does – as Meletus comes to learn. And he is no Sophist – because he is 'wise' in a higher sense. It is arrogance that he, one man on his own, undertakes to act as moral chastizer and that he, one man on his own, has a direct, connecting line to Apollo. And the Socrates, who – godless or not – looks forward to meeting Ulysses or Sisyphus in the beyond, speaks from the no man's land of irony and is exalted far above an indifferent trial – indeed also above life and death.

Politically Socrates also plays on two strings. He places himself above the parties – not only because he is the decent man, but because it provides him with a position as chastizer of democracy. That he did not perform as a politician is because this would have prevented him from fulfilling his mission; in that case he would have had to pay with his life years ago, for where 'the people' rule, law and justice are trampled under foot (31 D ff.; cf. 36 B). There are similarly grim undertones in his account of his round of visits to politicians, poets, and artisans. The artisans have respectable technical knowledge, but nobody he questions has the knowledge of justice and truth that they think they have – and which Protagoras attributed to all the people in a democracy. The cobbler should stick to his last, and everybody ought to confine himself to what he really knows. This is a frontal attack on democracy that is far more crucial than Xenophon's reservations about elections by lot. A direct line runs to Plato's division of labour in the *Republic* and to his view of politics as humbug and poetry as madness. The Platonic Socrates speaks with unheard-of pride and authority. My defence oration applies not to me but to you, he says (30D), and in Plato's staging the defence becomes an indictment of the judges, the Athenians, and the rest of us.

But what now if Socrates indeed were the only one to live his life in truth? The figure of Socrates that is delineated in Plato's *Apology* is a Socrates who follows truth and nothing else and who acts in the service of the god. Xenophon and Plato agree that Socrates' piety was his real motivation, and they agree that his inner voice, *to daimonion*, and the Oracle's answer are two sides of the same issue. As so often, this is an outward agreement. The strange concept of *daimonion* connects Socrates with ancient Greek religiousness. The word is derived from *daimōn*, that blend of divinity and abstract notion that from ancient times had demarcated the fate of individual man. Nobody has chosen to be who he is, but everybody is responsible for himself – this is inherent in Heraclitus' and Democritus' rational and in Aeschylus' poetical interpretation of the concept. Xenophon stands for old-fashioned religiosity, and hence Socrates' *daimonion* is not really a problem for him: it is evident that the gods, the all-wise ones, reveal their wisdom to those they wish to guide rightly. Plato's Socrates stands on the borderline between the old way of thinking and something revolutionary and new: a personal faith, which quite clearly does not conform with the state cult. The inner voice does not directly counsel but restrains – it has, for example, restrained Socrates from political life (31 D) but not from acting as he does during the trial (40 A). *To daimonion* is not in some vague moral sense a voice of conscience; it is the religious basis for Socrates' life. But the god does not impart his knowledge and does not deign to argue; he reveals, as in Heraclitus, and thereupon leaves man on his own – quite in the same way as in the famous oracular answer: Socrates himself must interpret and discover that he is wise because he knows nothing. The new lies in the god's having given Socrates a call – albeit an indirect one.

To Plato, Socrates' *daimonion* is indissolubly tied to Socrates' person – it goes with Socrates' other personal peculiarities, his strange appearance, his habit of stopping up and withdrawing into himself, etc. This is a characteristic that is allowed to remain; it cannot be developed – as Plato's Socrates can in other ways. But the demand for truth occasioned by it lives on and inspires both Plato and his Socrates.

This demand for truth is the nerve of the *Apology*. Truth is to be what one is and not to appear to be what one is not. Here again Socrates gives new shape to a motif with deep roots in the tradition. Philosophers, scientists, tragedians, and historians have all sought for truth behind appearance. Only the Sophists had sought human truth and human reality in the phenomenon. The Socratic truth rests on self-knowledge – to that extent Socrates continues the line from the great tragedians; but he makes knowledge an intellectual act and turns his back on the truth which the natural philosophers sought, because that is an external truth of no concern to man here and now. It goes without saying that the demand for truth cannot be honoured by pseudo-knowledge nor by technical ability, as Socrates must conclude whenever he questioned people. Actually he has not come across anybody who has met his demand of 'taking care of his soul'. None the less, the demand must be made. The means must be to do away with pseudo-knowledge, because it is pseudo-being – to that extent Socrates is a Parmenides of morality: true knowledge is true being; but personal knowledge and personal existence are his goals. Therefore he has to ask tough questions and unmask false knowledge of self, and therefore he has to adjust his arguments to the person to whom he is speaking. He helps his friends to find themselves; his enemies he attacks with irony and sarcasm, sometimes slyly; all meet the Socrates they are in need of. Socrates is the occasion, the 'midwife', not the teacher, for self-knowledge cannot be taught. It is possible to conclude directly from the *Apology* that knowledge is knowledge of one's own soul. Clearly knowledge is tied to existence, actions, and morality. Clearly knowledge is also tied to absolute values;

it is both a universal and personal matter. Behind such modes of thought lie paradoxes and philosophical perspectives.

Socrates often expresses himself in terse maxims. Some are directly referred to in the *Apology*; others are presupposed. But in the *Apology* they seem like dogmas, the sole warrant for which is Socrates' own person. Such maxims are: 'virtue is knowledge', 'take care of your soul', 'no evil can befall the good', 'no one acts wrong voluntarily', 'I know that I know nothing'. Behind them lies the old Delphic 'know thyself', which so to speak is Socrates' signature – also in Aristophanes and Xenophon. It seems as if there are stronger ties between Socrates and Apollo than the Oracle's answer, and apparently Socrates sought a foothold in ancient wisdom – there is evident resemblance between his maxims and those of the Seven Wise. Yet Socrates is no old-fashioned sage. His maxims are directly relevant to contemporary debates. The typical Socratic question, 'can virtue be taught?' was also asked by the Sophists, and Socrates discussed it with the Sophistic technique of argumentation. In his view of the soul as man's true self and of justice – the good consists in not wanting to act unjustly – he is in any case outwardly reminiscent of Democritus – even if he draws more far-reaching consequences. One may then ask what Socrates wants with his maxims. They can have an air of both paradox and tautology.

This pertains, for example, to the statement 'virtue is knowledge'. It is of course a paradox, if the statement is interpreted in strict intellectualistic terms. The counter-question presents itself readily – what about the morally weak man who knows the good but does not act accordingly? If the answer were that the morally weak has no knowledge, the paradox would seem to have been changed into a tautology. But this is apparently what the Platonic Socrates wants to get at. The called-for – and seemingly problematic – unity of virtue and knowledge is a leitmotif in all that Plato wrote and proved a challenge to Aristotle who attacks what he takes to be moral intellectualism in Socrates (Aristot. *Eth. Nic.* 1145 b 27); at the same time, however, he formulates a modified Socratic thesis: virtue is not knowledge, but implies knowledge (1144 b 28). In Stoicism the Socratic-Platonic demand lived on.

What does 'virtue' mean, and what does 'knowledge' mean? Apparently Socrates has the same frame of reference as the Sophists since without reservation he is able to discuss questions such as 'is virtue knowledge' or 'can virtue be taught' with them. There is a historical background for this agreement. Every Greek knows from Homer that the good man is he who 'knows good things', the cruel one 'knows cruel things' (cf., e.g. Hom. *Il.* XXIV 41; *Od.* XIV 433; XIX 248) – he who knows the good has it in his heart. At a time of upheavals, such as the end of the fifth century, such an inheritance of language and thought must be interpreted. A Protagoras must necessarily interpret as a utilitarian. The good is the expedient, which agrees pretty well with the fact that *aretē*, virtue or ability, in normal Greek usage signifies something – be it a tool, an animal, or a man functioning optimally and good for something (cf. Plat. *Gor.* 506 D). Knowledge thus means insight into the optimal use of something; in its broadest sense it is an ability to cope with existence; in modern terminology: 'knowledge how'. In this sense knowledge is practical and useful knowledge, and virtue must be a means, not a goal.

To Socrates moral knowledge is practical and useful. But that is not enough. Virtue is a goal, not a means, and one must know what virtue is in order to act virtuously. Socrates calls for a unification of theoretical knowledge and moral act, which probably goes beyond what the good man in Homer can come up with. Knowledge involves the whole person; goal and means coincide, and moral insight implies not only a moral judgement but also a moral life and a moral standard. It is a fundamental idea in the Socratic tradition that every human act aims at the good (cf. *Symp.* 205 A; *Gor.* 499 E; *Phil.* 20 D; Aristot. *Eth. Nic.* 1094 a 1), and inasmuch as the good is a final goal, it must necessarily be perfect. If it is an empirical fact that man strives for the good and a presupposition that the good is an intelligible absolute norm, it must follow that striving without knowledge is meaningless – man may strive for the seeming good, but what seems to be good is not necessarily good. Conversely, knowledge that may be true is in itself meaningless, if it does not oblige man in everything he does. Every intellectual dishonesty and all knowledge that does not simply oblige are pseudo-knowledge and prevent a life in truth. Most likely it is not just a strange accident that Socrates only encountered outward knowledge and never knowledge that is virtue at the same time. If virtue and knowledge mutually imply one another, knowledge is not something which one accidentally possesses or which happens to be true, but rather a manifestation of what one is. Nobody knows what the good is. Socrates is the wisest because he knows that he does not know it.

The Platonic Socrates likes analogies. He teased and provoked his listeners by speaking of pack asses, tanners, and blacksmiths whenever one might have expected loftier matters to be debated. The analogies with practical skill and craftsmanship – which nobody values more highly than Socrates – are indeed on the one hand meant to demonstrate the absurdity of making precise demands for professional ability in artisans, which one would never dream of making whenever the question is of man's relation to himself, to society, or to the values that make a man an 'able' citizen. On the other hand, such analogies are also meant to suggest their own limitations. Professional knowledge is neutral – it can be used, abused, or one can avoid using it. But one cannot distance oneself from moral knowledge, which is not a means to something else. Everybody is free to do as he wishes, in the sense that one can refrain from examining one's own life, from knowing oneself, and thereby relate oneself to the absolute good; but thus doing one runs away from one's own self. The good man, on the other hand, is determined by his moral knowledge; and indeed some sort of determinism seems to be implied: the good man will never do wrong and shall never suffer wrongs. And inasmuch as every man strives for what he considers good, no man can voluntarily do wrong. With this Socrates has not rejected, for example, Sophistic utilitarianism, but he has given the idea a radically new direction: at a higher level duty and utility coincide; it is always in man's own interest to do good, even though the consequences seemingly hurt him. A good man can never be harmed by a worse man. It is obvious that the Platonic Socrates has to provide arguments for the view that the new morality really is the only consistent one, if one thoroughly considers one's options for action. Again and again he returns to the provocative theses, 'nobody voluntarily acts wrong' (e.g. *Meno* 77 C ff; *Prot.* 345 D; *Tim.* 86 E) and 'no evil can befall the good' with the correlative that 'to do wrong is worse than to suffer wrong' (e.g. *Meno* 77 C ff.; *Gor.* 469 B ff.).

The individual will realize his own self if by self-knowledge he submits to an absolute norm. To the 'intellectual' Socrates there is nothing odd in demanding that the good man must be able to explain what the good is; in every discussion of moral values the question of the essence of virtue must take precedence over the question of whether virtue can be taught, for example. There is no way around such rational cognition. In one dialogue after another Plato has his Socrates ask how this or that virtue is to be defined; and behind the questions it is implicit that the virtues make up a unity: when virtue is knowledge of an absolute norm, there can be no partial virtue. But an ambiguous light is shed on the Socratic questions. The aim is an objective, true definition, but neither the ignorant Socrates nor his interlocutors ever arrive at the result. Questions are asked about the universal good, but they are asked of specific persons; the path of morality from *doxa* to *alētheia* runs not only in a theoretical sense from the particular to the universal; it is, so to speak, the person himself who must become true when confronted with the demand for absolute truth. Therefore a Socratic discussion becomes a strange mixture of personal appeal and abstract conceptual analysis. Socrates' victim might as well sooner than later realize that Socrates unscrupulously will take possession of his interlocutor's private person and that through a theoretical discussion he will be held responsible for his own life – here Plato can play on the ambiguity of the term *logon didonai*, which may mean 'define', 'account for', and 'render account of' (cf. e.g. *Lach.* 187 E; *Phaedo* 95 D; *RP* VII 531 E). Socrates' interlocutors and the reader must draw their own conclusions, as the discussion seemingly comes to an end without any result. And in the dialogue itself there is always one additional point: the person and his special habitus must be taken into account; more is said than appears to be said – often hinted at by Socrates' famous irony, which neither confirms nor disproves an assertion, but reveals a new perspective or a disproportion between ideology and truth, between person and knowledge. Unlike romantic irony, Socratic irony is not an expression of the free spirit's distancing; nor is it a mere display of the odd fact that pomposity and frivolity live as next-door neighbours. Through irony Socrates can give a signal to whoever can listen; he can do no more than that, for his form of communication is indirect.

Socrates' indirect form of communication – and his ignorance – imply that though he can examine the consequences of a hypothesis, he cannot himself conclude deductively with any degree of certainty; he has nothing to deduce from. He must turn to everyday language and all its oddities, traps, and occasional insights, and his form of argumentation is particular and rhetorical. In a later chapter a closer account will be provided of the technique of argumentation that Plato has Socrates employ in his dialogues; here it is enough to note that its aim, not its form, is different from the Sophists'. When Socrates uses everyday language – in his own plain and simple way – we ought to remember that language, *logos*, denotes speech, argument and statement. When the truth is not a given, language is not an external means of communication; the entire linguistic context – speaker, time, and place – must be considered, and the linguistic paradigm becomes the probing conversation – the dialogue; the function of language as a social phenomenon promoting knowledge becomes more important than the question of its nature – for example, whether it depicts correctly or exists from nature or by convention. Language is not something alien nor one particular person's property but is the medium by which man expresses himself and comes into his own as a moral and intellectual being and as a member of society. It is a warrant that individual man does not live in a void; in language 'one renders account', and hence discussion is a more genuine linguistic vehicle than a speech or a book, which can only account for themselves. Socrates, the master dialectician, makes a show of his midwifery that provokes others to deliver their spiritual issue (cf. *Theaet.* 149 A ff.); language is, then, not so much the expression of thought as it is the precondition of thought. Socrates is the philosopher of questions who teaches others that an answer depends on one's being able to question one's own presuppositions.

Now, it is one more Socratic paradox that a particular argument ideally must lead to an objective conclusion, for in fact the Socratic technique of asking questions and Socrates' famed art of midwifery do not lead to subjectivism. In the midst of his own relativistic – and to Socrates this means nihilistic – age, he wishes to re-establish the concept of an absolute truth. It is not truth itself but man's relation to truth that is questioned. Plato's Socrates knows that he knows nothing, and thus he presupposes already at this point that knowledge exists. While he has no objective knowledge of truth nor any objective method, he has, nevertheless, a concept of objective truth. The content of the absolute good – 'virtue in itself' – he cannot determine, but he stubbornly presupposes *that* an absolute truth and an absolute motive for acting accessible to knowledge do exist. Therefore he can with certainty point to the precondition for a philosophical inquiry, although he is ignorant of the outcome. Socrates' fundamental certainty cannot be verified; but it is this that to posterity has made him stand as the founder both of normative moral philosophy and of conceptual thinking, which is to say that for the tradition that builds on him he laid down the directive basis for knowledge and morality. He transformed Sophistic eudaimonism and utilitarianism into absolute morality. *Aretē* stands not only for that which is good for something or someone, but for that which is good in itself, and – to use a frequently quoted Cicero phrase (Cic. *Tusc. Disp.* V 10) – Socrates led philosophy from heaven down to earth in the sense that moral insight must be realized in the concrete situation. What has later been called 'practical reason' builds on this unification of the universal and normative with the concrete. But Socrates is also an innovator in epistemology. Knowledge of 'virtue in itself' presupposes the existence of a universal concept, which, precisely because it is unchangeable, can be applied to any particular case whatsoever.

The old and the new meet in the pious Socrates who in the midst of perhaps the greatest spiritual crisis of the Greek world laid the foundation for 'morality' (Hegel) and invented 'the concept' (Schleiermacher). He is more conservative than a flighty natural philosopher and more progressive than an incarnate Sophist. By confronting the individual with a *De te fabula narratur* he created the idea of the self – the human soul – as an autonomous being who realizes himself in his relation to a normative truth. By his call for self-knowledge he shifted the philosophical focus and reformed past traditions. The Platonic Socrates is conservative in the sense that he – as is abundantly clear in the *Apology* – is tied to his city and his god. He is also tied to the greater rational order – something that Xenophon interpreted in his own way. It is still the god who is wise and man who must find his place in the cosmos. Man becomes good thanks to his knowledge of the good, and there is congruity between man and the world. What is new is that Socrates made morality rational. Thus man is no longer first and foremost a citizen in a city state; faith is given a different content, and no longer is there room, for example, for the poetical experience of tragedy or for the tragic hero's acceptance of a fate he does not understand. Nietzsche realized this (*Die Geburt der Tragödie*), and so did Aristophanes who harshly criticized wishy-washy modern tragedy in *The Frogs*, pointing out that 'Socratic babbling' and the high art of tragedy could never be made to agree (Aristoph. *Ran.* 1491 ff.).

In a way the Socrates of the *Apology* speaks for himself. Yet every reader of Plato will know what perspectives lie behind. These perspectives have been adumbrated in the preceding – as an outline of the Socrates who inspired Plato. This – we are led to believe – was the real Socrates. In his other works Plato allowed his Socrates to develop further. Socrates, the pious rationalist, confronted man with a demand for unity of will and intellect, morality and existence. This may be a demand that cannot be met, and it may be a faith in a fundamental congruity between man and world that is lost today. But Plato's whole work may be seen as a grand attempt to meet this demand. It implies that Plato must let his Socrates reflect on his own presuppositions. How can it be demonstrated that man is a rational being who discovers his own identity in his relation to an absolute good? How must a society be constituted so as to be a reflection of the good and not turn into everybody's war with everybody? How is it possible to obtain objective knowledge if man is trapped in pseudo-being? What is the status of the concept if it is to warrant knowledge, value, and existence? In Plato's staging, Socrates is the ever-tireless questioner who with an enigmatic smile starts from the beginning in each dialogue. Yet he must grow as an ethical and political thinker; he must become an epistemologist and metaphysician on a grand scale.

OTHER SOCRATICS. ARISTOTLE'S SOCRATES

Plato's Socrates did not have a doctrine in the traditional sense. On the other hand, several of those who heard Socrates did have one. Some applied the Socratic inspiration to practical ethics; others gave it a theoretical direction. The differences between these doctrines, which to us are known only fragmentarily, are so striking that they can only be explained if we see Socrates – as did Plato – as a catalyst; in his discussions or by his personal example he helped each of them to arrive at an answer that suited him. If we did not know Socrates' 'art of midwifery', or maieutics, from Plato or were unacquainted with the outlook of the Platonic Socrates, it would be incomprehensible that such different personalities could invoke him. Socrates did not have disciples in the usual sense of the word, and, characteristically, these so-called Socratics all had some connection with other contemporary currents and apparently only developed certain Socratic features. We know in what manner Xenophon felt himself confirmed by Socrates in his old-fashioned view of life. In the inner circle of Socrates' friends and adherents – several of whom witnessed his death (cf. Plat. *Phaedo* 59 B ff.) – we find 'Pythagoreans' and followers of the Eleatics or the Sophists. Several of them must – in the longer perspective – be considered forerunners of Hellenistic thought, and it is worth noting that there are Socratic traditions that by-pass Plato.

Euclid of Megara (c.twenty-five years older than Plato) – the Socratic who seems to have been closest to Plato (cf. the 'dedication' in the *Theaetetus*) – was, according to the tradition, influenced by the Eleatics. To him the good was apparently a metaphysical reality, which he determined as a unity manifesting itself in different forms: insight, god, reason, etc. but without an 'opposite' (Diog. Laert. II 106 ff.). This can be interpreted as a fusion of Parmenides' monism with basic Socratic thoughts: virtue is a unity, cognition is dependent on an ontological-normative principle, and the highest – true reality – can only be related to the apparent, not to a principle of the same order. However uncertain such an interpretation may be, it is apparent that Euclid, like Plato, was interested in drawing metaphysical conclusions from the basic Socratic concept. It is reasonable to remember the role that 'the idea of the good' was to play to Plato.

As already mentioned, Antisthenes, a disciple of Gorgias and nearly thirty years older than Plato, became an eager member of the Socratic circle. His linguistic deliberations, probably his most original contribution to philosophy, belong in a Sophistic context, but in spite of persistent – and perhaps justified – attempts to think of him as a central philosophical figure, it does not seem easy to chart the connection between linguistic philosophy and logic on the one hand and a Socratically inspired ethics on the other. The ethics Antisthenes learned from Socrates is a strict, intellectual eudaimonism (cf. Diog. Laert. VI 11 ff.; Antis. frg. 70, 80, 101 Caizzi). Virtue is happiness, and virtue can be learned. Therefore, in any given situation the wise man will acknowledge the good; Socratic strength of character and an ascetic conduct of life are the sole requirements. Virtue consists in action; once learned, insight into virtue cannot be lost; and the wise man is self-sufficient and independent of conventions (*nomoi*), passions, and material needs (cf. Xen. *Symp.* IV 34 ff.). Following a Sophistic pattern, Antisthenes found his ideal of the wise man personified in such heroes as Ulysses and Heracles (frg. 15; 22 ff.). He is mentioned as the founder of the School of Cynicism – an important historical presupposition for Stoic ethics. Antisthenes exploited the Socratic message in a quite concrete manner. Yet it is not surprising that there is a direct line from the Socratic to the Stoic ideal of the wise man; the wise man is the ideal person who has fully met the Socratic demand.

But it is more surprising that Epicureanism could also claim a disciple of Socrates, Aristippus (c.435–365) – according to tradition yet another founder of a school: the Cyrenaics, who in turn inspired Epicurus – considered pleasure the absolute good, because it is an immediate experience that pleasure is the only thing sought for its own sake (cf. Diog. Laert. II 87 ff., Aristip. frg. 169 Mannebach). An uncertain source (Sext. Emp. *Adv. math.* VII 191, Aristip. frg. 217) attributes scepticism concerning our possibilities of knowing the external world to Aristippus; our cognition is exclusively tied to introspection, and this means that feelings – pleasure and pain – are the sole certain criteria. At first sight this may seem an odd blend of Protagoras' epistemology, Democritus' ethics, Socrates' demand for self-knowledge, and the Socratic thought that the absolute good is happiness for the individual (cf. Plato's *Protagoras* on Socratic 'hedonism', here p. 168). That which connects such an ill-matched couple as the ascetic Antisthenes and the hedonist Aristippus is the idea of the wise man who is independent thanks to his insight into the good. They differ from the Platonic Socrates, because unhesitatingly they can determine this good – here there is no trace of Socratic ignorance.

Nowhere in Plato's dialogues is there direct mention of the views of his 'fellow-Socratics'; he rarely refers to living persons. The dialogues are a possession forever, and Antisthenes and Aristippus, for example, perhaps did not in Plato's view have a claim to eternity. Still, it is more than likely that they are active back-stage. But a few isolated instances aside, we have no chance of catching possible allusions, and the more or less fanciful attempts that have been made in this regard do not invite presentation here. However, perhaps in opposition to other views of Socrates, it looks as if a consensus gradually was established in the Academy concerning what was to be considered Socrates' central message. And probably it was felt desirable to go behind Plato's exploitation of his Socrates in his more ambitious dialogues. With Plato as the purported author, a 'Socratic Primer', the so-called first *Alcibiades* dialogue, has been transmitted; but already on stylistic grounds Plato himself cannot have been the author, even though the author most likely was an Academy member. He tried to perform the trick of fashioning the Platonic Socrates *in usum Delphini* and found support in the *Apology*. His attempt is no masterpiece, yet successful in the sense that this dialogue became widely used as an introduction to the study of Plato in Antiquity, not least by the Neoplatonists.

The young Alcibiades – the bad conscience of all Socratics – wants to become a great politician. Socrates takes him aside ([Plat.] *Alc.* I 103 A ff.) and subjects him to heavy-handed psychoanalytic treatment. He has perceived his dubious character and shows him that he has no idea of politics, nor of right and wrong. In other words, Alcibiades is ignorant. It is too bad to lack insight, but worse not to know that one is ignorant (117 E). But worst of all is it not to take care of oneself (119 A) and not to heed the Delphic 'know thyself', even though that is no easy matter (124 A; 129 A). But to know oneself is to know one's soul, for the soul is the man (130 C), and the soul's virtue is wisdom (133 B). Without self-knowledge there is no knowledge whatever, and he who does not know right from wrong tends badly to his life and will become unhappy (134 A). The argument is conducted with the utmost care and seriousness; it is crystal-clear and has steady reference to horsemen, cobblers, and farmers. The Socratic ingredients are there, but one may feel that Socrates himself is missing.

One of Plato's students wanted to provide an independent and objective account of Socrates. Aristotle did not know Socrates personally, but thanks to his twenty-year stay at the Academy he was of course able to obtain knowledge we do not have. It goes without saying that Aristotle was familiar with the Platonic Socrates and, for example, knows of Socratic ignorance (Aristot. *Soph. El.* 183 b 6) and Socrates' tie to Delphi (Plut. *Adv. Col.* 1118 C; Aristot. Περὶ φιλοσ. frg. 1 Ross); as mentioned, in his own ethics he is in a basic sense in a dialogue with Socrates. But when – in the *Metaphysics* – he wishes to see Socrates in a historical perspective (*Met.* 987 b 1 ff.; 1078 b 17 ff.), it is evidently important for him to make his way behind hagiography and as soberly and precisely as possible point out Socrates' enduring achievement. He is the first who clearly distinguished between a Platonic and a historical Socrates. Socrates' field was ethics, he says, and here two things can safely be attributed to him: inductive argument and definition of universals. Thus Socrates' investigations concerned the universal, but – unlike Plato – he did not hypostatize it, we are told. What is essential is that Aristotle looks for a Socrates behind Plato. But this hardly makes him a primary source for knowledge of the 'historical Socrates'. In fact he does not tell us anything that we do not already know. But his assessment is of more than common interest. Induction and universal definitions are to Aristotle himself pre-conditions for all scientific knowledge, and actually he credits Socrates with founding the scientific method – which partially became muddled in Plato's doctrine of ideas.

Aristotle is the first in a long line of occidental thinkers after Plato who wanted to evaluate Socrates but at the same time – just like the first generation of Socratics – let themselves be challenged by him. A study of the history of the Socrates figure down through the ages would be a commentary on the self-perception of Western thought. There is, for example, a great distance between Kierkegaard's Socrates – the 'existing thinker' – and Nietzsche's – 'the thinker of reflection'. But all interpretations agree that with Socrates a new ideal of man appears in the world; he signals a new age, sometimes a 'fall'; Socrates has constantly been the occasion of unrest and self-examination. The Socratic thought of a rational morality and a conceptual cognition that is always normative is also a direct appeal to a self bound to a superior order. I want to know something about you and me, says Socrates in the *Protagoras* (Plat. *Prot.* 331 C).

PART III

PLATO

12

LIFE, WORKS AND POSITION

——— •◦• ———

Plato (427–347) was descended from a distinguished family. He was brought up in accordance with the ancient traditions of Attic nobility and was by temperament an aristocrat. On his mother's side he was related to the tyrants Critias and Charmides, but after he had met Socrates and had become disaffected with the aristocratic as well as the democratic regimes that he knew in Athens, he abandoned all ambitions for a career in politics, which, given his family background, might have been expected. In a more profound sense he never relinquished his political commitment, but it is evident from his works that he chose a life of contemplation rather than let himself become corrupted by political intrigues (cf. Plat.*Gor.* 521 D ff.; *RP* VI 496 D). Furthermore, there is an inherent truth in an anecdote of a later date which claims that Plato tried to become a poet but burned his tragedies after he had met Socrates (Diog. Laert. III 5). A Socratic adherent could not allow himself to be compromised by the pseudo-knowledge of poets or the corruption of politicians. Plato's writings are sustained by visions of the true life and true knowledge, but there is also resignation, occasionally even bitterness, and as he grew older an elusive sense of distance becomes apparent. It seems credible that the history of his own life provides some explanation for this.

Plato did not witness Athens at the height of her power, but evidently he saw in the Periclean democracy the seed of that political and moral decay that he was to encounter at close quarters during the Peloponnesian War (cf. *Gor.* 515 E ff.). He died ten years before King Philip of the Macedonians delivered the final blow to the Greek city states.

The death of Socrates was the shattering event that determined the course of Plato's life. His own commentary on it has been preserved for us in his so-called *Seventh Letter*, which here is accepted as genuine. It must have been written after 354, in other words when Plato was a very old man. First Plato discusses the unhappy events that occurred during the Athenian Tyranny (*Ep.* VII 324 B ff.). He had thought that the tyrants would realize their proclaimed intentions and guide the state to 'the path of justice', but was shocked to see the consequences of dictatorship, among them especially the tyrants' treatment of Socrates, 'one of my old friends, the justest man then alive'. He turned down a request to make common cause with the dictators and thus broke away from his own social circle. Subsequently democracy was reintroduced, and Plato acknowledges that in the beginning 'great consideration' was shown; but the execution of Socrates deprived him of his last illusions. Profoundly disappointed and morally outraged by both modes of government, he abandoned all further political ambitions.

Following the execution of Socrates, Plato and other Socratic adherents sought refuge with Euclid of Megara (Diog Laert. III 6), although we do not know if they did so for reasons of safety. Afterwards he is said to have undertaken extensive journeys during which he became acquainted with the Pythagorean Archytas from Tarentum. Thrice he visited Syracuse (probably in 388–7, 366 and 361), where he became tragically involved in the intrigues at the Tyrant's court (18 ff.). During his first stay he became close friends with Dion, a relative of the Tyrant Dionysius I, after whose death at the instigation of Dion he was summoned to serve as the political mentor to the tyrant's son and successor, Dionysius II. Two attempts to influence Dionysius were made and both were unmitigated disasters. Indeed, Plato's life seems to have been endangered. Dionysius II failed to live up to Plato's expectations, and Plato became involved in complex struggles for power, which led to the murder of Dion in 354. It is probably impossible to reconstruct the exact course of events in Sicily, and Plato's retrospective defence – in the *Seventh Letter* – is not the most reliable of sources; furthermore his talents as a practical politician may have been limited. It is, of course, tempting to imagine that the author of the *Republic* wanted to exploit a probable political opening and that he was attracted to the idea of an alliance between a philosopher-legislator and a hopeful young absolute ruler (cf. Plat. *Leg.* IV 710 C). Nevertheless, he can hardly have imagined that with one stroke he would be in a position to realize his ideal state, 'the state of heaven', as he called it. It is apparent from other letters attributed to Plato (*Ep.* V; VI; XI) that other members of the Academy were recruited – as were the Sophists – as political advisors in several cities. If Plato wrote these letters, it is worth noting that he constantly advocates political moderation. At the very least his experiences in Sicily provided him with first-hand knowledge of the political game and a tyrant's mentality (further explored in *RP* VIII 562 A ff.).

In all likelihood Plato founded the Academy shortly after his first Sicilian journey (c.385?, Diog. Laert. III 7) – the first genuine European scholarly institution – which with but few interruptions existed until AD 529 when it was closed down by the Emperor Justinian. It has been thought that it was organized as a religious community whose members were united in their worship of the Muses. This may have lent the institution legal status, and, if so, it may help to account for the fact that the Academy served as a framework for the Platonic tradition for so many centuries – however differently interpreted. Plato lived and studied with his pupils; the Academy appears to have functioned as a quite undogmatic home for different kinds of study, and prominent scholars, such as the mathematician Eudoxus, were affiliated with it. There is no mention of the Academy in the *Seventh Letter*, but there are occasional, although oblique references in the dialogues to the curriculum and the internal discussions (cf. Plat. *RP* VII 521 C ff.; *Parm.* 130 A ff.). From the sparse sources one can also conclude that mathematics, astronomy, the natural sciences, rhetoric, logic, politics, and metaphysics were subjects of study. Plato's own teaching, including a renowned lecture on the good, will be discussed later.

Shortly before the Academy was founded, another school which explicitly disapproved of scholarly theorizing, had seen the light of day. The programme of this competing school indicates perhaps better than anything else what Plato turned against when he established his ideal of knowledge and education. The earlier school had been founded in 390 by Isocrates, who was to attain an incredible age (436–338). He who had been born in the time of Pericles was as an old man able to correspond with the future Alexander the Great. Like Plato, he kept away from political life, but – again like Plato – he educated political advisors, and in his essays, which were couched as fictional speeches, he was a vigorous spokesman for his own educational programme, just as Plato implicitly was in his dialogues. Isocrates had been a pupil of the old Sophists (Gorgias, Prodicus). Clearly he was also influenced by Socrates. In politics he was a warm advocate of the unification of the Greek city states against the arch-enemy, the Persians, and when he had become an old man, it was for that reason that he supported Philip, the King of the Macedonians. He adhered to the nobler side of Sophistic rhetoric, but 'the art of contradiction' was not his chosen field. What he taught he called philosophy (Isoc. *Ant.* 181). In his view philosophy is a practical matter consisting in whatever action is called for at a given moment (266). Man is a product of culture, and, as with Gorgias, the special world of man is that of language; language (*logos*) conveys cultural and moral values, and every action is in principle a linguistic one. Isocrates' aim was to educate the soul (*paideia*, cf. 180) and to develop the ability to speak in political assemblies of the beautiful and exalted for the benefit of the commonwealth (276 ff.). An active human life is indeed identical with a life in politics: a life in word and action. The prerequisites for becoming an able orator (192) are natural ability (*physis*), experience (*empeiria*) based on formal rules that can be learned, and that *paideia* which enables the speaker to act in consonance with a virtue that all acknowledge (cf. 84). But it is misleading to maintain that virtue *per se* can be taught (274) and equally wrong to believe that it is humanly possible to arrive at the truth. It is possible to persuade about the probable, and the philosopher knows that he must take his point of departure in the belief (*doxa*) that hits the mark and not put his trust in theoretical insight (*epistēmē*) into absolute truths (271) for the actual circumstances are always more complicated than the theory (184); it is better to entertain beliefs (*doxai*) about useful things than to have insight (*epistēmē*) into what is useless (*Hel.* 5); it is vain to speculate on whether the world is made up of one or more elements, or, indeed, whether it exists at all (3); and difficult subjects such as geometry and astronomy may be employed in order to train the intellect, but one should not allow oneself to be stuck for a lifetime in such niceties (*Ant.* 265 – cf. Callicles in Plat. *Gorg.* 485 D ff.; *RP* VI 487 D). All of this may seem like turning Plato inside out, and that is no mere accident.

In fact Isocrates attacks on two fronts: one target is the 'bad' Sophists who lie when they claim to know the truth (Isoc. *Adv. Soph.* 1) and talk nonsense when they deny the possibility of contradiction (*Hel.* 1); the other is the specious thinkers (Plato) who claim that all virtues constitute a unity that may be understood by means of *epistēmē* (ibid.). None of these can be called philosophers. Both of Isocrates' targets are – in the derogatory phrase of the day – eristics, and Plato is a constant object of his scorn. Year after year the two competitors exchanged carefully worded barbs, and indeed Plato did not hold back (cf. *Gorg.* 462 B about the art of rhetoric as empirical;

RP V 480 A on lovers of wisdom and 'lovers of beliefs', *philosophoi* and *philodoxoi*). In the *Phaedrus* (279 A; cf. *Euthyd.* 305 C) he has Socrates, the idol of both adversaries, send greetings to the 'young Isocrates' who certainly is not without some talents – if only he would put them to better use.

Isocrates represents the rhetorical ideal of education, just as Plato represents the philosophical one. Both continued the debate they had inherited from the days of the Sophists and Socrates, even though they observed a proper distance from the society they spoke about. None the less, the conflict between the two men has persisted – even down to our own time when Isocrates' ideals indirectly have been of great importance in the teaching of the liberal arts.

WORKS

We do not know when Plato began to write. Although he may have written dialogues before the execution of Socrates, they seem to have been written against the ever-present backdrop of the fate of Socrates. There is reason to believe that all of Plato's published works have been preserved, and indeed some dialogues whose authenticity was disputed already in Antiquity are included in the oeuvre. In the tradition the dialogues were divided into groups of four, a classification credited to the astrologer Thrasyllus at the court of the Emperor Tiberius (shortly after the Birth of Christ, cf. Diog. Laert. III 56 ff.; Alb. Εἰσαγωγή IV), although probably of earlier date. Other classifications are also referred to (Diog. Laert. III 49 ff.; Alb. Εἰσαγωγή III). Furthermore we know that the Alexandrians occupied themselves with Plato's text. It seems probable that an authorized version had already been made by the Academy – at the latest in the third century BC – and this may help to explain why the text has been transmitted so well. The classifications of Antiquity were made according to thematic and aesthetic criteria. There was no interest in any chronological division, nor does it seem that much was known about it. The only certain point of information is that the *Laws* was Plato's last work, edited posthumously by one of his students (Diog. Laert. III 37; cf. Aristot. *Pol.* 1264 b 26).

Plato's works have a strangely anonymous character. The writer withdraws and disguises himself behind Socrates or other personae; Plato, the person, only receives mention twice, once as present at the trial of Socrates, and once as absent when Socrates died, because he was 'most likely' ill at the time (*Apol.* 34 A; 38 B; *Phaedo* 59 B). Many dialogues lead nowhere, and when a conclusion is drawn, we do not know whether the author supports it, for a writer of fiction must, in Plato's own words (*RP* III 393 C), withdraw himself and adapt his language to the person he allows to speak. This 'indirect form of communication' constituted a problem already for the commentators of Antiquity (cf. e.g. Olymp. *Vit. Plat.* VI).

Few philosophers have had such pervasive influence on all subsequent thinking as did Plato, nor has anybody else been interpreted so variously: every age and every philosophical school has its own Plato. Seemingly it is possible to find a rationalist, a sceptic, and a mystic in the dialogues, and apparently also both a dogmatist and an open-minded thinker. In consequence, any interpretation of Plato must be more tentative than that of any other thinker, and for many interpreters it has been difficult to distinguish between Plato and Platonism, between the dialogues themselves and the impact they had in later times. Aristotle's view of Plato and the Neoplatonic-Christian interpretations have had especially pervasive consequences for almost all later readings of Plato.

The early nineteenth century marked the beginning of the modern way of reading Plato, with Schleiermacher and Hegel as the principal figures. Briefly, they may be said to represent the two fundamental positions of modern times: hermeneutical sympathy and distance as opposed to direct discussion and evaluation. To Schleiermacher Plato's dialogues constituted a reflection of one basic position, expressed in each dialogue in a particular way. Here there is a certain similarity to the late Neoplatonists, including the view that each dialogue should be considered as an independent unity of form and content. Hegel, on the other hand, was in search of a philosophical system proper behind the literary form. He was looking for that stage in the development of human thought at which the universal rather than the particular manifestation was considered the essence of things. From a historical perspective this was a stage preceding the emancipation of 'the subject', although to Hegel the historical must always remain a part of a systematical context. The tension arising between a literary, historically determined reading and a philosophical debate that disregards historical demarcations has remained with us ever since.

Towards the end of the nineteenth century an interest in biographical, evolutionary history was added, which was typical of the period. No longer was the question asked about how Plato's thought unfolded itself in his works or system. Instead it was asked how Plato, the man himself – and thereby his work – had developed, and accordingly the chronology of the works assumed a significance it had not had before. The point of departure was a series of stylistic-linguistic analyses (begun in 1867 by Lewis Campbell). On the supposition that the *Laws* was Plato's last work it seemed possible to group the dialogues according to their greater or lesser stylistic similarity with the *Laws*. By means of such detailed analyses, supplemented by the sparse concrete knowledge available for establishing a chronology in the dialogues themselves, a classification was arrived at, which made possible a reconstruction of an inner philosophical development, whereby seeming contradictions between the dialogues might be explained. The Platonic chronology is still most often regarded as relatively well-established on this basis, in the sense that the dialogues allow for an arrangement in groups, usually called the early, middle and late dialogues – although not so precisely that an absolute dating or a certain sequence can be demonstrated within each group. Most often it is thought that the middle dialogues belong to the period after Plato's first journey to Sicily and that the late dialogues were written after c.370. The only dialogues that still seemed to have a relatively uncertain chronological place were the *Cratylus*, *Phaedrus* and *Timaeus*.

This new point of view led in the beginning of this century to a number of monumental treatises on Plato's development, today justly considered classics. And in spite of all differences, agreement prevailed among Plato scholars about two points. It has been maintained that if anything was certain it was the chronology, and, following the Schleiermacher tradition, most scholars identified Plato himself with the Plato of the dialogues. In recent years this consensus has been challenged.

According to a German school of interpretation, the dialogues are not the main concern in Plato's work as a philosopher. Plato intended his dialogues for a wider public, but in fact their philosophical contents can only be understood as being derived from the 'esoteric Plato', a systematic 'doctrine of principles', which Plato presented during his Academy teaching. About this we have only a few hints, even though it was to have decisive historical importance as a sort of Platonist undercurrent, which among other things became the presupposition of Neoplatonism. Inasmuch as the Platonic 'system' was laid down quite early, the chronology of the works was not of decisive significance. This is a theory that turns many accustomed thoughts upside down. It is indeed justified that attention has been focused more than hitherto on the indirect sources of the 'hidden' Plato, but several of the far-reaching conclusions may be challenged on both methodological and factual grounds (see more specifically, p. 255). The Platonic dialogues must still be considered our principal source for understanding Plato.

But in recent years doubt has also been expressed in other respects about the accepted Platonic chronology and about the picture of Plato's development, which gradually had become a tradition.

The group of the late dialogues still stands unchallenged, for the stylistic and factual arguments are convincing, and external criteria exist for assigning this group to the period after c.370 (cf. a reference to contemporary events in *Theaet.* 142 A). On the other hand, the chronological distinction between early and middle dialogues is debatable. Individual dialogues may have been written over extended periods – the *Republic*, for example – and a given dialogue may have been revised – as we know is the case with the *Theaetetus*. It should be added that the stylistic criteria are less than certain. In fact, without its being made explicit, an utterly different type of criterion has been applied in genetic Plato scholarship. The so-called early dialogues are aporetic – which is to say that Socrates apparently never arrives at any result – and the dialogue form is a lively one; Socrates' mode of debate is depicted with all conceivable nuances; and the reader has the sense that he is witnessing a genuine conversation. In the middle dialogues, on the other hand, the great classical dialogues, Socrates seems in a quite different sense to have a 'doctrine' of ideas and of the ideal state. Consequently it has been thought that the Socrates of the early dialogues gets very close to the 'historical' Socrates, while the Socrates of the middle dialogues functions as Plato's voice – it was not until this point in his life that Plato had conceived of the doctrine of ideas. In the late dialogues the figure of Socrates often retreats, and therefore it has been concluded that there was a steadily increasing distance between Plato and Socrates.

This picture is hardly tenable. Every Platonic dialogue is a work of fiction, and we have no guarantee that Plato at any given moment strove to give a 'correct' picture of Socrates. Any one dialogue is a world unto itself – it is in the nature of fiction that one must begin anew every time and that the author does not tell us of everything on his mind. There are clear links going backwards from the 'early dialogues' to the *Apology*, but in the first place the Socrates of the *Apology* is not readily identifiable with the 'historical' Socrates, and, secondly, there are at least as many links with the dialogues of maturity. There is such a sure and deliberate line in the 'early' dialogues that it cannot simply be a question of 'a doctrine of ideas in the bud', but rather of an anticipation of themes that the author himself knows very well, and it is a question whether the great classical dialogues in a more profound sense are not just as aporetic as they are dogmatic. If so, the traditional chronology has not thereby been disproved as a hypothesis, and in certain instances relatively certain chronological assumptions may be made. Thus the *Phaedo* and the *Symposium* seem to be nearly contemporary; the *Meno* must have been written before the *Phaedo* (cf. *Phaedo* 73 A) and presupposes at least the general mode of thinking in the 'early dialogues'; and the *Republic* in its final form is probably later than the *Phaedo* and the *Symposium*. But it is at least as likely a hypothesis that several of the early dialogues were written at the same time as the middle dialogues so that they deliberately advertise and refer to the latter. It goes without saying that such a theory cannot be proved, but it is an attractive one. Thus the indisputable difference between the 'early' and 'middle' dialogues will be thematical, not necessarily chronological.

Still, considered as a rough grouping by subject matter, the traditional classification of Plato's dialogues remains useful as an initial means of finding one's way.

One group (formerly: the early dialogues) is aporetic and polemical. In addition to the *Apology* and the *Crito*, a number of minor dialogues belongs to it, in which the question is how a virtue or a normative concept may be defined: the *Euthyphro*, *Laches*, *Charmides*, *Lysis* and *Hippias Major* (although the authenticity of this work occasionally has been doubted). The first book of the *Republic* is often thought to belong to this group. The two great dialogues, the *Protagoras* and the *Gorgias*, present a confrontation between Socrates and the Sophists, while problems of a far-reaching epistemological nature are raised in the *Meno*. By virtue of their aporetic or ironic, paradoxical forms, the *Hippias Minor*, *Ion*, *Euthydemus* and *Menexenus* belong in this group (though the authenticity of the last-mentioned has been questioned at times).

The second group (formerly: the middle dialogues) comprises the familiar classical dialogues: the *Phaedo*, *Symposium*, *Republic* and *Phaedrus*. They treat the metaphysical, ethical, epistemological-logical aspects of the doctrine of ideas in connection with anthropology and politics and are contrasted to the pseudo-knowledge of rhetoric and poetry. The *Cratylus*, which deals with language, has some affinity with this group. The most extensive dialogue in this group, the *Republic*, was at some later date divided into ten books.

It is still justified to label the last group the late dialogues. It comprises the *Parmenides*, *Theaetetus*, *Sophist*, *Statesman*, *Timaeus*, *Critias* (an incomplete work), *Philebus* and *Laws* (listed in a supposed chronological sequence, the *Laws* apparently left unrevised). Within this group there are two series, which is to say continuous discussions with the same circle of participants: the *Theaetetus-Sophist-Statesman* (an announced continuation, the *Philosopher*, was never written) and the *Timaeus-Critias*. Socrates does not participate in the *Laws*; in the *Parmenides*, *Sophist*, *Statesman*, and in the *Timaeus-Critias* others lead the discussion, although Socrates participates or is present. The *Parmenides* marks the introduction of a profoundly new direction of thought within the framework of the doctrine of ideas, which was further developed in the other late dialogues – with respect to a theory of knowledge and of language in the *Theaetetus*, *Sophist* and *Statesman*; to natural philosophy in the *Timaeus*; to ethics in the *Philebus*; and to politics in the *Statesman* and *Laws*. The longest dialogue in this group and in all Plato's works is the *Laws*, which at a later date was divided into twelve books with an addition, the *Epinomis*, probably written by the editor of the

Laws. In this group especially there is an affinity with what we know elsewhere about Plato's oral teaching.

In addition, in the Platonic corpus some minor dialogues have been transmitted, which must be considered spurious (for example the first *Alcibiades* dialogue, the *Clitophon*) without necessarily being deliberate frauds. Most of them are imitations of Plato's minor Socratic dialogues, and some were presumably written long after his death. A number of epigrams and the collection of thirteen letters have also been transmitted. The authenticity of these letters has been disputed, and some are obviously not genuine; but in any case, the sixth, seventh, and eighth letters are usually considered authentic. In the present work an explicit position has only been adopted with respect to the *Seventh Letter*, which is accepted as genuine.[1]

THE DIALOGUE FORM

In the *Seventh Letter* Plato comments on his indirect method of communication. On 'the matter itself' there is no treatise by him, nor will one ever appear, he remarks (*Ep.* VII 341 C ff.), but after many discussions and much social intercourse 'it suddenly emerges in the soul – as when the leaping spark ignites the candle and then continues to blaze'. He who possesses true insight will be unable to impart it to others, for 'the most serious lies concealed in the most beautiful place inside him' (344 C). In the *Phaedrus* (274 C) Socrates relates a tale about the relationship between the spoken and the written word. Once upon a time there was an old Egyptian divinity named Theuth who was a great inventor. He invented arithmetic, astronomy, the game of dice, and then he discovered writing as well. He went joyfully to King Thamus and presented his discoveries. But the King asked him of what use these discoveries were, and concerning writing he declared that it would do greater harm than good. It would only serve as an external reminder for those who were already in the know, but not as an internal one. It is always impossible to query the written word, for it can only answer with the same string of words once again. But the word, which builds on insight and by discourse is impressed upon the soul of the student, will always endure, know whom to address itself to, and will know when to remain silent. Whoever has insight into what is just, beautiful and good will never seriously commit himself to the written word. Nevertheless it may be amusing for him to play with words and tell stories about justice and much else besides.

This is, of course, a programmatic declaration. Knowledge comes from within and may come about through discussion, but – despite what professional paedagogues would maintain – it is not possible to implant an item of knowledge in a soul, which

---

1   There are no unambiguous linguistic arguments for or against authenticity. As to the historical background, a forger would hardly have had access to the necessary details, and the restrained anger and apologetic strain point to the principal himself, to Plato. As to the philosophical section, a forger would probably have stuck more closely to indisputably 'orthodox' Platonic points of view. There are indeed close connections with general Platonic modes of thought, but also a considerable degree of originality – which is what one would expect from Plato.

was not there before (*RP* VII 518 B). It is also a characterization of a Platonic dialogue in which the author amuses himself by 'playing with words'.

These two passages also tell us something about that remote Plato who possesses some core of knowledge that he will never communicate to others and who after all refuses to be responsible for his dialogues. The reader never knows where Plato is to be found; after apparently marking time in long tenuous passages, we are suddenly confronted with compressed and cryptical ones in which something is being said and more obviously is intimated. In the late dialogues we are not infrequently told that everything has been a jest after all (cf. *Parm.* 137 B; *Tim.* 59 C; *Leg.* III 685 A; IV 712 B), and in the *Laws* this is even made to include man as a plaything of the gods; it is, as we are told, our task to tend to human affairs, even though they do not merit serious consideration (VII 803 B ff.). Sometimes it is as if Plato distances himself from his dialogue by means of a complicated system of reports, as for example in the *Symposium* and the *Parmenides*, in which one person reports what somebody else has reported about what a third person has heard discussed by Parmenides and Socrates. The second reporter in this series is able to remember verbatim all of Plato's most complex dialogue, but now he prefers to take care of his horses. As we know, numerous dialogues arrive at no conclusion; at times Socrates keeps his opinion to himself even after having arrived at a most exalted conclusion (cf. *Phaedo* 107 B); and often we are told that what is most important will have to await another time (*Prot.* 357 B; *Phaedr.* 246 A; 274 A; *Soph.* 254 C; *Tim.* 48 C; 53 D). Apparently Plato does not care whether the spark will catch. He knows what he knows, indeed more than his Socrates knows, and he takes his reader to the limit of the dialogue with a strange mixture of cunning ambiguity and direct appeal, which in his last work is not without a misanthropic note.

This, to be sure, is all so simple. A dialogue is a drama, most likely – also – intended to be read aloud; a playwright does not reveal who he is; and of course a Socratic adherent can only employ the Socratic method and demonstrate how a certain person is bound to see his own chain of thought followed through to its conclusion for better or worse. The earlier thinkers who are included in the dialogue are dealt with indirectly in like manner, and so is the reader who stands apart, although he is none the less compelled to 'render account'.

But of course the dialogue is no ordinary drama. There are two constant and unusual actors: the argument, or *logos* itself, and Socrates. The argument is in control of the participants, including Socrates, and leads them wherever it wishes (*Theat.* 191 A; *Prot.* 333 C; *Lach.* 194 A; *RP* VI 503 B). *Logos* may lead one astray, but he who mistrusts *logos* abandons himself to the distorted world of the Sophists (*Phaedo* 89 D; cf. *Meno* 86 B); it is just as fatal to adhere to Socrates and not to truth (*Phaedo* 91 C; *Symp.* 201 C). It has often been intimated that Plato's late dialogues ceased to be dialogues, for now there are no longer so many debates, and only one person teaches, while another agrees with him. But this view ignores the fact that *logos* is a character in the dialogue that is able to unfold itself in questions and answers and is also able to pursue its own course, albeit always without a safety net. The argument finds its beginning and end aporetically, without Plato being able to do anything about it.

Therefore the Platonic argument is always of the 'if – then' type, and it is always important to bear in mind what are the explicit or implicit presuppositions upon which the argument is built. Some presuppositions are simply ill-founded, some turn out to be insufficient, and in most dialogues the course marked out at the point of departure is altered significantly: the original question must be asked once more in a new and unforeseen context.

But Socrates is familiar with the argument and knows from the outset how everything will end. Most often we only know him from what he says and what he does. He speaks only rarely about himself. If we would know about Socrates we must turn to other participants in the dialogue. Socrates' adversaries attack him: Meno compares him with an electric ray paralysing its prey (*Meno* 80 A), and Callicles mocks him because he is tattling in a corner with some youths instead of performing manly deeds (*Gorg.* 485 D). Against this we have the eulogy of Socrates by the drunken Alcibiades in the *Symposium* (215 A ff.) – Socrates is the only man to make him, Alcibiades, ashamed of himself.

If one abstracts from the customary grouping of Plato's dialogues and instead follows Plato's own directions, a surprising picture of the development of the person of Socrates presents itself. In terms of fiction the *Phaedo* immediately follows upon the *Apology* and the *Crito*, which is to say that there is no distance between the Socrates of the *Apology* and that Socrates who speaks of ideas and the immortality of the soul in his spiritual will. Nor is there anything that prevents the Socrates who attacks Athenian democracy in the *Apology* from being the founder of the ideal state. In the *Parmenides* a very young Socrates is humiliated because he has not thoroughly mastered the doctrine of ideas. It seems credible that he did master it in the *Phaedo* – fifty years later. But nevertheless Socrates has his limitations. That is what Diotima tells him in the *Symposium*, and he himself says so in the *Republic* (*Symp.* 210 A; *RP* VI 506 D).

The picture of Socrates changes in the late dialogues. In a famous passage in the *Theaetetus* (149 A ff.) Socrates speaks of his art of midwifery; but the very fact that he speaks about himself brings about a certain distance, which is reinforced by an equally famous passage in the same dialogue (172 B ff.) in which he speaks of the true philosopher who strives to make himself god-like. Socrates is speaking here, but he is no longer the humble servant of god. As late as in the *Theaetetus* it is Socrates who presides, as he does in the *Philebus* – a dialogue on ethics. But in the *Parmenides* he is taught dialectics by Parmenides, and in the late dialogues, which have epistemology or natural philosophy as their subjects, he allows himself to be instructed by some strange, wholly or partially anonymous persons who seem to hint at inspiration from the Eleatics (the *Sophist*, *Statesman*) and the Pythagoreans (the *Timaeus*). Evidently he has something to learn, even though he is present as a silent auditor and thus is a warrant that the continuity is unbroken. It is announced that the dialogue sequence of the *Theaetetus-Sophist-Statesman* will be followed by a crowning dialogue on philosophy, at which Socrates himself presumably will preside (cf. *Pol.* 257 A ff.). This dialogue was never written. Surely it is no accident that there is an intimation of a Socratic conclusion – nor that Socrates never puts it into words. Nor is it an accident that Socrates is absent in the *Laws*.

It goes without saying that a Platonic dialogue was written at a certain point in time, unknown to us, but the date of the dramatical context is equally important. Plato is always at great pains to make the externals of the dialogue historically correct, and there are but few anachronisms; great care has been taken with the uses of reported or dramatic forms. Of course the discussions are fictitious, but, the late dialogues aside, the participants, even the less prominent ones, are precisely characterized. The dialogues belong to a by-gone past that is not glorified, and yet a glow of nostalgia remains for those days before the catastrophe – the defeat of Athens and the death of Socrates. At the same time Plato accomplishes the feat of allowing Socrates to discuss problems of the fourth century in a fifth-century setting.

Plato pursues a deliberate 'principle of economy'. Only that is said that is appropriate to the specific situation and persons, but, as in normal discussions, loose ends and 'digressions' may occur, and sometimes these are the most important. Especially in the late dialogues there seem to be peculiar breaks in the composition, a tension between external form and inner structure. All levels of style are represented: the formal argument, the humorous, and the lofty poetic. The late dialogues often display a strangely artificial filigree style imparting an overall effect of exalted dignity.

Philosophy consists in somebody's philosophizing, and Plato's mode of presentation is adjusted to the presuppositions of the participants as well as of the reader. So was Protagoras', and sometimes Plato – as did Protagoras – uses images or myths in cases where he might have been able to express himself directly – as for example in the tale of Theuth and Thamus. In other cases Plato will make his reader his confidant – up to a certain point. For example, in the *Republic* (III 414 B ff.) there is discussion of a 'founding myth', which, being 'true' fiction, can inculcate loyalty towards the republic in the citizens by means of a tale of symbolic truth, but one which fails to represent the whole truth as perceived by the philosopher. In such a case the reader learns more than the citizen in Plato's republic.

Yet full knowledge can never be directly communicated, and of course this is reflected in Plato's indirect mode of communication and in his own special use of imagery. Here there is no resemblance with Protagoras. Plato always respects an argument – as far as it goes – whether hypothetical or not, and in so far as the presuppositions of his interlocutor allow. But philosophy consists not least in reflections about the presuppositions for reflection itself, and the philosopher can 'rub' arguments against each other until truth shines forth (IV 435 A). Yet reflection can never justify itself. To Plato there are some ultimate presuppositions for knowledge and existence. They may be accessible to the mystic's insight, and such an insight may be the precondition for rationality; yet there is no substitute for reflection, nor any pseudo-reflection concerning that which goes beyond rationality. Here Plato uses imagery and could do nothing else. As in the major images in the *Republic*, he is able to employ allegory when his aim is to show a how, not a why. But often he uses myth – the untranslatable myth.

MYTHS

A Platonic myth is not just simply a tale of gods and heroes as in tragedy or epic poetry, but a poetic image, a tale which exploiting all stylistic levels speaks of that which cannot be told in rational terms. In the *Phaedrus* there is a famous myth about man's contemplation of the most exalted, and the semi-mythical Diotima speech in the *Symposium* corresponds to this. Best known are perhaps the so-called eschatological myths that form the conclusions of the *Gorgias*, *Phaedo* and *Republic*, which is to say myths that 'deal with' the punishment and reward of the soul in a world after death but thereby make man responsible for his present life: god is without blame, and the choice is man's own (*RP* X 617 E). At the symbolic-poetic level these myths tell us that existence is governed by a higher justice, and hence they may be read as deliberate counterparts to the ambiguous tragedy, which Plato attacked from the beginning to the end of his writing life. But the message of the myth cannot be transferred to a rational, argumentative language. It must speak in quite different manner about the immortality of the soul – if the myths are read literally they may directly conflict with the rational presentation.

The cosmological myths constitute another type. Unlike the Presocratic philosophers, Plato cannot speak of the beginning of the world nor about human life in the earliest times in a 'scientific' language, for that cannot be employed about something of which nobody knows anything. But the myth may tell us about how it might have been. In the *Statesman* there is a mythical presentation of a cosmic world cycle. The entire *Timaeus* is a 'myth'. The subject of this dialogue is physics or natural philosophy, which according to Plato cannot be argued exactly, and which therefore only can be made the subject of a 'probable account'.

These myths are quite different and hence require different interpretations. Such a 'scientific myth' as the *Timaeus* may very well be interpreted rationally on the premises indicated by the myth itself. But those myths that deal with man's relationship with the most exalted or his fate in the world beyond are poetry of ideas and must be read on poetic rather than philosophic premises. Myth and rational knowledge have each its own limitations, and evidently there are limits to what Plato wishes to confide to his reader.

PLATO'S PHILOSOPHICAL VISION

Without doubt Plato considered his philosophy – as do we – a synthesis of earlier thinking. Socrates' contemporaries and the generation immediately preceding Plato have a certain indirect role to play. This applies for example to Antisthenes and Democritus, even though the latter is never mentioned. But first and foremost Plato looks backwards to the great old masters – Heraclitus, Parmenides, the Pythagoreans – in order to rethink them in his own setting. Here biographical information avails little – for example, his acquaintance with Archytas or Aristotle's telling us that as a young man Plato had been 'acquainted' with Cratylus (*Met.* 987 a 32). In those passages in which Plato mentions or alludes to his predecessors he uses them freely in order to think his way through to general philosophical positions. Seen in its entirety, Plato's thought continues the old tradition: the world is not what it immediately appears to be; there is a true nature, *physis*, which makes its appearance in the visible one, which makes unchangeable knowledge possible, and which is normative, also for man. Given this position Plato cannot go along with the 'tragic' view of life, for true reality is not hidden. He must turn against old-fashioned fatalism; against the subjectivity and utilitarianism of the Sophists, which in his view are delusions; and against a mechanical view of nature, which, as in Democritus, renders nature blind and purposeless. Opposed to this stand the grand, almost archetypal founders of the philosophical tradition. Plato is able to give new life to Heraclitus' thoughts about *logos*; he is the first to draw metaphysical consequences from Parmenides' work – although without considering the empirical world an illusion for that reason; and he is inspired by the Pythagoreans' view of the soul and of philosophy as a special way of life; like the Pythagoreans, he considers mathematics a paradigm of the unchangeable true knowledge he seeks for. The midwife in this renewal of the tradition is, of course, a Socrates who also thinks metaphysically and epistemologically. From the basic presupposition that the world is rational, can be known, and is good, Plato looks for answers to questions about the nature of the world, the nature of morals, and the conditions for knowledge and language. Often the questions are more important than the answers, for often it will turn out that questions that are posed unreflectedly depend upon unclarified presuppositions.

One concept gives coherence to all of this: the concept of idea, *eidos* or *idea* in Greek. Usually Plato shuns technical terms, and *eidos/idea* often retain their everyday meaning of visible form or shape. But already in Plato's own time this word had achieved a semi-terminological status, for example in the Hippocratic treatises and in Democritus (cf. Plut. *Adv. Col.* 1111 A), where the phrase *hē atomos idea*, the indivisible shape, is applied to his smallest unit of matter, the atom (Plato uses the same term for his own smallest unit, the indivisible idea, cf. *Soph.* 229 D.). In modern philosophy the word has been knocked about a good deal; links can be traced back to the Platonic tradition, even though they are difficult to discern in the later meanings: conceptual contents (Descartes, Locke and Hume) or concepts of reason (Kant).

It is customary to speak of Plato's doctrine of ideas – and for that reason that term is also used in the present work. But in Plato there is no doctrine proper in the unambiguous sense that Thales, for example, had a doctrine claiming that water is the source of everything. To him the concept of idea serves to clarify what we all presuppose whenever we wish to find our place in the world either theoretically or practically. Thereby ideas become the precondition for any doctrine whatsoever. 'The doctrine of ideas' is in fact not dealt with at any particular length in the Platonic oeuvre, and nowhere is there an attempt to prove it, because the final presuppositions cannot be proved; they can only be used. Plato is very reserved when it comes to providing precise answers to such current questions as for example: what does the world consist of? What constitutes the good? The purpose of philosophy is to reflect on the possibility of description and explanation. It is also for this reason that Plato's dialogues have an 'if – then' structure. And this calls for the counter-question: 'what – if not?' In the *Parmenides* we are told that whoever denies the existence of ideas for each existing thing will 'have no thing on which to fix his thought, and indeed he will destroy all possibility of discourse' (*Parm.* 135 B). This is hardly the appropriate language for somebody with a theory to defend against another theory. Such a counter-question lies behind most of the dialogues, although it may find different formulations: what if true knowledge does not exist, nor meaningful language, nor autonomous morality, nor an ordered world? The unstated answer is, of course, that in that case the world would dissolve into chaos. Yet, for Plato it is implicit in this answer that ontology, epistemology and ethics deal with real objects and that knowledge and morality are closely related. Of course one may disagree about that, but understanding is precluded if one misreads the questions which the doctrine of ideas would seek to answer.

To Plato some presuppositions must be taken as certainties, if anything whatsoever is certain: ideas must exist, man's self is his soul, and man is bound by absolute morality. To his 'enemies' he must show the consequences of rejecting such presuppositions. To his friends he simply refers to that which 'we are always speaking about', that which 'we believe', or the like (cf. *Phaedo* 64 C; 100 C; *RP* VI 507 B).

Above all, most philosophers reveal their basic stand by their understanding of the concept of 'concept'. To put it anachronistically, the idea is Plato's interpretation of what a 'concept' is. But an idea has real existence, or rather, it is that which exists without qualification; it is the intended object of cognition – not the content of consciousness nor the form of knowledge – and therefore it is not possible to distinguish between concept and conceptual correlate in Platonism. But even in this sense the Platonic idea did not emerge out of a historical void. Just as is reason in Anaxagoras, the ideas are 'separate' and unmixed; and just as with being in Parmenides, they exist eternally and immutably, and they exist in themselves (cf. Arist. *Met.* 1078 b 31 on the hypostatization of ideas). The radically new is that ideas exist beyond time and space, that there is a plurality of ideas, and that everything existing in time and space has dependent existence. That the idea is not a 'something' that is, can be seen in Plato's frequent use of synonyms, such as 'what is', that which 'really' or 'truly' is, or that which is 'in itself' (*auto kath'hauto*) and is homogeneous (*monoeides*). This entire vocabulary – which is also reminiscent of Parmenides' – of course serves merely as a formal determination of the idea *qua* idea; it is a vocabulary of the second order. Such a determination had been sufficient for Parmenides' One Being. On the other hand, the numerous ideas of course do not merely constitute a formal or numeric plurality; but their contents can only be determined by their self-identity and their relation to other ideas.

An idea is not the concept *about* something but the quintessence *of* something. Therefore the formal determinations are nothing but incomplete predicates. There is nothing that 'is' without being something definite. Thus the idea of justice is that which 'really' or 'in truth' is just, not a concept that may be applied to just actions but rather an entity – Plato may simply call it a 'thing' (*Prot.* 330 C; 349 D) – the existence of which guarantees that actions may be called just. Here Plato can exploit (or be guided by) the Greek idiom in which the just (*to dikaion*) may be used both about that which is just and about justice as a concept. If anything is beautiful it is beauty itself, as we are told emphatically in the *Phaedo* (100 C), and there are many analogous examples showing that apparently an idea may be predicated of itself (cf. *Hipp. Maj.* 289 C; *Prot.* 330 D; *Euthyd.* 301 B; *Meno* 87 D; *Symp.* 210 E; *Phaedo* 74 B; *Soph.* 258 B). This 'self-predication' and the reification that it seems to express were objectionable to Aristotle who saw in them an unwarranted blend of substance and universal (cf. e.g. *Met.* 991 b 1; 1039 a 2), which must have fatal consequences, because the idea *qua* substance would be predicated of itself by virtue of its being a universal. Yet on Platonic premises such criticism is irrelevant. The idea is not predicated of, but identical with itself; it is predicated of the phenomenon or the thing (substance, in

Aristotle's terminology) providing information about the thing. Accordingly, the thing is explained by the idea; by virtue of its self-identity the idea is self-explanatory. Ideas can be spoken of, but not explained by means of a set of higher concepts; a determination of their contents – a definition – has to be tautological.

The fact that there is no congruity between thing and concept will always remain a philosophical problem; none the less an individual can only be described by concepts, and concepts are universal. What then is the relationship between thing and concept, and what is the status of concept? In terms of language the relationship between thing and concept can be stated in a simple subject-predicate sentence. Of course the subject designates the thing, and without reflection one would say that the predicate attributes a property to the subject. But what does that mean? Plato would not have felt satisfied with such a formula, and since it is his intention to legitimate everyday language about what is the case he cannot either, as Antisthenes did, allow the missing identity between subject and predicate to cancel the possibility of predicative sentences. The subject only aquires meaning by the predicate, and the predicate stands for the idea – for example justice itself or piety itself. Semantically speaking, a Platonic idea is simply identical with the content of the predicate. But to Plato there is an intimate connection between the spheres of language and reality, and, speaking in modern terms, he never distinguishes entirely between meaning and reference; thus the predicate actually functions as a proper name designating something, the idea, which has status as both the intended object and the real object; a predicate statement implies an existential statement about the predicate. We cannot say, for example, that Socrates is pious without presupposing that piety exists. This is of course a continuation of Parmenides' thought about the connection between true statement, true thought, and true existence, and of course this raises the problems of the relationship between name and sentence, of negative statements, and of false statements – problems that had not been solved at the time and that nobody had succeeded in dissolving – but which Plato began to examine in his *Sophist* dialogue. The decisive perspective lies in the question of what the predicate stands for and in Plato's conclusion that a language about things is only possible if a language of ideas is possible. We cannot speak of individual objects or of instances of concepts without being able to speak of concepts, and all talk of concepts presupposes their existence – a single idea corresponds to the several phenomena to which we give a particular name, as we are told in the *Republic* (*RP* X 596 A; cf. *Phaedo* 102 B; *Parm.* 130 E; Arist. *Met.* 987 b 8). But when a language of ideas is a precondition for a language about individual objects, it has the radical consequence that statements about things actually refer to ideas. The thing is not prior to its properties nor to its essence, but the other way around. The incongruity between thing as subject and idea as predicate depends on the thing's being dependent on but not identical with the idea.

It will be seen that Plato's logical and semantic position is ontologically based. A language about the world of things is dependent on a language of ideas, because ontologically the thing is dependent on the idea, as is evident, for example, in the *Phaedo* (100 C ff.) where Plato presents a theory of predication on an ontological basis: a thing is what it is by virtue of its relation to the idea, and language reflects this relation. But then what is the relationship of the world of things or phenomena to ideas? The world of phenomena – whatever appears (*phainetai*) to sense perception – is composite, imperfect, and subject to constant change; everything that exists in time and space is a conglomerate of several elements in a state of constant flux – as in Heraclitus – which never realizes a perfect norm of self-identity, and its existence is contingent. For example, to one observer two logs may seem of equal size, of different sizes to another; a horse is never just a horse without also seeming either beautiful or ugly; an act is never simply just, for it may also be described in other ways; and any given object or state of affairs might have turned out differently. Nevertheless, the world of phenomena is not one of utter chaos. We live in a world of things that are in a certain state, and this world can – at least to a certain degree – become known, and such knowledge can be expressed in language. Without a modicum of stability and without definite, identifiable patterns or structures, existence would be impossible, and language and knowledge would break down. In the last resort the subjective and relativistic world of Protagoras would be a monstrosity and a nightmare. But in fact there is a fairly ordered world, and this is a fundamental, empirical point of departure – for Plato as well as Democritus – which can only be doubted by confused or destructive minds. Still, the material world cannot be explained by means of a principle that in itself is material and hence subject to a determination by time and space. The material presupposes the immaterial, just as the relative presupposes the absolute, the composite the non-composite, and the imperfect the perfect. It is this absolute, non-composite and perfect which Plato calls an idea. It is irreducible and immaterial, and its existence must be presupposed as a warrant for the existence and cognizability of the world. This is not to say that ideas must exist because phenomena exist; rather, the phenomenon can only exist because the idea exists. Because the phenomenon exists we may immediately conclude that the idea exists as a necessary condition. It is possible to imagine a world composed only of ideas, but a world of phenomena without a world of ideas would be impossible.

In other words, Plato cannot accept a nominalistic or conceptualistic view, which reduces the idea to an object in the mind or to a concept that conveniently imposes order on human knowledge of the external world. In Plato's view this would be tantamount to leaving this crucial question unanswered: why is the world an ordered world and why is it a cognizable world? The thought must be of an object, which is to say of something [existing] (*Parm.* 132 B). The idea must exist as the supra-sensory and supra-personal objective reality, which is a precondition for the world of appearances.

This has further consequences for Plato's view of the relation of phenomenon to idea, and here one recognizes the same features as in his logico-semantic theory, which after all is another aspect of the same theory. It is often maintained that Plato had a 'two-world doctrine': the world of phenomena is a world in constant flux, and the world of ideas is a world of supra-sensory and self-identical ideas. Such a characterization, which ultimately has its roots in Aristotle, may find support in several Platonic statements but is so brief that it can be misunderstood. Plato was no dualist in the sense that his universe can be divided into two independent realms with doubtful mutual connections. One might imagine a chaos as opposed to the ideas – but this is indeed a mere construct or limiting concept and occasionally Plato himself sought to give a sort of abstract description of such a chaos (*Parm.* 158 B ff.; 164 B ff.; *Theaet.* 181 B ff.; *Tim.* 47 E ff.). The world of phenomena, on the other hand, is structured or formed matter with the idea as the 'pattern' or 'paradigm', as it is sometimes rendered in Plato's metaphors. This implies on the one hand that the idea is transcendent, existing independently in itself, but on the other that one idea manifests itself in the several phenomena or 'copies' and to that extent is immanent in the thing. The phenomenon in its turn has a dependent existence. A thing is what it is by virtue of the idea, for the thing 'strives' to realize the idea, which functions as a norm, a paradigm, or a 'cause'. The thing 'has a share in' or participates in the idea; without ideas the world of things would be an amorphous mass and an event or an act would be an unstructured and aimless muddle. Here it is necessary to treat Plato's imagery with care, for here — as elsewhere — it serves to delimit what can be put in words. In our day nobody would probably demand a clear-cut explanation of how a concept may be instantiated, yet, ever since Aristotle, such an explanation has been demanded of Plato in connection with his 'theory of participation' (*Met.* 987 b 14; 991 a 22). Plato is careful to point out the difference between the self-identity of the idea (the beautiful is simply beautiful) and the dependence of the phenomenon (the beautiful thing is beautiful because it participates in beauty — cf. *Phaedo* 100 D), and he concerns himself with the dialectics between the unity of the idea and the multiplicity of the phenomena. Yet a theory that would literally account for the relationship between phenomenon and idea would require another set of concepts behind phenomenon and idea, an idea behind the idea — there are many beautiful things in the world, which for Plato may be 'explained' by the idea of the beautiful, but no theory could explain the explanans.

The dependent existence of things might also be misunderstood. The phenomenon exists on another level and in a different manner than the idea — frequently called the Platonic graduation of existence. But Plato himself does not entertain the peculiar view that something may exist more or less or may be the case to a greater or lesser degree. A thing exists, just as does an idea, and the essential nature of the thing is the same as that of the idea, although the thing does not exist of necessity and is not — as is the idea — identical with its nature. One of the most frequently discussed passages in Plato — the 'Simile of the Line' in the *Republic* (VI 509 D ff.) — aims to illustrate this relationship between mode of existence and — in later terminology — essence. Just as the subject can only be conceived of in terms of its predicate, so a thing is only intelligible by means of a reduction to those properties and ideas that constitute the essence of the phenomenon, wherein the phenomenon participates and whereby it 'appears'. In this sense Plato comes close to dissolving the thing into an aggregate of properties so that the thing *qua* thing ceases to be subject to strict philosophical cognition. Strictly speaking, we can only know a horse in so far as it exemplifies the nature of 'horseness', but not to the extent that it is this particular horse. Accordingly, a certain scepticism is closely tied to Platonic idealism — not with respect to the existence of the individual, but rather with respect to the possibility of comprehending an individual as an individual. The individual can only be known indirectly.

In Plato's so-called middle dialogues (foremost among them the *Phaedo* and the *Republic*) the main thrust is upon a demonstration of the ontological and epistemological dependence of the phenomenon upon the idea, upon the idea as our 'point of orientation' for understanding the world. In the late dialogues (especially the *Sophist*) the emphasis is elsewhere, on an analysis of the very concept of being, or on the word to 'be', on the interdependent relationship of ideas, and on the implications and other logico-metaphysical relations that must constitute the language of ideas, which makes it possible for us to understand particular states of affairs.

It is impossible to attain truth without attaining being. This crucial sentence, inspired by Parmenides (*Theaet.* 186 C), is the key to Plato's 'ontological' concept of truth and to his epistemology. It is possible to imagine a world of ideas without a world of phenomena, but the other way around is inconceivable. In the same manner one might imagine a world of ideas without an intelligent mind, but cognition without ideas is inconceivable. The dependence of cognition on object implies that cognition, just as its object may be perfect and direct as well as imperfect and indirect. From Plato's rigorous demand of philosophical knowledge, *epistēmē* – that at all times and of necessity it must be true – it follows that its object can only be that which is unchangeable and exists of necessity, the idea itself. The phenomenon on the other hand can only have contingent existence, and no knowledge exists concerning contingent objects, because judgements about contingent objects might be false. Therefore the phenomenon can only be the object of that cognition – *doxa*, or belief – which may be true or false; and it would be an epistemological blunder to confuse the belief which happens to be true but which cannot 'account for itself' with perfect knowledge. In Plato *doxa* frequently has the connotation of that cognitive state which purports to be necessarily true without being so. The two concepts, *epistēmē* and *doxa*, demonstrate the close connection between ontology and epistemology, and accordingly Plato combines two problems, which to most people today seem separate, and indeed a linking of them produces latent difficulties, even on Plato's own premises: on the one hand there is the question of the relationship between cognition and its object – cognition as an 'ability' that is directed towards an object – and on the other hand the question of why and how an opinion, which happens to be true, may be turned into legitimate knowledge that necessarily is true (in modern terminology: 'justification of right belief'). Here, once again, there is a shift of focus in Plato's dialogues. The ontological dependence of knowledge is especially emphasized, for example in the *Phaedo* and the *Republic*, while the question of legitimation of true knowledge is the focus of the *Theaetetus* – even though such a change of focus in no way indicates a change in basic position (cf. *Tim.* 29 A).

Behind Plato's discussions of the two cognitive states lie two themes that deserve to be singled out. One is a reinterpretation of the old dictum that 'like is known by like', which Plato rephrases so as to make the soul akin to the ideas or to the 'matter itself' (*Phaedo* 78 B ff.; *Ep.* VII 344 A) – and just as the ideas are the 'matter itself', the soul 'of itself' knows the ideas (*Phaedo* 79 D). This is a deliberately chosen reformulation of an archaic inheritance. It is an empirical fact that a close relation between knowledge and reality is possible. But unless the soul on its own were of like nature with that which it knows, such a relation could never be established, and the consequence would be total scepticism, like that of Gorgias, erecting an insurmountable barrier between reality, cognition, and language. The basic position finds expression in Plato's thought of man's possibility of knowing a priori – as for example in the semi-metaphorical theory of the *Meno*, *Phaedo* and *Phaedrus* concerning man's 'recollection of the ideas': by recollection one becomes aware of something that one in fact already knew. And this frees Plato from scepticism with respect to the possibility of adequate cognition of rational truths and from subject-object dualism.

Another feature that motivates Plato's theory of knowledge is the Socratic call for unification of theoretical and practical knowledge. This may be recognized in his presupposition that that which is the object of knowledge at one and the same time is something absolute and something present and available in a concrete set of circumstances. The idea may be recognized on its own but also by means of the thing; a moral quality, such as justice, is not only an abstract norm but a norm realized in action, and the good is both a transcendent principle and a quality attached to every moral action and to all existence (cf. *RP* VI 505 A). Theoretical knowledge and practical knowledge – *Gebrauchswissen* in Wolfgang Wieland's terminology – have been woven into each other, and frequently it is difficult to see whether philosophical knowledge – *epistēmē* – refers to an immediate, intuitive acquaintance with the object of knowledge, to an ability to use that knowledge, or to a sort of knowledge that may produce sentences – in modern terms the question is of *knowledge by acquaintance*, *knowledge how*, and *propositional knowledge* or *knowledge that*. This does not necessarily mean that Plato is unfamiliar with such distinctions. Rather it means that only he who knows 'the matter' directly is able to use his knowledge so that he can act accordingly and formulate true sentences *about* it. The direct contact with an ideal object is the basic presupposition for any theory of knowledge, because the concept must be grasped before sentences about the concept can be produced. Therefore demands are also made of the person who comes to know; the direct contact of knowledge does not in itself produce true sentences, and indeed true sentences randomly let loose in the world are not informative about their own theoretical presuppositions nor about who might be able to make use of them. This is yet another reason that Plato's own sentences – his dialogues – are left incomplete.

Such demands of knowledge are strict, for they mean that neither practical nor theoretical knowledge in and of themselves are valid, and they can probably only be realized on the ideal level. Behind this, of course, lie the Socratic concept of truth and those paradoxical Socratic maxims – for example that virtue is knowledge – which make it plain that cognition immediately has both a metaphysical and an ethical dimension and that all cognition in the end depends on knowledge of the good as objective reality and as absolute norm for performing any act. The world of ideas is orderly, rational, and knowable: it is normative, and hence it is 'good'. The world of appearance – the world of the phenomena – is an approximate realization of this ideal in another medium – that of time and space. Hence the good is at the same time a moral and metaphysical concept, and its opposite, the morally and metaphysically evil is hence – probably as in Euclid of Megara – surely an unavoidable and destructive fact, even though not a principle of the same order; evil is lack of goodness and rationality. This has consequences for man who is a member of a larger world and obliged by his allegiance to it. By virtue of his true self, his soul, and rationality, man is 'akin' to the ideal world, and just as is reason, so the true self of man is immortal.

Yet man is a dual being who is also bound to his body and to the material world of the phenomena. It is the privilege and curse of man that he is a free being, himself responsible for realizing his ideal nature by means of reason and moral act or for being misguided by his material nature towards the seeming good. Thought and desire, *logos* and *erōs*, are crucial determinants in the Platonic anthropology, and ideally these two concepts represent two sides of the same issue – as it, for example, appears in the two companion dialogues, the *Phaedo* and the *Symposium*. None the less, they are neutral concepts. *Logos* may lead one astray – as in the case of the pseudo-knowledge of the Sophist, the demagogue, or the poet – and *erōs* may mislead as it degenerates into lust and love of self – both dealt with in the *Phaedrus* and the *Republic*.

Man is not first and foremost an individual with individual rights. He is a rational being, a citizen of a greater commonwealth, and also a member of a political community, which ideally must be a copy of the macrocosmos. If the state primarily exists to serve the individual – to enable every member to do as he wishes, not as he must and ought to do (that which is 'his proper task') – it would be reduced to a mere mechanism arbitrating between personal and egoistical special interests. But thereby the obligation to an absolute moral world founded on the ideal world would be betrayed, and the egoistical man is actually an unfree person, not his own, a mere butt of circumstance. From different points of view, in the two major works dealing with politics, the *Republic* and the *Laws*, Plato examines the pre-conditions for a state that is to conform with moral order and realize the best life for her citizens. His political thought is morally committed: he looks towards a state inhabited by good citizens, and happiness – including individual happiness – is nothing on its own but the outcome of the virtuous life. It is the task and nature of man to realize the common social ideal, but this requires an insight not given to all. Government must hence be entrusted to those who have insight. Philosophers should serve as rulers with authority and responsibility for those who do not know. As is well-known, precisely this, more than anything else in Plato, makes the *Republic* provocative – and often offensive – to the modern reader who takes it that it is the purpose of the state, in so far as possible, to provide a frame guaranteeing individual liberty: Plato seems to have placed the common man under the administration of the philosopher. But doubtless the *Republic* was also provocatory reading in Plato's own time, and doubtless these provocations were deliberate, which may obscure the fact that even the *Republic* adheres to the overall fundamental Platonic scheme of if – then. The crucial thesis of the dialogue is this: the happiest man is he whose goodness and justice are the greatest (IX 580 C). If this thesis is true, it must require an analysis of the concept of justice as a condition for a good human life in a well-ordered society, and such an analysis is constantly contrasted to a tentative ideal construct. This dialectical interplay is extremely complicated, and the provocations should neither be explained away nor taken on their face value without further reflection. If and how the ideal model can be realized is an open question in the *Republic*. It is, however, the theme of Plato's 'legal state' – the *Laws* – which may be read as a far more substantial challenge than the *Republic*. Socrates is not a participant in the *Laws*.

Plato's republic is authoritarian in the sense that the individual unconditionally is subject to moral authority and thereby subject to those persons in the ideal republic who must be presupposed to have moral insight. The modern reader, feeling offended because Plato and his Socrates — not only in the *Republic* but in all the dialogues — place the cause above individual self-determination, may wonder that the same Plato by his indirect form of communication pays 'that single individual' the greatest compliment an author can pay to the personal integrity of his reader: he urges him to think for himself without forcing specific moral injunctions or formulated 'truths' upon him. Plato poses many riddles of this kind for his reader: with respect to both epistemology and morality he unseats the individual for the sake of the universal; but at the same time nobody can depict a situation or a man with the same empathy as he. He banishes the poets, yet is himself the greatest maker of Greek prose; he looks upon the world as an ordered system but has no personal philosophical 'system'; and he advocates asceticism and yearning for the world beyond (the *Phaedo*), yet finds the highest beauty in the present life (the *Symposium*). Furthermore, the ideal Platonic philosopher may seem strangely contradictory and Protean: the philosopher or dialectician is he who takes the comprehensive view of knowledge (*RP* VII 537 C); the philosopher is he who — as in the Mysteries — beholds pure truth purged of human folly (*Phaedo* 67 B); the philosopher is free, but his freedom renders him helpless in the world (*Theaet*. 174 C); and it is the philosopher's duty to govern, whether he wishes to or not (*RP* VII 499 B; cf. V 473 C; VII 519 E).

Such riddles are not entirely insoluble; but interpreting Plato is certainly not without problems. In all likelihood the historical Plato was not what we would call a harmonious person. The Plato accessible to us reveals himself most clearly in the presupposition that sustains all the dialogues: the notion of an absolute truth and a Socratic demand for truth must be taken seriously. In its consequences this Socratic starting point leads to a series of theoretical and practical ethical questions, sometimes to unforeseen challenges. Plato's dialogues do not provide answers to these questions in any finite form, but with the concept of idea as a guiding line, the pre-conditions for answers are analyzed. The starting point is maintained without compromise.

13

WHAT IS VIRTUE? CAN VIRTUE BE TAUGHT?

———•◄•———

In the beginning of the *Protagoras* (310 A ff.) Socrates is awakened early in the morning by an eager young friend, Hippocrates, who would like to enrol as a student of Protagoras who has just arrived in the city. Now he asks Socrates to introduce him to the great man. Socrates takes his time and asks him what he would hope to gain by becoming a student of a doctor or a sculptor, for example? To become a doctor or a sculptor, of course. And what would he like to learn from Protagoras? Does he want to become a Sophist? No, replies the young man, god forbid. What then does he want to learn? Well, he would like to become an able speaker. If so, what can Protagoras teach people to speak about? Hippocrates doesn't really know. But, if there were something physically wrong with Hippocrates, he would summon friends and acquaintances so that they might discuss his case, yet the subject would merely be his body: is he truly prepared to surrender his soul, his dearest possession, to a stranger without the least idea whether the soul will benefit or be damaged? Nevertheless Socrates gives in. The two men pay a visit to Protagoras to learn from his own mouth what it is that he teaches.

This passage yields a good deal of information. It tells us something about a young Athenian of social standing and about his ambivalent attitude towards the Sophists: he would like to study with a Sophist in order to advance his career, although there is something socially degrading about Sophistry as a profession. Above all, the passage shows us something about Socrates, his way of arguing, and his personal concern for the young Hippocrates who must learn to care for his soul. Behind it we sense the principal theme of the entire *Protagoras* dialogue, the concept of *aretē* – what is virtue, and can virtue be taught? Socrates and the Sophists agree about the questions, but they disagree about the meaning of 'virtue' and about what it means 'to teach'.

In a number of dialogues Socrates asks for the 'definition' of a virtue or some other normative concept. He asks about piety in the *Euthyphro*; about courage in the *Laches*; about self-discipline (in Greek: *sōphrosynē*) in the *Charmides*; about justice in the first book of the *Republic*; about friendship in the *Lysis*; and about beauty in the *Hippias Major*. These dialogues constitute an effective answer to the charges of godlessness and the seduction of youth. Viewed together they are a catalogue of acknowledged Greek virtues and basic aesthetic-moral concepts.

Everywhere Socrates phrases his question in the same way: What is x? The existence of 'x', this or that virtue, is presupposed, and Socrates aims to prove that a given virtue is an absolute norm and that all virtues in the final analysis constitute a unity. In and of itself this is merely a formal determination of virtue, but it is apparently a necessary precondition for the substantive determination of the contents, which the ignorant Socrates never arrives at. It is also characteristic of these dialogues that a certain method of argument is followed, which has both a universal and personal aim: it must be possible to provide a universal and bullet-proof definition of the concept in question; but it must be provided by the particular person here and now – leave Gorgias out of it, since he is not among us, but do tell me what you yourself think about the good, as we are told in the *Meno* (71 D). Socrates engages in discussion with an individual on the latter's presuppositions. And the characteristic Socratic fusion of theoretical and practical knowledge can be seen in the fact that it is Socrates' interlocutor who himself has to vouch for a universal assertion. Universal sentences are formulated, these sentences are talked *about*, and the talk is directed *to* one person who must learn to know for himself. At one level the argument pretends to objectivity, while at another it is particular and rhetorical. Socrates' evident joy in teasing and mystification does not make the interpreter's task easier.

Formally this mode of argumentation is not different from that of the Sophists, and a Socratic dialogue presupposes that the reader is familiar with the technique, although not with Socrates' use of it. Plato often opposes the Sophistic 'art of contradiction', 'eristics', to Socratic dialectics (cf. *Meno* 75 C; *RP* V 454 A). Yet Socrates owes a good deal to the Sophistic question-answer technique – including tricky argumentation (cf. Aristotle's description of Sophistic arguments *ad hominem, Soph. El.* 170 a 12). The difference lies in the form of knowledge Socrates aims for and in his demands for correct answers. An analysis of the Socratic technique of asking questions must take into account three things which are frequently intertwined: the actual course of the argument; principal remarks about method; and Socrates' purpose in arguing as he does with a particular person who is before him – and of course he never speaks directly about this. As a fourth element one might add the discreet hints intended for the reader, which are beyond the ken of the interlocutor.

In the discussion between Socrates and Hippocrates, Socrates makes use of inference by analogy: one can learn something from a doctor or a sculptor, ergo one must also be able to learn something from a Sophist – but what? Such inferences by analogy are included in Socrates' arsenal of arguments, as for example in the *Republic*: the arts of medicine and of cooking 'provide' something – what does justice 'provide' (*RP* I 332 C ff.)? Inductive arguments constitute the type of argument which Aristotle specifically attributes to Socrates. An example from the *Gorgias*: medicine is taken to effect a cure, a sailor plies his trade in order to make money – therefore, one performs acts to obtain a benefit that lies outside the act itself (*Gor.* 467 C). Another example comes from the *Protagoras*: good is the opposite of evil, high is the opposite of low; ergo everything has its opposite (*Prot.* 332 C; other characteristic examples: *Hipp. Min.* 365 D ff.; *Prot.* 349 E ff.; *Euthyd.* 279 D ff.). Analogy and induction are related types of argument (cf. the complex blend in *Hipp. Min.* 373 C ff.). Socratic inductions proceed from lesser universal sentences from which more universal ones are inferred. The argument by analogy is an incomplete induction in which the universal sentence or rule that establishes the analogy is taken for granted (cf. Arist.

Anal.pr. 69 a 13). These types of argument are obviously weak ones, for one cannot be assured that the induction is complete nor that the analogy is valid. It is evident that this does not bother Socrates. He is content whenever his opponent explicitly or silently agrees with him, and if not, he calmly changes tactics (cf. Plat. *Charm.* 165 C ff.). Analogy and induction are *ad hoc* and *ad hominem* arguments, stages in a more deliberate plan to summon forth some pre-knowledge or, quite often, to refute the interlocutor.

A Socratic refutation (*elenchus*) – or, exposure of pseudo-knowledge – has several historical antecedents: the Sophistic art of contradiction (to make the weaker cause the stronger), *reductio ad absurdum* argumentation (for example, Zeno) and late Presocratic inferences from hypothetical premisses. Often an *elenchus* will be complex and contain several stages, and often it takes up an entire dialogue (the *Euthyphro* is a good example; other characteristic examples: *Lach.* 192 C ff.; *Charm.* 167 B ff.; *Gorg.* 497 D ff.). The questioning of Meletus in the *Apology* (27 A ff.), a fairly brief passage, shows how inferences by analogy are built into an *elenchus*. The following is a condensed paraphrase:

> Meletus maintains that Socrates does not believe in the gods but in 'demonic voices'.
> Does anything exist concerning men, without the existence of men? No.
> Anything concerning horses, without the existence of horses? No.
> Anything concerning flutes, without the existence of flutes? No.
> Anything concerning demons, without the existence of demons? No.
> Demons are of course either gods or the offspring of gods? Yes, of course.
> If Demons are gods, Meletus would accordingly maintain that Socrates does not believe in gods but in gods.
> Are there offspring of gods but no gods? No.
> If Demons are the offspring of gods, Meletus maintains in other words that Socrates does not believe in gods but in gods.

This pattern of argumentation is operative, also when an innocent interlocutor attempts to define a virtue. Here Socrates can point out that the answer brings about contradictory consequences (p implies q, but something is wrong about q (cf. *Euthyph.* 6 E ff.)), or, more frequently, that it is at variance with commonly accepted points of view – especially those of the interlocutor – hitherto considered certainties. To paraphrase Gregory Vlastos freely: Socrates puts a question. One answers p, and p of course implies q; yet everybody says r; of course there is nothing odious about that, except that r implies s, and q and s are not boon companions; ergo s implies not-q, which implies not-p; if so, should we say p or r?

The outcome of an *elenchus* is rarely settled by logical necessity. What is decisive is that the person NN, given his moral character and stock views, is defeated by it. Socrates is not at all reluctant to trap his opponent. Meletus, for example, should never have agreed that demons are either gods or the offspring of gods, but Meletus is Meletus, after all, and so he is trapped. Quite often Socrates makes use of obvious fallacies (for example, *Prot.* 331 A, where contraries and contradictories are confused), and on occasion an apparently valid argument is constructed on ambiguous words (for example *Gorg.* 474 C). If we consider that Socrates' argumentation is everywhere personal, it is of course quite difficult to decide whether he himself is aware of his *faux pas* and whether a correct logician is always hidden behind the tactician. Yet, in a few instances it is possible to do so, as for example in the passage cited above from the *Protagoras*, for it is apparent from the *Euthyphro* (*Euthryph.* 11 E ff.; cf. also *Prot.* 346 D) that Socrates is perfectly aware of the flaw. Yet in most cases the question cannot be decided, and one has to concentrate on Socrates' tactics and ask what effect his arguments have on NN. Then it will often be seen that questionable arguments or ambiguous phrases crop up at the decisive turning points in the discussion and make it clear that NN – given his personal point of view – must consider the argument before him valid or accept an ambiguous concept as univocal (cf. *Charm.* 161 B on 'doing what is one's task'; *Prot.* 351 B on 'living well' in the sense of 'enjoying oneself' or 'living morally'; cf. *Gorg.* 495 E; *Hipp. Min.* 375 C).

In other words, from one point of view an *elenchus* is particular and destructive. But that is not the whole truth. In several cases Socrates advances some important methodological considerations that enable the interlocutor to improve on his own definition, even though he never reaches the end of the road. The definition must not be circular (*Meno* 79 D), and identity must be established between *definiendum* and *definiens*, as is made clear with great paedagogical precision in the successive attempts to define courage in the *Laches*. Here the first attempt at definition is too narrow (190 E ff.), the second is too broad (192 B ff.), and the third lacks specification of *genus* (194 D ff.).

The attempts to define piety in the *Euthyphro* are equally instructive. Here it is insisted that the definition must denote the essence of piety, not some derived property (*Euthyph.* 11 A ff.), and we are confronted with principles of conceptual inclusion: if that which is pious is 'a part' of what is just, the *genus* – justice – must have greater extension than the *species* – piety. This is the first formulation of a demand to distinguish between *genus* and *differentia specifica* (12 C ff.).

Such logical principles seem elementary to us, but obviously they take Socrates' interlocutors by surprise. Still, their greater error is to attempt a definition by means of simple enumeration. Meno, for example, is asked to define *aretē* (*Meno* 71 E ff.; cf. for example *Theaet.* 146 C ff; *Euthyph.* 6 D). To him this is a simple task. The *aretē* of a man consists of this and that, and in like manner he can define the *aretē* of a woman, a child, or a slave. Socrates is still not satisfied, for he wants a definition of the common denominator (*eidos*) that makes everything cohere. Of course he is just as contrary when Euthyphro explains that piety is that 'which I do now' (*Euthyph.* 5 D), or when Hippias defines beauty as a 'beautiful' girl (*Hipp. Maj.* 287 E). In other words, Socrates wants neither a definition by enumeration, nor an ostensive definition, nor, certainly, a nominal definition that would be merely lexical. What he requires is what we call a real or essential definition (cf. Arist. *Top.* 101 b 39). To him, however, it is probably not crucial to distinguish between the several types of definition but merely to understand the one reality that appears in many phenomena. For example, if we know what is the essence of justice we are also able to identify just actions. This is not as simple as it looks. Naturally we have more or less certain prior knowledge about the *definiendum*, for otherwise we would be unable to decide whether for example *definiens* and *definiendum* cover the same ground. The looked-for definition that is never attained would hardly provide us with totally new knowledge nor would it only clarify the meaning of words. The ideal definition will signify that we have attained a conceptual hold of more or less diffuse or latent pre-knowledge, and the knowledge of the essence of the thing will cause us to treat our opinions and actions rationally. While summoning our pre-knowledge we may be aided by inferences by analogy and induction. Nevertheless, tanners and shoemakers are only helpful up to a certain point. Socrates changes course as soon as the issue is a conceptual determination proper; just like Aristotle, Socrates is aware of the limitations of inference by analogy and induction. Induction may furnish a useful preamble, but only in so far as it provides a non-inductive insight (which has been called 'the principle of counter-inductiveness'). Hence, such an insight is possible in principle.

Socrates also has more to say about the nature of that which he is in search of, the *definiendum*. He does not ask why just men are just but about the 'cause' that makes just men just (*Prot.* 330 C ff.). Nor does he ask what it is that is beautiful, for beautiful things may be beautiful in one respect and ugly in another. He asks instead about beauty itself, which by its existence causes beautiful things to be beautiful (*Hipp. Maj.* 288 A ff.). In the *Euthyphro* he speaks about that one idea (*eidos/idea*), which by virtue of its self-identity makes pious acts pious and serves as a paradigm for our understanding of pious acts (5 D; 6 D ff.; cf. *Lach.* 191 E; *Meno* 72 B ff.; 75 A; *Gorg.* 497 E; 506 C). In the *Lysis* (219 C ff.) there is an analysis of *to philon*, that which is kind, amicable, treasured, or the like. Apparently this concept has several meanings (something may be treasured or someone may be kind) and may be relative (to something or for someone), and something may be 'dear' to us, because it is a means to something else. But all of these meanings must presuppose the existence of something absolute, something that in a primary sense is 'dear' to us. In such passages a vocabulary is at work that is well known from the classical doctrine of ideas and from the theory of participation, which characterizes the idea as idea; the self-identical idea is the epistemological criterion for the identification of individual phenomena, and ontologically it is a precondition for the mode of existence of the phenomenon.

When it is often claimed that in these Socratic dialogues Plato did 'not yet' have a doctrine of ideas, it is because here there are no far-reaching conclusions concerning the metaphysical status of ideas and about the relationship between the world of ideas and the world of phenomena, such as we do find in the *Phaedo* and *Republic*, for example. But it is hard to sustain such a claim. Evidently the Socratic theory is so well known that his Sophistic adversaries can parody him (cf. *Euthyd.* 301 A), and the passages cited above are not accidental, half thought-out casual remarks. The concept of idea is introduced as an explanatory cause concerning the same problems that are more elaborately examined in the classical dialogues; both with respect to terminology and subject matter the argument is conducted on the basis of one coherent theory. The dialogues can rightly be read as prolegomena to such a theory – whether they are 'early dialogues' or not.

Socrates also has something to say about his formal demands of a definition and of a 'concept', and on this basis it is possible to construct corrected and steadily improved attempts at definition. But, as we know, a final answer to the question 'what is x' is never provided – not even in Plato's classical dialogues, which deal in depth with the metaphysical and epistemological prerequisites for an answer, but no more than that. A Plato dialogue is always a prologue, a challenge to the reader. Whenever the unsuspecting reader believes that now he is getting close to a final definition of some virtue, Socrates discovers new difficulties, and in the end the discussion must, alas, be discontinued. A brief dialogue, the *Clitophon*, has found its way into the Platonic corpus, which on stylistic grounds cannot be by Plato. It is telling that here Clitophon, the title person, vents his irritation with Socrates who always advocates virtue and decent living, although he never says what virtue is. If Clitophon cannot get a clear answer he will enrol as a student of Thrasymachus – which would be a shame, but what else can he do (*Clit.* 410 C)?

Perhaps Clitophon is remembering that in the *Euthydemus* Socrates, in evident contrast to the juggling Sophists, clearly and simply is able to argue that virtue is knowledge – though not saying anything about what kind of knowledge (*Euthyd.* 278 E ff.). Perhaps he is thinking instead of a dialogue like the *Charmides*, in which Socrates firmly establishes thorough systematic confusion. The subject of this dialogue is self-discipline (*sōphrosynē*), and, as fate and Plato would ironically have it, the interlocutors are Charmides and Critias, the tyrants-to-be. Here the following definitions are presented:

1   decent and proper behaviour (*Charm.* 159 B)
2   the ability to be ashamed (160 E)
3   to 'do one's task' (161 B)
4   to act morally (163 E)
5   to know oneself (164 D)
6   knowledge of good and evil (174 B).

Apparently these present a nice, orderly progression from unreflected common-sense considerations to Socratic conclusions. None the less, Socrates topples the card-house consistently by advancing more or less quibbling objections.

But Clitophon may have overlooked something: for example, that although Charmides and Critias probably have learned some Socratic *bon mots* from hear-say, they fail to understand them. Yet, regardless of the argument these *bon mots* ought to provide him with matter for further reflection, and so should the fact that the final conclusion – just as in the *Laches* (194 D ff.; cf. *Phaedo* 69 A ff.) – suggests that all virtues constitute a unity based on knowledge, which is why it is in fact impossible to begin by calling for a definition of any one particular virtue.

Most likely Clitophon and others with him also overlooked the hints that Socrates often provides in passing about the proper understanding of his key concepts. In the *Euthyphro* (10 A ff.) we are, for example, told that what is pious is not pious because it pleases the gods – in the later philosophical tradition this is called ethical voluntarism (in John Duns Scotus, for example, the will of god as the highest authority justifies morality). Instead we are told that the gods are pleased because the pious is pious. In other words: virtue justifies itself.

A more intricate concept, indirectly clarified, is the concept of knowledge. In an enigmatic passage in the *Charmides* (166 E ff.) Critias proposes that self-knowledge must be knowledge of what one knows – knowledge of knowledge. Here one ought not to expect that the aim, in a Kantian sense, is to arrive at transcendental-philosophical considerations about objectless self-reflection or apperception. None the less, this dialogue does pose the question of preconditions for knowledge, and it is indeed possible that the hidden argument goes beyond Socrates' reach. Anyway Socrates always maintains that all knowledge must have an object; but on Critias' premisses knowledge of knowledge becomes a meaningless duplication of simple objective knowledge. What Critias apparently fails to grasp is that in the concluding definition it is implied that knowledge of the good legitimates the object-knowledge of the specialist by involving his own person so that he can make use of his special knowledge. But thereby knowledge of the good becomes object-knowledge of a special kind. It is not directed at factual matters but at something that anchors the specialist's knowledge by making him aware of what he knows. By the end of the dialogue Socrates is conversing more with his reader than with Critias, but the debate is undeniably more than usually opaque.

Those passages in which Socrates in obvious parody confronts his competitors' understanding of the concept of knowledge are really more transparent. This is, for example, the case with the *Euthydemus*. It is also true of the tiny dialogue *Ion*, which deals with poetical knowledge and which may be read as a prologue to the more elaborate criticism of poets in the *Republic* and the *Phaedrus* – and also as a commentary on the *Apology*. Socrates does not adopt an aesthetic point of view in any of these works. Instead he deals with poetry as if it would claim to convey rational knowledge. Yet, to a large extent, this was indeed the case: from ancient times the poet had been accorded the status of teacher of the wisdom of life, and poetry – as Homer's, for example – was recited orally and not 'read'. This means that the rhapsode reciting an epic poem is tied directly to a higher world, to universal wisdom, which, not least thanks to the mythical action and the formulaic language of the epic, is something other and more than a 'communication' or literary fiction. Homer continued to be used as moral mentor – for example in Athenian elementary education – but as poetry gradually lost its erstwhile role, it became 'literature'. Other genres served to impart knowledge, and recitals degenerated and became mere hollow performances. It is in this context that Plato blames poetry, which pretends to impart rational knowledge but in fact works by suggestive, emotional means. Ion was a rhapsode, which is to say that it was his job to recite Homer, and it is easy for Socrates to demonstrate that neither Ion nor Homer possesses 'professional' knowledge about such technical matters as are dealt with, for example, in the *Iliad*. According to Socrates (*Io* 533 D ff.), the source of poetry is divine inspiration, which by some sort of magnetic attraction transmits itself to the listeners, in other words through the poet and the rhapsode but not through the text. The god has his own hidden wisdom, but his interpreters – the poets and rhapsodes – do not 'know' what they are transmitting, and the listeners are prey to constant emotional influence. In Plato's eyes matters were not improved by the fact that others – the Sophists – had begun to interpret poetry, for this was carried out according to haphazard allegorical principles in such a way that the interpreter in fact only interpreted himself – as parodied in the

Protagoras (338 E ff.). An arbitrary interpretation of an arbitrary inspiration can never constitute knowledge.

In the *Hippias Minor* the Sophistic concept of knowledge is parodied to an amazed and not very perceptive Hippias. The subject is the interpretation of Homer. Who is the better man – the brave Achilles or the cunning (lying) Ulysses? Hippias prefers Achilles, but Socrates has his doubts. He who lies deliberately has knowledge about that which he lies about, but knowledge is 'superior' to non-knowledge; accordingly it is better to lie deliberately than to lie against one's will, as Socrates states in his conclusion (*Hipp. Min.* 371 E.) that apparently flagrantly contradicts his own famous maxims. But actually Socrates here only does what he did in the *Charmides*. He is building on alien premises, which is to say that 'knowledge' simply may be identified with the specialist's knowledge – for example, the liar's 'special knowledge' about the true and the false. But on the other hand, if the precondition for 'special knowledge' is a binding insight into the good, this conclusion of course becomes invalid. It is left to Hippias and the wondering reader to ponder this possibility.

THE *PROTAGORAS*, *GORGIAS* AND *MENO*

As we see in the *Ion* and in the *Hippias Minor*, Socrates is able to conceal himself. In the *Protagoras* and *Gorgias* – the two major encounters with the Sophists – it is easier for us to follow his strategy, which is an argument *ad hominem* that hypothetically accepts the premises of the opponent. In the *Protagoras* this is carried out in order to suggest or demonstrate that properly considered these premises will lead to Socratic conclusions and in the *Gorgias* to bring the confrontation to its bitter end. It is hardly surprising that along the way Socrates shows how he can make the weaker cause the stronger.

In the *Protagoras* Socrates, as usual, only formulates his own position indirectly, but in the *Gorgias* he speaks polemically and, for once, without concealment. Protagoras is an opponent worthy of his respect and justly is even allowed to object to Socrates' technique of argumentation (*Prot.* 350 C ff.; 331 B ff.; cf. *Theaet.* 166 A ff.). This dialogue is perhaps the best drama from Plato's hand. The characters are precisely delineated, and all the modes of debate and argumentation of the day are put to work: Protagoras' manifesto (314 C ff.); the presentation of the problem (319 A); Protagoras' myth (320 C ff.; cf. p. 94); and the debate between Protagoras and Socrates, which uses the Sophist-Socratic question-and-answer technique (328 D ff.; 348 C ff.), interrupted by an *interludus* (334 C ff.) and an interpretation by the two opponents of the poet Simonides (338 E ff.) – on the part of Protagoras a paedagogical form of presentation, on the part of Socrates a parody. As usual Socrates manages now and then to slip in some of his own basic views and sometimes obtains courteous approval from Protagoras: goodness is an absolute term (343 D); only god is good (344 C); nobody deliberately acts evilly (345 D); whoever knows the good will not act evilly (352 C).

The principal theme of the dialogue is contained in the two related questions: 'what is virtue?' and 'can virtue be taught?' These are questions that naturally may be asked on both Sophist and Socratic premises, but inasmuch as the two parties understand something different by 'virtue' and 'knowledge', it is Socrates' task to demonstrate that Protagoras' utilitarian and pragmatic position is untenable and that his premisses ought to lead to Socratic conclusions. Socrates questions Protagoras about the logical relationship between the traditional virtues (328 D ff.; 348 B ff.), which one by one were accorded their own lesser 'Socratic' dialogue. Are these virtues different or do they constitute a unity? According to Protagoras, they 'resemble' one another without being identical, which is an answer that one might well imagine would please Socrates. Nevertheless he attacks. It is one thing that his counter-attack is based on a flagrant fallacy (331 A, see above) but quite another that Protagoras is unable to provide an adequate reply because he cannot furnish an exact definition of *aretē*, nor, consequently, of the particular virtues – and this despite the fact that he is a professional teacher of civic virtue.

Always keeping his final goal in mind, Socrates focuses on his conclusion – well known from the *Laches* and *Charmides* – that all virtues constitute a unity and that knowledge or insight are a warrant for this unity. In agreement with his own presuppositions Protagoras is forced to agree (352 C). But Socrates proceeds: all are not as decent men as Socrates and Protagoras, and many would maintain that man allows himself to be led by pleasure rather than knowledge. Then follows an analysis of the consequences of this: one will often pursue immediate present pleasure without reflecting that later it will lead to greater pain. Therefore the adherents of the principle of pleasure must consider what in the long run provides the greatest amount of pleasure ('the hedonistic calculus'). But this can only be accomplished by means of knowledge and with respect to an absolute standard ('the art of measuring', 356 D). Accordingly the conclusion must be that even the man who considers the virtues as a means to a goal, pleasure, must rely on knowledge about something absolute as his guide. This applies to the acknowledged hedonist, but also to the utilitarian – such as Protagoras – who considers the virtues as a means to human well-being and who therefore in Socrates' eyes really is a hedonist in a civilized disguise.

It is evident that Socrates does not – as has sometimes been claimed – stand by his own argumentation. He carries a hedonistic argumentation to its utmost limits and emphasizes that he is arguing on behalf of others, not on behalf of himself. Just as he does in the lesser dialogues on particular virtues, he stops here at a reference to the concept of absolute knowledge. Nevertheless, he does note (357 B) that 'at some other time' we must examine the nature of this knowledge. Is there perhaps a higher pleasure tied to knowledge and truth? In any case, here Socrates – as in the *Charmides* – dispenses enough mystification to make the attentive reader wonder.

So does Protagoras. To him Socrates is a dangerous opponent, because formally they can agree about quite a lot – for example that there is a connection between knowledge and morality. Yet, in Plato's staging, he is helpless when confronted with the conclusion that knowledge of virtue presupposes an exact definition and an absolute standard. Therefore he ought to become a Socratic follower or at the very least cease to teach civic virtue. In the beginning of the dialogue Protagoras maintains that virtue can be taught, but Socrates doubts it. At the conclusion they seem to have exchanged positions (361 A) – and the whole dialogue is, as Kierkegaard puts it, a feud between two bald-headed men who finally find a comb (*On the Concept of Irony*, Princeton ed, 1989, II, 55). Behind this ironic surface are hidden two

understandings of the concepts of 'virtue' and 'knowledge' and therefore two interpretations of the statement 'virtue is knowledge'. Furthermore, the conclusion that
utilitarian relativism is a logical impossibility is hidden under the surface as well.

In the *Gorgias* Socrates removes his mask. The lesser dialogues about the particular
virtues and the *Protagoras* attack conventional and relativistic morality, the *Gorgias*
non-morality, which to Socrates is identical with immorality. Such a position is typically voiced in the statement 'might is right', and the theoretical basis is the morally
uncommitted rhetoric that – as with Gorgias – may be used for just about everything. Whereas the *Euthydemus* and *Hippias Minor* parody the Sophistic concept of
knowledge, the brief dialogue *Menexenus*, where Socrates parodies official political
rhetoric, is an adjunct of the *Gorgias*. The latter is a final reckoning concerning attitudes to life and is a bitter dialogue pervaded with allusions to the subsequent fate of
Socrates (cf. *Gor.* 486 B ff.; 521 B ff.).

The avowed theme of this dialogue is the question (447 A ff.): what is rhetoric? It
has been constructed as a drama in three acts, during which the ideology of power
becomes ever more apparent – notably as the sole logical counterpart to Socrates'
understanding of morality. Act One (449 C–61 A), in which Gorgias himself is
Socrates' respondent, poses the question whether rhetoric should know about good
and evil. Act Two (461 B–81 A), where the Gorgias student Polus is the interlocutor,
deals with the thesis that it is better to suffer injustice than to act unjustly. In Act
Three (481 B–522 E) the debate is between Socrates and Callicles (see p. 115) – and
the subject is how to organize one's life.

The dialogue is so constructed that Gorgias, a tired, somewhat burnt-out
authority, is not held directly responsible for the conclusions drawn by his more rabid
students. Yet it seems likely that the historical Gorgias would not so willingly have
made the concessions elicited from him by Socrates in the dialogue: that the political
rhetor concerns himself with justice and injustice; that his art must depend on
knowledge and not merely on belief; and that the rhetor who 'knows' what is right
must be just himself, just as the ideal architect and the ideal physician cannot but
build houses or cure men (454 B ff.; 460 B ff.). These are concessions that undeniably
seem at odds with Gorgias' initial position that rhetoric is the art of persuasion and of
gaining influence by the power of the word (452 E ff.). Indeed late Antiquity, which
was so devoted to the anecdotal, was able to relate how the ageing Gorgias on
having read the dialogue exclaimed: 'How beautifully Plato is able to lampoon'
(Athen. 505 D).

In fact, Polus does protest on Gorgias' behalf (*Gor.* 461 B ff.). Rhetoric, he says, is
an empirical science which enables the practitioner to become powerful and do what
he pleases. This is a more vulgar version than Gorgias' initial thesis and is illustrated
by an evidently much-favoured example, that of the tyrant who may do as he wishes
and therefore is the happiest of men (470 D ff.). Given this outlook, it is of course
worse to suffer injustice than to commit it, and when Socrates maintains the opposite, it is sheer nonsense. But also Polus is trapped by Socrates: certainly it is 'worst'
to suffer injustice but it is 'most dishonourable' to commit injustice, as he concedes
(474 C). Then Polus is trapped by the simple substitution of 'worst' for 'most dishonourable'. This mode of argumentation is of course unfair on Socrates' part, but what
is interesting is that Polus necessarily must be trapped: to be sure, he is an egoist,

but in his somewhat limited universe vice pays tribute to virtue – what matters is a good reputation and so to pay one's dues to convention. Probably Polus was far from the only one to embrace such an ambiguous position. Clearly Socrates wishes to show the necessity for making an unambiguous choice. Naturally he has made his: justice is an unconditional good, also for the individual, and there can be no difference between a subjective and objective good. Thus the criminal is the most unhappy of men unless he is punished, and if his punishment is just, it is a good.

At this point Callicles interrupts. He is uncompromising – one might call him the idealistic egoist. Although Socrates and Callicles are irreconcilable opponents, there is a strange sympathy between them, because neither will compromise. Callicles says that Socrates turns all existence upside-down, and in this he is undeniably right (481 C). He also turns *physis* and *nomos* upside-down by referring to justice as if it were 'nature' and not 'convention' (483 A). But nature decrees that the strong man must rule, which is to say that he should be able freely to satisfy his desires. Socrates, of course, has various comments – for example, that the many are obviously the 'stronger' (488 D). But the main argument is an analysis of the concept of pleasure. In itself pleasure is insatiable ('the hedonistic paradox' (493 A)), pleasure and pain are not absolute opposites (497 A), and there are good as well as evil pleasures (499 B). All in all, the concept of pleasure can only be assessed in the light of a superior principle, the good. The pleasing must be sought for the sake of the good, and this requires expert knowledge (500 A ff.). Each of the two men has his own natural law.

The analysis of the concept of pleasure is of course an instructive commentary on the indirect discussion in the *Protagoras*; but while Socrates is able to win Protagoras to his side – however reluctant he is – Callicles explicitly disagrees (501 C), and from this point on Socrates speaks for himself. As early as in the discussion with Polus he gradually began to abandon his customary manner, but towards the end of the dialogue he does so completely in order to advance his own gospel without any concealment whatsoever. He is pointed and incisive. What is at stake is the conduct of one's life (500 C). Happiness must depend upon virtue and knowledge and on nothing else. The good man acts unconditionally justly, and thus the virtues constitute a unity (507 A ff.); it is impossible to be partially good; and he who fails to live a virtuous life takes leave of the greater commonwealth of men, of the gods and mankind, indeed of heaven and earth. Mercilessly Socrates distances himself from any sort of illusory knowledge: from the verbal magic of the poets and rhetors with their insidious flattery of their audience (502 B ff.) and from the politicians who never did mankind any good. It is Socrates himself who is the true politician (521 D), and he speaks as a witness to truth with an assurance that is an evident extension of the *Apology*. Regardless of what will happen to him, a good man can never be hurt by a bad man (521 B), and the worst misfortune would be to arrive in Hades with a soul disfigured by crimes (522 E). The *Gorgias* is probably the first Platonic dialogue to end with an eschatological myth (523 A ff.): the soul is judged on its deeds in the world beyond. This is the mythical expression of the main thought of the dialogue: an unjust life is its own punishment.

Seemingly Socrates is only partially successful in the *Gorgias*. Elsewhere, using his indirect form, he was able to guide his interlocutors towards Socratic conclusions, but Callicles refuses to be convinced. The true message of the dialogue is probably double-sided. We are shown what the consequences will be if we do not acknowledge an absolute, binding morality, and the provocative conclusion is that there is no middle road between the ideal demand and a life of corruption.

While Socrates draws the merciless consequences of his ethical message in the *Gorgias*, in the *Meno* he draws some crucial epistemological consequences on the basis of questions that are formulated or suggested in the lesser 'Socratic' dialogues and the *Protagoras*. As in the *Protagoras*, at issue is *the* problem: can virtue be taught? This is a question that is equally significant on Socratic and Sophistic premises, but it leads of course to widely different answers. To a Sophist this question is roughly equivalent to the question of how to become 'able' enough to obtain those goods one desires or to realize those goals one has set for oneself. Meno understands the problem in this way, but Socrates must see the question in light of that morality which he pleads for in the *Gorgias* and in light of his own special understanding of the concepts of 'virtue' and 'knowledge'.

The *Meno* begins by asking the traditional question in a form that apparently had been in fashion since the days of Protagoras (Prot. DK B 3; cf. Isocrates): can virtue be taught, must it be acquired by practice, or does it depend on natural talent? (*Meno* 70 A). To both Socrates and the Sophists it is the first part of the question that is to be debated. Socrates elaborates on some familiar matters – for example, he asks what must be demanded of a correct definition; and he declares that one must know what virtue is before one can examine whether it can be learned and that all virtues constitute one unity. And despite Meno's somewhat primitive initial position, Socrates succeeds in making him agree that the good does not consist of being successful and that external goods are of value only if 'used' correctly – and so what is good and just in itself must be better than for example honour, power or wealth (73 C ff.; 87 D ff.).

Then suddenly Meno asks how one can seek something one does not know (80 D). Although Meno is not exactly overly bright, Socrates chooses to discern some far-reaching perspectives in his question; in fact it is the fundamental problem behind his search for definitions. According to Socrates, it is possible to learn something that one knows already in a certain sense – a latent knowledge that may be made present. Rightly considered, the sum of knowledge is a unity, just as the object of knowledge, reality, constitutes one grand coherence (cf. *Gorg.* 508 A); if one really knows one thing, strictly speaking one knows everything (cf. *Pol.* 277 D). And man knows everything, strictly speaking, for the soul of man is immortal, and the soul is constantly – before and after birth – in a state of 'having known' (*Meno* 81 D; 86 A). To attain knowledge will therefore mean to recollect knowledge – perhaps from a former existence – to become aware of what one always knew.

Now, naturally the ignorant Socrates cannot without further ado proclaim that the soul is immortal; this is something he has been told by priests (the Orphics) and other wise people, but of course he cannot be certain (81 D; 86 A). On the other hand, he is certain that knowledge is recollection (*anamnēsis*), and this he can demonstrate. This is shown by his asking the right questions of an ignorant slave whom he thereby enables to figure out how to double the size of a square (82 B ff.). At first, of course, the slave gives the wrong answer, but gradually he is led to the correct one (the square of the diagonal). The slave has recollected a knowledge he always had.

Disregarding the question of whether the slave learned the Pythagorean theorem in the beyond, one can concentrate – as Socrates does in the *Meno* – on the epistemological aspect. In this case, what does recollection mean? And what does the example of the slave demonstrate? At first glance it seems as if Socrates simply gets the correct answer from the slave by asking leading questions. But the point is: how is this possible? It is only possible because the slave possesses the pre-conditions for reasoning mathematically; nobody can equip him with these pre-conditions, nor has he acquired them empirically, for the drawn square is only a means to a 'recollection'. In the terminology of later ages the slave possesses 'innate ideas' or a priori knowledge.

The example shows the difference between internal understanding and external learning. The mere opinion – the belief, which, like the slave's first answer, is false, or which happens to be true – is different from that certain knowledge that can be legitimated by a rational account (98 A). This can only be provided by him who understands, and not by him who has merely been told something: I might have had the road to Larissa pointed out to me, but strictly speaking I only know it if I have walked it myself (97 A). In the same way, somebody may have told me how to double a square, but I can only understand it – transform true belief into certain knowledge – by virtue of some knowledge inherent in me, which enables me to formulate the correct answer. Thus Socrates demonstrates that all knowledge presupposes a priori pre-knowledge and he provides the criteria for certain knowledge. Thereby new perspectives on the Socratic concept of self-knowledge are also revealed.

According to Socrates, it is not until this basis has been established that one may ask whether virtue can be taught. It can, but only on the presupposition that virtue is knowledge (87 A ff.) – and if knowledge is 'recollection'. Thus familiar chords are struck, albeit in a new way. As is proper and fitting, the dialogue is concluded aporetically – if virtue is knowledge, it is after all strange that nobody is able to teach virtue (89 E). So we had better at some other time examine what virtue or the good is, in and of itself (100 B). But in the first place, the concept of knowledge has been given a new dimension, and secondly, Socrates has launched a method borrowed from mathematics: conclusion from a presupposition (*hypothesis*). This is the positive pendant to the *elenchus* method, which breaks down presuppositions; yet, strictly speaking, it is this method that ideally lies behind every Socratic debate.

With respect to both of these points, the *Meno* may be seen as concluding Plato's 'early dialogues' and as an introduction to the classic dialogues. But – irrespective of the date of composition – it applies to all 'the early dialogues' that they focus on the concepts of virtue and knowledge and on the fundamental questions: 'what is virtue?' and 'can virtue be taught?' They have thematic unity and deliberately seem to point towards those farther-reaching consequences, which in the classical dialogues are drawn from the connection between the key ethical concept of *aretē* and the key theoretical concept of *eidos*.

14

IDEA AND MAN

————— •◦• —————

THE 'CLASSICAL' DOCTRINE OF IDEAS

In a crucial passage in the *Phaedo* Socrates describes his development as a philosopher (96 A ff.). Apart from the question of the historical veracity of this 'autobiography', what is decisive is that Plato states precisely where and when his Socrates is compelled to make a break with traditional natural philosophy. What is being discussed is the cause for the coming to be and perishing of things. Socrates relates that as a young man he was quite preoccupied with the question of how natural philosophy could provide answers to such questions, and he commences with a standard materialistic explanation, which for example allows 'the hot and the cold' or the elements to be the causes of non-materialistic phenomena such as perception or consciousness. Now, by means of mystifying questions his aim is to show what it is that such a theory fails to provide answers for. To be sure, it may explain how one grows by eating and drinking. But if one man is a head taller than another, is the head then the cause of both greatness and smallness? And why does one plus one equal two? If one adds one and one, the result will be two; but that is also the case if one entity is broken in the middle.

Having achieved the desired confusion, Socrates guides the discussion to another level: now he uses Anaxagoras as his example in order to show what the latter cannot provide answers for (97 B ff.). For Anaxagoras did indeed maintain that reason is the cause of all things, and this appealed to Socrates who was anxious to have it explained to him that everything in this world is arranged rationally, which is to say in the best possible way. It is for example not enough to be told that the earth is the centre of the world; Anaxagoras should also be able to explain why it is best that it is to be found there. Great was Socrates' disappointment when it turned out that Anaxagoras was unable to use his theory for anything and instead took refuge in purely mechanical causal explanations. Socrates is sitting in his prison – and in that situation a mechanical-physical explanation about how to sit is of little use, since the real cause is that the Athenians have sentenced Socrates to die and that he has chosen not to escape. Socrates does not reject a mechanical explanation, but he demands a two-fold causal explanation in which the mechanical explanation is a necessary but insufficient condition for making a teleological cause effective – for of course it is a precondition for 'sitting in' prison that one knows how to 'sit'.

Plato was later to treat this two-fold causal concept more elaborately in the *Timaeus*. Here it will suffice to note that while we only use the two-fold causal concept in psychology and philosophy of action (seen as a physical event an action has causes, but the person who performs the act also has grounds or a motive for acting), Socrates demands that the entire physical world must be considered in teleological categories. It must be made plausible that the world is 'good' and that it does not merely follow the law of necessity.

Of course Socrates cannot simply explain why the world is constituted as it is. Therefore he chooses 'the second-best course' (a proverbial saying, 99 C), and this turns out to consist in accepting the doctrine of ideas as a presupposition (*hypothesis*, 100 A ff.). Apparently he does not provide an explicit explanation of the sense in which the doctrine of ideas fulfils his teleological programme; he wishes to show how the doctrine of ideas can be used, but as is his wont he gives the argument an unexpected twist.

Socrates' interlocutors are indeed familiar with the doctrine of ideas, know how a self-identical idea manifests itself in a plurality of individual phenomena, and earlier in the dialogue there is a provisional sketch of the implications of the theory. Something exists that is just, beautiful or good 'in itself', but this is not accessible by sense perception, only by pure reason (65 D ff.). These ideas are pre-conditions for the existence and recognition of the phenomenal world (74 A ff.). From our experience of the sensual world we are familiar with association by resemblance as a psychological mechanism: seeing x we recollect y because x resembles y. However, the resemblance may be asymmetrical, as in the case of picture and original. And if we now proceed to ask what it is that in any case establishes a relation of resemblance, we are thereby asking about the prototype of such an asymmetrical relation. Two logs can only appear 'of equal size' provided that an absolute standard exists: an idea of 'equality', which itself cannot be measured by the 'equal'. Evidently Socrates is not at this point interested in the special problems that arise by assuming ideas for relations; what does interest him is that a relation in the phenomenal world presupposes a standard in the world of ideas, and when he chooses 'equality' as his example it must be because 'equal' is a universally applicable predicate. It is one of those concepts that makes it possible for the world of phenomena to present itself as a structured and coherent order. The two logs of equal size – the phenomena – are the occasion, not the cause of our understanding the concept of equality. In other words, the knowledge of ideas is not causally dependent on the sensual world and does not depend on a process of abstraction, for in an absolute sense no phenomena are 'equal' – and hence we must previously have possessed the notion of the absolute standard, which re-emerges in our consciousness as 'recollection' (*anamnēsis*). Accordingly the idea becomes an a priori precondition for the phenomenon, not merely for our knowledge of the phenomenon but for the existence of the phenomenon – for inasmuch as no sense objects are absolutely 'equal', they 'strive' towards a norm. Furthermore, things are subject to change both in relation to other things and in relation to themselves. Here we clearly see an application of the theory of 'recollection' and a priori knowledge, familiar from the *Meno*; but now the theory becomes directly tied to the doctrine of ideas so that the idea is understood as an epistemological and ontological precondition for the phenomenon. It is likewise clear that the doctrine of ideas cannot explain the contingency – which relies on uncertain experience – that makes these two particular logs appear of equal size to a given observer; but it can explain what this means and the reason for their appearing of equal size.

Ideas are uncompounded and immutable, and also for this reason they have priority over the phenomena which are compounded and mutable and hence can be broken down into constituent parts (78 B ff.). The phenomenon is dependent on the idea, but it should also be noted that no distinction is made between physical and phenomenal object (74 A ff.). The thing is viewed simply as it appears or presents itself to somebody (*phainetai*), and therefore the world would be reduced to a Protagorean world (90 C), were it not for something superior, the ideas, which at least makes it certain what appears. It is irrelevant to object that the two logs might in fact be of identical size, for about such problems it would only be possible to reach empirical consensus.

This is the theory that Socrates in a general form makes into a *hypothesis* on his 'second-best course' (99 D ff.). The beautiful, for example, exists in itself, and this presupposition implies that by the beautiful all beautiful things are beautiful (cf. *Hipp. Maj.*). Socrates is too naïve to understand other specious explanations of something as beautiful, but he perseveres in claiming that it is beauty itself that is causal, and as to the rest he does not want to quibble about words – whether the phenomenon participates in the idea or whether the idea is present in the phenomenon. Simply and naïvely he also insists that when one person is a head taller than another, it is tallness and not the head that is the cause; furthermore, two is two not because of any addition or division but because of 'twoness'. With vociferous *naïveté* he thus manages to state what he wants to explain or not explain by his theory. He affirms the duality of the transcendence of the idea (*chōrismos*: separation, in Aristotle's wording) and its immanence (*methexis*: the participation of the phenomenon) and thereby he introduces his theory of participation. Indeed he insists that the very act of participation can only be described metaphorically. In other words, it cannot be justified with reference to some superior conceptual level. Finally, it is clear that the doctrine of ideas is not a theory concerning causal relations in the empirical world. 'By the beautiful all beautiful things are beautiful' is a maxim sounded like a fanfare, even though it is of course void of empirical information. It indicates the condition for empirical information.

Among other things this theory can be used to solve the Sophists' and Antisthenes' problem concerning a simple subject-predicate sentence (102 A ff.). A thing has several properties, and a particular subject has several predicates. The example that Socrates chooses is this: Simmias is shorter than Phaedo but taller than Socrates. This is an example, which, like that of 'equality', may confuse us because relations seem to be treated as simple properties. To Plato the two-place predicates 'is taller than' and 'is shorter than' express properties of Simmias, for example as he is seen in relation to Phaedo and Socrates, but they refer to ideal 'tallness' and ideal 'shortness', which accordingly must be understood as non-relational concepts. For this very reason Plato apparently finds seemingly 'opposite' predicates particularly suitable for showing that any given predication expresses something relative and contingent in the phenomenal world while referring at the same time to something absolute in the world of ideas (cf. *RP* VII 523 C). There is no contradiction in Simmias' being both 'taller' and 'shorter', and thereby he becomes distinguishable from other individuals in the same way as if he were 'white', 'just', etc. The subject has different, perhaps 'opposite' predicates, and the predicate is not identical with the subject. This is the linguistic-logical counterpart to the individual's participating in several ideas in different ways. The ontological concept of participation thereby legitimates a theory of predication, in which 'is' as a copula is transformed to 'participates in'. Antisthenes' problem has been solved, but without the proposition being considered a linguistic-logical unit.

Ideas, on the other hand, do not have properties and therefore they cannot 'change' properties. The 'tall itself' and the 'short itself' will continue to be opposites; but things in the phenomenal world change properties – what is tall becomes short, and what is tall in one respect is short in another. In other words, the thing is a physical substratum for changeable properties (*Phaedo* 102 D ff.; cf. 70 D ff.). But 'the tallness in us' can never cease to be tall, although we are told metaphorically that it may withdraw or perish; 'the tallness in us' is clearly not a metaphysical intermediate between idea and phenomenon, but simply the idea in so far as it is 'present' or appears in the phenomenon participating in it – the tall is tall and 'tall' means 'tall', whether it refers to a person or to the idea, 'tallness itself'. In this manner Plato's Socrates is able – as it has often and perhaps too simply been stated – to make Heraclitus and Parmenides 'agree'.

The thing can accordingly only be known by its properties – the ideas in which it participates – these properties are changeable, and so the thing is seemingly reduced to an aggregate of properties. Although not stated very clearly, it does seem to be implied (102 C) that a thing must have at least one essential property or participate in one idea in order to be that particular thing. So Simmias must at least be a human being in order to be Simmias. However, there is more emphasis (103 C ff.) on the fact that certain concepts necessarily imply other concepts with the result that there is no need to stop at the 'naïve' thesis that the beautiful is beautiful by beauty. For example, 'three' implies the concept of 'uneven' but not the opposite, and thus 'even' is precluded – just as 'fire' implies 'heat' but precludes 'coldness'.

Still, there is no question of new empirical knowledge, for the whole section is an analysis of concepts as precondition for the description of the world, thus indicating that such an analysis is necessary for the very formulation and understanding of empirical propositions – the understanding of the status of the idea in relation to the phenomenon is also indirectly a demonstration of a teleological cause.

Plato has his Socrates declare (100 A ff.; 101 D ff.) that he assumes the doctrine of ideas as a presupposition (*hypothesis*). In one respect he draws the consequences of this presupposition: a theory of participation, a theory of predication, and a theory of conceptual implication. In other words, he demonstrates the dependence of the phenomenon on the idea and the mutual connections of the ideas. In another respect he reflects on his theory as a method, and in this way the *Phaedo* also continues where the *Meno* left off. The hypothetical method is what Socrates always practised: to draw the consequences of a given presupposition; and his method is a pure analysis of concepts in contrast to the methodical combination of deduction and empiricism of the late Presocratic philosophers. At the outset it is examined whether these consequences lead to logical inconsistencies – whether they 'disagree' with each other (cf. *RP* IV 437 A). Not until the next step can it be considered whether a given *hypothesis* is a consequence of a more general one. This agrees perfectly with the practice in any Socratic dialogue. More specific logical rules are not provided – they should rather be inferred from Socrates' actual procedure – and it is unimportant whether a *hypothesis* applies to a concept or to an existential proposition about the concept – for example whether one proceeds, as in the *Phaedo*, from 'the beautiful' or 'the good' or from such propositions as 'the beautiful exists' or 'the good exists'.

The *hypothesis* examined in the *Phaedo* is not subjected to further verification. It is justified by its results. This is not surprising, for the chosen *hypothesis*, the doctrine of ideas, is in any case the most universal. It goes without saying that the doctrine of ideas could never be verified by any superior presupposition, and therefore this very *hypothesis* leads to strange self-reference; the method of *hypothesis* as such presupposes the existence of concepts – in fact, the doctrine of ideas. This self-reference must necessarily attach itself to the ultimate precondition of thought.

The doctrine of ideas is elaborated on in the 'metaphysical' sections of the *Republic*. Here there is special emphasis on the relationship between ontology and cognition, and it is in these passages that Plato probably comes closest to a 'systematical' presentation of his theory. In an introductory passage (*RP* V 474 B ff.) he speaks of that one idea (the just, the good, etc.), which manifests itself in a plurality – although here always associated with bodies and actions mutually connected. Now, the philosopher – the lover of wisdom – is the man who yearns for knowledge of the idea; ordinary people merely take pleasure in beautiful objects. They love, for example, to watch a play or listen to music. Actually their yearning is also for the beautiful itself, but they believe that the beautiful is identical with its manifestations, and therefore they have bound themselves to the sensual world and live out a life of dreams. Their mode of cognition cannot render an account of itself. On the other hand, the philosopher has transformed belief into certain knowledge. While sensual perception is contrasted to rational knowledge in the *Phaedo*, here in the *Republic* – as in the *Meno* – the contrast is between belief (*doxa*) bound to sensation and rational knowledge, which makes perceptual knowledge possible and demonstrates its dependence.

All cognition is intentional or bound to an object. Plato relies on two further sets of premises. One is that there is analogy between perception and knowledge. The statement 'I see x' is constructed with a direct object. Likewise, 'I know x' implies a direct acquaintance with an object, an idea, and this grasping of the object is a precondition for that-clauses or propositions about the object ('I see that x is y' and 'I know that x is y' – in the Greek it is possible to say 'I know x that it is y'). The other is that any kind of cognition is an 'ability' (*dynamis*) dependent on the object – inasmuch as there is a perceptual or rational cognition, it follows that there is also an object of cognition, and an object of cognition is a real object.

The connection with Parmenides is evident: what really and truly is, is a precondition for what really and truly is known. The connection with the Sophistic theory of knowledge, derived from Parmenides, is likewise evident – it is impossible to know a nothing. Surely this adherence to tradition is deliberate, and therefore it is all the more effective when Plato breaks with Parmenides on one important issue: the sensual world is not an illusion. What is crucial is the relation between cognition and object. There is one absolute and certain knowledge (*gnōmē* or *epistēmē*) which as its object has that which is in an absolute and unqualified sense, the ideas, and in the same way non-knowledge corresponds to that which in an absolute sense is not. But right in the middle between these two extremes there is another cognitive faculty, that of belief or opinion (*doxa*), which is not infallible and the object of which both is and is not, the phenomenal world where what is big may appear small and where nothing is constant.

This model of the correlation between cognitive states and their objects clearly indicates its own limitations. It illustrates true or incomplete cognition, but it cannot say anything about meaningful propositions concerning non-existing objects nor about false cognitions. According to the model both should perhaps be considered non-knowledge, but such matters are not discussed. In other respects the model is not as restrictive as it immediately appears to be. What is directly exposed is knowledge and belief as the optimal modes of cognition of the ideal and the phenomenal world respectively, but that does not preclude the existence of a *doxa* of ideas and an *epistēmē* of phenomena in a secondary sense. Those who find beauty in drama or music believe that they have adequate cognition of the beautiful, which really is to say that they have a *doxa* about ideas. If they realize that there is a mode of cognition, *epistēmē*, superior to *doxa*, they must also realize that they could never have anything but opinion or belief about the beautiful play, even though they would indeed, as in the *Meno*, be able to transform *doxa* into *epistēmē* with respect to the beautiful *in* this or that particular play. The philosopher, on the other hand, immediately has certain knowledge (*epistēmē*) about the beauty that manifests itself in the play – just as in the *Phaedo* he is able to know 'the tallness in us' – but he will never have infallible knowledge of the phenomenon, of a play as a phenomenon, for example. The model may conceal the two motifs in Plato's epistemology. But that the *Meno* and the *Phaedo* should be born in mind is apparent from the three famous images which are prepared for in this passage.

These three images have a universal aim. The first, 'the simile of the sun', illustrates the ultimate condition for the existence and intelligibility of the world by means of a metaphor of light, which in the Platonist tradition has remained as an expression of the highest principle, or the absolute. The second, 'the simile of the line', concerns the structure of the world that is open to human apprehension. The third, 'the simile of the cave', deals with man's place in the cosmos. No more fundamental subjects can be imagined, and this of course is the reason for the use of images instead of explicit language. To be sure, each image may be interpreted allegorically so that there is correspondence between each element of the image and the element of the subject to be illustrated. But of course an image cannot account for what it is that makes it an image; if only for that reason, something more will remain, which can only be hinted at, and it is wise to take Plato's own reservations seriously (cf. VII 534 A). The reader is not confronted with a compressed Platonic catechism, and there are details which only with difficulty fit the imagery. The images are preludes, not conclusions.

The first simile (VI 502 C – 9 D) considers the cosmos an ordered whole determined by the highest principle, the idea of the good, and it makes it clear that knowledge is dependent on this cosmic order. The highest knowledge is that of the idea of the good, as Socrates says (505 A), and he adds that his partners have heard this frequently, just as on more than one occasion they have heard that one idea corresponds to several phenomena. But what is the good? When it is a question of particular virtues, people may prefer appearance to reality, but nobody strives for what is seemingly good instead of the truly good, even though it is of course possible to interpret the good in different ways. Some believe it is pleasure, although this leads to self-contradiction (cf. the *Protagoras* and *Gorgias*). Other, more refined spirits – presumably Plato and his Socrates – identify the good with knowledge – but knowledge of what? Of the good? This is an obvious allusion to the basic theme in 'the early dialogues', for example the aporia in the *Charmides*.

Socrates cannot provide a clear-cut answer to the question of what the good is; but by means of an image he is able to speak of the offspring of the good. The good in the intelligible world corresponds with the sun in the visible one. With its power the sun creates everything living in this world and makes it possible for us, with light as the medium, to sense visual objects. Similarly, the idea of the good is the progenitor of the objects of thought, the ideas, and it enables us to know them – in the light of truth. Were it not for the good as a *tertium quid*, there would be no connection between subject and object of knowledge. Thus something has been said about the 'offspring' of the good but nothing about the nature of the good. The sun is the cause of sensory knowledge and of the generation of the sensory objects but is itself not generation. Similarly, the good causes the existence of the ideas and their intelligibility but is in itself beyond being (*ousia*).

Accordingly, the good is presented as a transcendent principle. This means that to us it assumes a double aspect appearing already at the linguistic level. It is called 'beyond being', but also the eminently being (VII 518 C), which we probably must take to mean that it is not simply beyond existence – most likely *ousia* never has that meaning in Plato – but rather that contrary to everything else that has being its being is indefinable. The relationship of the good to the ideas is analogous with that of the particular idea to the phenomenon. Yet, while other ideas can be defined in the light of the good, the good itself can only be understood rationally as the principle of something else (cf. 517 C). It is 'beyond being', because it is the basis of being, and therefore it can only be 'defined' by being abstracted from everything else (534 B). Elsewhere (the *Symposium, Phaedrus*) Plato describes insight in the highest principle – the good or the beautiful – in a poetic-mythical language, and in so far as the good – the principle of rational thought – allows itself to be grasped directly, the mystic's intuitive insight into that which he does not 'know' offers the only way ahead.

But for rational knowledge the essence of the good is a limiting determination. As the simile of the sun shows, it is the warrant for existence and knowledge, and its essence can only be determined ambiguously – for example as 'knowledge of the good'. The effect of the good, however, lets itself be known. It manifests itself on all cosmic levels and is – as are other ideas – both transcendent and immanent, although the analogy with other ideas is incomplete. It applies to any given idea – and thereby indirectly to any given 'thing' – but also to cognition and knowledge that they are empty concepts unless they are 'good'. For example, the idea of the just includes the quality 'good', which is to say that insight into the just is beneficial, and what is good is useful (VI 505 A). Thus the good is not some additional designation of objects or concepts – for in that sense it is not an object, but is simply that which causes the world to be orderly and the single elements in the world to be meaningful. Thus the good is both a limiting concept and a 'something' that everywhere manifests itself.

The good is a formal designation as long as it is not seen in relation to something else: 'the highest good' does not allow of determination. In recent philosophy the good has also often been considered as something indefinable, and it has been noted – as did Plato – that the concept of 'good' has its own special logic: there may be degrees of 'goodness' and something may be good for something or in itself; but in the world of experience there is nothing that is simply good: the man is morally good or the axe is good for cutting. From this Aristotle concluded that the good has 'several senses' (this as early as in the *Topics* 106 a 4 ff.). To Plato the fact that in all areas there are degrees of perfection implies not only a highest degree but also that a transcendent good must exist in itself.

Many basic Socratic-Platonic thoughts – and Socratic paradoxes ('virtue is knowledge', the unity of the virtues, that the good exists although never defined) – gain a new perspective by means of this philosophy of transcendence. Hence, in introducing the simile of the sun, Socrates begins by saying that he will elaborate on that about which they agreed beforehand. They agree that the good is 'the highest knowledge', that the ideal world is 'good', and that there is correspondence between cognition and existence. The argument does not start *ex nihilo*, and nothing is deduced from the existence of the good. Rather, it is the other way around: the existence of a good world presupposes the existence of 'the good in itself'. This 'good in itself' appears to rational knowledge as the foundation of being, as a pre-condition, but it is independent of consciousness and hence is not dependent on a transcendental consciousness; it is altogether essential to remember that throughout Antiquity it is hardly possible to speak of a transcendental philosophy in the Kantian sense.

Any interpretation of 'the idea of the good' is notoriously difficult as well as uncertain. The difficulties are not only owing to the issue itself nor merely to the relationship between mystical and rational knowledge. The terminology and frame of reference also pose problems. Plato deals with the good as a first principle and yet as an idea that is described with the usual vocabulary of the doctrine of ideas; at the same time this frame of reference is violated ('beyond being'). Analogous difficulties adhere to a series of key concepts in the late dialogues, especially the *Sophist*.

In the simile of the sun, the visible world is used as an image of the intelligible world. The simile of the line (*RP* VI 509 D-11D), on the other hand, illustrates the very relation between the image and that which it depicts. One must imagine a line divided into two uneven sections, and each is divided according to the same ratio:

According to Plato's instructions a/b = c/d = (a + b) / (c + d) whence it follows implicitly that b = c. Algebraic symbols are really more apt than the geometric illustration, which was more natural to Plato, for it is apparent that it is of minor importance whether a or d is the longer. What is decisive is the fact that certain proportions are established, which here, as often in Plato (cf. *Gor.* 508 A; *Tim.* 31 B ff.), is the formal expression of a rational cosmic order. Of course a mathematical image cannot indicate more than the formal relation between 'neutral' entities, but the assigned values are far from neutral, and so there is not entire agreement between the image and that which is depicted. Plato carefully indicates what each section of the line represents (on this, cf. *RP* VII 533 D ff.), and it turns out that each section represents both an ontological and an epistemological category. Schematically the 'filling in' may be indicated as follows:

Epistemological categories   *Ontological categories*

Knowledge (*epistēmē*)	Dialectical or philosophical knowledge (*noēsis*)	d	Ideas as objects for philosophical knowledge	The intelligible world (*to noēton*) or being (*ousia*)
	Discursive (mathematical) reasoning with hypothetical point of departure (*dianoia*)	c	Ideas as objects for discursive (mathematical) reasoning	
Opinion (*doxa*)	Assumption	b	Sensory objects 'things'	The visible world (*to horaton*) or the world of becoming (*genesis*)
	Illusion	a	Mirror images or shadows	

The assigning of epistemological categories to ontological ones is a consequence of the simile of the sun and of the earlier section (V 474 B ff.) in which it was concluded that there is an intermediary area between absolute being and non-being, and that an epistemological intermediate category, *doxa*, between knowledge and non-knowledge corresponds with this. Hence the line illustrates the two areas that are the objects of respectively perfect and imperfect cognition. The earlier section also allowed for the possibility of a connection between one level and another – given certain conditions it would be possible to transform *doxa* into *epistēmē*. These are the two principal motifs that sustain the line simile. In part, the line indicates that there are different levels of being to which there are corresponding states of cognition, and in part the line may be read vertically – the repeated proportions establish a continuity and illustrate how one moves from one kind of cognition to another, from a lower degree of 'truth' to a higher one; the subordinate minimal ontological levels are probably meant to clarify this epistemological ascent (the relation between a and b and between c and d).

The line is itself an image which, among other things, illustrates the very concept of image. The relation between image and original is familiar from the phenomenal world (cf. the *Phaedo*), and the metaphysical point is that an image has a two-fold status: it is a medium depicting something other than itself. The lowest section of the line, mirror images (a), is of course something in itself – for example a mirror or a pool – but it appears at first sight as something else, as physical objects (b), and so the corresponding form of cognition is illusory – if it identifies the image with the physical object. If we imagine beings who are only able to perceive mirror images, they will of course think of their cognition as the only true one; but their comprehension of reality will change if they are confronted with the world of things and thus come to see their former cognition as illusory. The ordinary man finds himself belonging in section b without reflection accepting the world of objects as the real world. But the relation between an imaginary world and a world of objects now becomes a paradigm of the relation between the entire phenomenal world and the world of ideas (a + b and c + d). If one has knowledge of ideas, he will recognize that sensory objects are 'things' as well as images of more 'true' objects, ideas, and he will have transformed *doxa* into *epistēmē* – to that cognition which can 'account for itself'. In other words, his attitude is like that of the lover of wisdom, the philosopher, as opposed to that of the lover of drama or music. An analogous relation is valid in the intelligible world – even though the analogy is incomplete. A mathematician (a geometer) occupies himself with intelligible objects (c) and will 'depict' them as visual figures, but he will not be able to justify his knowledge. It is only the philosopher who is bound to possess unqualified knowledge of true reality (d). At all other levels men will believe that they have true knowledge – without its being so.

If we read the line 'horizontally', it will depict different levels of being. But, in fact, this only becomes meaningful by a 'vertical' reading which reveals that the images everywhere reproduce the same original, the essence of a thing – the idea. In its pure form it appears only in the uppermost section (d), and there it is directly recognized; but on the lower levels it appears in another medium and is therefore only recognizable in veiled form. The thing exists as well as the idea does, but in a different way; however, the thing's essence or nature is identical with the idea. A bed, for example, is of course a thing, but it is a copy and thereby essentially identical with the ideal bed which the artisan has 'reproduced' in his own material (X 596 A).

It is presupposed at all levels that the object has real existence and that it can be recognized with a greater or lesser degree of clarity. The ontological classification does not apply to objects as they are 'in themselves', independent of an observer. It applies to the mode of appearance of the object or to the intentional object, and indeed it is apparent that a mathematician or a philosopher, for example, perceives the same object in different ways. The line simile presupposes the 'pre-established harmony' between subject and object of knowledge, indicated in the sun simile, and thus it is the same epistemological model as that in the *Phaedo* and in the preliminary section of the *Republic*.

Directly, the line simile only illustrates the world that is accessible to rational cognition. There is no room for pure nothingness or non-cognition and only for false cognition, in so far as it is considered imperfect cognition. Nor is the idea of the good reproduced, for the good transcends the line at the same time as it legitimates it and must be presupposed at every level. The simile is also limited in the sense that it only depicts the relation between physical objects and their intelligible paradigms; moral qualities, for example, must in principle be explicable in the same way, even though probably it could not easily be reproduced schematically.

No other science than mathematics occurs in the line simile, and of course this is understandable, for mathematics was (is?) the only science which as a closed conceptual system concerns itself with idealized objects; yet at the same time it is related to physical objects. Only 'things' appear in the lower sections, and the limitation of the line therefore also explains that only that science is taken into account which can be employed in an idealized description of the physical world. Perhaps that is the reason why sections b and c are equal, for inasmuch as the empirical world is described mathematically, the subject matter of mathematics will coincide with that of physics. This, of course, does not mean that the mathematician believes that his objects are physical. In Plato the 'good' geometer is aware that he only employs drawn figures as illustrations (cf. VI 510 D), and his arithmetician becomes angry (VII 525 E; cf. *Phil.* 56 D ff.) when anybody treats his numbers as 'commercial numbers' or wishes to break up his concept of unity, as if it were a thing.

But mathematics is not philosophy or dialectics. The latter is Plato's main concern, and here he develops the hypothetical method further (*RP* VI 510 B ff.). This is the method employed by mathematicians when they proceed from presuppositions (*hypotheseis*) that are considered given – such as numbers, figures, and angles – and draw conclusions from them. As so often, there is no distinction between objects and propositions about objects, and there are no further rules of inference, even though it is clear that Plato adumbrates what has later been called the axiomatic method: inference from unproven axiom to proven theorem.

The passage is the oldest surviving discussion of the foundation of mathematics, but it has a wider aim. Plato does not blame the mathematicians for working as they do within their own science. But he does maintain that such a science is a closed conceptual system that relies on unexplained epistemological assumptions. The philosopher or the dialectician does not confine himself to proceeding from assumption to conclusion. He justifies his assumption (*hypothesis*) by perceiving it as a special case of a higher presupposition, and in this way he ascends to a higher principle without further presuppositions (*to anypotheton* = the idea of the good). As he ascends, he is working tentatively, but having reached the highest principle, he can descend once more and subsequently draw his conclusions with certainty – not on the basis of hypotheses, for now he adheres to the world's own structure, and his conclusions are anchored in insight into the ideas and their mutual relations. Probably this is a generalized mathematical procedure (cf. *Meno* 86 E; Aristot. *Eth. Nic.* 1095 a 32 on 'the ascent and descent' as a general Platonic method of principle; see also pp. 258 and 412). But in contrast to the mathematician, the philosopher can arrive at an absolute point of departure, and he does not employ images: he moves in a universe of pure ideas.

In the *Phaedo* Plato left open the possibility of conclusive verification of a hypothesis. In the *Republic* it is now maintained that there is an ultimate criterion for verification, a first principle, which turns a hypothesis into certain knowledge. This first principle guarantees that there is – as we were already told in the *Meno* – systematic coherence between all knowledge and all that exists. Looked at more closely, what does this mean? Here Plato is not particularly informative – and indeed it is evident that the presupposition for knowledge cannot itself become known and certainly not be proved. It can only be 'grasped' intuitively (*RP* VI 511 B). Plato's dialectician has no expertise to add, for example, to the mathematician's, and of course he cannot deduce all human knowledge from one ingenious basic formula. He can, however, discover the conditions for knowledge. It is also characteristic that Plato does not say that the philosopher 'knows' this or that which might be formulated linguistically. He does speak about what the philosopher can do: he can 'use' his knowledge ('*Gebrauchswissen*') and, thanks to his dialectic, 'noetic' insight into concepts and their relations, he is for example able to account for the mathematician's discursive, 'dianoetic' thinking. Such knowledge presupposes that the world is one system, which in principle allows itself to be known in the light of a first principle. But this is an ideal which probably has never been realized – not by Plato and certainly not by Socrates. Plato lets him point out that he is only able to speak in images. He does not know whether his presentation is exactly true, 'but I do maintain that there is such a truth to be perceived' (VII 533 A).

The line simile does not prove anything. It illustrates what must be presupposed, *if* certain knowledge exists.

The last image, the cave simile (514 A-21 B; cf. the interpretation 532 A ff.), illustrates man's place in the world. Some persons are in chains in a cave and can only see the rear wall of the cave. A number of objects are paraded behind them, and these are illuminated and thereby their shadows appear on the wall. Clearly the prisoners will perceive the shadows as real objects, and some of the brighter ones will formulate an 'empirical' science, which is to say that they will remember that 'object' x usually is followed by 'object' y. Suppose now that one of the prisoners is unchained. Naturally he will be blinded at first, but gradually he will be able to understand what is object and what is image. This process, in which that which seems real is revealed as illusion, is repeated. The freed prisoner is led out of the cave into the real world, and once again habituation will be required before he understands what are images and what are real objects. It is not until the very last that he will understand that the sun is the cause of all things. As in the sun simile, the physical world is thus once more an image of the intelligible, and it is itself imitated by an 'under'-world. Unlike the other two similes, this third contains a political dimension. He who has perceived the truth is obliged to return and share his knowledge with his fellow prisoners – even though he will be ridiculed, and perhaps even risks being hauled into court – as we are told in one of the many allusions to the fate of Socrates.

Plato states expressly (517 B) that the cave simile should be compared with the earlier similes. The four stages of the freed prisoner's road to knowledge accordingly correspond to the four sections of the line. The resemblance to the sun simile is likewise clear. But the perspective is new, and there are elements which do not seem to fit immediately but are left to the reader to ponder: in the cave simile ordinary men – the prisoners – do not perceive the physical objects directly but perceive only illusions; transferred to the symbolism of the line simile, they would be found in the lowest section of the line; nor is there any continuity between the cave and the 'real' world. One can only guess at the answer. The thought of man captive in a cave is an allusion to Empedocles, but it is probably more significant that the simile in its entirety is permeated by political undertones and by a terminology of violence: the prisoners are chained, unknown powers manipulate them – who has enchained them, and who orders the series of objects to be paraded behind them? and the freed prisoner (Socrates? Plato?) encounters aggression. Is the explanation perhaps that the line simile speaks abstractly while the cave simile reproduces a factual situation in which man is subjected to indoctrination and a suppressive and false ideology? Or is it the individual himself who stands in the way of his own possibilities? In such a situation the liberation of man will be a laborious journey from Empedocles' cave to another world. The condition for liberation lies in man himself.

LOGOS AND ERŌS: THE *PHAEDO, SYMPOSIUM, PHAEDRUS* AND *CRATYLUS*

The doctrine of ideas is, so to speak, the ontological backbone of Plato's classic dialogues. In each of these it is seen in relation to the world of man, but in different perspectives. In the *Republic* the discussion deals with political man, and this relation will be dealt with in the following chapter. In the other dialogues – the *Phaedo, Symposium* and *Phaedrus* – the discussion concerns the individual, the possibility of his 'caring for his soul' or losing his identity. Principal themes in Plato's anthropology are the immortality of soul, its kinship with the ideal world, and the two forces that determine the life of an individual, his intellect or *logos* and his desire or *erōs*. Just as Plato's macrocosmos is divided in two, so is his microcosmos, man. He has an ideal nature and is also the product of his society, character, circumstances in life, and his will. But it is a special feature of man that he is in control of his own life. Man is not what he is immediately. He has the possibility of becoming what, ideally speaking, he has always been or of becoming perverted and crippled. The two forces, *logos* and *erōs*, are neutral, but they can be used or abused.

The *Phaedo* describes Socrates' last hours while he talks with his friends in the prison, and, as he himself remarks, this is his 'Second Defence' (*Phaedo* 69 E). Now he is able to speak freely, which means that he can draw his final conclusions and in his person well-nigh complete the entire philosophical and religious tradition. The composition of the dialogue has been thought out in every least detail, and already from the outset the presentation is conducted on two levels. On a symbolic level Socrates stands as the ideal philosopher behind a consistently realistic level of description that culminates in the sublime simplicity of the death scene where the great physician of the soul asks Crito to sacrifice a cock to the God of Medicine (118 A). Most of Socrates' friends are present, but the two most important participants in the discussion are the 'Pythagoreans' Simmias and Cebes – thereby the connection is established with the thinker who above all others combined knowledge, existence and morality. But this is not done without the use of thinly veiled irony, for it is Socrates who as the true 'Pythagorean' must teach the other two what their doctrine really means – in Socratic terms.

The subject of the dialogue is 'the immortality of the soul' and this turns out to be tied closely to the doctrine of ideas. A number of arguments are advanced to show that the soul is immortal, but none of them is a definitive proof. Socrates reserves his position (107 B; cf. 114 D), and as a whole the dialogue ought to be read with an ear to over- and undertones. It is aporetic, and, like 'the early dialogues', it builds on one quite specific presupposition that leads to conclusions which neither the participants nor the reader might have expected. The dialogue voices what has often been considered a flight from this world, although this probably has less to do with a longing for death than with a life preparing one for death. Above all, it is not readily evident what form of immortality is in fact being advocated, and the myth which concludes the dialogue throws its own light on the rational argumentation.

Just as the doctrine of ideas is included as an unalterable epistemological presupposition – 'that which we always speak about' (76 D; cf. 65 D) – the argument is conducted on the basis of a specific understanding of human nature: man consists of body and soul, the soul is an independent substance, and death consists in the separation of the soul from the body (64 C; cf. *Gor.* 524 B). Without reservation Simmias agrees, but the reader who might have a different idea of death and the relation between body and soul has been given a hint that this dialogue was hardly written for him. Perhaps the interlocutors have failed to understand what they actually have agreed to, for they air alternative views: the soul could be conceived of as the harmony of a lyre, that is as an epiphenomenon dependent on the existence of the lyre (85 E ff., Simmias); or one might conceive of the relation between soul and body as a constant renewal of the body – so that in the course of one man's life he has several 'bodies' – while the soul remains constant, but is dissolved at death (87 B ff., Cebes). Both proposals are rejected with reference to the *hypothesis* of soul and body which has been accepted once and for all.

The theme of the dialogue is seen from three angles: that of the ideal philosopher in the person of Socrates; the perspective of religion and morals; and the perspective of epistemology and metaphysics (cf. Olymp. *In Phaedonem* 1). Behind all the arguments the person of Socrates is a warrant for the immortality of the soul (cf. *Phaedo* 77 A ff.; 85 A) – in the words of Kierkegaard, he ordered his whole life around an 'if': if there is immortality (*Concluding Scientific Postscript*, Princeton ed, 1992, XII, 1,

201). Socrates is a man of god, a *daimonios* in Greek, that ideal philosopher who lives his life with awareness of death. He knows (66 A) that in this life the body, the senses, and the material world prevent the soul from knowing what in truth is, but it is his belief that in the beyond he will stand face to face with truth – it is not granted to the impure to behold the pure (67 B). But the purgation of the philosopher is the Socratic insight, *phronēsis,* which depends on one's inward self, and this concept throws light on the ever-present question of the unity of the virtues (68 C ff.): the traditional civic virtues consist of actions that are owing to disposition and acquired skills; they bring hope and fear with them; the 'virtuous' man is subject to external conditions, and one may be brave but not just. True virtue, *phronēsis*, on the other hand, depends on one's inner self, and that is indivisible. The philosopher's *erōs* is a love for *phronēsis* (68 A).

This twist of the traditional understanding of virtue is connected with Socrates' reinterpretation of traditional religious views. The religious purgation (*katharsis*), familiar from the Mysteries and Orphism, is transformed into the philosopher's *phronēsis*, and a quite different religious tenet, the thought of the soul as a vital principle, is exploited in a new way in Socrates' philosophical anthropology. It is often said that Plato was 'influenced' for example by Orphism; but it would perhaps be more correct to say that he uses religious inspirations in his own context, in the same way as he 'uses' the old philosophers.

But *phronēsis* is the virtue of reason, and the philosopher will never 'mistrust' the argument (89 D). The rational arguments are constructed step by step so that the circle steadily expands, but the pervasive theme is the relation of the soul to true reality, the ideas. The first argument (69 E ff.) – which is logically deficient and which *expressis verbis* is supplemented later on (103 A) – attaches itself to traditional philosophical and religious inheritance: the idea of existence as a constant shift between polar opposites (Heraclitus) and the Orphic belief in the transmigration of the soul. What remains of these ideas of the eternal recurrence is one thought, which Socrates imperceptibly sneaks in: the soul in itself exists forever even though subject to constant changes between life (in this world) and death (life in the beyond). This argument is further explored in the following one (72 E ff.), in which Cebes 'reminds' Socrates that he has a theory of recollection (*anamnēsis*). The epistemological side of this argument – that the soul has a priori knowledge of ideas as precondition for empirical knowledge – implies that the soul has a mode of existence independent of the empirical world, that it has a latent 'memory' of the ideas. It is an old point of dispute between interpreters whether the *anamnēsis* theory is to be read literally or metaphorically, in other words whether Plato considers it as a conclusive argument for the existence of the individual soul before birth. Inasmuch as this argument is also a link in a tentative chain, the question can only be answered on the basis of a complete evaluation of all the arguments. Yet what Socrates stresses in the conclusion of his *anamnēsis* argument cannot be unimportant: the belief in the pre-existence of the soul (that 'our soul' exists before 'we' are born) stands or falls with the existence of the ideas. The third argument (78 B ff.) – on the kinship of the soul with the ideas – follows this way of thinking. Like the idea the soul is invisible, uncomposed and unchangeable – and hence primary in relation to the phenomena. But the soul *is* not an idea: it has kinship because he who knows must be kin to that which is known.

The final argument for the immortality of the soul (105 B ff.) includes the major section on the doctrine of ideas as a *hypothesis* – which is to say that it is inserted in a frame, which in a universal context deals with the conceptual pre-conditions for any thought of something coming to be or perishing. Once more Plato builds partly on the ancient Greek thought of the soul as a principle of life and partly on the concept of *phronēsis* as an expression of man's moral and intellectual autonomy. The argumentation is notoriously difficult, among other things because it is presupposed that the soul is 'akin to' but not identical with the idea – which enables Plato to transfer the logic applying to the idea to the soul without establishing any identification. Undeniably this is a procedure that demands a precariously balanced walk on the part of the reader. It follows from the section on conceptual implication that 'snow' essentially implies 'cold' but excludes 'heat'; this must of course be valid both with respect to 'ideal' snow and to snow as an empirical phenomenon; but as a phenomenon snow may melt, i.e. cease to exist, even though snow is cold for as long as it does exist. Since the soul is a principle of life, it will essentially imply life and exclude death. Yet this not only means that the soul is deathless for as long as it animates the body, but also that it is simply immortal – without qualifications. While 'snow' – in this world – may disappear, 'soul' will never be compatible with death. The detailed but intricate argument prepares for the question whether there is a distinction between individual souls and an 'All Soul'. In other words: does this argument pertain to the immortality of particular souls or does it not? Two things should be noted: the first is that Socrates carefully avoids answering the question directly, but instead affirms (106 D) that in any case it must be true that god, the very idea of life (life is accorded the status of idea, the soul is not), and that whatever according to its nature might be deathless never can perish – and 'soul' is 'deathless'. In the second place (107 B), Simmias finds it impossible to challenge this argument, but human frailty still leaves him in doubt about such major questions, and Socrates agrees and concludes by asking his friends to continue the investigation – if humanly possible.

What is it, then, that Socrates urges his friends and readers to think about? Behind the seeming 'proof', the latest argument – like the many versions of the ontological proof of god's existence of later times – conducts knowledge to its ultimate limit: we must in all cases presuppose a first principle, a primary *causa essendi et cognoscendi*, and the soul's essence is founded on that. This agrees with the thread in all the arguments as a whole: at the outset there is an explicit discussion about individual immortality (cf. for example 71 E), but gradually more stress is laid upon the identification of soul and *phronēsis*, or reason, and the rational argumentation thereby intimates that it is reason as such that is immortal. Such a reading implies that immortality lies beyond time and space, in the same way as eternity lies beyond time to Plato. If so, it is really metaphorical to speak of a life before birth or after death, and, if so, the *anamnēsis* theory must be read metaphorically – as a way of saying that by recollection the soul is led back to its proper place. This in turn means that the question of individual immortality fades away – as it did for Empedocles and in the Pythagorean tradition with which Plato associates himself. The concept of immortality has been given a new focus.

Such a conclusion is seemingly contradicted by the myth that follows upon the discursive portion of the dialogue (107 C ff.). As in the *Gorgias*, here the individual souls are rewarded or punished in the beyond for their deeds in this life. But the relation between *logos* and *mythos* is not a simple relation. There are things that we are only able to imagine mythically or symbolically, and apparently it is within this framework that the thought of individual immortality and a life after death belongs. In the *Phaedo* myth Socrates also produces a full cosmology, no less – and thereby anticipates the 'scientific' myth in the *Timaeus*. On the philosophical level such a cosmology is out of place; there it would be as inadequate as would the explanations of the natural philosophers. But in its own language the myth can speak both of this world and the beyond and of the transmigration of souls from one world to another, until at last they come to rest. *Logos* and *mythos* offer each its own interpretation of the Socratic 'take care of your soul', and the levels of symbol and thought do not allow of mediation. The philosopher orders his life around an 'if', and the message of the myth is that you must act *as if* you must render an account after death, while the argument states that soul is reason.

That the essence of soul is reason does not preclude that our souls in 'this life' are affected by the material world and the inclinations of the body (cf. 66 B). This theme emerges as a principal one in the *Republic* and in the myth of the *Phaedrus*, and it is included in the late dialogues (cf. *Phil.* 33 D ff.). But thereby Plato has not abandoned his basic view of the soul's 'essence'. Yet the later dialogues elaborate further on the idea that is merely hinted at in the conclusion of the final argument of the *Phaedo* that 'soul' is a life-giving principle, which can appear both in the individual soul and in a cosmic 'all-soul'. In the *Symposium* there are also precursors of this development.

It can hardly be doubted that the *Phaedo* and the *Symposium* are roughly contemporary. Both dialogues deal with man's relation to the highest, the *Phaedo* from the perspective of death, the *Symposium* from the perspective of life. The *Symposium* treats of *erōs* – and, as Kierkegaard remarks in his *Concluding Unscientific Postscript*: 'Here Love apparently means existence or that whereby life is in everything, the life that is the synthesis of the infinite and the finite' (Princeton ed., 1992, XII, 1, 92). Cicero may be right that Socrates brought philosophy down to earth from heaven. The *Symposium* shows that it is not far from earth to heaven. The dialogue describes a drinking bout celebrating the tragic poet Agathon who had won first prize at the feast of Dionysus. The participants – a select group of educated Athenians – agree to take turns in speaking in praise of Eros, and Plato uses a technique familiar from 'the early dialogues', for example the *Charmides*: each speaker introduces a topic which might be read Socratically, but it is only Socrates who can endow the topics with coherence and substance. The first speaker, the trained rhetor Phaedrus (*Symp.* 178 A ff.), devotes himself to myth and poetical quotations in order to praise Eros for the virtues he encourages between friends and in society. Pausanias (180 C ff.) spiritualizes Eros. In and of himself Eros is neither good nor evil – everything depends on the form of Eros followed by man. There are two types of love, the vulgar, which is mere appetite, and the celestial, sublimated love between man and boy, which pursues ideal goals. At this point it ought to have been Aristophanes' turn, but either wine or Pausanias has temporarily rendered him *hors de combat* thanks to the most commented-upon case of hiccups in world literature. In his place the doctor Eryximachus speaks (185 E ff.). He introduces Eros as a cosmic concept. All of nature is a drama of opposing forces. The exalted Eros of whom Pausanias has spoken can bring about harmony between the forces; the lower leads to moral corruption. Eryximachus speaks from his medical experience, and it is appropriate for him to include Heraclitus. Now Aristophanes is ready (189 A ff.). He speaks of man, not nature. Nowadays men are only half men, but that was not the way it was of yore. Then men were round as balls, had two faces and four arms so that they rolled along like wheels. But this caused them to be impudent, and therefore Zeus cut them in two right down the middle, as one would split a hard-boiled egg with a string of hair. This is the reason that all of us long for our original nature; but should we find our other half we would also retrieve lost happiness of soul and body. Now it becomes Agathon's turn (194 E ff.). He is the master of the ornate style. He intends to deal not merely with the deeds of Eros, but will begin with his essence before proceeding to his deeds – a fine Socratic idea, as it were. But his speech is empty *l'art pour l'art*, a poetical wreath of odourless flowers, and thus it serves as a suitable lead-in for Socrates.

Socrates of course is helpless. He cannot make a speech, but – as did Hesiod and Parmenides before him – he does have a muse by the name of Diotima who, to be sure, is invented. She taught him how to become a Socratic and led him on to the highest Mysteries. He then reports what Diotima told him (201 D ff.). As he did in the *Phaedo*, Plato in the Diotima speech – which strictly speaking consists of two discussions – reshapes current religious ideas. To the modern reader it is important to remember that any given power in the world or in human life is divine; god (Eros) and force (*erōs*) are inseparable. It is likewise a matter of course that between gods and men there are intermediary beings, demons, who govern men's fate. But Plato's use of these ideas is not a matter of course.

Preceding his speech proper, Socrates asks some innocent questions of Agathon (199 C ff.). Eros is desire, but one does not desire that which one already owns. Desire is relative to something or directed at something. It is pretty and right to say, as Agathon does, that Eros is a force that permeates the whole world; but as Eros is desire, he cannot be perfect, as Agathon said. What is Eros' object? The beautiful and the good. But what does that mean?

This is what Diotima instructed him about. Eros is desire for the beautiful and the good, but it does not follow that he is either ugly or evil. He is in between, just as there is an intermediary state between knowledge and ignorance – the right opinion (*orthē doxa*), that conviction which, as in the *Meno*, cannot justify itself. Nor is Eros either mortal or immortal; he is a demon, a being who creates the grand coherence in the world by connecting gods to men, and the man who realizes this is a man of god, a *daimonios*; he who does not is a Philistine. There is of course an explanation for this, for Eros was conceived by Porus (he who knows a way out) and Penia (poverty or want) and he takes after both parents. He is always on the go, for he always feels want. None the less he finds a way out. He desires what he does not have: beauty, but to desire the beautiful is the same as desiring the good and the true – that this is the goal of all human endeavour is undoubted by all, including Diotima and the author of the *Republic*. To possess beauty, goodness, and knowledge is to possess happiness, and beyond happiness there is nothing. Perhaps it is impossible for man to possess eternal happiness, for man is a mortal and changeable being. Not only are the components of the body subject to constant replacement – as Cebes said in the *Phaedo*. Soul and consciousness are also constantly changing in content, so that the old man is no longer the same as the child. Nevertheless man strives for immortality and he strives to conceive and create in beauty. This takes place in procreation in which man survives himself in his offspring; but man also strives for spiritual offspring: fame and honour, the poet's work, and, most beautiful of all, the just state. Can this really be so, asks Socrates? Yes, indeed, replies Diotima.

But there is yet one higher immortality, a beholding, as it is called in the language of the Mysteries – although it is uncertain whether Socrates can become initiate (209 E ff.). There is a step-by-step progression from bodily beauty to the highest beauty, from the beauty that appears in a plurality to that one beauty that abides in itself, is eternal, perfect, and immutable. He who loves bodily beauty will see that beauty which is common to all, he will see the beauty in the many bodies, and he will progress to the beauty of the proper conduct of life and to the beauty of all forms of knowledge, until at last he stands face to face with pure beauty: not something that is beautiful in one respect and ugly in another, not a beautiful face nor a beautiful thought, but that one beauty on which he expended so much effort. He who beholds the beautiful with eyes that are allowed to see and who lives with it will not create idols of the good, for he has not grasped some image. He has been granted the truth and he will create true goodness. Would not such a man be loved by the gods, and would not he, if anybody, achieve immortality?

This then is what Diotima said. But once more we return to terra firma. The drunken Alcibiades enters noisily and delivers his eulogy of Socrates (215 A ff.). It is one thing that Socrates' connection with the dubious aristocrat could not be defended more effectively than by the rejected lover's own words. The place of the speech in the overall composition of the *Symposium* is another matter. Diotima may be right: Socrates cannot be initiated in the highest Mysteries; yet in Alcibiades' speech he emerges as the man of god, the man who is a *daimonios*. Thus here there is also a link with the *Phaedo*, which already is clear through Diotima's conceptual universe.

Gradually all the others had fallen under the table (223 B ff.); only Agathon, Aristophanes and Socrates were awake and Socrates tried to persuade his two companions that he who can write a good tragedy can also write a good comedy. Then these last two fell asleep as well. Socrates covered them and left. He spent the rest of the day as usual.

The Diotima speech is sustained by the sudden insight of mystical vision, and thus in its own language it can speak about that which in the sun simile in the *Republic* lies beyond rational knowledge. In the *Republic* the highest principle is called the Good, in the *Symposium* the Beautiful, and elsewhere Plato speaks of the One. To rational thought these are limiting determinations, but aesthetical, ethical and metaphysical categories converge in the mystical insight in one principle, which may be approached variously – in the Diotima speech, for example, via the unity between the Beautiful, the Good and the True. But whenever a mystical insight is put into words, it implies an interpretation, and this of course applies also to Diotima's speech. The beautiful is considered the highest principle giving the entire cosmos coherence and meaning. But thereby something is also said about man's position. The Platonic mystic does not devote himself to passive, enjoyable contemplation. He 'creates in beauty', just as does the philosopher in the cave simile who is obliged to transform his knowledge into political action. The connection between a lower and a higher world is not disrupted: it is the same beauty that manifests itself in physical love and love of knowledge and which at the highest level stands completely revealed – as the good in the sun simile or the 'pure' in the *Phaedo*.

Accordingly it is probably misleading to say that Plato for example sublimates sexuality. Individual love has its place in the overall scheme, but, as everywhere in Plato, the individual only acquires value via the universal – two lovers become victims of the same delusion as do the lovers of drama in the *Republic*, if they believe more in Aristophanes than in Diotima. He who only exists as an individual is, according to the Diotima speech, a Philistine (203 A) when contrasted with the person whose existence is determined by love of the beautiful. Intellectually man does not have his own private personality (207 D ff.): the contents of consciousness is a flickering jumble that comes and goes, and the soul only gains identity by directing its efforts towards an eternal object. In the *Symposium* the concept of immortality is a telling comment on the problem of individual immortality in the *Phaedo*.

Platonic mysticism is not anti-rational. On the contrary, mystical insight justifies the rational, and, conversely, the path to insight into the beautiful goes via the philosopher's knowledge, *epistēmē*. In the simile of the sun in the *Republic* – indeed as early as in the *Charmides* – the good could actually not be distinguished from knowledge of the good. And just as the good and the beautiful constitute a unity, so, from an ideal point of view, *logos* and *erōs* should converge, as we see in the *Phaedo* and the *Symposium*. In the *Republic* (VI 490 A ff.) it is said of the philosopher that he is not free from his labour pains until through *erōs* he comes to 'grasp' the essence of all things with that ability of the soul with which it is proper to grasp being. Only then will he beget insight and truth.

The *Phaedrus* deals with the relationship between *logos* and *erōs*, the constitutive forces of the soul. This occurs in several dimensions. 'Speeches' – *logoi* – are made on *erōs* and there is discussion of the educative function of *logos*. Stylistically, the dialogue has wide scope. There are everyday conversations, literary pastiche, strict deductive argumentation, and the lofty style of myth. These deliberately fashioned breaks make it exceedingly difficult to date the dialogue on formal criteria, and there are connections with respect to content both with the *Phaedo*, *Symposium* and *Republic* and to the late dialogues (the *Sophist*). Yet there is general consensus about placing it later than the *Symposium* and the *Phaedo* and probably also after the *Republic*. In the Diotima speech in the *Symposium* we find ourselves in a world free of conflicts and follow the happy lover on his way from the lowest to the highest Mysteries where the initiated experiences the union of beauty and wisdom. Here human possibilities are developed without constraint, the inspired poets are not held in check, for they create in beauty, and the politicians create just societies. In the *Republic* human passions are transformed into philosophical knowledge by means of paedagogical devices resting on a close intellectual analysis of the soul. In the *Phaedrus erōs* is, for better or worse, a chaotic force encompassing everything – from the height of human achievement to defeat and perversion. Of itself this *erōs* is a blind instinct, an obsession, or an appetite.

The dialogue takes its beginning with the interlocutor Phaedrus – familiar from the *Symposium* – who recites a speech by the rhetor Lysias (*Phaedr.* 230 E ff.) in which it is argued that it is to the advantage of the beloved for the lover to establish a relationship based on mutual interest, which is to say on rationally determined calculation. The *erōs* he recommends is therefore actually not *erōs* at all, for true *erōs* is a disease (231 D). It is easy for Socrates to show that Lysias' speech is a mere *tour de force*. Then (237 B ff.) – 'with his head covered' – he delivers an improved Lysias speech in which he adopts Lysias' idea of *erōs* as a contractual relation but indirectly shows that this turns *erōs* into disguised appetite and reduces the beloved to an object.

It should not be expected that Socrates would now speak of love of the beloved for his own sake. What he does is to give *erōs* a metaphysical foundation; only thereby can true love between two lovers be created. He retracts his first speech and – with head uncovered – he delivers another (243 E-57 B). It is the high point of the dialogue describing true *erōs*. It is true that *erōs* is madness: it is a divine rapture, which, like prophecy, incantation and poetry, leads man to act without knowing whither divine inspiration will lead him. Yet the soul has the possibility of arriving at insight into the gift of the gods, and therefore Socrates intends to analyze the soul.

Seemingly abruptly follows a strict deductive proof of the immortality of the soul (245 C ff.). It takes Socrates beyond the arguments in the *Phaedo*, but nevertheless it presupposes the cosmic perspective of both the *Phaedo* and the *Symposium* and the thoughts of the soul as a life-giving principle. And an expression, 'all soul', which may mean 'universal soul' and 'every soul' is used deliberately (cf. 246 B). 'All soul' is immortal, for everything that moves of itself is immortal and the soul does not transfer motion; rather it moves of itself.

Formally, this proof is valid, but the truth of it must of course depend on the truth of the premises. Then follows yet another abrupt stylistic shift in which Socrates proceeds from argument to myth, the Platonic pendant to Parmenides' flight to heaven.

The myth presupposes the definition of 'soul' as self-moving mover and exploits the thought that 'soul' can have both universal and individual manifestations. To be sure, we cannot define the essence of soul, but the soul may be compared with a charioteer driving a team of two winged horses. In the case of the gods both horses are of noble breed; but with men one horse is noble and pure (good desire), the other is coarse and impure (appetite), and the charioteer (reason) has a hard time managing his horses when one strives upwards and the other downwards. 'All soul' governs the soulless; if perfect, it controls the entire universe in its rotation around the earth; but the soul that is pulled downwards loses its wings, tumbles to earth, and assumes an earthly body.

Easily and effortlessly the souls of the gods follow the rotation of the heavenly vault in one grand procession, and there, beyond the circumference of heaven, they behold pure being, true justice, and everything which in truth is, as well as the knowledge which does not unfold itself piecemeal. When they have refreshed themselves by this sight, they stable the horses and feed them with ambrosia and water them with nectar. But the souls of men find it difficult to follow. Very few are the equals of the gods, and most are drawn downwards by the coarse horse, dress themselves in human bodies, and, depending on their deeds, are sentenced to rebirth from one bodily shape to another for millennia. But the soul which retains a recollection (*anamnēsis*) of the beyond will be able to discern the one idea in earthly plurality (249 C), and he who encounters beauty in bodily form will also recollect true beauty, so that the wings of the soul grow again (250 E ff.; 253 C ff.) – but this requires a struggle with the appetite of the coarse horse. Only pure *erōs* recalls true mutual love in the beloved in the light of beauty.

The *Phaedrus* myth is poetry on a principal philosophical theme, and the similarities with the view of the soul in the *Phaedo* and the *Symposium* are greater than the differences. But it is not an allegory: the details of the image live their own lives in the universe of the myth and hence should not be interpreted pedantically. It does no good to speculate on the relation between the souls of the gods and the 'all soul', nor to interpret by interpolating an 'astral religion' or a doctrine of a tri-partite soul, nor to wonder about how to view the 'idea' of knowledge. But it is worthwhile to note that *anamnēsis* in the *Phaedrus* unambiguously is a poetic metaphor and that the thought of reincarnation and judgement, as always, finds its home on the symbolic level of the myth. Most important are the cosmic perspective ('all soul') and the contrast between the pure and the fallen soul, which lies behind the message of reincarnation in the myth.

Until now there have been speeches about *erōs*, but in the last part of the dialogue Socrates takes a step backwards and asks what speech – *logos* – is. It is possible to speak falsely and truthfully, as in the first part of the dialogue, and speech is no neutral act: it convinces and it 'guides souls' (*psychagōgia*, 261 A; cf. 271 C). But what constitutes true or false logos? This is not a question of technique to be studied in the current rhetorical manuals, which one by one are given their come-uppance (266 C ff.). It is correct that the speaker must know the right moment to speak, the audience to be addressed, and the subject to be spoken about (272 A). But such a prescription is to be taken seriously, and this means that true rhetoric and philosophy coincide. The speaker must know the nature of the soul but cannot do so without knowing the nature of the world (270 C); his speech must of itself be an organism (264 C); but the true *logos* must follow the structure of reality, as it is discovered by the dialectical method (265 D ff.; cf. 273 E). The dialectician sees one unifying idea in diversity, and on the basis of it he is able to proceed in the opposite direction: to divide into subordinate ideas, for he follows nature's own articulation and does not hack piecemeal, as does the clumsy butcher. Here there is a reminiscence of the ascent and descent of dialectics, as in the *Republic*, but at the same time the so-called *diairesis* method is announced, which is treated thoroughly in the *Sophist* and *Statesman*.

The dialogue is concluded with the section on the relation between the spoken and written word and with the bitter-sweet greeting to Isocrates.

In the *Phaedrus logos* is dealt with as part of Plato's anthropology and paedagogics, and the question is asked what *logos* can bring about for better or worse. But *logos* may also be considered theoretically, which to Plato means metaphysically. *Logos* means word, sentence, speech, language or argument, but what does this imply? Like *erōs*, *logos* is directed to reality, but what is *logos* in itself? As he begins his final argument in the *Phaedo* (99 D ff.), Socrates says that following his disappointment with Anaxagoras he sought refuge in *logoi* as the second-best course – which is to say that he understood that reality does not permit itself to be understood directly, but only by means of the argument – and on this basis he established the *hypothesis* that something beautiful exists 'in itself'. Such a *logos* can say something true or false about reality, and the truth value of the argument can be tested; the truth of reality cannot be tested. Socrates says that *logos* is an image of reality, but it is an image which has the possibility of being more true than physical objects – which to Plato are images as well. The concept of 'image' is central, and that it is something other and more than a metaphor appears for example in the 'image' of the line, which is an image of the second degree. While physical objects merely depict the ideal reality in the phenomena, *logos* is more true, because even the most elementary linguistic expression depicts the universal. The dual nature of the image is recaptured in language. It is something in itself, but it depicts – speaks of – something else. Inasmuch as language does not speak of itself, it presupposes something that precedes language. There is a wordless cognition – for example the intuitive insight into the good – but *logos*, the second-best course, is a precondition for cognition.

The nature of language and its relation to reality are the subject of the *Cratylus*. Like the *Phaedrus* it is difficult to date – there are points of connection with the *Phaedo*, but also with the late dialogues, primarily with the *Sophist*. The dialogue presupposes the lively Sophistic discussion on language – first and foremost Prodicus and Antisthenes. Still, Plato only uses his precursors in order to crystallize some principal 'model theories', here connected with the fashionable concepts of *nomos* and *physis*. By analyzing the consequences of these theories, he shows that they are untenable; his own hinted-at conclusion rests on other premises, and, as opposed to for example Antisthenes and Euthydemus, he insists that there are false speech and false 'names' (*Crat.* 385 B). Nevertheless, on decisive points he operates within the traditional frame of reference: in one sense or another it is the function of language to depict. Although sentences are said (431 B) to consist of 'substantives' or names (*onomata*) and 'verbs' (*rhēmata*), 'the name' is in principle considered the smallest linguistic unit, and hence a sentence is only a sum of 'names'. Furthermore, here – as in the *Phaedo* – there is no distinction between meaning and reference. Accordingly language must refer to real objects. The declared theme of the dialogue is the problem of 'the correctness of the name', which is to say: what does a 'name' represent?

One of the interlocutors, Hermogenes, stands for a *nomos* theory. In other words, the relation of language to reality is arbitrary; the other and the more stubborn, Cratylus, believes that language reflects the nature of things (*physis*), and he makes use of some current Sophistic catch phrases: all names are correct in so far as they are names, and one cannot lie because one cannot say that which is not. Socrates ties these theories to two progenitors: Protagoras and Heraclitus, and – as he does later in the *Theaetetus* – he shows that the two theories only apparently conflict. If one draws the most radical conclusions, they will lead to the same – unacceptable – result. A radical Protagorean theory (385 E) will state that every man has his own language, and, if so, communication is impossible. A radical Heraclitean theory (440 B) will imply that reality is in constant flux; yet if there is no minimum of stability in the world, cognition – and with it language – will have no object. Thereby linguistic communication is also rendered impossible. By modifying the two theories it is in a certain sense possible to maintain both that language depends on agreement (a moderate Protagorean theory) and on similarity with reality (a moderate Heraclitean theory – cf. 435 C). But agreement about what and similarity with what?

In the discussion with Hermogenes Socrates tries to pinpoint what language is in itself. The true word expresses the nature of things; the false does not. Therefore language is employed to say what is and what is not (385 B). To speak constitutes an act, and language is a means of communication (387 B ff.); it is in other words essentially a tool: just as the weaver fashions his shuttle with the aim of using it for something, so the 'giver of names' – he who originally fixed the meaning of names – must have something to refer to. Let us suppose that the name-giver has acted arbitrarily, and, if so, we may read anything whatever into the meaning of the words, as is shown in a protracted section, in which Socrates (perhaps polemicizing against somebody?) disports himself with the most strange etymologies (391 E ff.). Nor does it help to assume that words can be reduced to minimal units of vocal imitation – the bleating of a sheep is not the 'name' of a sheep (423 C). If language is regarded as convention and nothing else, the presumed 'name-giver' accordingly would have to be operative in a void. If it is created by agreement, it must be an agreement with regard to something pre-linguistic, which it 'depicts'.

In his argumentation against Cratylus Socrates goes further. Language cannot simply depict the thing; and so, if we have no other criteria, language as image can be interpreted by just as arbitrary etymologies as before (437 A), and if the name as image is identical with the thing, we would be unable to distinguish between thing and image; language would become an autonomous structure; and one name could only be assessed with the other name as its criterion. Therefore we must be precise about what we understand by image. That the name is an image means that it is a sign that clarifies a state of affairs (433 D). On the one hand a sign is fixed by convention – not by natural similitude – but on the other hand a sign refers to something outside itself. The designated cannot be in constant flux: the sign must represent something that is knowable and hence communicable. Consequently the does not represent the physical thing, which is constantly changing: the tic correlative of the sign, its meaning, must concern only that with immutable e: the ideas. Language must presuppose that something exists, which for is beautiful or good in itself (439 C), and the correctness of language can erore only be determined by the dialectician who knows 'the matter'.

Several conclusions can be drawn from the *Cratylus*. Language is a system of 'names' or signs that by convention depict ideal entities, which transcend language. It is nevertheless impossible to step out of language and judge of the relation between sign and reality from some third point of view. For example, a name-giver cannot give names at will, but must have a language at his disposal prior to this. Therefore language must consist in the interplay between the linguistic expression and the pre-linguistic contents; it can never be reified and considered an object in itself preventing access to reality, for reality is already present in the language, and true language is thus transparent, an image of that which is being spoken of. If the dialectician can assess 'the correctness of the words' – and perhaps establish informative 'etymologies' – this must be carried out within the framework of language itself, but not by means of a language about language operating in a void. The relation between ideas is the precondition of the actual language. This thought is elaborated further in the *Sophist* where Plato also seeks to go beyond the limitation that attaches itself to the *Cratylus* where language can be reduced to a sum of 'names'.

The *Cratylus* provides a commentary on the brief remark in the *Phaedo* to the effect that *logoi* give a better picture of reality than physical objects do. Furthermore, there are parallels between the *Cratylus* and the theory of participation and predication of the *Phaedo*. In both cases the discussion is of an asymmetrical relation between original and image that precludes intermediates.

The *Cratylus* contains the first philosophy of language left to us. Not until recent years has it been acknowledged that here problems are formulated that have been basic down through the history of semantics and philosophy of language, even if Plato's frame of reference had been abandoned.

15

THE GOOD CONSTITUTION
OF STATE AND MAN

——•❖•——

In the *Gorgias* the life of corruption was opposed to a life of morality as the only logical alternative. The consequences are drawn in the *Republic*, a *magnum opus*, five times as voluminous as any of the other classical dialogues and seminal in the history of political thought, provocatory in its plan, and to this day the subject of discord. This is no political manifesto aiming for the reform of existing societies and constitutions. It depicts the 'perfect state' without regard to feasibility. The theme of the dialogue is the concept of justice, traditionally the social 'virtue' *par excellence*, but to Plato fully as much an 'individual' virtue. The economic, social, or legal aspects of society are not Plato's main concern. The basic perspective of the *Republic* is a moral one, and the dialogue builds on the one presupposition that absolute justice is a reality and that it is possible – on the ideal level at least – to establish a just human and social life as a counterpart to existing societies, which only reflect egotistical selfish interests. As is normal in a Greek context, there is no distinction between state and society, and in fact the Greek title, *Politeia*, contains both meanings; but Plato expands the concept so that it also applies to 'the constitution of our inner self' (*RP* IX 591 E; cf. X 608 B).

The bitter tone of the *Gorgias* is found once again in the *Republic*. With clear reference to Attic democracy, the state – Athens – is compared to a ship whose owner (the people) by and large is a kind-hearted fellow, although without insight and therefore an easy prey to all sorts of charlatans who without the least bit of knowledge of navigation vie with each other to become navigators (VI 488 A ff.). Or the state is compared with an unruly wild beast to which dubious flatterers pay token obedience (493 A ff.). What does the idealist – the philosopher – do in such a situation? He may very well be tempted to play the game, but the perverted idealist becomes the worst demagogue (490 E ff. – Alcibiades?), or he can retire from politics with his dignity intact and await some future miraculous change (496 D ff. – Plato?).

Such passages voice the moral indignation, familiar from the *Gorgias*, which inspires the entire *Republic*. But modern readers, who feel themselves the target of the direct appeal in the *Gorgias*, often become indignant when they see what this leads to in the *Republic*: are slavery, the dissolution of the family, eugenics, euthanasia, and censorship necessary ingredients in a 'moral' society? It is not advisable to seek a way out by smoothing and explaining away; Plato wanted to challenge, and his modern critics – including both liberals (Karl R. Popper) and Marxists – have probably acted more in his spirit than those humanist interpreters who have preferred to concentrate on the good and the beautiful.

To a large extent modern Plato criticism has been inspired by the experiences of World War II, which with one stroke placed Plato's *Republic* in a new light. Now it was no longer merely an interesting historical document, but a stumbling block occasioning impassioned debate. To Popper, Plato is the father of the modern totalitarian state, whether Fascist or Marxist: the power state is everything, the individual nothing. If so, it fades into the background why Plato considers 'tyranny' the worst form of government. A typical Marxist interpreter will consider Plato's *Republic* a false ideology, an attempt to legitimate the interests of those who own; but one wonders whether the proprietary classes of the fourth century would have felt secure with a spokesman who would abolish the private property of the elite and divide the economic and political power in such a manner that 'the lower classes' in fact would be in charge of production? Whether present-day criticism comes from the political right or left, it addresses itself to the same issue: in Plato's state the individual has no rights and is suppressed by a self-appointed elite. But as it is formulated, such criticism is rarely sufficiently thorough. The picture is a complex one, and the real issues are so fundamental that they are easily distorted by rash conclusions *ex post facto* that also fail to question modern conceptions.

Plato is of course a child of his times. Most likely he was inspired by the Pythagorean communities, but on many points he is bound by the traditional social structure. Necessarily his society is a city state, a relatively small economic unit, which in so far as possible is self-sufficient and, of course, politically independent (cf. IV 423 A ff.), and he can conceive of nothing but his good little state in a constant state of war. That which in the common opinion held a city state together was the autarchy concept; in Attic democracy the individual citizen was understood to be his own master in a state that was its own master. If some are free, others must be unfree, and the commonwealth must be on guard against them. The free citizens are united by a feeling of 'concord' or 'common will' – as in Pericles and Democritus. But where Pericles' emphasis is on freedom of speech, for example, and on every man's doing 'what he wishes', Plato's centre of gravity is elsewhere: what is decisive is that the state constitutes a unity (V 462 B), and such a unity depends on there not being conflicting economic interests – in other words, no significant difference between rich and poor (IV 421 D). Plato opposes economic privileges, but he is no believer in any social principle of equality and much less in the individual's rights as an individual. It is so self-evident that there are slaves in his state that they are only mentioned in passing (433 D; cf. *Leg.* VI 777 B: slavery is a practical necessity). It is equally self-evident that nobody values manual labour (*RP* IX 590 C). Traditionally a city state could be governed by a single person (a monarchy), by an upper class (an oligarchy), or by 'the people' (a democracy), and there were lively discussions about the advantages and drawbacks of these constitutional forms (cf. Her. III 80 ff.). Plato distances himself from this discussion.

The explanation of this admixture of conservative and revolutionary thoughts can be found in Plato's anthropology and in his special concept of freedom, which deviates radically both from that of his own time and from the ideals of his modern critics. As is clear in the *Phaedo*, *Symposium* and *Phaedrus*, the individual is to Plato's Socrates not an autonomous person merely by being a person: man gains his identity by relating himself morally and intellectually to transcendent absolute ideals. In the same way the freedom that consists of acting in accordance with one's inclination is a dangerous illusion. Freedom consists solely in realizing the ideal – man must 'do his task' – which does not solely mean fulfilling one's place in society. Above all, it means to act as a morally responsible individual. The individual only has worth by his relation to truth, and the same applies to state and society. Certainly man is a social being living in a city state, but the state is not some supra-individual entity, and it is not different from nor greater than the sum of its inhabitants (*RP* IV 435 E); in his analysis Plato is therefore able to play individual and society against each other in the light of truth. Socrates is the spokesman in the *Republic*, and the Socratic maxim 'virtue is knowledge' should be taken at its full face value as a guiding line for both the individual and the state.

In the moral and political discussions of the day it is less frequently asked how the ordinary man should conduct his life; the question is rather about the ideal type – which to the Sophists means the 'skilful' or perhaps the clever, while to Plato, the philosopher, he is the ideal person with full insight. But undoubtedly Plato believed that he was also thinking of the ordinary man's welfare. Human beings are not all alike, and most are in need of the help of others – the philosophers. In the ideal society, in which complete concord prevails, the ordinary man becomes happy by relying on the philosopher's intellectual authority. Plato knows very well that existing societies build on suppression: the ruler must keep his slaves in check, and it is only with the power of the state behind him that he can be sure that they will not rebel (IX 578 D ff.). In the ideal society, however, the role of master and serf has been reversed; here the noble regent serves his subjects:

> Every man is best served by being governed by the divine and the rational – at its best when a man has this as part of himself; if not, it must be imposed by some external power. The goal is that all, governed by the same divine reason, in so far as possible lead their lives in mutual equality and friendship.
> (590 D; cf. V 463 B; IX 547 C)

All that is controversial in Plato's state is contained in this quotation. Plato does not make his task so easy that he constructs an ideal state where all are equally wise; he concedes the fact that people are indeed different. But he maintains the ideal that knowledge of truth necessarily will bring about happiness and concord for all. Here one might ask – as did Aristotle (cf. *Pol.* 1261 a 10 ff.) – where the border in fact lies between the utopian and the realistic, and undeniably the question is reinforced when one finds that methods of coercion are employed in the ideal state, 'the state in heaven' (592 B). But of course the decisive questions in connection with Plato's state are whether there is one knowable 'divine truth' and whether it is possible to construct a society that corresponds with the ideal. Plato's answer to these questions is not quite unambiguous – as a good Socratic, he never, for example, did define truth.

An assessment of Plato's state must take into account both the radical and the complex and ambiguous – perhaps naïve – in his basic conception. But it should also consider the hidden Platonic counter-question: what if truth and justice are not absolute criteria? And consider the refined and cunning in the composition of the dialogue: from current problems gradually and unawares we arrive at Socratic-Platonic conclusions that throw new light on the point of departure.

THE CONSTRUCTION OF THE STATE: BOOKS I–V

In many respects the first book of the *Republic* has the appearance of an 'early dialogue', and it is often assumed that it was written as an independent one. Whether or not this is so, it seems appropriate for Plato to let it serve as the introduction to his great work. The inner connection with the other books is evident, and the placement of it as an introduction shows clearly how issues from an 'early dialogue' can be developed and how a typical fifth-century discussion can serve as a prelude to what in Plato's view is a timeless debate on the nature of justice. First we are introduced (I 328 C ff.) to the wealthy and worthy old Cephalus and his son Polemarchus in whose house the discussion takes place. Both are noble representatives of old-fashioned morality, the *kalokagathia* ideal with its roots back in Solon: one must live honourably, which is to say observe law and justice, speak the truth, pay everybody what is his, help one's friends and injure one's enemies. When one has reached the age of Cephalus one realizes that it is best to go to the grave with a clean conscience – who knows what awaits after death? Socrates finds no difficulty in showing that such external morality will lead to inconsistencies – for example, is it always in the best interest of one's friends to speak the truth? It was this moral view that was wiped out by the Sophists, and indeed it is the Sophist Thrasymachus who with much ado interrupts the discussion (336 B ff., see p. 115): the old morality is humbug; what is called justice is mere camouflage of the stronger's suppression of the weaker; might is right; and Thrasymachus' hero is the strong and ruthless egoist. Although Socrates is able to trap Thrasymachus in contradictions, what actually occurs is a close parallel to the discussion with Callicles in the *Gorgias*: Socrates can suggest some of his own basic ideas, but Thrasymachus withdraws in a huff, and so there is no genuine debate.

Seemingly Thrasymachus is the absolute opposite of Cephalus and Polemarchus. But both views actually express a utilitarian morality, in which the question is what actions are most rewarding for the individual in the long run. This point of view is unsatisfactory to Glaucon and Adeimantus, Plato's brothers, who from the beginning of the second book assume the role of Socrates' interlocutors. They are not egoists, but they want arguments and – in good Socratic manner – they want to know what is the essence of justice and how to counter the claim that it is good to act unjustly, bad to suffer injustice (II 358 B ff.). Glaucon illustrates the problem by means of an ancient tale about the Lydian Gyges (359 D ff.) who could make himself invisible and thereby managed to seduce the queen, kill the king, and assume royal power – in other words the familiar example of the man who is granted the possibility of acting unjustly on a vast scale; but in its own way it is also a comment on Antiphon's view of morality. In this way the several aspects of current fifth-century views have been presented in their proper order. Why should Gyges not act unjustly?

Glaucon himself makes his question more precise (357 B ff.). There are, says he, three kinds of goods: those we desire for their own sake, those we strive for for their own sake and for the sake of the consequences, and those we desire solely for their consequences. Where will Socrates place justice? In the second group replies Socrates without hesitation. In other words, justice must be sought for its own sake and because it makes the individual happy. With this 'both-and' Socrates sets himself apart from most modern discussions of morality. The good is first and foremost something one strives for, not something one must perform, and it is no concern of Socrates to discuss whether acts should be called moral with reference either to a concept of duty or to consequences of acts. He wishes solely to justify morality in itself and does not doubt that morality and happiness cohere: the good or the just has intrinsic value and is thereby beneficial for the individual. There can be no difference between objective and subjective good. Now Socrates undertakes to defend his position, and the entire remainder of the *Republic* is an attempt to meet this obligation.

He does not simply advance any definition of justice. What he wants to do (358 D) is to throw light on justice for the individual by means of an analogy with justice in the state, for capital letters are easier to read than small ones! Surely this is not an argument, but of course there must be some connection between social and individual ethics. To understand the entire *Republic* it is important to remember that Socrates makes use of a plausible analogy; he does not want to deduce one form of morality from another, and all the rest of the dialogue is indeed a constant interplay between a tentative construction of a model of society and the problem, which the model is intended to illustrate: the concept of justice.

Socrates begins by wondering how the state came into existence (369 A ff.). It emerged as a simple agrarian state that would ensure material necessities. Hence the purpose of the state is economic, and this has the social consequence of necessitating a division of labour. It is practical that some work the land, that some fashion tools, and that some conduct trade – but this is not all that important, for it is a small and frugal state, and therefore the inhabitants are satisfied with little; they are diligent, healthy, pious, and happy. – But this is a state of pigs, argues Glaucon (372 D). – Well, replies Socrates, then we must allow the state of pigs to develop, we must introduce civilization, luxury, and cultural products. But luxury leads to greater demand, and demand leads to aggression. Therefore we will need a military, and thus a new class has been introduced.

Here Platonic irony is at work of course. Plato has, to be sure, quiet sympathy for the simple and primitive but not for the luxurious state, which is the unavoidable consequence whenever the state is exclusively based on economic needs. Nevertheless, this is apparently the basis on which 'the ideal state' is constructed. The account is evidently intended as a parallel to the Protagoras myth, although something is missing: Socrates has 'forgotten' the social contract as well as law, justice, and morality, the guarantors of the survival of society. Apparently it is important for him to keep the categories apart: a society is either built on egoistical needs or on morality. At present all existing societies are 'luxury states', and it would be romantic utopianism to pretend that these sad realities do not prevail. The task then must be to 'purge' the 'inflamed' state (cf. III 399 E), and not until this has happened, will it be possible – as a thought-experiment at least – to speak of the perfect state (IV 427

E; V 472 D). It cannot be founded in a vacuum; Plato looks for a simple rational model which he erects segment by segment with consideration of the factual realities, although on a new foundation, the foundation of morals. The state must become an organic unit in which 'concord' is the foundation and not an expedient superstructure – only thereby can special interests and conflicts be prevented. In such a state, with everything depending on the rulers' moral habitus, only a minimum of regulatory legislation will be necessary (cf. IV 425 B ff.). The only thing that Plato is able to transfer from his 'historical' account is the idea of a division of labour, but this is, on the other hand, an important connection: as society now is, the division of labour is the product of the accidental distribution of power. If it can be justified by human nature, it will not occasion any problems: some will take care of the production of vital necessities, but these people require little attention. They can be left in peace and quiet, provided that there is not too great a difference between rich and poor. Others must 'guard' the state, and everything depends on their being educated properly.

Consequently the education of the future 'guardians' occupies a major part of the dialogue. The purpose of paedagogics is the forming of character – a scientific education only comes afterwards – and here Plato is able to build on the traditional Attic education, which aimed for the building of character first and acquisition of knowledge later (II 376 E ff.); but it must be revised and education is the task of the state. Full knowledge is acquired in freedom, but it presupposes an attitude, which the half-grown student does not have. Hence he must be guided, and, since, according to Plato, there are unlimited possibilities of forming man, the curriculum must be closely supervised. The student must be formed in body and soul, but education in the liberal arts is the more important – the physical is dealt with relatively briefly, mainly in connection with compulsive military service for eighteen- to twenty-year-olds (III 403 C ff.).

The education of character consists of inculcating the right attitude in the student, and one is formed by what one learns. As in traditional education, here the young must learn poetry and music; both are dealt with in detail (poetry: II 376 E–III 398 B; music: 398 C ff.), especially poetry. It is never too early to begin to learn. Already in early childhood children should listen to elevating, moral fables (II 377A). And in subsequent teaching one should refrain from all poetry that does not build on the tenets that god is good and not the cause of evil (379 A ff.); that only the morally good is beneficial; that injustice always leads to corruption (III 392 B). The poets had always been considered guides, but they must be true guides to the good life. But surely, there are few of those – one needs only to think of Homer's accounts of the gods and the tragedians' of the darker side of the mind. Plato's famous – and notorious – strictures against poetry make for quite a complicated phenomenon. As the literary artist that he himself was, he undoubtedly had ambivalent feelings (cf. X 595 B), but this does not mean that his position is inconsistent. He has written poetically about 'the beautiful' (the *Symposium*); he knows the poet's inspiration – divine rapture – which leads him he knows not whither (*Phaedrus*); and he has written myths. But it holds for poetry as all other human activity that it only gains value in light of the good; pure aesthetic enjoyment is an illusion, and it is always fatal to mistake illusion for reality.

The central concept in Plato's criticism of the poets is *mimēsis*, a concept only with difficulty translatable as 'imitation' or 'representation' which has played a major role in the later history of aesthetics. It can reflect the intimate connection between dance, music, and poetry in choral dancing and choral lyrics (later, tragedy), in which a person directly 'represents' a role. In a narrow sense Plato uses it about dramatic poetry (392 C ff.), but in a wider sense the word covers that whole universe of fiction in which the poet, 'the representer' (be he actor or rhapsode), or the audience is drawn into the magic circle of divine inspiration, as we see depicted in the *Ion*. Now, if one has the idea – as did Plato – that one identifies with the role one 'represents' or impersonates (395 C ff.), it is of course morally dangerous to remake oneself into a pseudo-person – perhaps even a person of dubious character – and it is even more serious if one does so in order to curry favour with the public (cf. *Ion* 535 E). In other words, Plato reacts against the emotional effect of art in this sense of *mimēsis*, against its capacity to replace reality with illusion – as in Gorgias' 'Poetics'. In this context it is natural to deal with poetry along with music, which was held to have direct influence on character (cf. *Leg.* II 667 B; VII 816 C ff.).

In a different context (*RP* X 595 A ff.; cf. *Soph.* 264 D ff.) painting – including the recently discovered effects of perspective – is a paradigm closer to hand, namely when it comes to evaluating poetry as knowledge. Here *mimēsis* – and this is probably a deliberate narrowing down of the term – is only considered as 'imitation', i.e. as imitation of nature, for if poetry claims to provide knowledge, this can only come about by copying nature. But inasmuch as 'nature' – physical reality – in itself is an image of true reality, poetry is accordingly an image of an image. Hence poetical 'knowledge' is worth very little. Of course Plato, the poet of myth, knows very well that art essentially is not representational, but whenever art claims to impart knowledge it must on Plato's premisses be considered simple imitation and hence insufficient.

For both psychological and epistemological reasons Plato wishes to subordinate poetical insight to philosophical *paideia*, and in fact the poets were no longer the sole guides to 'wisdom'; philosophy and science had their own modes of argumentation. Plato must turn against the old form of arguing to be found in Homer who lets a paradigmatic narrative work as a universal rule, and he makes full use of his stylistic skills to present a deadly boring account of the marvellous introductory scene in the *Iliad*, thus showing that very little remains, if the emotional context is removed (cf. Hom. *Il.* IX 529 ff.; I 12 ff.; *RP* III 390 E; 393 C). Everything is dislocated if the poem pretends to argue or inform. It is a different matter that in propaedeutic education Plato finds the good old tales useful, provided that they have symbolic truth value.

Therefore he uses 'true' myths and fables in his education. In Plato's ideal state everybody must strictly observe the truth – except in cases where the professional must employ a white lie in the interest of a higher truth, which for example occurs in a doctor's relation with his patient (III 389 B). All inhabitants in Plato's state require a major unifying national symbol, a symbolically true fable (sometimes mistakenly translated as 'noble lie'), a myth of the state (III 414 B ff.), which may go like this: you have all come from the soil of the earth and therefore you are brothers; yet when god created you, he mixed gold into the make-up of some (the rulers), silver into that of others (the warriors), and iron and bronze into yet others (the agrarians and artisans). This is not an argument but a mythical truth, and every state requires true myths, which are just as indispensable as in the education of the young.

There is of course a division of labour in any state. What is radical in Plato is that all men are identified with their profession. To him this is a natural consequence of men's different talents (cf. II 370 A), and it is emphasized time and again that from society's point of view the division of labour is the only rational measure and must be fully effectuated: the common good has priority over the personal good; individual happiness depends on that of the state; the citizens must jointly say 'mine' and 'not-mine' (IV 419 A; V 462 B ff.), for wherever everyone strives for personal happiness, the outcome is discord and in fact unhappiness for the individual. The consistent division of labour brings about a tri-partite class division: the working population, the auxiliaries, and the rulers. The lowest class – the agrarians and artisans – in fact make up the economic basis of society, but they are most kindly expected to be content with sustaining the two upper classes in return for being governed with wisdom and care. It is only gradually revealed (III 412 B ff.) that the ruling class is divided in two, the auxiliaries and the real rulers. First and foremost, the auxiliaries have military and lesser administrative tasks – they are to function as watchdogs, fierce towards strangers and protective of their own people (II 376 A). The rulers must have the best possible intellectual and moral qualities (IV 484 B ff.). One cannot inherit one's place in society; the auxiliaries and rulers are selected after strict examination and are regularly checked (III 413 D).

The auxiliaries and the rulers must devote their entire lives to the service of the state, and therefore care must above all be taken that they do not become distracted by private interests – whether money or women. In order to prevent these dangers Plato introduces the most utopian elements in his state, regardless of the fact that on certain points he probably was inspired by the state of affairs in Sparta, a fossilized military encampment, which exerted a strange magnetic attraction on Athenian critics of democracy. In the first place, the two upper classes may not possess private property, and they must live a communal life sharing housing and meals (416 D; V 457 B ff.). It is of decisive importance to keep economic and political power separate, and, as production is in private hands, it is misleading to call the Platonic state communist merely because the leading classes share the same material conditions of life.

In the second place, there is to be equality between men and women (451 D ff.), which is to say that women can also become auxiliaries or rulers – usually women are not as well equipped as men, but in principle there is only biological difference between the two sexes, according to Plato. He presents his ideas as something quite revolutionary, but although the position of women in Athens was far from enviable, this thought cannot have taken an Attic public by surprise (cf. p. 114). Probably, however, Plato did not think as much of the rights of women as of their duties. Women are unused resources and they are made equal on the conditions of a male society. Plato did not entertain a romantic attitude to women nor to love between man and woman, and it is indeed consistent that family life is dispensed with for auxiliaries and rulers (457 B ff.). The specific prescriptions adhere to their own grotesque logic: eugenic selection of partners, organized couplings with cunning rules intended to prevent parents from knowing their children – as all belong to one greater family – and the exposure of deformed children.

The *raison d'etat* seems to precede everything. Still, it is not all that uncomplicated. The entire construct of a model state was a tentative answer to the question of human justice. The aim was not some utopian state but an analysis of the concept of justice. How does it look if we proceed from the capital letters to small ones?

Seemingly Plato has a simple answer ready to hand. If the state is to have a moral basis, the division of labour must be morally justified, i.e. with reference to traditional civic virtues: wisdom, courage, self-discipline (*sōphrosynē*), and justice – the so-called cardinal virtues (IV 427 D ff.) – and fortunately it turns out that these virtues can be attributed to social classes or functions. Wisdom resides in the rulers, and courage in the auxiliaries (429 A ff.). Self-discipline, which consists of keeping lust and desire in check, must be present in all classes, and justice can then be considered the proper relation between the social classes as expressed in the phrase 'to do one's own task' (432 B ff.).

Once the analogy between state and man has been established, the virtues must be both social and individual. Society is neither more nor less than the sum of its members, and just as the virtues can be related to the social structure, so they must also correspond with the psychological constitution of man (434 D ff.). Now, man has several psychological functions, and psychological inclinations may, as we know, conflict. How can one psyche come into conflict with itself? Of course one cannot attribute opposites to one object in the same respect and at the same time (436 B – cf. Aristotle's principle of contradiction). But just as a top spinning around itself in the same spot in one respect is in motion and in another at rest, so there is nothing strange about the 'same' soul's wanting to do several things at once, provided that the differing inclinations are attributed to different elements or 'parts' of the soul. In fact, the soul has three 'parts' (439 D ff.): reason – corresponding with the virtue of wisdom; vigour and energy – corresponding with the virtue of courage; and finally desire that is kept in check by self-discipline. In other words, one finds the same tripartition in man as in the state, and, as in the state, in man it is also justice that guarantees that each part of the soul 'does its task'. In other words: reason governs the other two parts of the soul, just as the wise rulers govern the state (441 C ff.). Wherever injustice prevails each part strives for mastery; this will lead to civil war in the state – two states in one state – and to psychic conflicts in man (423 A; 444 B).

The schematic surface conceals both problems and important points. In the first place, the parallel between state and individual is only completed by the perfect state and the perfect individual, the wise ruler. A member of the working population may perhaps, now and then, perform a brave or wise act, just as the auxiliary in a bright moment may be wise, even though this is not a part of his nature, and accordingly the lower classes are in a manner of speaking amputated individuals. Plato's answer would probably be rather heavy-handed: in fact only the wise man is perfect, although this does not preclude that the others can be happy under the authority of the wise.

But there is, all in all, something strange about the schematics. The several virtues present themselves all too readily at the convenient moment. The 'definition' of justice is a typical persuasive definition and is far from living up to a Socratic definition. For how can the essence of justice consist in a relation? Plato knows that he has not defined justice (435 A). We find ourselves at a provisional stage where nothing else is possible but – by 'rubbing the arguments against each other' – to investigate whether the analogy between state and man seems productive. A proper definition of the essence of justice requires a lengthy detour (435 D; cf. V 472 B; VI 504 B).

Furthermore, the concepts of 'virtue' and 'soul' seem un-Socratic at first sight. What has happened to *phronēsis*, that Socratic insight which warrants the unity behind the traditional virtues, and what about the belief in the indivisible soul in the *Phaedo*? In the passage in the *Republic* there is in fact a shift in the content of these two concepts below the surface. We commence with the 'civic virtues' (cf. e.g. *RP* IV 430 C), which is to say with those acts that make society functional, but this does not reveal the essence of a particular virtue, nor virtue considered ideally. Something similar applies to the tri-partite soul, which hardly signals a principal change in Plato's view of the soul. Indeed he has more in mind. Empirically the soul has to be described by its psychic functions, and from that point of view the three parts of the soul are nothing but the functions or patterns of human behaviour. But on the ideal plane the soul is identified with reason, and in the conclusion of the passage the empirical frame of reference is abandoned (443 C ff.): reason creates unity out of multiplicity, and thereby the concepts of morality and of justice will also be altered in their contents. An act-centred ethics has been replaced by an agent-centred ethics; virtue is no longer dependent on external action but on the inner man, and morality is no longer a question of which acts to perform, nor a question of duty, but of the constitution of a man who acts morally. Hence 'to do one's own task' does not mean merely to tend to one's profession, but to act as a moral being.

That being so, it is possible – at least provisionally – to provide an answer to the problem that was introduced in Book II: if 'inner justice' is an expression of psychic harmony, to act justly will be its own reward – to do otherwise would land one in conflict with oneself.

It now looks as if we have two loose ends. On the one hand there is a rigoristic and wilful construction of an 'ideal state' in which rational principles replace the egotistical *laissez faire* of the state of luxury – apparently regardless of the individual. On the other hand, we have an analysis of the relation between social and individual ethics with emphasis on the individual's – the philosopher's – moral integrity. Apparently the concept of man has not been determined exhaustively, neither man as a social creature nor as an individual. And: justice has not been analyzed thoroughly enough.

'THE STATE IN HEAVEN' AND THE DECLINE OF THE STATE: BOOKS V–X

Plato does not present the problem in such a direct manner. He returns to the 'ideal state' that has now been constructed, and he asks whether it can be realized (V 471 C ff.). Hitherto the focus has only been on the ideal paradigm, which has been worked out 'playfully', as we are characteristically told (VII 536 C). It is stressed that a realization can only be an approximation to the ideal – practice is more remote from 'reality' than theory, but with that modification the 'ideal state' will be realizable, provided that one reform is effectuated: either the philosophers become rulers, or the rulers become philosophers (V 473 B; cf. VII 540 D). We must think of this taking place by means of a *coup d'état* whereby the philosopher for once and for all can 'clean the slate' (VI 501 A) and rusticate all inhabitants more than ten years of age (VII 541 A)! It is left unsaid whether such a *coup* is a realistic possibility. In the reality of theory it is decisive that government is entrusted to those who are above self-interest and who therefore do not wish for power (520 D).

It is not until now that we are given an explanation for the division of the upper classes. To use the language of the allegory of the cave, the future philosopher-rulers must be led up into the light and then be compelled to return to their fellow prisoners, and they must – in the symbolism of the allegory of the line – submit to an education leading from the next-highest to the highest sector, from mathematics to dialectics. Plato envisions an elitist education that is to follow the basic character-building curriculum with numerous 'tests' along the way. The philosopher-to-be must study mathematics from the age of twenty to thirty, then dialectics for five years, and following that he is to be trained in practical administrative matters for fifteen years. Thus, at the age of fifty he has matured as a philosopher-ruler – and in due time he will journey to the Blessed Isles amidst praise and respect (VII 537 B ff.).

The education in mathematics is described in an immediate sequel to the main metaphysical section of the *Republic*, and thereby it is an indication that it is intended as a guide to knowledge of the ideas and the good. This education, which surely reflects Academy teaching, and which formed the basis of the *quadrivium* of Hellenistic and medieval education, includes arithmetic, geometry (with the sub-branches of plane geometry and stereometry), astronomy, and the theory of harmony or music. It is, in other words, a clear progression from more to less general mathematical disciplines. Yet it is not for the sake of mathematics that the future philosopher-ruler should submit to this curriculum; rather it is because mathematics can 'draw the soul upwards' towards the intelligible (523 A ff.) – mathematics deals with idealized objects, and, if properly pursued, it will occasion reflections about the presuppositions of its own conceptual apparatus and method. Plato provides an example: we sense immediately a finger as a finger, this does not call for further reflection. But it will do so, on the other hand, when we consider that one object in one respect is a unity, in another a plurality, that the finger may be called both large and small, etc. The example recalls the *Phaedo* and shows that number and relational quantitative concepts are well-suited for reflection.

In his examination of the several mathematical disciplines, Plato constantly stresses that the issue is about intelligible objects and pure rational thought. Astronomy, for example (528 E ff.), is not an empirical science, and observation will not lead us far unless it is sustained by theoretical insight into that 'reality' that lies behind: the eternal laws of motion.

What Plato is aiming for is that balance between empiricism and theory, which alone makes the phenomena comprehensible. According to tradition, Eudoxus' explanation of the movement of the planets (see p. 328 and p. 414) is indebted to a Platonic exhortation to 'save the phenomena' (cf. Simpl. in Aristot. *De caelo* 488, 18 ff., Heiberg).

There is no section on the teaching of dialectics.

Whether or not philosopher-rulers will ever appear in the real world, it is clear that the ideal philosopher in his person is a warrant that the perfect state is based on the idea of the good. It is true that justice – civic virtue – is never defined, but in the metaphysical sections we have traversed 'the long detour', and from the analogy of the sun we know that justice is an empty concept unless it is based on the good (*RP* VI 505 A; cf. VII 540 E). Through knowledge of the good the discussion has been led to a higher level. Does this mean that the construction of the state that was laid down with such self-assurance – although without any firm foundation – now in a manner of speaking is legitimated retroactively? Furthermore, does this mean that the two loose ends – man as individual and man as social creature – can now become one? The answer is ambiguous, and Plato is not overly communicative.

To know the good was no straightforward matter, and one should not expect that the perfect state might be constructed by a simple deduction from the idea of the good. Besides, there is something else. Plato does not employ the designation 'idea' about his perfect state. It is, rather, a pattern existing in heaven (IX 592 A) – no matter whether censorship and the exposure of children take place there. The idea of justice is the subject of this dialogue. The construction of a model state depends on technical ability, a practical knowledge that attempts to transfer theoretical insight into the essence of justice to the fragile world of humanity. When the philosopher returns to the cave he must attempt to make the best of what he encounters. The analogy of the human being and the state is here an heuristic principle that may contribute what it can – with reason as guide and with the certainty of the good as an inspiration. Socrates himself labels his state construction a 'myth of argument' (VI 501 E; cf. VII 536 C).

The composition of the *Republic* is like the dialectical path in the simile of the line and like the philosopher's going up into the light and back down into the cave. The development of the concept of justice illustrates the stages of the 'ascent': first comes civic virtue, then psychic harmony, and finally metaphysically justified 'virtue'. 'The descent' of Books VIII and IX consists of an examination of what will happen if the perfect state declines – in other words a description of injustice. It goes without saying that any change in the perfect state will be detrimental (cf. VIII 545 D). The description of the decline adheres to this hypothetical process but is in fact systematically worked out, and indirectly it provides Plato with an opportunity to evaluate existing Greek forms of constitution according to a norm. In the perfect state the philosopher is an ideal person who by definition always acts for the good. But if the rulers no longer live up to the ideal, a process of moral degeneration will ensue. The perfect state is corrupted at the very moment when harmony and mutual social concord are destroyed by private interest. In the first place, this is due to personal ambition, and secondly to economic considerations and the introduction of rights to private property. Of logical necessity the state will gradually become divided into two or more 'states' at war with one another, and the like will pertain to the individual, because reason no longer governs aggression and ambition, and by and by, as the state no longer constitutes a natural unity, parasites will appear – 'the drones' – who are contemptuous of society and use it only for their own benefit. The individual stages in the decline are: timocracy, in which the ambitious ('the auxiliaries') suppress the working population (545 D ff.; in 544 C Sparta is cited as an example); oligarchy, in which a wealthy upper class confronts the proletariat (550 C ff.); democracy, in which all social norms are abandoned (555 B ff.); and tyranny, the criminal, totalitarian society, in which one person makes himself the master and enslaves all society as well as himself (526 A ff.). The descriptions of democracy – Athens, of course – and tyranny contain especially thorough social and psychological analyses. It is said that in a democracy everybody is free and can do 'what he wishes'. This sounds attractive, but it is an unprincipled freedom, a freedom to nothing, in which the politicians pander to 'the great beast', but one in which everybody is in fact at war with everybody else. In such a situation the strong man can seize power supported by all those who are dissatisfied and frustrated. But the outcome will be a society characterized by total dissolution, suppression, and fear, and the tyrant – the standard example of the day of the 'happiest man' (Gyges) – will himself become the least free of all as he surrenders to his own thirst for power and constant fear of his subjects. To the modern reader this depiction of the development from corrupt democracy to dictatorship seems chillingly far-sighted, and whoever has read the description of the Platonic tyrant will find it difficult to understand how the author could be regarded as an advocate of the totalitarian state.

The real challenge in Plato's time and in our own lies of course in the fact that Plato's 'ideal state' is based on a special view of man that subordinates both man and state to one concept, the concept of the good. Thereby the totalitarian state is precluded, but so are also, for example, pluralism and individualism in the modern sense, and history seems annulled. Plato seeks for a balance between state and individual, which to the modern reader seems to curtail the individual's rights; a reader from Antiquity may very well have been surprised that the power of the state must be legitimated from a legal point of view. But the idealized and realistic elements in the construction of the state come into conflict with each other: the ideal philosopher is justice incarnate; he is in a manner of speaking the spokesman of the idea, and he is always right; his subjects are ordinary people who must be guided to the good life. For this reason as well, it is reasonable to ask what Plato's own position is with respect to the construction of the state or to his 'myth of argument'. The ideal state could only come about on the presupposition that the ruler and the philosopher were united in one person – undeniably an utopian presupposition. Near the end of the section about the decline of the state we are told that the perfect constitution may exist in heaven, and that it may serve as a paradigm for the man who wants to lay down the perfect constitution in his inner self (IX 592 B).

This conclusion does not come as a surprise. In the course of the examination of the types of constitution there is steadily more emphasis, not on democracy and tyranny but on democratic man and tyrannical man, and Plato concentrates on an appeal to the individual, which is powerfully expressed in the sentence: 'Ariston's son judges that the happiest man is he whose goodness and justice are the greatest' (580 C) – Ariston's son: in the context this son is Glaucon. But Plato was Ariston's son as well, and this is probably as close as we get to a direct message from the remote Plato himself. The discussion has returned to its beginning. Twice Glaucon and Adeimantus have been provided with what they wished for, the rationale that explains why justice has its goal in itself and 'pays off'. The first time, this was carried out on a provisional empirical basis: the harmonious man creates unity out of his 'tri-partite' soul. The second time – after the metaphysical books – a just human life is founded on the idea of the good, just as true *erōs* was treated metaphysically in the *Phaedrus*. In both cases there has been a shift away from an act ethics to an agent ethics: the just man is he who in his inner self conforms with the good.

In the last books of the *Republic* the dual nature of man is emphasized. Empirical man is filled with conflict – he is like a fabled beast, combining a many-headed monster (desire), a lion (aggression), and real man (588 C ff.), or like Glaucus, the sea-god, with his body fearfully wounded and covered with mussels, seaweed, and grass that conceal his original nature (X 611 C). The ideal human being is real man. He only is related to the divine, and only he has the possibility of becoming happy.

The tenth book is often seen as an appendix and may seem constructed with brittle mortar. First comes the section on poetry as imitation (595 A ff., see above), then follow two sections, which, supported by extremely lax arguments, establish two theses. The first states that man's soul is immortal, that the soul may be disfigured but never destroyed by injustice, and that in the perspective of eternity, life on earth is but a brief episode (608 C ff.). The second states that goodness is its own reward, and Socrates – who paid with his life – asks if we do not know that the good man in the long run is rewarded in this life (612 B ff.)? So much for anybody who would demand a tangible 'reward'.

Finally follows a myth (614 B ff.) that does not know of an 'ideal state'. There was a man, Er, who was allowed to return to life in order to tell of the fate of the souls in the underworld. In vivid and terrifying detail he tells how the souls – having suffered the punishments they deserved or having received their just rewards – must choose another life on earth. They choose freely, but he who chooses must take the blame himself. God is without blame. And the soul that has chosen is bound to his fate by the law of necessity (617 D ff.). Many are tempted and choose a life in outward splendour, but it would be wiser to do as Ulysses (620 C) and choose a life in quiet withdrawal in the knowledge that what matters is how one uses one's talents.

As is the case with the *Gorgias* and the *Phaedo*, this myth is in strange contrast to the rest of the work. If it is read literally, it undeniably works as stale utilitarian moralizing. We are not far from Cephalus' pedestrian presentiments about the possible final reckoning in the beyond. And the relationship between freedom and necessity is reminiscent of the fatalism of a tragedy. Yet, as is characteristic of an eschatological myth, there is one clear-cut imperative, which makes its way through the ambiguous symbolism: the choice is your own, and you are responsible.

But the myth of the *Republic* is more than usually filled with contrasts. Along the road on this long walk we have heard of a 'myth of the state'; the construction of the ideal state has been called a 'myth of argument'; and in the end, as a contrast to dangerous poetry that leads one astray, we are provided with a symbolically true Platonic myth, which *sub specie aeternitatis* appeals to both Cephalus and Socrates. Plato is indeed the master of indirect communication.

What remains unaffected by the concealed reservations is the metaphysical basis for a moral and social life; the analysis of justice and injustice; the establishment of an agent morality; the appeal to the individual; and, most important, the basic vision of this work – the ascent to the ideal world and the return. Yet there are ambiguities which surely are different from and more than artful compositional devices. There is the contrast between argument and myth, the focal shift between the good constitution of state and man, the interplay between the ideal model and realism, and perhaps there is latent discord in the overall construction of the work – between contemplative and political man. The bitter conclusion is that the perfect state is only a heavenly paradigm – the philosopher must live his life in internal exile and long for a miracle.

Probably Plato's thoughts about the state – including his ethics and paedagogics – did not constitute a harmonious whole. Most of his dialogues are conspicuously apolitical – they concern the ideal philosopher and are addressed to the ideal reader. Both are found everywhere and nowhere. Yet Plato could not be content with speaking abstractly to his reader without regard to time and place. His political commitment was too firmly rooted. Like his infamous uncle, he wanted to steer the state on to the path of justice – although in a manner different from that of Critias: a happy social life must depend on rational principles. After the *Republic*, Plato had the choice between pure thought or the role of the sage who conceives of a deliberately utopian state. The late dialogues show that he chose both.

16

THE LATE DIALOGUES: KNOWLEDGE AND BEING

——— •◆• ———

The years after c.370 saw the last phase of Plato's work. In this period the dialogues are more 'technical' than the classical ones, and surely they reflect more clearly the debates at the Academy. Without surrendering his basic philosophical position, Plato undertook in these dialogues a series of profound analyses going beyond the conclusions arrived at or suggested, for example in the *Phaedo* or the *Republic*. The dialogues signal renewed interest in the Presocratic tradition – primarily the Eleatics and the Pythagoreans – and gradually Socrates ceases to be the leader of the debate, although his authority remains unchallenged.

The *Parmenides* and *Theaetetus* can be thought of as roughly contemporary, although the *Theaetetus*, judging from a 'reference' in it to the *Parmenides* (183 E), seems to have been concluded later. Each of the dialogues deals with one basic problem. In the *Theaetetus* the question is: what is knowledge? In the *Parmenides* the question is about the basis of metaphysics, the One and Being. In both cases the discussion is about concepts which Socrates has presupposed throughout – or which have been lost in ambiguity. What is the precondition for existence? How can knowledge be known? We cannot expect the two dialogues to solve insoluble problems but rather to analyze the implications of the questions.

THE *PARMENIDES*

The *Parmenides* is Plato's most cryptic dialogue. To the Neoplatonists it was a bible, and owing to Neoplatonic interpretation it has exerted considerable direct and indirect influence. There is no consensus among modern scholars, and the reason lies in the text itself. Plato has carefully plotted the difficulties in this dialogue – a discourse between the ageing Parmenides, his student Zeno, and a Socrates only about twenty years old. It is concluded by Parmenides conducting a strict dialectical demonstration, which with all its riddles is left without commentary.

In chronological terms the discussion might have taken place, but of course it is fictional from beginning to end. The principal characters are Plato's two great teachers, a Parmenides who apparently has become a Platonist in his old age and a very young Socrates who is about to be taught Socratic insight by Parmenides (and Plato).

The dialogue falls into two parts, which formally are sharply divided. The point of departure is Zeno's famous treatise, which, according to Plato, comes 'to the rescue' of Parmenides by reducing the supposition of plurality *ad absurdum* (*Parm.* 127 D ff.). There is special allusion to one partial argument, which concurs well with what we otherwise know of Zeno's treatise. If there is a plurality of 'existing things', these will be both 'like' and 'unlike', which is a clear-cut self-contradiction. From an orthodox Eleatic point of view x cannot be 'like' (y) and at the same time 'unlike' (z).

However, the young Socrates has a solution to the problem, which both legitimates the existence of a plurality and normal predicative sentences. He distinguishes (128 E ff.) between a world of sensible phenomena and a world of ideas. The idea of likeness can never become unlike, but there is nothing to prevent the same phenomenon from participating in likeness in one respect and unlikeness in another. A man, for example, is both one and many – he has a back, a stomach, etc. But if it can be shown that the ideas can be predicated of each other, so that the 'like', for example, in itself is 'unlike' and thereby many, then there is indeed cause for amazement. In other words, the twenty-year-old Socrates is very familiar with the doctrine of ideas and the theory of participation, which the seventy-year-old Socrates presents in the *Phaedo*, and indeed the *Phaedo* is the concealed frame of reference in the following.

The discussion between Zeno and Socrates is, however, merely an introduction to a critique presented by Parmenides (130 A ff.). The young Socrates is unable to defend himself. Indirectly he is taught that there is a difference between having a theory and understanding it – a lesson he was later to make use of.

Parmenides' criticism is quite schematically constructed. First he asks Socrates for which entities he is prepared to assume ideas. Are there only mathematical and ethical ideas? Or, are there also 'neutral' ideas, for example of natural species, or ideas of 'less worthy' topics, such as filth? In other words, the question is about the relation between the universal and the normative in the doctrine of ideas, which is perhaps the most challenging question that can be asked of Socrates and Plato. The young Socrates cannot come up with an answer, and Parmenides proceeds to another crucial problem, that of the one idea *vis-à-vis* the many phenomena. He examines the concept of participation point by point:

1   Does a phenomenon participate in the idea as a whole or only in part of the idea (130 E ff.; cf. *Phil.* 15 B)? In both cases the idea becomes separated from itself, as it would be divided and distributed among the individual phenomena – of course on the presupposition that ideas are conceived of as material entities, 'things', on the same level as phenomena, and provided that participation is a material relation. It is discreetly suggested that there is a way out of the dilemma (*Parm.* 131 B), and Parmenides himself is helpful in conducting it *ad absurdum*: if the phenomenon x is 'big' or 'small' because it participates in a part of 'bigness' or 'smallness', then it is accordingly big by virtue of the small, small by virtue of something that is smaller than 'the small'.

2   If the idea – on the same presupposition – were a member of its own class, this would lead to equally absurd logical consequences (131 E ff.): suppose that any big 'thing' is big by virtue of participation in something else – 'bigness', and suppose that the 'big itself' is big; in that case if 'bigness' is put on equal footing with big 'things', it should participate in something other than itself, and then there would be a new 'idea of bigness', by virtue of which any big 'thing' and 'the big itself' are big – and so forth *ad infinitum*. One of the premises of the argument – that the phenomena participate in the idea and therefore are different from it – is an orthodox Platonic one, but the other – the 'self-predication' of the idea – calls for a comment. The sentences 'x is big' and 'the big is big' have the same linguistic form, but to Plato they have different logical structures. The first sentence, in which 'is' functions as a copula, can, according to the *Phaedo,* be transformed into 'x participates in the big', while the second denotes an identity. And obviously Plato did not consider the argument conclusive (cf. *RP* X 597 B; *Tim.* 31 A; cf. also the argument in *Parm.* 150 A).

3   The first two objections imply an extreme, materialistic view of the concept of idea. The young Socrates now changes course and proposes a conceptualistic explanation (132 B ff.): perhaps the ideas exist only as thoughts in the mind. But Parmenides refutes him immediately – just as his historical namesake undoubtedly would have done: a thought must be a thought about something that is, and the world cannot consist of thoughts about thoughts. Socrates' proposal is the oldest formulation of a 'nominalist' understanding of concepts; but on the premises of the time – not on Plato's only – it must be rejected without further ado.

4   The idea is not a 'thing', nor is it a thought. Is it perhaps an ontological entity of a higher order (132 C ff.)? Socrates proposes that the idea is a pattern, the phenomena likenesses. Once more Parmenides refutes him: two entities are alike by virtue of a third, and consequently there must be a new entity that warrants the likeness of idea to phenomenon – and so on in an infinite regress, similar to the one we saw above. This refutation presupposes once more that idea and phenomenon are entities on the same level, and it fails to take the asymmetrical relation between copy and original into account, even though this had been heavily stressed in the *Phaedo*. In fact, Plato never abandoned the thought of the idea as a paradigm for the phenomenon (cf. *Tim.* 29 B; 52 A).

These four objections must in the view of the defenceless young Socrates make participation a suspect concept, and so Parmenides can spell out the corollary (*Parm.* 133 A ff.): there can be no connection between ideas and phenomena; ideas are related to ideas; phenomena to phenomena; and knowledge is either correlated to ideas or to phenomena – the continuity in the simile of the line seems broken.

Parmenides commences his criticism with a genuine Platonic problem, but as the thumbscrew is gradually turned, he dextrously slips in an interpretation of the doctrine of ideas, which Plato would never have condoned. Why does he do so?

Some of the explanation can be found in internal Academy debates, about which we are partly informed. Apparently they had the same point-by-point character, and we can surmise that the debaters did not slavishly confine themselves to orthodox

Platonic answers. For instance, the thought of 'literal', material participation was advocated (by Eudoxus, cf. Alex. Aphr. in Aristot. *Met.* 97,27 ff. = Aristot. Περὶ ἰδεῶν, frg. 5 Ross). The dilemma of the self-predication of ideas must have been discussed with the idea of man as exemplification, which is why it was called 'the third man' in Academy jargon (cf. *Met.* 990 b 17; 1039 a 2; *Soph. el.* 178 b 36; Alex. Aphr. in *Met.* 83,34 = Aristot. Περὶ ἰδεῶν, frg. 4 Ross). That the problem of participation in general has been a subject of debate is evident from Aristotle (cf. *Met.* 987 b 13; 991 a 22). The field of application of the ideas was also debated, and attempts were made to prove the doctrine of ideas (see p. 261). Plato must have had ample reasons to speak, and this also because the series of questions requires a proof of the doctrine itself, which, according to the *Phaedo*, is an impossibility.

It is one thing to allow Parmenides to demonstrate how not to read the *Phaedo*: the idea is neither a material entity nor a phenomenon of consciousness; participation is not a symmetrical relation; and one should not expect the fundamental theory – the doctrine of ideas including the theory of participation – to be justified by a theory of similar type. But it is another matter how to read the *Phaedo*? Is there no way of answering the questions that have been raised? Is there perhaps some 'meta-theory' that can throw light on the ultimate presuppositions: is the doctrine of ideas merely a postulate, or must it simply be abandoned?

Parmenides himself denies this latter possibility. He concludes his criticism of Socrates with unambiguous approval of the doctrine of ideas (*Parm.* 134 E ff.): difficulties of the sort he has just discussed may make an untrained mind doubt that ideas exist. But if one denies the existence of the ideas, the possibility of dialectics is destroyed. The doctrine of ideas is necessary, but the solution of the problems that the theory raises demands extraordinary insight, and the young Socrates has launched his theory without sufficient theoretical training (135 C). Reluctantly Parmenides takes upon himself the 'laborious game' to provide a sample of such training by means of an analysis of 'his own *hypothesis*': the One is (137 B) – which is to say an examination of the concepts of unity and being, the most fundamental concepts for the historical Parmenides and perhaps for Plato as well.

What language do we use when we speak about ideas? In the Platonic universe one cannot speak of a phenomenon without reference to an idea, and an idea is essentially defined by 'being' and 'being one' in an unqualified sense. What directly holds good for ideas, holds good indirectly for phenomena, and next to 'unity' and 'being' other formal terms and concepts will appear, which not only are parts of but preconditions for language and knowledge, indeed for saying that something exists. Any given entity and any given 'something' must be 'one', 'being', 'identical' (with itself), 'different' (from something else), etc. Such primitive or elementary concepts are indefinable, but it must be possible to demonstrate their mutual dialectics, their way of functioning in language and cognition, and to Plato this includes their metaphysical status. Such an analysis will perhaps turn the discussion of participation into a pseudo-problem or show that the problem must be formulated in a manner different from Socrates' and Parmenides' in their debate.

Parmenides hints (135 E) that he will include the ideas in his investigation, but he does not say how he will do so. Instead he concentrates on the formal aspect, and he adopts Zeno's procedure, although in an improved version (cf. 136 A). When one speaks about the One, one must also speak about the other: 'the One' implies its own complement, 'the not-one', and if one poses the sentence 'the One is' as a *hypothesis*, one must also negate the *hypothesis*. Of each of these presuppositions one must furthermore ask about the consequences for the One in itself and in relation to its complement and about the not-one in itself and in relation to the One. Thereby eight formal positions are produced, corresponding to the eight partial arguments – often called hypotheses – which two by two constitute the second and more extensive part of the dialogue.

Each series of arguments or 'hypothesis' follows the Eleatic practice of confronting a 'subject', 'the One' or 'the not-one' with a set series of 'predicates' arranged as pairs; thus the question is asked whether the One can be predicated with 'part/whole', whether it is limited or unlimited, whether it is placed in space (in itself or in something else), whether it is in motion or at rest, whether it is 'identical' or 'different', 'like' or 'unlike', and whether it exists in time (whether it is 'older' or 'younger'). 'The predicates' belong to the set Eleatic conceptual apparatus but have at least equal Platonic relevance: they are not concepts of things, but quite general formal concepts, frequently relations; and time and space are considered along with concepts that are not of necessity temporally or spatially bound. To us this is conceptual analysis, but to both the Eleatics and Plato this is tantamount to ontological or metaphysical analysis. 'The One' or 'unity' does not signify the concept of unity but that which in an unqualified sense and simply is one. But what is said about the simply One must hold good for everything that in a derived sense might be one – in Platonic terms: for both the world of ideas and the world of phenomena.

Strictly speaking, the labels 'subject' and 'predicate' are misleading. When Parmenides for example asks if it 'befalls' the One to 'become like', one should not imagine a well-defined subject, which may or may not have 'like' as predicate, but – metaphysically-logically – an entity that is 'like' by virtue of the fact that it is. Exactly such conceptual relations would have astonished the young Socrates, and he cannot make use of his theory of predication on a level that is so fundamental that 'subject' and 'predicate' are not fixed concepts. The agreement with the 'signs' of Being in the historical Parmenides are, on the other hand, evident.

The text does not – as in a normal Platonic dialogue – inform us of the reaction of the interlocutors. We are merely presented with the stripped-down arguments – for example, as in Euclid's *Elements* – which are only interrupted when a new interlocutor, ironically enough called Aristotle, says 'yes' in the right places. The seeming conclusion of the dialogue goes like this: 'Whether the One is or is not, it seems that both the One and the not-one in themselves and with respect to one another both are and are not, both appear and do not appear to be everything in every way' (166 C). This 'conclusion' alone should make it understandable that agreement about the interpretation of the second part of the *Parmenides* has never been reached: it has been read as a parody on Eleatic argumentation, as an exercise in logic – perhaps as an exercise in how to spot fallacies – as an account of a first principle with derived metaphysical levels (this is the 'Neoplatonic' reading), or as metaphysics in general. Of course these possible interpretations can be combined.

Each series of arguments draws conclusions from an assumed presupposition and that corresponds with the form of insight, which, in the simile of the line, belongs in the next-highest section. Throughout there are precise indications of the meaning to be attached to the original *hypothesis*, and with this stipulation in mind it is hardly possible to characterize any single argument as invalid. However, it is invalid when the final conclusion presupposes that all deductions have had unequivocally identical premisses so that actual disjunctions are seen as conjunctions – but after all, this was what Zeno did. And within one deduction – most strikingly perhaps in the second *hypothesis* – there are notable leaps from a 'metaphysical' entity to an entity in time and space – perhaps also as in Zeno? Perhaps because the whole universe – including the phenomena – has to be taken into consideration?

It is also in agreement with Eleatic practice that the series of arguments are presented as antinomies – whatever one hypothesis confirms is denied by the next. And it turns out that the basic hypothesis – 'if the One is' – leads both to the conclusion that it does not exist at all and that it is a plurality or 'everything in every way'. Clearly, this may be interpreted as a 'game', as Parmenides himself calls it, or as a parody of the Eleatics – coming from the mouth of Parmenides himself. But there is more to the text than a good jest or parody will warrant, and also quite a lot that points to Plato himself.

The following attempt at interpretation, which of course is as controversial as all others, relies on the assumption that the antinomies are meaningful and that behind the formal structure of the dialogue lies a hidden structure of contents – if so, a mode of procedure that is characteristic of most of Plato's late dialogues. It can hardly be denied that throughout certain patterns of thought are perceptible behind the formal structure. Only a few principal points will be mentioned here.

The relation between the first and second hypotheses is crucial. The first hypothesis (137 C-42 A) interprets the initial thesis so that unity only can be related to itself. Thereby being is excluded, but furthermore all the remaining formal characteristics are thereby excluded as well, both the positive and negative. The One cannot be conceptually related, for example to likeness and unlikeness, and it cannot exist in time and space. But then it cannot be related to itself either; it cannot even be in the sense that it is one; and it is not knowable (141 E). Accordingly the chosen presupposition cancels itself – although apparently only if unity is thought to exist in time and space.

So the second hypothesis – the most extensive in the investigation (142 B-55 E) – presupposes a connection between unity and being. 'The One' can be *one* without being, but it can only *be* one by having being. In a 'One being', unity and being will imply one another so that the two concepts have the same extension but are conceptually distinct. In other words, the starting point is two 'entities' in one: but at the very moment when there is more than one 'entity', the possibility exists of a combination of entities and consequently of a plurality. The 'original' unity can in this manner be multiplied in an infinite series of numerically different unities. If there is a One being, there is a multitude, and if there is a multitude, there is a number. In this way the concept of number is definable from the concept of plurality (143 C ff.; cf. *Soph.* 238 A). But if there is a plurality of unities, there is also a plurality of formal characteristics; the One being pulls the entire series of formal characteristics along – one is entitled to speak not only about limited and unlimited, like and unlike, etc., but also about being in time and space, and about knowable being.

Two points are of special interest: in the first place, the paradox that the One being at least conceptually presupposes pure unity, which according to the first hypothesis could not exist – without the One nothing exists at all, we are told later (*Parm.* 166 C). This was a principal point according to 'Neoplatonic' interpretation (Plotinus, Proclus), which identified the concept of unity of the first hypothesis with the good in the *Republic*, in other words with a transcendent first principle beyond time and space and beyond knowledge and being. The interpretation is wrong, inasmuch as nothing is *said* in the first hypothesis about an unknowable first principle. But if it is correct that the other hypotheses presuppose such a principle, then the first hypothesis is the logical place for it. In the second place, the concepts of unity and being cannot be defined by the other formal concepts; they imply them. One concept cannot be deduced from another, but if unity and being exist, conceptual relations *eo ipso* exist.

Apparently it is necessary to accept a double antinomy: the unity that *is* presupposes the unity that *is-not*, and if being *is* one, there will also be many; unity implies non-unity or 'otherness'. Thus Parmenides has provided himself and the young Socrates with matter for reflection. Are there 'Platonic' perspectives?

In the course of the second hypothesis we are furnished with a close analysis of the relation between one and many, identity and difference, whole and part, finite and infinite, and this analysis is elaborated on from other angles in the later hypotheses (cf. especially the third hypothesis, 157 B-9 D). It seems to be a principle (formulated in 146 B) that a given unity can be related to itself – be 'identical' – or to 'the other' – be 'different' – but that it can also be considered as a whole consisting of parts, or as a part of a whole – the whole is one, the part is also one, and *qua* whole the whole is more than its parts. A whole is a finite structure. It is one *qua* structure or system, although it consists of a finite number of independent unities. These unities may stand in certain relations to one another, but they can also be related to an infinite multitude without number – the 'something' that may become a finite multitude. The text only speaks abstractly, but the terminology that is used is basic to the formal language of the doctrine of ideas: an idea is a One being in itself, it joins a system of ideas, and it is related to an infinite multitude, which may 'become', but which not simply 'are' (phenomena). Consequences of this kind are drawn in later works by Plato (the *Sophist*, *Philebus* and *Timaeus*).

But further specification is required. An appendix has been added to the first and second hypotheses (155 E-7 B). The purpose of this is apparently not to cancel the contrast but to point to a paradox, which must be accepted if one wishes to consider the two hypotheses complementarily valid. The unity of the first hypothesis can be transformed into that of the second hypothesis; in the second hypothesis everything seems to participate in everything, even though it is also implicit that something 'becomes' something. The One can pass from non-existence to existence, from motion to rest, from, for example, 'like' to 'unlike'. How does such a shift take place? It may seem to take place in time, but this leads to all those paradoxes that adhere to the relation between continuity and discontinuity, which we know from Zeno. How does the present become the past and the future the present, is time relative or absolute, can an entity pass from state x to state non-x for a stretch of time when it is both x and non-x? The transition must take place in a non-fixable moment, the 'sudden' (*to exaiphnēs* – 156 D), which is a precondition of time, but lies beyond time as a sequel of past, present, and future. Accordingly, being is not bound to a time *in which* something happens. 'The sudden' is a limiting concept, but it is a precondition for any change whatsoever – both with respect to placement in time and space and change of predicate. Thereby the concept has relevance both for a theory of predication and for a theory of physics. Aristotle was to make use of the latter.

The hypotheses, which assume that the one is not, make a series of distinctions between non-being, understood absolutely, and conditional being. Something can simply not-be, but it can also not-be in the sense that it can be determined what it is that it is not (the fifth hypothesis, Plat. *Parm.* 160 B-3 B). In part this means that it is possible to distinguish between being and essence, and in part that what is not – as we are told more elaborately in the *Sophist* – can be in the sense of 'being different from'. Finally, the not-one or the 'other' can be considered something that is only related to itself; then it is separated from unity and is only something other than something other (the seventh hypothesis, 164 B-5 E). It is consequently an entirely undetermined multitude, pure matter, or outright chaos. Plato returns several times to such a pseudo-world (see p. 223 and p. 242) – his phenomenal world would look like that, if it were not determined by the ideas.

There is no direct discussion of idea and phenomena anywhere in the text. But behind the scheme of argumentation there is a gradual discovery of an interplay between elementary concepts or formal conditions for both ideas, phenomena, and participation, which cannot allow themselves to be described unambiguously in a language presupposing ideas, phenomena, and participation. If one in spite of this attempts to express oneself in discursive argumentation anyway, it must be done hypothetically, and the outcome will be the 'laborious game', which among other things contains the ironic point that Zeno's antinomies are valid on a higher level. He who understands the laborious in the game will be able to see the world suspended between a principle, that unity which in itself is unknowable and non-being, and the 'otherness' that in itself is matter or nothing. The principle can only be 'understood' by means of that for which it is a principle, 'matter' only by means of that for which it is matter – in both cases a world in which unity implies plurality and plurality unity, in which being is related to not-being, finite to infinite, unity to being, being to becoming, and time to being and not-being. Parmenides has criticized himself, the young Socrates has been told why the debate in the first part of the dialogue must go astray, and readers of the *Phaedo* have been furnished with a commentary on the unprovability of the doctrine of ideas. Something suggests that curious members of the Academy also were given answers to some questions; after having learned that everything is everything and nothing, they may have stopped asking questions of their master.

THE *THEAETETUS*

The *Theaetetus* (completed after 369) is the only dialogue by Plato in which the contents are exclusively epistemological. The *Parmenides* discusses the doctrine of ideas and its ultimate presuppositions; in the *Theaetetus*, on the other hand, nobody appears to have heard of ideas. The two dialogues, each in its own way, prepare for the other late dialogues – especially the *Sophist* – but formally the *Theaetetus* is the last aporetic-Socratic dialogue. Socrates poses his famous 'what is x' question, and seemingly the dialogue reaches a totally negative conclusion.

Theaetetus, a young mathematician who appears to have contributed decisively to the understanding of incommensurables (cf. *Theaet.* 147 C ff.) and in whose memory the dialogue is written, is asked by Socrates what knowledge is. He attempts three successive definitions:

1   Knowledge is perception (151 D-86 E).
2   Knowledge is true belief (187 A-201 C).
3   Knowledge is true belief accompanied by an account (201 C-10 D).

Each of these attempts is treated as a Socratic-Platonic *hypothesis*; all are rejected, but they give rise to a thorough analysis of the concepts of perception (*aisthēsis*), opinion or belief (*doxa*), knowledge (*epistēmē*), and their epistemological status. As in a Socratic dialogue, the reasoning is conducted on non-Platonic premises, but throughout Socrates shows that the proposed definition will bring about yet more fundamental questions. Orthodox Platonic views are permitted to break through directly in only one passage. This happens abruptly, as a deliberately chosen contrast to the assumed premises, in a famous 'digression' (172 B-7 C) on the true philosopher who strives to become god-like, as far as is humanly possible.

Seemingly without ground Socrates ties the definition proposed first – that knowledge is the same as perception – to Protagoras' *homo mensura* sentence (151 E ff.; cf. p. 103), but it soon becomes clear how Protagoras can be exploited: his theory is interpreted – probably correctly – in an individualistic-relativistic direction. Things are to me as they appear to me. Next 'is perceived by' is substituted for 'appears to'. Thereby the formation of beliefs and judgements of value are excluded for the time being, and the focus can be directed on the ambiguous word 'appears': what appears to whom, and what do perceptual judgements signify in a world in which perception and the objects of perception are the only things seemingly in existence? From the very beginning the problem is given a special turn, as Socrates obtains Theaetetus' approval for yet one more fundamental premiss: knowledge is infallible and its object is what is. The argumentation that follows aims indirectly to demonstrate that this premiss must be interpreted on Plato's – not Protagoras' terms, and hence Theaetetus' concurrence on this point is actually the pivot of the following.

If knowledge, as Protagoras conceives of it, is to be infallible – i.e. true – and reproduce reality, what is, one must be able to conclude from relativistic knowledge to a world in constant flux. Such a world would look like that of Heraclitus, and therefore Plato combines Protagoras' theory of knowledge with Heraclitus' ontology. This is of course a dialectical combination, which investigates the consequences of a certain line of thought, and with respect to Protagoras Socrates suggests unambiguously that he is not paying too much attention to historical veracity – he will make Theaetetus privy to the 'secret doctrine', which Protagoras had reserved for himself only (152 C; cf. 155 D).

First, the aim is to construct a theory about what sense-perception is on the given presuppositions (153 D ff.; 155 D ff.; 182 A ff.). It is only secondly that it is possible to ask whether such a theory of sense-perception can claim to explain true knowledge. Sense-perception must depend on a relation between the perceiving person or the sensory organ and the perceived object. Both these entities are considered as objects on the same level. Thus the perceiving subject is a physical object like all others, and sense-perception is a special case of the general structure of the world, which is to say, a relation between two objects, which themselves are 'relative' as well as fluctuating. Any object whatever is subject to motion, but in order for sense-perception to come about, it is necessary to presuppose an interaction between the perceived object and the perceiving subject, a process or force (*dynamis*) whereby object affects subject, and subject is directed towards object. The motions of these two may be coordinated or made to 'meet', and at this meeting the eye becomes a 'seeing eye' and its object – not 'whiteness', but a white thing (156 E). The eye as perceiving eye and the thing as perceived thing thus only come to exist due to the act of perception. The general conclusion is (159 E ff.) that nobody can have the same perception twice, that the same object will not be perceived identically by two persons, and that perceiver and perceived cannot exist independently of each other.

Let us assume that this theory of sense-perception – however unclear it may be – is able to account for true knowledge. It turns out to be impervious to criticism on a number of points, many of which have been incorporated in the established stock of epistemological dilemmas in the history of philosophy. Point by point Socrates asks (157 E ff.; 161 B ff.; 163 A ff.): is the perception of the sick man just as true as that of the healthy man? Are dreams and hallucinations true? Why is Protagoras wiser than a pig? What does it mean to 'know' a foreign language – is there a difference between apprehending sounds and letters and 'understanding' the language? Is memory not knowledge? If you close one eye and open the other, will you in that case both know and not know?

Most of these objections – big as well as small – can be refuted on the basis of the preceding. If one believes, for example, that there is identity between a Socrates in ill health and a Socrates in good health, one has failed to understand the implications of the theory radically enough (cf. 166 B). It is not a question of personal identity but of a series of isolated, analogous sensory situations, or – as in the case of memory – of situations that are analogous with sensation. Only two of the objections cannot be answered in this way: the difference between hearing and 'understanding' a language, and the question of why some are wiser than others. But these two objections go beyond the question of the truth of perceptual judgements.

The last question is answered in the grand defence oration, which Socrates has Protagoras deliver, where in all likelihood the historical Protagoras once more is allowed the floor (p. 105). Here Protagoras accounts for his theories of beliefs and judgements of value, for his relativistic theory of truth, and for its ethical and political consequences. Socrates' direct refutation consists of the self-refuting argument and the reference to expert judgements of what will be advantageous in the future (171 A ff.; 178 B ff.). But there are other answers to Protagoras. First, there is the 'digression' (172 B ff.), in which we – in the midst of the argument which presupposes that the advantageous can be substituted for the good – suddenly are confronted with the Platonic philosopher's understanding of the good. Secondly, it should of course be noted that Protagoras' political theory, in which the 'wise' is able to persuade the less wise, presupposes a personal identity that has just been denied. This counter-argument cannot very well be directly formulated, for it builds on Protagoras' 'secret doctrine', in other words on what Protagoras according to Plato ought to have meant. In a dialectical context, however, the argument remains valid.

Thus opinion and belief cannot be derived from perception, and therefore it can of course not be the case that perception is identical with all knowledge. Yet Protagoras is not refuted with respect to the particular perception. Is the act of sensation itself a cognitive act, or does it at least convey knowledge? Are we allowed to formulate 'protocol sentences' concerning what we experience at a particular moment (cf. 179 C)? With this question Socrates returns to the Heraclitus theme, and, as is his custom, he also makes the 'Heraclitus' position as pointed as possible (181 B ff.). The theory of sense-perception presupposed an object and a sensory organ in a state of constant flux, but it follows from this that the sensory image also must be subject to constant change. If everything is constantly in a state of becoming, there will be no moment when something 'is'. Nor will there be a moment when knowledge is not instantly transformed into non-knowledge, and it will be impossible to formulate any knowledge linguistically – we cannot say 'is', 'mine', 'this', 'man', or 'stone' (cf. 157 B). We cannot even say that 'something', for example, becomes 'white', and it is utterly impossible to speak of 'white' as an instance of the quality 'whiteness' – which Plato apparently stresses, for he creates the word 'quality' in order to emphasize his point (182 A). In other words, an ontological break-down leads to the break-down of knowledge and language. A world without a minimum of stability is a chaos, which corresponds to the pseudo-world depicted in the seventh hypothesis in the *Parmenides*. The point of departure was that knowledge should be infallible and have what is as its object. It was not the intention to show that knowledge is non-knowledge and being non-being. According to the radical theory of sense-perception, sense-perception is therefore non-knowledge.

But Plato cannot very well reach such a conclusion without acceptance of the theory of sense-perception, which he himself has constructed, as an adequate description of sensation as a process – there would be little sense in an argument that demonstrates that a wrong theory of sense-perception cannot explain knowledge. The extreme 'Heraclitus theory' stands for a view, which today would be called phenomenalism or neutral monism – only sense data but not things or persons exist. But that was not the way the argument began. The introductory presentation of the theory of sense-perception was characterized by a certain *chiaroscuro*, and the relation between physical objects and phenomenal objects was left strangely adrift (cf. Theophrastus' criticism, *De sens.* 60 ff.) – presumably as in the case of the historical Protagoras: there is a physical object and a physical 'person', but they are described only as entities that can 'become' objects of perception and subjects of perception. The lack of clarity ceases if subject and object only exist in relation to each other, but then the consequence will be the phenomenalist position which traps Protagoras but is unacceptable to Plato. Are there other possibilities?

While the model of perception in the *Theaetetus* is described in wholly abstract terms, it is exploited and made concrete in a theory of vision in the *Timaeus* (45 B; 67 C; cf. 61 C). Here the existence of physical bodies is presupposed. They are constantly emitting particles, which, with light as the medium, encounter particles from the eye, whereby the visual image comes about. According to this version of the theory, 'primary qualities' reside in the thing, while 'secondary qualities' come about in the very act of sensation, and there are clear parallels, for example with Democritus' theory of sensation. It looks as if one is confronted with a causal theory of perception of John Locke's type. But there are differences. Plato's model presupposes an interaction between subject and object, and, as the theory is presented in the *Timaeus*, it clearly emerges as a physical-physiological theory that can account for the physical substratum of sensation without further-reaching epistemological claims. The theory discovers a necessary but insufficient condition for sense-perception, and if one attempts to deduce knowledge from the experience of sense data, the result will be a phenomenalism that refutes itself. In the *Theaetetus* Plato's criticism does not as much refer to the fact that a causal theory precludes certain knowledge of the thing in itself, as to the need for the supplementation of it. Knowledge presupposes a degree of stability on both the object- and subject-side. What does this imply?

This leads to the conclusion of the first part of the dialogue (*Theaet.* 184 B ff.). Socrates emphasizes that we do not perceive with, but through the sense organs. In order for anything whatsoever to be perceived as an object, the single sense experiences must be correlated and interpreted. Thereby an important distinction is introduced between passive sense experience and interpretation of sense data, perception (cf. the distinction in German between *Empfindung* and *Wahrnehmung*). But this is a conceptual distinction: in the actual situation of sensation, the immediate sense-perceptions will always be connected with interpretation – in other words, a 'movement' from subject to object. However, it is not sufficient to create a synthesis of the passive sense impressions. Even the most elementary sensation – for example of the qualities hard and soft – can only be interpreted with the aid of a number of concepts, 'common concepts' (*koina*), which have universal applicability but no correlative in sense experience itself. Being and non-being, likeness and unlikeness, identity and difference, unity and number, are furnished as examples. Every sense object is acknowledged as 'being', 'one', 'different' (from others), and 'identical' (with itself). In the *Parmenides* such concepts were analyzed as metaphysical presuppositions. In the *Theaetetus* they stand as pre-conditions for experience, but they transcend experience. At the same time these concepts do have existence independently of consciousness. Here there is no talk – as with Kant – of forms of knowledge, but of objects of knowledge. Knowledge is, as always in Plato, dependent on being, and therefore it is generally concluded: it is impossible to attain truth without attaining being (186 C) – and to know the being (*ousia*) of a thing is not only to know that it exists, it is to know what it is, its essence. Hereby the introductory *hypothesis* has been rejected: under no circumstance is knowledge perception.

The epistemological analysis in the first part of the *Theaetetus* does not refer directly to ideas; but, as in the *Parmenides*, the pre-conditions that have always been implicit in the doctrine of ideas are analyzed. It is shown that even the most elementary cognition has a priori pre-conditions, and therefore this section can be read as a de-mythologized *anamnēsis* theory: perception is still the occasion but not the cause of knowledge. Plato does not formulate a new theory of knowledge in the *Theaetetus*, but nevertheless he uncovers new epistemological perspectives: it is not until now that he has provided an analysis of the process of sense-perception itself and of rival epistemological models, and by the 'common concepts' he refers not only to the doctrine of ideas but also points out what in any case, regardless of the special conceptual content of particular ideas, constitutes sensory cognition. Indirectly he has thereby also thrown light on that which he earlier had called 'the soul's kinship' with the ideas: we can only know by virtue of direct access to concepts that are independent of experience. This implies that a principal problem in a causal theory of perception to Plato recedes and becomes a pseudo-problem: we can know the essence of the thing, but not the thing as 'thing' – it exists as a physical thing, but to us it will always be something that 'appears' (cf. the *Phaedo*). 'Protagoras' must be correct in claiming that a subject of perception and an object of perception are subordinate to the act of perception, but to Plato it is possible to interpret the act of perception by virtue of an independent 'stable' standard. These fundamental positions were continued in Aristotle's theory of knowledge.

Sensation is dependent on interpretation, and interpretation is 'belief'. Ought one perhaps to identify knowledge with true belief (*alēthēs doxa*)? That is Theaetetus' next proposal (187 B), and it is examined in the second part of the dialogue – again in such a way that the main concept, *doxa*, is kept free from Platonic associations and simply stands for any opinion whatsoever that can be expressed in a judgement. Of course Theaetetus' proposed definition raises at once the question about how to distinguish between true and false belief. This problem is expressly not dealt with in the theory of predication in the *Phaedo*, nor in the theory of knowledge of the *Republic*, but a fatal point in the Parmenides tradition and in Sophist linguistic theories (Antisthenes) was precisely that false belief was dismissed as non-belief. This is where Socrates begins. In other words, again he reasons on alien premises that may be summarized under three points:

1   knowledge means to 'be acquainted with',
2   to one object corresponds one piece of knowledge,
3   one cannot think a nothing.

These are three sides of one principle that forms the basis of a radical theory of naming. By his analyses Socrates demonstrates where the fault in this principle lies, and he prepares for the answer, which is provided in the fully developed theory of language in the *Sophist*.

If one proceeds from the second point listed above, one might think that false belief consists in the wrong correlation of object and knowledge. But such a mistake is impossible on the given premises. False belief presupposes that one is thinking something not-being (189 A), but that is precluded by the third point, and false beliefs cannot exist in any way whatsoever, when true belief (knowledge) or non-belief (non-knowledge) are the only alternatives, and when knowledge means direct acquaintance with the object (as in point one). I will never maintain that 'horse' is the same as 'cow', and if I 'know' in the sense of 'being acquainted with' Socrates and Theaetetus, then I cannot 'not-know' Socrates and Theaetetus, and therefore mistaking them for one another is impossible (cf. *Crat.* 429 D).

This theme is played upon from all angles and backwards and forwards: the problem is made more complex, but the premisses are not abandoned. Not only can one perception not be mistaken for another if I 'know' two objects of perception. On the supposition that memory – as in the first part of the dialogue – is analogous with perception, I cannot either mistake a perception of Theaetetus for an image in my memory of Socrates (*Theaet.* 193 C ff.), and, all in all, I cannot mistake formerly acquired knowledge for present knowledge (197 D ff.). Furthermore, I have no access to any criterion that can determine whether I am actually in possession of 'knowledge', nor whether that which I believe is 'knowledge' actually is 'non-knowledge'.

The most decisive objection is that on the assumed premisses one can only account for simple identification of objects. It cannot be explained that I have a false belief *about* an object. I can 'know' the sign 12, but I do not for that reason have to know *about* 12 that it is $7 + 5$ (195 E). This is the first time that Plato – indirectly but unambiguously – points out the difference between *knowledge by acquaintance* and *knowledge that*, and of course it is no accident that it occurs in connection with the problem of false judgements. In the *Republic* Plato himself built on the direct correspondence between knowledge and object. The problem of false judgements – and of all judgements whatsoever – was not touched on. Nor would it have been possible to explain it. When it appears here, Plato apparently sees it as an extension of his former view, not as a break.

It is not until the *Sophist* that it is revealed how Plato connects the two views. But that he still believes that direct acquaintance with the matter at hand is a precondition for producing true judgements about it can be seen in the last section of the second part of the *Theaetetus* (201 A ff.). If a judge pronounces a correct sentence on the basis of true testimony at a trial, the judge is in possession of true belief, but the witness of *epistēmē*, true knowledge – which is the same point as in the *Meno*, where we learn about the difference between knowing the way to Larissa from one's own experience and from hear-say. Accordingly, the *Theaetetus* passage contains two conclusions: the principle of one-to-one correspondence cannot explain true knowledge, and true knowledge is different from true belief.

Hence it is consistent that the last part of the dialogue begins (201 C ff.) with the willing Theaetetus proposing the last definition: knowledge consists of true belief accompanied by an account or explanation (*logos*). As it happens, Socrates has 'dreamed' of such a view, and so he is immediately able to account for its implications. The theory has surprising similarity with Antisthenes' epistemology, and so, for the third time, Socrates reasons on alien premisses. Everything consists of irreducible elements, and thus knowledge consists in the enumeration of the elements; but each single element is only accessible to immediate sensation. Thus one can perceive the elements but only 'know' their relation. Of course Socrates rejects the theory (202 C ff.). If an element is unknowable, the sum of elements is likewise unknowable, and if the relation is a new irreducible element, it is likewise unknowable. With an example, frequently employed by Plato in the late dialogues, we can know a syllable if we can know the elements (letters) it consists of – and, according to the theory, this we cannot do. For surely, it cannot be that the whole is different from and more than its parts? On the premisses of the theory this cannot be so, and here Socrates desists. Yet, from a Platonic point of view the whole might very well be more than the sum of its parts. That has been shown in the *Parmenides*, and the idea is pursued in the *Sophist* as well.

But there is one more thing. An account or explanation can never legitimate itself. It only moves the problem elsewhere if *logos* is considered the phonetic expression of thought (206 C). The same is the case if the theory of the enumeration of elements (206 E) is expanded – for if nothing is known about the whole to which the elements belong, it is impossible to identify them as elements. Nor does it help (208 B) to suppose that a justification consists in identifying the special characteristic of each thing – for whence do we know it and how will knowledge thereby become other than true belief?

Accordingly the disheartening conclusion must be that Theaetetus and Socrates cannot say what knowledge is (210 A). This may occasion two considerations. First, one cannot ask the traditional Socratic question if the question is of knowledge, for any sort of question presupposes that one possesses knowledge. Second, one might after all wonder at the rejection of Theaetetus' third proposal, for in the *Meno* it was explicitly established that certain knowledge differs from true opinion in that it can be justified by an account. But there is no self-contradiction here. When there is true knowledge, it can be justified by a *logos*, but no *logos* can in itself decide whether there is true knowledge. It is no mere paradox to deduce the moral from the *Theaetetus* that there is knowledge when there is knowledge. Of course it prevents further questions about what knowledge is, but it does not prevent questions about what can be known or about how knowledge works. In the *Sophist* it turns out that the investigations of the *Theaetetus* are useful. And in a larger perspective the dialogue has been of far-reaching importance: one line runs directly to Aristotle's basic position that demonstrative knowledge presupposes preceding knowledge; another to the Hellenistic discussion of truth criteria.

THE *SOPHIST*

The *Sophist* builds both on the metaphysical dialectics of the *Parmenides* and on the epistemological analyses of the *Theaetetus*, but these are not the subjects of the dialogue. Nor does it deal with the relation between phenomenon and idea, as do the classic dialogues. The doctrine of ideas is presupposed. The main subject of the dialogue is the logico-metaphysical relations between ideas, and a certain general set of concepts turns out to be necessary to understand and describe these relations. The 'interweaving' of ideas under investigation emerges as an absolute precondition for knowledge and language, and the concrete results obtained contribute decisively to the solution of the questions that had been the curse of all earlier theories of knowledge and language – including Plato's own: how to explain the existence of negative statements and of false statements?

The ignorant Socrates can of course not advance such theories. The leader of the discussion is a somewhat abstract, anonymous person – the Stranger from Elea – but Socrates is present, and presumably he draws his own conclusions. Apparently the aim is to bring Socratic and Eleatic thought in line with one another, and this is formally stressed by the presentation of the *Theaetetus, Sophist* and *Statesman* as a series of continued discussions. Socrates chairs the first, aporetic discussion, while 'the Stranger' is in charge in the two following, which seem rather more like demonstrations than debates. A continuation, the *Philosopher*, is advertised (cf. *Soph.* 217 A ff.; 253 C; *Pol.* 257 A ff.), where Socrates would be the natural president. But it remains as a suggestion, which anybody can pursue for himself according to his abilities. What is announced is a characterization of three types of men, the Sophist – the man who can create illusions; the statesman – he who can govern in this frail world of ours; and the philosopher. So, only the first two points on the agenda are accomplished.

As a dialogue, the *Sophist* operates on two levels. The avowed purpose is to define a Sophist. A Sophist creates illusions, but how is one to define a person who produces something that is not? What is 'that which is not'? A constant motif in the dialogue – as so often before – is the concept of image. What is an image, and how can it depict both truly and falsely?

The Stranger throws himself headlong into an attempt to define the Sophist by using a special definitional procedure, which, by repeated division of superordinate concepts, arrives at the indivisible concept or the indivisible idea (*to atomon eidos* – 'the conceptual atom'), a definiendum, which accordingly is defined by its place in a conceptual system. First he looks for a sample definition of a neutral subject – an angler (*Soph.* 218 D ff.) – and then he sets about defining the Sophist. But as the Sophist is the master of illusion, he constantly withdraws and occasions no less than six provisional definitions (221 C-31 B). Here the Sophist appears in various strange disguises. The recurrent criteria of division are that the Sophist produces something, that he produces by 'imitation' – *mimēsis* – of reality, but that his imitation is false.

The procedure employed – the method of division or the *diairesis* method (*diairesis*: division) – is announced in the *Phaedrus*. It consists in the dialectician's finding one general or superordinate idea through an indefinite plurality of data – be they phenomena or indistinct concepts. This idea he subdivides according to certain rules and in conformance with nature's own articulation. In its basic structure this is a hierarchical classification, which has been practiced all the way down to the theory of classification of the present age, and which is familiar from for example botany, zoology, or library science. In modern terminology, one would say that a given class is divided into sub-classes by means of successive criteria of classification so that a system of classes appears, which is included in the superordinate classes. The traditional view – and Plato's as well – is, on the other hand, that concepts are divided. In scholastic terminology the superordinate concept is called *genus* (family) and is classified into more or fewer stages of *subgenera*, until one reaches the 'indivisible' concept, *infima species* (the 'lowest' or ultimate kind), which is superior only to individuals. The criterion of classification, which must not be contained in a superordinate genus, is called *differentia specifica* (the difference that 'creates' species). Classical demands of a hierarchical classification are that at every stage it must be exhaustive – so that subgenera or species have the same extension as genus – and that it must be exclusive – which means that subgenera or species mutually exclude each other, so that at each stage the division ideally should be binary, i.e. a division into two opposites (the principle of dichotomy). A modern system of classification will most often be a hypothetical construction made for a stipulated purpose; but to Plato the division ought to adhere to nature's own structure, which of course makes the requirements harder. It means that in principle competing classifications ought not to be constructed.

In Plato's earlier work there are suggestions of a *diairesis* method (cf., e.g. *Euthyph.* 11 E ff; *Gor.* 463 B ff.); the problem is latent in the discussions of virtue as a unity consisting of several parts, and the method can be considered a concretization of the dialectician's 'descent' in the *Republic*. But it is not until we have the assistance of the Stranger that the promises of the *Phaedrus* are met. Among other things, there is in the *Statesman* the demand that a classification must be exhaustive and exclusive (*Pol.* 262 A ff; cf. 263 E; 266 D). It also appears (*Phil.* 16 C ff.; cf. *Pol.* 285 A; *Soph.* 253 B ff. – cf. below) that a system of classification or a *diairesis* structure should follow natural divisions and that it is considered metaphysically as a whole/part structure in the sense of the *Parmenides*. The entire structure denotes the extension of the system, but it has been constituted as structure by means of the intension of the superordinate concept.

In his opening definitions the Stranger does not lose himself in either technical rules or in speculations about the metaphysical basis of a *diairesis*. On the contrary, the six attempts at definition are remarkably arbitrary. They provide rich opportunities for satirizing the Sophist who seems to be everything without being anything, and this discreetly suggests that there is a difference between ideal procedure and the humanly feasible. In a larger context the definitional attempts emphasize the precarious question: what is an illusion, and how can something 'be' non-being (237 A)?

In successive order the Stranger attempts to determine that which is not in any way whatsoever, that which seems to be, and that which fully is. Socrates also did this in the *Republic*, but here the aim is different, and the middle category – that which is and is not – does not have the same signification. Where the *Republic* investigates the ontological relation of dependence between phenomenon and reality, the subject of the *Sophist* is the relation between language and reality. As in the *Phaedo* and *Cratylus*, language reflects reality, and it is characteristic of the Stranger's position that he infers from linguistic usage to the metaphysical reality that legitimates language.

That which is not in any way whatsoever – the absolute nothing – cannot be spoken about (237 B ff.), for language must – as with Parmenides – deal with something, and therefore the very expression 'the absolute non-being' refutes itself. None the less, it is not a logical absurdity but a stumbling block, with which logic, metaphysics, and language can do nothing, but which must be acknowledged.

What is it then that seems to be – not, as in the *Republic*, the phenomenon but the image the Sophist creates in words, which 'is' an image, but 'is not' that which it depicts (239 C ff.)? It is not something that *really* is, but it is *really* an image. The Sophist of course will deny the existence of images and stick to his old slogan: one can neither speak nor think a nothing. Thereby we are back with the problem from the second part of the *Theaetetus*, and this can only be solved if the non-being in one sense or another is being. The Stranger is forced to attack his own teacher, 'Father Parmenides'.

But the question of what seems to be is of course dependent on the question of true being. The Stranger shows himself to be so conversant with Platonic techniques that by means of a retrospective survey of the philosophical tradition he is able to sketch some possible answers that are contrasted. The first contrast is between pluralism and monism. All the good old natural philosophers with Heraclitus in the lead (cf. *Theaet.* 152 Eff.) agree that being is actually a plurality (*Soph.* 242 B ff.) – using a standard example, it may be the hot and the cold. But what is implied by such an answer? Are the hot and the cold actually not two but one thing, or is being some third entity besides heat and cold? This the ancients did not take the trouble to explain to us.

Confronting the pluralists stands the monist Parmenides in lonely majesty (244 B ff.; cf. *Theaet.* 183 C ff.). When Parmenides maintains that being is one, he is implicitly saying that unity is a plurality, as the Stranger reveals in a condensed paraphrase of Plato's *Parmenides* – especially the second hypothesis. The indirect conclusion is that, properly considered, Parmenides' being must be a Platonic whole/part structure, i.e. a plurality. Consequently being can neither be explained from a purely monistic nor a purely pluralistic position.

On the background of the Parmenides discussion the Stranger is next able to take the discussion to a superior level by confronting materialists with 'friends of ideas' (*Soph.* 246 A ff.). This resembles the mythical battle between giants and gods, during which the giants tear down everything from heaven, grasping rocks and trees, and acknowledge only that which they can touch and feel. Meanwhile the gods defend themselves from their heavenly heights and declare that only the disembodied, the object of thought, has existence. All else is only becoming, not being.

It is only possible to speak with 'improved' materialists (246 E ff.). In other words, what is dealt with is a typical attitude and only indirectly is there reference to specific persons, even though Democritus might have filled the role as a civilized materialist quite well. Such a materialist must concede that for example moral qualities or insight are immaterial. But if being includes both something material and immaterial, there must be a common criterion for being as such. Such a criterion is the concept of *dynamis* – the ability to affect or be affected by something – briefly, a process that does not necessarily take place between material entities.

Having dealt with the materialists, the Stranger turns to 'the friends of ideas' (248 A ff.). These are not simply identifiable persons – such as Plato – but rather some perhaps imagined adherents of a doctrinaire 'Platonism' reminiscent of the philosophy advocated by the young Socrates in the *Parmenides*. These friends of ideas must also presuppose a form of *dynamis*, which is not merely a process between phenomena, but one that includes immutable ideas. At the very least they must consider knowing as a *dynamis*, an interplay between subject and object – which comes as no surprise to the attentive reader of the *Republic* and *Theaetetus*. In its entire extension being must therefore comprise not only the immutable ideas but also change, life, soul, and insight (248 E) – phenomena are not mentioned. Are we really to believe that the universe is void of life and insight, that without thought it stands immutable in aloof grandeur? It was at this point that the final argument in the *Phaedo* could be carried no further.

The conclusion must be that the improved 'Platonists' must behave like the child who replies 'both' when offered a choice between the left and the right hand. In its full extension being must comprise both the mutable and the immutable.

Yet such a conclusion is not without problems (249 D ff.). If being comprises both the mutable and the immutable, it must in itself be a third entity – for being is different from that which 'has' being – and apparently one is mired, as were the natural philosophers who identified being with the sum of the hot and the cold. The Stranger must come to the not very comforting conclusion that at this point we do not know what being and non-being are. He can build up aporias as ably as any Socrates.

In the following, and constructive part of his investigation the Stranger deals first with the relation between being and non-being – as it turns out with a view to explain negative statements. Behind all the paradoxes he arrived at in the preceding, he has described precisely the Platonic universe, a world that comprises both the mutable and the immutable and in which unity implies plurality. But not all sides of this universe are investigated. For example, he no longer asks what is mutable and what is immutable, but deals with the implications of such concepts, regarded as concepts. It is this transition from an extensional to an intensional point of view that renders him immune to the criticism that he had directed at the natural philosophers. His subject is the relation between ideas, which in agreement with good Platonic thought is considered a logico-metaphysical relation. It is also sound Platonism to consider language an access to reality. Language is not an independent object of investigation, and linguistic analysis and logic of being cohere.

The traditional problem of participation – the relation between phenomenon and idea – is considered solved, and therefore it seems trivial and a little comical when people who have absorbed learning late in life (probably an ironic reference to Antisthenes) wonder that one phenomenon may have several predicates (251 A; cf. *Phil.* 14 D). The problem is that some ideas are compatible and others necessarily incompatible. So 'motion' is incompatible with 'rest', but they are both necessarily 'being' (*Soph.* 251 C ff.; cf. 254 D). Different terms are employed about this 'blending' of ideas. Earlier, the most precise term, *methexis*, denoted participation, and the concept of participation has thus been expanded. Yet, while the relation between phenomenon and idea is contingent, the relation between ideas is necessary.

The prototype of relations of ideas is hierarchical, i.e. the *diairesis* system, which clearly is considered a Platonic whole/part structure. According to the Stranger it is the task of the dialectician to discover *one* whole consisting of *many* parts, in such a manner that genus comprises subgenera and species (the total extension of the system), while one species through higher level ideas is united in a whole yet still distinguishable from other species of the same level (253 D). Since only the intelligible world is under consideration, a finite number of concepts are mutually related, but each by itself is one metaphysical entity; 'below' the system an infinite number of particulars must be presupposed. The participation relating subordinate concepts to superior ones is necessary, asymmetrical, and transitive, and in its entirety the system is intensionally devised. Up to this point one is able to use modern terminology, but in Plato one never finds any distinction between concept and class. An idea still stands for being x 'itself', not for the concept of x, and genus is no more void of content than is species.

In order to describe this structure, the dialectician must employ a 'meta-language', which is to say that he must be able to speak of ideas as ideas, and he must employ a conceptual apparatus that can be applied to every *diairesis* system without it itself becoming a part of it – he must be able to see that special ideas cause 'normal' ideas to be compatible or incompatible (253 B). If 'motion' and 'rest' are considered the totality of everything in motion or at rest (252 D), the extension of being would thereby be exhausted but the concept of being would not. 'Motion' is incompatible with 'rest'. Both participate in but are not identical with being. In order to describe this relation we need the concepts of 'sameness' and 'difference'.

According to the Stranger's formulation, we need five 'highest genera' (254 B): 'motion', 'rest', 'sameness', 'difference' and 'being' – in other words concepts that are familiar from the *Parmenides*. The last three appear as 'common concepts' in the *Theaetetus*. Opposing Aristotle, the Neoplatonists (cf. Plot. VI 2,1 ff.) understood these five concepts as Platonic 'categories', which is somewhat misleading inasmuch as the concepts do not serve to delimit a given entity from any other, but indicate the pre-conditions for such a delimitation.

Quite clearly the five concepts are not of the same type. 'Motion' and 'rest' exhaust being and are mutually exclusive. But the other three concepts – which are the concepts to be used in the following – are formal predicates of any given idea. Therefore they must be considered meta-concepts or 'highest genera' in the strictest sense. The concept of being, which in Plato probably never simply meant existence, must – as in the second part of the *Parmenides* – necessarily imply a relation of identity and difference. The Stranger formulates this as a principle: everything that is can be said to be in itself or as being in relation to 'other things' (*Soph.* 255 C). In the tradition preceding Neoplatonism this principle (which should be compared with *Parm.* 146 B; cf. p. 219) was with greater justification considered a Platonic 'doctrine of categories' (c.f., e.g. Diog. Laert. III 108). If applied to the traditional Platonic universe, this means that an idea can both be considered in itself and in relation to other ideas, while a phenomenon exclusively is related to something other than itself.

These three concepts are indefinable formal concepts or meta-concepts that have the same extension – everything that has being – but differ in content. They are pervasive with respect to concepts of objects arranged in a *diairesis* system; each of them is reflexive; mutually they are symmetrical. Inasmuch as any entity is what it is, it is at the same time related to other entities. We should not – as the Stranger stresses – be amazed that 'motion' for example is both 'the Same' – namely, as itself – and not 'the same' – namely, as the Same. On the linguistic level this distinction corresponds with identifying judgements (including definitions) as opposed to predicative judgements.

If the conceptual relations are seen as participation, it is possible to expand the rule of transformation whereby one could, in the *Phaedo*, translate 'is' as a copula to 'participates in'. The Stranger advances a number of examples (255 E ff.), which may be presented as follows (the → signifies 'is transformed to'):

'Motion is not rest' → 'motion participates in the Different with respect to rest'.
'Motion is' → 'motion participates in Being'.
'Motion is not the same' → 'motion participates in the Different with respect to the Same'.
'Motion is the same' → 'motion participates in the Same with respect to itself'.
'What is, is not (other things)' → 'what is participates in the Different (with respect to other things)'.

'What is, is (itself)' → 'what is participates in the Same (with respect to itself)'.

From modern points of view there are evident shortcomings in the entire proceeding. The three highest concepts appear as meta-concepts, but they are none the less treated as if they were components in the system they describe (they are called 'highest genera') and as any idea: they are hypostatized; the possibility of 'self-predication' is therefore also retained for these concepts, and there is a gradual transition between concept and instance. All are necessary consequences of Plato's basic metaphysical position, but the hypostatization of relational concepts, such as 'the Same' and 'the Different' necessitates that on yet another meta-level he must insert a new relational phrase ('with respect to') in order to be able to account for two place predicates. Just as it is impossible to legitimate the concept of participation by a hypostatized concept, so it is impossible to legitimate this phrase – and indeed Plato never tried to do so.

But what is the purpose of this entire apparatus? According to a number of interpreters – mainly those writing in English – the problem is to what extent Plato manages to distinguish between existential, copulative, and identifying applications of 'is'. The theory makes possible a clear distinction between predicative and identifying statements (cf., e.g. 256 A); but it is more doubtful whether Plato wanted to single out existential statements (cf., e.g. 254 D contrasted with 259 B).

Yet such distinctions in meaning are not the avowed aim. Rather, it is by means of linguistic usage to arrive at an understanding of logico-metaphysical relations, which in their turn can explain linguistic usage. On the linguistic level Plato's point apparently is that the basic sentences stated can be transformed by means of the concept of participation, and it is all-important that thereby one can transform 'is not' to 'is different from'. By this Parmenides has been refuted (258 C ff.): it is the case that that which is not, is, and thus negative statements are possible. It is not illegitimate to maintain that what is is many things and that it 'is not' even more (259 B).

The theory is valid with respect to the point in which Plato is interested in the *Sophist*, which is that of negative predication with the subject having definite reference. The possibility of statements about non-existing subjects which can be conceptually determined is touched on in the *Parmenides* (the fifth hypothesis) but not in the *Sophist*, and the Stranger himself remarks (258 E) that a non-existing subject, which in no respect can be conceptually determined, a pure nothing, still eludes every attempt at analysis. The *Sophist* does not speak about the contrast between being and nothing, but about the contrast between being 'this and that' and not being 'this and that'.

Parmenides has been refuted, but not so the Sophist, for the existence of false statements has not been accounted for. But it turns out that it is possible to do so on the background of the theory of negative statements. Yet some supplementary premises are called for. From a Platonic point of view false statements are only possible if they express a pseudo-being, and thereby we are back with the metaphor that sustains the *Sophist* and so many other Platonic dialogues, the concept of image. It is affirmed that the 'interweaving' of the ideas has turned out to be the precondition for language (259 E) and thereby also for thought expressed in language (cf. 263 E; *Theaet.* 189 E). It applies not only to the basic sentences analyzed in the preceding, but to all sentences, that they presuppose that some ideas are compatible, others not – and 'compatibility' is a concept that is not confined to relations within a *diairesis* system; the idea, 'man', and the idea, 'understanding', are compatible, for example, even though they do not stand in a mutual hierarchical relation. Inasmuch as phenomena essentially are instances of ideas, the interweavings of ideas must consequently be presuppositions for ordinary every-day sentences, in which one, for example, ascribes a predicate to a particular subject. At this stage, in other words, the phenomenal world is included.

Language is a system of signs that stand for something, or an image that may depict truly or falsely, and it must – this was already presupposed in the *Phaedo* and *Cratylus* – also have a structure itself. Let us begin by looking at the latter. A statement consists of elements, but it holds good for linguistic elements as well as for the elements of reality that not all combinations are possible. 'Walks runs sleeps' is not a statement; 'man understands' or 'a man understands' is one (*Soph.* 262 C). The simplest possible statement consists of two elements (261 C ff.): a 'name' (*onoma*) that has reference to an object and a 'verb' (*rhēma*) that says something about a subject. What is revolutionary in this linguistic theory, which indirectly has been prepared for in the *Theaetetus*, is that a statement says something *about* something. It does not consist of elements, each designating an object; one element – the subject – has reference, the whole statement does not designate, but it communicates or clarifies a state of affairs (cf. *Crat.* 433 D). Thereby distinction is made between meaning and reference, and statements about existing subjects are thereby legitimated. Likewise it is a characteristic of a statement *qua* statement that it can affirm or deny (*Soph.* 263 E).

Because it is the nature of language to maintain something about something, it can state about that which is that it is or that it is not (262 E ff.; cf. *Crat.* 385 B) – and in the latter case a nothing is not being said; something is being said that is different from that which is the case. Thereby truth and falsehood are defined as properties of statements, but whether a statement is true or false depends on something non-linguistic, on whether it is in accordance with the facts – whether the image depicts reality or not. But that is hardly the whole matter. The Stranger advances two statements as examples: 'Theaetetus sits' and 'Theaetetus flies'. The first statement may be true or false and the second is necessarily false. It appears from the Stranger's staccato-like commentary that he does not find special problems in deciding when the first statement is true – whether there is correspondence with reality or not can be determined at once merely by looking at Theaetetus. What is of interest are the introductory remarks about the interweaving of ideas as precondition for language – what it is that makes it *possible* for a statement to be true – and surely it is a point that in both sample statements the subject is a proper name; it must also be possible to account for a language of particulars. The Stranger presents the problem and leaves the conclusion to the reader. But on the basis of the whole contextual background it is in fact possible to draw the conclusion: Theaetetus is an instance of the idea 'man'; what can be said about 'man' can also be said about Theaetetus. 'Man' is compatible with 'sitting', not with 'flying'. Consequently the first statement may be true, the second cannot be. If the predicate for example were the species under which the subject belongs, it would be possible to conclude that the statement necessarily is true – this would apply to the statement 'Theaetetus is a man'.

It was not the Stranger's task to show what is necessarily true but to show that it is possible to make a meaningful, false statement – for that is what the Sophist does. Accordingly, he can return to the beginning and reveal the Sophist's dark soul by means of a breakneck definition, which in an enormous *diairesis* scheme places him as a hypocritical manufacturer of illusions (*Soph.* 264 D).

17

THE LATE DIALOGUES: NATURE, MAN AND SOCIETY

———— •◆• ————

In Plato's *Republic* there is latent tension between man as a contemplative being and as a member of society. In the late dialogues this is made fully explicit. The *Parmenides, Theaetetus* and *Sophist* deal with the foundation of metaphysics and epistemology and are addressed to theoretical man. The continuation of the *Sophist*, the *Statesman*, attempts to translate theoretical philosophy to practical philosophy, a theory of state. Nevertheless, the contrast between the statesman and the philosopher persists.

Apparently Plato in his later years conceived of an ambitious project, which from new points of view was intended to place man in the transitory world of time and space; man belongs in society but also in the physical world, and he has a history. Nothing certain can be said about that world that is merely an image of the ideal one. But that which cannot be known with certainty can be described by an account of what might be the case, by means of the 'as if' of the myth.

THE *TIMAEUS* AND *CRITIAS*

Timaeus, the principal speaker in the dialogue that bears his name, is said to have come from Southern Italy. Most likely he is not a historical person. While the Stranger from Elea represents one Italic tradition – the formal, logico-metaphysical one from Parmenides – Timaeus represents another, the teleological science of Pythagorean ancestry, and is presented as an expert in astronomy. In the *Timaeus* Socrates meets Timaeus, the politician Hermocrates, and the older Critias, the grandfather of the infamous Critias, and accordingly Plato's great grandfather. In dramatic terms these dialogues can be dated to some time before the Peloponnesian Wars with their misery caused the world to be out of joint.

Socrates begins the *Timaeus* (*Tim.* 17 A ff.) with a summary of an account of the perfect state, which he presented the day before. This summary is strikingly similar to Plato's *Republic*, although with one significant difference. In compendium-like form we learn of the division of labour, the education of the guardians, equal rights of women and the economic community. But the summary stops with the fifth book of the *Republic*; there is no reference to the metaphysical sections or to the description of the decline of the ideal constitution of the last books; nothing is said about justice, and there are no philosopher-rulers; Socrates speaks only about his construction of the state, not about its justification. He says himself (19 B) that to him his model of a state seems like a schematic picture without life and movement. But the others might help out. Timaeus will describe man's place in nature, Critias will relate the story of how Athens in long by-gone days realized the Socratic state; but Hermocrates' assignment is lost in uncertainty. Perhaps he was to outline how the ideal state could be established in present-day Athens. That great vision was never realized. The *Timaeus* was completed; the *Critias* never became more than a mere fragment; and the 'Hermocrates' was never written. Evidently Plato once more changed his point of view when he came to that part of the project that deals with the theory of the state. The *Laws* pick up where the *Critias* ends, but not on the premisses of myth.

For centuries the *Timaeus* was Plato's most widely read dialogue. We know that already Plato's own students debated it, and in Antiquity it was diligently commented upon, the first commentator being the Academic Crantor (*c.* 300). It was of decisive importance in the Academy tradition, and in the Stoic tradition as well. To the Neoplatonists it and the *Parmenides* were the most important Plato dialogues. Cicero translated parts of the *Timaeus*, and through major periods in the Middle Ages Calcidius' incomplete Latin translation with commentary (fourth or fifth century AD) was the only known Platonic text. The principal astronomic work of Antiquity, Ptolemy's *Syntaxis*, was not translated from the Arabic until the twelfth century, and the *Timaeus*, which represents a less advanced stage in the development of Greek astronomy, was long the normative model for the picture of the universe of the Middle Ages – for better or worse. Among other things, nobody realized the subtle interplay between myth and 'science' in the dialogue, and accordingly everything was understood as authoritative truth.

The *Timaeus* deals with astronomy, physics, and physiology, and the dialogue includes and reshapes elements from the entire tradition of natural philosophy – for example Empedocles, Anaxagoras and Democritus – but the Pythagorean ideal of science is its most profound inspiration. The aim is a synthesis that adjusts the empirical knowledge of the day to a basic teleological view, and this synthesis is of course Platonic in every respect. The physical world mirrors a rationally determined and morally good order; there is intimate correspondence between the macrocosmos and the human microcosmos; and in the spirit of good Pythagoreanism scientific and religious positions are united in the form of the myth.

Timaeus begins his account in a pompous, majestic style (*Tim.* 27 D ff.; cf. 51 B ff.). He asks what it is that always is but has no becoming, and what is it that always becomes and has no being? The first can be apprehended by rational thought and is always in the same state; the second by belief and sensation void of reason, it becomes, perishes, and never has real being. This world is the transitory world of becoming. It must have a cause and a 'first beginning' (*archē*). It is only about the eternal world of reason that we are able to say: 'It always was'; it will hold true for the material world that 'it has become'.

To find the father and creator of this world is an onerous task, and if he has been found, it is impossible to communicate this to everybody, as we are told next. But we may ask whether the master builder of the world created the world with the eternal or transitory as his model. Because this world is beautiful and the creator good, his model was the eternal, the unchangeable, which is understood by thought. It would be sacrilege even to speak about the alternative.

Such a prose hymn does not invite debate or argumentation for or against. As always, Plato indicates what must be taken for granted before it is even possible to begin reasoning – but never before in such high-flown language. On crucial points the passage stays within Platonic orthodoxy – the *Republic*, for example. But what is new is the discussion of the 'creation' of the world. The world is an ordered chaos, created on a model, but not as perfect as the model. The concept of 'creation' is clearly intended to explain the relation between phenomenon and idea; thereby – in Aristotelian terms – a *causa efficiens* has been introduced next to the idea as the formal one, matter as the material cause of the existence of the phenomenon, and this cause is symbolically expressed by the master builder (Demiurge) or 'Father' who creates the world – not from nothing, but by ordering a chaos. Although Plato had earlier toyed with the thought of such a Demiurge (*RP* X 596 C; *Soph.* 265 C), it is not until now that he becomes the universal creator and warrant that the world is 'good'. It has always been a fundamental Platonic thought that the world is good because rational and ordered – which does not preclude that metaphysical or ethical evil are real (cf. *Theaet.* 176 A); but it does turn evil into a lack of order, and precludes its being a principle on equal footing with the good. This thought is now tied to a story of creation and to a creator, elevated into religious language. But this is not a god like the divinities in tragedy who carelessly do with the world as they please according to their own unfathomable will. He wants the world to be rational and he will never break the eternal laws (cf. *Tim.* 41 A). Who and what he otherwise is is lost in the twilight of the fable. But it is essential in Plato's last works that faith and thought lend authority to each other.

It has of course been discussed whether the story of creation should be taken literally – has there actually been a time when the world was chaos? The question was debated already by Plato's own students (cf. Aristot. *De caelo* 279 b 33; Procl. in *Tim.* 1,280), and it is clear that during the Middle Ages one could without much difficulty identify the demiurge with the Christian Lord of Creation. But there can hardly be any doubt that the story of creation in the *Timaeus* is a symbolic expression of a non-temporal metaphysical relation between model and copy. Time – we learn (*Tim.* 37 C ff.; especially 38 C; cf. 34 B) – only came into being at the very moment of creation, and the chaos of 'becoming' is simply a timeless basic fact. The expressions used by Timaeus – 'that which always was' and 'that which has become' – are fixed predicates for the world of ideas and the world of phenomena respectively; the phenomenal world is always a something that has 'become'. Now, as Timaeus in the following develops his thought about the rationality and goodness of the world, he indirectly provides the answer, which the young Socrates could not come up with in the *Parmenides,* to the question whether the ideas are both universal and normative. He also picks up the thread from the *Phaedo,* in which the old Socrates criticized the natural philosophers for their inability to provide a teleological explanation of the world. It will be seen that there are other points where the *Timaeus* pursues earlier Platonic hints.

One thing is what we, according to the *Timaeus*, simply are to believe. Quite another what we must believe in order to speak about the sensory world in any way whatsoever. As the temporal world – to use the favourite Platonic metaphor – is an image of the eternal world (29 B ff.), it follows that we can never speak exactly about this world. We can only speak in images about an image. There is no science about the sensory, and therefore only a 'likely account' (*mythos*) can be provided – the special feature of the dialogue as 'scientific myth' is accordingly that the premises must be uncertain. But if the premises are accepted, the further conclusions must be rational. Amid all the seriousness there is also room for saying that physics is a diverting hobby for philosophers (59 C).

The master builder's model was the eternal, for he was good and without jealousy. He wanted this world to be as good as possible. Therefore he created the world out of chaos, for he considered order best (29 E). In other words: it was possible to create an approximately good world, and therefore it was created. That is what we have to believe. But what must this 'likely account' additionally presuppose? Of the visible nothing is more beautiful than that which is endowed with reason, and only soul can participate in reason (*nous*). Hence the world must be animated, the soul must have reason, and in his providence the god has accordingly created the world as a depiction of what it 'truly is to be' a being endowed with reason (cf. 39 E). This means that the model not only consists of unchangeable rational ideas but also of the essence of life, soul and thought. This is an allusion to the *Sophist*, but the *Phaedrus* myth and the final argument in the *Phaedo* are also in the background. The world of the *Timaeus* is a rational, living organism, and the best possible world can only be one, for the model is one, and the universe comprises everything that can exist in bodily form (31 A ff.). Most clearly reason is discernible in the movement of the heavenly bodies.

The master builder, or the Demiurge, is not lord of reason nor of the fact that 'the stuff' of the world is an inert, irrational mass without properties. But to some extent he can impress reason on matter, and this he can do by means of soul, which – as always in Plato – has intermediate status: it can apprehend rational truths, although it is bound to the stuff; it is the principle for movement, which means that it makes movement orderly and 'rational'; and therefore the soul has a physical function as well. The world has extension and is moved, and consequently it has a body; it is ordered, and consequently it has a soul. But soul and body may, so to speak, be interwoven, as the active presupposes the passive, and the passive the active. Now, an explanation of 'the creation' of the world must – speculatively – lay down what would be rational and 'beautiful' and what would be the simplest possible explanation; but thereafter it must be demonstrated how such a rational plan is congruent with observable facts. Rationality presupposes coherence, i.e. proportion, for only proportion can create unity from plurality (31 C). The prototype of proportion is to Plato the continuous geometrical progression. A simple geometrical progression from integers via square numbers to 'three-dimensional' cubic numbers is therefore assigned to the relation between the four elements, which is what the three-dimensional body of the world consists of. More elaborate proportional series are assigned to the movements of the cosmic soul, i.e. the rotation of the heavenly bodies (35 B ff.), and the same numerical relations determine the diatonic scale. As in the

Republic, the mathematical disciplines are connected; as with the Pythagoreans, the mathematical proportions are the language of the universe. The more specific details are, to be sure, more than obscure, but the aim is clear: a simple, explanatory mathematical model that renders motion intelligible. The given frame is the then current view of the world: a spheric universe in which the moon, the sun, the planets, and the fixed stars move with the earth at the centre (cf. also the astronomic section of the myth in the *Republic*, X 616 B ff.).

The body of the world comprised all four elementary bodies (earth, water, air and fire), and the Demiurge shaped them as a ball, because the spheric shape is the most beautiful and most perfect three-dimensional figure, which contains all figures (*Tim.* 33 B). When this body is set in steady circular motion around its own axis, the simplest, most perfect, and therefore most rational motion of the universe takes place. A rational motion presupposes a soul, and therefore the Demiurge equipped the body of the world with a soul moving by itself. But the cosmic soul cannot only devote itself to an undisturbed, self-sufficient, rotary motion; the motions of the firmament are more complex, and the cosmic soul must have a more complex structure.

The Demiurge created the cosmic soul (35 A ff.) from the following ingredients: Being, the Same and the Different, but each of these ingredients can be both divisible and indivisible, and the cosmic soul as a whole is therefore a unity consisting of six components. Readers of the *Parmenides, Theaetetus* and *Sophist* will most likely be amazed to encounter these well-known concepts as elements in a cosmology. Yet the symbolism is not incomprehensible: the cosmic soul is a tie between the phenomenal and ideal world (divisibility and indivisibility), and being, identity, and difference are the most basic pre-conditions for anything existing.

The Demiurge created a circle of the Same with the centre and radius like those of the celestial sphere. This circle was placed on a level with the celestial equator and set in uniform motion from east to west (36 B ff.). Thereby a spherical motion came about, which explains the regular paths of the fixed stars as well as the entire westward rotation of the celestial sphere. Next the Demiurge created a circle of the Different, which according to geometric proportions he divided into seven parts corresponding with the moon, the sun and the five known planets. These circles acquired eastward motions, they differed in speed and counteracted the regular rotation of the celestial sphere. Hereby it would be possible to 'save the phenomena', in other words to explain the apparently diverging motions of the seven heavenly bodies by means of a combination of uniform circular motions with the earth as the centre. The course of the sun along the ecliptic could directly be explained in this manner. Seemingly Plato imagined that a refined version of the model could be applied to the more complex, retrograde motions of the planets (38 D). It is not clear whether he was familiar with Eudoxus' theory (see. pp. 328 and 414) when he wrote the *Timaeus*. But it is certain that the account of the *Timaeus* carries out the programme of combining astronomical observation with theory that had been formulated in the *Republic*. In his day there were a considerable number of observations, which Plato knew, and his theory seeks to explain them by means of two principles: the principle of 'the most beautiful' and the principle of the simplest possible description.

But the theory is not merely physical. The same fundamental factors – Being, the

Same, and the Different – manifest themselves in the heavenly motions and in human cognition (36 E ff.). The cosmos and man are formed alike, and therefore we are able to observe the rational, circular motions in heaven and can profitably transfer our observations to the circular motions in our own soul (47 C). But the celestial bodies and the cognition they incorporate follow a definite plan of before and after, that of time. Time – day and night, the course of the year – is simply a consequence of the motions in heaven (37 C ff.). In the language of the myth: when the Father beheld his work, he was pleased, and he created time as an image of eternity. In eternity there is no before or after, only an eternal 'is'; the world of becoming, on the other hand, is always determined by 'was', 'is', and 'will be'. According to this account – which should be compared with the analysis of the concept of time in the *Parmenides* – time is an orderly sequential succession determined by the model, eternity.

Although the universe and man are of the same nature, there is a difference between the celestial and earthly regions – the celestial bodies are immortal and their rational motions always the same. On earth some events are dependent on those in heaven, while others are accidental and heterogeneous. This is immediately apparent to observation as a simple fact, and in the entire tradition from Plato to the break-through in modern science with Galileo and Newton there is therefore a sharp distinction between the supra-lunary and sub-lunary regions. In the *Timaeus* Plato presents this distinction in a special way, where he – as in the astronomical sections – expands on ideas from the myth in the *Republic*.

The Demiurge created the divine heaven, but it was also possible to create a terres-trial world populated by mortals, and since this was possible, it was done: the Demiurge himself created the divine in man, but left the rest to the lesser gods – the stars (41 A ff.) – for he himself has no share in the evil of the world (42 D). Therefore the lesser gods created man and put a soul in his body. But what was left over of the stuff of creation was not of prime quality, the rational proportions had become disor-dered, therefore man's circular motions became defective (44 D; 43 D), and the soul was drawn downwards by matter. Man became a mortal being, subject to regularly occurring reincarnations according to the law of necessity: the way in which indi-vidual man conducts his life determines the form in which he will be reborn (42 B ff.). Nor could the human body become perfect (44 Dff.). Reason was given its seat in the head, which, so far as possible, got the spherical shape of the cosmic body. But in this terrestrial world a head cannot roll helplessly around without being hurt, and therefore it was equipped with suitable growths – the limbs – and care was taken that the lower functions were accorded seats in the body, sufficiently removed so that they did not disrupt the rational contemplation of the head (cf. 69 D). But one precious gift was given man so that he could unite his reason with that of the macro-cosmos: sight, which by rays of vision unites the human eye with the heavenly light. On the technical level there are connections with the theory of sense perception in the *Theaetetus*, while on a higher level the light metaphor of the sun simile in the *Republic* is exploited.

The world created by the lesser gods – the sub-lunary world – is not only rational. It is a world that has not been created from nothing, but has been formed. Form and structure are not given with matter, but have been received. Any description of the physical world must therefore move at two levels, and it must – as already suggested in the *Phaedo* – employ two causal concepts: the teleological and the mechanical, 'accessory' causes (46 C ff.). The quintessence of teleological causes is reason (*nous*), the quintessence of mechanical necessity (*anankē*), chance (*tychē*) or 'the random cause'. In other words, on the one hand we have necessary but insufficient preconditions for the creation of a relatively ordered world and on the other that order which is impressed on a formless stuff. At the creation reason had to 'persuade' necessity in order for the world of becoming to resemble its ideal model as closely as possible (48 A ff.). With the creation of man as a rational being Timaeus therefore breaks off, and in a sense he starts all over again (47 E-69 A). Now he sets off 'from below', which is to say that the physical world is considered in abstraction from the teleological aspect, and form and structure are introduced only gradually, so that by the by we come to the world we know – still in the 'time sequence' of the myth. For the first time what is investigated is not only what an image represents, but also what physical entity it is that is capable of receiving images – and thereby what is examined is a precondition of participation. We commenced with presupposing the idea as the original and the phenomenon as the copy, says Timaeus (48 E ff.). Now we must add a third entity, which is that which depicts.

This third entity is unintelligible in itself. It is a delimiting concept that can only be known by means of a sort of 'bastard reasoning' (52 B). It is both that in which something is and that from which something is formed. This means that it can both be considered as space and as prima materia, formless stuff. The Platonic space is neither an absolute space, nor – as with Democritus – a void in which the body moves, but – as with Zeno – a sort of receptacle, the site of the things that are subject to becoming and annihilation (52 A). When considered as stuff without contours, it may be characterized by a series of approximate metaphors – it is the site of necessity; it can be likened to the 'nurse of becoming' (49 A) or to a waxy matrix (50 C). In the primordial state of chaos (52 D ff.) pseudo-bodies, pseudo-elements, and pseudo-qualities move irregularly according to mechanical principles in the receptacle of space and in such a manner that like seeks like, although everything has only seeming, non-real existence, for all kinds of proportions and measures are missing. Laws of nature in the modern sense are alien to Plato.

This is yet another version of the Platonic chaos. In the *Parmenides* (the seventh hypothesis) it was considered from the metaphysical point of view and in the *Theaetetus* from the epistemological. In the *Timaeus* it now appears in a physical context. But there are surely some hidden polemics in the *Timaeus* account. Democritus' name is never mentioned. But all things considered, Plato also wanted to show that an ordered world could never arise on Democritus' premises – a material world, which only follows the law of necessity and mechanical principles of movement, is and remains a chaos. But the physical world is not like that: the god has acted and given structure to matter. Against the physical atomism of Democritus, Plato provides a mathematical, non-materialist theory (cf. the juxtaposition in Aristot. *De gen. et corr.* 325 b 24). It is implied that there are two components in the physical world: stuff and structure, and the theory meets both Plato's call for structure and for a teleological causal explanation.

Plato sees it as his task to reduce physical bodies to regular solids, i.e. crystals determined by number (*Tim.* 53 C ff.). The 'most beautiful' three-dimensional bodies, which at the same time are determined by simple numeric relations, are the five polyhedra, or 'Platonic' bodies, the construction of which was probably known in the Pythagorean tradition, and which were studied by Theaetetus (cf. Eucl. XIII, prop. 13 ff.). These polyhedra, which are delimited by congruent, equilateral plane figures and which can be inscribed into or circumscribed by a sphere, are now related to the four elements that already existed without order in the pre-cosmic chaos. The tetrahedron, the pyramid that is delimited by four equilateral triangles, is adjusted to fire; the octahedron (eight equilateral triangles) to air, and the icosahedron (twenty equilateral triangles) to water. The cube (six squares) is adjusted to earth. Finally, the last polyhedron – the dodecahedron, which is delimited by twelve equilateral pentagons and in form resembles the sphere most closely – corresponds with the world at large. Now use is made of the fact that the three polyhedra listed first are delimited by the same figures. This means that the individual particles can be broken down and recomposed. Three of the elements can in other words be interchanged, while the cubic form of earth prevents earth from participating in this transformational process.

This already shows that Plato's theory of atoms – unlike that of Democritus – was not a physical one. The regular polyhedra are ideal solids, not physical bodies, but these are not indivisible (*atoma*) either. They are composed of simple plane triangles, which explain the form of matter but not its nature 'in itself'; these geometrical 'atoms' are immaterial, and it is suggested (53 D) that perhaps they may be derived from superior metaphysical principles. And they can be broken. The equilateral triangles – which delimit particles of fire, air, and water – are composed of two congruent right-angled isosceles triangles, the sides of which are in the relation of $1:\sqrt{3}:2$, and the squares that delimit the cube of the earth are composed of two congruent, right-angled triangles, the sides of which are in the relation $1:1:\sqrt{2}$. The point of this further complication is presumably double-sided. Partly, it becomes possible to operate with a limited number of basic numbers, while consideration is given to the incommensurable relation between sides of even quite simple triangles, for the world cannot – as with the Pythagoreans – be described as a relation between integers, and therefore irrational basic numbers must be built into the theory. Furthermore, it is also possible to compose similar figures of different sizes from a varying number of atomic triangles. This explains (58 C ff.) why there are several phenomenal varieties of the elements: there are, for example, several kinds of 'water' or liquids.

Naturally this theory is imaginative, and it is expressly presented as a fantasy – observing the rules of reason that also apply to fiction. There are crucial similarities with the astronomical theory. In both cases basic, arbitrary choices are made with respect to proportions and 'basic numbers'. The criterion for these choices is that which is 'the most beautiful', simplest and most rational – on the presupposition that the world is constructed in conformance with mathematical principles and can be described *more geometrico*. Yet the conclusions that are drawn on this basis are not arbitrary. The theory of astronomy can, however, be connected with an established empirical science, but there was no science dealing with the nature of matter; nor were there means either to verify or falsify Plato's theory of matter. Experimental chemistry was unknown, and no science dealt with the movement of terrestrial bodies – the cinematics known by Plato is in principle identical with that of Democritus: bodies encounter one another, press against each other, or are joined, and – the ancient principle that 'like seeks like' aside – neither Plato nor Democritus assumed that there were forces at work from a distance. Logically enough, Plato concluded that astronomical motions must be owing to the fact that the heavenly bodies are endowed with reason, while the motions of terrestrial bodies are accidental and therefore must be ascribed to necessity, not to reason. Admittedly Plato's theory is just as speculative as other theories of the day. Still, it can account for more phenomena than rival theories. While Empedocles' four elements cannot be mutually transformed, this is possible with three of Plato's, and so a vision belonging to the old tradition of natural philosophy – for example, those of Anaximenes and Heraclitus – could be rationally vindicated. Both the transition of elements into each other and the 'varieties' of the elements provide more possibilities of explaining empirical facts than does the Democritus theory. First and foremost, Plato's theory can render an explanation of structure and form, which Democritus found difficult to provide. This is, of course, the cornerstone of the Platonic construction: the physical world consists of a substratum that evades cognition, and yet it is receptive of forms that *per se* belong at a higher metaphysical level. Consequently, a physical description must consist in a reduction to immaterial entities. Agreement with the fundamental principles of the doctrine of ideas is self-evident. The wider perspective is the idea of a mathematical description of nature. Plato himself carefully pays heed to the limits of what can be rationally explained. His successors through the centuries have all too frequently confused 'a likely account' with an authoritative doctrine.

With regard to basis and aim, Plato's theory of atoms is radically different from that of Democritus. Yet, after it has been established that bodies may be formed by the blending of elements, Plato is in fact able to stick quite closely to Democritus. This applies not least to the distinction between primary and secondary sense qualities (61 C ff.). The natural stuffs and the individual bodies are determined by the basic forms and their combinations and by the mutual transformations of the elements – thereby the primary qualities come about. The secondary qualities – and thereby the world as a sensed world – depends, as with Democritus, upon an interplay between physical objects and the constitution of man's sense organs. So in the *Timaeus* the physical substratum for sense-perception is described, while it falls outside the scope of the *Timaeus* to draw the epistemological conclusions. That Plato here chooses quite different paths than those of Democritus is seen in the *Theaetetus*.

The treatment of the sense qualities ends the account of the way in which it is shown how reason step by step persuades necessity to create a cosmos out of the chaos of nature. In this way the two main lines in the dialogue converge: the downward path from reason to necessity and the upward path from necessity to reason. Then follows a final section (69 A ff.), which describes the creation of the 'mortal parts' of the human soul and the creation of the human body by an interaction of reason and necessity. This section is concluded with a brief treatment of the lower living creatures – women, land animals, birds, and fishes (90 E ff.). The principal theme is in other words what we would call anatomy and physiology, and here Plato makes use of many sources – above all contemporary medical science, which mainly was founded on observations of the courses of diseases, dissection and the theory of the harmonious blend of those forces and elements that are a precondition for health. Inescapably the section has an odd effect on the modern reader who must accustom himself to the idea that, for example, the circulation of the blood and the functions of breathing and nerves were unknown. Plato is at pains to spice up his presentation. The gods have, for example, given man a long intestinal canal so that food may be stored for some time – otherwise the greedy human beings would spend time eating and drinking instead of dealing with philosophy.

The overall motif is of course the double level of description, the relation between mechanical and teleological causes. Hair, for example, consists of excretions from the scalp that are created to protect the head. The mouth with teeth, tongue and lips is created from an ingenious mixture of hard and soft matter, which serves both lower and higher purposes, ingestion of food and the articulation of words – the servants of reason (75 D ff.). Most important of all: man has been given his body to house the noblest part of the soul, reason or man's guardian spirit (*daimōn*) – as we are told with an echo from Heraclitus (90 A ff.). And he who refuses to be guided by desire coming from the unreason of necessity, will know how to care for his soul. By contemplation of celestial reason he will attain the highest human happiness.

Following Timaeus, it should now be Critias' turn – likewise in the form of myth – to place man in history, but, as has been mentioned, only the beginning of this dialogue was written. What Critias relates is true and certain, for his account goes back to the wise Solon who in his turn had obtained it from Egyptian priests (21 A ff.), and he even has written sources at his disposal (*Critias* 113 B). The account deals with a major war about 9000 years ago, when Athens saved Europe from becoming enslaved by a great realm far westwards in the ocean, Atlantis – quite as Athens much later was to save Hellas from the great Persian realm. Soon afterwards, one of those major natural catastrophes occurred, which at intervals devastate states and societies. The old Athens perished, and Atlantis was swallowed up by the ocean (*Tim.* 25 D). Now, the old Athens (*Critias* 110 C ff.) was – strange to tell – governed exactly like the ideal commonwealth, which Socrates describes in the beginning of the *Timaeus*. It was a frugal society, the rulers lived by themselves, all property was shared, and the state was justly, piously, and well ruled. Atlantis (113 B ff.) was a monarchy, a major realm with immeasurable riches, thriving commerce, and inexhaustible natural resources. Originally it had been a good and law-abiding society, but gradually covetousness and thirst for power gained the upper hand (121 B), and the great realm became aggressive. And here the text ends, just as Zeus is about to interfere.

One can conjecture on the reason why the *Critias* was left unfinished. What Plato had in mind concerning man and society probably did not well fit the fictional form of myth. The problem is not how things might have been, but how they are or ought to be.

THE *PHILEBUS*

The *Philebus* deals with what is good for man. It is an ethical dialogue, and Socrates leads the discussion. But if the dialogue – as is most likely – was written after the

'Eleatic' dialogues and the *Timaeus*, it shows that Socrates has been an attentive but independent listener. He has learned metaphysics from the Eleatics and cosmology from Timaeus, but his main concern then and now is that it is the good that rules in the cosmos and in the life of man. He now attempts to place the good in a metaphysical-cosmological context.

Socrates does not – as in the *Republic* – ask about the good itself, but – as did Aristotle later – about the good for man, or, happiness (*Phil.* 19 C; 11 D). He presupposes the standard Academy formula that the good is that which everybody strives for (20 D), and – as in the *Protagoras* or *Gorgias* – it is his task to reject the claim that the humanly good consists in pleasure or enjoyment (*hēdonē*), a position that in fact was advocated at the Academy (Eudoxus, cf. Aristot. *Ethic. Nic.* 1172 b 9). In the dialogue this position is advocated by a certain Protarchus who acts as the spokesman for Philebus, an invented person after whom the dialogue is named. The latter is such an out-and-out hedonist that he cannot even take the trouble to argue on his own behalf. In the course of the discussion Protarchus is reduced to a docile auditor of Socrates who masters the didactic mode of presentation as ably as the Stranger in the *Sophist*. Socrates' initial thesis (*Phil.* 11 B ff.) is that the good consists in reason and right belief.

The feeling of pleasure is a concept with several meanings (12 C ff.), and therefore it is mandatory first of all to determine what it means that something can be unequivocally determined. As in the *Sophist*, it is rejected that there are special problems connected with characterizing a particular by several predicates; the problem of one-many is to be posed in general terms (14 C ff.). In a system of ideas – 'monads', as they are called – each idea is a unity determined by its place or its 'number' in a whole. The ability to know this is owing to a gift from the gods, communicated by ancient sages – the Pythagoreans (16 C ff.) – who passed on the learning that all which is one and many is composed of the limiting and the unlimited (*peras* and *apeiron*). Wherever there is an unlimited continuum, a more or less, or 'an excess and defect', one can determine a measure. A man is not simply large, but has a definite size; what is high and low in pitch may be arranged on a scale; a number can make an indefinite quantity finite (cf. 23 C ff.; *Pol.* 283 D). A *diairesis* system is one finite plurality delimited *vis-à-vis* an indefinite plurality – the phenomena – and not until every unity has been assigned a 'number', can one let it 'pass into to the unlimited' (*Phil.* 16 E). Clearly there are references to the *Parmenides*, *Sophist* and *Timaeus*.

But in the *Philebus* the intention is not to reduce phenomena to ideas or matter to structure. The theme is man's life here and now in 'this mixed life' (20 C ff.) and the universe in which man lives ('everything that now is', 23 C) is a becoming or a process directed at being (*genesis eis ousian*, 26 D; cf. 27 B). Therefore the discussion that alone aims at ideas – 'monads' – is discontinued; with a *Phaedo* phrase, one must choose 'the second-best course', for there is need of an expanded, formal conceptual apparatus. Socrates poses four formal constituent parts of our world: the limit, the unlimited, the mixture and the cause of the mixture (23 C ff.). 'Mixture' does not merely, as in the world of ideas, apply to the joining of the limited and the unlimited but to the basic circumstance that in our world and our life several ingredients are included; and continuous striving for being in such a 'mixture' presupposes a *causa efficiens*, the rational cause that guides becoming towards being. In the mythical language of the *Timaeus* this cause is personified in the Demiurge, and in the *Philebus* reason is also the lord of heaven and earth, and it is the cause of the good in the mixed life (26 E ff.). It is mirrored in weak human reason, for the microcosmos is a reflection of the macrocosmos.

As an explanatory model this conceptual apparatus is steadily connected with the basic theme of the dialogue, the good for man. The good is perfect, self-sufficient, and everybody strives for the good. But Socrates has 'dreamed' that the good is neither pleasure nor reason (20 B ff.) – he has perhaps dreamed of the *Republic*; perhaps the good in the *Republic* is a dream in the human world; it is likely that the good, in the vocabulary of the *Philebus*, must be identified with the limit, the absolute that determines everything that is. But the good for man is an approximation; in the mixed life pleasure and reason presuppose each other, and hence the rest of the dialogue investigates pleasure and reason as ingredients in the good life with respect to the relative value of these concepts in relation to the absolute good. In several respects this investigation is the point of departure for Aristotle's ethics – even though Aristotle clearly distances himself from the metaphysical framework.

The feeling of pleasure must be a 'mixture' – not only is pleasure connected with pain, and a momentary pain may be connected with the expectation of some future greater feeling of pleasure, but pleasure cannot, as is remarked with a reference to the *Sophist* (53 D; cf. *Soph.* 255 C), belong to the class of things that exist in themselves; it is a feeling related to something else and strives for something else. Pleasure is always pleasure at something or enjoyment of something, and pleasure is closely related to the cognitive faculties of the soul; it is a feeling that in a manner of speaking presupposes a two-way dependence. The harmonious constitution of the body – a key concept in the medical science of the day – is a precondition for pleasure (*Phil.* 31 B ff.). But pleasure is not some passive feeling. A person enjoys himself, and is in other words conscious of the pleasurable. Thereby pleasure is connected with feelings, needs, anticipation and hope; the soul judges what is going on in the body; a conscious need implies that the person senses and recalls the circumstances that can satisfy the need; and – as shown in the *Theaetetus* – sense-perception implies interpretation and belief (*doxa* – 32 B ff.). But the judgement that expresses such an opinion may be true or false, and therefore there are also true or false feelings of pleasure (36 C ff.). Seen as a whole, pleasure is accordingly a complex phenomenon, but pure pleasure – which does not permit pain – appears in connection with the aesthetic experience of beauty and in connection with reason.

Perhaps pleasure may thus be considered an epiphenomenon to reason, and perhaps reason is thus, as Socrates began by maintaining, identical with what is good for man? Yes and no. In several passages it is suggested (21 E; 33 B; 43 D) that pure reason is above pleasure and pain. But we are also told that a life in pure reason is a divine prerogative, which therefore must presuppose that man transcends himself as a man of flesh and blood. Human reason is akin to but not identical with the cosmic reason, which causes the 'mixed' life. Therefore human reason is also tied to a life in pleasure and pain. To this must be added that human reason has an intentional structure: it is directed at beauty, proportion, and truth (64 A ff.); but reason is purer than pleasure, because its object is right measure, the absolute that delimits the unlimited.

In the 'mixed life' we can only reach 'the threshold of the good'. Here there can be no talk of one good for man but of a class of goods arranged according to their rank. First comes that which is in itself, the final objects of man's striving and knowledge: measure and the beautiful. Thereafter – in third and fourth place – reason and right opinion, i.e. that knowledge that is directed at being. Finally, in fifth place come pure pleasures, which are epiphenomena to reason (66 A ff.).

It is not denied in the *Philebus* that the philosopher – as in the *Republic* and the *Theaetetus* – may become 'godlike', but the discussion only concerns the man who is bound to the 'mixed life'. What consequences must be drawn if this 'human man' is considered as a social being? Here we cannot remain stuck with the ambiguous conclusion of the *Republic*, a perfect society balancing between utopia, construction and possibility. Furthermore, the myth has proved itself to be an unsuitable form of presentation.

THE *LAWS*

In the *Statesman* – which chronologically surely precedes the *Philebus* – it is still a presupposition that the state should be governed on the basis of wisdom and insight. Ideally one person, the king, who possesses absolute wisdom, will be the ablest ruler, and he will be above the law, because the law can only provide general rules but is unable to predict the concrete cases to which it will be applied (*Pol.* 293 C ff.). But in the real world such an ideal person does not exist. The existing constitutions – monarchy, oligarchy and democracy – can be lawful or lawless. Among the societies that are bound by law, monarchy ought to be preferred. Among lawless societies, on the other hand, the preferable is anarchistic democracy, for here the individual exercise of power will always be curtailed (291 C; 302 D ff.). Yet the state of law is the best approximation to the ideal constitution, and tyranny is the worst thinkable form (301 E ff.).

In the *Laws* Plato accordingly gives shape to a concrete and detailed legislation for a new city state, a colony intended to be built on Crete (*Leg.* III 702 C). There are reminiscences both of the account in the *Republic* of the origin of civilization and of the myth in the *Timaeus–Critias* – which besides had already been prepared for in a cosmological 'myth of history' in the *Statesman* (268 D ff.): long ago when the gods ruled on earth, everything was pure enjoyment, but ever since the gods withdrew, countless natural catastrophes have occurred in the history of mankind, and every time man has had to begin all over again in a constant cyclic chain of events (*Leg.* III 670 A ff.; IV 713 C); small contented agrarian societies have developed into greater more or less inflamed city states. But the myth is now transferred to another framework: a set of authoritative rules provided by a sovereign legislator (Plato). In such a context it is obvious that Socrates cannot undertake the role as Plato's spokesman.

The *Laws* – Plato's most extensive dialogue – is the work of an old man, and, according to the tradition transmitted from Antiquity, the dialogue was edited by a student (Philippus from Opous, Diog. Laert. III 37), which seems most plausible. The dialogue lacks a final touching-up, and although the main outline is clear enough, there are a great number of digressions, hints and repetitions. The style has become mannered, drawn-out, and yet it is abrupt; the presentation is pedantically meticulous but is nevertheless distant and strangely blurred. The work reflects the experiences and resentments accumulated during a long life; it is Plato's last message, but it is formulated as if through a veil. The author is remote, far from the reader, the addressee is humanity, those human beings who are as toys in the hands of the gods: the task is to take charge of man's affairs, but he is not worth much trouble (*Leg.* VII 803 B ff.; cf. I 644 D; *Ep.* VII 344 C).

The frame of the dialogue is a simple one: on a long, long summer day an unnamed Athenian, a Spartan and a Cretan are walking to the grotto where Zeus at the dawn of time gave King Minos the laws of the Cretans. They discuss the legislation of the new colony that is to be built. They are three old men in discussion, sedate, weighty, and with exquisite urbanity, although sometimes their voices are a little squeaky. The anonymous Athenian leads the discussion, frequently expressing himself in authoritative monologues, with which the two others concur with deferential respect. Surely the Athenian is not Plato, but it is beyond doubt that he makes ample use of Platonic sources.

We speak to men, not to gods, we are told (*Leg.* V 732 E). Hence it is only the second-best state that is debated (739 B; VII 807 B) – the state of heaven is a different matter. It is often said that the Plato of the *Laws* is a resigned man, and sometimes that he has become more tolerant and realistic. It all depends. He has not changed opinion since he wrote the *Republic*, and he was never an optimist. The *Laws* deal with the adjustment of the ideal to an imperfect human world.

In a society of men there should be no authority above the law, but the law should not be dictatorial. It must win the acceptance of the citizens (III 690 C) and consider the welfare of all. Worst are one-man rule, conflicting interests, and civil war. No existing society can live up to these demands, neither Sparta nor Crete – the home of two of the interlocutors – which, although they have respectable conservative constitutions, too much emphasize courage and military might and thereby neglect peace, friendship, and amity (I 628 A ff.). Yet the most frightening examples of the going astray of constitutions is the Persian monarchy, in which a despot rules over slaves, and the Attic democracy, in which freedom means unruliness, the fight of all against all (III 694 A ff; 698 A ff.). Both one-man rule and majority dictatorship are to be avoided, and friendship, insight, and freedom should be the guiding principles (693 B; 701 D); but the traditional types of constitution actually represent only party governments, not constitutions (VIII 832 B). Accordingly the best solution is what later came to be called 'the mixed constitution', one which – according to the Athenian – is partially in effect in Sparta, i.e. a mixture of democracy and oligarchy, a balancing of power, which imparts stability to society, because the interests of all groups of inhabitants are heeded (IV 712 E ff.).

When the Athenian is speaking about the balance between the groups of inhabitants, he is of course thinking of the citizens. As in the *Republic*, it is presupposed as a matter of course that there are slaves and immigrants without political rights. In other words, the traditional division into classes and the traditional, parasitic, economic paradigm is maintained – Plato never saw any problems with this, and where there are no problems, there is nothing to defend.

Slaves take care of heavy physical work, such as farmwork, and the immigrants work as artisans and conduct trade, a discreditable occupation that should be curtailed as much as possible (cf. VII 806 D; XI 920 A). The citizens on the other hand should not be distracted by manual work, but neither should they devote themselves to a *dolce far niente*: they have enough to do in governing and in being governed (VII 807 A). But, as in the *Republic*, women are to have – almost – the same status as men. Yet, and this is innovative with reference to the *Republic*, society is dependent on private property and family life – the state of law is the second-best state (V 739 A ff.). Agriculture is the principal occupation (736 C ff.; cf. XII 949 E); and the state must be large enough to defend and feed itself, but no more than that. The land is divided into 5,040 lots of equal size – a number that is divisible by many divisors and hence most agreeable to Pythogoreans and administrators – and if one includes everybody on two legs, men, women, children, immigrants and slaves, one probably arrives at a total population of a middle-sized provincial town. These lots of land must never be subdivided or sold, for the size of the population must be kept constant – something which of course causes certain problems (V 740 B ff.). The economic basis of the state is in other words to remain unchanged. All in all, it is a principle that in the good state any change is bad (VII 797 A). Another fundamental principle depends upon the difference between arithmetical and geometric proportion: there is – 'arithmetical' – equality before the law, but everybody does not have the same share of goods; in the second-best state all are rewarded according to their merits, and in accordance with this principle of equality – 'distributive justice' according to Aristotle – four owning classes are introduced (V 744 B ff.; cf. VI 756 E ff.). Yet there is a fairly tight upper limit to the extent of personal possessions, and it is forbidden to charge interest (V 742 C). Plato's upper class is intellectual, not economic, and economic considerations are a necessary evil that has to be kept in check.

If the principles of constancy and geometric equality are adhered to, the good agrarian state will be a healthy and stable state. But such a state must of course be on guard against foreign contamination. Travel abroad is only permitted in exceptional cases, and aliens must be kept under close supervision, except in the case of very distinguished visitors (XII 949 E ff.; 952 D ff.).

This is the economic and social basis for legislation and administration. The governmental apparatus (VI 751 A ff.) – civil servants, popular assembly, council, and people's courts – corresponds by and large with that of Athens, although with significant additions. There are for example 37 'guardians of the law' who are granted extensive authority. The 5040 households are not under-administrated, and it is clear that all citizens at some point will hold public office. Yet a complex electoral system (752 D ff.) ensures that the upper classes have relatively great influence – thereby both the 'principle of equality' and the 'principle of the balance of power' are adhered to. All officials can be held responsible in law, for example by the use of a special body of officials supervising the officials (XII 945 B). For although the law is only an imperfect reflection of reason itself, the law is sovereign in a human state; it is the backbone of society, and – unlike the *Republic* – it is clearly stated that the common good takes precedence over that of the individual (IX 875 A ff.; IV 714 A; V 740 A; IX 923 A). But law is not some dead prescription. The Socratic principle that nobody acts unjustly against his will and that man must care for his soul is fundamental in Plato's legal philosophy. Hence persuasion is better than punishment, and every law must be furnished with an introduction explaining the intention with it (IV 720 E ff.; IX 860 C ff.). Whenever the legal system is activated, ample opportunities for appeal are provided (VI 761 E; XII 956 B).

In many respects the Platonic laws can be considered an improved version of Attic practice, but his philosophy of law is his own and its impact has been considerable. The particular laws (civil law mainly in books VI–VIII and XI, criminal law in book IX) ensure the individual's legal rights with all available means. But that is not all. Not only is human life regulated in all details – even down to theft of figs and unpaid artisans' bills (VIII 844 D; XI 921 B) – and not only does Plato seem to presuppose that everybody will be in litigation with everybody in the state of concord, but all human life is subject to rigid control. The private life of citizens is no mere 'private matter' (cf. for example VI 772 E ff. on the choice of spouses), and the law explicitly encourages informing; there is also a 'secret police', a corps of young men who report everything suspicious to the authorities (762 B). Capital punishment is used in the not infrequent cases when the criminal is thought to be harmful to society. This applies not least to moral violations, and religious intolerance is a basic feature of Plato's state of law.

Whence derives the apparent contradiction between 'peace, friendship, and concord' on the one hand and control and inquisitorial supervision on the other? The explanation can already be found in the *Republic*: the individual is nothing, morality everything. There exists a natural law, a set of absolute moral norms, which – however incompletely – find expression in human laws. If such a natural law did not exist, law and order would be meaningless words, and one might as well choose Gyges as one's ideal. It is the unconditional duty of the citizen to observe the ideals that lie behind the legislator's prescriptions. Otherwise he will have no possibility to live as a free moral being. Life is too serious an affair to leave to men's own management.

The basic moral point of view means of course that education is of decisive importance, and the director of education – 'the minister of education' – is assigned a crucial role. The specific rules (VII 788 A ff.) are fairly similar to those of the *Republic*, but it should be especially noted that a kind of universal compulsory education is called for. As in the *Republic* poetry is subject to censorship; literature must edify; and it would for example be a good idea (811 C) to let young people read the *Laws* (!). Ordinary basic education does not include higher mathematics or studies in philosophy. Nevertheless, free men are to become acquainted with important things, such as incommensurables and planetary motions (817 E ff.) – in other words with the main points in the mathematical cosmology of the *Timaeus*. There are greater perspectives in such a decree than one might immediately think.

How can morality be determined and how can it be justified? It is done indirectly. In the *Laws* there is no metaphysical section like that in the *Republic*. The dialogue does not deal with philosophers, nor is it written for philosophers, but for the sort of men to whom the 'myth of state' of the *Republic* is addressed. This means that the symbolic truth familiar from Plato's myths must be accepted as the literal truth without hesitation, or at least as the truth man can understand. What everybody can recognize and everybody must consider is the reason – and thereby the goodness – that is manifest in the universe as a whole, in the 'visible gods' – the stars – and what matters is the implantation of this reason in the soul of man. Thus the basis of the state of law is cosmic religion, linked to the traditional religious ideas – the *Phaedo* went beyond that – and to piety, for example to the god in Delphi. Purgation of religious contamination is an important element in murder trials (cf. IX 864 C ff.). As in the myths, there is reference to punishment in the life hereafter – for this is a story believed by many (870 D; cf. X 904 A ff.), and it is expressly stated (VIII 838 D) that the particular provisions for punishment can be masked as religious sanctions. As with the Pythagoreans, symbol and reality have been fused. Whether there is a higher truth hidden behind this religiosity cannot be known by the crowd, perhaps only by the few men of divine nature (cf. XII 951 B).

The state of law is a theocracy, for in the state of law it is god who is the measure of all things (IV 716 C), and atheism is the worst crime against the state. An atheist acting in folly must be imprisoned for five years, during which time the authorities must try to make him think better of his ways. But if he stubbornly persists he must die. The man who is an unbeliever with evil intent must be isolated from everybody in a prison far from the beaten path, and his body is to be left without burial beyond the borders of the state (X 908 E ff.).

There are three heresies: that the gods do not exist; that they do not care about humanity; or that they can be affected by sacrifice or prayer (885 B). Behind these heresies, says the Athenian, there will often be a theory, and that theory turns out to be a sort of common denominator for the entire tradition of natural philosophy and Sophistry. The world in itself, they would say, is material; and it is in every respect subject to chance (*tychē*). All cultural institutions, on the other hand, are dependent on man's art and skill (*technē*), and consequently there is no natural justice.

Opposed to this stands the cosmic religion, which unites the cosmic soul with man's and claims that the universe is governed according to a rational plan and that soul is primary to matter (892 A). According to the Athenian such a claim can be explained scientifically, and he proceeds to a sort of resumé of the cosmology in the *Timaeus* and of the doctrine of the 'allsoul'.

In an important – and of course cryptic – passage (893 B ff.) the several forms of motion and change in the universe are examined, and two conclusions are drawn. In the first place, that the steady circular motion in one place is the basic one, because it is regular, unchangeable, and an expression of reason (cf. 898 A). In the second place, that something (matter) is moved, while something else moves on its own and thereby moves everything else – and what moves on its own and hence is alive is the soul (cf. 896 C ff.). The heavenly bodies move in regular circular motions, and their motions are transplanted to the earthly world, they are 'rational', and therefore the cosmic soul is 'good' – as opposed to an 'evil soul' that must be supposed to be responsible for the disorderly, chaotic motion in the world (896 E; 897 C – it is probable that the 'evil' soul corresponds with the necessity of the *Timaeus*). In continuation of the *Phaedo* and *Phaedrus*, for example, the soul, the cosmic soul as well as individual souls, is hence conceived of both as a vital principle and as the seat of reason, and all mental activities – not only reason, but also opinions and feelings – are prior to matter and its properties. Whether the apostate atheist will feel himself convinced must be left to surmise, but Plato believes that on his own premises he has performed a stringent demonstration on an empirical basis. The existence of 'visible gods' gives proof of the articles of faith: the soul precedes the body, and the heavenly bodies are rational (XII 966 D).

Far-reaching doctrinary consequences are drawn in the appendix to the *Laws*, the *Epinomis*, which surely is the work of a student, Philippus of Opous. What matters to the Athenian is to make the unbelieving man remember that 'the universe does not exist for your sake; you exist for the sake of the universe' (X 903 C). It is this message that gives the Athenian – and Plato – the position of guardian of mankind, messenger from the divine world.

In the state of law itself the role of intermediary between the divine and the human is taken care of by a special institution – the 'nocturnal assembly', as it is called in a sinister-sounding phrase. It merely means that the assembly consists of busy men who meet before dawn (XII 960 B ff.) The nocturnal assembly is in fact the highest authority of the state of law, even though its formal status is lost in mystification. It is its task to preserve the state intact, to receive reports of all the affairs of the state, to improve the law if necessary, to possess moral insight, and to communicate this knowledge. If this divine assembly can be created, we may go forth and found our colony, as we are told on the last page of the dialogue (969 A ff.).

The nocturnal assembly is not – as the rulers in the *Republic* – an assembly of philosophers, for the state of law is not the optimal, divine state, and the cosmic religion is merely a symbolic truth. Both the *Timaeus*, *Philebus* and the *Laws* are enacted in a world, which is only half-way real. We find ourselves on the 'threshold of the good'. It is hinted in all three dialogues, including the *Laws*, that there is a reality behind the veil. The stellar gods can be seen by all, and everybody can understand that they are souls endowed with reason; but we human beings will probably never be able to understand reason itself fully, we are told (X 897 D). The members of the nocturnal assembly have most likely not beheld the idea of the good, but in accordance with sound Socratic spirit they can explain why the virtues constitute a unity (XII 963 C ff.), and in one single sentence in this great work it is stated that they can see the one idea in a plurality and account for the sense in which it is a unity, in which sense it is a whole (965 C).

In one place (VII 817 B) the Athenian asks what the reply should be if tragic poets arrive in the state of law and offer to show their plays. Here is the reply: 'Most honoured strangers. We ourselves according to our abilities are poets of the most beautiful and best tragedy. Our entire state is an imitation (*mimēsis*) of the most beautiful and noble life, and that, we claim, is the most truthful tragedy'.

18

PLATO AND THE EARLY ACADEMY

—— •◆• ——

THE *SEVENTH LETTER*

There is only one passage where Plato speaks about philosophical subjects in his own name: a few pages of the *Seventh Letter* (*Ep* VII 341 B-4D), and those pages are of course especially interesting. But one should not expect Plato to express himself here without reservation and directly. The occasion of the passage is the superficial venture by Dionysius II into philosophy, and its purpose is precisely to explain that the 'matter itself' cannot be communicated directly (341 C ff.) – neither in written nor oral form. Only he who is 'akin to the matter' will be able to understand it. After lengthy dialectical investigation and philosophical debates 'it may come about that insight and understanding of every single thing shines forth, if one bends one's effort as much as humanly possible' (344 B).

Platonic mysticism cannot be communicated, but Plato's reasons for the indirect mode of communication can, and such reasons are provided in the *Seventh Letter* in which the pre-conditions for knowledge are dealt with briefly. Here (342 A ff.) three means to acquire knowledge are mentioned: name (*onoma*), explanation (*logos*) and image (*eidōlon*); as a fourth in the series is listed insight or knowledge itself (*epistēmē*), and as a fifth that which truly has being, the object of knowledge. The example of a circle is advanced: it has a name that can be explained by a definition, and it can be depicted. Neither of these elements are identical with true knowledge of the circle; nor is the knowledge identical with the circle itself. It is clear that it is superior to name and explanation – the name is arbitrary, and the definition may be false. But the concept of image has no fixed relation to name and explanation – as always in Plato both name and linguistic formulation may be called images, but so can a drawing and the physical object itself.

On the one hand, the three means to acquire knowledge and knowledge itself emerge as reflections of the matter itself – as in the ancient tradition, knowledge is an ontological phenomenon (cf. *Phil.* 66 A; *Leg.* X 895 D). On the other hand (*Ep.* VII 343 A ff.), there is of course, as everywhere in Plato, difference between reflection and reality. Explanation and name – language in short – are conditions for intersubjective knowledge and hence do not merely express individual cognition. But not only can language express false cognition: it is itself something different from that which is spoken about – as demonstrated in the *Phaedo* and *Cratylus*. As in the *Theaetetus*, it is only knowledge itself that can determine whether an explanation is 'true'. Language as well as any image may misrepresent reality – a circle that has been drawn will for example never be perfectly circular, and an explanation may confuse quality with essential property (343 B).

The fourth moment, insight – knowledge, reason, and true belief (342 C ff.) – is the surest, but insight is a mental phenomenon and therefore also intentionally determined by something other than itself. It is, however, a state that may lead onwards so that insight participates in the fifth, the matter itself. It is this true knowledge that may suddenly emerge in the soul like a blazing candle (341 C ff.; 344 A ff.). But it is a precondition that the soul is akin to the matter, and that the three means – name, explanation and sensory images – 'rub' against each other in the course of dialectical scrutiny (cf. *RP.*IV 435 A). He who has acquired such insight will never forget it, and it will enable him to distinguish between false and true in reality as a whole – *das Wahre ist das Ganze*; but such an insight can never be put into words. It judges for itself whether language is true, and it is not a species of knowledge on a par with other kinds. Insight cannot be communicated – and, after all, was not that the moral of the *Theaetetus*?

As in the great images of the *Republic*, the basic insight is intuitive, but this is not mere mysticism. The good in the *Republic* is known by its function; both the *Republic* and the *Seventh Letter* refer to that insight that legitimates any other insight and causes something to present itself as true and real. The subject is the totality of insight, and by this is of course not meant the sum of empirical or specialist knowledge but the insight that – in the language of the *Republic* – renders hypothetical knowledge true. In this sense knowledge of one thing implies knowledge of everything.

In this brief 'excursion' it is suggested that true insight implies knowledge of an inherent coherence in reality, of some 'first principles' (344 D ff.). It is also hinted that nothing is briefer than the truth of the 'matter' – to the philosopher. But of course it would be fatal for anyone to believe that it can be acquired at second hand and that it can be simply formulated – which is what Dionysius II apparently believed. But it seems that others both in Antiquity and in our times have so believed.

THE 'UNWRITTEN DOCTRINES'

Aristotle speaks of Plato's 'unwritten doctrines' (Aristot. *Phys.* 209 b 15). Undoubtedly he refers to Plato's teaching at the Academy. Especially in Aristotle, but in other ancient writers as well, there is a significant but fragmentary tradition, which must be assumed to refer to this teaching; it is not easily comprehensible, but on this basis scholars in this century have attempted to reconstruct an esoteric Platonic 'doctrine of principles'. The idea is that in the dialogues Plato adopted a mask, while it must be assumed that orally he expressed himself more directly. Now, Plato's reservations apply to both the written and unwritten word, and so it is not very likely that he would have imparted what was residing 'in the most beautiful place inside him' in his lectures. To this must be added that the main lines in 'the doctrine of principles' in fact can be recognized in the dialogues, and thus it seems more reasonable – as in the preceding pages – to place the main emphasis on them. Here it will be seen how Plato makes use of a theory of first principles or elementary concepts – an elementary theory, as it might be called in analogy with Kant. It will also be seen – something modern 'esoterics' often overlook – that the 'doctrine of principles' is not simply presented as a theory about this and that, but rather as more or less disguised reflections on the fundamental concepts that are necessary for the formulation of any theory.

The point of orientation in all Platonic philosophy is the doctrine of ideas. Ideas are irreducible entities, in so far as they account for every phenomenon and are the pre-conditions for existence and knowledge. A wordless, intuitive insight lies hidden back of the ideas; yet it is also possible to speak formally about the ideas and about the relation between the world of ideas and the phenomenal world in a sort of meta-language. This comes about as soon as one, for example, asks what it means that an idea is one, self-identical, uncomposed and unchangeable, that it manifests itself in a plurality of dependent phenomena, or that several ideas constitute one whole. Plato's usual way of thinking implies that he cannot speak about formal concepts without hypostatizing them as some kind of super-ideas, which means that formal concepts, in Aristotelian terms, are considered substances not predicates (cf. *Met.* 1040 b 16; 1053 b 9 ff.). But since formal concepts or principles are substances to Plato, the ideas are reducible to principles – in so far as one can abstract from the idea as the quintessence of something and instead considers it an entity that is one, self-identical, etc. Accordingly, the principles become constitutive elements in the ideas, and because ideas are principles for phenomena, the elements of the ideas will mediately be the elements of the phenomena.

From the very beginning the idea of an indefinable highest principle is implicit in Platonism – virtue and the good, the beautiful or the one. And the correlative of such a principle – a plurality dependent on unity – is likewise implicit. In the great images in the *Republic* there is a tinge of a formal-abstract metaphysical system. In the *Parmenides* the formal concepts that determine such a system are set up against each other in a dialectical play based on an Eleatic conceptual apparatus. In the *Philebus* the abstract theory is once more touched on briefly, but here with the use of a Pythagorean conceptual apparatus. In the *Theaetetus–Sophist–Statesman* the theory is applied to epistemology, logic and metaphysics, in the *Timaeus* to physics by means of the key concepts of being, identity, and difference.

Behind these different angles of approach a certain view of the first principles is discernible: at all levels of existence there will be a determining factor, which wholly or in part makes an infinite continuum or a piece of matter finite, a unity that manifests itself in plurality and implies an 'otherness'. In several places allusions to special points in an underlying theory are perceptible. Numbers and proportions, for example, are considered as especially privileged, abstract expressions of rationality – numbers are assigned to structures of ideas in the *Philebus*, proportions constitute the physical world in the *Timaeus*. There are also seemingly accidental formulations, which in fact betray themselves as rules, as for example the principle of the relation between whole and part (Plat. *Parm.* 146 B, cf. p. 219) – which lies behind the many instances in which a syllable is used as an example of a whole that is different from and more than its parts (cf. *Theaet.* 202 E ff.; *Soph.* 253 A ff.; *Pol.* 277 E ff.; *Tim.* 48 B; *Phil.* 17 A) – or the principle of the relation between absolute and relative being (*Soph.* 255 C, cf. p 232).

There can be no doubt that the general theory is identical with that 'doctrine of principles', the 'esoteric' or 'unwritten doctrines', which Plato – according to concurring testimony in secondary sources – presented at the Academy, especially perhaps in a legendary lecture 'On the Good', which may indeed have been a series of lectures. Plato's students – Aristotle among them – took notes at this lecture (cf. Simpl. in Aristot. *Phys.* 453,22 ff., Diels), but the reports are but indirect and preserved in fragments in later paraphrases. Furthermore, it seems as if Plato did everything in his power to discourage intruders (cf. Aristox. *Harm. el.* II 30, Meibom).

On certain points – especially concerning the relation between ideas and numbers – the indirect transmission provides more details than the dialogues, but this indirect information is often so confusing and self-contradictory that it would be difficult to make sense of them – if they could not be elucidated by the dialogues. This is connected with the fact that the main source, Aristotle, is clearly hostile. Often it would be difficult to determine whether he is speaking about Plato or about his fellow students, Speusippus and Xenocrates. He presupposes a knowledge that is not ours, and whenever Aristotle is aggressive, he is a far from reliable source. Add to this that many indirect sources have a doxographic form, and that this levelling genre often can give the impression of Plato's 'esoteric doctrine' as a strange, rigid system. Without doubt Plato expressed himself more technically at the Academy than in the dialogues. Without doubt he also thought that the world is a systematically coherent whole; but the dialogues are one long protest against the formulation of a doctrinaire philosophical system. The *Parmenides* demonstrates that the principles cannot simply be described in the language which they themselves legitimate. In itself the 'doctrine of principles' is almost as uninformative and formulaic as the battle-cry that 'by the beautiful all beautiful things are beautiful'. It is a theory that should be used to illuminate and apprehend the principal philosophical problem: what it means to grasp a multitude of data conceptually, and what it is that determines a conceptual connection. This comes about by means of a set of elementary concepts, but the Platonic dialectician is not so much a person who 'knows' as a person who 'is able to'. He can adopt a comprehensive, overall view, and he can perceive the particular in the general (cf. Plat. *RP* VII 537 C; *Phaedr.* 265 D; *Soph.* 253 D).

The theory is intended to explain a hierarchically-ordered universe in which a given level is based on a principle of superior order. The principle is uncompounded, while that for which it is principle is compounded and hence secondary (cf. *Phaedo* 78 C), and an inferior order implies a superior one, though not vice versa (cf. Aristot. *Eth. Eud.* 1217 b 10 ff.; *Met.* 1059 b 30 ff.). Therefore a superior order will exist unconditionally, a lower one conditionally, and the principle will be the cause of the derived and exist implicitly in it as idea in phenomenon, as unity in plurality (*Parmenides*) and as structure in matter (*Timaeus*). One might think that a higher level did exist, that a lower did not. The most superior principle, unity, is in itself indefinable. That to which this principle accords existence and structure – the pure possibility that in different contexts in the dialogues appears as the 'Platonic chaos' – was apparently in technical terminology called 'the great-and-small' or 'the Indefinite Dyad', which is to say that as an indefinite continuum it moves in two directions so to speak – towards a more and a less. The two principles are not co-equals.

One principal source is Aristotle's 'history of philosophy' in the first book of the *Metaphysics* (987 a 29 ff.; cf. Alex. Aphr. in *Met.* 55,20 ff., Hayduck). Here Aristotle almost treats the 'doctrine of principles' as the most important part of Plato's philosophy. He considers Plato as a follower of the Pythagoreans, but with the difference that the Pythagoreans did not distinguish sharply between the principle and that for which it was principle, while Plato distinguishes between hierarchical levels and makes things exist by participation (*methexis*) in ideas or numbers. Plato's motivation for so doing also becomes clear thanks to – perhaps rather in spite of – Aristotle's reluctant summary: there is no identity between the thing and the universal by which it is recognized. Aristotle's point is that because the ideas are the causes of 'the other things', the elements of the ideas must be the elements of everything, and these ultimate elements are then unity and 'the great-and-small'. Consequently 'the great-and-small' is an element in ideas and numbers, which implicitly are identified with ideas. This line of thought corresponds with that of the *Parmenides* and *Philebus*, and Aristotle quite rightly points out that Plato considers unity as substance not as predicate for something else, which is to say that it has reality in an unqualified sense.

In a brief but weighty summary (Theoph. *Met.* 6 b 11 ff.) Theophrastus, Aristotle's student, shows himself to be aware of the dialectical connection between the principle and 'the other things', and he is able to describe the dialectical procedure in a manner that corresponds with the 'ascent' and 'descent' in the *Republic*: phenomena are reduced to ideas, ideas to numbers, and numbers to 'the principles'. The reverse process goes from principles to what they are principles for. Both Aristotle and Theophrastus deal with the reductive and deductive procedure in a purely schematic way; unity and 'the Indefinite Dyad' are considered equal principles, and it is only implicitly clear that the reduction and abstraction that are spoken of are different in their several stages: reduction from phenomena to ideas is an abstraction from contingent and material facts; on the other hand, reduction from ideas to higher principles is an abstraction from contents. On the basis of his fundamentally empirical view, Theophrastus notes that to him it seems awkward to study abstract principles in isolation instead of concentrating on the variegated world, which the principles are meant to explain. But such criticism is probably addressed to some of Plato's students rather than to Plato himself, for – in Theophrastus' view – Plato was aware of both issues.

The theory pertains to the dialectical relation between continuity and discontinuity (on this see Porph. ap. Simpl. in Aristot. *Phys.* 453,31 ff., Diels), between stuff and structure, and between conditional and unconditional being. To the theory of reduction was tied a development of the 'doctrine of categories' familiar from the *Sophist*, which is to say the principle of autonomous versus relative being, where autonomous being is tied to the concept of unity, while relative being is tied to the Indefinite Dyad or plurality, and in which 'the Same' and 'the Different' were parts of the set terminology (cf. Alex. Aphr. in Aristot. *Met.* 256, 13 ff., Hayduck; Diog.

Laert. III 108). This model of reduction is of course first and foremost intended as a formal description of the relation between phenomena, ideas and principles; but the structure was recognized in partial contexts, for example in the dimensional sequence of physical body → stereometric body → plane → line → point (cf. Aristot. *Met.* 1085 a 7; 1090 b 5 ff.).[1] It is a favourite example 'paraded' by the Academy, as has been said, and it shows how an inferior level implies and is determined by a superior one while existing in its own right at the same time: the line could not exist without the point, but the point could exist without the line. On the other hand, there is transition from point to line. The line does not emerge by an addition of points; something has been 'added', i.e. linear extension; the principle of linear extension is called 'indivisible lines' in Academy jargon (cf. Aristot. *Met.* 992 a 22; 1083 b 13; cf. the indivisible triangles of the *Timaeus*).

The most controversial point of the theory is the relation between ideas and numbers, according to general Greek thinking understood as integers after 1. The main source is Aristotle (especially *Met.* 1080 a 12 ff.), but he expresses himself so unclearly and polemically that here consideration is only given to that which is relatively comprehensible from the dialogues. According to Aristotle, Plato distinguished between mathematical numbers and ideal numbers, and, according to Aristotle, both were assigned special ontological status (cf. 987 b 14). The ideal numbers were associated with ideas (*vide infra*). The mathematical numbers, which consisted of unchangeable units, were placed between phenomena and ideas, because they are eternal like the ideas, but multiple like the phenomena (each number has many instances). It is correct that Plato speaks of mathematical numbers as composed of equal units and that on behalf of the mathematicians he protests against considering such numbers 'commercial numbers', i.e. so and so many cows, horses, etc. (cf. Plat. *RP.* VII 525 E). The mathematical numbers are the objects of calculation, and they are instances of ideal numbers – but in his dialogues Plato never attributed a special form of existence to them, and undoubtedly it depends on a misunderstanding when modern scholars often take the second-highest section of the line simile to be evidence in this respect. Here there is no talk of a special category of objects, but of objects that are understood in a special way. An instance of an idea can never to Plato have intermediate status between idea and phenomenon, and to hypostatize an instance of idea would create insurmountable ontological complications (cf. *Phaedo* 102 D ff., see pp. 155 and 175). Mathematical numbers are thus reflections of intelligible numbers. Considered by themselves, they are cardinal numbers, which is to say that they are abstractions or properties of countable quantities. The most thorough discussion of numbers *qua* cardinal numbers is provided by Plato in the *Parmenides* (cf. p. 218).

There is a difference between the number of a quantity (10 cows) and the number whereby one counts (cf. Aristot. *Phys.* 219 b 5), but according to Plato's general mode of thought, a mathematical number must also be an instance of an ideal number. The idea of two-ness is different from the number that consists of two units:

---

1   The schema has a Pythagorean background, see p. 40; Sext. Emp. *Adv. math.* X 259 ff. is a late 'Pythagorean' source, not quite reliable, cf. p. 516.

2 is 2 by its two-ness, not by addition or division (*Phaedo* 101 B). As a hierarchy of ideas is also a countable quantity, numbers can consequently be assigned to ideas. Tradition sometimes has it that ideas have numbers, sometimes that they are numbers; but if we judge by the Plato of the dialogues, this confusion can be done away with: an idea *is* a number, if one abstracts from its contents; and it *has* a number if it is considered a substantive determination. But as ideas only are formal entities in a secondary sense, while the numbers are so primarily, the ideal number must in formal ontology be superior to the ideas. Hence the order of progression becomes: phenomenon – idea – ideal number – unity.

It is already inherent in this that there is no common idea for ideal numbers, and this has been emphasized in the sources. Since ideal numbers are concepts, they cannot be subjected to calculations – they are 'not-addable' – and since they are arranged in an order of priority, they cannot have a common genus, for there is no sequitur of 'before' and 'after' between species (cf. Aristot. *Eth. Nic.* 1096 a 17). Nor can the ideal number – *pace* Aristotle (cf. *Met.* 1084 a 3; b 37) – 'be created' in any other way than by combining unity and the Indefinite Dyad, although of course mathematical numbers can 'be created' by arbitrary calculations. It is another matter that the first ten numbers – in sound Pythagorean spirit – often have been accorded an especially privileged status (1084 a 12): not only is 10 the sum of the first four numbers, to which are assigned respectively point, line, plane and body, but in a decimal system the first decade will be primary, because it is repeated in all the following. The relation between ideal numbers is fixed, because ideal numbers have an order of priority, and to Plato proportions are as basic as they were to the Pythagoreans (cf. the *Timaeus*). Accordingly, analogous series of numbers will be determined by a definite proportion and a basic number or a 'first number' (not a prime number, as Aristotle's *Met.* 987 b 34 is often rendered), and all numbers other than 'first numbers' may be said to have been 'created' as members of the series in question. The most basic series would of course be the series of natural numbers, an arithmetical progression beginning with 1.

Where Plato himself apparently used his theory of principles dialectically – in light of his vision of the one in the many but well aware that the final truth cannot be formulated – his students must have looked on the matter differently, and this in fact holds good for Plato's philosophy as a whole. In the history of philosophy it is not an unknown phenomenon that the ideas of a great and visionary thinker can only be further developed by systematization or protest. Already to the first generation of Platonists Plato's philosophy must have seemed a grandiose vision of a system with many loose ends. The Plato who speaks by concealing himself had to be made transparent, unambiguous, and usable. A Platonic 'scholasticism' arose. From the very beginning, the proper interpretation of the *Timaeus* was debated – including the relation between the god of creation and the transcendent first principle. In a wider perspective the intermediate position of the soul between idea and phenomenon must remain a problem, and so also must the very question of the relation between the ideas and their status. Evidently it proved difficult to maintain the dual Platonic position: that ideas are irreducible, substantive determinants as well as reducible within a formal ontology. The need for a distinction between a vocabulary of the first and second order must become urgent. It is in connection with this discussion that the distinction between universal and substance emerges – which of course was to have fatal consequences for the doctrine of ideas.

We know something about the discussions about ideas – partially from Plato's undeniably indirect contribution (the *Parmenides*) and partially from an early Aristotelian treatise, *On Ideas*, later exploited in condensed form in his *Metaphysics*. It has been preserved in fragmentary paraphrases in the commentary of Alexander of Aphrodisias on the *Metaphysics*. These probably tell us more about Aristotle than Plato. There is an enumeration of some 'proofs' of the existence of ideas (Alex. Aphr. in Aristot. *Met.* 79, 3 ff, Hayduck = Aristot. Περὶ ἰδεῶν, frg. 3, Ross; cf. *Met.* 990 b 9 ff.; 1079 a 4 ff.), of which the most important are: (1) the argument 'from the sciences' (the sciences must have objects, but they cannot be identical with physical objects); (2) the argument of 'one over many' (many objects have a common predicate, and this must exist); and (3) 'the argument of thought' (thoughts must have objects). Aristotle notes that the arguments prove the existence of universals – not of ideas – and he adds that if they are valid, ideas must exist for artefacts, negations, memories, and relative terms – which 'we' (does this 'we' refer to Aristotle himself or to Platonists in general?) are not prepared to accept. Aristotle's version of the 'third man' criticism and of the entire problem of participation belongs in the same context (cf. p. 216). This fragmentary text is an early testimony to the new understanding of the concept of 'concept'. As to Plato's reaction – the *Parmenides* aside – we only know that he maintained the doctrine of ideas.

A number of names of Academy members have been preserved – among them those of two women (cf. Diog. Laert. III 46). The school attracted prominent mathematicians (Eudoxus and Theaetetus), and there were also trained astronomers – Philippus of Opous and Heraclides Ponticus among them. The most prominent philosophers were Speusippus, Xenocrates and Aristotle.

In addition to mathematics and astronomy, a broad field of sciences was pursued: systematic classification (*diairesis*) in the field of biology (Speusippus), semantics (Speusippus and Aristotle), theory of argumentation and rhetoric (Aristotle), and ethics (among others Eudoxus).

It is an open question to what extent Plato directly participated in the internal debates. But there are several testimonials to the considerable tolerance that prevailed within the Academy walls. The Plato, who in the *Laws* would regulate the life of the ordinary man from cradle to grave, was clearly quite liberal with students and equals, and it is more than likely that several of Plato's students – not only Aristotle – had arrived at very unorthodox positions even in Plato's lifetime. Both Speusippus and Aristotle abandoned the doctrine of ideas, and Eudoxus thought that ideas were materially inherent in things and that pleasure was the highest good (see pp. 216, 246 and 372).

We are not very well informed about the organization of the Academy, nor of its political role or other activities, even though something may be gathered indirectly from the doxographic tradition concerning particular Academy members. But the Academy was well known, and probably public lectures were given. We encounter Plato as the target of comedy – even though in a manner more gentle than that accorded Socrates. The One, which is not even one, and the good, which nobody knows what is, were ready objects of ridicule (Diog. Laert. III 26). The comedian

Epicrates has furnished a vivid picture of the study of natural sciences at the Academy (Epicr. frg. 11, II 354 Edmonds): Plato is standing with his colleagues and students in profound contemplation of a gourd, the species of which they intend to determine. 'This is a round vegetable' according to one of them. 'A species of grass', opines another, while yet a third ventures 'a species of tree'. A physician – Common Sense – happens to come by and demonstratively breaks wind. Nobody is infuriated, the students pay no attention, and mildly and gently Plato asks, 'Should we not attempt to determine the species of this gourd?'

SPEUSIPPUS AND XENOCRATES

Plato's nephew Speusippus (c.410–339) succeeded him as leader of the Academy. He developed the Platonic doctrine of principles in a radical and unorthodox form and constructed a strictly formal 'mathematical' ontology, the special features of which have not become recognized until recent years, thanks to thorough studies and the finding of new material. Still, the evidence is scant – and, in the case of Aristotle, so polemical that it is well-nigh incomprehensible (especially the *Metaphysics*, book N).

Speusippus' ontology (cf. Aristot. *Met.* 1028 b 21 ff.; 1072 b 30 ff.; 1075 b 37 ff.; 1090 b 13ff. = Speus. respectively frags. 33 a; 34 a; 33 e; 50 Lang; essential supplementary material in Iambl. *De comm. math. sc.* IV) is a strict hierarchical system with unity as a formal and plurality as a material principle, so that at every subordinate level a new dimension is added, whereby the principles at every level appear in a specific context. In themselves unity and plurality are empty concepts; if being is added, numbers will appear as the fundamental, real structural elements; if extension is added, spatial magnitudes will appear; if movement is added, the cosmic soul emerges; and finally, if stuff is added, sensible bodies appear.

This is an evident tightening of the scheme of principles. What is to be explained is an underlying structure and not the substantive determinations, which at every stage are considered 'accretions' – Aristotle compared Speusippus' system with a bad tragedy consisting only of episodes.

But more far-reaching consequences are drawn from the first principles as empty. As is the case with pure unity in the *Parmenides*, the first principle is unknowable, and surely there is not only structural agreement, but also a historical connection with Neoplatonism: unity is above being, but it is the cause and source of everything existing, as we are told in a quotation transmitted in Latin (Procl. in Plat. *Parm.* interpr. Guillelmo de Moerbeka, Klibansky/Labowsky, p. 40; cf. Aristot. *Met.* 1092 a 9 = Speus. frg. 34 e). It follows that the One is above reason or the Demiurge of the *Timaeus* (cf. frg. 38 (Aetius)), and evidently the creation of the world in the *Timaeus* is considered a non-temporal process. Furthermore, that the principles are empty means that the One is not identified with the good – for then plurality would be 'evil'. The good can only be understood as perfection on a specific hierarchical level (cf. Aristot. *Met.* 1072 b 30 ff.; 1092 a 11 = Speus. respectively frgs. 34 a and e) – a consequence that undeniably distances Speusippus from Plato.

But the most far-reaching consequence is probably that Speusippus abandoned the doctrine of ideas and thereby also the thought of ideal numbers as distinguished from 'mathematical' numbers. This clearly ties in with the basic view that the principles are not determinations of content but structural ones. A principle is a substance, although, as subsequently in Aristotle, a substance cannot also be a universal. Speusippus was arguably the first to identify the universal as a logical concept (cf. Diog. Laert. IV 2). The ontological correlative to universals are resemblances among things. But there is a system in these resemblances, and they may be arranged in a *diairesis* system. Speusippus worked diligently at scientific classification – he was among those to identify Epicrates' gourd – and the majority of the surviving fragments come from a comprehensive work on 'Resemblances' (Speus. frg. 5–26). Here he seems to have imposed order on a considerable amount of biological material. In his attempt at a universal science he followed Plato so literally that, as he saw it, total empirical knowledge was a necessary precondition for all partial knowledge – one must be able to define everything existing in order to define a man or a horse (cf. Aristot. *Anal. post.* 97 a 6 ff.; Philop. ad. loc. 405,27 = Speus. respectively frgs. 31 a and c).

Finally, Speusippus was a pioneer contributor to semantic theory. He systematized the several types of signification (frg. 32 a–c) – and this classification must be considered as separate from the ontological classification of 'resemblances'. The main types are synonyms (one name used with the same signification), homonyms (one name with several significations), and paronyms (linguistic derivatives). Aristotle adopted these principal distinctions (Aristot. *Cat.* 1 a 1 ff.). Furthermore, it seems likely that he was also inspired by Speusippus in other fields (biology, universals, and the critique of the doctrine of ideas).

Xenocrates (395–14 BC) succeeded Speusippus as leader of the Academy, and his death marked the end of the generation who had heard Plato speak. Tradition has it that he was noble, earnest, and slow-witted, which is indeed credible. Evidently it was important to him to return to Platonic orthodoxy. But in so far as it is possible to determine from the sources – there are no direct quotations, even though quite a few accounts and allusions have survived – the outcome was unhappy. When he was in doubt, Xenocrates was a man of compromises who filled in gaps in order to arrive at a coherent system. There is nothing that indicates originality, but much that suggests a fairly one-track mind without Plato's sense of the ambiguously veiled or of that which cannot be said. On the other hand, he apparently did have great importance as the conveyor of tradition – the view of Plato in middle Platonism seems basically to have come from him, and it is more than doxographically interesting that Zeno, the founder of Stoicism, as well as Epicurus are said to have been in his audience (cf. Diog. Laert. VII 2; X 13).

It is typical for the time that like Aristotle, Xenocrates felt a need to divide philosophy into disciplines (Sext. Emp. *Adv. math.* VII 16 = Xenocr. frg 1 Heinze), and his division – into physics, ethics, logic – was to prevail in Hellenistic times. In his voluminous oeuvre were included (Diog. Laert. IV 13) several works on classification, cognition, dialectics and linguistic expression (*lexis*). If they had been preserved, they – as well as the few Speusippus fragments – would surely have thrown interesting light on the background for Aristotle's *Rhetoric*, *Topics*, and doctrine of categories, and in a wider perspective perhaps also on the background for Stoic logic and semantics. As things stand, we can only be certain that Xenocrates maintained the Platonic 'doctrine of categories' as an ontological correlative to logic – probably in deliberate opposition to Speusippus' *Resemblances* and Aristotle's *Categories* (cf. Xenocr. frg. 12). Xenocrates' extensive work on ethics may have influenced Stoicism.

In Xenocrates' metaphysical system (frg. 34 = Aristot. *Met.* 1028 b 24 with parallel *loci*) Unity and the Indefinite Dyad were primary principles. In hierarchical order followed next: ideas and numbers, geometrical objects, heaven (the cosmic soul), and the sensible sublunary world. The system appears to be a compromise between Plato and Speusippus. The ideas – which Xenocrates defined as eternal models for natural species (Xenocr. frg. 30) – have been restored to their former dignity, but the more precise relation between ideas and numbers is not discernible, and apparently Speusippus' – and Aristotle's – distinction between universal and substance seems not to be taken into account (cf. Aristotle's criticism, *Met.* 1083 b 2; 1090 b 20 ff.).

Xenocrates is praised for having constructed the most complete system of derivation (Theoph. *Met.* 6 b 7), and probably this refers to the detailed working out of the common Academy scheme of dimensional sequence. He seems especially to have been interested in the theoretical minima as constituents at every hierarchical level ('indivisible' lines, triangles, etc.; cf. Xenocr. frgs. 37–8 and 41–9). Concerning this point, Xenocrates perhaps inspired Epicurus.

The system reveals Xenocrates' predilection for the *Timaeus*. Nor would it, for example, be easy to understand his definition of the soul as a 'self-moving number' (frg. 60) without familiarity with the *Timaeus*, and this applies also to a combination of epistemological categories, the myth in the *Phaedrus*, and the cosmology of the *Timaeus*, which suggests a strangely literal imagination (Sext. Emp. *Adv. math.* VII 147 ff. = Xenocr. frg. 5). As a whole the *Timaeus* is considered an illustration of the doctrine of principles, and therefore the dialogue cannot describe a creation in time (frg. 54). The special orientation towards the *Timaeus* has the result that Xenocrates does not – as did Speusippus – concern himself with unity as an empty first principle. But in relation to the world, unity is transcendent: it is identified with god (the Demiurge) and reason (frgs. 15–6). Side by side with Aristotle's theology it apparently became the point of departure for the doctrine in later Platonism that the ideas were the thoughts of god.

Xenocrates was not only interested in the *Timaeus* from a philosophical point of view. Like the author of the *Epinomis* (most likely Philippus of Opous; cf. [Plat.] *Epin.* 984 C ff.) he expanded the astral religion of the *Timaeus*, but he went well beyond the *Epinomis*. According to the doxographic tradition (Xenocr. frg. 15 (Aetius)), he identified unity with 'the Father' of the *Timaeus* and with Zeus, and below them he assigned the traditional gods their systematic places, each with his own metaphysical function. Apparently he wanted to create a synthesis of philosophy and religion. As the doxographic source remarks, he 'translates' Plato. Traditional religion was – as later with the Stoics – interpreted allegorically, philosophy mythically – with the risk near to hand that the result was neither interpretation of Plato, nor philosophy or religion.

That this is not a question of a 'paedagogical' mode of presentation and even less of Plato's subtle interplay between a religious and philosophical dimension appears from the fact that Xenocrates – once again there is resemblance with the *Epinomis* –

developed a detailed doctrine of demons, the intermediary beings between gods and men (frgs. 23–5 (Plutarch)). This is another amazing synthesis: on the one hand popular religion, on the other a one-dimensional reading of Plato, which without further ado connects the Diotima speech with the reflections on the necessity of intermediary proportionals between extremes in the *Timaeus*.

It was not the formalism of Speusippus but the mediocre orthodoxy of Xenocrates that became the main conveyor of the tradition. In a more profound sense it was perhaps the third of Plato's prominent students, the rebellious Aristotle, who was a 'Platonist'.

PART IV

ARISTOTLE

19

LIFE, WORKS AND
POSITION

———— •◆• ————

Aristotle (384–322) was born at Stageira, an Ionian colony on the Chaldike peninsula near the kingdom of Macedonia. His father was personal physician to Amyntas III, king of the Macedonians and the grandfather of Alexander the Great. Aristotle's destiny, like that of his father, was closely tied to the Macedonian royal family. As the son of a physician, Aristotle may have been predisposed to empiricism. In any case he was by birth fairly highly placed on the social scale and seems to have been well off. Nevertheless, he had two handicaps in Athens: he was an immigrant without rights of citizenship, and he was – no doubt with good reason – considered 'a friend of the Macedonians'.

When he was seventeen years old (367) Aristotle went to Athens to study at Plato's Academy, and he was to remain there for twenty years until the death of Plato. Undoubtedly he taught at the Academy – probably rhetoric and logic especially – and of course he must have participated in Academy debates on the idea and the universal, on classification, logic, and ethics. He earned for himself the soubriquets of 'Reason' and 'the Reader'. At the time of Plato's death Aristotle was no mere nonentity. Quite early on he must have signalled his independent critical attitude to Plato as well as to Speusippus and Xenocrates, although we do not know precisely when and how; it seems that he was never a lover of formal ontological systems, and he complains that nowadays philosophy has become far too mathematical (Arist. *Met.* 992 a 32). Aristotle does not shy away from direct and militant polemicism, but his inclination to hold contrary views within his own group should for example be contrasted with a frequently quoted passage in the *Nichomachean Ethics* (*Eth. Nic.* 1096 a 13, cf. *Phaedo* 91 B) where he begins his criticism with a subtle twist of a *Phaedo* quotation: the philosopher must honour truth more than he does his friends. In a poem written after Plato's death he maintains that evil men do not even have the right to praise Plato, for Plato was the only mortal who by his life and work showed that a good man also becomes a happy one. Such is not the lot of any man living today (Olymp. in Plat. *Gorg.* 196, 30 ff. = frg. 2 Ross). Here he quotes Plato once again (Plat. *Leg.* 660 E).

Soon after Plato's death Aristotle left Athens, although probably not, as has been supposed, because he had been disappointed in not being appointed Plato's successor. The choice of Speusippus – a reputable philosopher, Aristotle's senior by some twenty-five years, Plato's nephew, and an Attic citizen – probably did not seem unnatural. The reason must more likely be sought in political affairs: Macedonia was expanding her territory in northern Greece, and the anti-Macedonian party was in power in Athens. In any case, Aristotle received an invitation from a prince in Asia Minor, Hermeias, a devoted Platonist. He became a close friend of Hermeias (whose relative he married) and settled in the town of Assos with other Platonists. He also seems to have cooperated with Hermeias in political affairs, and his Assos residence must be seen as one of several instances of Academy members functioning as political advisors. From Assos he continued to the near-by island of Lesbos where he began a cooperation with Theophrastus that was to last for many years. The years at Assos and Lesbos seem to have entailed intense work; in his zoological works Aristotle records many observations from these regions.

It was perhaps at the instigation of Hermeias that Aristotle was summoned to Macedonia in 343 by King Philip to be the tutor of the king's thirteen-year-old son, the later Alexander the Great; but probably he stayed there for only three years. Although little is known about it, the relationship between the philosopher and the boy who was later to rule the world has inevitably stirred the imagination ever since Antiquity. Still, it is apparent that the two men had very different political ideals. While Alexander forged an empire, Aristotle in his *Politics* confined himself conservatively to the framework of the city state. Tradition has it that after Alexander had acceded to the throne, Aristotle advised him to treat the Greeks as friends and equals and the barbarians as dumb beasts. But tradition also adds that Alexander did not heed the advice and treated all alike (Plut. *De Alex. virt.* 329 B). There is at least some inherent truth in such a tale.

In 338 Philip of Macedonia defeated the Greeks at Chaeronea, and two years later he was murdered. The Greeks rebelled. In a lightning attack Alexander subdued them, made Aristotle's friend Antipater the governor of Greece, and commenced his conquest of the Orient. Given these circumstances, Aristotle who had been living abroad – for a while in his native town – was able to return to Athens (c.335). Here Xenocrates had in the meantime been chosen leader of the Academy, and Aristotle began to teach in the public gymnasium, the Lyceum. It is debatable whether he established his own 'school' in a legal sense, but he did found an institution that later became known as the Peripatetic School (*peripatos*: an ambulatory suitable for discussions). He organized projects of research with his students and – this was unusual – established a substantial library for study and instruction.

The news of Alexander's death in 323 led to immediate rebellion in Athens, and confronted with this renewed anti-Macedonian tide, Aristotle elected to flee to Chalkis where his mother's family held property – for he did not want to be responsible for the Athenians transgressing a second time against philosophy (of course a reference to the death of Socrates, Ael. *Var. hist.* 36). He died the following year, perhaps an embittered man. In his will he appointed Antipater his executor (Diog. Laert. V 11).

WORKS

Today there is general agreement that Aristotle wrote a considerable number of his treatises before Plato died and that he had then, at the age of 37, in all important respects arrived at his basic philosophical views. But this agreement is of recent date, and the special features and unique history of transmission of the Aristotelian works make it impossible to reconstruct a definite chronology. As other members of the Academy probably did, he wrote dissertations with a view either to publication – the exoteric writings – or for internal use – the esoteric writings: compendia-like manuscripts of lectures intended for colleagues (cf. Aristot. *Eth. Eud.* 1217 b 22). To the latter group belong also private annotations and the like. Fate was to decide that the exoteric writings were lost, and today we know them only fragmentarily or as paraphrases. The esoteric writings alone have been preserved. This means that although we do possess everything that Plato published, even though we have only indirect acquaintance with what he taught, the opposite is the case with Aristotle. Thus any comparison of the two depends on writings that belong to utterly different genres, and accordingly our perception may easily become distorted.

Several of the exoteric writings, famous in Antiquity for their style (cf. Cic. *Acad.* II 119), were dialogues. The inspiration must of course have been Plato, but Aristotle put the dialogue to very different uses, as did Cicero when he subsequently imitated Aristotle's model. These must have been educational, popular treatises, in which each participant acted as spokesman for a particular point of view, and in which Aristotle himself furnished the conclusions and presented his own positions (cf. Cic. *De fin.* V 10 ff.). Among these dialogues there is special reason to stress two: the *Eudemus*, which dealt with the immortality of the soul and is datable to shortly after 354, and the voluminous *On Philosophy*, which contained a survey of the history of philosophy, a critique of Plato's doctrine of the ideas, and a cosmological and teleological survey. The date of this work is uncertain. Yet the most important of the exoteric writings, the *Protrepticus* or *The Exhortation* (i.e. to philosophy), is not a dialogue but the reply to a programmatic treatise by Isocrates, from about 350, in which the latter explicitly had attacked the 'useless' philosophy of the Platonists. Aristotle's main thesis is that intellectual and moral knowledge belong with each other and that theoretical knowledge is normative – also in practical politics.

Not all the esoteric writings have been preserved (cf. catalogues from Antiquity, such as Diog. Laert. V 22 ff.). From the Academy days we have for example lost *On Ideas*, previously mentioned (p. 261), and the record of Plato's lecture *On the Good*. This is also true of the collections of working notes Aristotle brought together or had others compile for him so that they might serve as the bases for comprehensive dissertations: on doxography (e.g. on the Pythagoreans and Democritus); records of winners of performances of tragedies; and, above all, a compendium presenting no fewer than 158 Greek constitutions. Only one of these, that of Athens, has survived, rediscovered on a papyrus roll in 1891.

However, Aristotle's main esoteric works have survived. Usually they are classified as follows and are here provided with their traditional Latin titles.

Logic, rather than being considered a proper philosophical discipline, is a formal tool (*organon*) applicable to all subjects (cf. Aristot. *Top.* 108 b 32; '*organon*' did not become a fixed term until later (cf. Alex. Aphr. in Aristot. *Top.* 74, 29)). Aristotle distinguishes between formal logic and the theory of argumentation. The writings on formal logic can be arranged in a definite sequence based on content. First comes the *Categories* (*Categoriae*), which deals with the single terms of a given proposition. Then follows *De interpretatione* (Greek: *Peri hermēneias*, properly speaking: 'On Interpreting'), on propositions, which is to say simple subject-predicate statements. Finally, there is the *Analytics* (*Analytica*), in which the subject is inferences or syllogisms, i.e. the logical relationship between subject-predicate sentences. The *Analytics* contains two parts. The first, *Analytica priora*, discusses logically valid inferences; the second, *Analytica posteriora*, focuses on inferences with necessarily true premises and on definitions. The latter constitutes a presentation of Aristotle's ideal of deductive science. The principal work about the theory of argumentation or informal logic is the *Topics* (*Topica*; from '*topos*': place), which deals with the art of selecting arguments in accordance with their classes, 'places', and the drawing of conclusions based on probable or accepted premises. One pamphlet, *On Sophistical Refutations* (*De sophisticis elenchis*), is related to this work and analyses fallacies. The *Categories* was formerly, probably unjustly, considered spurious. There can be no doubt that the *Topics* is an early work, and so probably are the *Categories* and the *De interpretatione*. All in all, it seems likely that Aristotle's thoughts on logic took shape during his Academy days.

The principal work on natural philosophy, the *Physics* (*Physica*), contains weighty analyses of time, space, motion, and continuity. Not infrequently the first books are thought to have been written at the Academy. *On the Heaven* (*De caelo*) deals with cosmology. *On Generation and Corruption* (*De generatione et corruptione*) is concerned with qualitative natural processes, the transition of elements into one another. One particular work, the *Meteorologica*, deals with meteorology and other phenomena of the sublunary heaven. The biological writings have a more empirical character, and most of them are thought to have been written at Assos and Lesbos: the *Historia animalium* is a vast collection of biological observations, exploited in the *De partibus animalium*, a systematic treatise on the parts and organs of animals; the *De motu animalium* and the *De incessu animalium* discuss the movements of animals; and the *De generatione animalium* deals with generation. Within the Aristotelian classification a small important treatise, *On the Soul* (*De anima*), belongs in principle to his biological writings. A number of less important treatises, collectively known as the *Parva naturalia*, are associated with the *De anima*. There is a collection of *Problems* (*Problemata*), which, although spurious and from a later period, none the less gives a rather good picture of the working methods at the Lyceum.

The *Metaphysics* is an editorial title indicating that the metaphysical discourses were placed after those on physics, probably because metaphysics was regarded as a natural sequence to physics. Aristotle himself uses the terms 'first philosophy' and 'theology'. In its present form the work is a compilation of several treatises, but this in no way precludes the possibility that a coherent metaphysical theory lies behind it.

To Aristotle there is a close relationship between ethics, including the philosophy of action, and politics. Three works or lectures on ethics remain: the *Ethica Nicomachea*, *Ethica Eudemia* and *Magna Moralia*. In the course of transmission some of the books have come to be repeated in the first two of these works. The authenticity of the *Magna Moralia* is disputed, but in any case it must have been the work of a trained Aristotelian and may in fact have been written on the basis of lecture notes. The *Politics* (*Politica*) appears as the immediate continuation of the *Ethics*. The essay on the 'Constitution of Athens', cited earlier, is apparently one of several extensive preliminary studies.

Finally there are lectures on rhetoric (*Rhetorica*) and poetics (*Poetica*). The first books of the *Rhetoric*, which have rhetorical argumentation as their subject, are considered early and are closely affiliated with the *Topics*. The *Poetics* has survived only partially, and what remains deals almost exclusively with tragedy. Other works on literary aesthetics have been lost.

All in all, the esoteric works cover a vast field. In all likelihood, before Aristotle, only Democritus had dealt with so many different subjects. Aristotle examined almost all aspects of contemporary knowledge. Probably, it is no mere accident that we have no mathematical treatises; but Aristotle was well versed in current mathematics and used mathematical argumentation as a paradigm for his theory of science (*Analytica posteriora*). He never wrote special treatises on epistemology; his theory of knowledge has to be inferred, mainly from his logic, metaphysics, and psychology. Botany is one of the few more specialized fields that he seems to have left alone. Aristotle is rightly considered the father of logic and biology. But he also turned ethics into an autonomous discipline, and indeed the concept of practical reason is Aristotelian. His *Physics* is epochal in considering natural philosophy a genuine philosophical discipline, and here he is in disagreement with Plato. If one accepts the general consensus, it can be concluded that as early as in the Academy years Aristotle emerged as an independent logician and natural philosopher, and so by then he must have adopted an independent general philosophical position. His claim to originality is indeed not confined to special fields of investigation. His epistemology and metaphysics would be unthinkable without their Platonic background, but nevertheless they represent a turning point in Greek conceptual thought, and his terminological apparatus set the standard for posterity. As will be seen from the preceding survey, one indication of Aristotle's originality is the fact that the several philosophical and scientific disciplines are treated separately, each demanding its own methods and modes of analysis. Neither logic nor metaphysics, physics or ethics pose similar questions: different questions will produce different answers. This does not imply that there is a lack of unity in Aristotelian philosophy, but rather that it does not present that closed systematic character that was taken for granted by both adherents and opponents down through the history of philosophy. Aristotle remains both a philosopher and 'the father of science'.

Now and then Aristotle refers in his esoteric treatises to his own exoteric works, and on occasion he incorporates something from the exoteric in his esoteric work. This reminds us that we do not possess all of Aristotle's work and explains his often compressed style. What is left to us are not private working papers, but something intended for others to read, and those readers seem to have been so well informed that Aristotle could expect them to possess considerable prior knowledge. On the other hand, there are passages and even entire works that were evidently addressed to a less sophisticated circle: the *Categories* and the *De interpretatione* are textbooks; the introduction to the *Physics* as well as the early chapters of the *Metaphysics* are carefully planned paedagogical introductions; and the *Nicomachean Ethics* also seems to have been intended for a wider audience. Here and there, for example in the 'theological' book of the *Metaphysics*, one senses why Aristotle was admired in Antiquity for his stylistic brilliance, but as a rule there are no stylistic pretensions. The style does, however, reveal that here we are not reading mere notes by several hands, but one man's work. The presentation is matter-of-fact, compact, and at times indeed abrupt. None the less, it retains a certain charm. While the reader is left on his own by Plato, Aristotle includes him in the process of his reasoning. Again and again the same problem is seen from yet another angle, new arguments are tested, rejected, or contrasted with others. Long passages are tentative or aporetic, and often Aristotle proves himself to be more adept at formulating a problem or analyzing it than he is at solving it. Even though the line of thought is of course directed towards arriving at a definite end, and though Aristotle often magisterially declares that now this or that problem must be considered solved, what is really important is the manner in which it is solved as well as the context in which it is posed. Viewing him in this way provides a different picture from that of former times, when he was considered dogmatic and authoritative. That said, Aristotle was not an amiable writer, for as a polemicist he was biting and occasionally sarcastic. His analytical abilities may be matchless, but he does not possess Plato's talent for and readiness to join and participate in another person's way of thinking. A special feature of his style is the scholar's joy in hidden quotations, a certain dry, understated sense of humour, and an abhorrence of the sentimental. Sometimes one senses a note of resignation, a *tristesse*.

Evidently Aristotle lectured several times on the same subject, as we see especially in the *Metaphysics* and the two series of lectures on ethics. It will not do to think of an Aristotelian treatise as a completed final whole, for on several occasions Aristotle re-examined the same text and made corrections and additions. Accordingly the same 'work' may belong to different dates, and parts of it may be loosely connected. Therefore references from one work to another are not a reliable means of establishing a chronology, and the uniformity of style makes chronological dating on formal grounds equally impossible. Even where it is possible with a greater or lesser degree of certainty to observe a compositional hiatus, these cases do not necessarily indicate a change of mind, and it should be noted that although Aristotle did introduce changes or emendations, he did not reject earlier treatments of the same subject. Hence it is evident that his way of working presents scholars with special problems.

It is owing to a strange set of circumstances that Aristotle, unlike the Presocratics, the Sophists, and the old Stoics, was not inscribed in the annals of the history of philosophy as an enigmatic maker of fragments. For more than 200 years the public at large knew only of his exoteric works while but a few specialists, such as Epicurus and the older Stoics, in all probability had access to the esoteric work. But in the first century BC Aristotle's literary inheritance was found hidden in a cellar in Asia Minor (Strabo XII 1, 54 ff.; Plut. *Sulla* 26), and a Peripatetic, Andronicus of Rhodes, undertook a complete edition – probably in the second half of the first century BC. This was the first historical 'rediscovery' of Aristotle. Andronicus must have been a careful and reverent editor, for he edited and collated several related texts, and apparently included everything he found. Yet the fact that we can still identify lacunae and 'loose' transitions shows us that he must have refrained from revisions, attempts at harmonizing, or the like. So we do have Aristotle's text, although it may be difficult in specific instances to determine whether we have a text arranged by Andronicus or by Aristotle himself.

The Andronicus edition gave birth to an Aristotelian renaissance, even though the exoteric writings, not included in his edition, gradually were forgotten and left out of the Aristotelian canon. Still, interest in Aristotle was rekindled, and during the Roman Empire it occasioned extensive and valuable commentaries that have survived in several cases (Alexander of Aphrodisias and late Neoplatonist commentators, such as Simplicius, cf. p. 567). Our Aristotle text is indirectly derived from the Andronicus edition, and it is he who must be credited with the very existence of an Aristotelian tradition in Western philosophy.

Like Plato, Aristotle has left such a profound mark on all subsequent philosophy that it is impossible to distinguish between the history of Aristotelianism and the general history of philosophy. Furthermore, just as Plato is not identical with Platonism, so Aristotle is not identical with Aristotelians of other times – although this is not the place to trace the complex history of Aristotelianism.

Still, it ought to be mentioned that Hegel was just as important to the modern, especially the German understanding of Aristotle, as he was to the modern understanding of Plato, because whether Hegel provoked his opponents or inspired his adherents, he came to serve as a needed corrective to the traditional but one-sided view that Plato and Aristotle were antagonists: Plato, the idealist, confronted with Aristotle, the empiricist. Hegel, who feels congenial with Aristotle, emphasizes the kinship between the two Greek philosophers. To both the concept expresses the being of a thing, but while Plato considered the concept 'abstractly', it was 'concrete' and 'speculative' to Aristotle. It is concrete, because the thing is captured in all conceptual aspects – by means of that which Hegel calls 'total empiricism'. It is speculative, because the thing exists only in its essence or in its concept. Reality is rational, but this does not imply an inert self-identity, but *Tätigkeit*, motion and change. Yet Hegel blames Aristotle for not having created a fully developed system and for allowing reason to consider itself an object. He voiced his own close affiliation with Aristotle when he concluded his *Enzyklopädie* with a quotation from Aristotle's 'theology' on reason that thinks itself. The quotation is provided without commentary, and thus it provokes the reader to perceive for himself the difference in the similarity between Hegel and Aristotle.

Probably Hegel's most important contribution was that he brought about a revaluation of the Aristotelian 'system', for until then it had been taken for granted by the entire Aristotelian tradition that Aristotle should be thought of as a systematist. Yet it is not particularly difficult to point out systematic self-contradictions, and even today it is often considered a main problem – 'Aristotle's dilemma' – that on the one hand he attributes real existence only to particular entities, believing on the other hand that the objects of science are perpetual and unchangeable. One interpretation of this is that in epistemology he was a Platonist but that in natural philosophy he was an empiricist. But the case is not that simple, for Aristotle is not a Platonist in one field and an anti-Platonist in another. He himself is fully aware of 'his dilemma', which, surely, is not his alone.

The image of a dogmatic Aristotle that had become entrenched in the long course of the tradition has changed in this century. Especially in British and American scholarship it has been found more rewarding to investigate how Aristotle actually practised philosophy than to ask whether his 'system' adds up to a coherent whole. Quite a different response to Aristotle appeared in Werner Jaeger's book, *Aristoteles, Grundlegung einer Geschichte seiner Entwicklung* (1923), in which – at this surprisingly late date – he introduced *Entwicklungsgeschichte* into Aristotelian scholarship. The influence of this book was epochal, and suddenly Aristotle was dusted off and revealed as a man of flesh and blood. For about thirty years Jaeger's views were universally accepted, but then it became apparent that his position was hardly tenable. Today only a few would agree with Jaeger without reservations.

It was Jaeger's thesis that Aristotle's esoteric writings – our Aristotle, in other words – constitute the final phase in a development. Aristotle began as a committed 'Platonist', but on Plato's death he broke with Platonism and became an 'Aristotelian'. His writings reveal a gradually increasing disavowal of Plato. Jaeger built his views on a close study of the fragments of the 'exoteric' writings, and he considered *On Philosophy* as the turning point and as a clearly anti-Platonic manifesto. In the esoteric writings he thought it possible to excavate successive layers that would explain apparent self-contradictions. Strangely, he failed to examine the writings on logic, the only area in which it is possible to demonstrate a development with any reasonable degree of certainty.

There are several reasons why Jaeger's position is untenable. In the first place, the *Protrepticus*, his principal evidence, is not unambiguously 'Platonic', for it contains a good deal of 'Aristotelian' terminology and thought. In the second place, it is not possible to draw firm chronological conclusions on the basis of the esoteric writings. It seems that linguistic-stylistic criteria have proved applicable only to artistic prose and not to matter-of-fact prose like Aristotle's. Jaeger *has* shown that Aristotle's lectures are frequently the final product of editorial collations of several segments, but he has not shown *how* the layers can be arranged chronologically. His own criterion – that the 'Platonizing' sections must be the earliest – is in fact a *petitio principii*, for this was the very thing to be proved. In the third place, 'Platonism' versus 'Aristotelianism' sets up a far too unsubtle contrast. Platonism is a great number of things, and Platonic modes of thought lay behind everything Aristotle ever wrote. On the other hand, his critical position had already been clearly stated while Plato was still alive. Jaeger's enduring achievement lies in his decisive contribution to our understanding of the form of the esoteric writings, and thanks to him it is hardly feasible to consider Aristotle a rigid systematist any more.

Regardless of the discussion for or against Jaeger, Aristotle plays an important part in recent philosophical debates, and he enjoys the privilege of being equally highly regarded on both sides of the Channel. His basic position does indeed have points in common with phenomenology as well as with British ordinary language philosophy and philosophy of action.

THE COPERNICAN TURNING POINT

In his *Metaphysics* (1028 b 2 ff.) Aristotle declares that the crucial question philosophers have asked at all times and always will continue to ask it this: what is being?

He adds that this is synonymous with another question: what is *ousia*? The word *ousia* is really untranslatable. It is derived from *einai*, to be, and in daily parlance it means 'that which is one's own' (property) while in standard philosophical terms it means 'primary' or 'unchangeable being'. In Plato this is tantamount to 'nature' or 'idea'; in traditional Aristotelian terminology it is 'substance'. In other words, what Aristotle says is that the eternal question asked by philosophy is this: in a fundamental sense what is 'being'? Is it one or many, material or immaterial? His own provisional answer is that it is that which immediately is present as being, which is to say the particular thing here and now. But this is of course only a provisional answer that calls for new questions: what is a thing? What is implied by attributing being to a thing? How can an object be recognized as being this and not that?

Much, however, is contained already in the preliminary answer. Aristotle speaks less about 'primary being' than about that which has primary being, and this ties in with what might be called anti-reductionism. The world and the things in the world are nothing but what they claim to be, for things are not 'really' atoms or other material elementary entities, but neither are they hypostasized concepts or ideas, and the world is not contingent. At first glance it may seem surprising to encounter such views in an Academy member, and indeed we may here speak of a 'Copernican Turning Point', which changes the meaning of both the real and the concept. Nevertheless, Plato and Academy discussions are prerequisites. Generally speaking, Aristotle agrees with Plato that reality is rational and reason real, and he also shares the formal view of the Academy 'doctrine of categories' that some entities have independent and others dependent being (cf. *Met.* 1019 a 1 ff.). This doctrine of categories is important for an understanding of Aristotle's turning point. To Plato only ideas exist 'in themselves', phenomena only if ideas exist; but to Aristotle it is the thing that is the ontological crux of the matter, and so the properties of the thing are relative to the thing itself. Accordingly the idea is no longer that reality which 'appears' in time and space but rather a superfluous complication. In spite of this decisive shift, Aristotle and Plato share a fundamental problem: there is a difference between thing and concept, for the individual thing is a particular, whereas the concept is a universal. Yet it is only by virtue of the concept that we are able to say that anything is what it is, or, in Aristotle's special terminology – which may well be disconcerting to a novice reader – that something is a 'this something' or a 'this such'. Or, again in Aristotle's terms: is there a difference between being something and what it is for something to be? In other words, is the thing identical with the definition or the essence of the thing?

In such formulations lie both 'Platonism' and objections to Plato. Let us deal with the objections first. It is not possible to grasp the essence of a thing by reducing it to something else – to ideas. And if one does so anyway, the consequence is self-contradiction: for the idea must either be a universal – and the universal is, according to a standard Aristotelian definition, 'that which is said about many' (e.g. *De int.* 17 a 39; cf. *Met.* 1038 b 11), which is to say that it does not have its own real existence but is a concept *of* something – or the idea must be a 'thing' of a superior order, in other words an individual or substance with an especially privileged form of existence, in which case it cannot at the same time be the universal under which the thing – and hence the idea itself – is subsumed. Reduced to a formulaic phrase: ideas cannot be 'causes' and independent substances (997 b 3 ff.) at one and the same time. As mentioned before, at this point there is formal agreement between Aristotle and Speusippus. The latter had also distinguished between substance and universal, but he had presupposed the existence of metaphysical substances with real existence, even though he did not accord real existence to universals. Aristotle denies that there are 'super-things' – whether they are called ideas, numbers, or principles. But he does agree with the distinction itself, and it is instructive to remember that it was students of Plato who introduced a distinction that broke with the Platonic interpretation of the concept of 'concept'. A systematic analysis of the relationship between independent and dependent modes of existence ('the doctrine of categories') led to a more acute reading of the very concept of substance and thereby to a critique of Plato himself. Formal concepts can hence no longer be considered substances, and, above all, it is no longer possible, as Plato had insisted both in his 'doctrine of principles' and in his 'theory of ideas', to maintain that that which is an entity *per se* can manifest itself in a plurality. Aristotle, and for that matter Speusippus, have to ask: a plurality of what? Aristotle is unable to accept a veiled Platonic world of phenomena, which both is and is not, and he arrives at the conclusion that the idea or the principle becomes one entity among several and that an explanatory instance of a thing has the same form of existence as that which is to be explained. Formally, this is Platonism directed against Plato himself.

In his treatise *On Ideas* Aristotle had already maintained that the fact that science deals with unchangeable objects does not imply the existence of ideas, but only that universals exist (cf. *Anal. post.* 77 a 5; 85 b 19) and that a universal is not a substance. The concept of idea is confused, for the idea can never become a 'model' for something else, and participation thus becomes an empty metaphor – which Plato had never bothered to explain (*Met.* 987 b 13; 991 a 22; *Anal. post.* 83 a 33). In brief, all the objections in the first part of Plato's *Parmenides* become relevant at once.

Thus Aristotle is able to refute the doctrine of ideas point by point (*Met.* 990 b22 ff. with a parallel passage 1078 b 31 ff.; cf. 1038 b 6 ff.), and he does so frequently and bitingly: to introduce ideas is nothing but to double the number of things to be explained; a given thing participates in several ideas, but if ideas are substances, there will be several substances in a single substance. Within Socrates there will be both 'Socrates', 'man', and 'living being' (cf. 1038 b 29), but the same idea will likewise be split up and found in several substances (cf. 1039 a 26 ff.). On the other hand, it does not help that ideas exist 'separately' – the formula of 'X itself', man himself, for example, is a chimera, because man himself and this particular man have the same definition (*Eth. Nic.* 1096 a 35; cf. *Met.* 997 b 8). If there is a connection between idea and phenomenon, there must also be a common element that warrants the connection (cf. 'the third man' argument). Finally, the idea cannot explain how an individual substance – the thing – can be altered (cf. *De gen. et corr.* 335 b 7 ff.).

These arguments constitute an extensive *tour de force*, and it is evident that they are based not on Plato's but on Aristotle's own understanding of what a substance – *ousia* – is. The arguments show that in order to come to terms with Plato, Aristotle was forced to establish his own premisses and also that in a manner of speaking he chose to read Plato literally. This is, for example, what he does in his reading of the *Timaeus* (cf. *De caelo* 280 a 30; *De gen. et corr.* 329 a 13 ff.): Plato thought that the world had been created in time, for he says so in the *Timaeus* – Aristotle cannot accept such a 'mythical truth', just as he cannot in consequence accept, for example, the *anamnēsis* theory. Similarly, the concept of participation is not a clear-cut one, for nothing can be accomplished with 'poetical metaphors'. Platonic imagery must simply be rejected, but that means that Plato's basic metaphor of the world as an image must be rejected as well. The same applies to the dialectics between unity and plurality, being and not-being. Aristotle does make use of some details, for example from the *Parmenides* and the *Philebus*, but he never refers to the metaphysical dialectics in these two dialogues. The world is not a 'manifestation' of metaphysical structures but a collection of things that can be determined conceptually, and a given thing cannot simply be reduced to its properties. Aristotle is not interested in the metaphysical conditions for defining man, for example; instead he is interested in determining how man – or any other *infima species* – in fact may be defined and thereby become distinguishable from other objects. Natural objects are given priority, and general concepts are only of interest in so far as they can be employed for purposes of concrete description. Aristotle's new view permits him to use concepts as explanatory tools without hypostatizing them. This is not only a break with Plato but with all earlier Greek thought as well.

Nevertheless, 'Platonism' lies hidden behind the explicit criticism, and in fact one learns a lot more about Aristotle's attitude to Plato by investigating how he works with and reshapes Platonic problems when he does not directly confront Plato. A thing is what it is, in so far as it can be defined – in so far as it is a 'this-such'. The proper locus of the concept is the thing and the human mind; yet Aristotle is not a naïve realist, a sensualist, nor a conceptualist. His 'Platonism' consists above all in his claim that the concept is not derived from the thing, for thing and concept are ontological entities that presuppose each other. The concept is not to be found in heaven, but neither is the thing anything in and of itself. Aristotle's basic question is a Platonic one: what is the essence of a thing, and in what manner does an essential characteristic distinguish itself from an accidental one? A couple of examples will show how Aristotle here builds on and reshapes Plato. In one instance (*Met.* 1031 a 28 ff.; b 18 ff.), he says that it is superfluous to assume ideas, for if they did exist they would be identical with the essence of things, and existence and essence must coincide. Here Aristotle rejects on the one hand the distinction between levels of existence and the identity of essence while maintaining on the other hand that the thing only exists and only is intelligible by virtue of its essence. Paradoxically it might be said that he wanted to purge Platonism by doing away with the theory of ideas. Another example (1041 b 11 ff.): a thing exists thanks to its structure or – in Aristotle's language – its form, and this form is something other and more than the material parts of the thing; a house is not merely a pile of bricks. Aristotle illustrates this with a favourite Platonic example: a syllable is different from and more than the sum of its letters. Here he uses the Platonic dialectic between wholeness and part, but does so in a description of a single thing, not in the description of a structure that brings idea and phenomenon together. It is crucial to get a conceptual hold of 'this-something', and therefore *infima species* is not only the most complete definition of the thing; it is indeed that which makes the thing into a 'this-something'.

Aristotle's position is further clarified in his semantics and theory of knowledge.

Language has its own structure for Aristotle as well as for Plato, but it reflects factual reality. It is transparent. Language is not reified and is not an obstacle between us and reality. On the contrary, language is a means of cognition, for through language reality is understood, and one important task of philosophy is to clarify everyday language. But while the reality that language discovers is the ideal one to Plato, to Aristotle it is the concrete world. Aristotle himself summarizes the main points in his theory (*De int.* 16 a 3): the written sign stands for what is spoken, the sound or the spoken language is an arbitrary symbol of a state of soul or mind, in other words of concepts, and therefore there are several actual languages. But the arbitrary sound is a mark of one identical concept, and concepts resemble real things. This means that the decisive dividing line is not between the linguistic sign and reality but between the expression and its content; between the linguistic content — the concepts — and reality there is formal identity. On the one hand this guarantees intimate agreement between what is contained in the mind and the external world — the external world poses no problems for Aristotle — but on the other hand this is not to be taken to mean that every component part of language is a mere copy of the physical object. There is a difference between meaning or signification and reference (*Met.* 1006 b 15). 'White' and 'man' do not denote each its own 'thing'. They are linguistic terms, each with its own signification, and if I say 'the man is white', this means that I can say *about* the man that he *is* white. 'White' is not identical with the 'thing' man but a property the man may have, and to that extent there is reference to something real. Viewed in this way, language is an analysis of reality: in language the thing is determined by the concept without coincidence between thing and concept.

Behind this lies the basic Aristotelian metaphysical thought that the world I perceive — the phenomenological world — is not essentially different from the world as it objectively is. But the objective world is not simply identical with the world that is perceived immediately. Here it is interesting to compare Aristotle's attitude to epistemological scepticism with that of Plato. According to Plato man is able to understand rational truths, because the soul is 'akin' to ideas, while physical objects on the other hand never can be recognized as physical objects only. Indeed Aristotle's position is not very different in this respect, even though the conceptual framework has been changed. Confronting the die-hard sceptic who advances arguments well known from the *Theaetetus* — objects perceived from the distance look different if perceived at close hand; the sick man's perception is different from that of the healthy, etc. — Aristotle's retort is surprisingly nonchalant (*Met.* 1010 b 1 ff.): all that is called for is verification. Nobody, actually in Libya but dreaming that he were in Athens, would set out for a concert in Athens once he had woken up. Behind this lies a more subtle argument. If the real world were identical with that of the senses, the sceptic would be right (cf. 1010 a 1 ff.); but such is not the case. I have access to some criteria whereby I can evaluate my sensory perceptions. It is subjectively certain that this wine tastes sweet to me; it is objectively certain what the property 'sweet' is and that this property does not change. In like manner I may be in doubt whether this is a triangle (*Anal. post.* 71 a 26); but supposing that it is a triangle, I know that the sum of the angles is equal to two right angles (cf. *Met.* 1087 a 18). I would not be so certain if the world and my consciousness were not after all isomorphic, and thus under normal circumstances of observation I will have relative certainty that I am applying my criteria correctly to my sensory experiences. Yet there are infinite possibilities of perceiving a particular, and one may grant the sceptic a certain margin of uncertainty with respect to identification of the particular; but one cannot doubt that there are objects that can be described in a certain way. None of us possesses each his own world, for the existence of the public world is evident (cf. *Phys.* 193 a 1), and it would be a logical absurdity to assume that the world might in principle be different from that which we inter-subjectively are able to speak about. The world is as it is, and the world is rational.

According to the Aristotelian model of perception, man is not – as was his lot in the Cartesian tradition – confronted with an alien world, but is already *in* the world. Therefore the act of perception – or any other single act of cognition for that matter – is not a dubious relation between a familiar subject and a mysterious unknown object. Perception includes at one and the same time a subject and an object, and since I have prior access to the essence of the object, the pure sensory experience may be interpreted and corrected, for I know that there is an objective, intelligible world. In this there are points of clear agreement with the *Theaetetus* (cf. *Met.* 1010 b 30 ff.).

The world consists of objects that are intelligible, not as they are, one by one as individual objects, but as they are by virtue of their essence, and the essence of a thing exists in the thing itself and in my recognition of the thing. This is constant – not because there are eternal separate ideas, but because each member of a species has the same essence that is perpetually reproduced in time and space. There is no such thing as 'man himself' – rather, 'man begets man', as we are told in a favourite phrase (for example in *Phys.* 194 b 13 and in *Met.* 1033 b 32).

As we know, the so-called Debate about Universals of the Middle Ages arose out of a discussion about what sort of existence Aristotle had ascribed to the concept – whether it resided in the mind or in the thing. The full weight of such a question is only felt when a sharp distinction between subject and object is generally presupposed – which it is not in Aristotle. Yet the debate is understandable, for there is some apparent lack of clarity in Aristotle himself. In his critique of Plato, Aristotle must distinguish between substances and concepts referring to something – universals without real existence but under which individual objects are subsumed. Apparently concepts must be interpreted in this way if they are to be applied to a plurality of phenomena. But to Aristotle this would be a derived application of concepts that does not work when the concept is considered formally identical with the essence inherent in the thing. This problem leads to complications in any detailed reading of the *Metaphysics* – simply because Aristotle, without ever saying so explicitly, distinguishes between universal and essence. The universal is a single concept that may apply to multiple objects, and the essence of a thing is neither singular nor multiple.

To this must be added that to Aristotle mind is really nothing but the sum of recognized objects (cf. *De an.* 429 a 18 ff.). There are objects of reason and objects of sense, and the object of reason is inherent in the object of sense. Aristotle's anti-reductionism forbids him to attribute real existence to ideal objects, and this has consequences for his view of the ontological status of mathematical objects. As a matter of course Aristotle refuses to acknowledge the existence of ideal numbers and finds it wrong to reduce physical entities to mathematical ones. On the contrary, mathematical entities are abstractions from physical ones, and the mathematician treats his objects *as if* they had real existence and as if they were separate from physical objects (cf. *Phys.* 193 b 31 ff.; *Met.* 1026 a 7 ff.; 1061 a 28 ff.; 1077 b 17 ff.). No ideal geometrical figures 'exist', but the surface, of a body for example, does have geometrical form; nor do numbers 'exist' except as abstractions from quantities, which is to say that Aristotle concurs with Plato's understanding of numerals as designations of quantities but has no use whatsoever for Plato's ideal numbers.

PRINCIPLES AND METHODS

All of this must of course have consequences for Aristotle's understanding of the concept of principle – the basis for any science that cannot be proved (*Anal. post.* 76 a 31) – as well as for Aristotle's method. In the contemporary philosophical tradition he was up against two radically different types of method. One was the scientific method, which had evolved during the later stages of natural philosophy and according to which material events were explicable by means of non-sensory, material basic elements; the other was the Platonic conceptual-analytical method of hypothesis and the doctrine of principles, which, in Speusippus at any rate, was aimed at a universal science. In the formal sciences, mathematics and formal logic, Aristotle was able to employ a deductive method. But for the purposes of a philosophical-scientific description of reality it can at best be used as a means to present knowledge that has already been reached by some other path. Here Aristotle is unable to employ either the reductionism of natural philosophy or that of the Academy. He adopts the entire Academy vocabulary: principles, causes, elements (cf. *Phys.* 184 a 10 ff.; *Met.* 1012 b 34 ff.; 1070 a 31 ff.), but while a principle is a metaphysical cause to the Academy that determines the existence of lower entities, to Aristotle it is an explanatory factor. He would in fact have been able to use the celebrated argument paraded by the Academy (cf. 1017 b 17), but he would not have considered it a metaphysical deduction (cf. p. 259). A principle has no special privileged form of existence, for it 'exists' only with regard to that which it is meant to explain. A principle is always a 'principle of something' (Wieland, cf. *Phys.* 185 a 4). Principles and methods must therefore adapt themselves to the subject that is to be explained, and explanations do not proceed from principles. Rather, they are established with the aid of principles. Such principles may be formal – as is for example the principle of contradiction – or substantive, regardless of whether they are couched as sentences or concepts; here Aristotle's usage may, like Plato's, be somewhat vacillatory (cf. *Anal. post.* 99 b 15 ff.), and one must also be absolutely certain whether the principles are valid in general or only in the specific sciences (cf. 75 a 38). It follows from this that the philosopher cannot derive conclusions from pre-existing, well-defined principles, for they are recognizable together with that which they explain; thus cognition has a certain circular structure. It is the task of the philosopher to seek out principles, and this means quite simply that philosophy consists in finding causes and in explaining *why* this or that is the case, and not merely – as with experience – to find *that* this is the case (89 b 21 ff.; *Met.* 981 a 28). Whoever has arrived at such a philosophical insight is omniscient in the sense that he knows the general that causes the specific (982 a 8) – a telling contrast to Plato's dictum that the philosopher 'knows everything'. His logic aside, all of Aristotle's works represent a search for universal or specific principles that may explain the factual knowledge that we already possess to a greater or lesser degree. The process itself – the search for clarification by means of conceptual analysis and argumentation *pro et con* – may be called dialectical by Aristotle (*Top.* 101 a 36); however, if one imagines the ideal situation, in which the philosopher has attained his goal, he will no longer reason dialectically (cf. 155 b 9) – but in fact this would be a borderline situation and perhaps an elusive goal.

Philosophy should not constitute reality but so describe it that it can be understood. The world that Aristotle wants to describe lies phenomenologically before us, for our world is *the* world. The phenomena – *ta phainomena* – are the point of departure, and this means everything that is included in our prior understanding of the world and in our everyday language whenever we speak without reflection about the world. 'World' is here used in its broadest sense to comprehend both the physical and human worlds, including for example moral standards, social structure, and tradition. Accordingly, *ta phainomena* refer not only to the world of experience and scientific data, such as astronomical observations (cf. *Anal. pr.* 46 a 17 ff.) or the circumstance that winged snakes exist in Ethiopia (*Hist. an* 490 a 11), but also to common beliefs (*endoxa*), or a consensus (cf. *Eth. Nic.* 1172 b 369) – each of us can contribute our little bit to the truth, and such a storehouse of knowledge and perception cannot simply be wrong (*Met.* 993 b 1). This is of course particularly true of the earlier philosophers, for all philosophers devote themselves to the same cause (cf. 983 a 33 ff.).

Aristotle explains his procedure as follows (*Eth. Nic.* 1145 b 2 ff.): on the basis of *ta phainomena* one must discuss all problems – the *aporiai* – that present themselves, and by providing solutions to these *aporiai* one must, if possible, seek to confirm common beliefs. It may be that some must be corrected, but a reasonable result has been obtained if most, or at any rate the most authoritative ones, have been confirmed. This is not a means to acquire new knowledge, nor is it a prescription for reforming the world, for there is no doubt that the method favours both moral and political conservatism. Yet it is probably not to be understood quite as ingenuously as it is phrased. The language of philosophy and the matter of philosophy are inseparable, and philosophical reflection consists in making a pre-philosophical experience explicit by means of conceptual and linguistic analysis. This does not necessarily mean that everything that has gained acceptance is right, but merely that the philosopher will be working in a void unless his analysis is anchored in that which people in fact believe or have believed. This is also the reason why Aristotle almost always introduces his treatises with a survey of his philosophical predecessors – albeit on his own terms, though rarely as polemically as in his personal break with Plato – and with an aporetic section as well: what answers have been provided to the questions we ask, and where do the problems lie? The entire first book of the *Metaphysics* is a 'history of philosophy', and another whole book is devoted to *aporiai*. Two examples from the *Ethics* may serve to illustrate his method. In his discussion of voluntary acts (1109 b 30 ff.) Aristotle begins with a tentative definition, which both has a philosophical point to make and is in agreement with the current ideas about responsibility: voluntary acts are acts performed neither under compulsion nor in ignorance. Next he musters every imaginable counter-argument and proceeds to analyse each of them thoroughly. The upshot is that he is able to hone and legitimate his own definition. But the basic theme of the *Ethics* is a careful demonstration of the fact that the true meaning of the concept of happiness fails to correspond with the concept as frequently used.

In more theoretical terms Aristotle says (*Phys.* 184 a 16 ff.; cf. e.g. *Met.* 1029 b 3 ff.) that one should proceed from that which is 'more familiar to us' to that which is 'simply' or 'according to nature' better known, which is to say that explanatory principles take logical precedence over phenomena. By 'induction' (*epagōgē* – cf. *Top.* 105 a 13; 156 a 5) from an indeterminate number of data, which are immediately present, one recognizes the universal in the particular in such a way that the universal legitimates or explains *ta phainomena*. This is not a reduction to principles with factual existence but a recourse to epistemic principles that already 'are present' in the world they are meant to explain. Structurally speaking, however, the procedure is the same as the standard Platonic one, also in the sense that there is no strict inductive 'method', and the Academy terminology persists (e.g. 'better known according to nature'). Aristotle himself is quite aware that he is reshaping a Platonic method, for, as he remarks, Plato was right in always asking us if we are on our way towards or away from first principles (*Eth. Nic.* 1095 a 32). It is one thing to construct a theory and quite another to use it, but it is the laying down of a theory that is the very core of philosophy.

That one cannot know the principles of explanation a priori means that the method must always depend on the particular subject, and therefore Aristotle normally includes some important considerations about method along with his historical and aporetic introductions – and here the introductions to the *Physics*, *De anima* and *De partibus animalium* are of special interest. In any science it is a fundamental precondition that we cannot take our point of departure in a definition of the essence of this or that, for it is precisely that definition we are in search of. For this reason it is impossible to arrive at conclusions deductively, and hence the Platonic method of *diairesis* – which Aristotle often uses himself – can only communicate but not bring knowledge about (cf. *De an.* 402 a 10 ff.; *Anal. pr.* 46 a 31 ff.). Thus one will usually need to resort to inference from attribute to substance, from function to essence, and from effect to cause – in short, from phenomenon to explanatory principle (cf. *De an.* 402 b 21; *De part an.* 640 a. 14)).

The essential point is that every subject matter must be grasped conceptually from as many angles as possible – which is what is meant by Hegel's 'total empiricism'. Therefore there are several levels of description, which are complementary but not necessarily causally related, and it is important to remember that a given descriptive level is not metaphysical or structural. A biologist, for example, must not only study the organs that constitute a living creature; he must also ask why living creatures are not mere physical entities among other physical entities. In other words, he must ask what is understood by the vital functions (*De part. an.* 640 b 29). A phenomenon such as anger can be described physiologically, for anger consists in blood and heat boiling around the heart, but also psychologically, for anger is a wish for revenge. A house exists in order to provide shelter against the elements, but it also consists of a certain material, it has a certain shape, and has been built by a master builder (*De an.* 403 a 29 ff.; cf. *Met.* 1043 a 15). In some ways this investigative strategy is commonplace, but Aristotle's strength lies in asking good commonplace questions.

In his 'investigative strategy' Aristotle makes use of certain schematic types of questions. He systematizes in order to arrive at concrete conceptual delimitations and, unlike Plato, he does not wish to reveal general preconditions of any description. An important device for asking questions is the categories, which, differing from the Academy doctrine of categories, are a systematization of simple predicative sentences about definite subjects. It aims to penetrate beyond the linguistic to the logical form, and, inasmuch as language reflects reality, something will thereby be said about that subject which is accorded a predicate – the thing which is a conveyor of properties. In this way a series of irreducible classes of predicates is established (see p. 294).

Another device concerns the very question of the cause of a phenomenon, and indeed this type of questioning is at least as important and is independent of the question of categories. In Aristotle's view there are four causes: the formal, the material, the efficient and the final (cf. *Phys.* 194 b 16; see p. 319; *Met.* 1013 a 24 ff.); in scholastic terminology these were the *causa formalis, materialis, efficiens* and *finalis*. The application of this technique of questioning can be seen in the example cited earlier: a house has matter or a stuff, it has a form and a purpose, and it has been made in a certain way. The four 'causes' are equals – none of them can be reduced to any of the others – but together they provide an exhaustive description of the phenomenon. The word 'cause' is not to be understood in its modern sense, for in fact it is only the efficient cause that corresponds to cause as used in the modern natural sciences. The Aristotelian causes are not necessary and sufficient conditions allowing for a given effect to follow from a given cause. They are modes of description and conditions for an object's becoming what it is. The combination of stone, plus master builder, plus house plan, plus purpose will not of itself produce the house; but if the house does in fact exist, the necessary conditions must also have been present. Other circumstances are incidental – such as the name of the master builder, his height, or his musicality. Aristotle often uses artefacts as his examples, for to him an artefact is a paradigm of the way nature works, and it is aptly chosen, in so far as in an artefact the four causes are real separate conditions for the existence of the artefact. In a natural product, on the other hand, the four causes are still conceptually separate, even though three of the causes in fact will often coincide (cf. *Phys.* 198 a 24). The form of an oak tree fulfils its purpose in itself, and it is the oak tree itself that grows. But nature has her own purpose as has the artisan with his work. Everything considered, living creatures are prototypes of nature, and everything in nature strives to fulfil a purpose, to realize its own specific form. This is a special shift in focus with respect to the Platonic concept of teleology: every object and nature in her entirety have their purposes in themselves. It is quite conceivable that there is a closer affiliation with Speusippus' teleology than Aristotle cares to reveal (see p. 262).

Aristotle has a certain predilection for thinking schematically. But a scheme is something to be filled in, and to Aristotle it is a point of departure rather than a conclusion. It may help in coming to terms with a problem, but often it points to something beyond that. It is, for example, possible (*Eth. Nic.* 1102 a 26; cf. 1138 b 35; *De an.* 431 a 8 – see p. 337) to divide the soul schematically according to its several functions, but if one keeps the scheme in the mind's eye one sees a continuous series of overlappings stretching from the 'vegetative' part of the soul to the rational, and not until then is it possible to grasp the real point (cf. p. 334 on biological classifications).

FORMAL CONCEPTS AND PLURALISM

Everything considered, the most important element in Aristotle's philosophical method is his development of a conceptual apparatus that is uniquely well suited as an analytical tool. Translated into Latin, many of these concepts became the nucleus of what might be called a shared vocabulary of Western philosophy. 'Substance', 'essence', 'form' and 'matter' are examples. Translated into modern languages, several came to colour daily usage, as we see in such words as 'matter', 'necessity' and 'accident', 'reality' and 'possibility'.

Some of these concepts may stem from common usage at the Academy, but there is no doubt that Aristotle himself established most of his own terminology. It is tailored to his purposes and is, besides, fully developed in the treatises that have survived – apparently already in the *Protrepticus*. The conceptual apparatus is given its special character by the fact that Aristotle, unlike Plato, did not reify. A concept may represent anything whatsoever. Thus a predicate, for example, does not necessarily designate a certain 'reality' but rather an aspect of something. On the other hand, a concept does stand for some feature of reality.

Certain concepts may be fixed metaphors, as for example 'matter', which in the Greek is *hylē*, literally 'wood' (i.e. 'stuff', as in 'timber'; but Aristotle simply recasts it to mean 'matter'). With special virtuosity he exploits the possibilities in the Greek language of substantivizing for example adverbs and prepositions. Thus 'time', 'space' and 'relation' may be expressed by substantivizing 'when', 'where', and 'relative to something' (cf. *Cat.* 1 b 26 ff.). A substantivizing of 'of' and 'from' can also be exploited terminologically (cf. *Met.* 1023 a 26 ff.). In this way Aristotle is able to achieve a high degree of precision, while his terminology at the same time retains its associations with everyday language. He removes a word from its normal context and turns it into an abstract term. An important and quite subtle example is his terminological use of the little word *hēi* (Latin: *qua*), which means 'in respect of', 'in so far as', or 'by virtue of'. With this word he is able to examine a certain aspect of a subject abstracted from other aspects and he is not ontologically obliged to reify it. A mathematician does not speak of a line 'in respect of' its being physical, and so, in other words, mathematical objects are abstractions from physical ones (*Phys.* 194 a 9). It is possible to speak of an object *qua* its being moved; of honour, wisdom, and pleasure *qua* their being goods (201 a 28; *Eth. Nic.* 1096 b 23). A similar manoeuvre can of course be carried out by other means. To cite a standard example (e.g. *Met.* 1025 b 31): it is possible conceptually to isolate 'concavity' from 'nose' in 'snub-nose'. Or

Aristotle distinguishes between what is said 'simply' or with qualification (cf. *Eth. Nic.* 1139 b 2; 1148 a 11), or between numerical unity and conceptual or definitional plurality: a sound is one event, but conceptually (literally: with respect to being) a sound is both something that sounds and something that is heard (*De an.* 425 b 2). Conceptual flexibility is arrived at by simple linguistic means.

Of course Aristotle does not need to create a special terminology in order to express simple object concepts such as 'man' or 'horse'. But he does need a special set of formal concepts or conceptual tools whenever he wishes to speak of object concepts. Such concepts are void, unless they are filled in with respect to given objects. In this way Aristotle avoids the difficulty that confronted Plato as a consequence of his dealing with formal concepts or 'principles' in the language used for object concepts. Aristotle has no phrase for 'formal concept', but quite early on he must have been aware of the differences between vocabularies of the first and second order (cf. *Top.* 137 b 7). Aristotelian formal concepts are furthermore quite flexible, because the contents they are meant to describe are not univocal. Formal concepts express different points of view about 'what is' – and, in a standard phrase, we are told that 'what is' may be said 'in several senses' (e.g. *Met.* 1003 a 33). If 'what is' first and foremost is a thing, we may question the very concept of thing – what makes a thing a thing? – and we may ask: what is the structure *of* a thing, what is essential *about* a thing, how can a thing arise or be altered, and how can a thing be classified?

The formal concepts needed for answers to these questions, of which many are arranged in pairs, lead directly to the core of Aristotle's philosophy. The most important ones will be mentioned here (retaining the traditional Latin terminology).

Substance and accident. To Aristotle the world consists of things endowed with properties. But, what is a thing? What is it that establishes identity between the infant and the old man? In fact, what is it that makes the thing the same, even though all its component parts have been replaced in the course of time? How can we distinguish between words denoting 'things' and 'mass-words'? For example, when does a lump of snow become a snowman? Is a thing characterized by its properties or will something remain of it if all properties are removed? Do certain properties determine whether the thing is this thing? Is a hand a thing or a part of a thing? What lies behind the distinction between thing and property in everyday language is that something exists in itself in such a way that it is 'separate' and so that one may point to it. But something else has derived existence, for it can only exist, if something exists in a primary sense. In daily speech 'man' is something that exists in a primary sense; 'white' is a property that presupposes that 'man' or another subject that is 'white' exists. Here Aristotle must distinguish between that which in traditional terminology is called substance and accident (Greek: *ousia* and *symbebēkos*),[1] where substance denotes that which exists in itself and accidence the contingent. But that

---

1 The correct etymological translation of *ousia* is *essentia*, and Cicero is said to have so reproduced it (Sen. *Ep.* 50,6). *Substantia* is a translation of *hypostasis*, 'supporting' or 'basis'. Augustine used *substantia* and *essentia* synonymously (cf. Aug. *De Trin.* V 2,3). It was not until Boethius (c.AD 500) that *substantia* became the only word used (*Contr. Eut.* 3).

which exists in itself is not just simply a thing. It is also the conceptual designation of the thing as a thing – the thing exists as this thing of this kind. This means that the concept of substance is a formal one, and that Aristotle lets his use of it depend on the context (cf. the summary in *Met.* 1042 a 24 ff.). Without reflection substances may be considered as things with properties about which something is said – as we see in the *Categories*. But it is not so simple if the concept is applied to a natural object subject to motion and change, or, in other words, to a thing that alters its properties – as we see in the *Physics*. Finally, in the *Metaphysics* the very relationship between thing and concept creates further complications, and here 'substance' denotes the concept that designates the thing as thing. In a qualified sense it is also possible to take it to mean that which has the possibility of becoming this thing – as for example the mass of snow that has not yet become a snowman. What is decisive is the way in which there is a need for the concept of something that has priority of existence. When the concept of substance is accorded the thing, it means that all designations other than the substantial ones must be considered accidental. This pertains, for example, to quality and quantity. It implies a differentiation of concepts that is alien to Plato, such as a colour for example, which does not exist in the same way as does a physical object. Primary existence is accorded to the natural species, natural objects, or living creatures (cf. Xenocrates).

Form and matter. Aristotle found the problem of change unsolved by Plato. In order to account for the way in which an object may change – how 'something' can become another 'something' – he needs the correlative concepts of form (*eidos*) and matter (*hylē*), which are two of the Aristotelian 'causes'. According to the traditional terminology, which is adhered to here, *eidos* is translated as 'form', but actually we are victims of a centuries-old terminological tyranny, for Aristotle himself uses the same word as that which in Plato is translated as 'idea'. Hence this is not a question of a new term but of a reinterpretation of an old one. Whenever a thing changes, something must remain that is constant during the process of change, something to or from which the thing is changed. Aristotle frequently uses a bronze ball as his illustration (cf. *Met.* 1033 b 1 ff.). A bronze ball has been fashioned from something, bronze is its matter, and the matter is constant. The shape of the ball is thus the 'form' the bronze receives, and the form itself is also constant. In Aristotle 'form' may stand for a great deal – sometimes so much that the concept suffers a loss of precision. It may be the visible form (often called *morphē*), the ball. But often it is impossible to distinguish between the structure, function and purpose of the thing. The form of a knife is what makes it usable for cutting, and, in the example cited earlier, the form of a house is determined by its purpose. This means that 'form' most often has to do with something non-sensory – a complicated example is that of the soul, which is the form of man, in other words that which makes man something different from and more than mere flesh and bones, etc. (*De an.* 412 a 16 ff.). Nor does matter need to be sensory matter. A generic concept (*genus*) may for instance be considered the 'matter' of a subordinate one (*species*): we shall never meet a living being that is only a 'living being' and not, for example, a man as well, and so 'living being' is the 'matter' for a complete description of 'man'. The thing is an entity or a whole (*synolon*) consisting of form and matter, but form and matter are not separate parts, but rather aspects and constituent elements in the thing, as is the surface of a table that cannot be separated from the table. In yet another sense form and matter are relative concepts. In a bronze ball, bronze is the matter, but the bronze from which the ball is made had its own form and its own matter; similarly, one can imagine that the bronze ball will be reshaped into other forms, and to that extent it is itself matter. In this way the whole world may be viewed as a hierarchy of matter and form. But the existence of such relative concepts implies for Aristotle that it is possible in the final analysis to speak of matter in an absolute sense (often called *prima materia*) and of pure form. Both are limiting concepts. Matter will never be present in an absolute sense but must be conceptually presupposed. To Aristotle pure form is identical with god, the unchangeable being who is a precondition for something to be formed. In the large cosmic format there are significant structural resemblances to the Platonic universe (the *Timaeus*), but Aristotle's principal emphasis is on the description of the individual phenomenon as constituted by form and matter.

Matter is the conveyor of or substratum (*hypokeimenon*) for form. This flesh and these bones are a man; the thing is the substratum for further determinations of form, such as: the man is musical. An individual cannot *qua* – 'by virtue of' – individual be defined (*Met.* 1039 b 20), for it is the form that causes the individual to exist as an individual of this kind, that makes it not merely a 'this something' but a 'this such' (1033 b 23). The individual – the unity of form and matter – is perishable. The bronze ball has been fashioned and will cease to be, although the matter as such and the form as such are eternal (cf. 1033 a 24 ff.). God is pure form, but in our world form does not exist 'separately', for then it would be a 'super-thing', as is the Platonic idea. Physically, form exists by constant reproduction ('a man begets a man'). Accordingly, inasmuch as there is formal identity between structure and concept, between the thing as an existing object and the thing as intelligible object, this means that the form also exists in the mind – the soul is 'the seat of the forms' (*De an.* 429 a 27); as an intelligible phenomenon – which may be expressed by one conceptual determination – the form is a 'this' and 'separate' (*Met.* 1042 a 29). If the Aristotelian form looks both like an ontological and a mental phenomenon it is owing to the fact that the content of the mind is determined ontologically. In the physical world there is a multiplicity of identical forms, but in the mind the corresponding form is only one.

Actuality and potentiality. The concepts of form and matter serve to describe the conditions for change. The process of change itself (*Met.* 1045 b 26 ff.; 1065 b 5 ff.) is described by means of the concepts of actuality, reality or activity (*energeia*), and potentiality or possibility (*dynamis*).[2] Aristotle himself notes that strictly speaking these concepts cannot be defined (cf. *Met.* 1048 a 25 ff.) but that their meaning may be understood by means of a series of analogous examples: a block of stone may become a statue; he who is asleep may wake up; the master builder may build the

---

2   In some cases Aristotle finds it necessary to add more subtle nuances to his concepts. The concept of *entelecheia* (complete reality) emphasizes that a process has fulfilled its purpose, and *hexis* (*habitus*, state) designates a firm disposition to actualization. A person who can see, for example, is disposed to look at something (cf. *Met.* 1050 a 23; *De an.* 412 a 22 ff.).

house; and the house may be built by the builder. From such examples it is clear that *dynamis* can signify both 'ability' and 'possibility', as in the ability a man has to do something (the sleeper who can wake up) and in the possibility that is realized through the interaction of two entities (when the builder builds the house he realizes his own potential to build and the potential of the house to become built). Now the point is that a thing or a stuff (bronze, for example) cannot become just anything. It has certain possibilities in certain respects, and a possibility may be actualized or not actualized – it is, so to speak, either positive or negative – and, since a possibility is always a possibility *of* or *for* something, the concept of actuality logically precedes the concept of potentiality. The possible and the actual will have the same definition: the house that can be built is defined in the same way as the house that has been built. Hence the concepts do not denote differences of essence but of modes of existence. The scheme of actuality/potentiality is closely tied to the concept of *kinēsis*, movement, or, in a wider sense, process, which is the 'movement' from possibility to actualization. Aristotle examines this concept closely both in physical and metaphysical contexts and in virtuoso manner he exploits the meaning of the process verbs. A process may have its purpose in itself – as for example 'to see' and 'to live' – or the purpose may be the completion of a process – as for example 'to look at something', 'to learn geometry', 'to go on a diet' – and in formal terms movement is defined as the actualization of a potentiality (*Phys.* 201 a 10).

It is evident that the concepts of actuality and potentiality are closely connected with form and matter. The fact that bronze is the matter of the ball informs us that the bronze has the possibility of becoming a ball. The difference between the two conceptual pairs is that while form and matter are static tools of analysis, actuality and potentiality are concepts of process. Actuality and potentiality have wider fields of application and may, for example, be applied to man's use of his cognitive abilities, and it goes without saying that the two conceptual pairs will behave in logically different ways: form may exist in the mind as apprehended form, whereas a process cannot exist in anything, although reason, for example, may be made actual when it is engaged in cognition. Ultimately, coincidence occurs: pure potentiality coincides with *prima materia*, and the pure act is the pure form or god.

Essence. To Aristotle the standard scientific question is the old Socratic 'what is X' question, which means that a question is raised about the essence of a thing. The answer can be expressed by means of a definition, and a definition applies to both thing and concept; the definition of a particular man is identical with that of the species; and in this there is agreement with Plato's position. The essence of a thing is of course something that the thing possesses, but it is only identical with the thing to the extent that the thing is identified with its concept. Form and matter, actuality and potentiality, are concepts that constitute the thing as thing or as a thing subject to change. The essence indicates what a thing of a certain type is, but not whether the thing exists. The essence of a thing may comprise both form and matter, as when a man is defined as 'a two-footed living being', and in the same way it may include actuality and potentiality. Nor, strictly speaking, does the answer to the 'what is X' question have to be a definition of the essence of a thing. Aristotle is able to ask about all aspects of a thing or a subject without being ontologically obliged to reify that which he is asking about. A substance as well as a quality, a sensory organ as well as a sensory faculty can be defined, regardless of the fact that the substance is the conveyor of qualities and that the sensory organ and the ability to sense are numerically one. For example, the essence of a colour can be designated as a quality, even though the colour has no independent existence. Essences without instances (such as a chimera) can also be defined, but the prototype of an essence is the essence that belongs to an existing object, and it is impossible to imagine an object without essence, because it is impossible to imagine an object about which one could not ask the question 'what is X? (cf. *Anal. post.* 89 b 25 ff.). If a thing were to be understood as the sum of co-equal properties, and if there were nothing that primarily characterized the thing, the concept of thing would disintegrate. Once again, the terminology is instructive. The point of departure may be the question, 'what is man?' The answer will of course pertain to the essence of man, which Aristotle recasts as 'what-it-means-for-a-man-to-be-a-man'. This formula presupposes an ontological 'something' (man) and states that conceptually we define this something in terms of – *qua* – man, and not, for example, in terms of being tall, white, or a grandfather, for there is a difference between numerical unity and definitional plurality. Whatever one wishes to define or designate conceptually may be expressed by 'being X', whereas Plato's formula had been 'X itself'.[3] The priority of the thing is made clear in the *Categories* where the thing itself is called 'the primary substance' (*ousia*), while 'the secondary substance' designates the essence.

Genus and species. An essence is expressed by a definition, and the definition indicates the family or genus to which a thing belongs (Latin: *genus*; Greek: *genos*) and the subordinate kind or species (Latin: *species*; Greek: *eidos*). These concepts – genus and species – were inherited by Aristotle, but he refined them. Infinite complications have arisen from the fact that *eidos* can be rendered as both form and species. Nor does Aristotle himself always distinguish between the two meanings. But genus and species are in principle universals (*universalia*, singular: *universale*; Greek: *to katholou*, 'what is said about many'), i.e. logical concepts that indicate the extension of those objects that fall under the concept. Form, on the other hand, is in modern parlance primarily an intensional concept that corresponds with the structure of the thing. Aristotle distinguished implicitly but not consistently. If *eidos* is read as referring to intension, it has ontological relevance. Conceptually it is a 'this something' and can be related to the concept of substance. If it is read with reference to extension, it has no ontological status – Plato had blundered by confusing the individual with the universal.

Form has priority over matter, actuality over potentiality. Form, actuality and essence provide three approaches to a conceptual determination of substance. In certain circumstances, which are carefully explored in the *Metaphysics*, the three may converge and be identified with substance. The incongruity between thing and concept leads Aristotle to take a dual position, although this does not necessarily pose

---

3   The answer to the question 'what is X?' Aristotle calls 'what it was (i.e. "what it turned out to be") in order for X to be X'. By even further reduction this is called 'to be what it was' (*to ti ēn einai*). This technical formula is in Latin translated by *essentia*, but this does not, alas, capture what is contained in the Greek, apart from the fact that it is etymologically a translation of *ousia*.

an insoluble 'dilemma': on the one hand, only things have *real* existence; on the other, the thing is defined both epistemologically and ontologically by its concept, and concepts are inter-subjective. The ultimate precondition for concepts that makes the world intelligible is reason, which is divine and coming to man 'from outside' (*De gen. an.* 736 b 28). God himself is pure actuality and pure form.

Aristotle's conceptual apparatus is finely adjusted to a pluralist description. Corresponding to the pluralist description at which he aimed, each of his works deals with one area of reality or with one 'science', and this is reflected in his classification of the sciences.

As stated earlier, logic is a tool rather than a science. The sciences proper are divided into three main groups (cf. *Met.* 1025 b 25 ff.): theoretical sciences (*theōria*: contemplation); practical sciences (*praxis*: action); and sciences concerned with human productions (*poiēsis*: production). There are three theoretical sciences: physics concerns itself with objects that exist independently, which consist of form and matter and are movable; mathematical objects are immovable and abstractions from matter; the superior theoretical science is metaphysics, the subject of which is immovable substances without matter – first philosophy or theology according to Aristotle's terminology. The practical sciences are those of ethics and politics. The last principal group is made up of rhetoric and poetics – but it should be noted that there is no 'science' dealing with the making of artefacts.

The distinction between theoretical and practical philosophy has prevailed until modern times. In the theoretical sciences man is an independent observer of the world, although this in no way renders these sciences 'neutral'; but in the practical sciences man is concerned with himself. In the theoretical sciences it is possible to arrive at a high degree of generalization and precision, because the focus is on what exists of necessity. In the human world, on the other hand, the philosopher can only speak about what happens for the most part. Certain patterns of action do exist, but they are bound up with changeable human life and its specific circumstances, and therefore the practical sciences cannot achieve the same degree of precision as the theoretical sciences – Aristotle cannot consider moral philosophy and politics exact sciences that reveal laws of nature. *Praxis* and *poiēsis* signify human activities with different intentions. Man's ethical and political life depends upon that act which has its own inherent purpose (*praxis*), while a 'production' (*poiēsis*) has an extrinsic purpose in the 'product'; we exist in order to exist, and we produce something in order to use it. Finally, it is part of Aristotle's theory of science that accidental events do occur; these are not without cause but they cannot be predicted. Such events cannot be dealt with scientifically, for it is not even possible to speak about what 'happens for the most part'.

In a more profound sense the distinction between theory and practice consists in the difference between the life contemplative and the life political. The difference between *praxis* and *poiēsis* is one of goal and means, and this is essential for Aristotle's view of man. Man is not a productive but a cognitive being, and he is an ethical and political being who creates his own life.

What follows will be a presentation of each of these 'sciences'.

20

LOGIC AND THEORY OF SCIENCE

—— •◆• ——

In his conclusion to his lectures on informal logic or theory of argumentation (Arist. *Soph. el.* 183 b 15 ff.) Aristotle declares with justified pride that he has established an entirely new discipline. With even greater justification this characterization might be applied to his syllogistics, the main portion of the formal logic. Plato's logic was a logic of being, in which logic and metaphysics were inseparable. But Aristotle's logic in its fully developed form is formal and concerns itself with the formal validity of logical inferences, which is to say with the relation between judgements, regardless of their content. On the one hand such a formal logic is thus delimited and set apart from metaphysics or science, and on the other hand from psychology. Formal logic does not examine how we think but deals with those abstract rules that are valid for correct thinking – whether anybody is thinking or not. From a modern point of view it is particularly significant that Aristotle refrains from any form of 'psychologism'. Furthermore, since the Middle Ages a distinction between formal logic and linguistics has been generally accepted. Linguistics concerns itself with the actual structure of language, logic with the logical form of the linguistic expression and with the truth value of propositions. Aristotle himself does not always distinguish explicitly between linguistics and logic – in his time linguistics had not yet become an established science. Yet he was well aware that logical form and linguistic form are not readily identical, and in his syllogistics he does in practice maintain a distinction between the two. It reflects his understanding of the special nature of formal logic that he does not include it in his scientific system.

In many respects the so-called classical or traditional logic is a systematization of Aristotle's. In standard presentations of classical logic one accordingly finds three principal sections: on terms, on propositions and on syllogisms. Put another way: first the component parts of a judgement, then the simple judgement and finally the relationship between judgements. This systematization relies on the sequence of the *Categories*, *De interpretatione*, *Analytics*, which for paedagogical reasons were canonized during the Roman Empire. To these are often added sections dealing with definition, classification and axiomatics. Finally, formal logic will be distinguished from informal or rhetorical logic, which deals with the manner in which arguments may be constructed most convincingly (*Topics* and *De sophisticis elenchis*).

As is well known, far into the nineteenth century it was thought that classical logic, like Euclid's *Elements*, constituted a perfect system to which nothing could be added and from which only a few particular subtleties might be deducted (cf. Kant, *Kritik der reinen Vernunft* B VIII), and it is likewise well known that this view is incorrect. Nor is it correct simply to identify 'classical logic' with Aristotelian logic. In 'classical logic', which is a rather vague designation often applied to all logic that precedes Boole, Frege and Russell, important elements (hypothetical and disjunctive syllogisms) go beyond Aristotle, and the traditional way of presenting syllogisms departs on essential points from Aristotle's (see below). Nor has logic always been distinguished from psychology. Finally, Aristotle's writings about logic are not a closed system, for the completed theory was not formulated until he wrote the *Analytics*. In the other works it is possible – and this is unique in the surviving oeuvre of Aristotle – to follow the development of a theory in the making. Thus in the *Categories* the single terms are not considered as terms belonging in a syllogism, and the concept of a purely formal logic has not yet emerged. This small treatise deals in fact with both logic and metaphysics and is indeed an able introduction to both subjects. In the *De interpretatione* we can see Aristotle working to emancipate logic from a general philosophy of language, but not even here is a syllogistical theory presupposed. In the *Topics* it is apparent as an ideal, although the theory has not yet found its firm and final form. In these, the earliest writings, one senses clearly the common Academy background. But the keystone – the *Analytics* – was probably in place during the Academy days, and by that time Aristotle had arrived at his sharp distinction between formal and informal logic. In the present chapter this distinction is observed, and it has proved relevant to follow the traditional sequence. So doing it is possible in the field of formal logic to move from the lesser to the more complicated, also in the sense that the *Categories* and the *De interpretatione* are textbooks – we are able to see how the components bit by bit become incorporated in a coherent theory.

THE *CATEGORIES* AND *DE INTERPRETATIONE*

In the early Middle Ages Aristotle's *Categories* and *De interpretatione*, translated into Latin, were his only writings on logic known in the Western world. Together with Porphyry's introduction from the third century AD and Boethius' commentary on this from about AD 500 they constituted the 'old logic', *Logica vetus*. *Logica nova* (the *Analytics*, the *Topics* including the *De sophisticis elenchis*) did not become known until the Aristotelian renaissance during the thirteenth century. It was the interpretation of *Logica vetus* that occasioned the breakthrough in medieval thinking, which is known as the 'Debate about Universals'.

Naturally, the background for Aristotle's *Categories* is 'the doctrine of categories' of the Academy with its distinction between autonomous and relative being. It is within this framework that Aristotle performs his radical shift from a formal metaphysical theory to a description of the particular object. That which exists of itself is hereafter taken to be the thing and its essential properties; that which exists relatively as accidental properties which can be ascribed to the thing. Next Aristotle deliberately abstracts from all problems about the concept of thing – what makes a thing a thing, how a thing may be altered, etc. – and asks what we are able to say about a thing that is present here and now. This means that the thing can be directly equated with substance and that substance is conceived of as a substratum (*hypokeimenon*) for further determinations; metaphysically it is the bearer of properties, logically it is the subject to which predicates may be assigned. Aristotle himself has described the situation we have to imagine (*Top.* 103 b 29): suppose that we have a man in front of us and ask, 'what is this?' We may then reply, 'this is a man' or, 'this is a living being', and thus the essence of the man has been indicated. But we might come up with other replies and may for example specify the man's size, colour, or other, secondary determinations. It will in other words be clear that some descriptions presuppose others – that the man is white presupposes that he is there, but no type of secondary reply can be reduced to any other; that the man is white does not say anything about the man's size.

Simple subject-predicate sentences are employed in our answers. If we now systematize these answers, the result will be a table containing the possibilities of description of any given object. This means that we systematize the predicates, and an Aristotelian category is an irreducible class of predicates. It is a presupposition that language is a means of cognition. Therefore, thanks to the categories, we are enabled to learn something about the thing by analyzing how we speak of the thing.

Aristotle commences with some terminological remarks, introducing (*Cat.* 1 a 1 ff.) the concepts of 'homonym' (in scholastic terminology: equivocal), 'synonym' (univocal), and 'paronym' (denominative). He has taken over these three concepts from Speusippus, but he uses them differently, for the concepts do not apply to the linguistic sign, the word, but to the thing *qua* signified. Homonymous entities are accordingly to be understood as entities with the same name but with different definitions, as for example a real human being and a picture of a human being. Synonyms are entities with the same name and the same definition – the name 'animal' signifies the same, whether it is applied to 'man' or 'cow'. Paronyms are linguistic derivations, not in any etymological sense, but, for example, as when we say that the man is 'white' because he possesses 'whiteness'. It is obvious that one will get into a logical mire unless one relies primarily upon univocal entities (synonyms).

The objects under investigation are the smallest component parts of the proposition, which, as is characteristic for the fusion of linguistic, logical, and ontological points of view, are defined as 'things' [properly, existing entities], which are 'said' without combination such as 'man' and 'runs' as opposed to the combination (the sentence) 'the man runs' (1 a 16). But 'things' may be 'said' in several ways (1 a 20 ff.): (1) something may be 'said of' a subject without 'being in' the subject. The universals 'man' or 'living being', for example, are said of the individual, 'man'. In the terminology that is employed in the *Categories* secondary substances (species and genus) are said of primary substances (individuals), inasmuch as the individuals may be subsumed under universals (cf. 2 a 11 ff.). (2) Something may 'be in' a subject without being 'said of' it, where 'is in' does not mean 'is part of', but 'is an inherent property of'. It is a particular accident, as is for example 'the white' in Socrates, which is in, but not said of Socrates. (3) Something may both be 'said of' and 'be in' a subject, and this is the case with universal accidents. Thus a universal such as 'white' will always presuppose – 'be in' – a subject, at the same time as 'white' may be said of (the white in) Socrates. (4) Something is neither 'said of' nor 'is in' the subject – simply because it is the subject itself, the "primary substance", for example the individual man or the individual horse. This classification may be reproduced in a table:

	Not in a subject	In a subject
Not said of a subject	Primary substance (Socrates) = subject	Particular accident (the white in Socrates)
Said of a subject	Secondary substance (man, living being)	Universal accident (white as a quality)

It will be seen that the two criteria for classification apply respectively to the particular versus the universal and to substance versus accident. As a predicate the universal will be stated about the particular, the subject; the accident will presuppose the existence of the substance and will accordingly be an additional description of the substance. But the secondary substance will also be related to the subject or the primary substance, and accordingly the subject can only be characterized negatively in our table as a substratum for properties, a subject for predication.

The table is certainly not without problems. The main question is of course whether one is dealing with things, concepts, or names, or, in other words, whether the classification should be understood ontologically, logically, or linguistically; and the terminology employed – 'things' may be 'said of' or 'be in' a subject – provides little precise information. As early as in Porphyry's time the *Categories* were used as a manual in elementary logic, and therefore it was important for Porphyry and those commentators who relied on him to emphasize that the treatise dealt with logic, not with linguistics, and that it remained neutral with respect to wider metaphysical problems. The formula that he arrived at and which was to become the norm for medieval thinking was a sort of compromise: the *Categories* deals with simple linguistic utterances – not as linguistic phenomena but in so far as they signify things and concepts (cf. Porph. in Arist. *Cat.* 58, 5 ff.; Simpl. in Arist. *Cat.* 13,12 ff.). In a logical context, however, Porphyry refuses to decide about that which was to become the main issue in the Debate about Universals: whether the universals (genus and species) have real existence (Porph. *Isag.* 1, 8 ff.: cf. Boeth. in *Isag.* Porph. II 1, 10 ff.). He himself and later commentators interpreted on the basis of their differentiated terminology, and the distinction they made between 'concept' and 'thing' probably owes more to the Stoics than to Aristotle. An unprejudiced reading of Aristotle himself must lead to the conclusion that there is no distinction between logic and metaphysics. The aim of the treatise, however, is clearly not linguistic. The purpose is by means of standard linguistic formulations to arrive at the logical form. This appears from the assertion that a primary substance, such as Socrates, could not function as a predicate – which linguistically of course is quite feasible ('this man is Socrates', cf. Arist. *Anal. pr.* 43 a 34) – but the point of the passage is that 'Socrates' can never be a property of anything. It is Socrates himself who has properties.

Now, if one studies what is said essentially about Socrates – without 'being in'

Socrates – the following sequence could be established: Socrates – man – living being. Here 'man' (species) is said of Socrates and 'living being' (genus) of 'man', and a transitive relation will readily be seen: that which is predicated of 'man' is also predicated of Socrates (*Cat.* 1 b 10 ff.). Analogous series of abstractions – proceeding from the less to the more general – could be constructed for the accidental properties (predicates) which 'are in' and are said of Socrates. In series such as these there would be a lower limit, the individual (for example Socrates), which can only function as subject, not as predicate, and an upper limit, the universal predicate, which cannot function as a subject and of which nothing accordingly can be predicated. Such an irreducible predicate is called a category, and by means of an analysis of ordinary language Aristotle is able to establish ten such categories. Next to the central category of substance (for example 'man' and 'horse') he mentions (1 b 25 ff.) quantity ('four feet tall'), quality ('white'), relation ('greater' or 'lesser'), place ('in the market place'), time ('yesterday'), position ('seated'), 'having' ('wearing shoes'), performing ('cutting'), and being affected ('to be cut'). The evident aim of such a systematization is the description of a certain individual in a certain situation, which is intended to be as exhaustive as possible in order to distinguish this individual from other individuals.

Aristotle never explains why just these categories and not others exist. This is not what interests him, for what is decisive is the procedure itself that leads to a separation of one central category from other accidental ones. It is telling that the complete list of ten categories appears only in one other passage (*Top.* 103 b 22 ff.). Elsewhere Aristotle is content with the first six categories just listed. Undeniably there is something casuistical about the whole undertaking. The last – 'the lesser' – categories are linguistically complex and could perhaps be reduced to others (thus 'position' is considered a relation in *Cat.* 6 b 11), and, in any case, it would be difficult to set up a series of abstractions, for example for 'having' with precisely defined species and genera. To this must be added that relation in principle is considered a category that behaves in the same manner as the others do – regardless of the fact that Aristotle is not unaware that relation is a two-place predicate (cf. 6 a 36 ff.).

It is now possible to adapt the categories to the formal table above (only one representative of the accidental categories – quality – is stated) in the following way:

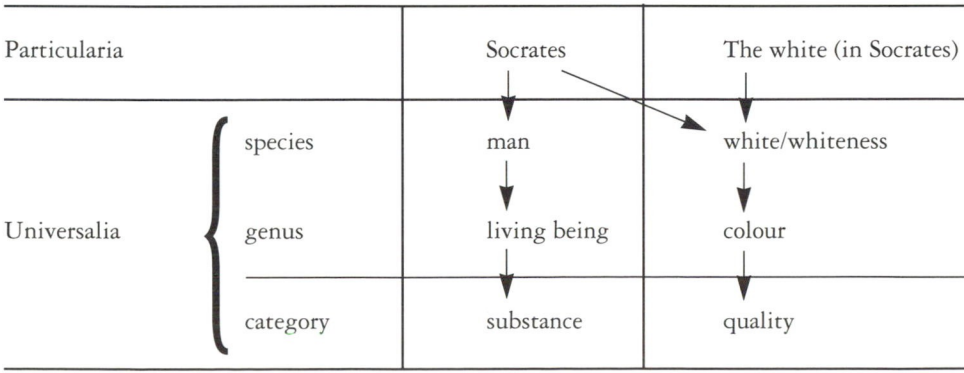

Particularia		Socrates	The white (in Socrates)
	species	man	white/whiteness
Universalia	genus	living being	colour
	category	substance	quality

This table demonstrates a dual intention with the entire fabric. One may choose to deal with the accidental categories in analogy with the category of substance – which means that quality is predicated of colour, which is predicated of whiteness, which is predicated of the white in Socrates. So, throughout the whole series a transitive relation appears, exactly as in the category of substance. Aristotle is of course aware that the table may be read in this manner, by means of which it is possible, for example, to determine the essence of an instance of whiteness (cf. *Top.* 103 b 27 ff.; *Met.* 1030 a 17 ff.). But this is not what is most important in the *Categories*. That is to systematize what may be stated about Socrates, and about Socrates we may not only say what he is but also what accidental properties he possesses. The categories of accidence can be stated about a primary substance, but they cannot be mutually predicated. What can be predicated about Socrates is, however, not the property designation ('whiteness') but the paronym ('white'), and the transitive relation is inapplicable (Socrates is not a colour – cf. *Cat.* 2 a 29; 3 a 15; 10 a 27). 'White' is used as homonym about the white in Socrates and about Socrates.

There is a clear anti-Platonic tendency in the table as a whole. It is not un-Platonic to distinguish between essence and property; but the consequences that Aristotle draws from this are not Platonic. The accidental categories refer to the category of substance, but this means that although 'being' can be predicated of any category, it is not predicated in the same sense. In the *Metaphysics* it is a crucial point to examine the central instance of being, the substance. In the *Categories* it is sufficient to conclude that 'being' cannot act as a common genus for all the categories, because it is not an unambiguous concept. 'Being' is – unlike Plato's view – a predicate; it is a predicate with a universal field of application, but it refers to one central meaning. In a way it is the concept of being that makes the table cohere, but as being cannot be expressed synonymously, the concept does not have a rubric in the table itself; 'substance' and 'quality', on the other hand, have the same meaning when predicated of the concepts that fall respectively under the substance and quality categories. It applies to being – as to other concepts with universal fields of application, such as unity, truth and (perhaps) goodness – that they 'transcend' the categories, which is why they were called *transcendentalia* in medieval terminology.

Every category must necessarily comprehend both particulars and universals. The category of substance thus comprises both the primary substance (Socrates) and the secondary substance (species and genus), the secondary substance being a conceptual determination of the primary. Here as well it is the task of metaphysics to investigate the very problem of the relation between thing and concept, and once again Aristotle in the *Categories* confines himself to saying the least possible. He says (3 b 10 ff.) that the primary substance in an unqualified sense signifies a 'this'; the secondary substance, on the other hand, marks off a qualification – not as in the other categories an accident but the kind of a 'this'. Species has a higher degree of substance than does genus, because it is more informative (2 b 7 ff.).

The principal idea in the *Categories* is the basic distinction between substance and accidence. Accidental designations presuppose primary substances and accordingly would not exist, if primary substances did not exist (cf. 2 b 5). This, of course, does not mean that substances can exist without accidents – for example, a man who does not have a certain size or certain qualities. But accidental designations are transient;

the designation of the essence of a man *qua* man is, on the other hand, necessary. Nor does it mean that primary substances are imperishable – but to explore what it means that substances come into being and perish lies beyond the scope of the *Categories*. A substance is further characterized by there not being degrees of substances (3 b 33) – one cannot be a man to a greater or lesser degree – and by there not being contrary opposites to substances; but substances can 'receive' contrary predicates – a man may be large in one respect and small in another (cf. 3 b 24; 4 a 10; cf. Plato). The last point was to be important in the theory of substance in the *Physics*.

Aristotle's treatment of quantity (*Cat.* 4 b 20 ff.), relation (6 a 36 ff.), and quality (8 b 25 ff.) in some respects (quantity) anticipates the more thorough investigations in the *Physics*, but hardly provides anything decisively new concerning the concept of category itself. The last chapter of the *Categories* – in the Middle Ages called *Postpraedicamenta* – are *disjecta membra* on such concepts as contraries, priority and motion, which he deals with more fully elsewhere.

Like the *Categories*, the *De interpretatione* is a textbook, which means that there is no room for discussion in it. The subject is the sentence as the minimal logical unit, and there are clear connections back to Plato's *Sophist* and, in part, to the *Cratylus*. The treatise begins with a concentrated presentation of Aristotle's semantic theory (16 a 3 ff., see p. 280), and thereby offers a far more differentiated understanding of the relation between linguistic expression, concept and reality than in the *Categories*. Unlike the *Categories*, the *De interpretatione* does not include metaphysical problems. The point of departure is that language designates something arbitrarily constituting the linguistic expression as a sign or symbol.

The minimal element of language is the word, and in a sentence there must be – as in Plato – at least two kinds of words: name (*onoma*) and verb (*rhēma*). This does not refer to grammatical parts of speech but to parts conveying meaning. Both name and verb signify by convention; the name has direct reference (16 a 19 ff.), but the verb states something about the subject and in addition signifies time (16 b 6 ff.). In its most elementary form a sentence is a union of name and verb. It is defined (16 b 26 ff.) as a spoken sound signifying something and consisting of elements that also signify in separation. Only sentences can have truth value (cf. *Cat.* 2 a 4 ff.), but this is not true of all sentences; it is only true of those that – indicatively – assert that something is the case or is not the case, which is to say judgements or statements (*apophansis*: a statement-making sentence) and not of prayers, for example, nor – one might add – of commands or questions. This is an important distinction that implies that Aristotle must consider for example the logic of imperatives as belonging to rhetoric. It should be noted, however, that his distinction is based exclusively on the question of the truth value of a sentence. While he distinguishes in his semantics between concept and linguistic expression, he does not expressly distinguish between the linguistic form of a judgement and its content (proposition), and this means that he is still bothered by the old problem with sentences about contingent facts being sometimes true and sometimes false (cf. 4 a 22 ff.).

Any judgement – understood by Aristotle as a statement-making sentence – can affirm or deny, and it can – in modern terminology – be atomic or molecular (*De int.* 17 a 8 ff.), which is to say that it can be single or be broken down into single statements by means of connectives. The ideal would be an atomic statement, and such a statement is true, if it states about what is the case that it is the case, and about what is not the case that it is not the case; if not, the statement is false (17 a 26; cf. *Met.* 1011 b 26). This definition of 'true' and 'false' – which goes back to Plato – is often considered a formulation of the theory of correspondence for truth, which is to say that a true statement corresponds with or has the same structure as the fact to which the statement applies – which in Aristotle rather should be formulated in such a way that truth is a property of sentences and a function of reality (cf. *Cat.* 14 b 9 ff.; *Met.* 1051 b 6 ff.). Of course hereby nothing has been said about the possibility of demonstrating the correspondence with reality, but Aristotle apparently considered it a problem that the truth value of judgements about contingent facts cannot always be decided with certainty. Furthermore, in the *Metaphysics* (1051 b 17 ff., see p. 359) – once again like Plato – he concerns himself with the precondition for true and false statements as able to 'combine and separate' that which really is combined or separated (S is P, S is not P). It appears that to Aristotle a 'correspondence theory' of truth is founded on a concept of evidence; but in a textbook like the *De interpretatione* there is no need to go beyond a logical analysis of sentences.

After the specification of what a sentence is and what makes a statement true, three main problems remain in the *De interpretatione*: (1) the quantity of a sentence and, cohering with this, the relation between contrary and contradictory opposites; (2) the question whether statements about contingent future events have fixed truth value – which is to say, a flagrant example of the relation between truth value and verifiability; and (3) some basic deliberations on modal logic.

The first point (*De int.* 17 a 38 ff.) so to speak shows Aristotle on his way towards his fully elaborated formal logic. As usual, he searches for the logical structure behind the linguistic expression. But language can make things tough for him: the fact that there is no indefinite article in the Greek makes him understand an expression such as 'man' as ambiguous: it may mean 'man' as a concept and may thus be equivalent with 'every man' or it may mean 'some man'. Therefore he operates with 'indefinite' statements and uses a classification of singular, universal, particular and indefinite statements. But he considers singular statements as analogous with universal ones and indefinite statements as equivalent with particular ones (cf. *Anal. pr.* 29 a 27) – and in the *Analytics* both categories have been left out. Already in the *De interpretatione* what is decisive are the two divisions that cross each other: universal and particular, affirmative and negative statements (cf. the classification in classical logic of categorical propositions into A-, I-, E- and O-propositions) to which are connected the introduction of quantifiers, in the *De interpretatione* terminology, 'every' (A-propositions), 'some' (I-propositions), 'no' (E-propositions), and 'not every' (O-propositions). Against this background and on the assumption that the truth of an affirmation implies the falsehood of the negation, Aristotle is able to establish precise definitions of contradictory and contrary opposites: contradictory statements affirm and negate the same about the same (*De int.* 17 a 33); contrary statements cannot both be true, but their opposites can. Through his analysis of linguistic form Aristotle thus established a principal point in the classical logic of propositions – in more recent textbooks often illustrated by the so-called square of opposition. The theory is further expanded by a not altogether successful adumbration of the difference between copulative and existential propositions (19 b 19 ff.). It is only at one point – the obstinate indefinite statements that are without definite quantifiers – that he arrives at an untenable conclusion, because he considers two 'opposite' indefinite statements as contradictory and not as sub-contrary. This induces him to remark that one cannot always assign a certain truth value to contradictory opposites.

It is this problem that in still more intricate form shows up in statements about contingent future events (*futura contingentia*, 18 a 28 ff.). It was Aristotle who formulated the principle of the excluded middle (cf. *Met.* 1011 b 23 ff., see below). If this principle also holds for future contingents, does it not mean that right now it is true that an event will or will not occur in the future? And does it not imply that everything is predetermined in such a way that the outcome will be a fatalism that cancels the possibility of accidental events or of events determined by man's interference? To use Aristotle's famous example: is it true now that a naval battle will take place tomorrow – or is it true now that no naval battle will take place tomorrow? This is an explicit formulation of the problem of determinism, and it has been the subject of thorough discussions both among medieval and modern logicians.

The question throws light on Aristotle's understanding of the concepts of truth and necessity. He could have interpreted his own theory of correspondence purely formally so that the statement that 'p' respectively is, was, or will be true, provided that it is, was, or will be the case that p. So, the formal conditions for truth would be the same for past, present and future events (the statement 'a naval battle will take place tomorrow' is true, if a naval battle does take place tomorrow), and so no problem of determinism would arise. But apparently Aristotle thinks of his theory of correspondence 'realistically', not formally, which means that a statement about a future event only can be true, if it is already now determined that the event will take place. Thus he does not distinguish between logical and factual necessity but combines conditions for truth and conditions for verification.

Nor is it of course always possible to verify past or present events. But what is decisive to Aristotle is that an event that has occurred is necessary in the sense that it cannot be changed, although not in the sense that it occurred of necessity – such as for example astronomical events. From this he seems to draw the conclusion that statements about contingent events do not acquire truth value until they have taken place. But with respect to future events, it is only the tautological disjunction itself that has fixed truth value, because it is not necessary – in the sense of being predetermined – for the event to take place. One of the disjuncts will be true, but which one is uncertain – it is necessarily true that p or not-p; it is not necessarily true that p, or necessarily true that not-p.

Probably Aristotle's deliberations should be seen as part of a discussion with the Megarians about the concepts of 'possible' and 'necessary' (cf. *Met.* 1046 b 29 ff., see p. 358; *De int.* 22 b 10 ff.) where it was Aristotle's position that 'necessary' implies 'possible' – not the other way around. All in all, such discussions are presumably the background for the sections of the *De interpretatione* on modal logic. Aristotle's understanding of modalities probably never reached full clarification, but in the *De interpretatione* he takes the first steps towards modal logic. Thus he asserts (21 a 34 ff.) that the negation of 'it is possible that p' is 'it is not possible that p', and not 'it is possible that not-p'; on the contrary: 'it is possible that not-p' is implied by 'it is possible that p'. In the same way the negation of 'it is necessary that p' is 'it is not necessary that p', not 'it is necessary that not-p' – here the last statement is naturally not implied by the first. It is a crucial observation that the negation of modal statements applies to the whole statement – the statement 'that p' is not changed – and Aristotle is in fact working with confirmed or negated modal operators. In the *Analytics* he draws further conclusions with respect to modal syllogisms.

THE *ANALYTICS*

The *De interpretatione* might have pointed towards a system of propositional logic. But this was not to be; Aristotle's finished logical system is a subject-predicate logic. This is found in the *Analytics*, which deals with deductive reasoning or syllogistics, i.e. with inferences from two premises to one conclusion. In a simple or assertoric syllogism valid inferences are examined without regard to the truth value of the conclusions; an apodictic or demonstrative syllogism is true, however, because it builds on true premises; a dialectical syllogism examines what consequences can be drawn from hypothetically assumed, contradictory premises (*Anal. pr.* 24 a 22 ff.; cf. *Top.* 100 a 27) – the differences between these three types depend on the truth value of the inference, not on its form. In the *Analytica priora* the investigation is of valid inferences; hence the subject is the form of the syllogism. The *Analytica posteriora*, on the other hand, is Aristotle's theory of science. Here he examines which inferences are true, and hence the subject is the content of the apodictic or scientific inference. The dialectical syllogism is investigated by informal logic, which is to say in the *Topics*. Finally, formal logic is concerned with propositions that always are valid or true, informal logic also with statements about contingent facts. In the title, the *Analytics*, lies hidden – as is so often the case – an adapted Academy terminology; but to Aristotle *analysis*, 'dissolution' or 'reduction', does not mean a reduction to metaphysical principles but to basic forms of inference or to the premises for a given inference. The decisively new in Aristotle's logic lies partly in his distinction between logical form and logical content and partly in his introduction of letter notation for variables, which makes the language of logic far more precise and expedient. But he does not make use of logical formalizations proper.

Aristotle is at great pains to exclude all non-logical problems from syllogistics. It is the task of formal logic to investigate what propositions follow from others. The logicians' field of work is the relation between categorical subject-predicate sentences; logic is a logic of concepts and classes, and an extensional point of view is adopted, which precludes more ambitious problems of natural philosophy and metaphysics – the logician works with statements and unambiguous (synonymous) terms; he must master a specific formal procedure and has need of quantifiers, negations, and connectives; it is not his task to ask, for example, what is implicit in the fact that a thing can be essentially determined. But hardly any system of logic can avoid being indirectly ontologically loaded, and this of course applies to Aristotle's as well: the relation between subject and predicate corresponds to the relation between thing and properties, and it is presupposed that the world consists of things that are furnished with essential or accidental properties.

Aristotle himself defines a syllogism as an argument (*logos*) in which something is presupposed in such a way that something else necessarily follows from it (*Anal. pr.* 24 b 18; *Top.* 100 a 25). Although this is an excellent definition of deductive argumentation, it is too broad in relation to the field that Aristotle's syllogistics does in fact comprehend.

In a syllogism are included three terms (*Anal. pr.* 25 b 32; cf. 26 a 21): the major term, which is the predicate in the conclusion, and which appears in one of the premisses (the major premiss); the minor term which is the subject in the conclusion, and which appears in the other premiss (the minor premiss); and the middle term, which appears in both premisses and warrants the logical connection between the major and minor premisses. Traditionally, one can, for example, construct the following syllogism:

All men are mortal
Socrates is a man
———————————————
Socrates is mortal

These three propositions constitute an inference, and the conclusion is true if the premisses are true. But Aristotle's formulation is essentially different from that of traditional logic with respect to four points:

1 Syllogistics is concerned only with those terms (genus and species) that can act both as subject and predicate (43 a 25 ff.; cf. *Categories*). A singular term cannot act as predicate and does not meet the demand of a strict syllogism that it must assert something that is always the case. The most general terms – the categories or the first principles of the individual sciences – cannot act as subjects in a syllogistic demonstration, because they are themselves the presuppositions for a demonstration. – In the example provided above, the singular term 'Socrates' should accordingly be replaced with, for example, 'all Greeks'.

2 In the *Analytica priora* Aristotle always inserts letters for variables. If the example is changed accordingly, a scheme of argument or a rule of inference – not an inference – is formulated. A rule of inference is not an argument and consequently has no truth value, even though a correct rule of inference of course is valid.

3 In the *De interpretatione* normal everyday language is adhered to, so that the subject is placed first and connected with the predicate by means of the copulative 'is' ('every S is P'). In the Analytics, on the other hand, subject and predicate are interchanged so that the artificial form 'P belongs to every S' comes into use. This has the following consequence:

Traditional formulation	Aristotle's formulation	
All M are P	P belongs to every M	P: Predicate
All S are M	M belongs to every S	M: middle term
		S: subject
All S are P	P belongs to every S	Normally Aristotle uses the first three letters of the alphabet

Hereby the middle term in fact comes to stand 'between'. Aristotle's reason is probably that the linguistic formulation is unambiguously to designate subject and predicate.

4 However, in the great majority of cases Aristotle expresses himself conditionally. Accordingly, the formulation should be changed once more – now to the corresponding conditional:

If P belongs to every M, and M belongs to every S, then P will belong to every S (cf. e.g., 25 b 37).

Unlike a rule of inference, a conditional has truth value. – Though it has sometimes been so supposed, the frequently employed conditional formulation probably does not mean that an Aristotelian syllogism is not a rule of inference, only that in the *Analytics* the discussion is *about* rules of inference.

As is the case in classical logic, Aristotle divides all syllogisms into figures according to the placing of the middle term – the middle term can be subject in the one and predicate in the other premiss (1. figure, cf. 25 b 32), it can be predicate in both premisses (2. figure, cf. 26 b 34), and it can be the subject in both (3. figure, cf. 28 a 10). In cases where the middle term occupies different positions in the premisses, Aristotle does not distinguish between it being subject or predicate in, respectively, the major and the minor premiss (cf. 41 a 13), and therefore he only acknowledges three figures. In classical logic, on the other hand, a fourth figure was added – which Aristotle, by the way, was not unfamiliar with in practice (cf. 29 a 19 ff.).

It is well known from classical logic that each of the premisses and the conclusion within each figure may have a different quality (affirmative or denying) or a different quantity (universal or particular propositions). Each link can accordingly be an A-, E-, I- or O-proposition, and inasmuch as there are three links, there will in each figure be sixty-four possible combinations or 'moods'. The example cited above is the first mood of the first figure (*Barbara* in medieval mnemo-technical artificial terminology), which is to say that all three links in the syllogism are universally affirmative (A-propositions). This mood occupies a favoured place in Aristotle's system. In part, it illustrates the logical transitivity between species, subgenera, and genus that is discussed in the *Categories*; in part, it probably tells us something about the genesis of the Aristotelian syllogism: if one imagines a Platonic *diairesis* 'translated' into extensional language, it is this very mood that will appear.

But the other valid moods in the first figure also enjoy special status. In the three figures Aristotle examined no fewer than 148 moods and found fourteen valid – among these, four in the first figure (AAA-, EAE-, AII-, EIO-propositions – *Barbara*, *Celarent*, *Darii* and *Ferio* in medieval terminology. Cf. 25 b 26 ff.). These four moods are called perfect, which means that they are inferences, the validity of which, according to Aristotle, are evident;[1] to this should be added that it is only in the first

---

1 It is on the basis of these moods that the principle of *Dictum de omni et nullo* was formulated during the Middle Ages: what is affirmed or denied about a whole can be affirmed or denied about any part

figure that it is possible to draw conclusions within all four types of judgement. Aristotle demonstrates next that the valid moods of the second and third figures can be reduced to the perfect syllogisms – and, in the final analysis, to just two of these (*Barbara* and *Celarent*), which accordingly gain axiomatic status (cf. 29 b 1 ff.). This comes about partially by the use of rules of conversion (cf. 27 a 5 ff.; 28 a 18 ff.; b 11 ff.) and partially by the use of *reductio ad absurdum* arguments (e.g. 27 a 36 ff.).

Aristotle examines in detail under what conditions it is possible or impossible to draw valid conclusions (cf. 25 b 26 ff.), and in a summary (41 b 6 ff.) some basic points are established: at least one of the premisses must be affirmative; at least one must be universal; a universal conclusion requires universal premisses; and one premiss must be negative, if the conclusion is to be negative.

Purely assertoric propositions have no modal factor; apodictic propositions state that something necessarily must be the case; problematic (a later technical term) propositions state that something possibly is the case. Aristotle thoroughly examines modal syllogisms in which there are apodictic and problematic premisses (29 b 29–40 b 16), and the intention is to delimit the apodictic propositions upon which a scientific theory must be built. The main principle (cf. 34 a 5 ff.) is that the necessary follows from the necessary, the possible from the possible. At certain points (cf. 30 a 17 ff.) disputable conclusions are drawn, which were contested already by Aristotle's own students (see. p. 401), and today Aristotle's modal logic is assessed variously. It is a pioneer work, and Aristotle's presentation suffers from the absence of a propositional logic.

Aristotle's definition of the modalities themselves has also been criticized, but it is hardly profitable to discuss whether they should be understood to refer to propositional contents or to objects (*de dicto* or *de re*), and clearly they have physical and metaphysical connotations. 'Possible' is defined as that which neither is necessary nor leads to something impossible (32 a 18), and thus it seems that, somehow, it is dependent on 'necessary' (cf. *De int.* 23 a 18); the expression may apply to both 'contingent' and 'potential', which is unfortunate, because 'contingent' is incompatible with 'necessary', although 'potential' is not. 'Necessary' – one of the most intricate Aristotelian concepts – can be understood relatively or absolutely (*Anal. pr.* 30 b 31 ff.). Relative necessity is relative to the premisses in a syllogism, which means that it is the entailment between premisses and conclusion. Absolute necessity is really not-logical; it is the relation that connects subject with predicate in a proposition in which the predicate follows from the essence or definition of the subject, or in a proposition in which the predicate indicates a property that must always be attributed to the subject ('man is a living being', 'the sun rises in the morning', 'the natural motion of a stone is a fall' – cf. *Anal. post.* 73 a 21 ff.).[2]

Aristotle's syllogistics is a consistently thought-out deductive system. But of

of the whole. The principle was not formulated by Aristotle (25 b 32 is the closest approximation), and since it includes singulars it falls outside the scope of the *Analytics*.

2   There are other kinds of relative necessity than the 'logical' – for example, the unchangeableness of contingent, past events (yesterday's naval battle) and compulsion. To this should be added 'hypothetical' and 'simple' necessity (see p. 320).

course this does not preclude that – in modern views – shortcomings and lack of clarity can be demonstrated within the framework of the system itself. It is for instance debated whether the basic elements – the individual terms – stand for classes or concepts, and the system does not account for 'empty classes', i.e. classes without existing members; this is connected with the fact that Aristotle does not operate with existential quantifiers – he simply presupposes that existing entities are being discussed. Nor does he take into account that there are valid syllogisms with a weaker conclusion than could have been drawn (for example AAI in the first figure).

Still, the system has more significant limitations. It only deals with subject-predicate propositions of the type in which the middle term 'mediates' the conclusion – thereby precluding relational propositions. But what is most important is the very limitation inherent in subject-predicate logic itself. Aristotle does not deal with propositional logic, in which the variables are propositions, not terms; and as propositional logic is both more basic and has wider extension than does subject-predicate logic, the outcome is that syllogistics in no way can claim to deal with all deductive logic. Yet Aristotle cannot make do without principles from propositional logic, without their being formulated or included in the system. For example, in general he knows very well that the truth of the consequent does not imply the truth of the antecedent (cf. *Soph. el.* 167 b 1; *Poet.* 1460 a 20), and in the *Analytics*, theorems from the propositional logic are not infrequently presupposed, as for example in the proof of the theorem that the predicate in a universal, affirmative proposition can be converted to the subject in a particular affirmative one (*Anal. pr.* 25 a 20 ff.). Sometimes Aristotle can even 'inadvertently' let letters designate variable propositions (34 a 5 ff.; 53 b 12 ff.). Not least with respect to *reductio ad absurdum* arguments he touches naturally on hypothetical arguments (40 b 25 ff.); yet, although he gets close, he never conceives of hypothetical syllogisms as an independent type next to the categorical ones. This was left to his students Theophrastus and Eudemus. As is well known, it was the Stoics who first formulated a coherent system of propositional logic. That Aristotle was not induced to do so, even though he did use laws of propositional logic, may be owing to deliberate choice: it is a subject-predicate logic and not the propositional logic that corresponds with the Aristotelian universe of objects equipped with properties.

Deductive logic implies drawing conclusions from certain premisses, but in Aristotle's theory it is not requisite that syllogistics must render account of the way in which the premisses are set up. There is in fact no 'method' for setting up universal sentences; empirical generalization, or induction in the modern sense, is never complete and will always presuppose some prior knowledge of the universal that is looked for in the particular (cf. *Anal. post.* 71 a 30; 92 a 37). Aristotle often speaks of a counter-part – or, rather perhaps, a preamble – to deduction, and he designates it with a word that normally is translated as induction (*epagōgē*). By this is understood the passage from the particular to the universal (cf. *Top.* 105 a 13; 156 a 5); but it is not a formal method, rather a dialectical-paedagogical procedure whereby a person is 'led' to see the universal in a group of *particularia* intuitively (cf. *Anal. pr.* 67 a 23; *Anal. post.* 71 a 21). If it is acknowledged beforehand that all members of a collection fall under a given universal, an Aristotelian induction can be constructed in syllogistic form (*Anal. pr.* 68 b 8 ff.) – but otherwise 'induction' is irrelevant for syllogistics. There are points of resemblance with the Platonic dialectician who immediately 'sees' the idea in random multiplicity (Plat. *Phaedr.* 265 D ff.) and with the Platonic Socrates who will realize 'the universal' through, but not from, induction.

In the *Analytica priora* syllogistics is presented as a system, but there are no reflections on it as a system. This occurs in the *Analytica posteriora*, which describes Aristotle's ideal of scientific deduction, the demonstrative or apodictic science, in which the syllogistic argument depends on necessarily true and unchangeable premisses, and in which the basic scheme is *Barbara*, the basic mood in the first figure, where all links are universally affirmative (cf. Aristot. *Anal. post.* 79 a 17). It is an axiomatic system that deduces theorems from evidently true premisses and axioms. As his paradigm Aristotle clearly used mathematical argumentation (cf. 71 a 3), familiar to us from Euclid's *Elements*, which, some twenty years after Aristotle's death, summarized earlier textbooks that Aristotle must have known (see p. 411); but Plato's 'hypothetical method' also played a background role. The agreement with Euclid can already be seen in the terminology, even though there are minor divergencies. Where Euclid speaks of 'common notions', Aristotle – as do we – uses the designation 'axioms' about general presuppositions (72 a 17 ff.; 76 b 14). Corresponding to Euclid's 'definition' and 'postulate', we have Aristotle's 'thesis' (*thesis*), which is either a definition or a '*hypothesis*' defined as a definition accompanied by an existential assertion (72 a 20 ff.; 76 b 27 ff.). The first 'principles' of the system, the axioms, are pre-conditions for proof, and therefore cannot themselves be proved. As an example of an evident axiom, Aristotle offers the following statement: 'if equals are subtracted from equals, equals remain' (76 b 20; cf. Eucl. *El.* I Not. comm. 3). But there are two fundamental axioms: the principle of contradiction – 'the same attribute cannot at the same time belong and not belong to the same subject with respect to the same' (*Met.* 1005 b 19) – and the principle of the excluded middle, or of bivalence – 'it is necessary to deny or affirm the same about the same' (1011 b 23; cf. *Anal. post.* 71 a 14). In other words: 'A cannot both be B and not-B', and 'A must be either B or not-B'. The two principles are equally basic – one cannot be deduced from the other. The third fundamental principle of classical logic, the principle of identity, was not formulated by Aristotle, but is silently presupposed.

It is no accident that Aristotle did not formulate his two basic principles in his writings on logic, but did so in the *Metaphysics*, for to him they are not merely logical principles but principles that hold true for every object in the world; hence he considers it a matter of course that the principle of contradiction is equally valid for things, opinions about things, and statements about things (*Met.* 1005 b 19; 1011 b 13). This is clear-cut testimony to the close connection that in the final analysis exists between logic and ontology, and on this point there are basic similarities between Plato's 'logic of being' and Aristotle's 'formal logic'. It is also worth noticing that to Aristotle only one axiomatic system can exist: that which corresponds with reality. An axiomatic system is not an arbitrarily chosen system and therefore it is not – as in modern axiomatics – possible for an axiom in one system to be a theorem in another.

Demonstrative knowledge can only be valid for universal, necessary and eternal connections (*Anal. post.* 74 b 5; 75 b 21; cf. *Eth. Nic.* 1139 b 22 ff.). This is an extremely strict deductive ideal of science – indeed so strict that it only has ideal status. In practice the apodictic method can only impart knowledge acquired by other means, and in his own writings Aristotle does in fact, as has been mentioned, employ other methods. One might believe that the method could only be used in purely formal sciences – in logic itself and in mathematics. But Aristotle is an essentialist, and this means that the attributes that pertain to a thing by virtue of its essence will pertain to it by necessity and always. The problem is not whether there are metaphysical truths but how it is possible to find true definitions that express the unchangeable essence of a thing.

The first book of the *Analytica posteriora* deals with the nature of demonstrative knowledge; the second with definitions. All demonstrative knowledge presupposes pre-existing knowledge (*Anal. post.* 71 a 1); for not all knowledge is provable – if one demands proof of the first principles, one will either end in infinite regress or in a circular proof, and thereby one would in fact render every form of knowledge impossible (72 b 5 ff.). But does this not mean that one both has knowledge and is in search of it; if so, asks Aristotle (71 a 29), is one not then confronted with the so-called Meno paradox (see p. 171) that either one knows everything, or else that one can never learn anything? Plato's answer was that man possesses a pre-existing knowledge, which is a precondition for particular knowledge. Aristotle's answer is a characteristic variant: I have a universal knowledge which I can use, provided that I am acquainted with a fact – for example, 'here is a triangle' or 'the principle of contradiction is valid' – and with the meaning of the words. If this is a triangle, I 'know' for example the sum of the angles of this triangle (71 a 19; cf. *Met.* 1087 a 15). This universal knowledge is potential in relation to a given empirical material and is not dependent upon a complete induction. Hence knowledge is not an unambiguous concept, and Aristotle lists four forms (*Anal. post.* 89 b 23 ff.). We can know:

1 *that* something is the case – that the predicate P belongs to the subject S;
2 *why* this is the case – why P belongs to S;
3 *that* something exists; and
4 *what* this something is – i.e. its essence and definition.

Points one and three are knowledge from experience – with all the uncertainty that may attach itself to this form of cognition. Points two and four are scientific knowledge; but even so, it is only point two that indicates demonstrative knowledge proper, the inference from premisses to a conclusion. This form of cognition presupposes experience and definition; and the *that* of existence precedes the *what* of essence.

Experience depends on sensation, and hence sensation is a necessary condition for demonstrative knowledge (cf. 81 a 37), although of course far from sufficient, for there is no science of the particular or the accidental (87 b 30 ff.; 19 ff.). An unavoidable precondition must therefore be indisputable premisses, and indeed Aristotle has very rigoristic demands of the premisses (71 b 25 ff.): they must be true – that is to say correspond with facts; they must be primary and irreducible; they must be prior – in the standard formula: be better known 'according to nature'; and, finally, they must indicate a reason or a cause (Aristotle does not distinguish between logical relation (reason-consequence) and real relation (cause-effect)). Furthermore, it not only holds good that the premisses must be universally true and that the predicate thus must be true for every instance that stands as subject; it must also be the case that the relation between subject and predicate is an essential one – the subject must by virtue of its nature possess this and that necessary attribute (73 a 21 ff.; cf. *Met.* 1029 b 13 ff.). Man is necessarily a living being; the definition of a triangle presupposes both the definition and existence of the line. It is only when these strict conditions are met that it is possible to speak of what cannot be otherwise – everything else is accidental. By their requirements of the premisses, apodictic syllogisms are distinguished from assertoric and dialectical syllogisms.

A demonstrative proof must hence presuppose three elements (*Anal. post.* 75 a 40 ff; 76 b 11 ff.): one – universal – subject; those attributes that are ascribed to the subject in the conclusion; and the basic premisses – principles, as Aristotle often calls them – that make the conclusion possible. These basic premisses can either be the quite general axioms or the axioms or definitions that are presupposed in any particular science (cf. 76 b 2 ff.). A proof that is true in one science cannot be transferred to another genus, i.e. to another science, unless one of the sciences is superior, the other subordinate to it (such as, for example, geometry and optics – cf. 75 a 37 ff.: erroneous transition to another genus, *metabasis eis allo genos*, is Aristotle's counterpart to the modern concept of category-mistake).

To Aristotle a 'first principle' is the basis of any science that cannot be proved (76 a 31); yet there is some ambiguity in his terminology, because what he has in mind is partly that by which one makes inferences (the general axioms, such as for example the principle of contradiction) and partly that from which one makes inferences (fundamental definitions of *summa genera* in one particular science). This is a lack of clarity that now and then creates complications by confusing validity with truth.

What an apodictic science can provide and cannot provide can be seen in the following example (78 a 26 ff. – in which the syllogistic formulation of classical logic is used for the sake of convenience):

1 Celestial bodies that do not twinkle are near
   Planets do not twinkle
   ———————————————
   Planets are near

2 Celestial bodies that are near do not twinkle
   Planets are near
   ———————————————
   Planets do not twinkle

Both are valid syllogisms of the first figure. The second differs from the first because the terms in the major premiss are converted, whereby the minor premiss and the conclusion exchange places. However, it is only the second that is an apodictic syllogism; for the first only shows *that* something is the case ('planets are near'), while the second informs us *why* ('planets do not twinkle *because* they are near'). In other words, the second demonstrates the cause, and in Aristotle's terminology the cause is provided by means of the middle term ('nearness'). The example shows at the same time that an apodictic syllogism communicates some knowledge by means of a proof. It does not create new knowledge. The truth of the conclusion is naturally contained in the premisses, and whether the premisses are true is determined by the empirical science of astronomy. Regardless of Aristotle's insistence that the premisses must be true by necessity, he will thus in practice often be obliged to suppose that an empirical generalisation holds good. The premisses are not analytically true, but in Aristotle's view the second syllogism probably states something essential about planets, which can be 'grasped' through systematic observation.

To Aristotle the middle term becomes identical with cause, and, as has been mentioned, 'cause' has very wide signification, so that even 'causes' of an essence are spoken of. This occurs in the second book of the *Analytica posteriora* in which Aristotle to as great extent as possible seeks to construct an answer to the question 'what is S?' (definition and essence) as analogous with the question 'why is S P?' This is feasible when it is a question of the definition of an event, for example a lunar eclipse (90 a 5 ff.). Here the answer will actually be the same if one asks what a lunar eclipse is and why it takes place. It becomes more far-fetched when the question is of essences proper – is man, for example, mortal 'because' he is an animal and 'because' animals are mortal? In a scientific theory a nominal definition – knowing the meaning of the words – is not sufficient, because one can define non-existent objects (92 b 4 ff.), and it is a real definition that is looked for. Such a one can in certain cases be identical with the conclusion of an apodictic syllogism and can hence be established by means of the middle term – this applies, for example, to the lunar eclipse (93 a 30 ff.). But insight into real essences can only depend on immediate cognition of evidence (93 b 21 ff.).

But this raises far-reaching problems. Demonstrative knowledge depends on pre-existing knowledge, and pre-existing knowledge depends in part on experience and in part on insight into 'first principles'. Aristotle deals with the question in the famous concluding chapter of the *Analytica posteriora* (99 b 15 ff.), which without doubt is intended as a rational alternative to Plato's '*anamnēsis*-theory'. Aristotle asks how we can gain insight into the first principles – and one must remember that 'first principles' both stand for general axioms and for the highest genera in a given science. We cannot be acquainted with these principles from birth without knowing it. On the other hand, it cannot be acquired knowledge either, for what is involved is the very presupposition for acquisition of knowledge. Aristotle takes it that sensation and 'induction' from objects of experience are a necessary but not sufficient condition for grasping the first principles. Many sense perceptions are stored as memory; several memories of the same thing are retained as one experience, which is to say as a practical, implicit knowledge of universals. This implicit knowledge can now be made explicit through the intellectual intuition of the first principles by reason (*nous*). Hence such an intuition is not derived from but completes pure sense perception and practical experience. It makes theoretical knowledge about universals and 'art' (*technē*) possible, 'art' being general knowledge as a precondition for productive activity.

This is a psychological account of the genesis of theoretical knowledge that is not at odds with but supplements the epistemological answer provided to the Meno paradox: theoretical knowledge is a precondition for scientific knowledge in individual cases. However, the role of *nous* in the cognitive process calls for further commentary. Discursive knowledge – dianoetic or apodictic knowledge – provides the scientific answer to *why* something is the case, yet presupposes *that* something is the case. This *that* can only be 'grasped' by an intuitive cognitive act; such 'grasping' is a precondition for both sense perception and knowledge of principles and also for both theoretical and practical knowledge. Sense perception is bound to the particular, but in my very act of perceiving an individual I perceive it as being of this or that kind – as a 'this-such' – which means that I 'grasp' the universal in the particular. In the same way practical insight – *phronēsis* – will immediately take a concrete situation to be of this or that kind. On the basis of a systematical examination of sense perceptions – 'induction' – I will be able to make my knowledge of universals and of the general first principles explicit in the same way as habituation and experience will be able to render my ethical knowledge explicit. Such an 'induction' and such a 'habituation' will be a necessary precondition for apprehending the general first principles and at the same time it will imply an immediate intellectual intuition. Sometimes Aristotle reserves the term *nous* for intuitive insight into the most general first principles; sometimes – more informatively – *nous* also designates the insight that this object or that situation is of this or that kind. Thus *nous* provides insight into those facts or principles that cannot be proved but are pre-conditions for proof and so to speak constitute the starting and final points of discursive cognition (cf. on this 73 b 7; 87 b 29; *Met.* 1036 a 6; *Eth. Nic.* 1098 a 31; 1139 b 27; 1142 a 25; 1143 a 35).

The intellectual awareness of immediate evidence frees Aristotle from the problems that normally are tied to induction and it frees him from deriving rational truths from sense perception. The presupposition for such a view is of course that reality and the human mind – as in Plato – in the final analysis are isomorphic. Hereby one ends up with epistemological and metaphysical questions that are alien to logic, and Aristotle does in fact deal with those questions in another context.

THEORY OF ARGUMENTATION

Dialectical argumentation, which Aristotle deals with in the *Topics*, analyzes the technique of argumentation that makes it possible to discuss any given problem that might become the subject of debate (*Top.* 100 a 18 ff.). This form of argumentation is that of rhetoric, but formally it does not differ from demonstrative science, as it is described in *Analytica posteriora*. Syllogisms are employed in both cases, and the same rules prevail for the validity of a syllogism; but where the scientific – or apodictic – syllogism proceeds from necessarily true and irreducible premisses, the dialectical syllogism rests on probable or generally accepted premisses (*endoxa*). The dialectical 'induction' proceeds from 'similarities' and employs plausible inferences from analogy (*Anal. post.* 71 a 5; *Top.* 100 a 27; 105 a 10). It follows from this that demonstrative science has a limited field of application, while the dialectician can argue about everything. But his premisses are hypothetical; a concrete debate with alternative possible inferences is presupposed.

Tradition has assigned the *Topics* a place as a supplement to the *Analytics*.

Undoubtedly this reflects the view that Aristotle himself arrived at; yet it should not be overlooked that the *Topics* probably was written first.

Already in the *Topics* Aristotle is able to formulate his standard definition of a syllogism (see p. 294) and can distinguish the dialectical syllogism from the apodictic; but apparently syllogistics is not yet a strictly axiomatic system. No mention is made, for example, of the middle term, nor of moods and figures. On the other hand, the doctrine of categories is fully completed (103 b 20 ff.).

In the *Topics* there are many traces of Academy discussions. This pertains to questions about the forming of concepts and about definition, for example semantic ambiguities, similarities and dissimilarities in things themselves, and the relation between genus and species (105 a 20 ff.; 121 a 10 ff.; 151 b 28 ff.). It applies also to those very subjects that are used as examples (the doctrine of ideas: 113 a 25 ff.; 137 b 3 ff.; ethical problems: 116 a 3 ff.). The author of the *Topics* distances himself from the doctrine of ideas, although he is still working in the shadow of *diairesis* thinking. But first and foremost it is Aristotle's understanding of the concept of dialectics itself that is important: to Plato dialectics is the path to truth, Aristotle emancipated demonstrative science from dialectics, and to him dialectic argumentation concerns the probable (cf. *Met.* 1004 b 22 ff.).

The *Topics* presupposes a certain paradigmatic situation, which directly points back to the heritage from Sophistic and Socratic techniques of argumentation (*Top.* 155 b 3 ff.): a questioner, A, is competing with a respondent, B, and they are to follow a definite procedure. A asks for the definition of a subject, x; B answers p; as this point A has the task of justifying not-p by making B arrive at problematic or self-contradictory consequences from p (159 a 15 ff.). The purpose is not eristics but training in logic – also in making 'the weaker case the stronger'; the argumentation must be valid, but questioner and respondent have predetermined roles. The questioner should defeat the respondent by leading questions, hidden points, traps, etc.; the respondent should demonstrate that the question was at fault; both parties profit by referring to *communis opinio*. Such an exercise is valid beyond itself; not only is it training for a debate with an opponent, it is also a paradigm of how to debate a problem with oneself. And not least the philosopher has need of dialectical argumentation when he is seeking 'principles', which is to say when he seeks to establish the basis of a scientific discipline (101 a 25 ff.; cf. 155 b 7 ff.). It is in this manner that Aristotle himself employs the dialectical method in his philosophical writings; when he says (105 a 35 ff.) that the dialectician should proceed from what people in general believe, or from what the philosophers – or the most important of them – have thought, he is providing an apt self-characterization.

The presupposition for every technique of argumentation is the ability to define the subject precisely and to find 'places' – *topoi*, i.e. general views – and a paradigmatic argument. The major part of the *Topics* constitutes a series of detailed rules for this. They are casuistic but subordinated to a certain scheme that orders the material. A predicate can characterize a subject in one of four ways (101 b 38 ff.) in that it (using medieval terminology) can designate:

1   definition
2   proprium
3   genus
4   accident

The definition designates the essence of the subject, and in a definition definiens and definiendum are convertible ('man is a living being endowed with reason'). Proprium means a quality that is specific for the subject without being included in the definition; if the predicate designates a proprium, the subject and the predicate will accordingly be convertible, but the predicate is not essential ('man can learn grammar'). Genus is a part of the definition and thus says something essential, although it is not convertible with the subject ('man is a living being'). But an accident is no part of the definition, nor is it convertible with the subject ('this man is musical'). In the later tradition these four designations are called *praedicabilia* (modes of predicating). Sometimes differentia has been added, which is the 'difference' by virtue of which one species is distinguished from another species under the same genus ('man is rational'), but Aristotle deals with this concept along with definition (143 a 29 ff.). Mistakenly, however, the tradition from Porphyry added species – for species stands for the subject. Clearly each of the praedicabilia requires its own procedure of argumentation. It is equally clear that they can be employed in any category, and thus the praedicabilia and the categories cross each other and are mutually irreducible methods of classification. The categories are classes of predicates that delimit a given subject from another one; the classification by praedicabilia is a formal classification of modes of predication, which is metaphysically indifferent to what it is that has primary being; in the context it is of no interest to Aristotle that from metaphysical points of view one could problematize for example the relation between essence and proprium or between proprium and accident.

Within this framework Aristotle's standard question is: what do the expressions that we use mean? Before we know that we cannot evaluate an argument, answer the opponent's questions, or put him in his place. A few examples will demonstrate the technique (109 b 33 ff.). Problem: 'can one wrong a god?' Ask: 'what does 'to wrong' mean?' If it means 'deliberately to damage', one cannot wrong a god, for a god cannot be damaged. New problem: 'is the good man envious?' Ask: 'what does 'envy' mean?' If it means 'being ill at ease with an honest man's success', the good man is not envious, for then he is not good. Variant of the problem: 'is the indignant envious?' – Ask: 'what do 'envy' and 'indignation' mean?'- If 'envy' still means 'being ill at ease with an honest man's success' and 'indignation' means 'being ill at ease with a dishonest man's success', the answer is given. In these examples accidental predication is analyzed, and it is presupposed that all agree about what is compatible or incompatible with, for example, to be 'a god' or 'a good man'. Most often, but not always, *communis opinio* is accepted as the starting point (110 a 14 ff.): 'healthy' means 'what contributes to good health'; but it is up to experts to decide whether this medicine contributes to good health. In other words: the dialectician analyzes concepts on a pragmatic base, it is not for him to ponder, for example, what makes an expert an expert. One can easily find examples of this technique of argumentation in Aristotle's own philosophical investigations.

The *De sophisticis elenchis* can be considered an appendix to the *Topics*. Like the *Topics*, it presupposes a debating situation, although the aim is far wider than the solution of 'Sophistic refutations'; it is an analysis of formal fallacies and fallacies in discourse in general. The treatise had far-reaching influence in Antiquity and the Middle Ages and has left its marks even on modern textbooks. The background for it must be looked for in the Academy and in the encounter with the Sophists (cf., e.g. Plato's *Euthydemus*).

According to Aristotle all paralogisms can be traced back to misinterpretation of what a refutation is (*ignoratio elenchi, Soph. el.* 168 a 17 ff.). But the treatise does not aim at a systematic classification proper. In catalogue form different paralogisms are presented and dissolved, and it goes without saying that the catalogue is far from complete (cf. 170 a 20 ff.). At a superior level there is nevertheless a systematic classification of fallacies dependent on linguistic ambiguities and fallacies exclusively derived from logical errors. The most important linguistic ambiguities (165 b 24 ff.; 177 a 9 ff.) are ambiguous termini ('homonyms', cf. the example from the *Theaetetus* about 'knowing' a language – if the middle term in a syllogism is homonymous, the syllogism is invalid) and poly-semantic expressions ('one can walk when one sits'). Distinction is made between the following types of false conclusions that do not depend on language itself (166 b 28 ff.; 179 a 26 ff.):

1   Confusing accidental with essential properties ('Coriscus is different from Socrates; Socrates is a man; ergo: Coriscus is not a man').
2   Confusing relative with absolute expressions (fallacy *secundum quid et simpliciter*: 'an Indian is black but has white teeth; ergo: he is white and not-white'). (1) and (2) are not mutually sharply delimited.
3   *Ignoratio elenchi* in a more narrow sense, i.e. misinterpretation of a given definition ('2 is the double of 1, not the double of 3; ergo: 2 is both double and not-double').
4   A circular argument or *petitio principii* (cf. *Top.* 162 b 3) begs the question, which means that the same assertion – perhaps in different form – both appears as premiss and conclusion ('being is indivisible because it cannot be divided'; 'the soul is immortal because it cannot perish' – these are constructed examples). A *petitio principii* is fallacy in discourse, not a logical fallacy in the strict sense.
5   Erroneous conversion of antecedent and consequent (*fallacia consequentis*; 'the man who has a fever is hot' and 'the man who is hot has a fever'). It is informative that this main point in propositional logic is dealt with in the informal logic.
6   Irrelevant statement of cause, for example that A is the cause of B because A takes place before B (*post hoc ergo propter hoc*).
7   'Several questions as one' ('A is good, B is not-good; is A + B good or not-good?').

The *Topics* and its complement, the *De sophisticis elenchis*, are the last spin-offs from the Sophistic-Socratic technique of argumentation, but the two treatises also break new ground by providing analyses of arguments instead of lists of paradigmatic arguments and fallacies. The question-answer procedure has been made a science, and rhetoric has been given a theoretical foundation, emancipated from strict formal logic. Seen in an historical perspective, the *Topics* has been of far-reaching importance in law, politics, and ethics, in which dialectical and hypothetical argumentation are a necessity. Also moral debates and certain literary genres (speeches, historiography, but also poetry) were in late Antiquity, the Middle Ages and the Renaissance often structured according to *topoi* or 'sources of arguments' and normative, standardized examples, paradigms.

21

NATURAL PHILOSOPHY
AND PSYCHOLOGY

——— •◆• ———

Aristotle considered his lectures on natural philosophy and natural science a unity (cf. Aristot. *Meteor.* 338 a 20 ff.). The *Physics* deals with the fundamental principles, the *De caelo* with cosmology and astronomy, the *De generatione et corruptione* with the four elements, and the *Meteorologica* with the region between the moon and the earth. Last in the series comes the treatment of animals – in other words, the biological writings. Halfway outside it stands the essay on the human soul (the *De anima* with the appendices of the *Parva naturalia*). Such a programme implies not only that within the same systematic framework one moves from the more to the less general, but also that the focus is shifted from philosophical to scientific reflection. The *Physics* is pure natural philosophy, the *De caelo* and the *De generatione et corruptione* are philosophical deliberations that presuppose Aristotle's cosmology and his theory of the elements; the biological writings are the only ones that rest on systematic observation. It has quite often been maintained that thanks to his enormous authority Aristotle made science come to a stand-still for almost 2000 years: how much better had it not been if the tradition from Democritus had been allowed to continue? – and occasionally he is somewhat resentfully blamed for not taking Galileo and Newton into account. Classical physics arose from an encounter with Aristotelianism; but Aristotelianism and Aristotle are not necessarily the same. Whenever basic Aristotelian concepts – form, matter, entelechy, etc. – are understood as 'forces' that 'work' as independent entities in the thing itself and not as a descriptive conceptual apparatus, and whenever the Aristotelian causes are understood as causal thinking in the modern sense and not as structural thinking, Aristotle's intentions are clearly misapprehended. His natural philosophy is not merely out-dated 'natural science'; his is another project: to discover concepts that make possible a description of the world as it appears phenomenologically to immediate observation. Planned experiments under idealized – artificial – conditions with a view to establishing exact natural laws and predictions of future events or possible mastery of nature lie not only beyond what is possible for him but are also beyond his aim. Yet his basic position in no way precludes systematized observation – as can be seen clearly in the biological writings, which compel the admiration also of a modern historian of science. While most of his other scientific views can be dismissed as erroneous, his reflections and his arguments within natural philosophy are not for that reason without interest as philosophy. The

Physics is a seminal work of natural philosophy which cannot for any reason be assigned to a collection of curios in the history of science.

THE *PHYSICS*

In his natural philosophy Aristotle is everywhere faithful to his basic principle: to describe and explain *ta phainomena*. Already with this he places himself clearly in the contemporary debate. On many points he continues the main tendencies in the old natural philosophy – this applies, for example, to the concept of nature itself – and on other points he exploits Platonic ideas in his own original way. Yet he must emphatically reject every physical reductionism; nature – *physis* – is to be explained from itself, which is to say by a physical theory (cf. *Met.* 995 a 16). Plato's mathematical atomism in the *Timaeus* must hence be rejected. Democritus' physical atomism is more acceptable (cf. *De gen. et cor.* 316 a 10 ff.; *De caelo* 309 a 1 ff.), because it explains nature by minima in nature herself. Yet his theory is also untenable, because physical atoms are a construction. Therefore Aristotle must assert a third position next to those two dominant theories: a mathematical description of nature and a physical corpuscular theory. There is one theory that Aristotle must totally reject: that of the Eleatics who simply deny the existence of the physical world. Only to accept one principle – that of being – is absurd because a principle is always a principle of something (*Phys.* 184 b 25 ff.). Physics has to investigate *what* nature is (193 a 1 ff.); to doubt *that* it is indicates advanced confusion. The point of departure for physics is the immediate fact that there are natural things, subject to motion and change (185 a 12).

Nevertheless, Aristotle is the last thinker to feel it incumbent on himself to settle with Parmenides. It is correct that nothing can come into being from nothing and that nothing perishes in nothing, but from this it does not follow that nothing comes into being, perishes, or is changed. As in Plato, Parmenides is opposed to 'the pluralists' who think of everything as an interchange of opposites (188 a 18 ff.). The conclusion is that the simplest model must operate with three 'principles', a substratum and a positive and negative determination: that which the substratum becomes or does not become (189 a 28 ff.). But the argumentation is Aristotelian, not Platonic. It is a clear and paedagogical demonstration of how the Aristotelian basic concepts of their own accord, so to speak, crop up in a description of nature.

We must legitimate the way in which we speak about nature, and therefore the method depends on linguistic analysis (189 b 30 ff.). Let us proceed from three statements from everyday language:

1   A man comes to know music.
2   Not-knowledge of music becomes knowledge of music.
3   The man who does not know music comes to know music.

Here, clearly, what is described is the same, but the very fact that there are three expressions of the same occurrence reveals an underlying conceptual structure. Something in the process remains constant: the substratum 'man'; as is shown in the

Categories, this substratum can receive contrary designations of form – the positive form 'knowledge of music' or the negative form 'not-knowledge of music'. These 'forms' preclude but also define each other, and the substratum cannot become anything whatever. The three 'principles' – the substratum and the positive and negative forms – make it possible for something to come into being (knowledge of music) and for something to perish (not-knowledge of music). But this is not a coming-into-being or perishing in an unqualified sense, for man remains; man does not come into being, nor do the qualities as such, but 'man with knowledge of music' comes into being *qua* 'man with knowledge of music', and not-knowledge of music becomes a knowledge of music *qua* a property of 'man'. Thus Parmenides has been refuted, and the principle of contradiction has been observed (191 a 22 ff.).

But the man who comes to know music does not live forever (190 a 31 ff.); it may seem as if 'man' in an unqualified sense comes to be. But this is only apparently so, for man's coming to be can be described by an analogous conceptual structure: a certain matter receives a certain form – in medieval terminology, a *forma substantialis* – the human form. And so it is man as a unity of form and matter who can receive further formal determinations; for in relation to these determinations 'man' is substratum or matter. What matter is in an unqualified sense – that which is only substratum – can only be understood by analogy (191 a 7; 192 a 31).

By nature exist living beings and lifeless objects consisting of 'simple bodies', the four elements (192 b 8 ff.). These natural products share the characteristic that they have 'the principle of motion in themselves', which is to say that by their own nature they have a certain disposition to motion and change. Within certain limits living beings control their own motions; lifeless objects will 'of themselves' move in a certain direction: a stone will fall down, fire will rise. But living beings display more complex behaviour: an acorn becomes an oak tree, a child becomes adult; all living beings are born, reach a point of culmination, and die; in the course of their development they will by nature assume a certain form – to be an oak tree or a man. Furthermore, living beings possess the ability to reproduce themselves; by generation new individuals of the same kind are created.

Aristotle has a tendency to consider the most complicated or the most highly developed as prototypes for the objects he examines. Thus living beings often simply stand for natural products; lifeless objects are merely less complicated, and are therefore often described in the same language – the stone 'strives to' fall, as the acorn 'strives to' become an oak tree. This common feature of natural products becomes especially clear if they are compared with artefacts. A man-made product will not of itself behave as an artefact but as the material from which it was made: man begets man, but a bed does not beget a bed – if a bed made of wood begets anything, it is a tree that sprouts (193 b 8).

But there are also similarities between artefacts and natural products, for art imitates nature, and the making of man-made products can therefore illustrate nature's own achievements. What man achieves by art, nature produces by itself (194 a 21 ff.; cf. *De part. an.* 641 b 12); yet human 'art' perfects nature's work (*Phys.* 199 a 16). In both cases it is a question of matter being formed for some purpose. The difference is that the artisan deliberately selects his material, while nature brings forth her products from a material that is already there; a natural process fulfils a purpose without being a deliberate act and without outside interference.

The structural similarity between artefacts and natural products makes it possible for Aristotle to apply his four causes in both areas without difficulty, so much so that they appear most readily with respect to artefacts: the sculptor gives this bronze this form in order to make this statue. In nature there is no independent sculptor, and the form of the oak tree coincides with its purpose – which is to say that the oak tree is considered at that stage of its growth at which it optimally has realized what it means to be an oak (cf. 194 a 32). The four causes, however, only indicate the necessary pre-conditions for a thing's being what it is. It was accidental that the sculptor's name was Polycletus, and accidental causes elude scientific analysis.

The history of Aristotelianism – and anti-Aristotelianism – shows that the analogy between artefacts and natural products is not chosen particularly aptly. It is not Aristotle's intention to have nature act in accordance with some subtly devised plan, nor as a godfather who works everything for the best. On the contrary, he has little sympathy with the mythical master builder in the *Timaeus*. Aristotelian teleology – which in the final analysis unites *causa finalis*, *formalis* and *efficiens* – is, to be sure, normative: it is 'better' to be an oak than an acorn, and it is 'better' to be a fully developed oak tree than a scrawny one. But this 'better' refers to the empirical fact that the natural processes follow a certain pattern, and 'good' means 'in agreement with nature's normal course'. The artisan acts deliberately; nature follows a plan without planning, and its 'plan' can be more or less successful. The problem in Aristotelian teleology is how far the analogy between the artisan's deliberate planning and nature's normal course extends.

As mentioned (see p. 285), the Aristotelian causes differ basically from modern causal thinking. It is not Aristotle's intention to show that A necessarily will cause B but that A *has* caused B. From that point of view, mechanical and teleological causes will be entwined: the diet caused the man to become well; he went on a diet to get well. The question is, of course, whether diets can function as paradigms for all natural processes. The *causa efficiens* is the Aristotelian cause that comes closest to the modern causal concept – but, in agreement with Aristotle's retrospective understanding of causality, it should be taken to mean the cause or chain of causes that gave rise to the event x. No event is without a cause, but to Aristotle this does not imply a strict physical determinism, nor, consequently, a common point of departure from which one in principle should be able to predict all events – there is no such point of departure, if only for the reason that the world is eternal. A certain chain of events can be traced back to a certain initial state – for example a human decision – but no farther (cf. *Met.* 1027 a 29 ff.; *De part. an.* 640 a 6), and different causal chains can coincide, whereby unpredictable – accidental – events will come about. In our world only few events follow a necessary course; the possibility of accidental events will almost always be present, and one can only ascertain what 'most often' happens.

A man is beaten up because he left home; but he might have stayed at home (*Met.* 1027 b 1 ff.). A man throws a stone and happens to hit his neighbour; he might have refrained from throwing the stone, but once done, he cannot prevent the regrettable outcome (*Eth. Nic.* 1114 a 17); the acorn would have become an oak tree, if the pig had not uprooted it; if rain had not spoiled the crops, the harvest would have been good (cf. *Phys.* 198 b 21). In the first two examples, the chain of events can be led back to a human act; the person had a motive – accordingly a cause – for his act, although he could have acted otherwise. The latter two examples show that one natural chain of events can affect another.

When Aristotle proceeds to generalize, he considers *causa efficiens* a necessary but insufficient precondition for effectuating the *causa finalis*, and here he is in close agreement with Plato (see p. 173 and p. 242). If B is present, A must necessarily have been present; if A is present, B will become present, unless unforeseen or abnormal circumstances interfere – this is what Aristotle understands by 'hypothetical necessity' (199 b 34 ff.).

But could one imagine that all natural events have only mechanical causes – in Aristotle's terminology: that they come about by simple necessity without any efficient cause whereby necessity and chance would coincide? Here Aristotle turns against the tradition of natural philosophy – that is to say that all physical events can be explained by mechanical interaction (198 b 10 ff.) and perhaps even that the world as a whole has come into being by chance (for example, the vortex theory of the fifth century, 196 a 33). But first and foremost he attacks Empedocles' evolutionist explanation of the emergence of life; and he confines himself throughout to examples from biology (198 b 16 ff.). Here the final causes are, in a manner of speaking 'palpable', but apparently these examples are intended as illustrations of all natural processes that follow a fixed pattern. Did man get teeth *in order to* bite, or did teeth come about by some fortuitous coincidence *so that* we can bite? To Aristotle there is no doubt that teeth came about for a purpose. If the opposite were the case the world would appear as the chaotic, original state in Empedocles – dismembered arms and legs, many-headed cows, vines with olives, etc. But the world does not look like that. The species are constant, and every individual strives to realize his natural form. Such striving may succeed or fail but is a striving towards a specific purpose and a specific structure, which cannot be explained mechanically. We can demonstrate the 'most often' in nature in the development of living beings – just as it is 'most often' hot in summer and cold in winter.

Just as Plato does not entertain an idea of natural laws in the modern sense, so with Aristotle. It is clear that his way of thinking is in close accord with the fundamental project: to describe the present world phenomenologically – and the world, as it is present to us, is a world where nothing occurs at random (cf. *De caelo* 271 a 33). Accidental causes are therefore only accidental in relation to teleological causal chains. There is an infinite number of purely accidental causes – for example, that the master builder was musical – but these are pseudo-causes (*Phys.* 271 a 33). Elsewhere Aristotle has a predilection for explaining accidence with a sort of 'as-if-teleology'; this applies for example to luck: x is collecting money for a festival; unexpectedly he meets y; then he 'accidentally' obtains y's contribution to the festival (196 b 33; cf. 199 b 20). This coincidence depends on the crossing of two causal chains, but it takes place *as if* the outcome were intended. In other cases the outcome is misfortune, as is, for example, the rain that ruins the crops. Most likely Aristotle never aimed for an explanation of all contingent events according to such a model; at any rate he was certainly aware that there are phenomena that only are owing to 'simple necessity' – for example, that one has blue or brown eyes (*De gen. an.* 778 a 32; cf. *De part. an.*

677 a 18). But such phenomena are marginal; the main focus is on explaining accidence as deviation from a teleological, normal course of events.

The four causes are the working tools of natural philosophy. What is to be elucidated by these formal concepts is the phenomenon of motion, for motion is common to all physical objects; a physical object is an object that can be moved or changed. As in the earlier tradition, Aristotle thinks of 'motion' very broadly so that the concept not only comprehends locomotion but every change from one state to another. The different forms of change can be assigned to four of the categories. A substantial change means that the object x comes into being or perishes; qualitative change that x changes property; quantitative change that x becomes larger or smaller; and locomotion is a change in space from one place to another. Substantial change, however, occupies a special position, and Aristotle concentrates on the three other types that adhere to the same structure: a substance passes from one state to another; man for example exchanges the quality 'not-knowledge of music' with the quality 'knowledge of music' (*Phys.* 201 a 2 ff.; 225 b 5 ff.; 226 a 23 ff.; 225 a 7 ff.). Nevertheless the prototype is a movement from one place to another.

It is not Aristotle's intention to lay down cinematic laws but to arrive at a conceptual hold of what we mean when we say that an object is moved or changed. However, as he himself says (201 b 33), it is quite difficult to answer the 'what is X question' with respect to motion (cf. Zeno). Still, it is evidently Aristotle's intention to make the concept of motion intelligible and philosophically manageable.

To Aristotle motion and change are inseparable from the object that is changed or moved (200 b 32), but they are not properties next to others. The reason is that they are a precondition for an object's obtaining or losing properties and for its passage from one opposite to another (cf. 229 a 7). Motion is continuous; a continuum is infinitely divisible; and motion takes place in time and space (200 b 16 ff.). Consequently an investigation of motion must include these other concepts that by and large turn out to have parallel structures. Just as motion to Aristotle is not 'a something' in itself, so he never reifies continuity, divisibility, time and space, not even as abstract mathematical entities; they are considered as the forms under which motion appears or as bound to a thing. That which above all makes the analysis of this whole complex of concepts difficult is the old problem of incongruity between continuity and discontinuity. Although Aristotle's physics as a whole and in detail may be read as one big protest against Plato, here, to a large extent, he is able to make use of him – especially Plato's *Parmenides* (cf., e.g. Plat. *Parm.* 138 B ff.; 156 C ff.). But Aristotle rids himself completely of Plato's metaphysical superstructure and concentrates on a concrete object changing in time and space. Thereby the same conceptual structures acquire a wholly new perspective.

The fundamental problem already turns up when Aristotle applies the scheme of actuality and potentiality to motion. Motion is defined (Aristot. *Phys.* 201 a 10; cf. 202 a 7; 251 a 9) as the actualization of what exists potentially, in so far as it exists potentially – which is to say that it is neither simple potentiality nor simple actuality but in some sense both: a continuous process from potentiality to the actuality for which the potentiality is a potentiality (cf. *De an.* 417 a 14 ff.).

A movement always proceeds from something to something else and presupposes an interaction or contact between two entities: the mover and the movable (*Phys.* 202

a 3 ff.). But the movement itself is one; accordingly, movement as actuality is common to the two entities. There is only difference in definition – depending on the same event's being described from the one point of view or the other: the teacher instructs the student, and the student learns from the teacher (202 b 1). A movement is continuous, but it must in any case presuppose finite limits in two dimensions: a beginning and an end, and a mover and something moved.

Now, in what sense is a continuum infinite? What does 'infinite' mean? Concepts are neither finite nor infinite, but in some sense – directly or indirectly – 'finite' and 'infinite' can be predicated about the physical world. Nevertheless, no physical entity can exist that in fact – actually – has infinite extension (204 b 4 ff.), for the idea of a physical substance of infinite extension is inconsistent with the concept of substance itself: it would not be possible for something to exist 'next to' such a substance, nor could it exist 'in' a place, and its 'parts' could not be counted (cf. Parmenides).

Nevertheless, we use the predicate 'infinite' about time, divisibility of finite magnitudes, and the sequence of numbers (206 a 9 ff.). The sequence of numbers has a lower limit – 1 – but not an upper one; a finite magnitude has an upper limit, but not a lower one, it can be infinitely divided. But time has neither an upper nor lower limit (cf. 207 a 33 ff.). A quantity is hence infinite, inasmuch as one can always pick out one part after another (cf. 207 a 7). This means that infinity does not mean that there is nothing 'outside', but that there is always something 'inside'. Two things are decisive: in part, that infinity is always potential, for a division is never completed, and therefore infinity can never be actualized (206 a 16 ff.; cf. *Met.* 1048 b 9 ff.), and the infinite can never be a 'this' or a substance (*Phys.* 206 a 30). On the other hand, every other potentiality can be actualized (this bronze can become this statue), and with this it is stated in Aristotelian terminology that the finite and the infinite have different logical structures. In part it follows that divisibility always presupposes someone able to divide, and 'countability' someone able to count. The parts and their numbers are not present until division or counting has taken place.

Infinity is tied to division of finite magnitudes (207 b 21 ff.), but the concept of infinity attracts other concepts that also have a continuum structure and are assigned to bodies. Number is always a property of quantity and thus only exists when parts of a quantity are counted. Motion presupposes the traversal of a distance (= an extension). Time presupposes motion. These derived conceptual structures are not 'things'; they are modes of appearance of the thing to experience, but they are not mental constructs. In other words, a continuum structure implies extension, divisibility, motion and time, and a phenomenon as complicated as motion can only be measured as relative to time and extension.

Locomotion takes place in space, and space is therefore one of the concepts that follows from things being in motion (*Phys.* 208 a 27 ff.; 211 a 12 ff.). But inasmuch as Aristotle wants to avoid any reification of the conditions for motion, Aristotelian space, like the Platonic, is not an autonomous entity; it is neither absolute space nor empty space, and, in the precise terminology, it is called place (*topos*), not space (*chōra*). Aristotle considers place some sort of container – an 'immovable vessel' (212 a 15). But it is not, as in Zeno, a thing containing another thing; nor is it, as in Plato's *Timaeus*, a limiting concept comprehending space and *prima materia*. The Platonic model should rather be looked for in the *Parmenides* (cf. Plat. *Parm.* 145 B ff.).

A phenomenological description of 'place' must take the empirical facts into account (Aristot. *Phys.* 210 b 32 ff.; cf. 208 a 29 ff.; 209 a 7 ff.): a thing is in one 'place', i.e. it is surrounded by something; the 'place' of a thing is neither larger nor smaller than the thing itself; two things cannot be in the same place; and things — objects or elements — can exchange places, which is why thing and 'place' cannot be identical. In addition, the elements have their 'natural place' — no isotropic space exists, rather an absolute 'up' and 'down' — a simple consequence of heavy elements seeking downwards and light elements upwards. 'Place' is hence defined as the inner, immovable boundary of that which surrounds a given magnitude (212 a 20). In consequence (212 b 8) the universe as a whole cannot be in a 'place', for then it would be surrounded by something, an object or a reified space.

That Aristotle rejects empty space — i.e an unfilled region (208 b 26) — as a precondition for motion may in part be owing to a principle of economy (214 a 26): motion can be explained without a void. In part, the concept itself is in his view self-contradictory — to Aristotle Democritus' paradox that 'nothing exists' must be an absurdity, and if space is 'something', it would break with the thought that space only can be understood relatively (see also p. 331).

Just as little as an absolute space exists, just so little does absolute time, an independent duration in which something takes place. Time is even more unreal than place. While place is assigned to a physical body, time is, so to speak, dependent on a second level: time is assigned to motion, which in turn is dependent on a physical body (219 a 3 ff.). Therefore the predicates 'before' and 'after' are more primitive concepts than the concept of time itself. Apart from the fact that they may be used about logical priority, they are primarily used about an object that is 'before' or 'after', i.e. in front or back of another; the second time around they are used about motion and not until afterwards about time. And, all in all, time has a strangely unreal character (217 b 32 ff.). Time consists of past, present and future, but the past no longer is, the future is not yet, and the present consists of a segment of the past and a segment of the future.

Nevertheless, events can be ordered in a sequence of time; a given segment of time can be related to a 'before' and 'after'. This is made possible by 'the now', a concept not included in time (cf. 233 b 35 ff.) but related to time as the point is to the line. In a certain sense 'the now' is self-identical — that is if it is thought of as constant in relation to time as sequential. However, if the sequence of time is thought of as constant, 'the now' steadily moves, and time can then be divided by means of several 'nows'; in this way 'the now' will both render time discontinuous by dividing it and continuous by uniting two time segments in the same point (218 a 8 ff.; 219 b 9 ff.); at any point in time 'time' will both begin and end (222 b 1).

Any segment of time, however brief, is in itself a stretch of time, but it is delimited by two 'nows', and such a limited stretch of time makes it possible to measure time. Since time is dependent on motion and since measuring presupposes numbers, time can be defined as 'the number of motion with respect to before and after' (219 b 1; 220 a 24). Here number is not to be understood as an abstract standard of measuring but rather as a measuring unit related to 'motion' and to 'before and after', which means that time is measured by arbitrarily chosen segments of time itself; time is counted by means of units of time, just as horses are counted by 'horse units'

(219 b 6; 220 b 20; cf. *Met.* 1053 a 24); and as time is the number or motion, the contents of time, motion, are also counted by time units.

But does this mean that time only exists if somebody is counting time units, that time in other words would not exist if mind did not exist (*Phys.* 223 a 21 ff.)? If Aristotle simply answered yes to this question, time would be a pure form of intuition in the Kantian sense. But his answer takes a different direction: if mind did not exist, and if only mind were able to count, motion would still exist as an ordered succession, and as time is the number of motion, time would exist as countable, not as counted. Time is dependent on motion, and motion exists independently of a subject.

Two conclusions may be drawn from time's being dependent on motion: partly, that what is not subject to motion – concepts, for example – does not exist in time (cf. 221 b 20); partly, that a given segment of time corresponds with a given segment of motion – the duration of a journey can be related to the length of the route (220 b 22 ff.). But this also implies that time and motion are not identical. Motion is both temporally and spatially extended; furthermore, time is the same even though the movements are different (223 b 1 ff.), which explains why a rapid or slow movement can be measured by the same time, just as one can compare seven dogs and seven horses. In the final analysis both motion and time are – as in Plato's *Timaeus* – founded in the primary motion, the circular motion of the universe (223 b 18 ff.); the first motion has a circular, non-linear structure, and the eternity of time therefore depends on the eternity of the completed circular motion. But eternity still means eternal duration; Aristotle does away with Plato's metaphysical distinction between time and eternity.

After the analysis of time Aristotle is enabled to provide a closer analysis of motion as continuum. The continuum concept itself can be formally described by means of some other concepts (226 b 18 ff.; 231 a 21 ff.). B 'follows after' A if something of the same kind does not stand between A and B in a series in which A and B are included; A and B are 'in contact' if they have a point of contact in common (cf. *De an.* 427 a 9 ff.; *De mot. an.* 698 a 14 ff.); A and B constitute a continuum if they are both included in a series and have a point of contact in common. The series of numbers is a discontinuous series, in which the individual members 'follow after' one another without the possibility of a number being inserted between any given number and the following one. A series of points is also discontinuous; yet it will always be possible to insert a point between two others; but regardless of the density with which the points are placed, they will never be in contact. The line, on the other hand, is a continuum; its individual parts follow after each other and are in contact. But any given part of a continuum will also itself be a continuum; the line consists of line segments, not of points. Furthermore, a continuum is finite but infinitely divisible; one can never arrive at indivisible minima, and consequently a continuum can only be measured by another continuum.

The continuum concept itself is abstract, for 'continuous' is always a predicate of a definite kind of continuum. One such is time, and the incommensurability between continuous and discontinuous has appeared quite clearly from the distinction made in the analysis of time between time as measured time and the 'now' as the indivisible instance, which does not measure but makes measurement of time possible. Time is dependent on motion, and motion is a very complex form of continuum because it can be measured in time and spatial extension. What extension, time and motion are in themselves does not permit definition; they are phenomena that are immediately given in experience. They can only be grasped indirectly by measuring them against each other (*Phys.* 232 b 20 ff.). These analyses make it possible to refute Zeno (233 a 21 ff.; 239 b 9 ff.; 263 a 4 ff.; cf. 240 b 8 ff.): a continuum does not consist of atomic minimal particles; it is infinitely divisible but never infinitely divided. Actually, it is finite; potentially, it is infinite. It is true that an unlimited distance cannot be traversed in finite time, but a distance is not unlimited because it is infinitely divisible. Finite magnitudes are traversed in finite time (cf. 237 b 23 ff.).

Yet Aristotle has his own paradoxes about motion. A continuum can only be divided into continua, and motion can only be divided into segments of motion. An object moves and has moved (237 a 11 ff.), but there is no moment at which the motion begins or finishes, only a now where it has begun or has finished, for an atomic now cannot at the same time be in motion and not in motion (cf. 235 b 16 ff.). The transition from motion to rest or from rest to motion accordingly does not take place in time (238 b 23 ff.). This concept of transition corresponds with the concept of 'the sudden' in Plato's *Parmenides*, and is probably the single point that most clearly shows Aristotle re-shaping Plato's metaphysical conceptual framework into natural philosophy. A movement is normally directed at a purpose outside the movement itself, and the purpose cannot be described inside the frames of movement *qua* movement. But there is an exception in the case of the 'complete' motion, which is that motion in which the purpose is inherent in the motion or act itself, where motion and actualization coincide (I am living and I have lived; I am perceiving and I have perceived – *Met.* 1048 b 18 ff.; *De an.* 431 a 4 ff.; *Eth. Nic.* 1174 a 13 ff.). Such a motion has exactly the same structure as the 'incomplete' motion (I am building a house in order *to have* built the house – cf. *Phys.* 201 b 32); it is of course also finite – I do not live forever – but here it is irrelevant to ask what lies outside the course of events. The ethical basic concept of *praxis* is one such 'complete' motion – a noble example of how Aristotle can apply a thought structure from natural philosophy to an entirely different field.

Aristotle always asks what is the ultimate precondition for the phenomenon he is discussing. This also occurs in the last book of the *Physics* where he investigates how to explain that motion does exist. His aim is by means of an argument for the eternity of motion to demonstrate that an unmoved mover exists. All objects in the physical world are either in motion or at rest, and this state of constant transition cannot have come into being, because such a coming into being would itself be a transition, and, furthermore, the eternity of time implies the eternity of motion (250 b 11 ff.). A further premiss is that everything moved is moved by something else and that every motion comes about by contact between mover and the moved (254 b 7 ff.; cf. 241 b 24 ff.; 243 a 3 ff.). That everything moved is moved by something else is evident with respect to movement by compulsion, but natural movements also begin from certain initial conditions; with respect to voluntary movements one has to distinguish between the soul as mover and the body as moved, and, anatomically even, between mover and moved in a living being (*De mot. an.* 698 a 16 ff.).

It is one thing that the chain of events and changes is infinite in time. It is quite another that the chain of pre-conditions for motion is not infinite nor occurs in time. Aristotle provides an example himself (*Phys.* 256 a 6): the stone is moved by the stick that is moved by the hand that is moved by the man. It is one and the same movement, for the several 'movers' move at the same time. But considered as a limited sequence, such a motion has a first mover, the man. If this example is transferred to the sum of all motions – the universe as a whole – there must in an absolute sense be an unmoved first mover that often through many intermediate links transmits the motion to the last link; however, an intermediate link cannot be an intermediate link without the presence of a first and a final link. An infinite regress is impossible according to this model: it is necessary to come to a halt (257 a 6; cf. *Met.* 994 a 16).

How is one now to think of the first motion and the unmoved first mover? The first motion must be eternal, which is to say continuous, and among primary motions only the circular one fulfils this condition. The linear motion cannot be eternal in a finite universe, and quantitative and qualitative changes are derived movements moving reversibly between two opposites, such as for example large–small, wet–dry (*Phys.* 260 a 20 ff.; 265 a 13 ff.).

The first mover – who causes the first motion, the circular motion – must be eternal and one (258 b 10 ff.). That it must be one follows, strictly speaking, only from the principle of economy. That it must be eternal is proved by the very existence of the universe. In the earthly world there is something that is moved, something that is not moved, something that becomes, and something that perishes. But this process can only continue forever, if both the first motion and the first mover are eternal. In other words, the inference is from the existence of contingent events to the necessary existence of something eternal. Furthermore, the first mover must be indivisible and without extension (266 a 10 ff.), for nothing finite can have infinite effect and everything divisible and everything extended can be moved. In the *Metaphysics* (1071 a 3 ff.) it is added that the unmoved mover must be pure form and pure act – because everything that exists materially or potentially can be moved or changed.

Of course this argument is out and out speculative, but fortunately enough the speculation can be justified empirically. All of us have the circular motion in view every day – the celestial rotation. But we cannot espy the unmoved mover; so it is clearly metaphoric language when Aristotle 'places' it 'in' or 'outside' the limit of the universe (*Phys.* 267 b 9; *De caelo* 279 a 18 ff.; *De mot. an.* 699 a 12 ff.). In a physical sense there is nothing outside space; the unmoved mover transcends space because it is a metaphysical entity. Here Aristotle's mode of expression is reminiscent of that of the unfortunate Xenocrates (Sext. Emp. *Ad. math.* VII 147 ff. = Xenocr. frg. 5, Heinze).

Ultimately, the celestial circular motion has the same function to Aristotle as to Plato. But clearly Aristotle's unmoved mover is deliberately opposed to Plato's theory of the soul as a self-moving mover. It is likewise clear that the idea of the unmoved mover leads directly to Aristotle's metaphysics and theology; and indeed several of the arguments in the last book of the *Physics* were employed in the series of medieval proofs of god's existence, which – like the 'five ways' in Thomas Aquinas – would demonstrate the existence of god from the existence of the physical world. In Aristotle, however, the argument is not really a proof of god's existence. The very fact that something exists implies that there must be a first principle for its existence. Aristotle's question is what such a principle would be like in order for the world to function as it does; and it is telling that he stops at the border of physics. The *Physics* points forwards to the *Metaphysics* but does not concern itself with metaphysical problems. Nowhere in the *Physics* is the unmoved mover identified with god. But nobody reading Aristotle's minor works on natural philosophy can doubt that there are religious undertones behind the physical theory of the unmoved mover – with his usual matter-of-fact attitude Aristotle suggests that his theory uncovers the real meaning behind the ideas in popular religion and mythology about the divinity of celestial bodies and of the universe (*De caelo* 270 b 4 ff.; *De mot. an.* 699 a 27); but in one passage he goes so far as to have god 'act' (*De gen. et corr.* 336 b 31), and, as in the *Metaphysics*, god's activity is characterized as eternal life (*De Caelo* 286 a 9; cf. *Met.* 1072 b 26).

COSMOLOGY AND THEORY OF ELEMENTS

The modern reader of Aristotle's natural philosophy will hardly feel bothered by the distance in time when he confronts the weighty analyses of the concepts of time, space, and continuity. This is not the case with Aristotle's cosmology and theory of elements, which in the main are dealt with in the *De caelo* and the treatise on substantial change, the *De generatione et corruptione*. The reason that these writings provoke a certain uneasiness nowadays is not only the banal one that Aristotle did not know what we know or believe we know, but also that he – just as did the old natural philosophers – undertakes most daring, speculative generalizations based on everyday observations, which often are more rash and untested than they ought to be or might be. To this should of course be added that Aristotle was prevented from conducting the advanced experiments that are a prerequisite of modern natural science. Still, it is not merely a question of missing presuppositions. After Galileo, experimental natural science builds on an idealized view of nature that deliberately ignores a number of factors in immediate experience. It is no coincidence that here one could find inspiration in the Platonic tradition – not in Aristotle and – most certainly not – in the Aristotelian epigones. Aristotle proceeds in a very different manner when he combines conceptual analysis and direct observation of *ta phainomena*. He found himself confronted with the same task as Plato: to reflect philosophically on the results that had been reached in an existing science, that of astronomy, and to establish a speculative theory of matter without support in any existing 'science' but with a background in the tradition of natural philosophy. But there are marked differences between Aristotle and the *Timaeus*. Aristotle wants to explain nature from nature herself and is therefore opposed to a reduction to mathematical structures; where the mythical form of the *Timaeus* reflects the view that an exact natural science is impossible, Aristotle apparently has no such scruples. Yet he knows that he is speaking as a layman about astronomy (*Met.* 1073 b 10), and he emphasizes that his cosmology is a theoretical construct (1072 a 8 ff.; cf. *De part. an.* 645 a 4; see p. 361). It is on these premises that Aristotle's cosmology should be judged.

The celestial bodies move in regular circular motions, and their motion is eternal. Such a motion is not found in the sublunary world, and as motion is a property of the moved object, this means that the celestial bodies consist of another sort of matter than the four elements known on earth. To a simple motion there is a corresponding simple stuff, to this stuff, the natural motion of which must be circular and uniform, Aristotle gave a name that had gained an honoured status in the poetical and early philosophical tradition: ether, *aithēr* (*De caelo* 268 b 11 ff.) – in later terminology, the *quinta essentia*, the fifth essence (or the fifth element).

This theory is tied to scientific astronomy, which is to say to Eudoxus (see p. 414) who described the motion of the celestial bodies as concentric circular motions with earth as the permanent centre and who by means of an elegant mathematical construction explained the apparently irregular orbits of the planets by breaking down their complicated motions into several combined circular motions. Now, when Aristotle interprets this theory – with modifications by the slightly younger astronomer Callippus – in the light of his own philosophy (cf. *Met.* 1073 a 14 ff.), he must presuppose one unmoved mover for each circular motion. This does not agree with the theory that according to the principle of economy there ought only to be one unmoved mover – but the razor-sharp balance between physics and metaphysics probably makes it possible to maintain that a physical analysis leads to the assumption of several unmoved movers that metaphysically can be reduced to the first in the series (cf. *De gen. et corr.* 337 a 20; *Met.* 1074 a 35.).

But that is not the sole difficulty. Eudoxus' theory was a mathematical model and no more than that. But Aristotle's aim was to make the theory mechanically relevant. He wanted to deal with actual reality – in his view mathematics did not concern itself with real objects – and therefore he attached the celestial bodies to physically existing, transparent spheres. In order for motion to be transferred from outer to inner spheres, the individual spheres had to be in physical contact. But the result was that the number of spheres and thereby of unmoved movers had to be increased in order to counteract the transmission of an outer to an inner especial planetary motion. In Eudoxus' system one had to calculate with twenty-seven spheres. Callippus increased the number to thirty four. Aristotle was forced to set the figure at fifty six, including the outermost sphere of the fixed stars. Outside the sphere of the fixed stars there is nothing; only one universe or 'heaven' can exist – which follows from the theory of space. But Aristotle seeks to legitimate it further by a series of arguments that are more sophisticated than convincing (*De caelo* 276 a 18 ff.; *Met.* 1074 a 31 ff.).

Even more sharply than did Plato, Aristotle distinguished between the supra- and sublunary regions of the universe. This was a simple consequence of what he observed and – we can add – his ignorance of the law of gravitation. What he observed were the regular motions of the celestial bodies; such motions were unknown in the earthly region, and consequently it was unthinkable that the same forces were at work above and beneath the moon. The model does of course make it difficult to explain the connection between the two regions of the universe. It is not easy to comprehend that the events on earth are dependent on the celestial bodies (the passing of the seasons, for example), even though they obey other laws. The explanation (*De gen. et corr.* 336 a 14 ff.) builds on the *Timaeus*: in so far as the sun in its course along the ecliptic follows the motion of the fixed stars, it is the cause of the four seasons; in so far as it deviates, it causes earthly motions to be irregular, although they occur permanently. This is no happy explanation; but on Aristotle's premisses it would be worse to be left without a reasonable explanation of the regular motions of the celestial bodies.

The sublunary region is in fact divided into two: one is the area between earth and the moon – dealt with in the *Meteorologica* – where phenomena such as wind and weather, lightning and thunder, and comets (!) are explained according to methods that correspond completely with those of the old tradition of natural philosophy; the other is earth itself. But common to both areas are the two natural motions 'upwards' and 'downwards' to which the corresponding qualities are 'light' and 'heavy' (*De caelo* 268 b 21 ff.; 308 a 34 ff.). In a universe constructed like the Aristotelian one these motions can only be finite, and as the universe has a centre and the sublunary sphere is delimited, 'heavy' and 'light' must be absolute designations: if the natural motion is not prevented, some stuff will tend towards the centre and some towards the periphery. There will always be natural movements upwards and downwards; they will never continue infinitely.

Terrestrial bodies are composed of the four elements, each with its own natural motion. In a spherical universe there must be a centre and, consequently, one element, earth, whose natural motion is the absolute downward motion, i.e. towards the centre, or, the 'natural place' of earth (286 a 13 ff.; cf. *De gen. et corr.* 330 b 30 ff.). Earth must, we are told, have a 'contrary', fire, with an absolute 'upward' motion toward the limit of the sublunary region. Between these two opposite poles two 'mean proportionals' are inserted, air and water that have their own 'natural places', respectively below fire and above earth. The line of thought – a typical *post hoc* rationalization – is not suited to convince modern readers. More interesting is the very fact that Aristotle has recourse to the elemental doctrine of the old natural philosophy – more specifically, Empedocles'. Once again his motive is to systematize what he registers from immediate observation. Bodies can have a solid state ('earth'), a liquid state ('water'), an airy state (air, smoke and steam), and an igneous state; these states move in a 'natural' direction and can be transformed into each other.

Natural philosophy must be able to explain how this can be. Plato attributed geometrical structures to the elements. Aristotle's physics, on the other hand, is fundamentally a continuum physics and a quality physics. The universe is a plenum, a continuum of stuff; and, as a continuum cannot be reduced to minimal entities, it can only be described qualitatively at the fundamental level; the elements must be considered qualitative transformations of a stuff without properties, the *prima materia*. This means that although the elements are basal states, they can be reduced to the qualitative determinations of an underlying stuff (338 b 26 ff.). There are four primary qualities, arranged in pairs as contraries: 'cold/warm' and 'wet/dry'. These qualities are then assigned to the elements as follows: 'cold' + 'dry' $\rightarrow$ earth; 'cold' + 'wet' $\rightarrow$ water; 'warm' + 'wet' $\rightarrow$ air; 'warm' + 'dry' $\rightarrow$ fire. A shift of qualities thereby makes it possible for one element to change into another and – contrary to Plato's theory – all elements can mutually be transformed. The underlying thought is the same that already was presented in the beginning of the *Physics*: a substratum that receives contrary determinations of form. There it was also suggested that a substratum that only is a substratum is a limiting concept, and that is exactly what *prima materia* is; it is never empirically present. Aristotle rightly emphasizes that his theory of the elements differs from Plato's in principle. None the less, he assumed a

Platonic 'dualism' and this produces a latent tension in his entire natural philosophy: on the one hand, the world is materially a plenum and a continuum in which the elements can exchange places and a region can be filled with greater or lesser intensity of stuff (*Phys.* 208 b 1); on the other hand, it presents itself as a world of isolated, autonomous entities, substances. This is owing to matter's being structured by form. Form is inherent in the material thing, not in matter *qua* matter, and only rudimentarily in the four elementary bodies. This splitting up of the world, where form or structure on the basal level, so to speak, comes from the outside, probably implies a greater agreement with Plato than Aristotle would have cared for.

Probably no physical body consists exclusively of one element. Physical objects consist of mixtures, and the proportion can be altered by a number of processes – putrefaction, heating, concoction, tempering, etc. – as described in a supplement to the *Meteorology* (378 b 10 ff.), which most generously has been called Aristotle's treatise on chemistry. The most complex physical objects – living beings – consist in part of qualitatively unlike parts, organs and in part of like parts, the *homoiomerē*, tissues that qualitatively are unalterable – regardless of how much they are divided (389 b 23 ff.; *De part. an.* 646 a 12 ff.).

DYNAMICS

Aristotle's combination of immediate observation with speculation is a consequence of his basic position that natural philosophy should presuppose 'that' and explain 'why' – the Aristotelian 'why'. Broadly speaking, modern natural science has achieved its results by refraining from explaining 'why' and by concentrating instead on a description of 'that' or 'how'. Here, as is well known, carefully planned and ordered experiments have been of decisive importance. The arranged experiment has no place in Aristotle's project in natural philosophy; he does not even find it worthwhile to check what to him were evident, observable facts – which Galileo quite justly criticized in his famous refutation of the Aristotelian theory of the free fall (Galileo, *Dialogo sopra i due massimi sistemi del mondo*, I 106 ff.). Aristotle's natural philosophy is an interesting example of how far one, on his presuppositions, could come towards a phenomenological description of nature; but not least the cosmology and the theory of elements reveal the chasm that separates him from modern principles of natural science. Nevertheless, there is one area of physics in which Aristotle – also from the point of view of natural science – was a pioneer, even though his concrete results are unacceptable. This concerns his special theory of motion, dynamics. In the old tradition motion was explained by the principle of 'like seeks like' or generalization from the observation of thrusts, pushes, or the like. It follows from Aristotle's general position that motion is a most complex phenomenon that must be understood as the joint work of several factors. Now, it is one thing that he was ignorant of the law of gravitation, of the difference between gravitational and inertial mass, and of the concepts of acceleration and momentary velocity and that with oddly lop-sided perspicacity he rejected the laws of free fall and of inertia. But it is crucial that he introduced the concept of force as a quantifiable entity in the theory of motion. In agreement with his ideal of science, Plato was concerned with cinematics, which is to say that he wanted to describe motion mathematically. It agrees with Aristotle's ideals that in his description of motion he introduces the physical concept of force; this opens the way for a quantitative causal explanation, dynamics. Aristotle did not anywhere present dynamics as a separate discipline; yet it is possible to extract a consistent theory.

His special doctrine of motion rests on two basic views that have already been brought up. In part, everything moved is moved by something else; in part, there are three forms of motion: the natural, the compulsive and the voluntary (cf. *Phys.* 254 b 12 ff.). Voluntary motion is of course special for living beings and defies the possibilities of physical description. The natural motion 'up' and 'down' is the basic one (*De caelo* 300 a 23), but most clearly of all the motion by compulsion shows the general principles: here it is evident that the moved is moved by something else; the natural object does indeed have the principle of motion in itself, but motion comes about through some external cause.

As no forces working from afar exist, all movements must take place by direct contact. This is immediately apparent with respect to compelled motion: the horse pulls the cart, the man pushes the stone. From such examples Aristotle formulates the basic law that velocity is directly proportional to the moving force, inversely proportional to resistance (*Phys.* 249 b 30 ff.; 215 a 29 ff.). But observation shows that there are borderline cases: if 100 men can pull a ship in a given time, it does not follow that one man can pull the ship in 100 times as much time: there must altogether be some limit, no further specified, to how a given force can overcome a given resistance (250 a 15 ff.) – this is as close as Aristotle gets to the concept of inertial mass. Still, it is more difficult to reconcile for example a missile motion with the basic Aristotelian law that refuses to acknowledge inertia. An object that is thrown continues to move, also after the contact with the mover has ceased. Aristotle is compelled to explain the phenomenon by claiming that the initiating force is transferred to the air, which thereafter for some time functions as 'mover' (267 a 2 ff.). A late Aristotle commentator, Philoponus (sixth century AD), presented the more advanced theory that the force is transferred to the thrown object itself and that it decreases during the course performed by the object (Philop. in Aristot. *Phys.* 642, 3 ff.). This so-called impetus theory – which was continued in the Middle Ages by Ockham and Buridanus – can be considered a stage on the way to understanding the concept of inertia.

If the law of dynamics is transferred to natural movements, it means that the greater the body, the faster it will move towards its natural place: fire upwards, earth downwards (cf. *De caelo* 277 b 3 ff.; 290 a 1 ff.; 309 b 11 ff.). During the free fall, where force equals weight, a heavier body would accordingly move more quickly than a lighter one (cf. 273 b 3) – Aristotle was not aware that air resistance is so minimal that it normally can be disregarded; and, as we know, it was precisely by experiments with the free fall that Galileo demonstrated that Aristotle's theory was untenable.

But it is informative to study how he employs his law of motion in his argument against empty space. If empty space existed, it would from one point of view mean that an object would fall infinitely quickly in a vacuum in which no air resistance would counteract the weight; from another, that heavy and light bodies will fall with the same speed – both conclusions are clearly absurd in Aristotle's opinion (*Phys.* 215 b 12 ff; 216 a 17 ff.). To him it seems equally absurd that a body moving in a vacuum would never be able to stop (215 a 19). Accordingly, these three consequences are on Aristotle's presuppositions self-refuting thought experiments. But they are very astute thought experiments – the latter two in fact anticipate Galileo's law of the free fall and the law of inertia. It is something more than a mere curio in the history of science that these two laws are formulated but rejected – in a nutshell it shows the difference between the two conceptions of nature.

BIOLOGY

In modern times Aristotle, the biologist, enjoys a considerably greater reputation than does Aristotle, the physicist. This is owing to the enormous material – c.500 species of animals – that partially was gathered by Aristotle himself and his students and partially stems from written sources, interviews with experts, apiarists, fishermen, hunters, etc. Yet it is probably especially owing to a series of original observations that were not confirmed until recent times and to sureness of method and classification. Naturally enough, there is much that Aristotle did not know – he was as ignorant as Plato about the circulation of blood and the functions of the respiratory system and the nerves; the theory of elements and the doctrine of the function of the hot and the cold led to speculative constructions that are remote to us; and it seems, for example, a peculiar step backwards that the heart is made the central sensory organ (*De part. an.* 656 a 29 ff.; *De sens.* 439 a 1; *De juv.* 469 a 5). The idea that certain lower animals arise 'spontaneously' from mud (*De gen. an.* 762 a 8 ff.) builds on current popular belief. But there are hosts of acute observations and specific investigations – great and small: it is Aristotle who found out that whales were mammals (*Hist an.* 489 a 34 ff.); he provides detailed reports of embryological investigations – among them, as in the Hippocratic writings, of the development of chicken embryos (561 a 3); he can with equal expertise tell of flesh-eating fishes, of the social lives of bees, and of the missing gall bladder of elephants (564 b 15 ff.; 623 b 4; 506 b 1); clearly he performed dissections. Most of the material is presented in the *Historia animalium*; a summary is provided in the treatise on animal organs (*De partibus animalium*). Two problems were of special interest to Aristotle and led to special treatises: how can the continuation of the species be secured by reproduction (the larger treatise, the *De generatione animalium*), and how can the movements of animals be described physiologically (the lesser treatises, the *De incessu animalium* on motory organs and the *De motu animalium* on the mechanics of motion). The *De generatione animalium* is typical in uniting physical observation and reflections on how hereditary characteristics can be transferred – how is the soul propagated? 'The explanation' is notorious: man contributes with form, woman with matter, just as the artist impresses the form of his work in the stuff (*De gen. an.* 730 b 6 ff.).

This is but one example showing that Aristotle's biological method in principle is not different from that which he employs in his cosmology and theory of elements. In both cases it is a question of a combination of systematized observation and speculation, and what is being asked is still not only how but also why. The difference is simply that there is a much greater and more varied material available in biology to the person who will and can observe. Aristotle notes this himself (*De part. an.* 644 b 22 ff.) in a committed and warm defence of biology as a science: certainly the celestial bodies are more divine; but there is nothing unworthy in nature; its beauty and regularity show themselves also in the small details that perhaps at first sight can seem out-and-out repugnant.

This defence of biology is surely evidence that Aristotle also in this field saw himself as the founder of a new science. This is justified – but it does not mean that nobody before him was interested in zoological classification. Speusippus was, although his concern was with a formal and an a priori universal science. Aristotle distances himself from such a position. He uses – successfully – the Academy method of classification, *diairesis*, but sharply criticizes rigid principles of dichotomy (642 b 5 ff.; 644 a 12 ff.) – a *diairesis* does not bring about knowledge, but orders empirically known stuff in a practical manner. Aristotle's considerations of method are everywhere empirical and pragmatic – even though the aim is more ambitious. It is clear that the purpose is to find the 'causes' and 'principles' of the phenomena; it is the essence that determines the phenomenon, but the points of departure – what is known to us – are and remain the phenomena themselves (640 a 10 ff.; 645 b 1). It is useless to superimpose a theory on the facts (cf. *De caelo* 306 a 5); the theory must concur with the observed phenomena (*De gen. an.* 760 b 31). Often Aristotle simply constructs his method according to what is most practical: it is not reasonable to examine animal species one by one if general features can be ascertained once and for all (*De part. an.* 639 a 12 ff.) – which of course does not mean that the essence is established before the detailed analysis.

The purpose of a biological investigation is a pluralistic description. A description of an organ, for example, must take into account stuff, structure, composition and function – in Aristotle's language: the material, the formal and the final causes (642 a 14; cf. 640 b 29 ff.). This has consequences for the choice of classification method. A classification only fulfils its *raison d'être* by being expedient in a given context, and hence several classifications are conceivable. One might classify according to animals that are oviparous and animals that are viviparous, etc. (*De gen. an.* 732 a 25 ff.). But many other criteria are possible (*Hist. an.* 487 a 11 ff.): way of life and habitat (animals on land, in air and water), foods (carnivores, herbivores), wild and domestic animals, social habits – men, bees, ants and cranes, for example, are social animals – or character – lions are noble, snakes wily, elephants even-tempered, peacocks egocentric, men can deliberate.

Finally, one can classify according to the structure and function of the organs. This determines Aristotle's basic classification (cf. 490 b 7 ff.; 505 b 25 ff.; *De part. an.* 685 b 29 ff.). In the first stage animals are classified as with or without blood – corresponding to vertebrate and invertebrate animals; in the second stage the classification is according to modes of procreation (animals giving birth to live progeny resembling themselves, oviparous animals, animals that produce grubs, animals that come to be 'spontaneously'). Then follows a classification according to the special structure of the individual organs. This scheme is primarily interesting because it is not bound by hierarchical rigidity of classification – there may be overlappings. Thus there are both egg-laying animals with or without blood. In this way all animal species can be placed in a continuous series ascending from the lower species via fishes, birds, oceanic mammals, and terrestrial mammals to man. This can be exploited in two ways.

In the first place this can be done when one poses the question of nature's why – that is to say when one draws the philosophical consequences of empirical observation. The series of natural species constitutes what has been called the Aristotelian *scala naturae* (nature's ladder). Every species is unchangeable; every individual reproduces the special characteristics of the species; and the species are constant (*De gen. an.* 731 b 31 ff.; cf. *De an.* 415 a 26 ff.). But there are 'transitional forms' – for example, between plants and animals (*De part. an.* 681 a 10 ff.; *Hist. an.* 588 b 4 ff.).

The *scala naturae* denotes a steadily increasing degree of complexity. Since the species are constant, this cannot be interpreted in terms of evolution – as, for example, in Empedocles. It is interpreted in terms of perfection – involving the basic concepts of simple necessity, hypothetical necessity, and finality: every species has its purpose and function, and certain pre-conditions must be fulfilled for the purpose to be realized in a certain matter; the more complex the structure, the higher the place of the particular species. Matter is structured with regard to the formal and the final cause – which would coincide in biology – but these structuring causes are not inherent in matter (*De part. an.* 639 b 11 ff.; 642 a 1 ff.; 645 a 27 ff.; *De gen. an.* 731 b 24 ff.; 788 a 29 ff.). Nature acts as planner, and nature does nothing in vain (*De part. an.* 639 b 30 ff.; 658 a 8 ff.) – metaphysics deals with what is; natural science with the actualization of what ought to be. It is this that the biologist must be able to demonstrate point by point: bones and sinews exist 'for the sake of' flesh, which primarily is the seat of sensation (653 b 30 ff.), animals with horns have their horns in the most appropriate place (553 a 35 ff.), the body exists for the sake of the soul (645 b 13 ff.). Put in the extreme: man is not intelligent by virtue of having hands – that part of the body that is his tool *par excellence*; he has hands because he is intelligent.

In the second place, the *scala naturae* is a flexible conceptual scheme that can serve as the basis for intersecting comparisons of the several organs. Like all physical objects, living beings are composed of elements at the most basic level, next follow the uniform tissues, *homoiomerē*. Most complicated are the individual organs consisting of heterogeneous parts (646 a 12). Mere classification of the organs is, however, not sufficient (655 a 28 ff.). Aristotle was the first who by anatomical comparison made use of the important distinction between homologous and analogous organs – that is to say between such organs that, like arms, wings and fins, have the same anatomical structure and such that, like lungs and gills, have the same function (644 a 23 ff.; 645 b 1 ff.; 653 b 35); he has studied blood circulation and skeleton as special 'systems' in the individual organism (654 a 32 ff.); and he has studied the division of tasks among the organs within the various species (683 a 22 ff.). An especially intricate problem is how the soul can affect the body. It presupposes a special life principle, vital heat, and a special air-like substance, *pneuma* or breath of life, analogous with the ether (*De gen. an.* 736 b 35) – a decidedly awkward explanation; but among other things Aristotle evidently was in need of a stuff with the same function as that of the nervous system.

PSYCHOLOGY

On the *scala naturae* man occupies the highest step; no species can be placed next to man who possesses the most complex constitution, for man is endowed with reason (cf. *Hist. an.* 490 b 18). None the less, the *scala naturae* is a continuum, and man's physical and psychic constitution corresponds in all other respects with that of animals (cf. 588 a 3 ff.). This has consequences for Aristotle's psychology – presented in the *De anima* and supplemented with the *Parva naturalia*, which investigates specific problems. Aristotle based his psychology on a biological basis. Yet the very fact that man is a rational being means not only that in this respect he transcends the animal kingdom – and thereby the biological basis (cf. *Met.* 1026 a 5) – but also that man's other psychic functions acquire a special perspective: his behaviour is determined not by instinct but by reason. Accordingly the *De anima* deals with psychology from man's point of view. Still, the *De anima* does not treat of all sides of Aristotle's view of man. The treatise depicts the naturally-given basis for the conduct of human life. The subject of the *Ethics* and *Politics* is the question of how man, on this basis, can create the optimal life in mutual intercourse. The *Metaphysics* gives an account of the object of man's activity as a contemplative being.

The introduction to the *De anima* is one of the most noble examples of how Aristotle in a few pages is able to lay the foundation of a wholly new philosophical discipline. He begins with a few considerations of method which clearly place the *De anima* in line with the biological writings (*De an.* 402 a 10 ff.). Plato is not mentioned, but between the lines one senses Aristotle's wish to distance himself radically from his psychology. There is no common method for all the empirical sciences. No deductive standard method is applicable – neither the apodictic, Aristotle's own, nor the *diairesis* method, that of the Academy; the reason is that a deductive method presupposes a prior knowledge of essence, and in the empirical sciences the purpose is precisely to discover an explanatory principle or an essence. Therefore – as in biology – one must begin with what is 'more familiar to us' (cf. 413 a 11), which is to say that one must proceed from the soul's attributes to its essence. Nor can one a priori presuppose that the soul has 'parts' (402 b 1 ff.; cf. 411 b 5 ff.; 432 a 22 ff.); it is necessary to start with the soul's functions.

Yet there is a prior knowledge that can be used as a basis, which is that man is a psycho-physical unity (403 a 3 ff.). With the possible exception of thinking, all psychic processes – joy, anger, hate, etc. – will have physical, accompanying phenomena; nor will perception only be tied to pleasure or pain but to a series of complicated physical events, for example, in the sense organs. It is probably the fundamental view of man as a psycho-physical unity that is the radically new in Aristotle's psychology. He introduced the concept of person in the sense that man does not consist of soul + body; he is an animated body. It is not the soul that is angry, just as it is not the soul that builds houses; it is the person who feels or comes to know by means of the soul (408 b 11 ff.).

Aristotle ties this basic view to the traditional Greek one of the soul as a vital principle (413 a 20 ff.), that which makes man not merely a physical object with a certain structure but a being that is born and dies, takes nourishment, multiplies, moves, senses and knows. It is the soul that is the cause of the difference between a dead and a living body (cf. *De part. an.* 640 b 30 ff.). Aristotle's idea of the psycho-physical unity leads to a break with the Pythagorean-Platonic understanding of the soul as an alien guest in the body's prison.

Aristotle tests his basic view in a detailed examination of earlier thinkers (*De an.* 403 b 20 ff.) and their understanding of the soul as mover and the seat of sensation. Clearly he cannot share Plato's view of the soul as a cosmic self-moving mover; indeed he explicitly criticizes the *Timaeus* (404 b 16). But to a like degree he criticizes a materialist and an idealist view, and he is able to employ the same argument: in both cases the soul becomes a person inside the person – Democritus' atoms of soul, for example, behave like mercury sluggishly moving inside the body (406 b 15 ff.; 409 a 31 ff.). Aristotle does not see himself as either materialist or idealist, and hence he cannot consider the soul an epiphenomenon to bodily processes either – as Simmias had tried to do in the *Phaedo* (407 b 27 ff.).

The physical and the psychic are two aspects of man; there is of course an inter-play, but one aspect is not causally dependent on the other. Aristotle considers the psycho-physical processes as a unity, but at the same time he is deliberately operating with two descriptive levels: one is physical, the other psychic. It is a profoundly orig-inal approach to the soul-body problem which means that he does not have to reduce psychic phenomena to physical ones or vice versa – the price of regarding physical and psychic events as parallel is of course that the mutual relation between the two series of events often must be left unexplained. The Aristotelian view of the relation between soul and body almost of itself calls for the formal concepts of form/matter and actuality/potentiality. This conceptual apparatus allows for possibilities that go beyond Plato's explanation of the interplay between soul and body (cf., e.g. Plat. *Phil.* 38 A ff.). It is used in many contexts and with great virtuosity in the *De anima*, most often precisely and in an illuminating way, even though occasionally in such a complicated manner that more becomes blurred than clarified.

The soul is the form of the body (Aristot. *De an.* 412 a 16),[1] and as so often happens, the formal, final, and efficient causes converge (cf. *De an.* 415 b 8 ff.), for the soul is both essence, end and principle of motion. But the soul is also activity: it causes man to act. As designation for activity Aristotle here uses the special term, *entelecheia*, complete actuality, for the soul makes man complete; it is not merely an actualization (*energeia*) of any potentiality. When the soul is related to its special kind of matter it can therefore be defined as the first entelechy of a natural body that potentially possesses life and is furnished with organs (412 a 27; b 5; cf. 414 a 27). Both the definition and the somewhat acrobatic conceptual scheme that lies behind

---

1 Form is a concept with several applications, and it makes Aristotle's precise formulation more complicated than is really necessary. *Qua* form the soul is in fact also called substance, i.e. a substance is here – as in the *Metaphysics* – taken to be the immaterial constituent of an object consisting of form and matter, that which is predicated of matter. In its relation to matter the soul is accordingly form, as an essential determination of 'what-it-means-to-be-a-man' substance (cf. *Met.* 1035 b 14; 1043 b 2; cf. p. 355). This is not a particularly fortunate application of the concept of substance in a work that does not acknowledge a person inside a person. The reason must be that the substantial form of the body is not to be construed as the external structure (*morphē*) but as the quintessence of all manifestations of life – what distinguishes the living from the dead.

it[2] can be misunderstood. The soul as entelechy has often been interpreted vitalistically, so that the soul was understood as a mystical force inside the body – but this is precisely what Aristotle objects to; here, as everywhere, his formal concepts are not hypostatized entities but a descriptive apparatus: the person is described as living. Aristotle himself warns against another possible misunderstanding (414 b 20 ff.): the definition must include all vital manifestations in all living beings, and therefore it is so general that its real informative value is more than doubtful. Nor is it Aristotle's last word, it marks out the frame for the analysis that follows, and in fact Aristotle proceeds to a systematization of the functions that are observable in living beings.

Now a special form of *scala naturae* appears (414 a 29 ff.): plants as well as animals take nourishment and multiply – they have a 'vegetative faculty'; in addition animals can sense, and the faculty of sense perception is closely tied to the feeling of pleasure and pain and thereby to impulses to action, to 'motion'; only man is also furnished with the faculty of reason. In his closer reflections on this step-like sequence, Aristotle demonstrates his predilection for ascertaining structural similarities as well as differences in a divided continuum – just as he does in the biological writings. The sequence differentiates between and connects plants, animals and men, and the most complicated being, man, occupies the highest step: perception (414 b 33 ff.; cf. *Eth. Nic.* 1102 a 32 ff.) does imply vegetative functions – but not vice versa – and reason does imply perception – but not vice versa. The structural similarity manifests itself in there being an activity at all three levels linking a subject with an object, although in different ways. Nourishment brings about a physical change in both subject and object: when I eat an apple, something physical happens to both the apple and to me. Perception is also a relation between subject and object, but without physical changes – apart from the fact that the sensory organ perhaps undergoes a qualitative change: when I look at an apple, the apple does not change, although something does occur between the apple and me. Thinking and reasoning do not imply matter; a subject and an object of thought are presupposed, but not two physical magnitudes: I may think of the concept of apple without having an apple before me.

Aristotle makes short shrift of the vegetative functions (416 a 19 ff.) – a closer analysis belongs to biology. Perception, on the other hand, is a very complicated phenomenon in which Aristotle gradually includes the behaviour of the entire perceiving being. He operates with two basic models: in part the parallel courses of physical and psychic events; in part the relation between activity, subject and object. The former model includes the formal concepts of form and matter; the latter actuality and potentiality.

The details in the description of the physical events between object and subject

---

2   'First entelechy' is yet another quite complicated term – the subject itself is complex. The concept of *entelecheia* is here connected with the concept of *hexis*, disposition, so that the distinction between active and passive is employed at two levels. Just as knowledge can both signify an ability and the employment of that ability, the soul's entelechy can be understood both as a disposition (the first entelechy or *hexis*) and as an employment of the disposition (the second entelechy): both the man who is asleep and he who is awake are alive; the sleeper can accomplish what the man who is awake in fact does accomplish. Accordingly the first entelechy is actuality relative to a natural body furnished with organs, potentiality as relative to the actualization of its disposition.

and in the perceiving person (418 a 20 ff.) may perhaps – as in the case of Democritus – only be of interest in a catalogue of curiosities in the history of science – for example, that the heart is the central sensory organ or that the impressions on sense and imagination are 'transported' by the blood (*Insomn.* 461 a 25 ff.). The fundamental position is that sensation presupposes physical contact. Such physical contact is most clearly present in the basic and most primitive sense, that of touch (*De an.* 413 b 4 ff.; 414 b 33 ff.). A 'medium' must be presupposed for sight and hearing (418 a 26 ff.; 419 b 4 ff.) – air or water, for example – which mediates the contact or 'the motion' from object to subject. From a philosophical point of view this is not essential; nor is it decisive whether one for example thinks with the head or the heart. What is decisive is Aristotle's attitude to the psycho-physical problem itself. On the physical level it is clearly a question of causal efficacy: a stimulus from a sense object affects a sense organ (cf. 417 a 14 ff.); if the stimulus is too intense it may harm the sense organ and thereby the sense faculty; and special circumstances can for example cause an after-image (425 b 24). But the process of sense perception as a whole is not considered in this way. The course of physical events is a substratum for the psychic, as is matter for form; the physical impact is – as in Plato – the occasion of and not the cause of the sense experience itself. It may well fade into obscurity how, for example, the blood can transport a sense image to the heart, and it is true that Aristotle no better than anyone else can provide a plausible explanation of how physical events suddenly can 'come to be' psychic experiences. But the problem is not as fatal for him as it is in a strict causal theory of perception: perception is not a one-dimensional course of events.

Perception is also a psychic activity directed at an object; as in the *Theaetetus*, it includes an explicit or implicit judgement about the sense experience. Aristotle states directly that perception is like an affirmation or denial (431 a 8 ff.). Every sense judges of its special object – for example, 'this is red' – and such a judgement is always, or practically always true (418 a 11 ff.; 428 b 18; 430 b 29), which must mean that it is true that I sense something red and almost always true that objectively something red is present. Several senses can have sense objects in common: primary sense qualities such as movement, size, and extension (418 a 16 ff.; *De mem.* 450 a 9 ff., which adds time). Finally there are 'accidental' objects of perception, which is to say interpreted sense objects: I can, for example, on the basis of several sense qualities judge that this is Diares' son (*De an.* 418 a 20) – such a judgement or a judgement about 'common' sense objects may be true or false (428 b 19 ff.). However, this is not to be taken to mean that the total perceptual experience is secondary to the elements present in the individual senses. The perceptual act applies primarily to the entire sense situation (cf. 426 b 23; *De sens.* 449 a 8) – which then can be analyzed in its elements; therefore a 'common sense' must be presupposed, which coordinates the individual senses and makes an identification of objects possible (*De an.* 425 a 14 ff.). It is not least important that sense awareness must also be presupposed; man cannot sense without at the same time being aware *that* he senses (425 b 12 ff.; *De somno* 455 a 16 ff.) – it is not a reflection about sensation but an immediate awareness of sensation *as* sensation; it corresponds with empirical apperception in Kant. Every human activity, not only sensation, is accompanied by such a continuous awareness of itself (*Eth. Nic.* 1170 a 25 ff.): I see, hear, walk, perceive, think, live, and I am aware of all of this at the same time. As for every other basic vital manifestation, it holds true for sensation that it is a process that includes the purpose in itself, not a process directed towards an end (cf. above, p. 325, about 'complete motion').

My awareness that I sense cannot, however, be separated from what I sense. The sensing subject, the sensed object, and the sense act mutually presuppose each other. The same applies to the physical and psychic parallel courses: the sense organ is influenced physically by the object while the sensing person at the same time judges of the object. These two 'basic models' are worked into a common phenomenological description. That physical objects exist, even when they are not sensed, is as certain as the existence of sense organs and sensing persons prior to the sense process. In the sense process the physical object is actualized as sense object, and the faculty of sense is actualized as sensation (*De an.* 426 a 15 ff.; *Met.* 1010 b 30 ff.). The sense organ is of course physical, but the ability to sense is not. Sensation, on the other hand, is a unity, and therefore a phenomenological description of this unity can consider organ and faculty as only differing in definition – they are not two different things, but a non-physical function with its location in a physical thing (*De an.* 424 a 24 ff.). The same mode of description can be extended to the sense act, the process that connects sense object with sense subject. Object and subject are of course separate physical entities, but the sense act is common; a sound, for example, is produced by an object and is perceived by a subject; something is sounding and something is hearing; but the activity is one and the same phenomenon (425 b 26 ff.; cf. 426 a 15; 420 a 19). In this respect sense perception is accordingly a special case of motion in general. This subtle application of the scheme of actuality/potentiality respects the factual separation of physical entities and opens at the same time for the possibility of a differentiated description of the psycho-physical sequence of events.

Even greater perspectives in the Aristotelian conceptual apparatus appear when the act of sense perception is interpreted by means of the concepts of form and matter. When I perceive an object, I do not absorb it at a gulp; I take in the sensory form of the object without its matter, just as a piece of wax receives an imprint (424 a 17). This metaphor can be misinterpreted (cf. the corresponding image for intellectual cognition, 429 b 31) – the soul is not a *tabula rasa* in the sense that it is only passively receptive of forms. On the physical level it receives a sense impression or an image (431 a 15) – but, to use a modified quotation from Thomas Aquinas (Thom. Aq. *Summ. theol.* I 85, 2), the image is not that which I perceive but that whereby I perceive, which is to say that the image does not direct attention to itself but towards what it depicts (cf. Aristot. *De mem.* 450 b 21). As both commentators from late Antiquity and Hegel insisted (cf. Them. in Aristot. *De an.* 78, 7; Philop. in Aristot. *De an.* 437,9; Hegel, *Gesch. d. Philos.*, Jub. Ausg. XVIII, 378 ff.), the wax metaphor does not in fact apply to the material side of the process but to an isomorphism between soul and perceived object – corresponding to the common activity – and to the soul's active interpretation of sense data in agreement with a *logos*. The physical event is still the occasion for, not the cause of perception, and the sensible forms are not essentially different from intelligible forms – they are forms *qua* sensed. But what is it that makes it certain that the soul perceives by means of an image and that the image is not a distorting intermediary between person and reality? It is the fact that the soul and the external world are formally identical. In the thing form exists with matter; in the soul as perceived form (Aristot. *De an.* 429 a 27); and the soul is identical with its contents. In itself the soul is nothing (429 b 31), potentially it is everything; and this potentiality is actualized through cognition, whether intellectual or perceptual – the intellect is the form of forms and sense the form of objects of perception (431 b 20 ff.; cf. 418 a 3; 431 a 1), and the objects of thought are included in the objects of perception (432 a 3). This actualization of formal identity means that Aristotle has no 'problem of the external world' and no interest in 'private' psychic phenomena, and it makes possible the 'grasping' of the universal in the particular, which is dealt with in different contexts both in logic and metaphysics (see p. 311 and p. 351). The soul cannot 'err' with respect to the form itself, but it can undertake a false identification and for example judge that this is Diares' son. John Duns Scotus characterized the thinking in this way: it is not the mutability of perceived objects that causes knowledge, but their nature; and the nature of mutable things is immutable (Duns Scot. *Op. Ox.* III 4, art. 3).

'Theory of abstraction' is the label that the medieval tradition affixed to Aristotle's understanding of the act of perception – by a complicated mechanism the soul abstracts the intelligible forms from a given material of experience. But in Aristotle there is no complicated mechanism, nor is it a question of the formation of concepts but of cognition of concepts – not of abstraction but of an actualization of a potentiality that already is at hand. Here, as elsewhere, Aristotle should not be identified with Aristotelianism.

Perception occupies an extremely important place in Aristotle's psychology, and hence perception should not really be considered in isolation. This means not only that the entire field of perception – subject, object, act of perception – should be included, but also that perception epistemologically is tied to intellectual cognition and that it is closely connected with all other human behaviour. In the concrete situation perception immediately provokes a feeling of pleasure or pain, which in its turn provokes a desire to attain or avoid something and leads to an act. All this could be expressed in judgement-like statements: this is an x (a perceptual judgement), I like x, I want to attain x, I act (Aristot. *De an.* 431 a 8 ff.; *Eth. Nic.* 1139 a 21 ff.). Now, what governs this process? The object of a person's desire – a real or seeming good – is the final cause, on a small scale an unmoved mover (433 a 26 ff.). On the subject side both a rational and desiring element are included, although the two elements cannot be separated. The act is initiated by desire (*orexis*) which sets the goal together with practical insight that realizes the situation and finds the means (433 a 9 ff.). This analysis of human actions is an essential basis of Aristotle's ethics.

Practical insight is of course only one function of intellect. Intellect can also be directed towards pure theoretical knowledge, and here as well there is close connection with perception. The continuity between perception and intellectual cognition is established by means of the concept of *phantasia*, imagination. All cognition comes about by means of mental images, *phantasmata* – what appears (*phainetai*) – and *phantasia* is the ability to perceive these images. An image is derived from a sensed impression, but although *phantasia* is an epiphenomenon to man's cognitive faculties, it is not identical with perception, belief, or knowledge. *Phantasia* is not perception, for in opposition to perception I myself can recall an image in my memory; or it may present itself – in dreams (427 b 16 ff.; 428 a 5 ff.; *De mem.* 450 a 25 ff.). Nor is it identical with belief, which is true or false, or with knowledge, which is always true. *Phantasia* is most often false, or rather: *phantasia* has no truth value, for I can imagine something without claiming that it is true; in the imagination the sun, for example, comes to have a one-foot long diameter, but I do believe that it is larger than the inhabited world (*De an.* 428 a 5 ff.; b 1 ff.). Nor is thinking imagining, but thinking cannot take place without images (431 b 2; 432 a 10). In other words, *phantasia* is a psychological, not an epistemological concept.

Evidently Aristotle wants to keep two things apart (cf. 429 a 12): it is one thing to ask how thinking takes place – that is a psychological question; it is something else to ask what thinking is 'in itself'. With the latter question one transcends psychology, for in itself thinking goes beyond man as a biological being.

The structural similarity between perception and thinking – the function of reason – consists in both cases in a unification of subject, object and act. As has been mentioned, this may be expressed in such a way that soul – by means of sense perception or intellectual cognition – potentially is everything and in itself nothing. Through cognition the soul is formally identified with its object – which is Aristotle's version of the fundamental thought in Greek idealism: according to Parmenides being and thinking are the same; according to Plato soul is akin to ideas. But when soul perceives the form, it is not identified with the entire object – the perceived object exists outside soul and is composed of form and matter; it is a 'this in a this'; only the form is perceived. Intellect – *nous* – on the other hand, cannot be affected by any external object, and hence one may think independently of an external object's being to hand or not. Nor is *nous* dependent on material organs: it is immaterial and therefore incomposite. Consequently the formal identity is complete: the soul is the seat of the forms. The identity between subject, act, and object is likewise complete: when thinking is actualized, intellect will have itself as object (429 a 13 ff.; cf. 417 b 16 ff.).

Now, if one were to ask how thinking takes place, the answer would be two-fold, depending on the cognitive mode and the object of cognition (430 a 26 ff.; cf. 429 b 10 ff.). The intellect can think discursively – dianoetically – about composite objects. Such an act of thinking occurs in time and can be formulated as a judgement that is either true or false and composed exactly like the state of affairs to which the judgement pertains (see p. 300). But a presupposition for such discursive thought is the existence of an immediate, non-temporal knowledge of objects, which are or are considered incomposite. A continuum – for example a line – can be traversed section by section, but it can also immediately be grasped in its totality. An essence – what it is to be an x – is an incomposite object, which simply is and which is grasped with immediate evidence. An essence is not a judgement – therefore it is neither true nor false – but the grasping of essences makes judgements possible, as for example a definition or an identification of an object. Within the mode of perception, the immediate grasp of an essence corresponds with the perception by each individual sense of its own special object (cf. 430 b 29). In a psychological context Aristotle hereby arrives at the very ontology of cognition – the relation between intuitive and discursive thought – which is a fundamental feature in logical and metaphysical contexts (see p. 311 and p. 359.).

But with this Aristotle can also ask: what is thinking 'in itself'? – thinking as pure actuality regardless of who is thinking? He formulated his further thoughts about this 'active intellect' quite tersely, and it has occasioned widely different interpretations. Once again it is important to stay clear of the complicated metaphysics of cognition which medieval Aristotelians – especially Thomas Aquinas – erected on the basis of Aristotle. It is better to realize what kind of philosophical problem Aristotle himself tries to solve on his own terms. Concepts and relations between concepts appear to exist inter-subjectively, independently of individual man. By means of his cognitive faculties, man has access to this conceptual world, although he does not master it. Still, it is not so much the contents of thought – *what* we think – that is problematic for Aristotle; rather it is the very fact *that* we think. Even this is beyond our control. In the physical world contingent motion presupposes an eternal, necessary motion and a mover. Thinking is a kind of motion; human thought functions momentarily, but thus must presuppose a necessary, eternal 'pure' thinking. Aristotle formulates this within his scheme of actuality/potentiality (430 a 10 ff.). The human intellect is potentially everything, and as potentiality – or as 'passive intellect' – it is subject to the influence of possible thought objects. In and by the actualization of this possibility the thought object, the thought subject and the thought act become a unity – an identification that transcends Plato. Aristotle says that intellect (*nous*) as actuality creates everything, just as light actualizes potential colour. This does not mean that this 'active intellect' creates this or that thought object; it means rather that – as the light in Plato's simile of the sun – it makes it knowable. The 'active intellect' then makes partial or deficient – human – knowledge possible. Man is mortal, and to man pure intellectual knowledge is only present partially and momentarily – I grasp the essence of this object in such a manner that my intellect becomes identical with its content. But this cannot come about unless thinking or intellect 'in itself' exists eternally, is unaffected, 'separated', and independent of man, as the warrant of all knowledge whatsoever. Man is not immortal, but the active intellect, to which man has access, is so.

Aristotle goes no further in the *De anima*. He harbours an unmistakable reluctance to speak of the divine, and indeed further-reaching metaphysical perspectives have their proper place in the 'theology' (see p. 360 ff.). In the *De anima* he does the same as in the *Physics*. He shows that psychology, like physics, reaches a limit, a point at which the special science points beyond itself towards a divine, transcendent principle, which in the final analysis turns the world into a systematic totality.

22

METAPHYSICS AND THEOLOGY

———— •◆• ————

'By nature all men desire to know' (*Met*. 980 a 21). With this famous dictum Aristotle begins his *Metaphysics*. The apparently simple sentence is loaded with Aristotelian terminology. It claims that knowledge is the final cause of human desire (*orexis*), and that this desire is inherent in human nature. It is an essential determination of man that refers to a *praxis* – an activity that has its purpose and meaning in itself – and this purpose is realized by the free, reputable man who is his own master (982 b 26).

Knowledge or wisdom (*sophia* – 981 a 25) combines intuitive reason with *epistēmē*, the demonstrative science of the necessary truths, and it is distinguished from rationally founded skills and from practical insight (*technē* and *phronēsis*), as Aristotle goes on to state (981 b 25; cf. *Eth. Nic*. 1139 b 14 ff.). Theoretical knowledge or *sophia* is elevated above all practical undertakings and is the highest knowledge, for it is directed at the highest object, the first principles of nature, which are necessary and therefore must become the object of the most exact knowledge (*Met*. 982 a 25). Knowledge of the highest object is knowledge of the divine. But is it not hubris for man to concern himself with the divine (b 28)? No, for the godhead is without jealousy, and insight into the divine is the most honourable for man – as we are told in two concealed quotations from Plato (from the *Timaeus* and the *Theaetetus*, see p. 239 and p. 221). Behind this lies Aristotle's own anthropology: man achieves the highest when he transcends his humanity.

The exercise of *theōria*, theoretical knowledge or knowledge for its own sake (*Met*. 982 a 15), is a *praxis*; but the contents of *theōria* on the other hand – the question what the highest knowledge is knowledge of – is not. The goal of theoretical science is truth; the goal of practical knowledge is action (cf. 993 b 20).

The *Analytica posteriora* ended by asking how one attains insight into the first principles. The *Metaphysics* begins by asking the same question; metaphysics begins where logic ends. The connection is established by means of the schematic account of the path of knowledge from sensation to memory, from memory to experience, from experience to theoretical knowledge, and the 'art' that is based on general knowledge (980 a 27 ff.; cf. *Anal. post*. 99 b 15 ff.). But in the beginning of the *Metaphysics* not much is said about the role of intuitive reason – *nous* – for this is the main subject throughout the rest of the work. On the other hand, more is said about experience, implicit general knowledge, which for example enables the artisan to cope with a situation and a practical problem. This knowledge makes him more able than the theorist in practical affairs, but the theorist is 'all-knowing' in the sense that he knows the universal causes so that he not only can identify the 'that' of nature but also its 'why'. His knowledge is about what comes first 'according to nature', which is the most certain knowledge but also the most difficult, because the universal is farthest from the particular that is present in immediate sense perception. Wonder is the point of departure for the philosopher's rational explanations; but in the past it was also the starting point of the 'mythologists' – rational thought is heir to myth.

The introduction to the *Metaphysics* is clear and immediately understandable; evidently it is addressed to the ordinary, educated reader – and it is in fact adapted from the exoteric pamphlet in defence of philosophy, the *Protrepticus*.

The rest of the *Metaphysics* does not possess the formal virtues of the introduction. The *Metaphysics* is a very difficult work, and, as left to us, it is evidently heterogeneous; several different lectures have been combined, perhaps by Aristotle himself, perhaps by Andronicus, and a provisional table of contents may be to the purpose (traditionally the individual books are designated by Greek letters). The first book – A – is Aristotle's 'history of philosophy'. Here he discusses his philosophical predecessors with one basic question in mind: to what extent did these earlier thinkers prepare the way for the basic Aristotelian scheme of concepts, the four causes? According to Aristotle, the earliest natural philosophers only paid attention to the material cause; the later ones had a vague inkling of the other three – Empedocles stutters hopelessly, but in fact he is on the right track (*Met.* 985 a 4 ff.; cf. 993 a 17), and Anaxagoras speaks like a sober man amidst foghorns (984 b 15 ff.). Major parts of A are devoted to the confrontation with Plato and the Academics (987 a 29 ff.; 990 a 33 ff.; cf. 1078 b 7 ff.): 'we' Academics have abandoned the real task of philosophy to seek the causes of what is manifest to perception (992 a 24). This polemic has its own special character; however, when it comes to other philosophers one should not be led astray by the somewhat condescending style. Aristotle's 'history of philosophy' is a philosophical debate on Aristotelian premises, and it is at the very least also a compliment to the old 'primitive' lovers of wisdom from whose tradition Aristotle sees his own questions arise. To A is added a minor appendix, α, probably the work of a student (Aristot. *Met.* 993 a 30 sch. Brandis). It contains clear and in places beautifully phrased formulations of basic Aristotelian principles.

B is a collection of 'aporias'. It is an important text because – often with a point of departure in the Academy – it provides Aristotle's own formulations of the principal metaphysical problems and thereby prepares for the 'solutions' presented in the later books. It is not until Γ that the subject of metaphysics is determined; otherwise the book primarily deals with the principle of contradiction. Δ is an independent text – a 'dictionary' of basic Aristotelian concepts and – as is characteristic for Aristotle – takes the form of a survey of the different 'meanings' a given concept may have in given contexts. E begins once more by asking the question about the nature and subject matter of the 'first philosophy'. Z–H–Θ constitute a coherent, difficult, and central investigation of 'being as substance'. I once again breaks off with an analysis of the concept of unity and related concepts. K – which it is unlikely that Aristotle wrote himself – consists in part of a compilation of some of the earlier books and in part of excerpts from the *Physics*. In Λ follows Aristotle's theology. As a contrast to this the last books, M and N deal with the Academy theories of supra-sensory first principles. These books, which especially review Speusippus and Xenocrates critically, do not make for easy reading, which is due not only to the difficulty of the subject and because other sources are scarce; Aristotle's basic, hostile position does not contribute to clarity.

It will immediately be seen that as a work the *Metaphysics* is no carefully constructed unit; but here no attempt at chronological placing of the individual parts will be made. It is a quite different question whether the scattered treatises represent one underlying theory. What follows has been written from the point of view that such a theory in fact exists – an Aristotelian 'metaphysics'. But it is hoped that it should also be clear that such a theory can be challenged and why. For obvious reasons, a continuous book-by-book examination does not recommend itself. The account will seek to extract a coherence between the following three main problems: what is the subject and task of the 'first philosophy' (books Γ, E and I)? – What is implied by assigning 'being' to the concept of substance (the connected books Z, H and Θ)? – In what sense can the metaphysics be called theology (book Λ)? Books A, M and N have been considered in different contexts in the preceding; K can only be used as a secondary reference text; and B and Δ will be consulted steadily.

WHAT IS 'BEING'?

What is being and what does 'is' mean? This is the subject of metaphysics. But what is implied by the question, and is there one 'science' that can provide the answers? It may look as if there is a dilemma. Each science deals with one particular delimited area of reality but presupposes that something is and presupposes some universal 'causes' and 'principles' that precede the science in question. These causes and principles can be formally dealt with in logic; if they cannot be dealt with 'really' – that is, if they do not hold for something that in a fundamental sense is – then the individual sciences have no ontological basis, and then it is impossible to speak about the world as a coherent whole. But can a specialized science treat of the universal, and is 'is' an unambiguous concept (*Met.* 996 a 18 ff.; b 26 ff.; 997 a 15 ff.; 25 ff.; *Eth. Eud.* 1217 b 34)?

There is a science of being (*Met.* 1003 a 21 ff; 1025 b 3 ff.). Unlike other sciences, it does not concern itself with a region of reality but with that which is, in so far as (*qua*) it is (*to on hēi on*). Mathematics abstracts from the real object, physics deals with changeable objects *qua* changeable, and metaphysics concentrates on this one basic fact: the object 'is'. This means that 'being' cannot be taken as an abstract concept apart from 'that which is', the time-honoured translation 'being *qua* being' is therefore misleading, nor is there mention of existence in contrast to essence. Aristotle speaks – in modified modern terms – of 'the being of that which is', and he belongs so much to the older tradition that to him 'to be' will always mean to be something definite (cf. 1006 a 28). But in the *Metaphysics* he focuses on a series of ontological basic determinations, which for every object follows from the fact that it is. The subject matter of metaphysics is the highest and the most universal, for there is nothing besides being. It concerns itself with that which the specialized sciences presuppose and is therefore superior to them – also to logic, which must presuppose for example essence and definition. Inasmuch as 'being' is investigated as a metaphysical concept, it can come as no surprise that Aristotle does not care that 'is' logically can have several meanings or can be used in different ways (in modern parlance, the existential, copulative or identifying 'is').

Nevertheless, it is decisive that 'what is' also in a metaphysical sense 'is said with several meanings', as we are told in a standard formula (1017 a 7 ff.; 1003 a 33; 1026 a 33 ff.; 1028 a 10 ff.). 'Is' can be used accidentally – the master builder may be musical, the physician may be his own patient – but there is no science about accidental being (1027 a 29 ff.).

There are, however, three other pertinent 'meanings' of metaphysical relevance. 'Is' can be used in connection with the categories – i.e. in the determination of the essence of a thing (the category of substance) or its secondary properties (the other categories); it can be applied to modes of being, which is to say to actuality or potentiality; and it may be used in the sense of 'being as truth'. In other words, one can ask what a thing is, what it can become, and what may in truth be said about it; and if one succeeds in making the structure of these questions clear, one has thereby – according to the basic Aristotelian view – uncovered an ontological, basic structure. They are three different questions but must necessarily be connected.

But the matter is not settled merely by establishing different 'meanings' – different usage, that is to say – of the word and concept of 'is'. If that were all, the project of a general investigation of 'that which is in so far as it is' would be doomed to failure at once. Being is not an unambiguous concept and it cannot function as *summum genus* or as a superordinate concept above a series of parallel species. Thus it is not a synonymous concept, nor is it homonymous (cf. 1003 a 33 ff.; 1060 b 31 ff.) in such a way that there is no connection whatsoever between the different 'meanings'. There are other concepts that similarly lie between synonyms and homonyms, so to speak. 'Healthy', for example, may refer to 'health', 'man', 'medicine', or 'way of life'. But it has one central meaning, 'a sound state of health'. In just the same way, 'what is' has reference to one central instance, that of substance – which is already implicit in the enumeration of the several 'meanings': there is no question of properties, unless a bearer of properties is presupposed, nor is it a question of actuality and potentiality or of truth unless the substance is presupposed as that which is actualized or as that about which something is true.

Thus different conceptual applications have reference to a central instance. Aristotle himself has no term for such a conceptual structure; in modern interpretations expressions such as 'focal meaning' and '*pros hen*' structure (modelled on '*pros hen*': with respect to one – 1003 a 33; cf. 1030 b 3; 1043 a 37; *Eth. Nic.* 1096 b 27) are employed. Often this conceptual structure is considered an innovation in the *Metaphysics*. But there is no reason for that – already in the *Categories* it was the sustaining conceptual scheme; that it is not found in the *Analytics* is for the sound reason that a syllogism must build on synonymous terms. But that the same scheme is to be found in the *Categories* and the *Metaphysics* does not mean that it has the same content in the two treatises. The matter becomes complicated the moment one asks whether a 'thing' adequately meets the demand of the concept of substance for self-identity and independence.

Γ and E have in common that they determine the subject of metaphysics as 'that which is in so far as it is' and introduce the idea of a primary instance of 'being'. But E goes somewhat further. This occurs in a section that is taken to be the Aristotelian *locus classicus* for the classification of the sciences (*Met.* 1025 b 18 ff.). Among the theoretical sciences physics is concerned with independent autonomous substances that 'have the principle of motion in themselves'; but these are substances that are not separated from matter. The objects of mathematics are immaterial and most often immovable – but they are abstractions. Now, if there are independent ('separate') and immovable substances, they must belong to a special science, and in that case this science must be called first philosophy or theology; in the opposite case, physics will be first philosophy.

The passage – perhaps the most commented upon and debated in the entire *Metaphysics* – is remarkable for two reasons. In the first place it is formulated with the greatest caution – *if* there are independent and immovable (and hence immaterial) substances. Presumably there can be no doubt that 'if' should be replaced by 'since', but so far that has not been shown to be the case. Nor is anything said about the nature of incorporeal substances, and it is left up in the air whether there are one or several incorporeal substances (cf. 1064 a 33).

In the second place – and this is the more important – one may ask how one then is to understand the relation between metaphysics as the science of that which is, in so far as it is, and metaphysics as theology, the science of the eternal and divine. Is metaphysics general ontology or theology? In the later tradition a distinction came to be maintained between *metaphysica generalis* and *metaphysica specialis* (the terminology is presumably as late as the seventeenth century). In modern times many have thought that the two views are incompatible – that Γ represents one metaphysical project and E another. But Γ and E are not incompatible, and Aristotle himself provides a commentary. He says that one may ask (1026 a 23 ff.) whether the first philosophy is universal or deals with one particular 'nature'. The answer is that if there is one immovable substance, the first philosophy will have it as its object and be universal, *because* it is first. In other words: one can only study that which is in so far as it is, if there is something that 'is' in a primary sense and warrants that something else 'is'. In fact both Γ and E have prepared for this conclusion – through the idea of a primary instance of 'being'. This is first brought to bear in a familiar area: the substance that is the precondition for further determinations. Then, secondly, it is applied to a primary substance that warrants the existence of physical substances. It is a general Aristotelian thought that the prototype explains the general type (cf. 1003 b 16 ff.), and in its final consequence it means that nothing can exist unless something exists in a primary sense. This view has been of seminal importance in the entire European metaphysical tradition. It may be criticized as ambiguous and inconsistent, but there cannot very well be doubt about the nature of Aristotle's metaphysical programme. The main problem in the *Metaphysics* is not whether there are two projects but whether and how the one project is carried out.

Aristotle's prolegomena to what a metaphysics should deal with allows for several approaches. One can, for example, examine the very general concepts that – like being – must be included in a metaphysics, so to speak before one introduces the idea of a primary instance; by itself such an examination would be a *metaphysica generalis*. Being can be predicated of everything, although not in the same way. In the *Categories* the concept of being functions as a sort of limit, as a predicate which may be stated of everything within each category but which transcends the table of categories, because it is not stated synonymously about the categorial designations themselves. Transcendent concepts – the *transcendentalia* – were dealt with systematically in the medieval tradition, most subtly by John Duns Scotus (*ens, unum, bonum, verum* and *aliquid* are the concepts most frequently termed *transcendentalia* during the Middle Ages). Aristotle did not deal with the transcendent concepts in a completed, systematic form, but it is important to him to establish that there are concepts with the same structure as being. This is first of all the case with the concept of unity – to which he devoted a special book, I (1052 a 15 ff.; cf. 1015 b 16 ff.): everything that is is one. It is also the case with truth, about which we are told that everything relates itself to truth as it relates to being (993 b 30). The good is also mentioned as *transcendentale* (*Eth. Nic.* 1096 a 19), but this concept presumably occupies a special position: everything that is is not simply good, but 'good' can be predicated in all categories. To the central concept of unity are tied such concepts as plurality, identity, difference, similarity, dissimilarity (cf. *Met.* 1004 a 9 ff.; b 27 ff.; 1054 a 20 ff.; 1056 b 3 ff.).

Most of these concepts play a significant role in Plato's metaphysics – precisely because they have universal applicability and therefore make it possible for anything whatsoever to exist and be known. Aristotle's interest lies elsewhere. In evident opposition to Plato, he emphasizes (1053 b 16) that unity and being are not substances but predicates. This means that unity and being are not pre-conditions for existence but designations of something existing. To Aristotle the general concepts cannot sustain an independent metaphysics; they refer to concrete entities – in the final analysis to what in a primary sense is or is one. It is of no metaphysical interest that something is identical with itself or different from something else (1041 a 14).

Unity and being are the most universal predicates, and hence they cannot, strictly speaking, be defined (998 b 22), for a definition presupposes a *differentia specifica*, which itself must be and be one. It is, however, intuitively clear that the two concepts have different contents but that they are convertible (cf. 1053 b 24). They have the same extension, for they are applied to the same objects: 'man' is equivalent with 'one man' and 'one existing man' (1003 b 23 ff.), but they have different meanings. In his analysis of the concept of unity Aristotle therefore distinguishes precisely between what unity is predicated of and 'what-it-means-to-be one'. To be sure, unity cannot be defined, but the meaning of the word can be determined formally (1052 b 15 ff.). To be one means to be indivisible and to be a 'this such' – in other words, to be something that can be determined, whether with respect to space, form, numerical or conceptual unity.

These most general predicates refer to that which they are predicated of, and thereby a 'general metaphysics' refers to a metaphysics about primary instances or substances. This connection also appears in the general axioms. As has been mentioned, both the principle of contradiction and the principle of the excluded middle are ontologically based, and hence these principles are formulated in the

Metaphysics. The principles that apply to statements or opinions about things are the same as those that apply to the thing itself, and accordingly Aristotle can easily formulate the principle of contradiction ontologically, psychologically, as well as logically (1005 b 19; 23; 1011 a 19 ff.). The principle of contradiction is treated at most length (1005 a 19 ff.). The principle of the excluded middle can be accounted for by analogous arguments; the two principles are apparently considered complementary and equally evident.

The principle of contradiction was anticipated by Plato (Plat. *RP* IV 436 B, see p. 206), and it is indeed clear that Aristotle also in his further argumentation builds on him, especially on the arguments of the *Theaetetus* against Protagoras (cf., e.g. Aristot. *Met.* 1010 b 12). To Aristotle Protagoras stands as the chief spokesman for the view that everything is true, but this is self-refuting: if everything is true, everything is false, and if everything both is and is-not, everything is true (1009 a 6 ff.). If Protagoras is right in claiming that one can deny and affirm the same about the same, man would be identical with a man-of-war or a wall (1007 b 20). Antisthenes' linguistic theory is also criticized without its author being mentioned. What matters are not particular persons but a position that leads to the cancellation of the concept of truth.

The argumentation takes the form of a debate with an imagined opponent – we may call him Protagoras or, simply the 'Sceptic'. A non-hypothetical first principle (note the 'Platonic' terminology) must exist, Aristotle maintains, which is valid for everything 'that is in so far as it is'. It must be a principle which makes any form of knowledge possible and which itself is beyond any doubt. The principle of contradiction is such a principle (1005 b 5 ff.). Inasmuch as it is a precondition for knowledge and thereby for proof, it cannot itself be demonstratively proved; it can only be demonstrated by indirect proof. How can it be demonstrated to the imagined opponent? By making him open his mouth to say something meaningful – if he won't do that, he is no better than a plant. If he expresses himself in language, he must presuppose that language is comprehensible, and it is only that if the expression has definite truth value – which is to say that he presupposes the principle of contradiction.

Normal linguistic usage could not be explained by Antisthenes' picture and element theory. But it can be explained if the particular word has one or only a limited number of definable meanings, and if – as in Plato's and Aristotle's linguistic theory – there is a distinction between meaning and reference (1006 a 28 ff.). If 'to be a man' means the same as 'not to be a man', language would be meaningless, and a meaningless language would – according to Aristotle as well as to Plato – be a mark of ontological chaos. On the other hand, the function of language as meaningful communication cannot merely be accounted for by a theory of reference (1006 b 11 ff.). If 'white', 'musical' and 'man' refer to different things, we would never be able to say of a man that he is white or musical. If the three terms refer to the same thing, 'white', 'musical' and 'man' will 'mean' the same, and then everything means everything. As language in fact does function, each of the three terms has its own meaning; they can indicate something about one and the same subject, and thereby something true or false is stated.

Now, if one pursues the directions of language itself, it will turn out – with or without the Sceptic's sanction – that language itself points to an Aristotelian conceptual structure. We know from the *Categories* that what is predicated of the species 'man' is also predicated of the individual man, while that which is predicated of a quality cannot be predicated of the object that possesses this quality. Language presupposes that in principle there is a difference between 'being man' and 'being white' and therefore it compels us to distinguish between essential and accidental designations. If this distinction did not exist, the whole world would consist of accidents of accidents, and such a world would be a not-world.

The argumentation shows how the Aristotelian conceptual structure grows out of his own linguistic theory. The fictitious Sceptic himself is not given occasion to indicate how far he is willing to follow suit. This is Aristotle speaking, and he is allowed to say what the Sceptic ought to think. He should reflect, for example, that he himself is acting in accordance with the principle of contradiction (1008 b 12; 1010 b 9). It is true enough that the wine is sweet to one person and sour to another (1010 b 3 ff.); but if one specifies to whom, when and under what circumstances something comes about, the concept of truth has not been made relative – the phenomenal object is not identical with the real object (1011 a 21 ff.).

But one thing is what the Sceptic would feel inclined to say, another that serious men can find themselves in doubt – is the world not in a continual flux, as the natural philosophers thought, and does this not mean that no absolute concept of truth exists (1009 a 22 ff.)? And what is the criterion for the normal person's being right in claiming that the wine objectively is sweet, and the sick person wrong in claiming that it is sour (1009 b 1)? If immediate sense perception were the only form of cognition, scepticism would be the consequence. But there are other ways to attain knowledge, and once again the Aristotelian conceptual apparatus is helpful. The natural philosophers overlook the distinction between actuality and potentiality – everything in the sensory world cannot become just anything (1009 a 32 ff.), and both the natural philosopher and the serious sceptic overlook form, the constant element in every change (1009 a 37; 1010 a 25).

Thus the discussion about the principle of contradiction provides Aristotle with an occasion to define clearly his own epistemological basic position – he does so briefly, although in a way he never did elsewhere (1010 b 15 ff.; cf. p. 280). The special sense object is always true – it is true that 'sweet' now appears to me; the identification of the sense object can lead astray – perhaps this wine is objectively not sweet, although I believe so; but I have a criterion – I know what 'sweet' is and this knowledge is also infallible; I know the conditions for maintaining that something is sweet, and the existence of a sensory world presupposes the existence of an objective world. When I maintain that the wine is sweet, I presuppose that objectively it may be the case that the wine is sweet, and the concepts whereby I interpret the sensory world are unambiguous and objective.

WHAT IS 'SUBSTANCE'?

The sections on the universal predicates and the principle of contradiction have reference to a primary instance of being, in other words to the concept of substance.

Books Z, H and Θ are devoted to an investigation of this concept. Yet from a metaphysical point of view it is a concept that is fraught with difficulty. To Aristotle substance, *ousia*, means that which has independent being, but such a definition is only a formal one. It applies not only to the concept of substance but to the other basic Aristotelian concepts as well that they are formal concepts. This means that they are context-dependent concepts, but not that they are purely mental phenomena without ontological status. These concepts do not simply refer to 'things' in the real world but to features of it. In the *Categories* the concept of 'primary substance' stands for 'physical thing', because physical objects in this work are simply considered as independent, unchangeable, real objects about which something may be stated or 'in which' something is. In the *Physics* the ontological fixed point – the substance – is a physical object that can be moved and changed; but in order to explain motion and change, substance must be seen as a changeable unity of form and matter. In the *Metaphysics*, however, the very concept of thing is debated; the subject matter to be discussed is what it means in any case that a thing 'has' a structure or is 'determined' by a concept. The thing is not identical with its structure or with its concept, but its structure or its concept is that independent and unchangeable factor that makes the world intelligible, and consequently structure and concept meet the formal demands of a substance.

With this an attempt has been made to adumbrate the problem by means of modern terminology; but Aristotle does not speak of concept and structure but of substance, essence and form, genus and species. In the more simplified conceptual universe of the *Categories* only the concepts of substance, genus, and species appear, although the metaphysical problem is already implicit in this treatise (*Cat.* 3 b 10, see p. 298). Genus and species are universals, but what is predicated of the primary substance is not universality but the contents of the universal, that whereby a particular is subsumed under a universal – essence, in Aristotle's more subtle terminology. It is already latent in the *Categories* that a thing – a 'primary substance' – cannot be a thing without at the same time being 'of this kind'; thereby the later formula, a 'this-such' (*tode toionde*, *Met.* 1033 b 23, cf.*De an.* 412 a 6) has already been anticipated. The *Metaphysics* does not examine the thing as thing but rather that concept or that structure that makes a thing a thing; hence it is not an indication of a new theory of substance but of another approach when Aristotle in a metaphysical context – to the amazement of many – can identify essence or form with 'primary substance' (*Met.* 1032 b 2; 1037 b 2). Here, as everywhere, the conceptual apparatus is formal and depends on context.

The problem is of fundamental significance to Aristotle, if for no other reason than because 'things' are what to him primarily have real existence, while what primarily is known are universals. This is not necessarily an insoluble paradox. But it is characteristic for Aristotle that he himself formulates it in the most pointed paradoxical manner possible. This occurs in the aporetic book B (999 a 24 ff.; b 24 ff.; 1003 a 5 ff.). If only individuals exist, we are told, no knowledge exists, for knowledge is about the universal. If, on the other hand, the universal has real existence, one ends up in a Platonic mire – substances existing besides substances, or as substances within substances. The paradox depends on a sharp distinction between individual – a 'this' – and universal – 'a such'. The task in the books on substance is to demonstrate that this sharp distinction is a simplification and that the concept of 'concept' is a complex phenomenon.

It has sometimes been claimed that Aristotle believes himself able to solve the problem by means of a simple application of the scheme of actuality and potentiality – this to be taken to mean that universal – scientific – knowledge is potential, while its application – the knowledge of the individual – is actual (on this, cf. 1086 a 30). To use an example from the *Analytics* (*Anal. post.* 71 a 17 ff., see p. 308): my general knowledge of triangles can be 'applied' to this triangle. It is true that knowledge of individual phenomena are actualized in this way. But thereby the problem has not been solved; not all knowledge is knowledge of 'things', and the question of the onto-logical status of concepts remains. Accordingly the metaphysician still has a major task ahead of him.

Now, it is not Aristotle's intention to arrive at some surprising solution that suddenly makes everything fall into place in a new systematic whole – that is not his style. He is no metaphysical systematist, such as for example the German idealists or Thomas Aquinas, whose youthful work, the *De ente et essentia*, is an instructive example of how the Aristotelian concepts could be adapted to metaphysical system-atics. In his books on substance Aristotle applies his whole conceptual apparatus metaphysically and plays one concept against another, but does not do so to solve a puzzle but to clarify a given basic fact: the incongruity between thing, form and essence and the necessity, none the less, to connect them with each other. To a great extent the more detailed argumentation turns out to depend on the familiar thought that a given concept has a wide area of application, although there is a central meaning to which all other applications of the concept are related.

The point of departure is the physical thing. In so far as a physical thing has inde-pendent existence, it can be called a substance, *ousia*; but this is no informative metaphysical answer. One must make a detour by first determining the concept of substance formally and its content afterwards. If anything is to be called a substance – i.e. if it is in a primary sense – it must meet two criteria: it must be a *tode ti*, a 'this', in other words be a numerical unity, and it must be *chōriston*, 'separate', which is to say that it must have independent existence (*Met.* 1028 a 10 ff.). This is a speci-fication of what was always inherent in the concept of substance – definition and knowledge of the other categories presuppose definition and knowledge of substances, and the substance 'exists' prior to its properties. But thereby has not been said that a substance can simply be identified with a physical thing. Something can only be a 'this' if it has an essence, and since the essence in itself is also a numerical unity, a 'this' will not simply be identical with a physical thing. Similarly, as Aristotle frequently emphasizes, something can be 'separate' in two ways – either 'simply', as the physical individual exists as a numerical unity in time and space, or in definition and conceptually, as essence or form exists independently for thought. Therefore, when Aristotle, offering a sort of key summary, arrives at the final deter-mination of the concept of substance, he does so with reference to contexts: there are sensible substances consisting of form and matter; matter can become a 'this' and is therefore potentially a substance; form is substance in so far as it is a 'this' by defini-tion and in so far as it is by virtue of form that the thing is this thing (1042 a 24 ff.; cf. 1039 b 20; 1070 a 9; *De an.* 412 a 6). It is the latter 'filling-in' of the concept of substance that is of interest to the metaphysician. To him it is the primary instance of 'being'.

But there is a long way to go before one can arrive at this conclusion. For the time being (*Met.* 1028 b 33 ff.) Aristotle offers four possible fillings-in of the concept of substance: substance may be thought of as essence, as universal, as genus, or as substratum. And substratum (*hypokeimenon*) can even have three meanings: form, matter, and the composite of form and matter. It is only gradually revealed what is the role assigned to these concepts. This takes place in the complicated analyses in the books on substance; in the following an attempt has been made to systematize their main contents. It is clear that Aristotle pursues two paths. In part he eliminates some of 'the candidates' to the title of substance, because they do not meet the formal criteria laid down; in part he demonstrates that the concepts of essence and form must converge with the concept of substance on the presupposition that the question of what primarily exists is asked from a metaphysical point of view.

Once again the *Categories* presents the preliminary problem. Here simple subject-predicate sentences are dealt with. In other words, the question is: what is implicit in saying 'something about something' (*ti kata tinos*)? The problem is simple if an accidental category is stated about the substance – then the substance is something basically known that can acquire or lose transient properties. But if the predicate states the essence of the subject, what then is the subject itself, that about which something is stated? The question is hinted at in the *Categories*, made explicit in the *Physics*, and is the main problem in the books on substance in the *Metaphysics*. In the *Categories* the concept of substratum was unproblematical; it could be identified with substance, because substance was simply considered as subject for predication and bearer of properties. In the *Metaphysics* it is a different matter.

The problem is posed in the *Metaphysics* (1028 b 36 ff.) by a combination of main ideas in the *Categories* and the *Physics*: substance – the sensible physical object – is a unity of form and matter; substance – the substratum – is that about which something is stated. Hence the three 'significations' of substratum: matter is substratum for form, the unity of form and matter for accidental properties, and the substantial form may underlie further formal determinations. But from a metaphysical point of view the model is unsatisfactory. In a metaphysical sense the unity of form and matter is not substance, because metaphysically substance is primary; the composite is both logically and metaphysically secondary in relation to the incomposite (1029 a 30) – and so the meaning of 'substance' which is basic in the *Physics* is left out. It is true that the substantial form may serve as a substratum for further determinations; but what is essential about the formal concept is not that under certain circumstances it can have something predicated of it, but that it itself is predicated of something. Therefore form cannot be termed a substratum, but perhaps a substance. Inversely, matter is substratum, but only potentially substance. Hence metaphysics must distinguish between the concepts of substance and substratum.

What is the outcome if substratum is identified with matter, i.e. with that about which something is stated but which is not something definite (1029 a 10 ff.)? In that case the substratum is not substance, and hence matter is not so either, for matter is neither a 'this' nor 'separate'. What is matter then? Let us imagine that we gradually remove all properties from a thing. What remains then? A something that is a nothing. In other words, it would be fatal for the concept of thing, if a thing were considered to be x equipped with the properties of a, b, c . . . n.

This is of consequence for the concept of matter itself. Matter may be considered relatively. In that case it is always matter *for* something and thereby – as mentioned – potentially a substance. In this signification matter can both pertain to physical stuff and intelligible 'stuff' – pure spatial extension is, for example, not-sensible, 'intelligible' matter for the circle, and a semi-circle exists potentially 'in' the circle (cf. 1036 a 11; b 32). On the other hand, if matter – as in the preceding argument – is considered absolutely, then it is a limiting concept. In the greater cosmic context the so-called *prima materia* is such a limiting concept; but at all levels matter can be considered *qua* matter – which is to say absolutely – and viewed in this way, matter is indefinable, unknowable, and undetermined, *aoriston* (1036 a 9; 1037 a 27). Since matter is indefinable, each particular physical object is only definable by virtue of its form, which, however, is not special for any particular individual. As an individual consisting of changeable matter, the particular object is therefore also indefinable (1039 b 20ff.); every numerical plurality contains matter, and on this basis the doctrine of 'the principle of individuation' (cf. 1074 a 34) was formulated in the Middle Ages (Albertus Magnus). But numerical plurality is indefinite, whereas a definition is finite; it is a 'this', and therefore a 'this' is not to Aristotle identical with an individual *qua* individual; an individual is only a 'this' in so far as it is an entity of 'this kind'.

The examination of matter and substratum has shown that it is not that about which something is stated that from a metaphysical point of view should be called substance; this means that the model from the *Categories* is inapplicable. It is not the subject but the predicate in a subject-predicate sentence that is of interest. The predicate stands for a concept, but the sense in which it does so is not unambiguous. In the sentence 'Socrates is a man' 'man' may stand for the universal under which a number of individuals are subsumed; but it may also stand for an essence, for what essentially signifies Socrates; and, finally, the form is the characteristic of Socrates, which makes it possible to distinguish him essentially. According to Aristotle's standard definition a universal is 'that which is said about many' (*De int.* 17 a 39; *Met.* 1038 b 11), but thereby the formal criteria for a substance are not met: to be a 'this' and to be 'separate'. Consequently, genus and species – considered as universals – must also be eliminated. In his discussion about whether the universal can be called substance (1038 b 6 ff.) Aristotle launches some of his harshest attacks on the doctrine of ideas – for an idea is in Aristotle's opinion both substance and universal, which is to say an individual within an individual or an individual distributed to several individuals. What is interesting in an Aristotelian context is not the polemics but the thought behind it: a concept can be understood in two ways – in modern terms, it can be understood either extensionally or intensionally. A conceptual content or a conceptual intension is finite and therefore a numerical unity, regardless of the fact that it can be applied to a plurality; but this does not apply to the extension of the concept. The intensional application is primary, and in metaphysics it therefore takes precedence over the question of 'one-many'. Aristotle expressly defines *universalia* and *particularia* extensionally; otherwise he makes the reader's task an extremely difficult one, because he never formulates his distinction explicitly. But he does carry it out in practice, in spite of his own terminology, as it were (but see also 1035 b 27).

Matter, understood as absolute, and the concept, understood extensionally – i.e. the universal – are eliminated, and the combination of form and matter are secondary. Essence and form remain.

The essence – 'to-be-what-it-was' – is expressed by a definition, but anything within any given category can be defined, and accordingly it has an essence; the question 'what is x?' can be asked about any subject. But since substance is the central instance of 'being', there must also be a narrower meaning of essence, the essence of substance, and this meaning must be the basis for derived essential definitions. In his analysis of the primary meaning of 'essence' (1029 b 1 – 32 a 11) Aristotle once again makes use of his process of elimination – which can be compared with the eidetic reduction in Husserl's phenomenology.

In the first place, all secondary categories are excluded (1029 b 15 ff.; 1031 a 19 ff.): 'to be you' is not the same as 'to be musical'; that a surface is white does not say anything about what a surface is. With special energy Aristotle denies the existence of one essence for the combination of substance + accidental category – for example, 'white man'. Now, of course a substance will always be equipped with accidental properties; the man is, for example, white; but it is evidently important – as in the discussion of the principle of contradiction – to distinguish between denotation and connotation, between the thing and its essence; it is not man's essence to be white. Aristotle is furthermore at pains to emphasize (1030 a 17 ff.) that he wants to isolate essence in a primary sense; he does not preclude that in a derived sense there are essences for qualities or for white men.

In the second place, matter must be eliminated if one wishes to isolate pure primary essences: 'snubness' is the same as 'curvature' *in* noses (1030 b 28 ff.), and one can abstract from noses, if one wishes to carry through a reduction to incomposite essences. Strictly speaking, it is only substance understood as essence that is definable (1031 a 1 ff.). What this means is elaborated on in two conclusions that seemingly are at odds with each other: only species have essence (1030 a 12), and the individual is identical with its essence (1031 a 15; b 18). The individual can never be identified with genus, for genus is an abstraction, while the essential determination of species is the complete essential determination of the individual (cf. 999 a 29). The two conclusions show that Aristotle abstracts from species as a universal and from the individual in its infinite aspect as bearer of properties (cf. 1037 a 27; 1040 a 2). In other words, what remains is essence as conceptual intension. An individual and its species are defined in the same way (cf. 1032 a 5). The separation between universal and particular is hence secondary.

In this way essence meets the formal demands of substance. Essence is conceptually 'separate' and conceptually a 'this'. But it can never have independent, real existence, as is stressed in one of the most informative discussions of the Platonic idea (1031 a 28 ff.). If, for example, the idea of the good exists as a real entity, which is good, the idea of the good would be different from the essence of the good, and in that case the idea would not be recognizable, nor would the essence exist.

Essence is a conceptual determination *of* the thing; form is the structural element *in* the thing which at the same time as intelligible form exists in the mind. In a broad sense essence covers a larger area than form, because everything – including the unity of form and matter – can be essentially determined (cf. 1033 a 4), while form always is opposed to matter.

The closer analysis of the concept of form (1032 a 12 – 4 b 19) is conducted in the same way as the analysis of essence, and it concludes that the central meaning of form must coincide with the central meaning of essence. Here Aristotle also adheres to the procedure of elimination. Form in the strict sense – *forma substantialis* – is no accidental determination; by virtue of the formal determination the thing is this thing. And form must of course be distinguished from the matter for which it is form. Matter is eternal, the form is eternal, the thing is perishable, but it is the form that determines matter; consequently the form is the substantial element in the thing. It is a 'this in a this' or a 'something in something else' (1030 b 18; 1036 b 23; 1037 b 3); but in isolation the form is the same as the incomposite essence. A circle taken simply is the same as 'being a circle', the soul taken simply is the same as 'being soul'; but 'man' can be reduced to the substantial form 'soul', 'snubness' to 'curvature' (1036 a 1; 1037 a 28; 1043 b 2).

To the mind form is a numerical unity and indivisible – a 'this' and 'separate' – and thereby it meets the formal criteria for substance (1032 b 6; 1034 a 8; 1042 a 29). That it – in the extra-mental world, in the things – at the same time is a numerical plurality is from an intensional point of view without importance. Just as essence is the same in the universal and in the individual, form and thing as having form have the same definition (1035 a 7; cf. 1032 a 23). In itself the form is a *tode* (a 'this'); seen in relation to the thing it is a *toion* ('a such'). Like essence, form can have no independent, reified existence; but the thing, on the other hand, can only be a 'this' if it is 'a such' at the same time – hence the famous formula of 'a this such' (1033 b 19 ff.).

The result of the parallel analyses of essence and form is accordingly that the concepts converge (cf. 1032 b 1; 14) and that both meet the formal criteria for substance. Metaphysically considered, essence, form and substance are the same. But such can only be the outcome, if substance in a primary sense is the element in the thing that constitutes it, if one in the same way looks for the primary sense of the concepts of essence and form, and if concepts are viewed intensionally. The conclusion is given with the premises; the important thing is to realize that the thing is different from its concept or its structure but cannot exist without its concept or structure.

The examination of essence and form makes it possible to return to the starting point (1041 a 6 ff.). What does it mean to say 'something about something'? In other words: what ontology legitimates a simple subject-predicate sentence? The subject-predicate sentence was the model that was taken over from the *Categories*, and according to the *Analytics* science consists of answering the question: why does the predicate P belong to the subject S? No serious metaphysical problem arises with accidental predicates but does so with the essential determination of the subject. This was where the model turned out to be inadequate – if, but only if, the subject and not the predicate was identified with substance. What is it in fact that takes place in an essential determination? That the substantial form or essence is predicated – not of the thing but about the matter. It is not interesting to find out that a man is a man, but a reformulation in subject-predicate form is interesting: this flesh and these bones are a man. Form and essence are not some new element in addition to the material elements; it is a super-imposed structure that causes the material elements to be something different from and more than an aggregate – the whole is more than the sum of its parts, just as the syllable is different from and more than the sum of its letters. It is no accident that here a favourite Platonic image is employed. The entire reduction of the subject to the conceptual content of the predicate is Platonism, although of course a Platonism that is adjusted to another framework – as one is soon given to understand.

Whenever one applies a form-essence to a matter or substratum, one says 'something about something'; the form-essence is the 'cause of' the matter's being a certain thing, but it itself appears as an irreducible and simple 'this', and there is no cause for the cause. But is one unable to say 'something' *about* the form-essence? Certain forms present themselves immediately as composite – 'snubness' is an always ready example. But in a certain sense something can also be said about pure form-essences. According to the *Analytica* the question 'what?' precedes the question 'why?', and the answer to a 'what?' is a definition. A definition has the same linguistic form as a normal subject-predicate sentence, but it does not have the same logical form, because the subject and predicate are identical; there is nothing 'super-imposed', and therefore the 'something about something' formula does not apply. None the less, problems arise. A definition does in fact consist of several parts; but does this not mean that every definable form or essence is composite, and in that case how can it be a numerical unity, a 'this' that simply is present?

A definition defines species by means of genus and differentia. But if so, does not the definiendum – species – become dissolved in its constituent parts (1037 b 8 ff.; 1043 b 10; 1045 a 7 ff.)? No, because the parts of the definition are integrated in a whole that is different from and more than the sum of its parts; to that extent it is therefore considered in the same way as is the unification of form and sensible matter. If the specific form warrants that 'man' is not merely a collection of flesh, bones, etc., species is the unifying factor that causes the concept of 'man' to be not only 'animal' + 'two-footed' + 'featherless'. Genera and differentiae can therefore be considered as matter for species – in analogy with the 'intelligible' matter, which, according to Aristotle, is presupposed for mathematical objects. A genus – 'living being', for example – does not exist in itself, only as matter for this living being – 'man', for example.

With this Aristotle distances himself from the Platonic understanding of a *diairesis* scheme. To Plato every step in a definition – and thus every link of a *diairesis* – has independent existence as an idea, even so much so that the intensity of being increases with the degree of universality; a man is in fact 'animal' + 'footed' + 'two-footed' + 'featherless' and it is the superordinate concept that unifies the subordinate ones. Aristotle turns the scheme upside-down; as he says (1038 a 19), it is the last differentia that is the substance of the thing, i.e. species brings about unity, and since genus does not refer to independently existing entities, it is superfluous information to call man both 'footed' and 'two-footed' (cf. *Cat.* 2 b 7 ff., see p. 298).

It is in other words the specific form – or the form-essence – that to Aristotle is the ontological centre – both when seen in relation to sensible matter and its elements and in relation to 'conceptual' matter and its elements. And this specific form is not a concept that differs in essence from the thing. Now, since form is not an element beside others, this means that if all material elements (*materia proxima*) – physical and intelligible – are present, the substance is potentially present. The form does not contribute a new conceptual determination but actualizes the potentiality so that substance actually is a 'this' and 'separate' (*Met.* 1045 b 21).

Thus actuality and potentiality have been introduced – not as new conceptual determinations but as modes of existence, as the set of concepts that describes the process that constantly realizes the conceptual and structural constants.

A good deal of the treatment in the *Metaphysics* of the concepts of actuality and potentiality is a summing-up of what has been said in other contexts – mainly in the *Physics*, but also in the works on logic and psychology – and hence only a few important points shall be discussed. The transition from possibility to reality does not occur of necessity; but if something is present as real, it must necessarily have been potentially present – which is to say that temporally possibility precedes reality. Yet, in logic and ontology, reality implies possibility (one can conclude from *esse* to *posse*, but not from *posse* to *esse*). If one could conclude from possibility to reality, the world would follow a strictly determined course, which in fact it does not do, as Aristotle stresses in a debate with the Megarians, the spokesmen of hard determinism (1046 b 29 ff. – see also *De int.* 22 b 10 ff.; here p. 301).

This way of thinking agrees handsomely with Aristotle's teleological view of nature and with his concept of hypothetical necessity. Aristotelian teleology implies that every process aims at a goal. It will hold true for natural processes that a potentiality can be actualized or not be actualized – favourable external circumstances are a necessary and sufficient precondition for realizing the possibility. Human acts, on the other hand, imply a rational choice – here the external circumstances are a necessary but not a sufficient pre-condition, and man has not only the choice of acting or not acting: he can act in different ways (*Met.* 1047 b 31 ff.). Finally, a human act can be described as an 'incomplete' or 'complete' motion – the act can have its purpose outside or inside itself (1048 b 18 ff., see p. 325).

Actuality and potentiality are operative at all levels of the world, and the concepts serve to describe a world of events that are not determined but directed at a goal. The difference between actuality and potentiality can only be described by analogies from experience, for there is no difference in definition (1048 a 25 ff., see p. 290). It follows from this that potentiality is a deficient mode of existence; the actual is primary in relation to the potential (1049 b 4 ff.). It is true that possibility precedes reality in time – the egg precedes the hen – but species also has temporal precedence – the hen precedes the egg; a man begets a man; and actuality is ontologically primary – actuality is the realization of the pre-existing formal and final cause. Disregarding the fact that actuality and potentiality are determinations of being, not of essence, a parallelism accordingly appears with respect to the earlier examinations: essence is primary in relation to accident, form in relation to matter, actuality in relation to potentiality. This, as will appear, will be of importance for Aristotle's theology.

What exists in a primary sense – substance – can be determined as essence and form, and it exists actually. But it also exists as truth – Aristotle shares the view of the tradition that truth in a fundamental sense is an ontological determination.

'Being as truth' was in fact one of the 'meanings' of being, which the metaphysician according to Aristotle's programme should investigate – he goes so far as to say that this is the most important – and truth is a *transcendentale*. His investigation of being as truth occupies only a brief chapter in Θ, the last of the books on substance (1051 a 34 ff.). Seemingly without motivation it follows the treatment of actuality and potentiality, but yet it presupposes it, although there are even closer connections with the treatment of form and essence. Actually the chapter forms a conclusion to all three substance books; it deals with a fundamental question of both epistemological and ontological relevance. Lines of thought from other Aristotelian works are also summed up in the chapter.

The Aristotelian definition of truth based on his 'correspondence theory' is formulated in the *De interpretatione* (*De int.* 17 a 26 ff.) and in a couple of passages in the *Metaphysics* this standard definition is repeated or alluded to (*Met.* 1010 b 23; 1011 b 26; 1027 b 18). The character of the *De interpretatione* does not allow further-reaching questions. But the *Analytics* is concluded with a presentation of immediate intellectual intuition as a presupposition for demonstrative knowledge (see p. 311). In psychology it is presupposed that there are incomposite objects recognized immediately as a precondition for discursive thinking (see p. 341); and the ontological course of the substance books has also led to the pure, incomposite form-essences as the last presuppositions that elude simple predication (to say 'something about something') and 'of which neither inquiry nor teaching is possible' (1041 b 9). As examples of pure essences – without sensible or intelligible matter – Aristotle mentions in one passage the categorial concepts of substance, quality, etc. themselves (1045 b 1). But clearly it is not his intention to provide a catalogue of pure essences (cf. 1037 b 1). The intention is to point out *that* there are objects of cognition that are apprehended intuitively through sense perception or intellect (cf. *De an.* 430 a 26 ff.) and that this apprehension is a precondition for 'dianoetic cognition'. These objects can in fact also become known discursively – through a definition – but, as has been demonstrated, there is a 'something' that holds the definition together, and this something must be present with evidence; there must be a concept before I state something about the concept – every statement about, for example, 'red', 'curve', or 'man' presupposes an intuitive familiarity with 'red', 'curve', or 'man'. I can only claim that the wine is sweet if I know what 'sweet' is.

Aristotle begins by recapitulating his definition of 'correspondence'. Truth and falsehood depend on combination and separation in a judgement that corresponds or does not correspond to what is really combined or separated. It follows from this that the same judgement may be true or false, if it pertains to contingent facts. Judgements concerning necessary facts are on the other hand always true or false. The truth value has its 'ontological place' in the mind (cf. *Met.* 1027 b 27), but it is dependent on the fact itself – you are not white because I truly think that you are white.

But what is the precondition for such a theory of truth? That incomposite entities exist. In a statement the predicate is incomposite and therefore not true in the same way as the statement is true – it is true that the table is white; in this sense 'white' has no truth value (cf. *Cat.* 2 a 8; *De an.* 430 a 26; *Met.* 1027 b 27). It is 'true' not by virtue of a mental act, but because it is simply present as something that can be grasped by 'touch' and which merely can be 'said'. What holds true for the linguistic expression applies of course to the content – to the essences to which the predicate refers. They do not come to be nor do they cease to be, and therefore they exist for ever actually, not potentially. One can of course – in a definition – say something *about* these essences, and a definition is true or false. But about the essence in itself it is not possible to be in error; one may be acquainted with it or not, but it is never false. An essence is not present *in* the mind but *for* the mind, because it is present in reality. It can be apprehended or 'touched' by human reason (*nous*), because *nous* is adjusted to the cosmic structure and because it is an ontological mark of essence that it is intelligible. But an essence is not in an absolute sense an epistemological or an ontological entity.

What, then, is essence 'in itself'? There are profound similarities with Plato as well as a clear Platonic note in the entire line of thought. But with respect to one decisive point Aristotle strikes out on his own: he does not hypostatize essence, and he never asks what it is 'in itself'. This is perhaps the most telling expression of the Aristotelian principle of economy. There is no reason to duplicate the things to be explained. Essence is substance in the sense that it makes the thing an intelligible thing, it is not a special entity nor a mystifying *tertium quid* beside or above thing and mind: rather, it is a basic fact that makes a direct intercourse of subject and object possible. There is no reason to ask further questions.

Aristotle's chapter on 'being as truth' opens the way for a new understanding of concepts, but it is at the same time the copingstone of a long historic development. There are roots going back to Antisthenes' idea of knowledge as a direct contact with an object, although, undeniably, this has become more subtle when it no longer applies to any cognition whatsoever and its linguistic expression but instead to the precondition for cognition and language. To Plato this precondition was the idea; to Aristotle it would only bring about confusion to imagine an idea that *has* an essential determination. It is not only his criticism of Plato but also his own conceptual apparatus that build on this presupposition. The 'phenomenological reduction' is not a reduction to hypostatized concepts.

THEOLOGY

But precisely this produces complications, in brief the relation between metaphysics and theology. Aristotle constructed his books on substance in conformance with a firm basic scheme: in the same way as substance understood as thing is primary to accident, so the substantial element in the thing – its form and essence – is primary to the thing itself. With this he bridged the chasm between thing and concept that was a main question of the aporias in B. But he has not yet taken the last step and fulfilled the programme of E: to account for one independent ('separate'), eternal, and immovable substance upon which depend the changeable physical objects, one divine first substance that warrants a general metaphysics about that which is in so far as it is. The pure form-essences are not independent substances with real existence, they exist *in* the thing and *for* the mind, they are primary as causes for the existence or intelligibility of a thing, but a cause is the cause for or a principle of something; in the books on substance the thing has been conceptually grasped but has precisely not been reduced to concepts. The thing continues to be thing and is not a manifestation of a higher level of being. With this decisive point Aristotle cut himself off from constructing a major metaphysical system culminating in a highest idea or an absolute concept. If the world nevertheless is a coherent system and if there is a warrant for this totality – god – then god cannot merely be a principle. He must be a substance – the primary one – with real existence, a substance that sustains the world as a world of intelligible physical things. The road to the Aristotelian god does not course through a metaphysical hierarchy of concepts; most directly it goes through physics. But Aristotle's metaphysics and theology are indissolubly entwined. It is no path without thorns – but inconsistencies and unresolved questions cannot justify the assumption of two conflicting theories conceived of at two different points in time; indeed there are hints in the books on substance of their being preparations for further examinations (cf. 1041 a 7; 1050 b 6).

What seems most strange to a modern reader is that Aristotle's theology combines physics, cosmology and metaphysics; the universe as a whole is presupposed to be rational and living, and the celestial bodies are considered especially privileged rational beings. But in Aristotle's milieu this was not strange. Not only does Plato in the *Phaedo* claim that god and the very idea of life itself shall not perish and in the *Sophist* that the universe must comprise change, life, insight and thought (cf. p. 188 and p. 230). It is also a main point – in the *Timaeus* – that all motion in the end is owing to a self-moving first mover, the cosmic soul (cf. *Phaedr.* 245 C; *Leg.* X 894 E). Aristotle accepts the idea of a first mover, but rejects a self-moving first mover. Still, all in all, his theology is based on debates in the Academy. In its structure Aristotle's theology is most closely aligned with Xenocrates', though with respect to contents he frees himself of any hierarchical-metaphysical model.

All the individual sciences presuppose a first philosophy or theology according to Aristotle; the several areas of existence converge towards one highest principle. In the individual sciences one can be led to the point where it is realized in what sense a highest principle must be presupposed. But to the human intellect it is not easy – it is perhaps impossible – to ascertain what this first principle is 'in itself'. If one were able to describe it with the same degree of certainty as one can describe the individual phenomenon, a more superior descriptional apparatus would be presupposed, a principle behind the highest. Probably Aristotle cannot be wholly absolved of reifying his concept of god, of speaking of it as an object accessible to objective description. But it is a sort of quasi-language; he is aware that his concept of god is a limiting concept and that strictly speaking one can only speak about it in so far as it is operative in the world. So one must proceed by analogy, not by strict proof. Hence he stresses the tentative and probable in his way of thinking – it is a possible explanation, says he, but if it is false, one would have to fall back upon the basic stuff of the natural philosophers – an explanation that is no explanation – or the mythologists' 'chaos and dark night' (*Met.* 1072 a 19; cf. a 8). As has been mentioned, Aristotle is cautious, reserved, extremely brief – hence obscure – in speaking about divine reason that 'comes from the outside' (*De gen. an.* 736 b 28). Therefore it is difficult to determine precisely not only what he wants to say, but also what he does not want to say. He can write tersely and briefly, on occasion with a strangely pedestrian argumentation, but in spite of the extremely abstract nature of his concept of god, now and then he comes close to the lofty style of religious pathos.

In the *Physics* Aristotle argued that the existence of a physical world in motion presupposes the eternal circular motion of the heavens, which in turn presupposes a non-spatial unmoved first mover. His psychology leads to the notion of a super-personal reason (*nous*), to pure thought that always exists actually – as distinguished from human thought that only momentarily is actualized – a mode of thought in which object and subject coincide in the very act of thinking and in which there is no external object outside thought – no external thought object, no individuals whatso-ever, and therefore no universals. Man has access to this thinking, but only through a world of sensible individuals, and man is also a person in an external world; god is, we must believe, identical with pure thought. Most remarkably these two motifs are combined already in B (*Met.* 999 b 1 ff.). But how are they to become combined in the unmoved mover that 'thinks itself', and how can this come about without at the same time introducing a metaphysical conceptual system? Already Aristotle's pupils seem to have had their troubles (cf. [Aristot.] *MM* 1212 b 37; Theophrastus, see p. 402). It is no wonder that the uncertainty has endured even in modern Aristotelian research.

Much of this uncertainty, which of course also adheres to the present interpreta-tion, is owing to Aristotle's lapidary way of expressing himself. Undoubtedly much is also owing to the tradition. In the course of late Antiquity, Aristotelian theology was incorporated in Neoplatonic metaphysics (see p. 515) – presumably under the influ-ence of the Xenocrates heritage. This implies that intellect – *nous* – is not only conceived of as a unity of thought object and thought subject but also as containing the ideas; and the ideas were – thanks to the creative act of the cosmic soul – exem-plary causes and source of the material world; they were 'god's thoughts', a notion that was developed further in the Christian tradition. Today the Christian interpreta-tion is rejected almost unanimously – Aristotle's god was not a personal god acting freely. Nevertheless, the Neoplatonic interpretation still has long-term effects, even though it cannot be right – Aristotelianism is not a hierarchical metaphysical system in which steadily higher concepts lead on to the highest. Aristotle combines meta-physics and cosmology in a manner that may have been understood in Antiquity but is alien to a modern interpreter to whom the Aristotelian cosmology is a by-gone phenomenon.

Already in his account of actuality as prior to potentiality (*Met.* 1050 b 6 ff.) Aristotle in evident agreement with the *Physics* says that if there are eternal substances existing by necessity, they cannot exist potentially. Everything that is contingent – things in the sublunary world – must exist by virtue of what actually and of necessity exists, i.e. the celestial bodies, their motion and the eternal mover.

That such substances do exist we know from the *Physics*, and here the theology, Λ, takes its point of departure. We are told (1069 a 30 ff.; b 3 ff.) that three kinds of substances must exist: the perishable, sensible and movable objects in the sublunary world; the eternal, sensible and movable celestial bodies; and the eternal, unsensible and immovable one. It should be noted that here the criterion for a substance is that it is simply 'separate' (1070 b 36), not conceptually separate.

The argument for an unmoved mover is provided first (1071 b 3 ff.): the existence of perishable substances points to the existence of eternal ones; the steadily varying motion in the earthly region points to the eternal uniform circular motion of heaven, and this in turn presupposes an immaterial, unmoved mover, for a first mover cannot be moved by anything else. Here the argument is of course conducted on presuppositions that are not ours: the concept of substance, the existence of an eternal circular motion, the principle that all that moves is moved by something else, no inertia, and no infinite regress. What is decisive is the way in which the unmoved mover is characterized: it cannot exist potentially, for then it would possibly not-be; it cannot be material, for then it would be changeable and then it would be composite. Consequently it is pure actuality and pure form. In all phenomena known to us actuality corresponds to potentiality and form to matter; they are correlative concepts. Pure actuality and pure form are limiting concepts that pertain to a transcendent substance. But these concepts are not hypostatized; they characterize a substance and accordingly are still formal concepts. Yet it ought to be noted that the unmovable mover is not called pure essence. The unmovable mover can hardly have an essence – as did the concept of god in medieval Aristotelianism – for an essence defines one entity next to another.

How does the first mover move (1072 a 23 ff.)? It itself cannot be moved, for in that case it would be changeable. Hence it cannot be a *causa efficiens*; it moves as a *causa finalis* because it is an object of desire. We are familiar with such a form of motion from our own world. An object of desire is a small, unmoved mover and so is a thought object; but one can desire a seeming good, whereas the thought object is a genuine good and therefore the true object of desire.

Here there is reason to pause, for within these few lines Aristotle seems to perform two immense, sudden transitions, which can only be understood against the background of his entire philosophy and not from the surface of the condensed style. In the first place, here we encounter the perhaps most daring generalization in his whole thought: the transfer of the teleological mode of thinking to the entire world. In the second place, we have suddenly leapt from physics to thinking and metaphysics. Naturally enough this is partially based on the antropomorphic line of thought that the physical motions of the celestial bodies are due to their being endowed with reason. But that is not all. To Aristotle reality is rational and reason real, which is to say that reason and reality basically are ontological categories. Given this fundamental view, one can try to ponder what function the Aristotelian god must have. Plato's universe is warranted by ideas + a moving principle, the soul. Aristotle must connect the two views. His god is to account for motion – and to make motion intelligible is a principal point of Aristotle's whole philosophical undertaking. But motion is no mere mechanical process. Motion and change in our world consist in a steady interchange of constant forms; forms are structural elements in objects but are at the same time intelligible and must therefore ontologically and epistemologically have one ultimate pre-condition. Physically the constancy of the forms is manifest by 'a man's begetting a man' and epistemologically by self-identical form-essences. The Aristotelian concept of god is a precondition for the existence of such a world. The world does not exist because god created it; god exists because the world exists.

Gradually Aristotle is approaching the highest principle, that upon which 'depend the heavens and the world of nature' (1072 b 13 ff.). Its actuality consists in the highest form of life, and the highest form of life is thought. Once again Aristotle moves from the empirical human world to the highest principle, which only in the end (1072 b 25) is identified with god. Pure thought we know only as a reflection during a few blissful moments. God, on the other hand, is always identical with thought – not with the passive element that is receptive of its objects but with thinking as pure actuality uniting subject with object. This is a life in pleasure, and Aristotle concludes: 'for the actuality of thought is life, and God is the actuality of thought'.

But wherein consists pure divine thought – *noēsis* (1074 b 15 ff.)? The question involves some problems, as Aristotle remarks in the mundane style he also has at his disposal. Pure thought (*nous*) is incomposite; it is without matter; it cannot be potential – for thereby it would be dependent on an external, higher thought object. Therefore pure thought thinks itself; it is 'a thinking of thinking' (*noēsis noēseōs*). Perhaps it is best understood as the very act of thinking as opposed to thinking of this and that (cf. the phrase 'the form of forms', *De an.* 432 a 2); for it is emphasized that in pure thinking one can only distinguish formally but not really between thought and what is being thought about. Aristotle makes a comparison with sensation: sensation is directed at external objects but is at the same time accompanied by an awareness of sensation. But as thinking, on the other hand, is not directed at external objects, its object will coincide with consciousness of thinking – and accordingly it is neither a question of a reification *of* thinking nor of a reflection *about* thinking. Again Aristotle reminds us that from the world with which we are familiar we are acquainted with the identity between the act of thinking and the object of thought – this is true of the artist who holds the form of the work of art in his consciousness before he impresses it on a stuff, and it is true of the theoretical sciences where the act of thinking is the same as the object of thought. From these momentary experiences of thinking that are known to man one can by analogy conclude about god's pure thought.

Aristotle draws an analogy between man and god, but points out the difference at the same time. The Aristotelian god is not a person and does not permit an interpretation in terms of 'psychologism'. For this reason alone the famous formula by Thomas Aquinas – knowing himself god knows everything (Thom. Aq. in Aristot. *Met.* XII 11,2614) – is invalid. Man's highest knowledge is of contents – reason grasps or 'touches' this or that form-essence; structurally this means – as everywhere in Aristotle's epistemology – that subject and object are given with the thought act. As in the *De anima* it is this structure that corresponds with pure reason or divine thought. That god knows himself must mean – in modern terms – that god's knowledge is void of contents; god is pure actuality and pure form. This implies that the pure form-essences are not deduced from the nature of god but exist in their own right – whereby a striking similarity with Speusippus' system emerges. It is not the function of god to constitute a world consisting of an odd number of things, each with its own essential characteristics but to sustain the structure of the world. Himself immovable, god is the warrant for the existence of motion; himself the form of thought, god is the warrant that something can be thought. The Aristotelian god is the metaphysical precondition for knowledge and existence; he is not a self-reflecting consciousness nor a transcendental ego in Kant's or the later Husserl's sense; yet one can perhaps call Aristotle's theology and – despite all the differences – Plato's 'doctrine of principles' transcendental philosophy on Greek premises. The weakness of Aristotelian theology is not that god apparently thinks without thinking of anything; nor is it primarily to be found in the tension between a *metaphysica generalis* and a *metaphysica specialis*. It derives rather from Aristotle's wanting both to separate and tie conceptual metaphysics and cosmology together. On the one hand he wants to isolate form-essences as irreducible intentional objects; on the other hand he considers reality as a cohering totality that can be described by a primary philosophy that also legitimates a conceptual metaphysics. The tension is, so to speak, built into the basic project.

In a concluding chapter (Aristot. *Met.* 1075 a 11 ff.) Aristotle asks whether the principle for structure and order is transcendent or immanent in the world. The answer is: both; but this answer is to be understood in a special way, which Aristotle illustrates with a famous image. The ordered world can be likened to an ordered army; order can be found in the army but only because it has a commander who is superior to the army – as Homer puts it: 'the rule of many is not good; one ruler let there be' (Hom. *Il.* II 204). With this image Aristotle indirectly indicated that the existence of god is not a question of proof: the ordered army shows immediately that there is a general. It is characteristic of Plato's pupil, Aristotle, that he directly identifies world order with the metaphysical good that exists in itself and everywhere. Although Aristotle's god is a very abstract and formal entity, he is also the object of reverence, as can be seen in the famous core passage in his theology:

> On such a principle, then, depend the heavens and the world of nature. And it is a life such as the best which we enjoy, and enjoy but for a short time, for it is ever in this state, which we cannot be, and its actuality is also pleasure, even as we too find the highest pleasure in waking, perception, and thinking, and hence in hopes and memories. And thinking in itself concerns that which is best in itself, and thinking in the fullest sense concerns what is best in the fullest sense. And thought thinks itself because it shares the nature of the object of thought; for it becomes an object of thought by touching and thinking its object, so that thought and the object of thought are the same. For that which is capable of receiving the object of thought or its essence is thought. But it is active when it possesses this object. Therefore the possession rather than the receptivity is the divine element which thought seems to contain, and the act of contemplation is what is most pleasant and best. If, then, God is always in that good state in which we sometimes are, this compels our wonder; and if in a better state this compels it yet more. And God is in a better state. And life also belongs to God; for the actuality of thought is life, and God is the actuality of thought; and God's self-dependent actuality is life most good and eternal. So, this is our verdict that God is a living being, eternal, most good, so that life and duration continuous and eternal belong to God; for this is God.
>
> (*Met.* 1072 b 13 ff.; after W.D. Ross and Richard Hope)

ETHICS AND POLITICS

—— •◆• ——

'Every practical skill and every methodical inquiry, every action, and every choice apparently aims at some good; hence it has rightly been declared that the good is what all things aim at' (Aristot. *Eth. Nic.* 1094 a 1 ff.). Aristotle's principal work on ethics, the *Nicomachean Ethics* once again opens with a general statement. It is Aristotle's version of a basic view in the entire Socratic tradition (cf. p. 130). Although he distances himself in many respects from Plato, the Socratic inspiration is at the core of his ethical thought.

Read as a description of human acts, the statement may look like a tautology (cf. 1172 b 35) – that human acts aim at some good, could that mean anything but that human acts aim at something desirable? Yet within the Academy tradition this truism conceals some crucial questions: how to distinguish between the seeming and the truly good; for whom is the good good?

Read as a determination of what moral philosophy is, the statement can – at least in our day – seem more controversial. The ethics of modern philosophy is dominated by a utilitarian tradition, by a Kantian ethics of obligation, and by the view going back to Hume that moral judgements express feelings, not cognition. Both Plato's and Aristotle's ethics cross these lines of demarcation. This is precisely why there have recently been clear tendencies to include Aristotle in the debate. Plato's ethics seems perhaps too rigoristic or utopian. Aristotle's ethical naturalism, on the other hand, appears the more attractive.

Aristotle is in fact an ethical naturalist. As a moral being man is determined by what he is as a natural creature, by what his biological features are. Nature determines man's possibilities for action; ethics deals with how these possibilities are to be used, and therefore ethics is closely connected with a philosophy of action. But, just as little as Plato's, is Aristotle's concept of nature normatively neutral; inasmuch as man by nature is what he is, it follows that something is good for man because it concurs with his nature. Aristotle has no scruples with 'the naturalistic fallacy' and simply concludes from 'is' to 'ought'. To him there is therefore no conflict of principle between obligation and inclination, and it hardly serves any purpose to ask whether he is an adherent of deontological or consequential ethics; the problem is to realize which natural inclinations are 'good'. Man should not follow his duty contrary to nature but cultivate his inner nature so that no conflict arises. Aristotle's is an agent ethics in the same sense as Plato's: what is decisive is not whether this or that action is good, but that the good man will perform good acts. The good act depends on man's moral habitus and the concrete situation in which he finds himself. This does not preclude a normative ethics, but it does preclude a rule ethics – there is something that is good in the given situation, but rules do not provide much guidance, because they are general; therefore a formal determination of a categorical imperative – as in Kant – cannot be provided. On the contrary, Aristotle can confuse his reader by coming up with seemingly void directions: one should act as the good man would act; a moral action should be praiseworthy, noble, good, and as right thinking dictates (cf. the deliberately void definition of 'the noble', *Rhet.* 1366 a 33 ff.). This does not mean that Aristotle confines himself to referring to moral linguistic usage – here he also collides with modern distinctions: he would seem to adhere to meta-ethics as well as to normative ethics, which is to say that he analyzes moral linguistic usage in order to draw normative consequences. He is an ethical cognitivist without a rule ethics.

The opening sentence of the *Nicomachean Ethics* probably reveals what is most important: the good is not something man has to perform but something that man strives for and therefore performs. Thereby 'good' is not simply an ethical concept. But Aristotle undertakes to demonstrate – as did Socrates and Plato before him – that the ethical good is the real good. What man strives for is happiness – *eudaimonia*; but when Aristotle's ethics frequently is called eudaemonism, one has to exclude Kantian connotations: happiness is not pleasure and is not opposed to duty. To Aristotle happiness is natural self-realization, but it is tied to moral norms and obligations to other men and to the society to which man belongs. Ethics and politics are closely connected: it is worthwhile for individual man to attain his own happiness, but nobler and more divine to attain it for the commonwealth (*Eth. Nic.* 1094 b 9). Tension may exist between individual and social ethics, but the goal of both is happiness.

Aristotelian 'eudaemonism' is not far removed from Socrates' opening thesis in the second book of the *Republic* (see p. 202): the true good is desirable for its own sake, *because* it makes the individual happy. The objective good and the subjective good coincide.

Aristotle is considered the founder of practical reason. Even though he certainly shares the honour with Socrates, it is in any case true that in his classification of sciences he marks off ethics and politics as special fields: they are practical sciences in which man relates himself to his own acts, *praxeis*. As has often been mentioned, a *praxis* is an act that has its purpose in itself; among much else, this means that a man's life – as an individual and as a citizen – has its meaning in itself; a moral life does not depend on anything else. In the first place some methodical consequences can be drawn (*Eth. Nic.* 1094 b 11 ff.; cf. a 25; 1098 a 20): human life is variable; it is not possible – as in the theoretical sciences – to attain exact knowledge of necessary facts; at the most one can speak about what most often happens; and the practical sciences can therefore only state something without precision and in outline – this naturally does not mean that one in a particular situation should content oneself with this or that act as being approximately right, but rather that all generalizations are uncertain. Here more than ever it holds true that we must take our point of departure in what is 'known to us'. But to commence with what is most 'known to us' implies that we have an intuitively certain point of departure for the understanding of first principles. Epistemologically induction and sense perception constitute such a point of departure; ethically it is experience and habituation (1098 b 3).

There are perspectives in this that go beyond a theory of science. Ethics pertains to human life and is therefore no mere neutral inquiry which accidentally has ourselves as its object. There is something awkward in lecturing on ethics, for its aim is not knowledge but to become better as human beings (1095 a 5; 1103 b 27; 1179 a 35; cf. 1143 b 22). Nor can one simply impart ethical knowledge; ethical knowledge requires experience in life and is therefore no proper subject for young students (1095 a 2; cf. 1143 b 13). A remark like this shows that a great deal of Aristotle's ethics consists in a rational scanning of general wisdom of life and reflections on pre-philosophic experience accumulated through generations. It makes profound sense that '*ta phainomena*' in ethics includes current ideas and norms that the philosopher must seek to account for (1145 b 2 ff.; 1172 b 36 – cf. p. 283). It may turn out to be necessary to break with traditional ideas, but they cannot be thought away.

There are several versions of Aristotle's ethics. The exoteric early work, the *Protrepticus*, which is known to us only from fragments and paraphrases, has a special status. The main aim of this treatise was apparently to show that a life without rational insight is meaningless. Reason (*nous* and *phronēsis*) is the divine element in man; pure reason is the highest human activity, and without reason practical life – ethics and politics – will also come apart at the seams. It looks as if the treatise contained many Platonic reminiscences, but the Socratic-Platonic 'other-worldliness' was given a twist. It is possible that the *Protrepticus* concluded with a familiar Platonic theme: one must philosophize or depart this life – everything but philosophy is empty vanity (Προτρ. frg. 110 Düring). But indeed one should not turn one's back on life: the truth is the most important of all and hence practical life should be governed by insight into truth (frg. 46 ff. Düring). The *Protrepticus* hardly provides firm bases for the idea of a development in Aristotle's thought (see p. 276), partially because it lies outside its scope to distinguish precisely between theoretical and practical knowledge. Aristotle never abandoned the main point of this treatise.

Three esoteric versions of the Aristotelian ethics have been preserved. The *Magna Moralia* is presumably the work of a student. The *Eudemian Ethics* and the *Nicomachean Ethics*[1] must both be considered authentic; but the relation between the two versions is complicated, which can be seen from the fact that books V–VII of the *Nicomachean Ethics* in the transmission are identical with books IV–VI of the *Eudemian Ethics*. The mutual relation between the two ethics has been the subject of thorough debate since Werner Jaeger's day, but no chronological consensus has been arrived at. In the present book the point of view is that the *Nicomachean Ethics* appears to be the more mature and elaborate version. This work – which probably is aimed at a wider audience – is carefully outlined and has stylistic qualities rare in the

---

1 The name of Aristotle's father and of his son was Nicomachus; both a friend and a student of Aristotle were called Eudemus. The titles may indicate dedications or names of editors.

Aristotelian oeuvre, and – apart from the above-mentioned partial coincidences with the *Eudemian Ethics* – it is only possible to point to one decisive problem of transmission: there are – with loose ties to the context – two differing discussions of the concept of pleasure (VII 11–14 and X 1–5). The supposed differences in content between the two Ethics do not seem evident, apart from the fact that the *Eudemian Ethics* contains no independent discussion of contemplation. In what follows, the *Nicomachean Ethics* serves as the main text.

WHAT IS HAPPINESS?

To Aristotle it is natural to begin by asking what people generally consider good for man (*Eth. Nic.* 1095 a 14 ff.; b 14 ff.). Everybody immediately identifies the good with happiness (*eudaimonia*), and happiness means to live well and do well, as we are told with a current but ambiguous formula: originally and commonly it means 'to lead a good life'; to Plato and Aristotle it means 'to live a morally good life'. This twist in meaning can of course only gradually be made explicit. Initially it is sufficient to point out that the formula as used in daily parlance is not very informative, for it is well known that opinions differ about the more precise nature of happiness. Some find happiness in pleasure or enjoyment, others in honours gained – which we would call success – and still others consider the contemplative life happiness. Later it turns out that the concepts of 'pleasure' and 'honours' will gain a more refined signification thanks to closer philosophical reflection. But in any case it cannot be right to identify them immediately with happiness. He who seeks pleasure or honour can never have enough, and hence there will always be something superior to both pleasure and honour. Despite Aristotle's sensitivity to popular wisdom, he must in other words depart from it on a quite fundamental level. The current ideas about happiness are inconsistent – hence not wisdom of life – and cannot pass an exacting philosophical examination. As the good or happiness is what everybody strives for, it only makes sense on the assumption that happiness is something absolute, the content of which can be determined.

But what about the contemplative life? Once again Aristotle withholds his own conclusion. He begins with a discourse with Plato – not specifically about the contemplative life, but about the nature of the concept of the good. The debate with Plato (1096 a 11 ff.) as usual takes the form of criticism but is introduced by a very handsome expression of respect and devotion (cf. p. 269); and it is apparent that the passage is equally a debate conducted by Aristotle with himself. As can be seen in the theology, Aristotle does not in any way wish to reject the thought of a universal metaphysical good, but he must deny that what is good for man can be deduced from the metaphysical good; it is indeed the more humble task of the moral philosopher to seek the good for man – as was Plato's intention in the *Philebus*; Aristotle can in fact use Plato's questions but not his answers. The good is a complex concept – the good is good *for* something or somebody, and has different meanings in the different categories; hence, like being, it is a *transcendentale*. If one accepts the idea of the good, the concept will accordingly be either broken up or void of content. The carpenter or the physician does not look for the good 'in itself' but for that which aids him in his work, and the moral philosopher must similarly ask what is good for man; he cannot use the idea of the good, nor can he use a universal (cf. *Eth. Eud.* 1218 b 7 ff.), and this all the more so because neither an idea nor a universal governs action. What is needed is the concept of the good as the aim of human life. But what would characterize such a concept? Something must connect the several meanings of the word. Aristotle is noticeably cautious in his answer (*Eth. Nic.* 1096 b 26 ff.). The good is not a homonymous concept. It may be a *pros hen* concept; there may only be an analogy between the several 'meanings' of the concept. One might have expected that – as in the *Metaphysics* – we should look for a primary instance to which all other instances of the good are assigned. That Aristotle chooses to leave the question suspended probably shows that he wants to point out that the moral philosopher should not speak about the world at large. The function of the passage is aporetic – the good must be assigned to this or that for which it is good, but it must remain an unambiguous concept. It is the task of the moral philosopher to solve this dilemma.

In the human world the good must be an absolute concept and must function as final cause – the very concept of the good presupposes a standard and a goal. Provisionally Aristotle had already formulated this idea on his own terms (1094 a 4 ff.; 18 ff.): some activities are superior to others – politics is the more important social activity; to make bridles is subordinate, but after all also a useful social activity – and some activities have their purpose in themselves while others do not. Here the concept of an absolute good is at least presupposed. Just as the archer aims at his target, so we must ask what the good is, and this is tantamount to asking what happiness is.

As Aristotle – throughout the rest of his *Ethics* – seeks to hit his target, he follows exactly the same procedure as in his books on substance in the *Metaphysics*: the concept of happiness must be formally determined prior to any attempt to determine its content. Happiness must be that for the sake of which everything else is done (1097 a 18 ff.). More specifically, two formal criteria must be met: happiness must be the final goal (*to teleion*), and happiness must be self-sufficient (*autarkes* – cf. the terminology of the *Philebus*, e.g. 67 A). All acts aim for a goal, and it is possible to distinguish between means and goal. A certain course of action may have one final goal – in or outside the act itself – but the same act can be considered a means in another context. So, the absolute, final goal is not the sum of all imaginable goals of action – for that is infinite – but the goal that cannot be thought to be a means; hence there is nothing to prevent a given action from being carried out both for its own sake and for the sake of happiness. The second criterion – happiness as the self-sufficient – is closely related, but here Aristotle employs current political ideas of what it means to be 'self-sufficient' or to be one's own master (the ideal of autarchy): no single individual is sufficient unto himself, but the 'self-sufficient' life is to be found in intercourse with others – in the family and in the common life of free citizens. Such a self-sufficient life comprehends all human goods. It holds true about both the 'final' and the 'self-sufficient' that they are concepts with a special logical structure: it is not a question of one good as superior or on a par with other goods but of *the* good that creates unity of and coherence between all other goods (cf. [Aristot.] *MM* 1184 a 15 ff.). The concept of the good has the same structure as the concept of form.

A formal determination of the good or happiness can, however, go further than the listing of purely abstract criteria (*Eth. Nic.* 1097 b 22 ff.), and here Aristotle also follows a familiar path: to proceed from function to essence; one can ask what function (what *ergon*) applies specifically to man. The answer is that specific for man is reason. Man is not only a vegetative and perceiving creature; he is also a rational creature; to employ reason 'rightly' and 'well' is synonymous with 'the good' *for* each particular man. It is inherent in human nature that there is a common good for all men. Hence man's specific function lies in the soul's activity (*energeia*) in accordance with reason.

The further argumentation (1098 a 7 ff.) may surprise the modern reader, but on Aristotle' presuppositions – which concur with Greek ideas in general – it is natural. To function well is an *aretē* – man's virtue and 'ability'. This dual meaning permits Aristotle to move effortlessly from the descriptive to the normative: to fulfil one's function as a player of the lyre means that one is a good player of the lyre; to fulfil one's function as man means to be a good man – and thus the path is opened for interpreting the concept of *aretē* as a moral quality. Hence, what is good for man is not only an active life in accordance with reason, but an active life in accordance with virtue (*aretē*), and if there be other virtues – then in accordance with the best. This formal determination contains three key words: activity, reason and virtue, and it has been arrived at by a three-stage argumentation. First by an abstract determination by means of formal criteria, next by reference to human nature, and finally by a smooth – and natural – transition from the descriptive to the normative.

What is good for man is an activity, but a life-long activity – one swallow does not a summer make (1098 a 18). This not only means, as Solon said (1100 a 10; cf. Her. I 32), that nobody can be praised as happy until after his death. It also means that nobody can be happy, unless his whole life, every single moment of it, were a good life. An activity (*energeia*) is exactly a 'complete motion', i.e. it has its purpose in itself, and the part is qualitatively equal to the whole. In the human sphere such an activity is known as *praxis*, and happiness is hence the good *praxis*, *eupraxia* (Aristot. *Eth. Nic.* 1098 b 22 ff.; cf. 1140 b 7). Thus *eupraxia* is the concept whereby Aristotle reinterprets the common-sense idea of happiness as living and doing well (1098 b 9 ff.).

This is an activity in accordance with virtue and man's special 'virtue', reason. But happiness is not simply identical with virtue; virtue is a necessary, not a sufficient precondition for happiness (cf. 1101 b 10 ff.). To understand what happiness is, it is therefore necessary to understand what virtue is, but this in turn requires a review of man's biology and psychology (1102 a 5 ff.; cf. 1097 b 33 ff.). As the most superior natural being, man is equipped with a 'vegetative soul', a 'perceiving soul' and a 'rational soul' – three functions of the soul and not three souls inside the soul. In the *De anima* it was shown (see p. 340; cf. p. 380) that perception is not an isolated phenomenon, but a faculty that is closely tied to desire, striving and rational conduct. This can now be transferred to a description of man as an acting creature. Vegetative functions are totally irrational; they are unconscious and are therefore irrelevant for the study of human acts. The perceiving soul, on the other hand, is not irrational. Perception is a cognitive act. But the striving, the acting, and the awareness of pleasure and pain, which are connected with perception, also contain a cognitive element, and it is this which is of interest to the moral philosopher. An animal acts seemingly rationally, but does so only instinctively. Man, on the other hand, is aware of his acts and can control them. Therefore there is a connection between that rational element in the 'irrational part' of the soul, which merely desires to satisfy needs, and the true 'rational soul', which can direct an act and – in the end – plan a course of life. The irrational part of the soul can be made to 'obey' the rational soul – so that it does not end up with the head wanting to go to the left and the legs to the right. Human desires and emotional impulses can be made subordinate to reason, and if that process is successful, man as a rational being can also become a morally responsible being. The 'virtues' of the truly rational soul are by Aristotle called intellectual virtues, or rational virtues. The virtues that transform desire and inclination into a firm moral character are called character virtues or moral virtues.

Book I of the *Nicomachean Ethics* is thereby concluded. It is Aristotle's prolegomena to a philosophical ethics. But Book I deliberately confines itself to a formal determination of the concept of *eudaimonia*. The special conceptual structure thus delineated can be underlined by a comparison with a concept that in many ways has the same structure, albeit with a quite different function in Aristotelian ethics: the concept of pleasure (*hēdonē*). Indeed, pleasure was also one of the candidates for a determination of the contents or meaning of happiness.

As previously mentioned, there are two discussions in the *Nicomachean Ethics* of this concept. The latter is clearly the more subtle; it corrects some of the findings in the former, and with great probability it can be considered the later. Here Aristotle also builds on Plato's *Philebus*. Like Plato he stresses in part that there are both good and bad feelings of pleasure – in itself the concept is neutral – and in part that one cannot just feel pleasure; one will always take pleasure *in* something – in the same way as one will always be happy *about* something. For this reason alone it cannot be right to maintain – as Eudoxus apparently did (1172 b 9 ff.) – that pleasure is the good that all men strive for. What is needed is a clarification of what gives pleasure.

At this point Aristotle breaks with Plato by substituting his own concept of activity (*energeia*) for Plato's metaphysical concept of 'mixture' – according to the *Philebus* pleasure was 'mixed' with insight, expectation, etc. – and this is no mere quibble about terms. In his first discussion of the concept of pleasure it is merely important to Aristotle to define pleasure as an activity (1153 a 14). In the second he examines closely what is here to be understood by the concept of activity, and he defines pleasure as an epiphenomenon to an activity.

The closer account of the concept of activity in connection with pleasure (1174 a 13 ff.) is probably the most informative analysis of how the notion of a continuum, understood as a 'complete motion' that has its purpose in itself, can be transferred from the physical to the human sphere. An activity naturally takes place in time, but it does not aim at a termination *in* time, and hence time is basically irrelevant. The purpose of the activity resides in the activity itself – I am seeing and have seen, I am understanding and have understood, I am living well and have lived well, I am living happily and have lived happily (see p. 325). The activity is a whole in which every single part qualitatively is like the whole. If I rejoice, the rejoicing is not fixed to a certain point in time – if I say that I rejoice now but not in two minutes, I no longer rejoice.

To that extent the feeling of pleasure and happiness have the same structure. But pleasure is an epiphenomenon, and pleasure can accompany any activity whatsoever (cf. 1175 a 21 ff.). Pleasure completes an activity, as the flower of youth supervenes on those in the full bloom of their age (1174 b 34; cf. 1104 b 4). Pure pleasure or pure enjoyment accordingly accompanies the highest form of life – god's life is always pleasure, and the greatest human pleasure is an added benefit to the life that is best for man as a species (cf. 1176 a 3 ff.).

Pleasure can only be determined as an epiphenomenon; happiness, on the other hand, is an autonomous activity, the highest one, and its contents can be determined. Both pleasure and happiness have their purpose in themselves, but only happiness is 'self-sufficient'.

THE PRACTICAL LIFE

The question of how to define happiness cannot be answered until one has analyzed what human activity or action is in itself and what is meant by the 'virtuous' man's being able to direct his acts with the aid of reason. Until this point it has been ascertained on biological-psychological bases that human acts can be rational, that man accordingly does not only act mechanically from desire and instinct. But that presupposes that man – at least within certain limits – can act voluntarily, that in a given situation he might have acted otherwise. To Aristotle indeterminism is a simple presupposition, a matter of experience, and on several occasions he applied this fundamental view to a broader metaphysical, physical and logical context (cf. p. 301 and p. 358). Aristotelian indeterminism does not imply that there are events without cause but that some series of events can be traced back to human decision, and in his discussion of *futura contingentia* it is not Aristotle's intention to argue for indeterminism, but to draw the logical consequences of the invalidity of determinism. Indeterminism is immediately implied in *ta phainomena* – which for example can be seen from the fact that criminals are punished; in the common view man is considered a responsible being.

A continuous analysis in the *Ethics* (*Eth. Nic.* III 1–5) combines the question of what voluntary actions are with the question of the structure of human actions. Aristotle never speaks of free will but of voluntary acts – he may say that a man is desiring, striving, or wishing, but the idea of will as an autonomous psychic phenomenon can probably not be found until in Seneca and subsequently in Augustine. To Aristotle the problem is to ascertain what lies 'in our power', as it is called with a phrase that was to become a standard formula in Hellenistic philosophy (1112 a 31; 1113 a 11; 1114 b 29).

Voluntary acts have their 'principle' in the agent (1111 a 23). But the actual definition is negative: an involuntary act is an act due to compulsion or ignorance (1109 b 35). This definition, which is also frequently used in modern debates, of course raises the question of which acts are to be ascribed to compulsion or ignorance. This provides Aristotle with an occasion for a thorough analysis of borderline cases – is it 'voluntary' to carry out a tyrant's command under the threat of reprisals; does a drunken man act 'voluntarily' (1110 a 4 ff.)? The former example appears really debatable to him; not so the latter – it is voluntary whether one drinks or does not, and one ought to know that voluntary acts can have unintended consequences. Put more generally: once one has acquired an unfortunate behavioural pattern, it is perhaps impossible to change; but this is no excuse, for one is responsible for one's own character (cf. 1114 a 12 ff.). The various examples serve to legitimate what one in fact holds a person responsible for, what in fact is 'praised or blamed'. It is telling that it is from this position that Aristotle – quite peripherally – decides on 'modern' arguments against indeterminism or against a person's responsibility: if external circumstances can excuse any and all acts, nobody can be held responsible for anything; if a person's bad character is due to heredity, the same argument applies (1110 b 8; 1114 b 3). Aristotle's position is a common-sense compromise between old-fashioned ethics (a man is what he does) and current legal practice: extenuating circumstances can be brought up. It follows from this that the Socratic position, as Aristotle understood it, must be rejected: if nobody voluntarily acts evilly, nobody will voluntarily act well either (1113 b 2 ff.).

The very concept of human acts implies that man – within certain limits – can act freely. A voluntary act presupposes a rational choice (*proairesis*) with respect to a goal; a rational choice presupposes deliberation (*bouleusis*), and deliberation presupposes several possibilities of action. The more precise analysis of these concepts (1111 b 4 ff.; 1112 a 18 ff.) uncovers the structure of human acts as opposed to behaviour solely determined by instinct and desire. The model of description adopted by Aristotle is in itself neutral; what he wishes to demonstrate is how one finds the means to attain a certain goal, and in that respect it is of less importance whether the goal is morally good or bad. But of course nobody would set a goal for himself that he does not consider good (1113 a 15 ff.) – which is a consequence of the good being defined as that for which everybody strives. But moral man will strive for the objective good; amoral man for that which seems good to him.

The agent is not an abstract person but a person with a certain character; and virtue is a mark of character. Now, if one proceeds from philosophy of action to ethics in a narrower sense, one must accordingly examine the concept of virtue. Aristotle begins from the bottom, as it were, with the moral virtues. At the outset the analysis is conducted phenomenologically; it is left open in what sense the moral virtues 'obey' the rational soul, the intellectual virtues. By themselves the moral virtues are not irrational, but they do not express a reflected rational attitude.

Virtue is not – as for example sense perception – a natural faculty; a man is formed or moulded, and he is himself responsible for the result. Intellectual virtues are acquired by teaching; the moral virtues by training and habituation (1103 a 14 ff.) – evidently Aristotle attributes far greater importance to environment than to heredity. To become habituated to a particular form of behaviour, the forming of character, requires time, and this also means that a strange circular structure is attached to the moral virtues: we become just by performing just acts; we act justly because we are just (1103 b 6 ff.; 1105 a 17 ff.). This fundamental paradox cannot be resolved, nor should it be. As acting persons we are from the outset bound to the life of action; moral life is a *praxis*, not a reflection about *praxis*.

This also means that it is only in a vague sense possible to specify wherein the moral act consists – it is dependent on the person and the situation, but both person and situation are particular and do not permit exact, general rules (1103 b 34 ff.). Aristotle's constant, seemingly empty statements that one should act as right thinking (*orthos logos*) dictates or as the good man would act (cf. e.g. 1103 b 32; 1105 b 5) follow from his premisses. The notable – and often misunderstood – concept of 'virtue in the mean' should also be understood on this background (cf. 1104 a 10 ff.; 1106 a 24 ff.). The expression 'mean' was derived from the metaphysical vocabulary of the Academy. The choice of this term is probably not particularly fortunate, for indeed it does not have any metaphysical relevance to Aristotle. He uses it as an abstract phenomenological descriptive term – independent of the contents of the individual virtues and without the banal connotation of 'the golden mean'. In every situation there will be one act that is right, although many will be wrong; in many respects one can do too much or too little – in this sense courage lies in the 'mean' between cowardice and foolhardiness, although thereby nothing has been said about what would be courageous in a given situation. Aristotle applies the concept at two levels. It can be used descriptively as a rule-of-thumb criterion in a general classification of virtues, and in his examination of the individual moral virtues Aristotle uses it as such a loosely tied ordering principle. There are more far-reaching perspectives in his second application of the concept, for here he also speaks about the mean as 'relative to us' (1106 a 28 ff.; cf. 1104 a 7). Here the expression is used as a sort of abbreviation stating that every act depends on unique circumstances: the ethical mean consists in avoiding extremes and acting at the right moment, under the right circumstances, *vis-à-vis* the right people, with the right motives, and in the right way. This means that an ethical act unambiguously is related to a specific person in a specific situation which it is the person's own responsibility to assess – it is not the same that is right for all and sundry at all times – just as little as Milon, the wrestler, is to be allocated the same meat ration as a tiny fellow. The Aristotelian mean is relative to the concrete.

The conclusion of these deliberations is that virtue is a disposition (*hexis*) to act rightly; with proper regard to the several bordering concepts it can then be defined as a disposition tied to choice and the mean which is relative to us; it can be determined rationally in such a manner as a man with moral insight would determine it (1106 b 36).

But this way of thinking creates problems. One can ask whether it makes morality subjective – a question which will be dealt with later. But there is a further problem. On the one hand morality is related to individual man – to a state of character, not to acts – and is not formulated in a set of rules. On the other hand morality consists in the exercise of virtue, and virtues are not abstract – they concern the relation between persons, are relative to social norms, time and place, and people have certain ideas about the contents of the virtues. There is nothing that indicates that Aristotle saw a serious problem in norms changing from one society to another – in practice he seems to have felt quite comfortable with the norms that in fact prevailed in his own milieu. But the relation between a social ethics and an individual ethics, between prevailing morality and the individual's moral character, is a main point in his moral thinking. A determination of virtues cannot be carried out abstractly, and Aristotle accordingly gave his examination of the individual virtues the form of a descriptive charting of current moral ideas and used 'virtue in the mean' as his practical ordering principle. This extensive discussion, which fills two and a half books (*Eth. Nic.* III

6–7), can therefore be considered an ordering of given data of experience – *phainomena* – and be seen as parallel to the great collection of constitutions that was the basis of the *Politics*. But this is not all.

It is not surprising to find analyses of acknowledged 'civic virtues' such as courage (1115 a 6 ff.) and 'self-discipline' (*sōphrosynē* – 1117 b 23). It is more surprising that Aristotle's delight in precise, detailed analysis makes him include not only some moral attitudes that seem rather to have to do with polite behaviour than with virtues (1126 b 11 ff.) but also some virtues that he apparently invented himself. They contribute to the general picture of the Attic ideal of the gentleman but at the same time show that Aristotle did not merely provide a systematized report on current norms. He is interested in coming up with typical positions; his investigations sometimes come close to being impressionistic studies in character; and on occasion he undertakes a reforming of unreflected moral ideals. The individual virtues will not be examined here; it is more reasonable to concentrate on the central – perhaps a little awkward – question of the extent to which Aristotle performs as a neutral observer – and the extent to which he himself believes in his virtues. The question is quite complicated and can be illustrated by looking at one individual 'virtue', magnanimity (*megalopsychia* – 1123 a 34 ff.).

The magnanimous is a strange man. He possesses all civic virtues, has deserved the highest distinctions, and knows so himself. He expects to receive honours, although they are far beneath him. He is a *grand seigneur* – gives most generously, receives reluctantly. He regards the vicissitudes of life as petty, staunchly confronts danger, and conducts himself with dignity; his pace is measured, his voice deep. What is one to do with such a mixture of hero and caricature? Aristotle describes him with an immobile poker face – without irony and without awe. But he does say that magnanimity is the ornament of all virtues, and this person would in fact neatly fit into Aristotle's *Politics*; so it may be that only we with our ballast of Christian humility find this strange. It has in fact often been thought that here Aristotle's own aristocratic ideal slips out – without philosophical varnish. But probably it is not all that simple. The magnanimous personifies the ancient ideal of autarchy in the extreme – of all people, he is his own master. But he is not much more than that: honour is the central concept to him, but he does not possess the important virtue of *sōphrosynē*; everything considered, he is quite unaffected by loftier Aristotelian ideals of practical and theoretical reason, *phronēsis* and *theōria*. Can the answer be that Aristotle is experimenting – that he is bringing out a certain type and leaving it to the reader to make up his mind whether he likes the man or not? Is the magnanimous merely an example of the ambiguousness that necessarily must attach itself to the civic virtues, as long as they are considered in isolation without connection with the real virtue, *phronēsis*? Yes and no. What is interesting about the magnanimous is that he exemplifies the tension that manifestly exists between Aristotle's ethics and politics.

One might expect the section on justice to provide a clearer answer to the question of social ethics versus individual ethics and to the question of Aristotle's own view of the virtues. Justice is simply *the* social virtue that in itself comprises all the others, and therefore it is not surprising that one whole book (*Eth. Nic.* V) is devoted to justice. It is evident that Aristotle cannot – as could Plato – account for justice metaphysically; the concept of justice must be based on actual social reality; justice pertains to relations in the state, and the different applications of the word are dependent on what relations are being discussed.

Aristotle begins by distinguishing between two types of justice, the universal and the special. Later it turns out that this distinction does not cover all angles from which the concept can be considered. Universal justice (1129 a 3 ff.) is what is aimed for by legislation, for legislation touches on all aspects of human life in Aristotle's opinion and likely enough in the opinion of most Greeks. Special justice (1130 a 14 ff.) deals with the distribution of external goods – honours and money. It characterizes both forms of justice that they are not virtues without qualification, because they concern the relation to 'the other' (1130 a 13; b 1). It may of course sound surprising that virtues should have nothing to do with one's 'neighbour', nor is this the intention. The intention is to show that above all a virtue without qualification concerns man's inner, moral *habitus*, while universal and special justice are concerned with institutionalized rules for the relation between citizens. Justice as virtue *per se* and social justice have identical extension but different contents.

Special justice concerns the distribution of external goods only (1131 a 10 ff.). Here Aristotle advocates so-called 'distributive justice'; as he himself says – once more using terminology taken over from the Academy – one should adhere to a geometrical proportion: if a person, A, has been more deserving than another person, B, A should correspondingly receive that much more of the goods available for distribution. But if it is a question of rectificatory re-establishment of the *status ante* (1131 b 25 ff.) – typically by means of a court decision – the arithmetical proportion obtains: if A and B are guilty of the same offence they must receive the same punishment. The two principles – also used in Plato's *Laws* – thus combine reward according to merit with equality before the law, but to Aristotle it is in both cases a question of equality: it would be unequal if there were not agreement between merit and reward. These two principles have been of far-reaching significance even down to the most recent debates about social justice.

The rule of arithmetical proportion applies in principle also to business contracts and the private exchange of goods (1132 b 2 ff.; cf. *Pol.* 1257 b 17 ff.), and thus Aristotle became the godfather of economic theory. The problem on which he focuses is that it is difficult to find a common denominator for the exchange of goods: how many shoes correspond to a house? Shoes and houses are in fact incommensurables, and when their worth is measured in money, this is strictly speaking an arbitrary denominator. None the less, there is a criterion for 'a just price', which is demand – in other words, not a property of the goods themselves but a property imposed by society. Accordingly Aristotle bases the exchange-value of goods on their value in use. Money is a useful symbol of value in use; but if money itself becomes an object of exchange, dangerous perspectives open up, the accumulation of capital for its own sake and in the final analysis usury.

From other points of view political justice can be discussed (*Eth. Nic.* 1134 a 17) – but it varies according to the different constitutions of democracy, oligarchy, and tyranny. Behind the positive law that builds on convention, there is, however, a natural law that everywhere is uniform at all times (1134 b 18 ff.; cf. *Rhet.* 1373 b 1 ff.). Thus Aristotle summarized earlier debates about the relation between conventional and divine law (see p. 113) and laid the foundation for the debates about natural law of later times.

As will be seen, Aristotle does not at all confine himself to the purely descriptive in his analysis of justice as it manifests itself in society; and in a number of areas his analyses have served as the basis for later discussions. But an analysis of social justice still captures only the external side of the concept. Justice is not merely a question of the distribution of external goods, nor of legal equality; justice as virtue concerns the inner man. The tension between the two sides of justice appears for example in Aristotle's concept of 'the equitable' (*Eth. Nic.* 1137 a 31 ff.; cf. *Rhet.* 1374 a 26 ff.; compare with *aequitas* in Roman Law, equity in British Common Law) – and here he also continues and refines Plato's thinking (*The Statesman, Laws*). Social and legal justice must necessarily be expressed in general rules; but what in a given situation is right cannot directly be deduced from a rule; it depends on moral insight. The law is to be used with consideration of what is equitable in the particular case, and it will always hold true that no rule is sufficient in itself. In that sense morality is above the law.

It seems to be Aristotle's position that in social life every deliberation about what is right and wrong must build on the premises which existing societies provide or can provide. Moral concepts are reflected in the norms of a given society, but it is not a question of identity. Ethics deals with the good man, politics with the good state; but ethics is founded on the concept of virtue, and virtue immediately places man in his social context; thus ethics and politics are connected, even though they still belong on two levels: external frameworks, institutions and rules on the one hand, and inner attitude and moral insight on the other, are not the same. Hence it will hold good not only with respect to justice but to all virtues that as social beings we are bound by prevailing norms, even though man's identity as a moral being has not thereby been determined.

The set of problems implied in the concept of justice can be made clearer by consideration of Aristotle's examination of friendship, for friendship is a concept that ties social relations, family relations, and morality together; how much importance Aristotle attributed to friendship appears immediately from the fact that two books (*Eth. Nic.* VIII–IX) are devoted to the concept. Friendship and justice concern the same – good relations between men – but friendship is the more fundamental: among true friends there is no need of justice, but the just society cannot exist without friendship or 'concord' (*homonoia*) – the concept which according to traditional ideology (Pericles and Democritus, for example) was the precondition for the good society (*Eth. Nic.* 1155 a 22 ff.; 1159 b 25 ff.). This implies that if all were true friends, it would be possible to live in an anarchic society, and in fact Aristotle stresses that between true friends there is no need of an external standard of values, as there is in regulated social relations (cf. 1158 b 29 ff.). Friendship is the true relation with 'the other' or one's 'neighbour'.

Friendship is a natural necessity and is 'noble' in itself, which is to say that it serves no higher purpose. It may not be a virtue, but it implies virtue and is – like the exercise of a virtue – an *energeia* (1155 a 3 ff.; 1157 b 5 ff.). Yet true friendship is rare. Friendships based on utility or pleasure – for example pleasure in somebody's ready wit – serve other ends and are therefore inconstant. True friendship, on the other hand, is enduring, exists for the sake of the friend himself – for one's friend is one's other self (1169 b 6) – and can only exist between good men who are equal in virtue (1156 a 7 ff.).

The happy life is an activity, but no man can live in isolated self-sufficiency (autarchy), and therefore cohabitation with friends is part of the good life (1169 b 3 ff.). The good man feels for his friend as he does for himself, but true friendship presupposes personal integrity, that one has a true relation to oneself. In real friendship altruism and egoism will therefore coincide; when one seeks 'the noble' for a friend one seeks it for oneself (1166 a 1 ff.). There is therefore a true self-love, which is the basis for the good common life in which everybody gives and receives according to his ability. Happiness does not consist in friendship, but no man can achieve happiness on his own; he who acts 'nobly' does so in harmony with himself and others and with awareness of 'the noble', and man's 'true self' is reason – but reason is a common property (1168 b 28 ff.; cf. 1164 b 2 ff.).

True friendship is only to be found among equals; friends are equals because of virtue and reason. But there are also social and role-determined aspects of friendship – in fact this is a necessity in every society. It is one thing that only mature men are suitable for friendship – old people are testy and acquire no friends, the young are too tempestuous and allow themselves to be duped by whoever comes along (1158 a 1 ff.), but more importantly, friendship in the real sense can only come about between social equals. 'Concord' does, to be sure, bind the different population groups together; but friendships between persons of different social status will almost always be friendships of utility. The exceptions are rare, but do occur – Aristotle goes so far as to say that it is possible to be friends with one's slave, not *qua* slave but *qua* man (1161 b 2; cf. 1177 a 8) – a remarkable example, but a solitary swallow.

But there is one case of natural friendship between unequal parties: family life. The relations between family members can – more or less playfully – be compared with the different types of constitution. The father is like a king to his son, and the father–son relationship is therefore analogous with monarchy; the husband rules his wife like an aristocrat; the relationship between brothers is analogous with democracy. But those types of constitution have their deviations: monarchy can become the worst of all, tyranny; aristocracy can become dictatorship by the few; democracy can become general licentiousness. If family relations in like manner deteriorate, all can see the fatal consequences (1160 a 31 ff.; 1158 b 11 ff.).

Within these patriarchal frames Aristotle can entertain handsome thoughts, not least with respect to the friendship between husband and wife (1162 a 16 ff.). The books on friendship do perhaps show more than anything else the vast scope between the ideal and timeless on the one hand and on the other the temporal and socially determined – in Aristotle's eyes the naturally determined.

When all is said and done, friendship is only an external good, albeit the highest one (1169 b 10). Friendship presupposes good character, just as the good social order presupposes the good man. But the good man is not only a man who by habituation and education has acquired a firm character. In the final analysis the moral virtues consist only in the cultivation of natural faculties whereby moral man comes to 'obey' reason. From an ethical point of view reason is identical with the intellectual virtue which governs a life in action, *phronēsis* or the practical insight that makes man conscious as a rational moral being. The man who only possesses moral virtues will perhaps act morally well but not with moral insight. But moral insight also presupposes good character. This reflects the fundamental duality: on the one hand moral life is conditional, for man is dependent on society, tradition and friends, and virtue cannot be abstracted from these external conditions. On the other hand, virtue is internalized; the external framework is only good, if the man is good. *Phronēsis* is accordingly related to political wisdom as is friendship to justice: the two concepts have the same extension, but are still not identical (1141 b 23 ff.). And it is true in Aristotle, as in Plato, that the good man will act well; good acts do not in themselves have moral value.

Aristotle begins his analysis of *phronēsis* with a reminder that the morally good person acts in conformance with 'the mean' and as right thinking dictates. What lies in these concepts? Apparently they are void of contents; it is possible to define one concept by the other, but that does not get us much further. How are they then to be defined? If one expects a strict determination in the form of a rule ethics, one will of course miss Aristotle's basic intention. Apparently the answer lies in a closer examination of the way *phronēsis* works. This requires a preliminary distinction between practical and theoretical reason. Until now it has merely been stated that reason is the guiding part of the soul. But reason can either be directed at unchangeable or changeable objects; it can be theoretical or it can be oriented to practice. The goal of theoretical reason is truth; the goal of practical reason is truth bound to desire.

This is an important statement, but in order to understand it, it is necessary to take a step backwards (1139 a 17 ff.). From nature's hand man has three basic faculties: reason (*nous*), sensation (*aisthēsis*) and desire or inclination (*orexis*). In a manner of speaking these can cooperate in pairs. If one, in the abstract, considers man only as a cognitive being, one has need of sensation and reason; on the combination of these two faculties depend the theoretical sciences and logic, and the outcome is a judgement that may be affirmative or negative, true or false. If one combines sensation with desire, one finds oneself on the animal level. As is often emphasized, perception, the feeling of pleasure and pain, and the whole behavioural pattern are here tied closely to each other; and the actual behaviour might find expression in judgement-like statements. However, human behaviour is something different and more: it is a deliberate behaviour, an action or *praxis* that depends on a choice (*proairesis*) and deliberation (*bouleusis*) and aims at something to be achieved. Here *nous* and *orexis* are combined so that reason guides and desire is guided, cultivated, or formed for action, and here a judgement could also be formulated, which is implicit in the action: a rational action has a rationale. In itself reason cannot initiate an action, but the choice that determines the action depends on the unbreakable unity of reason and desire, and hence Aristotle calls this unity desiderative reason or rational desire. This is the unity that ties the moral virtues with the practical intellectual virtue, prudence or *phronēsis*. *Phronēsis* implies character, and character implies *phronēsis*.

Phronēsis is the only intellectual virtue concerning human acts – according to modern views it is therefore strictly speaking the only intellectual virtue whatsoever; the other intellectual virtues are 'abilities'. Aristotle delimits *phronēsis* carefully in relation to these other virtues: the experience or technical ability, *technē*, which aims at producing something (*poiēsis* – 1140 a 1 ff.); demonstrative knowledge or *epistēmē*

(1139 b 14 ff.); the insight of theoretical reason into first principles, *nous* (1140 b 31 ff.); and finally to the combination of *epistēmē* with *nous*, wisdom or *sophia* (1141 a 9 ff.). Naturally, the main focus is on the relation between *phronēsis* and *sophia*, and it can provisionally be determined as follows: *sophia* concerns the highest, which is above man, the universal and invariable – in fact the metaphysical good; *phronēsis* concerns the human good, the variable which can be made the object of deliberation; it pursues a goal realizable in a *praxis*; it knows both the universal and the particular. *Phronēsis* can hence be defined as a true and reasoned disposition to act with an aim to what is good or bad for man (1140 b 4).

The man who possesses *phronēsis* – *ho phronimos* – aims for an action, and an action presupposes deliberation, choice, and an intention with the act, so that the agent discovers the means to the goal. Aristotle has accounted for all this in his description of a neutral course of action. But *ho phronimos* does not undertake any odd action, nor is he merely skilful or clever at finding means (1144 a 23). First, his action has its purpose in itself – it is a *praxis*. Second, his action is a good action, *eupraxia*; he carries out the realizable good, *to prakton agathon* (1139 a 34; 1140 b 7; cf. 1097 a 23). *Ho phronimos* deliberates the means to effectuate the good. But is this not a modest role to assign to practical reason? Should *ho phronimos* not also determine the goal; ought he not to ponder what is the right goal? Let us deal with the latter first. It is a question that Aristotle never asks directly, because to him – as to Plato – it is self-evident that in a given situation there is one, and only one right action, as the good man comes to see. Whoever realizes the good will never doubt the goal, only the means – in Plato and Aristotle the good man will never find himself in a conflict like Antigone's.

The former question is connected with the latter. Aristotle explicitly states (1144 a 7; 1145 a 5) that the moral virtues define the goal; *phronēsis* finds the means. Yet he also says (1142 b 33) that *phronēsis* realizes or 'grasps' the goal. This division of labour between moral virtues and *phronēsis* is in fact not surprising. In the moral man character and moral insight are united – desiderative reason and rational desire. It is of course in practice the whole man who sets the goal, deliberates, and chooses the means. But if one were to distinguish conceptually between character and reason, it is clear that *phronēsis* represents the intellectual aspect – deliberation and insight – while the good intention – to 'set a goal' – depends on character.

What is meant by *phronēsis* 'realizing' the goal? It is an insight that consists in *ho phronimos* understanding the present concrete situation because by virtue of his experience he can see that it is a situation 'of this kind'. The particular and the universal are therefore bound to each other (1141 b 14). In itself an action is of course particular; but if the world consisted only of atomic events, every possibility of action would be cancelled. The act must necessarily be related to a general purpose or be considered an instance of something general. *Phronēsis* is reason aimed at practice. Practical and theoretical reason aim at different objects, but reason – *nous* – is in its essence one and the same: the faculty of intuitive insight. Sometimes Aristotle narrows the designation *nous* down so as to apply to the insight into first principles by theoretical reason. In this sense theoretical reason is opposed to practical reason, which intuitively 'grasps' the particular situation (1142 a 23). But in its basic signification – insight – *nous* is active both in the perception of particulars as being 'of this kind' and in the insight into first principles (cf. p. 310). Hence theoretical and practical reason have the same structure (1143 a 25 ff.): in perceiving that 'this' is a triangle I know something universal about 'this'; in perceiving this situation I know what must be done. The object of *phronēsis* is what must be done now; but what must be done now can only be understood if one has insight into the universal in the particular. The difference between theoretical and practical reason is accordingly in part an object-determined difference, in part it is dependent on theoretical reason's being exclusively cognitive, while practical reason comprehends the whole man as an individual who has insight and acts in certain situations.

Aristotle expresses this relation between the particular and universal in human acts formally in what is called a practical syllogism. The practical syllogism (*De an.* 434 a 16 ff.; *De mot. an.* 701 a 7 ff.; *Eth. Nic.* 1144 a 31 ff.; cf. 1141 b 18 ff.) consists of a universal, imperative major premiss (one ought to perform act x in situation y), a singular, indicative minor premiss (this is situation y), and a singular, imperative conclusion (I ought to undertake act x) – which Aristotle simply identifies with the act (I perform x). A variant can include the deliberation of means to a given goal (x is a good thing; y is a means to x; I perform y). Just like Aristotle's scheme for a course of action, the practical syllogism is of course in itself neutral. But to *ho phronimos* the major premiss will stand for the objective good – which is also good for him; the minor premiss for a correct understanding of the situation. Whoever is without *phronēsis* (cf. 1142 a 21; 1146 b 35; 1147 a 25) will – in formal terms – commit an error in the major premiss (he pursues the apparent good) or in the minor premiss (he misunderstands the situation).

The practical syllogism raises two questions. First: is it not a blunder to identify conclusion with action? No, because there is no question of a theoretical deliberation that subsequently in a mysterious manner results in action – a thought cannot initiate an act. The practical syllogism presupposes the act, not the other way around; it provides the rational justification that in a way is built into every act. The good man acts as he does because of his character, and this act will at the same time agree with right thinking.

Second: does not an act's being based on a general principle mean that Aristotle ends up in a rule ethics anyway? No, for the major premiss is not a rule which can be formulated once and for all and be readily available. The intimate connection between the universal and the particular appears from the fact that *phronēsis* comes to understand what must be a general precept in *this* situation. The conclusion can be universalized, but it is still bound to the concrete – *to prakton agathon*.

Aristotle's conclusion concerning *phronēsis* takes up the relation between moral character and moral insight (1142 b 22 ff.). *Phronēsis* pertains to the just, the noble, and the good for man, but so do the moral virtues. What more does *phronēsis* provide? If *phronēsis* is knowledge, how can knowledge make us good? Either we are already good or we are not – the purpose was to do the good, not to know about the good. The answer lies already in the point of departure: moral insight and moral character mutually imply each other; one cannot be good without *phronēsis*; one cannot have *phronēsis* without virtue (1144 b 30 ff.). Moral man's desire is for the good and is accompanied by insight into the good that creates moral conscience and responsibility.

This conclusion is surely reached in a standing dialogue with Socrates and Plato. It implies a partial departure from Socrates, as Aristotle understood him: virtue *is* not knowledge, virtue *implies* knowledge (1144 b 17 ff.). And the interplay between naturally determined desire and reason signals a departure from Plato. Still, it is also a continuation of the Socratic-Platonic inspiration. The man who is simply good is not virtuous in one area and not in another; perfect virtue (*hē kyria aretē*) implies all virtues because it is founded in man's nature, and this perfect virtue is *phronēsis* (1144 b 2; 16; 1145 a 1; cf. Plat. *Phaedo* 69 A; see p. 187). Whoever does not possess *phronēsis* can very well possess what Aristotle calls natural virtues; he can for example be naturally disposed to courage but not to 'self-discipline' (1144 b 2 ff.; 32 ff.). On the other hand, whoever possesses genuine virtue also possesses all civic virtues. This throws retrospective light on the treatment of the civic virtues or the moral virtues. If the moral virtues are present in isolation they are merely natural talents cultivated by education, and such virtues are frail and transient; if they are illuminated by insight, *phronēsis*, they are transferred to a higher level. Then they express true virtue.

Aristotle does not contest the existence of the metaphysical good, but contrary to Plato he does not believe that the good for man can be derived from the metaphysical good. The focal point in his ethics is not so much the concept of *the* good as the concept of the good *man*, the ideal person who in the given situation grasps the objectively good and acts according to his insight. What objectively are seen as good or 'noble' acts can only be defined quite stereotypically: to die for one's country, do well by one's friends, etc. (cf. *Rhet.* 1366 a 23 ff.) – what is decisive is the acting person who of course will die for his country and do well by his friends, because he is who he is. But the ideal person also lives in this world, and he is not – as the Stoic hero – indifferent to suffering: it is, as Aristotle remarks, nonsense to speak about being happy on the rack (*Eth. Nic.* 1153 b 19). And a certain number of external goods – good health, economic and social status, honour, friends – are pre-conditions for the happy life (cf. 1099 a 33; 1123 b 20; 1153 b 17; 1178 b 3; *Pol.* 1323 a 24). In this respect as well, the good man is placed in the midst of life and is subject to its conditions. But it is his attitude to the world that is decisive. Whoever merely does what he should and obeys the law is not virtuous (*Eth. Nic.* 1144 a 13); he may very well understand how to make use of the external goods correctly, but only he who possesses perfect virtue will manage the goods so that what in itself is only 'good' or 'useful' becomes 'noble and good' (*Eth. Eud.* 1248 b 8 ff.). He lives the good life that renders man autonomous and happy as a human being.

Like nearly all Greek ethics, Aristotle's is concerned with the ideal person. But he is rare, and it should be possible to account for why it is that most men fail to live up to the ideals. To Aristotle out-and-out evil or moral depravity are pathological borderline cases. What interests him is the incontinent person who does not act as he knows he ought to – the good that he wills but does not perform (1145 a 15 ff.). If one takes Socrates at his word it is impossible to act evilly if one has come to know the good. And yet we know that this is possible (1145 b 21 ff.).

But when Aristotle tries to solve the problem, it turns out that he is a Socratic and an intellectualist a good deal of the way. Behind his arguments are two basic positions: everybody in fact desires what appears good for himself, and the truly good will never be without insight into the objectively good. Accordingly the attempt is made to explain incontinence as insufficient ability to reason (1146 b 8 ff.). The principal thought is that one can omit acting on the knowledge one in fact does have – the drunkard knows very well that it is wrong to drink, but he has 'forgotten' it. Disorder has crept into his practical syllogism, but perhaps his faults are covers for sinister psychic repressions.

For of course Aristotle knows that there are psychological realities behind 'false judgements'. One can judge falsely in momentary recklessness or because one's character is generally weak (1150 b 19 ff.; 1152 a 27 ff.), but it is a question of judgement, and Aristotle could have concluded that there are therapeutic possibilities in making an implicit judgement explicit. He does not do so – for it is habituation not arguments that prepares the way for moral insight (1158 a 18). But it is remarkable that he considers incontinence a sickness that – in principle, at least – is curable. The inferior part of reason should be made to 'obey' true reason.

THE THEORETICAL LIFE – AND MAN'S DOUBLE IDENTITY

In the last book of the *Nicomachean Ethics* – to which there is no counterpart in the *Eudemian Ethics* – Aristotle returns to the first book. The life in happiness has turned out to consist of actions – *praxeis* – in conformance with virtue (1176 a 30 ff.). No determination in the form of prescriptions for action is provided; instead there is a closer determination of what is to be understood by perfect virtue and by *eupraxia*. The formal criteria have been met – a life in agreement with perfect virtue is a final and self-sufficient goal – and the formal definition (1098 a 16) has also been filled in.

But still, man has a double identity; he can transcend himself and attain the divine by virtue of pure reason, *nous*, for *nous* is the divine 'self' in the individual, in so far as man is more than human (1178 a 1; cf. 1168 b 31). The double identity is in full agreement with Aristotle's anthropology, and this is why also the *Ethics* concludes by referring to the transcendent and divine. Contemplation or *theōria*, the exercise of wisdom or *sophia*, is hence the highest happiness and man's loftiest activity – if he transcends the human (1177 a 12 ff.; cf. 1144 a 4; 1141 a 26). We may only have access to reason and pure thought in a few, happy moments, but with the divine element in us we should, in so far as possible, strive for immortality – that is the message at the end of the *Ethics*, just as it was in the beginning of the *Metaphysics*. It is clear that *theōria* eminently fulfils the demands of a happy life in book I – it is independent of all external factors in practical life; he who lives the contemplative life and cultivates the divine in himself is beloved by the gods (1179 a 22 ff.); no pleasure is greater than that which attends the contemplative life (1177 a 25). But it is likewise clear that one demand in book I cannot be met: if there are several virtues, man must live in conformance with the best (1098 a 17). Man is a composite creature, and the practical virtue cannot simply be reduced to the theoretical one.

The relation between the two highest forms of life is paradoxical – which Aristotle stresses already by his language: the real man is he who transcends the human. But man's nature is paradoxical – he has his place in practical life but also belongs elsewhere, and this, it would appear, is a contrast that is not to be glossed over. The man seeking the contemplative life is of course also a man of flesh and bones; he has his needs and participates in moral and political life (1178 b 5), and with his friends and people of similar persuasion he partakes of the theoretical. It is hardly Aristotle's problem how one in fact arranges matters with one's dual identity on the odd gloomy Monday; ethics is not concerned with applied psychology. His errand is the very contrast between the two 'lives'. If man is considered as an ethical and political being, there can be no doubt that the life based on internalized virtue and *phronēsis* is a wholly happy human life.

On the other hand, if man is considered a contemplative being, practical life becomes secondary, as Aristotle says (1178 a 8). Then it is the task of *phronēsis* to prepare the way for *theōria* (1144 a 8; cf. *Eth. Eud.* 1249 b 16 ff.). It will in general hold true that *phronēsis*, moral goodness, and experience in life are preconditions for the contemplative life. But *phronēsis* is not logically subordinated to *theōria*, and it is nowhere stated that one can learn practical wisdom by contemplation. When it comes to what is good for man, *ho phronimos* is sovereign.

The *Nicomachean Ethics* leads to a confrontation of the two ideals of life, but in the last chapter (*Eth. Nic.* 1179 a 33 ff.) the reader is faced with yet another surprise. Here the gates are effectively shut against the great visions, for there is a difference between man's ideal and empirical nature, and with respect to the latter Aristotle is not in any way wrapped in illusion: his view of men as they mostly are is certainly no more optimistic than Plato's. This final chapter takes an overall view of the entire ethical tradition and is rife with hidden and direct quotes: the wise Solon – the apple of Aristotle's eye – Pindar, Democritus, the Sophists, Isocrates and Plato are all there, expressly quoted or alluded to. How can we become good men, Aristotle asks once again, and then he pursues a current way of asking the question, which goes back to the Sophists and has proven decisive for his own approach (Prot. frg. DK B3; Isocr. *Ant.* 192; cf. Aristot. *Eth. Nic.* 1099 b 9 ff.): are we good by nature, or do we become so by habituation or by teaching? If nature is the more important – as in the old ethics of nobility – ethical education is of course meaningless. There are probably not many who can cope with intellectual instruction – with arguments. What about the training of character – habituation? Might there not be a need to nourish the student's soul so that he by habit will be disposed to noble deeds – and noble hate, just as the soil is cultivated to nourish the seed (cf. Ant. frg. DK B60)?[2] If it is a question of the forming of character, we shall above all need legislation, for it is the task of law to provide a firm frame for education and to chastize. Only the few are susceptible to rational arguments, and only the few allow themselves to be guided by what is noble; chastizement and admonition are on the other hand efficient arguments (Arsitot. *Eth. Nic.* 1179 b 31 ff.). Such is the transition from ethics to politics, a transition without illusions.

2   The modern meaning of 'culture' is derived from this image.

POLITICS

Aristotle's ethics deals with the inner conditions for human happiness, his politics with the outer framework, public life, and thereby with the distribution of external goods. If *phronēsis* is one step removed from the highest happiness, politics is removed by two. In the *Ethics* political and social life are taken up – primarily in the sections on justice and friendship and in more stylized form in the examination of individual moral virtues – although only as a sort of reflection, the outward expression of the highest ethical virtue, *phronēsis*. To be sure, politics is the superior science, the purpose of which is to lay down the conditions for happiness, but in itself the political life is not happiness (cf. *Eth. Nic.* 1094 a 28 ff.). As Aristotle moves from ethics to politics, the stage changes, and the shift is from the ideal to the practical-empirical level; it is characteristic of his methodical rigidity that as the premisses are bound to the concrete political world so are the conclusions. Reason is of course to govern in the community as well as in the human soul. The distinction between the obeying and the leading parts of reason and between practical and theoretical reason are presupposed (*Pol.* 1324 a 25 ff.; 1325 b 14 ff.; 1333 a 16 ff.), but such distinctions only appear if they have social relevance; the focus is on finding a rational social model, not on asking what reason is, and when *phronēsis* is sometimes used, it is – as in the *Protrepticus* – in the broad basic sense of reason or insight in general (cf., e.g. 1289 a 12).

To Aristotle, as to Plato, the city state is the natural frame for political life, but Aristotle feels much more at home with *de facto* moderate, conservative norms and with the Attic ideal of the gentleman. Himself a bourgeois and a newcomer with connections to the Macedonian monarchy, he identified himself much more with his milieu than did Plato, the aristocrat and prophet. There are many striking points of resemblance between the *Politics* and especially the *Laws*, but Aristotle's attitude is different. He feels personally engaged in his subject matter, and his method is empirical. Politics is the art of the possible, and the best constitution possible is found by investigating actually existing constitutions – the empirical background for the *Politics* is, as has been mentioned, an analysis of 158 Greek constitutions undertaken by Aristotle himself and his students. Only one of these preparatory works – on Athens – has been preserved and it is thought to be Aristotle's own work. The examination of Athens was probably especially extensive, but nevertheless it seems possible to draw some general conclusions from the nature of this work: a very careful historical and systematic presentation with a wealth of details, but throughout also evaluating and reasoning.

This working method is quite different from Plato's, and Aristotle's critique of Plato's political thought is in fact aimed at the utopian and unrealistic, most especially the abolition of private property and family life (1261 b 16 ff.) – to Aristotle two pillars of society. The Platonic state is an artificial unity that fails to respect the actual difference between individuals; Plato took no interest in the role of the common man; it is dangerous to invest one class with power (1261 a 14 ff.; 1264 a 13 ff.); not only will the inhabitants of Plato's state not be happy, but the result of the whole undertaking will be the opposite of what was aimed for – strife and civil war (1264 b 15 ff.; a 24). Plato is never commonplace, as Aristotle remarks, but it is difficult always to hit the right mark, and he is too much given to digressions (1265 a 10; 1264 b 39).

Aristotle's ethics is elitist yet seeks for the universally valid through the temporally determined; but in the *Politics* one can feel oneself placed in a closed universe, one that is indeed very dated, and at times out-and-out provincial. The Greek city state is not only the centre of the world — the world outside Verona is alien and barbaric — but it is a city state that only exists for the sake of an upper class of male citizens. The position of the head of the house is patriarchal, women have no civil rights, slaves are the property of their masters — and a 'living tool' — barbarians are inferior, and strictly speaking tradesmen ought not to be citizens (1259 a 37 ff.; b 18 ff.; 1253 b 23 ff.; 1327 b20 ff.; 1328 a 21 ff.). As it for example appeared in his analysis of friendship, within this framework Aristotle has quite differentiated points of view; but that the framework is universally valid is not in doubt. It is only with respect to one point that he seems to have been affected by the emancipation movements of his day, namely in his view of slaves. In the *Ethics* he distinguished in remarkable manner between the slave *qua* slave and the slave *qua* human being. But in principle he retains slavery as an institution — as did Plato. The motive is economic: if all tools could work of themselves when told to, there would be no need of slaves; but since the world is as it is, slavery is an economic necessity (1253 b 33 ff.) — an almost anachronistic acumen. If one does not have machines one will have to have slaves. But apparently Aristotle also felt that another justification was urgent: some human beings are, he thinks, by nature destined to be slaves; they are physically well equipped but intellectually inferior, and hence they are better off living at the slave level — it is nature's order that some are destined to lead, others to obey, just as the soul rules the body, and as reason has a 'leading' and an 'obeying' part. The conclusion is that it is necessary to distinguish between natural slavery and unnatural slavery — prisoners of war, for example (1254 a 17 ff.; 1255 a 3 ff.).

On a number of points Aristotle thus follows traditional points of view. Perhaps there is nothing surprising in that, but it almost seems atavistic that his horizon is entirely confined to an idealized version of the city state. While he was writing the *Politics*, his pupil, Alexander the Great, was seeing to it that the days of the city state were numbered. No doubt Aristotle realized this, and one can imagine that the *Politics* was written in protest: whether or not the old world was fading, it was nature's intention that men should live in *polis*-communities.

That this was Aristotle's position can be seen in the introduction to the *Politics*. Here it can also be seen that his ideal was not unreflected. Just like all other phenomena, state and society must be explained teleologically. Human communities are determined by nature, for by nature man is a social being (*zōion politikon*) — he who of his own volition stands outside society is either a scoundrel or a god (1253 a 2; cf. 29). The basic, naturally given relations (1252 a 24 ff.) between humans exist between man and woman and between master and slave. On this basis the family is constituted as a social and economic unity; if one next includes several generations and ramifications, the family becomes a village, and a reasonable number of villages become a community. In this sense the community is secondary to the family, but as man can only flourish in a community, community as the final cause is primary in relation to the individual and the family. What binds the community together are language and the feelings of justice and injustice.

It is a standard scheme in Greek political thought to explain the nature of society through a fictive reconstruction of its coming into being. The prototype of this mode of presentation is of course Protagoras' myth; Plato used the model in the second book of the *Republic* – but did so in order to take it to the limit of parody and break away from it. In many respects Aristotle is closer to Protagoras, but he too left his own impression on the traditional freight: what is decisive is the teleological way of thinking. It also enables him to maintain that it is the Greek city state that represents the final stage, but this of course does not oblige him to explain why all communities have not developed into city states.

Certain key concepts lie behind Aristotle's special analyses, which, as in the *Ethics*, connect the normative with the descriptive. What first and foremost bind the state together are justice – by Aristotle understood as the proper combination of equality before the law with distribution of external goods according to merit; concord (*homonoia*) – from ancient times a basic concept in political theory; friendship and the concept of autarchy – the ideal of the free (male) citizen who is his own master in a state that is not too big, and which is also its own master (cf., e.g. 1253 a 37; *Eth. Nic.* 1167 b 2; *Pol.* 1262 b 7; 1253 a 1). Taken together these ideals aim at democratic relations within an elite.

Like so many other Aristotelian works, the *Politics* is heterogeneous as transmitted to us; probably it is a collection of treatises, some of which are unfinished. But their contents constitute a whole. A state is the sum of her citizens, but a citizen is not simply a person living in a particular city – slaves are not citizens, settlers from the outside (metics) have only limited legal, private rights; the citizen in the real sense is accordingly only the man who participates in judicial decisions and in government (1275 a 22). This is of course only a formal definition. It depends on the constitution who has these rights, and here Aristotle uses the classical division of constitutions into three types: monarchy, aristocracy and majority rule. And like Plato he adds three deviant types: tyranny, oligarchy, and mob rule (democracy). In the good constitutions the rulers govern for the sake of the subjects, in the bad for the sake of themselves (1279 a 22 ff.; cf. *Eth. Nic.* 1160 a 31 ff.; see p. 379). It is also in agreement with Plato (the *Statesman*) that Aristotle considers the ideal monarchy as the best of all forms of government and majority rule as the worst, although tyranny is the worst and democracy the most tolerable deviant. Now, the ideal monarch is a somewhat utopian figure, so in practice one can disregard kingly rule (cf. *Pol.* 1288 a 15 ff.). A descriptive analysis of the types of constitution will primarily aim to show how a given form of constitution can best be sustained (1304 b 19 ff.). Here the question is not whether the constitution is good or bad, and Aristotle goes so far as to give the tyrant good advice about how best to stay in power (1313 a 34 ff.).

But if one asks about the best possible constitution, the traditional scheme will turn out to be insufficient (1279 b 11 ff.). It is a classification for the sake of convenience that exclusively asks whether government is in the hands of one, a few, or the many. But reality is not that convenient. A given constitution will always reflect the social and economic structure of that society. An oligarchy is governed by wealthy men, a democracy by the poor, and if one wishes to find the best possible constitution one must therefore stabilize the relation between rich and poor rather than speak abstractly of the few or the many. A necessary precondition for a good constitution is therefore that economic possibilities be created for a strong middle class; that is the only thing that can prevent the state from breaking down into two factions (1295 a 25). Therefore poverty must be opposed – not by subventions, such as the diets paid in Athens as fees for political tasks, but by securing land and employment for the poor (1320 a 32).

Such a social programme is rather unique in the world of Antiquity. Equally original is the observation that constitution and state are not the same and that the political system is dependent on the social and economic structure. But it is an observation that causes Aristotle to moderate his ideals. His true ideal is aristocracy, the state where literally the best men rule (cf. 1276 b 37; 1279 a 35), but in general there are not many good men, and moral aristocracy easily degenerates into moneyed aristocracy or oligarchy – and a capitalist society is certainly not Aristotle's preference. Therefore one must compromise and have regard for the economic and political interests of all social groups. In practice the best possible state hence becomes a mixture of oligarchy and democracy, called *politeia* by Aristotle. This simply means constitution, but in practice it stands for the 'good' majority rule with added elements of oligarchy and subject to the law: *politeia* is the constitutional form in which the people govern for the common good (1279 a 37). In such a commonwealth the people will collectively have better political judgement than each particular individual by himself, and in contrast to a rule by experts the good democracy will have regard for the interests of all – it is like a Dutch treat where all contribute to the common success (1281 a 42 ff.). This is a handsome declaration of confidence in democratic principles, and not only notable for its concealed departure from Plato.

But to Aristotle the good democracy does not mean economic and political equality. He refers to a political theorist from the fifth century, Phaleas, about whom one would like to know more (1266 a 39 ff.), who advocated political equality based on economic equality. To Aristotle this is utopian and wrong. His concept of justice implies judicial equality but political and economic inequality – within certain limits. This is not only a practical compromise but an acknowledgement of the fact that people are manifestly different, which is why full equality that ignores merit would be inequality (cf. 1280 a 7 ff.; see p. 377 on distributive justice): rights and goods should be distributed according to the 'geometrical proportion'. If one imagines the economic base – the strong middle class – as established, the next question is how that constitution should look which would bring about the best possible and most stable commonwealth. Where should political sovereignty be invested? The legislator – a fictive person who frequently appears in Greek political thought in agreement with the practice that was often observed when colonies were established – must take into account three factors that guard the political and judicial life of the commonwealth: the authority that lays down the general policy, the executive and the judicial authority (1297 b 35 ff.). This distinction was of some importance in Montesquieu's tripartite division of power, but the correspondence is imperfect, and it is not an innovation; it is modelled on the actual distribution of power between the people's assembly, the magistrates, and the courts of law in Athens.

The good legislator will strive for a distribution of power among the three 'authorities' of state. Of even greater importance is the compromise between democracy and oligarchy which he must strive for when he makes provisions for appointing magistrates: a combination of universal franchise with a property census for eligibility, which can be arranged by more or less cunning methods (1300 a 9 ff.; 1320 b 22 ff.). In all his decisions the legislator aims at a 'mixed constitution' – which is to say a mixture of oligarchy and democracy which respects both wealth and liberty, both 'quality' and 'quantity' (1293 b 30 ff.; 1296 b 17), and which accordingly, in the terminology of the *Ethics*, aims for 'the mean' (1295 a 35 ff.). Such a 'mixed constitution' will not only create a stable balance of power; it will also, in so far as possible, conform with Aristotle's ideals of justice. It is immediately clear that both the way of thinking and the concrete provisions are very close to Plato's *Laws*.

This mixed constitution or *politeia* is an expression of the politically feasible. But it is not the ideal. The last books sketch the ideal state – yet it remains a loose sketch; the great visions are not Aristotle's main concern. He remarked earlier (1276 b 16 ff.) that the good citizen is not necessarily identical with the good man – under a bad constitution the opposite is the more likely. But in the ideal state what is good for the state and for the individual should converge (1325 a 16 ff.). The external framework must be an agrarian state, for the wealth of nature comes from the soil, and it must be dependent on private property and family life. The state should not become absorbed in excessive trade and capitalism; it must supply its own need for foods and otherwise produce a reasonable measure of external goods, which requires a suitable number of slaves and foreign residents who in all other respects should be kept at a suitable distance (1325 b 33 ff.; 1326 b 26 ff.; 1328 a 21 ff.). The citizens – the elite – should not be burdened with work, for to work is not to live. But among themselves the elite live as equals – nobody has the sole claim – as in Plato – to insight or government; the young must learn to obey, but adults must take turns to govern and be governed (1332 b 23), for sovereignty is collectively invested in the citizenry. The citizen should combine freedom with responsibility and have sufficient leisure (*scholē*, 1333 a 33 ff.); only in this way is he able to practice perfect virtue (1332 a 7 ff.), which is to say to exercise *praxis* or *theōria*. From a political point of view the two forms of self-sufficient activity do not conflict (1325 b 14 ff.; 1331 b 39 ff.; 1333 a 16 ff.).

The *Politics* deals with the preconditions for human happiness; its main focus is ethical. Therefore it is as self-evident to Aristotle as it is to Plato that education is a public responsibility; it is decisive that the future citizens be educated correctly (1337 a 34 ff.). In the ideal state the authorities must regulate but not do much censuring. It is important that the free citizen not become a slave to practical technicalities or expert knowledge, and education is therefore an all-round training in the liberal, character-building disciplines – and the more useless such disciplines are, the better for the free man (cf. 1338 b 2).

The difference between Plato and Aristotle is manifest: to Aristotle education is not determined by lofty metaphysical ideals; the key phrase is all-round liberal education – as in the old enemy, Isocrates. The free citizen is an educated person, and the ballast provided by education is his to make use of – in *praxis* or *theōria*. This difference between master and disciple is not only one of differing views of paedagogics. Aristotle's view of man is another: man does not acquire his identity from some higher reality; he is not like a puppet, a toy of the gods. God is not the measure of all things, and there is no need of either philosopher-rulers or a nocturnal assembly. His ideal of education is liberal-humanist, and his citizens are free, confident men, who unfold their own character. To Aristotle himself there is no doubt that this free citizen only can live in an almost archaic *polis*. But it is a question whether his view of man's double identity does not also carry wholly modern perspectives with it: the educated private individual living his inner life in a society that assures external welfare.

Aristotle's political thinking does not work like Plato's – as a challenge. None the less, the *Politics* has had its *Wirkungsgeschichte*. This is owing to the refined examination of politics as the art of the possible. Aristotle's classification of constitutions were normative until the eighteenth century. But to this should be added that with great acumen he asked the questions of the relation between liberty and equality, between the common good and sovereignty, of the connections between the political, economic and social structures of society, and of how to delegate power without society breaking down in cliques and factions.

24

RHETORIC AND POETICS

—— •◦• ——

Aristotle designates the human activity that by means of professional experience (*technē* or 'art') aims to create or produce something by the word *poiēsis*. Of course he knew of no conflict between man and technology. But his distinction between *poiēsis* and *praxis* demonstrates a subtle understanding of the difference between professional skill on the one hand and moral judgement on the other. A *poiēsis* delivers a product with man as the *causa efficiens*. In part this means that the form exists in the human consciousness before being 'transferred' to a given material and in part that artefacts differ from natural products, because the relation of form and matter is arbitrary – a statue can be made in marble or bronze. The making of artefacts belongs of course to that region of the world where things 'could happen otherwise'. But – as opposed to ethics – it is possible to set down general rules; the artisan knows how to proceed to obtain his desired result.

Naturally, every human society is dependent on production. But not all technical skills are of interest to the free man – nor to Aristotle. Within the vast field covered by the concept of *poiēsis* there are only two areas with which Aristotle concerned himself scientifically; both have to do with verbal art. It is possible to present general rules and provide a scholarly account of rhetoric and poetry. Poetics is – in modern terminology – a purely aesthetic discipline; essential aesthetic factors are present in rhetoric, but the rhetor uses the word performatively – he aims at a certain judicial or political decision.

RHETORIC

Rhetoric is interdisciplinary with points of contact to dialectics on the one hand and to ethics and politics on the other (*Rhet.* 1356 a 25; cf. 1354 a 1). Both dialectics and rhetoric are formal disciplines; both have everything and nothing as their subject, because their proper concern is the argument, or the speech itself, and the subject of a speech may be anything whatsoever. Put in modern terms, dialectics is a theory of argumentation, rhetoric a theory of communication.

Rhetoric is applied dialectics; the speaker is to make his arguments plausible to a certain audience. Hence rhetoric may be defined as the ability to observe the means of persuasion available in a given case; the speaker is not to persuade of just anything but to point out what are the persuasive factors (1355 b 26; 9). It is clear that rhetoric – as opposed to dialectics – presupposes that something is to be decided, and a decision presupposes the possibility of a choice – nobody can ponder what is unavoidable, a decision is bound to a concrete situation, but as an art rhetoric can only provide general rules to be exploited according to the special demands of the particular case (1357 a 4; 1356 b 28). Finally, rhetoric is concerned with the different social functions and can thus be considered a formal tool of what we would call social science – in Aristotle's classification of sciences: ethics and politics. The speaker must on the one hand know his subject and master logical thinking and on the other be prepared for the inability of his audience to comprehend a too complicated argument – which of course is something the politician knows how to exploit (1356 a 22; 1357 a 1; 1401 b 31.).

Aristotelian rhetoric has double roots; one is Plato, the other the Sophistic rhetorical tradition. In the *Gorgias* (Plat. *Gor.* 453 A ff.) Plato had attacked rhetoric as actually practised: it was not an art, he maintained, but nothing more nor less than demagoguery. In the *Phaedrus*, on the other hand, he drew a picture of ideal rhetoric as necessarily converging with philosophy – knowledge is to be communicated, and the true orator should, like the philosopher, use his insight to instruct: he must know the truth and he must be able to 'guide souls', which is to say understand to whom he is speaking and when to be silent and when to speak (*Phaedr.* 259 E ff.; 265 C ff.; 271 C ff.; cf. p. 194).

In his *Rhetoric* Aristotle includes the Platonic demand for psychological insight, but he reinterprets the demand for truth: it is not the orator's task to know a higher truth but to determine when an argument is true; one cannot apprehend the probable if one does not apprehend the true (Aristot. *Rhet.* 1355 a 14). Aristotle wants to give rhetorical practice a theoretical foundation, and thus he places himself midway between lofty Platonic intentions and current practical manuals, which he actually does not respect very much (1354 b 16). It is probably also justified to consider Aristotle's *Rhetoric* as a deliberate countermove against Isocrates' position and his whole ideal of education.[1] Aristotle's *Rhetoric* signals the final separation of philosophical and rhetorical argumentation. His conception of rhetoric as a special mode of expression in its own right has been important in the Latin-Roman tradition – in cooler northern countries there may not be much regard for formal education but rather a wide-spread tendency to agree with Plato's *Gorgias* in which rhetoric is considered varnished humbug.

Formally the *Rhetoric* is closely related to the *Topics*; in both the argument proceeds from probable or universally recognized points of view. The difference is not due to the form of the conclusions but to the fact that rhetoric aims at what a certain audience can cope with or must be assumed to accept, and therefore rhetorical

---

1   Probably Aristotle attacked Isocrates already in an early dialogue, the *Gryllus*. It is likely that as early as in his Academy days he lectured on rhetoric, but the *Rhetoric* as it is known to us is surely a final redaction of several lectures. From Aristotle's time a manual on rhetoric in more traditional style has been preserved (*Rhetorica ad Alexandrum*), which incorrectly has been transmitted among the Aristotelian works.

argumentation can – in some cases ought to – be somewhat less pointed, even though of course valid. The rhetorical syllogism – the enthymeme (*Rhet.* 1356 a 35 ff.; 1395 b 20 ff.) – should proceed from what is well known; sometimes a self-evident premiss may be omitted so that formally the conclusion has only one premiss and thus there are similarities with the maxim or general statement (the gnome), which merely states a rule, appeals to prejudices, and is suitable for elderly or rustic people (1394 a 19 ff.) – such is the humble lodging Aristotle assigns to the oldest philosophical form of argumentation. A special kind of enthymeme is the conclusion from 'signs' or circumstantial evidence, that is to say from effect to cause. If y is present, x has been present. A variant: since Socrates was wise and just, the wise are just (1357 a 33 ff.; 1359 a 7; 1402 b 14). The enthymeme is the rhetorical syllogism; in rhetoric the inference from the example or paradigm (cf. *Anal. post.* 71 a 5) corresponds to 'induction', but rhetoric does not use a complete induction, nor does the inference proceed from particulars to universals, but from one particular (the example) to another: Dionysius is a budding tyrant when he asks for a bodyguard, for so did Peisistratus (*Rhet.* 1357 b 25 ff.; 1356 a 35 ff.; 1393 a 25 ff.).

More important than the form of argumentation are the contents. Aristotle follows the tradition in distinguishing between the political oration that concerns decisions about events to come, the occasional oration or eulogy that concerns the present, and the forensic oration that seeks to unravel past events (1358 b 6). Naturally, the orator must possess the necessary familiarity with the special circumstances of the case, but it is just as important that he is familiar with generally accepted values to which each of these types of oration must refer. The political oration (1359 a 30 ff.) presupposes familiarity with such concepts as 'happiness' or welfare, 'good' and 'evil', 'expediency'; the occasional oration (1366 a 23 ff.) presupposes familiarity with the virtuous and beautiful; and the forensic speech (1368 b 1 ff.) presupposes familiarity with justice and injustice, positive law and natural law, and with the psychological motives that make people act unjustly. The examination of these normative concepts can to some degree be read as a popular application of Aristotle's *Ethics* and *Politics*. But it is a coarsened one; the purpose is to enable the speaker to appeal to the actual preconceptions of his audience. In speaking of happiness, for example (1360 b 4 ff.), it is indeed possible to distinguish between physical, mental and external goods, although it would probably be unwise to burden the Popular Assembly with a lecture on *phronēsis* and *theōria*.

The demand for general and special knowledge is – outwardly – an extension of the *Phaedrus*. This is also true with respect to the consequences that must be drawn from an oration's implying three factors (1358 a 36 ff.): the speaker, the subject, and his audience. The speaker should above all come across as a person of unblemished character, know his subject, and be a psychologist. The last presupposes thorough familiarity with the feelings and affects (*pathē*) he wishes to produce, and he should know human character (*ēthos*) in general. The greater part of the second book (1377 b 16–91) is a catalogue-like examination of, for example, anger, fear, compassion, friendship, the peculiarities of the young and the old, or the influence of power and wealth on character. Here again it is an examination that shuns the really profound; it is a question of applied psychology – although it presupposes a general education: Aristotle has a predilection for supporting his points with quotations from tragedy.

The *Rhetoric* is a manual. In the first two books the purpose is to show how the rhetor can 'find' what he has to say (*heuresis* in Greek, *inventio* in Latin). This is achieved by systematizing current – general or specific – *topoi* or 'places', the sources for argumentation or standard arguments. In this respect the *Rhetoric* can also be considered an applied *Topics*. An example (1393 b 15): the man who has beaten his own father will also beat his neighbours – this, we are told, is an example of an argument that concludes from the rarely to the frequently occurring.

The first two books of the *Rhetoric* can among other things be used as a source for Greek public morality. The third book deals with the arrangement of a speech and with its style (*lexis* in Greek, *elocutio* in Latin terminology); modern stylistics is a true-born child of this side of rhetoric. The principal demands of style are that it must be clear and appropriate and stylistically commensurate with the subject (cf. 1404 b 1 ff.). Aristotle's remarks about metaphor may be of special interest: with its unexpected form it is indeed an especially precise means of communication (1410 b 6 ff.).

POETICS

It was probably not until the time of Cicero that political conditions again permitted the employment of Aristotle's *Rhetoric*. The *Poetics* had to await the Renaissance before it could lay down a tradition and become normative – frequently in a way that likely would have surprised Aristotle. Like the *Rhetoric* the *Poetics* deals with the art which by means of the word aims for a certain effect – the poet 'guides souls' as does the orator; but what is aimed for is not decision or act but aesthetic enjoyment. And the *Poetics* differs from the *Rhetoric* by dealing with the finished work, wheras the *Rhetoric* is a manual on how to write speeches.

Apparently Aristotle wrote several exoteric treatises on aesthetics, among them a dialogue *On Poets*. These writings are lost. The preserved work, the *Poetics*, is esoteric and its transmission was perilous. Furthermore, we only have the first book, the main subject of which is tragedy. To all appearances a second book on comedy also existed. The book that is preserved for us does not have a polished form and it can be difficult to decide whether we confront a lecture manuscript or some personal working notes. It is a small pamphlet with compositional gaps. Still, the contents are weighty.

The central concept in Aristotle's literary aesthetics is *mimēsis*, 'imitation' (cf. Aristot. *Poet.* 1447 a 13 ff.; 1448 b 4 ff.). Aristotle never defines the concept, but to him it is clearly the concept that delimits the field of aesthetics. Pictorial art, dance, music and fictional literature 'imitate', and the urge to imitate is congenital. But what is meant by 'imitate'? Plato had deliberately used the connotation of 'copy' in his criticism of poetry, but in his critique of the poets he did not evaluate art as art. Aristotle was not Plato, and in the course of the roughly forty years that separate them, times had changed. Aristotle never asks whether a tragedy is 'true'. The old idea that the poet held a monopoly on knowledge – and thus became the philosopher's competitor – was dead and buried, and the artistic experience had become aesthetic. To Aristotle it must have been an obvious task to establish a new 'discipline' also in this area – the aesthetics of literature. His *Poetics* describes what it is that makes a literary work a work of art and what it ought to be in order to be good art – it is only in this oblique way that he provides 'rules' or 'prescriptions'.

He does not mention Plato, but it is certain that his understanding of the *mimēsis* concept is in deliberate opposition to the Platonic one. Art exists in its own right, and it is evident that if *mimēsis* constitutes art, it can never signify a photographic or naturalistic 'imitation'. Art does not imitate slavishly; the artistic illusion stylizes, it may idealize, and the fictional universe of art has its own strict logic; the work of art has a 'meaning' that a random bit of everyday life of course does not have. Thus, when Aristotle uses *mimēsis* as a common designation for artistic expression, 'imitation' is most often a misleading rendition. An actor, for example, 'imitates' a fictive person in the sense that he acts or represents this person. 'Representation' or 'illusion' can in certain instances be adequate translations; the element of 'imitation' that is left is due to the fact that the work of art is an 'as-if world' that might be true.

Mimēsis can in fact be carried out by different means – colours or forms, rhythm, language, or harmony (1447 a 17 ff.) – or in different ways – a literary work can, for example, present itself as the poet's account, or the characters can act directly (1448 a 19 ff.). But what is most important is 'the object of imitation' (1448 a 1 ff.), which is to say the theme of the work of art – typically the actions of human beings. Of course every artistic genre has its own conventions and possibilities, but the branches can be combined – a tragedy, for example, consists of music, dance, and speech. In literary art it is natural for Aristotle to establish an aesthetics of genre, but it is remarkable that first and foremost he defines a genre by content – 'the object of imitation' – not by form; a didactic poem, for example, is not simply poetry (1447 b 13 ff.). As is characteristic for him, Aristotle imagines that a given genre in the course of time will find its perfect form (1449 a 7), and he is in no doubt that tragedy culminated in the fifth century, nor that tragedy is a loftier and more perfect genre than its predecessor, the epic (1461 b 26 ff.).

Aristotle narrows down his real subject – tragedy – by means of a definition, and, as so often, the definition is an introduction to the closer analysis, not a conclusion. The definition goes as follows:

> Hence tragedy is an imitation of a serious action and, as having extension, complete in itself – in language embellished with artistic ornaments, each kind brought in in the separate parts of the work – performed by acting persons, not in a narrative form – and which, by arousing pity and fear, completes the purgation of such emotions.
>
> (1449 b 21 ff.; after Butcher and Bywater).

Then, on the basis of the definition, six elements are mentioned, which must be present in tragedy (1450 a 9 ff.): plot, character, style, thought, spectacle and musical composition. But the definition also mentions the effect on the audience: to bring about pity and fear, to complete an aesthetical purgation. Of the six elements, style (*lexis*) and musical composition concern the means of imitation, the spectacle concerns the way. The most important elements by far are the three concerning the object of imitation: plot (*mythos*), character (*ēthos*) and thought (*dianoia*), where *dianoia* is subordinate to *ēthos*, *ēthos* to *mythos*. It may seem as if this is a rather heavy-handed systematics, but it expresses a carefully thought-out theory. It is not strange that 'the thought' is subordinate to character – for by this is not to be understood the poet's 'thought' with his work, but the thoughts that the characters' voice, which accordingly are important links in the representation of the characters (cf. 1450 b 4 ff.). It is more important that *mythos* is superior to *ēthos* – for a tragedy is not primarily a study of character. It depicts a course of events, something that happens to the hero, and which, to be sure, follows an unavoidable course, because the hero is who he is; but it is not an unfolding of his psychic habitus – in tragedy the hero confronts his destiny, as one might say in a vocabulary that might be too pompous for Aristotle's taste.

Hence, says Aristotle (1450 a 38), the plot or myth is, as it were, the soul of tragedy. In speaking of *mythos* Aristotle does not mean myth as the stuff of tragedy, but rather the structured action or plot that constitutes tragedy as a work of art. He is not interested in the psychological process that precedes the tragedy: that the poet intended this or that, that he expresses his own mental experiences, or that he 'finds' a subject that he can 'form'; the aesthetic focus is on the work as a work. Here it is decisive that the poetic universe is different from real life. Tragedy is concentrated reality; nothing must be superfluous; events are not only to succeed each other but are to follow from each other (1452 a 12 ff.). Therefore the fable is to have a quite firm structure in which all the links are to be logically connected. A tragedy should have a beginning, middle and end (1450 b 21 ff.; cf. 1449 b 12 ff.) – which is to say that it should begin without logical presuppositions and end when the course of events has reached its necessary and unavoidable end. Aristotle calls for the unity of action – not as in French Classicism, which claimed him as authority (Corneille, Boileau-Despréaux) also for the unities of time and place. The action is to show how events must ensue with probability or necessity: the knot is tightened, the catastrophe or 'reversal' (*peripeteia*) comes about, often by a 'recognition' (*anagnōrisis*) – the characters recognize each other, or, on a more profound level, the hero recognizes the truth (1452 a 22 ff.; 1454 b 19 ff.; cf. 1455 b 24 ff.). It is especially effective if the audience comes to know before the hero does so – which can be effectuated through the action, by tragic 'irony', or simply because the mythical stuff is already familiar. In fact, what is decisive in Greek tragedy is not that the audience experiences something unanticipated but that the hero does so; what is probable and necessary in itself is to him improbable or unthinkable, indeed at times also to us. The subtle interplay between what occurs on stage and in us finds its prototype in Sophocles' *Oedipus Rex* – which not unreasonably was Aristotle's favourite tragedy.

All this means that the hero must have a certain, fixed character. The representation of character is of course to be consistent (cf. 1454 a 26 ff.); it should be obvious that a person who is of this or that kind will act in this or that way (1451 b 8). A person who in every situation acts rightly will not be a tragic hero – *ho phronimos* would cut a rather tedious figure in a tragedy. The focus of tragedy is on what in the *Ethics* are interesting marginal cases: individuals who – perhaps innocently – cannot grasp the consequences of their acts. Oedipus is once more the prototype of the tragic hero – both morally and intellectually he is better than average, but he is also stubborn, he does not have full comprehension of his situation, and he is in error (*hamartia* – 1453 a 7 ff.). What does it mean that the hero errs or 'goes wrong'? In the post-Aristotelian tradition – Corneille, for example – it is often taken to mean that the hero has committed a moral error, a 'sin' that must be exonerated. This is clearly not Aristotle's intention – there may be moral undertones in Aristotle, but the main emphasis is on the hero's not having full knowledge of himself or his situation and therefore erring. Ancient tragedy itself – *Oedipus Rex*, for example – voices something different from both the moralizing and the Aristotelian interpretation: the tragic hero does not sin; objectively, he draws guilt upon himself; subjectively, he is guiltless.

It is a very important factor in Aristotle's aesthetics of tragedy – as in his *Rhetoric* – that he takes the effect on the audience into account: tragedy does not play on the entire emotional register but should cause fear (*phobos*) and pity (*eleos*), as they traditionally are translated (*Furcht und Mitleid* in German, following Lessing). 'Terror' and 'woe' would better convey the elementary emotional states, which at the very least are also thought of. What is essential is that it is a question of the emotions in us – the audience – produced by the course of action – the tightening and undoing of the knot (1452 b 30 ff.; 1453 b 1 ff.). What unites the tragedy with the audience are 'fear' and 'pity', not just any odd state of anxiety, dread, shock, or terror, nor, as Lessing thought, the spectator's compassion and brotherly love; the well-composed tragedy brings about an emotional cleansing – an aesthetic pleasure (1453 b 11) or a purgation (*katharsis* 1499 b 28). To be affected by a tragedy is in itself an emotional experience, but it presupposes the intellectual side of the matter – that the tragedy has coherence and falls into place. That the tragedy ends in grief of course does not prevent the artistic experience; what matters aesthetically is the intense experience of a compressed reality that moves both intellect and feeling and thereby creates insight. The insight that Oedipus buys so dearly lifts and takes possession of the spectator.[2]

From a philosophical point of view, wherein does artistic insight consist? Aristotle considers the question in a quite brief passage that marks the high point of the *Poetics* (Aristot. *Poet.* 1451 a 36 ff.). Poetry, he says, is more 'philosophical' than history. The latter deals with factual, particular sequences of events – what Alcibiades did and what happened to him. Tragedy, on the other hand, deals with the universal, which is to say with what might happen because it is either probable or necessary. This is an excellent formulation. It describes how tragedy – or poetry in general – affects the spectator by showing the universal in the particular in a compressed and conspicuous manner, which only is possible in an idealized fictional universe. Measured by the yardstick of practical life, the aesthetical experience is perhaps only a surrogate;

---

2   The word *katharsis* has occasioned endless deliberations. The statement can either be taken to mean that the feelings of fear and pity are purged, or that we are purged *of* (or *from*) fear and pity. The latter has led to the interpretation that fearful people by some sort of homeopathic therapy can be brought into balance by the production of fear (cf. *Pol.* 1341 b 33 ff.). However, this somewhat prosaic interpretation fails to explain *katharsis* as an aesthetic concept. Probably the meaning is that the action produces an elementary state of 'terror' that is cleansed or becomes settled with the undoing of the knot. It is both a purgation *of* and *for* chaotic feelings (cf. Plat. *Soph.* 226 D ff. on the purging *of* the soul and *for* the soul's illness). In some measure the learned debate forgets that '*katharsis*' is an elementary aesthetical experience familiar to all – before one begins to explain it.

perhaps art does not change our real lives, but it does provide an insight that is paradigmatic and universal because it is experienced as something that really might be so. Art is philosophical, because it shows the universal by the concrete, and philosophical and artistic insight are therefore of the same kind. Aristotle's delight in tragedy is due to the fact that he is an aesthete and a philosopher in one person; he is not merely a philosopher who happens to possess aesthetic sensibility.

Aristotle wanted to found a discipline of aesthetics. His errand was to consider the literary work as an autonomous entity, to analyze the structure that makes a work of art a work of art, and to demonstrate the interplay between work and audience. This errand precludes moralizing and it precludes psychologizing.

If Aristotle's *Poetics* is considered in relation to earlier Greek views of literature, it is safe to say that here we come upon a revolution. The very creation of aesthetics as an independent 'discipline' implies a distancing from literature: it is a kind of second-hand experience and something to be analyzed. Literature provides a special form of cognition through its own medium; it is not a total interpretation of existence that philosophy must contest. Nevertheless, to the tragedians themselves poetry was a total interpretation of existence. A distance has arisen between Aristotle and the tragedy, which he understands on the premises of an aesthetic observer. The great tragedy lay in the past – it was one hundred years older than Aristotle. Yet this is no mere distance in time. It can be sensed that Aristotle has become a reader – it is not necessary to experience the effect of tragedy in a performance (1450 b 18). One notices that the myth has become a suitable literary subject – the poets concentrated on certain myths because so many woeful things happened to quite a small number of mythical families (cf. 1453 a 17). But primarily one should note that Aristotle never speaks about guilt, offence, fate, let alone gods. To him tragedy does not concern itself with hidden, gigantic powers that determine man's life. It is concerned with what happens to a man who errs because he does not known his own situation.

Perhaps this little treatise, the *Poetics*, depicts Aristotle himself in concentrated form: the last of the 'Hellenes', the first among the moderns.

25

THE EARLY PERIPATETICS

————•◆•————

Aristotle was both an empiricist and a systematist. It proved difficult to maintain this balance in the Peripatetic School; early Aristotelianism turned to specialized studies and empirical research, and – in opposition to the new Hellenistic systems and partially in opposition to the Academy – the school became an undogmatic community of scholars marked by scepticism towards philosophical synthesis. This may have contributed to bestowing gradually on Aristotle's conceptual apparatus the status of a neutral, general philosophical vocabulary, which it has had until recent times.

An important reason for this atypical development lies with Aristotle himself and in the working method at the Lyceum: collective scientific projects with joint gathering of empirical facts, and to some extent joint authorship or working papers in which the individual writer is less prominent. Another undoubted reason is Theophrastus (c.370–c.285), Aristotle's slightly younger friend and long-time collaborator, who succeeded him as head of the Lyceum. He had heard Plato in his youth (Diog. Laert. V 36) and as the head of the Lyceum for many years he was a critical witness to the emergence of Epicureanism and Stoicism. He was a tireless empirical scholar, but sceptical of any synthesis, and he considered systematism with noble, aloof reserve. Like Aristotle, Theophrastus was a polyhistor. His oeuvre – which reflected both esoteric and public lectures – was voluminous (cf. V 42 ff.), and – like Aristotle – he lectured on every philosophical subject, often probably with Aristotle's lectures as the base, although he was not unoriginal. Apparently Theophrastus never made a break with fundamental Aristotelian views, even though indirectly he aimed his aporetic scepticism at Aristotle himself.

Among Aristotle's students and fellow workers Theophrastus and Eudemus were probably closest to him. Presumably they collaborated on several projects. Their logical investigations were especially important. To an even higher degree than Aristotle, they aspired to turn logic into a formal discipline free from ontological ties.

In syllogistics they worked with rules of conversion (Alex. Aphr. in Aristot. *Anal. pr.* 31, 4 = Eud. frg. 10 a Wehrli), and to the four valid moods in the first figure, which Aristotle had acknowledged, Theophrastus added five more, which subsequently by conversion were assigned to the fourth figure (69, 36). In modal logic they presumably interpreted 'possible' as 'potential', not as 'contingent', and unlike Aristotle they maintained that the conclusion in a syllogism with premisses of different modality follows the weaker premiss (220, 9; 124, 8 = Eud. frg. 16; 11 a). Finally, in addition to their studies of modality they worked with hypothetical syllogisms (Philop. in Aristot. *Anal. pr.* 242, 14 = Eud. frg. 22) – an important link between Aristotelian and Stoic logic, because a hypothetical syllogism of the normal type within propositional logic is formulated as a *modus ponens*.

A special project in the Lyceum was devoted to the history of philosophy and science. Theophrastus wrote the history of natural philosophy (*Physikōn doxai*), Eudemus that of mathematics, and a certain Menon that of medicine. Theophrastus' work was for better or worse to be influential by constituting the basis for the doxographic tradition, especially with respect to the Presocratics (see p. 6) – his method was to focus on the history of topics, and the Aristotelian conceptual apparatus was his obvious foundation. It is true that this was also Aristotle's working method. But where Aristotle often enters into a substantial discussion with his predecessors, in the hands of Theophrastus the method tends instead to degenerate into a dissection, and it goes without saying that it was to have quite unfavourable effects on the compendia that relied on Theophrastus without including his arguments. The method can be seen in the preserved section on sensation. Theophrastus proceeds by subject matter, not persons, and within a particular topic the individual philosophers are paraded and must fend for themselves as best they can – on Theophrastus' premisses. The strength of the method is that it not only uncovers – real or supposed – inconsistencies in the individual philosophers; it also brings out the aporias inherent in the subject matter itself. The weakness is, of course, that the philosophers which are dealt with are never allowed to speak for themselves – a disheartening example in this respect is the treatment of Democritus' theory of vision (Theoph. *De sens.* 50 ff.). Somewhat more stimulating is the comparison of Democritus' and Plato's views of the ontological status of sense objects.

The task is not to ascertain the ultimate truth but to bring questions and aporias into the open. This might be called Theophrastus' motto. The positive side of his procedure is to be found in his writings on natural science. A couple of minor treatises on mineralogy and meteorology have been preserved. But the main works are the preserved botanical treatises, *Historia plantarum* and *De causis plantarum*, of which the former – like Aristotle's *Historia animalium* – presents and discusses a comprehensive material, while the latter – like Aristotle's *De partibus animalium* – has a systematic character. Aristotle had not dealt with botany; hence it was natural for Theophrastus to take up the subject. Aristotle was the founder of zoology, Theophrastus of botany.

The empirical basic position is evident and is in fact formulated explicitly – sense perception is the basis of scientific knowledge, and theory should agree with observed facts (*De caus. plant.* I, 1; II 3, 5). Therefore Theophrastus was extremely cautious when it came to teleological and speculative explanations, and he stresses the difficulty in establishing precise definitions and firm classifications (*Hist. plant.* I 3, 2 ff.; 5; 1, 1). One example is his reserved attitude to the theory that plants – and animals – can come to be 'spontaneously'; yet he does not break with it (*De caus. plant.* I 5, 1 ff.). Of course his empirical attitude follows in Aristotle's wake, but it also implies a discreet departure from the speculative element in Aristotle's biology; everywhere he emphasizes the positive 'facts' at the expense of doctrinaire theorizing – a favourite word, *skepsis*, investigation, often comes to contain an element of doubt and reservation, which through Greek Scepticism has given the word its modern meaning.

Naturally Theophrastus must to a very high degree muster his 'scepticism' with regard to metaphysics. A 'metaphysical fragment' has been preserved, which characteristically enough is not an account of metaphysics but an examination of some of the questions raised by metaphysics. It is evident that Theophrastus rejects the formal metaphysics of the Academy, which contributes nothing to an understanding of actual reality (*Met.* 6 a 14 ff.). He argues from Aristotelian metaphysics and accordingly does not reject it. What he does is to point to a series of questions that must be 'investigated' (cf. 11 b 24), even though there are many inquiries that hardly can lead to clarification (8 b 13); one senses reservation about the capacity of human cognition to understand its own presuppositions (cf. 9 b 11; a 10 ff.). Theophrastus does not doubt the existence of first principles – rather our capacity to know how they work (4 b 11 ff.) – nor the existence of a first mover; but to understand how it works is not easy (5 a 14 ff.). In principle he adopts a teleological point of view; but why is there so much that is not ordered for the best (6 b 23 ff.)? Soberness, honesty and a certain worried caution characterize these marginal metaphysical notes.

To judge by the indirect transmission, Theophrastus' ethics – which was quite influential in Hellenistic times – was of the same nature. His common sense forbade him to adhere to a too rigoristic ethics – which for example does not acknowledge the importance of external goods for happiness (cf. Cic. *De fin.* V 12; 77). In addition he apparently stressed man's biological kinship (*oikeiotēs*) with animals (cf. Porph. *De abst.* III 25). With this word Theophrastus probably did not anticipate the Stoic idea that individual man by virtue of his 'kinship' with other men has absolute responsibility for the whole human race. His aim is the whole animal world, and his attitude is descriptive.

Among Theophrastus' 'ethical' treatises a small pamphlet, the so-called *Characters*, has been preserved. It may surprise by revealing a well-developed sense of humour, which does not exactly sparkle in the other treatises. The work consists of thirty brief and lively sketches of human types, all equipped with more or less innocent vices; they are not scoundrels but comical because they offend against good manners (the babbler, the miser, the insolent, the superstitious, etc.) and there are clear points of resemblance with contemporary, so-called New Attic comedy (Menander). These unpretentious descriptions of manners cannot be called philosophy but reveal the Aristotelian by the interest in human types familiar from Aristotle's *Ethics* and *Rhetoric* – they are clearly defined types; the miser, for example, is only miserly, nothing else. We cannot know whether Theophrastus had other intentions than merely to relax. One notes that he refrains from any kind of moralizing – it is the remote ironist who depicts the foibles of trifling people and otherwise suspends his judgement.

Reservations, but no break, seem to sum up Theophrastus' attitude to Aristotle. The other collaborators – several of them not much younger than Aristotle either – were even less systematically bound to the master. Dicaearchus (born c.375), who mainly occupied himself with ethics and politics, wrote a now lost account of Greek cultural history, and his formulation of the theory of 'the mixed constitution' (cf. Dic. frg. 7 Wehrli) was influential, not least on Cicero. Aristoxenus who had a 'Pythagorean' past was a specialist in the theory of music. Both held highly unorthodox psychological views (frg. 5–12; Aristox. frg. 118–21 Wehrli), as they – almost like Simmias in the *Phaedo* – considered the soul an epiphenomenon to the body. This implies that reason is not immortal either. The slightly younger pro-Macedonian politician Demetrius of Phaleron devoted himself to rhetoric and was probably more of a man of letters than a scholar. As a ruler in Athens he made it possible for Theophrastus – who like Aristotle was a metic – to acquire land, which means that at least from this time on the Lyceum can be considered a legal institution (cf. Diog. Laert. V 39). When Demetrius was banished from Athens he became affiliated with the library in Alexandria – one of several links between the Lyceum and Alexandrian scholarship.

But the most original figure belongs in the second generation. Straton of Lampsacus, Theophrastus' successor as head of the Lyceum (c.340–c.267), was a natural philosopher – nicknamed 'the physicist' – and in Antiquity he is a rather unique example of a thinker who seeks to accommodate his natural philosophy to scientific observation and not vice versa. His dislike of speculation is for example apparent in a detailed criticism of the arguments for immortality in Plato's *Phaedo* (Strat. frg. 122–4 Wehrli, Olymp.). But above all he pursued his own paths in his relation to Aristotle. It is surprising to find an 'Aristotelian' as an opponent of teleology, of the unmoved mover, of the dualism of form/matter, and of the division of the world into a sublunary and a supralunary region. Instead he poses 'natural explanations' (cf. Cic. *Acad.* II 121 = frg. 32 Wehrli), more exactly, a blend of mechanical and dynamic physics – with evident exploitation of the Atomistic tradition, a materialistic view of nature that finds the same laws or 'forces' in the universe as a whole. Aristotle's physics is the starting point, but otherwise there is not much left of Aristotle – excepting of course the very impetus to empirical investigation.

Physics calls for at least three basic concepts – space, time and motion. Straton was – as the first? – an adherent of both absolute space and absolute time, which is to say that the concepts of space and time are not, as in Aristotle, dependent on the entities that exist *in* space and time. Space is absolute in so far as it has the same extension as the finite universe; in itself it is empty, and the universe must be considered filled-in space (frg. 60, Simpl.). Time is also absolute; it is defined as the measure of motion and rest, which is to say that it is not, as in Aristotle, an assignation *to* motion – both motion and rest occur *in* time (frg. 79 a, Sext. Emp.; 76 Simpl.). Motion is a continuum (as in Aristotle) and hence infinitely divisible – as matter also is (frg. 70, Simpl.; 82, Sext. Emp.).

In his special physics Straton shows how he can simplify the Aristotelian conceptual world by renouncing the metaphysical background. There is for example no reason to assume that both upward and downward motions exist by nature; it is sufficient to attribute weight to all elements, understood as the tendency to seek towards the centre of the universe (frg. 52, Simpl.). Furthermore, Straton elegantly combines an Atomistic doctrine with the Aristotelian plenum theory. In theory matter is infinitely divisible, but physically it occurs in the form of particles. The universe as a whole is filled-in space; but there is neither a void outside nor in greater regions of the universe; space 'in itself', however, is empty; vacua can be artificially created, which can be demonstrated by experiment. And the passage of light through air and water shows that there are vacua on the microscopic level (frg. 65 a, Simpl; 65 b, Hero; 64, Hero).

The basic materialistic view also permits Straton to adopt the simplification of ignoring the Aristotelian concept of form. It complicated Aristotle's physics (see p. 330) that on the one hand he considered the universe a continuous plenum and on the other let matter be structured by the immaterial form. Straton's theory of particles and his view of matter rid him of this dualism. The forming principle is so to speak inserted in matter itself, for any given matter is equipped with 'qualities' or 'forces' (*dynameis*) – i.e. with certain properties that determine its behaviour (frg. 43, Sext. Emp.; 49, Plut.). The basic 'forces' are our old friends 'the hot' and 'the cold'; and probably the concept of force can aptly be modernized to 'energy'. The materialistic mode of thinking implies a simplification of Aristotelian quality physics.

In several respects Straton is a unique figure. But of course he belongs in a context. His base was and remained Aristotelian, but it is rather more important that he was contemporary with Epicurus and Zeno, the founder of Stoicism; the sources are not explicit, but it is possible to point to parallels, and it is unthinkable that there was no exchange of thought among contemporary philosophers in Athens. Speculations about absolute space and time are common property, and Straton's view of matter and his theory of *dynameis* bring him close to Stoicism. Still, parallels to Epicurus are – at least outwardly – more easily discernible.

Straton, too, had ties to Alexandria, for he taught the later King Ptolemy Philadelphus (Diog. Laert. V 58). In the Lyceum he concentrated on research, and he seems to have neglected popularization, which had been among the activities of the school since Aristotle's time. The Lyceum declined after his death. The Aristotelian renaissance in the first century BC, which was connected with Andronicus' edition of the esoteric Aristotle led to renewed interest in Aristotle's work but not to the establishment of an Aristotelian systematism. The importance of the early Peripatetics pertains to two fields. They influenced the development of philosophical scepticism and the development of Hellenistic science. The road from Aristotelianism to emancipated science was via Alexandria.

PART V

HELLENISTIC PHILOSOPHY

26

SCIENCE AND PHILOSOPHY

——— •◆• ———

In late Antiquity the word *hellēnismos* signals the essence of Greek culture, more especially the effort to cleanse and protect the 'pure' Greek language – it is not until post-classical times that a common Greek literary language (*koinē*) was formed on the basis of the Attic tongue. Towards the end of the ancient world the word can simply be used about paganism as opposed to Christianity. 'Hellenistic' did not come to designate the period from the death of Alexander the Great to the Roman Empire (Augustus) until one century ago.

In the course of only eleven years (334–23) Alexander had turned the world upside-down. With his lightening campaign he had created a monarchy, a world empire extending from Greece and Egypt in the west to the borders of India in the east. This not only caused the fall of the Persian Empire but also the demise of the Greek city state; it brought about a cultural assimilation between west and east which perhaps would have come about in any case, but which now followed a sudden and violent course. New metropoles – most importantly Alexandria in Egypt – were founded as administrative and trading centres; a Greek upper class, Greek military, and Greek merchants settled throughout the Near East. The new common market led to increased prosperity, and in cultural fields the borders were opened as well; there was a larger reading public than before; several authors not of Greek origin now appear in Greek literature – a famous example is the founder of Stoicism, the Phoenician Zeno.

The political history in the era after Alexander is monotonous. His generals and successors – the Diadochi – divided the vast realm among themselves and were constantly at war with each other. They established dynastic monarchies, first and foremost the Ptolemaic Realm in Egypt and the Seleucid Realm in the east. The political unit was not a city with its surrounding lands as in the Greece of yore, nor a national state in the modern sense, but a state that solely was held together by the absolute ruler and his bureaucracy and military. In Egypt and the Seleucid Realm the rulers could simply continue an ancient tradition of despotism, and to the average inhabitant it probably meant little that the ruler and his administrative apparatus were now Greek. Formally, constitutions were introduced for the individual cities according to the Greek model, but the real political power was not there. Still, in the old Greek region relative independence might be achieved from time to time, and the dream of liberty persisted, although it seldom amounted to much more than municipal self-government; liberty had become an abstract concept.

In ideology and religion the Hellenistic kings legitimated themselves by a ruler cult – the king was divine and was worshipped as a god. In the Orient this was once again merely a continuation of ancient traditions. But in the original Macedonia the new ideology did not stand a chance among the old warriors. It can seem more surprising that it became accepted relatively painlessly in Greece proper.

In many respects the general view of life changed profoundly. The old city state with its ideal of autarchy was built on inequality. To Plato and Aristotle this inequality was a matter of course, and it was likewise a matter of course that the good state in so far as possible should be isolated from the alien world haunted by the Barbarians. If it is possible to speak of a common Hellenistic 'view of life', it consists in a combination of cosmopolitanism and individualism – which perhaps found its most beautiful expression in Stoicism. Before the ruler all were equal; politics had become a remote affair, and the individual no longer had his natural place in the city; he had recourse only to himself – but such were the conditions for everybody, and the idea of a community of all mankind was therefore not remote. Another aspect of the same issue was a feeling of rootlessness and alienation, a search for happiness – or salvation – in inner exile or in the personal religious experience. Traditional religion could not satisfy this need, but the oriental mystery religions could; with their initiations into a higher reality and with the hope of a better life in the beyond they appealed to the individual and to everybody, regardless of place and social status. The increasing interest in astrology and the worship of *Tychē*, fate or chance, are also characteristic – already in the fifth century (Euripides) there had been a tendency to deify the incalculable vagary of life itself: if life is capricious, so is the divine.

Philosophy, too, considered its highest goal the finding of happiness for the individual without regard to external conditions. But where religion appealed to the emotions, the new philosophical systems were emphatically intellectualistic; reason was man's noblest possession, the way to personal integrity and peace of mind. There are religious dimensions, for example in Stoicism, but in general it is true that philosophy and religion pursued their own paths. In spite of the mark of uniformity that is characteristic of Hellenistic times, the era is nevertheless marked by a certain splitting up into separate cultural domains. Literature, for example, branched off in two directions: an elitist literature for connoisseurs side by side with popular literature for a larger public. It is no accident that it was in precisely this period that science became specialized and emancipated from philosophy. One can point to basic attitudes in Hellenistic science that have their roots in the philosophical tradition, but it was in Hellenistic times that science was cultivated for the sake of science itself – just as art became *l'art pour l'art*. The natural unity between philosophy and science that is fundamental to Aristotle no longer existed; scientific results were no longer adapted to a philosophical overall view as a matter of course. From a scientific point of view this can be considered progress – the third and second century BC mark the high point in the history of ancient science. On the other hand, this meant that science was the business of only a very few specialists, and the impact of professional science on philosophy was also quite modest. Hence, in the following only some main trends in the history of science will be discussed with a view also to late Antiquity, which in all essentials was to continue the Hellenistic tradition.

It was part of the new kings' cultural politics to establish state-supported libraries and institutions staffed by scholars on state salaries. This was an innovation with wide perspectives. To the ruler it was undoubtedly a status symbol; to scholarship it opened for hitherto unknown possibilities – to posterity it meant nothing less than the rescue of major portions of classical literature. The most important by far of these 'academies of science' or 'universities' was the Museion in Alexandria, founded close to 280 BC by Ptolemy I, perhaps on the initiative of Demetrius of Phaleron and in any case with clear links back to the Lyceum. Somewhat later the important library at Pergamon was established. At times the Museion suffered a turbulent fate, but it endured until 270 AD, and at its height it contained c.700,000 scrolls. The learned poet Callimachus (died c.240 BC), who was affiliated with the library, wrote a major annotated library catalogue, which also functioned as a kind of normative history of literature. The major part of known literature was collected, edited on the basis of the best manuscripts, and annotated. In addition there were studies in prosody, grammar, etc. It can justly be claimed that textual criticism and philology as sciences were founded in Alexandria (cf. p. 4). The list of librarians contains prominent philologists and natural scientists, and thereby the special fields of study at the Museion have been indicated.

Mathematics, including astronomy, and medicine, are the two oldest independent sciences and the two branches of science in which the Greeks can boast the most significant results. From early on there were fruitful mutual exchanges between philosophy and mathematics – one need only think of the Pythagoreans and Zeno – but it is not possible to tell who gave and who received, for example in developing the deductive, axiomatic method. Medicine, on the other hand, often found itself in conflict with philosophy, and the relation between philosophy and early medicine is a good example of the interplay between speculative and empirical ways of thinking (see p. 79 ff.).

MATHEMATICS

In the period until the middle of the fourth century BC there are two epochal events in the development of Greek mathematics into a rational science. One is the discovery of incommensurables, the other the founding of an idealized geometry. At first, the discovery of incommensurability was detrimental to the Pythagorean ideal of science (see p. 43), but it provided the impetus for an intensive study of what we call irrational numbers, and here Theaetetus seems to have played a decisive role – precisely in what respect is unclear. The sources for this very fruitful period in the history of mathematics are all in all more than sparse. But in the introduction to Plato's *Theaetetus* (147 D ff.) one is, for example, allowed a glimpse of the work on establishing a general theory of incommensurability, which shows at least one thing: the work was carried out with a geometrical, not an arithmetical conceptual apparatus. Incommensurability cannot be expressed by means of natural numbers but can be illustrated geometrically; the geometrical concept of quantity is more comprehensive than that of arithmetic, and, after the discovery of incommensurability, Greek mathematics apparently deliberately employed a geometrical rather than an arithmetical language ('geometrical algebra'). 'Irrational' numbers were expressed by the relation between finite lines, not by means of infinite series such as our decimal fractions. The 'geometrization' of mathematics meant that complicated tasks could be solved without introducing a new concept of number proper – nor were fractions considered numbers but numerical relations. On the other hand, this produced a divide between algebra and geometry that left its marks on the philosophical debate about the relation between continuous and discontinuous quantities, which was not overcome until the advent of Descartes' analytical geometry.

Apparently the crisis of mathematics led to a discussion of the mathematical – which is first and foremost to say the geometrical – conceptual apparatus itself: of the special character of mathematical objects. Undoubtedly geometry was originally considered a simple tool for measuring natural bodies, but a philosophical reflection had to question the status of this tool, and the development proceeds from natural to idealized geometry. Protagoras had denied the existence of not-sensible geometrical objects (see p. 104), and Democritus had presumably considered geometrical objects as constructions analogous with natural ones (see p. 72). Plato, on the other hand, strenuously maintained that mathematical objects are ideal objects with independent supra-sensory existence. He probably did not make original mathematical discoveries but exploited the mathematical knowledge of his time philosophically, and he was of great importance as a mathematical theorist. From his polemical tone (cf. the difference between 'commercial numbers' and mathematical numbers, drawn circles and the circle 'itself') it can be concluded that the new approach probably did not then prevail fully. But this became the case after Plato. To Aristotle it was a matter of course – his view of geometrical objects as abstracted, idealized objects that are treated *as if* they have real existence does not challenge idealized geometry as such. In the seventh book of Plato's *Republic* (see p. 208) an enduring systematization of the mathematical disciplines was established, and a programme of mathematical studies set down: astronomy, for example, should penetrate behind the observed phenomena to an ideal model that explains the phenomena by means of theoretical constructs. It is a misunderstanding to imagine Plato at war with empirical observation proper. What he wants to do is to 'save the phenomena' by means of a scientific theory. It is likewise a misunderstanding to think that he blamed the mathematicians *qua* mathematicians for working from a hypothetical starting point. The mathematicians should do nothing but what they are doing: undertake deductions on the basis of unproved presuppositions and given concepts. But there is a difference between the dialectician's and the mathematician's handling of concepts.

In the Academy both the philosophy of mathematics and mathematics as science were studied. The then most prominent mathematician, Eudoxus of Cnidos (c.408–355) who also was active in several philosophical areas, belonged to Plato's circle. Especially with respect to two points he obtained significant results in pure mathematics – and both have to do with the discovery of incommensurables. In the first place, he formulated a theory of general proportion that determines the conditions under which two given magnitudes can be said to stand in the same relation as two other given magnitudes. Without introducing a new concept of number (the real numbers in modern terminology) he formulated the theory in such a way that it is valid for commensurables as well as incommensurables and in geometry, arithmetic and harmonics. His second main contribution – which is related to the theory of proportion – is the formulation of the so-called method of exhaustion, which makes it possible to use arbitrarily small magnitudes. The theory specifies the conditions for an infinite convergence, but Eudoxus characteristically did not operate with infinitely small magnitudes; instead, he 'saved' the numerical concept by using steadily decreasing, arbitrarily small limiting values. The method of exhaustion, which perhaps builds on Democritus and was further developed by Archimedes, is the ancient parallel to modern infinitesimal calculus. It can for example be employed in an approximate measurement of the area of a circle.

Euclid's *Elements* united idealized geometry and the theory of numbers in one grand deductive system, which until the discovery of the 'non-Euclidean' geometries in the first half of the nineteenth century simply was considered *the* axiomatic system for geometry. The whole early tradition is included in the work. Thus Eudoxus' theory of proportions is incorporated (Eucl. *El.* V; the theory applied to geometrical magnitudes in VI), and the method of exhaustion is employed in the determination of area and volume (XII; cf. X 1); one book deals with incommensurables on the basis of Theaetetus (X); and the 'arithmetical' books (VII–IX) build on the Pythagorean theory of numbers. Euclid's *Elements* is also the keystone of a development in the sense that earlier textbooks preceded it. We know the names of several authors of such manuals (Procl. in Eucl. *El.* I, 66, 18 ff. Friedlein) and can also infer their existence from Aristotle's *Analytics*. Euclid flourished around 300 BC, presumably in Alexandria. How independent he was of his predecessors is debatable, but it was certainly not he who conceived of the idea of one comprehensive axiomatic system for all geometry.

It is said of Euclid as of several of his predecessors that he was a 'Platonist' (68, 20 ff.). This is information that probably should be taken with a pinch of salt – the source is Neoplatonic (Proclus, fifth century AD) – but there is no doubt about the connection of the mathematical tradition with the Academy; at least there is this much truth to it: Euclid behaves as Plato says a mathematician should behave. He is – as his predecessors surely also were – a mathematician, not a dialectician; he builds on philosophical presuppositions without being or wishing to be a philosopher. The definition of fundamental concepts such as 'point' and 'line' (Eucl. *El.* I, def. 1; 2) points directly back to the Academy, and the same goes for the definition of the simplest basic concepts within the theory of numbers (VII, def. 1; 2; the remarkable definitions – def. 3–4 – of 'part' and 'parts', for example, can be compared to Plat. *Parm.* 153 D): Euclid considers a number a multitude composed of indivisible unities just as does the 'good' mathematician in Plato's *Republic* (*RP* VII 525 E, see p. 183). Further-reaching philosophical speculation, for example on the relation between unity and plurality or on ideal numbers, is irrelevant to Euclid.

Of greater importance is probably Euclid's method itself, the axiomatic ideal which he took over from his predecessors. In itself the method goes far back – presumably to the Pythagoreans. It had served as paradigm for the generalized Platonic theory of method, the *hypothesis* method, and the tradition of Antiquity is probably correct in claiming that the Platonic doctrine of method in its turn retroactively affected mathematical procedure. Euclid's 'Platonism' is clear, for example, from the fact that he never presents existential propositions. As did Plato's mathematicians, he posits instead 'hypothetically' odd and even numbers, figures, angles, etc. (cf. VI 510 C) – 'let there be . . .' (two straight lines, for example) is a standard formula in the language of Euclid as well as in later mathematics.

There are also at least structural resemblances between the dialectical ascent and descent of the *Republic* and mathematical 'analysis' – i.e. the reduction of a given problem to a known theorem – and mathematical 'synthesis' – i.e. the deductive proof from a known theorem. Euclid is mentioned among the authors of these methods (Papp. *Coll.* 634, Hultsch), but it was indeed more than mild exaggeration when eager Platonists claimed that Plato had invented them (Procl. in Eucl. *El.* I, 211,18 ff., Friedlein). But Euclid's text, the *Elements*, only uses the synthetic, i.e. the deductive, method. As with 'induction' in Aristotle, analysis is obviously a preliminary, heuristic procedure. It is not presented to the reader; Greek mathematics bestowed the heritage on posterity that the mathematician presents his final proof without accounting for how he arrived at it.

Aristotle's *Analytics* belongs to the same tradition as Euclid. Euclid's *Elements* is a geometrical, Aristotle's a logical, axiomatic system; the close connection between the two has been discussed as has also their terminological agreement (see p. 307). Euclid proceeds from definitions, five postulates – valid in geometry – and five 'common notions', which is to say axioms valid in all fields (Eucl. *El.* I, init.). The definitions, for example, concern 'point', 'straight line', and 'surface'. The postulates concern geometrical constructions; for example: a straight line can be drawn from any point whatsoever to any point whatsoever, and all right angles are equal to one another. Several determinations of 'common notions' are familiar from Plato and Aristotle; for example, equals added to equals make up equals, and the whole is greater than the part. The individual proof then rests on these presuppositions or on previously proven theorems. First the problem to be solved is formulated, presented, and specified; the proof follows, generally expressed in the form of geometrical constructions; and finally the formulation of the problem is repeated – now as a proven theorem. The crucial are the formulation of the problem, the proof, and the conclusion (cf. Procl. in Eucl. *El.* 203, 1 ff.), where the proof clarifies the entailment between axioms (postulates or common notions) and theorems. As in Aristotle's *Analytics*, there is need of a subject, a statement about the subject, and some specified rules of inference that warrant the correctness of the statement. A *reductio ad absurdum* has the same logical structure as the direct proof but demonstrates the contradictory to an assumed supposition – by this method Euclid demonstrates for example that the number of prime numbers is infinite (Eucl. *El.* IX 20).

Traditionally the main demands of an axiomatic system are that it must be complete, which is to say that it does not build on unspoken premisses, that it must be free of contradiction and be independent, which means that no axiom can be deduced from others. But what is not demanded is that the system should 'reproduce' reality. It is often difficult to decide whether a given system meets the three demands. For centuries it was the general view that Euclid had in fact realized the ideal. That is not so; the demand for completeness is not strictly observed. There are only a very few and unclear indications in Antiquity of anybody's doubting that

Euclid's *Elements* was the only valid axiomatic system of geometry (see p. 439), but it was discussed whether the system was wholly independent. These discussions focused, in Antiquity as well as later, on the so-called parallel postulate (I, post. 5; cf. def. 23; one critique is reproduced Procl. in Eucl. *El.* I, 191, 21 ff.), which implies that through a given point outside a given straight line one and only one straight line can be drawn, parallel with the given. Euclid used the postulate to deduce several theorems (cf. Eucl. *El.* I 28; 31; 32). Later it was shown that the order could be reversed: the parallel postulate could be deduced from one of the theorems, if this were accepted as axiom; but it was also shown that it cannot be deduced from Euclid's other axioms. Hence the system is independent on this point. However, this very discussion did demonstrate that by omission of the postulate it was possible to construct non-Euclidean geometries.

Side by side with Aristotle's syllogistics, Euclid's *Elements* is the noblest example in Antiquity of an axiomatic system. From the point of view of methodology and the history of ideas, Euclid's *Elements* is the most important work in Greek mathematics. This is not to say that he was the greatest Greek mathematician. The most prominent mathematical genius of Antiquity was Archimedes of Syracuse (287–12) who was equally active in pure mathematics, mathematical physics, and as an engineer, celebrated in admiring anecdotes as probably nobody else in the history of mathematics ('give me a place to stand, and I will move the earth'; 'do not disturb my circles'). In pure mathematics he provided an approximate determination of the relation between the periphery of the circle and its diameter (π), and he exploited the method of exhaustion (corresponding to modern integral calculus) in his works on measuring the quadrature of the parabola and the volume and surface of the sphere. In mathematical physics (statics and hydrostatics) Archimedes invented the science of equilibrium of solids and fluids, and, for example, formulated the principle of the lever (statics prop. 6, Arch. II, 132, 13, Heiberg (*De aequil.*)), which specifies the conditions for the equilibrium of commensurables and the 'Archimedean principle' (hydrostatics prop. 7, II 332,21 (*Corp. fluit.*)), which asserts that a body immersed in a fluid and heavier than it will lose as much of its own weight as that of the fluid displaced. With statics and hydrostatics Archimedes contributed essentially to a mathematical description of nature, and he took over Euclid's methods in his axiomatizing of mathematical physics. This implies a strict deductive method of proof, which – as in Euclid – does not betray how the theorems are discovered. But it is unique that Archimedes elsewhere (II 426, 3 ff. (*Eratosth.*)) did provide such information. He used 'mechanical methods' to discover pure mathematical theorems. Such methods can be useful, but according to Archimedes they should not be incorporated in the demonstration proper.

Among other mathematicians, mention should be made only of Eratosthenes of Cyrene (ca. 275–194) who employed purely geometrical methods to measure the size of the earth and of Apollonius of Perga (ca. 262–190) who did important work on conic sections. Both performed their principal work in Alexandria, where Eratosthenes, also a prominent philologist, was head librarian.

The axiomatic method and the idealized conception of geometry bind the philosophical and the mathematical traditions together – at least in the early phase. But beyond that there are not many ties between philosophy and mathematics. Surely it is not much to the point to ask about Archimedes' philosophy. He is the spokesman of an emancipated, deductive science existing in its own right, and he probably had little philosophical motivation for quantifying physics, even though the ideal in principle is Platonic (the *Timaeus*) and not Aristotelian.

ASTRONOMY

The Platonic programme of 'saving the phenomena' by means of mathematical theory found its most handsome formulation in Eudoxus' astronomy. The main features of the theory have been presented earlier (p. 328): an explanation of the motions of the celestial bodies based on a combination of uniform circular motions with the earth as the centre. The most difficult problem was that of the planetary motions, for not only – as reflected in the *Timaeus* – was the task to account for the daily motion of the planets, which follows the rotation of the heavenly sphere (the sphere of the fixed stars) and for their eastward motion along the ecliptic but also to account for the inclination of the planetary paths in relation to the ecliptic and for the retrograde planetary motion. The problems were sought resolved by assigning four spheres to each of the planets, so that the motions of the outer spheres are transferred to the innermost one. The system was purely mathematical, and most subsequent astronomical theories continued this Platonically-inspired view – thus one can also speak of an 'idealized' astronomy. Aristotle's physical interpretation of the model is a deviation.

The geocentric theory was indeed dominant but not sovereign. The Pythagoreans

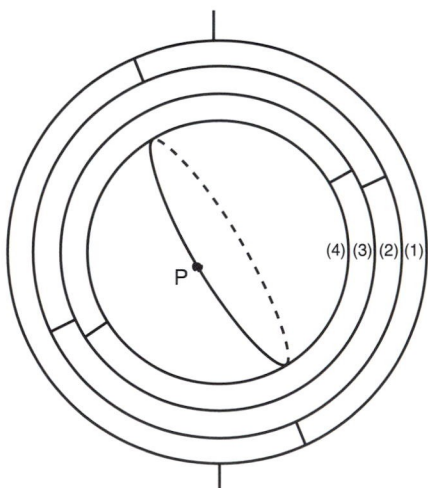

The motion of a planet according to Eudoxus' theory of concentric spheres. It will be seen that each of the four spheres assigned to the planet (P) has its own rotational axis.

From G.E.R. Lloyd, *Early Greek Science: Thales to Aristotle*, London, 1970, p. 88.

had assumed a spherical universe with the 'central fire' as the centre, and a student of Plato's, Heraclides Ponticus, had proposed a geo-heliocentric system. A fully helio-centric 'Copernican' system was, however, construed by Aristarchus of Samos (c.310–230, a student of Straton of Lampsacus) – just as Eudoxus' system a hypothet-ical mathematical construct that did not implicitly claim to explain the nature of reality (cf. Arch. II 218, 7 ff. (*Aren.*); the criticism summarized in Ptol. *Alm.* I 7 (I 24 Heiberg)). According to Aristarchus the sphere of the fixed stars and the sphere of the sun were immobile, while the earth – like the planets – moved in a circle with the sun as the centre while at the same time rotating daily around its own axis. Aristarchus' model was simpler than Eudoxus' but was not accepted. The Stoic Cleanthes found it offensive for religious reasons (Plut. *De fac.* 923 A), but most likely the – more or less weighty – scientific objections meant more: the theory was not in agreement with 'observable' facts – heavy objects seek towards the centre of the earth, which consequently must be the centre of the world (the basic Aristotelian view). According to Aristotelian dynamics, the earth would by virtue of its weight move with such great velocity that all living creatures and other 'loose' objects would have fallen off long ago and would be moving freely in cosmic space; finally, and not least important, the theory presupposed a not-observed shift in the angle between two sight lines to the same celestial body (the parallax).

However it was necessary to develop Eudoxus' theory further. The apparently irregular motion of the sun that causes the seasons to be of unequal length remained unexplained, and the retrograde motions of the planets were still problematic. With a view to resolving this, two equivalent models were constructed: the theory of epicy-cles and of eccentric circles (cf. Ptol. *Alm.* III 3 (I 216 ff.)). The author of the theories was presumably Apollonius of Perga; they were further developed by the influential astronomer Hipparchus (born c.190 BC). The theory of epicycles assumes that a given planet moves in a smaller circle (the epicycle) the centre of which moves in a larger circle (the deferent). The combination of these circular motions should then yield the desired result. But this can also be achieved by the other theory, according to which the celestial body is in motion on a circle with a centre outside the earth (eccentrically). The fact that the two theories are geometrically equivalent – and that one hence in every case can choose the simpler model – is once more testimony that astronomical theories were considered as mathematical models, not as descriptions of 'actual' reality. The theory of eccentric circles is simpler because it operates with one motion, while the epicyclic theory calls for two; nevertheless it has the 'unaesthetic' drawback that the centre of the universe, the earth, is not the mathematical centre of the motions of the celestial bodies.

Many centuries after Euclid had summed up the geometric knowledge of his time, Ptolemy of Alexandria (presumably dead soon after 160 AD) wrote a major compre-hensive treatise on astronomy (the *Syntaxis mathēmatikē*, 'Mathematical Collection', which by a medieval distortion of an Arabic title became known under the name of the *Almagest*); a major work on geography has also been preserved. Ptolemy's *Almagest* was the work that transmitted the final stage of ancient astronomical knowledge to the Middle Ages; it became known in the west in the twelfth century and was from then on the standard work on astronomy – not only until Copernicus, but even as late as Tycho Brahe and Kepler. Ptolemy aimed for an encyclopedia of all the natural

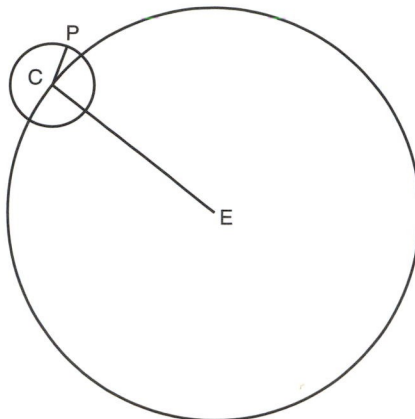

This figure shows the motion of a planet according to the theory of epicycles. P is the planet, C is the centre of the epicycle, and E is the earth.

From G.E.R. Lloyd, *Greek Science after Aristotle*, London, 1973, p. 62.

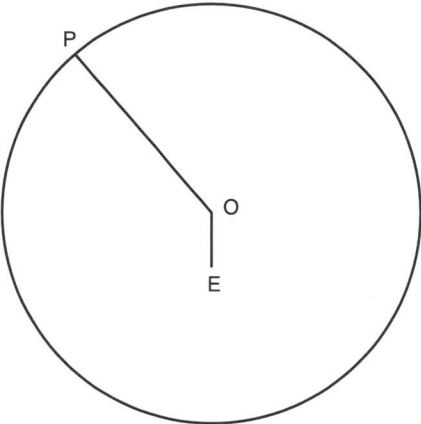

This figure shows the motion of a planet according to the theory of eccentric circles. P is the planet, O is the centre of the deferent, and E is the earth.

From G.E.R. Lloyd, *Greek Science after Aristotle*, London, 1973, p. 62.

sciences. It was also his avowed intention to fit the natural sciences into a broader philosophical framework – more precisely an eclecticism marked by Aristotelianism (I 1 (I 4 ff.)); but in practice he was – like Archimedes – free of philosophical ties. It was as an empiricist and with the assistance of the hypothetico-deductive method that he summed up the development of an idealized mathematical astronomy. His general picture of the world can be seen in the beginning of the *Almagest* where he says that he will account for five principal points: that heaven is spherical and moves like a sphere, that the earth is similarly spherical, that the earth is the centre of the universe, that the earth is related as a point to the sphere of the fixed stars because of the great distance, and that the earth is unmoved (I 2 (I 9 ff.)). It is evident that the universe – as in the entire astronomical tradition – is considered finite.

Although Ptolemy depended on the tradition – especially on Hipparchus – he was a quite original astronomer. He improved the technique of observation and established a very detailed catalogue of the stars (VII 5 (II 38 ff.)). In theoretical astronomy he employed both the epicyclic theory and the theory of eccentric circles, but he introduced a number of further constructions in order to achieve the greatest possible agreement with available observations. Thus he added to Hipparchus' theory of planetary motions by introducing the so-called equant. According to his standard model the planet moves on an epicycle with its centre in a deferent, the centre of which does not coincide with the earth (a combination of the two traditional methods). Furthermore, the centre of the epicycle does not move with uniform speed on the deferent but relative to a point (the equant point) that is different from the centres of both earth and deferent (the motions of the planets are described in books IX–XIII, see especially IX 5–6 (II 250 ff.)).

In this way a high degree of precision was achieved – although at a price. Not only did Ptolemy's system in general become fairly complicated and unwieldy; the device of the equant must also be seen as a break with the ancient principle of uniform circular motions. Ptolemy's whole system was a system of mathematical constructs, and his abstract, hypothetical astronomy could not very well meet the Aristotelian demand for physical relevance. The more simplified Ptolemaic 'world picture', which lived side by side with his abstract description during the Middle Ages, has been characterized as a popularized version of Ptolemy. But in one form or another Ptolemy came to dominate medieval astronomy. Copernicus' break with the geocentric view was not a break with the other presuppositions of the tradition.

MEDICINE

Like astronomy, medicine became a highly developed special science in Hellenistic times and was characterized by extensive use of experiments and dissection – sometimes vivisection. Herophilus and Erasistratus (both first half of the third century BC), for example, undertook thorough investigations of the anatomy of blood circulation and of the nervous system; Erasistratus discovered that the heart functions like a pump, and he distinguished between sensory and motory nerves. But he did not arrive at a correct understanding of blood circulation nor of the functions of the two 'nerve systems'.

Throughout the history of Greek medicine there was a lively discussion about the relation between theory and practice. This discussion of method dates back to the Hippocratic writings, and since medicine as opposed to deductive mathematics is an empirical science, the two disciplines stood in different relation to the philosophical tradition in the course of their development. In the first phase mathematics and philosophy are closely related. Idealized mathematics is philosophically inspired, but as mathematics gradually became established as a special science with a fixed method, the basis of the discipline was no longer radically in dispute. Otherwise with medicine. In its origin medicine is a practical discipline, and in the Hippocratic writings one encounters philosophy as a disquieting partner and opponent. Plato could make use of the mathematical mode of thinking as paradigmatic for metaphysics and so could Aristotle for logic. But medicine deals with the changeable world where things 'might happen otherwise'. The theoretical discussions of method, often of a philosophical nature that already emerged in the Hippocratic writings continued, and down through time medicine was influenced by differing epistemological views. A mechanical-materialist view is represented, for example, by Erasistratus and the Atomistically oriented Asclepiades (first century BC); another movement stuck to the old Hippocratic view of medicine as nature's aid; man was considered a unity of soul and body, and human nature depended on an interplay between certain opposing forces – this could enter into a fruitful alliance with Aristotelian ideas. The contrast between a preponderantly theoretical and a preponderantly practical attitude resulted in two schools – 'the dogmatists' who with an old epistemological formula sought the 'hidden' causes and 'the empiricists' who relied on the immediately given, the patient's immediately observable symptoms. There is a clear connection between 'the empiricists' and philosophical scepticism.

The most important figure in the medicine of late Antiquity was Galen of Pergamon (129–c.200 AD) who rose to become court physician to the Emperor Marcus Aurelius and who left a very substantial oeuvre. Like Ptolemy, he stands as one who consummated a long tradition; as Ptolemy was the astronomical authority of the Middle Ages, so Galen was that of medicine – until Harvey discovered the double circulation of the blood. Galen was also marked by the philosophical eclecticism of his day; but while philosophy to Ptolemy mostly constituted the backdrop, it was to Galen of decisive importance in his practical, scientific work. To him Hippocrates was the great medical authority; Plato was accorded the rank of *président d'honneur* of philosophy, though he probably found Aristotle more suitable for life in this world. Galen was an outstanding logician. He contributed independently to relational logic (cf. Gal. *Inst. log.* 38, Kalbfleisch), and his main interest was in a practical, applicable theory of proof, where he especially concerned himself with the relation between categorical and hypothetical syllogisms and with the axiomatic basis for a philosophy of science (32 ff.; 38 ff.). He was inspired by both Aristotelian and Stoic logic.

Galen was a hot-tempered writer who knew his own worth. With harsh polemicism he turns against the empiricists and against purely mechanical-materialistic medicine; Erasistratus was his constant whipping boy. Mechanical causes are – in the proper Platonic spirit – necessary but insufficient, and Galen clearly adheres to a teleological observance, for nature does not act blindly (*De nat. fac.* III 15). One ought to return to Hippocrates' view of nature and of man as an organic whole (I 13). It is the whole patient, not merely his liver or kidneys, that is to be treated. In elaborating on his basic thoughts Galen tied the Hippocratic humoral pathology (II 8–9) to Aristotle's doctrine of the elements and to his general conceptual apparatus. The physician is to search for the causes, nature's hidden 'forces' (*dynameis*), which one can infer from their effect (*ergon*) or activity (*energeia* – I 2). These 'forces' are the four bodily fluids, which – like the four elements – are composed of the Aristotelian elementary qualities (I 3; II 4). Disease depends on a disproportion among the 'forces', and since man is a psycho-physical entity, it follows that the famous four temperaments will be given disproportionate weight from one of the bodily fluids: the sanguine temperament (blood), the phlegmatic (slime), the melancholy (black bile), and the choleric (yellow bile) (II 8).

For Galen a special problem was what it is that enables a living being to live. From his point of view it must be some kind of stuff that possesses the property of sustaining life. Influenced by Aristotle and the Stoics, he believes that such a stuff, *pneuma* or breath of life (cf. II 6), exists and is transported through the arteries. This theory is not only wrong; it is also philosophically unsatisfactory – as it was in Aristotle. The theory – which was maintained for centuries thanks to Galen's authority – perhaps shows even more than does the theory of the four bodily fluids that from modern points of view Galen can hardly be said to have found a satisfactory balance between speculation and empiricism. However, his empirical knowledge was impressive. The most valuable aspect of his scientific attitude is probably the wish to respect man as an organic whole.

TECHNOLOGY

In accounts of the history of science in the ancient world it is traditional to ask why applied natural science was of so little importance. Of course mechanics and technology did exist. Also as an engineer Archimedes was a natural talent – he employed the principle of the lever in practice, invented 'the endless screw' and widely-acclaimed cunning war machinery. The Hellenistic period can also boast a series of pneumatic inventions, uses of the pulley, mechanisms for the lifting of water (the water snail or 'the Archimedean Screw'), etc. – in addition of course to technical implements that had been known since time immemorial, such as the use of hydraulic power. In some measure technical inventions were of benefit, for example in agriculture, but otherwise technology was not used for much besides war and entertainment. Steam power, for example, was known although not systematically exploited. Why was there no development of a technical culture – an exploitation of natural forces with an eye to mass production, industrialization and profit? Traditionally many different answers are advanced: a widespread fear to challenge higher powers by interfering with nature (but were all afraid of the gods' wrath?), little call for machinery in a slave society (yet there was not always abundance of cheap labour), and a general scorn of manual labour, at least after Plato and Aristotle (but how wide-spread was this outside the elite?). All are reasonable but insufficient answers. A better one may be that it is our technological culture that is in need of an explanation. The deliberate effort to master nature is a unique phenomenon, characteristic of recent Western history; in this respect the ancient world does not differ from cultures outside our own.

PHILOSOPHY

Philosophy had a greater public than did science, even though it never did become everybody's dish. An outward expression of the difference between philosophy and science was that while the sciences were cultivated in the new, great metropoles – primarily Alexandria – Athens continued to be the capital of philosophy. Hellenistic philosophy is centred in Athens; it was here that the Epicurean and Stoic schools were founded, and here a philosophical and educational milieu continued to exist; and unlike the scientists, the philosophers were not dependent on political potentates. It may be to the purpose to take a look at the state of philosophy in Athens in 300 BC. In the Academy the metaphysical systems of Speusippus and Xenocrates belonged to the past – even though most philosophers had 'heard' Xenocrates. The head of the school, Polemo (died c.276), was primarily concerned with ethics – a sign of the times. The same applies to Crantor who, to judge by all we know, was the first commentator on Plato. The leadership of the Academy was assumed by Arcesilaus, presumably in 273, and thereby began a new era, that of Academic scepticism (see p. 472 ff.). Theophrastus resided at the Lyceum. For years he was held in unanimous esteem, but as the last Aristotelian polyhistor he was not a man for the new times. With Straton the character of the school changed. Yet one should also take other currents into account in and outside Athens. The enigmatic Pyrrho (ca. 365–270) was later considered the founder of Scepticism (see p. 471), and, besides, the non-Platonic Socratic tradition – i.e. the tradition from Euclid of Megara, Antisthenes, and Aristippus (see p. 133 ff.) – was in no way extinct. In all branches of philosophy there were rich possibilities to establish connections back behind Plato and Aristotle to the older tradition and above all to the great ideal figure, Socrates.

These possibilities were exploited by the new philosophical schools. Epicurus founded his own school in 306 BC; a few years later Zeno of Citium founded the Stoic school; but one cannot at this time speak of a genuine sceptical 'school'. Even so, certain features were common to Epicureanism, Stoicism, and Scepticism. From a formal point of view it was not Aristotle's but Xenocrates' classification of philosophy that was adhered to – which is to say a tripartite division into epistemology (including logic), physics, and ethics. The ideal was a consistent universal system where it was possible with epistemology as the point of departure to comprehend the fabric of the physical world and, with it as the basis, human nature – i.e. to draw ethical consequences of man's place in the world. With logical certainty one should be able to unroll the system from one end, as it were. The possibilities of human cognition is the presupposition, insight into the nature of the world the means, and happiness the goal. The Hellenistic schools had different answers to basic philosophical problems, but the questions and the frame in which they were asked were to a large extent common property, and hence they carried on a lively debate with each other in which they often relied on certain fixed, standardized types of argument. They agreed about what they disagreed about.

The Hellenistic mode of philosophizing is a systematic approach, which departs from Plato and Aristotle in several respects, and much of Hellenistic philosophy must be understood as a reckoning with these two giants – with due consideration of earlier traditions. Plato and Aristotle could not be thought away, but in general the break with Platonism and Aristotelianism is owing to an empirical-naturalistic basic outlook. One should begin with the concrete and immediate. This appears clearly in epistemology, now an independent discipline. The three Hellenistic movements all build on sensualism, which is to say that they share the view that if there is true cognition, it must depend on sensation – in short, they acknowledge the initial thesis of Plato's *Theaetetus* but reject the refutation. As Epicurus states it: if all sense experiences are rejected, there is no basis for rejecting those sense experiences that are considered false (Epic. *Rat. Sent.* 23). In the same way the Stoics say that he who rejects one sense impression must do so with reference to another (Sext. Emp. *Adv. math.* VII 259). Here it is implicit that concepts and intellectual knowledge are derived from sensation. If there are criteria for true sense perception – as 'the dogmatists', i.e. the Epicureans and Stoics thought – then sure intellectual knowledge is possible; but if there is no criterion, it is impossible – the sceptical view. This is a radical break with the Platonic-Aristotelian position, according to which man has direct access to concepts and intellectual truths. Plato and Aristotle can permit themselves a certain scepticism with respect to the possibility of valid sense perception of individuals. On the other hand, an Epicurean or a Stoic is not bound to a vast metaphysical apparatus, but – in the terminology of the day – he is obliged to establish criteria for the truth of individual sense data; failing this, scepticism is the only respectable epistemological position.

A sceptic should refrain from 'dogmatizing' about the physical world. But to Epicureans and Stoics it was natural that sensualism was tied to a materialistic view of the world. If intelligible objects – ideas, forms, or essences – have no autonomous existence, it is the physical object that is given beforehand, and if the physical world – as the Stoics thought – follows a rational course, reason must, so to speak, be built into matter. In all Hellenistic philosophy it is important to study causal connections; it is at this time that the problem of determinism became a main problem in philosophy.

However, epistemology and physics are of no worth, if one cannot by this path achieve happiness or peace of mind (*ataraxia*) for individual man. A naturalistic ethics is a rooted tradition in ancient moral thinking. But it is a special characteristic of Hellenistic ethics that it tries to reconcile man with the greater cosmic course of events on which the individual has no influence – to achieve inner harmony despite external circumstances. Nevertheless it is possible to use the Aristotelian heritage extensively. For man it is a question of understanding what lies 'within our power'. On this depends the possibility of happiness, and the very concept of happiness is of Aristotelian inspiration, even in a radical version: happiness is the highest good for man; it is a realization of his true nature and it is an absolute concept that does not allow for a more or less. It is characteristic of Hellenistic naturalism that discussions on ethics commence with a purely empirical, descriptive examination of what in fact is the natural driving force behind human acts. What dictates an unspoiled human being's natural, instinctive behaviour? To use one of the standard questions beloved by Hellenistic philosophers: what instincts can be observed in an infant ('the cradle argument')? If this question is answered, it is possible to proceed and ask what characterizes the adult, rational man and ask how man develops rationality from instinct. The answer to that question will then of itself lead to a determination of happiness, for man is to live 'in accordance with nature' – both nature at large and man's own nature; happiness completes what is embryonic in man's biological nature. But happiness presupposes rational insight into the world. The happy man and 'the wise' are, ideally, the same person. Man must understand.

Inasmuch as ethics and the proper determination of happiness are considered the goal of philosophy, and inasmuch as happiness in one sense or another consists in inner independence, it is natural to connect this with the individual's position in the new political situation after Alexander the Great, which has been described in the beginning of this chapter. Outward losses must be made up for in the inner man. 'The spirit of the age' is real enough but never a *deus ex machina*, and although many common features of Hellenistic thought have their background in man's new position in an alien world, it is difficult to explain for example sensualism and materialism by the irremediable loneliness of the soul. Nor did the sensitivity to the vagaries of the external world present itself all at once; there are never abrupt paradigmatic shifts in philosophy. First, the special ancient form of 'eudaemonism' is not of Hellenistic origin. It is part and parcel of the tradition (Socrates and his associates as well as Democritus); the same is true of 'the wise' as the ideal person (the Socratics, Aristotle). Perhaps the most typical 'Hellenistic' sage lived before the Hellenistic age – the legendary Cynic Diogenes (c.400–325 BC) who shocked the establishment by breaking with conventions, quitting society, and living according to an ascetic ideal (see p. 442).

Secondly, however much Hellenistic philosophy aims to liberate the individual from the misfortunes of this world, its strict intellectualism is no facade. The appeal is to human reason, and it will appear from the following that the new intellectual freight of the Hellenistic age – a long way down the road – is a reworking of old questions.

27

EPICURUS

——— •◆• ———

When the life of man lay foul to see and grovelling upon the earth, crushed by the weight of religion, which showed her face from the realms of heaven, lowering upon mortals with dreadful mien, 'twas a man of Greece who dared first to raise his mortal eyes to meet her, and first to stand forth to meet her: him neither the stories of the gods nor thunderbolts checked, nor the sky with its revengeful roar, but all the more spurred the eager daring of his mind to yearn to be the first to break through the close-set bolts upon the doors of nature. And so it was that the lively force of his mind won its way, and he passed on far beyond the fiery walls of the world, and in mind and spirit traversed the boundless whole; whence in victory he brings us tidings what can come to be and what cannot, yea and in what way each thing has its power limited, and its deep-set boundary stone. And so religion in revenge is cast beneath men's feet and trampled, and victory raises us to heaven.

(Lucr. *De rer. nat.* I 62 ff.; trans. Bailey)

This exalted eulogy honours Epicurus. It was written more than 200 hundred years after his death by the Roman poet Lucretius, one among many enthusiastic adherents. After Pythagoras (and Empedocles?) Epicurus is probably the only philosopher in the West who gained the honour of being worshipped – almost – as a god, the saviour who had freed mankind from fear and terror. He himself is not without responsibility for this image. He had not only a philosophy but a message and he liked to present himself as an autodidact: nobody had taught him anything; he himself had found the truth. Yet he was more than a self-appointed guru. In his school – Epicurus' 'garden' – he realized his own ideal of life, to live with his friends and students in restful peace and joy, unaffected by the noise of the world. His like-minded friends met him with devotion; he is praised for his mildness and unselfishness (cf. Diog. Laert. X 9 ff.), and preserved letters to his circle show both his charm and warmth (cf. 5 ff.). He has often been underrated as a philosopher; as a psycho-therapist he surely cannot be overrated.

Not everybody considered Epicurus a mild and wise father-figure and guardian of the truth. Lucretius' contemporary, Cicero, evaluates him coolly as a philosopher: as a rule Epicurus, according to Cicero, follows Democritus, but when he tries to be inde-pendent he makes a fool of himself; his physics is queer and his ethics inconsistent, and he does not understand logic (Cic. *De fin*. I 17 ff.). Apparently the Epicureans were never really accepted – they considered 'pleasure' as the goal in life and virtue as a means not as a goal, and therefore they were not socially acceptable. Internally the school was dominated by its founder even as late as the second century AD, when it faded. At times – especially in Italy in the first century BC – it had quite widespread influence. Some particular points were indeed developed further and refined, but while the other schools were constantly in a state of development from one generation to the next, the Epicurean truth had been laid down once and for all.

Epicurus (341–271) was born on Samos, probably in quite modest circumstances; his father was an emigré Attic citizen. Already in his school years he realized his call to philosophy – because his teacher could not explain what existed 'before' chaos in Hesiod (Sext. Emp. *Adv. math*. X 18) – and from then on he absorbed whatever knowledge came his way. Among other things he became acquainted with the Democritean tradition thanks to the Atomist Nausiphanes, whom he later disavowed as heartily as he could (Diog. Laert. X 8).

What he disliked in Nausiphanes – the jellyfish, as he called him – was presumably that he advocated a strictly deterministic interpretation of Democritus' materialism. Freedom of will was probably not a serious problem for Democritus himself, but in the course of the fourth century it had become a problem, and an Atomist must choose: either he must adhere to a merciless mechanical causality or he must – like Epicurus – seek to build the possibility of freedom into the materialistic system (cf. the polemics against 'the physicists' belief in destiny, Epic. *Men*. 134). Following what was evidently intense philosophical activity in his home region, Epicurus went to Athens where he founded his own school in 306. It was a sort of philosophical commune open to all layers of society of both sexes, where the master with his friends practised what they taught. Surely it was not an institution of learning of the same nature as the Academy or Lyceum, but the reason for Epicurus' settling in Athens was undoubtedly his wish to make his mark in the stronghold of philosophy.

Epicurus' work was extensive. It was written, so to speak, at different levels adjusted to what the addressees might grasp. *On Nature*, his principal philosophical work, in thirty-seven books, was apparently aimed at an inner circle. Only the title was known until excavations at Herculaneum in the eighteenth century by sheer good fortune led directly to a big Epicurean private library from the flourishing period in Italy in the first century BC. Among other things, papyrus remains of *On Nature* were found but were not well preserved; their condition since then has not improved. The preserved material has not yet been fully edited, but it seems only to throw new light on particular points. One – not preserved – treatise on epistemology and method, which following Democritus' model was entitled the *Kanon*, probably also belonged in the more exclusive part of his oeuvre. Beyond this Epicurus found it important to present basic views in the form of compendia, letters, and collections of aphorisms. Here there are also gradations and he stresses that the student should memorize main points or apophthegms in order to prepare himself well for all the vicissitudes of life (cf. *Her*. 36; *Men*. 135). That which is intended for beginners is written in a handsome ornate style, while the writings to more advanced readers are in a compact professional style laden with terminology but without stylistic pretensions. Our principal source is the tenth book of Diogenes Laertius' history of philosophy. He quotes three letters *in extenso* – *The Letter to Menoeceus* (the most important basic features of the ethics, a handsome work of paedagogics written in noble style), *The Letter to Herodotus* (the main points of physics for the more advanced and without stylistic pretensions), *The Letter to Pythocles* (on astronomy – the authenticity of which probably unjustly has been disputed), and a collection of aphorisms ('Principal Doctrines' – *Kyriai doxai*). Anyway, Diogenes Laertius had access to a good source, especially on epistemology and method. Sextus Empiricus is another good indirect source with the addition, of course, of Lucretius. Cicero provides some information from the point of view of an opponent.

Although Epicurus himself would probably protest, it is a good general rule of thumb that he continues Democritus and that his innovations are either determined by the new Hellenistic view of epistemology and ethics or by a wish to come to terms with Aristotle's criticism of the old Atomism. Epicurus had to find a way out of the controversy about the divisibility of matter and about the existence of the void; but he also let himself be influenced by Aristotle's epistemology, by his view of the preconditions for voluntary acts, by his understanding of the concept of happiness and the concept of pleasure (*hēdonē*), and by his thoughts on friendship. Perhaps it is especially in this confrontation with Aristotle that Epicurus shows his face as a philosopher. The basis is and remains Democritus. This applies to his ethics as well. There are, to be sure, lines back to Aristippus' hedonism, but Democritus' ethics seems to be the more important basis.

In Lucretius' eulogy Epicurus appears as the conqueror of religion, that is the fear of unreliable gods. This is genuine Epicureanism. Another fear that Epicurus conjured away was the fear of death. In *The Letter to Menoeceus* – which, without mention of the atomic theory, briefly, clearly and handsomely states his ethical message – these are also the two leitmotifs. Epicurus does not deny the existence of the gods but attacks on two fronts: in part against the philosophical concept of god (Plato, Aristotle, the Stoics), which is closely connected to a teleological view, in part against the fear of popular belief in the wrath of the gods and their wilful interference in the events in the world – which is to say that he opposes chance or *Tychē* (134; cf. *Her.* 76). To the modern reader this provides an interesting insight into faith and superstition in those groups of society, which the surviving literature otherwise does not tell us much about. Epicurus counters the fear of death in a beautiful apophthegm, which surely deliberately alludes to Socrates' defence oration: when we are, death is not; when death is, we are not (*Men.* 125: *Rat. sent.* 2; cf. Lucr. III 830; Plat. *Apol.* 40 C).

Epicurus confronts the fearful man who is plagued by self-created troubles and lets himself be affected by ill fortune with the rational man who calmly rests in himself and exploits the good things in life that are always to hand (Epic. *Men.* 127 ff.). Such a man seeks what lies 'in our power' and ignores the rest. He seeks the pleasure that consists in freedom from pain and knows that his basic natural needs are small and easy to satisfy. He laughs at destiny and realizes that what happens of necessity eludes our control and that what happens by chance is inconstant, whereas what lies in our power is subject to no other masters. Such a man possesses immortal goods; god-like he moves among men (135).

EPISTEMOLOGY

An insight such as this is acquired through philosophy, and philosophy begins with epistemology. While the starting point of the old Atomism lay in the theoretical problems of the divisibility of matter, which the Eleatics had raised, Epicurus – like the other Hellenistic philosophers – begins elsewhere: how can one prove that certain knowledge exists? The basic elements are the same as in Democritus: an infinite number of atoms moving in an infinite void that is the precondition for motion (*Her.* 39). And Epicurus also takes over the basic axioms of the old Atomism: nothing comes from nothing, nothing perishes in nothing, the universe is eternally the same, and nothing exists outside the universe (38; cf. Lucr. I 146 ff.). But basic axioms as well as events below the sense threshold belong to what Epicurus – once more in agreement with the tradition – calls 'the hidden'. How does one arrive at the 'hidden' from the evident? Democritus' answer – the old Anaxagoras formula: 'through the phenomena that which is hidden can be seen' – is one with which Epicurus did not disagree. But he cannot give intellectual knowledge priority over sense perception. Sensation is not 'bastard' knowledge, and the phenomenon is true. In this also lies a methodical distancing from Aristotle. If sensation is the given starting point, one cannot employ an abstract, formal logic conceived in airy nothing. Demonstrative, apodictic knowledge is not only superfluous but misleading. The Epicurean *kanon* is bound to concrete sense phenomena, and hence 'logic' is closely tied to physics – no *organon* exists besides the science of the real world (Diog. Laert. X 31).

Sensualism is the given epistemological basis, and the primary epistemological question is: what are the criteria for truth? There are three criteria (X 31 ff.; cf. Epic. *Her.* 38; Sext. Emp. *Adv. math.* VII 203): sensation (*aisthēsis*), i.e. the immediate experience of what is provided by the senses; emotion (*pathos*), a sort of inner sensation, which is to say the immediate experience of pleasure or pain; and the concept that is directly derived from sensation (*prolēpsis*). As a fourth criterion is sometimes added the contested concept of *epibolē tēs dianoias*, the immediate apprehension or focusing of thought, which must mean the deliberate direction of thought towards and the grasping of its object. A *prolēpsis* is derived from sensation, an *epibolē tēs dianoias* is considered as analogous with deliberate sense observation. The criteria all pertain to something incontestably evident (*enarges*) and are the bases for true cognition.

At first sight it may seem confusing that it is maintained both that sensation is irrational (*alogos*) and is always true, but that is owing to the simple fact that 'true' in Epicurus and in the Greek tradition in general (Plato, Aristotle) is both a logical and an ontological concept; it is a property of a judgement and it stands for what exists or is simply present (cf. VIII 9). When it is claimed that immediate sensation or feeling is always true, it means that it is incontestably true that a given sense experience now is present for me. But Epicurus puts more into it than that I am actually sensing what I sense; to him it not only means that no sense experience can be refuted (Diog. Laert. X 32) and that all sense experiences are equally valid, but also that what I sense has real existence. According to the theory of sensation, which Epicurus adopted from Democritus, sense objects are minimally thin images (*eidōla*) that are steadily emitted from the physical bodies (cf. Epic. *Her.* 46 ff.). This means that sense objects are not mental but physical entities with the same status as physical 'things', and physical things are defined as something that can move or be moved (cf. 67; Lucr. I 440; cf. p. 446). This in turn also implies the radical consequence that dreams and hallucinations refer to objects having the same reality as all other sense objects (Diog. Laert. X 32). Emotions are explained according to a quite analogous model – they have a real, physical basis, the atomic constellation within the person.

Now, 'pure' sense experiences and 'pure' emotions are of course not sufficient ingredients in an epistemology, but they must constitute the point of departure. If I see a cow I must be able to identify it as a cow so that I can make the judgement that 'this is a cow' (33). The predicate stands for a concept, and the concept must be universal. How is such a concept formed and how is it employed? Here Epicurus follows what might be called his standard procedure: to accept the theses that are rejected in Plato's *Theaetetus* (here the second part of the *Theaetetus*) and approach the Aristotelian thought structures as closely as possible. A simple object concept (a *prolēpsis*) such as the concept of a cow is formed by a kind of storing of sense experiences in the memory that together form the universal – in other words, the Aristotelian scheme without rational intuition. Whenever the concept has been formed, it may be applied to sense experiences, which is to say by a simple object identification. In this sense the concept exists before the thing – *prolēpsis* means 'preconception' – I cannot identify the cow without knowing what a cow is – once again an Aristotelian reminiscence. The simple object concept – *prolēpsis* – is evidently true; although perhaps it is not evidently true that this is a cow, but that a cow is a cow.

The theory raises several questions. First, what ontological status do simple concepts have, and how can it be explained that I can conceive of something without a sense object being present? Here Epicurus undertakes a daring but consistent inference by means of an analogy from sense objects to intelligible objects – where one may perhaps suspect an echo from Democritus. Sense objects have extra-mental existence, and so do intelligible concepts (Epic. *Her.* 49; cf. Lucr. IV 749 ff.). This means that in the external world not only sensible *eidōla* but also an infinite number of very fine atomic constellations will be present, lying below the sense threshold and comprehensible by the mind. Thought objects are physical entities, and any thought object whatsoever is immediately available in the external world. It is merely a question of the mind's 'choosing' to direct its attention at thought object x and thereby excluding thought object y. It is this deliberate 'direction' towards a thought object that is called *epibolē tēs dianoias*, and in the field of sensation there is an analogous concept, *aisthētikē epibolē*, which explains that I look *at* something – not just passively see (cf. Epic. *Her.* 38; 50).[1]

Another difficulty is the question of correct object identification – by virtue of what is it justified to employ a *prolēpsis* about a cow to this or that sense experience?

---

1 The model can directly explain how one can think of physical objects that are not to hand. However, it is not easy to manage in connection with reflections about for example basic axioms and basic concepts, and indeed Epicurus seems to have operated also with a theoretical cognition independent of *epibolē* (cf. Περ. φύσ. 31,17 ff., Arrighetti (book XXVIII)), but it is unclear how he did so.

More precisely, what is the relation between sense object (*eidōlon*) and physical object? It can be illustrated by well-known examples: from the distance the square tower looks round; in the water the straight oar looks as if broken; the wine is sweet to one person, sour to another (cf. Sext. Emp. *Adv. math*. II 79). Of course the problem goes back to Plato's *Theaetetus*. To Epicurus the sense object itself is 'evident'; it is present or it is not present, and it is always 'true' – as are the special sense objects in Aristotle. My judgement or belief *about* a given object (*hypolēpsis*, supposition – cf. Diog. Laert. X 34) can on the other hand be true or false. Concerning this point Epicurus is not far from Aristotle's 'correspondence theory' of truth (cf. Sext. Emp. *Adv. math*. VII 210).

The reason for one's having true or false beliefs about physical objects is easy to provide. It is of course a physical one and rests on the *eidōla* theory (cf. Lucr. IV 216 ff.). A given physical object – the tower, for example – steadily emits images of itself: since such an image – an *eidōlon* – is physical, it is exposed to outside influences on its way from the physical object to the observer, and the greater the distance, the more numerous the sources of error. The image of the tower will become worn down or in other ways be distorted from the distance; in extreme cases images can coalesce so that they form a picture of a not-existing physical object – a centaur, for example. Now, if I judge: 'I have a sense experience of a round tower' or 'I have a sense experience of a centaur', I judge truly – for my judgement corresponds with a physical reality (*eidōlon*). But if I say: 'here is a round tower' or 'here is a centaur', I may judge falsely of a physical object (the thing).

This in turn has consequences for Epicurus' epistemological method (Epic. *Her*. 39 ff.; 50 ff.; Sext. Emp. *Adv. math*. VII 21 ff.; Diog. Laert. X 32 ff.). In some cases there is irrefutable, positive testimony (*epimartyrēsis*) that my judgement is true – Epicurus does not doubt, for example, that I can formulate a true judgement about a physical object if I am standing right next to the square tower; here there is evidence (*enargeia*). In other cases my judgement must await verification; but that is possible – I see the tower in the distance but cannot formulate a true judgement until I reach it. But there are cases in which verification by infallible observation either for practical reasons or in principle is impossible; this is in a broad sense what is called 'the hidden' or the unseen. Here it is sufficient if there is no contrary evidence (*ouk anti-martyrēsis*) – cf. 'the principle of economy' in Democritus – and one must have recourse to inferences by induction or analogy. In some cases it does not matter that one is prevented from a clear decision – I shall probably never know the number of grains of sand in the Sahara, and moreover I do not care. Epicurus' delight in provocation can be seen from the fact that he assigns astronomical phenomena to this category (Epic. *Pyth*. 85 ff.; *Her*. 76 ff.). Regardless of the astronomers' tales, we can never inspect the planets and the sun as closely as we can in the case of the tower. Therefore the only correct position is to acknowledge a plurality of possible explanations. That is indeed more than sufficient as long as we do not allow our peace of mind to be disturbed by superstitious notions of celestial events. This is an interesting 'realistic' commentary on the hypothetical constructions of contemporary astronomy. And Epicurus plays his ace by saying that as far as we are concerned we should maintain that the sun has roughly the size that it appears to have (*Pyth*. 91; Cic. *De fin*. I 20). It may be that it is 'improper' to say something like that, but, as

Epicurus writes (Diog. Laert. X 6): 'My friend, Set all sails and flee from all culture'. Finally, there are fictive objects, such as those of mathematics and metaphysics, which there is no sensible reason to worry about. This includes for example, also Aristotelian logic. There is a need for analogy and induction from sensation and not for deduction from definitions of non-existent essences.

Yet there are areas of existence in which it would to the highest degree disturb our peace of mind if we could not make certain inferences about the hidden. This is true of the basic axioms as well as the basic elements in the atomic theory themselves: if things could come into being from nothing and perish in nothing, the world would either be chaos or not exist.

There is no counter evidence to the effect that the world does not consist of atoms moving in the void; if this were not so, the world would not look as it does – the void must exist as the necessary precondition for motion; atoms must exist as warrant of the constancy in the world (cf. Sext. Emp. *Adv. math.* VII 213 ff.; Epic. *Her.* 41; Lucr. I 146 ff.). Not only is there no contrary evidence; the theory of atoms itself is the only possible explanation of the world's being as we perceive it. The only alternative to the theory of atoms is scepticism, but scepticism is self-refuting, because it presupposes the certain knowledge that I know nothing (cf. Lucr. IV 469 ff.). Concerning the behaviour of the atoms, it can be deduced by analogy from the visible to the invisible world (cf. I 422). The similarity with Democritus is striking – but so is the difference. The main question in Democritus is how rational cognition can be directive in a materialistic system. The paradox of the Epicurean system is that it is on the one hand strictly sensualistic and on the other that it must account for the physical basis (the theory of atoms) by pure rational inference.

All knowledge is formulated in words, and language is, or ought to be, a tool to impart knowledge. In the debate about whether language exists by nature or by convention, the Epicurean linguistic theory (Epic. *Her.* 75 ff.; cf. 38; Diog. Laert. X 33; Lucr. V 1028 ff.) occupies the middle road. In its origin language was a natural product in the sense that in men – and animals – it reflects an immediate emotional reaction to the external world; to that extent language is onomatopoetic. But as the cultural development gradually proceeds, language acquires a cognitive function as a means of communication. This does not come about by deliberate decision; language knows no legislator; as a means of communication it is a social product, and so it depends on a kind of unconscious collective convention. The phonetic sign (the sound) is contingent in relation to its signification; the sign should as precisely and unambiguously as possible represent or stand for the concept (*prolēpsis*) that is directly derived from the thing itself, and thereby *prolēpsis* comes to link the linguistic expression and the objective empirical world – *prolēpsis* is necessary in order for us to identify an object correctly and give it an unambiguous linguistic designation. But if language is to achieve its optimal cognitive function, it must be purged. Actual language is often ambiguous and metaphorical; it is still burdened by its origin as emotional expression, and it can contribute to erroneous interpretation of the relation between sensation and *prolēpsis* (cf. Epic. Περ. φύσ. 31, 10 (book XXVIII)). A meaningful language must therefore be led back to the primary, 'unambiguous' concept, and in a given case a clear, unmistakable expression must be created – Epicurus was himself an assiduous creator of terminology. Accordingly the theory emphasizes that language is to reproduce 'facts' – a metaphysical language, for example, refers to a pretentious nothing and a poetical language only to 'inner' facts, emotions. The focus is on the single linguistic designation – the word – but the theory has little to say about the sentence or proposition as a linguistic unit. As in Aristotle's semantics, in Epicurus the relation between expression and content is arbitrary, and there is formal identity between concept and 'reality'. The difference consists in 'concept' and 'reality' not having the same meaning in Epicureanism and Aristotelianism.

Frequently Epicurean epistemology recalls Platonic questions; on one point after another it has been modelled on Aristotelian patterns. Epicurus' transformation of Aristotle points everywhere in the same direction: language and thought are to be freed of every metaphysical dependence; ontology has to stick to the positive, empirical and concrete.

PHYSICS

To Democritus as to Epicurus it is incontestable that a world exists in which bodies are in motion. An explanation of this fact should be looked for in the 'hidden' causes, which is to say that it should be looked for by a rational procedure that explains the available facts and is irrefutable; it is on this that the atomic theory rests. The void is – as in old Atomism, but not as in Plato and Aristotle – a necessary condition for motion, and hence it exists. But the argument for the existence of atoms is not that indivisible entities must exist; rather, that constant material elements must exist behind the mutability of the world of things and that therefore indivisible entities must exist (Epic. *Her.* 39 ff.; 54).

The further conclusions (41 ff.) all follow the same pattern: *ouk antimartyrēsis* combined with a demonstration that the negation of Epicurus' theses would lead to absurdity. In contrast to the dominant view in ancient philosophy and science, it is assumed that the universe is unlimited. Democritus thought so, and Epicurus supports it with an anti-Aristotelian argument: a limit presupposes something beyond the limit, or, as Lucretius picturesquely describes it: move to the limit of the universe and throw a spear; whether it continues on its trajectory or is thrown back, there must be something beyond the limit (Lucr. I 968 ff.) – an argument that presupposes a very graphic world picture. As the universe is unlimited, it must follow that space is infinite, but also that there must be an infinite number of atoms; otherwise it would be impossible for atoms to meet and form bodies. And as there is an infinite number of atoms, there is nothing to prevent the existence of an infinite number of worlds resembling or not resembling our own (Epic. *Her.* 42;56). However, the number of atomic forms is not infinitely great but incomprehensibly great; otherwise some atoms would appear above the sense threshold, which would be absurd. Epicurus agrees with Democritus that atoms per definition can never be sensed. But it is an innovation that they therefore must be small – again an argument that presupposes a quite graphic model.

The atoms are compact, solid and qualitatively identical pieces of matter in perpetual motion. They must necessarily have a certain form and a certain size, but, contrary to Democritus, Epicurus believes them to be furnished with weight (54). Apparently Aristotle made him uneasy. In Aristotle's spheric universe there is a natural downward motion towards the centre of the universe – heavy bodies have weight – and a natural upward motion towards the periphery of the universe; Straton had introduced the simplification that in a finite universe there is only need of one natural motion, the downward motion. Epicurus agrees, and thereby he breaks with Democritus to whom the atoms in the original state move chaotically among each other. Why can Epicurus not accept this? He probably believed that he ought to counter Aristotle who criticized Democritus for not having 'explained' motion; and probably he thus partly sought to explain motion by a 'principle' in matter itself (weight) – as did the Aristotelian tradition – and partly to reduce composite motions to one primary motion (along the straight line). Still, his universe is not finite and has no centre, and the 'downward' motion must therefore be understood as relative to an imagined observer (60); the decisive is that the primary motion is uniform. Another point is important. Aristotle had denied the existence of the void, among other things because it would lead to the 'absurd' consequence that heavy and light bodies would move infinitely quickly and at the same speed in a *vacuum* without resistance. Epicurus took him at his word (61). It is in fact the case that 'heavy' and 'light' atoms fall equally quickly in the void and move 'as swift as thought'.

The idea of the vertical fall of atoms at the same speed through the void is astute, but it leads to the complication that they will never be able to meet and form bodies, if that were all. But there is more – for in fact atomic composita are formed and by them sensible bodies. Hence it is necessary that the atoms occasionally deviate from their course so that on the basic level there are not-determined events that break with the 'law of fall'. There is no need for vast, dramatic deviations that would be contradicted by sensation. A not-determined, 'free' swerve (Greek: *parenklisis*, Latin: *clinamen* or *declinatio*) in a minimal unit of time and a minimal unit of space is sufficient to start a chain reaction. Strangely enough, this swerve is never directly mentioned in the extant texts by Epicurus himself. But it is a necessary correlative to the idea of weight and of uniform motion 'downwards', and the entire later tradition – the Epicurean as well as the anti-Epicurean and the doxographic – agree about attributing this theory to Epicurus. The main source is Lucretius (Lucr. II 216 ff.; cf. Cic. *De fin.* I 19; *De nat. deor.* I 69; *De fat.* 22; Diog. Oen. 32, Chilton; Aet. I 12,5; 23,4). In a special way, according to the tradition, the theory connected Epicurean physics and ethics (see below).

Atomic composita are formed according to the pattern in the old Atomism – atoms can clash or become entangled and form bodies (Epic. *Her.* 43). But inasmuch as not all atomic forms fit each other, the outcome is not a chaotic pell-mell; to judge from Lucretius (cf. Lucr. I 173; 560 ff.; II 700 ff.), a certain 'secret' limit to the possible combinations has been established in ordered worlds – apparently this is intended to explain the weak point in Atomism that in fact bodies of uniform type are formed. But any composed body whatsoever is of course unstable – it comes into being and perishes. It participates in a perpetual interaction with the surrounding world and it exists as a body for as long as there is balance between the atoms that are taken in and those that are emitted by the body, for example as *eidōla* (Epic. *Her.* 54). Inside the body – below the sense threshold – the individual atoms will have their own forward and backward motion, just like particles of dust in a sunbeam, which is how Lucretius illustrates it in a famous image (Lucr. II 111 ff.). But the body as such will have its own – sensible – motion; a heavy, compact body with few cavities will move more quickly than a porous, light body with many cavities. Hence composed bodies move at different speeds (cf. Epic. *Her.* 62).

Epicurus distinguished closely between the properties that belong to the atoms themselves and the properties that belong to atomic composita, and he exploited this difference with greater virtuosity than Democritus. Only atoms are in possession of unchangeable properties – form, size and weight. An atomic compositum has other properties, but they are objective, nor, as in Democritus, is there any parallel with, for example, Locke's distinction between primary and secondary qualities (68 ff., cf. 40). The properties of composite bodies are of course perishable, and it is clear that they have no real existence (Plato), they are not immaterial but inherent in bodies (Aristotle), and they are not corporeal in themselves (the Stoics). In fact, only physical bodies have real existence, for only that has real existence which can move or be moved, and properties are not movable; hence they are epiphenomena. But macroscopic objects have two kinds of properties: in part such as cannot be removed without the object's perishing (*ta symbebēkota*)[2] – the size, form, weight and, for example, colour of the thing – and in part such as can be thought away without the thing perishing – for example, the fact that somebody is a slave or is rich (*ta symptōmata* – or accidents, cf. Lucr. I 449 ff.).

Two things are immediately striking. In the first place, form, size and weight are imperishable properties of atoms and perishable in things. In the second place, colour appears in the series of *symbebēkota*, for a thing will necessarily have colour, even though the colour may change. All that can be sensed has objective existence; consequently colour does not come about in the meeting of sense object and sense subject but in certain external atomic constellations; here Epicurus can exploit the fact that atoms in a compositum are steadily in motion and hence change relative position (cf. Plut. *Adv. Col.* 1110 C). Lucretius furnishes precise examples: the sea can change colour – it can be blue or foam with white – and the tail of the peacock can shimmer in several nuances (Lucr. II 766; 806; 973). It is on the given premisses an interesting solution that shows Epicurus' wish to place as much as possible in the external, objective world.

Time is a special type of accident (Epic. *Her.* 72). To Aristotle time is a property of a property. In Epicurus' conceptual framework time also acquires an almost unreal character. It is unreal inasmuch as we never can form a clear concept (*prolēpsis*) of time. It is real as a 'form of intuition' – with intuitive certainty we experience that events take place 'in' time.

The point of departure of old Atomism was the question of divisibility, and it

2   This is a telling transformation of Aristotelian terminology. *Ta symbebēkota* (what is present with something else) means accidents to Aristotle, which is to say the contingent properties of a thing. In Epicurus it designates the properties a thing must have in order to exist as this thing, because such properties are accidental in relation to those of the atoms. To Aristotle it is the thing, to Epicurus it is the atoms that exist primarily, and therefore Epicurus needs two kinds of 'accidents'.

raised the complicated question whether Democritus considered the atoms physically indivisible but theoretically divisible. Epicurus does not ask the question of divisibility until the second time around – but he does, on the other hand, ask it with customary provocatory radicalness (56 ff.; cf. Lucr. I 599 ff.; 746 ff.). He is again forced to take Aristotle's criticism of the old Atomists into consideration, and again he seeks to exploit him in his own way (cf. Simp. in Aristot. *Phys.* 925, 17 ff.). It is clear that when atoms have different forms and sizes they are in theory divisible. But there must, maintains Epicurus, be a limit also to theoretical divisibility; there must be theoretical minima in the atom. These minima within the atom are physically inseparable from the atom but function as common measuring units for any given atomic form. Epicurus' argument for the existence of such minimal units shows that he was staunchly unaffected by contemporary mathematics. He revives the old thought that if a finite entity is infinitely divisible, it is both nothing and infinitely large. This is a bad argument in the service of an interesting cause. What Epicurus wants to do is at all costs to guard against an Aristotelian continuum world, against, as he says, 'making everything weak' – in a world in which everything, however theoretically, is divisible, only a nothing is left. Hence finite minima must exist.

A division of a minimum is not even thinkable. Every assertion about the atomic world must rely on analogies from the sensible world. The eye cannot see anything smaller than a sensible minimal point – so Epicurus claims; by analogy the mind cannot 'see' anything smaller than a theoretical minimal point. Since one cannot either by sight or thought distinguish anything smaller than a minimum, it does not exist, for thought is constructed like reality, and what cannot be comprehended by any of the criteria for truth does not exist.

A physically discontinuous world must also be theoretically discontinuous. To Aristotle a line is infinitely divisible into sections, but it cannot consist of points without extension (Aristot. *Phys.* 231 b 25 ff.). Epicurus chose the alternative: the line consists of minima – points – with extension. If theoretical minima are assumed, one does away with the Aristotelian paradoxes of continuity and discontinuity; one is rid of the distinction between actuality and potentiality, and the fact that so doing one does away with idealized geometry is surely only an improvement. This way of thinking has the further consequence that 'infinite' only can be a predicate of space, time, and the number of atoms.

The notion of theoretic, atomic minima leads logically to a generalization of the atomic theory. As there are minimal measures of material extension, temporal and spatial minima must also exist, and thus minimal unities of motion must also exist: a minimal unity cannot move continuously in time and space. The atoms move 'as swift as thought', but their motion must be composed of minimal 'jerks' – thus the swerve from the straight line should also be thought to take place in a minimum of time and space. This means that Epicurus once again accepts what would be an absurdity to Aristotle: if time were composed of atomic unities, says Aristotle, one could not at any given moment say that a body is in motion but only that it has moved (240 b 8 ff.; Them. in Aristot. *Phys.* 184, 9 ff.). Epicurus' generalization of the atomic theory is perhaps the most interesting example of the results he could achieve by turning Aristotle upside-down.

The human soul must necessarily be material (Epic. *Her.* 63 ff.) – it can only be corporeal because it is able to move or be moved, to affect or to be affected (67). The soul must be able to sense and to reason, which is to say that the mind must be able to be directed to sense objects and intelligible objects; it must be able to feel, which is to say be aware of inner atomic states; and it must be able to move the rest of the body. For this a quite intricate combination of different kinds of atoms is required. What is probably most important is, according to Lucretius (Lucr. III 94 ff.), that a distinction is needed – reminiscent of Aristotle – between a 'guiding' rational soul (*animus*) and an 'obedient' part of the soul (*anima*), the function of which is to sense and move. Epicurus, like Democritus, is unconcerned about how physical events can be transformed to psychic experiences; nor is he apparently interested in the human 'self' – what sort of entity, for example, it is that 'decides' this or that, or chooses to direct its attention to one object or another. He would probably have considered such questions pseudo-problems; psychic phenomena are only accidents to physical ones; the soul atoms are physical; they are in immediate contact (*sympatheia* in Stoic-sounding terminology, Epic. *Her.* 64) with the rest of the complicated human organism – and a contact can only be material.

Democritus had stressed the distinction between an atomic original state, the creation of worlds within an infinite universe, and finally man's creation of his own world. Such a distinction is of course also presupposed by Epicurus, but he seems not to be particularly interested in a detailed cosmogony – he considers Democritus' vortex passé (*Pyth.* 90) – and with respect to the development of human civilization it appears from the preserved texts (cf. *Her.* 75 ff.) as if he first and foremost concentrated on the origin and development of language. On the other hand, in Lucretius (Lucr. V 925 ff.) one encounters detailed interest in the gradual development of mankind towards civilization. The background is evidently the old theory of cultural optimism, which, for example, had found a late advocate in Diodorus Siculus (see p. 94). But in Lucretius a characteristic turn takes place from optimism to ambiguity; material progress can very well lead to psychic decline; technical ability, the use of fire, and the invention of language, for example, have undoubtedly made existence easier – and man more effeminate. There are also other factors. Man is in principle an egoistical being – and there is no reason that he should be anything else. Therefore cultural institutions are first and foremost a means to check personal interests. But cultural development can foster aberrations leading man astray: this is, for example, the case if justice is considered a goal rather than a means, or if man lets himself be guided by wealth, empty status symbols, or desire for social standing. The greatest misfortune of human culture is that it has led to delusions about the gods, created in man's own imagination, and to fear of their wrath or an inescapable fate.

It is of course remarkable that Epicurus acknowledges the existence of the gods (Cic. *De nat. deor.* I 43 ff.; cf. Epic. *Men.* 123). The gods exist, for their existence is acknowledged by all peoples, and knowledge of the gods is evident – which is to say that since the existence of the gods is universally acknowledged it can only be owing to irrefutable knowledge of god, which must depend on the fact that we receive *eidōla* emitted from the gods. The concept of the gods (*prolēpsis*) is consequently also evident – and it is part of the concept of the gods, likewise by *consensus omnium*, that they have human figures, that they live eternally, and that they are happy. But there are false ideas (*hypolēpseis*) about the gods: the philosophical-teleological concept of god and popular belief; they are equally fatal. Existence means physical existence, but since the gods are immortal, they cannot have the same form of existence as sense objects; indeed they cannot be known by sensation but by the mind, and they are 'quasi-corporeal', which is to say that unlike sensible, physical objects they consist of extraordinarily fine atomic constellations in which there is a constant balance between the atoms leaving the quasi-bodies and those taken in by them. So the gods must be constituted physically, and in an infinite universe there is no counter-evidence of such beings existing in remote celestial regions (*intermundia* in Lucretius). These gods are happy, for they live in peace and pure joy. This is implicit in the true concept of god, but that is precisely why the gods do not interfere in human affairs and precisely why the false suppositions, which attribute deeds, wishes, needs and ordinary officiousness to the gods, are refuted – all of them being at odds with true happiness and belonging to weakness (*Rat. sent.* I).

If Epicurus had wished to do so, he could of course have disputed the existence of the gods and explained the concept of god in analogy with, for example, the idea of centaurs. Since he does not do so and accordingly must find housing for the gods in his material universe, it is, we may imagine, because he has a paedagogical errand: it is unprofitable to contest gods *tout court*; but one can turn religious ideas in the right direction. Thereby the gods acquire a paradigmatic function: they possess the happiness that man by right insight can strive for – to live *like* a god among men.

ETHICS

Insight into nature – which is to say the atomic theory – is a precondition for man's achievement of happiness. It may not be a necessary precondition – apparently busy travellers can make do with a collection of aphorisms or with *The Letter to Menoeceus*, even though in this work Epicurus does say a good deal more between the lines than a novice might comprehend. But whoever understands that nature has its own laws can rid himself of baseless fear of death and the gods, and thus he can concentrate his psychic energy on matters upon which he does have influence. It is wholly sufficient to create a life for oneself in inner freedom, independent of the external world, which in itself is neither good nor evil and which is not determined by a higher purpose or a providence. But man's forging of his own happiness presupposes that he has what we call free will, and that again presupposes that natural events do not adhere to a strictly predetermined course.

In *The Letter to Menoeceus* (*Men.* 133) Epicurus says that some things occur of necessity, some things by chance, but that some things lie in our power. But what does lie in our power? To Aristotle voluntary acts are those that are performed without compulsion or from ignorance. Epicurus cannot disagree. But with his mechanical, materialistic basic view he is to a higher degree than Aristotle obliged to account for the fact that not all human acts are the result of external circumstances or heredity. From our sparse sources it does indeed appear (Περ. φύσ. 34, 27; cf. 24 ff.) that he distinguished between causes 'within ourselves', man's original constitution, and the necessity that is owing to the surroundings and that which 'penetrates', as it is called in Democritean terminology. What surrounds us and 'penetrates' are of course atomic structures from the outside. The 'original constitution' must be man's congenital atomic structure, and it can be altered so that gradually a more or less firm disposition is developed – character in Aristotle. Epicurus' whole argumentation for the existence of causes 'within ourselves' (26 ff.; cf. 21 ff.) is – as in Aristotle – pragmatical: in ordinary language and in our daily doings we presuppose freedom of will; nobody lives as if the world were strictly predetermined. It is apparently on this point that Epicurus distances himself from the old Atomism as he understood it – or as the jellyfish Nausiphanes took it to be. It is not necessary to live according to necessity, and whoever enforces the law of necessity is unable to criticize anyone who denies it – from necessity (*Sent. Vat.* 9; 40; cf. Περ. φύσ. 34, 28). Such is the basic thought as formulated in aphoristic form. But how is human freedom reconcilable with the theory of atoms?

Strangely enough, the Epicurean texts left to us are silent on this point. On the other hand, the later tradition – adherents as well as opponents – is not silent. There is agreement that the connection between physics and ethics relies on the not-determined swerving of the individual atom. The opponents took inexhaustible delight in the fact that Epicurus ostensibly bases human freedom on the discretion of the atoms, but apparently that did not upset later vulgar Epicureanism (Diog. Oen. 32). It is however clear that a theory that turns man over to spontaneous atomic motion (chance) is just as awkward as a theory that assigns everything to determinism (necessity). Our principal source, Lucretius (Lucr. II 251 ff.; cf. Philod. *De sign.* 36,11) does in fact have something different to say. For him the swerve is a necessary but not a sufficient condition; the not-determined atomic motion corresponds with free will – unlike Epicurus, Lucretius, the Roman, has a word for 'will' (*voluntas*) – which is to say that it is the necessary physical substratum for the working of will. Lucretius illustrates it with a famous image: when horses are released in a race their will will spread to their limbs, and not until then will they spiritedly tear along. Although the theory of the atomic swerve does not appear in our Epicurus texts, it must surely be presupposed – also as a connective link between physics and ethics. Lucretius' explanation should be considered the orthodox one.

But the theory does not 'explain' free will, and there is much to suggest that in the final analysis Epicurus held the same view as Aristotle: freedom of will is a basic fact that is not in need of justification; what is to be explained are the physical preconditions for man's acting freely, for his being able to control or exploit not-determined atomic motions. This corresponds to the theory of *epibolē*, which likewise presupposes that the mind can 'choose' what it will direct its attention to, and such a choice is tied to action (cf. Lucr. IV 877 ff.). Like Democritus, Epicurus apparently saw no need to explain thinking *qua* thinking or will *qua* will. It is sufficient that there are special atomic constellations – the soul – that can think or will.

The purpose of life is pleasure, enjoyment, or well-being – *hēdonē* (Epic. *Men.* 128 ff.; cf. Cic. *De fin.* I 29 ff.). Everyone can observe that animals, infants and uncorrupted souls seek pleasure and shun pain; this is an empirical fact, and empirical facts take precedence over rational arguments; hence there is no occasion to prove that people act as they do. In light of the general naturalism of the times it means that man not only seeks pleasure but *must* seek pleasure; pleasure is happiness.

Pleasure and pain belong among the truth criteria, and every feeling of pleasure is *qua* pleasant feeling a good, although not just any pleasure should be chosen. A momentary pleasure can lead to greater pain later, and in turn a momentary pain can lead to greater pleasure later. It is the task of reason to weigh the pros and cons and carry out a 'hedonistic calculus' (Epic. *Men*. 129 ff.; Cic. *De fin*. I 32 ff.) regarding optimal pleasure. With this, familiar old notes are sounded (cf. Plato's *Protagoras*), but Epicurus differs from both Plato and Aristotle in his view of the role of reason: to him it is evident that reason should serve the primary need, that of pleasure. Such a calculation is in fact not difficult to carry out (Epic. *Men*. 127; *Rat. sent*. 29; Cic. *De fin*. I 45 ff.). There are natural and necessary desires that demand to be met, but they do not exceed simple daily needs. Furthermore, there are natural desires that are unnecessary; but the unnatural and unnecessary desires are the most dangerous. They are products of human folly that knows no limit, and these false desires – for wealth, success, etc. – therefore lead to boundless self-made suffering. The proper calculus consists in reason's curing the mind of false pleasures – empty yearnings are replaced by true ones; fear of the gods or of death is replaced by sure knowledge of the world and the nature of the soul.

A simple hedonism is threatened by the paradox that every enjoyment calls for more; the very need for enjoyment is never satisfied ('the hedonist paradox'). Apparently Epicurus had encountered such a hedonism that strives for constant, momentary satisfaction among the Cyrenaics who invoked Aristippus, the old Socratic. Epicurus distanced himself from Aristippus and again he found his weapons in Aristotle's arsenal. What he can make use of is Aristole's thought of pleasure as an *energeia* that has its purpose in itself, an activity the strength and value of which are on the qualitative level in which the temporal is irrelevant – the qualities of life do not depend on the length of life. On the other hand, what he cannot use is the thought of pleasure as an epiphenomenon to something else, pure pleasure as an epiphenomenon to happiness. Pleasure is simply happiness, and happiness is, as Aristotle had said, something absolute to which nothing can be added and from which nothing can be subtracted. Hence pleasure is impervious to outside influences that come and depart leaving wounds in the soul. There is no intermediary between pleasure and pain – for an emotion is not neutral. There are, however, two kinds of pleasure and pain. A feeling of pleasure is pleasure 'in motion' – as in Aristippus – i.e. a feeling of pleasure *in* something. Such a feeling of pleasure can be true but is risky – it is bound to an external object, is thus not independent, and it steadily demands external satisfaction. But then there is also the 'static' pleasure that is defined negatively as freedom from disturbance of the mind and pain in the body (Diog. Laert. X 136 ff.; Epic. *Rat. sent*. 3; Cic. *De fin*. I 37). This is an absolute state beyond momentary moods; in it the external influence can only be varied – it can neither be increased nor be reduced – since the sole warrant of happiness is man himself. It is not difficult to achieve that independence of mind that makes it possible not to need a delicious meal when there is none, but to enjoy it all the more when it chances to be there (Epic. *Men*. 130). And acute physical pain does not endure (*Sent. Vat*. 4). But there are things that are more difficult to master: sex never helped anybody; one should be happy, if it does no harm (51, Diog. Laert. X 118).

Soul and body are tied together, but there is a difference between psychic and bodily pleasures (cf. Cic. *De fin*. I 55 ff.). Bodily well-being is the most basic, which

Epicurus of course chose to express in a way that ensured optimal scandal: the joy of the stomach is the root of all goods; here also wisdom and refinement have their source (Epic. frg. 227, Arrighetti (Athen.); Περ. τέλ. 22,1 Arrighetti). Nevertheless, the psychic pleasures are of greater importance. A bodily pleasure belongs only to the moment – just as a physical pain is of short duration – but by virtue of memory and anticipation the soul can extend the psychic goods throughout life (Diog. Laert. X 137; Epic. *Rat sent.* 18 ff.; Cic. *Tusc. disp.* V 95).

A life in pleasure is not irreconcilable with a virtuous life. On the contrary. In order to administer one's life well one is in need of the mother of all virtues, wisdom (*phronēsis*); and, as in the whole Socratic tradition, it is claimed that *phronēsis* implies all other virtues (*Men.* 132; *Rat. sent.* 5; Cic. *De fin.* I 42 ff.). In practice Epicurus is a traditionalist. Conformism is expedient, but the virtues have no value in themselves; they are necessary as means not goals – 'the handmaidens of pleasure', as Cicero calls them (II 69). They are necessary to promote the good life, and whoever has offended will destroy his peace of mind with the thought that sooner or later he will be found out – never do anything that will make you afraid if your neighbour were to find out, as we are told (Epic. *Sent. Vat.* 70; cf. *Rat. sent.* 35). In other words, Epicurus is an adherent of the moral philosophy that Socrates was asked to contest in the second book of the *Republic*. Platonic-Aristotelian virtues can be repolished and used, but they are a means and thus express an egocentric ethics. The relative character of the virtues is perhaps seen most clearly with respect to justice (31 ff.). There is no justice 'in itself'; justice signifies a 'contract' between men about not doing harm and not being harmed; accordingly it concerns the common good that indirectly is also to the advantage of the individual. If the law no longer serves that purpose, one can in good conscience break it.

That Epicurus' ethics is egoistical of course does not mean that he is pondering his neighbour's misfortune. Other people are part of the life of every individual, but only to the extent that coexistence with others furthers the goal of life, the individual's inner independence (cf. frg. 218 (Clem.)). This is not the case with politics, which is why the wise man shuns all public life and lives in the hidden (cf. frg. 551, Usener; Plut. *Non posse* 1128 A ff.; Epic. *Rat. sent.* 7). But in one area of life pure egoism and pure altruism converge: in friendship. It should be superfluous to point out that here Epicurus had also been taught by Aristotle: the true friend is one's alter ego – or as Epicurus has it: the greatest blessing owing to wisdom is possession of friendship (27). With his friends the wise man can realize the good life, make himself master in his own house, and turn his back on the noise of the world. He laughs, philosophizes, and manages his household all at the same time (*Sent. Vat.* 41.). But he is also helpful: the philosopher who does not alleviate human suffering uses empty words (frg. 247, Arrighetti (Porph.)). All the over- and undertones in Epicurus' message are present in the words of Metrodorus, his favourite student:

> I have anticipated you, Fate, and repelled all your sinister plots. Indeed we shall never surrender ourselves as prisoners to you or any other incident. But when our hour comes, and we must depart, we shall spit on life and on those who vainly cling to it. We shall leave with a magnificent song of triumph and cry out that our lives were well lived.
>
> (*Sent. Vat.* 47)

LATER EPICUREANISM

Epicurus' wisdom did not allow for many modifications, nor did his personal authority invite new thinking; one senses only sporadically some further development.

In one regard, however, the appetite is whetted – but unfortunately no more than that. Epicurus did not acknowledge mathematics, and hence it is interesting to learn of 'Epicurean mathematicians', first and foremost Zeno of Sidon (c.150 BC) who apparently attacked Euclid (cf. Procl. in Eucl. *El.* I 199 ff., Friedlein); but it is uncertain whether the attack merely concerned deficient proofs of details in Euclid or whether the aim was to undermine Euclid's whole system – in other words whether Zeno wants to point to an 'alternative' geometry.

In other respects the textual basis has been more favourable. This brings us to the Epicurean renaissance in Italy in the first century BC. Here a prominent name is that of the Greek Philodemus by whom several papyrus texts have been preserved, found along with the Epicurus fragments in Herculaneum. Thereby we are provided with fragmentary knowledge of Philodemus' apparently extensive oeuvre, among other things with a work on piety that supplements our knowledge of Epicurean theology. From the other preserved texts mention should here be made of some points concerning Epicurean theory of science and linguistics. One of these works deals with inductive logic (inference from 'signs'), apparently in opposition to the Stoics who represent the formal logic rejected by the Epicureans – especially a logic that only permits inferences by formal contraposition. According to the Epicurean argument it is for example permissible to infer from the sentence 'the men we know are mortal' that 'men are mortal everywhere' – provided that there is no 'counter-evidence' and provided that 'men everywhere' stands for the same kind of beings as those we know (Philod. *De sign.* 16 ff.; 33, de Lacy). The example suggests an interest in inductive inference with full knowledge of 'the problem of induction' – an interest which brings Epicurean logics close to the empirical-undogmatic one of the Sceptics. Such an heuristic method might have been exploited scientifically, but neither Epicureans nor Sceptics did so. But strictly speaking it is not surprising that the two parties could meet in practice.

Philodemus also concerned himself with linguistics. The orthodox theory (see p. 429) holds that language in its origin expressed emotions but functions as a means of communication by referring to facts – which is why philosophical and scientific language should be purged of ambiguity, puns, and the like. But the original function of language survives in poetry, which accordingly is justified as expressions of emotion, which is to say as a purely aesthetical phenomenon void of truth value – in other words a theory of literature as art for art's sake exclusively. Rhetoric, on the other hand, pretends to communicate facts but actually aims to capture feeling (cf. Philod. *Poet.* V 77 ff., Jensen; II 265, Hausrath; *Rhet.* I 156 ff., Sudhaus). The extent to which this Epicurean aesthetics can be attributed to Epicurus himself is unclear.

Titus Lucretius Carus (c.94–55) is of course the most prominent figure in Italic Epicureanism. There are but few points of resemblance between Philodemus, the typical Greek scholar, and the poet Lucretius, one of Rome's greatest, a loner who is spokesman of no milieu and atypical in every respect – according to Philodemus' aesthetics, he ought never to have written a didactic poem. In the preceding his *On the Nature of Things* (*De rerum natura*) has been used as a main source; indeed there is no reason to doubt that he faithfully transmits orthodox Epicureanism and fully masters his philosophical material. Although he cannot be called an independent thinker, yet, as the poet of one of the most sublime didactic poems in world literature, he is indeed profoundly original. In six songs Epicurean physics is presented in dignified hexameters and in a lofty, deliberately old-fashioned style that combines missionary fervour with poetical vision and profound passion. The other aspects of the system are not dealt with explicitly, but epistemology is included, and the ethical aim is the nerve of the whole poem: to liberate man from the fear of death and the scourge of religion – in the end, to rid man of his fear of himself (cf. Lucr. III 1068). Lucretius' message is Epicurus'. Still, the tone is different: not only did Lucretius, the Roman, for example have other religious experiences than Epicurus; there is also a mile-wide difference between the rationalist observer, Epicurus, and the poet of passion, Lucretius – one may for example compare Epicurus' half ironical cool advice to young people in the throes of erotic pain with Lucretius' fight to the death with the woes of love (IV 1058 ff.).

Lucretius' creative imagination is congenial to his subject. With great virtuosity he can illustrate 'the hidden' with the well known; the poetical metaphor functions as a perfect Epicurean analogy. Details in his poem were probably not perfected at his death, but the structure is fully finished, and the ordering, which is independent of every school tradition, is at least outwardly clear: two cantos on the universe, two on man, and two on the development and perishing of the world. Yet it is a subtle composition that contains more profound layers than the surface ones.

Lucretius makes it no secret that he preaches sublime egoism (II 1 ff.): it is delicious to observe others in troubled waters, if one oneself is safely ashore, but nothing is sweeter than to behold those who tear hither and thither on turbulent paths, while one oneself lives in peaceful regions fortified by wisdom. What is delightful is not the distress of others but one's own freedom that enables one to assist also those who are lost. Here Lucretius – as he frequently does – weaves in a hidden Epicurus quotation that is rare because it allows an inner uneasiness to be voiced: face to face with death we all inhabit an unfortified city (Epic. *Sent. Vat.* 31). But the quotation is turned around so that Epicurus' wisdom becomes the soul's true fortress.

It has been shown (Diskin Clay) that the concealed composition of the poem gradually conducts the reader from his own presuppositions to salvation – full insight into nature as she appears to eye and thought (cf. Lucr. I 148: *naturae species ratioque*). But it is a harsh insight that demands that one can come to terms with the corruptibility of all things: only atoms and the void exist; all else is subject to death and annihilation. Symbolically this is expressed in a subtle interplay between the introduction and the end of the poem (I 1 ff.; VI 1138 ff.): in the beginning an allegory is presented on nature's gentle, peaceful idyll; the conclusion is a terrifying account of the plague in Athens – modelled on Thucydides. This is wayward nature in her extreme opposites. Between these two extremes lies Epicurus' message that raises the reader above the whims of nature, frees him from being enslaved by fate, and permits him to live in a fortified city – if he is able enough, that is. The poem brings the glad tidings, and yet it ends with pestilence and death. Certainty of salvation and despair lie close to each other in Lucretius.

Epicureanism survived for some time into the age of the Roman Empire. Plutarch still found it urgent to write anti-Epicurean pamphlets, and in the second century AD there was yet another Epicurean missionary, Diogenes of Oenoanda in Asia Minor; he let a vast inscription containing the main points of Epicurus' doctrine be carved in stone so that as many as possible might have a share in the truth. Diogenes is often a good source for the history of Epicureanism, but rarely for its contents. This late disciple of Epicurus would hardly have troubled his master; he was faithful and insignificant.

Thereafter Atomism received no attention for a long time. In medieval Aristotelianism (especially in the fourteenth century, Nicolas of Autrecourt) the possibility of natural minima (*minima naturalia*) was a subject of discussion. But the path to the old Atomism was opened when Lucretius was rediscovered in 1417 and Diogenes Laertius was translated into Latin in 1470. Then followed the decisive turning point in the seventeenth century when Gassendi with his studies on Epicurus (Diogenes Laertius' tenth book) revived Atomism in his battle on the one hand with the Aristotelians and with the Cartesians on the other. Thanks to the physicist and chemist Robert Boyle, a scientific corpuscular theory in the modern sense was constructed.

28

EARLY STOICISM

—— •❖• ——

All human beings are born free and equal in dignity and rights. They are
endowed with reason and conscience and should act towards one another in
the spirit of brotherhood.
(The United Nations Declaration on Human Rights, adopted 1948, Article 1)

Tous les hommes sont égaux aux yeux de la raison et de la justice. Il ne faut
point altérer cette vérité éternelle.

(Robespierre, April 19, 1793)

Nihil est profecto praestabilius, quam plane intellegi, nos ad iustitiam esse
natos, neque opinione sed natura constitutum esse ius.

(Cicero, *De legibus*)

Zeno of Citium at Cyprus, the founder of Stoicism (335–265), arrived in Athens
in 313 after a perilous voyage (Diog. Laert. VII 2 ff.). In Athens he happened by
a bookseller and heard him reading Xenophon's *Memorabilia* aloud to himself. Zeno
was fascinated by what he heard, and asked where one in our day could find such a
splendid man as Socrates. 'Follow that man', said the bookseller, pointing to the
Cynic Crates who just then was passing in the street. Thereafter, as we are told, Zeno
joined Crates, even though he adopted more decent manners than his master's. In
301 he founded his own school – which is to say that he lectured in rooms in the Stoa
in the market square (*stoa*: colonnade).

Crates (VI 85 ff.) was a student of the notorious Diogenes (c.400–325) who
earned his fame for all eternity by living in a barrel and speaking familiarly to
Alexander the Great (cf. 38). He practised extreme asceticism, rid himself of all
conventions, and lived the life of a dog (*kyōn*: a dog). To posterity Diogenes stands
as the figurehead of the Cynics, but the later tradition is probably correct in maintaining that in all essentials the Cynics continued Antisthenes' ethics. Thereby the
succession from Socrates to Zeno was established, and the bookseller anticipated the
judgement of history when he pointed to the leading Cynic of his day as a Socrates
redivivus. Diogenes – and with him the other Cynics – first and foremost showed
their ascetic attitude to life in practice, and surely it was part of their strategy to

provoke established society. The purpose was to 'adulterate the coinage', as Diogenes said with a subtle allusion to his father's being incarcerated as a coiner (20; 71). A closer justification for this *'Umwertung aller Werte'* is hidden behind countless anecdotes of witty replies in grotesque situations; yet the main way of thinking is clear enough: social status, wealth, reputation, seeming good fortune, tradition, and custom (*nomos*) mean nothing (72). Man is to return to nature (*physis*) and its simple demands; what matters is inner freedom, the freedom to speak and act as one wishes, freedom from affects (cf. 38; 69; 71). Reason dictates such an attitude and in it virtue consists; whatever does not contribute to a virtuous life is worthless, *adiaphoron* (24; 73; 104 ff.).

It is the single individual who is to live in inner independence; the idea of the free citizen in the free state has been orphaned. Diogenes – himself a refugee without civic rights anywhere – proclaimed himself a 'citizen of the world', a cosmopolite (63). Society in the traditional political sense is an illusion; but a community of the wise, the brotherhood of the wise, does exist (72). Still, there are indeed few wise – quite literally Diogenes walked about 'looking for a man' with a lamp in hand (41). There is a chasm between the few who are wise and the many who are fools, but in principle all can attain virtue and wisdom, regardless of rank and class (72). To the Cynics not all men were of equal worth, but they do have the same possibilities – Crates imagined a utopian land of bliss where all were friends (85); still, to the Cynics social commitment was of little concern.

Cynic philosophy is a practical doctrine about how to conduct one's life with a greater appeal to the ordinary man than that taught by the distinguished philosophers in the Academy or Lyceum, and the Cynic ideals continued their life side by side with the school traditions (Bion of Borysthenes, Teles from the third century BC). As late as the Roman Empire there were 'cynic' mendicant philosophers and preachers of philosophy. A main representative of late Stoicism, Epictetus, could present the 'Cynic' as the ideal type of philosopher (Epict. *Diss.* III 22).

A youthful work by Zeno was called the *Republic* (*Politeia*). It has been lost, but mention of it elsewhere probably shows something about Crates' influence on his young student (cf. Diog. Laert. VII 33; 121; 131). The title is somewhat provocatory, for apparently it did not deal with the state as a political institution but with an anarchic community of men and women with equal rights living in common and in friendship, without money, laws and family life. Evidently Zeno drew on Plato's ideas about the common life of the rulers and on Aristotle's vision of the ideal friendship that renders regulated societies superfluous. But above all, his thoughts should be seen in the context of the Stoic theory of man's place in the world at large (see below).

It is also stated (24 ff.) that Zeno 'heard' the then most prominent Megarians, Stilpon and Diodorus Cronus. We do not know all that much about the Megarians – strictly speaking hardly a school – but precisely at this time they seem to have played a significant role in the background. Interest seems in some degree to have shifted from the general metaphysics of Euclid of Megara to formal logical questions, although a too clear-cut borderline between metaphysics and logic should not be imagined – after all, the two had been closely connected in Socrates. The

Megarians continued the late Eleatic logic – which among other things implies that they operated with propositions, not with terms – and in the Sophistic-Socratic technique of argumentation they would have been able to find rich matter for theoretical considerations of paradoxes and fallacies. A series of logical 'riddles' are attributed to Eubulides, Aristotle's contemporary (cf. II 108) – the best known paradox is that of the 'liar' (Cic. *Acad.* II 96): NN maintains that he lies; if he speaks the truth he lies; if he lies he speaks the truth. Other paradoxes, for example 'sorites' (*sōros*: a heap – how many grains of corn are needed to enable one to speak of a 'heap' of corn? – 49; cf. Diog. Laert. VII 82), depend on linguistic vagueness and are comparable to the fallacies discussed by Aristotle in the *De sophisticis elenchis*.

The interest in logical paradoxes is taken over by the Stoics. More important are probably the Megarian deliberations about the modal concepts of possibility and necessity. We have glimpses into Aristotle's debate with contemporary Megarians (see p. 301 and p. 358) and can see that neither distinguished between de facto and logical modality; if something is logically possible, it is also *de facto* possible. The controversy concerns whether the possible necessarily is actualized, which is to say whether all events are strictly determined. After Aristotle, Diodorus Cronus – indirectly – voiced the Megarian position by formulating three propositions (the so-called master argument, *ho kyrieuōn*, Epict. *Diss.* II 19,1):

1   Everything that is past and true is necessary.
2   The impossible does not follow from the possible.
3   Something is possible that neither is nor will be true.

Diodorus considered these propositions incompatible. He could accept the first two, but denied the third, and hence he formulated his own definition of the possible as that which either is or will be true (cf. Cic. *De fat.* 17). The three theses are Aristotelian, and Diodorus' intention was evidently to demonstrate an inconsistency in Aristotle. He can accept that an event in the past is necessary in the sense that it is unalterable; nor does he object to the second thesis. By rejecting the third he hits at the weak point in Aristotle: the question of truth value in statements about the future. What is true tomorrow must in Diodorus' view also be true today, and what is possible today will be actualized in the future. With this Diodorus distances himself from Aristotle's concept of potentiality and voices a strictly deterministic position. The formulation of the Diodorus theses clearly shows an oscillation between logical and metaphysical modes of thought, which, in this respect, is also characteristic of Aristotle. The discussion is simply about 'the true', 'the possible', and 'the necessary'. Matters are not made clearer by some modern translators who with misguided helpfulness insert 'propositions about . . . '. At issue is a metaphysical debate with logical implications. It has quite wide perspectives. In the first place, we are informed about the background for the Stoic notion of the world as a chain of strictly determined events. Secondly, the debate anticipates the discussion of the truth value of conditionals, which gradually led to the separation of metaphysics from logic (see below). The Megarians inspired Zeno and the Stoics after him to a particular form of formal thinking (propositional logic); the Stoics were also affected by Megarian monism, and they were compelled to clarify the relation between logic, language and reality.

As apparently was customary among young students of philosophy in the fourth century, Zeno consulted many authorities. In the Academy he may have listened to Xenocrates and certainly to Polemo (Diog. Laert. VII 2). This means that he must have witnessed the discussion of the proper understanding of the relation between symbolic thinking and doctrine in the late Plato. The *Timaeus*, especially, must have preoccupied him, and the idea of an alliance between philosophical and religious thinking must have appealed to him, albeit in the spirit of Xenocrates rather than of Plato. Naturally Zeno had not only heard of but indeed studied Plato – he wanted, for example, to provide a counterpart to the *Republic*. His relation to Aristotle is a little different from that of Epicurus. The important thing was not so much to decide on particular arguments, but rather to think one's way through – perhaps reinterpret – basic positions systematically.

In a survey of the spiritual ancestors of Stoicism one name especially should be singled out: Heraclitus. The Stoics' understanding of Heraclitus does, to be sure, contain an aspect of allegorical interpretation. But it is essential that Stoicism considers itself as perfecting an ancient tradition, and it is no accident that a demythologized Heraclitus, as it were, appears again and again, not only in details but in the basic view: the world is a unity of tensions held together by *Logos* or reason, in which all men participate and which therefore is accessible to anyone who can see for himself.

With this, some constituent elements of a general pattern have been indicated. But one should not conclude that Stoicism was an eclectic philosophy. The pattern is to be understood in itself, and the Stoics were justly proud of the systematic coherence of their doctrines (cf. Cic. *De fin*. III 74). Any given part of the system presupposes the whole: the world is a unity and can be known as a coherent unity. The common features of Hellenistic school philosophy have been presented earlier. Despite the widely differing answers, the point of departure, the problems, and the way of asking questions were to a large extent the same in epistemology, natural philosophy, and ethics, and all agreed that the goal of philosophy was human happiness, inner freedom and independence, but that the goal could only be reached by understanding the nature of the world and of human cognition. Nevertheless, the difference between Stoicism and, for example, Epicureanism is of course striking. It is not insignificant whether one believes that happiness consists in pleasure or virtue, and the two schools differ fundamentally in their view of man's place in the world. To Epicurus – as to the old Atomists – man himself created his own meaningful existence in an alien world in itself without value. The Stoics, on the other hand, adhere to what might be called the main line in Greek philosophy that culminates with Plato and Aristotle: the world is rational, it is teleologically constructed, and man must – as a conscious rational being – adjust himself to the greater order. It has rightly been pointed out that there are two key concepts in Stoicism, which really are two sides of the same issue. These are the two Heraclitean concepts of *logos* and *physis*. Both concepts are – and must be – ambiguous. The universal *logos*, which governs the world and turns everything into a meaningful unity, is necessarily distinct from the deficient reason of individual man, which although a part of the grand *logos* all too often fails and must be inculcated and guided to the right path. The concept of *physis* likewise has two levels of meaning, a normative and a descriptive one: the totality or ideal nature and individual man's actual nature, which must be purged in order for ideal nature to be realized in the individual. It was important to the Stoics to understand this tension with certain, quite specific assumptions in mind. One of the most important is that inasmuch as the world is one rationally determined whole there can be no chasm between spirit and matter. The world is material, but matter is everywhere permeated by spirit. Only that has real existence which can affect or be affected – as was repeatedly affirmed by all the important Stoics (Diog. Laert. VII 134). This is a Platonic formula (Plat. *Soph.* 247 D, see p. 230), but it was reinterpreted by both Epicureans and Stoics to mean that only physical bodies meet the criterion. To Epicurus it was solely a question of mechanical processes among material bodies. To the Stoics on the other hand, physical entities contain both an active and a passive principle; a body is not dead stuff. Man is also a piece of matter permeated by spirit. But he has a special position because he is not only part of the greater order; he can become conscious of that order, and from this follows the obligation that is inherent in the formula 'to live in accordance with nature'.

Unlike Epicureanism, Stoicism is not dependent on one person. The school underwent developments and can boast a series of prominent figures until it – roughly as did Epicureanism – died out towards the end of the second century AD. It is customary to divide Stoicism into three periods: early Stoicism (Zeno, Cleanthes and Chrysippus), middle Stoicism (from the middle of the second century to the first century BC, the main representatives being Panaetius and Posidonius), and late Stoicism (during the Roman Empire: Seneca, Epictetus and Marcus Aurelius). The last two periods have each its own special features that will be discussed in their chronological contexts. During these later periods the main focus is on ethics, even though the system *per se* was preserved as it had been promulgated in the first part of the history of the school – without doubt there were not a few particular differences between individual Stoics; but to be a Stoic meant to adhere to a certain view of existence as a whole. This basic position goes back to Zeno whose work covered all philosophical disciplines – although apparently with lesser emphasis on logic (cf. Diog. Laert. VII 4). Zeno's successor as head of the school, the somewhat younger Cleanthes (331(?)–232), likewise wrote a considerable number of treatises (174 ff.). His main interests were apparently theology and natural philosophy, but he was overshadowed by his predecessor as well as by his successor, Chrysippus (c.280–7) who began as a student of the prominent founder of the Sceptical Academy, Arcesilaus (see p. 472 ff.), but was then 'converted' to Stoicism, which he defended in constant polemics with the Academics. His oeuvre, which is said not to have paid attention to form and style, was extremely voluminous – he is reputed to have written no fewer than 705 'works' (= scrolls; 189 ff.; cf. 180). Apparently Chrysippus not only worked out the detailed Stoic 'dialectics' (semantics, epistemology and logic); in all matters he became the great systematist of Stoicism, the author of what later came to be considered Stoic orthodoxy. The systematic character of Stoicism resulted in the school's also having its heretics – the most prominent probably being Zeno's student Ariston of Chios who in his radical ethics was almost more Stoic than orthodox Stoicism.

Now, one thing is the internal history of Stoicism and Stoicism considered as a phenomenon of the past. Something else is the enormous indirect impact of Stoicism – and perhaps especially of Stoic ethics – on the entire Western cultural tradition. A few headings will suffice: the influence of Stoicism on Neoplatonism and Christian ethics, its influence on Renaissance Humanism, on natural law, and on the concept of human rights. If the names of some major figures in the history of philosophy are to be mentioned, those of Spinoza and Kant seem close to hand.

But this is an indirect influence. Not one single treatise from early or middle Stoicism has been preserved – the 'classicistic' tendency of late Antiquity with its favouring of Plato above all others had a fatal influence on the nature of the transmission. Hence the systematic coherence in Stoic philosophy must be reconstructed on the basis of fragments, paraphrases and critical assessments. It goes without saying that this puts us at a disadvantage – also because many sources are hostile. One should constantly bear in mind that crucial parts of the whole presumably are not present to us at all or exist only in distorted form. Furthermore, the sources often only tell us that 'the Stoics' say this and that, which most often – but not always – has reference to Chrysippus. Hence an account of Stoicism can only exceptionally single out an individual Stoic's position. Naturally it is in many cases possible to conclude backwards from the preserved, late Stoics – from Seneca, Epictetus and Marcus Aurelius – but often they are not interested in technical details. Philo of Alexandria and Plotinus are examples of non-Stoic philosophers who on several points let themselves be inspired by Stoic thinking. However, among the non-Stoic philosophers there is probably special reason to single out Cicero who skilfully exploited Stoic material and who – without himself being a Stoic – often reports sympathetically. Plutarch, the author of a series of anti-Stoic treatises, also provides valuable information. Diogenes Laertius apparently used several sources, some of which were quite well informed. Sextus Empiricus is as usual a balanced and knowledgeable reporter but of a critical persuasion. The late commentators on Aristotle can be useful. Finally we have the summaries in the form of doxography and compendia – as always derivative and poor informants. It is a motley gathering – in certain cases several sources must be pieced together; in others it may be to the purpose to follow one or two.

EPISTEMOLOGY, SEMANTICS AND LOGIC

Like Epicurus, the Stoics adhered to Xenocrates' tripartite division of philosophy – into logic, physics and ethics (Diog. Laert. VII 41), which is to say the basis, nature and form of cognition; the world in which man lives; and man himself. Each part of philosophy presupposes the others. Seen from the point of view of man logic is fundamental, and 'logic' covers a very large area. Rhetoric was considered a part of logic, but its most important branch is 'dialectic', which in our terminology comprises epistemology, semantics, and grammar as well as logic in a stricter sense. These are not randomly brought together. Dialectic as a whole concerns what is true and false (42); it is the insight that mirrors the universal *logos* that governs the physical world and determines the moral law for man. Hence it is – like the Epicurean *kanōn* – a part of philosophy proper and not a tool applicable to philosophical subjects – as it is in Aristotle. Physics and ethics can simply be called a kind of dialectic (83), and dialectic – reason – is the virtue that comprehends all virtues (46).

All animals can receive sense impressions and utter sounds, but only man is by disposition a rational being who can articulate his experience of the world as a logically coherent whole (Sext. Emp. *Adv. math*. VIII 275). This comes about by means of signs. According to Chrysippus, dialectic is concerned with that which signifies and that which is signified (*ta sēmainonta* and *ta sēmainomena* – Diog. Laert. VII 62). Now, a sign can in part be a – material – sense impression (*phantasia*) representing a physical object and in part be linguistic, which is to say that the sign is a statement about something. Further, the linguistic sign in turn has two aspects: as expression it is material, a sound that signifies; it also has an aspect of content, the meaning of the linguistic expression or the 'sayable' (*lekton*), which is signified by the sound and is immaterial – because it does not meet the conditions for what it means to have real existence. The more specific implications of these distinctions will be discussed later. What is decisive here is that to the Stoics human cognition is a reflection of reality – partially the reality that presents itself through the sense impression, partially the reality as it is structured and articulated by human thought. Hence there is both an element coming from the outside – sensation that constitutes the basis for cognition – and an active element, man's interpretation and ordering of the material for cognition. It is important that these two elements are interwoven already in the simplest process of perception.

Thus Stoic epistemology is based on a representative or causal theory of perception. But this does not lead to the sceptical conclusion that man only has access to sense data, not to the objects causing sense data; Stoic epistemology contains an element of naïve realism. Knowledge must depend on sensation, but sure knowledge does exist – if only for the reason that the human *logos* does not differ essentially from the universal *logos*, which it reflects. Scepticism is to a Stoic – as to an Epicurean – self-refuting; one cannot know that one does not know (Cic. *Acad*. II 17; 44).

Like the Epicureans, the Stoics are sensualists. But while the Epicureans maintain that all sense experience is true, the Stoics recognize the existence of false sense impressions. In practice the difference is not as great as it may look – an Epicurean must from sense impressions make inferences about the 'truth' of a physical object, and therefore he must, like the Stoic, examine whether a given sense impression represents a physical object correctly or not. There is the further similarity that cognition cannot rely on a priori knowledge of Platonic ideas or Aristotelian essences; concepts are dependent on sensation, and the individual thing has ontological priority. This is mirrored in the intense epistemological debate between the Stoics and the Sceptical Academics. An Academic will maintain that two objects of the same type can present themselves in such a way that no difference can be discerned. The Stoic position, on the other hand, is that two particular entities can only be individual by virtue of an individual difference that in principle can be known (Plut. *De comm. not.* 1077 C; Cic. *Acad.* II 40; 85; Sext. Emp. *Adv. math.* VII 252).

Sensation depends on an interplay between passive sense experience and interpretative or 'active' sensing, perception; the two factors can be separated conceptually, not actually. Inherent in the very act of perception lies – as in Aristotle – a latent judgement, and the Stoics continue both the Aristotelian view of conceptual application and of the psychological genesis of cognition (see p. 308 and p. 310 ff.). Cognition comes about gradually (*SVF* II 83; Aetius; cf. Diog. Laert. VII 52 ff.; 61; Cic. *De fin.* III 33; *Acad.* I 42; Sen. *Ep. mor.* 120,4). At birth the soul is a *tabula rasa*. A sense impression – a *phantasia* – is 'imprinted' on the soul; it can be retained as memory, and several memories constitute experience – a scheme of thought that is akin to Hume's 'impressions' and 'ideas'. On the basis of this, simple object concepts are formed, which is to say concepts that are directly and naturally derived from sensing – *prolēpseis* or preconceptions as they are called with a borrowing from Epicurean terminology (cf. Cic. *De nat. deor.* I 44). From a combination of these concepts – by analogy, association, or the like – one subsequently is able to form more comprehensive concepts (*ennoiai*: one might for example think of genera). Finally there are the so-called common concepts (*koinai ennoiai*), a sort of meta-concepts or concepts that are prerequisites for the systematization of knowledge (for example the good or the very notions of science, meaning (*lekton*), or logical coherence). These concepts are neither directly nor indirectly derived from sensation, but they are not 'innate ideas' either; they are dispositions of human cognition – and therefore they are 'common' – but this disposition is only developed at the instigation of experience. Hence all concepts are secondary to sensation, and they do not, as with the Epicureans, have extramental existence. Although the scheme is indebted to Aristotle, the interpretation of 'concept' is un-Aristotelian. It should also be noted that while *phantasia* in Aristotle is an epiphenomenon to cognition, it is the base of cognition to the Stoics. The Stoic theory of the formation of concepts is more psychologizing than the Aristotelian.

The question of the application of concepts can be formulated in two ways: wherein consists true cognition, and what ensures that we are in possession of true cognition? It is in other words – as in all Hellenistic philosophy – a question of the criteria for truth. Apparently there was disagreement about the precise formulation of the criteria for truth (cf. Diog. Laert. VII 54), but the general line of thought is clear (49; cf. Sext. Emp. *Adv. math.* VIII 397): the basis is the sense impression (*phantasia*); but not every *phantasia* is true; the soul gives its assent (*synkatathesis*) to the cognitive impression (*phantasia katalēptikē*) whereby a 'grasping' (*katalēpsis*) of the sense object occurs, which then gives rise to scientific, rational cognition (*epistēmē*), in which the human *logos* is active. Using one of the images beloved of the Stoics, Zeno put it as follows (Cic. *Acad.* II 145): a hand with stretched-out fingers corresponds to *phantasia*; a bending of the fingers to assent; the closed hand to the soul's 'grasping'; and the firmly clenched fist to knowledge. The image designates steadily greater sharpness, but otherwise does not say much about what is implied in the individual concepts that constitute cognition.

A *phantasia* is an 'impression' in the soul – here the Stoics used the Aristotelian image of the seal that stamps the wax (Diog. Laert. VII 45); but the image is to be understood literally, for something material happens to the soul: according to Chrysippus it undergoes a qualitative change (Sext. Emp. *Adv. math.* VII 229; 373). The concept of assent marks the transition to the active part of sense perception, to that which depends on the perceiving person (VIII 397); the soul strives to make the external world 'its own' (*oikeion* Cic. *Acad.* II 38). But not every assent is correct; a mere opinion – a 'weak' assent – can be false (cf. Sext. Emp. *Adv. math.* VII 151). In order to 'grasp' the real object or what in fact is the case, there is need of a *phantasia kataleptikē* (VIII 85; cf. VII 397). A *katalēpsis* is, as in Zeno's image, a 'grasping' or 'apprehension' (cf. Cic. *Acad.* I 41), and a *phantasia kataleptikē* is according to Zeno a sense impression imprinted by the real object, in conformity with it, and of such a kind that it could not arise from a not-real object (Sext. Emp. *Adv. math.* VII 248; 402; Cic. *Acad.* II 18). The last link in the chain is then the knowledge – *epistēmē* – that makes simple 'grasping' explicit – and thus it has the same function as *nous* in Aristotle. It consists in reason's – *logos'* – insight into what is true and false; it can be formulated as a logical inference; it cannot be called into doubt by arguments; and in its entirety knowledge is a system of articulated cognition (Diog. Laert. VII 47; Cic. *Acad.* I 41; *SVF* I 68, Stob.).

This whole chain of thought was constantly bombarded by the Academic Sceptics, and a lengthy passage in Sextus (Sext. Emp. *Adv. math.* VII 227 ff.) shows how the Stoics honed the particular links: what does it mean that a sense impression is imprinted, that it is convincing, that it is true; in what circumstances does a picture of the external world present itself so that it is possible to comprehend the object without 'obstacle'?

But with this no answer has been provided to the question of cognitive certainty – and it was on this point that the Academics constantly pressed the Stoics (see p. 473). Here the sources seem strangely silent, but the account of the structure of cognition can none the less provide an indirect answer. It is of course not sufficient to maintain that true knowledge exists if one cannot explain how true knowledge is attained. The Stoic theory of cognition presupposes – as in Aristotle's 'correspondence theory' concerning truth – that true cognition builds on conformity between the cognitive impression and the physical object. But it appears from the above that other elements are included as well. True knowledge is not present until reason has structured the sense impressions. Initially *prolēpsis* is used for simple object identification, but then the general and systematizing concepts (*ennoiai* and *koinai ennoiai*) come into use. With the aid of these concepts it is possible for reason to form a coherent system of knowledge, free of contradiction – it is recorded (Diog. Laert. VII 54) that some 'old Stoics' considered the good old Aristotelian concept of *orthos logos*, right thinking, as a criterion of truth, and *orthos logos* can here be rendered as coherence. In modern terminology the Stoics seem therefore in a strange way to combine a theory of correspondence with a theory of coherence. The correspondence between sense impression and object is a physical-ontological phenomenon. However, to the Stoics 'coherence' is not a concept that merely guarantees compatibility within a closed system. Human reason is a reflection of the universal reason that rules the world. By nature man is adapted to making the world 'his own', and consistent rational cognition – in the final analysis knowledge of the whole world as one system – is therefore per definition knowledge of the external world. The epistemology is dependent on the basic Stoic vision.

A sense impression is a physical 'imprint'. A concept is likewise corporeal – in so far as it is a structuring of the human soul; but the content of the concept is a 'meaning' (a *lekton*); it is inter-subjective and independent of the person who thinks; and it is incorporeal inasmuch as it does not honour the demand of real existence – such incorporeal entities exist, but only because they presuppose the existence of corporeal entities. The same duality of corporeal and incorporeal is found in the concept of truth itself, which, as we know, is ambiguous in the Greek tradition. 'True' is a property of a judgement or a proposition, and a judgement is an incorporeal *lekton*. 'Truth', on the other hand, refers to a state of mind and is hence corporeal. 'True' propositions can be uttered by fools. To possess the truth is, on the other hand, strictly speaking the privilege of the sage, of the man whose soul is entirely pervaded by knowledge of the universal *logos* (Sext. Emp. *Ad. math.* VII 38 ff.; cf. *SVF* II 913, Stob.; Marc. Aur. IX 1).

These distinctions have wide perspectives. Reality can be mirrored or present itself in several ways. *Phantasia kataleptike* is a sign coming from the outside that reproduces reality for the observer. The linguistic sign, on the other hand, is the result of the working by the human mind on the received material; it expresses our understanding of the world as a rational system. In the mouth of the sage, language can reproduce reality correctly, but language is not reality. This means that language no longer – as in Plato and Aristotle – is transparent; it exists as a structure in itself; it can be studied as an independent object; and a closer study of language will in turn uncover a distinction between linguistic and logical form. Language has several levels. The lowest-ranging is sound (*phone*), then follows the articulated sound (*lexis*), and finally the articulated sound with meaning (*logos* – Diog. Laert. VII 55 ff.; 59); a *logos* is said and its meaning is stated (57). Here it should only be mentioned that the Stoics did pioneer work in the field of pure linguistics – the famous grammarians of Antiquity (for example Dionysius Thrax, Varro, Donatus, Priscianus) built on them – that they for example established a detailed classification of parts of speech, and that they studied case, mood and tense (58; 63 ff.).

Here, however, the most important thing is Stoic semantics. It embraces three constituent parts (Sext. Emp. *Adv. math.* VIII 11 ff.): the signifying (*to semainon*), the signified (*to semainomenon*), and external reality, that which is the case (*to tynchanon*). The linguistic expression (*to semainon*) and that with which language deals (*to tynchanon*) are corporeal. The signified or the meaning (*to lekton*) is on the other hand incorporeal since it can only exist in connection with something else, the linguistic sign (*logos* – Diog. Laert. VII 57; Sext. Emp. *Adv. math.* VIII 70). Stoic semantics is a theory about the relation between these three elements. In contrast to Epicurus, the Stoics react against Aristotelian semantics. To Aristotle, the essentialist, there is formal identity between the content of language and reality. But the Stoics are conceptualists; concepts do not exist in the external world, and their scheme must therefore look very different:

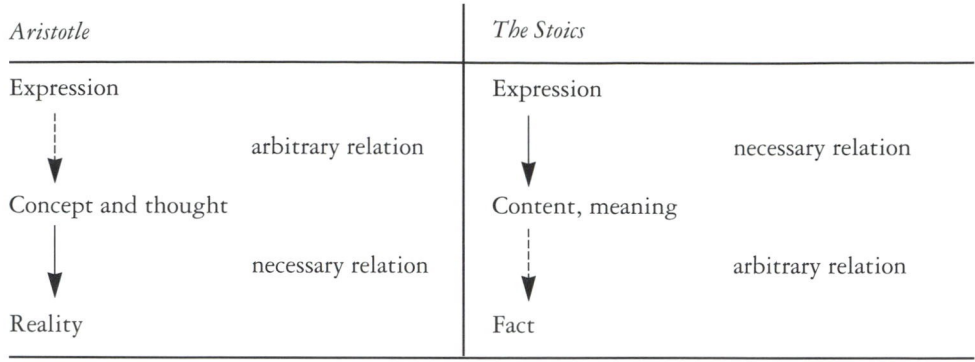

Aristotle		The Stoics	
Expression		Expression	
↓	arbitrary relation	↓	necessary relation
Concept and thought		Content, meaning	
↓	necessary relation	↓	arbitrary relation
Reality		Fact	

Contrary to Aristotle but in agreement with modern structural linguistics, expression and content correspond for the Stoics, but there is no direct relation between meaning and reality (what is the fact); language deals *with* reality.[1] To Aristotle the dividing line runs between expression and content, to the Stoics between content and fact. Furthermore, Stoic semantics allowed them to distinguish more precisely than Plato and Aristotle between meaning and reference (cf. *Sinn* and *Bedeutung* in Frege). According to the Stoics there are complete and incomplete meanings. 'Writes', for example, is an 'incomplete meaning'; it is a predicate (*katēgorēma*) with universal signification that says something about something. 'Socrates writes' is a complete meaning. The subject denotes or points to a material object; but the sentence does not point to; rather, it deals with an object and has signification (Diog. Laert. VII 63 ff.; cf. Sext. Emp. *Adv. math.* VIII 70; Sen. *Ep. mor.* 117,13). There are reminiscences of Aristotle, but the Stoics distinguish between a statement ('Socrates writes') and its content (the proposition),[2] and so doing they can solve the old conundrum of the same statement being now true, now false. A concept also has meaning but is unambiguous whereas the word is ambiguous: the word 'dog' can refer to something that barks, to something in the sky – the Dog Star – or to a philosopher – the Cynic (Sext. Emp. *Adv. math.* XI 29; cf. *SVF* II 152, Gellius).

A denotatum is a material object. What a material object is in itself is an ontological question that belongs to physics. It is, however, possible to undertake a classification of denotata, in so far as they are pointed to by a deictic sign. To do so the Stoics formulated a theory, which later came to be called the Stoic doctrine of categories. The transmission is more than uncertain, but apparently it is a theory that is in opposition to both Aristotle's doctrine of categories and 'the doctrine of categories' of the Academy, which already can be seen in the fact that a Stoic 'category' must be understood as a class of objects *qua* denoted. There are four categories (Plot. VI 1,25 ff.; Simpl. in Aristot. *Cat.* 66, 32 ff. = *SVF* II 369; 222, 30 ff. = *SVF* II 378;

---

1   Yet, in the process of forming words the relation does not seem to be arbitrary (cf. Orig. *CC* I 24; Aug. *De dial.* 9). But the subject of semantics is the use of words, not their origin.

2   They are furthermore able to distinguish between 'proposition' and 'speech act' (cf. Plut. *De Stoic. repugn.* 1037 D).

165, 22 ff. = *SVF* II 403): the substratum (*to hypokeimenon*), quality (*poion*), state (*pōs echon*), and relation (*pros ti pōs echon*). The basic category is the substratum, that which is simply pointed to – the corresponding linguistic sign would be a demonstrative pronoun. But there is nothing that only lets itself be pointed to. It is possible to describe any material object whatsoever as an object equipped with a certain set of properties (qualities) that characterize it as this object, permits identification, and warrants object identity. The Aristotelian category of substance presumably belongs in the Stoic category of quality – but the Stoics avoid the Aristotelian problem of substance 'stripped' of properties. However, a material object also has shifting predicates – that belong to the third category, the object in a certain state. To this category belong several of the Aristotelian secondary categories. Finally, the fourth category – relation – is designated by incomplete predicates, which when they are filled in distinguish the object from others – the Stoic category of relation thus demonstrates a significantly greater understanding of relational predicates than the Aristotelian. Different 'categories' do not designate differing objects but steadily more differentiated linguistic determinations of one and the same material object. Now, material objects and their properties do not exhaust everything that simply 'is present'. *Koinai ennoiai*, for example, are present as objects for the mind but have no real existence. Therefore the Stoics in this and other contexts operate with a sort of superior concept, which is simply called 'something' (*ti*), which is to say everything about which it is possible to say anything at all. The categories can be said to constitute a sub-class under this superior concept.

Stoic logic in the narrow sense is inseparably tied to the semantics. In both cases it is a question of *lekta*. That which corresponds to logic in the modern sense does not, however, concern the relation between *lekton*, linguistic sign and reality but the formal structure of a *lekton* and the formal relation between *lekta*; as in Aristotle, it is the logical form that is sought for behind the linguistic form. But while Aristotle's logic is a subject-predicate logic presupposing a world of objects instantiating specific types and furnished with properties, Stoic logic is a propositional logic – corresponding to the Stoic understanding of the world primarily as a chain of events in a physical plenum, and an object is always an individual, not an instance of a type. In fact subject-predicate logic is a special case of propositional logic, but in Antiquity it was often believed that they were two competing systems. For ages Stoic logic was considered a sterile, formalistic system; it was not until this century, against the background of recent advances in logic, that it became clear that Stoic logic signalled a quite significant achievement. There are roots going backwards – first and foremost to Eudemus' and Theophrastus' investigations of hypothetical syllogisms and late Eleatic and Megarian logic; but as a whole the Stoics' system of propositional logic is original, and as a coherent system it should be credited to Chrysippus. In modern accounts Stoic logic is often treated as a closed, formal system. This is not quite right. The purpose is to find valid rules of inference and forms of proof that can assist us in finding our way in life – in the final analysis with regard to moral philosophy – and one should always bear in mind that the human *logos* is a depiction of the universal; it has its own laws, but in the end it conforms with the greater order.

The basic logic unity is the proposition (*axiōma*) that differs from other utterances (questions, imperatives) by being true or false and by affirming or denying (Diog.

Laert. VII 65; Sext. Emp. *Adv. math.* VIII 71 ff.). This is quite reminiscent of Aristotle, but a proposition is a *lekton*, i.e. not a statement but the content of a statement. Stoic formalization does of course use propositions – not concepts or terms – as variables and throughout it treats negations as operators separate from the proposition itself (cf. 89).

A distinction is made between simple and non-simple propositions – in modern terminology: atomic and molecular propositions, and the non-simple proposition consists of two or more simple ones that are combined by means of a connective (Diog. Laert. VII 68; Sext. Emp. *Adv. math.* VIII 93 ff.). The simple proposition is the basic form of a complete *lekton*; and also in other ways the analysis of simple propositions shows the close connection with semantics. The most precise simple proposition is called 'definite', which is to say that it consists of a simple denoting element and a predicate ('this man is walking'). An indefinite proposition has an undetermined subject ('someone is walking'); an intermediate form has a proper name as its subject ('Socrates is walking') – in other words the old standard example of a proposition about contingent states of affair that seemingly change their truth value. The truth value of indefinite propositions and of the intermediate form depends on the truth value of the definite proposition (if it is true that 'Socrates' or 'someone' is walking, it is also true that 'this man' who is walking can be pointed to); the truth value of the definite proposition depends on a *phantasia kataleptike*, in other words on a simple correspondence (96 ff.; cf. Diog. Laert. VII 70; Sext. Emp. *Adv. math.* VIII 100).

Several types of non-simple propositions are enumerated (Diog. Laert. VII 69; 71 ff.). The most important – familiar from modern logic – are the conjunction, the disjunction and the conditional. The Stoics should not only be credited with having established these forms of proposition; they also studied their criteria of truth closely. A conjunction is only true if both or all conjuncts are true (Sext. Emp. *Adv. math.* VIII 125). The disjunction is usually taken to be exclusive, and hence it is true, if one of the disjuncts is true and the other false (282; cf. *SVF* II 220, Galen who gives testimony that there was awareness of inclusive disjunctions). The truth value of such non-simple propositions accordingly depends on the truth value of the propositions of which they are composed – which means that they are understood to be truth-functional and allow for the making of truth tables. The introduction of truth functions is an essential feature of Stoic logic – which with respect to one single point (the conditionals) can be traced back to the Megarians.

Of the non-simple propositions probably the conditional was the most interesting to the Stoics – and as is well known, the interpretation of the truth value of conditionals is contested today as well. Apparently they began (cf. Diog. Laert. VII 71 ff.) with the actual language, more precisely with the meaning of simple connectives that signify one form or another of entailment. 'If' indicates the conditional proper; 'since' indicates that the antecedent is evidently true; 'because' indicates the antecedent as cause. The conditional was of special interest to the Stoics, because it most directly mirrors a world of individual events linked according to definite laws; it is character-istic that they – as did Ockham later – transformed universal, categorical propositions into conditionals in order not to sneak in an unnecessary bit of Aristotelian metaphysics (thus 'man is mortal' is transformed into 'if something is a man, that thing is mortal', Sext. Emp. *Adv. math.* XI 8). We are able to follow a continuous debate begun by the Megarians and continued by the Stoics; apparently it was a debated *cause célèbre* – we are in any case told that the crows on the Alexandrian rooftops cried out about the question of the truth value of conditionals (I 309).

Four different interpretations are recounted, three of which are essential (VIII 112 ff.; *Hyp Pyr.* II 110 ff.; cf. *Adv. math.* VIII 245). The participants in the debate all agreed that the conditional is true, when the consequent follows from the antecedent, but the question is what this means. The Megarian Philo claimed that a conditional is false only if the antecedent is true and the consequent false; in the other three cases it is true ($p \rightarrow q =_{def.} \neg(p \wedge \neg q)$). This means that Philo considered the conditional a truth function; his view corresponds with what today is called material implication, and it can be formulated in a truth table. What interested Philo was not the contents of propositions, but only which propositions are formally incompatible. Diodorus Cronus – slightly older – represents a more orthodox Megarian position. He does not regard the conditional as a truth function, but includes the time factor in order to account for laws of nature. He maintains that a conditional is true, if, and only if, it is not possible at any moment for the antecedent to be true and the consequent false. According to his interpretation, a conditional is an empirical generalization that permits inferences about laws in the actual world.

Now, it is well known that interpretations of conditionals, when confronted with ordinary language, often lead to paradoxes. This was also acknowledged in the Megarian-Stoic debate. In Philo's view the following conditionals are for example true: 'if the earth flies, the earth has wings' (false antecedent, false consequent), 'if the earth flies, the earth exists' (false antecedent, true consequent). 'If it is day, I am discussing' is, according to Philo, a true conditional, unless I do not discuss. To Diodorus it is false, for it is not at any given moment true that I do discuss. Still, Diodorus' version can also produce paradoxes: 'if atoms do not exist, atoms exist' is in his view a true conditional.

The third on the list was in all likelihood Chrysippus. According to him, a conditional is true if denial of the consequent is logically incompatible with the antecedent ($p \rightarrow q =_{def.} \neg \Diamond (p \wedge \neg q)$). In other words, cohesion is presupposed between consequent and antecedent – thus precluding the Diodorus paradox. Chrysippus' interpretation is intensional; it corresponds with modern-day strict implication and precludes the use of truth tables. It is an interesting expression of Stoic thinking in general. On the one hand Chrysippus distances himself from a truth-functional view that abstracts from the content of the conditional; on the other he cannot go along with Diodorus, for it is important to him to maintain that something may be logically possible but factually impossible (see below). The conditional can therefore not be considered an empirical generalization.

Of course the Stoics' doctrine of inference corresponds with Aristotle's syllogistics. Like Aristotle, they operate with two premises and one conclusion in a simple inference. Nevertheless, on the whole the differences are greater than the similarities. Chrysippus is presumably the author of a systematic presentation of the five so-called indemonstrable schemes of argument (Diog. Laert. VII 79 ff.; Sext. Emp. *Hyp. Pyr.* II 156 ff.; cf. *Adv. math.* VIII 223 ff.) – which of course does not mean that he 'discovered' these types of argument.

The schemes of argument look like this:

Scheme 1

	Schemes of argument or rules of inference		Corresponding standard arguments
	Modern formalization	Stoic quasi-formalization	
1. Modus ponens	p→q p q	If the first, the second. But the first Therefore: the second	If it is day, it is light But it is day Therefore: it is light
2. Modus tollens	p→q ¬q ¬p	If the first, the second Not: the second Therefore not: the first	If it is day, it is light Not: it is light Therefore not: it is day
3. First premiss: negated conjunction	¬(p∧q) p ¬q	Not both: the first and the second But the first Therefore not: the second	Not both: Plato is dead and Plato is alive But Plato is dead Therefore not: Plato is alive
4. First premiss: exclusive disjunction	p ∨ q p ¬q	Either the first or the second But the first Therefore not: the second	Either it is day or it is night But it is day Therefore not: it is night
5. First premiss: exclusive disjunction	p ∨ q ¬q p	Either the first or the second Not: the second Therefore: the first	Either it is day or it is night Not: it is night Therefore: it is day

(From a combination of 4 and 5 it appears that the disjunction is exclusive.)

As in connection with Aristotle, it should be remarked that a rule of inference of course is not true, whereas the conclusion in the corresponding standard argument is true, if the premisses are so. A criterion for the truth of an argument is that it is possible to construct a true conditional with both premisses as an antecedent and the conclusion as consequent (*the principle of conditionalization*). Accordingly (cf. Sext. Emp. *Hyp. Pyr.* II 113; *Adv. math.* VIII 233; 414 ff.):

Scheme 2

Standard argument according to scheme I:	Transformation according to the principle of conditionalization:
If it is day, it is light But it is day ——— Therefore: it is light	If it is day it is light, and if: it is day, then: it is light

The transformation clarifies the entailment that is implicitly accepted in the first formulation.

The five indemonstrable schemes of argument are evidently valid. Corresponding to Aristotle's reduction of valid moods in the second and third figure to the 'perfect' syllogisms in the first figure, the Stoics formulated rules for the reducing of complicated arguments to the five simple ones (229 ff.) that are but incompletely known.

A Stoic standard argument usually states a rule as a first premiss; in the second an evident, particular state of affairs is pointed out; then a conclusion is drawn, which refers the particular state of affairs to the rule. The pendant in Aristotelian syllogistics is the middle term that points out the cause. Both Aristotle and the Stoics stress the difference between the merely valid argument and the demonstrative proof: Aristotle demands of a scientific explanation that it should uncover the essential cause that is 'better known according to nature'; the Stoics seek to account for the empirically present, concrete event – and for this the first scheme of argument, the *modus ponens*, is best suited.

They discussed how one could proceed from a merely valid argument to a true proof that really explains something (300 ff.; 411 ff.; *Hyp. Pyr.* II 134 ff.). The most precise Stoic definition of the scientific proof – which surely is owing to Chrysippus – states that an argument is a proof if it is both valid and true and leads to a non-evident conclusion (*Adv. math.* VIII 314). A standard argument such as

If it is day, it is light
But it is day
_____

Therefore: it is light

is valid; it is also true, if the premisses are true. Still, it does not reveal something non-evident – for it is evident that it is light, if it is day. On the other hand, the following argument meets all conditions for a proof (*Hyp. Pyr.* II 140; *Adv. math.* VIII 306):

If sweat is discharged from the skin, invisible pores exist
Sweat is discharged from the skin
_____

Therefore: invisible pores exist

Here the conclusion is non-evident (*adēlon*, 'hidden', is the tradition-laden terminology (cf. *Hyp. Pyr.* II 97 ff.)). Sweat is a 'sign' that pores exist – not a 'commemorative sign', such as when we from repeated experience know that where there is smoke there is fire, but an 'indicative sign', which is to say that the empirically observed refers back to a non-perceived cause (cf. 99 ff.). Such a sign is the basis for empirical science – characteristically enough, Aristotle is reserved with respect to an inference from 'signs', because it is an inference from the probable that does not indicate any necessary conceptual connection (Aristot. *Anal. post.* 75 a 33).

One can ask in what sense this entire apparatus can function in an actual process of research. The answer must be that by such means one cannot acquire new knowledge but is enabled to formulate already acquired knowledge, so that a 'non-evident' conclusion gains logical form – exactly the same as was the case with Aristotle's 'explanation' of why the planets do not twinkle. Science provides the material; the logician formulates a law and does so by means of an empirical generalization that follows Diodorus' pattern: as this skin discharges sweat, it has pores – for at all times a law obtains that can be expressed in the form of a conditional. The theory of proof concerns the factual world; the theory of argumentation concerns the logically possible and the logically necessary. It is apparently this distinction that was the point behind Chrysippus' interpretation of conditionals.

PHYSICS AND THEOLOGY

Stoic natural philosophy – physics – rests on the basic thought that the world is a material unity, a living being, pervaded by *logos*; and as man is part of nature, he also participates in *logos*; human reason is a reflection of the universal one, but not identical with it. The Stoics can easily accept and further develop the idea of the *Timaeus* that the world is an animated organism in which reason everywhere pervades matter, but not, on the other hand, the idea of an intelligible world beyond that of sense nor that of the Demiurge as a mythical go-between between the two realms – the Stoics' *cosmos* corresponds, roughly speaking, to the created world of the *Timaeus*, but the Stoics leave out pure ideas and pure reason. The relation to Aristotle shows perhaps best how Stoic physics arose. Naturally, the Stoics cannot accept a transcendent, immaterial concept of god nor the notion of forms and essences as the fundamental, immaterial connecting link between man and the external world. On the other hand, they are, for example, able to make use of Aristotelian teleology, and they can exploit and transform Aristotelian terminology. What is most important is, however, their reinterpretation of the concept of substance in light of the basic monist vision. To Aristotle the world consisted of things – substances – equipped with properties, and substances order themselves in certain types that instantiate invariable forms and essences. The Stoics cannot think like that. To them the world consists primarily of events in a plenum, which is to say that the very concept of thing is problematic; a 'thing' is not sharply delimited from other things; it is causally and physically dependent on other things – ultimately on the world as a whole – and hence the world is primarily a chain of cohering events. All individual events are equally 'interesting' – even the very least event occurs in agreement with nature (*physis*) and reason (*logos*), said Chrysippus (Plut. *De Stoic. repugn.* 1050 A ff.). So, only one thing meets the Aristotelian demand for the independence of substance, and that is the world as a whole. The world is one substance, and it is a material substance. With these two essential presuppositions one can – if not take over – yet exploit the Aristotelian vocabulary. Furthermore, the Stoics could – like Straton – point to the latent ambiguity in Aristotle that the world is both a continuum and a world of separate, independent substances. This latent ambiguity is cancelled in Stoicism.

The Stoic doctrine of the world can naturally be divided into two parts. In part there is the doctrine of those principles and general concepts that must be presupposed in a description of the world – corresponding to Aristotelian meta-physics – and in part there is the actual description of the world – by and large corresponding to Aristotelian physics.

The Stoic world is material, and the criterion for whatever has material existence has been mentioned several times: only that has real or physical existence which can affect or be affected, and this criterion can only be fulfilled by three-dimensional magnitudes that can be touched (Diog. Laert. VII 56; Cic. *Acad.* I 39; *SVF* II 358, Philo; 359, Clem.). It has also been mentioned that according to the Stoics something incorporeal exists and that the concept 'something' comprises both the corporeal and the incorporeal. For this the Stoics were widely mocked during Antiquity, but there is of course nothing odious about an avowed materialistic philosophy that also operates with non-corporeal, conceptual entities dependent on corporeal objects. The Stoics acknowledge four incorporeals: *to lekton*, place, void and time. The definitions of place, void and time are quite reminiscent of Aristotle: place is the region of the world that is occupied by something corporeal; void is that which is not occupied by something corporeal (*SVF* II 503, Stob.; 504, Aet.; Sext. Emp. *Adv. math.* X 3). Now, the world is a plenum and hence there is no void in the world. But the concept of the void is possible, and since the world is one substance or one individual, it is delimited by something; consequently the void exists outside the world (Diog. Laert. VII 140). Time is a characteristic of motion – and so presupposes the existence of a world – and its unreal character is manifest from the fact that neither past nor future exists, nor does an instantaneous now (*SVF* II 511, Philo; Plut. *De com. not.* 1081 C ff.). It appears that place, void and time in the Stoics – as in Aristotle – are concepts that approach Kant's forms of intuition, although primarily they are given with the existence of the world rather than with consciousness. As has been mentioned, concepts, considered psychologically, have real existence, while in logic – considered as *lekta* – they are incorporeal. A special case is that of the 'common concepts', which are not derived from the world of sense. It is a mark of the Stoics' persistent call for consistency that 'good' as quality is corporeal, 'goodness' as a universal incorporeal – 'good' belongs to persons and to perceptible acts, while 'goodness' on the other hand cannot be perceived but is a concept formed by the mind (*De Stoic repugn.* 1042 E; Cic. *De fin.* III 33; Sen. *Ep. mor.* 120, 4). It may be added that the concepts of principles employed in ontology in themselves are incorporeal, even though they do of course refer to something corporeal (Diog. Laert. VII 134).

The material world is pervaded by *logos*. Hence, although it is a unity, it has two aspects – the active and the passive principle (*to poioun* and *to paschon*), as they are called with designations that go back to Plato's *Sophist* (see pp. 230 and 446). *Logos* is the active principle; the passive, that which is acted upon, is matter. But nothing exists that is only matter – *prima materia* is an abstraction as in Aristotle. In fact, matter is always present in one state or another, and such a bit of matter is denoted by the third of the categories (*SVF* I 86, Calc.; 87 Stob; Diog. Laert. VII 134; Plot. II 4, 1).

Physics in the more narrow sense deals with events within the one substance. Here the immanent, structuring principle appears in different ways and can therefore be given different names that actually stand for several aspects of the same thing: fire, breath (*pneuma*), god.

The simplest constituents of this material world are the four elements. But they are not separate; as in the Aristotelian continuum physics, they continually pass into each other; the difference is merely that the notion of the continuous transition can be conducted with greater consistency, because there is no room for the Aristotelian form-essences. Two of the elements – fire and air – are 'active', the other two 'passive', but fire has a special status. Everything comes from fire and returns to fire – this sounds remarkably Presocratic, and the tie to Heraclitus is of course deliberate. But this does not imply that fire 'means' the same to the Stoics as to Heraclitus. Fire is primary in the sense that everything can burn – everything 'returns to' fire. But the decisive point is probably that fire manifests itself as heat and as energy – two absolute pre-conditions for the functioning of the Stoic universe as a continuum of matter in motion. As the active structuring element of the world, fire is in fact identical with god (*SVF* II 418, Nemes.; 413, Stob.; Cic. *De nat. deor.* II 25; III 35; Aug. *De civ. Dei* VIII 5).

Pneuma – consisting of air and fire – is another manifestation of *logos* as structuring principle. The concept is Aristotelian, but while it stands for a not particularly successful attempt to unite the material and the immaterial spheres in Aristotle, it leads a better life in the conceptual context of the Stoics. *Pneuma* is responsible for the coherence found at all levels of nature. At the lowest level we find what we call inanimate physical objects. Ranking higher are the plants with their vegetative functions; then follow the animals, and finally man, the most complicated structure – man can sense, desire, and think (Plut. *De Stoic repugn.* 1053 F ff.; *SVF* II 458, Philo.). Here, naturally, there is an Aristotelian scheme at the base, but it has been transformed, inasmuch as an 'object' is not an isolated, delimited magnitude, but a certain region of the universe characterized by a specific form of 'coherence'. A precondition for such structurings of the world is the mixture of the elements (*krasis*), a complete ('chemical') interpenetration of two stuffs (water mixed with wine, for example), so that it is meaningful to say that two things are in the same 'place' (cf. Diog. Laert. VII 151). This of course presupposes infinitely divisible matter; matter has no minima (150).

A physical 'thing' is, then, a region of the material universe, a structuring brought about by *pneuma* by a balance of opposite tensions (*tonos*: tension) so that the thing appears as a unified (*hēnōmenon*) bit of matter (Sext. Emp. *Adv. math.* IX 78; Alex. Aphr. *De mixt.* 223, 25, *SVF* II 441). The terminology is deliberately close to Heraclitus'. What the Stoics wish to emphasize by reviving such notions as a 'unity of tension' is that a thing is a 'tensional field' – on the one hand a more or less stable structuring of matter, on the other an event that is related to all other events within the real substance, the world; a 'sympathy' exists between the individual parts of a structured whole – in the final analysis between the individual structures and the whole world (Sext. Emp. *Adv. math.* IX 80; Cic. *De fat.* 5).

The world is the sole autonomous individual in an Aristotelian sense. But an individual is not only delimited spatially; it is also delimited temporally. Here as well the Stoics believe themselves able to follow the trails back to Heraclitus – 'the world is an eternal living fire, which is kindled in measures and extinguished in measures'. The world arose from fire and will perish in fire when the possibilities laid down at its creation have been exhausted. But only one world exists, which means that the possibility of what will come into existence has been determined once and for all. At the conclusion of one cosmic sequel in the universal conflagration (*ekpyrōsis*), only that sequel can be repeated, and indeed Socrates and Plato will be reborn ad infinitum (Diog. Laert. VII 142; 157; Cic. *De nat. deor.* II 118; *SVF* I 107, Stob.; II 625, Nemes.; cf. 596 ff.). Strictly speaking, here it is not a question of an infinite number of identical events, but of the same event, which in the medium of time reappears in an infinite number of sequels.

The Stoic god, then, is identical with the one existing substance, the world. He may be spoken of in quite Neoplatonic terms as him who creates everything from himself and to whom everything returns; or, as in the *Timaeus*, he can be called the Demiurge, the master-builder (Diog Laert. VII 137 ff.). But this is imagery, for god is immanent in the world; he, if anything, is matter in 'a certain state' – and his existence can immediately be known by the man who is able to look at the world as a rational whole. Just as did the Epicureans, the Stoics emphasize that the notion of god is present in all men; the disagreement lies in the question of what he is like (Cic. *De nat. deor.* II 12 ff.) – and here they came up with what was later called the physico-teleological proof: god's existence appears from the order of the universe. Divine order shows itself most clearly in the motion of the heavenly bodies (43); brief reflection will show this to be the best of possible worlds (45). God is identical with world order, the world is rational, a rational living being, but god should not be looked for in the beyond.

As mentioned, it is also a continuation of an Academy trend that the Stoics pay a lot of attention to the harmonizing of philosophy and religion. True philosophy is in fact also true religion. Ancient mythological ideas contain a true core, provided that they are not taken literally; hence the Stoics work out an allegorical method that extracts the 'real' contents of the old myths; the gods are personified concepts, and the myths are (mis)readings of the forces that make the world an ordered whole that can be recognized by the trained observer (59 ff.). The spokesman of Stoicism in Cicero's *De natura deorum* is an excellent exponent of this philosophical reinterpretation of transmitted religion, which evidently is to be understood as the Stoics' appeal to the religiousness of ordinary people.

It is a part of Stoic religiousness that god rules the world by his providence (cf. II 73 ff.); the sequence of events that he has prescribed aims at making the world the best possible one. This not only means that god takes care of man, but also that nature exists for the sake of gods and men (133) – for as a rational being, man is the only creature akin to the divine. The Platonic-Aristotelian view – that man exists for the sake of the universe – may best accord with the general position in Antiquity: it is not fitting for mortals to interfere in nature's order. The Stoic view, on the other hand, implies that nature is a means in man's hands – a view that undoubtedly was to have profound significance for the history of Christian, Western thought. That man, at least in principle, has kinship with god can also be seen in god's plan – still in principle – being knowable to man from ancient times, to wit by omens and divination (II 7 ff.; *De div.* passim; Diog. Laert. VII 149). Divination and astrology are indeed most honourable sciences – it is of course human to err, but what god himself has intimated can be interpreted correctly. Rightly practised, divination is an exact science of the coherence between phenomena temporally remote from each other; it is a science that can predict what is preordained (Cic. *De div.* I 72 ff.). But apparently god does not always manage everything for the best. Man is responsible for his own wickedness, but cosmic evil and the misfortunes that are inflicted on man without his own fault are links in the greater plan. In a universal perspective, apparent misfortunes serve a higher purpose, which individual man cannot comprehend, and the very concept of the good presupposes the concept of evil (Plut. *De com. not.* 1065 B; Marc. Aur. V 8). In Neoplatonic and Christian staging, this was to become a very influential theodicy argument – and here as well there are clear reminders of Heraclitus.

The most famous expression of Stoic religiousness is Cleanthes' hymn to Zeus (*SVF* I 537, Stob.), in the form of a cult hymn addressed to the one and omnipotent Lord of Nature, Zeus of the many names. Nothing occurs in the world that eludes divine law and the greater harmony. Only the fool fails to comprehend the greater coherence; he is without the insight that can bring him happiness. Somewhat different notes are sounded in a prayer Cleanthes addressed to Zeus (527, Epict.): 'Lead me, oh Zeus and thou, oh Fate, along the path thou hast ordained for me. I follow without hesitation. Should I resist in evil – yet I must follow'.

Behind these solemn words, problems lie hidden: god is omnipotent; the law of the universe is inviolable; in folly or evil man may resist but is still subject to god's will. What is the relation between the will of god and human will? This is one of the greatest problems in Stoicism.

The first link in this chain of thought is god's 'omnipotence'. God has determined the cosmic sequence of events – and since he is immanent in the world, he 'is' also the cosmic sequence; whenever there is talk of the world as created *by* god or of god's having an intention *with* the world, a great deal of metaphoric language is employed. At the creation of the world god planted 'seminal principles' (*logoi spermatikoi*), which *in nuce* contain the later sequel (Diog. Laert. VII 135; *SVF* II 1027, Aet.). This means that the course of events has been determined by god's voluntary act (cf. Cic. *De nat. deor.* II 43; 58). With an aim for the best god has chosen the best of all possible worlds – but he might have chosen otherwise; something can be logically possible but actually impossible, as Chrysippus emphasized. Hence from a human point of view it is meaningful to say that the possible is what can be realized – unless prevented by external circumstances (Diog. Laert. VII 75; Cic. *De fat.* 13ff.; *SVF* II 959 = Alex. Aphr. *De fat.* 176, 14); but from a cosmic point of view Diodorus' understanding is correct: that is possible which will become real. One can now consider god's ordinance as providence (*pronoia*, Latin: *providentia*), but if the course of events is considered an unbreakable causal nexus, the term fate (*heimarmenē*; Latin: *fatum*) is employed. Fate is the divine *Logos* governing the course of events and causing the past to have happened, the present to be happening, and the future to happen (*SVF* II 913, Stob.; 943, Calc.; Cic. *De div.* I 125). All events are causally determined, and by virtue of the cosmic 'sympathy' all events in the world, even the least, do cohere. Does this not only mean that everything has a cause but also that every event could not happen otherwise (cf. *De fat.* 18 ff.)? In other words, were the Stoics adherents of strict determinism or even of fatalism?

If one proceeds to the second link in Cleanthes' prayer, this does not seem to be so: man may resist and act in folly. If it were meaningless to claim that man can act freely, every possibility for an ethics would be obviated, and the main intention with all Stoic philosophy would be rendered vain. It is a little misleading to speak of the question of 'free will' in the Stoics. Like the entire Greek tradition, they do not operate with a concept of will. There is no talk of will as an autonomous element in the human psyche but of man's capacity for willing this or that, of his capacity for acting voluntarily. The Stoics were in the same situation as the Epicureans, and like the Epicureans they sought to a far higher degree than Aristotle to distinguish between external compulsion, individual man's constitution or character – inner 'compulsion', and that which nevertheless 'lies within man's power', which is to say his environment and heritage as opposed to freedom. But their analysis of the whole set of questions was surely more profound than that of the Epicureans.

In modern discussions of the freedom of will one encounters a view that occasionally is furnished with the strange appellation of 'soft determinism'. The main features of this view are that the logical opposite of freedom is compulsion, not necessity; the logical opposite of necessity is chance, not freedom. Whoever acts freely, precisely does not act by chance; he has a cause or a motive for his act, and he might have acted otherwise if he – in the Aristotelian formula – were not prevented by compulsion or ignorance. It is possible that a 'cosmic intellect' could determine that in a given situation he could only act in one way. But in the concrete situation this changes nothing for individual man – his wish or decision is equally much wish or decision and hence becomes part of the determined sequence. The Stoics illustrate this by a refutation of a famous fatalistic argument, called 'the lazy argument' (Cic. *De fat.* 30; Orig. *CC* II 20): a sick man might as well not fetch the doctor, for if it is predetermined that he will get well, he will get well, and if it is predetermined that he must die, he will die – regardless of what else he may do. As demonstrated by the Stoics, this is clearly a fallacy: in both cases it is 'co-fated' whether he sends for the doctor – if he does not do so, that is what has been predetermined. The point is palpably clear in the following anecdote: Zeno punished a slave who had stolen from him; the slave objected that fate had determined that he must steal. To this Zeno replied that fate had also determined that he should be given a drubbing (Diog. Laert. VII 23).

Here as in so many other areas the Stoics had a predilection for expressing themselves in anecdotes or images. Two images are especially instructive. One deals with a dog that is tied to a cart and is pulled along, whether it will or no. The dog can, in other words, choose the necessary or it can resist, but the course of events cannot be altered (*SVF* II 975, Hippol.). In other words, freedom consists in the inner attitude, not in the freedom to choose this or that. This is designated by a key word – one of the terms that recurs in all parts of Stoic philosophy, the concept of *synkatathesis*, assent (cf. Epict. *Diss.* IV 1, 69). It is inner freedom that is decisive. External circumstances do not matter; man's freedom consists – as in Spinoza – in recognition of the necessary, and hence there is no contrast between freedom and necessity. On the contrary: man is free if he takes his fate upon himself, if it is man's own 'self' that acts (Diog. Laert. VII 121). If you will, you are free, says Epictetus (Epic. *Diss.* 117, 28).

But is man's 'assent' also predetermined; is there no field in which man can choose one act instead of another? The Stoics' adversaries simply considered them fatalists. But this is contradicted by the second image. It goes back to Chrysippus himself

(Cic. *De fat.* 43) and compares man with a cylinder. If the cylinder is pushed it will roll – such is the nature of the cylinder. If man is affected from the outside, he will likewise act according to his nature – and we ourselves are the masters of this act; it depends on us (*to eph' hēmin*). Now, according to its nature a cylinder can only act in one way, but man is equipped with reason and can at least assent or not assent. But there is more behind this. Chrysippus distinguished (41 ff.) between two kinds of causes of action: partly the immediately antecedent 'auxiliary' causes – the cylinder is pushed – partly the primary or proximate causes – the cylinder rolls, man acts. These primary causes lie within ourselves.

Within certain limits we have different possibilities to act: we can choose virtue, and we can – as in Cleanthes' prayer – choose evil, i.e. omit to follow reason. Hence the slave is to receive a drubbing, and hence man is responsible; he can justly be 'praised or blamed', as also Aristotle said (Alex. Aphr. *De fat.* 196, 24; cf. Diog. Laert. VII 89). What we choose is, however, to a large extent dependent on who we are. My actions are, to be sure, at the moment dictated by my character, but I am also responsible for that; for in the long run character can be altered. I am the one who acts, whether or not I have been formed by bad influences (*SVF* III 224–5, Clem.; 229, Calc.; Plut. *De Stoic. rep.* 1048 C; Alex. Aphr. *De fat.* 181,13 ff. = *SVF* II 979).

How can this be reconciled with the third point in Cleanthes – that everything is subject to god's will? There is nothing self-contradictory in a man's being able to will what is predetermined, and when man acts well or ill he acts according to his own *logos*, which in the final analysis is in agreement with the greater, universal *Logos*. The difficulty left to the Stoics is that the divine *Logos* unites everything for the good, while the human *logos* can err; but at the same time it is still part of the greater *Logos*. The Stoic solution – for example exploited by Augustine and Boethius (cf. Aug. *De lib. arb.* III 4 ff.; *De civ. Dei* V 9 ff.; Boeth. *Cons.* V 6) – undoubtedly assumes that there is a difference between pre-knowledge and predetermination. God knows beforehand – or always – that the individual man will act in this or that way; he has predetermined that man should be able to act according to his nature. In this consists man's special position as superior to all other living beings.

Man's privilege shows itself in his being able to fail; indeed most often he does so. Like everything else, the human soul is in steady interaction with the surroundings, but unlike all other living beings, man as a rational being has self-consciousness, and by his reason and through his acts he seeks to make the world 'his own'. In the idealized, marginal case – that of the sage – one can imagine an identification with the greater *Logos*, but actually the human soul is limited, a *microcosmos* reflecting the greater *kosmos* on its own conditions.

When the Stoics speak of soul and reason, all of it can sound quite ethereal. But we should not forget that they solve the 'psycho-physical' problem by maintaining that it does not exist: the soul is corporeal, but a very complex piece of matter pervaded by *pneuma* (Diog. Laert. VII 156), a tensional field unified in a special way. Furthermore, the highest activities of the soul – the ability to receive sense impressions, to 'assent', to perceive, to think, and to desire, all of which are located in the 'guiding' part of the soul (*to hēgemonikon*, cf. *SVF* II, Aet.; Diog. Laert. VII 157) – are corporeal. This idea is carried through consistently. As properties of particular persons, virtues and vices are corporeal; the same applies to affects such as cruelty, anger, envy, which immediately can be observed in facial expression, gesture, blushing, etc. (Sen. *Ep. mor.* 106,5 ff.). Where Aristotle operates with a parallelism between psychic and physical phenomena, the Stoics assume identity.

ETHICS

In spite of the fact that all events in the world are subordinated to a strict causal nexus, man can act voluntarily. Human reason is literally akin to universal reason – they are made of the same 'stuff'. These two facts form the basis of Stoic ethics. The principal Stoic idea is that man develops into a free moral being – if, and only if, he becomes conscious of himself as a rational being. And he attains happiness – if, and only if, he acts in agreement with god's providence. The morally good is intimately connected with the two basic concepts of reason, *logos*, and nature, *physis*. Human reason and human nature are imperfect, but perfectible. Like all Hellenistic ethics, Stoic ethics is intellectualistic and naturalistic, and the concept of nature is both descriptive and normative. If one begins with a neutral description of what man in fact is, it will be seen that at a higher level this implies naturally given norms. The sage who understands the 'is' of nature also understands its 'ought to' – he lives in agreement with nature (Diog. Laert. VII 87; cf. *SVF* I 179, Stob.), and to him there is no difference between his own nature and universal nature.

The Stoics share the naturalistic basic view with Aristotle, but not the intellectualistic one. Stoic ethics – a naturalistic-teleological agent ethics – has its background in Aristotle, but the Stoics radicalize, systematize, and transform the Aristotelian heritage in a new context. This can perhaps be seen most readily in the Stoic view of the concept of happiness, the highest good. Like Aristotle, they approach the concept formally; it is the state to which nothing can be added and from which nothing can be subtracted. But to the Stoics – as to Epicurus – this precludes anything of relative value – the external goods in Aristotle. Where virtue to Aristotle is a precondition for happiness, virtue or 'the noble' is to the Stoics simply that in which happiness consists – which corresponds with Epicurus' definition of happiness as pleasure.

Epicurus subordinates reason to pleasure; the Stoics follow Aristotle and make reason superior. But where Aristotle bases moral life on an interplay between good character and practical reason, rational insight is to the Stoics the only decisive factor; there is no difference between virtue and reason. So the highest good can be determined both as virtue and rationality, and whoever lives virtuously and rationally lives 'in accordance with nature'. How can this position be justified?

The point of departure is descriptive-naturalistic. Man strives by nature to attain something, and this striving or impulse (*hormē*) is – in the proper Aristotelian spirit – immediately connected with assent (*synkatathesis*) and action (III 377, Clem.; 171, Stob.; Plut. *De Stoic. rep.* 1037 F). What human impulse aims for is more clearly explained by means of the key concept of *oikeiōsis*, appropriation – a man appropriates something to himself and adjusts himself to something so that it becomes his own and belongs to him (Diog. Laert. VII 85; Cic. *De fin.* III 16). The two concepts of *synkatathesis* and *oikeiōsis* are familiar from other parts of the Stoic system, and the wide perspectives in the concept of *oikeiōsis* will be clear if one considers that all parts of the world exist in mutual interaction. Every human being is a part of the world, but man can become conscious of his position, and through reason he can make the world his possession. At the outset man makes his self his 'possession', but subsequently he includes family and friends in his care (*cura* in Cicero). The circle is increased to include his society and all mankind, and at last the whole world is made the property of man.

In all essentials the line of thought is preserved in Diogenes Laertius and Cicero (Diog. Laert. VII 85 ff.; Cic. *De fin*. III 16 ff.) – each of them evidently reproducing good Stoic sources. Both accounts begin with the unadulterated, unreflected state of nature that can be observed in the child. Immediately after birth the child will feel an impulse to preserve its own self; it seeks for what is in agreement with the instinct for self-preservation – good health, nourishment, etc. (*prima naturalia* in Cicero, corresponding with external goods in Aristotle) – and to shun whatever is inimical to the sustenance of the self. It is a fact that the child acts like an egoist – and ought to do so, for that is what nature has ordained for the child. However, the pure instinct for self-preservation is already tied to self-consciousness (*syneidēsis, sensus sui*) and to an ability to select and reject, to seek whatever belongs to the self, and set a goal for itself.

With this the Stoics naturally distance themselves from the Epicurean position according to which pleasure is man's primary purpose; they follow Aristotle and claim that pleasure is a by-product without a purpose in itself.

But man is not – as is the animal – a creature exclusively bound to desire. Gradually, as the child grows older it becomes aware of itself as a rational being. The 'natural' life for the adult person is thus a life in agreement with reason. But this implies a life in agreement with virtue, a life in which man by living in agreement with his individual nature lives in agreement with universal nature and in which he obeys the common law, reason – which with an Aristotelian term occasionally may be called 'right thinking' – that governs everything and is identical with Zeus.

In Diogenes' account the main emphasis is on the teleological side of this development. Man has a certain nature and a place in the greater whole, which determines the goal for the individual's life. Cicero – or his source – stresses the decisive transition from desire to rationality, from egoism to virtue and this transition is also naturally determined. What makes the several stages of the development cohere (20 ff.) is that whatever is in agreement with nature or contributes to fulfilling her primary demands has value (*axia*). At the first stage, whatever serves to sustain life has absolute value. But gradually, as human reason develops, the emphasis changes. Gradually one gains insight into nature's coherence, into the fact that one is a link in this coherence, and into the fact that the highest good – that which alone has value in itself – is full insight, which in an absolute sense brings man into agreement with nature. It is not until reason develops that it is meaningful to speak of morality, and moral acts in themselves do not even represent the final stage. Insight and action cohere; it is not the act but the state of mind that builds on insight that has value (cf. 32 ff.); the final goal is not moral acts but moral man. The coherence in the development from the instinct of self-preservation to morality can be expressed by the concept of 'appropriation' (*oikeiōsis*) and 'to live in accordance with nature'. But the contents of these concepts change as the egoistical man gradually develops into a moral man – at the highest level egoism and altruism will converge, as in Aristotle.

There are several lines in this pilgrim's progress. Man aims constantly to preserve his 'self', but the understanding of the human self changes – not in such a way that original self-preservation is considered a past stage, but rather in such a way that what was simply valuable at the outset – *prima naturalia* – now has only relative value. It is at the same time a shift from a descriptive to a normative and from a subjective to an objective point of view – what is valuable is not what is in 'my' interest but what is in everybody's interest. And there is, finally, a development in man's consciousness of his own self. The final point is the concept of 'the noble' (*honestum* in Cicero). This is and must be an absolute concept (26 ff.; 33; 36 ff.) – as in the entire Socratic tradition 'virtue' implies all virtues; wisdom is its own end (24). Virtue manifests itself in a 'care' for all men, but since it depends on full insight into the nature of the world – and thereby into man's own nature – virtue in an absolute sense is identical with perfect happiness – also for the individual (26; 45 ff.). Whoever fails to act from virtue acts in conflict with himself, and the virtuous man can only act in accordance with a 'categorical imperative'. However, unlike Kant but like Aristotle, moral man, according to the Stoics, acts in full agreement with his nature; there is no conflict between duty and inclination.

Only 'the noble' (*to kalon, honestum*) is good (Diog. Laert. VII 10; Cic. *De fin.* III 21), we are told with a standard formulation. But the noble is an absolute concept; he only is 'sage' who has gained full insight into the noble (Diog. Laert. VII 127). It is possible to stick to this one point of view – as did 'the heretic' Ariston of Chios (Cic. *De fin.* III 50 ff.) – and indeed it was the position of the Cynics; but this implies that one rejects all of ordinary, social life on a blue Monday. There are not many sages in the world – there may be none – and only very few acts can unconditionally be called good. Therefore it is essential for orthodox Stoicism to stick to the dual aspect of the concept of 'nature' and draw the ethical consequences from it: the concept of nature, understood as absolute, implies an absolute norm, but individual man here and now has an imperfect nature and is in need of guidance in his daily doings. To the child there are certain acts that are of value simply – acts that preserve the self. To the adult these acts have only relative value – which is to say that in a strict sense they are void or indifferent (*adiaphora*): either one is sage or one is not; the man with his head just under the water surface will drown as promptly as he who lies at the bottom of the sea (48). In another sense it is nevertheless not an indifferent matter whether imperfect man approaches virtue or not. Therefore there are actions that are meaningful as means to the goal and actions that simply must be performed.

On this basis probably already Zeno formulated a rule ethics (Diog. Laert. VII 103 ff.; Cic. *De fin.* III 50 ff.; *SVF* III 128, Stob.). There are objects that have positive or negative or neither positive nor negative value (*axia*): such objects are respectively preferable (*ta proēgmena*) or not preferable (*ta apoproēgmena*) – or they are neutral. Psychic or bodily properties, such as skill, moral progress, or good health and external goods, such as wealth or reputation, ought to be preferred.

Correspondingly, there are actions of obligation or duty (appropriate actions: *ta kathēkonta, officia* in Latin) that are morally binding; the opposite acts are morally reprehensible, and here as well there is a neutral intermediary area. Thus moral evaluation makes its appearance here, and it is characteristic for Stoic anthropology that duty towards oneself and other men forms a synthesis. What are termed appropriate actions is everything that also in the current moral view are duties: to honour one's parents, help one's friends, support one's native country, etc. It holds good for all such obligations that only general rules can be laid down, but that in particular cases rational justifications can be provided (Diog. Laert. VII 107; Cic. *De fin.* III 58). Whether an act in fact is good, will, however, often depend on the circumstances, and in a given situation it may be right for example to maim oneself or sacrifice one's property (Diog. Laert. VII 109).

But the good is not simply identical with the valuable; the merely valuable is indifferent, and the act that in a real sense is a good (*katorthōma*, right action; Latin: *recte factum* – *SVF* III 500–3, Stob.; Cic. *De fin.* III 58 ff.) is above rules. It depends on the right state of mind and springs from the inner man. Seneca says:

> An action is not right, unless the will be right, for from this springs the action. And the will is not right, unless the state of mind be so; from this springs the will. The state of mind, finally, is only perfect, if it perceive the laws of life and weigh what should be judged about every single case.
>
> (Sen. *Ep. mor.* 95, 57)

Elsewhere he says (*De ben.* III 18) that the good action depends only on the state of mind, not on rank or position. In other words, only the sage acts morally rightly in a real sense – but on the other hand he will do so with unerring certainty. Normally his acts will also be in agreement with current views of moral duties (*kathēkonta*); yet it follows that one cannot decide merely on the basis of the act itself whether it is morally perfect or a merely appropriate act (*SVF* III 511, Clem.), just as it follows that an act should be judged on the intention rather than the result.

It is often said that the Stoics advocated a double ethics: one for the exceptional person, the sage, another for the ordinary man. That is only half of the truth. What is decisive is that they distinguished firmly between an agent ethics and a rule ethics. As they so often did, they also radicalized Aristotle here. Like him, they based the whole of ethics on a paradigm, a fictive, ideal person – *ho phronimos* in Aristotle, the sage in the Stoics. Such a perfect moral person can with intuitive certainty decide what the situation calls for and hence he meets the demand without hesitation. In Aristotle act, character, and reflection – practical reason – are intimately connected. Stoic ethics constitutes a monolithic unity that depends on rational insight – assent and adjustment to the whole cosmic order. Epicurus' philosopher is the equal of the gods; the Stoics' sage has the insight of god, and full moral insight does not differ from full theoretical cognition.

The Stoic sage is an ideal type; he is as rare as the Phoenix bird that lets itself be reborn once every 500 years (Sen. *Ep. mor.* 41, 1). But since the entire Stoic ethics is built upon the ideal demand, the sage has a necessary function as an *exemplum*. There are no degrees of wisdom, and the sage thus represents the directive ideal: he lives the life of a citizen, shares in family life, in politics, etc.; just like Kierkegaard's ethical man he lives incognito – nobody looking at him from the outside can tell whether he acts from duty or the right state of mind. But he is never wrong, possesses all virtues, is free, and everything belongs to him (Diog. Laert. VII 121 ff.; cf. *SVF* III 548, Stob.; 557, Stob.). He is never knocked down by blows of fate and is above external vicissitudes and inner passions; he lives in 'apathy' (*apatheia*), freedom from passion – he is untouchable and is free from, for example, compassion (cf. Cic. *Tusc. disp.* III 14 ff.; Diog. Laert. VII 123). To this extent he may remind one of 'the magnanimous' in Aristotle (cf. Diog. Laert. VII 128; see p. 376), but he is no upper-class gentleman; his calm of mind is his sole possession. One favoured Stoic *topos* would have offended Aristotle: the sage who retains his tranquillity and is happy on the rack (cf. Cic. *De fin.* III 42). But Plato would not have been offended; it is a true Socratic thought that nothing can harm the good man.

The Stoics liked to stress the sage's exceptional position in paradoxical form (cf. *Par. Stoic.*). Since he always perceives the right, he can act contrary to prevailing norms; in exceptional cases cannibalism and incest are, for example, permissible (*SVF* III 743 ff.), and the sage masters his own life to such a degree that he can calmly commit suicide, if that is what the situation calls for (Cic. *De fin.* III 60). He is raised above passions and affects, for passions (*pathē*) are only diseases of the soul that show that human reason has been led astray; they are 'wrong judgements' (Diog. Laert. VII 110; Cic. *De fin.* III 35; *Tusc. disp.* IV 29; Plut. *De virt. mor.* 441 C; 446 F). Philosophy is the true psychotherapy that can turn 'wrong' judgements straight (*SVF* III 444, Lact.; 471, Galen).

There are clear points of similarity with the Cynics. But the difference is that the Stoic sage takes his place in communal life. And he cares for his fellow men, includes them in his care (*cura*). There is certainly a fathomless chasm between the sage and the fool, but all men are equal; not all are wise, but all men are endowed with reason, and reason is common property. This is why justice and moral law have their foundation in nature herself (Cic. *De re publ.* III 33; cf. Diog. Laert. VII 128). All men are brothers with equal rights; we must take care of our fellow man, because he is a man (Cic. *De off.* III 27); men and gods inhabit a common city, the whole world, in which the individual has obligations to the commonwealth and to the weak (*De fin.* III 64; *SVF* III 323, Philo) – there is no denying that the distance is vast to the Epicureans' 'fortified city'.

Cosmopolitanism and natural law, the thought of men's common rights – and common obligations – is surely the most remarkable part of Stoicism's legacy to posterity. The basic idea is already present in Zeno's *Politeia* (cf. Plut. *De Alex. virt.* 329 A), but in its encounter with the Roman world it was refined and made more profound in theory as well as practice. Cicero puts it this way:

> Of everything discussed amongst the learned, this occupies the uncontested first place: full realization that we are born to justice, that law does not depend on beliefs but on nature. This clearly appears, if one has human society and the commonwealth in mind. Nowhere does one find a similarity so striking as that which binds us humans to each other. . . . For it is certain

that reason, the only thing that raises us above the brutes, . . . is common; although we may be unequal in learning, we are equal in ability to learn.

(Cic. De leg. I 28 ff.)

29

SCEPTICISM

—— •◆• ——

Almost from the very beginning it is possible to speak of sceptical currents in Greek philosophy. Xenophanes can be called the father of Scepticism, and with some justification Heraclitus has been counted among its ancestors. But scepticism is many things. An important tradition in Greek thought considers intellectual cognition certain, yet is sceptical about the possibility of valid sense cognition. This 'tradition' includes such different names as Parmenides, Democritus, Plato and Aristotle. A typical 'rationalist' counter-attack against general scepticism is the Aristotelian argument: even if I have no certain knowledge that this is an x, I know what it means to be x.

Confronting this were the epistemological subjectivism and relativism, often *en bloc* attributed to the Sophists. This is a simplification, although it is true that Gorgias represents an anarchic scepticism as it were, and that the principal Sophist, Protagoras, must be considered a main figure in the history of Western scepticism. Protagoras – but also empirical medicine with its disrespect for the speculative – are the most important precursors of Hellenistic Scepticism. Its more specific development was largely determined by the opponents: they were the ones to furnish the premises to be contested.

Scepticism is often marked by a certain resignation: certain knowledge is desirable but unattainable. This is not the way of it in the Hellenistic age. Here Scepticism is not a regrettable necessity but a precondition for peace of mind or *ataraxia* – the key word of the day. As in all Hellenistic philosophy, epistemology and moral philosophy are linked to each other, but here in a manner that can be quite surprising.

Apparently this is true already of Pyrrho (c.365–c.270), whom a later tradition considered the founder of Scepticism. Only about twenty years younger than Aristotle and barely a generation older than Epicurus and Zeno, he stands at the threshold of Hellenistic philosophy; to us he seems to be quite close to the form of scepticism that Plato and Aristotle fought against. But he is an obscure figure; he wrote nothing, and the fact that from the first century BC he was considered the 'saint' of Scepticism makes it mandatory to be careful of concluding backwards from later 'Pyrrhonism'. He seems (Diog. Laert. IX 61) to have come from the Democritus tradition and to have studied Megarian logic; to this is added the information, no further specified, of ties to Indian and Persian philosophy. He did not found a real school; our best source is his 'student' and spokesman, Timon of Phlius (c.320–c.230), who is transmitted fragmentarily; in a number of satiric poems he attacked the 'dogmatic' philosophers of his time.

The clearest and most credible resumé of Pyrrho's views goes back to Timon (Aristocl. ap. Eus. *Praep. Ev.* XIV 18, 2). Here we are told that whoever seeks happiness should bear three questions in mind: the nature of things; what attitude to adopt to things; and the outcome of such an attitude. Things are immeasurable and indeterminable, and hence neither our perceptions nor our beliefs can be true or false. Accordingly we should refrain from every judgement; in every case we should not say 'is' rather than say 'is not', 'both is and is not', or 'either is or is not'. If we adopt this attitude we will not only avoid assertions; we will also attain peace of mind (*ataraxia*).

Thus neither sensation nor reason provides us with reliable information about things, and to every assertion about the nature of things corresponds – as in Protagoras – a counter-assertion (Diog. Laert. IX 114; 106). The so-called *ou mallon* argument (*ou mallon*: 'no more') is employed, i.e. 'no more p than q, therefore neither p nor q' – an argument with roots in the old 'principle of economy' (Anaximander, Democritus, and, later, Epicurus); but in the staging of Scepticism it is no longer used as an argument of probability (cf. 76).

But this scepticism has its limitations. In ancient thought there is no radical doubt about the existence of the external world, and a Pyrrhonian Sceptic may doubt our cognitive possibilities but not the existence of things – just as Protagoras in Plato's *Theaetetus* did not doubt the existence of the wind, but asked whether it was hot or cold. No true or false judgements exist about the actual nature of reality, but about my understanding of reality (*to phainomenon*). In other words, it is a question of the same distinction between physical and phenomenal objects that we know from Protagoras, and the concept of truth is not simply cancelled. I do not claim that honey is sweet, but I do assert that it appears sweet, as Timon said, using a stock example, and Pyrrho is reputed to have said that he let himself be guided by the phenomena (*ta phainomena* – 105 ff.).

If one rejects judgements about reality but accepts judgements about the phenomenon, one will in addition attain peace of mind, which is the real purpose of philosophy (107). This is a quite remarkable assertion, which – as in Epicurus – must imply that disturbance of the mind is owing to fruitless speculation about problems we can never solve. This also applies to value judgements, and when all is said and done Pyrrho was apparently a moralist rather than an epistemologist: what is generally considered valuable is in fact worthless (cf. Cic. *De fin.* II 43; IV 43). With such thoughts he sounded the basic chord of all Hellenistic moral philosophy. We do not know whether he entertained more precise moral views; but we do learn that 'some Sceptics' considered mildness to be the purpose with life (Diog. Laert. XI 108).

ACADEMIC SCEPTICISM

Preumably Arcesilaus (c.315–242) – *inter alia* a student of Theophrastus – assumed the direction of Plato's school in 273. Thereby Scepticism gained entrance to the

Academy, and Arcesilaus was later considered the founder of the so-called middle or sceptical Academy (Diog. Laert. IV 28; Sext. Emp. *Hyp. Pyr.* I 220; cf. Cic. *Acad.* I 17; *De or.* III 67). Although it can hardly be doubted that he was affected by Pyrrhonian scepticism, he considered himself first and foremost the heir of the dialectical, questioning, and ignorant Socrates, and, to all appearances, he differed from Pyrrho by emphasizing epistemology. Where epistemological scepticism to Pyrrho was subordinated to the purpose of philosophy – *ataraxia*, to Arcesilaus *ataraxia* was an epiphenomenon to suspension (*epochē*) of judgement and belief (cf. Sext. Emp. *Hyp. Pyr.* I 232); his main interest was in the dialectical interplay between pro et con. In the general philosophical tradition the opposite of belief or *doxa* was always certain knowledge (*epistēmē*); but to Arcesilaus it was well-founded scepticism. Now, a basic sceptical position can be formulated as self-refuting – whence do I know that knowledge is uncertain – and one can imagine that Arcesilaus' student, Chrysippus, joined the ranks of the enemy, the Stoics, precisely because he thought that at the very least the concept of certain knowledge must be maintained. It appears that Arcesilaus was familiar with the problem; he stressed that he – in contrast to Socrates – did not even *know* that he knew nothing (Cic. *Acad.* I 45).

Otherwise one should probably be very cautious about claiming that Arcesilaus believed this or that. Like Pyrrho – and Socrates – he wrote nothing, and we only know him as an anti-Stoic. The Stoics claimed that true cognition or knowledge depends on a 'grasping' (*katalēpsis*) that comes about by the assent (*synkatathesis*) of the soul to a cognitive sense impression (*phantasia katalēptikē*). But, says Arcesilaus (Sext. Emp. *Adv. math.* VII 153 ff.; cf. Cic. *Acad.* II 59; I 45), in part any assent is a judgement, and hence cognition must take place already at that stage at which the soul assents; and in part no sense impression exists that might not be false; a true and a false sense impression can be fully identical. Accordingly the Stoic criterion of truth collapses; on the Stoic presuppositions there is in fact no true cognition. Furthermore, it is inconsistent for the Stoics to consider the soul's 'grasping' a cognitive act *between* assent and knowledge, for according to their own understanding there is no intermediate stage between the fool who 'opines' or assents to anything whatsoever and the sage who 'knows'. Since 'opinion' (*doxa*) is unfounded and 'knowledge' on the Stoics' own premises is unattainable, the Stoic 'sage' should draw sceptical conclusions from his own premises and suspend his judgement.

Inasmuch as morally right human action – still according to the Stoics – is determined by insight, 'the sage' cannot invariably act rightly; he can only pursue what seems reasonable (*eulogon*) to him, which is to say that he must be able to provide a rational justification without certainty of its truth (Sext. Emp. *Adv. math.* VII 158). 'To provide a rational justification' is to the orthodox Stoic the definition of an appropriate action (*kathēkon*). With polemical finesse Arcesilaus suggests that there is no difference between the appropriate action and the sage's absolutely right action (*katorthōma*). The sage must be satisfied with a rule ethics building on arguments of probability.

Stoic epistemology and Stoic moral philosophy are self-refuting. That is what Arcesilaus wishes to demonstrate – no more than that. His criticism has relevance only for an epistemology of the Stoic type; hence one becomes curious to know whether he entertained other – 'positive' – beliefs. One ancient tradition replies affirmatively. Arcesilaus' scepticism applied to cognition of particulars – i.e. phenomena – and his debate with the Stoics merely constituted the outworks – a Socratic's maieutic prologue to the pure Platonic doctrine, which he reserved for an inner circle, as we learn (*Hyp. Pyr.* I 234; cf. Cic. *Acad.* II 60; Aug. *Contra Acad.* III 17, 38). At first this sounds like a tall tale, and it is indeed customary to reject it – but perhaps one should not feel too sure. We only know Arcesilaus as an anti-Stoic; but we do know that he thought himself the heir not only to the 'sceptical' Socrates but to the entire Platonic tradition (cf. Plut. *Adv. Col.* 1121 F). The most apt characterization is probably furnished by the contemporary Stoic Ariston of Chios. According to him, Arcesilaus was a Plato in front, a Pyrrho from behind, and a Diodorus Cronus (i.e. a dialectician) in the middle (Sext. Emp. *Hyp. Pyr.* I 234).

Arcesilaus' student Chrysippus became a Stoic, but Chrysippus himself also acquired a critic among Academic sceptics, Carneades (c.215–129), who was later called the founder of the 'new Academy' (I 220). As had become proper for a good Sceptic, he wrote nothing. But he is famed as a dialectician; during a celebrated embassy to Rome in 155 with one Stoic and one Peripatetic colleague he caused a sensation by 'advocating' justice one day and 'speaking against' it the next – the Hellenization of Roman intellectuals was indeed well under way, but the public was probably not yet accustomed to the 'pro-et-con' technique that had been familiar to the Greeks since Protagoras' day (Lact. *Inst.* V 14, 3 ff.; cf. Plut. *Cat. mai.* 22). There is nothing in the tradition suggesting that Carneades entertained a secret doctrine. And, as will appear from the following, modern scholars are, as much as were the Romans, at a loss to understand what Carneades 'really meant' – and, by the way, so was his closest student Clitomachus (Cic. *Acad.* II 139).

If there could be doubt about what Carneades 'meant', there is no doubt about what he did – he fought the Stoics in general and Chrysippus in particular with their own weapons. He did so on a wide front, point by point. As in Arcesilaus' refutation of Zeno, the most essential was epistemology. But where Arcesilaus confined himself to referring the Stoic 'sage' to *epochē*, Carneades went further.

Apparently he began with a critique of Zeno's definition of *phantasia katalēptikē* (Sext. Emp. *Adv. mat.* VII 402 ff.), and with this the battleground was marked off. Carneades concedes to Zeno that a cognitive sense impression is imprinted by the real object and is in conformity with it; but he disputes whether a sense impression can ever be of such a kind that it could not be derived from a non-real object. Then follows a series of standard sceptical arguments: perception can in certain – external or internal – circumstances be uncertain; exactly identical sense impressions may exist, etc. (cf. Cic. *Acad.* II 84). All are well-trodden paths, and the conclusion is of course clear: there is no sure 'grasping' of a real object; there is no sure criterion of truth (cf. II 48). But Carneades does not stop with this. Suppose that something like a *phantasia* does exist – so the argument continues. Such a sense impression has both an objective and a subjective side; it can – objectively – reproduce the actual object truly or falsely; it can – subjectively – appear true or false to an observer (Sext. Emp. *Adv. math.* VII 167 ff.). Thereby Carneades distinguished clearly between condition for truth and criterion of truth. Let a given sense impression be ever so true in an objective sense; we have no possibility of determining when that is the case. This means that a comprehension or 'grasping' in the Stoic sense is impossible, but it does not mean that a sense impression cannot be more or less acceptable (Cic. *Acad.* II 99 ff.).

Carneades proceeds on the basis of this concept of the acceptable (*to pithanon*). The concept has a certain similarity with *to eulogon* in Arcesilaus, but where *to eulogon* is act-directing and belongs in the discussion of morality, Carneades' concept is purely epistemological. According to Carneades there are degrees of probability; some sense impressions are more acceptable than others, and the empirical data – the sense impressions – can be tested systematically in order to eliminate sources of error so that one can achieve a result that – although in principle uncertain – cannot be challenged in practice. One should only realize that even the most everyday indentification of objects is an extremely complex affair: to say that this man is Socrates implies deliberation of a long series of factors – height, colour, figure, way of speaking, gestures, etc. (Sext. Emp. *Hyp. Pyr.* I 227 ff.; *Adv. math.* VII 176 ff.). It is this kind of a systematic testing with which the Stoics sought to adapt themselves within their more and more elaborate theory of convincing and true sense impressions comprehended 'without obstacle'. But whereas an orthodox Stoic will maintain that either there are absolute cognitive sense impressions or else no cognition at all, Carneades will deny the alternative (Cic. *Acad.* II 36).

What, then, did Carneades 'mean'? According to some modern scholars his sole aim was for an *reductio ad absurdum* of Stoic views. According to others he constructed a 'positive' epistemology. He may, however, have been on a two-fold mission. On the one hand, he makes inferences on Stoic premises, which must have been fatal for every dogmatic Stoic who demands absolutely certain knowledge. On the other hand, he does in fact construct an empiristic theory of science that may be highly acceptable from other points of view. Considered from that angle, quite striking parallels within Hellenistic philosophy present themselves: partially the Epicurean interest in inductive logic, and partially – and especially – the Peripatetic 'scepticism' that goes back to Theophrastus. But it must be conceded that only the Aristotelians seem to have influenced the science of the times directly. Of course the Stoic theory of science occupies a special position: empirical generalizations about 'non-evident' causes – all within the framework of a dogmatic, epistemological system. Theoretically the distance between a Stoic and a Carneades is great, in practice perhaps less so.

In other respects Carneades seems only to have had polemical intentions in his debate with the Stoics. He is said to have undermined the whole foundation of logic by asking the Stoics how they would deal with the Megarian paradoxes (the *sorites* paradox and 'the liar', see p. 444) and with the old conundrum of the truth value of propositions about contingent future events, and he appears to have pointed out to them that a proof of the non-evident demands a proof of the proof (Cic. *Acad.* II 91 ff.; Sext. Emp. *Adv. math.* VIII 340 ff.). If such questions look as if they make the concepts of true and false relative, what then remains of logic? Now, it would be rather precipitate to believe that Carneades, the logician, wanted to do away with logic. The point is more likely this: what remains of Stoicism if it constructs a concept of absolute truth but cannot realize the ideal in the formal science of truth?

The question of the truth value of propositions about the future points to something more essential. Here Cicero provides a very valuable report of Carneades' points of view (cf. Cic. *De fat.* 17 ff.). It is not merely a question of formal logic but of the entire relation between logic and reality and between fate and free will. Aristotle adopted indeterminism as a given fact and from this he inferred that affirmative or negative statements about future events have undetermined truth value (see p. 301). To Diodorus Cronus, what is possible is that which is or will be true – if it is true that an event will occur, it has also been predetermined. To the Epicureans, not all events are strictly causally determined, and consequently statements about the future do not have fixed truth value. Chrysippus' attitude is more intricate (see p. 455 and p. 462 ff.). What is logically possible may in fact be impossible. Since all propositions are either true or false, this must also hold good for propositions of actual events – including future ones – regardless of our not knowing the truth value, and hence we must have recourse to inference from the logically possible or by empirical generalization. But, in principle, propositions about the future are either true or false, simply because the future – as in Diodorus – is predetermined. Not only is the statement 'Scipio will die' true, but so is the statement 'Scipio will be murdered in his bed' – of course presupposing that this is what has been predetermined. On the one hand a strict causal nexus obtains, which has been determined once and for all; on the other hand this does not preclude the existence of free will according to Chrysippus. These – mutually discordant – views do agree that logical truth is tied to physical causality.

Carneades cuts through the discussion (23 ff.). He says in the first place that everything has a cause but that this does not preclude that some causes lie in ourselves, for it is evident that some actions must be led back to free will. More generally, there is – using modern language – a difference between necessary and sufficient conditions: in some cases, a will necessarily cause b; in other cases it can only *ex eventu* be determined that a has caused b. This means that strict determinism is invalid, and consequently there is no reason – as in Chrysippus – both to distinguish between primary and secondary, 'auxiliary' causes and to include both causal types in a predetermined course of events. In the second place Carneades denies that a fixed truth value of propositions about the future implies strictly determined causality; there is a difference between conditions for truth and conditions for verification. Propositions about the future have the same truth value as propositions about the past; they are true or false without this having deterministic consequences. This clear distinction between logical truth and physical causality signals a notable departure from both Aristotle and the Stoics, and it is difficult to imagine that Carneades' argumentation 'only' was intended to put the Stoics in their place.

It goes without saying that Carneades also must turn against the Stoic faith in divination (*De div.* II); on the whole he argues against the Stoic concept of god. One whole book in Cicero's main work on the philosophy of religion (*De nat. deor.* III) probably reproduces his arguments. There is no satisfactory reason to assume that the world is endowed with reason, that the stars are gods, that god has created the world, or that he has endowed man with reason – so, why does he permit them to abuse reason? Strictly speaking, only the 'negative' is maintained: the Stoics cannot argue for their concept of god. But it is difficult not to think that Carneades also here 'meant' something. His whole criticism of the Stoics seems in the end to reflect the view that the world is a world of empirical facts and contingent events without room for a creator, a god, or a teleology. Everything in the world occurs naturally – without the normative overtones usually sounded in the Greek concept of nature.

This concurs with the fact that Carneades also attacked the Stoic doctrine of natural law. Here Cicero – as usual our main source – perhaps exploits what Carneades said on the second day of his famous embassy to Rome. Law, maintained Carneades, is a product of society – which means that only positive law exists and that it rests on the principle of mutual benefit, i.e. a social contract (*De re publ*. III 13; cf. Lact. *Inst*. V 16, 3). Consequently individual man is not by nature just (Cic. *De re publ*. III 18). Natural virtues simply do not exist, and justice can very well come into conflict with wisdom: he who owns a slave or a house with shortcomings would be wise to sell his property without telling the buyer – but this is not just (Lact. *Inst*. V 16,5).

It is debatable whether Carneades had a moral philosophy. Apparently – like everybody else at the time – he assumed that the purpose of human life is to attain the goods nature herself indicates – perhaps he was convinced of this; perhaps he only said so for the sake of the argument (Cic. *Acad*. II 131). What he in fact did accomplish (*De fin*. V 16 ff.), we would perhaps call meta-ethics, a scanning of what one can believe when one speaks of morality within a naturalistic ethics. He established a catalogue of all possible ways of filling in the concept of the highest good, including possible combinations – whether or not anybody in fact did adopt these theoretical possibilities. Thereafter anybody could select whatever suited him from the stock. One may ask whether Carneades here acts the dialectician or the empiricist – and, when all is said and done, that is the question that must serve as the heading for any interpretation of this strange man. In any case, his classification of beliefs about the good might invite eclecticism or formalism. That invitation was to become partially accepted.

THE 'PYRRHONIAN' REACTION

In any case, in the days after Carneades an eclectic *rapprochement* between the Academics and the Stoics took place, which can be said to characterize official philosophy in the first century BC (see p. 484 ff.). This provoked a reaction, inasmuch as Aenesidemus (first century BC, exact dates unknown) who probably broke away from the Academy, proclaimed a 'return' to Pyrrho. At that time nothing much concrete can have been known about Pyrrho, so it was probably just the name the new Scepticism could exploit. Principally we know Aenesidemus through Sextus Empiricus who lived as late as the end of the second century AD. We have two of his works preserved *in extenso*: partly a shorter account of the basic views of Scepticism (*Hypotypōseis Pyrrhōneoi* – *Outlines of Pyrrhonism*), partly a detailed confrontation with 'dogmatic' philosophy and epistemology (in fact two works: *Against the Dogmatists* and *Against the Professors*, both works being usually cited by the Latin title of the latter, *Adversus mathematicos*). These works are constructed as an extensive arsenal of arguments against 'dogmatic' views in all fields whatsoever. Whoever – contrary to the intention – reads it consecutively may weary as good points change place with a display of more or less empty arguments in which the conclusion is given in advance;

but this is a deliberate tactic – everybody ought to get what he needs (cf. Sext. Emp. *Hyp. Pyr.* III 280). Behind the deliberate schematical form Sextus can be both witty and sarcastic; on rare occasions he gets angry.

Sextus was a physician and belonged to the so-called empirical school (see p. 418); undoubtedly he also incorporated material from the Scepticism of the Roman Empire, which we know but little about, but in all essentials he probably reproduces Aenesidemus; attempts to uncover differences between Aenesidemus and Sextus have not proved very fruitful. Sextus' work is marked by considerable independence, formal proficiency, and thorough familiarity with the whole philosophical tradition; but it is noteworthy that his work reproduces a philosophical discussion that in his day was more than three hundred years old.

'Pyrrhonian' Scepticism returns to the concept of *epochē* and to the connection between *epochē* and *ataraxia*; in other words, it is emphasized that Scepticism in its aim is a philosophy of life. Scepticism, says Sextus, is the attitude whereby one by advancing equally weighty arguments for and against (*isostheneia*: equipollence) is led to the suspension of beliefs and thereby to peace of mind (I 8 ff.; 25 ff.).

But it is not only in its general aim that the new Scepticism distinguishes itself at least from Carneades. Within epistemology in a narrower sense Carneades had maintained that with greater or lesser certainty we can speak about objective reality. To Aenesidemus and Sextus this is a betrayal of the cause. We must simply desist from speaking about the physical object and confine ourselves to the phenomenon. On the other hand, it is not called into doubt that something real 'appears' to an observer (13 ff.; 19 ff.). It is not doubted that men, towers, or honey exist in the actual world but indeed that honey for example is sweet or the tower square (cf. 20; 32).

It is a general presupposition that true cognition, if at all possible, must depend on agreement between sense impression (*phantasia*) or phenomenon and physical object (*to hypokeimenon*, the underlying or the substratum) – to that extent 'Pyrrhonian' Scepticism is in accordance with Stoicism – but such an agreement can never be demonstrated; it is also presupposed that sense cognition is a necessary condition for intellectual cognition. Hence the truth of intellectual cognition cannot be demonstrated either (22; *Adv. math.* VIII 60). The general sceptical strategy consists, then, in opposing phenomenon to phenomenon, thought object to thought object, or thought object to phenomenon (*Hyp. Pyr.* I 31 ff.; *Adv. math.* VIII 40 ff.).

Since no *tertium quid* exists whereby one can compare phenomenon with physical object, and since sense cognition is a presupposition for all other cognition, certain cognition is in fact already precluded. But Aenesidemus preferred to proceed pragmatically. This takes the form of ten modes or 'tropes' (methods leading to the suspension of beliefs). They have been preserved in Sextus and in contracted form in Diogenes Laertius (*Hyp. Pyr.* I 36 ff.; Diog. Laert. IX 79 ff.), although it is possible that reformulations were undertaken after the days of Aenesidemus. The first seven tropes are constructed according to the same basic scheme: different sense impressions disagree with each other; it is impossible to tell which is correct; it is impossible to decide what a physical object is like according to its own nature (cf. Sext. Emp. *Hyp. Pyr.* I 59 ff.). Point by point it is ascertained that different animals have different sense experiences, that the same holds true for different people, that the different sense organs report differently, that sense experience is dependent on subjective factors (sickness, hallucination, etc.) or on objective factors (the tower may appear to be round from the distance, square at close quarters), that sense experiences are never manifest in themselves but are affected by, for example, climatic conditions, and that the same stuff can appear different in great and small quantities. Each point is backed up by an extravagant store of more or less striking examples. It is a recurrent point that any sense impression whatsoever is relative to the observer, to the circumstances of observation, and to external circumstances. This is generalized in the eighth trope (135), which asserts that all sense impressions and conceptions are relative. The last two tropes have a different character; they are respectively concerned with different evaluations of rare or frequent events and differences in moral views, customs, and habits.

Aenesidemus and the Sceptics after him not only maintained – this was a commonplace – that passive sense experience in itself has no truth value (*Adv. math.* VIII 43) but that truth simply does not exist (*Hyp. Pyr.* II 88 ff.; *Adv. math.* VIII 17 ff.; 40 ff.). This is an assertion that should be taken *cum grano salis*. A Sceptic will not deny that it is true *that* I have a sense experience, and in his whole way of arguing he relies on a logical concept of truth – the ten tropes presuppose for example that p and q cannot both be true, if they are incompatible (cf. VII 392). In agreement with a deeply rooted tradition, truth to Aenesidemus means neither more nor less than correspondence with objective reality (XI 221) – and, considering the given premisses, the assertion is thus not all that amazing.

Since we only have access to the phenomenon and not to the thing itself, it is a reasonable inference that we cannot explain the known – the phenomenon – with the unknown – the thing. But inasmuch as the thing in one sense or another is assumed to be the cause of the phenomenon, does this in turn mean that although causes exist, they are inaccessible to us and that we accordingly must make do without causal explanations? 'The Pyrrhonists' do not ask the question in this way. They follow their customary procedure and conduct the battle on enemy soil. According to Sextus (*Hyp. Pyr.* III 14) all dogmatists must agree on defining cause as that which by its activity produces an effect. And Aenesidemus untiringly established eight 'tropes' against the dogmatists' causal explanations (I 180 ff.); but we are expressly told that this is an attack on the dogmatists. In other words, it is not simply directed against the causal concept as such. These tropes are – like the ten against certain cognition – a fairly unsystematic, pragmatic classification; but two fundamental views can be singled out. In the first place, the evident cannot be explained by the non-evident, such as god, souls, or atoms (cf. *Adv. math.* IX 195 ff.). In the second place, the dogmatists' actual procedure is criticized: they select one of several possible causes (the addressee undoubtly being Epicurus); they provide an explanation that in fact explains nothing; they explain what is obscure with the obscure; they build on unproven hypotheses and their own hobby-horses; and they cannot rely on any *communis opinio*. What is criticized here is that the dogmatists do not perform their work ably enough; these are not arguments against the causal concept as such. The first type of argument is, however, more far-reaching.

What, then, does a Sceptic from the School of Aenesidemus himself think about the concept of cause? Sextus furnishes the official answer (*Hyp. Pyr.* III 17 ff.), which – of course – states that one should suspend one's judgement. The reasoning is perhaps more important than the answer. On the one hand the contradictions in the concept of causality itself are pointed out: it is a relation between entities that mutually explain each other; cause is explained by effect, effect by cause, and there is no way out of that circle. On the other hand, the world does in fact appear as an ordered sequence of events in which not anything whatsoever can follow from anything whatsoever. To a Sceptic of Sextus' cast there is a way out of the dilemma, provided only that the question is formulated correctly. One should not explain the evident with the non-evident, and one should not imagine that 'things' or 'principles' according to their nature cause this or that. What one should do is to have recourse to the world one can say something about, which is to say a world of phenomena that in given circumstances seem to follow a certain order.

One can also approach the same problem from another angle, that is to say by analyzing the concepts of 'sign' and 'proof'. According to the Stoics there are two main classes of signs (see p. 457): the 'commemorative' in which one concludes in general from experience that sense object x accompanies sense object y ('no smoke without a fire') and the 'indicative' in which one by empirical generalization makes inferences about a non-perceived, 'hidden' cause ('sweat is discharged from the skin' is an indicative sign of 'the skin has invisible pores' – or an Atomistic example: 'motion exists' is an indicative sign of 'a void exists'). Obviously the Sceptics must reject the indicative sign, which is an inference from the evident to the non-evident – akin to shooting at a target in the dark (II 97 ff.; *Adv. math.* VIII 145 ff.; 325; for the examples, see 306; *Hyp. Pyr.* II 140; *Adv. math.* VIII 277). But on the other hand they have no objection to the commemorative sign in which one infers to that which temporarily is non-evident but which is known from experience to accompany an evident event – one infers, for example, from smoke to fire (156). But it should be noted that thereby one does not say anything about it being the nature of fire to produce smoke; one only says something about what usually is part of an ordered temporal sequence.

It is implicit in the above that the demonstrative proof is rejected and also that here the artillery is aimed at the Stoics. According to the standard Stoic definition (see p. 457; *Hyp. Pyr.* II 134 ff.) one arrives deductively at a non-evident conclusion in the demonstrative proof. Here the Sceptic must object on two grounds. In the first place, he must ask what makes the premisses true, i.e. what is the basis for a proof: it can only be a hypothesis based on induction or a universally acknowledged unprovable presupposition; but as neither is acceptable, the outcome will be an infinite regress or a circular proof (*Adv. math.* VIII 367 ff.; *Hyp. Pyr.* I 168).[1] Like the concept of causality, the concept of a demonstrative proof is self-contradictory. In the second place, Sextus of course attacks the non-evident conclusion, which in Sextus' version characteristically enough is incorporated in one of his favourite parade arguments: one cannot prove the evident with the evident, nor the non-evident with the non-evident, nor the evident with the non-evident, nor the non-evident with the evident;

---

1 The latter citation is part of a passage that reproduces five general 'tropes' leading to *epochē* and is attributed to 'late sceptics', perhaps to a certain Agrippa (164 ff.; Diog. Laert. IX 88 ff.). Ostensibly it is as usual the Stoics who are the targets, but, as can be seen, Aristotle is also under attack.

ergo the demonstrative proof does not exist (II 177 ff.). Of course only two of the possibilities are of interest. On Sceptical presuppositions it is clear that the non-evident cannot prove the evident. But why can the evident not prove the evident? Because here it can never be a question of 'proof'. But to maintain that x follows y is not a proof.

Sextus and those of his mind of course do not challenge the existence of valid deduction nor the possibility of the negative proof of which they themselves are the masters. They claim that the truth of the premises cannot be proved and attack the hypothetico-deductive method they find expressed in the Stoic theory of science. But so doing they also indirectly attack both the tradition of natural philosophy that followed Anaxagoras' ancient dictum: through the phenomena the hidden is seen (cf. I 138) and the Aristotelian view that in nature one can uncover universal, necessary and eternal connections. But the Sceptic has something to put in their stead: he uses the phenomenon as the 'criterion' (cf. 22), as Sextus says. He does not deny the existence of objects independent of human experience and is to that extent no phenomenalist. But his world is nevertheless one of phenomena, and that is sufficient for him. Sextus does not concern himself with what might lie behind the phenomena, but the relation between phenomena can very well be a subject of inquiry; he often stresses that Scepticism is synonymous with 'investigation', and in his view a Sceptic can very well deal with science (cf. 3; 18). Hence his ideal must be an extreme empiricist theory of science; the Stoics' theory of science builds on the indicative sign, Sextus' on the commemorative. According to Carneades science may speak with greater or lesser certainty about reality; according to Sextus one can only speak scientifically about the phenomenon. But it is also true of Sextus that the distance to actual science is considerable. Philosophers in Hellenistic times and late Antiquity took care of the theory of science; by and large science proper took care of itself.

Regardless of how far-reaching ambitions Sextus may have had as to the theory of science, it is apparent that his main emphasis is elsewhere. The anti-metaphysical 'positivism' which he and – despite theoretical differences – also Carneades represent has an important aim: to reveal traditional philosophical questions as pseudo-problems and traditional concepts as self-contradictory. Scepticism relies on common sense, he thinks, and thus it can be used in daily life and as a means to attain happiness. With a passion that is rare for him he turns against those who claim that the Sceptics abolish 'the phenomena' (19 ff.) or the 'commemorative' sign (*Adv. math.* VIII 156 ff.). Similarly his sarcasm is directed against those philosophers who from higher metaphysical or dialectical motives set about to prove the evident: that things move, that snow is white, or that we do not have horns and against those who prove the absurd – he enjoys referring to Diogenes who refuted the Eleatic arguments against motion by walking back and forth (*Hyp. Pyr.* II 244). Once one has rid oneself of the philosophers' pseudo-problems and once one – by *epochē* – has refrained from 'opining' about objective reality, one will achieve the peace of mind – *ataraxia* – that is life's goal: then one lives in a quite ordinary world – that of the phenomena – in which snow is white, honey usually sweet, and where there is smoke from a fire. *Ataraxia* enters unexpectedly and utterly by itself (I 28).

The two connected concepts of *epochē* and *ataraxia* are decisive to Sextus and are the main concepts in the introductory chapters of *The Outlines of Pyrrhonism*, and that is perhaps the passage where he most clearly reveals his own personality. Here the two most important questions are whether Scepticism is self-refuting and how one can be led to *ataraxia*. The former question had already been a preoccupation for Arcesilaus. Sextus' solution is a radical one. He believes that Scepticism is not self-refuting for the simple reason that *epochē* implies that one altogether gives up 'opining', i.e. to pronounce a judgement. There are, says Sextus (2 ff.), three main types of philosophy: the dogmatists of course believe they have found the truth; the Academic Sceptics, from whom Sextus would like to distance himself, believe according to him that the truth cannot be found (cf. 220 ff.); the Pyrrhonian Sceptics, on the other hand, do not 'believe' anything, not even that the truth cannot be found – perhaps somebody will find it some day. And when they employ their standard formulas, for example 'no more' (p than q) or 'I determine nothing', they do not 'believe' these statements; they merely state what appears to them. All in all, a real Sceptic is a man who like a historian merely reports what appears to him (*to phainomenon* – 14; 4). This applies to sensation as well. Of course a Sceptic accepts a sense impression *qua* sense impression; it is a fact that I, for example, am affected by 'white' (I am 'whitened'). But this is not something I 'believe'; it is not true or false, as is the case on the other hand with the perceptual judgement that 'this object is white' (13; *Adv. math*. VII 293; 344). Therefore it holds good for the most elementary sense situation as well as the most abstract discussion that the Sceptic never 'believes'; he merely reports that this or that appears so to him. This is of course the weak point in Scepticism of Sextus' type. One can ask whether there is any real difference between saying 'it appears to me that p' and saying 'I believe that p'.[2] Although the problem apparently bothers Sextus somewhat, he does 'believe' that he has solved it.

Epochē is a necessary precondition for *ataraxia*, or, couched in technical terms, one can only have an ethical criterion if one abandons an epistemological one; for whoever has an epistemological criterion must believe that something has or does not have real existence, and he must, according to Sextus, also believe that something objectively good or evil exists that can be known. The Sceptic, on the other hand, has the phenomenon as criterion, and this frees him from making objective value judgements. If the dogmatist has an accident, he will be doubly injured: by the misadventure itself and by the belief that it is evil by nature, whereas the Sceptic who merely allows things to happen gets off with half the pain; nor is he disturbed – a clear parallel to Epicurus' psychotherapy (Sext. Emp. *Hyp. Pyr*. I, 21; 29). But the sceptic does not merely sit idly by. He trusts to common sense and lives his ordinary human existence in safe, illusion-less calm. Just as he remains impervious to the philosophers' arid and meaningless subtleties, he remains untouched by absolute judgements of good and evil; he sticks to accepted customs (23) – a dangerous conformism?

To Sextus Scepticism consists in dissolving pseudo-problems; philosophy is a means, not a goal. In his main work he uses an image, which Wittgenstein made

---

2 This was of course also criticized in Antiquity, for example in the late Peripatetic Aristocles who wrote a refutation of Scepticism (cf. Aristocl. ap. Eus. *Praep. Ev*. XIV 18, 12).

famous – Sextus himself was perhaps inspired by Plato's *Symposium*: the Sceptic can use philosophical arguments as a ladder; when he has climbed up, he can throw away the ladder (*Adv. math*. VIII 481; cf. Plat. *Symp*. 211 C; Wittgenstein: *Tractatus* 6.54).

Ancient Scepticism has had a far-reaching *Wirkungsgeschichte*. Cicero has been studied in all ages and thereby – and through Augustine's criticism – Academic Scepticism became well known. Sextus became known in fifteenth-century Italy and was a main source of inspiration for Renaissance Scepticism (Montaigne, Charron). Here – and later in Gassendi, in the British empiricists, and even as late as Kant – again and again one comes upon standard examples, arguments and questions deriving from the Scepticism of Antiquity. The frame of reference may have changed, but one of the constant factors has been the relation between epistemological scepticism and moral scepticism.

30

GREECE AND ROME

——— •◦• ———

Towards the end of his life when Cicero (106–43 BC) wrote his work on the foundation of morals, the *De finibus*, he began the last book (Cic. *De fin.* V 1 ff.) with a recollection from his grand educational journey to Greece in his youth. He finds himself in Athens and with good friends he makes for the Academy. All the sites are permeated by the glorious past, and the great ancients appear to their mind's eye: Plato, Sophocles, Pericles and Demosthenes. Cicero's friend, the Epicurean Atticus, is also allowed to send a quiet thought to the outsider in the garden. This is an evocative picture on the verge of sentimentality and nostalgia. A Roman of Cicero's cast and social position was probably marked by a certain ambivalence: he had received his literary and philosophical education from the subjugated Greeks, but he also acknowledged his Roman heritage; as a citizen in a world-wide realm he was called to an active life in the service of the state and of civilization. A Greek, on the other hand, could only live in the past. Philosophy had become an eclectic, epigone philosophy; the great questions had been asked and the answers had been provided. The basic attitude was that one should not get lost in subtleties such as the debate between Stoics and Academics, but rather that all good forces – which is to say Stoics, Academics and Peripatetics, but not, of course, Epicureans – should join in cherishing common values.

Many Romans might of course be mentioned as mediators between Greece and Rome, among them the lonely Lucretius or the learned Varro. But Cicero was the principal actor in the cultural process of amalgamation that was to determine Europe's history ever afterwards. He had received a thorough and all-round philosophical education. He 'elected' to become an Academic and was close friends with his two teachers, Philo of Larissa (c.160–80 BC) who headed the Academy after Carneades' student Clitomachus and Antiochus of Ascalon (c.125–68 BC) who directed the Academy during Cicero's studies in Athens (cf. *Brut.* 306; 315; *Acad.* II 113).

Philo belonged to the Carneades tradition and disputed the possibility of certain knowledge; but the fact that nothing is certain does not mean that everything is equally uncertain – whether he went further than Carneades on this point cannot be ascertained (18; 32 ff.; Sext. Emp. *Hyp. Pyr.* I 235). Antiochus went considerably further.

Both considered themselves guardians of 'old' Platonism, as was typical of the time. But where Philo probably – like Carneades – considered himself heir to the questioning Socrates, Antiochus stood for a very far-reaching syncretism. He proclaimed a return to the 'old Academy': Socrates was the starting point for all true philosophy; there was no essential difference between Platonism, Aristotelianism and Stoicism; and teasingly Cicero called him a true-born Stoic (Cic. *Acad.* I 13 ff.; II 15 ff.; 132). Like everybody else he considered the criteria of truth and the determination of the good the main issues of philosophy (29), and his Stoicizing attitude appears for example in his claim – advocated in debate with Philo – that at least some sense impressions can be known as true (49 ff.; 11; 111). He concedes to Plato this much that perception itself is uncertain, but in his view of the formation of concepts and of the dependence of reason on perception he follows Stoic paradigms (I 30 ff.; II 30 ff.). The same imprecise eclecticism appears in the ethics. According to Antiochus the purpose of ethics is to perfect man. He prefers Aristotle and common sense to the orthodox Stoic concept of the absolute good, but is nevertheless utterly dependent on the basic Stoic scheme according to which the instinct for self-preservation is the point of departure for morals and on Stoic ideas of natural law (*De fin.* V 24 ff.; 65 ff.; *Acad.* II 131 ff.). Antiochus was no impressive thinker, but he was influential. When Cicero was young the Academy did not stand for any philosophical innovation; old problems were re-examined and diluted. But Cicero showed his philosophical common sense by sticking with Philo, the teacher of his youth; he could not accept Antiochus' compromises. His basic attitude is a Carneadean probabilism in unorthodox form, which does not claim to possess the truth but deliberates for and against with an aim to the reasonable and likely (64 ff.; 125 ff.). This attitude, which Cicero already voices in a youthful work on rhetoric (*De inv.* II 9 ff.), could of course also be called eclecticism; but it avoids muddling the philosophical concepts and makes possible an unbiased evaluation, free from systematic pretensions.

The cultural Hellenization of Rome had begun long before Cicero's time. The famous philosophical embassy in 155 BC was no isolated event. Just at the time when Greece was subjugated (168) and Rome's position as a world power was consolidated by the destruction of Carthage (146), it became important to the Roman elite to adopt a position vis-à-vis the increasing Greek influence. The elder Cato had received a Greek education but wanted to protect the special Roman character. The head of one of the most distinguished families, the prominent politician Scipio Africanus the Younger (c.185–29) – Cicero's great idol – advocated an accommodation of Greek and Roman ways and gathered a circle of Greek writers around him. In politics he represented Roman imperialism; it was he who left Carthage in ruins; he was the one to manage Roman policies in the East; he struck down dangerous resistance in Spain; on the home front he resisted Tiberius Gracchus' reform policies; and all in all there could be no doubt of his humanity. What he wanted from his Greek friends was – at least also – a moral and ideological legitimation of Rome's position as a super-power and of his own political views: the preservation of the traditional Roman constitution, especially the powerful position of the Senate, and thereby of the upper class. He got the wished-for assistance. Two Greeks in the Scipio circle are of special interest: the historian Polybius and the Stoic Panaetius.

Polybius (c.203–120) wrote a history of the world covering the period from c.220 to 145, i.e. from and including the second Punic war to and including the ruin of Carthage. Major parts of his work have been preserved. Thucydides was his great model, and his interest, like Thucydides', was in power politics and military confrontations. The new in his work was that in depicting Rome's expansion, he also depicted the history of the civilized world and – although otherwise without philosophical inclination – that he wrote on the basis of a universal theory of history. The question he asked was how it could come about in a mere fifty years or so that Rome became master of most of the civilized world. He had two answers. One was a theory of constitutional forms derived from a common Greek tradition – with roots back to Plato. Thus he operated with the three familiar 'good' constitutions – monarchy, aristocracy, democracy – and the three deviants – tyranny, dictatorship by the few, dictatorship by the many. He next assumed that a given constitution contains the seed of its own dissolution and that the development is decided by power and abuse of power in a steady cycle (Pol. VI 3 ff.). Every constitution, every people, and every state have their time, but from a universal perspective there is nothing new under the sun. His second answer was that the possibility exists for delaying – perhaps halting – the development. This can be done by means of the 'mixed constitution' – once again a familiar concept in Greek political thought – which in a stable and harmonious way combines the three good types of constitution. Such a stable constitution is in fact to be found in the natural evolution of Rome's constitution (11 ff.), and the good mixed constitution will reflect a stable relation between the classes of the people. Undoubtedly this theory pleased Scipio, and surely it was not unwelcome to him that the theory harbours moral undertones: the stability of a society depends on its morals; Rome is endangered if the ideals of her fathers – *mos maiorum* – are betrayed.

MIDDLE STOICISM

The moral ideals were provided by Panaetius (c.185–09), the founder of what has later been called Middle Stoicism. He introduced Stoicism to Rome in a form acceptable to the Roman upper class. We have practically no direct quotations left by him – the indirect main source is Cicero – but nevertheless it is reasonably clear what he stood for. The epistemological debate with the Academics, which had been going on for generations, was of no interest to him; it was Stoicism as a philosophy of life that occupied him, and he did as did Antiochus after him: he claimed a common Socratic point of departure for Stoicism, Platonism and Aristotelianism (cf. Cic. *De fin.* IV 79) concerning essentials. But the syncretism he formulated did not – as did Antiochus' – consist in a general levelling of views but in a practical philosophy with the main emphasis on ethics and political thought. This meant that some of the more radical and provocatory Stoic doctrines must be sacrificed. In physics he abandoned for example the theory of 'conflagration' and maintained – like Aristotle – that the world is eternal (Philo *De aet. mund.* 76). But the decisive was that he broke with the absolutist ethics of orthodox Stoicism; virtue was not the only thing of value; the 'external goods' were also – as in Aristotle – important. The sage does not live in out-and-out apathy; man has both emotions and intellect (cf. Diog. Laert. VII 128; Gell. XII 5; Cic. *De off.* I 101). This means that the very idea of 'the sage' is undermined and that ordinary human life cannot be dismissed as 'indifferent' (*adiaphoron*). It is characteristic that a main work – employed by Cicero – deals with 'duty' (*kathēkon*); what is of interest are rules for practical life, not the ideal sage's 'right action' (*katorthōma*, cf. *De fin.* IV 23).

When the ethical 'dualism' of the Stoa is abandoned or at least is pushed into the background, and when man first and foremost is considered a social creature, political problems arise that already had been latent in early Stoicism. All men are equal, and consequently the ideal must be a classless, anarchic society, as already in Zeno's *Politeia*. But this is indeed 'only' an ideal or utopian. Actually men live in specific societies with specific laws and constitutions, and it is one's duty to participate in this life in the specific society. What, then, should a Stoic do? What realistically can be striven for will often be a constitution with the stable balance, which is best guaranteed by the 'mixed constitution', but not even that is always possible. In principle a Stoic advocates the abolition of slavery, the emancipation of women, etc. But he must live in the society in which he is placed, and there he must try to realize the ideal as circumstances permit. What then is possible or expedient can of course be interpreted differently, as was indeed the case on Roman soil. One can trace Stoic influence in the second half of the second century both among 'democrats' and 'conservatives'; the democratic reform policies of the Gracchi – to Cicero mere demagogical bluster – aimed at a more equal distribution of land and were in all likelihood influenced by Stoicism (Plut. *Tib. Gracch.* 8). How the question looked from the conservative side can be seen in a passage in Cicero (Cic. *De off.* I 21), probably based on Panaetius, where we are told that although private property is not warranted by nature, it is still the inviolable foundation of existing society.

Panaetius was a 'right-wing Stoic', which is to say that he was persuaded that not only the power but also the moral responsibility for the stability of society should be vested in the upper class. On this basis he constructed a humanistic ideal of a gentleman. The 'magnanimous' (cf. Aristotle) is he who realizes nature's goal and deflects injustice; without regard to danger and adversity he pursues the moral ideal – thereby distinguishing himself from the mob, as Cicero reports his thinking (65 ff.). This ideal can only be realized by one who possesses the outer and inner – moral and intellectual – qualifications. At the same time, it is an ideal of the sterling personality who by serving the commonwealth brings his own nature into agreement with common nature, the noble and the proper.

Panaetius' student Posidonius (c.135–50 BC) headed an independent Stoic school at Rhodes. Cicero was his student during his grand tour to Greece and valued him highly. As usual he absorbed what he could without letting himself be trapped body and soul. While Panaetius was your man for practical philosophy, Posidonius was a theorist – and as such something of a loner attempting to combine science and Stoicism in one grand unity. Such an effort was a rarity in those days and his enormous oeuvre was comparable with respect to extent and variety of subjects to Democritus' and Aristotle's. Today he is only known from bits of fragments and more or less reliable reports in other authors – which for a while in this century caused him to be considered the *éminence grise* who conveniently might be responsible for all the ideas for which one lacked the original sires.

Posidonius must have had the devouring curiosity of an old natural philosopher. For a considerable time he stayed among the Celts and Teutons to conduct ethnographical studies; he travelled the length and breadth of the Mediterranean area and northern Africa in order to make observations in natural science. He studied history, ethnography, geography, geodesy, tides, earthquakes, mineralogy, mining, meteorology and astrology, apart, of course, from having opinions about logic, criteria of truth, ethics, fate and god. His work must have been a strange mixture of enormous collections of data and unbounded imagination. One grand vision inspired the whole: the thought of the world as a cohering, animated organism (Diog. Laert. VII 138 ff.) – an old Stoic idea with a background in Plato's *Timaeus*, which Posidonius seems to have provided with a commentary (cf. Sext. Emp. *Adv. math.* VII 93). His purpose was to demonstrate that *logos* was the working force in the whole universe, in the great and the small, in the development of the physical world, and in the history of mankind. This was a continuation of the early Stoic idea of 'cosmic sympathy', the coherence and cooperation between even the smallest phenomena and events that seemingly are temporally and spatially separate. The theory may be called vitalism, and 'life-force' was apparently a key concept; it is that spiritual force which at all levels of the world causes matter to assume more or less complex forms of unity (cf. Cic. *De nat. deor.* II 83 ff.; Sen. *Nat. quaest.* V ff.; Diod. Sic. II 51 ff.; Sext. Emp. *Adv. math.* IX 78 ff.).

The world is an organic whole, but there are hierarchical levels that depend on the degree to which matter has been pervaded by *logos*. Man is a microcosmos, an intermediate being between spirit and stuff. Affects and passions are expressions of man's dependence on matter and cannot – as in Chrysippus' intellectualistic view – be dismissed as 'wrong judgements' (Pos. frg. 150 a ff. Edelstein/Kidd, Galen). But through reason the soul is related to the divine *Logos* with which it is united after death in the ethereal regions of the universe (cf. Sext. Emp. *Adv. math.* IX 71 ff.; Cic. *Tusc. disp.* I 42 ff.). Both with respect to his 'realistic' psychology and his belief in the immortality of the soul Posidonius thus breaks with classical Stoicism and instead seeks his models in the Platonic tradition. In a wider perspective his *logos* doctrine and his hierarchical metaphysics have been seen as one among many sources of Neoplatonism. Like probably most of his contemporaries, Cicero was impressed with Posidonius' system, but most often he uses it only on solemn occasions.

CICERO

Marcus Tullius Cicero was no great original thinker, but his philosophical judgement was reliable and he was a genius as a mediator. He left his personal mark on the tradition he inherited, and this turned out to have far-reaching effects on the history of ideas. As a mediator he was no mere spokesman of a somewhat arid school philosophy.

By profession Cicero was not a philosopher; to him as to every Roman of the upper class, philosophy was synonymous with an all-round liberal education; what mattered was an active career as a lawyer and politician – two sides of the same coin. He lived during the last century of the Roman republic. This implies that Rome's position as a world power had long ago become an established fact but also a constant state of internal and external discord, social tensions, anarchy and civil wars in which those in power often could ignore the constitution (Marius, Sulla, Pompey, Caesar). What made the political machinery function were personal alliances between the leading families and individuals (*amicitia*: friendship in the political jargon) and the client system, which is to say the mutual dependency of the patron who provided legal protection and economic assistance and the client who delivered his vote in return. The sustaining factors were in other words favours and returns – in fact an advanced mafia system. Cicero had no objections to the system in and by itself – provided only that the constitution remain in force, the social classes be reconciled, and the leaders have the same moral habitus as in Scipio's golden age. Undoubtedly this was a short-sighted political ideal; but behind day-to-day politics, dimensions of a different kind were implicit.

Throughout his career Cicero sought to pursue his political ideals, as far as his abilities and temperament would allow, and it should not be overlooked that there is an intimate connection between his speeches and theoretical writings, between practice and theory – something he stresses himself (*De div*. II 7; *De nat. deor*. I 6; *De off*. I 3). He came from a wealthy family of the *equester ordo* (the knighthood class), which meant that to the finest families he was an upstart (*homo novus*). Nevertheless, his career as a lawyer and politician developed with surprising rapidity. By 63 BC he had become a consul, and in that capacity he 'revealed' and defeated the so-called Catiline conspiracy, a feat he himself never underrated. In effect Cicero was without influence for long periods – he possessed neither Pompeys' nor Caesar's statesman-like qualities, and the masked dictatorship was profoundly alien to him. Still, after the murder of Caesar (44), Cicero was once again to play a principal part in trying to restore the Senate's erstwhile authority. But he was killed during the purges carried out by the so-called Second Triumvirate. From Cicero's political activities and his correspondence, in which we can follow him from day to day, we come to know him as an emotional person often marked by indecision. But he also had political flair, and his modern critics have been inclined to overlook the fact that he died for his cause and that he was one of the few politicians of his day who in fact had ideals.

By and large Cicero's theoretical work belongs to two periods. During his politically inactive years he wrote his main work on rhetoric, the *De oratore* (55) and his works on political philosophy, the *De re publica* (54–1) and the *De legibus* (presumably only soon afterwards and perhaps unfinished). The philosophical work proper was written during an amazingly brief period during the last years of his life. First came two books, now lost – a consoling essay (the *Consolatio*) written by Cicero to himself on the death of his daughter Tullia, and the *Hortensius*, a call to philosophy, which had Aristotle's *Protrepticus* as its model and which many centuries later came to serve as Augustine's initiation in philosophy. Then, one after another, followed the other writings. To some extent they can be grouped systematically. The *Academica* presents the fundamental epistemological discussion. The main work on moral philosophy is the *De finibus bonorum et malorum* (On the Ends of Good and Evil); practical ethics is dealt with in the *Tusculanae disputationes*, which examines various subjects belonging to individual ethics; in the treaty on duties (the *De officiis*) Cicero discusses social ethics; in addition the brilliant small treatises on old age and friendship may be noted. The *De natura deorum* is the main work on the philosophy of religion; works on divination (the *De divinatione*) and on fate (the *De fato*) are related to it.

Cicero himself states that his purpose is not to present new views but rather to transfer Greek philosophy to Roman thought and to Latin – at once an ambitious and modest undertaking (cf., e.g. *De fin.* I 1 ff.) carried out with Cicero's stylistic mastery. One aspect of this was the creation of a Latin terminology of philosophy – which subsequently became the common property of Western thought. Here Cicero's guiding principle is the idiomatic and precise etymological translation (e.g. *poiotēs*: *qualitas*; *idea*: *species*; *phantasia*: *visum*; *katalēpsis*: *comprehensio*, cf. *Acad.* I 25; 30; 40 ff.; II 145). Another aspect is the use of Roman *exempla*; heroes from Rome's ancient history have under conditions of unimaginable deprivation and without the least hesitation performed noble deeds and saved their native country – thus in wondrous ways combining old Roman virtue (*virtus*) with the highest Greek ideals (cf. e.g. *De fin.* II 73). Cicero employs the dialogue form, and his interlocutors are for the most part noble Romans past or present – and readily furnished with heroic ancestry. The model, however, is not Plato but Aristotle's lost exoteric writings. This means that every person stands for one philosophical position, which is presented in the form of a lecture; then Cicero in most cases provides concluding comments. This is a form that excellently suits Cicero's purpose: to present *pro* and *contra* in a sceptical search for truth. Exceptions to this normal procedure are the *Tusculanae disputationes*, in which a teacher authoritatively answers questions from a student, and the *De officiis*, in which Cicero addresses his son Marcus directly; in practical ethics he can in fact speak more directly and didactically. Here it is not so much the Academic Sceptic suspending his judgement; rather, when Cicero speaks of his personal philosophy of life the basic mood is that of undogmatical Stoicism.

One can speak of three principal motifs in Cicero's view of life: his humanitarian ideal, his scepticism with respect to philosophical doctrines, and his Roman patriotism. The three motifs are of course interwoven throughout.

Humanitas is a Ciceronian concept that is inherited by all subsequent 'humanism' – in the Renaissance, in the Age of Enlightenment, and in our own time. Cicero did not invent the word, but he has given it a special content. Nor is it a word that he presents as a particularly revolutionary concept; it appears with a naturalness that imparts a special colouring to 'interesting' concepts. The precise meaning of the word is as difficult to delimit as the modern concept of 'humanity' – for the simple reason that the modern concept with all its over- and undertones is Ciceronian. The word applies not simply to man's 'nature' but to human dignity and culture – including both bookish learning and, in old-fashioned parlance, goodness of heart – to generosity and magnanimity (*liberalitas*), to piety (*pietas*), to considerateness, and to the natural exercise of congenital talents (cf. *De or.* II 72; 86; *Tusc. Disc.* V 66; *De off.* III 41; 47). All meanings point to 'the human' as having its purpose in itself. The word is opposed to what is mere duty and what is merely useful (cf. 30; 89) and is not directly used in connection with the theory *about* man – shared by Cicero – that all men are connected with each other in a community of rights and obligations (cf. I 50 ff.). However gladly Cicero would establish the ties with the old Roman paragons, it is difficult to make them 'humane'. Roman *virtus* consists in performing one's duty to the state, not in developing oneself as a person. Cicero himself stresses that it is not easy to combine old Roman *gravitas* with *humanitas* (*De leg.* III 1).

If Cicero's ideal – contrary to his intention – differs from the ancient Roman ideal, it also differs from the Greek. The Greek model for the concept of *humanitas* is Panaetius' ideal of personality, but *humanitas* is not a Greek concept. In the Greek one can say *philanthrōpia* – love of mankind – or *paideia* – education, but one cannot say 'humanity'. This is probably connected with the strong tendency in Greek moral thought to intellectualistic idealization: the focus is not on 'man' but on 'the wise'. What is interesting here is that Cicero also effortlessly can think in a Greek way about 'the wise' just as he would dearly like to think in both Greek and Roman ways about virtues and duties.

Cicero's ideal of humanity can, however, only be realized by a politically active upper class, by the independent aristocrat who as orator and politician combines his practical activity with good breeding, as Cicero depicts it in his main work on rhetoric, the *De oratore*. The ideal of *humanitas* is a practical ideal realized in act and speech. Speech is the noblest expression of man's nature; through speech one man influences another; and thought does not become the property of individual man until it is formulated – which is why form and content are tied to each other (cf. Cic. *De or.* I 33). But true rhetoric presupposes political liberty – *humanitas* and *libertas* cohere (30). Hence the good orator is identical with the good man (*vir bonus*) who combines lofty morality with psychological empathy and with the breeding and learning that are fitting for a civilized gentleman (II 85; I 68; 72). Cicero cannot accept the schism between philosophy and rhetoric that goes back to Plato and Aristotle on the one hand and to Isocrates on the other (30 ff.; III 72). To him Plato is an idol, but when, for example, he speaks of philosophy as the mother of all arts (I 91), it is actually Isocrates' view of philosophy as general education that lies at the base, and in searching for great Greek models, he mentions the outstanding rhetors from the times of liberty, Pericles and Demosthenes (III 71).

The relation between philosophy and rhetoric is the main theme in the *De oratore*, and the debate between the interlocutors first of all considers whether rhetoric is based on breeding and humanity or whether it is a technique and special discipline. Of course the rhetorical technique is examined – the classification of cases according to their kinds, the art of finding arguments (*inventio*), argumentation, disposition, form and style – but the technique is not the main object. Aristotle's *Rhetoric* is a manual on a practical discipline; Cicero writes about an attitude to life, and the interlocutors in his dialogue are prominent politicians who present and discuss experiences accumulated through their lifetime as leaders of the most powerful state in the world.

Of course Cicero's sceptical attitude appears first and foremost in the dialogues dealing with fundamental theoretical questions. Here the positions of the philosophical schools are summarized and discussed, and indeed these treatises are a main source for our knowledge of Hellenistic philosophy. In the preceding they have been used as sources for Epicureanism, Stoicism and Academic Scepticism, and hence only one question shall be asked here: does Cicero show independence with respect to his subject matter, and if so, to what degree? For a long time it was considered appropriate to answer in the negative. That is not the case today and for good reason. Cicero's independence as mediator and reporter can be seen especially in the *Academica*, the *De finibus*, the *De fato*, and his own position in an apt self-characterization (*De nat. deor.* I 12) in which he declares that he will not deny that something is true but deny the existence of any criterion of truth. But something can have such a degree of probability that one can conduct one's life according to it. With considerable consistency Cicero himself adhered to the line he lays down here. When he juxtaposes several positions, this is not a manifestation of philosophical paucity but of a philosophical programme. The dialogue form is well suited to asking the questions dialectically, and it is exploited in such a way that the real dilemma almost always becomes clear. The personal evaluation then appears indirectly from the ordering and more directly from the concluding comments – and a questioning, sceptical conclusion is indeed also a conclusion.

In the *Academica* and *De finibus* there is a consistent sceptical line. The *Academica* – the main epistemological work – sticks throughout to Philo in his debate with Antiochus; Cicero steers clear of the dominant eclecticism of his day in which all cats are grey. He emphasizes that we must choose between the Stoics and the Academics; both sides cannot be right (*Acad.* II 132). This view is found again in the *De finibus*, the work dealing with the foundations of morality, the determination of good and evil. The basic, common Hellenistic scheme is accepted – that the highest good consists in the perfection of man in agreement with nature. A presentation and a critique are provided of respectively Epicureanism (*De fin.* I–II), orthodox Stoicism (III–IV), and Antiochus' syncretism (V) – with the point that Antiochus can be used to criticize the Stoa, and Stoicism to criticize Antiochus. Once again the conclusion is that either one must maintain that virtue is the only thing needful or that the wise is not unconditionally happy, and that the 'external goods' belong with happiness (V 77 ff.).

Antiochus represents an untenable middle position; the Stoics are in a way consistent, but their theory is too rigoristic to be acceptable. To this extent the conclusion of the *De finibus* is sceptical, but it is a form of scepticism that makes it possible for Cicero to sound different chords in his practical ethics.

The explicit position in the philosophy of religion is, as stated in the beginning of the *De natura deorum* (I 11), also sceptical, and in the *De divinatione* and in the *De fato* divination and belief in fate are indeed unhesitatingly dismissed. But Cicero is clearly affected by Posidonius' thoughts of the cosmos as a unity governed by a divine providence (III 95; cf. *De div.* I 9) that in the end legitimates morals and human society. To this is added a third element: respect for transmitted religious ceremonies as social institutions and as expression of reverence for whatever we cannot rationally comprehend (cf. II 148; *De leg.* II 16). This is no convincing systematic whole; what are essential are probably the Roman's conservatism and the humanist's somewhat reserved undogmatic religiousness.

Cicero's theoretical scepticism permits an engagement in practical ethics and political philosophy. Man has the possibility of natural self-development; but this can only be successful with respect for others and in intercourse with others in agreement with 'virtue' and with reverence for the world order in which man himself is but an insignificant pawn. Here both Stoic and Academic elements are clearly involved, but what is crucial is how Cicero uses his sources as a humanist and as a Roman.

To translate the ideals into a guideline for everyday life is what he – at least also – understands by philosophy. In the *Tusculanae disputationes* (V 1 ff.) a justly famous laudation of philosophy as a basic moral position is to be found. The work is constructed as a dialogue between teacher (Cicero) and pupil, in which it is the teacher's task to refute a series of pessimistic theses about general human, concrete issues: death is an evil; pain the greatest evil; the wise can give himself over to worries; the wise is not above being affected; virtue is not sufficient for a happy life. Now, as these theses are refuted, it is evident that the result can be classified as practical Stoic morality. But the manner in which they are refuted is not unimportant. Two examples will illustrate the method. Death is not an evil, for either the soul is immortal and related to the divine (I 27 ff.) or it perishes with the body (82 ff.). Regardless of whether one might believe the former or the latter, death is no evil. The wise is above being affected, for either affects are an illusion or it is demeaning to give in to affects; the wise gives in to affects in neither case (IV 58 ff.). The practical, ethical appeal lies of course in the validity of the conclusion, even though one as a Sceptic cannot solve the constructed dilemma. This appeal has had a significant effect down through the centuries, and it is on it that the work should be judged. It is not a Stoic manifesto but an exploitation of Stoic thinking as a directive ideal.

The work on social ethics, the *De officiis*, and the works on theory of state, the *De re publica* and the *De legibus*, tie the link to the *De oratore*. The *De officiis* – Cicero's last philosophical work, written during the chaotic months after Caesar's death – has also had far-reaching effects, not least during the Enlightenment. The Greek model is Panaetius, as Cicero himself acknowledges (*De off.* I 6 ff.). The subject of the treatise is the concept of *officium*, duty or obligation – in other words, the Stoic concept of *kathēkon*, appropriate action. Cicero begins (7 ff.) by stressing that he does not intend to speak of the absolute moral concept of *katorthōma,* but of duty, the act for which rules can be provided. The principal Stoic distinction between the sage's right action and the everyday obligatory act thus fades into the background, and it is apparent that Cicero in contrast to classic Stoicism assigns an independent moral value to the obligatory acts. The schism between absolute morality and duty is replaced by the relation between the morally right (*honestum*) and the useful (*utile*) – as in Panaetius – and rightly considered, the purpose of the treatise is to show that these two concepts must converge (cf. III 20).

Virtue consists in an active rather than a contemplative life (cf. I 19), and nature herself has indicated the framework and purpose of an active human life – here the standard Stoic scheme is adhered to (11 ff.): the original instinct for self-preservation is developed into the care of one's fellow man and insight into the rational coherence of the world. But man's life is enacted in his society, and hence the good life consists in rational morality in a given society: human society is the commonwealth of all, although with strict observation of the decrees of civil law (51). Herein, of course, lies a number of problems: the relation between natural law and positive law, between rights and obligations, especially between property rights and the obligation to one's fellow man.

Of course one encounters in Cicero the thought of natural law in a Stoic formulation based on the idea of the commonwealth of all men by virtue of man's common possession, reason; natural law is both descriptive and prescriptive. The world follows a certain regular course, which obliges individual man; natural law bids us to do what is right and shun what is wrong. It is independent of time and place, and since it is in agreement with nature herself, it is inherent in man's nature (*natura/nata* – cf. *De re pub.* III 33; *Pro Milone* 4, 10). Cicero next transfers the relation between natural law and positive law to the concepts in Roman Law of *ius gentium* (international law) and *ius civile* (civil law), and this identification has been significant for the entire development of natural law, among other reasons because it had the effect that Roman Law in its later form was strongly influenced by basic Stoic thoughts (see p. 512). Civil law differs with different peoples, but it should reflect natural law (*De off.* III 69).

The relation between individual and society and between rights and obligations contains matter for conflicts – in modern terms the conflict between equality and liberty. Cicero can wholly subscribe to the Stoic command for one man to have an obligation to another (*cura*). But this can only come about in a state of law, and in a state of law the individual's rights as a private person must be unconditionally respected. This applies above all to the rights to hold property (cf. II 73; 85); if legally acquired rights are not protected, the result will be bondage, chaos and demagoguery – as witnessed during the unprincipled revolts of the Gracchi (72; 85). Furthermore, any society is in need of a firm structure and of leaders. But only he is a leader who has the right morality and who – in Plato's words – feels an obligation towards those whom he rules (I 85). Cicero goes quite far in his demands for consideration of the socially lowly, for example the slaves (cf. 41), but he does not wish to reform society, and in many respects his concept of freedom implies an elitist way of thinking. What is essential is a society in which everyone has the place he deserves and where justifiable interests are in balance (56). Undoubtedly Cicero follows Panaetius, but there are also clear connecting links back to Plato's *Laws* and to Aristotle. It can be seen that Cicero has but little sympathy with utopian Stoicism. It can also be seen that he does not perceive any decisive conflict between the Stoic concept of absolute equality and the Stoic call for human and social obligation, which to him implied human and social inequality.

As a whole, the *De officiis* deals with the free gentleman's obligations to society, to his equals, and to those below him. The elements that best warrant an optimal society with internal equilibrium are the traditional 'virtues': wisdom or knowledge of the true (*veri cognitio* 18 ff.), the sense of the human commonwealth that comprehends justice and benevolence (*iustitia* and *beneficentia*, 20 ff.), courage and *magnanimitas* (61 ff.), and *moderatio* (93 ff.). These virtues are the basis for the functioning of the state of law. They may conflict with each other (152; III 35 ff.), but if they are kept in proper balance, the outcome will be that there is no opposition between the morally right and the useful (*honestum* and *utile*) – which are the subjects of the last two books of the *De officiis*. The most important of these social virtues is the sense of concord (I 157), and hence the two concepts included in this sense, *iustitia* and *beneficentia*, are important. Justice partially consists in not harming anybody unless provoked by injustice, partially in exploiting the common for the common goal and the private for one's own ends. This definition unambiguously stresses the principle of the inviolability of the individual and the difference between the public and private sectors.

Still, justice is not enough. The second concept, comprising liberality, benevolence, and generosity, leads us directly to everyday Roman life. Characteristically, the main treatment of this subject is to be found in a passage concerning how the leader or the politician wins honours, respect and devotion (II 30 ff.), for to render services and good offices (*beneficia*) in the proper way is a useful form of unselfishness. Here the ideal of the client system is reflected. The true leader not only performs his duty (*officium*), but by dextrous generosity he acquires 'friends' who are personally bound to him. This way of thinking is really at loose ends in Stoicism but certainly not in the realities of Rome.

In the *De officiis* Cicero failed to make a stream-lined system out of his humanist ideal. Yet the great popularity of the work in later times is perhaps not least owing to the fact that here practical ethics is treated in a concrete, realistic context.

The *De officiis* deals with the moral foundations of the state and the *De re publica* with the state as an institution. Major parts of the latter work were rediscovered in 1819; until then only the end, *Scipio's Dream,* had been known. This work applies Greek theories to Roman affairs, and, as the most 'Roman' of Cicero's philosophical works, it is without doubt also the most original. The dramatic setting is c.130, and the principal character – Cicero's spokesman – is Scipio who appears as the ideal statesman personifying the best of ancient Rome, the good constitution and regard for inherited customs (*mos maiorum*). Cicero's main sources also belong to Scipio's circle – he himself mentions Polybius and Panaetius (*De re publ.* I 34). One might also mention Dicaearchus and, earlier, Aristotle and Plato. An essential background is of course the Stoic doctrine of natural law.

The work is clearly inspired by Plato's *Republic*, just as the *De legibus* corresponds with the *Laws*. Politicians should – as in Plato – be philosophers, but the concept of philosophy should of course be read in a Ciceronian rather than in a Platonic sense; all in all there are probably greater differences than similarities in Plato's and Cicero's states. Unlike Plato's, Cicero's state is no fictive, ideal paradigm elevated above time and place (cf. II 52); it is in no way a Stoic utopian state, but rather an idealized version of the actual Roman state. Hereby is implied that the philosopher-ruler above all must be an active politician and not – as in Plato – a philosopher who also has the duty to rule (cf. I 2).

A state, says Scipio, is constituted by a people (*res publica* = *res populi*), but a people is no mere haphazard group of men; it is rather a society based on common laws and the principle of usefulness, and it lies in man's innate nature to form societies. Cicero operates with the three types of constitution, monarchy, aristocracy, democracy and their deviants (35 ff.) and also with the transition from one form of constitution to another. In principle he follows Polybius' theory of cycles, but he is in fact more inspired by Plato's account of the gradual decay of the state (65 ff.), and, unlike Polybius, he is not very interested in abstract laws of the historical course of events; in his view of history the individual plays a more prominent part – it was for example an individual, Brutus, who changed the course of history by exiling Rome's last king who was only a king in title but in reality a tyrant (II 44 ff.). In other words, a development can be halted, and the people, or their representative, have the right to overthrow a ruler who does not act in the interest of the people. Among the 'good constitutions' monarchy is ideally the best – as also Plato and Aristotle believed –

but the danger that the king will become a tyrant is too great, and in fact the best and most stable constitution is therefore the mixed one (I 69 ff.). All are familiar tones. But it is worth noting that Cicero does not even think of the anarchic, Stoic utopian state.

The mixed constitution is not a remote ideal; it has been realized in Rome, to be sure not in Cicero's own confusing days, but probably in Scipio's and certainly in the early times of the Republic (II 52 ff.). The liberty of the people – the democratic element in the constitution – is ensured by the popular assembly. The senate has the aristocratic prerogatives and the consuls those of the king (cf. 56). It is Polybius' view, which Cicero here provides with flesh and bones. In the Roman constitution the various organs of power keep each other in check; but Cicero is not dissatisfied with the prevailing aristocratic dominance – it is the Senate that has the decisive influence, and it is probably only for the sake of the principle that he acknowledges the authority of the popular tribunes to cancel decisions by the Senate (cf. *De leg.* III 23 ff.). The ideal of the mixed constitution – which had been realized in the good old days – can be implemented in practical politics; Cicero's own practical guideline was from first to last the concord between the classes – *concordia ordinum* (cf., e.g. *In Cat.* IV 7, 15 ff.). But it presupposes two things: the good statesman and justice implying care for one's fellow man. The good statesman – a Scipio – can be called 'the governor of the state' (*rector*, *princeps* or *moderator rei publicae*; *De re pub.* II 51; cf. V 8 ff.). Yet this does not mean a dictator or sole ruler, but rather the statesman who within the framework of the constitution can ensure the welfare of the state because he possesses the moral qualities and authority which Cicero later described in the *De officiis*. Cicero plays on two strings: the institutional frame and that *vir bonus* who gains influence thanks to his character.

The basis of the constitutional state is justice and this in the final analysis means natural law, the law that is common to all, because all partake of reason. Cicero deals with natural law in the only fragmentarily preserved third book of the *De re publica* and in the first book of the *De legibus*. In the remainder of the *De legibus* – which perhaps is unfinished and in any case transmitted incompletely – Cicero wishes to show how the decrees of positive law can be deduced from natural law, and here, not unexpectedly, he finds agreement with the old Roman legal tradition (cf. *De leg.* II 23). In the *De re publica* the analysis of natural law (*De re pub.* III 33 ff.) effectively follows after a report of Carneades' arguments 'against justice' (8 ff.). Here as well Cicero transfers the ideals to the Roman reality. The ideal of the just society has been realized by Rome. It is the will of nature that the best rule and this legitimates for example the Roman conquests – for they are just wars fought to make amends for injustice and have led to greater happiness for the subjugated (34 ff.). A modern reader might find a certain discrepancy between ideal and reality. To Cicero it is rather a contrast between what Rome was and could become on the one hand, and on the other the Rome of his own time, ravaged by discord and civil war.

The last perspective in Cicero's thoughts on law is that the positive law to be found in Rome is derived from natural law, which in turn is an expression of the cosmic order. This occasions a cosmic vision – *Scipio's Dream* (*Somnium Scipionis*) – which concludes the *De re publica* (VI 9 ff.). Here Cicero exploits Posidonius, but this can only be done by imagery, and indeed Scipio's dream is a deliberate counterpiece to the final myth in Plato's *Republic*. Scipio dreams that his late father, the famous Aemilius Paulus, the conqueror of Greece, in a place far from earth is initiating him into the secrets of the universe. Earth is a small part of the whole universe, and yet it is the centre of the greater cosmic system, the eight celestial spheres. In this life man has his place on earth, but the soul is immortal, and whoever has performed pious and just deeds in the service of his country – like the great statesman – will posthumously be rewarded with eternal life in the heavens above (13 ff.). In this bombastic, pathetical vision Greek learning becomes part of Roman national pride; the national is united with the cosmic; and man's mini-world is seen as a reflection of the *macrocosmos*.

On the earthly level and in the given situation Cicero's visions were unrealistic. The civil wars ended with the emergence of Octavianus Augustus as *princeps* – but in a very different sense from that envisioned by Cicero. By then he himself had died for the ideals he believed in.

PART VI
LATE ANTIQUITY

31

IMPERIAL ROME

— •◆• —

In 31 BC Caesar's adopted son, Caesar Octavianus – upon whom a few years later was bestowed the honorific 'Augustus', the venerable – became the sole ruler of the Roman Realm. From then and until his death in 14 AD, he laid the groundwork for the Roman Empire; in reality Rome became a monarchy. Augustus was probably one of the most effective pragmatists in political history. Economically and militarily independent of the Senate, he dextrously arrogated the real power to himself while at the same time ostensibly protecting the old constitution and its institutions. By a combination of conservatism and reform politics he brought about social stability and order in the administration of the provinces – two of the fundamental problems during the last days of the Republic. First and foremost he provided the Roman Empire with internal and external peace – a peace that was to last for 200 years.

Augustus exploited a general wish for peace, and in his cultural politics he played on the intense Roman national pride. Cicero was not the only one who considered the old noble Romans ideal figures. To the Romans history had more direct significance for the present than it did to the Greeks. The – idealized – past was a moral *exemplum*; the great ones of the past had lived so that the present could perfect Rome's predestined call. These thoughts found expression in the literature of the day – Livy, Horace and above all Virgil, the national poet – and Augustus was a patron of literature with a ready eye to the importance of the myth of state in daily politics.

The line of succession was not secured constitutionally, however. Augustus had seen to it that the imperial dignity would descend in his own family, but intrigues at court and murders were the order of the day in that anything but happy family, and Augustus' provision ceased with Nero's death (68 AD). Then followed the Flavian dynasty with a number of extraordinarily able rulers ('the good Emperors'), where the Emperor secured the succession by adopting his successor. This period lasted until the death of Marcus Aurelius Antoninus (180); thereupon it became clear how powerful the army was. Different units of the army proclaimed their own emperors ('the Soldier Emperors'); in quick succession emperors were overthrown, and only a few had a modicum of political format.

The political development corresponds to the economic and social ones. The first two centuries or so were marked by economic progress – not least in the provinces. But in the long run it did not last. The more profound causes of 'the decline and fall of the Roman Empire' – and thereby of the fall of the ancient world – probably cannot be fully accounted for, but the symptoms – at least in the West – are clear: inflation and partial transition to a natural economy, social and ethnic tensions, internal discord, external wars – against 'the Barbarians' – and a steadily increasing economic decentralization, which the imperial bureaucracy by and by could not withstand. During the last centuries of the Empire the major landed estates became self-supplying and thus increasingly independent administrative units – the basis for the medieval feudal system. Towards the end of the third and the beginning of the fourth century Diocletian and Constantine succeeded in retarding but not in stopping this development. At the same time contrasts between east and west became apparent. The eastern parts of the Empire were and were to remain marked by Greek language and culture; in the west the upper class was as a rule bilingual, but the lower classes were not, and gradually the cultural unity that characterized the early centuries faded into the background. Furthermore, the western provinces in particular suffered from economic stagnation and from 'Barbarian' incursions. In 395 the Realm was divided. In 476 the Western Empire disintegrated in the course of the great migrations; 'Antiquity' was replaced by 'the Middle Ages'. The Eastern Empire, on the other hand, continued until the Fall of Constantinople in 1453. Nevertheless, it was a Christian Roman Realm that disintegrated in 476 and a Christian Roman Realm that was destroyed in 1453.

Augustus provided the basis for prosperity and stability but not for liberty. During the good years many may not have felt this a major deprivation, but as living conditions worsened, more and more sought inner freedom as a substitute for the loss of the external one. Philosophy and literary and aesthetic studies could only satisfy the few, and official religion was something external, an official institution that could not meet more profound needs. However, many found their place in the Oriental mystery cults, where all were equal before the divine and where all could be united in their yearning for release and unification with the divinity. Especially important were the Egyptian cults of Isis and Osiris and the Persian Mithraic cult. Even though the mysteries have no philosophical contents, mystical piety and experiences were combined with elements from Greek philosophy, especially Platonism, in the so-called Gnostic movements. It holds true in general that as times gradually grew more harsh, pessimism and the urge to escape this world increased; the period from the second to the fourth century has justly been called 'an age of anxiety' (E.R. Dodds). Frustration and a general sense of absurdity and alienation probably characterize this age more than any other in Western history – including our own. This was the period during which Christianity became a world religion by degrees.

Philosophy had a much smaller public than the new religious movements. The first two centuries of the Empire cannot boast any real philosophical innovation. The major philosophical systems had been transmitted from classical and Hellenistic times; they were first and foremost considered as different forms of philosophies of life, as different 'lives' – which among other things means that philosophy 'competed' with religion; and outside the learned circles the more theoretical questions were probably thought to be more or less obsolete. In this spirit the satirist Lucian (second century AD) wrote a brilliant caricature of the school philosophies in a dialogue in which assorted philosophical 'lives' are offered at auction – most of them go for very little. To this should be added that the borderline between philosophy and generally edifying writing is blurred; philosophers and lay preachers were working side by side. The ancient confrontation of philosophy with rhetoric had also been softened – among other things of course for political reasons. Rhetorical writing during empirical times – often collectively called 'the second Sophistic' – consisted in part in a purely formal technique of declamation, in part in the use of the rhetorical form to communicate an edifying message. Thus the Cynic ideal of life was popularized by Dion of Prusa (born c.40 AD). A characteristic example of superstition and escapism in the average man in late Antiquity are the legends concerning the Pythagorean moralist and worker of miracles, Apollonius of Tyana, later considered a pagan 'saint'.

Nevertheless, the serious philosophical tradition still persisted, and especially Stoicism could boast of philosophers with considerable general appeal. The Epicureanism and Scepticism of the times followed the patterns laid down in Hellenistic times – and hence they are treated in that context in the present work. Aristotelianism stuck in essentials to the esoteric paths; the two traditions that characterize the period are Stoicism and Platonism, which were both, towards the end of the period, absorbed in Neoplatonism; but during the first two centuries each had its own face – the three great Stoics of the Empire, Seneca, Epictetus and Marcus Aurelius gave the Stoic ideal of man a special form of enduring importance; Platonism transmitted a metaphysical tradition, the importance of which was at least as far-reaching.

There were, naturally, significant similarities between the two currents. Posidonius and Antiochus had not lived in vain, and the doctrinal differences were perhaps less important than the difference in attitude. A Stoic and a Platonist share the conviction that man is part of the universe, that the human microcosmos reflects the greater order. The difference consists first and foremost in the Stoic's denial of a higher transcendent reality; if man lives in accordance with his own reason, he also lives in accordance with nature as a whole. The Platonist, on the other hand, assumes a hierarchical order; the world is not what it immediately seems to be; man finds himself in finding a higher reality. In contrast to Stoicism, this brings Platonism into close contact with the religious currents of the times. Hence there are differing strands in the Platonism of the Empire. There is an esoteric Platonism; it can be a learned one, or it can degenerate into rather barren schematics; but in any case it preserves the outlines of a system. In many ways this tradition is interwoven with the so-called Neopythagoreanism in which the religious dimension none the less is more prevalent. Plutarch, an independent Platonist, has affiliations with the school tradition. Philo of Alexandria – at one and the same time an isolated figure and yet typical of the time – unites Jewish religion with Platonism, in part also with Stoicism. Mention should finally be made of Platonic influence on Gnosticism – and on Christianity.

LATE STOICISM

Seneca was a prime minister and Epictetus was born as a slave; Marcus Aurelius was the Emperor. Rank and position were not important in Stoicism, but the sage's relation to society must necessarily play a decisive role – not only because Seneca and Marcus Aurelius were placed at the centre of power. It is not surprising that the Empire Stoics did not directly continue the middle Stoa, which indeed was intimately connected with the political ideals of the last phase of the Republic. The mixed constitution had become precisely as utopian as Zeno's *Politeia*, and in early Stoicism it was indeed also a substitute for the ideal. The events of the latter years of the Republic could only be used in a romantic worship of the champion of liberty who uncompromisingly fought the tyrant – examples: Cato the Younger who opposed Caesar and Brutus who murdered him.

Instead the return was to the early Stoa. The Empire Stoics did not at any time break with the theoretical foundation laid down by Zeno and Chrysippus. But epistemology and logic, for example, were not the main issues; it was the moral view of Stoicism that individual man should find himself in accordance with reason. But early Stoic orthodoxy also implied that the individual should participate in society if nothing prevented him (cf. Diog. Laert. VII 121), and it is an essential feature of Stoicism that one should be able to adjust to changed political circumstances without compromising oneself. The Empire was a given reality that could not be altered, but already in early Stoicism the just monarchy was considered an acceptable – although not ideal – form of government (cf. 131). Hence the task was, as far as was feasible, to contribute to the monarchy's having as humane a content as possible. It was only when this was impossible that the Stoic was allowed to withdraw to 'the inner man'; in given circumstances suicide was a permissible last way out. There are traces of Stoic ideology not only in the everyday politics in the days of the Republic but also during the Empire – and this goes not only for Seneca and Marcus Aurelius. In the first century AD there was among senators a 'Stoic opposition' to imperial tyrants; it did not consist of armed revolt but of passive resistance and disobedience, and at times it markedly bothered the despot (cf., e.g. Tac. *Ann.* XIV 12; XVI 21 ff.).

But to participate in social life is after all secondary in relation to the only decisive, the need for man to develop himself. In moral philosophy the Stoics of the Empire do not break with the old dogmas either, but in them the Stoic ideal of man is nevertheless given new dimensions and new depth. Each in his own way, the three great ones contribute their part: Seneca by analyzing the human will in the fight with affects and passions; Epictetus by stressing human freedom; and Marcus Aurelius with his reflections on the agreement between human and cosmic reason.

Lucius Annaeus Seneca (4 BC–65 AD) – 'the humanist at the court of Nero' – was born in Spain and came from a wealthy family of the equestrian order. He became the teacher of Nero, the future Emperor; when Nero at the age of seventeen did become Emperor, Seneca became his 'prime minister' – which is to say that he was accorded a role that has not been the lot of many philosophers down through history and that he was faced with the greatest challenge a Stoic could receive: to govern a world-wide realm. He accepted the challenge – as was a Stoic's duty – and subsequently his career went completely according to the book. During approximately the first five years of

Nero's rule he had the opportunity to exercise a beneficial influence, and these were notoriously good years marked by humane government. But Nero grew to become almost the cruel despot personified, intrigue and murder flourished, and for a while Seneca had to balance and perhaps share the responsibility for some of the misdeeds; but no longer able to influence events, he sought – in vain – to obtain his dismissal 'in grace'. *De facto* he did retire, but gradually the situation came so much to the head that Nero ordered him to commit suicide. Seneca obeyed. He did what a Stoic must do: assume responsibility, 'stand firm with shouts or silence' (Sen. *De tranq. an.* IV 6), and end one's life when all paths are closed.

One might think that thereby Seneca attained the status of a Stoic saint. That is far from the case. Already his contemporaries accused him of hypocrisy – he preached independence of external goods but was himself enormously wealthy. And in modern times it has often caused deep indignation that Seneca, the moral preacher, dirtied his hands by committing himself to the corrupt court and the depraved Emperor. Why did he simply not quit? Seneca has indirectly answered the first indictment (*De vit. beat.* XVI 1 ff.): he is no sage but just an ordinary man, and besides it is the inner attitude that is decisive, not whether one happens to be rich or poor; it is a proper Stoic reply, correct as far as it goes. The second indictment is the more surprising; it is often voiced by learned men who fail to understand that the moral purity of the writing desk could not be directly transferred to the Court of Nero. Would it have been morally better if Seneca had failed to explore the possibilities he did in fact have?

A commentary on Seneca's attitude is to be found in a treatise entitled *On Clemency* – the *De Clementia*. It was written for a very young Nero, presumably soon after his enthronement. Learned or naïve readers have rich opportunities to wax indignant; seemingly there is no end to the virtues possessed by the neophyte Emperor. But a closer reading will show something different: apparently the young man is in need of good advice anyway, and there is evident worry behind the picture outlined of the cruel ruler. Seneca exploited – courageously? – the possibilities available to him to address His Imperial Majesty. He wants, he says (*De clem.* I 1, 1), to hold up a mirror to Nero – this is the first 'mirror for princes' – and then follows all the flattery. What Seneca in fact does is to show Nero a picture of the ideal prince that Nero ought to be. In Seneca's view the good monarchy is based on nature (cf. *Ep. mor.* 90, 4 ff.). The good prince heeds nature's law and is distinguished from the tyrant by his clemency; the cruel prince neglects the norms of nature and becomes a prisoner of his own abuse of power (*De clem.* I 19, 1; 3, 3; 11, 4; 13, 2). The good king is the soul of the state, the state his body, and he is the serf of the state (5, 1; 8, 1) – as is the philosopher in Plato's *Republic*.

After all, the relation to the monarch is only a special case – although it is of course of urgent interest to Seneca personally. It is important that the monarch rule the state with clemency but more important how the individual rules himself and lives with others. Whoever does ill by himself breaks the law of nature, just as does the cruel king. Considering the political realities, it is understandable that no social ethics is to be found in Seneca corresponding to Cicero's *De officiis*. His ethics moves in the sphere of private life – the relation to family, friends and social circle – or confines itself to the quite general, the relation to other people regardless of social position. Ethics may benefit from practical rules, but only if the moral act is founded on inner attitude. On the other hand, an abstract categorical imperative is worth little unless related to the particular situation and the particular person here and now (cf. *Ep. mor.* 94; 95; *De ben.* II 16, 1). Within this ethics the old Stoic distinction between *kathēkon* and *katorthōma* fades away; and compared to the one decisive issue, outward knowledge or useless erudition must be rejected (cf. *Ep. mor.* 88, 1; *De ben.* VII 1, 4). Seneca himself cultivated natural philosophy in the manner of Posidonius, but in itself scholarship has no purpose.

What is the most important of all? To have gained the greatest victory of all, the victory over one's own faults – many have conquered cities, few themselves – to rise above the threats and promises of chance, to arm oneself against misfortune, to meet prosperity and adversity head on, and not to strive for the good that someone else must yield (*Quaest. nat.* III, praef., 10 ff.).

In abbreviated form this is one of Seneca's formulations. It is orthodox Stoicism with the focus on individual man's 'victory over himself' – the man who is harmed but unbowed (*De const. sap.* III 3). It may be read as a programme that was realized in Seneca's considerable oeuvre, which regardless of genre is marked by a rhetorical, sometimes turgid, long drawn-out style, interspersed with well-turned epigrammatic points and antitheses with a direct emotional appeal. A major portion of his work is – misleadingly – called dialogues; some are 'consolations'; many are diatribes – a popular genre among Cynics and Stoics and consisting of a personally formed, rhetorical address to a named or fictive addressee who can ask questions or object. The contents are virtues and vices and general conditions of life – for example providence, firmness of mind, the brevity of life, clemency, the happy life, peace of mind, beneficent acts. Next to these moral essays there are the *Moral Letters*, perhaps Seneca's main work, a treatise on natural philosophy (*Quaestiones naturales*), and a long series of tragedies. Regardless of form, genre, and subject matter, questions of moral philosophy are the sustaining element in the whole oeuvre.

Man is to raise himself above chance or *Fortuna*, which means to make himself independent of external conditions. As a good Stoic Seneca of course knows that rightly considered nothing occurs by chance – everything occurs according to the decree of providence (*providentia*) or fate (*fatum*), and to that extent there is no divergence between chance or fate (*De ben.* IV 8, 3; 7, 2). But he is not interested in the theoretical problem in early Stoicism of how free will relates to fate; what does interest him is that *Fortuna* is an expression of man's understanding of the world as a series of fortunate or unfortunate accidental events which one cannot influence (cf. *Ep. mor.* 107, 7). What matters is the attitude to external events, and this lies within man's power; good and evil are inherent in the inner man – and whoever is tried by *Fortuna* is tried in order to grow in firmness and justice (*De prov.* III 4 and *passim*).

Man is only seemingly at the mercy of *Fortuna*; he is likewise only seemingly at the mercy of the affects, the destructive forces within himself. According to early Stoicism affects are 'wrong judgements'. By nature man is disposed to reason and hence lives in agreement with nature, provided that reason permeate all conscious manifestations of life. By nature the human soul is therefore a unity; but this unity is disrupted if reason is perverted. On this Seneca constructs a very differentiated psychology which in its basic view is optimistic: by nature man is good; to live a happy life is therefore really quite simple, but most men pursue the far more difficult path of destroying the natural psychic harmony (*De ira* II 13). The possibility of self-destruction is available to men, but not to animals which are not equipped with reason (I 3, 4); therefore man lives life with risks that are unknown to animals. Immediate impressions and feelings are automatic, but an affect such as anger is not an immediate impulse; it implies the 'assent' of the soul, but 'assent' implies both will and reason (II 1, 1 ff.); by virtue of man's having both free will and reason he is responsible for his own life. To Seneca the battle is not between reason and emotion but between the natural self on the one hand and perverted reason and perverted emotion, the affects, on the other.

Nothing is more easy and nothing more difficult than being oneself – to be 'sage' as the old terminology has it. Most men lack the courage to be themselves. They succumb to *Fortuna* and the affects; they construct defence works and enclose themselves in a pseudo-world; they repress their desires so that they are turned inwards; they are in steady flight from themselves, as Lucretius said (*De tranq. an.* II 10; 14). Whoever is in conflict with himself lives a life of tedium and nausea (*taedium, nausea* – I 17 ff.); he pursues an inclination not his own, lets himself be led by false hopes, and his realization of his own self is thwarted. The difficult – and simple – is to have the peace of mind that rests in itself, to be friends with one's self, to be kindly disposed towards one's self, or to lay claim to one's self (cf. *De vit. beat.* II 3; *De tranq. an.* II 4; *Ep. mor.* 1, 1). Seneca depicts the tyranny of 'the affects' with gaudy colours in his tragedies that are often called gory. They follow the traditional myths, but the subject is not of gods who treat men badly, nor – as in Classical French tragedy – of heroes who pursue virtue and duty and fight against their own inclinations. In Seneca's tragedies there are no heroes. They deal with the 'pure' affects, with self-consuming passions and self-delusion leading to cruelty.

Seneca's psychology does, to be sure, lie within the framework marked out by the early Stoa, but his analysis of inner conflicts and repressions is an innovation, and it is strikingly modern. It is a psychological, individual ethics appealing to everybody. Each man has responsibility for himself and for all; a slave is as much a human being as anybody else (cf. *De ben.* III 28, 1). Hence, when Seneca speaks of the mob, there is no social disdain. He is thinking of the difference between whoever is himself and the many who behave as the wind blows (cf. *De vit. beat.* II 1 ff.). All have equal possibilities – what makes you good depends on yourself (*Ep. mor.* 80, 3) – and the decisive factors are the inner man, his attitude, and his good will (*De ben.* I 6, 1).

The good will – choice and assent – is of course also a main point in early Stoicism, but hardly anybody before Seneca had to the same degree considered will as a constitutive element in the human psyche. Will (*voluntas*) is not something between deliberation and act; one does not begin to will; one wills or one does not will (cf. *Ep. mor.* 37, 5); but one cannot become good unless one wills and wills wholeheartedly. Will cannot be taught – more likely it is will that determines intellect rather than the other way around (80, 4; 81, 13; 71, 36 ff.).

But the good will is connected with self-consciousness, conscience or *conscientia*, once again a psychological moral concept that Seneca stresses more than anybody before him. The tyrant is tormented by bad conscience that compels him into a vicious circle (cf. *De clem.* I 13, 3; *Ep. mor.* 97, 15); the good act, on the other hand, has no other reward than the good conscience (*De ben.* II 33, 3; IV 12, 4). One side of the concept of *conscientia* is self-consciousness and awareness of one's own acts – Seneca recommends that every evening one ought to ask oneself how much of one's badness one has rid oneself of and how many of one's vices one has resisted during the day (*De ira* III 36, 1 ff.; *Ep. mor.* 80, 10). This way of sitting in judgement on oneself could of course quite easily lead to self-centredness and narcissism – if the concept did not have another side as well: only he has a clean conscience who is in harmony with himself, and if one is in harmony with oneself, one is also in harmony with one's neighbour.

Seneca's individualistic ethics does in fact immediately imply a relation to one's fellow man. His humanitarian ideal differs from Cicero's in not concerning the 'educated' man well established in society but in concerning any human being in relation to any other. The view of benefactions (*beneficia*) and magnanimity demonstrates clearly that Seneca is not bound to the ancient Roman principle of favours given and received. A benefaction is exclusively performed in the interest of the recipient (*De ben.* IV 14, 2; *Ep. mor.* 81, 32); the magnanimous is he who benefits others, and humanity is caring for all one's fellow men (*De ben.* III 15, 4; *Ep. mor.* 88, 30). Seneca draws far-reaching consequences from the old Stoic idea of the fellowship of mankind (*societas* – cf. *De ben.* IV 18, 2). In one of his epistles he asks how we are to relate ourselves to others (*Ep. mor.* 95, 51 ff.). The negative, not to harm, is a modest demand. We are, says he, to extend a hand to the ship-wrecked sailor, point out the right way to the man who is lost, and share our bread with the hungry. Why? Because we are limbs of the greater body of the world, because nature has related us to one another, because it has inculcated love for one another as well as a need of fellowship in us, because it is nature's decree that it is a greater misfortune to do harm than to be harmed. Seneca concludes with a well-known quotation (from Terence, Ter. *Heaut.* 77): I am a man; I consider nothing human alien to me. The tenor of this and similar passages lies close to the New Testament, and hence it is not surprising that Seneca's Stoicism in later times could be understood as Christian.

Epictetus (55–135) came from Asia Minor and was a native speaker of Greek. He lectured, first in Rome and later – when the Emperor Domitian banished all philosophers – in Greece. Like his teacher, the popularizing Stoic philosopher Musonius Rufus, he used the oral diatribe form, which is to say that he did not – as did Seneca – develop the diatribe into literary art. He wrote nothing, but in straightforward language he addressed himself to laymen and students. We know several of his 'lectures' through presumably very reliable – possibly stenographic – reports by the historian Flavius Arrianus who also was the author of a preserved compendium of *The Discourses*, known as Epictetus' *Enchiridion* or *Manual*. *The Discourses* is by far the better source – not only because it is the more copious but because it reproduces Epitectus' form exactly.

Epictetus was a slave – subsequently freed – and it is surely no accident that all his lectures deal with the one concept of freedom. It is of course also a main concept for Seneca, but while Seneca's concern is with what the harmonious person frees himself from, it is crucial to Epictetus to understand the very fact that man is a free creature – whether or not he is outwardly free or a slave. Although his principal aim is the moral appeal to ordinary people with everyday problems, he accordingly – to a higher degree than Seneca – takes his point of departure in the early Stoa's ideas of what it is that lies 'in our power'. This does not mean that he engages in technical deliberations on the relation between 'determinism' and 'indeterminism' – in that he probably sees no problem; rather he sticks to the ancient connection between epistemology and morals. While Seneca arrives at a significant understanding of the human personality, Epictetus concerns himself with the human act itself.

Human freedom is owing to the fact that man by virtue of his reason is the only being who is conscious of the world and of himself and interprets the world and himself. Many activities are simple and object-directed but do not have themselves as objects; but reason can look upon itself and reflect backwards on itself as well as consider everything that lies outside itself – grammar tells us how to write a letter; yet, only reason can tell us whether we should write a letter to a friend (Epict. *Diss.* I 1,1 ff.). In the same way reason turns to the impressions we receive from the outside. We sense immediately – receive *phantasiai* – but it is reason that interprets or 'uses' what we receive. We also immediately have concepts such as good or evil (12; 22, 6 ff.). This 'use' of impressions and concepts is what frees man; it is what 'lies in our power' (1, 1 ff.; *Ench.* I 5). Everything else – not only external events and external 'goods' but man's own body – is 'alien' and of no concern to us. But our interpretation is not neutral; every interpretation is really a moral one; I have an opinion, I take a position, and I act. Now, there are several 'opinions' about for example the good, but the very notion of *the* good implies that there is one right norm or guideline (*Diss.* II 11, 12 ff.; cf. III 9, 1 ff.). Freedom rests on this norm, and a direct line runs from the impression that simply is present to the proper use of the impression and thereby to the freedom which consists in self-respect, faithfulness, and moral integrity and which precludes affects, pain, fear and confusion (IV 3, 7). The path runs from the 'alien' and the external to the inner man and the whole man. You must be one man, good or bad; you must choose between the outer and the inner (III 15, 13). He then is free who acts as he wills, unfettered by compulsion; whoever in an inner sense is a slave is prevented by what is alien, by desire or fear – all want what is right, but the unfree man does not realize it. On the other hand, 'to act as one will' means to know the right that one truly wills (cf. IV 1, 1 f.).

In other words, cognition, action and morality belong to each other. But so do cognition and will. That was the case in early Stoicism too; but, like Seneca, Epictetus stresses the element of will in human activity. To Seneca man is constituted by *voluntas* and *conscientia*. Epictetus places the main emphasis on the right choice. Here he has recourse to the Aristotelian designation for the right choice, *proairesis* – apparently because he finds the orthodox Stoic concept of *synkatathesis* too narrow. *Proairesis* is simply man's noblest characteristic (II 10, 1 ff.). On the one hand it is an intellectualistic concept – the right choice is as in the early Stoa the right judgement. On the other hand, the concept is also a moral and voluntaristic one. Only the right man makes the right choice from the right will. He does not let the external or alien decide but uses it as 'matter', which is to say that he chooses the thing, the thing does not choose him (I 29, 1 ff.; II 15, 1 ff.).

On many points Epictetus is closer to the early Stoa than Seneca – even though his focus may differ. But in one respect he chooses his own path entirely. That is in his religious feeling. When Epictetus speaks of man as a 'fragment' of god (II 8, 1 ff.) it is – superficially seen – orthodox language. But he goes much farther than the early Stoics who regarded religion as a symbolic expression of the philosophical truth. Epictetus' god is a personal god and no mere personification of a theological, pantheistic principle; but he shows no inclination to theoretical deliberations on the relation between god's transcendence and immanence. In proper conformance with Stoic thought he produces the 'physico-teleological' proof: we can infer god's existence from the expediency of the world. But this god is a god of creation; he has bestowed the world and life on us, and when we perceive the coherence of the world, we should be grateful and praise him (I 6, 1 ff.; 16, 7; 15 ff.). God has granted you life, he has granted you your own self to care for (II 8,22 ff.), and hence you are to observe god's will on your way through life (IV 1, 98 ff.; 7, 17 ff.; II 16, 42 ff.).

Morality is when all comes to all founded on this personal concept of god. Love of one's neighbour is a commandment – not so much because of the greater fellowship of mankind as because all men are created by god: your brother is descended from Zeus (I 15, 3). What god has given in our care is what 'lies in our power'. What we have in our power is to suffer injustice – but not to instruct. What some other man does with himself is not your affair; no man is the master of another (29, 60).

Seneca's ethics comes near to Christianity. Epictetus' does so too, but so does his concept of god, which underlies the ethics.

In many respects one encounters in Marcus Aurelius (AD 121–80, emperor 161–80) the same view of man as in Epictetus whom he regarded highly. But where the basic mood in Epictetus is one of gratitude for life, Aurelius is marked by resignation. 'Every morning when you wake up', says he (Marc. Aur. II 1), 'you are to tell yourself: today I shall meet officious, ungrateful, brutal, deceitful, and selfish people'. But, he continues, their evilness is due to ignorance. I have realized that the good consists in virtue, and therefore they cannot harm me; we are in the world to work together, and to oppose each other is to oppose nature.

This is the Stoic Emperor speaking. He was the last of the so-called good emperors, a Stoic wise man whom fate had given a heavy responsibility, disposed as he was to a contemplative life, though forced into an active one. Everything indicates that he did what was in his power to realize the Stoic ideal ruler, but he was to feel the need of considering the external world indifferent. The economy of the vast realm was in poor shape, there were incessant wars at the borders, and Marcus Aurelius was constantly forced to be on a war footing. In idle hours during wars against 'the Barbarians' in the Danube region – and without thought of publication – he wrote some reflections in Greek *to himself*, which show his strength of character, his humanity, his sense of duty – and his *Weltschmerz*. We live but for a little while, says he (V 33; cf. II 17); what is valued in life is empty, rotten and petty – small dogs biting each other; small children quarrelling and laughing, although they will soon cry. Fidelity and strength of character, justice and truth have long ago fled to Olympus from the wide earth (quote from Hes. *Op*. 197). What else should we do but praise the gods, help mankind and forbear? In different words (Marc. Aur. VI 10): either a mishmash of atoms entangled in each other or unity, order and providence; if the latter, I stand firm in reverence and derive my courage from the power that governs. Nobody can doubt that Marcus Aurelius stood firm.

Be careful not to *act* the Emperor, he admonishes himself (VI 30). To *be* Emperor means to assimilate oneself to the notion of a society based on equality before the law, freedom of speech, and a monarchy that above all respects the liberty of the subjects (I 14). No topical, political comments are to be found in Marcus Aurelius, but this is none the less a political programme resting on a general view of the world. Nature has destined man for a commonwealth, because all in common partake of reason, and men are born to help each other – even though they are in need of instruction or forgiveness (VII 55; VIII 7; 59; V 30). When Marcus Aurelius speaks of a 'commonwealth' he uses an expression that might as well be reproduced as 'society' (*koinotēs* – *societas* would be the Latin equivalent). He also has recourse to the old Stoic expression of the world as a 'common city', the highest city of which all other cities partake (III 11; IV 3) – of himself he says that he is a citizen in Rome and a citizen of the world (VI 44). The world is one, even though it appears as a plurality, and in its greater totality every man has his place in the common task, not only as a part but as a limb of the greater common body (XII 3; VII 13; cf. VI 42).

The individual is his own master; he harvests the fruits of his own deeds, but his soul passes through the whole world and penetrates into infinite eternity (XI 1). He may contribute to the whole if he is himself, i.e. if he recognizes that the leading part of the soul (*to hēgemonikon*) is autonomous because it comes from god (VII 16; III 9), that it is not the external world but judgements about it that can harm the inner man (VIII 47), and that other people are entitled to help and forgiveness – their mistakes are not your affair. Marcus Aurelius is able to summarize the moral demands in a sort of memorandum (XI 18; cf. XII 26): remember that you are born to protect the world, that whoever errs acts from ignorance, that you yourself also often do wrong, and that whatever harms you is not what the others do but what you believe about what they are doing; do, finally, remember that clemency can never be overcome, for clemency is humanity, as we are taught.

Behind such rules of life lies a more theoretical view of man. Man is composed of three parts: body, soul and reason (XII 3; cf. III 6). The body and the soul (*psychē* or *pneuma*, the perceiving soul or principle of life) are not one's own, so if man lets himself be led by these two, he loses his identity. But if man, on the other hand, follows reason or the intellect (*nous*) and lives in justice and truth, he has liberated himself from necessity. The particular concepts in such lines of thought are familiar from early Stoicism, but in the use of the concepts there is a shift in emphasis – this is true of the liberation from necessity and of the tripartition of the human person; there may be reminiscences of Posidonius, but in any case both aspects point forwards to Neoplatonism.

God is intellect or reason (*nous*), and he takes care of that part of man that is related to him. Hence individual man must meet providence with reverence and confident that whatever benefits the greater unity can never harm the parts (XII 2; II 11; X 6). Nor is there here a clear break with the early Stoa but a new tone, a religious fervour that belongs to Imperial rather than to Hellenistic times. Marcus Aurelius voices an intense cosmic religious feeling, but not – as Epictetus – a personal relation with god.

The death of Marcus Aurelius was the death of the last prominent Stoic. But Stoicism did not die with him. As has been emphasized several times, features of late

Stoicism live on in Neoplatonism. To this should be added a more or less concealed influence in other fields. The fact that Roman historians – for example Tacitus – extensively adopt a moral position in evaluating political events is most likely owing to Stoic influence. Stoic moral philosophy also influenced the brilliant work on rhetoric written by Quintilian in the first century AD (cf. Quint. *Inst. or.* XII), a landmark in the history of Western paedagogics and 'humanism'.

The influence on Roman Law was even greater – an influence that already had begun to make itself felt in Cicero's time (see p. 494). In its origin Roman Law – both private and public law – was a law for Roman citizens, but gradually, as the need for legal regulation primarily of trade with foreigners became urgent, 'an international law', *ius gentium* arose, a system of private law, understood as the laying down of legal rules pertaining to the intercourse between civilized nations. The Stoic influence became manifest at the moment these rules were interpreted as an expression of rights and obligations decreed by nature – *ius naturale*, the law of nature. Roman law developed gradually and casuistically as a system of *plebiscita, Senatus consulta*, Praetorial edicts, and – later on – Imperial edicts; to this should be added as a very essential factor, the legally binding *responsa* by prominent jurists. There were important jurists already in late Republican times, but the grand era of jurisprudence was in the second century AD (the most outstanding representative being Ulpian who lived around 200). In c.530 this vast body of material was codified in the *Corpus iuris civilis* at the instigation of the Emperor Justinian. This is divided into several parts, some of the most important being the general introduction, or the *Institutiones,* and the *Digesta*, which are excerpts of codified responsa delivered by jurists through the ages and provide excellent insight into general legal thinking at the time when jurisprudence was in full flower (not least Ulpian).

It goes without saying that the Stoic influence is most noticeable in the general sections on the philosophy of law. In one of these (*Dig.* I 3 ,2), side by side with statements by Roman jurists – can be found a quotation from none other than Chrysippus (which in turn builds on Pindar – Pind. frg. 169, Schröder):

> Law is king of all things – human as well as divine; it takes precedence over good and evil; it must govern and guide and provide rules of right and wrong for living beings whose nature it is to form societies; it must decree what is to be done and not to be done.

Here law means natural law, and already in the beginning of the *Digesta* (*Dig.* I 1, 1) it is ascertained that law (*ius*) is derived from justice (*iustitia*); law is 'the art of the good and the equitable' (*ars boni et aequi*). Its prescription is to live honestly, not to harm another person, and to pay everybody his due (1, 10); since all are related to each other, it is unjust for one man to injure another (1, 3).

In the Stoic view all living beings are subject to the same law, but only man has rights in the true sense, because man is equipped with reason (Diog. Laert. VII 86 ff.). This is expanded in Roman Law so that all living beings have natural rights (*Dig.* I 1, 1). But the question of human rights creates problems whenever the ideal (natural law) encounters the facts of life – problems that are familiar from Stoicism itself. In Roman law this can be seen from some learned jurist consults distinguishing between *ius naturale* – what nature teaches all men – and the positive legal order, *ius gentium* (I 1, 1; *Inst*. I 2, 1) while some do not (*Dig*. I 1, 9). The question of slavery is especially intricate. According to the law of nature all are free, but slavery is legally valid according to *ius gentium* – in other words to de facto law (*Inst*. I 2, 2; *Dig*. I 1, 4). It can even be formulated so pointedly (*Inst*. I 3) that *ius gentium*, contrary to nature, legitimates slavery. In other words, Roman Law adopts the Stoic view of man, including the problems caused by the state of affairs in existing societies. This ambiguous heritage was left to posterity.

SCHOOL PHILOSOPHY: PLATONIC, PYTHAGOREAN AND ARISTOTELIAN TRENDS

If one proceeds from the Stoic to the Platonic line – or, rather, the Platonic lines – of the Empire, the lack of social commitment is striking. Regardless of the political realities, the utopian state remained to a Stoic as a challenge somewhere in his mind; the Platonists, on the other hand – who as a rule belonged to the prosperous classes – apparently were unconcerned about the Platonic state – whether the best or 'the second best'. It is Plato, the metaphysician, who determines the tradition. The reason is of course that it is the transcendent, metaphysical world that is the true reality to these Platonists. A Stoic wants to live in agreement with nature; a Platonist strives – with a frequently employed *Theaetetus* quote (176 C) – to escape this world and make himself as god-like as possible. To most of the Platonists this does not mean that this world is evil. God is good and without jealousy, and therefore he created the best possible world as a depiction of the eternal one – as another, equally beloved quotation (*Tim*. 29 E) states. But nevertheless this world is but a shadow, and only he who knows true reality knows his true self. Such knowledge is not available to everybody: 'To find the creator and father of this world is an onerous task, and if he has been found, it is impossible to communicate this to everybody', as we are told in yet another quotation from Plato (28 C) cited again and again, which justifies the exclusive and esoteric side of the Platonism of the time. Although there are obvious common motifs in the Platonism of the time, the overall picture is hard to grasp. There is room for religiousness and intellectualism, for mysticism and rationality, and for exalted enthusiasm and a quite rigid Platonic scholasticism. The transmission is fragmentary, but from it we get a glimpse of what has been called a Platonic 'undercurrent', a hidden – partially perhaps oral – tradition, the main features of which undoubtedly go back to the old Academy but which often seem like echoes of a systematic philosophy no longer fully understood. All in all, it is an epigone philosophy that does not acquire new life until Neoplatonism. It is also an eclectic philosophy that takes in many elements from Aristotelianism and Stoicism, even though as a whole it is clearly considered a *philosophia perennis* that had been fully completed in Plato's writings. What matters is not to think in new ways but to preserve the 'right' Platonism. The difficulties this raises for the interpreter do not grow less by the frequent thinking in symbols – the borderline between what is true, what might be true, and what is symbolically true is not drawn in such a manner as to match a modern reader's expectations. Furthermore, it is not easy to isolate genuine Platonism from the religious currents influenced by Platonism.

The movement that conceived of itself as Pythagoreanism is nowadays normally considered part of Platonism. In the first century BC a wave of 'Pythagoreanism' inundated the ancient world, not least Rome and Alexandria. To a large extent – but not entirely – it may be explained as a reaction against the official Platonism presented by Antiochus of Ascalon in Athens. The movement had been prepared for by a series of frauds – to judge from fragments with less than sterling contents – treatises purportedly by good old Pythagoreans. Neopythagoreanism comprises both number mysticism, theosophy, belief in miracles appealing to wider circles (Apollonius of Tyana), and philosophy; but the name is a loose catch-all – what holds it together is a semi-religious belief in Pythagoras' wisdom. At a time of trust in authority and tradition it was an advantage that Pythagoras was so ancient and that one was not weighed down with too much knowledge of the historical person; his memory was veiled in a suitable aura of mysticism. The philosophical side of the movement is eclectic, but the main characteristic is Platonic, if only for the reason that the image of Pythagoras of the day came from Plato, the Academy and – partially – from Aristotle. Officially a Neopythagorean will maintain that Plato merely followed in the path of Pythagoras, but in general it holds true that a philosopher of these centuries who calls himself a Pythagorean is a Platonist. The Platonism in question is the Platonic doctrine of principles; a philosophically inclined Neopythagorean will to a higher degree than his Platonist colleague concentrate on a highest principle 'beyond being', and here it is possible to trace a line back to Speusippus. Leaving aside the pure, Neopythagorean mysticism of numbers, the interesting figures are Eudorus of Alexandria (c.40 BC) – who perhaps gave Neopythagoreanism a philosophical dimension – Moderatus (first century AD), and Numenius (second half of the second century AD).

By and large the more official Platonic line presumably goes back to Xenocrates, and thereby it inherits all the ambiguities attached to his system. The more precise connecting lines are obscure, but in any case the path runs from Antiochus' Athens to Alexandria, and here Eudorus was apparently once again an important figure. Whatever direction the line followed, gradually a scholastic Platonism was formulated, which is called middle Platonism with the high point in the second century AD. There seems to have been a school in Athens (Taurus and the anti-Aristotelian Atticus), but for us the best known figure is one Albinus or Alcinous who in the middle of the second century wrote a compendium of Platonism that is preserved.[1] It is an unoriginal manual but to us the best expression of middle Platonism as a system. Other middle Platonic texts have also been preserved (Apuleius, Maximus of Tyre); but of greater significance are some philosophers more loosely connected with middle Platonism: Plutarch, Celsus – the author of one of the earliest writings against Christianity (see p. 572) – and Calcidius who wrote a Latin translation with commentary on parts of the

---

1 Probably the author of the compendium was called Alcinous. But until quite recently he has been identified as the middle Platonist Albinus. As he is still most often referred to as Albinus, this name has been retained in the following.

Timaeus, which was normative in the Middle Ages – the latter is of considerably later date but builds on middle Platonism rather than Neoplatonism.

The two principal branches of the tradition – Neopythagoreanism and middle Platonism – have a considerable heritage in common. Eudorus, for example, has one leg in each camp. Most of the elements of the tradition seem to be present already at the beginning of the period, and the texts that by chance have been preserved for us are variations on common themes, which relate themselves first and foremost to the common 'hidden' transmission. Therefore, in what follows, it has not proved profitable to proceed strictly chronologically as if a given text were a response to an immediately preceding, known text. Some of the common elements of the official tradition will be presented first; then follows a presentation of some special positions and off-shoots.

The Plato of the period is an amputated Plato, but to a large degree it is this very Platonism of the Empire with its escapism and asceticism that came to determine posterity's view of what Platonism is. Faced with Platonic irony and ambiguities, the Platonists of the period do not really know what to do, and Platonic myths, for example, are not read as poetry but as veiled, symbolic truths. Everything is in a manner of speaking made one-dimensional; what was asked for was a system. The Plato texts of greatest importance as paradigms for the tradition are the metaphysical books of the *Republic* and the *Timaeus*. Within the Neopythagorean line the *Parmenides* should be added. And, finally, the Platonic 'doctrine of principles' constantly operates in the background.

The simile of the line in the *Republic* presents itself as a schematic resumé of the system as a system of hierarchical levels, in which the superior level is the paradigm and cause of the lower, and in which the summit or the ultimate precondition – the idea of the good – lies outside the system itself.

The *Timaeus* is interpreted as an application of this structure. Here three fundamental levels were found: reason (*nous*), soul (*psychē*), and matter. These levels can be found in both the world at large and in man (*macrocosmos* and *microcosmos*), but *macrocosmos* is primary – individual souls being off-springs of the cosmic soul. *Nous* is often directly equated with god, and the contents of *nous*, the ideas, are accordingly seen as god's thoughts. The soul occupies a middle position between reason and matter; reason is implanted in the soul, which governs the body. What is decisive is of course that the bodily world through the soul is structured by a rational principle that is not itself material. The mythical form of the dialogue is viewed as pure allegory and, in the orthodox view, it is part of the allegory that the world is depicted as created in time; but this is understood as a paedagogical expression of a process of creation that actually is timeless (cf. Plut. *De an. procr.* 1013 B). The latter is probably correct; but on the whole, the allegorical interpretation demands a heavy-handed translation from imagery to system, and here numerous problems present themselves, which already had been embarrassing in the old Academy. Is the Demiurge or the creator god merely a metaphor for reason whereby reason – *nous* – accordingly is both a creative principle and a principle that is transcendent in relation to the created? And what is the relation between this highest principle – god – and the opposite power, matter or necessity, which seemingly curtails god's power? – the physical world is the best *possible* world.

Whoever would systematize Plato was in fact threatened by two latent dangers. In the first place: it is good Platonism to believe that the good has no opposite and that evil or chaos is lack of structure and goodness, and yet there seems in the *Timaeus* to be a latent dualism between reason and necessity, which is uncomfortable in a would-be monistic system – and this danger also lurks in Stoicism, which was of no small influence on Platonism. In the second place there is the question of the dual status of the highest principle. In orthodox middle Platonism the inherited ambiguities are simply accepted, and so the problems remain – by and large as in Xenocrates. Special points of view are to be found among Neopythagoreans and will be discussed below.

If one takes an abstract point of view – and that is a favourite one in the Platonism of the day – one will tie the thought of the hierarchical levels and of the 'creation' of the world to the Platonic doctrine of principles. This is to say that unity – at times called the Monad – everywhere affects 'the Indefinite Dyad', the limiting affecting the unlimited and amorphous. But of course an abstract formulation like this does not solve the two problems.

The justification for imagining a world divided into levels in which the immaterial affects the material is to be found in the Platonic procedure of reduction. A 'Pythagorean' source provides a good impression of the line of thought and its formulation; it is a continuous account that is reproduced in Sextus Empiricus (Sext. Emp. *Adv. math*. X 248 ff.) but it can be supplemented from several other sources (e.g. Diog. Laert. III 107 ff.; VIII 24 ff. (Alex Polyh.); Simpl. in Aristot. *Phys.* 247, 30 ff., Diels (Hermodorus); see also p. 259). But although the substance is old, it is erroneous to use the text as a source providing direct access to the old Academy – primarily it throws light on the understanding of the tradition in the second century. It is a compendium-like account; some of the older stuff is undoubtedly diluted, and something new has been added. The process of reduction – the technical terms are abstraction and analysis (cf. Alb. Διδασκ. X; Cels. ap. Or. *CC* VII 42; 44) – goes from corporeal to incorporeal, from composite to incomposite, from dependent to autonomous existence, generally from the phenomenon to more and more formal principles void of substantial content – often illustrated by the old example of reduction of a physical body via surface and line to point. The doctrine of ideas is thus considered a special case of the doctrine of principles – phenomenon is reduced to idea, idea to principle. The underlying, purely formal structure is the relation between 'the Monad' and 'the Indefinite Dyad'. But this relation is not clarified; the two principles are regarded as co-equals, but at the same time the 'Indefinite Dyad' is also – in a more 'orthodox' Platonic way – presented as the unity in its 'otherness' (Sext. Emp. *Adv. math*. X 261), in other words as implied in the unity. The dualism still lies in ambush, and the author cannot be said to master his subject-matter.

The passage immediately proceeds to an account of the Academy 'doctrine of categories', in other words to the relation between independent and dependent being, which clearly is a Platonic inheritance. The theory is systematized and expanded – not always wholly clearly. It is notable, however, that 'negative' and 'relative' concepts are considered secondary to autonomous substances – an evident attempt to counter a crucial point in Aristotle's criticism of the doctrine of ideas. But the debate conducted in late Antiquity about whether it was the Academy doctrine of categories or that of Aristotle or the Stoics that was 'the right' one is at fault because the classifications rely on quite different criteria. The debate was introduced by Eudorus who defended the 'doctrine of categories' of the Academy against Aristotle (Simpl. in Aristot. *Cat.* 174, 14, Kalbfleisch).

As might be expected, Sextus' account (Sext. Emp. *Adv. math.* X 283) concludes with the physical application of the theory, which means that the line is tied to the *Timaeus*. The entire representation is not distinguished by its argumentation nor by its acumen, but it does uncover the contours of a system of doctrines that must be considered typical of the Platonism of the time.

Albinus was not a philosophical heavy-weight either, but for this very reason – one is tempted to say – his manual can provide a good picture of the time. To be sure, his compendium relies on the Xenocrates tradition – but, as with the 'Pythagorean' text, it is a monument to thoughts once thought by others. It is a complete survey of the Platonic 'system' into which is incorporated not a little from Aristotelianism and Stoicism – the entire presentation of logic, for example (Alb. Διδασκ. V ff.) is a mixture of Aristotelian and Stoic logic, which *en bloc* is attributed to Plato. In practice Albinus uses syllogisms of Stoic types as crystal-clear proofs of that which already was presupposed in his premises. Furthermore, one notes an extensive use of general Aristotelian concepts, also in fields that have nothing to do with Aristotle – thus testifying that Aristotle's terminology by this time had become common philosophical property.

The compendium begins by maintaining (I) that philosophy is a striving for wisdom, a freeing of the soul from the body leading the soul to the true, intelligible reality and to insight into the divine and human (cf. the Chrysippus quotation cited p. 512). The presentation proper commences with logic and dialectics; then follows theoretical philosophy (mathematics, doctrine of principles, theology, and physics) and, finally, ethics. Here only a few specific points will be touched upon.

The section on ideas (IX) is a good example of middle Platonic scholasticism. In relation to god, says Albinus, the ideas are his thoughts; in relation to us they are the first intelligible objects; in relation to matter they are measure; in relation to the world of sensation they are the paradigm; and in themselves they are substances.

This is a somewhat empty systematization of numerous traditional elements. Rather abruptly Xenocrates' formula (see p. 264) is introduced: the ideas are eternal models for natural species – whereby, for example, relations and 'negative ideas' are precluded. The idea as transcendent, eternal model is in Albinus called *idea*, while the idea as immanent in the phenomenon is called *eidos* – this is the Aristotelian form which, once again abruptly, makes its entrance (IV; cf. Sen. *Ep. mor.* 58,19 ff.).

Albinus' section on the concept of god (Alb. Διδασκ. X; cf. on this Apul. *De Plat. dogm.* I 5; Max. Tyr. XVII 5 ff.) is an impenetrable mystery. Somehow or other the Aristotelian concept of god is linked to the view of the ideas as the thoughts of god and with the Demiurge of the *Timaeus*, while at the same time the possibility is opened for a higher principle prior to reason. Many currents of thought wrestle with each other; the whole seems even more inadequate than the report of the doctrine of principles provided by Sextus' 'Pythagorean' authority.

On the other hand, Albinus does clearly reproduce three classical paths to knowledge of god. One – the *via negationis* – leads to knowledge of god by continuous abstraction and negation of every positive determination, for god is 'unsayable' – elsewhere in the tradition the first hypothesis in Plato's *Parmenides* is mentioned as examplification. The second path is the *via analogiae* – the paradigm is clearly the simile of the sun in the *Republic*. The third path – the *via eminentiae* (paradigm: the Diotima speech in the *Symposium*) – consists of the ascent from bodily to spiritual beauty and thence to the beautiful and good itself.

It is on the Neopythagorean outskirts of the tradition that deliberate attempts to solve the real problems are made. Eudorus maintained (Simpl. in Aristot. *Phys.* 181, 10 ff., Diels; cf. Alex. Aphr. in Aristot. *Met.* 59, 7, Hayduck) that a higher unity must exist mediating between unity and the 'Indefinite Dyad'. In other words, he confronted the problem, but his attempt at a solution is not a good one – it presupposes that the 'Indefinite Dyad' has status as an independent principle; to insert a mediating 'superior unity' is of course not a solution in itself.

A more stimulating treatment of the question is to be found in Eudorus' Neopythagorean colleague Moderatus. He distinguishes (Simpl. in Aristot. *Phys.* 230, 34 ff.) between three levels: the first One is beyond any being; the second is the fully being or intelligible, or the ideas; the third is the psychical that participates in the One and in the ideas. Finally follows matter, which does not participate in unity but receives order by an imprint. Thereby the One is not – as in Eudorus – a mechanical principle of mediation for two opposites. In itself and as principle it is beyond being and thereby beyond determination – as is the good in Plato's *Republic*; in the intelligible world it manifests itself as a union of being and unity; the soul is – as in the *Timaeus* – intermediate between the intelligible world and matter, which in itself is an amorphous chaos. It is a system that shows the One in itself and in its transformation to 'otherness'. Moderatus' more specific considerations are not known, but the line of thought occupies an important place in the history of the tradition. There is a clear connection back to Speusippus' metaphysics (see p. 262) and forwards to Plotinus, for Moderatus' tripartition corresponds to the three hypostases in Plotinus, and matter also has the same function. Thereby Moderatus' system is also in agreement with Plotinus' reading of Plato's *Parmenides* (cf. Plot. V 1, 8 – see p. 537). Moderatus anticipates the structure of Plotinus' thinking; this is likewise true of his combination of *Parmenides* motifs with *Timaeus* motifs. On the other hand, it is not possible to trace any direct connection with middle Platonism.

Thus both Xenocrates' and Speusippus' doctrines of principles had after-effects. So did Aristotle's. To posterity – from Plotinus (perhaps already from Albinus), down through the Middle Ages, and to some extent even until our own times – it seemed an established fact that what here is called the Xenocrates tradition on all essential points must coincide with Aristotle's theology. Intellect as containing the ideas, ideas as the thoughts of god, or identity between thought subject and thought object, does not all this point to the Aristotelian god who thinks himself? Undoubtedly the Xenocrates tradition let itself be influenced by Aristotelianism, but the identification is wrong in principle. Aristotle's god thinks neither ideas nor form-essences; god's self-thinking is void of substantial content; it is a 'transcendental' precondition for our being able to think conceptually in our way. And there was indeed an independent Aristotelianism during the Empire that cannot be enlisted in Platonism.

Aristotle suffered a strange fate during the Empire. Antiochus of Ascalon could still maintain that basically Plato and Aristotle meant the same. But the rediscovery of the esoteric writings in the first century BC inaugurated an Aristotle renaissance in the sense that the 'real' Aristotle now was read and known in all philosophical schools; gradually his conceptual apparatus and terminology became common philosophical property. But as an independent philosophy, Aristotelianism led a quiet life in the background. The greatest Aristotelian of the time, Alexander of Aphrodisias (c.AD 200), who held an Imperial chair in Aristotelianism, nevertheless testifies that Aristotelianism had not died out. Several of his commentaries on Aristotle have been preserved. They are the oldest known to us, and he distinguishes himself as perhaps the greatest of all interpreters of Aristotle. In addition some minor treatises have been preserved, in part against the Stoics (primarily the *De fato* against Stoic determinism).

One of his lesser works – *On the Soul* (*De anima*) – provides his version of Aristotle's epistemology and doctrine of intellect. On certain points he makes Aristotle more radical in a way that has influenced later times significantly; with respect to intellect he follows his master with certain clarifications (Alex. Aphr. *De an.* 80, 16 ff.; 106, 19 ff., Bruns). Man is from birth equipped with the 'passive intellect' – he is a *tabula rasa* (84, 25) – which is to say that actually it is nothing and potentially everything, since it is capable of receiving everything. This comes about by means of what in the Middle Ages was called abstraction – Alexander can be considered the author of 'the theory of abstraction', and his interpretation of the relation between the 'active' and the passive or 'possible' intellect determined the more specific developments of the theory in the Middle Ages. The intellect abstracts the forms which are inherent in matter and which are directly received by sense perception but is also able to distinguish between the simple form that makes the thing a 'this' and that whereby the thing is what it is – its essence (87, 5 ff.). But essence is a universal, and a universal only exists in so far as it is thought (90, 2 ff.). The process of abstraction is the cause of man's acquiring a knowledge that in a given case can be actualized – at this stage one can speak of an 'acquired intellect' or intellect as *habitus*.

Up to this point Alexander can be called a 'conceptualist'; he has also been called a 'materialist', by which is meant that only physical objects have real existence and that man in his capacity of man also is a physical object, a bit of matter furnished with a special form (the soul). But the soul has access to something that goes beyond man. Through intellectual cognition man experiences a momentary unity between the act of cognition and the object of cognition, which cannot be explained on the basis of the human constitution – what then makes it possible for it to come about anyhow? And, inasmuch as human intelligence by man's own nature is only a potentiality, what will then cause the process of abstraction to take place? The answer to both questions is that it is 'the active intellect', which – in Aristotle's phrase – comes to man 'from outside' (cf., e.g. 108, 22). In itself this active intellect – the first cause, or god – can only be determined as being identical with its object (cf. especially 87, 43 ff.; 108, 16 ff.; 109, 23 ff.). We experience this identity momentarily and as something alien; but god is essentially characterized by the identity between intellect and the intelligible (*nous* and *noēton*), and he does not receive his knowledge from the outside; He does not know this or that, but only himself – pure intellect is simple and only thinks the simple (109, 30). In its highest form intellect is supra-human and at the same time a formal limiting concept – as in Aristotle.

Plotinus was undoubtedly strongly influenced by Alexander's view of the unity of intellect and intelligible object – it is this identity that constitutes the so-called second hypostasis. But it is an irony of fate that at the same time he has the responsibility for – or the honour of – finally reconciling Xenocrates and Aristotle. This comes about thanks to a quite simple but radical reinterpretation. Where Alexander speaks of unity between *nous* and *to noēton* (the intelligible object as formal concept), Plotinus speaks of the unity between *nous* and *ta noēta* (the intelligible objects, which is to say the ideas). In this round-about way Alexander is the precursor of Neoplatonism.

PLUTARCH

In Neopythagoreanism, in official middle Platonism, and in Alexander of Aphrodisias, one comes upon the more esoteric and theoretical discussion of the highest principle. It is not always clear from these rather scholastic texts that what is at issue is an existential problem – to a good Platonist at least, it is an all-important tenet that man can know himself by knowing god. The many unresolved tensions of the times – not only in the very concept of god and in the problem of monism versus dualism but also the tension between philosophical and religious ways of thought – emerge clearly in the Platonist Plutarch (born soon after AD 45, died after 120) of Chaeronea in Boeotia. Major parts of his very extensive oeuvre comprising both scholarly and popular treatises have been preserved, and hence we are allowed to become acquainted with a real person. Plutarch came from a distinguished family and led the life of an *homme de lettres* in his noble, ancient native city. The fact that he was also a priest of Apollo in near-by Delphi is not merely a biographical detail.

Plutarch was learned, pious and conservative. As a writer he is charming – something which of course is not always synonymous with systematic lucidity. He was also troubled – in general because the world no longer was what it had been and in particular because religion had declined. He is famed for his ominous account of a voyage during which the helmsman at dusk suddenly is hailed by a voice in the dark: 'Make it known that the great Pan is dead' (Plut. *De def. or.* 419 B). Apollo has likewise suffered, and it bothered Plutarch that Delphi now was being overrun by touring groups and guides, while the oracle was not functioning quite as in the days of old (*De Pyth. or.* 395 A). What he looked for and found was universally valid philosophical wisdom back of religious myths and ceremonies. This applies for example to a strange inscription at Delphi consisting only of the letter E, which could occasion many stimulating interpretations; yet certain it was that concealed wisdom lay behind (*De E*).

Plutarch's extensive work falls into two groups: a series of historical biographies – in which Greek and Roman heroes are juxtaposed in pairs – and a series of philosophical essays called the *Moralia*. The latter partly comprises some polemical treatises against Epicureans and Stoics and partly a great number of treatises on moral philosophy, on philosophy of religion and on metaphysics – sometimes in the form of proper essays, sometimes in the form of dialogues. Some of the philosophical writings are intended for a wider public, others are more technical. Most of them move subtly back and forth between a rational and a symbolic mythical level. To Plutarch these two modes of expression are in fact two sides of the same issue. One should be aware, says he (*De Is.* 374 E), that a myth is not simply history; it is an allegorical expression of a universal truth which is to be extricated. On the other hand, he can also choose the opposite path, and here it is not merely a question of, for example, external imitation of Platonic myths. It is not possible to apply his own allegorical method unambiguously to himself and extract some doctrines that are doctrines only; rationality and symbolism are woven into each other. Behind his apparently naïve interpretations of myths can be discerned a certain sly reservation – this is for example true of his seven different readings of the letter E at Delphi. Among the many pedants of the day Plutarch in fact has the rare characteristic of being sly, and his naïveté has an air of cunning that is reminiscent of Herodotus' – whom by the way he did not like very much (cf. *De Her. malign.*).

Many of Plutarch's works deal with rather mundane ethical problems. But behind this lies on the one hand the Platonic conviction that man's task is to make himself god-like; on the other hand Plutarch accepts that man is after all a mixture of good and evil, reason and desire. Hence he cannot accept a rigoristic ethics – such as that of the Stoics; he is far more attracted to Aristotelian ethics. Virtue lies in the middle and above all manifests itself in kindness to others – *philanthrōpia* (cf. *De virt. mor.* 444 C ff.; *Ad Apol.* 120 A).

Plutarch's ethical position colours his biographies. Most often they are indeed idealized portraits, but he notes that no human life is blameless. We should not depict errors as evil but as an expression of virtue gone wrong, and in all humility we should be ashamed of human nature, which never produces a wholly pure and blameless character (*Cim.* 2). Human nature contains both good and evil, because the world as a whole does so – and ethics is therefore tied to metaphysics.

If one approaches Plutarch's metaphysics rationally, the resemblance to the *Timaeus* becomes clear at once – that work is indeed the subject of one of his weightiest treatises. The basic scheme (cf. *De gen. Socr.* 591 D; *De fac.* 943 A ff.; *De Is. passim*; *De Pyth. or. passim*) is intellect or reason (*nous*) – soul (*psychē*) – matter. Reason – or *nous* – is identified with god; in the language of the *Timaeus*, with the Demiurge. But god himself is independent of the world: he is real being, the totality of all ideas, the one and good, and he exists independent of matter and beyond time (*De E* 392 E ff.). Yet it is granted to man as if by initiation to make his way to that first, simple, and immaterial (*De Is.* 382 D). This is simply the Xenocrates model – with the possible inclusion of elements from Aristotle's theology. It is likewise traditional to view the process of creation as an interplay between the One and 'the Indefinite Dyad'.

Still, Plutarch has his own special views. God cannot be responsible for evil, whether in man or in the cosmos, and hence Plutarch is a convinced dualist: outside of god himself, good and evil are never separate (369 A ff.). This is his interpretation of reason and necessity as fundamental phenomena in the *Timaeus*. But in connection with an enigmatic Platonic passage (*De an. procr.* 1014 E; Plat. *Leg.* X 898 B, here p. 252) he can also speak of 'the evil cosmic soul'; evil is not merely something given with matter but a phychic reality. In the learned treatise in which he comments upon the creation of the soul in the *Timaeus* (*Tim.* 35 A ff.) he concludes – contrary to all other Platonists than Atticus – that the world is created in time and that the *Timaeus* accordingly is to be read literally (Plut. *De an. procr.* 1014 A ff.). God is good, and god created the world; but inasmuch as the world is imperfect, evil must pre-exist, and evil is bound to time. If god had not created the world and did not rule it with his providence, everything would fall back into the chaos described in the *Timaeus* (1014 E). Neither Plutarch's dualism nor his view of the theodicy problem is wholly consistent – but he is convinced that god in his providence keeps watch over the world, even though his paths are not always fathomable (cf. *De sera num.* 549 E ff.).

None the less, god is remote and the world is full of demons – beings between god and man. Here Plutarch unhesitatingly goes along with Xenocrates; he does so literally by the inclusion of suitable material from oriental religions (cf. *De def. or.* 414 F ff.). Much goes on in the world, which god simply cannot be troubled with, and therefore there are many kinds of demons loose in the lower regions of the world. Shakespeare made one of Plutarch's demons famous – the evil demon of Brutus, Caesar's murderer, who appears to him at night saying, 'We meet at Philippi' (*Brut.* 36).

This is a fateful account and no mere poetic imagery. We may view Plutarch as an embodiment of the dense superstitiousness of his time; he himself insists that he wants none of superstition (*De superst.* 165 E ff.; *De Is.* 378 A), although he certainly does acknowledge the concealed wisdom of symbolism and myth. He wrote a captivating treatise *On the Face in the Moon* in which he argues convincingly that on the moon there must be mountains and valleys and that she must have her own inhabitants. It turns out that the moon has a place in the universe corresponding to that of the soul. This quite literally, because the moon is the site of the freeing of reason from departed souls to become united with the sun; and the process also follows the opposite course: on the moon reason is implanted in the soul, which in turn is united with the body on earth (*De fac.* 944 B ff.). The entire cosmic, metaphysical drama can be formulated mythically. Plutarch did so in his treatise on Isis and Osiris. The Osiris of myth is the principle of the good, Typhon that of evil, and Isis is the intermediate goddess (*De Is.*). This does not mean that Plutarch forsook Apollo for the sake of the Egyptian cult of Isis. It means that the one and same god and the one and same providence are given different names by different peoples. Whoever understands the symbolism can look behind the veil. Yet one should take care not to slide into superstition or fall directly into the abyss of godlessness (377 F ff.).

So says Plutarch, and thus he voices the fusion of his time of philosophical and religious yearning in a world where not everything is transparent but where the soul's kinship with the divine is the firm base. Plutarch is courteously tolerant of all sorts of religious manifestations because he knows that they are only symbols expressing the real truth. The relation between truth and symbol appeared in a different way in a thinker like Philo who, although inspired by the Platonic tradition, at the same time was firmly anchored in a specific religion, Judaism, or in a religious movement such as Gnosticism in which the myth is the true mode of expression.

PHILO

Philo (c.25 BC–c.50 AD) belonged to the Jewish congregation in Alexandria. Thus he was born into two cultures, the Jewish and the Hellenistic, and he combined them in such a way that it is impossible to tell whether he first and foremost was a Jew or a Hellenist. His was probably not a unique case – we must take it that the Jews in the great Hellenistic cities, though orthodox and though most often living together, were strongly influenced by the surrounding culture. There were many Jewish settlements in the big cities, but they were united in the common religion and by the common holy site, the Temple in Jerusalem. Despite their geographic dispersal, the Jews constituted a significant, powerful factor in the Roman Empire, and the Jewish minority in Alexandria was a considerable one. Far-sighted emperors recognized the Jews as a useful population group and protected them; tyrannical emperors were offended because they refused to participate in the Imperial cult. What imperilled the Jews and later the Christians *vis-à-vis* the state was not really their monotheistic religion – by now paganism had only outwardly become polytheistic, and the 'philosophical' concept of god was monotheistic. The stumbling block was the worship of the Emperor – by the regime intended as an expression of loyalty to the state that in no way precluded other religious practices, but in other religions no scruples were entertained because of the addition of the Imperial cult to all the other outward ceremonies. Extensive pogroms in Alexandria were supported by the Emperor Caligula (37–41), and Philo was appointed head of a legation to the Emperor in order to placate him. This was not an undangerous mission – as appears from a dramatic account written by Philo himself (Philo *Leg.*, especially 178 ff.; 349 ff.). Fortunately for the Jews, Caligula was murdered soon afterwards.

Philo belonged to one of the most distinguished and wealthiest Jewish families in Alexandria, and with this went a responsibility, which the family apparently was used to living up to. The situation of the Jews could be precarious; the relations with the local authorities and the Emperor in Rome must be tended to with the necessary diplomacy. What Philo in fact thought about the master race – the Romans – can be deduced from his account of the legation to Caligula, published after the tyrant's murder and after the word had been set free – with respect to *his* misdeeds. Otherwise Philo recommended caution with the tyrants – in the veiled style that is the familiar vehicle of any suppressed minority (*De somn.* II 83 ff.). Circumstances forced Philo to be politically active, even though as a mystic he felt himself strongly attracted to a life of contemplation (*De leg. spec.* III 1 ff.; cf. *De vit. cont.*).

Without doubt Alexandria was the most cosmopolitan of cities in the Roman Empire, and Philo exploited the possibility of assimilating all sides of Greek culture – not just philosophy. Judging by everything, middle Platonism – and Neoplatonism for that matter – can be said to originate in Alexandria, and Philo's oeuvre alone shows that fundamental motifs in the Platonism of the following centuries already were at least familiar here. But this does not mean that he was presented with a firmly wrought system, and nothing points to one particular source of inspiration – for example, there is no apparent connection between Philo and Eudorus. Nor did Philo create a systematic philosophy. He exploited the Platonic hierarchical metaphysics – probably his principal philosophical source; he was influenced by

'Pythagorean' mysticism of numbers; and he was strongly inspired by Stoic *logos*-thinking and ethics. Stoicism and Platonism were, however, not two philosophical systems to him, but rather expressions of a perennial philosophy which it was crucial to connect with the truth embodied in the Jewish holy text, the Old Testament. He only knew this in the Greek translation, the *Septuaginta*, the most important part of which was the *Pentateuch*, which Moses of course had written himself. Philo found himself faced with exactly the same task as the early Christian thinkers who followed him – to connect pagan philosophy with Sacred Scripture, the philosophical way of thinking with revealed religion – thus, as it were, anticipating the entire philosophical state of affairs in the Middle Ages. For good reasons Philo was unable to look at it in this way, and he would certainly have denied that he was in fact undertaking something new. To him it was certain in advance that there could not be two 'truths' – one philosophical, the other religious.

How, then, does the philosophical truth relate to the religious one? The philosophers have quite simply 'borrowed' their wisdom from Moses (cf. *De aet. mun.* 18; *Quod omn. prob.* 57; *Quis her.* 214), and Moses' true – philosophical – meaning can be uncovered through an allegorical interpretation. The allegorical method that enjoyed such great triumphs in imperial times was not discovered by Philo – from ancient times it had been used to interpret Homer, and the Stoics used it to de-mythologize traditional Greek religion. In Philo, however, the method is anchored in the conviction that Moses chose the mythical-historical mode of presentation comprehensible to all; but he who truly can read will also be able to discern the philosophical truth behind it. Major parts of Philo's work consist simply of an allegorical-philosophical exegesis of the Mosaic Books – at times for Jews, at times for pagans. Everything Moses wrote – the most and the least important – has a figurative meaning. That the Lord God – as we are told in Genesis – creates heaven and earth means that He creates the intelligible and sensible world; it goes without saying that it is figurative language that God created the world in six days, for time is created along with the world; hence the world is not created in time, but Moses wishes to show us the mystical significance of the number 6; on the seventh day God did not rest; rather, He 'brought to rest'. That Genesis contains a dual account of Adam's creation is a clear reference to intelligible man versus earthly man; subsequently God created woman to be man's helpmate, for it is not good for man to be alone – no, because only God is the One (*Leg. all.* I 1 ff.; II 1 ff.; *De op. mun.* 69, 134). The whole history of the Jewish people – from the Creation, via the Egyptian Captivity, to the wandering through the desert to the Promised Land is one vast symbol of the soul's path to God.

It was Philo's firm conviction that his allegorical method is far more exact than the loose and arbitrary allegories that anybody can use for any purpose whatsoever. Credit is due not to him, Philo, but to Moses, for Moses used his figurative speech very deliberately; he knew that the world is always an image of a higher reality and that the most important events in the world – the history of Jewish deliverance – cannot only be read *as* a picture but is the *true* picture of the higher world. He also knew that the allegorical reading is at heart only figurative speech as well: an image of a truth that cannot entirely be put into words. It was with this knowledge that he provided the Law and recorded the books of the Old Testament that so justly bear his name. He was unlike other legislators who either proceed directly to specific decrees or make everything palatable by telling invented stories (1 ff.). Moses places the law in the framework in which it belongs, and hence he begins with the Creation of the World. He recounts in such a way that the initiated comes to understand that Genesis depicts how the transcendent God by His *Logos* first creates the intelligible world as the model and then the material world that reflects the intelligible one so that God's creative power everywhere forms passive matter according to unbreakable laws. In this world man also belongs in his own particular place, subject to the Kingdom of God. But all men are equal before God; they are inhabitants in 'a common city' – as the Stoics put it – which is governed by a common law, that of nature's *Logos* (*De Ios.* 28 ff.). To other nations man-made laws are added as a sort of appendix. Not so with the Jews, for the Law Moses received from God is directly derived from God's own *Logos* and is hence both a reflection of a higher reality and a genuine legal codex to be followed literally, because it is adjusted to visible reality, which is a true symbol of the real (cf. *Migr. Abr.* 89 ff.). The world's order follows from the creation of the world; Mosiac Law follows from the universal law – and that is why Moses wrote as he did. In this grand synthesis, created by Philo and Moses, there is surely no need to point out in greater detail that here God's creation and God's Law are indebted to Plato's *Timaeus*, the Stoic doctrine of *logos*, and Stoic ideas of natural law.

Now, if one asks about Philo's metaphysics in the strict sense – i.e. if one asks in Greek – the best overall presentation is to be found in the treatise *On the Creation of the World*, in which Moses' insight is depicted. God, whose nature – like that of Plato's god in the *Timaeus* – is to create, also watches over and governs His creature by his providence – like the Stoic god (cf. *De op. mun.* 10 ff.). But what is god like in himself? Here one encounters the answers familiar from later middle Platonism. God is 'the Monad' or the One, and he is the really being or the pure being – for he says of himself 'I am that I am' (*Quod Deus imm.* 11; *Quis her.* 187; *Quod det.* 160; cf. *Ex.* 3, 14). He is also – as later in Albinus – unsayable and hence can only be known through the *via negationis* (Philo *De somn.* I 67).

Prior to Philo, we know of no texts in which the intelligible world or the ideas expressly are called the thoughts of god (*De op. mun.* 20), but, as has been mentioned, this becomes a permanent element in the later tradition, and there is no reason to believe that Philo in fact was the first. Nor do we, after all, know whether he had predecessors in his way of tying Platonism to Stoicism by means of the *logos* concept – Posidonius provides at least a parallel – but the precise contents with which he invests the concept is probably special for him. God's creative power is infinite, but his power operates finitely – according to the receiving creature's possibilities (23). *Logos* is the designation for this creative power. In so far as *Logos* equals god's essence and god's thoughts, it is transcendent; in so far as it equals god's creativity, it is an intermediate link between god and the world (cf. 20, 31). Philo sees no disagreement between transcendence and immanence, and with Plato's simile of the sun in mind he is able to compare *Logos* with the sunrays that radiate from the sun and propagate its creative capacity – god sees by virtue of his own light (*Cher.* 97). Elsewhere he calls god the Father and *Logos* or the intelligible world god's first-born son who intermediates between the Father and the world, as the satrap intermediates between the Great

King and his people (*Quod Deus imm.* 31; *De op. mun.* 51; *Leg. all.* III 175; *De somn.* I 215) – in language that of course remarkably resembles The Gospel According to St. John, although with the not unimportant difference that Philo knows nothing of incarnation. From a technical viewpoint, his *logos* concept unites the Platonic world of ideas with the active *Logos* of Stoicism; but that is far from being the most important. God or *Logos* manifests himself in two 'powers', goodness – by virtue of which god created the world – and sovereignty, the divine power – by virtue of which he rules his creation. Tied to this appear two additional divine 'powers', mercy and the law (*Cher.* 27 ff.; *De fuga* 94 ff.). Hereby the Old Testament is connected to the *Timaeus*; this is not merely of doxographical interest, for it is the very nerve of Philo's thought: the Greek god of creation who is 'without jealousy' is identical with the merciful and all-judging God of the Bible. To this might be added that the Christian reader effortlessly should be able to recognize the relation between law and gospel in Philo's theology.

Philo was not the man to solve the systematic problems that later on vexed Platonic scholasticism. Neither the Bible nor the philosophical tradition enabled him to explain the relation between god's omnipotence and the existence of evil or matter, and his ideas of god and of *Logos* are often unclear and contradictory. What he accomplished was to give the Old Testament philosophical meaning and philosophy a religious meaning. As might be expected, in his view of mankind he draws on both sources. What is usually understood by a human being (*Cher.* 113 ff.) is something very elusive, a frail combination of soul and body. What is it that connects soul with body, and what is the identity of the self, that which holds the child and the old man together? The explanation is simple: we have only borrowed our selves; man's identity does not lie in the union of soul and body but in the spiritual world, and the spirit stems from god. Already in the account of the creation it is clear how god first made spiritual man, and then – as in the *Timaeus* – permitted the corporeal to be made by inferior powers (*De op. mun.* 134 ff.; 69; cf. *Gen.* 1, 26; 2, 7). Corporeal man is – presumably – subject to the law of necessity (cf. *De op. mun.* 61; *Cher.* 128). But man is a 'fragment' of god – as we are told with a Stoic term (*De op. mun.* 146); thanks to his spirituality he is related to the divine *Logos*, and hence god has granted spiritual man free will (*Quod Deus imm.* 47 ff.). To spiritual man the path lies open to the whole world – almost as Marcus Aurelius was to say later on. But Philo is able to go beyond the Stoics: whoever is replete with god and leaves his earthly self, his body, his senses and human language can arrive at the mystical, wordless knowledge of the divine truth (*De op. mun.* 69 ff.; *Quis her.* 68 ff.; cf. 259). Spiritual man can follow the path walked by Moses and the Patriarchs. Philo's mysticism sustains his whole thought. This mystical knowledge is the goal itself; as usual, one should not ask pedantic, systematic questions: apparently it is god who deals with man at the same time as man of his own volition approaches god; and apparently man comes to know god's glory without becoming wholly one with god.

There is nothing to indicate that Philo was read by later pagan philosophers – not even Plotinus betrays familiarity with him – but he exercised considerable influence on the Christian Alexandrian theologians – Clement and Origen.

GNOSTICISM

The ultimate goal for Philo is the mystical knowledge of god, *gnōsis*. This is the concept that occasioned the designation Gnosticism, a modern common designation for a number of related religious and theosophic currents that presumably arose in the first century AD and reached full flower in Egypt in the second century and in Persia in the third century. Although there are fairly large differences between the various Gnostic branches, the common characteristics still justify a common designation. The origin of Gnosticism is unknown, but it partakes of strong elements of oriental religions (among them Zarathustrianism) and frequently also of Hellenistic Platonism. The general mood of the time is perhaps more clearly voiced in Gnosticism than in the philosophical tradition proper, and it is and remains a religious rather than a philosophical phenomenon. There is a Christian as well as a pagan Gnosticism. Christian Gnosticism culminated with Basilides and the systematist Valentinus of Egypt (second century), known from polemical reports in the Church Fathers (especially Irenaeus). But in our own century a significant further number of independent Gnostic, Christian texts have been found (for example a number of apocryphal gospels). The most important contribution to pagan Gnosticism is the so-called *Corpus Hermeticum*, which was translated in the Platonic Academy in Florence in the fifteenth century where it was considered orthodox Platonism next to that of Plotinus and Plato himself, and it exercised considerable influence for the next two centuries, especially on Renaissance occultism. Mention can also be made of the Chaldean Oracles. The last great spokesman of Gnosticism is Mani from Persia (third century), the founder of Manichaeism that had far-reaching after-effects both in the Islamic and Christian world. The sustaining thought of Gnosticism is expressed in mythical personifications and a symbolic language that is not easily comprehensible.

The basic note is a profound feeling of the absurdity of human existence. Man has been thrust into an alien world that threatens to tie him to matter and to destroy the true – spiritual – self. The question is why man has entered this world and how he can find his way back to his native land. The answer is provided in mythical form. A common element is the belief in an unsayable, transcendent god – the 'unknown god' – who is beyond intellect (*nous*) but is the progenitor of *nous*. There is strong tension between spirit and matter – spirit or light are the good forces, matter or darkness the evil ones. This tension is often seen as an extreme dualism (as in Manichaeism); sometimes (as in Valentinus) a fall is assumed, where evil is owing to the renunciation of the good. In any case, the course of the world is considered a drama, a battle between good and evil forces, and this battle finds its expression, for example in Valentinus, in a complex system of higher or lower divine powers involving man in the greater cosmic drama – in Mani, but not in Valentinus, even to the extent that the victory of the good powers is dependent on whether man fights on the side of the good. There is in fact no difference between the cosmic drama and the drama in man himself. Man is in the power of evil but must fight to return to his spiritual home through *gnōsis* of the divine, which is to say come to be aware of the divine within himself.

Valentinus' system is often considered the classical formulation of Gnosticism. The one god, the forefather or the abyss, is unsayable, invisible, and unborn (Ir. *Adv. Haer.* I 1 ff. (*PG* 7, 445 ff.)); near him dwells silence. He exercises his power in the fullness of the spiritual universe, in the number of superior or inferior divine beings, aeons; but among these only the only-begotten, intellect, can know god. The fall consists then of the last aeon, *Sophia* or wisdom – Aeon no. 30 – desiring to know the abyss. This she cannot accomplish, but by her sin the world we know comes into being, created by a lower creator-god – the Demiurge (cf. I 5 (*PG* 7, 492)) – who in his folly creates a world bound to matter and darkness. He also creates man, but in man exists a spark of spirit and of the divine, and man and the spiritual world shall hence be redeemed – through the divine in man, symbolized by a redeeming aeon, the heavenly Christ. Some men (cf. I 6 (*PG* 7, 504)) – the pneumatics or the spiritual ones – carry redemption within themselves and are disposed to *gnōsis*; some – those of soul or the psychics – occupy an intermediate place between spirit and matter and carry the possibility of redemption or damnation within themselves; the great mass – the material ones or the hylics – are lost in matter.

In this – very simplified – paraphrase Platonic reminiscences are probably obvious, and the similarities with Philo should also be evident. It is more important to try to understand the real meaning of this mythical garb, especially perhaps of the myth of the fall. To us the various Aeons are a mythical garb, but to the Gnostics it was probably the other way around: the world of man is a reflection of the cosmic drama; the myth voices the archetypal. And here there is really no borderline between inner and outer, man and cosmos. When *Sophia* desires to know the abyss – as Adam and Eve would eat from the Tree of Knowledge – it is at one and the same time a question of god as the wordless deep of the world and of the deep – the unconscious – in man. The abyss cannot be known in the sense of becoming known rationally. Whoever commits the sin of wanting to understand the unfathomable – like the Demiurge who characteristically enough has become an 'evil' god – thereby creates a pseudo-world to which he is bound. Redemption is knowledge through the spirit – *gnōsis* – and this is knowledge of a special kind, a knowledge of god and a knowledge of the self – opposed to outward 'understanding'.

The Hermetic Writings lie somewhat closer to the Hellenistic philosophical tradition without being properly philosophical for that reason. They are not furnished with such a formidable mythological apparatus as Valentinus'; they are connected with no cult but intended for personal edification and self-examination. The corpus consists of several tracts presumably by several hands and written during the first to the second century, once more in Egypt. Not a few appear as the wisdom of the Egyptian god Thoth – in the Greek Thoth was also given the name of Hermes Trismegistus, 'the Thrice-Greatest Hermes' – but it is Hellenistic, not ancient Egyptian heritage.

Usually a divine teacher speaks to a disciple. This is also the case in the first tract, which will be the only one discussed here. The narrator receives a revelation from the divine Poemandres, the *Nous* who has proceeded from the highest god who rests in himself (*Corp. Herm.* I 1 ff.). Guided by him he beholds the universe, a vast light and a dreadful darkness that snake-like wreathes itself in the depths. The light is Poemandres himself, the divine intellect, or the archetype, whence proceeds the son of god, *Logos*, who at the bidding of god forms the starry heaven and all the elements, numberless powers that are made into one cosmos. Then god creates the first man in His own likeness empowered to rule nature (12 ff.). But man becomes enamoured of physical nature in which god's *Logos* is not present. By the fall man has become a dual being consisting of body and soul. But spiritual man can become liberated by ascending through the seven celestial spheres and by discarding his earthly body (24 ff.), and he finally attains *gnōsis* and becomes god. The tract concludes with a hymn to the holy god who by his *Logos* has created everything and is greater than the greatest (31).

On several points this vision does not differ from Valentinus' system. To Valentinus' complex hierarchy of Aeons corresponds in the *Hermetic Writings* a series of strangely contour-less figures and powers; nor do the Christian elements in Valentinus make any difference in the basic view. If the attempt is made – more or less successfully – to translate the symbols into prosaic words, important similarities with the philosophical tradition will be found as well: the first, unsayable principle, *nous*, *Logos* as creator, matter and evil, and man's dual position. The latent problems in the philosophical tradition are left wholly unexplained in the *Hermetic Writings*: what is the relation between the light and the dark to which god does not come, between god and the world, and between good and evil? In the *Poemandres Treatise* the world is created by god, even though it is subject to evil. Elsewhere in the *Corpus Hermeticum* (e.g. V) god's greatness is understood through his creation, the world. The invisible god is, thanks to the universal order, the most visible.

Gnosticism may be considered a condensed expression of a prominent mood in an 'age of anxiety', as a visionary reply to the question of how man finds his redemption from an alien world; in its own strange way it continues the soul-body dualism that on Greek soil is already present in Orphism. The impenetrable mixture of faith and superstition is likewise characteristic of the time as a whole. Nevertheless, Gnosticism has its own face. This is true not only of the mythical language, the sophisticated depth psychology, or the vision of the world as a drama in which man is a co-actor. Gnosticism differs from the mystery religions – with which it otherwise has much in common – by man's not receiving salvation from god; he has from the outset the possibility of redemption in himself; furthermore, Gnosticism is not necessarily tied to cult and rite. Even Christian Gnosticism differs from orthodox Christianity by being ahistoric: the Gnostics have no use for the incarnation, 'the God in Time'; the Christian Gnostics do indeed speak of the heavenly Christ but only reluctantly of the earthly one. The so-called anti-Gnostic Church Fathers fought a life-and-death battle with the Gnostic interpretation of Christianity and they insisted on a barrier between Gnostic and Christian orthodoxy. Finally – despite similarities – Gnosticism differs essentially from the philosophical tradition that culminated with Plotinus. Plotinus wrote a treatise against the Gnostics (Plot. II 9), in which he most firmly turns against the religious language and heavy freight of mythology. The many 'powers' and Aeons serve no serious philosophical purpose. Furthermore, he attacks the whole idea of a cosmic drama and a fall, and especially the dualism between good and evil, where matter lies in the power of evil. To Plotinus the physical world as well is an emanation of the highest principle, the One.

Philo is perhaps the one who most resembles the Gnostics, and he has sometimes been considered a kind of 'proto-Gnostic'. But here also the differences are greater than the similarities. Philo's philosophical-religious syncretism is far removed from the cosmic drama of Gnosticism.

NUMENIUS

In our transmission the Neopythagorean Numenius emerges as the figure before Plotinus who more than anyone else attempts to gather the threads. He is a 'Pythagorean' and so in a way he continues Moderatus, even though with significant alterations. He is influenced by Gnosticism and Hermetism – which partly appears from a semi-religious language (his metaphysical principles are consistently called 'gods') and partly in a quite far-reaching dualism, which still of course is also to be found in Plutarch. Thus he speaks of 'the evil world soul' and of two parts of the human soul, and he considers matter evil (Num. frg. 52, Des Places (Calc.)). Although not a Jew himself, he was familiar with Jewish thought and the Old Testament – which may be accounted for by his having been born in Syria. He finds much philosophical wisdom in the Old Testament, and of course we are reminded of Philo when he opines that Plato was 'a Moses who spoke Attic' (frg. 8 (Eus.)). But the philosophical contents of the preserved fragments point unambiguously to the Greek tradition. Like all Neopythagoreans he was in fact a Platonist – and wrathfully he attacked the 'apostate' Platonists of Academic Scepticism (frg. 27 ff. (Eus.)). It is Numenius' intention to think his way systematically through the philosophical elements of the tradition, and despite the religious language he avoids over-embroidered Gnostic symbolism.

Numenius came up with a precise formulation of what may be called the standard argument for the existence of immaterial principles. In a transmitted passage in which he employs the didactic dialogue form known from the *Corpus Hermeticum* (frg. 3–4a (Eus.)) he asks what being is. It cannot be corporeal, for matter cannot be explained by matter, which in itself is changeable, unstable, and chaotic. Being is precisely determined by permanence and stability and is hence immaterial. The argument is known in many variants before Numenius; in the last analysis it goes back to Plato's *Phaedo* (see p. 187), and later it can be rediscovered in Leibniz.

Pure being is called the first god. It is raised above *nous* and also above past, present and future (Num. frg. 5 (Eus.)); being is in other words conceived of as a *nunc stans*, but no principle precedes it. The more detailed formulation of the doctrine of principles is not quite transparent (cf. frg. 12; 13; 15; 16; 20 (Eus.)) – and that this is not merely owing to our transmission appears from the accusation against Numenius in late Antiquity of lack of clarity (cf. Porph. *Vit. Plot.* 17). The main line of thought can presumably be reconstructed as follows (cf. Num. frg. 22 (Procl.)): there are three 'gods'. With links to the *Timaeus* (Plat. *Tim.* 39 E), the first is called 'what truly is to be' a living creature; the second god is *nous*; the third, presumably the created world, corresponds to discursive thinking. These gods are hierarchically connected with each other, which is stated by their 'utilizing each other'. The first god is beyond *nous*, but he 'uses' the other, which is to say that he can transform himself into *nous,* the god who is aware of himself by thinking himself. *Nous* in its turn can 'use' the third god, which is to say that he can transform himself into the creator-god or Demiurge. What is essential is that there are not simply three separate gods; the three gods are actually one, related to each other and appearing in different manifestations as the intelligible world and the created world that can be known discursively. Here there are important points of resemblance with Plotinus. The basic structure corresponds with the three hypostases – although not as clearly as in Moderatus, because Numenius' 'first god' is not beyond being as is the One in Plotinus. However, to this should be added that the somewhat clumsy expression 'to utilize' corresponds to the metaphor of emanation in Plotinus. One can perceive a connection with Plotinus' thought that creation is a by-product of contemplation, and in other ways as well the notion of emanation is anticipated. Emanation is a figurative expression of the essential identity between everything that is and of the idea that all that is springs from the same inexhaustible source; in Plotinus and in later Neoplatonism this is often expressed in two formula-like phrases – to be found in Numenius (Num. frg. 41 (Iambl.); 14 (Eus.)): 'everything is in everything, but in each according to its mode of being'[2] and 'the divine is granted from the beyond without suffering diminution itself'.

In many ways Numenius points forward to Plotinus. In Platonic scholasticism – for example in Albinus – there is indeed room for mystical knowledge of god. But no middle Platonic text is in itself sustained by mysticism. It is, however, the case with Philo, in the *Corpus Hermeticum*, and in Numenius. In lofty language that may remind one of Plotinus', Numenius can speak of the mystical experience in which one distances oneself from the sensual, suddenly to stand face to face with the good, lonely with the lone, where there is nothing but an unspeakable and inconceivable divine solitude (frg. 2 (Eus)). One of Plotinus' treatises (Plot. VI 9, 11) ends with the words 'the flight of the lonely towards the Lone'.

2   Already Philo comes close to this idea (see above, p. 525).

32

PLOTINUS

———— •◆• ————

Plotinus (c.205–70) may be called the most prominent systematic metaphysician of Antiquity. Daringly combining Platonism, Aristotelian theology, and Stoic 'vitalism' he created a coherent 'philosophy of reflection', in which the absolute and infinite, the One, is reflected in the finite, in its totality, and of necessity – but in such a manner that the finite can reflect infinity. Via Augustine he was – indirectly – to have important influence on medieval philosophy. The Western world gained direct access to him through the Renaissance Platonist Ficino's Latin translation of 1492, which contributed to the reading of Plato in a Neoplatonic spirit during the Renaissance. Directly or indirectly, Plotinus' influence extends further – to the Cambridge Platonism of the second half of the seventeenth century, to German idealist philosophy, and to romantic poetry. Nicolaus Cusanus, Leibniz and Schelling are probably the most important thinkers who – although not Plotinians – have come closest to Plotinus' philosophical intentions.

Plotinus was a philosopher and a mystic. Probably this was a combination that at the time was the rule rather than the exception. But the way in which Plotinus tied the mystical mode of cognition to that of philosophy is special – also at that time. The mystical experience itself is probably everywhere the same. It cannot be communicated, for the 'unsayable' cannot be spoken of – or, as Plotinus himself put it: anyone who has experienced it for himself knows whereof I speak (Plot. VI 9, 9). Nevertheless, not a few mystics have attempted to communicate – in philosophy, art, or religion – and that implies a translation into a language that is tied to time and place. This is also true of Plotinus. He ties in with – is perhaps burdened by – a long philosophical tradition, which in a sense he completes. What is special for him is what might be called his intellectualistic mysticism. He distances himself as much as possible from the symbolic language of his time. In the style of his age he may call the highest principle 'god' or 'the father', but these are not symbols laden with significance: he distances himself firmly, for example from the mythical imagery of Gnosticism, and surely regards himself as the steward of a true Greek philosophical tradition that confronts oriental irrationality. There is no miraculous short-cut to knowledge of the highest. The path to what warrants philosophical reflection traverses philosophical reflection. In this respect – as in so many others – Plotinus feels himself to be the heir to Plato, and probably rightly so. Unlike the Christian mystics, for example, he is not bound to any religious truth. When he speaks of the highest principle – 'the One' – he uses the same language as that employed in the later metaphysical tradition about 'the absolute'.

Plotinus' most prominent student, Porphyry (c.233–305), edited his writings and furnished an introductory biography. This has been preserved and is an extremely valuable document that is strikingly modern in many ways. Biographical writing in Antiquity – Plutarch, for example – is most often idealizing and portrays the typical in an individual. Porphyry, on the other hand, furnishes a most lively characterization of Plotinus, the man himself – an interest in the individual, which one might perhaps not expect to find in a Neoplatonic environment.

Plotinus was born in Egypt. He cannot have been without means, and presumably his name is Latin, even though his mother tongue and his milieu undoubtedly were Greek. His general background is that of cosmopolitan Alexandria, where he among other things must have become acquainted with the *Hermetic Writings*. Porphyry tells us that he felt ashamed of his mortal frame and that therefore he was very chary with information about his childhood and early life (Porph. *Vit. Plot.* 1); yet we are told this much (3): it was not until he was twenty-eight years old that he began to be interested in philosophy. He attended one teacher after another, until he became a student of Ammonius Saccas – 'here is the man I sought', he said. We know next to nothing about this Ammonius Saccas; he was a Platonist – a middle Platonist or a Neopythagorean – but wrote nothing, and seems primarily to have been impressive because of his personality. Apparently he was a Socrates to Plotinus, and one may trace an inheritance from Ammonius in Plotinus' predilection for the oral form and the philosophical, maieutic dialogue, a sharp contrast to the practice of a typical middle Platonist. Plotinus transplanted Ammonius' spirit to his auditorium, as Porphyry tells us (14). Subsequently Plotinus participated in the Emperor Gordianus III's campaign against Persia in order to become acquainted with Persian and Indian philosophy (3). In this, however, he did not succeed; Gordianus III was killed (244), and Plotinus barely escaped himself. Thereupon he settled in Rome, where he became the centre of a sort of philosophical school. He must have occupied a quite significant position in Rome and was closely connected with the Emperor Gallienus, one of the few 'soldier emperors' to interest himself in cultural matters. Probably Gallienus supported Plotinus as part of his cultural politics, but he was weakened by incessant wars and struggles with the Senate opposition, and Plotinus did not succeed in his wish to establish a philosophical society – 'the Platonopolis' – under imperial auspices. He did not begin to write until he was about fifty (4), but writing was a by-product of the oral teaching and debates.

It is a warm portrait that Porphyry draws of his teacher. He often touches on Plotinus' kindness and psychological flair – which for example showed when Porphyry was entertaining thoughts of suicide (23; 11). One learns of the big and the small, for example that Plotinus probably was dyslectic, that he was fairly frail, that he was a practical man who assisted others in monetary matters, and acted as a ward for orphans (9; 2). The other side of Plotinus' character is of course also dealt with. Four times during the time Porphyry knew him, he had a mystical experience, and his dying words were: 'Try to bring the divine in you back into the All' (23; 2). What is perhaps especially informative is what we are told of Plotinus' attitude to magic (10). A malicious person had practised magic against him, but Plotinus was so well-versed in that art that he turned the magic back on the miscreant himself. Like everybody at the time Plotinus was convinced that occult forces existed – to him justified by the Stoic belief in 'sympathy' between all parts of the world – but he also believed that magic was confined to the visible world; whoever had his footing in a higher reality was immune (Plot. IV 4, 40 ff.).

Porphyry gives an excellent picture of Plotinus' teaching. There was an inner circle of students, which in addition to Porphyry himself included Amelius, a very diligent man, who acted the eternal footman and eagerly carried out all the tasks that Plotinus did not care for (Porph. *Vit. Plot.* 7). Apparently the public was allowed to attend Plotinus' teaching, which largely took the form of discussions. Porphyry relates how three days running he asked Plotinus about the relation between soul and body – which annoyed a member of the audience who had come to listen to a lecture. Soon after his arrival Porphyry ventured a contribution to the effect that intelligible objects exist outside the intellect – a view directly opposed to Plotinus' (18). Plotinus smiled and left the question to the ever-willing Amelius who promptly wrote a treatise on intelligible objects existing within the intellect. Porphyry wrote a rejoinder, Amelius issued a rebuttal, and finally Porphyry got the point.

When Plotinus presented his views, he did so with the utmost concentration. He liked to deal with questions and objections, but the words halted after the thought. This is precisely the form of presentation we find in his writings, which can also contain small fictive dialogues with questions and answers. It was Plotinus' students who persuaded him to write; his writings are not lecture reports or manuscripts but come very close to the oral form. It has been said of them that they are unsystematic treatises written on the basis of a system. When Plotinus was writing, says Porphyry (8), he had the line of thought concentrated in his mind beforehand; then he wrote at lightning speed as if he were copying a manuscript, and at the same time he was able, for example, to carry on a conversation. He did not check his manuscript – others could correct misspellings. The result is a treatise as we know it: a firm thought structure concealed in a loosely arranged form. It is always the same cause – the system as a whole – that is dealt with, but from different angles and in different variations, so that the system is never presented in one coherent argumentation; often the particular arguments must be augmented from the unspoken totality. The style is often poetical and suggestive, occasionally highly compressed; language is to impart something that it really cannot impart – and once in a while Plotinus' treatment of the Greek may remind one of Heidegger's use of German. Porphyry's characterization deserves to be quoted (14): 'Plotinus' style is concise, thought-laden, and terse; he is richer in thoughts than in words; often he writes inspiredly and passionately'.

Plotinus began to write in 253 and continued until his death. Porphyry stayed with him from 263 until 268, after which, on Plotinus' advice, he sought a change of environment because of his suicidal thoughts. Plotinus himself left it to Porphyry to publish his writings (24), but he did not fulfil his promise until late (c.300); in the meantime less reliable versions were in circulation, which in our transmission have left their traces as quotations in other writers. Porphyry's edition – our text – is a fine work of philology. The editor probably undertook revision of the wording, but on the whole he had a delicate touch. In his biography he gave very precise facts about the particular dates when the individual treatises were written (4 ff.) so that we are on very firm chronological ground – compared with other ancient writers. He did, however, arrange the writings on a systematic basis into six 'Enneads', groups, each consisting of nine treatises, and this is less than happy. The individual treatises can only with difficulty be ordered unambiguously, but Porphyry was so pleased with his systematics that occasionally he divided coherent treatises into two right down the middle; one particularly lengthy treatise was distributed over several Enneads.

We are in great debt to Porphyry for the information he provides (14) about the authors that were studied in Plotinus' 'school'. Evidently he found it superfluous to mention Plato, but he does, for example, mention Aristotle' *Metaphysics*, a series of middle Platonists, Alexander of Aphrodisias, and Numenius. With respect to the last of these, Plotinus was accused of plagiarism – understandably so, although without justification – and of course the faithful Amelius wrote a treatise in which he refuted the allegations (17). In his teaching Plotinus never got lost in detailed commentary; he captured the more profound meaning in a few words and then went ahead. Finally, Porphyry notes that in Plotinus' writings there is much concealed Stoicism and Aristotelianism (14).

PLOTINUS ON PRINCIPLES

In the preceding chapter a number of Plotinus' direct or indirect predecessors have been referred to. Hence there is no special need to single out differences and similarities, and Porphyry is correct in maintaining that Plotinus should not be interpreted doxographically. However, it is decisive to understand his place in the tradition in a slightly wider perspective, and so he wished to be understood himself. As a good Platonist Plotinus most firmly distances himself from every philosophical view that would explain the physical world by elements in the physical world itself – this applies to a materialistic corpuscular theory (Epicurus) or to a theory that finds the intelligible principles to be inherent in the material world (Stoicism). Just as forcefully he repudiates the basing of cognition on a causal theory of perception – be it an Epicurean, a Stoic, or an Aristotelian theory of perception, as Plotinus understood it. If cognition is dependent on the material it receives from the outside, no true cognition exists, and scepticism becomes the only acceptable escape (cf. Plot. III 8, 2; V 1, 1 ff.; III 1, 1; V 5, 2).

The remaining option is the main highway of philosophy that has its source in Plato and his more notable predecessors – Heraclitus, Pythagoras and Parmenides – a philosophy that presupposes that in its essence the world is immaterial and intelligible, accessible to human cognition. Plotinus is of course familiar with the problems that loomed as a perpetual threat to the Platonists of the Empire – the latent dualism and the question of the relation between the absolute and the world. These are problems that in the nature of things cannot be 'resolved' at a single stroke, but Plotinus differs from his predecessors by going behind every scholastic construction and tries instead for a philosophical elucidation of what in the most profound sense must be understood by the absolute or highest principle. He does so in constant dialogue with Plato. Plotinus distances himself from other philosophers and often assesses them with astute objectivity. But Plato is a part of himself; he is not to be judged or assessed; one has to understand the truth he perceived – frequently Plotinus merely says 'he' instead of 'Plato'. This does not mean that Plotinus is unaware of the difficulties in interpreting Plato. But they are the difficulties inherent in the subject itself. To Plotinus the reading of Plato coincides with his own reflections.[1]

All philosophy and science presuppose – in the terminology of Antiquity – 'principles' behind the world as it immediately presents itself. The special mark of the Platonic tradition is that these principles not only are explanatory principles, but that they have real existence, and that the physical world only exists as a reflection of the principles. Already Parmenides had said that thought and being are the same (cf. Plot. V 1, 8), and to Plotinus it is from him that the tradition takes its point of departure.

Two main approaches sustain Plotinus' notion of principles in his one-sided but consistent combination of Platonic, Aristotelian and – partly – Stoic ideas.

The first may be illustrated by means of one quotation from Plato and one quotation from Aristotle. In the *Sophist* (248 E; cf. *Phaedo* 106 D; here p. 230 and p. 188) Plato had asked whether change, life, soul and insight do not belong to being in its full extension. Plato himself saw the connection between thought and being as a kinship, not as an identity. But to Aristotle thought in its highest form was identical with its object, and in his theology he declared (Aristot. *Met.* 1072 b 27, here p. 364) that life is the actuality of thought, and the actuality of thought is god. Now, when Plotinus explicitly or implicitly joins these two quotations (cf., e.g. Plot. III 8, 8; V 1, 7; VI 6, 8; 7, 36), he is of course not acting as a historian of philosophy – for example, he ignores the fact that the Aristotelian god is a limiting, formal concept – but as a metaphysician. True reality – behind the visible – consists in the identity of being, life and thought. Ontology and epistemology coincide; a thought object immediately implies a thought subject and an act of thought, and any thought object immediately implies any other one. To the Stoics – and for that matter also to Plato and Aristotle – the visible cosmos was a living organism; Plotinus transfers this to the intelligible world; here 'life' exists in its highest potency. In the visible world there is also coherence – 'sympathy' in Stoic terminology – but it is a coherence between separate entities, a broken identity; and yet it holds true, as Plotinus says, that everything is boiling with life (12).

The second main view in Plotinus' notion of principles is that every being is one

---

1   Of course Plotinus had read all of Plato, but an examination of his quotations and allusions will show that by and large his Plato corresponds to the Plato of the middle Platonists and the Neopythagoreans. It is not the dialectical and ignorant Socrates who concerns him; nor is Plato's political philosophy discussed – surely all the Platonopolis Plotinus wished for was a refuge for philosophers, not a Platonic republic. Furthermore, major parts of Plato's epistemology and logic are only indirectly of interest. The most essential Plato texts are the *Parmenides*, *Timaeus*, and the metaphysical sections of the *Republic*. To this should be added the mythical-mystical passages of the *Phaedrus* and the *Symposium*, the argument for the immortality of the soul in the *Phaedo*, 'the digression' in the *Theaetetus*, and the metaphysical passages in the *Sophist*, *Philebus* and *Laws*. Finally mention should be made of Plato's *Seventh Letter* and of some cryptic remarks in the *Second* and *Sixth Letter* (Plat. *Ep.* II 312 E; VI 323 D), the authenticity of which is doubted today, but in which Plotinus found unambiguous allusions to the three hypostases.

(cf. 9, 1), which is to say that it has structure and is complete as that which it is – the physical world, the intelligible world, the physical object or the individual idea. Some entities are complete unities in themselves at the same time as they are related to other entities – Socrates or an idea is included in a totality of individuals or ideas. And inasmuch as every entity is one, it implies all other entities; every part implies, mirrors, or reflects the totality. But this occurs in different ways. A physical object implies the whole universe but does so as one object next to others and bound to others by 'the cosmic sympathy'; a thought or a thought object immediately implies the whole system of thoughts and thought objects. But prior to this distinction there is another more fundamental one, which is the distinction between that which simply is unity and that which has unity – or, as Plato puts it in the *Parmenides*, the difference between the One and the One being. Plotinus puts it in this way (V 1, 8; cf. 5, 9; VI 9, 3): Parmenides himself did not clearly perceive the difference between unity and being; Aristotle made the same mistake; but the Platonic Parmenides distinguished unambiguously between that which is only one (the first hypothesis), that which is one-many – the intelligible world (the second hypothesis) – and that which is one and many – the soul, the physical world, or the individual physical object. This is a unity consisting *of* a plurality of parts and can come into being or perish (appendix). Unity itself therefore differs from everything else by having no other determination than unity – and thereby it is principle for everything that *has* unity. Often when Plotinus uses the Platonic phrase that unity in itself is 'beyond being' (cf. e.g. V 5, 6; 4, 2) he does not mean that the One is nothing, but rather that it is not this or that – which not only is in agreement with Plato's thought in the *Republic* but with the general Greek view that 'being' (*ousia* – substance in Aristotle) means being something. Unity is not in itself, as Aristotle thought, a predicate; it is not a something that also is one – only he who is bound to the categories of the sensible world will be afraid that unity dissolves itself into a nothing (VI 9, 2 ff.; 5).

Therefore one must distinguish between three levels of existence that are bound together by the concept of reflection. That which *has* being relates to everything else; to relate means to turn towards something, to reflect in the widest sense; Plotinus calls such reflection contemplation (*theōria*). Any given entity, a 'something', is therefore primarily determined by its form of reflection; only secondarily does a something undertake something – 'contemplation' precedes 'creation', but 'creation' is a necessary product of 'contemplation' according to Plotinus. Now, 'something' can 'relate' to itself or to something else. Transferred to the world as a whole this means that only three levels are to be found – as Plotinus forcefully points out to the Gnostics (II 9, 1; cf. V 1, 3). First of all there is the highest principle that precedes reflection. This is the One that in itself only is one, but which is the ontological warrant for the existence of anything, which is what it is by *being* one. On the second level unity relates to itself by self-reflection – this is the intellect or *nous*, in which the subject is aware of its unity with the object, in which the thought object hence is not something external but rather is included in self-consciousness, and in which the one thought object or the one thought act includes all others. Finally there is the third level of reflection where the intellect is reflected by a further differentiation and individualization in time and space. Here unity relates or turns towards something other than itself – it is a world of individual entities which are recognized by discursive thought that places object x in relation to object y. But that which both makes every object and the totality of objects one is the soul, and therefore Plotinus calls this level the soul (*psychē*). Both on the levels of intellect and soul, consciousness or reflection thus precedes 'creation' of objects: the ideas exist in and by the unity turning towards itself; physical objects exist in and by unity turning away from itself. Hence at the levels of both intellect and soul, ontology and epistemology converge.

Plotinus calls a level of reflection or a mode of existence a hypostasis (*hypostasis*: foundation), something that exists in itself in so far as it has its own criterion for existence or reflection. But obviously it is not a question of three separate spheres. All levels are manifestations of the One, and at all three levels the world as a totality is viewed as unity or in the form of intellect or soul. The One is 'potentially' both intellect and soul (III 8, 10; IV 8, 6; VI 9, 5). Therefore the world can be understood statically and dynamically, as a process. A necessary connection between the three hypostases must exist; they must be transformable from one to the other; the intellect is subordinate to the One, the soul to the intellect and the One. Metaphorically this transition is called an emanation. Either Plotinus speaks of an emanation from the One as an inexhaustible spring or as a radiance like the sunrays emitted by the sun without the sun ever being extinguished (V 1, 6; III 8, 10), or he says that the One 'overflows' in its fullness (V 2, 1).

Each hypostasis covers the whole universe according to its mode of existence. And yet there 'is' something that has no form of consciousness and hence does not constitute a hypostasis but delimits the soul 'downwards', i.e. matter. In a certain sense it does not exist – as little as Plato's space-matter or Aristotle' *prima materia* is found anywhere. In the physical world matter is always present as formed matter, as the stuff that mirrors the world of the soul without itself having any form of reflection or autonomous existence. Matter is the outermost limit of the creative power of the One. To the extent that it is part of the physical world, it is also necessarily part of the good order that springs from the One. But if matter is considered in abstraction, it is a nothing and an evil that leads the soul to its destruction. This duality of course determines Plotinus' view of the relation between good and evil. But what is decisive for his position on this ever-present question is that matter is not – as in the Gnostics, Plutarch, or Numenius – an independent power. Nothingness is privation of something else or an 'otherness'. To be not-x is not a property in the same way as to be x. Plato had realized this in the *Sophist* when he identified not-being with difference (1, 2; II 4, 5; I 8, 3; 5; 7; 11; Plat. *Soph.* 255 E, here p. 233). If negation or nothingness were an independent power, the One would not be perfect.

Man contains the whole cosmos in himself. He is soul contained in body, and if he permits himself to be trapped by the body he will perish in nothingness. But the soul also contains the intellect and the One. Corresponding to the process of emanation, which indicates the continuous creation from the One to intellect and from intellect to soul – the downward path, there is also an upward path where the soul can identify itself with the intellect and the One. This path goes through self-knowledge.

The intellect is an image of the One; the soul is an image of the intellect. It goes without saying that the image-metaphor must be as essential to Plotinus as to Plato. The archetype appears in the image but in another medium; and an image is therefore both something in itself and something other than itself (cf. Plot. V 2, 1; VI 4, 10; V 1, 7; III 8, 1). The unity, beauty and harmony found in the world are not unity, beauty, or harmony in themselves but images. And as Plato had said, time is an image of eternity. Eternity as an abiding now belongs to the intellect and its life; the world of the soul unfolds in a perpetual series of before and after, as it unfolds in a series of separate individuals (III 7; cf. I 5, 7; Plat. *Tim.* 37 C ff.).

Language is a quite special kind of image (cf. Plot. V 5, 6; VI 9, 3). It is modelled on the physical world; it reproduces discursive thought, and its basic structure consists of subject-predicate sentences. If only for that reason the One is 'unsayable' – it neither has nor is a property. If one speaks of the One, the Aristotelian formula 'to say something about something' has no meaning; here one can only speak negatively and say what the One is not. Nor can language express the world of the intellect adequately, for discursive language separates and combines what in the intellect is a coherent whole. Language must always be metaphorical when it speaks of the One or the intellect. Plotinus makes use of this: in deliberate imagery he signals that he is expressing himself indirectly – he is a master at drawing concrete, sensible images which by their very lucidity point beyond themselves. The emanation metaphor is a good example, and Plotinus himself expressly declares that in itself the image is insufficient (5, 5). Elsewhere he may inject a discreet 'as if' or 'as it were'. When he speaks of the One as the well-spring of being, beauty, or goodness, he likes to place a *hyper* before them – the One is 'the hyper-being', 'the hyper-beautiful', 'the hyper-good'. In this way language is pressed to express what it, strictly speaking, cannot express – Plotinus' wilful treatment of the Greek language has its reasons. But it is characteristic of his rationality that he never – as did Plutarch or the Gnostics – allows image, symbol, or myth to stand on its own. He may use myths and interpret them allegorically, but this always happens as a paedagogical means, as a starting point for reflection proper, and he emphasizes that the myths are only an outward symbol (9, 9 ff.). He may also give a twist to the traditional professional language of philosophy – not least to Aristotle's 'common terminology' of form and matter, actuality and potentiality, etc. – for example when he considers the One as potentiality for the intellect or the soul as an actualization of the intellect (III 8, 10; IV 8, 5). Here potentiality (*dynamis*) is not – as in Aristotle – a mere passive possibility; Plotinus goes back to the original meaning 'power', and thus the word designates the 'power' of the superior hypostasis to create an inferior one.

As has been mentioned, Plotinus did not provide a complete presentation of his system. Occasionally one finds brief sketches of the system, but mostly in such a way that the reader has to insert some unspoken premises. A small treatise (V 4) thus presents the standard argument of the day for the existence of a highest principle: the composite must be derived from the incomposite, and the incomposite must be unborn, imperishable, and beyond any determination of being. At the same time the standard paradox is presented: the autonomous first principle exists in itself but must nevertheless be 'present' as principle for 'the other things'. It is an unspoken premiss that the incomposite must have an ontologically superior status *qua* principle, and the relation between the transcendence and immanence of the principle is not discussed. In its form this treatise is a specimen of a paedagogical argument that can remind one of middle Platonism. Often such a sketch-like presentation can show up as an interpretation of Plato. Plotinus can, for example, take his point of departure in the simile of the sun in the *Republic* and in the *Symposium* in order to follow the soul's path to the highest, and then suddenly shift to another stylistic level – in Porphyry's phrasing an inspired and passionate rendition of the soul's sudden vision: he whose lot it has been to come close to the good

> takes leave of all knowledge, he who until then was trained and had gained a seat in the beautiful. As long as he dwells there, he is thought (*noei*), but he is torn away as if by the wave of thought; as if up from the swelling sea he is elevated to the high, and suddenly he beholds without seeing how. But the vision fills his eye with light so that he sees nothing else by its aid; but the light is itself that which is seen, for then there is no object that is seen and no light that allows for seeing, not a thought nor a thought object. But these things are created afterwards by the beam of light and are alotted their being in the viewer. He himself is the light that merely creates the thought; it itself is not extinguished in the act of creation but abides in itself; the created comes into being because this is.
>
> (VI 7, 36)

What is characteristic in such a passage is not only the depiction of the mystical vision but also the complete agreement between experience and doctrine. Plotinus never uses mystical experience as a substitute for a theoretical presentation but as a complement that protreptically stimulates the reader to understand the theoretical reasoning by insight into his own self. If one can speak of a basic structure in Plotinus' frequently disconnected form it is precisely this double-sidedness of doctrine and experience where neither can stand by itself. Plotinus envisioned what he taught.

A good example of this basic way of presentation is the treatise *On the Good or the One*, which Porphyry placed at the end of his edition and which is often read as the standard presentation of Plotinus' thinking, even though this treatise also considers the totality from its own point of view (VI 9). The first half is theoretical. All beings exist by virtue of the One – as we are told at the outset. Then it is demonstrated how unity manifests itself in the physical world, in the spheres of the soul and of the intellect. Everywhere unity appears as the property whereby the soul is soul and the intellect intellect, but in itself unity lies beyond thought and passion; and having declared this, Plotinus alters course and demonstrates in the second half (VI 9, 7 ff.) that the entire metaphysical universe can be found again in man himself and that it is possible to gain insight into the highest by contemplation and concentration. This is the path from the outward to the inward and from the inward to the higher. Mythical examples can serve as guides – but no more than that. The all-decisive is that the seer finds himself in the seen, in 'the flight of the lonely towards the Lone' (11).

Since the days of romanticism the treatise *On Beauty* (I 6) has often been used as an introduction to Plotinus in general. This can distort the picture somewhat, for the normal in Plotinus is not the aesthetic but the metaphysical-psychological path towards the highest. And nevertheless the several paths do converge – as do knowledge and insight into the beautiful in Plato's *Symposium* – and hence the aesthetic path does in its own way contain the totality. The subject of the treatise is the meta-physics of the beautiful. Plotinus begins by showing that beauty in a work of art – like beauty in nature – does not depend on the corporeal itself nor on a particular kind of harmony in the work of art itself but on the ideal beauty laid down by the artist in his work. Therefore the work of art is a condensed image or symbol of the immaterial beauty experienced by the artist, which the viewer can experience anew if he abstracts from the bodily beauty and sees it as an expression of the beauty in his own soul and if he is able to proceed to the beauty in the intellect and to the highest, the beautiful in itself, which is another expression of the One in itself. One aspect of the treatise is accordingly the path to the high that proceeds from the outward to the inward – the path that the treatise not only demonstrates but itself follows. If the work is viewed as an aesthetic dissertation, it immediately becomes apparent that Plotinus silently is distancing himself from Plato – the work of art is not an image of an image three stages removed from reality; precisely as image or symbol the work of art can mirror real beauty. To this is then added the expressionistic aspect. The artist expresses a higher reality, and the viewer finds it anew in himself; the idea precedes its realization in matter and can be experienced anew in abstraction from matter. The reality of the work of art is a metaphysical reality.

A presentation of Plotinus cannot – as with the great Hellenistic systems – begin at one end and then let the other parts follow in natural consequence. As has been attempted in the preceding, with Plotinus one must begin with the whole and consider it in its relation to the form of the treatises; then one can consider the parts in light of the whole.

THE THREE HYPOSTASES

'The One is everything and yet not a one', is the way one Plotinus treatise begins (V 2,1). Elsewhere Plotinus says that the one is ineffable – i.e. we cannot define it – but we can speak *about* it – which is to say provide a tentative linguistic formulation (cf. 3, 13 ff.). That the One is everything means that it is present in everything else, 'the other'. But the sentence cannot be turned around; Plotinus is no Pantheist (cf. III 8, 9). That the One is not even a one means that it is not one thing next to others or a numerical unity (cf. with respect to the following: V 5, 4; 6; 12 ff.; VI 2, 17; 9, 3 ff.). Everything else is one by participating in the One; the One is simply one. It is beyond any determination and not a *summum genus* – for then its essence could be determined – nor is it an Aristotelian 'this' – for if so, it would be possible to deter-mine it in relation to something else. Although no determination can be attached to the One, Plotinus can nevertheless identify it with the good, as Plato had done – provided that the good in itself is not understood as *a* good that is predicated of the One. This identification is important, because it shows that Plotinus – as opposed to the Gnostics – maintains Plato's basic teleological view: the One is not an abstract nothing but the transcendent precondition for the world's being good inasmuch as it exists. Since it is not a 'something', Plotinus draws the logical consequence that it is infinite (6; cf. V 5, 6) – a clear but unspoken break with the earlier metaphysical tradition and thereby also with Plato.

Wherever Plotinus seeks to make the language delimit the one or the absolute without predicating anything of it, he is at pains to maintain a duality. In itself the One is transcendent and perfectly impervious to everything else. But it is also the power or goodness that produces everything; it is the precondition for both existence and cognition (cf. III 8, 9 ff.). It is evident that it is precisely when language is to maintain this duality that it comes up short; the flickering language employed by Plotinus is probably partially intentional. In the treatise *On Beauty* he can identify the beautiful with the One, although with reservations that suggest that the aesthetic path to the highest cannot stand on its own. And he can also emphasize (V 5, 12) that strictly speaking the identification is invalid, for also intelligible beauty is beauty *in* something. The One is the cause of beauty, just as it is the cause of thought – and yet Plotinus may also say that the One has 'as if' a sort of immediate self-consciousness (4, 2); the One is 'hyper-thinking', 'hyper-beautiful' – but also 'hyper-good' (cf. VI 8, 16; I 8, 2; VI 9, 6).

Plotinus' deliberately versatile play on the inadequacy of language appears clearly in a treatise *On Freedom and the Will of the One* (VI 8). When the One creates everything else, is this by virtue of free will? More precisely: can the Stoic phrase 'what is in our power' be applied to the One – or is it possible in Aristotelian manner to say that the One acts freely because it is not under compulsion? First one must realize that the One exists of necessity – and what the term necessity means. In approaching the One by depriving it of all determinations, one is not to imagine a kind of space from which one has removed all objects in order to place the One in it, for that would be to inquire about the One as if it were something alien, an object among others, which might not-be. The same is the case if one asks 'what is the One?' in the same way as one asks 'what is object x?', for that would be a question of the essence, quality, cause, or existence of the One, and that question cannot be asked. Why not? Because the One as opposed to the object is identical with its essence and is its own cause – *causa sui*, to use a concept that not least due to Plotinus later became the basis for the so-called ontological proofs of God's existence, in which the presupposition is that essence and existence coincide in God. Consequently it is not accidental that the One exists. Nor is it necessary in the sense that the One is bound by a power outside itself. So if we ask if the One does 'what is in its power', whether it acts freely or whether it has a will, the answer must be yes and no. No, if one infers by analogy from man: it is not the case that the One has certain options, that it acts in this or that particular way, but that it could have acted otherwise. Yes, if the freedom and will of the One simply are manifestations of its essence; then the One 'acts' freely and without compulsion but also of necessity, since it would be meaningless for it to 'act' in spite of itself (VI 8, 11; 13 ff.; 21).

That the 'freedom' and 'will' of the One merely are different linguistic expressions of its essence means that the One does not create with consciousness *of* its 'freedom' or its 'will'. It also implies that in fact it is meaningless to ask whether one could think of a world without the One or of the One without the world; that would be like asking whether the necessary is necessary. We can infer from the effect, the world, to the cause, the One. But as far as humanly possible one can and should also go the other way, for otherwise one would only arrive at the idea of the One from the – perhaps contingent – fact that the world exists. In the language of a later time: one would thus construct an aposteriori proof that would make God's existence dependent on the existence of the world. When Plotinus follows the path from the world to the One he can use arguments handed on by the tradition, which were obvious to the Platonists of the day: the composite presupposes the incomposite; motion and change presuppose an unmoved mover; the principle has a higher ontological status than that which is derived from the principle; if the principle is not absolute, something superior to the principle must exist. When Plotinus goes the opposite way, he speaks most often in images. The One can no more stop creating than the well-spring can stop springing; god has created the world, because he is 'without jealousy'. This way of thinking has both a metaphysical and a logical side, although Plotinus uses the metaphysical version most frequently. He takes his point of departure in tacitly conceding to the Stoics that a given entity is not simply an entity that merely is present; inasmuch as a 'thing' exists, it acts and creates something – being implies life. The next point is that a perfect entity necessarily must also act or create perfectly, which is to say that the One is not perfect unless it constantly creates everything that can be created; the possible must necessarily become actualized. The logical line of thought states that in order to be perfect the One necessarily implies plurality, the other or 'otherness'. A physical object or a concept has the otherness outside itself; being perfect the One must include the other in itself. The One must create the other or the not-one, because it is its nature to 'turn towards itself'. All Neoplatonic thinking or all thinking inspired by Neoplatonism rests on this paradox (cf. V 1, 6; 2, 1; 4, 1; IV 8, 6; 3).

It is one thing that creation necessarily takes place; it is another how it comes about. The world is eternal – the One and the intellect are beyond time; but in the hypostasis of the soul, being unfolds itself in the medium of time; but this creation is also a constant process, and since it takes place of necessity, it comes about without planning (cf. V 8, 7). Everything is in everything, the parts in the whole and the whole in the parts; the principle or *archē* appears in the particular or finite – in 'the other' – according to the nature of this other: the intellect relates to itself, the soul to something other than itself (5, 9; 8, 4; IV 9, 1). Creation is a process that continues by a constant differentiation and individualization all the way to the outermost limit, matter. The higher principle remains unaffected by the process of creation; it 'contains' the lower, and the lower cannot affect the higher – the sunbeams are dependent on the sun, the sun not on the sunbeams (cf. I 7, 1; VI 8, 18; III 8, 8). But that the lower exists is a necessity, for when unity exists, it is necessary also for 'otherness' to exist – the intellect and the soul has each its own otherness, and if 'the other' or the not-one were not, the One would only exist in undisturbed quietness (V 1, 1; 3 ff.).

Emanation and hypostasis are the technical terms attached to the process of creation. The two concepts are complementary. The lower hypostases have descended from the higher ones and are what they are by virtue of having their own special being, their special way of relating to unity. Emanation is really a misleading term – not only because it is a metaphor, but also because the process is two-directional. A given hypostasis exists only by relating to that from which it has proceeded. The intellect becomes intellect by relating to the One; the soul becomes soul by relating to the intellect (cf. 2, 1 ff.). Therefore there are in both the intellect and the soul three stages that express the static and the dynamic. The lower hypostasis has proceeded from the higher one (*proodos*: procession); it remains itself (*monē*: remaining); it 'returns' to its point of departure (*epistrophē*: reversion or turning back – cf. IV 2, 1; II 1, 1; V 2, 1).[2] The intellect or the soul is accordingly 'itself' when it finds itself on the balancing point between *proodos* and *epistrophē*, which is to say at the point where by cognition or reflection it 'turns towards' that which is the cause of its existence. This way of thinking is of course only meaningful when it is realized that every hypostasis is identical with the whole – although in a particular mode or in a particular form of reflection. Here Plotinus exploits Aristotle's psychology, in which *nous*, or soul, in itself is nothing but potentially everything. *Nous* becomes itself by identification with its object; the soul becomes soul by identification with the formal side of an external object. Plotinus develops this so that self-consciousness and consciousness *of* something are two aspects of the same issue, and he adds the special feature that the something against which intellect or soul turns is a higher hypostasis, which the intellect or soul appropriates as intellect or soul. *Epistrophē* comes about by *theōria* or contemplation, and tied to this is self-awareness, *synaisthēsis*, just as rational cognition or sense cognition in Aristotle is tied to awareness of cognition (cf. III 8, 1 ff.; V 1, 7; see p. 338). With regard to the relation between the One and the intellect, it makes no difference whether one says that the One creates the intellect by self-reflection or whether the intellect exists by contemplation of the One – as sight becomes seeing in the act of vision (V 1, 7; 2, 1 ff.; 3, 11; VI 7, 15). But if one says that the intellect contemplates the One, one is thereby saying that it contemplates as intellect (cf. III 8, 8).

'Everything strives towards contemplation'. Thus Plotinus begins a treatise which indeed has contemplation as its subject (1). But contemplation implies existence, and existence implies creation – activity or creation is a by-product of contemplation, and accordingly a given hypostasis not only 'relates upwards'; it also operates 'downwards'. The One 'creates' intellect, intellect 'creates' soul, and soul 'creates' the physical world – all by contemplation. That the physical world is a by-product of the soul's contemplation can be demonstrated empirically according to Plotinus. The physical world is not a random chaos of motions; the motions adhere to a pattern and are included in an order. Likewise the physical object has its intelligible model. In the aforesaid treatise, *On Contemplation* (4; cf. 3), Plotinus allows Nature to deliver a small monologue. What comes into being, says Nature, is that which I silently behold, a vision that assumes physical form. My contemplation creates the object of contemplation, just as the geometers draw their figures while contemplating. But I am not drawing; the figures delimiting the bodies fall, 'as it were', from my contemplation. In our terms, we would perhaps say that the intentional object precedes the real one.

In this way intellect and soul are also 'so to speak' a balancing point between contemplation and creation (cf. IV 8, 3). The continuous progression towards greater individualization is in itself 'natural'. Yet, if the part forgets itself, isolates itself from

---

2   The three concepts frequently appear in Plotinus but do not become fixed terminology until late Neoplatonism.

the whole, and allows itself to be captured by its own production, it becomes guilty of what Plotinus calls 'audacity' (*tolma*), which he explains by the 'first otherness' or a willing-to-be-one's-own (V 1, 1; cf. VI 9, 5; III 8, 8; 7, 1; IV 8, 4). It is a distortion due to self-assertion but results in alienation, and therein consists evil. Later we shall return to Plotinus' view of evil; suffice it here to point out that to Plotinus it is a question of distortion within the greater order. He does not – as did the Gnostics – entertain a dualistic view of the relation between good and evil.

Nous – the hypostasis of intellect – is the first differentiation of the One, the hypostasis where unity 'contemplates' itself and where it thereby – downwards – creates the further differentiation of the soul. *Nous* is both one and many (cf. 3) – really it is a unity, but formally a split between thought subject and thought object has taken place in *nous*. Herein lies an agreement with Aristotle and a distancing from him. Really, thought subject and thought object do coincide, but since in fact one can speak of subject and object, it is no longer possible to maintain – as did Alexander of Aphrodisias, for example – that *nous* is simple and incomposite (cf. V 1, 9; 3, 12). Inasmuch as self-consciousness and consciousness *of* something are two aspects of the same issue (cf. II 9, 1), this means that the self-reflection of *nous* directly implies a reflection about all intelligible objects – there are no intelligible objects outside *nous*, as Amelius demonstrated to Porphyry and as carefully described by Plotinus in a weighty treatise (V 5). Here again there is an ambiguous exploitation of Aristotle. As already mentioned, Plotinus combines the notion of the ideas as god's thoughts with Aristotle's self-thinking god – and that is not Aristotelianism; but it should not be overlooked that crucial Aristotelian ideas lie behind it: in rational cognition subject and object are united; in sense perception the perceived object is in itself outside consciousness, because the form exists *in* the matter. Now, since cognition and existence converge in *nous* – here life, being and thought are the same – this means that when we recognize *nous*, it is because with a higher level of ourselves we are *nous*, and to call the existence of thought objects into doubt is to question our own existence – a formulation that sometimes has been called Plotinus' *cogito* (V 3, 8; 8, 11). In *nous* there are no external objects; everything is a substantial unity. In the hypostasis of the soul, on the other hand, one entity relates – by magic – to the other, and this relation can, with the Stoics, be called *oikeiōsis*, an appropriation of or an adjustment to the other (III 8, 8). In the world of soul we perceive with light as the medium; in the world of intellect the light of cognition is found in the intellect itself (V 5, 7). The soul is surrounded by now this now that – at one moment Socrates, at another a horse; but in the intellect everything is one (cf. 1, 4) – as in the second hypothesis in Plato's *Parmenides*. The intellect emerges from the One by contemplating the One. Thereby the self-consciousness of the intellect comes into being; but thereby the intellect at the same time becomes conscious of what it contains, the ideas (cf. 7).

In the hypostasis of the soul matter is a precondition for the differentiation into physical objects. Plotinus is so much the heir to the tradition that he concludes that in the hypostasis of the intellect there must also be a precondition for the differentiation which already presents itself when the intellect by thinking itself is two – but it is characteristic for him that he combines two traditions: the precondition is, in Aristotelian terms, intelligible matter; in Platonic terms it is the 'Indefinite Dyad', the ideas and the numbers coming from the Indefinite Dyad (4, 2; II 4, 3). Of course such an intelligible matter is never present without form, but Plotinus feels himself obliged to presuppose a substratum for the formal plurality in *nous*. Another precondition for the one-many that constitutes the intellect is perhaps more interesting. The intellect is one in so far as it is a substantial unity; it is many in so far as it is a conceptual plurality. Here Plotinus needs certain concepts of reflection that can be applied in the analysis of the several aspects of the wholeness of the intellect. Such concepts must be universal; they cannot be dependent on a concrete conceptual content. Plotinus finds his concepts of reflection in Plato's *Sophist* (254 B ff.; see p. 232); they are the five 'highest genera': being, motion, rest, difference and sameness. *Nous* and any element within *nous* are being; but being is 'life' or motion – 'life is the actuality of thought'; it is also rest, for being is unalterably what it is; being finally comprises that which is identical with itself and different from something else. Plotinus calls these concepts of reflection 'categories', and thus he contributes to the debate of the time with a new 'doctrine of categories'. But it is a doctrine of categories of a special kind. The Aristotelian doctrine of categories, which Plotinus criticizes in detail (Plot VI 1), can only be applied to the sensible world where one object is determined in relation to another; Plotinus' categories, on the other hand, apply to the intelligible world (VI 2; cf. V 1, 4) – only by analogy to the sensible (VI 3).

Plotinus' 'categories' are a tool for analysis of the 'one-many' of the intellect, in which one thought object immediately implies the totality of thought objects in the same way as a theorem in geometry implies all geometry; and while we, in our understanding of the theorem, are bound to the progressive, discursive proof occurring in time, cognition in *nous* is intuitive, timeless and given with the theorem itself (cf. IV 9, 5). The thought object itself 'is' its own nature – in the intelligible world there is no difference between essence and existence, between the Aristotelian 'why' and 'that' – and by being itself it implies a plurality of other thought objects, as intelligible 'man' implies 'two-footed', 'living being', etc. (VI 7, 2; 9, 2). In the world of the soul one proceeds from genus to species, but in *nous* that which the soul divides in time is already divided (IV 4, 1; V 9, 9), and there truth is not correspondence with something else. But the truth of each particular thing is what the thing is (III 7, 4).

Plotinus does not speak much about ideas. He prefers to say 'thought objects' (*noēta*), and this already implies that what interests him is not so much ideas of this or that particular field of subjects but the ontological status of the ideas as elements in *nous*. Still, there is one remarkable exception. Plotinus assumes ideas for individuals – presumably not for all objects, but in any case for individual men (V 7; IV 3, 5), for the individual contains both the intellect and the One within himself and has his own form of eternity thereby. There must, says Plotinus, be a Socrates 'himself' who does not perish when the accidental union of body and soul that we call Socrates dies. Such an interest in the individual, especially in Plotinus, may seem surprising. Off-hand one might well expect that he only wanted to consider what is individual as something to be overcome. But it is not as simple as that. What is to be overcome is everything that is bound to matter. But in every man there is something that is not bound to matter; the manner of being intellect that is called Socrates belongs to eternity. Individual man is not only an instance of the idea of man but part of the greater whole of the intellect. With this something else is also implicitly stated. In middle Platonism ideas are – in agreement with Aristotle's interpretation of Plato – simply hypostatized universals. Plotinus of course also assumes ideas for the universal. But what is decisive to him is not the opposition of the universal and the particular but of the eternal and the temporal. An idea is first and foremost substance and act – *ousia* and *energeia* – it is 'life' and source of life.

The idea of the individual's eternity is undoubtedly connected with something else. Plotinus' combination of self-consciousness and cognition in the intelligible world is no mere theory. As always, to him self-consciousness implies direct experience. In his treatise *On Intelligible Beauty* (V 8, 4) he depicts in an inspired prose hymn – not how individual man experiences the eternity of the intellect, but how every part of the intellect comes to know itself by knowing everything in one, by beholding everything in its own light – as we are told with the 'light metaphor', which in Plotinus is no mere symbol. 'Everyone' – every part or every individual? – thus possesses everything in himself and sees everything in everything else; everything is everywhere, all is all, each and one are all, and the radiance is infinite. Probably it is only in his role as post-rationalizing interpreter that Plotinus distinguishes between the experience of the intellect and the experience of the One.

The hypostasis of the soul is the most differentiated one-many (cf. VI 2, 3). The soul is intermediary between intellect and matter, and by its contemplation it creates the physical world consisting of individuals – and, as appears from Plotinus' view of the eternity of the individual soul, this means that individuals unfold themselves in time and with matter as substratum. Like the intellect, the soul can turn both upwards and downwards (22). But it also has its own life, and it is not – as in Aristotle – bound to the stuff as the form of the body (IV 7, 85). The world of the soul unfolds itself in time and space; it is a world of discrete objects recognized by discursive thinking (*dianoia*), by the consciousness passing from one object to another. But the soul and its cognition are not dependent on the temporal-spatial; sensation in itself is a physical process, but sensation is – as in Plato – only the occasion, not the cause of cognition, and every judgement about sense objects is therefore an independent judging of physical processes (V 3, 2 ff.; III 7, 1; IV 3, 26), for the physical world is created by soul itself, and the soul can turn both upwards and downwards. Every soul should consider that it has created the entire world, and as long as it is aware that it is also an image of the intellect, it will not abandon itself (V 1, 2 ff.). It has bestowed unity and being on every thing according to its kind (VI 9, 1), but every creation or act is a by-product of contemplation, and therefore the 'higher part of the soul' remains in itself while the 'lower part' abandons itself in order to return to itself (III 8, 5 ff.). In its desire (*orexis*) for creation, the soul is directed towards the created, but never as something external. The soul's *proodos* goes as far as possible, but both when it rules the whole world and when it rules the individual parts, it rules it as a power from within, and Plotinus emphasizes that actually it is wrong usage to say that the soul is 'in' the body: the body – whether the body of the world or the individual body – is a product of the soul and therefore exists in the soul as does a fishing-net in water (IV 7, 13; 4, 11; 3, 9). In so far as the soul both is itself and can 'animate' a plurality of bodies, it is possible to say both that it is divided and that it is undivided – and therein lies no contradiction, for divisibility is a property of extended bodies (2, 1). If one says that the soul is undivided, one thereby says that the same substance is present everywhere where there is 'soul'; if one says that it is divided, one is speaking of the many bodies that have 'soul'. But it is also possible to say that the soul is 'divided in two' in another sense. The soul finds itself between the intellect and the world. Like everything else it must necessarily create – to ask why the soul creates the world is to ask why the soul is soul (II 9, 8). If it looks to the created, it must participate of the sensible; if it looks to its begetter, it thinks, and then its essence is *nous* (IV 8, 3; 7).

Plotinus stresses that in all its functions the soul is a unity; the whole is in the parts and the parts in the whole. But it is incontestable that the many functions assigned to the soul create difficulties; nor is there any doubt that the greatest difficulties in Plotinus' thought – considered as a system – are inherent in the third hypostasis. It is precisely here that he is burdened by a problematic tradition: the relation between the All-Soul or cosmic soul on the one hand and individual souls on the other; on the one hand, the soul is a reflection of the intellect; on the other, it is in contact with matter; the soul is both creator and guide of the body, and it is identified with discursive thinking. Plotinus goes quite far in speaking of different 'kinds' of souls, and he maintains that the 'higher part of the soul', as opposed to the 'lower', is unaffected by stuff. That he recognized the difficulties himself appears from the fact that – as always when he is in trouble – he plays several Plato quotations against each other (cf. 3,4; 7). But there is no doubt that behind the many different functions and manifestations of the soul he assumes one hypostasis of the soul. The hypostasis of the soul is and remains the mode of existence, in which that which is one relates to something outside itself. That Plotinus after all is able to stick to the unity of the soul is owing to the combination of a static and a dynamic view expressed in the complementary concepts of hypostasis and emanation. A hypostasis is not a sealed-off box, but a centre from which a form of consciousness can move in several directions. There are especially two areas in which modern interpreters – probably erroneously – have thought that Plotinus implicitly operates with further hypostases. At issue are the concepts of *physis* and *logos*.

The 'lower' part of the soul is occasionally called nature or *physis* (cf. 4, 13). This does not signify the totality of what in fact is present in the world but the soul as the power creating the world. Like all entities or levels in Plotinus's universe, nature creates of necessity, because it contemplates; and like all other entities, it is turned towards itself in self-contemplation and does not contemplate with an aim to create. Nature is the lowest part of Plotinus' universe capable of contemplation; hers is contemplation dim and dream-like (III 8, 4). But in spite of such formulations, nature is still not independent; she contemplates in her capacity as soul.

The power by means of which the soul or nature creates is often called *logos* by Plotinus. This is of course a Stoic concept, and Plotinus' use of it can be compared with Philo's, even though there are differences. Like the soul, *logos* has its source in the intellect and acts as nature's contemplation. It 'remains' in itself (*monē*) and is only able to affect matter because it – *qua* principle – has a different nature. Motion is in itself a property of matter; *logos* is structure and form (2 ff.; 5 ff.). In one of his later treatises (cf. 2, 11 ff.; 3, 1 ff.) Plotinus lays more stress on *logos* as a conveyor of structure and form, as the power proceeding from the intellect and the higher part of the soul that orders our world and makes it good (cf. especially 2, 16). Here he – nearly – treats *logos* as an independent actor, but none the less it remains true that *logos* essentially is a manifestation of intellect and soul.

Plotinus' entire philosophical system is an attempt to demonstrate how the infinite, the one, manifests itself in the form of the finite – in the intelligible world, in the world of soul, or in the sensible world – without being changed itself; infinity 'is contracted' in the finite, as Nicolaus Cusanus put it later on. As has already been mentioned, this idea leads to a number of seeming paradoxes due to the fundamental paradox of infinite-finite. In the first place, it is inherent in the concept of infinity itself that it contains the finite, and the finite is of course delimited – in Plotinus' language: there is a 'lower' limit. In the second place, it is also a consequence – at least of Plotinus' concept of infinity – that everything that can exist also must exist (IV 8, 3). The lower limit of the creative power of the one is matter; but a limiting concept is also paradoxical: it can only be understood in relation to that which it delimits. The world is not created in time; there was never a time when the world was not. Of the world 'before' creation it can only be stated metaphorically that it was a darkness of matter (V 1, 2). When he speaks of matter Plotinus, naturally enough, has recourse to the figurative language and line of thought of the *Timaeus*, and often he simply expresses himself by means of an interpretation of Plato. Matter is a necessary precondition for creation; creation consists in reason's 'persuading' necessity, and, as in the *Timaeus*, matter is called a 'receptacle' or a 'nurse' of becoming (cf. I 8, 7; III 6, 13). Thus matter is the 'something' that receives structure, form and order; but in itself matter is – still in the proper Platonic spirit – lack of form and to that extent not-being (II 4, 14 ff.).

Now, matter is never to be found 'in itself', and this occasions another paradox when matter is considered a – necessary – element in the created world. Matter receives form and order as if by an imprint – as already Moderatus believed; it itself has no reflection or self-consciousness, but is nevertheless, as Plotinus states in one passage (V 8, 7), the 'ultimate form', and in so far as the material world is a structured world, it is good (IV 8, 6). In so far as matter is the opposite of structure, it is evil – yet evil is still not an independent power, but a privation or a nothing. Plotinus retains this dual view. Matter is the cause of evil – both metaphysical and human evil: he is 'evil' who in 'audacity' would isolate his own self; he gains the opposite of what he wants; he is drawn towards not-being and finds himself in the power of affects, error and irrationality. Still, the world as a whole is not evil (I 8, 15; cf. III 9, 3).

Plotinus may affirm (II 3, 18) that without evil the world would not be perfect. But that is not all he has to say. His treatise against the Gnostics is one lengthy defence of the goodness of the world. *Kosmos* is an image of the intelligible world and therefore participates of the goodness of the idea. Whoever criticizes this world order does not know what he is doing; whoever despises it becomes evil – he encapsulates himself and cuts himself off from the intelligible world (II 9, 16 ff.; 8; 13). But the good man does not let himself be affected by external adversity; he is subject to god's providence and knows that his happiness lies in the beyond, not in the world below (9). If the Gnostics were right, the good man would have no home – a cosmic fall implies that the world is not an ordered whole, a *kosmos*, and in the last consequence it implies that every connection between the below and the beyond is disrupted (cf. 4 ff.; 10 ff.). To Plotinus the Gnostics are refuted by simple empirical observation. His 'fall' is the individual's *tolma*, taking place within the greater order.

But thereby the problem is of course not 'solved'. Plotinus considers this a good world – but only because it is a reflection of the intelligible world. He does not reject the existence of evil – but takes it to be privation *of* the good, as it is manifested in the cosmos. So metaphysical good and metaphysical evil do exist. But the relation between good and evil, as experienced by individual man, raises the question not only of human evil but also of human suffering and of human freedom and responsibility. All of this preoccupies Plotinus throughout his works. His concern for individual man's welfare, also in this world, is greater than one might perhaps suspect – even though there is no comfort to be found in the external world.

MAN

Plotinus often asks what man is (cf. I 1). In an early treatise, *On the Descent of the Soul into Bodies* (IV 8), he does so in a very concrete way. He asks himself what actually happens when, after having beheld the spiritual world, he returns and finds himself as a soul in a body. Who is he? As so often, he looks for help in the ancients (IV 8, 1). Heraclitus, Empedocles and Pythagoras said wise words, but they are very ancient and very obscure. What then does the 'divine' Plato say? Apparently he contradicts himself; in the *Phaedo* and the *Phaedrus* it looks as if he considers the union of the soul with the body a misfortune, but in the *Timaeus* a good. Then Plotinus takes a step backwards and reconsiders how the soul proceeds from the intellect and how the body is subject to the governance and care of the soul – when it contemplates the intellect, soul is intellect; it remains itself in self-contemplation; when it looks downwards it governs the world. But the world is not necessarily evil, and nothing prevents the soul from remaining in the intellect and at the same time governing the body or the world. However, it is necessary that the world exists – necessary and therefore good. It does not become evil until the soul – in 'audacity' – wants to be itself and lets itself be captured by the world where everything exists piece-meal and divided. What, then, is the conclusion of this, and how can one resolve the seeming contradiction in Plato (5)? The soul's descent into the body is a necessity. But, says Plotinus, necessity comprises free will. It is necessary for the soul to govern the body. But man is free if he wills the necessary; however, if his will is perverted, he is mercilessly abandoned to necessity; like the Stoic dog pulled behind the cart, man too has his inner freedom. The voluntary and the involuntary do not preclude each other. It is involuntary that the soul is subject to necessity – it is not the soul that decides whether it will create or no; but both the descent and what happens to the soul in this world are due to its own nature, which in turn is a link in the greater order. Perhaps individual man cannot 'help' doing what he does. But it is the man who acts;

therefore he is free, and therefore he justly incurs the responsibility and the punishment for his own deeds — as in tragedy, man is what he does. The soul that has the needful capability may acquire its experiences by familiarizing itself with suffering and evil. It must learn that on its own it is responsible for how it acts; but it can also learn that despite the noise and adversities of the world it has a higher identity; the path to the highest is always open; the soul is never entirely submerged in the body (8). What Plotinus says in this treatise about inner freedom and the path to the higher world is clear. The combination of freedom and necessity in this world is on the other hand less clear. Here he seems more harsh than any Stoic — can man in no way whatsoever determine his own acts in the below?

Plotinus explored the question of fate and human freedom and responsibility further in two other treatises. One, *On Fate* (III 1), is an early work and has the character of a technical school discussion of the philosophical views of others. The other, *On Providence* (III 2–3), stems from Plotinus' last years. It is by far the more significant, and its personal and earnest tone is surely connected with the fact that Plotinus wrote the treatise when he was marked by illness. There is no real contradiction between the two treatises, but the latter is far more carefully thought out, and it has been said of it that here Plotinus is thinking aloud.

To a large extent the treatise *On Fate* undoubtedly builds on a school tradition with which we have only very sporadic acquaintance. Among other things Plotinus here criticizes a form of Stoicism that seems fairly diluted; but we ought to bear in mind that according to Porphyry there is much concealed Stoicism in Plotinus; behind the criticism he is indeed highly dependent on Stoic thinking and terminology. Plotinus lets the views of the freedom of will of different schools file by on parade (III 1, 1 ff.): the Epicureans accomplish nothing more than the replacement of the compulsion of necessity with that of chance; seemingly the Stoics rescue free will, but in reality they subordinate both emotion and intellect to the predetermined causal chain, and Stoic reason — which Plotinus calls the world soul — cannot function as an independent cause inasmuch as the material cannot in a metaphysical sense be both cause and effect; in the same breath Plotinus advances a conspicuously down-to-earth criticism of astrology and divination. The criticism of these other views is focused on their destroying man's freedom, each in its own way. When Plotinus is to account for his own view of free will (8 ff.), a new point turns up. In the material world strict determinism in actual fact prevails — a necessity depending on an interplay of the Aristotelian concepts of *tychē*, chance, and *proairesis*, here best translated by 'will'. That is to say that everything in this world has a cause and in Plotinus' view consequently is predetermined; the seemingly accidental has a cause outside man; seeming inner freedom is psychologically determined. Opposed to this, Plotinus holds that man in a wholly different sense is a freely operating cause; the true nature of the soul is not bound by the material, empirical world, and if the soul follows its nature, it is raised above the causal chain and is in a real sense free — freedom means to realize what one in fact already is. A modern reader cannot help noting the agreement with Kant. In the context of Antiquity Plotinus is probably — *nolens, volens* — more of a Stoic than he would admit. But he can only rescue the 'Stoic' concept of freedom by linking it with the dual causal concept, familiar to him and us from Plato's *Phaedo* and *Timaeus*; Plotinus can only consider the Stoics' own distinction between primary and auxiliary causes a pseudo-distinction, because both causes operate in the material world. Man's true freedom is not subject to fate.

Now, this implies that unlike the Stoics Plotinus cannot consider *heimarmenē*, fate, and *pronoia*, god's providence, as two aspects of the same issue. He must call for a demarcation; *pronoia* – to Plotinus: the care of the intelligible world of the corporeal – is set apart from fate. But so doing he runs the risk of inserting a dualism by the back door. Is this world with its predetermined causal chain independent of *pronoia*? – one might well ask.

This question underlies the treatise on providence or *pronoia*. Now, in what sense is it possible for Plotinus to use this Stoic concept; how is it possible to speak of divine care or providence in a metaphysical system that precludes that the divine may have a plan, an aim, and a will? And how can this care be reconciled with the amount of suffering, discord, and evil in man's world? In contrast to the early works – *On Fate* and *On the Descent of the Soul into Bodies* – in this late treatise one senses an evident disquiet behind Plotinus' words, which adds a captivating dimension to the picture that one otherwise might form of him as a person. Throughout he has to speak from the presuppositions of his philosophical system. But he also interrupts himself with counter-questions: why does the good man suffer evil, and why does the evil man prosper? Not infrequently he replies with 'consoling' arguments: in an inward sense the good man is never harmed; the injustice that occurs in this life will surely be made up for in the next; nothing is so bad that it is not good for something else; everything has its place in the greater whole (2, 6 ff.). Some of these arguments can be supported philosophically, others only by mustering considerable philosophical forbearance. But they are not the main issue anyway.

Plotinus arranges his material clearly. First the issue is viewed from the universal angle, then from the individual one, and subsequently the conclusion is drawn. In his universal treatment of *pronoia* (1 ff.) Plotinus first ascertains two things: partly, not everything can be attributed to blind fate or chance; partly, it is not possible to conclude to god's *pronoia* by analogy from human volitional acts; a man can at least seemingly choose between one thing or another; god or *nous* – the words are interchangeable – does not choose and he does not plan; he acts according to his own nature and he does not act temporally. But it is necessary that he create; the individual things must be singled out, and everything must receive perfection according to its nature – plants are perfected with their vegetative soul, animals with their perceiving soul, and man with his rational soul. This spontaneous and necessary creation is in itself a 'care' or a providence that is manifest in the 'order' (*taxis – ordo* in Augustine), which this world receives. In itself the material world is a chaos, but out of chaos order is created through the *logos* that proceeds from *nous*. In *nous* itself there is no need of either ordering or providence; but in the material world there is something to be ordered, and here there is need of providence. What is ordered and embraced by providence is that which by its very nature is separate and remains in mutual discord. According to its own nature, matter is evil or privation; but evil is only evil for him who is evil himself; it is included in the order as an *exemplum* for the man who is good.

But why does the good man fare so ill? For what purpose all this quarrelling and discord? The section dealing with *pronoia* from the point of view of the individual begins in this way (6 ff.). Now, in the first place one should consider that in our mixed life – as we are told with an allusion to Plato – not everything can be pure and beautiful. Next, it is a part of providence not to reduce man to a pawn or a robot. In this world the divine has come to its 'otherness'; it does not direct man but lets him attain his degree of perfection, which is to say that it makes man a free, autonomous being who chooses his true self and thereby chooses the good himself. Providence does not prescribe that one should act well or evilly; it does prescribe the consequences of acting well or evilly – and Plotinus quotes Plato's words from the myth in the *Republic* (Plat. *RP* X 617 E, here p. 211; cf. *Leg.* X 904 B ff.): god is without blame; the blame lies with the man who chooses. Plotinus not only follows Plato; he also adopts a position close to that found before him in the Stoics and subsequently in Augustine: God does not predetermine evil but foresees it. Therefore the blame rests with him who chooses. It is true enough, as Socrates said, that the evil man acts involuntarily because he acts in ignorance – he chooses what he does not want and destroys what he loves (cf. Plot. III 2, 17; 10) – but it is still he who chooses, and therefore he can be punished – as was already stated in *On the Descent of the Soul into Bodies*.

It is *logos* which so to speak acts on behalf of *nous* or providence; *logos* accords men their lot in life, adjusted to their unequal possibilities (11 ff.). But can it be justified that *logos* permits evil? Yes. In the first place it is only the external man who suffers; the inner man is free (15 ff.). In the second place, *logos* uses evil but is not responsible for it (cf. 5) – evil, nothing or shortcoming, is not something that is distributed at the whim of higher powers, but something existing in advance by necessity as the 'downward' delimitation of the good but included in the order. Plato said (Plat. *Leg.* VII 803 C; cf. I 644 D, here p. 249) that man is a plaything of god; Plotinus gives a twist to this quotation. He compares life to a performance (Plot. III 2, 15 ff.). *Logos* has assigned the roles to every single individual, but we are the ones who play our parts – not in the sense that we have been furnished with some cues and are then permitted to act extempore. We have been assigned our parts fully scripted – but in agreement with our characters, and it is unfitting for him who has been assigned the villain's role to criticize the playwright. Interpreted: I belong in the causal chain as the person I am; seemingly I choose one thing instead of another, but who I am is fully determined by fate, even though I myself choose (3, 3). To this extent Plato's pessimism wholly prevails: we are puppets in the hand of god, but god is blameless.

None the less, man has a free will (4). This is not the freedom to act in this or that way, but a free 'principle' (*archē*) in man himself; I have the freedom to 'choose' to be my higher self. In his anthropology Plotinus does not distinguish first and foremost between soul and body but between a lower self which consists of the soul in its union with the body and a higher self, which is the soul in its capacity as intellect. And, as everywhere in Plotinus, the human world corresponds to the world at large. The world as a whole is good by its very existence; the individual parts – which each on its own may be good or evil – are good *as* parts of the whole, because the cosmos is and remains a unity *in* a plurality. These parts are not free; in isolation they can never become 'themselves'; they are determined by the multiple chain of internal and external causes, by fate. Confronting fate stands *pronoia*.

With this we are back at the question raised by the treatise *On Fate*. Plotinus seeks to draw the conclusion in a chapter (5), in which he includes both the cosmic and the human points of view. Fate or *heimarmenē* comes 'from below', providence or *pronoia* 'from above'. What comes from below is not preordained by *pronoia*, but *pronoia* makes 'use' of it and fits it into its order so that what occurs in the world as a whole occurs in agreement with *pronoia*. Man is bound to *heimarmenē*, and he is fully responsible for the errors he commits. If he acts rightly – i.e. exploits his true freedom – he does not act by virtue of himself but by virtue of *pronoia* – good acts belong to *pronoia*; bad acts do not. Like a physician *pronoia* prescribes the proper medicine; if we refrain from taking it, the fault is ours; if we do take it, the credit is the physician's. Since *pronoia* comes from above and hence is superior to *heimarmenē*, Plotinus would probably think that we have misunderstood everything if we ask whether it is 'predetermined' that we take the medicine.

This section – and the whole line of thought – lies close to Augustine's. In his distinction between *liberum arbitrium* and *libertas* (see p. 611) Augustine is undoubtedly influenced by Plotinus, and it is – almost – Augustinian for Plotinus to speak of *pronoia* – like grace – coming 'from above' as a precondition for man's ability to act freely. Almost, for Augustine's God is a personal God, separate from man. Plotinus finds his 'god' in man himself, in the 'higher' self that belongs to intellect.

That it is possible for man to attain real freedom is due to his having a double identity; the path from the external to the inner and higher is open to us, and on his presuppositions Plotinus can endorse Aristotle's dictum that in man there is something more than human. Every man is the intelligible world in 'contracted' form, and it is of course also for this reason that there is an idea for each 'spiritual' human being (cf. 4, 3). We are what we make of ourselves – we are in *nous* when we think intuitively and in the hypostasis of the soul when we think discursively; we are *nous* and we are not *nous*. 'We' are placed in the middle of the universe, and all three hypostases are in 'us'. But when Plotinus says 'we', he is as a rule thinking of the ordinary person, the man who finds himself in the point of balance of the soul, who has *nous* 'above' himself, sensation 'below', and 'we' think discursively. But the inner man can raise himself above this level and make himself one with the intelligible world. Then he does not think *of* or *about* justice, for example, but is illuminated by the just, which thinks itself in him (V 3, 3; 1, 10 ff.). Once more a transformed Aristotelian inspiration, and once more a source for Augustine.

That man is identical with his form of consciousness and so to speak can pass from one form to the next means that in man there is a – most often unexploited – potential. In Plotinus the unconscious therefore plays an important and fascinating role. Man has possibilities within himself which he normally does not use, the possibility to ascend from soul to intellect and from intellect to the One; he can hear 'the note from above' and ascend to the point where he no longer is a beholder looking at something, but where beholding and beholder are one (IV 8, 8; V 8, 11; 1, 12). When he returns to this earthly life he has deepened his insight and has become wiser also in matters of this world.

There is no shortcut to the experience of the grand silence beyond desire, thought, or consciousness (cf. VI 9, 11). On the contrary, it presupposes the most extreme effort – precisely of true desire, true thinking, and true consciousness. The reality beyond being is only reached by the man who has made himself one with the intelligible unity of life, thought — and being. The path to this goes through the purging of the whole man. Cognition is to know oneself, and knowing oneself is closely tied to the experience of beauty and goodness. It is not a passive experience exclusively. The beautiful and the good are also moral categories. Beholding the beyond is not knowledge, but knowledge precedes it; and cognition is our teacher. Milestones on the path towards the beyond are purgation, virtue and inner harmony, as Plotinus says in a passage in which he builds on Plato's *Symposium* (7, 36; cf. Plat. *Symp.* 211 C). With one of the famous Plato quotations, the goal is to flee from this world and become god-like; but Plato also said that the means is the purging that consists in virtue (Plot. I 2, 1; 3; cf. Plat. *Phaedo* 69 C). It goes without saying that in the beyond virtue is rather homeless — there one has nobody towards whom one can be virtuous. But nobody attains the highest good unless he become as 'good as possible' both intellectually and morally in this world, and unless he perceives the beauty and goodness in this world. When Plotinus uses the standard phrase of the time, 'the flight of the lonely towards the Lone', what he has in mind is not — as in most of his contemporaries — a flight from an evil and alien world, but rather a perfection of the possibilities that lie ready in this world. In that respect he is no mean Platonist.

33

LATE NEOPLATONISM

—— •❖• ——

Neoplatonism marks the final phase of pagan philosophy. As has been seen, it is a philosophical current that adopted many ideas from Aristotelianism and Stoicism. But this came about on the premises of Neoplatonism itself and without competition from the old philosophical 'schools' – real live Stoics, Epicureans, or Sceptics were no longer to be found. Three features characterize the last phase of ancient philosophy: systematism, belief in authority, and a combination of philosophical and religious thoughts, which surely had antecedents in the first centuries of the Empire and even earlier, in Plato's Academy, but which at this time emerges as a monolithic unity – of course not least because the competitor now no longer was another philosophical school but a religion, Christianity.

To some degree Plotinus was a source of inspiration for late Neoplatonism, but Plato remained the unshakable authority. However, in his field Aristotle was quickly seen as an authority who could walk hand in hand with Plato. After Plotinus the old idea was revived that Plato and Aristotle actually stood for the same. On their own presuppositions the late Neoplatonists reflected on the relation between the two great authorities in a far more astute way than for example Antiochus of Ascalon had done, and their interpretation remained unchallenged for ages. To them Aristotle and Plato represented two different but reconcilable cognitive stages. The era after Plotinus was to an even higher degree than the preceding marked by adherence to the tradition, and if one – in contrast to Plotinus – can call middle Platonism scholastic, this is even more true of late Neoplatonism. In this context scholasticism means that philosophical thinking was conducted within certain firm frameworks, in a certain way, and with obligation to an established transmission. But it does not mean that thinking was abandoned. It is not by chance that most of the writings of late Neoplatonism were commentaries – on Plato and Aristotle. New truths were not to be uncovered, but the truth that had been discovered was to be understood anew and be made meaningful. The scholasticism of late Antiquity is closely related to the medieval Western one, which was indebted to it. *Auctores* became authorities, but quite demanding authorities that were to be appropriated. It is true of both ancient and medieval scholasticism that original ideas must be excavated back of the outward form of the tradition and the system – it is another matter that there are perhaps greater distances between the giants of thought in late Antiquity than in the Middle

Ages. Many modern readers – and most often this means readers of secondary text-books – consider the last pagans decadents or epigones, and more or less peculiar at that. Nevertheless, especially Proclus was of decisive influence for the Middle Ages and the Renaissance, and he was to find an interpreter of genius in Hegel. The basic view, which they take to its ultimate consequence, is a 'philosophy of reflection': only the reality of thought is 'real', and thought is not a thought *of* something else; reality is self-reflection and what determines self-reflection. For these Neoplatonists 'thought ascends to the high when it descends into itself'.

The religious dimension is in agreement with the general tendencies of a time when demons and occult powers were ubiquitous. But the linking together of sophisticated metaphysics, doctrines of redemption, and magic that the philosophers stood for can seem bizarre. Yet it is not entirely a strange hodge-podge. On the one hand, a series of rites from all sorts of religions are accorded philosophical significance sated with symbolism; on the other hand, there is most often a sharp distinction between what are religious symbols with projected philosophical significance and what is philosophy with a religious background dimension. The motive for this linking together is partly the belief that both philosophy and religion lead to mystical insight, partly the conviction that the highest should engage the whole man, both intellect and feeling; insight into the highest is not an abstract act of cognition but a deeply personal matter. Behind this lies the yearning of the time for deliverance of the single individual who is redeemed by being freed from being this accidental individual. To this should be added the historical situation. In the course of the fourth century Christianity came to prevail. This was far from meaning that all were now Christians, but it did mean that from the third to the sixth century Neoplatonism – from being the self-evident position of the elite – was reduced to a hard-pressed position, forced into a confrontation with the new religion and forced to manifest itself as a philosophical religion displaying will and ability to combat the new by guarding the old. In philosophy Plato was the acknowledged authority with 'Pythagoras' as an obscure background figure. A religious need arose for sacred scriptures, and they were found in the previously mentioned *Chaldean Oracles* and in a series of – spurious – Orphic poems. Seen from our vantage point the marriage of philosophy and religion led to a philosophy with religious varnish or to a peculiarly anaemic, de-mythologized religiosity. But we must accept that the late Neoplatonists were profoundly religious people who – as did Plutarch – found what they sought for by a symbolic interpretation of transmitted and obsolete ancient religions. But the main thing was no longer to interpret the myths allegorically; rather it was to experience the religious services, the rituals, as symbols and to reach salvation by magic. A single feature can be mentioned as an example of the mood among the last Neoplatonists. Proclus lived in the fifth century at a time when the pagans irrevocably had been forced on the defensive. Apparently he himself felt that he was living during the last times. It is related (Mar. *Vit. Procl.* 19; cf. 28) that he lived each day in hectic activity. He wrote one major work after another; he taught himself half to death; he fasted at any given opportunity; he was incessantly sacrificing to all conceivable gods of any observation whatsoever – although of course with the exception of the Christian one; by virtue of his supernatural talents he cured the sick and performed miracles galore. Much was to be managed while time served. Not long afterwards – in 529 – the

Emperor Justinian forbade philosophical teaching in Athens, and thereby Plato's Academy ceased to exist.

PORPHYRY, IAMBLICHUS AND PROCLUS

The three principal figures of late Neoplatonism were Porphyry (c.233–305), Iamblichus (250–325) and Proclus (412–85).

Porphyry was a Syrian. Before becoming Plotinus' student, he studied at the stronghold of official Platonism in Athens and there presumably acquired a form of middle Platonism. Following his sojourn with Plotinus, he settled in Sicily where most of his writings saw the light of day. They were very numerous, but most have been lost. He wrote commentaries on Plato and Aristotle, a number of works with religious and ethical contents, edited Plotinus, and wrote a collection of *Sententiae* based on Plotinus. Best known in his own time was a polemic against the Christians (see p. 573) – which of course has not been preserved. The most influential part of his oeuvre is his elementary commentary and introduction (*Isagoge*) to Aristotle's *Categories*. He was famed for his overwhelming learning. As a philosopher he was hardly particularly original, and actually he was probably untypical inasmuch as he simplified Plotinus in the direction of monism instead of elaborating on a major system. His main contribution was as a moral philosopher, as a popularizing conveyor of Plotinus, and as a commentator. Through Latin translations he became the Neoplatonist who was to be of the greatest influence in the West – in part indirectly through Augustine.

Iamblichus – likewise from Syria and a student of Porphyry's – was on the other hand the philosopher of the East and indeed worked first and foremost in Syria. He quickly became known as the chief systematist of Neoplatonism; in his system philosophy and theosophy entered a firm alliance, and probably there is something programmatic in the fact that he regarded himself both as a Platonist and a 'Pythagorean' – he, as well as Porphyry, wrote *The Life of Pythagoras*, which is to say an account of the philosophical way of life. A major work, *On the Egyptian Mysteries*, the authenticity of which probably unjustly has been questioned, has been preserved. But, apparently his main philosophical contributions were incorporated in his commentaries on Plato and Aristotle – today only known fragmentarily and from quotations elsewhere. In one – preserved – *Protrepticus* he exploited both Plato and Aristotle. It was Iamblichus who was to have the greatest influence during the centuries immediately following. The Emperor Julian the Apostate belongs to the Iamblichus tradition – the 'apostate' Emperor who during his brief reign (361–3) sought to introduce Neoplatonic philosophy and religious views as the official ideology of the Roman Empire. A number of pamphlets and letters from him have been preserved. To the Julian circle belongs also Sallustius, the author of a pamphlet for laymen, *On the Gods and the World* – probably a manifestation of the religious politics of Julian.

In the fifth and sixth century Neoplatonism had two principal centres, in predominantly pagan Athens and in predominantly Christian Alexandria. The last great systematist, Proclus, belongs to the 'school' in Athens. Ultimately he built on

Iamblichus; we know but little about his immediate predecessors and teachers (Plutarch of Athens and Syrianus). A considerable portion of Proclus' extensive oeuvre has been preserved, including major commentaries on Plato's *Parmenides* (this commentary extends to and includes the first hypothesis), on the *Timaeus*, and on Euclid's first book, where Proclus shows himself as a gifted interpreter. A presentation of *Plato's Theology* is actually a reading of the *Parmenides*, although not in the form of a commentary. The main systematic work is *The Elements of Theology*, and to this is added *The Elements of Physics*. Some lesser treatises, among other things on providence, are only known in Latin translations.

Most of the late Neoplatonic writings reflect the teaching; through teaching a gradual introduction to Plato and Aristotle, the two authorities, was to be provided. Therefore it must be important to lay down a curriculum and establish firm principles for textual interpretation. The basic view was that Aristotle and Plato could be harmonized so that with Aristotle's logic a tool was provided for analysis of the sensible world, which in turn could be followed up by Aristotelian physics. It was in this spirit Porphyry wrote his elementary commentary and introduction to the *Categories* (cf. Porph. *Isag.* 1, 3 ff., Busse), and he performed his task so well that for more than a thousand years his interpretation was the indispensable introduction to philosophy altogether. After the introduction to Aristotle, the philosopher *in spe* could next read Plato, and thus by degrees be initiated in the higher metaphysical matters. It was Iamblichus who established the canonized Plato curriculum (cf. Anon. *Prol. ad Plat.* 26). The student was first to learn to know himself – and therefore he was to begin with the first *Alcibiades* dialogue, which was considered genuine. Then followed the other dialogues according to a fixed sequence proceeding from the easier to the more difficult dialogues; gradually one became acquainted with all philosophical subjects. Finally – as the climax – followed, not surprisingly, the *Timaeus* and the *Parmenides*. Whoever had mastered those had finished his training. As an outcome of this curriculum the metaphysical works known to us are only accessible with great difficulty; in contrast to Porphyry's *Isagoge* they are intended for the advanced student.

Myths and poetry were of course interpreted allegorically – and without Plotinus' reservations with respect to this method of interpretation. Porphyry also followed this practice (cf. Porph. *De antr. Nymph.*); on the other hand, in his learned commentaries he was strictly matter-of-fact. But apparently Iamblichus did not find his method satisfactory. How the relation between Porphyry and Iamblichus as commentators was viewed in the later Iamblichus tradition can be seen in Proclus who says that Porphyry commented on the detail, while Iamblichus commented as an initiate (Procl. *In Plat. Tim.* I 204, 24, Diehl). Iamblichus' main principle for the interpretation of Plato was that each dialogue should be understood according to its genre and from its intention or aim (*skopos*). Any given dialogue has one and only one aim; it is – in conformance with Plato's own demands of a 'speech' – one organism, which like a microcosm reflects one aspect of the universe at large; seeming digressions should be understood allegorically, because the different ways of describing the world in fact are analogous (19, 24 ff.; 77, 25 ff.; cf. Plat. *Phaedr.* 264 C). A Plato dialogue should in other words not be interpreted doxographically but from an understanding of the subject matter itself. We know Iamblichus' method from Proclus who in addition to surprising allegorical interpretations shows an impressive respect for the interplay between text, intention and subject matter.

Porphyry's *Isagoge* occupies a special position not only because of its unique historical importance, but also because it throws light on how the Aristotelian logic could find an independent place in the Platonism of the time. In the first place, the *Categories* was a well-suited basis for a course in philosophical propaedeutics, which could be followed up by a reading of the *Organon* in the traditional sequence (cf. Porph. *In Cat.* 56, 23 ff., Busse; here p. 293). But in the second place, Porphyry could make use of Plotinus' thought that natural language refers to the empirical world and that Aristotle's categories concern natural language. The categories are thus linguistic designations, but only to the extent that they designate 'things' (58, 3 ff.; 91, 7 ff.). With this it has not been said that the linguistic expression designates correctly, nor what 'things' are. Language does not actually designate the things directly either; it designates the concept which stands for the thing (cf. Dex. *In Aristot. Cat.* 7, 1 ff., Busse; Olymp. *In Aristot. Cat.* 19, 26 ff., Busse), and from this follows the Aristotelian tripartition: linguistic expression – concept – thing (*De interpretatione*). Now, both Porphyry's *Isagoge* and his commentary are elementary introductions, and hence he expressly desists from dealing with more far-reaching problems; he merely wants to provide an account of what the old Peripatetics said in a logical context (Porph. *Isag.* 1, 15). But undeniably there are problems – not only for a Platonist. In the first place there is the question of how the categories relate to the predicables (see p. 313): the categories refer to an ontological basic structure in which substance has priority; the predicables make up a formal classification equally valid within each category. Hence concepts such as accident and difference acquire diverging meanings within the two classifications. But the greater problem by far is what a thing is and what a concept is. Within the framework laid down it is sufficient for Porphyry to say that a thing or an individual is contained in its *species* and furnished with special attributes (7, 21 ff.). To ask what a 'concept' is is the same as to ask what ontological status genus and species have. This, declares Porphyry, he will not embark upon (1, 9 ff.), but he does point out where the problem lies: do genus and species have independent existence, or do they only exist in the intellect? If they have independent existence, are they then corporeal or incorporeal? And are they separate from sense objects or inherent in sense objects? Owing to Boethius this approach, as stated in these few lines, occasioned the dispute about universals in the Middle Ages. Probably only a Platonist would couch the problem as Porphyry did, and, being a Platonist, he naturally had his own view of the ontological status of the concept; still, in the given context, it is decisive to delimit logic from ontology, which is to say that logic is made a neutral discipline that is independent of ontology. This was to be of no little significance for the development of medieval logic.

If one proceeds from Porphyry's Aristotelianism to his Platonism – i.e. from his logic to his ontology – it is like coming to an entirely different world. To us there are few points of resemblance; to Porphyry it is probably a natural consequence of reality actually comprising several levels. To late Neoplatonists man has two possibilities for higher insight: in part a metaphysical-theoretical path – that of philosophy or 'theology' – in part a practical path that includes ethics or the doctrine of virtues and what is called theurgy, divine action, which is to say both man's ritual actions and the action of the divine with man. The two paths are connected, for man should not only speak about god; he should act. The virtuous act marks a purification of the soul; the 'divine action' consists in rites, magic and prayer, an active religious performance that in so far as possible aims for man's 'becoming god-like'; theurgy is the knowledge of the means whereby the divine influence can be affected. It relies on the belief that all divine powers are dependent on a highest divinity and thus mediate between man and the highest and that magic is the natural consequence of the coherence of everything. The question had to arise whether it was philosophy – theology – or theurgy that took precedence. Characteristically Porphyry gave first place to philosophy, while Iamblichus and his successors – among them Proclus – gave it to theurgy (cf. Olymp. *In Plat. Phaedonem* 123, 3, Norvin).

To Porphyry as to Plotinus the virtues are necessary pre-conditions for knowing god, but Porphyry places more emphasis on a virtuous and ascetic conduct of life. He established a classification of virtues (Porph. *Sent.* 32, Stob) leading from social life to the divine. It was characteristic of the time that virtues meant the perfection of the self; hence social obligations occupy a lowly place, and hence only few can be perfected: only the wise man prays in the right way (cf. *Ad Marc.* 16 ff.; 24; Aug. *De civ. Dei* X 29). Thanks to virtue the wise abstains from affects (Porph. *De abst.* I 33), and in contrast to the mob he is a vegetarian (IV 18) – the wise can achieve what the others cannot, but strict demands are made of him. Porphyry wrote an entire still extant treatise on abstinence. Apart from its preaching abstinence in general, it is an interesting testimony to the Platonist view that human beings as members of the greater order are also obliged towards other living creatures; animals have rights. Porphyry does not reject theurgy, but, as the learned intellectual he was, he did have reservations (cf. Aug. *De civ. Dei* X 9). It is also Porphyry, the rationalist who criticizes not only Christianity but also polytheism. He is, to be sure, ready to interpret not a few things allegorically, but he had several strictures on rites and on polytheistic practice in general, as he pointed out in a letter to an Egyptian priest, Anebo, a document known only in fragments from Iamblichus.

But Porphyry's religiosity is unmistakable, and he takes a major step beyond Plotinus – man can no longer accomplish very much on his own. Prayer is much more important to him than to Plotinus. But that is not all. Plotinus could speak of *pronoia* working from above – but divine 'grace' as a precondition for man's salvation plays a far more important role in the Neoplatonists who came after him. In the dispute with the Christians it becomes more and more important for the Neoplatonists to 'employ' Christian concepts with pagan signatures. Both Porphyry and Iamblichus call for faith, hope, and charity – to which is sometimes added truth – as pre-conditions for man's receiving divine 'grace'. The concepts were in all likelihood not derived directly from St. Paul's famous words, but they are important in the confrontation with the Christian opponents (Porph. *Ad Marc.* 24; Iambl. *De myst.* V 26; Procl. *In Plat. Tim.* I 212, 21; cf. Paul, 1 Cor. 13, 13). The difference lies of course in the fact that the Neoplatonist unlike the Christian is able to find the divine within himself. Correspondingly, a Neoplatonist practising theurgy will activate forces in the world itself, while the Christian sacraments signify God's intervention in the world order from the outside.

In his treatise *On the Egyptian Mysteries* – which takes the form of a reply from a high-ranking 'Egyptian priest' to Porphyry's letter to Anebo – Iamblichus attributes decisive importance to theurgy, precisely because knowledge of god comes from above. Philosophy or theology are necessary but insufficient conditions; man cannot on his own achieve initiation; contact with the divine is gained by prayer and symbolic acts, rites (Iambl. *De myst*. III 18; II 11; V 26). That theurgy is superior to theology does not, however, prevent Iamblichus from speaking in theoretical-metaphysical terms, as he also does in the treatise on Egyptian wisdom (I 2; VIII 2).

It had been a main point to Plotinus that only three hypostases were conceivable: the one, intellect and soul. From a systematic point of view this led especially to difficulties in subordinating the several functions of the soul under one point of view. However, this could be overcome, because every concept and every entity was viewed as dynamic, as a creative power interacting with other concepts and entities. The special mark of the intellect was the unification of being, life and insight, not as three entities in one but as three aspects of the same reality. This unity was reflected in the further differentiation of the hypostasis of the soul in time and space. To Plotinus' successors the choice apparently came to be between modifying the basic systematic structure or developing it further. Porphyry represented the first possibility, Iamblichus and his successors the second.

When Porphyry became acquainted with Plotinus, he had scruples, especially with respect to thought objects as elements in *nous* and with respect to the relation between soul and body. He was converted to Plotinus' position and maintained it. In principle he also maintained the doctrine of the hypostases, but what interested him was the inner connection between the hypostases, not their systematic separation. In its essence the soul was of the nature of intellect and without parts, and its unification with the body was only a 'relation' – in other words, not given with the soul's own nature (cf. Stob, I 365, 14 ff., Wachsmuth; 354, 7 ff.; Procl. *In Plat. Tim*. II 105,22). In the same way it is apparent that he reduced the distance between the first and second hypostases (cf. a partially preserved commentary on Plato's *Parmenides*, presumably written by Porphyry, Kroll, p. 599 ff.). Thereby Porphyry stressed one side of the Plotinus heritage. It agrees fairly well with the picture one gets of him as a man of practical ethics; to him the main point was not a metaphysical system in itself.

Iamblichus protested against this on behalf of systematics (cf. Procl. *In Plat. Tim*. III 334, 3 ff.), and the rigid monumental system for which he was responsible dominated all later Neoplatonism. The main principle was to insert special intermediate links between the hypostases or within the individual hypostasis in order thereby to delimit precisely all conceivable ontological and epistemological aspects and functions. They are considered as self-subsisting entities related to all other entities within a firm rational order – everything is in everything, but according to the nature of the recipient (cf. *El. theol*. 103). Further basic principles are that two unequal entities require an intermediate link, that every conceptual entity has a tripartite structure, and that the same superior structure can be recognized at every level of reality so that reality so to speak is structured both along vertical and horizontal lines (*In Plat. Tim*. II 313, 15 ff.; 215, 5 ff.; I 426, 20). Surely, at least the procedure makes exact conceptual analysis possible – one should only remember that the Neoplatonists are extreme realists, not conceptualists; the concepts exist in themselves, not because we think of them (cf. *In Plat. Parm.* 1054, 27, Cousin). Logical order coincides with real order, and what makes this system so difficult for the modern reader is not least that what to us is logical or conceptual analysis, to these Neoplatonists is ontology: wherever there is a conceptual distinction or a relation between concepts, an onto-logical entity with independent systematic rubrification is required. Here the living continuity between the single elements of Plotinus' philosophical universe becomes the victim of a vast filing system, and with good reason one can ask if it is really possible to explain a continuous movement of thought by inserting an intermediate link, thus thereby requiring more intermediate links.

Iamblichus' system was developed further, until it received its final form in Proclus' work on *The Elements of Theology*. It is impossible to decide what it owes to Iamblichus and what it owes to the school in Athens before Proclus. Hence Proclus' version will be the basis here – without the slightest ambition to present the system in its entirety. As to the contents, Proclus probably in all essentials builds on his predecessors; his own original contribution is first and foremost the method. Like Spinoza, he presents his system *more geometrico*, which is to say that his model is Euclid; he proceeds by a continuous series of theorems that are proved deductively. While he may be wordy in his commentaries, in his principal systematic work he is strict and so concise as to be obscure. His project is to grasp the whole of reality – undeniably not an unambitious one. It is executed with sophistication, but there is hardly any other more 'scholastic' work to be found in the history of philosophy.

The overall objective with the work is to demonstrate unity in plurality, identity in difference, and the whole in the parts, and the historical basis is, as already in Plotinus, first and foremost Plato's *Parmenides*, especially the relation between the first and second hypotheses. One should not expect to find information about partic-ular object concepts nor any empirical material. The subject is a metaphysical structure.

All that exists is one (*El theol.* 1 ff.). It is not simply one, but a whole or finite multitude, which, being finite, participates in the One. Of course Plato's *Parmenides* lies behind (see p. 219) when a distinction thus is made between the One, the finite whole that *has* unity and the indefinite multitude that has potential existence but does not exist, because all that exists is one. Using Stoic terminology, the existing unity is delimited from the One by being unified (*hēnōmenon*). In the concept of unity lies the identity between the One and being; the difference lies in the simply One as opposed to unity as predicate of being.

The relation between unity and plurality can be considered in several ways. It can be regarded causally (7 ff.; 56 ff.; 97 ff.). Just as the One is the cause of being, any unity whatsoever is the cause of more specified – and hence subordinate – entities, as genus is the cause of species. But the cause always 'contains' more than the effect and is therefore ontologically primary. It unfolds itself in a plurality and is – with a modified Aristotelian phrase (cf. Arist. *Met.* 1026 a 30) – universal because it is primary.

The relation can also be considered by means of the concept of participation. From the One proceeds the intellect, from the intellect the soul. More differentiated is the sequel: unity – being – life – thinking – soul – natural organisms with vegetative souls – inanimate bodies (cf. E.R. Dodds on Procl. *El. theol.* 58–9). The concept of participation serves to ensure the continuity in this process of unfolding. But to a systematist the Platonic notion of participation contains the difficulty that the idea is both transcendent and immanent. The problem is solved by assuming that every participation implies three elements: a superior, transcendent and self-identical one, in which nothing participates but which makes participation possible, the participated, and the participating entities (23–4; cf. *In Plat. Tim.* II 105, 16 ff. on Iamblichus). The participated mediates between the self-subsisting – which exists everywhere and nowhere (cf. *El. theol.* 98) – and the participating (cf. 28). Thus every conceptual entity has a tripartite structure – a translation into modern language has been ventured to the effect that the intension of a concept is transcendent, whereas the extension is the plurality of participating parts; the participated, then, will be the universal, embracing the parts as a whole of parts and inherent in the parts.

The dialectics of participation exemplifies an even more fundamental formal structure that is applicable to any conceptual entity whatsoever when considered by itself and in its function. It is the relation between *monē*, *proodos* and *epistrophē* (see p. 544). This structure is also a triad (40–43; cf. 9–10). The point of departure is the concept *qua* self-subsistent containing its possibilities of unfolding latently (*monē*). The possibilities are unfolded through *proodos* according to the proper nature of each thing (103) in such a way that the effected is the manifestation of the effecting and so that unity is manifest in difference. But by a reversion (*epistrophē*) the effect will return to the cause (25 ff.; especially 30–31; cf. *Theol. Plat.* III 9). The point is that a given concept has such a structure that it contains its potential realization in itself, unlike a physical entity that receives its existence from the outside (cf. *In Plat. Tim.* III 39,2).

What, then, is accomplished with this apparatus? It can be understood if one, for example, looks at the triad that constitutes the hypostasis of *nous*, the triad of being, life and thought. To Plotinus it was not decisive to systematize: to him the three aspects imply each other immediately. A Iamblichus or Proclus does not think like that. To them there is a unity of three distinct terms in which life mediates between being and thought (*El. theol.* 101–03; 138; *Theol. Plat.* III 14). The circular movement from being to thought breaks down the old idea of the unity of thought act, thought subject and thought object into its elements. It is a movement of reflection wherein the thinking subject attains self-consciousness by recognizing its content (cf. *El. theol.* 168). It is not misleading to employ Hegelian terminology and declare that the spirit becomes conscious of itself; indeed Hegel himself does voice his satisfaction with this whole way of thinking (Hegel: *Gesch. d. Philos.*, Jub. Ausg. XIX, p. 85).

The tendency to break down a conceptual complex into parts appears everywhere. Thus eternity and time are separate entities preceding intellect and soul respectively (Procl. *El. theol.* 52–5). An important example is the very principle of pluralization. At all levels of reality unity unfolds itself in a plurality. That unity implies plurality is a common Neoplatonic assumption; the problem for the late Neoplatonists is how to unfold this thought systematically – in other words, what intermediate links are required. There is a special one-many structure within both intellect and soul (cf. 166 ff.; 184 ff.). But preceding it there is a series of transcendent principles of pluralization – a number of entities or *henads* in which every specific plurality participates (113 ff.). The system is not very friendly to the reader nor particularly elegant, but performs a religious task. The Henads are gods, and the entire traditional, mythological corps of divinities are seen as the symbolic expression of the Henad system (cf., e.g. *In Plat. Parm.* 647, 9 ff.). It might be more correct to say that the system of Henads is the imperfect philosophical rationalization of religious reality, which more effectively is open to the person who in addition to theology and philosophy masters theurgy. The Henads bestow the highest divine reality on the whole universe (cf. *El. theol.* 128 ff.) and on those who know its secrets; and providence proceeds from the Henads (120). Proclus' religiosity is only indirectly apparent in the tight form of presentation in *The Elements of Theology*; directly it appears in the allegorizing hymns he wrote to 'the god' and the individual gods (*Hymn. in Deum Plat.* Jahn; *Procli opera inedita*, Cousin 1316 ff.), which he perhaps himself considered the weightier part of his oeuvre.

The gods hold the world together, because the divine is one. What it is that unites scholasticism with religiosity in the tradition proceeding from Iamblichus and culminating with Proclus can perhaps best be gathered from the long prose hymn to the Sun God written by the Emperor Julian 'the Apostate', no less. The sustaining element is the mediation between the heavenly and the earthly. To Julian both the transmitted Greek and Roman gods and the divinities of the mystic cults are symbolized by the sun. Hence he can combine the inheritance from just about everywhere with the symbolism in Plato's simile of the sun and with more primitive ideas of the sun as giver of life. But what is decisive is that one and the same divinity – in agreement with Iamblichus' theology – manifests itself at different levels of existence. The visible sun is a reflection of the sun that illuminates the intelligible world, and in turn it is the reflection of the highest 'sun', the One beyond *nous* (Jul. Apost. *Or.* IV 132C ff.; 138D ff.). It is a religious expression of 'sameness in difference' of late Neoplatonism, a connecting link between the divine and the earthly that answers a profound religious need of the time – probably intended by Julian as a counter-move to the Christian idea of incarnation.

THE AFTERMATH

The last representative of the school in Athens was Damascius (c.460–after 530), hardly a very outstanding philosopher. A major work – of course a commentary on Plato's *Parmenides* – has been preserved. The emphasis is on the mystical and religious side of the tradition and on the absolute transcendence of the one, which leads to scepticism with respect to the possibilities of rational cognition. The style is turgid and the line of thought rather nebulous. In 529 when Justinian forbade pagan teaching in Athens, Damascius and some of his colleagues took up residence with the Persian King Chosroes; this was not a success, and the exiled philosophers were permitted to leave – perhaps for Athens – but the Academy was not reopened.

There were of course connections between the school in Athens and the school in Alexandria, but the development was different in the two places. Metaphysical systematics belongs in Athens; in Alexandria the concentration was on the working out of commentaries. Most likely this is owing to external circumstances. In Athens – at the time a small, insignificant university town with a glorious past – the pagans enjoyed a relatively free position even as late as in the fifth century. But the Platonists in Alexandria had to adjust themselves to living in a preponderantly Christian city. They got their martyr – the female philosopher Hypatia who was lynched by the Christians in 415 – and apparently it was safer to write commentaries on the least dangerous Platonic dialogues and on Aristotle's uncontroversial logic and psychology. The main emphasis was in other words on the introductory studies in the Neoplatonist curriculum. The central figure was Ammonius (early sixth century) by whom some commentaries, in part as rendered by his student Philoponus, have been preserved. An essential task for him was to demonstrate the agreement between Plato and Aristotle – this holds good for the relation between ideas and universals, and it holds good for the Aristotelian concept of god, which he interpreted as both *causa finalis* and *causa efficiens*, whereby Aristotle was made to agree with the Neoplatonist scheme of reflection (cf. Simpl. *In Aristot. Phys.* 1363, 8 ff., Diels).

Ammonius' student Philoponus was a Christian; he was, to be sure, also a Platonist, but on decisive points he broke with the tradition. The contrast was no longer between the intelligible and the sensible world but between God and the world, and from this new basic position Philoponus attacked a series of doctrines that for ages had been considered evidently true. He rejected the Aristotelian distinction between the supra-lunary and the sub-lunary world (cf. *In Aristot. De caelo* 87, 29 ff., Heiberg). With his *impetus* theory he attacked a weak point in Aristotle's dynamics (the movement of a missile – cf. p. 331), and he attacked Proclus who in a treatise now lost apparently had maintained that the created world in the *Timaeus* must be eternal, because the ideal model is so – Philoponus wanted to make the revolutionary thought philosophically acceptable that God can create the world out of nothing.

The contrast between Christians and non-Christians among the Alexandrine Platonists ended with the Christians' victory, and, although the Neoplatonism of Alexandria ceased with the Arabic conquest in 641, influences from the Alexandrians continued both in Byzantine-Christian and in Islamic thinking. In Athens, on the other hand, Justinian's edict of 529 signalled an abrupt stop. Influences from the school in Athens followed more complicated paths.

In two ways late Neoplatonism became significant for the time that followed, partly through the writing of commentaries, and partly – rather indirectly – through Proclus. The Neoplatonists did not invent the commenting on Plato and Aristotle, but the importance of the genre during Neoplatonism is of course due to the overall backward-looking basic tendency in late Antiquity: the proper understanding of Plato – and of Aristotle to a very large extent – was the vital nerve of philosophy. The special place assigned to Aristotle in the teaching produced a great need for introductory commentaries, and after Alexander of Aphrodisias the interpretation of Aristotle passed into Neoplatonist hands. It goes without saying that Plato was the subject of commentaries. That they were written especially on the *Parmenides* and the *Timaeus* is equally natural. We are familiar with Proclus and Damascius and through them we are told a good deal about earlier interpretations; we can follow the discussion of the *Timaeus* that had been conducted since the old Academy, and we can see how the scholastic interpretation of the *Parmenides* had found its final form prior to Proclus.

The commentaries on Aristotle are usually more accessible. Much has of course been lost, but what is preserved constitutes c.30 compendious tomes in the standard modern edition. Impressive learning has been set down in these works, which as yet have been far from sufficiently studied; with respect to both subject and method they were to have normative importance for the understanding of Aristotle in the Middle Ages, in Byzantium, among Arab scholars, and, later on, in the West. Alexander of Aphrodisias was already an authority for Plotinus. Of Neoplatonist commentators there is reason especially to single out Porphyry, Themistius, Ammonius, Simplicius and Philoponus. Almost all commentators have in common the claim that there is fundamental agreement between Plato and Aristotle, as presupposed in Neoplatonist teaching. When Aristotle criticizes Plato, one should – as was frequently maintained – look for the meaning, not at the wording; then it would be seen that the disagreement is only superficial (cf., e.g. Simpl. in Aristot. *De caelo* 640, 27 ff.). But in the best commentators this is not synonymous with a distortion of Aristotle, nor does it mean that he is denied his say.

No interpretation of Aristotle, after Alexander, was to have greater influence than Porphyry's *Isagoge*. Themistius – a rhetor and man of letters (a 'sophist') of the fourth century and a friend of the Emperor Julian the Apostate – is the closest one can get to what at that time was an 'Aristotelian'. He was not an original thinker, but opened new paths by writing a series of frequently used Aristotle paraphrases (cf. his remarks on this, Them. *In Aristot. Anal. post.* 1, 2 ff., Wallies). Otherwise the careful sentence-by-sentence commentary predominated. Among the Alexandrians Ammonius was the most pre-eminent. Simplicius was among his students; he had also studied in Athens where he resided until 529 when he was banished with Damascius. Despite his Neoplatonic credo, he never wrote commentaries on Plato; to us he is the most important commentator on Aristotle from Antiquity after Alexander of Aphrodisias, not, however, because of his philosophical originality but by virtue of his vast erudition, sober-minded form of exposition, and impeccable documentation – it is thanks to him that many verbatim quotations from the Presocratics have been preserved. Several of his commentaries appear to have been written after his return from the King of Persia. At that point he had been forbidden to teach, and probably this was why he wrote his learned commentaries, which were intended to be read rather than taught. The quality of his work can be evaluated, for example by a comparison of his commentary on the *Categories* with the other remaining commentaries. To him as well the *Categories* constitutes the basic introduction to the study of Aristotle, and he shares the general Neoplatonic view that the study of Aristotle is preliminary to the study of higher matters (cf. Simpl. *In Aristot. Cat.* 438, 23, Kalbfleisch). Yet this does not induce him to let up on quality and thoroughness, as is already apparent at the outset in a meticulous *Forschungsbericht*, a discussion of the aim of the *Categories* and an astute examination of whether this treatise deals with words, 'things', or concepts (1, 3 ff.; 8, 9 ff. 9, 8 ff.).

Something symbolic can be read into the fact that the best known of the late Neoplatonists who were muzzled by Justinian were the dreamer Damascius and the scholar Simplicius. With Philoponus, the Ammonius student, a break occurred. A bitter war was waged between the revolutionary Philoponus and the traditionalist Simplicius.

By strange paths and at various times Proclus was to become important to posterity – indeed very important. The first time around he appeared in disguise, when an anonymous writer, today known by the imposing name of Pseudo-Dionysius the Areopagite, published a number of treatises in ca. 500, in which he, without mentioning Proclus, undertook the *tour de force* of 'translating' his metaphysics into a Christian frame (see p. 586). This work was also to affect the West.

The next time Proclus invaded the West was also in disguise, which is to say with *The Book on Causes* (*Liber de causis*), a twelfth-century Latin translation of an Arab compendium of Proclus' *Elements of Theology* – until Aquinas it was considered a work by Aristotle, which naturally caused a certain confusion in the understanding of Aristotle. The third time Proclus arrived in Western Europe, he came in his own name – through thirteenth-century translations. It is suggestive that Proclus thus became known in the West before Plotinus and before most of Plato, and his reputation endured until Leibniz.

It was Hegel who made Proclus fashionable for the last time (cf. Hegel: *Gesch. d. Philos.*, Jub. Ausg. XIX, 2. 71 ff.). One may think Hegel's Proclus more stimulating than Proclus himself and ought not to close one's eyes to the fact that a Hegelian 'triad' behaves in a different manner from Proclus' triads. But by virtue of his own thinking Hegel was able to uncover what is of philosophical relevance in Proclus: the intelligible world is a process in which the spirit does not relate to anything else, but becomes conscious of itself.

34

EARLY CHRISTIAN
THOUGHT

———•◆•———

The encounter of Christianity with ancient culture and the unification of the Judaeo-Christian and the Greco-Roman tradition – perhaps the most important event in the history of Western culture – is a process stretching over approximately three centuries, and when all is said and done, it is hardly meaningful to ask which of the two sides won out. They fought each other, adapted themselves to each other, and learned from each other, and the encounter meant that something new was created. Actually, it is only a half truth to speak of a cultural battle between two clearly defined opponents. To the *dramatis personae* it was certainly a confrontation where one had to choose sides. But one cannot choose one's own culture, and the Judaism from which Christianity sprang was already a mixed culture at the time of Jesus. The fact that the writings of the New Testament were written and thought in Greek and not in the native tongue of Jesus, Aramaic, shows that almost from the beginning the Christian message was 'translated' into and formulated in a common cultural conceptual world. Subsequently the process often pursued the opposite path – the late Neoplatonists, for example, are in no small measure influenced by Christian thought. It was not until the second and third century that philosophical thinking on a Christian basis began, and the debilitating Christological disputes of the fourth century are understandable only as attempts at a philosophical formulation of a non-philosophical faith. It is important to keep in mind that Christian thought and Christian philosophy are secondary to Christian religion, that Christian thinkers do not simply express the thought of the ordinary man and that Christian thought is no unambiguous concept. Christianity is new thinking, but not a new thinking formulated in a void.

The external history of Christianity in late Antiquity can be divided into three main phases. In the first – the time of the Apostles – Christianity spread from Palestine to the principal cities of the Roman Empire, first and foremost to Antioch, Ephesus and Alexandria in the East. But a congregation was also early established in Rome. The rapid dissemination would not have been possible without the lively communication between the cities of the Roman Empire and is also connected with the existence of Jewish communities in all major cities – the rural areas did not join until much later: first Syria, Asia Minor, and Northern Africa. Primarily we know of this entire missionary activity from the Epistles of St Paul and from the account in the Acts of the Apostles of his missionary journeys. However, the problem arose early on of the relation between Jewish and pagan Christians. Jesus fulfilled the promises of the Messiah in the Old Testament, but did this mean that the Christian message only was relevant for Jews and that baptized pagans were bound by Mosaic Law? Apparently this was the view of the first congregation. St Paul represented the opposite view: the Gospel was addressed to all men, and according to Pauline theology Mosaic Law had been replaced by 'the New Covenant'. This position prevailed. The destruction of Jerusalem in 70 was also a contributing cause of Judaic Christianity's never coming to play a decisive role. The future belonged to pagan Christianity. St Paul's theology became normative, and Christianity and Judaism were definitively separated.

The second phase – the second and third century – is internally marked by consolidation and institutionalization and externally by confrontation. The central element in the lives of the congregations was the service, during which one gathered for the confession and to hear the orally transmitted sayings by Jesus. Gradually these were written down – the four Gospels with their accounts of the sayings, life and acts of Jesus stem from the end of the first century. The Epistles of St Paul, the principal source for our knowledge of the earliest congregations, are older and were written only a brief generation after the death of Jesus. Already towards the end of the second century the writings that constitute our New Testament had acquired authoritative status, even though the final canonization of the New Testament in its present form stems from c.400. From the very first the Old Testament was also a sacred book to the Christians: the Christian faith was the fulfilment of the prophecies of the Old Testament, and hence it was of course important that the content of the faith be available in written form. But the oral transmission was at least as important. In the struggle for Christian orthodoxy it was essential to be able to point to an unfalsified 'Apostolic' tradition behind every written account. This tradition was safeguarded by the ministry, and hence the bishops were of special importance. Originally the congregations had been loosely organized, but gradually the church became an institution, and the bishops who conducted the divine services thus also came to take care of the proper Christian message; subsequently the assembly of bishops, the Synod or Concilium, became the highest regional authority. Scripture and tradition were necessary internally and externally – externally in the fight with Gnostics and pagans, and it is at this time – from the second century – that Christian theology takes its beginning. Its importance to the life of the ordinary Christian is probably limited, but it was important that Christianity not be swallowed up by Gnostic theology, and it was important for the Christians to find their own identity *vis-à-vis* the pagan tradition of Antiquity, all the more so as Christianity during this period acquired more and more adherents among the literate. Here two paths were open. It was possible – as did Tertullian – to reject every connection with the surrounding culture, or – as did Justin, Clement and Origen – to view Christianity as the true philosophy, as the fulfilment not only of the Jewish but also of the Greco-Roman tradition.

Like the Jews, Christians led dangerous lives. It was true that the state tolerated a plethora of religions, but a religion that considered itself the only true one must *eo ipso* already be suspect, and refusal to participate in the imperial cult was a crime against the state. At first the Christians were considered undangerous dreamers, but they were potential rebels. Marcus Aurelius still considered Christian martyrdoms theatrical fanaticism (Marc. Aur. XI 3). But locally the persecutions became an ever-increasing threat, and in the third century it was apparent to the state that Christianity was dangerous. Around the year 250 the Emperor Decius instigated the first realm-wide persecution; things were to become even worse under Diocletian who in 303–04 organized persecutions with disastrous consequences – at least in the East. Then ensued an abrupt turn-around. In 311 the Emperor Galerius issued an 'edict of tolerance' (cf. Lact. *De mort. pers.* 34, 1 (*PL* 7, 249); Eus. *Hist eccl.* VIII 17 (*PG* 20, 792)). It is a peculiar declaration from an absolutist ruler, for on the one hand it maintained that Christianity was deleterious, but on the other hand it affirmed that hitherto the policy of persecution had proved useless, wherefore the Christians were allowed to worship their god freely.

The next step was taken soon afterwards by Constantine the Great, and with this the last phase was initiated. In 312 Constantine had defeated an opposing emperor in Italy and proclaimed that the victory was owing to his being under the protection of the Christian God (cf. IX 9 (*PG* 20, 820). It may be difficult to judge of his personal motives, but his deeds testify to a firm political line. He was a usurper and was compelled to out-manoeuvre several competitors; to him it was decisive to legitimate his claim to be sole ruler, and in a state such as that of latter-day Rome with its intimate connection between religion and politics divine legitimation was a necessity. First he supported the cult of the Inconquerable Sun, *sol invictus*, but seemingly the sun was not of much help. By supporting the Christian God he gained several advantages at once. He got rid of persecutions requiring considerable resources, he took over control of an efficient bureaucracy, and he acquired an ideology. Hereafter it must be decisive for him to exploit this state of affairs so that he could gain control of the church, and not vice versa. He succeeded in this as well. Having defeated the last of the opposing emperors, the first ecumenical council, the Council of Nicaea, was held in 325. It was Constantine who convened the council and he who presided.

This was of course an entirely new situation for the church. Christianity had not become an obligatory state religion, but the Christian faith was supported by the Emperor, and suddenly the church was metamorphosed from an organization in opposition into a pillar of state with economic and juridical independence. The alliance between church and state was to be of decisive importance for both parties. In the Byzantine East this intimate connection was preserved down through the Middle Ages; in the West the result was centuries-long confrontations and reconciliations in the relations between state and church, between Emperor and Pope. With Constantine's ploy the church had gained a position of power with everything that followed from it: on the one hand, relief; on the other, a cause for moral self-reflection. The great expansion of the monastic movement of the fourth century was at least also a reaction against secularization. In theology the period is characterized by controversies about the natures of the Holy Trinity and Christ, especially as they took form in the fight with the Arians (see p. 583). Now such disagreements had also become a matter of state, and the Emperor participated eagerly. It might also be noted that the participants not infrequently displayed a highly developed flair for un-Christian intrigue.

Christianity did not come to prevail with one stroke thanks to Constantine. The majority of the whole population of the Roman Empire were probably still pagan, although we do not know much about the common man.

Nor did the upper class suddenly turn Christian, even though Christianity in the course of the fourth century gained more and more adherents among imperial officials. Probably Julian the Apostate had good reason to believe it realistic to re-establish paganism. He did not resume persecutions in the style of yore, but during his brief reign he tried to conduct a consistent cultural policy and to bring about a moral rearmament; he sought to learn from the enemy, from the Christians' firm organization, from their unshakeable faith and social care (cf. Jul. Apost. *Ep.* 36; 20; 22, Wright = 61a; 89a; 84a, Bidet-Cumont). But Julian only reigned for two years; the old-time worship was in a helpless state of decay, and the special Neoplatonic alliance between religion – conceived of more or less allegorically – and philosophy, which Julian had taken over from the Iamblichus tradition, cannot have had many opportunities to gain acceptance in the population at large.

In 380 the Emperor Theodosius issued a decree that made Christianity the official religion of the realm, the only cult permitted, that is to say. Thereby paganism was of course not done away with, but the coping stone had been laid for the development begun by Constantine.

ANTI-CHRISTIAN POLEMICS

It was probably around 170 that a Platonist named Celsus wrote a treatise entitled *The True Doctrine* (*Alēthēs logos*) in which he attacks Christianity. At the end of the 240s Origen wrote a lengthy refutation (*Contra Celsum*) in which he quotes Celsus extensively, and hence we are well acquainted with his views. He is probably to be considered a typical representative of the position held by the educated – apart from the fact that he betrays a very thorough knowledge of Christianity that certainly was unusual at the time. His philosophy is quite reminiscent of middle Platonism (Or. *CC* VII 42; 45), and to him philosophy, as is typical of the age, is theology or religious philosophy. God is transcendent, beyond knowledge and existence. It is the task of philosophy to make man god-like; but to find the creator and father of this world is onerous, and whoever has found him cannot impart his knowledge to everybody – as we are told in two quotations familiar from Plato. This is the true doctrine, and it is also an ancient one. Actually it has been available to wise men of all peoples, even though it is an exclusive doctrine only available to the few who are wise. The Christians place themselves outside the tradition already by maintaining that they alone possess the truth. Furthermore, they are uneducated, they constitute a secret brotherhood that actually is hostile to the state, and they are recruited from the dregs of society. It is, for example, outrageous that slaves and chambermaids propagandize in the nursery but are silent the moment the master of the house shows up, and it does no good for sinners to be given preferential treatment (III 44 ff.; I 1; III 55; 59 ff.). The Christian doctrine offends Celsus. Everybody may refer to unverifiable miracles; it is philosophically hopeless to imagine that God has created the world; it is blasphemy to declare that He has created man in His own image and that He became man Himself; and how can any man rise from the dead? It is altogether absurd to believe that the dead are resurrected in flesh and blood and that sinners are roasted on the Day of Judgement. The Christians worship a corpse – in fact Jesus suffered a miserable death, abandoned by everybody (cf. I 68; V 59; VI 60; 63; V 14; II 33 ff.; 54 ff.; VII 45). At one and the same time this is a showdown from the point of view of philosophy of religion, a cultural confrontation, and a battle between social classes. Later we shall see how Origen replied.

Christianity is irrational; the Christians wish to destroy society. These are the two enduring main indictments advanced with ever greater unease as the new faith grew stronger. Plotinus seems still relatively unaffected – he never mentions the Christians directly; probably his attack on the Gnostics (see p. 529) is primarily aimed at Valentinus, but in accusing the Gnostics of irrationality (cf. Plot. II 9, 6), he may very well also have had non-Gnostic Christians in mind. The situation changes after Plotinus, and surely it is with a polemical sting that the Neoplatonists add 'truth' to the triad of 'faith, hope and charity'. Porphyry's famous treatise against the Christians is known only in fragments, but it is clear that now the Christians have become the arch-enemy. By and large the same thing offended Porphyry and Celsus, but Porphyry cannot any longer dismiss the Christians as an uncouth minority. He may acknowledge Jesus as a 'sage', but the worship of Jesus as a god remains the stumbling block (cf. Aug. *De civ. Dei* XIX 23). What otherwise was special about Porphyry was that he – learned man that he was – practised philological biblical criticism; he pointed out late layers in the Old Testament and contradictions between the Gospels and in St Paul. (cf. Porph. *Adv. Christ.* frg. 12 ff., 30 ff., Harnack). For a long time Christian authors considered Porphyry their most dangerous adversary.

In a bitter treatise – preserved in fragments – the Emperor Julian the Apostate, who himself had been brought up as a Christian, attacked his mortal enemy, 'the evil fiction of the Galileans' (Jul. Apost. *Adv. Gal.* 39A, 318, Wright). As is typical of the Neoplatonism he represents, Julian begins by asserting that there is a natural, cosmic religion among all nations and behind the many different myths (52B; 69B, 320 ff.). Hence there is nothing wrong in the Jews having their own religion – but certainly in the intolerance inherent in their provincial God's having chosen a special people. Then he undertakes a comparison between the accounts of creation in Genesis and Plato's *Timaeus* (49A ff., 328 ff.), which, as might be expected, does not turn out to the advantage of Genesis. Thereafter, indirectly, he goes on to confront the envious, 'jealous' God of the Jews with Plato's god who was 'without jealousy' and was the god of the whole universe (115 D ff., 344 ff.; 155 C ff., 360 ff.). Now, has this envious and peevish God granted the Jews wisdom, culture, and power greater than that granted by the Greek and Roman gods to the whole world? – a question which is typical for an age that takes it for granted that the most powerful god is he who creates happiness and welfare. Even so, one has to concede that the Jews are consistent monotheists (cf. 306B, 406). But what of the Christians? They have taken over the worst from both sides and they are hopelessly inconsistent. Why do they find prophecies of Jesus in the Old Testament and maintain at the same time that their God has replaced the old covenant with the new; do they believe in one or three gods (209 D ff., 378 ff.)? The latter occasions a frontal attack on St John the Evangelist's doctrine of *Logos* – is Christ the word of God or is he a man (327A ff., 412 ff.)?

CHRISTIANITY AND PHILOSOPHY

Why did Christianity prevail? This is a question as impossible to answer as it is to state why the ancient world came to an end. But many connections and influences criss-cross each other; much lies in the *Zeitgeist*; first and foremost, Christianity and paganism are not static entities – paganism undergoes a development, for example from Celsus to Julian the Apostate; Christianity is interpreted by differing peoples with changing cultural backgrounds: the original congregation in Jerusalem, St Paul, the Alexandrine theologians, the Cappadocian Fathers, and the average, ordinary Christian. Much is – or at least in the course of time becomes – common thinking. To an ever greater extent pagan philosophy becomes religious; on a Christian basis a philosophy of religion is developed, which exploits the pagan one. Within pagan thinking one can trace an ever greater interest in the individual in spite of or rather comprehended in the cosmological, supra-individual way of thought that character-izes the entire philosophical tradition of Antiquity. The tendency is apparent in the three great Stoics, Seneca, Epictetus and Marcus Aurelius and in Plotinus, the premier Neoplatonist. The divine is found in man himself, but more and more it is emphasized that man has a dual identity, and more and more it is stressed that 'human' man in himself can do nothing; redemption is received from 'above'; the individual must rely on faith, hope and charity – and on truth. This also holds good for truth, understood as a pure, moral life.

The ancient thinker seeks for a world behind the present one, but not necessarily for one in contrast to it. There was every possible reason for pagans and Christians to understand each others' language and each others' yearnings – and all the greater reason for confrontation. The differences appear in the similarities.

Of the three attackers of Christianity, Celsus is in a way the man who sees most clearly. In any case he had a sure understanding of the external dividing lines. Christianity kept itself intact by its intolerance; the 'secret brotherhood' performed extensive social work but broke away from the elitist culture represented by Celsus; it won terrain among slaves and chambermaids – or as St Paul puts it: here there are no Jews or Greeks, bonded or free (Paul 1 Cor. 12,13). The Christian message is 'unto the Jews a stumbling block, and unto the Greeks foolishness' (1, 23).

The greatest stumbling block and folly was undoubtedly the Incarnation. The Jewish expectations of the Messiah and the idea of the life of Jesus as the fulfilment of the 'Old Covenant' were a matter of course for the early Christians, but that God became man must to a Greek or Roman be incomprehensible and blasphemic – if he had any literary or philosophical training. To the ordinary man it must have been something revolutionizing that God not merely was remote and transcendent but that He acted as a man among men. The idea of creation as God's act of will in time must also have been novel, and with it the thought, expressed in belief in the Resurrection, that God created man as a unity of body and soul – the soul was not, as in the philosophers, an alien guest in the body. New was first and foremost the radical belief in the grace of God – there were indeed parallels in late Neoplatonism, but Christianity did not show the path to man's higher self but to an entirely new life granted by that God who had also created individual man himself. To a Jew it must be a challenge that observance of Mosaic law was not simply the path to salvation (2 Cor. 3, 12 ff.) and to both Jews and pagans that man left to himself was completely bound by sin and that he could be redeemed – 'justified' – not by deeds but by faith alone (Rom. 4, 1 ff.). Man was both subject to the judgement of God and set free by His forgiveness, and the gospel of love – thou shalt love the Lord thy God with all thy heart and thy neighbour as thyself (Matth. 22, 37; Mar. 12, 30 ff.; cf. Paul. Rom. 13, 9; Gal. 5, 14) – was also unrealizable according to human measuring, yet at the same time a promise of the new life in which everything – in the words of the Sermon on the Mount (Matth. 6, 33) – shall be 'added unto' the believer. Back of these familiar formulations of the Gospel lie a new anthropology and a new concept of God, emphasized by the authoritative commands – 'Thou shalt . . . ', 'I say . . . '; this was also a challenge – at least to the Greeks and the Romans.

In contrast to mystery cults, Christianity laid claim to the whole man by a total demand and a total promise given through the Sacraments of Baptism and Holy Communion by the transcendent God. Through sermons and scriptural readings the Sacred history – from the Old Testament to the fulfilment in the New – was relived and appropriated by the individual as a member of the congregation. Inherent in this was also the new idea that the Christian faith was indissolubly tied to history – creation, incarnation and the last day. It is not, as has often been maintained, Christianity that introduced a 'linear' view of history; that could be found among the Romans (see p. 501), and apparently the phrase that 'the view of history of Antiquity' was cyclical cannot be erased. The new lies in the eschatological view of God's plan, as it manifests itself in history.

Of the writings of the New Testament the Epistles of St Paul and The Gospel According to St John can most directly be related to philosophical modes of thinking in the surrounding culture. But neither St Paul nor the author of St John's Gospel wishes to formulate a philosophy. They express their faith aided by the language and way of thinking that are the common property of well-educated persons of the day, and it goes without saying that the Jewish background is at least as prominent as the Greek one. That St Paul – naturally – was familiar with the yearning of the times for 'the unknown God' and that he knew how to exploit it is clear from his famous speech at the Areopagos in Athens, which follows upon a debate with 'Epicurean and Stoic philosophers' (Acta 17, 18 ff.). Indeed parallels can also be drawn first and foremost to Stoic popular philosophy, for example when St Paul acknowledges that all peoples have a natural knowledge of God and are familiar with a natural moral law (Paul Rom. 1, 19 ff.; Acta 17, 26 ff.; Paul Rom. 2, 14). But he also breaks with ideas like that: the Gospel perfects the Law and stands above every human law. And at the same time he attacks 'the wise': God has turned worldly wisdom into folly, and although the wise knew God, they 'glorified Him not as God, neither were thankful; but became vain in their imaginations, and their foolish heart was darkened' (1 Cor. 1, 20 ff.; 3, 19; Rom. 1, 21).

It is well known that St John's Gospel – as does Philo – exploits Stoic–Academic *Logos* thinking, which more or less was common property at the time. But here as well current thoughts were given a twist (John. 1, 1 ff.; cf. Paul. 1 Cor. 1,24). Christ is God's creative force or *Logos*, who was in the beginning, who was with God, and who was God. *Logos* is eternal as God but at the same time incarnate in Christ, and the *logos* 'that became flesh' is central in the teaching of the whole Gospel According to St John.

Two quotations from St Paul were to be especially important when Christian thinkers wanted to make philosophical reflections. One concerns natural knowledge of God; of the non-believers it is said that

> that which may be known of God is manifest in them; for God hath shewed it unto them. For the invisible things of him from the creation of the world are clearly seen, being understood by the things that are made, even his eternal power and Godhead.
>
> (Rom. 1, 19 ff.)

It is a quotation with a *Wirkungsgeschichte* that extends even to the medieval aposteriori proofs of God's existence (cf. Thom. Aq. *Sum. theol*. I 2, 2). The other quotation deals with the transcendence of God: 'For now we see through a glass, and in a riddle; but then face to face' (Paul. 1 Cor. 13, 12). Such a quotation may appeal to a Platonically tinted view of God, and it too has a *Wirkungsgeschichte* extending far beyond late Antiquity.

But whenever Christianity begins to formulate herself philosophically, problems in the New Testament naturally surface. This is first and foremost true of the issue of the Trinity, of Christ's nature, and of the question of predestination. St Paul's words about God as the potter who sovereignly fashions one vessel for honour and another for dishonour (Rom. 9, 20 ff.) is a crucial passage for Augustine, as it was later for Luther; but it calls for an interpretation as soon as it is confronted with the philosophical discussion of freedom of will, just as the question of the nature of God and Christ cannot simply be answered within the framework of Greek religious philosophy. To this can be added such questions as the creation of the world in time, the relation between soul and body, and individual immortality.

The process of confrontation begins in the second century. It was necessary to fight on two fronts, internally against the Gnostic understanding of Christianity, externally against Greco-Roman philosophy and education – the *paideia* – in general. The result was an orthodox, catholic theology. The earliest theological treatises are both apologetic and polemical – Christianity defending herself by attacking.

The Gnostic reinterpretation of Christianity must have been felt to be dangerous, because it removed some stumbling blocks – incarnation, the resurrection of the flesh, God's work of creation and plan with the world, for example, because it got close to Platonizing religious philosophy, first and foremost to the *Timaeus*, and because by its dualism it satisfied the generally felt wish to flee this world, which in no manner had left the Christian congregations unaffected.

The great enemy was Marcion (c.150) who was close to Gnosticism without being a Gnostic in the strict sense. He who placed himself at the head of an 'alternative' church, interpreted St Paul so radically that the difference between Law and Gospel precluded every connection between the Old and New Testaments. The God of the Old Testament, Jahve, was the strict God; he was the God of creation – the Demiurge – who had enforced his law on the world; but the God of the New Testament was the God of love; in fact He did not have anything to do with the other God but had sent Christ forth out of compassion for man (cf. Just. *Apol.* I 26; 58 (*PG* 6, 368; 416); Tert. *Adv. Marc.* I 2; III 24 (*PL* 2, 273; 384)). Marcion completely rejected the Old Testament. He also rejected any allegorical interpretation, and for this reason alone he could not in the harsh God of the Old Testament see any sacred promise of the God of the New Testament (cf. I 19 (*PL* 2, 292)).

To orthodox Christianity it must be the greatest possible challenge that God was not both creator and saviour, that the world or creation hence should in fact be irrelevant to God. Confronted with the Gnostics' claim that they possessed a secretly transmitted account of Christ, Irenaeus – who died soon after 200 and is one of the most prominent 'anti-Gnostic Fathers' – emphasized the Apostolic Succession, the faith transmitted from the days of the Apostles through the Church, in which the crucial point was the confession of faith in the triune God and the thought of God's plan for salvation to be completed with Christ coming again to 'restore everything' (cf. Ir. *Adv. haer.* III 1 ff.; 10 (*PG* 7, 844 ff.)). What is decisive is faith, not knowledge nor insight into God's nature (*gnōsis*).

The same notes are sounded in Tertullian (c.160–220), the first important Church Father whose language was Latin, a brilliant stylist and a merciless polemicist. Later ages have credited him with the formula *credo quia absurdum*, which is not quite authentic but conveys his view well. He also emphasizes the tradition, which the Jews forfeited, but which has become rooted in the Church (Tert. *Apol.* 21 (*PL* 1, 449); *De praesc. haer.* 13 (*PL* 2, 30)). But God's omnipotence and God's unity can also be seen directly from His work, the cosmos; He is invisible and yet visible; He is incomprehensible and can yet be comprehended in His grace (*Apol.* 17 (*PL* 1, 431)). Such a 'cosmological' proof of God's existence has connecting points not only with St Paul but also with pagan religious thought, and Tertullian also sees a connection between the Christian *Logos* doctrine and Stoicism (21 (*PL* 1, 457)). Yet, in the end, he totally rejects worldly wisdom. Whatever is of the good in pagan philosophy has been taken over from Moses but secularized and misinterpreted (47 (*PL* 1, 581)) – a standard argument in the polemics of the time, already familiar in Judaism (Philo). Another point was also to be a permanent element in Christian polemics. Plato said that it was difficult to find God – but, says Tertullian, even the most simple-minded Christian artisan knows his God. It is said that Christianity recommends the same virtues as the philosophers, but Christianity is not a philosophy. What do philosophy and the Christian have in common, what the disciples of Greece and Heaven, what he who destroys and he who constructs, what the thief of truth and its guardian (46 (*PL* 1, 580))? A Cicero or a Seneca speaks handsomely of enduring pain – but the philosophers' words do not win as many disciples as do the Christians' deeds, as Tertullian concludes his apologetic main work (50 (*PL* 1, 603)). You may mow us down, but we shall multiply!

JUSTIN MARTYR AND CLEMENT OF ALEXANDRIA

The other possible position for a Christian thinker was to adjust to the pagan tradition and consider Christianity the true philosophy. The first to do so was Justin Martyr (executed c.165). In a *Dialogue with the Jew Tryphon* he set himself the goal of debating both with Judaism and paganism. A purportedly autobiographical account (Just. *Dial.* 2 ff. (*PG* 6, 476 ff.)) explains how he – for the nonce – finds himself at rest as a Platonist, which is to say in the belief that happiness is to be found in the knowledge of the highest God (4 (*PG* 6, 484)). Then he meets an 'old sage' who in Socratic, maieutic manner makes him realize that Christianity is the true philosophy. The Platonists do not know that God created the world and the soul of every man, nor that Christ is the Redeemer (5 ff. (*PG* 6, 486 ff.)). In other words, the concepts of creation and incarnation are what distinguish Christianity from Platonism, although what is best in pagan philosophy anticipates Christianity (8 (*PG* 6, 492)). The old sage refers to God's plan of redemption, which, as is apparent to all, has been realized in history – and which is more telling than any theoretical argument.

In two apologetic treatises – addressed to the Roman Emperor – Justin then seeks to demonstrate that Christianity provides the truth that in imperfect form occurred to the philosophers. The main idea is a combination of the Platonic-Stoic *Logos* concept with St John's Gospel (*Apol.* II 13 (*PG* 6, 465)). The notion of God is congenital in all men, because all partake of *Logos*, which is both God's creative power and Christ Incarnate (6; 8 (*PG* 6, 453; 457)). St John's Gospel does of course have its Greek background, but Justin's interpretation gets close to being an *interpretatio Platonica*: the main emphasis is on *Logos* as cosmic principle, and Justin's ideas of the 'unsayable' God (cf. I 61 (*PG* 6, 421)) come very close to those of middle Platonism. This 'Hellenization' of Christianity was, so to speak, the price of presenting Christianity as a philosophy. But like Tertullian, Justin knows that even the ordinary Christian knows his God, whatever Plato might think (II 10 (*PG* 6, 461)).

What was begun by Justin was continued by Clement of Alexandria (c.150–215), even though he does not mention Justin directly. Clement wanted to formulate an ideal of Christian life or a Christian 'education' (*paideia*) and a Christian theology; both were an almost necessary task in an Alexandria saturated with Gnosticism. A Christian theology had to be a theology of creation demonstrating God's direct interference in the course of the world, known and knowable through the Apostolic tradition. In his fight against Gnostic dualism Clement could find support in pagan philosophy; in his interpretation of the Bible he made use of Philo. The philosophical background is the prevailing one of the day, which is to say middle Platonism with elements of Stoic popular philosophy. Clement's philosophical learning is not inconsiderable but can assume a compendium-like or doxographic character (cf. Clem. *Protr.* V ff. (*PG* 8, 164 ff.)). In his view of God's transcendence he is, like Justin, a middle Platonist, and to him the biblical account of the Creation is not far removed from that of Plato in the *Timaeus* (cf. *Paed.* I 8; *Strom.* V 9 (*PG* 8, 326 ff.; 9, 89)). In His transcendent form God is unknowable; the Son or *Logos*, on the other hand, can be known through the created world, and the incarnation is not much more than a special expression of God's immanence in the world (1 ff.; I 17 (*PG* 9, 9 ff.; 8, 795 ff.)).

In his *Exhortation* (*Protrepticus*) to the Greeks Clement attacks polytheistic worship of God and shows that good philosophy – especially Platonism – points forwards to Christianity; a subsequent treatise (*Paidagōgos*) contains moral prescriptions for the conduct of a Christian life. According to a programme of progression, Christian theology follows next – the purpose of which is to show man true insight (*gnōsis*), as it is tellingly called. In fact, however, this exists only as a collection of *Miscellanea* (*Strōmateis*), perhaps a kind of preliminary work. Yet, despite the form, this is Clement's principal theological work.

These writings delineate a steadily more profound insight and thus an education of the Christian as a man. The same plan can be followed in God's education of mankind. Philosophy is the Greek precursor of faith, as the Law is the Jewish one (5 (*PG* 8,717 ff.)), but, like the Law, philosophy only possesses partial truth (14 (*PG* 8,757 ff.)).

In the Christian process of education, Christianity and philosophy, faith and knowledge, must enter an unbreakable alliance. Faith is superior to worldly knowledge and is a presupposition for *gnōsis* or true knowledge of God, but *gnōsis* also presupposes philosophy and *is* philosophy (cf. II 4; I 10; VI 14; II 11 (*PG* 8, 943 ff.; 981 ff.; 9, 329 ff.; 8, 984)). This has consequences for the interpretation of the Bible in scholarly theology – dogmatics. The theologian has to understand the meaning hidden behind the letter of the biblical text, and this is done by the allegorical method, the hermeneutical method *par excellence* of late Antiquity, familiar to Clement from Philo. To a modern reader the method seems fairly arbitrary (cf. e.g. *Quis div.* 5 (*PG* 9, 609 ff.)). But seen with contemporary eyes it is a science, and Clement is well aware that a rational mode of interpreting the Bible must be formulated. The grand perspective in his theology is that Christianity is the doctrine of the creation of mankind and the individual, his education and redemption. It is God's purpose to save all mankind; He persuades, but does not compel, and the goal – the restoration of man – is most often arrived at after this life (*Paed.* I 9; *Strom.* VII 12 (*PG* 8, 236; 340 ff.; 9, 508)).

ORIGEN

The line laid down by Justin and Clement was completed by Origen (c.185–254), the most learned of the early Greek theologians and the creator of a genuine systematic theology. With him Christianity became the equal of pagan philosophy. Intensively but independently he exploited Greek thinking and he was able to criticize without being impeded by lack of expertise. He received his philosophical training from Ammonius Saccas – afterwards Plotinus' instructor (see p. 533). In his teaching, first at a school for baptismal candidates in Alexandria, which he quickly turned into a sort of university, and subsequently at Caesarea in Syria, he systematically lectured on all branches of philosophy as a preparation for Christian theology. His teaching included roughly the same profane authors as did Plotinus' (cf. Greg. Thaum. *Pan. in Orig.* 7 (*PG* 10, 1073 ff.); Eus. *Hist. eccl.* VI 18 (*PG* 20, 561 ff.)) but was apparently more systematically carried out. Major parts of Origen's very considerable oeuvre have been preserved. This is true of his main systematical work, *On First Principles* (*De principiis*), his answer to Celsus (*Contra Celsum*), and a series of sermons and biblical commentaries.

His major treatise against Celsus was written about seventy years after Celsus' attack, but much had happened during those seventy years. Origen was not like those unlettered Christians disparaged by Celsus. He is a cunning polemicist with a well-developed logical sense and is extremely well versed in philosophy. But what is most striking is that he does not really argue about the very concept of God. The truth of Christianity can, so he says, be legitimated on the basis of simple facts (cf. Or. *CC* I 2; 11; 23), which is to say that the truth of Christianity is to be found in the fulfilment of the prophecies of the Old Testament, in the Christian miracles, in the proliferation of Christianity, and in the Christians' pure morality. Strictly speaking, Christianity is in no need of a verbal defence – it is profoundly meaningful that Christ Himself remained silent when He was accused (*Praef.* 1 ff.). The notion of Christian morality plays a major role – here Clement's idea of the true Christian man is surely implicit. A good example of Origen's strategy is the section in which he refutes Celsus' theology (VII 42 ff.). Partly, his reckoning concerns attitude to life; partly, he encounters self-sufficient rational theology as opposed to the Christian one in which knowledge of God is only possible thanks to the Grace of God. The passage is replete with hidden quotations from the Bible and from Plato. In fact the philosophers have – using a Plato quotation – reached 'the threshold of the good', and the ascent of the soul in the *Symposium* corresponds to the words of St Paul on the invisible things of God being understood from the things that are made. But the downfall of the philosopher consists in his not living in agreement with his insight. He studies the most exhalted doctrines about God but afterwards abandons himself to idolatry – which, once again, is warranted by St Paul (Rom. 1, 22 ff.; cf. Or. *CC* VI 3). Add to this the philosopher's arrogance – it is onerous to find the Creator and Father of this world, Plato thought, but still, apparently, it is possible to do so. Yet even the most uneducated Christian knows that there is no way for man to find God 'unless helped by Him whom he seeks', and he knows – as Platonists ought to know – that now we only look through a glass and in a riddle, but then face to face (VII 38). In other words: the learned man uses the standard arguments of his day; he attacks the philosophers, not philosophy.

There are reasons for this, for concerning the nature of God, Origen is not in disagreement with Celsus. We cannot know God's nature directly, but we can deduce His nature from His creation, and we know that He is one, that He is the Monad: invisible, incorporeal, transcendent, reason, and yet beyond reason and being – for being participates in Him; He does not participate in being – and that He is omnipotent. The only thing He cannot do is to act against goodness and wisdom, for that is contrary to His nature (*De princ.* I 1,5 ff.; *CC* I 23; VII 38; III 70). A good part of the way this – God as the transcendent, incorporeal unity – is pure middle Platonism, and without scruples Origen can agree with the ancient Platonic formula that the purpose of knowing God is to become 'God-like' (*De princ.* III 6, 1). With Justin and Celsus he also shares the middle-Platonic reluctance to identify the 'unsayable' God in any positive way. To that extent Celsus and Origen have little to argue about. And yet there is this difference: Origen's God is an omnipotent, acting God who has revealed Himself to man. Natural theology may be employed, but it has a limit transgressed by the revealed *Logos*. Evidently Origen prefers the vagueness of middle Platonism to a more metaphysical system, such as that of Numenius – with whom he is acquainted (cf. *CC* V 7). He never tries to fit the Trinity into a Greek metaphysical system, and he never interprets God's voluntary act of creation as an emanation. Origen knows precisely when he is on speaking terms with the philosophers and when he is not.

When he speaks of *Logos* or the Son, it is not difficult to recognize the Greek tradition – and Philo – behind it. And yet Origen certainly signals a difference. He considers it an open question whether it is possible, for example, to call the Son the being of being or the idea of the ideas (VI 64); what is decisive is that *Logos* is God as He operates in the world, but how *Logos* precisely is to be understood eludes thought. *Logos* is at once creative reason, the Son of God, and Holy Scripture (cf. VII 42). *Logos* is identical with the Father, but also proceeds from the Father's will and assumes different forms, depending on the individual's capacity to understand; Jesus was *one* but he appeared to men in different forms (IV 16; II 64). Origen finds this notion of *Logos* in St John's Gospel, and it is used as his chief evidence in his confrontation with Celsus' theology. With this notion he steers clear of Greek metaphysical systems, but is nevertheless caught by Greek thinking on one point: he did not take the idea of incarnation literally; the Son proceeds in eternity from the Father; there was never a time when He was not (*De princ.* I 2, 9; IV 4, 1). In Origen's theology *Logos* is needed, but – strictly speaking – Christ is not.

Origen's principal dogmatic work, the *De principiis*, is divided into four main sections that deal with God, the world, the freedom of man, and revelation in Holy Scripture. Already this shows how much emphasis he places on biblical interpretation, as he does in his entire *oeuvre*. Apologetics and the philosophy of religion (*Contra Celsum* and *De principiis*) are not everything. At least as important – perhaps more so – are scriptural understanding and scriptural interpretation. Origen undertook thorough biblical studies – he taught himself Hebrew for example – and set down his learning in his commentaries on the Bible, which in turn found their way into sermons adapted to the laity. This distinction between scholarly theology and edifying exegesis corresponds exactly with his general hermeneutical principles. Indeed it is not easy to interpret Holy Scripture, and the Apostles only transmitted what was necessary; they left the rest to later generations (*praef.* 3). And it is evident that Holy Scripture – *Logos* – is addressed to both the learned and the rude. Hence it can be read in several different ways; distinctions must be made (IV 2, 4) between carnal, psychic and spiritual interpretations. The decisive dividing line runs between literal understanding – available to the simple – and the more profound meaning which it is the task of theology to extract, i.e. an interpretation relying on allegory and on a – so-called typological – juxtaposition of the promises in the Old Testament with their fulfilment in the New Testament. This does not mean that lay understanding is unacceptable in the eyes of God; it is true on its own terms but is and remains a figurative expression of a higher truth – it would not be unreasonable to recall Plato's myth of the state. Both take the ordinary man into account. But to Origen it is an even more pressing issue than to Plato to emphasize that all can live in truth, in spite of the fact that the truth cannot be known by all; and he needed a theoretical counterargument, for example, against Celsus, the intellectual aristocrat.

There is a high degree of reflection behind Origen's allegorical method (cf. *CC* I 42). He may be right in claiming that one interprets allegorically whenever one looks for a 'meaning' behind the textual wording – strictly speaking of any text whatsoever. But undeniably there are in Origen just as peculiar allegorical readings as in Philo or Clement.

From Holy Scripture man can learn of God's plan of salvation for mankind. God Himself is transcendent but works through *Logos*. His essence is goodness and, as in Plato's *Timaeus*, He creates from goodness (71); God's very goodness and omnipotence presuppose a creature, an object of goodness and omnipotence. But since God is also eternal, his act of creation is eternal; spiritual beings have always existed; only the physical world and with it man's world are created in time (*De princ.* I 2, 10; 4, 3; II 9, 1). God has granted His creature free will; He has willed that His creature shall will the good – or, in Stoic terms, assent to the good. Therefore it is man who errs; evil is in man, not – as in the Platonists – in matter, and man it is who of his own free will can return to the good (*CC* IV 3; *De princ.* III 5, 4; *CC* III 69; *De princ.* I 5, 2; *CC* IV 66).

God has willed that man shall will the good himself; yet man cannot gain salvation by his own volition. This means on the one hand that God is not responsible for human acts – He foresees what will happen because it will happen; it does not happen because He foresees it (II 20). On the other hand, man is in the care of God; man is led by God's providence (*pronoia*). In many respects Origen's thoughts on free will and providence are inspired by Stoicism; hence it is all the more important to him to distance himself from Stoic materialism; God's providence permeates everything in the world, but God is transcendent, He intervenes from the outside; and the world is not, as in the Platonists, divine in itself; it is only divine by having been created by God, and the physical world was created for the sake of man (VI 71; *De princ.* IV 1, 7; *CC* IV 99). By virtue of free will man is a fallen creature. God's plan of salvation – His providence – accordingly consists in educating man by employing his free will – without annulling it. Christ is the great educator, and education (*paideusis*) is the means to virtue (I 61; III 49). God's education of mankind is a drama in which the ultimate goal is man's final salvation or 'restoration' (*apokatastasis*), where God is all in all (*De princ.* III 6, 1 ff.; cf. on 'restoration': 3, 5; 5, 7; 6, 6). It is a lengthy process that may extend beyond the span of one man's life – thus Origen must presuppose a form of rebirth – and a new fall is thinkable after which the process is repeated (II 11, 6; III 6, 7).

Origen's cosmic drama differs – deliberately so of course – from that of the Gnostics by dealing with a fall within God's order. This is reminiscent of Plotinus; so is the thought that salvation comes 'from above' – but one should certainly step carefully. Plotinus' man is saved thanks to resources that after all reside in himself; not so Origen's. Just as in biblical exegesis, so in theology Clement is and remains Origen's precursor. Yet Origen's is not merely a more systematic intellect. He is far more reflective.

Was Origen then a Christian or a 'Hellene'? The answer would be as unclear as if one were to ask whether Philo was a Jew or a Greek, and these sharp categorizations are anachronistic. Origen's notion of God, his *Logos* philosophy, his thoughts on spiritual education, and his ideas of providence and free will are only thinkable within the framework of the Greek tradition, and not much is left of incarnation and the notion of man as a unity of body and soul. On the other hand, the world is created by God's deliberate act; in itself it is not divine; man does not save himself, but God has a plan for man that is enacted in history. The later development testifies to the difficulties of finding an appropriate attitude to Origen. His thinking was to be of decisive influence, especially in Greek theology. But he was also dangerous. As late as in the sixth century – at the Council of Constantinople in 553 – several 'Origenistic' heresies were condemned, for example, that the Son proceeds eternally from the Father.

THE CHRISTOLOGICAL CONTROVERSIES

That Origen became dangerous was owing to the fact that the debate on the Trinity and on Christ's nature became more acute in the fourth century. What was the relation between the Father and the Son and between Christ's divine and human nature? The question had already been a precarious one for a long time, but at the moment when Christianity had acquired official status it was necessary – certainly not least for the Emperor – to adopt an official position so that at any rate one could ascertain what was false doctrine. In this situation Origen must seem ambiguous; in his *Logos* doctrine Christ was both of the same substance as the Father and subordinate to Him. This had its own philosophical justification, but in the given situation what was called for were manageable and unmistakable formulas. Arius – a priest in Alexandria (beginning of the fourth century) – had maintained that the Father's perfect nature precluded that the Son was of the same substance as He, and he saw the 'persons' of the Trinity as different 'beings' (cf. Epiph. *Panar.* 69, 6 ff. (*PG* 42, 209 ff.)). His teaching became widely accepted – a couple of Emperors were 'pro-Arian' – and long after Arianism had been branded as heresy, it still had significant influence – several Teutonic tribes at the time of the Migrations were Arians.

The official counter-attack already came at the Council of Nicaea in 325. Here, Constantine presiding, it was decided that Christ, the Son, is of the same substance as the Father and that He is increate; the opposite view was expressly condemned (Socr. *Hist. eccl.* I 8 (*PG* 67, 72)). This, however, did not put a stop to the debate about whether Christ was of 'the same substance' as the Father or of a 'similar substance', and hence the Nicene Creed was confirmed at the Council of Constantinople in 381. What remained was the incarnation, the relation between Christ's divine and human nature. The problem had been a pressing one ever since the fight with Marcion and the Gnostics, and it remained an issue. In fact, it was logical either to stress Christ's divine nature – the Monophysite view (*monos*: one, *physis*: nature) – or to distinguish sharply between his two natures – the position of the Nestorians, which, long after it had been condemned, was maintained in the Orient, far beyond the borders of the Roman Empire. But there was no great interest in logic from official side; it was necessary to maintain both unity and difference, and the orthodox position was accordingly adopted at the Council of Chalcedon in 451, which affirmed that Christ was one 'person' with two 'natures', for the divine nature was of the same substance as the Father's, the human of the same nature as ours.

Behind these bureaucratic declarations lay political disputes, intrigues and compromises between clerical and imperial interests, and the result hardly lived up to the clarity and unambiguousness that might have been hoped for. To a large extent Greek philosophical terms and concepts are employed – 'substance' (*ousia*), 'nature' (*physis*), *hypostasis*, but also 'person' (*prosōpon*), which lies outside Greek metaphysical thinking. From a philosophical point of view the distinctions between these concepts are not pellucid. Probably this did not trouble many in the West; but in the East theology was far more philosophically oriented.

Philosophically the problem remained unsolved – probably also because it is indeed insoluble; it makes sense that the nature of the Trinity in Augustine – and in fact already in Origen – is viewed as a mystery; in the terminology of a later age, the Trinity cannot be known by natural theology. And surely the task of the three Councils was not philosophical; the reality that lay behind the more or less fortunate formulations was the mystery experienced during Holy Communion, and it was necessary to hold fast to the idea of the Incarnation: Christ had taken the human condition upon Himself, and He was divine. If either were denied, an unbridgeable chasm would open between God and man. To the average, unphilosophical man there were realities behind the façade.

EARLY BYZANTINE THEOLOGY AND ANTHROPOLOGY

The Trinitarian philosophy that began with Origen could not be satisfied by authoritative formulas, and the most significant theologians sought to go behind the concepts in order to uncover a rational coherence; but at the same time it was emphasized that rational understanding has its limits.

The trend-setting Greek philosophers of the fourth century – the Cappadocian Fathers (from Cappadocia in Asia Minor) – are Basil (c.330–80), his fellow student and friend, Gregory of Nazianzus (c.330–90), and his brother, Gregory of Nyssa (c.335–95). They were active between the Councils of Nicaea and Constantinople and contributed considerably to the final victory of the Nicene Creed, and they participated in the opposition against the heretical Emperor Julian the Apostate. Their background is in large part in Origen – though purged of offensive deviations – but they had also received a standard literary and rhetorical education, in Athens among other places, and had thereby acquired relatively broad familiarity with pagan Greek literature; thus they were well read in Plato and Plotinus but, strangely enough, seem unaffected by Iamblichus. Their learning hardly measures up to Origen's, but like him they must adopt a position with respect to the entire pagan ideal of the *paideia* – thus a small treatise by Basil has been preserved, which is addressed to 'young people' on how it is possible to read profane literature for moral benefit. Basil was the practical one among the three, active as a church administrator and as organizer of monastic life. His works demonstrate a remarkable interest in exploiting profane science to understand the concrete physical world as God's act of creation. Gregory of

Nazianzus was first and foremost an aesthete and a man of feeling, one of the most accomplished of the early Byzantine poets. The most profound thinker was Gregory of Nyssa.

On the one hand Gregory of Nyssa considers profane knowledge as a preliminary to faith (cf. Greg. Nyss. *Vit. Moys.*, *PG* 44, 360); on the other, he distinguishes sharply between faith and knowledge – more sharply than Origen. Natural theology can achieve a preparatory understanding of the world, which however can only be legitimated through faith; it can go so far as to demonstrate God's existence from His work (*Or. cat.* 12, *PG* 45, 44; cf. *Hexaem.*, *PG* 44, 72), and ordinary reflection and partial analogy with man will also show, claims Gregory in his principal systematical work (*Or. cat.* 1 ff., *PG* 45, 13 ff.), that God without the dissolution of His essential unity works through His word of creation – *Logos* – and His power – the Holy Ghost – so that He is one of substance but three persons or hypostases (3, *PG* 45, 17). The real essence of the Trinity is, however, impenetrable to human thought. We can – as in the later medieval tradition, for example in Thomas Aquinas – account for the existence of God, not for *what* He is. This is tied to Gregory's epistemological views in general. When he speaks of man as a natural being, he is consistently a sensualist. Sensation is the point of departure for all natural cognition (*Cont. Eunom.*, *PG* 45, 341), but nothing that can be sensed or thought has real existence (*Vit. Moys.*, *PG* 44, 333); only God possesses that. The 'names' whereby we call God – He is 'Wise', 'Just', 'Omnipotent', etc. – are inadequate (*In Cant.*, *PG* 44, 784). In fact we cannot predicate anything about God; we do not understand what it means that God is not wise, but Wisdom (781).

But we have not only been created as rational beings. Man is created in the image of God, and he has the privilege – unlike all other creatures – to turn to God or towards the world – we are what we make of ourselves, as in Plotinus (*Vit. Moys.*, *PG* 44, 328). The divine is in ourselves, and we can – again as in Plotinus – discard what is alien and return to our true nature (*De virg.*, *PG* 46, 372 ff.). Gregory finds his anthropology symbolically expressed in the account in Genesis (*De hom. op.*, *PG* 44, 177 ff.; *De an. et resur.*, *PG* 46, 29), and here he relies on Philo. God made spiritual man before corporeal man who is bound to sensation and discursive thought, and corporeal man is a fallen creature in so far as he lets himself be bound by sin and matter. But fallen man can be liberated from his body; he can be purged and return to his spiritual self. The final stage is the restoration – Origen's *apokatastasis* – of divine man, who, as an image of God, is able to behold Him (*De hom. op.*, *PG* 44, 148). This mystical path to restoration and knowledge of the unknowable (cf. *Vit. Moys.*, *PG* 44, 377) man cannot master; the highest knowledge presupposes faith, but is granted as an act of grace by God – God acts on the man who attains the highest insight (cf. 380 ff.; *In Cant.*, *PG* 44, 792; *In Steph.*, *PG* 46, 717). Like Philo, Gregory reads the Exodus account of Moses as emblematic of man's way to God. This is carried out in an exegetical treatise, in which the first half provides a literal and the second an allegorical interpretation of the biblical text.

All of this might well be called eclecticism. It combines Philo's exegetical method with Origen's doctrine of 'the restoration' of fallen man and with Plotinus' of the descent of the soul into the body and its return to a higher identity. Yet, it is more than that. Gregory has no use for Plotinus' doctrine of hypostases. His concern is not with the intelligible world nor with general metaphysics but with spiritual man. Augustine probably did not read Gregory, but nevertheless there are clear points of resemblance: the all-decisive to Gregory is man confronted with God and God's restoration of fallen man by an act of grace. Gregory's doctrine of man – his anthropology – is a direct consequence of his theology. To this should be added his distinction between faith and knowledge, between revealed and natural theology, which points directly forwards to the Middle Ages.

Man and God are the two poles around which the theological thinking of the times is grouped. One side of the issue, the anthropology, finds an interesting expression in a treatise on *The Nature of Man* (*De natura hominis*), written around 400 by Bishop Nemesius. This might also seem a specimen of eclecticism, but behind it lies a fairly firm thought structure. Man is a microcosmos, an image of the entire created world (Nem. *De nat. hom.* 1, *PG* 40, 533); as in Plotinus, he is composed of body, soul, and intellect (504); he occupies a middle position and can follow two paths, upwards towards God, downwards towards matter. A presupposition for this is that the human soul is an immaterial substance and that it, as Plato thought, is a self-moving mover, and thereby the Aristotelian view of the soul as the form of the body is precluded (2, *PG* 40, 537 ff.; 565 ff.). On this fundamental level Nemesius accordingly clearly chooses Plato's side rather than Aristotle's. But when he describes the human soul in its connection with the body he is an 'Aristotelian', strongly influenced by Aristotelian psychology and physiology, by Alexander of Aphrodisias, and by Galen. The eclectic aspect is really not surprising; more striking are the interests in man as a sensing being and in the human passions, where Nemesius with or without intermediate links ties himself closely to Aristotle's *De anima* and the *Nicomachean Ethics* (5 ff., *PG* 40, 612 ff.; 16 ff., *PG* 40, 672 ff.). Nemesius' anthropology comprehends what is human in all its aspects.

The combination of Platonic metaphysics with Aristotelian science is not in itself a problem for Nemesius. The problem is how to understand the union of soul and body, the supra-sensual and the sensual. It cannot be an outer unification of two substances; the solution is the Neoplatonic one, presumably with Porphyry as the source: the supra-sensual governs the sensual, and the soul governs the body, for, without itself being changed, a spiritual substance can penetrate a piece of matter (3, *PG* 40, 592 ff.); the intellect is in the soul and the soul in the body, but not as one stuff mixed with another.

To understand man's place between God and the world it is necessary to presuppose that man has a free will. If only it can be demonstrated that free will and God's providence do not exclude one another (39 ff., *PG* 40, 726 ff.), Nemesius can also here exploit the Aristotelian arsenal – more specifically the analysis of deliberation, choice and voluntary acts (29 ff., *PG* 40, 717 ff.).

About 100 years later the other main issue – theology – was given a special form in Pseudo-Dionysius the Areopagite. In many ways he continued and systematized the general Platonic tradition, especially that of the Cappadocians, but the decisive stimulus came from Proclus' metaphysics. Pseudo-Dionysius expands the thought of affirmative, symbolic, and mystical theology, familiar from the Platonic tradition cf., e.g. p 517–18) – and mystical theology, the wordless knowledge of the unsayable and hidden God, takes its point of departure in the denial of every predicate of God (*via negationis*). The 'names' we attribute to the divine are symbolic in the sense that we only 'name' the effects of God, not His essence. All this corresponds for example to Gregory of Nyssa's reinterpretation of Platonism. But Pseudo-Dionysius goes further. He takes over the whole Neoplatonic doctrine of emanation in the form Proclus gave it; creation is understood as emanation, and thus his system becomes metaphysical rather than theological. When he also says that the final goal is 'to become God-like', his words are surely more Neoplatonic than Christian (cf. Ps.-Dion. *Hier. coel.* III 2, *PG* 3, 165). Gregory's thought of created man as recipient in his relation to God has been replaced by a Neoplatonic identification with God. All of the spiritual world – and the church, so to speak the spiritual world in concentrated form – is an enormous hierarchy of divine powers that mediate between the one God and the visible world; actually it is a hierarchy of masked Proclus henads. The leitmotif behind the often fantastic symbolism is the dialectics between the one and the not-one, or 'the other' (cf. *De myst. theol.* 5, *PG* 3, 1044 ff., exploited by Nicolaus Cusanus, Nic. Cus. *De non aliud* I). And the basic structure is the movement *monē-proodos-epistrophē* and Proclus' parallel triad unparticipated-participated-participating. This basic structure is found everywhere in the intelligible sphere, but first and foremost in the relation between God and the world: God remains in Himself, everything proceeds from Him and returns to Him (*Hier. coel.* I 1, *PG* 3, 120).

The Areopagite exercised considerable influence on Byzantine theology (John Damascene) and through the Latin translation by John Scotus Eriugena also on the West. Nevertheless it is not in him that one finds the keynote of Byzantinism. It is not his 'de-Christianized' Platonism but Gregory's that determines the Byzantine view of God and man. Until and including the fourth century it is Eastern, not Western theology that is drawn to speculative thinking and debate. With Gregory the basic features of Byzantine theology were established; its contemplative character did not change essentially for centuries to come; what is called for is contemplation, not words. Western theology, on the other hand, was steadily renewed down through the Middle Ages. It is one that debates, searches and argues. Its source is Augustine.

35

AUGUSTINE

—— •◆• ——

'God and the soul I desire to know.' – 'Nothing else?' – 'Nothing else'.
(Aug. *Sol.* I 2, 7; cf. *De ord.* II 18, 47)

Thou hast created us for thyself, and our heart cannot be quieted till it may find repose in thee.

(*Conf.* I 1; cf. XIII 38)

These two quotations announce the leitmotif in Augustine's thinking – and in contemporary Greek theology. Both had learned from the Platonists – but it is not, as a Platonist would say, god and the world or god in man whom they desire to know. It is God *and* man. Like the Platonists, they sought to return to God, but to the God who made man as man. Still, there are notable differences between East and West. Augustine grew through crises and arrived at dearly-bought insight into man's nature and relation with God, which is remote, for example, from Origen's confidence that in the fullness of time God will 'restore' all men and become all in all. His background is in Latin Christianity; to him man is created 'for God', yet by himself he is but dust and ashes (cf. Aug. *Conf.* I 6) bound to nothingness and sin. God has made man but he is created of nothing – a contrast that is inherent in man's nature and one that lies behind Augustine's ideas about the relation between faith and thought, intellect and will, grace and predestination, love of God and love of self. Since man in himself is nothing, yet assigned to God, he can only know God's nature or work in the world through 'signs' or 'traces'. In Augustine this imparts a special character to the general thinking in symbols of the time. This world is a reflection of a higher one; the physical world can only be understood from the spiritual one, but it is understood indirectly through the direction of the will and the reading by the intellect of God's 'signs'. Augustine had an enormous talent for absorbing; elements in his thinking come from elsewhere, and – on the basis of the preceding chapters – a detailed demonstration of this should be unnecessary. His originality lies in the whole he constructs, which has been of immeasurable importance for the view of man and the concept of God in the West. The whole is not present from the outset. After the first crises and Augustine's conversion, the goal is constantly to become perfect in God. First the main emphasis is on knowing God by knowing oneself and by faith.

Later the main theme is restlessness of the heart and yearning for repose. Faith and grace, grace and predestination become the central concepts in this later phase. The standard theological questions of the time – the doctrines of the Trinity and the Incarnation – acquire a special ring in Augustine: the Trinity is a symbolic expression of existence altogether; the Incarnation is God's direct intervention in human life. Thereby both acquire an importance going beyond Origen's intellectualism and the formal dogmatics of the Councils.

Aurelius Augustinus (354–430) lived in a time of change. Having grown up in the tradition of the Western Early Church, educated in Latin profane literature, and a witness to the demise of the old world, he was, as perhaps nobody else, to give form to the medieval world of ideas. He was born in North Africa and as a young provincial he witnessed the rapid decline of the Roman Empire – class conflicts, inflation, ruinous taxation, adscription, abuse of power, secret police, legal anarchy. In his manhood the division between East and West became definitive; in 410 the Visigoths conquered Rome; the Empire came apart. There is an almost insistent symbolism in the Vandals standing twenty years later at the city gates – as Augustine lay dying in his diocesan residence in North Africa.

He was born in the small Roman colony of Thagaste in Numidia (the present-day Algeria) as the son of a Roman citizen, an impecunious landowner. Such a remote provincial town was marked by sharp ethnic and social contrasts. The native population – 'the Punics' – constituted a lower class; in the near-by North African mountains lived the nomads; but practically speaking there were no connections between the population groups. Within the ruling group, the Romans, the economic and social contrasts were also considerable. Augustine's father was a *petit bourgeois*, and it was only with great difficulty that he succeeded in giving his son an education in letters that opened the way to social advancement. It is of no little importance that Augustine did not come by his cultural ballast with ease; it is of even greater importance that he was a provincial – his life's work was in North Africa, and throughout his life he felt himself to be both a Roman and an African.

While Augustine's father did not mean much to him, his mother Monica did. She was a Christian, and her simple but uncompromising piety is a part of his spiritual background. He was closely tied to her; in the *Confessiones*, his autobiography, which is the source of our knowledge of Augustine's youth, she acts as his lodestar. She was his confidante and accompanied him when he went to Italy; the conversion of her son was her life's goal. Yet she was also an extreme busy-body in temporal matters – for example, she saw to it that Augustine broke a happy liaison of many years standing with a woman who was blocking his career.

Augustine received the best education available in Africa, which is to say that he studied 'the liberal arts', first and foremost grammar and rhetoric. His studies were finished in the provincial capital of Carthage. It was a narrow and not very up-to-date education. One read one's classics, Virgil and Cicero first and foremost, but not much else, and the teaching was purely formal. Characteristically, Augustine probably never learned enough Greek to read Greek texts in the original – already at this time the Greek and Roman cultures were worlds apart. In his Bible studies he used Latin translations,[1] and by and large he had only second-hand knowledge of Greek philosophy and theology – one must for example accept as fact that he seems not to be familiar with Gregory of Nyssa; hence agreements with the Cappadocians are not owing to direct influence. However, from the outset it is striking how much Augustine could accomplish with modest means; he was in a manner of speaking compelled to be original. Quickly he himself became a teacher of rhetoric in Carthage. In these years of his youth he formed life-long friendships with a circle of fellow students and pupils; this African 'junta' followed him to Italy and they appear as interlocutors in his early dialogues; like Augustine himself, some of them later became bishops in their native Africa. Augustine always lived with and thrived in the company of others; by nature he was an open and a thoroughly emotional man to whom friendship was a necessity of life.

After a brief period as a teacher in Rome, in 384 Augustine became a 'professor' of rhetoric in Milan, the Emperor's western residential city. This was a major advancement and the high point in Augustine's career. But also in another sense it marked the turning point in his life. Outwardly it had been a success until then, but he had found no inner satisfaction. While reading Cicero in his youth he had been called to philosophy by Cicero's *Exhortation to Philosophy* (*Hortensius*, see p. 489; cf. *Conf.* III 4); and to Augustine, as to the whole age, philosophy, literally translated, meant love of wisdom, which is to say of contemplative life. The spiritual awakening set in motion by Cicero's dialogue surprisingly made Augustine a Manichaean, and for nine years he was a warm adherent of this late, eclectic off-shoot of Gnosticism (see p. 527). Manichaeism, with its dualistic view of the relation between good and evil, the battle between light and darkness, provided him with a far better answer to the problem of evil than his mother's simple Christianity could do at the time; without profound philosophical ballast, as he was, he felt himself drawn to the Manichaeans who laid wholesale claim to 'scientific' answers to all questions. However, he discovered (V 7) that Manichaean learning was not very profound. This occasioned sceptical scruples, and once again he took refuge in Cicero – he had very little else to seek refuge in – this time the *Academica*, Cicero's report of the debate between the Stoics and the Academic Sceptics – in Augustine's time a mere 500 years old.

Then he went to Milan, and for the first time he encountered a cosmopolitan culture. Leading circles in the residential city were marked by a Christianity tinted with Neoplatonism. This was true not least of the powerful Bishop Ambrosius, the world's first real ecclesiastical magnate, who acted with great authority against the Emperor Theodosius. Ambrosius was also a learned man, schooled in Greek thought, especially in Origen's theology. He was a too remote figure for Augustine to become intimate with (cf. V 13 ff.; VI 3), but his sermons made a strong impression on him. This was true of the formally accomplished style, but gradually even more of the contents, the Platonizing Christianity, and, not least, of the allegorical method. It caused Augustine to read the Bible with new eyes. At the same time he was reading 'Platonic writings' (Plotinus and Porphyry) in a translation by Marius Victorinus, a

---

1   Only occasionally the translation that later became the authorized version of the Roman Catholic Church, the *Vulgata*, by one of Augustine's contemporaries, the learned Hieronymus, with whom he conducted an – at times volatile – correspondence.

highly regarded advocate of the current unification of Platonism and Christianity (cf. VIII 2), among other things well known for his attempt to unite the doctrine of the Trinity with the Neoplatonic doctrine of hypostases (cf. Mar. Vict. *Ad Cand.*, PL 8, 1023 ff.). Augustine himself relates (Aug. *Conf.* VII 20) that he read 'the Platonists' before renewing his Bible studies. But it is wrong to imagine that he became a Neoplatonist first and a Christian second. It was a Platonizing Christianity he encountered in Milan; it was a Platonizing Christianity to which he converted, and the difference between Christianity and a 'pagan' Platonism undoubtedly was clear to him from the beginning. It is incidentally worth noting that Augustine – the father of medieval 'Platonism' – probably never read Plato himself. The Aristotelian influence is also indirect – Augustine himself only mentions that he has read the *Categories* (IV 16), undoubtedly in Latin.

With his conversion Augustine overcame a personal crisis. He renounced a secular career and during the time before his baptism (387) he withdrew with his mother and his African friends to a country house at Cassiciacum, north of Milan. What attracted him was not a life of ascetecism but a life of *otium*, which is to say one devoted to philosophical and theological studies, described very charmingly in his earliest writings, the so-called Cassiciacum dialogues.

After his baptism he returned to Africa, but on the journey his mother died at Ostia, the port of Rome. He intended to continue the contemplative life in his native city, but a few years later, in 391, he was ordained and later made Bishop of Hippo Regius, the second-largest city in the province of Africa, even though it was far from being a metropolis. It was not very willingly that Augustine exchanged the theoretical life with the practical, but he never did anything half-heartedly; once he had been given the responsibility for the welfare of a congregation, he devoted all his energy to the new life. The diocesan dignity was no *sine cure* post. The conduct of divine services was onerous and so was the instruction of baptismal candidates. And in those uneasy times the Bishop also had an important civic function; for example, he had to act as judge in major and minor secular trials. At the same time Augustine organized a sort of monastic community, considerably more ascetically planned than the life in Cassiciacum; he conducted intensive Bible studies, and he participated energetically in general church politics. It is surprising that he nevertheless found time for very comprehensive literary activities. His writings, his work in church politics, and a very extensive correspondence gradually made him the grand old man of the African Church, and his influence extended far beyond insignificant Hippo and provincial Africa.

He remained in Hippo until his death. During this long period his religious fervour and piety deepened; gradually, although never entirely, the Platonic influence was weakened. He himself considered the time in Milan and Cassiciacum as preparatory for his restless heart's finding repose in the Hippo of realities. The realities were grim enough: caring for the church demanded care of the faith and fighting the heretics. Without doubt Augustine had an irenic temperament, but already the many titles in his oeuvre that begin with 'Against . . . ' show how much emphasis he – as did everybody in the golden days of theological schisms – placed on fighting false doctrine; and it was not least by virtue of his unique position that it came to be decided what in the judgement of history was to be considered false doctrine and what was not. First came the fight against the Manichaeans, then against the Donatists, then against the Pelagians. The Donatistic movement – named after Donatus (beginning of the fourth century) – went all the way back to the time of Constantine the Great and was tied to the state of affairs immediately after the victory of Christianity. What should be done about the priests who had failed during the persecutions? The Donatists' answer was that they had forfeited the right to administer the sacraments. The position that won out – and Augustine's – was that the holiness of the sacraments was independent of the individual priest's moral habitus. In its original form this was no longer relevant, but of course the question remained whether moral perfection could be demanded. In Augustine's time the Donatists had especially many adherents in Africa – many cities had both an orthodox bishop and a Donatist 'anti-bishop', and it looks as if the movement at this time had the character of a rebel movement in which 'the pure' turned against the establishment. Pelagianism – which took its name from a British monk, Pelagius, a contemporary of Augustine – was disseminated throughout the whole Western world. The Pelagians maintained man's absolute freedom – the message of the Gospels had no meaning unless the individual in full freedom could decide whether he wanted to follow it. It was an untraditional heresy. The Pelagians had no false doctrine of the Trinity nor of Christ's nature. But in this movement as well there seem to have been social and political undercurrents, and the Emperor became alarmed. All were equal before God – so the Pelagians claimed – and wealth was incompatible with the Gospels. According to this 'socialist' view, Augustine's doctrine of grace (*gratia*) was apparently interpreted in analogy with the old and still viable client system: the ruler bestows favour (*gratia*); his reward is loyalty (*fides* – faith). But, according to the Pelagians, God was not a ruler acting arbitrarily with his subjects (cf. Anon. *De div.* 6, 2 ff.; 12, 2, Caspari).

It was of fatal importance that Augustine in his fight against the Donatists felt himself compelled to invoke 'the secular arm', as did Luther after him. If the heretics could not be persuaded, they must be led back to the church by force (Aug. *Ep.* 133; 185 (*PL* 33, 509 ff.; 792 ff.)). It is uncertain how he viewed the social aspects of Donatism and Pelagianism; the decisive in his battle against the heretics is the view of God and man. The logical consequence of both Donatism and Pelagianism was in Augustine's opinion that man was autonomous in his relation with God; but to Augustine grace did not depend on human merit. The emphasis is on the consciousness of sin and on the individual's dependence on God; that determined the understanding of Christianity in the West after Augustine.

WORKS

Shortly before his death Augustine wrote a sort of annotated catalogue of his vast *ouevre* – the *Retractationes* ('Retractions' or, rather, 'Revisions'). It is arranged chronologically and thus provides a firm date for every work. Beyond this, it is valuable in showing how Augustine in old age assessed what he had written earlier. He explains and defends some points and dissociates himself from others – all in light of the pious orthodoxy he gradually had arrived at; he wishes, so he declares, to examine his writings with a judge's severity and make note of what offends him (*Retr.* prol. 1). The works – of which most by far, but not all, have been preserved – consist almost exclusively of occasional writings, which is to say of treatises occasioned by specific situations, whether polemical or addressed to specific persons on specific occasions. The first treatises are in dialogue form, as might be expected inspired by Cicero. They are written in an elegant, fluent, personal style. First come (386–7) the so-called Cassiciacum dialogues, which in written form mirror Augustine's discussions with his friends at Cassiciacum. They are addressed to the educated readers – one might think of the milieu in Milan – and show the Platonizing view of Christianity of the young baptismal candidate, which is not entirely approved of by the author of the *Retractationes* (I 1 ff.). Against Academic Scepticism and within the framework delimited by Cicero and the Hellenistic school discussions, Augustine seeks to find criteria for certain knowledge (*Contra Academicos*). A treatise on *The Happy Life* (*De vita beata*) also relies on the Ciceronian conceptual world and seeks to demonstrate that happiness and the good life are the life in God. Perhaps the most important of the dialogues, the *De ordine*, under evident influence from Plotinus, depicts the world as God's order, and here for the first time the question is asked about providence and evil. Connected to the Cassiciacum dialogues is the *Soliloquia*, in the form of a dialogue between Augustine and reason. Here he ponders what it means to desire to know God and the soul. These dialogues have rightly been called aperitifs; the common theme is that Christianity provides the answer to the questions posed by Cicero and 'the Platonists'.

During the next years followed a couple of lesser treatises on the immortality and incorporeality of the soul (the *De immortilitate animae* and the *De quantitate animae*), a presentation of 'the liberal arts' – the acknowledged basis also for Christian 'education' – of which, *inter alia*, the treatise on music (*De musica*) has been preserved,[2] and a dialogue on the teacher (*De magistro*), which through a penetrating analysis moves from philosophy of language to essential aspects of epistemology.

Because of the adverse circumstances, many of the most weighty writings after Augustine's ordination were written over several years. The dialogue *On Free Will* (*De libero arbitrio*) from 388–95 points both backwards to the earlier works and forwards to the later ones. From a philosophical point of view it is perhaps Augustine's most central work. The most important works on philosophy of religion are three: two brief treatises, *On True Religion* (*De vera religione*) from 389–91 – an apologetic discourse directed against the Manichaeans – and a manual on the Christian faith, the *Enchiridion* from 421, which is ordered according to the three main concepts of faith, hope and charity; and above all the great work *On the Trinity* (*De Trinitate*) from 400–16 in fifteen books, not occasioned by external instigation.

The *Confessiones* (397–401, in thirteen books) and the *De civitate Dei* (416–26, in twenty-two books) are rightly considered Augustine's principal works. *Confessiones* does not exactly mean confessions of secret sins; rather, the work is a confession to

---

2   The whole account of the liberal arts was never completed. Parts of the *De dialectica* (formerly considered spurious) that largely build on Stoic linguistic philosophy have been preserved.

God or an acknowledgement of faith in God. It is an autobiographical account of Augustine's inner development until his baptism, but viewed ideally it presents a life under God's guidance. The *Confessiones* is an epochal work in European literature, which sets itself apart from the narrow autobiographical genre by uniting self-analysis with an eternal perspective – in the most literal sense the work proceeds from time to eternity. The *De civitate Dei – On the City of God* – has been of as least as great importance to posterity. It constituted the ideological arsenal of the medieval theories of church and state. Here Augustine presents his views of society and history, but once again from an ideal point of view: the relation between two powers, the Earthly City and the City of God.

Side by side with these monumental works there are numerous polemical writings directed against heretics. The anti-Pelagian writings especially, are often of philosophical interest because of their treatment of the concepts of grace, providence, and predestination. A considerable number of sermons, addressed to different types of listeners, more directly tell of Augustine's Christian teaching and can be supplemented with the treatise on the teaching of 'uneducated' baptismal candidates (*De catechezandis rudibus*), which provides a valuable insight into his teaching of the Christian message to the laity. Often the sermons have the character of scriptural interpretation, and hence they have close connection with Augustine's major exegetical works, the most important of which is the commentary on Genesis, the *De genesi ad litteram* (401–15). Augustine set down his principles for exegesis – and with this the basis for Christian 'education' altogether – in his *De doctrina Chistiana* (397, completed in 426), a sort of counterpart to the youthful 'worldly' project on the liberal arts, the *artes liberales*. The first three books deal with biblical hermeneutics, the last one with the form of preaching, homiletics in modern terms; as a whole, the work can be called a Christian rhetorical manual. Finally, a very considerable collection of letters has been preserved, the subjects ranging from quite ordinary everyday problems to the main questions of theology.

Far from all the works have been mentioned in this lapidary survey. The vastness of the *oeuvre* alone necessitates a selection. But this is also necessary in a presentation of Augustine as a philosopher. His biblical exegesis, his sermons, and his polemics contain passages that also from a modern point of view can be called philosophical, but here they must by and large fall outside the field of vision. Nevertheless it is important to emphasize that hence the outcome must also of necessity give a one-sided – on some points perhaps distorted – picture of Augustine's work and thoughts as a whole. It is not the whole Augustine who speaks in the following pages.

Augustine expects his reader to have time at his disposal: not everything is said at once. Throughout lengthy passages the discussion moves back and forth with digressions and digressions on digressions in a constant movement from the emotionally laden and pathetic, via the elegantly subtle, to paedagogical, down-to-earth formulations and reformulations. Then all of it is suddenly interrupted by a *mise au point* taking the reader by surprise and placing the preceding in a wholly new light – in the oldest preserved work, the *Contra Academicos*, the decisive turn in the argument does not appear until the third and final book; the most important link in the so-called *cogito* argument (see pp. 602 and 614) is inserted in the *De libero arbitrio* (II 3, 7) by a linguistic surprise manoeuvre. It is not difficult to see that Augustine's style is rhetorical and that the professor of rhetoric takes it for granted that the reader is interested both in what is said and how it is said. In countries with Romance languages this stylistic tradition remains unbroken, and there no barrier exists between Augustine and his reader. It is a different matter in the more puritanical North where it is an immediate cause for suspicion if an author is able to express himself in perfect form and causes indignation if he plays on the emotions. Augustine masters the three classical stylistic levels: the plain style that teaches, the 'medium' style that delights, and the grand style that moves the reader. Not least in his sermons one can see how the style is adjusted to the addressee – not everything can be said to everybody in the same way. Also with respect to the style, it is surprising how much Augustine can do with his scant schooling. His secret is that the proper style is no accidental outer garment but a direct reflection of the thought (cf. *De doctr. Christ.* IV 6, 10). This marks a break with the formal practice of school rhetoric. Augustine's first philosophical revelation came when, in Cicero's *Hortensius*, he was conducted from the form to the content in the form. This was repeated when he was initiated into Christianity by Ambrosius' sermons (cf. *Conf.* V 13 ff.).

Augustine has a special talent for capturing and visualizing a situation and for characterizing a person with a few strokes; the characterizations in the Cassiciacum dialogues are far more lively than in Cicero, the stylistic model. At the same time he is able to operate deliberately on two levels of meaning without one annihilating the other – the famous account of his youthful theft of pears (II 4) is no less than an image of original sin or of sin for the sake of sin itself but is not therefore a flat allegory; in the same way a spring or a cockfight can have surprising symbolic value without thereby losing immediacy (*De ord.* I 3, 6; 8, 25); and the picture of a happy and carefree, inebriated beggar in Milan can better than many words describe Augustine's loathing of careerism (*Conf.* VI 6). Momentous, decisive events can also be so depicted that the inner finds outer expression: this is true of the masterly psychological account of Augustine's dully mechanical reactions after Monica's death (IX 12), and it is true of two of the most famous scenes in the *Confessiones*. The crisis preceding the conversion is resolved when Augustine in the Milan garden hears a child's voice: 'Take up and read, Take up and read!'; Augustine opens at a random passage in St Paul, and it becomes the direct occasion of his renunciation of the world (VIII 12). The other scene – a sort of mystical experience Augustine had with Monica at Ostia (IX 10) – also proceeds from the outer to the inner. It agrees handsomely with Neoplatonic theory, but the scene is wholly void of speculative theory; it is the perfect unification of form and content, which was Augustine's stylistic ideal. As a whole, the *Confessiones* also moves at two levels: it is an autobiography but at the same time a supplication to God and an encomium on God. Hence the narrative is everywhere interwoven with prayer to God and discourse with God – a stylistic device which directly voices Augustine's attitude to life and one which he used in all his works (cf. *Sol.* I 1, 2 ff.; *De Trin.* XV 28, 51).

It is not possible to distinguish between philosophy and theology in Augustine; philosophy is an attitude to life, and faith is the proper philosophy. This is the general view of the time, but in comparison with Greek theology, the close intimate connection in Augustine between faith and knowledge, *auctoritas* and *ratio*, may come as a surprise. Naturally, there are mysteries inaccessible to the intellect, but in general it holds good that faith both is a presupposition for reason and that the content of faith must be understood by means of reason – 'believe, that ye may understand' and 'if ye will not believe, ye shall not understand' (*crede, ut intelligas; nisi credideritis, non intelligetis*, cf., e.g. *De lib. arb.* II 2, 5 ff.; *Serm.* 118, 1, *PL* 38, 671 ff.; *De Trin.* VIII 5, 8), as he says several times. Faith seeks understanding, as it later was stated by Anselm (*fides quaerens intellectum*). Faith and reason are a 'double path'; faith precedes in time, but rational insight into the contents of faith is primary from a logical point of view – certainly provided that it has faith as its presupposition (cf. *De ord.* II 5, 16 ff.; 9, 26 ff.; *Contr. Acad.* III 20, 43). Of course one can believe without knowledge, and one can know without faith – as in secular science, *scientia*; but the knowledge that has faith as its presupposition – *sapientia* – is not only an intellectual cognition; it is an illumination of the soul, which engages the whole man; faith is the thinking that – using Stoic terminology – demands 'assent' (cf. *De praed. sanct.* 2, 5). That faith and knowledge cannot be separated in Augustine is connected with his overall refusal to isolate intellect, feeling and will.

AUGUSTINE'S BREAKTHROUGH

The most important event on Augustine's thorny path is undoubtedly his conversion from Manichaeism to Neoplatonizing Christianity. In Augustine's version in the *Confessiones* (IV 15 ff.; V 10; VII 3), Manichaean dualism conceives of the relation between good and evil, light and darkness in purely material categories. There are two substances: the unchangeable God, the 'Monad', and evil nature, the changeable or the 'Dyad'. Since evil is incompatible with God's unchangeableness and goodness, it is a nature outside the substance of God and in constant fight against the remote God. The world as a whole is in the power of evil, but there are men who are of the substance of God; quite literally they contain particles of light, and therefore they can return to the light. Confronted with this, Augustine can now in the first place ask what happens to the inviolability of the God of Light if He must put up with constant attacks by the powers of darkness (cf. VII 2). But it is far worse that evil, the 'mass' of darkness, in this way becomes a metaphysical reality outside man, for this means that whoever belongs to the race of God is not responsible for sin and evil; whoever feels himself chosen is therefore proud. What in retrospect deeply offends Augustine is that the Manichaean hero is free of responsibility, and his own greatest youthful sin is indeed that he spurned the consciousness of sin and responsibility. At the philosophical level Augustine was here aided by 'the Platonic' writings. In the first place he became aware that the unchangeable God is immaterial and without spatial extension, and the *Confessiones* profoundly describes his dawning 'metaphysical awareness', his understanding of the nature of the spiritual (cf. especially IV 15; VII 1; 10) – and apparently one had to go to Milan to experience such a philosophical awakening. In the second place he learned that evil is a shortcoming or privation (cf. 12 ff.). In a philosophical universe such as the Neoplatonic one the divine permeates everything, and therefore there can only be questions of degrees of goodness, not of an evil substance. As Augustine puts it himself: everything that exists is good in and by its existence. It can be corrupted and lose its goodness, but the loss of something –

sinning – is to become nothing, and if something loses all, it no longer exists. Accordingly, says he, it is good as long as it exists, and evil would not be evil, if no good existed. Augustine maintained this view of the nature of evil for the rest of his life (cf. *Ench*. III 11 ff.). The Neoplatonic doctrine of emanation and hypostases was, however, of no interest to him, and what he only found partially expressed in Neoplatonism is that individual man is responsible for his sin; it is man who is evil, not matter (cf. *De civ. Dei* XII 26). What he did not find anywhere at all was God's direct intervention in man's world.

What Augustine owed to the Platonists and what separated him from them he set down in a justly famous passage in the *Confessiones*, a stylistic masterpiece in the grand style. Augustine begins:

> There [in the Platonists] I read – although not in these words but with the same meaning and supported by numerous arguments – that in the beginning was the word, and the word was with God, and the word was God. This was in the beginning with God. Everything came into being by it, and without it nothing came into being. In that which came into being was life, and the life was the light of mankind; and the light shines in the darkness, and the darkness comprehended it not. Likewise, that though man's soul bears witness to the light, it is not itself the light; but the word, God himself, is the true light that illuminates every man who comes into this world; and that God was in this world, and the world came into being by Him, and the world knew Him not. But that He came to His own and that His own received Him not, but that all who did receive Him He empowered to become God's children, those who believe on His name – that I did not read there. There also did I read that God the Word was not born of flesh nor of blood, nor of the will of man, nor of the will of the flesh, but of God. But that the Word was made flesh and dwelt amongst us, did I not read there.
>
> (VII 9; after William Watts)

Thus continues this lofty rewriting of the beginning of St John's Gospel in antithetical, ornate style: 'there I read . . . ', 'that I did not find there . . . '.

In his day Origen had confronted Celsus with St John's Gospel, and he too had found the decisive dividing line in the Incarnation; but whereas Origen's concept of the Incarnation is somewhat de-mythologized, it is in Augustine accorded full value. In the Platonists he could not read that Christ came to God's children as if to His own, that He humbled Himself and became obedient even unto His death on the Cross. But he did find *Logos*, which is to say that he found the current concept of *Logos* as the creator of the world and as born of God; farther-reaching metaphysical systems – emanation and hypostasis – are nowhere referred to, and Augustine goes further than Origen in his translation of the Platonist material into a Christian conceptual world; in the passage there is not a single quotation from the Platonic writings – Origen had quoted Plato diligently; everything is constructed on direct or indirect Bible quotations, first and foremost St John's Gospel. It is of course a deliberate synthesis that Augustine builds, but it is also a transformation: though the human soul bears witness to the light, God Himself is the true light.

Although Augustine has no use for a metaphysical system, he is able to use a basic metaphysical structure. From the Platonists he had learned 'to return to himself' (10), to follow the path that goes inwards and upwards, from the body to the soul, from the soul to intellect and God, from self-knowledge to knowledge of God. The goal is truth (*veritas*): I found the unchangeable and eternal truth beyond my own changeable mind – for that is in truth, which remains unchangeable (17; 11). Without mentioning it, Augustine can here directly make use of Plotinus, more specifically his treatise *On Beauty*. In his Manichaean folly he had in an early, now lost work (on beauty, *De pulchro et apto*) only been able to see the beautiful as a harmony between corporeal forms – the view which Plotinus had attacked in the beginning of his treatise (Plot. I 6, 1; Aug. *Conf*. IV 15) – but now (VII 17; cf. *De ver. rel*. 32, 59) Plotinus can be used to the fullest extent in the description of the soul's *itinerarium*, which not only is the path towards God, but is a path that follows the world's own metaphysical structure, from lower to higher degrees of existence and truth. It was this metaphysics that made Augustine understand that the essence of evil is privation and nothingness (*Conf*. VII 11 ff.). Above the ladder of beings with dependent existence God stands as the only one who exists in Himself. Also in his later works Augustine is able to agree wholly with Platonism on this point: God is the source of being, truth and goodness (*De civ. Dei* VIII 9), He is the cause of existence, of knowledge, and of the moral order (4). The metaphysical ladder that opens for the mind's eye is the basis for Augustine's so-called proof of God's existence.

But: in Plotinus man could identify himself with God; to Augustine (cf. *Conf*. VII 10) there is no identity between the Creator and the created; man is confronted with the truth and with God, and in so far as he can know God, he can only do so as recipient and metaphorically; the world is not God, but an image of God. And God is not beyond being; He is an active and personal God, and 'He became flesh'. Augustine is aware that later Neoplatonists – Porphyry – knew grace; but they did not know the Incarnation (*De civ. Dei* X 29, 1). When all is said and done, the philosophers put their trust in their own power; they are proud. And just as did Origen, so Augustine musters the traditional quotations from St Paul: God's power and godhead can be seen from the creation of the world, but the philosophers have exchanged the incorruptible glory of God with idols (cf. *Conf*. VII 20; 9). Having read the Platonists, Augustine read St Paul (21).

The *Confessiones* was written ten years after Augustine's conversion. Is his description of his spiritual awakening a true one? To judge by the early writings the answer is: in all essentials, yes. The tone of the Cassiciacum dialogues is remote from that of the *Confessiones*; the serene perspective of the *Confessiones* is missing, but the perspective is not distorted. The main aim with the early dialogues is to guarantee certain knowledge – or at least the minimal amount of certainty that Augustine is in need of. Augustine needs to demonstrate that man is assigned to God, that his happiness is dependent on God, and that God's Providence manifests itself in the ordered world. In his confrontation with Academic Scepticism in the *Contra Academicos*, at the same time a confrontation with his own sceptical doubts, Augustine affirms the safe point of departure that at least logical tautologies are incontestably true (*Contr. Acad*. III 10, 22 ff.). We do not know whether one or several worlds exist, but we know that the disjunction is true: either one or several worlds exist; either the world is created or it is uncreated. We do not know whether we interpret our sense perceptions correctly, but it is incontestably true *that* this appears white to me (cf. *De ver. rel.* 33, 61). And that is fully sufficient; it means *that* a world exists and that *my* world is the totality of what I perceive. Truth exists, if a minimum of truth exists and is not dependent on whether I interpret my sense perceptions wholly correctly. In turn this means that the Academics are wrong in suspending every judgement. To refrain from 'giving one's assent' (*Contr. Acad.* III 15, 33 ff.) will paralyze every action. An action demands a norm; a norm demands that man at least has the possibility of knowing the moral truth as well. The Platonists have understood this (20, 43); to Augustine Christ is the warrant for the very existence of truth. Thus ends this dialogue, a sketch – that does not pretend to be more than a sketch.

Man's being directed towards God – the subject of the *De vita beata* and the *Soliloquia* – is a direction towards God as the unchangeable (*De vit. beat.* 2, 11). Whoever lives his life in the changeable lives his life in imperfection and deprivation; whoever lives morally well will 'possess' God who is goodness, wisdom, and truth (3, 17; 4, 28 ff.). This is a Christian transformation of the ancient ideal of the happy and perfect life and of the highest good, and the mature Augustine does indeed have his reservations – the perfect life cannot be realized in this world (*Retr.* I 2, 4). But it marks all the phases in Augustine's development that goodness and wisdom cohere. When he desires to know God and the soul in the *Soliloquia* – 'let me know myself, let me know Thee' (*Sol.* II 1, 1) – he is speaking of both intellectual knowledge of God through self-knowledge and of a knowledge that relies upon the three Christian virtues of faith, hope and charity (I 7, 14). Man should not merely recognize truth but be directed towards it, and to be directed towards truth is identical with being directed towards true existence. The truth he desires to know is the truth that adheres to what really is; falsehood pretends to being but is absence of truth, just as sin is absence of goodness (II 5, 8; 9, 16; 15, 29 ff.). Therefore truth is not a neutral concept; it is an ontological category that determines the content of a 'good' life.

'Let me know myself, let me know Thee' – self-knowledge cannot be conceived of without knowledge of God, and this is further pursued in the *De ordine*. To know oneself also means to understand one's place in God's order. The moral, epistemological, and ontological orders are several aspects of the same. Everything in this greater order (*ordo*) is dependent upon and assignable to God, the independent creator. But on the face of it man conceives of the world as a chaos, because he is 'unknown to himself' (*De ord.* I 1, 3) – but whoever, on the other hand, renounces the world of sense and lets the soul turn towards itself can know God in the world: the whole world is to be found in man's soul; it is not sensation but the inner man who is capable of understanding the external (cf. *De ver. rel.* 40, 74). The path via the inner man towards God reveals that God has created the world as a unity and a whole (*De ord.* I 1, 2 ff.), but it can only be understood if one so to speak shifts the focus from the narrowly human to the cosmic perspective that is latent in the soul. Not until then is it realized that everything has a cause and a purpose (4, 11 ff.). This does not mean that all things in themselves are elements in the order, but that they are subject to *ordo* by God's Providence (II 4, 11) and that nothing exists outside *ordo* (7, 21). This applies also to evil, which does not stem from God but is embraced by *ordo*, and God makes use of it in the greater whole (I 7, 18; II 7, 23 ff.). Hence man is to understand and follow *ordo*; to whoever can see, *ordo* manifests itself as a harmony in which both the whole and the details are determined by proportion, number and unity (I 9, 27; II 15, 43; 18, 47 ff.).

The *De vita beata* and the *Soliloquia* show the path from man to God; the *De ordine* shows God in the world. It is immediately evident to what a great extent this dual view – and not least to what great extent the very notion of *ordo* – builds on Plotinus; the theodicy argument is surely also derived from there. It is likewise apparent how Augustine could feel Plotinus' idea of the unity of the world as a liberation in his fight with the Manichaeans. But his Neoplatonism is a Christian one, even though he does not, as in the *Confessiones*, have direct occasion to mention the Incarnation, and even though he is probably more confident of man's possibility of achieving perfection than he was later on. Augustine found much in Plotinus, but the God he refers to in the *Contra Academicos*, to whom he prays in the *Soliloquia*, and who is the warrant for the happy life and the order of the world, Him he did not find there. The Cassiciacum dialogues reflect Augustine's breakthrough in Milan, but on the whole they are half-baked and – deliberately – provisional; motifs are sounded but not played through in full. Augustine himself mentions (17, 46) that the relation between evil and God's providence and omnipotence remains. The purpose of the *De ordine* is to point to the harmony in the world, hardly more than that.

The line from the Cassiciacum dialogues is continued in the following lesser writings. In one of the two small treatises on the soul, a series of traditional proofs of the immortality of the soul is reproduced (*De immort. an.*). In the other the main point is that the soul because it is an immaterial and unextended substance can 'contain' the whole world and that because it is equipped with reason it is suitable for governing the body (*De quant. an.* 5, 7 ff.; 12, 22). This means that the soul is a substance of a different kind from that of the body; yet it is the nature of the soul to be tied to a body. Augustine compares this to a circle that is defined by a centre without spatial extension and a supra-sensory principle of equality (cf. 14, 23). The point of this analogy is that it is the soul that gives proportion, number and unity to the body.

As we were told in the *De ordine* (II 15, 43), in the sensible world one can see the traces (*vestigia*) of supra-sensory proportions and principles. When Augustine at this time decided to examine 'the liberal arts', his guiding idea was precisely that through *scientia* one could be led from the material to the spiritual world. We can see this programme carried through in the last book of the treatise *On Music* (*De mus.* VI), in which the tonal harmonies – in the spirit of Pythagareanism – can be seen as 'traces' and 'signs', as reflections of supra-sensory harmonies and proportions; these incorporeal harmonies live as notes in the soul and point towards knowledge of the unsayable.

The weightiest treatment from these years of the concept of 'sign' is found in the dialogue *On the Teacher* (*De magistro*). It deals with the linguistic sign, with the relation between sign and signified, and with the reality behind the sign. It is an important treatise on the philosophy of language, but at the same time it introduces Augustine's budding epistemology. It is – directly or indirectly – strongly influenced by Stoic semantics, but with a single stroke the semantic discussions are placed in a new light. Within the framework of the philosophy of language Augustine's originality appears especially with respect to two points: the function of language and the nature of the sign. Initially one can determine the function of language as a means of communication – or, as Augustine puts it, to teach and to be taught and to retain what has been taught in the memory (*De mag.* 1, 1 ff.). But language can also be used in another way – mastered by Augustine himself – in prayer or in discourse with oneself, for example. Yet communication is not only by words; gesture is also language. The spoken language is a system of words, and the word is a sign; a sign consists of one element that signifies and one that is signified; but what it is that is signified is not all that simple, as Augustine demonstrates in a fine paedagogical analysis of a verse by Virgil (Verg. *Aen.* II 659; Aug. *De mag.* 2, 3 ff.). What does a preposition signify, and what is signified by the word 'nothing'? Further, some linguistic signs can signify actual reality, some signs can stand for other signs, maybe for themselves – in later medieval terminology one would here speak of names of first or second imposition (4, 7 ff.). Finally, the same word as part of a proposition can stand both for itself and for that for which it naturally is the sign – *suppositio materialis* and *suppositio personalis* in scholastic terminology. '*Homo*' (man) is both 'a name with four letters' and 'a living being', but if I say '*homo sum*' I am not saying that I am a name with four letters, and no lion will emerge from my mouth if I say 'lion' (8, 22 ff.). To understand a proposition is accordingly different from and more than mere knowledge of a group of words – speech (*locutio*) is more than words (9, 26).

All this means that language as a complex system of signs not only can be analyzed into sign and signified; it presupposes pre-existing knowledge of both sign and what is signified (9, 25 ff.). Epistemologically the latter is the decisive; knowledge of the signified is, as Augustine says, 'better' than the sign. If we possess prior knowledge, it means that it is incorrect to view language as a means of teaching. One can learn without signs, and the linguistic sign can actually – using a Platonic formulation – only remind us of what we already know (11, 36). Whence do we have that knowledge? By an illumination (*illuminatio*) of the soul. Sensible objects become known by sensation; the intelligible becomes known by reason (12, 39), but reason does not itself create its truth. Plato's answer to what constitutes a priori knowledge was that it is 'recollection'. Augustine's is illumination, which is to say the illumination of the soul coming from God. Christ is the 'inner teacher' who enlightens us about the truth of which we ourselves are not the masters (11, 38). This view of the relation between sign, concept, and truth goes far beyond Augustine's sources and forms the basis for his epistemology in general.

KNOWLEDGE OF GOD

The many and varied subjects in Augustine's earlier works are gathered in the 'proof of God's existence' in the second book of the *De libero arbitrio*. If any one single text by Augustine may be said to be a key to understanding his philosophical universe, this must be the one. It stands on the dividing line between the early and the later Augustine and is therefore also a good point of departure for understanding the philosophical parts of the later work. The general context – the question of freedom, sin and responsibility, which Augustine formulates as a question of whether free will, the source of sin, is created by God – will here be set aside for the time being; the first time around the focus will be on the account in the second book of the soul's progress from the outward to the inward and higher. It is through this that God's existence is accounted for by the intellect. That God exists is given with faith – but 'we desire to know and understand what we believe' (*De lib. arb.* II 2, 5). In pre-Christian philosophy one can hardly speak of proof of God's existence in the traditional sense, precisely because here there is no need to let the intellect examine something already assumed by faith.

Still, one can discuss what entitles one to speak of a proof of God's existence in Augustine, not only because it can be discussed what a proof of God's existence really means – what it means, for example, to 'prove' the condition for something being provable – but also because Augustine accounts for God's existence on the basis of a view of the world the correctness of which he never 'proves'. Undoubtedly Augustine is aware of this; the proof he furnishes is formally fully valid, but the truth of it is dependent on the truth of the premises. He reasons from his general metaphysics of knowledge, and the essential line of thought is perhaps rather recognition of God than the proof of His existence. If the term 'Augustine's proof of God's existence' is used, one would in later terminology call it an a posteriori proof, which is to say an empirical proof or a proof relying on the actual world order. Augustine is not interested in proving God's existence from the concept of God (the a priori proof of God's existence) nor in proving that God must exist in every possible world. It is a different matter that Kant's claim that every empirical proof of God's existence has a priori presuppositions (Kant, *Kritik der reinen Vernunft* B 619) is correct with respect to Augustine. Already in advance he has certain ideas about God's nature in any case.

Normally Augustine does not ask whether God is but what He is, and his answer builds on St Paul: God's invisible being is understood by what He has made. But this does not mean that God immediately lets Himself be known. In the *Confessiones* (Aug. *Conf.* X 6 ff.) he questions, for example, the earth, the sea, and all living beings, and they reply: 'We are not the God whom thou seekest' but 'He made us'. Not all men can see God through His work of creation; He is only visible to the inner man, to him who is able to ask correctly. This agrees with the *De ordine* and in a way also with the *De libero arbitrio*, but here he puts his question more profoundly and radically. The starting point is to establish the basis for certain knowledge and, on that background, the entire structure of Augustine's metaphysics of knowledge is gradually uncovered; the final point is the understanding of man and God, and within this frame 'the proof of God's existence' in the strict sense is established.

Can I be sure of anything? Yes. I can be sure that I myself exist, for I can err, and I cannot err without existing (*De lib. arb.* II 3, 7). This is Augustine's famous *cogito* argument, which undoubtedly strongly influenced the Cartesian one – often rendered as 'I think, therefore I am' (cf. Descartes, *Med.* II) – but with the difference that Descartes follows a stricter method than Augustine and that Augustine's *cogito* simply establishes man's existence, while Descartes through man's existence as a thinking substance wishes to account for the difference between soul and body. Yet there are also profound similarities: in neither Augustine nor Descartes is the 'I exist' a conclusion of a logical inference but a statement, which by analysis and self-reflection turns out to be indissolubly tied to the statement that 'I exist *as* a thinking, erring, or doubting being'. It also holds true both for Augustine and Descartes that the existence of God turns out to be the precondition for my existence.

In numerous passages Augustine provided variants of his *cogito*. The most complete formulation declares: nobody can doubt that a man lives, that he remembers, that he understands, that he wills, that he thinks, that he knows, that he judges (Aug. *De Trin.* X 10, 14 ff.). The reflexive aspect is frequently stressed: not only do we live; but we know that we live and we love our existence and our knowledge (*De civ. Dei* XI 26; other versions: *De vit. beat.* 2, 7; *Sol.* II 1, 1; *De ver. rel.* 39, 73; *De Trin.* XV 12, 21). Here there are several things to take note of: through introspection Augustine is immediately sure of the existence of the inner man in his full totality; it is an existence comprising intellect, feeling and will – *esse, nosse, velle* as the *Confessiones* has it – and these three elements are so interconnected that I *am* as a knowing and willing creature, that I *know* that I am and that I will, and that I *will* be and know (*Conf.* XIII 11). Introspection is thus not a reflection on myself as an object but self-reflection and self-awareness; I am aware of my vital manifestations – in the *De libero arbitrio* this is demonstrated already on the level of sensation (*De lib. arb.* II 4, 10). Finally, it is stressed – as in the *Contra Academicos* – that my world, which is to say everything I experience, is *the* world; the world exists inasmuch as I exist. One knows one's inner world; one does not know exactly how the external world is (cf. *De Trin.* 10, 16), but one knows with certainty that it is, and that it is not my own private imagination; as is shown in the *De libero arbitrio* (*De lib. arb.* II 7, 15 ff.), sensation and reason are private, but sense objects and rational objects are public, and this is a warrant against solipsism. Since my world exists there is no need – as in Descartes – for an extra argument for the existence of the external world. This is a view which – whether Augustine knew it or not – lies quite close to Aristotle's.

With his *cogito* Augustine placed man as a conscious being in a surrounding world. The further argumentation in the *De libero arbitrio* (3, 7 ff.; parallels are found in *De ver. rel.* 29, 52 ff.; *De Trin.* X 10, 13) depends on a special dialectic between some of the basic concepts that characterize human existence (Augustine's existentials, as it were). To exist is characteristic of all objects in the world, to live of all animals and plants, to understand of man alone. Life implies existence but not vice versa; reason implies life but not vice versa. Thereby a sequence emerges, which in the final analysis may also be indebted to Aristotle, but which Augustine gives a Neoplatonic twist: reason is 'higher' than life and life 'higher' than existence. The ontological sequence, existence-life-insight or reason, can be epistemologically supplemented: above the sensed objects that merely 'are' stand the senses; above the individual senses stands the interior sense that coordinates the elementary sense experiences and makes us aware of sensation, and both the senses and the interior sense are manifestations of life; above the senses and the interior sense stands reason. These sequences express what has been called the Neoplatonic principle of subordination and regulation: the lower cannot affect the higher; the higher, on the other hand, 'judges' of the lower (cf. *De lib. arb.* II 5, 11 ff.). The senses judge of the sensed object; reason judges of the senses. It should furthermore be noted that at the higher level – reason or insight – the two sequences converge: consciousness and being coincide.

Each of us is equipped with his own reason or *ratio*. Now, if anything can be pointed out that excels *ratio* and hence judges of *ratio*, and to which nothing is superior, then something above man has been demonstrated, and this means that the existence of God has been demonstrated – for God is simply defined, as later in Anselm, as *id quo nihil est superius*, that to which nothing is superior (6, 14). Thereby Augustine has clearly stated what he wishes to prove. He does not wish to prove the truth of his metaphysics of knowledge but that this metaphysics of knowledge is dependent on a first link. If there is something above man, which we do not master in the same way as our reason all by itself decides how to interpret our sense experiences, then God exists.

There is something above man – in two areas. One is number (8, 20 ff.). The notion of unity is not abstracted from sense experience, for any given physical object can be perceived by the senses as both one and many; it is acquired by illumination. If unity is given, the whole sequence of numbers is thereby given, and the relation between numbers is also given as independent of us. That $7+3 = 10$ is not something in our control, and we cannot change it as we like. Hence it is a truth superior to us and our private reason. It is evident that the line of thought draws on Pythagorean-Platonic sources and points back, for example to the *De ordine* and the *De musica*.

The other area where one can point to something superior to human *ratio* (9, 25 ff.) is wisdom (*sapientia*) and truth (*veritas*). Many are good arithmeticians, but there are not very many wise men; nor is there general agreement about what wisdom consists in. But there is agreement that wisdom exists and about certain formal statements as well – for example, that the worse stands below the better, that the incorrupt is better than the corrupt, that the eternal is better than the temporal. Accordingly here one finds invariable truths corresponding to the mathematical ones, and here as well they become known by illumination or by a notion impressed on our soul (*notio impressa*). And if there are truths, then 'truth' exists – as we are told with a typical Platonic inference – and truth 'judges' of our *ratio*. Truth is not the result of reflection; it exists beforehand and is the precondition for reflection (*De ver. rel.* 39, 72).

With this Augustine has proved what he wanted to prove; the proof of God's existence proper has been carried through by a valid *modus ponens* (cf. *De lib. arb.* II 15, 39). But the formal proof is not what is decisive. It is decisive that the two areas – numbers and truth – actually are two sides of the same issue. Augustine says (11, 32) that numbers and wisdom are consubstantial; they are of the same substance, and what this more closely implies is expressed in lofty, lyrical passages (13, 35 ff.; 16, 41 ff.). Wisdom and truth appear in numbers, in the very fact that the world has structure and form ordained by God's Providence, and truth or wisdom implies happiness and freedom – whoever knows truth is happy and is free, which is to say that he has realized his true existence. But truth is identical with God; hence man's real existence, his freedom and his happiness, comes from God. Thereby Augustine's whole conceptual world has actually been unfolded; man's existence is founded on the order created by God; it comprises both intellect and feeling, because God's order is both truth and goodness, and consciousness and being – knowledge and the object of knowledge – coincide.

It is evident how much Augustine owes to Plotinus and to Platonism in general – it holds good for 'the principle of subordination and regulation' according to which the higher affects the lower without being affected itself; it also holds good for the theory of illumination, which at heart is Platonism; it holds good for the idea that 'truths' imply 'truth', that the world is ordered and good, and that the spiritual is superior to the corporeal. But it is just as important to identify the differences. In the *Confessiones* Augustine says that the Platonists know where to go but do not know the way (*Conf.* VII 20). The differences appear throughout the argumentation. The starting point is Augustine's *cogito* and his methodical search for certainty. Plotinus also had his *cogito*: to doubt contemplation is to doubt oneself; and to him it was crucial that the intelligible objects are to be found in the intellect itself (Plot. V 8, 11; 5, 1, here p. 545). But what Plotinus wishes to do is to establish a metaphysico-epistemological certainty, cognition of essences by means of self-contemplation. Augustine seeks for an indisputable understanding of individual man in his totality – his will, intellect and feelings – before God. In doing so he makes use of the concepts of being, life and reason. These are Neoplatonist concepts, but Augustine uses them wholly in his own way. In Neoplatonism being, life, and reason designate the second hypostasis; perhaps inspired by Aristotelianism, Augustine sets up the sequence: to exist – to live – to understand, in which the concepts are not equal manifestations of one and the same metaphysical reality. He transforms a general metaphysics into an anthropological metaphysics; he has no need of any metaphysical doctrine of hypostases and none whatsoever of a first hypostasis beyond knowledge and existence. It is equally significant that to Augustine reason (*ratio*) is not a cosmic metaphysical concept. Every individual person has his own private *ratio*, and truth is superior to the individual's reason. Finally, the difference appears in the concluding point. Augustine maintains the duality of Man – God; the knowledge man acquires by understanding his true self and his higher identity is a knowledge received from God as an impression in the soul. After the synthesis in the *De libero arbitrio* Augustine is able with renewed vigour to seek for the truth about the soul and about God.

MAN – KNOWLEDGE AND WILL

In his view of man's ontological status Augustine must both dissociate himself from the Manichaean position in which man, like the whole world, consists of two incompatible substances warring with each other and from that of Neoplatonism in which the inner man is ultimately identical with God. In his early writings he had defined the soul as a substance equipped with reason and suitable for ruling the body, but he had also stressed that man is bound to die (Aug. *De quant. an.* 12, 22, see p. 600; *De ord.* II 11, 31). Later he would say that man is a rational being consisting of soul and body, or that the soul is tied to the body but is of another substance (*De Trin.* XV 7, 11; I 10, 20). Behind these formulations one may be aware of the 'technical' difficulties of adopting Neoplatonist elements to a Christian view. Augustine does not wish to contest that man is a unity of body and soul; the soul co-exists with the body; it would, as he says, be foolish to imagine the body as separate from man's nature (*De an. et ej. orig.* IV 2, 3, *PL* 44, 525; cf. *De civ. Dei* X 29, 2); and it must be maintained that the soul is not of God's nature (*De quant. an.* 34, 77). But it must also be maintained that soul and body are two substances, the soul ruling the body – the soul is, roughly as in Nemesius, in the whole body without being affected by it (cf. *De immort. an*. 16, 25). All of it is something of a compromise. But if this doctrine of two substances breaks down, the entire anthropological metaphysics breaks down as well.

Epistemology in the strict sense builds on this anthropology. It is evident that Augustine has to regard sense perception from the principle that the lower cannot affect the higher. What matters is the judgement of sense experiences, and reason is the judge. The physical process of sensation is not the cause of sensation, but the soul or reason is active in relation to the physical events. It is not the body that senses, but rather the soul that does so by means of the body; the attention of the soul is directed to what occurs in the body (*De gen. ad litt*. III 5, 7, *PL* 34, 282; *De quant. an*. 23, 41; cf. *De ord*. II 2, 6).

This means that sensation is a parallel process: on the one hand a series of physical events and on the other sense perception proper that pertains to the soul. Here there are points of similarity with Aristotelian psychology, although the underlying anthropology differs. Plotinus is, naturally enough, more important in the background of the picture.

But man is not the master of rational cognition proceeding from God. The eternal, unchangeable verities (*rationes aeternae*) are found in God as part of His essence (cf. *De civ. Dei* XI 10, 3; *De div. quaest*. LXXXIII 46, 2, *PL* 40, 30) – which is Augustine's version of the ancient thought of the ideas as the thoughts of God – they are models or exemplars of the truth created by God and manifest themselves in the world (sometimes this is called exemplarism). But man does not partake of God's essence, and hence human knowledge is a reflection of the divine, not – as in Malebranche's radical Augustinianism – identical with it. The eternal verities are above man (*De Trin*. IV 15, 24; XII 2, 2); they become known by illumination, through ideas impressed in the soul (*notiones impressae*) as for example described in the *De magistro* and in the *De libero arbitrio* (cf. 15, 24; VIII 3, 4). Once more, it is a consequence of the principle of the relation between the higher and the lower that man receives rational knowledge by a direct illumination in which God is the active and man the receiving part. Augustine's 'theory of illumination' – which of course has much in common with 'the doctrine of recollection' in Plato, even though Augustine dissociates himself from it (cf. XII 15, 25) – is clearly an a priori theory of knowledge in Christian form, and its influence during the Middle Ages and even later is considerable. In the Middle Ages it was opposed to the 'theory of abstraction', which was viewed as Aristotelian and asserts that experience is a necessary but insufficient precondition for cognition.

The theory of illumination should not be regarded as an isolated and normatively neutral theory of knowledge – everything in Augustine is value-laden. A *notio impressa* is both concept and norm; it is both an object of cognition and act-directing, and hence it illuminates both man as a knowing and volitional being. This inclusion of the entire man in the cognitive process is also very clear in Augustine's view of consciousness – or memory (*memoria*). *Memoria* is the quintessence of spiritual man's potential in its full extension. It is like an immeasurable space, which man only gradually and only partially can get to know – for man is not himself transparent. In a profound analysis in the *Confessiones* (*Conf*. X 8 ff.) Augustine uncovers layer upon layer in *memoria*. *Memoria* not only comprises the memory of sensations or events, but also science, wisdom, knowledge of intellectual truths, self-consciousness, and the will that makes use of the human potential, recollects what is half forgotten, and interprets the contents of consciousness and gives it direction to action (cf. also *De Trin.* XI 10, 17; XII 14, 23; XIV 11, 14).

Man's life is determined by the direction of his cognition and will. Augustine agrees with the profane tradition that happiness – or the perfect life – is what all strive for; but this happiness is not attained unless all the powers of the soul are directed to the truth in God – we are created for God (*Contr. Acad.* I 2, 5; cf. *De civ. Dei* X 1, 1; *Conf.* V 1). Knowledge of this world – science or *scientia* – is not objectionable to Augustine and can be employed in the service of a higher cause, as Augustine did himself when he began his presentation of the liberal arts. But often it is not particularly useful; in itself it does not lead to happiness; but wisdom or *sapientia* does so – the knowledge of the divine (cf. *De Trin.* XIV 1, 1 ff.; XII 14, 26 ff.). But since human wisdom is not identical with God's, it will not be perfected until after this life in the beholding 'face to face' (XIV 2, 4; 19, 25). Wisdom is God's nature; to man it is a directive ideal. This dividing line means that Augustine – despite many passages describing intense joy at experiencing the truth – hardly can be called a mystic, at least not in the same sense as his Greek colleagues, and he would himself most decidedly have distanced himself from interpreting his experience as a mystical union with God. His 'mystical' experience at Ostia with his mother (*Conf.* IX 10) is instructive. In his account he first proceeds along the Neoplatonic way from the inner towards the higher, but he and his mother only lightly 'touch' the truth, and the experience turns into a conversation about how it would be if 'somebody' could experience everything as being silent and God speaking directly, not through his creature.

All desire happiness; human wisdom consists in willing the good (*De lib. arb.* I 14, 30). More precisely, this means to observe God's eternal moral law that is written in the heart as a ring leaves its impression in wax – in other words, the Law of God is known by illumination (*De Trin.* XIV 15, 21; *De ord.* II 8, 25; *De lib. arb.* III 5, 17). The divine or eternal Law (*lex aeterna*) is found in God Himself; in the world order it is reflected in natural law (*lex naturalis*), which is both descriptive and prescriptive – both law of nature and moral law – and which man can know through reason (*Ep.* 157, 3, 15, *PL* 33, 681; *Contr. Faust.* 22, 27, *PL* 42, 418). Augustine does not always distinguish between *lex aeterna* and *lex naturalis*, but he does distinguish between divine and temporal law (*lex temporalis*), and with this conceptual apparatus he can transfer the entire Stoic thinking about natural law into a Christian frame of reference. The right temporal law – positive law – acquires its authority from the eternal one; the deficient will is set aright by temporal law, but temporal law does not denounce everything that according to the eternal one is sinful (*De lib. arb.* I 6, 14 ff.; 15, 31 ff.; 5, 13).

That human existence always is directed towards a goal is by Augustine expressed as man's being determined by his will and his love (*voluntas* and *caritas*), and these two key concepts are really identical (cf. *De Trin.* XV 20, 38 ff.). With the possible exception of Seneca, no thinker before Augustine emphasized the will as strongly as did he; one might almost say that he discovered will as an anthropological category.

Knowledge and wisdom are powerless unless governed by will; cognition is an act of willing. The radically new in this anthropology is readily apparent if one, for example, compares it with Aristotle's description of voluntary acts; the specifically Christian interpretation of the concept of will is made possible by the linking of will with love.

Just as one must distinguish between divine and human wisdom, so one must distinguish between divine and human will and love. Man is always directed towards something other than himself; God's will and God's love are one with His essence; God's substance is Love (17, 29; 19, 37); His love of man – first and foremost manifest in the Incarnation (*Conf.* X 43; *De Trin.* XV 17, 31) – is so to speak a love from abundance. While for example St John's Gospel first and foremost speaks of God's love of man, Augustine speaks rather more of man's love of God.

In man will and love are in themselves neutral concepts. They are naturally endowed; man does not choose his love or *caritas* in a void; the life of every man already has its direction or 'weight' – my weight is my love, says Augustine (*Conf.* XIII 9). Everything in God's *ordo* has its own place – or its weight – and since man is created by God, he also has his love, just as he has his entire nature from God. But while a stone has its own natural motion, and that is all, human 'motion' is far more complicated; man is conscious of himself and can work to affect his nature; he can will, which is something the stone hardly seems able to do (*De lib. arb.* III 1, 2). Human love is determined by its object; love in itself is neither good nor evil; but the just man loves the good (cf. *De civ. Dei* XIV 7, 2; *De doctr. Christ.* I 27, 28). On the other hand, if love is perverted, it becomes desire (*cupiditas*), which is to say that man is directed towards the earthly as an end in itself; hence the moral commandment is to shift the weight of desire to that of love (*De Trin.* IX 8,13; *Ep.* 157, 2, 9, *PL* 33, 677).

All commandments refer to the commandment of love, says Augustine in one of his dogmatic works (*Ench.* 32, 121), but only one goal of love is its own goal; only God can be loved for his own sake (*De doctr. Christ.* I 5, 5).

Love of one's self and of one's neighbour are, so to speak, derived commandments of love – love of one's neighbour, unlike love of God, is love of an equal but is only rightly directed, if it is a love of one's neighbour in God (III 10, 16; *Serm.* 336, 2, 2, *PL* 38, 1472). Augustine's concept of love is subordinated to his concept of divine law. Thereby he is probably more in agreement with Neoplatonism than with the New Testament. But the idea is not that love of one's neighbour is secondary – in the sense of being less important; the idea is that it only becomes possible by virtue of love of God. Only if one is directed rightly is it possible to love oneself and others.

The thought of loving something for its own sake or as a means to something else is by Augustine expressed by the words *frui* – to enjoy – and *uti* – to use (*De doctr. Christ.* I 3, 3 ff.; cf. *De Trin.* X 10, 13). These terms are also neutral in themselves – but one can use or abuse, and one can 'enjoy' that which one ought to 'use' (cf. *De lib. arb.* I 15, 33). One can make good 'use' of this world if it is done with regard to God; if one 'enjoys' it, one is the victim of *cupiditas*. The final goal for rightly directed man is the bliss or happiness of 'enjoying' God (cf. *De civ. Dei* VIII 8). Augustine's conceptual pair can be seen as a Christian reinterpretation of the Stoic concepts of *honestum* and *utile*, which Cicero had dealt with in the *De officiis* – that which in a real sense is 'useful' is not at odds with that which in an absolute sense is 'noble'.

GOD AND MAN: CREATION, PROVIDENCE AND FREEDOM

The concepts employed by Augustine to describe man's being directed towards God can also be used negatively – *caritas* can turn into *cupiditas*; the will can be perverted; one can 'use' and 'enjoy' what is wrong. This is – of course – because man is an imperfect being and that again is because he is created and, theologically speaking, is bound to original sin in his present state. What does it mean that the world order and man have been created? Whereby does the created differ from the creator? In this life we see as through a glass and in a riddle; we know that God is one with his being, for He has said, 'I am that I am' (*Ex.* 3, 14), but what He is is unsayable and incomprehensible to us – as in the Platonic tradition (Aug. *De Trin.* V 1, 1; VII 5, 10; *De ord.* II 16, 44).

Indirectly we know God through the world and the beings He created. Why did God create His creatures? In order that they might be, for to be is a good. Whereof has He created them? Of nothing (*De ver. rel.* 18, 35; cf. *De lib. arb.* III 13, 36). Everything created is good because created, but since it is created of nothing, the created is neither pure being nor pure nothing (cf. *Conf.* VII 11), and at any given moment the creature can fall back into the nothing whence it came.

In the beginning God created Heaven and Earth. In philosophical terms the Christian belief in creation means to Augustine that the world has a beginning in time and has been created once and for all. This he interprets by making use of Stoic inheritance. At the creation of the world God sowed 'seminal reasons' (*rationes seminales*) that in time develop into the beings and objects, which, each in its own time, emerge and thus proceed from potential to actual existence (*De civ. Dei* XII 26; *De Trin.* III 8, 13). Accordingly every thing develops from God's ordinance, and it is possible to distinguish between the primary causes laid down in the world at its creation – the beginning of the causal nexus, and the causal nexus itself, the secondary causes – laws of nature as it were – that regulate how things affect each other in the course of time; but there is nothing to prevent God at any given moment from arbitrarily interfering in a course of events – what are called miracles, although nothing compared with the miracle of the very existence of the world (*De civ. Dei* VII 30; *De Trin.* III 9, 16; *De civ. Dei* X 12). Hence time is the medium wherein the world unfolds and whereby one can measure relations between events in the created world; but time itself is created together with the world. It did not exist 'before' the creation of the world, and God Himself does not exist in time; He overlooks everything in one moment – hence it is not meaningful to ask what God did before He created the world and why it was created at this and not at that point in time (XI 5 ff.; *De lib. arb.* III 3, 6; *Conf.* XI 10 ff.).

All of this has consequences for Augustine's view of determinism, free will, sin and God's pre-knowledge and predetermination. How can the determinism that seems implied by *rationes seminales* be reconciled with man's ability to give his love or his will a wrong direction or with the fact that in Augustine free will is always a self-evident presupposition? Moreover, by virtue of what can man change the nature accorded him by God? Is not such a change also dependent upon and predetermined by God? The problem is one of the most difficult ones in Augustine's thought, and it is important to disentangle the various threads. If sin did not exist, something would be missing in *ordo* (*De lib. arb.* III 11, 32) – in this manner Augustine was able, more or less as was Plotinus, to make use of a traditional theodicy argument, and on other points he could also go along with Plotinus a good part of the way. That something would be missing implies in part that sin then, as with the Manichaeans, would be a power outside *ordo*, in part that *ordo* would miss that creature, man, who freely can choose the good. Sin comes from free will, in other words from man himself, not from God; it depends on deliberate choice, not on an inherent predisposition given once and for all: two persons of the same hereditary disposition may act differently in the same situation (*Retr.* I 15, 2; *De civ. Dei* XII 6).

Now, man can only fully be man in intercourse with God. Therefore his sinning means that he tears himself away from his true identity and his true freedom and so falls back into nothingness. Sin is perverted will (*perversa voluntas*, *De lib. arb.* II 14, 37) that consists in wishing to be sufficient unto oneself and thereby losing oneself, and therefore it is called *superbia*, 'audacity' or 'pride' (III 25, 76; cf. *De civ. Dei* XIV 3, 1) – again as in Plotinus (*tolma*). It results in one's becoming alienated from oneself – the concept of 'alienation' (*alienatio*) goes back to Augustine (*De doctr. Christ.* I 4, 4). But one only acts freely if one is free; one cannot in an abstract situation of choice decide whether to become alienated or not, and certainly not in the present state of mankind – after the Fall and in the state of Original Sin. Before the Fall man could freely and happily follow God's commandments (cf. *De civ. Dei* XIV 26), but the possibility of sin was present, because he is created out of nothing; the Fall and its fatal consequence of Original Sin that adheres to the whole present race consist in man's having forfeited his possibility of choosing the good on his own. With the Fall and Original Sin follows desire (*cupiditas*). If man were only left on his own he would be forfeit to the 'mass of perdition' (*massa perditionis*), as it is called in an almost Manichaean phrase (*De lib. arb.* III 20, 55 ff.; *De civ. Dei* XIII 12 ff.; XIV 10 ff.; *Ench.* 8, 26 ff.; cf. *De don. pers.* 14, 35, *PL* 45, 1014). If one undertakes the – risky – thought experiment of 'de-mythologizing' Augustine, it can be said that the good life – before the Fall – is an ideal state, but that man in fact – after Adam – is himself unable to choose what is right. The Fall is of course owing to man, not to God (cf. *De lib. arb.* III 24, 71). In other words, no man can become perfect on his own; in theological terms: only God's agency, the Incarnation, can restore human innocence.

With this the problem has been outlined but is far from sufficiently illuminated, and certainly it has not been resolved – whether or not Augustine did resolve it is another question. On the one hand, we encounter the classical problem – familiar from Stoicism – of determinism versus free will. On the other hand, there is the Augustinian problem: man is created by God, but is himself responsible for sin; Augustine can speak of man's directedness towards God, seemingly at least as if it were within the power of the individual; but on his own man is lost. The Manichaeans thought that some men are saved, others damned; the Donatists and

Pelagians, each in their own way, thought that perfection is humanly possible. What did Augustine think?

The theme of the *De libero arbitrio* is that sin comes from free will, and that free will, but not sin, comes from God, for free will in itself is a good, and all that is good comes from God. That all that is good comes from God is accounted for in 'the Proof of God's existence' in the second book, and the last book, the third, shows free will to be an element in God's *ordo*. It is clear in advance that God rightly punishes sin. In the course of the dialogue Augustine's view of what is free will is explored and spelt out. The problem that is posed (*De lib. arb.* I 2,4) is whence sin comes, or, more precisely, why God created free will, since it can be distorted into sin. The question is not asked whether we have free will – that is taken for granted in Augustine's universe where man can only be conceived of as a willing creature. Nor, of course, is the question asked whether God created sin – God did not create evil – quite apart from the fact that evil, a privation, cannot be created. Sin consists in surrendering to desire, and the cause of sin is perverted will (3, 8; 10, 21) – hence it resides in the state of mind, not in the act, and sin is not owing to external circumstances beyond man's control, if only because the lower cannot affect the higher (III 1, 2). Anyhow, that man has the possibility of sinning surely elevates him to a higher place in *ordo* than the creature without free will; but why did God create the precondition for sin? In order to make us free to act well, and this presupposes the possibility of our acting evilly; consequently free will in itself is a good (II 16, 47).

Just as reason by self-reflection can have itself as object, will is reflexive – one can will to will, which is to say that one can will to will what is good or will to will what is evil (I 12, 26; 14, 30; II 18, 49 ff.; cf. *De grat. et lib. arb.* 15, 31). To will does not simply consist in choosing one of several possibilities where one might just as well have chosen another. The choice is dependent on the state of mind – whether one wills good or evil. Hence to be willing to will does not mean that one act of will precedes another *ad infinitum* but that the concrete choice depends on the fundamental inclination of the will. Thereby two views of freedom or free will are delineated: *liberum arbitrium* – the free choice among several possibilities – and *libertas* – freedom, the freedom to will the good and thereby one's true self (cf. *Ench.* 9, 32). Genuine freedom is freedom to the good, *libertas*. If it is thwarted, only pseudo-freedom remains, that *liberum arbitrium* where the choice is determined by accidental external circumstances and by the perverted will that seeks freedom where it is not and instead finds the nothingness that no human being consciously wishes for (cf. *De lib. arb.* III 8, 22). *Libertas* does not cancel *liberum arbitrium* but gives it the right direction and is therefore its true pre-condition. But *libertas* does not present itself of its own accord. By himself man is powerless; the will to act for the good comes from God (15, 43 ff.). Such is the conclusion of the *De libero arbitrio*, but there the further implications are not pursued. What is implied is Augustine's whole doctrine of grace.

However, another problem is raised in the *De libero arbitrio* (2, 4 ff.; cf. *De civ. Dei* V 10). Like everything else in *ordo* man is encompassed by God's Providence; the acts of the individual are included in the great causal chain that in the final analysis depends on the *rationes seminales* planted in the world at the creation (cf. *De lib. arb.* I 1, 1; *De civ. Dei* V 9, 3). But does this not mean that all human acts are predetermined?

And since God of course knows beforehand how man will act, does this not also point to a strict determinism? Augustine's answer is and must be no. The answer betrays Stoic influence, perhaps mediated by Plotinus. Man's will is included in the great causal chain precisely as will and can therefore not be cancelled without self-contradiction. It is not a logical necessity that I will act in this or that way, regardless of the fact that it actually will happen – and still: I am the one to act and I am responsible for my acts.

God is of course not subject to any external necessity. Furthermore, his foreknowledge is not identical with predetermination. What God knows beforehand is exactly what we will do of our own free will. His foreknowledge presupposes the existence of free will, and foreknowledge has no greater influence on future events than recollection has on past ones (cf. *De lib. arb.* III 4, 11) – and one might perhaps add that as God is beyond time and overlooks everything in one moment, 'foreknowledge' in connection with God is strictly speaking a metaphor: God knows at once the totality of all human acts. What He willed was that man should act freely.

That grace is the precondition for the right will was what Augustine learned when he read St Paul after having read the 'Platonists' (*Conf.* VII 21 ff.; cf. *De grat. et lib. arb.* 4, 7 ff.). Where was my free will before, he asks in the *Confessiones*. He now knows that what mattered was 'not to will what I willed, but what thou willed' (*Conf.* IX 1; cf. X 29). In St Paul Augustine could both read that 'the good that I would I do not' and that the precondition for salvation is faith on man's part and grace on the part of God (Paul. Rom. 7, 19; 5, 1 ff.). By this he was led to understand that salvation does not depend on human merit. God grants His grace gratis (Aug. *De lib. arb.* III 15, 45, note: *gratia/gratuito*) and it is a precondition for the right will (15, 43; *De civ. Dei* XII 9, 1; *Retr.* I 9, 6). Whoever does not receive grace does not gain what he wishes (*De grat. et lib. arb.* 4, 7). Whoever does receive it, assents in full freedom, but grace is also the precondition for the good will and thereby for freedom or *libertas*, and this means that grace is not dependent on our merit, but our merit on grace (*Ep.* 217, 5, 16, *PL* 33, 984; *Ench.* 9, 32; *Serm.* 169, 2, 3, *PL* 38, 916). In this two things lie hidden: in the first place that despite the Pauline inspiration Augustine does not retain St Paul's radical distinction between grace and merit; and in the second place that grace and predestination are bound up with each other.

In St Paul Augustine could also read that God is like the potter who fashions one vessel 'unto honour and another unto dishonour' (Paul. Rom. 9, 14 ff.). Thus God grants his grace to whomsoever He wishes, and only few are chosen; the many are not saved, because they do not wish to be (cf. Aug. *Ench.* 25, 98; *Ep.* 217, 6, 19, *PL* 33, 985). In a late, condensed version of his doctrine of predestination (*Ench.* 8, 27 ff.; 9, 30 ff.) Augustine begins by affirming that God is both just and merciful. It is just that the sinner is punished; but God has also shown mercy, for He considered it better to create good out of evil than not to let it exist at all – as we are told, almost as in Plato's *Timaeus*. The continuation, however, is less Platonic. With original sin man forfeited the possibility of choosing freely – and if one has renounced one's freedom, it cannot be regained, just as little as a suicide can resuscitate himself; thus one is only free to sin (cf. *De lib. arb.* III 18, 52). The chosen ones are therefore made free – not by their own merit nor by their own free will but by the grace of God.

To this the Pelagians could voice several objections – and did so, even by invoking Augustine's own *De libero arbitrio* (cf. *Retr.* I 9, 3). One – be he Pelagian or not-Pelagian – could, for example, ask whether it is not pure Manichaeism to affirm predestination and thereby deny man's own possibility for merit, and whether the doctrine of predestination is not in conflict with the sharp distinction in the *De libero arbitrio* between foreknowledge and predestination. To a considerable extent Augustine is probably right in maintaining that there is no contradiction. His doctrine of predestination is not Manichaeism, for according to Augustine predestination does not preclude either free will or merit. One must realize precisely what it is that is predestined. All can be saved if they wish to be, but their will is determined by God, says Augustine (10, 2). It is the direction of the will that God predetermines; He does not prescribe the application of the will, but He foresees it. After all, Augustine therefore considers himself entitled to speak of man's merit and to establish a difference between willing the good and earning merit by the good will (cf. *De lib. arb.* I 14, 30), but it is a merit conditioned by grace, just as the free application of will is conditioned by grace (cf. *De grat. et lib. arb.* 6, 13). Grace precedes the assent of the will (cf. *De spir. et litt.* 30, 52, *PL* 44, 233), but thereupon man can earn merit by virtue of grace, and at that stage Augustine can speak of a sort of 'cooperation' between grace and good deeds (*De grat. et lib. arb.* 8, 20 ff.). The conclusion must – presumably – be that grace is a necessary but insufficient condition for man's acquiring merit and acting freely. This is hardly a Pauline conclusion, but is it tenable?

A comparison can be made with the Stoics and with Plotinus. Augustine shares the Stoics' view that human freedom is encompassed by the great causal nexus without thereby being annihilated. The points of resemblance with Plotinus are greater – and probably to many surprisingly great. Also in Plotinus 'man' is himself responsible for his errors, but if he acts rightly, this does not come about by virtue of himself but by virtue of divine providence. In Porphyry Augustine could also have become acquainted with the Neoplatonic doctrine of 'grace'. The difference between Augustine and Plotinus lies – as always – in the fundamental view of what man is and what God is.

Probably one cannot blame an imagined Pelagian given to slightly more elementary modes of thinking for believing that the dividing line between foreknowledge and predestination can seem a little Sophistic. The distinction can be found in both Augustine and Plotinus. But in practice Augustine is forced to a compromise to which Plotinus is not committed, a compromise between man's capacity and God's power; the difficulties lie in the concept of merit. Merit is demanded of man, regardless of the fact that the precondition for merit does not lie in the power of the individual; but Augustine cannot ignore the demand for human merit and good deeds without abandoning Christian morality. Plotinus can do so, because he has no need of an absolute distinction between God and man. To him the 'human' in man is simply helpless, but man is also a citizen in another world where he – almost as in Kant – is his own legislator. Augustine, however, cannot ignore the 'human' in man. His entire anthropology and theology are built on the two poles of God and man.

Augustine's doctrine of grace and predestination is a dual one; his message is both unmerited joy and judgement. Grace is bestowed gratis, but God decides sovereignly whom He bestows it upon – according to a higher justice unknown to us (cf. 23, 45). Realism may lie behind Augustine's view – actually only few are free in the real sense. Behind it also lies a stern reading of St Paul – which became no less stern when Augustine as a bishop felt himself responsible for the true faith. Predestination is without doubt the single point on which Augustine most markedly distinguishes himself from the Alexandrians' humane and idealistic Christianity (cf. Augustine's confrontation with Origen, *De civ. Dei* XXI 17).

THE TRACES OF GOD

That man is bound to God is in part expressed in Augustine's doctrine of grace and predestination and in part in the notion of cognition as recognition of God's 'traces' in man himself and in the world. To recognize God's traces means to recognize the dependence of the temporal on the spiritual, to recognize the spiritual through the temporal. God's 'traces' are a main theme, which here will be examined in three of Augustine's principal works, the *De Trinitate*, the *Confessiones* and the *De civitate Dei*.

Augustine's view of the Trinity is the official one that was adopted at the Council of Constantinople. This means that the Trinity is three persons but of one substance. To Augustine the substance precedes the persons, and everything predicated essentially of the Trinity is to an equal degree predicated of all persons (cf. *De Trin.* VIII 1, 1; *De civ. Dei* XI 24). In the doctrine of the Trinity lies an implicit distancing from a Neoplatonic doctrine of emanation; everything is immediately created by the Trinity: God made the world, by the Son, and in the Holy Spirit (*De ver. rel.* 7, 13; cf. *De lib. arb.* III 11, 33).

Here Augustine's doctrine of the Trinity will not be discussed further; what is crucial from a philosophical point of view lies in the application of it. Man is created in God's image (*De Trin.* VII 6, 12); this occasions Augustine to find 'traces' or 'images' of the Trinity at all levels of the nature of inner man. His uncovering of 'ternaries' in human nature is carried out with a high degree of imagination, but in such a way that his anthropology and his view of man's dependence on God are illustrated in steadily new perspectives. If one were to summarize his view of man in one 'ternary', it is probably the ternary of *esse, nosse, velle* – man is an existing, knowing, and willing creature (*Conf.* XII 11), and each of these three elements presupposes the other two. In the *De Trinitate* this basic thought is explored from many different angles. One takes its point of departure in the concepts of *esse, vivere, intelligere* (*De Trin.* X 3, 5 ff.; 8, 11 ff.). In the *De libero arbitrio* this vertical ternary was used to demonstrate man's place in the hierarchical *ordo*, introduced by the Augustinian *cogito*. In the *De Trinitate* the emphasis is on man as a reflecting creature, and thereby the presuppositions for the famous *cogito* are illustrated. That man exists, lives and understands can in modern terminology be expressed as transcendental presuppositions for any given human activity; they are three elementary facts that are always present 'beforehand', and by reflection man can always become conscious of them. The soul leaves itself and becomes alienated from itself if it views itself in analogy with external objects. It must – as in Plotinus – turn towards itself, not as something absent but as present, and the implicit self-knowledge – *nosse*, to know or to be acquainted with – can by reflection – *cogitare*, conscious thought – be made explicit. If this happens, the soul will realize that *intelligentia* – the intellect – immediately implies *memoria* (existence retained in 'memory') and *voluntas* (will). These three parts of the human self are in other words consubstantial; they constitute a ternary in a unity and thus they depict the archetypal ternary 'in' one: the Trinity (11, 17 ff.; cf. XIV 4, 6).

The starting point was the sequence of existence, life, and reason or intellect. The higher stage of this sequence has turned out to imply two other concepts at the same level (memory and will), and it is such a 'horizontal' ternary that in a real sense reflects the divine ternary in the inner man. But there are more ternaries that in this manner supplement each other. The ternary *memoria-intelligentia-voluntas* expresses self-reflection: what is in my consciousness (*memoria*) is the object of my under-standing (*intelligentia*) by virtue of my will (*voluntas*), and the three are inseparable. This ternary refers to self-consciousness, whereas consciousness in general is desig-nated by the ternary of mind-cognition-love (*mens-notitia-amor*, cf. IX 4, 4), and it reflects, Augustine maintains, the divine Trinity (the Father: *memoria*; the Son: *intelli-gentia*; the Holy Spirit: *voluntas* or *amor*; cf. XV 23, 43). There are numerous analogous ternaries in man. The systematic connection between them is probably of less interest than the very analysis of the structure of consciousness; by means of a steady shift of perspective it uncovers the directedness of consciousness towards the world, towards itself, or towards God.

The entire aim behind the analysis of the different forms of consciousness is the soul's dependence on God and its path to God. What is it that the soul uncovers through its self-examination (XV 10, 17 ff.)? Augustine calls it the inner, spiritual 'word', *verbum mentis*, the conscious content of self-consciousness, as it were (cf. IX 11, 16). It is a cognition, which – as in the *De magistro* – precedes the outward sign and which can only be expressed metaphorically and incompletely verbally. But man is created in the image of God, and hence *verbum mentis* is a reflection of the divine word (*verbum divinum*), which indeed also has its own outward expression – the word became flesh. Therefore human cognition can move from *verbum mentis* to *verbum divinum*; none the less it is only a matter of an analogy or faint reflection (13, 22, ff.; 20, 39 ff.); one thing is the matter itself, another the image. The trace is not identical with the maker of the trace; the human ternaries belong to man's nature; the divine Trinity *is* God (23, 43).

The *Confessiones* occupies – as stressed again and again – a unique place in European literature. The work revolutionizes – or creates – autobiography as a genre, and this comes about by the author's directing his consciousness towards himself. Now, it holds good for all of Augustine's works that truth is only to be found in self-knowledge but that self-knowledge is bound to the knowledge of God – if I desire to know the soul, I desire to know God. Authors of textbooks are most often quite pleased that Augustine discovered 'the self' or the consciousness of the ego, and it is understood that this makes him very modern. This is undoubtedly so, and what is new is that Augustine writes about Augustine, not about 'man'. But he did not write the *Confessiones* because he thought that his life and thoughts were especially inter-esting, rather because his life was paradigmatic of God's guidance of all mankind (cf. *Conf.* II 3); and he wrote his 'autobiography' as a confession to God. He moves masterfully on several levels – how this is carried out stylistically has already been suggested. He can relate how he prayed to God for chastity – only not just now (VIII 7) – and he can unfurl the most sublime visions. He can, as it were, converse with God – 'Good God! what is that which is wrought in man' (3) – and like very few others he can write about his God so that all else is silence. Etched in memory are the sharply delineated scenes that – in the great and the small – are symbolically condensed and thus stand out as landmarks in Augustine's history – from the notorious theft of pears, via the garden scene in Milan, to the vision at Ostia where Augustine's and Monica's threads of life finally and irrevocably are entwined in the shared experience. The two lines in Augustine's life are in fact symbolized in Monica, that enterprising mother figure but at the same time God's tool in the guiding of Augustine – for indeed Augustine is guided by God. Man is not transparent to himself; God knows what resides in man, that which not even his own spirit knows (X 5). This means not only, as it did in Augustine's early writings, that the soul is so great that it contains the whole world but also that the human soul is 'a vast wilderness so full of snares and dangers' (35): let men walk, let men walk that the darkness overtake them not; darkness conceals what resides in me (23; 32). If the 'subconscious' in Plotinus contains hidden resources, to Augustine it is full of dangers as well.

Augustine's life is a concealed guidance by God, a sign or a symbol; but a sign must be interpreted: it does not immediately declare what it is a sign of. The *Confessiones* ends with the conversion, the final point of God's guidance. But the autobiography was not written until ten years after the event. What Augustine has to say here about his philosophical views can without much difficulty be compared with the contents of his early writings. Yet, when he wrote the Cassiciacum dialogues he was not in a position to interpret his own life – nor was he probably interested in doing so. The interpretation did not mature until he returned to his native Africa and was enthroned as the Bishop of Hippo. What does it mean to interpret one's life? To store it in the memory. How does the memory interpret? In the dimension of time. What is time? An image of eternity that does not acquire its true meaning until seen in the light of Holy Scripture, God's revelation that translates the eternal verities into the language of time. Each in its own way, *memoria*, time and Holy Scripture are traces of God. Only by virtue of these supra-individual signs can the life of the individual be interpreted – also as a sign. The tenth book of the *Confessiones* deals with *memoria*, the eleventh with time, and the twelfth and thirteenth with Holy Scripture. These final books provide the autobiography proper – books I–IX – with a sort of retroactive perspective, the universal point of view that alone makes it possible to interpret the individual's life as a sign of God. But *memoria*, time and Holy Scripture are in themselves signs that call for interpretation, an appropriation in human terms, and a knowledge of the inner space of the soul, but a self-knowledge that transcends the analysis of the individual, accidental 'ego'.

Memoria, or recollection, stands at the intersection between the individual and the universal, and hence the tenth book forms the transition from the account of Augustine's life to the general reflections in the last books. One should bear in mind the broad significance inherent in Augustine's concept of *memoria*. It contains all man's understanding of himself; it is no mere reservoir of past events but of a sequence of events retained by consciousness as meaningful. Memory is at the same time consciousness of the verities above man, and memory is a trace of God – to me God is not to be found anywhere but in consciousness; God resides in my memory (24).

Time is the medium of memory. In his ontology and theology of creation Augustine affirmed that time was created contemporaneously with the world; it did not exist prior to the world, but by means of time we measure the relation between events in the world. What is time in itself? If nobody asks me what time it is, I know perfectly well. If someone does ask, I do not know (XI 14). Time seems to be unreal, because the past no longer exists, the future not yet; the present exists as a point only, and so it does not really exist either. Nevertheless we measure the motion of a body in time and we measure time itself; we measure time as an extension – although of what (16; 26)? What is decisive is probably that we ourselves do the measuring. Time exists in consciousness – the past as a memory, the future as an expectation; hence one finds in the soul a present with regard to the past and a present with regard to the future. It may be consciousness itself that we measure when we measure time as extension (18; 20: 26). With an example Augustine shows what it means that time is experienced time (27 ff.). Suppose that we sing the hymn by Ambrosius, the *Deus creator omnium* ('God, Creator of all things') – a hymn Augustine often returns to. We sing in the expectation of what is to come; gradually expectation turns into memory. But we only understand if we measure the parts of the hymn in relation to the whole. Exactly the same is the case with the life of individual man and the life of all mankind.

Since time exists as experienced time, it does not exist as objective time independent of consciousness, for example as an eternal circular motion or as the motion of the celestial bodies (23; cf. *De civ. Dei* XII 14, 1). But this does not mean that time exists only subjectively. God created time as the medium in which all men experience the world, as that which constitutes *memoria*. God Himself knows in eternity, beyond time (*Conf.* XI 31), but to us He has revealed the truth in time. The whole history of mankind is enacted in time, in the Sacred History – from the creation of the world, via the Incarnation, to the end of time – and this is why Christianity is a historical religion (cf. *De ver. rel.* 7, 13). We understand our own existence in time and we understand it thanks to Holy Scripture, which renders a temporal account.

In Holy Scripture God revealed the truth so that we see in a sequel of time what exists with God in timeless eternity (*Conf.* XIII 29). This means that the Bible also is a sign demanding interpretation. The Bible can be taken literally, but in so far as is humanly possible, the sign can be interpreted and reveal the true reality. God says something, but what He says must have meaning; I cannot believe that God speaks idly, says Augustine (24). Nor can I, says he, believe that he who wrote down God's words, Moses, was more stupid than I, and if I were to write down the story of creation I only wish I could do so as well as Moses did: speak so that all can understand what is written and so that those who are able to do so can perceive the hidden meaning (XII 26). The Bible is a revelation, but a revelation that is to be interpreted. 'In the beginning God created the heaven and the earth' (Gen. 1). But what do 'beginning', 'heaven', and 'earth' mean, and what does it mean that the spirit of God moved upon the waters? Did God first create a formless stuff and then an ordered world? Did He create of nothing? What does the Creation symbolize (Aug. *Conf.* XII 3 ff.)?

Augustine himself was a very meticulous and thorough exegete. Like almost all the Church Fathers he interpreted Genesis again and again. He has also accounted for the technical problems connected with scriptural exegesis. He did so in the first three books of the *De doctrina Christiana* where he exploits the aids of rhetoric and grammar – philology, we would probably say – in the service of biblical interpretation, but throughout from the point of view that what matters is to proceed from the linguistic sign to the matter behind it (*De doctr. Christ.* I 2, 2 ff.; II 1, 1 ff.). In the last two books of the *Confessiones* he also deals with the principles for higher hermeneutics. He begins by contrasting a series of different, more or less worthy, allegorical interpretations of Genesis. He concludes (*Conf.* XIII 12 ff.) by furnishing his own allegorical interpretation, where he moves brilliantly and with surprising ease from his 'conversational style' to a sublime poesy encompassing the entire Bible. Here Genesis anticipates the whole Sacred History; it is a symbol of wisdom, the Trinity, the Sacraments, the Heavenly Jerusalem, spiritual and carnal man; all can be read about in the Bible, and the whole Bible and the whole world are found in condensed form in the account of the seven days of creation, of 'the beginning', 'heaven', 'earth', and 'the spirit of God moving upon the waters'.

Augustine knows exactly what he is doing, and he reflects on it. A precondition for any interpretation is that the Bible is true and that it speaks to us in symbolic form. Since there are so many interpretations of Genesis, which one is true? Two kinds of disagreements can arise, says Augustine, whenever something is reported by signs from reliable reporters (XII 23): doubt can arise about the truth of what is reported – but that is impossible in the case of the Bible. Next, there can be doubt about the meaning of the related, and that is where the battle is fought. Now, if two interpreters fight about their 'true' interpretation, this is in the first place a manifestation of pride, and in the second it shows that they have failed to understand the conditions for interpretation (14 ff.). The truth is not unambiguously reproduced in the sign or the image, and thus, if one does not understand the issue, the wording cannot be understood. The truth is always greater than the sign; sometimes the truth of the text transcends that of the author – Moses. Hence, that there are several interpretations of the Bible means no more than that the Truth – which itself is one – is expressed in a way that can be understood variously, depending on men's ability to understand. The Truth of Genesis does not let itself be expressed once and for all; the text is always open, but he who understands in truth understands what Truth itself 'tells me in my inner ear with a strong voice' (15). It is on this background that Augustine can offer his own truth in the concluding poetical allegory – in which he, however, approaches the text considerably more freely than he does as a professional exegete.

The aspects of this discussion that point forwards to modern philosophical hermeneutics will not be pursued here. But something else will be. The allegorical method was a tried and trusted one in Augustine's time. But Augustine's reflections on the method and his application of it are new. He not only exhibits an arsenal of allegorical interpretations on which the reader may have his own ideas; he includes his own – and the reader's – person in the interpretation; *his* cognition is at stake, and the allegory is not an external literary form or 'scientific' method. It is human existence as a whole that is understood as an allegory in the *Confessiones*. In this world we know through a glass and in a riddle, and the *Confessiones* ends with a prayer that alludes to the beginning: our heart cannot be quieted till it may find repose in Thee. On each day while God was creating the world it became morning and it became night, but 'the seventh day is without any evening, nor hath it any setting' (XIII 36; cf. *De civ. Dei* XI 8).

In 410 the world came to an end. Politically speaking, the Visigoths' conquest of Rome was of little importance – the centre of power was no longer there – but psychologically it meant all the more that the centre of the world fell into Barbarian hands. It was asked who was 'guilty' of the catastrophe. In Rome the upper class – the senatorial families – were still preponderantly pagan, and thus the answer was close to hand: the guilt was with the Christians; the abandoned ancient Gods – for centuries the warrant of Rome's grandeur – were now taking their revenge; furthermore, the Christians' position was ambiguous. The Visigoths were Christian, albeit Arians. This furnished the external occasion for Augustine's great work, the *De civitate Dei*, *On the City of God*. He undertook the defence of the Christians, but as the work took form, the apologetic aim was altered to a presentation of Augustine's general view of history and society – or rather, to a presentation of God's traces in history and in society.

In his introduction (*praef.*) Augustine writes that with his work he will defend God's glorious city (*civitas Dei*), both as long as its people here in the temporal wander as exiles in the faith among the godless and when they have gained rest in the eternal dwellings. He will defend the humble people of God against the proud who desire to rule, the inhabitants of the earthly city (*civitas terrena*). With this the basic theme of the work has been announced; what it might more closely imply remains unstated for the time being. On the other hand, what is immediately apparent is the dual perspective between the eternal and the temporal, where the battle between the City of God and the earthly city is fought; but it is a battle that can only be understood in light of the eternal. Rightly considered, the same theme sustains the *Confessiones*. Here Augustine speaks from his own experience as an individual. In the *De civitate Dei* the theme is the same, but the point of view is not the individual but the collective, the development of all mankind. Of course this leads to a difference in the form of presentation; the intimate personal style of the *Confessiones* gives way to a more general, authoritative and objective style – the author of the *Confessiones* is Augustine, the man, that of the *De civitate Dei* is the Bishop of Hippo. But both works deal with how to interpret the traces of God, and in both the key to interpretation is Holy Scripture, the subject of the last two books of the *Confessiones* and in the *De civitate Dei* the ever-present horizon for understanding.

Augustine himself says (XV 1, 1) that the title is 'mystical', which is to say allegorical, and he refers to the mention of 'God's city' in *Psalms* (XI 1). It is apparent that with '*civitas*' he does not mean the state as an institution but a commonwealth or community of men bound to each other as 'citizens' by common will – this can or cannot be institutionalized. It is probably also permissible to recall the Stoics' 'city' that is common to all people. In fact, the interplay between the inner community and its outward manifestations marks the whole tension in the *De civitate Dei*.

The first ten books of the *De civitate Dei* constitute the apologetic part of the work, which takes the form of a general encounter, both with pagan religion and pagan philosophy. In the last twelve books the historical development of the two *civitates* is examined on the basis of Sacred history (cf. XVIII 1). First come creation and fall and the origin of the two *civitates* (books XI–XIV), then their development from Adam and Eve via Abraham and David to Christ (XV–XVIII), and finally the end and separation of the two *civitates*, the last day, the Judgement, and life eternal (XIX–XXII). The historical development is further subdivided into six periods corresponding to the six ages of man and the six days of creation, crowned by the Sabbath, the seventh day, or rest eternal. We live in the sixth period, in the time from Christ until the end of the world. Everything is considered from Sacred history; there God Himself has revealed His guidance, and there God's 'city' lives. This means that profane history – the rise, development and fall of secular empires – only is looked at in passing (XVIII 2 ff.).

The reckoning with pagan religion and philosophy actually reflects a general cultural encounter. When it is claimed that the conquest of Rome is owing to the abandonment of the ancient Gods, can it then be maintained that these Gods hitherto had granted the Roman Empire happiness? And when a comparison is made with lofty Christian morality, can it then be maintained that the old religion demanded moral purity (I–V)? Such questions are traditional in Christian apologetics and polemics. But they acquire their special character, partially because Augustine – probably with the learned Varro as his main source – includes a considerable amount of material from the history of pagan religion, today of great interest, but especially because he undermines the whole issue. It was a widely held view – familiar for example from Julian the Apostate's polemics against Christianity – that whoever observed the worship of the gods would be rewarded with happiness and power in this world. This is what Augustine contests. In the first place it implies – and this must have been a challenge to many contemporaries – that Rome had no special, privileged place in world history. In many respects Augustine was and felt himself to be a Roman, but Rome was merely one secular state among others. In the second place it implies that Augustine pursues a deliberately secularized view of history. Thus – in the third place – it indirectly illustrates his view of the City of God. This is not a state like all others, but a community transcending secular powers. Also for this reason everything is considered from the perspective of Sacred history. It is history of a different kind.

The reckoning with pagan philosophy is tied to the reckoning with pagan religion (VI–X). Augustine's knowledge of the history of philosophy in general is second-hand. The most important point is his discussion with 'the Platonists', which naturally enough contains a considerable amount of agreement (cf. VIII 1 ff.; X 1 ff.; 14; 23 ff.; 29). In the preceding there has been ample occasion to discuss Augustine's relation to Platonism, and the sections in the *Confessiones* are rather more profound; what matters in the polemical context of the *De civitate Dei* is that although the Platonists entertain a transcendent view of God, they turn against the Incarnation, and they have not rejected polytheism, even though they ought to do so according to their own handsome theories. All are familiar notes, but it should not be overlooked that throughout the *De civitate Dei* Augustine is conducting a background discussion with the philosophers. It surfaces frequently, perhaps most clearly in the treatment of what is the goal of life – according to the philosophers and to the Christians (XIX 1 ff.).

Now, in what sense is it possible to speak of a philosophy of history in Augustine? Certainly in the sense that history pursues a linear course; it is so to speak suspended between the beginning of time, the Creation, and the end of time, and the great intersection in this course is the Incarnation of Christ, also in the sense that the course is purposive, for history is governed by Providence (cf. X 15, 1). The two *civitates* have their origin in the Fall, and they are finally separated at the end of history where those predestined for salvation are divided from those predestined for damnation. What is special for Augustine – and for Christianity generally – is, as has been noted earlier, not the linear view of history as such, but the eschatological purpose of history.

Augustine does not have a philosophy of history in the sense that he constructs a reflected theory of the course of history within the eschatological frame. What we know, we know from Sacred history, and we can see the power of Providence in the fulfilment of the prophesies in the Old Testament. In Holy Scripture God has revealed the Truth to whomsoever understands how to read according to the spirit, not according to the flesh (XI 2). But beyond what God has wished to reveal, we know nothing (cf. XVIII 40). We see realms come and go, but we do not see the good rewarded and the evil punished. God does not act at random; He has His plan, but it is hidden from us (cf. IV 33; V 21) – just as it is hidden from us whom God has predestined for salvation or damnation. The traces of God in history are not unambiguous. Augustine can speak of history as a beautiful poem (XI 18), but it is not as with Ambrosius' hymn in the *Confessiones*, which we do know and where we accordingly can interpret the parts from the whole. Augustine does not have a theory of the concrete course of profane history but a theory of the forces that govern history.

Thus he does not have a theocratic view of history. The City of God is not a secular power, and here, in time, no genuine Christian state will ever exist. Augustine was familiar with a theocratic view of history; he had encountered it in Ambrosius in Milan, and he must have been acquainted with it through the church historian Eusebius, the official chronicler of Constantine the Great, who considered Constantine's realm as God's state on earth. It is the hidden irony of history that in the medieval battles between Pope and Emperor precisely the *De civitate Dei* was read as a theocratic manifesto. The Church was God's *civitas* on earth according to the Pope. But the Emperor was not without ammunition either; he could refer to what Augustine wrote about 'the just King', the secular steward of divine justice (V 24, cf. below). A purely idealistic interpretation of the contrast between the *civitas Dei* and the *civitas terrena* does, however, also seem to encounter difficulties. Augustine is fully capable of speaking of Rome as a *civitas terrena* or as the second Babylon (cf. XVIII 22). But he can also declare that Rome has been rewarded for her virtues (cf. V 15 ff.). What lies behind this seeming ambiguity? In any case not Eusebius' *naïveté*.

Every man is a member of a society or a community (cf. IV 3). But behind the societies created by men lies the community that will live after the flesh and that which will live after the spirit, and from men's appearance one cannot tell whether they belong to *civitas terrena* or *civitas Dei*, God's city in exile (cf. XIV 1; XV 1, 2).

The Heavenly City or the Heavenly Jerusalem is reflected in the earthly Jerusalem, and this means that the earthly city also encompasses God's City in exile; a part of the earthly city has its source in Heaven (*De civ.* XV 2). Hence the earthly city never shows itself in pure form; here on earth the two *civitates* are entwined, and not all members of the church are in fact members of the Heavenly City (I 35; XV 8). On earth the two *civitates* are subject to the same fate, but they do not have the same faith (XVIII 54). Therefore there is something good in *civitas terrena* and hence also in the Roman people (cf. XIX 24). The expression *civitas terrena* is accordingly deliberately ambiguous. Outwardly good and evil are mixed; if one looks at the ideal reality, there is a sharp dividing line between the earthly city and the Heavenly City in exile. The outward represents the inward, but the outward sign is ambiguous; we cannot immediately see what really is good and evil in this world, and hence it depends on an interpretation or differing points of view whether we, for example, call Rome a second Babylon or praise the relative virtues of the Romans.

In the course of history one can find archetypal representatives of the battle between the earthly and the heavenly city. This is true, for example, of the two pairs of brothers, Cain and Abel from Sacred and Romulus and Remus from profane history. Abel and Remus represent good, Cain and Romulus – both fratricides and founders of cities – evil (XV 1 ff.; 5). What to us probably first and foremost are conflicts in human nature, are in general to Augustine primarily mythical events in Sacred history, and so it was already in the first drafting of his view (cf. e.g. *De ver. rel.* 27, 50). The history of mankind is determined by the Creation and the Fall. Man was created in the image of the Trinity. Thereby he acquired his real identity, expressed in the ternary of 'existence', 'knowing', 'loving'; on the awareness of this ternary also relies the version of the Augustinian *cogito* to be found in the *De civitate Dei* (*De civ. Dei* XI 24 ff.). At the mythical level the fall of man is prefigured in the account of the fall of some of the angels from God (17; XII 1).

The cause of the Fall is evil or perverted will (cf. 6; XIV 5). Man chooses to live in self-assertion and not in obedience to God – *secundum hominem*, not *secundum Deum*; but the soul dies when abandoned by God, just as the body dies when abandoned by the soul, and man's misery consists in his revolting against himself by turning away from God (4, 1; XIII 2; XIV 15, 2). At the Fall man's will became thwarted; he lost his true freedom and his true love. Since this is the cause of the emergence of the *civitas terrena*, it is evident that precisely the same forces operate individually and collectively. The cause of the happiness or misfortune of the individual or the community depends on whether or not will and love are directed to God. On this – and on nothing external – depends the difference between *civitas Dei* and *civitas terrena*, and Augustine's view of the two *civitates* is therefore a direct consequence of his view of man. Pride (*superbia*) confronts humility (*humilitas*), *cupiditas* confronts *caritas* (cf. 13, 2; XV 7); the true goal of man's life is to be bound to God (cf. X 3). This is already inherent in the introduction to the *De civitate Dei*; in a central chapter (XIV 28) it is unfolded and summarized. Two kinds of love, says Augustine here, have created the two *civitates*: self-love amounting to contempt of God and love of God amounting to contempt of oneself. One city seeks its glory among men, the other its glory in God; one is guided by thirst for power, the other by love. And he adds that in the city where love is directed towards God men serve each other in love, the rulers by taking care of the subjects, and the subjects by obedience.

The latter raises the question of how to adjust oneself to the social and political life in this world where God's City in exile mingles with the earthly city. In theory Augustine's social thinking is revolutionary inasmuch as it establishes a new basis for the organization of societies; in practice he is conservative – for the same reason. He takes his point of departure in the Hellenistic discussion of the highest good – known to him from Cicero and Varro – which is to say in a discussion about social life and virtues in a world where man forges his own happiness (XIX 1 ff.). Augustine can agree with the general – in all essentials Stoic – view that human society encompasses the family first, then the state, then all humanity, and also with the traditional Roman view of the authority of the *pater familias* (3, 2; 16). What binds a people or a society together is justice, and Augustine offers an interesting discussion of Cicero's definition in the *De re publica* (see p. 495): a people (*populus*) is a society based on common laws and on common interest. But when one considers what Cicero himself or Sallust relates about circumstances in Rome, the 'Roman people' were not, notes Augustine, a people according to this definition (21, 1 ff.; cf. II 21). The definition can, however, be generalized so as to declare that a people is a group of rational beings concurring about what they love. According to this, Augustine's definition, the Roman people were a people (XIX 24). But the definition has now become so general that one must ask what it is the people in question love.

The decisive is of course that the members of the two *civitates* have each their own love or each their own goals in life: aiming for happiness in this world or in the beyond (20). The ideal of happiness here below is an illusion, and thus, although one does find virtues in the pagans, they are not true virtues; the worship of God is proof of true justice (25; 22). The citizens of the two *civitates* have the same earthly fate, but the Christians use what the pagans enjoy (cf. 14; 17). This world is never a goal in itself, and if one considers Augustine's application of classic natural law, this must imply that *lex temporalis* only is binding if derived from *lex aeterna* (cf. *De lib. arb.* I 15, 31).

In general, however, the secular order should be heeded by both parties, and in this world, determined by the Fall, slavery, for example, should also be accepted (*De civ. Dei* XIX 17; 15). But the earthly goods are exploited for different purposes. Citizens in the City of God in exile never lose sight of the true goal, and this of course applies to a special degree to the Christian prince. Augustine described the just Christian emperor, *imperator* or *rex justus*, in a famous passage that has been called his mirror for princes (V 24; cf. IV 3). That Christian emperor is happy who governs justly and shuns pride, who remembers that he is only a man, is obedient to God, is tardy in punishment, quick to forgive, and performs charity and mild deeds. Such a Christian emperor was Theodosius, Augustine's former employer – he is somewhat more reserved about Constantine (V 25 ff.). If there are just princes there are also just wars – but only if they aim for peace in God; wars to gain the goods of this world lead only to misery (XV 4).

Justice is an important concept in Augustine's social thought; peace is even more important. To a far higher degree than does justice, it points beyond social thinking in a narrow sense, and no other concept can reflect both the convergence of interests in this world and the difference between the two types of love that characterize the citizens of *civitas terrena* and *civitas Dei*. Where honour is the key word among the ancient Roman virtues, it is peace that matters to Augustine, and this can of course come as no surprise, indeed not when one considers that in his lifetime he had witnessed everything collapsing into war and chaos. By nature all men strive for peace (XIX 12), but the contents of peace depend upon the direction of man's life. Concerning individual man, one can proceed from the harmonious function of the body through peace of the soul to peace in God; in society, the path proceeds from earthly peace and concord to the peace of the Heavenly City.

Peace eternal is not achieved in earthly life (11; 4, 2); here on earth God's people are in exile; in this world the Christian's peace consists in walking in the faith; in the beyond it consists in the vision of God (26 ff.; cf. Paul. 2 Cor. 5, 7). The *De civitate Dei* concludes where the *Confessiones* ended: at the seventh day of Creation that has no evening and where God is beheld face to face (Aug. *De civ. Dei* XXII 30, 4).

Augustine lived during the transitional period between what we call Antiquity and what we call the Middle Ages. His development is almost symbolic of this transition. The first phase of his life concluded with his finding in Christianity the happiness dimly envisioned by the Platonists. The guiding thought for the Bishop of Hippo was that the Christian lives a life in exile. That inheritance he bestowed upon the Middle Ages.

ABBREVIATIONS
GENERAL

———— •◆• ————

ACA	Ancient Commentators on Aristotle, ed. R. Sorabji, London and Ithaca, NY, 1987–. Translations in progress.
ad loc.	ad locum, i.e. [commentary] to passage referred to.
ap.	*apud*, 'by', i.e. 'quoted by'.
Budé	*Collection des Universités de France, publiée sous le patronage de l'Assocation Guillaume Budé.* Greek or Latin texts with French translations. Steadily in print.
CAG	*Commentaria in Aristotelem Graeca.* Published by the Berlin Academy, 1882–1909. Greek text.
CAS	*Clarendon Aristotle Series.* Oxford 1962–. English translation with commentary.
CC	*Corpus Christianorum.* Turnhout 1954–. Latin texts.
CPS	*Clarendon Plato Series.* Oxford 1973–. English translation with commentary.
CSEL	*Corpus Scriptorum Ecclesiaticorum Latinorum.* Wien 1866–. Latin text.
DK	Diels/Kranz: *Die Fragmente der Vorsokratiker.* See Bibliography, section E I.
frg.	fragment.
GCS	*Die Griechischen Christlichen Schriftsteller der erstern Jahrhunderte.* Published by the Berlin Academy. 1897–. Greek text.
KRS	Kirk/Raven/Schofield: *The Presocratic Philosophers.* See Bibliography, section E I.
Loeb	*The Loeb Classical Library.* Greek or Latin texts with English translations. Steadily in print.
OCT	*Oxford Classical Texts/Scriptorum Classicorum Bibliotheca Oxoniensis.* Greek or Latin texts. Steadily in print.
PG	*Patrologia Graeco-Latina,* ed. J.P. Migne. Paris 1857–68. Greek text with Latin translation.

PL	*Patrologia Latina*, ed. J.P. Migne. Paris 1844–55. Latin text.
SC	*Sources Chrétiennes*. Paris 1941–. Greek or Latin text with translation and commentary.
sch.	scholion. Marginal note in the manuscripts.
SVF	*Stoicorum veterum fragmenta*, ed. Arnim. See Bibliography, section E, V, 28.

INDIVIDUAL AUTHORS
AND TEXTS

——— •◆• ———

Acta	Acts (The Acts of the Apostles)
Ael.	Aelianus
Var. hist.	*Varia historia*
Aesch.	Aeschylus
Ag.	*Agamemnon*
Pers.	*The Persae*
Prom.	*Prometheus*
Aeschin.	Aeschines (orator)
Aet.	Aetius
Alb.	Albinus (Alcinous)
Διδασχ.	Διδασκαλικός
Εισ.	Εἰσαγωγή
Alcm.	Alcmaeon
Alex. Aphr.	Alexander of Aphrodisias
De an.	*De anima*
De fat.	*De fato*
De mixt.	*De mixtura*
In Aristot. Anal. pr.	Commentary on Aristotle´s *Analytica priora*
In Aristot. Met.	Commentary on Aristotle´s *Metaphysics*
In Aristot. Top.	Commentary on Aristotle´s *Topics*
Alex Polyh.	Alexander Polyhistor
Anax.	Anaxagoras
Anaximan.	Anaximander
Anaximen	Anaximenes
Anon: *De div.*	Anonymous: *De divitiis*
Anon: *Prol. ad Plat.*	Anonymous: *Prolegomena ad Platonem*

Anon. Iambl.	*Anonymus Iamblichi*
Ant.	Antiphon
Antis.	Antisthenes
Apul.	Apuleius
De Plat. dogm.	*De Platone et eius dogmate*
Arch.	Archimedes
Aren.	*Arenarius*
Corp. fluit.	*De corporibus fluitantibus*
De aequil.	*De planorum aequilibriis*
Eratosth.	*Ad Eratosthenem*
Aristip.	Aristippus
Aristocl.	Aristocles
Aristop.	Aristhophanes
Av.	*Aves (The Birds)*
Eccl.	*Ecclesiazusae*
Nub.	*Nubes (The Clouds)*
Ran.	*Ranae (The Frogs)*
Aristot.	Aristotle
Anal. post.	*Analytica posteriora*
Anal. pr.	*Analytica priora*
Cat.	*The Categories*
De an.	*De anima*
De caelo	*De caelo*
De gen. an.	*De generatione animalium*
De gen. et corr.	*De generatione et corruptione*
De int.	*De interpretatione*
De juv.	*De iuventute et senectute*
De mem.	*De memoria et reminiscentia*
De mot. an.	*De motu animalium*
De part. an.	*De partibus animalium*
De sens.	*De sensu et sensibili*
De somno	*De somno et vigilia*
Eth. Eud.	*The Eudemian Ethics*
Eth. Nic.	*The Nicomachean Ethics*
Hist. an.	*Historia animalium*
Insomn.	*De insomniis*
Met.	*Metaphysics*
Meteor.	*Meteorologica*
MM	*Magna Moralia*
MXG	*De Melliso, Xenophane, Gorgia*
Περὶ ἰδεῶν	Περὶ ἰδεῶν
Περὶ φιλοσ.	Περὶ φιλοσοφίας
Phys.	*Physics*

Poet.	*Poetics*
Pol.	*Politics*
Προτρ.	Προτρεπτικός
Rhet.	*Rhetoric*
Soph. el.	*De sophisticis elenchis*
Top	*The Topics*

Aristox.	Aristoxenus
Harm. el.	*Elementa harmonica*

Athen.	Athenaeus
Aug.	Augustine
Conf.	*Confessiones*
Contra Acad.	*Contra Academicos*
Contra Faust.	*Contra Faustum*
De an. et ej. orig.	*De anima et eius origine*
De civ. Dei	*De civitate Dei*
De dial.	*De dialectica*
De div. quaest. LXXXIII	*De diversis quaestionibus. LXXXIII*
De doctr. Christ.	*De doctrina Christiana*
De don. pers.	*De dono perseverantiae*
De gen. ad litt.	*De Genesi ad litteram*
De grat. et lib. arb.	*De gratia et libero arbitrio*
De immort. an.	*De immortalitate animae*
De lib. arb.	*De libero arbitrio*
De mag.	*De magistro*
De mus.	*De musica*
De ord.	*De ordine*
De praed. sanct.	*De praedestinatione sanctorum*
De quant. an.	*De quantitate animae*
De spir. et litt.	*De spiritu et littera*
De Trin.	*De Trinitate*
De ver. rel.	*De vera religione*
De vit. beat.	*De vita beata*
Ench.	*Enchiridion*
Ep.	*Epistolae*
Retr.	*Retractationes*
Serm.	*Sermones*
Sol.	*Soliloquia*

Boeth.	Boethius
Cons.	*Consolatio*
Contr. Eut.	*Contra Eytychen*
In Isag Porph.	**Commentary** on *Porphyry´s Isagoge*

Calc.   Calcidius
Cels.   Celsus
Cic.   Cicero
  Acad.   *Academica*
  Brut.   *Brutus*
  De div.   *De divinatione*
  De fat.   *De fato*
  De. fin.   *De finibus bonourum et malorum*
  De inv.   *De inventione*
  De leg.   *De legibus*
  De nat. deor.   *De natura deorum*
  De off.   *De officiis*
  De or.   *De oratore*
  De re publ.   *De re publica*
  In Cat.   *In Catilinam*
  Par. Stoic.   *Paradoxa Stoicorum*
  Pro Mil.   *Pro Milone*
  Tusp. disp.   *Tusculanae disputationes*

Clem.   Clement of Alexandria
  Paed.   *Paidagōgos*
  Protr.   *Protrepticus*
  Quis div.   *Quis dives salvetur?*
  Strom.   *Strōmateis*

Corp. Herm.   *Corpus Hermeticum*

Dem.   Democritus
Dex.   Dexippus
  In Aristot. Cat.   Commentary on Aristotle´s *Categories*
Dic.   Dicaearchus
Dig.   *Digesta* (Part of *Corpus juris civilis*)
Diod. Sic.   Diodorus Siculus
Diog. Apol.   Diogenes of Apollonia
Diog. Laert.   Diogenes Laertius
Diog. Oen.   Diogenes of Oenoanda
Duns Scot.   Duns Scotus, John
  Op. Ox.   *Opus Oxoniense*

Emp.   Empedocles
Epic.   Epicurus
  Her.   *Letter to Herodotus*
  Men.   *Letter of Menoeceus*
  Περ. τέλ.   Περὶ τέλους
  Περ. φύσ.   Περὶ φύσεως.
  Pyth.   *Letter to Pythocles*

Rat. sent.	*Kyriai doxai* (Principal Doctrines)
Sent. Vat.	*Sententiae Vaticanae*
Epich.	Epicharmus
Epicr.	Epicrates
Epict.	Epictetus
Diss.	*Diatribes*
Ench.	*Enchiridion*
Epiph.	Epiphanius
Panar.	*Panarion*
Eucl.	Euclid
El.	*Elements*
Eud.	Eudemus
Eur.	Euripides
Bacch.	*The Bacchae*
Hec.	*Hecuba*
Hel.	*Helena*
Her. fur.	*Hercules Furens*
Hipp.	*Hippolytus*
Io	*Ion*
Med.	*Medea*
Troad.	*The Trojan Women*
Eus.	Eusebius
Hist. eccl.	*Historia ecclesiastica*
Praep. Ev.	*Praeparatio Evangelica*
Ex.	Exodus
Gal.	Galen
De nat. fac.	*De naturalibus facultatibus*
Inst. log.	*Institutio logica*
Gell.	Gellius
Gen.	Genesis
Gor.	Gorgias
Greg. Nyss.	Gregory of Nyssa
Cont. Eunom.	*Contra Eunomium*
De an. et resur.	*De anima et resurrectione*
De hom. op.	*De opificio hominis*
De virg.	*De virginitate*
Hexaem	*In Hexaemeron*
In Cant.	*In Cantica*

In Step.	*In Sephanum*
Or. Cat.	*Oratio catechetica*
Vit. Moys	*De vita Moysis*
Greg. Thaum.	Gregory Thaumaturgus
Pan. in Orig.	*Panegyricus in Origenem*
Her.	Herodotus
Heracl.	Heraclitus
Hero	Heron
Hes.	Hesiod
Op.	*Works and Days*
Theog.	*Theogony*
Hipp.	Hippocrates
De aëre	*De aëre, aqua, locis*
De arte	*De arte*
De corde	*De corde*
Epid.	*Epidemiae*
Hum.	*De humoribus*
Jusj.	*Jusjurandum*
Morb. sacr.	*De morbo sacro*
Nat. hom.	*De natura hominis*
Nat. puer.	*De natura puerorum*
Praec.	*Praecepta*
Vet. med.	*Vetus medicina*
Hippol.	Hippolytus
Hom.	Homer
Il.	*The Iliad*
Od.	*The Odyssey*
Iambl.	Iamblichus
De comm. math.	*De communi mathematica scientia*
De myst.	*De mysteriis*
Pyth.	*De vita Pythagorica*
Inst.	Institutiones (Part of *Corpus juris civilis*)
Ir.	Irenaeus
Adv. haer.	*Adversus haereses*
Isocr.	Isocrates
Adv. Soph.	*Adversus Sophistas*
Ant.	*Antidosis*

Hel.	*Encomium Helenae*
Johs.	The Gospel according to St. John
Jul. Apost.	Julian the Apostate
Adv. Gal.	*Adversus Galilaeos*
Ep.	*Epistulae*
Or.	*Orationes*
Just.	Justin Martyr
Apol.	*Apologiae*
Dial.	*Dialogus cum Tryphone*
Lact.	Lactantius
De mort. pers.	*De mortibus persecutorum*
Inst.	*Institutiones divinae*
Leuc.	Leucippus
Lib.	Libanius
Decl.	*Declamationes*
Lucr.	Lucretius
De rer. nat.	*De rerum natura*
Lys.	Lysias
Mar.	Marinus
Vit. Procl.	*Vita Procli*
Mar. Vict.	Marius Victorinus
Ad Cand.	*Ad Candidum*
Marc.	The Gospel according to St. Mark
Marc. Aur.	Marcus Aurelius
Matth.	The Gospel according to St. Matthew
Max. Tyr.	Maximus of Tyre
Melis.	Melissus
Nemes.	Nemesius
De nat. hom.	*De natura hominis*
Nic. Cus.	Nicolaus Cusanus
De non al.	*De non-aliud*

Num.	Numenius
Olymp.	Olympiodorus
In Aristot. Cat.	Commentary on Aristotle's *Categories*
In Gorgiam	Commentary on Plato's *Gorgias*
In Phaedonem	Commentary on Plato's *Phaedo*
Vit. Plat.	*Vita Platonis*
Orig.	Origenes
CC	*Contra Celsum*
De princ.	*De principiis*
Orph.	*Orphica*
Papp.	Pappus
Coll.	*Collectiones*
Parm.	Parmenides
Paul.	St. Paul
1 Cor	1 Corinthians
2 Cor	2 Corinthians
Gal.	Galatians
Rom.	Romans
Philo	Philo of Alexandria
Cher.	*De Cherubim*
De aet. mund.	*De aeternitate mundi*
De fuga	*De fuga et inventione*
De Ios.	*De Iosepho*
De leg. spec.	*De legibus specialibus*
De op. mun	*De opificio mundi*
De somn.	*De somniis*
De vit. cont.	*De vita contemplativa*
Leg.	*Legatio ad Gaium*
Leg. all.	*Legum allegoriae*
Migr. Abr.	*De migratione Abrahami*
Quis. her.	*Quis rerum divinarum heres sit*
Quod det.	*Quod deterius potiori insidiari soleat*
Quod Deus imm.	*Quod Deus sit immutabilis*
Quod omn. prob.	*Quod omnis probus liber sit*
Philod.	Philodemus
De sign.	*De signis*
Poet.	*Poetica*
Rhet.	*Rhetorica*
Philop.	Philoponus

In Aristot. Anal. post.	Commentary on Aristotle's *Analytica posteriora*
In Aristot. Anal. pr.	Commentary on Aristotle's *Analytica priora*
In Aristot. De an.	Commentary on Aristotle's *De anima*
In Aristot. Phys.	Commentary on Aristotle's *Physics*
Pind.	Pindar
Nem.	*Nemean Odes*
Ol.	*Olympian Odes*
Pyth.	*Pythian Odes*
Plat.	Plato
Alc.I	*Alcibiades I*
Apol	*Apology*
Charm	*Charmides*
Clit.	*Clitophon*
Crat.	*Cratylus*
Critias	*Critias*
Crito	*Crito*
Ep	*Epistles*
Epin.	*Epinomis*
Euthyd.	*Euthydemus*
Euthyph.	*Euthyphro*
Gor.	*Gorgias*
Hipp. maj.	*Hippias Major*
Hipp. min.	*Hippias Minor*
Io.	*Ion*
Lach.	*Laches*
Leg.	*Leges (Laws)*
Lys.	*Lysis*
Menex.	*Menexenus*
Meno	*Meno*
Parm.	*Parmenides*
Phaedo	*Phaedo*
Phaedr.	*Phaedrus*
Phil.	*Philebus*
Pol.	*Politicus (Statesman)*
Prot.	*Protagoras*
RP	*Republic*
Soph.	*Sophist*
Symp.	*Symposium*
Theaet.	*Theaetetus*
Tim.	*Timaeus*
Plot.	Plotinus
Plut.	Plutarch (of Chaeronea)
Ad Apol.	*Consolatio ad Apollonium*

Ad Col.	*Adversus Colotem*
Brut.	*Brutus*
Cato mai.	*Cato Major*
Cim.	*Cimon*
De Alex. virt.	*De Alexandri Magni fortuna aut virtute*
De an. procr.	*De animae procreatione in Timaeo*
De comm. not.	*De communibus notitiis adversus Stoicos*
De def. or.	*De defectu oraculorum*
De E	*De E apud Delphos*
De fac.	*De facie quae in orbe lunae apparet*
De gen. Socr.	*De genio Socratis*
De Her. malign.	*De Herodoti malignitate*
De Is.	*De Iside et Osiride*
De Pyth. or.	*De Pythiae oraculis*
De sera num.	*De sera numinis vindicta*
De Stoic. repugn.	*De Stoicorum repugnantiis*
De superst.	*De superstitione*
De virt. mor	*De virtute morali*
Non posse	*Non posse suaviter vivi secundum Epicurum*
Sulla	*Sulla*
Tib. Gracch.	*Tiberius Gracchus*

Pol.	Polybius
Porph.	Porphyry
Ad Marc.	*Ad Marcellam*
Adv. Christ.	*Adversus Christianos*
De abst.	*De abstinentia*
De antr. Nymph.	*De antro Nympharum*
In Aristot. Cat.	Commentary on Aristotle's *Categories*
Isag.	*Isagoge*
Sent.	*Sententiae ad intelligibilia ducentes*
Vit. Plot.	*Vita Plotini*

Pos.	Posidonius
Procl.	Proclus
El. theol.	*Elementa theologiae*
Hymn. in Deum Plat.	*Hymnus in Deum Platonicus*
In Eucl. El. I	Commentary on Euclid's *Elements, Book I*
In Plat. Parm.	Commentary on Plato's *Parmenides*
In Plat. Parm. interpr. Guillelmo de Moerbeka	Commentary on Plato's *Parmenides* in the interpretation of Guillelmus de Moerbeka
In Plat. Tim.	Commentary on Plato's *Timaeus*
Theol. Plat.	*In Platonis theologiam*

Prot.	Protagoras
Ps.-Dion.	*Pseudo-Dionysius the Areopagite*

De myst. theol.	*De mystica theologia*
Hier. coel.	*De coelesti hierarchia*
Ptol.	Ptolemy
Alm.	*Almagest*
Quint.	Quintilian
Inst. or.	*De institutione oratoria*
Sen.	Seneca
De ben.	*De beneficiis*
De clem.	*De clementia*
De const. sap.	*De constantia sapientis*
De ira	*De ira*
De prov.	*De providentia*
De tranq. an.	*De tranquillitate animi*
De vit. beat.	*De vita beata*
Ep. mor.	*Epistulae morales ad Lucilium*
Quaest. nat.	*Quaestiones naturales*
Sext. Emp.	Sextus Empiricus
Adv. math.	*Adversus mathematicos*
Hyp. Pyr.	*Hypotypōseis Pyrrhōneioi* (Outlines of Pyrrhonism)
Simpl.	Simplicius
In Aristot. Cat.	Commentary on Aristotle's *Categories*
In Aristot. De caelo	Commentary on Aristotle's *De caelo*
In Aristot. Phys.	Commentary on Aristotle's *Physics*
Socr.	Socrates (Ecclesiastical historian)
Hist. eccl.	*Historia ecclesiastica*
Solo	Solon
Soph.	Sophocles
Aj.	*Ajax*
Ant.	*Antigone*
OT	*Oedipus Tyrannus*
Philoct.	*Philoctetes*
Speus.	Speusippus
Stob.	Stobaeus
Strabo	Strabo
Strat.	Straton of Lampsacus

Tac.	Tacitus
Ann.	*Annals*
Ter.	Terence
Heaut.	*Heautontimorumenos*
Tert.	Tertullian
Adv. Marc.	*Adversus Marcionem*
Apol.	*Apologeticum*
De praesc. haer.	*De praescriptione haereticorum*
Them.	Themistius
In aristot. Anal. post.	Commentary on Aristotle's *Analytica posteriora*
In Aristot. De an.	Commentary on Aristotle's *De anima*
In Aristot. Phys.	Commentary on Aristotle's *Physics*
Theogn.	Theognis
Theol. arith.	*Theologumena arithmeticae*
Theoph.	Theophrastus
De caus. plant.	*De causis plantarum*
De sens.	*De sensibus*
Hist. plant.	*Historia plantarum*
Met.	*Metaphysics*
Thom. Aq.	Thomas Aquinas
In Aristot. Met.	Commentary on Aristotle's *Metaphysics*
Summ. theol.	*Summa theologiae*
Thras.	Thrasymachus
Thuc.	Thucydides
Verg.	Virgil
Aen.	*Aeneid*
Xen.	Xenophon
Apol.	*Apology*
Mem.	*Memorabilia*
Resp. Ath.	*Res publica Atheniensium (Constitution of Athens)*
Symp.	*Symposium*
Xenocr.	Xenocrates
Xenophan.	Xenophanes
Zeno	Zeno of Elea

BIBLIOGRAPHY

——— •◆• ———

(Within the individual sections editions and translations of text have been listed first in an order following the order in the expository text. Subsequently, secondary references are arranged alphabetically.)

A BIBLIOGRAPHIES

L'année philologique: Bibliographie critique et analytique de l'antiquité gréco-latine, Paris, 1928 ff.
The Philosopher's Index, Bowling Green, 1967 ff.
Platnauer, M. (ed.) *Fifty Years of Classical Scholarship*, Oxford, 1954; 2nd revised edn, 1968.
Totok, W. *Handbuch der Geschichte der Philosophie*, I, Frankfurt, 1964.
Ueberweg, see section C.

B ENCYCLOPEDIAS, DICTIONARIES, TERMINOLOGY

Cary, M. *et al.* (ed.) *The Oxford Classical Dictionary*, Oxford, 1949 (and later).
Edwards, N. (ed.) *The Encyclopedia of Philosophy*, I–VIII, New York, 1967 (repr. 1972).
Eucken, R. *Geschichte der philosophischen Terminologie*, Leipzig, 1879 (repr. Hildesheim, 1964).
Goulet, R. (ed.) *Dictionnaire des philosophes antiques*, I–, Paris, 1988–. Biography and history of texts.
Lalande, A. *Vocabulaire technique et critique de la philosophie*, Paris, 1976 (12. edn).
Paulys Realencyclopädie der classischen Altertumswissenschaft, ed. G. Wissowa *et al.*, Stuttgart and München, 1894–1980 (70 vols).
Ritter, J. *et al.* (ed.) *Historisches Wörterbuch der Philosophie*, I–, Basel, 1971 ff.
Wiener, P.P. (ed.) *Dictionary of the History of Ideas*, I–IV and index, New York, 1973–4.
Zeyl, D.J. (ed.) *Encyclopedia of Classical Philosophy*, Westport, 1997.
Ziegler, K. *et al.* (ed.) *Der Kleine Pauly: Lexikon der Antike*, I–V, München, 1975 (and later).

C GENERAL HISTORY OF PHILOSOPHY AND HISTORY OF IDEAS

Vogel, C.J. de (ed.) *Greek Philosophy: A Collection of Texts*, I–III, Leiden, 1950–9 (and later, Greek and Latin).

Bréhier, É. *Histoire de la philosophie*, I, 1–2, Paris, 1926–7 (and later, Eng. trans. 1963–5).

Copleston, F. *A History of Philosophy*, I, London, 1946 (and later).

Guthrie, W.K.C. *A History of Greek Philosophy*, I–VI, Cambridge, 1962–81.

Hegel, G.W.F. *Vorlesungen über die Geschichte der Philosophie*, I–III. *Werke, Jubil.ausg*, 17–9, Stuttgart, 1959 (1833–6).

Höffe, O. *Klassiker der Philosophie I*, 2nd edn, München, 1985 (1981).

Jaeger, W. *Paideia: Die Formung des griechischen Menschen*, I-II, Berlin, 1933–45 (and later. Eng. trans. 1945).

O'Connor, D.J. (ed.) *A Critical History of Western Philosophy*, New York and London, 1964 (and later).

Robin, L. *La pensée grecque*, Paris, 1923 (and later).

Röd, M. (ed.) *Geschichte der Philosophie*, I (Röd: *Von Thales bis Demokrit*), II (Graeser: *Sophistik und Sokratik, Plato und Aristotles*), III (Hossenfelder: *Stoa, Epikureismus und Skepsis*), München, 1976–85.

Routledge History of Philosophy, I: *From the Beginning to Plato*, ed. C.C.W. Taylor, II: *Aristotle to Augustine*, ed. D. Furley, London, 1997.

Ueberweg, F. *Grundriss der Geschichte der Philosophie* (orig. 1862), 12 ed., I (K. Praechter: *Die Philosophie des Altertums*), Berlin, 1926 (repr. Basel 1953). New edn., *Die Philosophie der Antike* III (H. Flashar *et al.*: *Ältere Akademie* (Krämer) – *Aristoteles* (Flashar) – *Peripatos* (Wehrli)), IV 1–2 (H. Flashar: *Die hellenistische Philosophie*, Basel and Stuttgart, 1983–94).

Zeller, E. *Die Philosophie der Griechen in ihrer geschichtlichen Entwicklung* (orig. 1844–52). New edn (by W. Nestle *et al.*) compl. 1923. Repr., I–III (6 vols.), Darmstadt, 1963.

D SPECIAL SUBJECTS (INCLUDING HISTORY OF SCIENCE)

Adkins, A.W.H. *Merit and Responsibility: A Study in Greek Values*, Oxford, 1960.

Annas, J. *The Morality of Happiness*, Oxford, 1993.

Barker, K. *Greek Political Theory: Plato and his Predecessors*, London, 1918 (and later).

Beare, J.I. *Greek Theories of Elementary Cognition*, Oxford, 1906.

Bocheński, I.M. Ancient Formal Logic, Amsterdam, 1951.

Dodds, E.R. *The Greeks and the Irrational*, Berkeley and Los Angeles, 1951 (and later).

Dover, K. *Greek Popular Morality*, Oxford, 1974.

Fraisse, J.C. *Philia: La notion d'amitié dans la philosophie antique*, Paris, 1974 (and later).

Fritz, K.v. *Philosophie und sprachlicher Ausdruck bei Demokrit, Plato und Aristoteles*, New York, 1938. Repr. Darmstadt, 1963.

Furley, D. *The Greek Cosmologists*, I–, Cambridge, 1987–.

Gagarin, M. and Woodruff, P. (ed.) *Early Greek Political Thought from Homer to the Sophists*, Cambridge, 1995.

Hamlyn, D.W. *Sensation and Perception: A History of the Philosophy of Perception*, London, 1961.

Kahn, C.H. *The Verb 'Be' in Ancient Greek*, Dordrecht, 1973.

Kapp, E. *Greek Foundations of Traditional Logic*, New York, 1942.

Kennedy, G. *The Art of Persuasion in Greece*, London, 1963.

Kneale, M. and Kneale, W. *The Development of Logic*, Oxford, 1962.

Lange, F.A. *Geschichte des Materialismus*, I, Leipzig, 1908.

MacIntyre, A. *A Short History of Ethics*, London, 1967.

Marrou, H.-I. *Histoire de l'éducation dans l'antiquité*, 6th edn, Paris, 1965 (1948), Eng. trans. 1965.

Natorp, P. *Forschungen zur Geschichte des Erkenntnisproblems im Altertum*, Berlin, 1884, repr. Hildesheim, 1965.

Næss, A. *Scepticism*, London, 1968.

Sabine, G.H. *A History of Political Theory*, London, 1937, revised edn 1963 (and later).

Sinclair, T.A. *A History of Greek Political Thought*, London, 1951.

Snell, B. *Die Entdeckung des Geistes: Studien zur Entstehung des europäischen Denkens bei den Griechen*, Hamburg, 1955 (and later), Eng. trans. 1953.

Sorabji, R. *Time, Creation and the Continuum: Theories in Antiquity and the Early Middle Ages*, London, 1983.

—— *Matter, Space and Motion: Theories in Antiquity and their Sequel*, London, 1988.

Steinthal, H. *Geschichte der Sprachwissenschaft bei den Griechen und Römern*, I–II, 2nd edn, Berlin, 1890 (orig. 1863).

Watson, G. *Phantasia in Classical Thought*, Galway, 1988.

Science and mathematics

See also Chapter 26

Cohen, M.R. and Drabkin, J.E. (ed.) *A Source Book in Greek Science*, Cambridge, MA, 1958 (and later). Trans. of selected sources.

Becker, O. *Das mathematische Denken der Antike*, Göttingen, 1957.

Dijksterhuis, E.J. *Die Mechanisierung des Weltbildes*, Berlin, Göttingen and Heidelberg, 1956.

Farrington, B. *Greek Science*, I–II, London, 1944 (and later).

Heath, T. *A History of Greek Mathematics*, I–II, Oxford, 1921. Later repr.

Lloyd, G.E.R. *Early Greek Science: Thales to Aristotle*, London, 1970.

Neugebauer, O. *The Exact Sciences in Antiquity*, Copenhagen, 1951 (and later).

Sambursky, S. *The Physical World of the Greeks*, London, 1956 (and later).

Taton, R. (ed.) *Histoire générale des sciences*, I: *La science antique et médiévale*, Paris, 1957. Eng. trans. 1963.

Toulmin, S. and Goodfield, J. *The Fabric of the Heavens*, London, 1962.

Waerden, B.L. van der *Science Awakening*, Groningen, 1954 (and later).

E BIBLIOGRAPHICAL GUIDE TO THE INDIVIDUAL CHAPTERS

Introduction

Diels, H. (ed.) *Doxographi Graeci*, Berolini, 1879, repr. 1965.

Diogenes Laertius *Vitae philosophorum*, ed. H.S. Long, I–II. *OCT*.

—— *Lives of Eminent Philosophers*, ed. R.D. Hicks, I–II, *Loeb*.

Mejer, J. *Diogenes Laertius and his Hellenistic Background, Hermes Einzelschriften*, 40, Wiesbaden, 1978.

Reynolds, L.D. and Wilson, N.G. *Scribes and Scholars: A Guide to the Transmission of Greek and Latin Literature*, Oxford, 1968.

West, M.L. *Textual Criticism and Editorial Technique applicable to Greek and Latin Texts*, Stuttgart, 1973.

Part I: Presocratic philosophy

Diels, A. and Kranz, W. (ed.) *Die Fragmente der Vorsokratiker: Griechisch und deutsch*, 6th edn, Berlin, 1951–2 (and later). Orig. 1903.

Kirk, G.S., Raven, J.E. and Schofield, M. (ed.) *The Presocratic Philosophers*, 2nd edn, Cambridge, 1983 (and later). 1st edn (by Kirk/Raven) 1957. Greek texts, Eng. trans. and commentary.

McKirahan, R.D. (ed.) *Philosophy before Socrates: An Introduction with Texts and Commentary*, Indianapolis and Cambridge, 1994.

Barnes, J. *The Presocratic Philosophers*, I–II, London, 1979 (and later).

Burnet, J. *Early Greek Philosophy*, 4th edn, London, 1930 (and later). Orig. 1892.

Fränkel, H. *Wege und Formen frühgriechischen Denkens*, München, 1955.

Furley, D.J. and Allen, R.E. (ed.) *Studies in Presocratic Philosophy*, I–II, London, 1970–75.

Gadamer, H.-G. (ed.) *Um die Begriffswelt der Vorsokratiker*, Darmstadt, 1968.

Hussey, E. *The Presocratics*, London, 1972 (and later).

Jaeger, W. *The Theology of the Early Greek Philosophers*, Oxford, 1947.

Mourelatos, A.P.D. *et al.* (ed.) *The Pre-Socratics*, Garden City, 1974.

Vernant, J.P. *Les origines de la pensée grecque*, Paris, 1962, Eng. trans. London, 1982.

I, 1: Myth, poetry and philosophy

Hesiodus *Theogony*, ed. M.L. West, Oxford, 1966. Greek text. Eng. trans. and commentary.

Burkert, W. *Griechische Religion der archaischen und klassischen Epoche*, Stuttgart, 1977. Eng. trans. 1985.

Cornford, F.M. *Principium sapientiae: A Study of the Origins of Greek Philosophical Thought*, Cambridge, 1952 (and later).

Fränkel, H. *Dichtung und Philosophie des frühen Griechentums*, New York, 1951, Eng. trans. 1973.

Frankfort, H. *et al. Before Philosophy*, Harmondsworth, 1949.

Guthrie, W.K.C. *The Greeks and their Gods*, London, 1950 (and later).

Kirk, G.S. *Myth, its Meaning and Functions in Ancient and other Cultures*, Berkeley and Cambridge, 1970.

Linforth, I.M. *The Arts of Orpheus*, Berkeley, 1941.

I, 2. Ionian natural philosophy

Kahn, C.H. *Anaximander and the Origins of Greek Cosmology*, New York, 1960.

I, 3. Heraclitus

Kahn, C.H. *The Art and Thought of Heraclitus: An Edition of the Fragments with Translation and Commentary*, Cambridge, 1979.

Heraclitus *The Cosmic Fragments*, ed. G.S. Kirk, Cambridge, 1954. Text, trans. and commentary.

Marcovich, M. *Heraclitus*, Merida, 1967. Text, commentary.

Heraclitus, *Fragments: A Text and Translation with a Commentary*, by T.H. Robinson, Toronto, 1987.

I, 4. The Pythagoreans

Burkert, W. *Weisheit und Wissenschaft: Studien zu Pythagoras, Philolaos und Platon*, Nürnberg, 1962. Eng. edn, Cambridge, MA, 1972.

Philip, J.A. *Pythagoras and Early Pythagoreanism*, Toronto, 1966.

Raven, J.E. *Pythagoreans and Eleatics*, Cambridge, 1948.

Vogel, C.J. de *Pythagoras and Early Pythagoreanism*, Assen, 1966.

I, 5. The Eleatics

Coxon, A.H. *The Fragments of Parmenides*, Assen, 1986. Text, trans. and commentary.

Diels, H. *Parmenides' Lehrgedicht, griechisch und deutsch*, Berlin, 1897.

Parmenides, ed. L. Tarán, Princeton, 1965. Text, trans. and commentary.

Lee, H.D.P. (ed.) *Zeno of Elea*, Cambridge, 1936. Text, trans. and commentary.

Calogero, G. *Studi sull'Eleatismo*, Roma, 1932.

Grünbaum, H. *Modern Science and Zeno's Paradoxes*, London, 1968.

Mansfeld, J. *Die Offenbarung des Parmenides*, Assen, 1964.

Mourelatos, A.P.D. *The Route of Parmenides*, New Haven, 1970.

Reinhardt, K. *Parmenides und die Geschichte der griechischen Philosophie*, Bonn, 1916.

I, 6. Post-Parmenidean natural philosophy

Bollack, J. (ed.) *Empédocle*, I–III, Paris, 1965–9. Text, trans. and commentary.

Inwood, B. *The Poem of Empedocles: A Text and Translation with an Introduction*, Toronto, 1992.

Lur'e, S. (ed.) *Demokrit*, Leningrad, 1970. Greek text, Russian trans. and commentary.

Bailey, C. *The Greek Atomists and Epicurus*, Oxford, 1928 (and later).

Cole, T. *Democritus and the Sources of Greek Anthropology*, Bronx, 1967.

Furley, D.J. *Two Studies in the Greek Atomists*, Princeton, 1967.

Kingsley, P. *Ancient Philosophy, Mystery and Magic: Empedocles and Pythagorean Tradition*, Oxford, 1995.

Langerbeck, H. Δόξις ἐπιρρυσμίη. *Studien zu Demokrits Ethik und Erkenntnislehre*, Berlin, 1935.

Mau, J. *Zum Problem des Infinitesimalen bei den antiken Atomisten*, Berlin 1954.

O'Brien, D. *Empedocles' Cosmic Cycle*, Cambridge, 1969.

Schofield, M. *An Essay on Anaxagoras*, Cambridge, 1980.

I, 7. Medical science

Hippocrate *Oeuvres complètes*, ed. E. Littré, I–X, Paris 1839–61. Text, trans.
Hippocrates, ed. W.H.S. Jones, I–IV, *Loeb*.
Heidel, W.A. *Hippocratic Medicine*, New York, 1941 (and later).

Part II: the great century of Athens

II, 9. Tragedy and view of history

Eschyle, ed. P. Mazon, I–II, *Budé*.
Sophocle, ed. A. Dain and P. Mazon, I–III, *Budé*.
Herodotus, ed. C. Hude, I–II, *OCT*.
Thucydides, ed. H.S. Jones and J.E. Powell, I–II, *OCT*.
Euripide, ed. L. Méridier *et al.*, I–VI, *Budé*.
Edmunds, L. *Chance and Intelligence in Thucydides*, Cambridge, MA, 1975.
Fritz, K.v. *Die griechische Geschichtsschreibung*, I and notes (II) Berlin, 1967.
Lesky, A. *Die griechische Tragödie*, 2nd edn, Stuttgart, 1958 (1937).
Myres, J.L. *Herodotus: Father of History*, Oxford, 1953.
Nietzsche, F. *Die Geburt der Tragödie. Werke*, ed. K. Schlechta, I, München, 1966 (1872).
Nussbaum, M.C. *The Fragility of Goodness: Luck and Ethics in Greek Tragedy and Philosophy*, Cambridge, 1986.
Romilly, J. de *Thucydide et l'impérialisme Athénien*, 2nd edn, Paris, 1951 (1947).
—— *La tragédie grécque*, Paris, 1970 (and later).

II, 10. The Sophists

Diels/Kranz – see Section I.
Sprague, R.K. (ed.) *The Older Sophists, a Complete Translation*, Columbia, 1972.
Classen, C.J. (ed.) *Sophistik*, Darmstadt, 1976.
Heinimann, F. *Nomos und Physis*, Basel, 1945 (and later).
Kerferd, G.B. *The Sophistic Movement*, Cambridge, 1981.
Newiger, H.J. *Untersuchungen zu Gorgias' Schrift über das Nichtseiende*, Berlin, 1973.
Romilly, J. de *Les grands sophistes dans l'Athènes de Périclès*, Paris, 1988, Eng. trans. 1992.
Untersteiner, K. *The Sophists*, trans. K. Freeman, Oxford, 1954.

II, 11. Socrates

Aristophane, ed. V. Coulon and H. van Daele, I (including the *Clouds*), *Budé*.
Xenophon *Memorabilia and Oeconomicus: Symposium and Apology*, ed. E.C. Marchant and O.J. Todd, *Loeb*.

Socratis et Socraticorum reliquiae, ed. G. Giannantonini, I–IV, Napoli, 1990 (1983).

Döring, K. (ed.) *Die Megariker: Kommentierte Sammlung der Testimonien*, Amsterdam, 1972.

Antisthenis fragmenta, ed. F. Caizzi, Milano, 1966.

Aristippi et Cyrenaicorum fragmenta, ed. E. Mannebach, Leiden and Köln, 1961.

Burnyeat, M. (ed.) *Socratic Studies*, Cambridge, 1994.

Cornford, F.M. *Before and after Socrates*, Cambridge, 1932 (and later).

Gulley, N. *The Philosophy of Socrates*, London, 1968.

Hackforth, R. *The Composition of Plato's Apology*, Cambridge, 1933.

Kierkegaard, S. *On the Concept of Irony*, Princeton ed., 1989, II (1841).

Maier, H. *Sokrates*, Tübingen, 1913.

Stone, I.F. *The Trial of Socrates*, London, 1988.

Vander Waerdt, P.A. *The Socratic Movement*, Ithaca, 1994.

Vlastos, G. (ed.) *The Philosophy of Socrates: A Collection of Critical Essays*, Garden City, 1971.

—— *Socrates: Ironist and Moral Philosopher*, Cambridge, 1991.

Part III: Plato

III, 12. Life, works and position

Platonis opera, ed. J. Burnet, I–V, *OCT*, 2nd edn, ed. E.A. Duke *et al.*, 1995–.

Platon *Oeuvres complètes*, ed. M. Croiset *et al.*, I–XIV, *Budé*.

Plato, ed. W.R.M. Lamb *et al.*, I–XII, *Loeb*.

The Dialogues of Plato, trans. B. Jowett, I–IV, 4th edn, Oxford, 1953 (1871).

The Complete Works of Plato, ed. J.M. Cooper and D.S. Hutchinson, Indianapolis and Cambridge, MA, 1997.

Isocrate *Discours*, eds G. Mathieu and É. Brémond, I–IV, *Budé*.

Allen, R.E. (ed.) *Studies in Plato's Metaphysics*, London, 1965.

Ast, F. *Lexicon Platonicum*, I–III, Leipzig, 1835–8. Repr. Darmstadt, 1956.

Bambrough, R. (ed.) *New Essays on Plato and Aristotle*, London, 1965.

Brandwood, L. *A Word Index to Plato*, Leeds, 1976.

—— *The Chronology of Plato's Dialogues*, Cambridge, 1990.

Bröcker, N. *Platos Gespräche*, Frankfurt, 1964.

Crombie, I.M. *An Examination of Plato's Doctrines*, I–II, London, 1962–3.

Des Places, É. *Lexique de Platon*, I–II, Paris, 1964 = *Budé*- edn XIV, 1–2.

Ebert, T. *Meinung und Wissen in der Philosophie Platons*, Berlin, 1974.

Festugière, A.J. *Contemplation et vie contemplative selon Platon*, Paris, 1936.

Field, G.C. *Plato and his Contemporaries*, London, 1930 (and later).

Friedländer, P. *Platon*, I–III, Berlin and Leipzig, 1928–30, 3rd edn, Berlin, 1964–75. Eng. trans. 1958–69.

Frutiger, P. *Les mythes de Platon*, Paris, 1930.

Gadamer, H.-G. *Platos dialektische Ethik und andere Studien zur platonischen Philosophie*, Hamburg, 1968.

—— *Kleine Schriften*, III, Tübingen, 1972.

—— *Die Idee des Guten zwischen Plato und Aristoteles*, Heidelberg, 1978.

—— *Dialogue and Dialectic: Eight Hermeneutical Studies on Plato*, New Haven, 1980.

Gosling, J.C.B. *Plato*, London, 1973.

Graeser, A. *Platons Ideenlehre*, Bern and Stuttgart, 1975.

Gulley, B. *Plato's Theory of Knowledge*, London, 1962.

Havelock, E.A. *Preface to Plato*, Oxford, 1963.

Irwin, T. *Plato's Moral Theory*, Oxford, 1977.

Krämer, H.J. *Arete bei Platon und Aristoteles*, Heidelberg, 1959.

Kraut, R. (ed.) *The Cambridge Companion to Plato*, Cambridge, 1992.

Kraut, R. *Socrates and the State*, Princeton, 1984.

Lee, E.N., Mourelatos, A.P.D. and Rorty, H.M. (ed.) *Exegesis and Argument. Studies in Greek Philosophy presented to Gregory Vlastos*, Assen, 1973.

Martin, G. *Platons Ideenlehre*, Berlin, 1973.

Moravcsik, J.M. (ed.) *Patterns in Plato's Thought*, Dordrecht, 1973.

—— *Plato and Platonism*, Cambridge, MA, 1992.

Natorp, P. *Platos Ideenlehre*, Leipzig, 1903, 2nd edn, 1921.

Oehler, K. *Die Lehre vom noetischen und dianoetischen Denken bei Platon und Aristoteles*, München, 1962.

Prauss, G. *Platon und der logische Eleatismus*, Berlin, 1966.

Raven, J.E. *Plato's Thought in the Making*, Cambridge, 1965.

Ritter, C. *Platon, sein Leben, seine Schriften, seine Lehre*, I–II, München, 1910–23.

Robin, L. *Platon*, Paris, 1935.

Robinson, R. *Plato's Earlier Dialectic*, 2nd edn, Oxford, 1953 (1941).

Robinson, T.M. *Plato's Psychology*, Toronto, 1970.

Ross, D. *Plato's Theory of Ideas*, Oxford, 1951.

Ryle, G. *Plato's Progress*, Cambridge, 1966.

Ræder, H. *Platons philosophische Entwickelung*, Leipzig, 1905.

Stenzel, J. *Zahl und Gestalt bei Platon und Aristoteles*, 3rd edn, Darmstadt, 1959 (1924).

—— *Studien zur Entwicklung der platonischen Dialektik von Sokrates zu Aristoteles*, 2nd edn, Leipzig, 1931 (1971). Eng. trans. 1940.

Taylor, A.E. *Plato: The Man and his Work*, London, 1926 (and later).

Thesleff, H. *Studies in Platonic Chronology: Commentationes humanarum litterarum*, 70, Helsinki, 1982.

Tigerstedt, E.N. *Interpreting Plato: Stockholm Studies in History of Literature*, 17, Stockholm, 1977.

Vlastos, G. (ed.) *Plato: A Collection of Critical Essays*, I–II, New York, 1971.

—— *Platonic Studies*, Princeton, 1973.

Wedberg, A. *Plato's Philosophy of Mathematics*, Stockholm, 1955.

Wieland, W. *Platon und die Formen des Wissens*, Göttingen, 1982.

Wilamowitz-Moellendorff, U.v. *Platon*, I–II, Berlin, 1919.

Wyller, E.A. *Der späte Platon*, Hamburg, 1970. Norwegian edn, Oslo, 1984.

III, 13. What is virtue? Can virtue be taught?

Allen, R.E. *Plato's 'Euthypho' and the Earlier Theory of Forms*, London, 1970. Trans. and commentary.

Plato *Hippias Major*, trans. with commentary and essay, P. Woodruff, Oxford, 1982.

Plato *Protagoras and Meno*, trans. W.K.C. Guthrie, Harmondsworth, 1956 (and later), Penguin Classics.

Plato's Protagoras, Indianapolis and New York, 1956. Jowett's trans., revised M. Ostwald, intro. G. Vlastos.

Plato *Protagoras*, C.C.W. Taylor, Oxford, 1976. Trans. and commentary. *CPS*.

Plato *Gorgias*, E.R. Dodds, Oxford, 1959. Greek text, intro. and commentary.

Plato *Gorgias*, T. Irwin, Oxford, 1979. Trans. and commentary. *CPS*.
Plato *Meno*, R.S. Bluck, Cambridge, 1961. Greek text, intro. and commentary.
Sprague, R.K. *Plato's Use of Fallacy*, London, 1962.
Tuckey, T.G. *Plato's Charmides*, Cambridge, 1951.

III, 14. Idea and man

See also Chapter 12

Plato's Phaedo, R.S. Bluck, London, 1955. Trans., intro. and commentary.
Plato's Phaedo, ed. J. Burnet, Oxford, 1911 (and later). Greek text and commentary.
Plato *Phaedo*, D. Gallop, Oxford, 1975. Trans. and commentary. *CPS*.
Plato's Phaedo, R. Hackforth, Indianapolis, IN and New York, 1955. Trans., intro. and commentary.
Plato *Phaedo*, C.J. Rowe, Cambridge, 1993. Greek text and commentary.
Plato *Symposium*, K. Dover, Cambridge, 1980. Greek text and commentary.
Plato *The Symposium*, trans. with comment R.E. Allen, New Haven and London, 1991.
Plato's Phaedrus, R. Hackforth, Indianapolis and New York, 1952. Trans., intro. and commentary.
Plato *Phaedrus*, trans. with intro. and notes A. Nehamas and P. Woodruff, Indianapolis, 1995.
Derbolav, J. *Platons Sprachphilosophie im Kratylos und in den spätern Schriften*, Darmstadt, 1972.
Ficino, M. *Commentaire sur le Banquet de Platon*, ed. R. Marcel, Paris, 1956 (1469).
Heidegger, M. *Platons Lehre von der Wahrheit*, Bern, 1947. The 'metaphysical' sections of the *Republic*.
Rosen, S. *Plato's Symposium*, New Haven, CT, London, 1968.

III, 15. The good constitution of state and man

Adams, J. *The Republic of Plato*, with critical notes, commentary and appendices, I–II, 2nd edn, Cambridge, 1963 (ed. D.A. Rees). Orig. 1902. Greek text.
Plato *The Republic*, the Greek text, ed. with notes and essays B. Jowett and L. Campbell, I–III, Oxford, 1894.
Plato *The Republic*, trans. F.M. Cornford, Oxford, 1941.
Plato *The Republic*, trans. H.D.P. Lee, Harmondsworth, 1955 (and later). Penguin Classics.
Annas, J. *An Introduction to Plato's Republic*, Oxford, 1981.
Bambrough, R. (ed.) *Plato, Popper and Politics: Views and Controversies*, Cambridge, 1967.
Barker, E. *The Political Thought of Plato and Aristotle*, London, 1906. Repr. 1959.
Cross, R.C. and Woozley, A.D. *Plato's Republic: A Philosophical Commentary*, London, 1964.
Else, G.F. *Plato and Aristotle on Poetry*, ed. P. Burian, Chapel Hill and London, 1986.
Levison, R.B. *In Defense of Plato*, Cambridge, MA, 1953 (and later).
Moravcsik, J. and Temko, P. (ed.) *Plato on Beauty, Wisdom, and the Arts*, Totowa, 1982.
Murdoch, X. *The Fire and the Sun: Why Plato Banished the Artists*, Oxford, 1977.
Murphy, A. *The Interpretation of Plato's Republic*, Oxford, 1951.
Nettleship, R.L. *Lectures on the Republic of Plato*, London, 1898 (and later).
Popper, K.R. *The Open Society and its Enemies*, I, *Plato*, London, 1945 (and later).
Reeve, C.D.C. *Philosopher-Kings: The Argument of Plato's Republic*, Princeton, 1988.

Vicaire, P. *Platon critique littéraire*, Paris, 1960.

White, N.P. *A Companion to Plato's Republic*, Oxford, 1979.

III, 16. The later dialogues: knowledge and being

Allen, R.E. *Plato's Parmenides: Translation and Analysis*, Minneapolis, 1983.

Brumbaugh, R.S. *Plato on the One: The Hypotheses in the Parmenides*, New Haven, 1961. Text, trans., commentary.

Cornford, F.M. *Plato and Parmenides*, London, 1939 (and later). Intro., trans. and commentary to Parmenides' poem and Plato's *Parmenides*.

The Being of the Beautiful: Plato's Theaetetus, Sophist and Statesman, trans. and with commentary S. Benardete, Chicago, IL, 1984.

Burnyeat, M. *The Theaetetus of Plato*, trans. M.J. Levett, Indianapolis and Cambridge, 1990.

Cornford, F.M. *Plato's Theory of Knowledge*, London, 1935 (and later). Trans. and commentary to the *Theaetetus* and the *Sophist*.

Plato *Theaetetus*, J. MacDowell, Oxford, 1973. Trans. and commentary. *CPS*.

Plato *The Sophistes and Politicus,* ed. L. Campbell. Oxford 1867. Greek text and notes.

Plato's Statesman, J.B. Skemp, London, 1952 (and later). Trans. and commentary.

Bostock, D. *Plato's Theaetetus*, Oxford, 1988.

Frede, M. *Prädikation und Existenzaussage: Platons Gebrauch von " . . . ist . . . " und " . . . ist nicht . . . " im Sophistes*, Göttingen, 1967.

Meinwald, C.C. *Plato's Parmenides*, Oxford, 1991.

Rosen, S. *Plato's Sophist: The Drama of Original and Image*, New Haven, 1983.

Vogel, C.J. de *Een keerpunt in Plato's Denken*, Paris and Amsterdam, 1936.

Wyller, E.A. *Platons Parmenides in seinem Zusammenhang mit Symposion und Politeia*, Oslo, 1960.

III, 17. The later dialogues: nature, man and society

Cornford, F.M. *Plato's Cosmology*, London, 1937 (and later). Trans. and commentary to the *Timaeus*.

Plato *Philebus*, trans. with intro. and notes D. Frede, Indianapolis, 1993.

Plato *Philebus*, J.C.B. Gosling, Oxford, 1975. Trans. and commentary. *CPS*.

Hackforth, R. *Plato's Examination of Pleasure*, Cambridge, 1958. Trans. and commentary to the *Philebus*.

Plato *The Laws*, trans. J. Saunders, Harmondsworth, 1970 (and later). Penguin Classics.

Gadamer, H.-G. *Idee und Wirklichkeit in Platos Timaios*, Heidelberg, 1973.

—— *Platos dialektische Ethik und andere Studien zur platonischen Philosophie*, Hamburg, 1968.

Morrow, G. *Plato's Cretan City*, Princeton, 1960.

Taylor, A.E. *A Commentary on Plato's Timaeus*, Oxford, 1928.

Vlastos, G. *Plato's Universe*, Oxford, 1975.

III, 18. Plato and the early Academy

Lang, P. *De Speusippi Academici scriptis. Accedunt fragmenta*, Bonn, 1911. Repr. 1965. Collection of frgs (Greek).

Speusippo *Frammenti*, ed. I. Parente, Napoli, 1980. Frgs with Italian trans. and commentary.

Heinze, R. *Xenokrates: Darstellung der Lehre und Sammlung der Fragmente*, Leipzig, 1892. Repr. 1965. Collection of fragments (Greek).

Cherniss, H. *The Riddle of the Early Academy*, Berkeley and Los Angeles, 1945.

Edelstein, L. *Plato's Seventh Letter*, Leiden, 1966.

Findlay, J.N. *Plato: The Written and Unwritten Doctrines*, London, 1974.

Gadamer H.-G. *et al. Idee und Zahl. Studien zur platonischen Philosophie*, Heidelberg, 1968.

Gaiser, K. *Platons ungeschriebene Lehre*, Stuttgart, 1963 (and later). With a collection of frgs. (Greek).

Krämer, H.J. *Die ältere Akdademie*, see section C, Ueberweg.

—— *Arete bei Platon und Aristoteles*, Heidelberg, 1959.

—— *Der Ursprung der Geistmetaphysik. Untersuchungen zur Geschichte des Platonismus zwischen Platon und Plotin*, Amsterdam, 1964 (and later).

Merlan, P. *From Platonism to Neoplatonism*, The Hague, 1968.

Morrow, G.R. *Studies in the Platonic Epistles, with a trans. and notes*, Urbana, 1935.

Robin, L. *La théorie Platonicienne des idées et des nombres d'après Aristote*, Paris, 1908. Repr. 1963.

Wippern, J. (ed.) *Das Problem der ungeschriebenen Lehre Platons*, Darmstadt, 1972.

Part IV: Aristotle

IV, 1. Life, works and position

Aristotelis opera, ed. I. Bekker, I–V. I–II: Aristotle's text (Greek). III: Latin Renaissance translations. IV: Scholia. V: frgs and H. Bonitz, *Index Aristotelicus*. Berlin, 1831–70. Repr. 1960.

OCT, Budé and *Loeb*, see the individual sections.

The Works of Aristotle, trans. into English, ed. W.D. Ross, I–XII, Oxford, 1908–52 (and later). Revised edn J. Barnes, Princeton, 1984.

A New Aristotle Reader, ed. J.L. Ackrill, Princeton, 1987.

Aristotle *Selections*, trans., with intro., notes and glossary, T. Irwin and G. Fine, Indianapolis, and Cambridge, 1995.

Aristotelis fragmenta, ed. V. Rose, Lipsiae, 1886. Greek.

Aristotelis fragmenta selecta, ed. W.D. Ross. Greek text. *OCT*.

Aristoteles *Protreptikos*, ed. I. Düring, Frankfurt, 1969. Text, German trans. and commentary.

Ackrill, J.L. *Aristotle, the Philosopher*, Oxford, 1981.

Allan, D.J. *The Philosophy of Aristotle*, Oxford, 1952 (and later).

Aristote et les problèmes de méthode, ed. S. Mansion, Louvain, 1961.

Articles on Aristotle, ed. J. Barnes, M. Schofield and R. Sorabji, I–IV, London, 1975–9. I: *Science*. II: *Ethics and Politics*. III. *Metaphysics*. IV: *Psychology and Aesthetics*.

Autour d'Aristote: Recueil d'études de philosophie ancienne et médiévale off. à A. Mansion, Louvain, 1955.

Barnes, J. *Aristotle*, Oxford, 1982.

—— (ed.) *The Cambridge Companion to Aristotle*, Cambridge, 1995.

Berti, E. *La filosofia del primo Aristotele*, Padova, 1962.

Bonitz, H. *Index Aristotelicus*, see *Aristotelis opera*, Bekker.

Cherniss, H. *Aristotle's Criticism of Presocratic Philosophy*, Baltimore, 1935.

—— *Aristotle's Criticism of Plato and the Academy*, Baltimore 1944 (and later).

Düring, I. *Aristotle in the Ancient Biographical Tradition*, Göteborg, 1957.

—— *Aristoteles. Darstellung und Interpretation seines Denkens*, Heidelberg, 1966.

Düring, I. and Owen, G.E.L. (eds) *Aristotle and Plato in the mid-fourth Century*, Göteborg, 1960.

Flashar, H. *Aristoteles*, see section C, Ueberweg.

Jaeger, W. *Aristoteles: Grundlegung einer Geschichte seiner Entwicklung*, Berlin, 1923. Eng. trans. 1934 (and later).

Lear, J. *Aristotle, the Desire to Understand*, Cambridge, 1988.

Lynch, J.P. *Aristotle's School*, Berkeley, 1972.

Moraux, P. *Les listes anciennes des ouvrages d'Aristote*, Louvain, 1951.

—— (ed.) *Aristoteles in der neueren Forschung*, Darmstadt, 1968.

—— (ed.) *Frühschiften des Aristoteles*, Darmstadt, 1975.

Moravcsik, J.M.E. (ed.) *Aristotle: A Collection of Critical Essays*, London, 1968.

Oehler, K. *Ein Mensch zeugt einen Menschen*, Frankfurt, 1963.

Ross, W.D. *Aristotle*, London, 1923 (and later).

Wieland, W. *Die aristotelische Physik*. 2nd edn, Göttingen, 1970 (1962).

IV, 20. Logic and theory of science

Aristotle *The Organon*, ed. H.P. Cooke and H. Tredennick, I–II. *Loeb*.

Aristoteles: Categoriae et liber de interpretatione, ed L. Minio-Paluello. *OCT*.

Aristotle's Categories and De interpretatione, J.L. Ackrill. *CAS*. Trans. and commentary.

Aristotle *Prior and Posterior Analytics*, ed. W.D. Ross, Oxford, 1949 (and later). Greek text and commentary.

Aristoteles *Analytica priora et posteriora*, ed. D. Ross and L. Minio-Paluello. *OCT*.

Aristotle *Posterior Analytics*, J. Barnes, Oxford, 1975. *CAS*. Trans. and commentary.

Aristoteles *Topica*, ed. D. Ross. *OCT*.

Becker, A. *Die aristotelische Theorie der Möglichkeitsschlüsse*, Berlin, 1933 (and later).

Dancy, R.M. *Sense and Contradiction*, Boston, 1975 (and later).

Hager, F.P. (ed.) *Logik und Erkentnislehre des Aristoteles*, Darmstadt, 1972.

Hambruch, E. *Logische Regeln der Platonischen Schule in der aristotelischen Topik*, Berlin, 1904.

Hintikka, J. *Time and Necessity: Studies in Aristotle's Theory of Modality*, Oxford, 1973.

Łukasiewicz, J. *Aristotle's Syllogistic from the Standpoint of Modern Formal Logic*, Oxford, 1951 (and later).

McCall, S. *Aristotle's Modal Syllogisms*, Amsterdam, 1963.

Owen, G.E.L. (ed.) *Aristotle on Dialectic: The Topics*, Oxford, 1968.

Patzig, G. *Die aristotelische Syllogistik*, 3rd edn, Göttingen, 1969 (1959).

Rijk, L.M.de *The Place of the Categories of Being in Aristotle's Philosophy*, Assen, 1952.

Waterlow, S. *Passage and Possibility: A Study of Aristotle's Modal Concepts*, Oxford, 1982.

IV, 21. Natural philosophy and psychology

Aristotle *Physics*, ed. W.D. Ross, Oxford, 1936 (and later). Greek text and commentary.

Aristoteles *Physica*, ed. W.D. Ross. *OCT*.

Aristotle *The Physics*, ed. P.H. Wicksteed and F.M. Cornford, I–II. *Loeb*.

Aristotle *Physics*, books I and II by W. Charlton, Oxford, 1970. *CAS*.

Aristotle *Physics*, books III and IV by E. Hussey, Oxford, 1983. *CAS*.

Aristoteles *De caelo*, ed. D.J. Allan. *OCT*.

Aristotle *De caelo*, ed. W.K.C. Guthrie. *Loeb*.

Aristotle *On Coming-to-be and Passing away (De generatione et corruptione)*, ed. H.H. Joachim, Oxford, 1922 (and later). Greek text and commentary.

Aristote *De la génération et de la corruption*, ed. C. Mugler, *Budé*.

Aristotle: Histora animalium, I–VI, ed. A.L. Peck. VII–X, ed. D.M. Balme. *Loeb*.

Aristotle *Parts of Animals*, ed. A.L. Peck. *Loeb*.

Aristotle *De partibus animalium I and De generatione animalium I, II, 1–3*, D.M. Balme, Oxford, 1972. *CAS*.

Aristote *De la génération des animaux*, ed. P. Louis. *Budé*.

Aristotle *De anima*, ed. R.D. Hicks, Cambridge, 1907. Text, trans. and commentary.

Aristotle *De anima*, ed. D. Ross, Oxford, 1961. Greek text and commentary.

Aristoteles *De anima*, ed. W.D. Ross. *OCT*.

Aristotle *De anima*, D.W. Hamlyn, Oxford, 1968. *CAS*. Books II and III and parts of book I. Trans. and commentary.

Aristotle *Parva naturalia*, ed. W.D. Ross, Oxford, 1955. Greek text and commentary.

Blond, J.M. le *Logique et méthode chez Aristote: Étude sur la recherche des principes dans la physique aristotélicienne*, Paris, 1939.

Cassirer, H. *Aristoteles' Schift "Von der Seele" und ihre Stellung innerhalb der aristotelischen Philosophie*, Tübingen, 1932 (and later).

Furley, D.J. *Two Studies in the Greek Atomists*, Princeton, 1967.

Heath, T. *Mathematics in Aristotle*, Oxford, 1949.

Kullmann, W. *Wissenschaft und Methode: Interpretationen zur aristotelischen Theorie der Naturwissenschaft*, Berlin, 1974.

Mansion, A. *Introduction à la physique aristotélicienne*, Paris, 1913 (and later).

Modrak, D.K.W. *Aristotle: The Power of Perception*, Chicago, 1987.

Moreau, J. *L'espace et le temps selon Aristote*, Padova, 1965.

Nussbaum, M.C. and Rorty, A.O. (ed.) *Essays on Aristotle's De Anima*, Oxford, 1992.

Nuyens, F. *L'évolution de la psychologie d'Aristote*, Louvain, 1948.

Seeck, G.A. (ed.) *Die Naturphilosophie des Aristoteles*, Darmstadt, 1975.

Seidl, H. *Der Begriff des Intellekts (νοῦς) bei Aristoteles*, Meisenhaim am Glan, 1971.

Solmsen, F. *Aristotle's System of the Physical World*, Ithaca, 1960.

Waterlow, S. *Nature, Change, and Agency in Aristotle's Physics*, Oxford, 1982.

Wedin, M.V. *Mind and Imagination in Aristotle*, New Haven, 1988.

Weiss, H. *Kausalität und Zufall in der Philosophie des Aristoteles*, Darmstadt, 1967 (1942).

Wieland, W. *Die aristotelische Physik*. 2nd edn, Göttingen, 1970 (1962).

IV, 22. Metaphysics and theology

Aristoteles *Metaphysica*, ed. W. Jaeger. *OCT*.

Aristotle *Metaphysics*, ed. W.D. Ross, I–II, Oxford, 1924 (and later). Greek text and commentary.

Aristotle *The Metaphysics*, ed. H. Tredennick. *Loeb*.

Aristotle *Metaphysics: Books M and N*, J. Annas, Oxford, 1976. *CAS*.

Aristotle *Metaphysics*, trans. R. Hope, New York, 1952 (and later).

Aristotle *Metaphysics: Books , Γ, Δ and E*, by C. Kirwan. Oxford 1971 (and later). *CAS*.

Aristoteles *Metaphysik Z, Text, Übers. und Komm.*, M. Frede and G. Patzig, I–II, München, 1987.

Aubenque, P. *Le problème de l'être chez Aristote*, Paris, 1962.

—— (ed.) *Études sur la Métaphysique d'Aristote*, Paris, 1979.

Boehm, R. *Das Grundlegende und da Wesentliche. Zu Aristoteles' Abhandlung "Über das Sein und das Seiende"* (*Met.Z*), Den Haag, 1965.

Furth, M. *Substance, Form and Psyche: an Aristotelian Metaphysics*, Cambridge, 1988.

Gill, M.L. *Aristotle on Substance: The Paradox of Unity*, Princeton, 1989.

Hager, F.-P. (ed.) *Metaphysik und Theologie des Aristoteles*, Darmstadt, 1969.

Happ, H. *Hyle: Studien zum aristotelischen Materie-Begriff*, Berlin, 1971.

Irwin, T. *Aristotle's First Principles*, Oxford, 1988.

Jaeger, W. *Studien zur Entstehungsgeschichte der Metaphysica des Aristoteles*, Berlin, 1912.

Lloyd, A.C. *Form and Universal in Aristotle*, Liverpool, 1981.

Loux, M.J. *Primary Ousia: An Essay on Aristotle's Metaphysics Z and H*, Ithaca, 1991.

Owens, J. *The Doctrine of Being in the Aristotelian Metaphysics*, 3rd edn, Toronto, 1978 (1951).

Reale, G. *Il concetto di filosofia prima e l'unità della metafisica di Aristotele*, Milano, 1961 (and later). Eng. trans. 1976.

Stallmach, J. *Dynamis und Energeia*, Meisenheim, 1959.

Tugendhat, E. Τὶ κατά τινος. *Eine Untersuchung zu Struktur und Ursprung aristotelischer Grundbegriffe*, Freiburg, 1958.

IV, 23. Ethics and politics

Aristotle's Ethics, ed. J.L. Ackrill, London, 1973. Selections, trans. with notes.

Aristotle *The Athenian Constitution, The Eudemian Ethics, On Virtues and Vices*, ed. H. Rackham.*Loeb*.

Aristoteles *Eudemische Ethik*, F. Dirlmeier, Berlin, 1962 (and later). In *Aristoteles: Werke in deutscher Übersetzung*. Trans. and commentary.

Aristotle *Eudemian Ethics*, books I, II and VIII, M. Woods, Oxford, 1982. *CAS*.

Aristoteles *Ethica Nicomachea*, ed. I. Bywater. *OCT*.

Aristotle *The Nicomachean Ethics*, trans. T. Irwin, Indianapolis, 1985.

Aristoteles *Nikomachische Ethik*, F. Dirlmeier, Berlin, 1956 (and later). In *Aristoteles: Werke in deutscher Übersetzung*. Trans. and commentary.

Aristote *L'éthique à Nicomaque*, intro., trad. et comm., par R.A. Gauthier and J.Y. Jolif, I–II, 1–2, Louvain, 1958–9 (and later).

Aristoteles *Magna Moralia*, F. Dirlmeier, Berlin, 1958 (and later). In *Aristoteles: Werke in deutscher Übersetzung*. Trans. and commentary.

Aristote *Politique*, ed. J. Aubonnet, I–. *Budé*.

The Politics of Aristotle, ed. W.L. Newman, I–IV, Oxford, 1897–1902 (and later). Greek text and commentary.

Aristoteles *Politica*, ed. W.D. Ross. *OCT*.

Aristotle *Politics*, books III and IV, R. Robinson, Oxford, 1962. *CAS*.

Aubenque, P. *La prudence chez Aristote*, Paris, 1962.

Bien, G. *Die Grundlegung der politischen Philosophie bei Aristoteles*, Freiburg, 1973 (and later).

Cooper, J.M. *Reason and Human Good in Aristotle*, Cambridge, MA, 1975.

Engberg-Pedersen, T. *Aristotle's Theory of Moral Insight*, Oxford, 1983.

Fortenbaugh, W.W. *Aristotle on Emotion*, London, 1975.

Furley, D.J. *Two Studies in the Greek Atomists*, Princeton, 1967.

Hager, F.-P. (ed.) *Ethik und Politik des Aristoteles*, Darmstadt, 1972.

Hardie, W.F.R. *Aristotle's Ethical Theory*, Oxford, 1968 (and later).

Joachim, H.H. *Aristotle: The Nicomachean Ethics, a Commentary*, ed. D.A. Rees, Oxford, 1951.

Kenny, A. *The Aristotelian Ethics*, Oxford, 1978.

—— *Aristotle's Theory of the Will*, London, 1979.

—— *Aristotle on the Perfect Life*, Oxford, 1992.

Keyt, D. and Miller, F.D., Jr, *A Companion to Aristotle's Politics*, Oxford, 1991.

MacIntyre, A. *After Virtue: A Study in Moral Theory*, London, 1981 (and later).

Monan, J.D. *Moral Knowledge and its Methodology in Aristotle*, Oxford, 1968.

Mulgan, R.G. *Aristotle's Political Theory*, Oxford, 1977.

Ritter, J. *Metaphysik und Politik: Studien zu Aristoteles und Hegel*, Frankfurt, 1969.

Rorty, A.O. (ed.) *Essays on Aristotle's Ethics*, Berkeley, 1980.

Sorabji, R. *Necessity, Cause and Blame: Perspectives on Aristotle's Theory*, London, 1980.

Stewart, J.A. *Notes on the Nicomachean Ethics of Aristotle*, I–II, Oxford, 1892.

Urmson, J.O. *Aristotle's Ethics*, Oxford, 1988.

IV, 24. Rhetoric and poetics

Aristote *Rhétorique*, ed. M. Dufour, I–III. *Budé*.

Aristoteles *Ars rhetorica*, ed. W.D. Ross. *OCT*.

Else, G. *Aristotle's Poetics: The Argument*, Cambridge, MA, 1957 (and later). Greek text, trans. and commentary.

Aristoteles *De arte poetica*, ed. R. Kassel. *OCT*.

Aristotle *Poetics*, ed. D.W. Lucas, Oxford, 1968. Greek text and commentary.

Aristotle *The Poetics*, trans. S. Halliwell, London, 1987. With commentary.

Bernays, J. *Zwei Abhandlungen über die aristotelische Theorie des Drama*, Berlin, 1880. Repr. 1968.

Halliwell, S. *Aristotle's Poetics*, Chapel Hill, 1986.

Rorty, A.O. (ed.) *Essays in Aristotle's Poetics*, Princeton, 1992.

—— (ed.) *Essays on Aristotle's Rhetoric*, Berkeley, Los Angeles and London, 1996.

IV, 25. The early Peripatetics

Wehrli, F. (ed.) *Die Schule des Aristoteles: Texte und Kommentar*, I–X and suppl. 1–2. Basel 1944–59 (and later). Fragments: Greek text and commentary.

Theophrastus *Opera quae supersunt*, ed. F. Wimmer, I–III, Lipsiae, 1854–62. Repr. 1964.

Stratton, G.M. *Theophrastus and the Greek Phsysiological Psychology before Aristotle*, London, 1917 (and later). *De sensibus*, text, trans. and commentary.

Théophraste *Recherches sur les plantes (Historia plantarum)*, ed. S. Amigues, I–V. *Budé*.

Theophrastus *De causis plantarum*, ed. B. Einarson and G.K.K. Link, I–III. *Loeb*.

Theophrastus *Metaphysics*, ed. W.D. Ross and F.H. Fobes, Oxford, 1929. Text, trans. and commentary.

Theophrastus *Characteres*, ed. H. Diels. *OCT*.

Théophraste *Caractères*, ed. O. Navarre, I–II, Budé. Vol. II: commentary.

Bocheński, I.M. *La logique de Théophraste*, Fribourg, 1947.

Steinmetz, P. *Die Physik des Theophrastos von Eresos*, Bad Homburg, 1964.

Wehrli, F. *Der Peripatos bis zum Beginn der römischen Kaiserzeit*, see section C, Ueberweg.

Part V: Hellenistic philosophy

V, 26. Science and philosophy

See also section D, Science and mathematics

Long, A.A.and Sedley, D.N. (ed.) *The Hellenistic Philosophers*. I: *Translations of the Principal Sources with Philosophical Commentary*. II: *Greek and Latin Texts with Notes and Bibliography*. Cambridge, 1987.

Euclides *Opera omnia*, ed. J.L. Heiberg and H. Menge, I–VIII and suppl., Leipzig 1883–1916. Greek text, Latin translation.

Euclid's Elements, trans. T. Heath, I–III, Cambridge, 1908. Repr. 1956. With intro. and commentary.

Archimedes *Opera omnia*, ed. J.L. Heiberg, I–III, 2nd edn, Leipzig, 1910–5 (1880–81). Greek text, Latin trans.

The Works of Archimedes, trans. T. Heath, Cambridge, 1897 (and later).

Claudius Ptolemaeus *Opera quae extant omnia*, ed. J.L. Heiberg, I–II, Leipzig 1898–1907. Greek text.

Claudius Ptolemaeus *Handbuch der Astronomie*, ed. K. Manitius, I–II, Leipzig, 1963. Trans. with commentary.

Galenus *Opera omnia*, ed. C.G. Kühn, I–XX, Leipzig, 1821–33. Greek text.

Galenus, ed. H. Diels *et al.* (not completed), Leipzig, 1918–. *Corpus Medicorum Graecorum*, V 4, V 9, V 10.

Galen *On the Natural Faculties*, ed. A.J. Brock. *Loeb*.

Galenus *Institutio logica*, trans. J.S. Kiefer, Baltimore, 1964.

Annas, J. *Hellenistic Philosophy of Mind*, Berkeley, 1992.

Barnes, J, Brunschwig, J., Burnyeat, M. and Schofield, M. (ed.) *Science and Speculation: Studies in Hellenistic Theory and Practice*, Cambridge and Paris, 1982.

Brunschwig, J. and Nussbaum, M.C. (ed.) *Passions and Perceptions: Studies in Hellenistic Philosophy of Mind*, Cambridge, 1992.

Dihle, A. *The Theory of Will in Classical Antiquity*, Berkeley and Los Angeles, 1982.

Dijksterhuis, E.J. *Archimedes*, Copenhagen, 1956.

Giusta, M. *I dossografi di etica*, I–II, Torino, 1964–7.

Green, N.P. *Alexander to Actium: The Historical Evolution of the Hellenistic Age*, Berkeley and Los Angeles, 1990.

Hicks, R.D. *Stoic and Epicurean*, London, 1910.

Krämer, H.J. *Platonismus und hellenistische Philosophie*, Berlin, 1971.

Lloyd, G.E.R. *Greek Science after Aristotle*, London, 1973.

Long, A.A. *Hellenistic Philosophy*, London and New York, 1974 (and later).

Nussbaum, M.C. *The Therapy of Desire: Theory and Practice in Hellenistic Ethics*, Princeton, 1994.

Pedersen, O. *A Survey of the Almagest*, Odense, 1974.

Schofield, M., Burnyeat, M. and Barnes, J. (ed.) *Doubt and Dogmatism: Studies in Hellenistic Epistemology*, Oxford, 1980.

Schofield, M. and Striker, G. (ed.) *The Norms of Nature, Studies in Hellenistic Ethics*, Cambridge and Paris, 1986.

Walbank, F.W. *The Hellenistic World*, London, 1981.

V, 27. Epicurus

See also section I, 6.

Epicuro *Opere*, ed. G. Arrighetti, 2nd edn, Torino, 1973 (1960). Text, Italian trans. and commentary. Incl. papyrus-frgs.

Epicurus *The Extant Remains*, ed. C. Bailey, Oxford, 1926 (and later). Text, trans. and commentary.

Epicurea, ed H. Usener, Leipzig, 1887 (and later). Texts.

Philodemus *On Methods of Inference (De signis)*, eds. P. de Lacy and E. de Lacy, 2nd edn, Napoli, 1978 (1941). Text and trans.

Lucretius *De rerum natura*, ed. C. Bailey, I–II, Oxford, 1947. Text, trans. and commentary.

Lucretius *de rerum natura*, ed. C. Bailey. *OCT*.

T. Lucreti Cari De rerum natura libri sex, ed. C. Giussani, I–IV, Torino, 1896–8.

Diogenes Oenoandensis *The Fragments*, ed. C.W. Chilton, London, 1971. Trans. and commentary.

Asmis, E. *Epicurus' Scientific Method*, Ithaca and London, 1984.

Bignone, E. *L'Aristotele perduto e la formazione filosofica di Epicuro*, I–II, Firenze, 1936.

Boyancé, P. *Lucrèce et l'épicurisme*, Paris, 1963.

Clay, D. *Lucretius and Epicurus*, Ithaca and London, 1983.

Cronache Ercolanesi, Napoli, 1971–. Edns and discussions of papyrus frgs.

Farrington, B. *The Faith of Epicurus*, London, 1967.

Festugière, A.J. *Épicure et ses dieux*, 2nd edn, Paris, 1968 (1946).

Kleve, K. *Gnosis theon: Die Lehre von der natürlichen Gotteserkenntnis in der epikureischen Theologie*, Oslo, 1963.

Manuwald, A. *Die Prolepsislehre Epikurs*, Bonn, 1972.

Mitsis, P. *Epicurus' Ethical Theory*, Ithaca, 1988.

Rist, J.M. *Epicurus: An Introduction*, Cambridge, 1972.

V, 28. Early Stoicism

Arnim, H.v. (ed.) *Stoicorum veterum fragmenta*, I–IV, Leipzig, 1903–24 (and later). Greek and Latin texts. Vol. IV: index (by M. Adler).

Hülser, K. (ed.) *Die Fragmente zur Dialektik der Stoiker*, I–IV, Stuttgart, 1987–8. Texts, trans. and commentary.

Baldry, H.C. *The Unity of Mankind in Greek Thought*, Cambridge, 1965.

Barwick, K. *Probleme der Stoischen Sprachlehre und Rhetorik*, Berlin, 1957.

Bréhier, É. *Chrysippe et l'ancien Stoicisme*, 2nd edn, Paris, 1951 (1910).

Brunschwig, J. (ed.) *Les Stoiciens et leur logique*, Paris, 1978.

Christensen, J. *An Essay on the Unity of Stoic Philosophy*, Copenhagen, 1962.

Dudley, D.R. *A History of Cynicism*, London, 1938.

Edelstein, L. *The Meaning of Stoicism*, Cambridge, MA, 1966.

Engberg-Pedersen, T. *The Stoic Theory of oikeiosis*, Aarhus, 1990.

Erskine, A. *The Hellenistic Stoa: Political Thought and Action*, London, 1990.

Forschner, M. *Die stoische Ethik: Über die Zusammenhang von Natur-, Sprach- und Moralphilosophie im altstoischen System*, Stuttgart, 1981.

Frede, M. *Die stoische Logik*, Göttingen, 1974.

Graeser, A. *Zenon von Kition*, Berlin, 1975.

Inwood, B. *Ethics and Human Action in Early Stoicism*, Oxford, 1985.

Long, A.A. (ed.) *Problems in Stoicism*, London, 1971.

Mates, B. *Stoic Logic*, Berkeley and Los Angeles, 1953 (and later).

Pohlenz, M. *Die Stoa: Geschichte einer geistigen Bewegung*, I–II, Göttingen, 1948 (and later).

Rist, J.M. *Stoic Philosophy*, Cambridge, 1969.

Sambursky, S. *Physics of the Stoics*, London, 1959.

Sandbach, F.H. *The Stoics*, London, 1975.

Sloterdijk, P. *Kritik der zynischen Vernunft*, I–II, Frankfurt, 1983.

Watson, G. *The Stoic Theory of Knowledge*, Belfast, 1966.

V, 29. Scepticism

Sextus Empiricus, ed. R.G. Bury, I–IV. *Loeb*.

Sextus Empiricus *Outlines of Scepticism*, trans. J. Annas and J. Barnes, Cambridge, 1994.

Annas, J. and Barnes, J. (ed.) *The Modes of Scepticism: Ancient Texts and Modern Interpretations*, Cambridge, 1985.

Barnes, J. *The Toils of Scepticism*, Cambridge, 1990.

Brochard, V. *Les sceptiques Grecs*, 2nd edn, Paris, 1923 (1887).

Burnyeat, M.F. (ed.) *The Sceptical Tradition*, Berkeley and Los Angeles, 1983.

Stough, C.L. *Greek Skepticism*, Berkeley and Los Angeles, 1969.

V, 30. Greece and Rome

Polybius, ed. W.R. Paton, I–VI. *Loeb*.

Panaetii Rhodii fragmenta, ed. M.v. Straaten, 3rd edn, Leiden, 1962 (1952).

Posidonius, ed. L. Edelstein and I.G. Kidd, I–II, Cambridge, 1972–88. Texts and commentary.

Cicero *Academica*, ed. J.S. Reid, London, 1885. Text and commentary.

Cicéron *De fato*, ed. A. Yon. *Budé*.

Cicero *De finibus bonorum et malorum*, ed. I.N. Madvigius, 3rd edn, Hauniae, 1876 (1839). Text and Latin commentary.

Cicéron *Des termes extrêmes des biens et des maux (De finibu)*, ed. J. Martha, I–II. *Budé*.

Cicero *De finibus bonorum et malorum, libri I-II*, ed. J.S. Reid, Cambridge, 1925. Text and commentary.

Cicero *De natura deorum*, ed. A.S. Pease, I–II, Cambridge, MA, 1955–8. Text and commentary.

Cicero *De officiis*, ed. H.A. Holden, Cambridge, 1879. Text and commentary.

Cicéron *Tusculanes*, ed. G. Fohlen and J.Humbert, I–II. *Budé*.

Büchner, K. (ed.) *Das neue Cicerobild*, Darmstadt, 1971.

Fritz, K.v. *The Theory of the Mixed Constitution in Antiquity*, New York, 1954.

Glucker, J. *Antiochus and the Late Academy*, Göttingen, 1978.

Hirzel, R. *Untersuchungen zu Ciceros philosophischen Schriften*, I–III, Leipzig, 1877–83.

——— *Der Dialog*, Leipzig, 1895.

Hunt, H.K. *The Humanism of Cicero*, Melbourne, 1954.

Merguet, H. *Lexikon zu den philosophischen Schriften Ciceros*, I–III, Jena, 1887–94. Repr. Hildesheim, 1960.

Reesor, M.E. *The Political Theory of the Old and Middle Stoa*, New York, 1951.

Reinhardt, K. *Kosmos und Sympathie: Neue Untersuchungen über Poseidonios*, München, 1926.

Süss, A. *Cicero: Eine Einführung in seine philosophischen Schriften*, Wiesbaden, 1966.

Part VI: Late antiquity

VI, 31. Imperial Rome

Sénèque *Lettres à Lucilius*, ed F. Préchac and H. Noblot, I–V. *Budé*.

Seneca *Moral Essays*, ed. J.W. Basore, I–III. *Loeb*.

Seneca *Naturales quaestiones*, ed. T.H. Corcoran, I–II. *Loeb*.

Seneca *Tragedies*, ed. F.J. Miller, I–II. *Loeb*.

Epictetus, ed. W.A. Oldfather, I–II. *Loeb*.

Marcus Aurelius *The Meditations*, ed. A.S.L. Farquharson, I–II. Oxford, 1944 (and later). Text, trans. and commentary.

Marc-Aurèle *Pensées*, ed. A.I. Trannoy. *Budé*.

Philostratus *The Life of Apollonius of Tyana*, ed. F.C. Conybeare, I–II. *Loeb*.

"*Albinos*", ed. C.F. Hermann. Plato *Dialogi*, VI, Lipsiae, 1921 (1853).

Alcinoos (= Albinos) *Enseignement des doctrines de Platon* (Διδασκαλικός), ed. J. Whittaker and P. Louis. *Budé*.

Alexander Aphrodisiensis *Commentaria in Aristotelem*, ed. M. Hayduck *et al.*, *CAG*, I–III, Berolini, 1891–1901. Trans. in *ACA* (in progress).

Alexander Aphrodisiensis *Scripta minora*, ed. I. Bruns. *Supplementum Aristotelicum*, II, Berolini, 1887–92. Greek text.

Alexander Aphrodisias *On fate*, ed. R.W. Sharples, London, 1983. Text, trans. and commentary.

Plutarch *Moralia*, ed. F.C. Babbitt *et al.*, I–XV. *Loeb*.

Philo Alexandrinus *Opera quae supersunt*, ed. L. Cohn and P. Wendland, I–VI, Berolini, 1896–1915. Greek text.

Philo, ed. F.H. Colson *et al.*, I–X. *Loeb*.

Calcidius *Timaeus a Calcidio translatus commentarioque instructus*, ed. J.H. Waszink and P.J. Jensen, Londinii and Leidae, 1992. *Corpus Platonicum Medii Aevi*, Latin text.

Numénius *Fragments*, ed. É. des Places. *Budé*.

Dörrie, H. *Der Platonismus in der Antike, I: Die geschichtlichen Wurzeln des Platonismus. Text, Übersetzung, Kommentar*, ed. A. Dörrie, Stuttgart, 1987.

The Pythagorean Texts of the Hellenistic Period, ed. H. Thesleff, Åbo, 1965.

Corpus Hermeticum, ed. A.D. Nock and A.-J. Festugière, I–IV. *Budé*.

Corpus Iuris Civilis, ed. T. Mommsen and P. Krüger, I–III, Berlin, 1911–29 (and later).

Armstrong, A.H. (ed.) *The Cambridge History of Later Greek and Early Medieval Philosophy*, Cambridge, 1967.

Aufstieg und Niedergang der römischen Welt. Geschichte und Kultur Roms im Spiegel der neueren Forschung, ed. H. Temporini and W. Haase, II 36, 1–2: *Philosophie. Platonismus, Aristotelismus*, Berlin, 1987. In progress.

Bonhöffer, A. *Die Ethik des Stoikers Epictet*, Stuttgart, 1894.

Bowersock, G.W. (ed.) *Approaches to the Second Sophistic*, University Park, 1974.

Bréhier, É. *Les idées philosophiques et religieuses de Philon d'Alexandrie*, 3rd edn, Paris, 1950 (1907).

Dillon, J. *The Middle Platonists*, London, 1977.

Dodds, E.R. *Pagan and Christian in an Age of Anxiety*, Cambridge, 1968.

Festugière, A.-F. *La révelation d'Hermès Trismégiste*, I–IV, Paris, 1950–4.

Gersh, S. *Middle Platonism and Neoplatonism: The Latin Tradition*, Notre Dame, 1986.

Goodenough, E.R. *An Introduction to Philo Judaeus*, 2nd edn, Oxford, 1962 (1940).

Griffin, M.T. *Seneca, a Philosopher in Politics*, Oxford, 1976.

Jonas, H. *Gnosis und spätantiker Geist*, I, 3rd edn, Göttingen, 1964 (1934), II 1–2, Göttingen, 1954–65.

Leisegang, H. *Die Gnosis*, 5th edn, Stuttgart, 1985 (1924).

Maurach, G. (ed.) *Seneca als Philosoph*, Darmstadt, 1975.

Moraux, P. *Alexandre d'Aphrodise*, Paris, 1942.

—— *Der Aristotelismus bei den Griechen von Andronikos bis Alexander von Aphrodisias*, I, Berlin, 1973.

Nock, A.D. *Conversion: The Old and the New in Religion from Alexander the Great to Augustine of Hippo*, Oxford, 1933 (and later).

Russell, D.A. *Plutarch*, London, 1973.

Sørensen, V. *Seneca the Humanist at the court of Nero*, Chicago, 1948. Trans. from Danish (orig. 1976).

Thesleff, H. *An Introduction to the Pythagorean Writings of the Hellinistic Period*, Åbo, 1961.

Witt, R.E. *Albinus and the History of Middle Platonism*, Cambridge, 1937 (and later).

Wolfson, H.A. *Philo*, I–II, Cambridge, MA, 1947.

Zintzen, C. (ed.) *Der Mittelplatonismus*, Darmstadt, 1981.

VI, 32. Plotinus

Including Neoplatonism in general

Plotinus, ed. A.H. Armstrong, I–VII. *Loeb.*

Plotin *Ennéades*, ed. É. Bréhier, I–VI. *Budé.*

Plotins Schriften, ed. R. Harder, I–VI, Hamburg, 1956–71. Text, trans. and commentary.

Plotini opera, ed. P. Henry and H.-R. Schwyzer, I–III, Paris and Bruxelles, 1951–73. Greek text.

Plotinus *The Enneads*, trans. S. MacKenna, 3rd edn, London, 1962 (1917–30).

Plotinus *Ennead V 1, On the Three Principal Hypostases*, a commentary with trans., ed. M. Atkinson, Oxford, 1983.

Armstrong, A.H. *The Architecture of the Intelligible Universe in the Philosophy of Plotinus*, Cambridge, 1940. Repr. 1967.

Beierwaltes, W. *Denken des Einen. Studien zur neuplatonischen Philosophie*, Frankfurt, 1985.

Blumenthal, H.J. *Plotinus' Psychology*, The Hague, 1971.

Bréhier, É. *La philosophie de Plotin*, Paris, 1928 (and later). Eng trans. 1958.

Emilsson, E.K. *Plotinus on Sense-Perception: A Philosophical Study*, Cambridge, 1988.

Gerson, L. (ed.) *The Cambridge Companion to Plotinus*, Cambridge, 1996.

Graeser, A. *Plotinus and the Stoics*, Leiden, 1972.

Hadot, P. *Plotin*, Paris, 1963.

Harris, R.B. (ed.) *The Significance of Neoplatonism*, Norfolk, 1976.

Inge, W.R. *The Philosophy of Plotinus*, I–II, 3rd edn, London, 1929 (1918).

Lloyd, A. *The Anatomy of Neoplatonism*, Oxford, 1990.

Rist, J.M. *Plotinus, the Road to Reality*, Cambridge, 1967.

Sleeman, J.H. and Pollet, G. *Lexicon Plotinianum*, Leiden, 1980.

Theiler, W. *Die Vorbereitung des Neuplatonismus*, Berlin, 1930 (and later).

Wallis, R.T. *Neoplatonism*, London, 1972.
Whittaker, T. *The Neoplatonists*, 4th edn, Cambridge, 1928 (1901).
Zintzen, C. (ed.) *Die Philosophie des Neuplatonismus*, Darmstadt, 1977.

VI, 33. Late Neoplatonism

Oracles chaldaiques, ed. É. des Places, *Budé*.
Porphyrii Isagoge et in Aristotelis Categorias commentarium, ed. A. Busse. *CAG*, IV 1. Berolini, 1887.
Porphyrius *Isagoge*, ed. E.W. Warren, Toronto, 1975. Trans. and commentary.
Porphyrius *Opuscula*, ed. A. Nauck, Lipsiae, 1886.
Porphyrios *Gegen die Christen*, ed. A.v. Harnack, Berlin, 1916. Frgs, Greek text.
Iamblichi Chalcidensis in Platonis dialogos commentariorum fragmenta, ed. J.M. Dillon, Leiden, 1973.
Jamblique *Les Mystères d'Égypte*, ed. É. des Places. *Budé*.
—— *Protreptique*, ed. É. des Places. *Budé*.
Iamblichos *Pythagoras*, ed. M.v. Albrecht, Zürich, 1963. Text and trans.
Proclus *The Elements of Theology*, ed. E.R. Dodds, 2nd edn, Oxford, 1963 (1933). Text, trans. and commentary.
Proclus *Théologie Platonicienne*, ed. L.G. Westerink and H.D. Saffrey, I–VI. *Budé*.
Proclus *In primum Euclidis Elementorum librum commentarii*, ed. G. Friedlein, Lipsiae, 1873.
Proclus *Opera inedita*, ed. V. Cousin, 2nd edn, Parisiis, 1864, repr. Frankfurt, 1962. Orig. 1821–7. Includes the commentary to Plato's *Parmenides*.
Proclus *Commentarium in Parmenidem, pars ultima adhuc inedita interprete Guillelmo de Moerbeka*, eds R. Klibansky and C. Labowsky, Londinii, 1963. *Corpus Platonicum Medii Aevi*, Latin text, Eng. trans.
Proclus *In Platonis Rem publicam*, ed. W. Kroll, I–II, Lipsiae, 1899–1901.
Proclus *In Platonis Timaeum*, ed. E. Diehl, I–III, Lipsiae, 1903–6.
The Works of the Emperor Julian, ed. W.C. Wright, I–III. *Loeb*.
Saloustios *Des Dieux et du Monde*, ed. G. Rochefort. *Budé*.
Damascius *Traité des premiers principes*, ed. L.-G. Westerink and J. Combès, I–III. *Budé*.
Ammonius *Commentaria in Aristotelem*, ed. A. Busse, *et al.*, *CAG*, IV 3–6, Berolini, 1891–9. Trans. *ACA* (in progress).
Themistius *Commentaria in Aristotelem*, ed. M. Wallies, *et al.*, *CAG*, V, Berolini, 1899–1903.
Simplicius *Commentaria in Aristotelem*, ed. J.L. Heiberg, *et al.*, *CAG*, VII–XI, Berolini, 1882–1907. Trans. *ACA* (in progress).
Philoponus *Commentaria in Aristotelem*, ed. A. Busse, *et al.*, *CAG* XIII–XVII, Berolini, 1887–1909. Trans. *ACA* (in progress).
Beierwaltes, W. *Proklos: Grundzüge seiner Metaphysik*, Frankfurt, 1965.
Bidez, J. *Vie de Porphyre*, Gent, 1913 (and later). Includes frgs of *De regressu animae*.
—— *La vie de l'Empereur Julien*, Paris, 1930.
Hadot, I. (ed.) *Simplicius, sa vie, son oeuvre, sa survie*, Berlin, 1987.
Dalsgaard Larsen, B. *Jamblique de Chalcis*, I–II, Aarhus, 1972. Vol. II: testimonies and frgs.
Sambursky, S. *The Physical World of Late Antiquity*, London, 1962.
Sorabji, R. (ed.) *Philoponus and the Rejection of Aristotelian Science*, London, 1987.
—— (ed.) *Aristotle Transformed: The Ancient Commentaries and Their Influences*, London, 1990.

VI, 34. Early Christian thought

Porphyry, see section VI, 33.

Julian the Apostate, see section VI, 33.

Irenaeus: *PG* 7.

Tertullianus: *PL* 1–2.

Tertullianus *Opera*, ed. P. Borleffs, *et al.*, I–II, Turnhout, 1954. *CC* 1–2.

Tertullian *Apologeticum*, ed. C. Becker, 2nd edn, München, 1961 (1952). Text, trans. and commentary.

Tertullien *Traité de la prescription contre les hérétiques*, ed. R.F. Refoulé and P. de Labriolle, 1957. *SC* 46.

Iustinus: *PG* 6.

Clemens Alexandrinus: *PG* 8–9.

Clemens Alexandrinus, ed. O. Stählin, I–IV, 1905–36. *GCS*.

Clement of Alexandria *The Exhortation to the Greeks: The Rich Man's Salvation*, ed. G.W. Butterworth. *Loeb*.

Origines: *PG* 11–7.

Origines *Werke*, ed. P. Koetschau, I–XII, 1899–1941. *GCS*.

Origène *Contre Celse*, ed. M. Borret, I–IV, 1967–8. *SC*, 132, 136, 147, 150.

Origen *Contra Celsum*, trans. H. Chadwick, Cambridge, 1953 (and later).

Origenes *Vier Bücher von den Prinzipien*, ed. H. Görgemanns and H. Karpp, Darmstadt, 1976. Text, trans. and commentary.

Eusebius Caesariensis: *PG* 19–24.

Eusebius *Werke*, ed. I.A. Heikel, *et al.*, I–VIII, Berlin, 1902–56. *GCS*.

Basilius Caesariensis: *PG* 29–32.

St Basile *Aux jeunes gens: Sur la manière de tirer profit des lettres helléniques*, ed. F. Boulenger. *Budé*.

Gregorius Nazianzenus: *PG* 35–8.

Gregorius Nyssenus: *PG* 44–6.

Gregorius Nyssenus: *Opera*, ed. W. Jaeger, *et al.*, I–, Leiden, 1952– (1921–).

Grégoire de Nysse *La création de l'homme*, ed. J. Laplace and J. Daniélou, 1943. *SC* 6.

Grégoire de Nysse *Traité de la virginité*, ed. M. Aubineau, 1966. *SC* 119.

Grégoire de Nysse *Vie de Moise*, ed. J. Daniélou, 3rd edn, 1968 (1941). *SC* 1.

Nemesius: *PG* 40.

Nemesius Emesenus *De natura hominis*, ed. M. Morani, Leipzig, 1987. Text.

Dionysius Areopagita: *PG* 3–4.

Denys l'Aréopagite *La hiérarchie céleste*, ed. R. Roques, G. Heil and M. de Gandillac, 1970 (1958). *SC* 58.

Andresen, C. *Logos und Nomos: Die Polemik des Kelsos wider das Christentum*, Berlin, 1955.

Campenhauser, H.v. *Griechische Kirchenväter*, Stuttgart, 1955 (and later).

Campenhauser, H.v. *Lateinische Kirchenväter*, Stuttgart, 1960 (and later).

Chadwick, H. *Early Christian Thought and the Classical Tradition. Studies in Justin, Clement and Origen*, London, 1966.

—— *The Early Church*, Harmondsworth, 1967 (and later).

Daniélou, J. *Origène*, Paris, 1948. Eng. trans. 1955.

—— *Platonisme et théologie mystique: Essai sur la doctrine spirituelle de St. Grégoire de Nysse*, 2nd edn, Paris, 1953 (1944).

Harnack, A. *Lehrbuch der Dogmengeschichte*, I–III, 4th edn, Freiburg, 1909. Repr. Darmstadt, 1964. Orig. 1886–90.

Ivánka, E.v. *Plato Christianus: Übernahme und Umgestaltung des Platonismus durch die Väter*, Einsiedeln, 1964.

Jaeger, W. *Early Christianity and Greek paideia*, Cambridge, MA, 1961 (and later).

Koch, H. *Pronoia und Paideusis. Studien über Origenes und sein Verhältnis zum Platonismus*, Leipzig, 1932.

Momigliano, A. (ed.) *The Conflict between Paganism and Christianity in the Fourth Century*, Oxford, 1963.

Roques, R. *L'univers Dionysien*, Paris, 1954.

Wolfson, H.A. *The Philosophy of the Church Fathers: I: Faith, Trinity, Incarnation*, 3rd edn, Cambridge, MA, 1970 (1956).

VI, 35. Augustine

Augustinus: PL 32–47. Text of the Maurist edn, 1679–1700.

Oeuvres de St. Augustin. Bibliothèque Augustinienne, Paris, 1947–. Latin text, French trans., commentary. Not yet completed. Appears in the following series: 1. *Opuscules*, 2. *Dieu et son oeuvre*, 3. *La grâce*, 4. *Traités Anti-Donatistes*, 5. *La Cité de Dieu*, 6. *Lettres*, 7. *Exégèse*, 9. *Homélies*. Planned series: 8. *Enarrationes in psalmos*, 10. *Sermones*.

The Complete Works of Saint Augustine, ed. J.A. Rotelle, London, 1994–.

Augustinus *Confessiones*, ed. L. Verheijen, Turnhout, 1981. *CC* 27.

St Augutine's Confessions, revised trans. W. Watts (1631), I–II. *Loeb*.

Augustinus *Contra Academicos; De beata vita; De ordine; De magistro; De libero arbitrio*, ed. W.M. Green and K.D. Daur, Turnhout, 1970. *CC* 29.

Augustinus *De civitate Dei*, ed. B. Dombart and A. Kalb, I–II, Turnhout, 1955. *CC* 47–8.

Augustine *The City of God*, ed. G.E. McCracken, I–VII. *Loeb*.

Augustine *De dialectica*, ed. B.D. Jackson and J. Pinborg, Dordrecht, 1975. Text and Eng. trans.

Augustinus *De doctrina Christiana; De vera religione*, ed. J. Martin and K.D. Daur, Turnhout, 1962. *CC* 32.

Augustinus *De doctrina Christiana*, ed. G.M. Green, Wien, 1963. *CSEL* 80.

Augustinus *De libero arbitrio*, ed. G.M. Green, Wien, 1956. *CSEL* 74.

Augustinus *De magistro; De vera religione*, ed. G. Weigel and G.M. Green, Wien, 1961. *CSEL* 77.

Augustinus *De Trinitate*, ed. W.J. Mountain and F. Glorie, I–II, Turnhout, 1967. *CC* 50–50 A.

Augustine *Select Letters*, ed. J.H. Baxter. *Loeb*.

Marius Victorinus *Traités théologiques sur la Trinité*, ed. P. Henry and P. Hadot, I–II, 1960. *SC* 68–9.

Andresen, C. *Bibliographia Augustiniana*, 2nd edn, Darmstadt, 1973 (1962).

—— (ed.) *Zum Augustin-Gespräch der Gegenwart*, I–II, Darmstadt, 1975–81.

Bohlin, T. *Die Theologie des Pelagius und ihre Genesis*, Uppsala, 1957.

Brown, P. *Augustine of Hippo: A Biography*, London, 1967.

Cayré, F. *Initiation à la philosophie de St. Augustin*, Paris, 1947.

Courcelle, P. *Recherches sur les Confessions de St. Augustin*, Paris, 1950.

Gilson, É. *Introduction à l'étude de Saint Augustin*, 4th edn, Paris, 1969 (1929). Eng. trans. 1960.

Hessen, J. *Augustins Metaphysik der Erkenntnis*, Berlin, 1931, 2nd edn, 1960.

Hölscher, L. *The Reality of the Mind. Augustine's Philosophical Arguments for the Human Soul as a Spiritual Substance*, London, 1986.

Holte, R. *Béatitude et sagesse. St. Augustin et le problème de la fin de l'homme dans la philosophie ancienne*, Paris, 1962.

Kirwan, C. *Augustine*, London, 1989.

Markus, R.A. *Saeculum: History and Society in the Theology of St. Augustine*, Cambridge, 1970.

Marrou, H.-I. *Saint Augustin et la fin de la culture antique*, 4th edn, Paris, 1958 (1938).

O'Connell, R.J. *St Augustine's Early Theory of Man. A.D. 386–391*, Cambridge, MA, 1968.

—— *St Augustine's Confessions: The Odyssey of Soul*, Cambridge, MA, 1969.

—— *The Origin of the Soul in St. Augustine's Later Works*, New York, 1987.

O'Daly, G. *Augustine's Philosophy of Mind*, London, 1987.

O'Meara, J.J. *The Young Augustine*, London, 1954.

Portalié, E. *A Guide to the Thought of St Augustine*, London, 1960. Trans. from French (orig. 1902).

Rist, J.M. *Augustine: Ancient Thought Baptized*, Cambridge, 1994.

INDEX